The *Three Books of Occult Philosophy* is the single most important text in the history of Western occultism. Occultists and magicians have been drawing upon its vast storehouse of magical lore for five centuries, although they seldom if ever credit their source. For example, Francis Barrett's *Magus* is a wonderful book only because it is made up of a direct plagiarism of *part* of the *Occult Philosophy,* with some additional material attributed to Agrippa (the apocryphal *Fourth Book of Occult Philosophy)* thrown in at the end. The Golden Dawn systems of the Kabbalah, geomancy, elements, and seals and squares of the planets are all taken in large measure from Agrippa. Though countless writers have borrowed from the text, the *Occult Philosophy* has never been reprinted in its entirety, except in limited facsimile editions, since 1651.

The reason the book has not been made into a new edition is simple—it required a herculean effort to correct the hundreds of errors, most of which were reproduced in both the English edition of 1651 and the Latin edition in the *Opera* of around 1600. These errors could only be corrected by understanding the material completely: not only what was present in the text, but what *should* be, and *should not* be, present.

For the first time in 500 years (first Latin edition, Antwerp, 1531), the seals, sigils, and magic squares of the planets, which are universally used in modern magic, are correctly given, and their structure and construction fully explained. For the first time the complex Hebrew tables of the practical Kabbalah are accurately drawn. For the first time the geomantic figures are corrected and truly represented.

Agrippa drew upon the Egyptian, Greek, Roman, Arabic and Jewish writers who had gone before him. The *Occult Philosophy* is the most complete repository of Pagan and Neoplatonic magic ever compiled. The countless references to magic in, and exhaustive quotations from, classical literature lead the careful reader through the ancient world of the occult and provide the basis for what amounts to a doctoral degree in classical occultism. This book is the source, and represents the crossroads between the ancient and modern worlds of magic.

In addition to the value of Agrippa's text, the copious notes make difficult references understandable, give the origin of quotations, and expand upon many of them, so that Agrippa's work is not only available but accessible as well. All the herbs, stones, beasts, monsters, gods, spirits, places, stars, symbols, ancient writers, and occult practices mentioned by Agrippa are set forth in the notes using the same sources that were available to Agrippa himself to illuminate them. In this way the reader is given valuable insights into the thought processes of Agrippa.

An extensive set of appendices on such subjects as the elements, the magic squares, the practical Kabbalah, geomancy, the humors, and the Soul of the World provide background on the more important matters treated in the text. The Biographical Dictionary gives a short biography of each of the hundreds of writers and historical figures referred to by Agrippa, and the Geographical Dictionary does the same for the rivers, nations, cities, mountains, and other places, many of which no longer exist or now carry different names. The General Index will prove invaluable to all serious readers, as it allows immediate reference to every topic touched upon in the text, notes and appendices.

All occultists and magicians need this book, because the corrections contained in its pages render obsolete many of their magical names and sigils. Without it they cannot know if they have accurately drawn a square, or correctly spelled the name of a spirit. Likewise, it is a necessary reference tool for all scholarly students of the Renaissance, Neoplatonism, and Western Kabbalah, the history of ideas and sciences, and the occult tradition.

LLEWELLYN'S SOURCEBOOK SERIES

Three Books of Occult Philosophy

written by Henry Cornelius
Agrippa of Nettesheim

Completely Annotated, with
Modern Commentary

The Foundation Book
of Western Occultism

Translated by James Freake

Edited and Annotated by
Donald Tyson

2003
Llewellyn Publications
St. Paul, MN 55164-0383, U.S.A.

FIRST EDITION
Sixth Printing, 2003

Library of Congress Cataloging in Publication Data
Agrippa von Nettesheim, Heinrich Cornelius, 1486?–1535
    [De occulta philosophia. English]
    Three books of occult philosophy / by Henry Cornelius Agrippa of Nettesheim, completely
annotated with modern commentary ; translated by James Freake ; edited and annotated by
Donald Tyson.
       p. cm. — (Llewellyn's sourcebook series)
    "The foundation book of western occultism."
    Includes bibliographical references and indexes.
    ISBN 0-87542-832-0 : $29.95
    1. Magic—Early works to 1800.   2. Occultism—Early works to 1800.
I. Tyson, Donald, 1954–   . II. Freake, James. III. Title. IV. Series.
BF1600.A3613   1992
133—dc20   92-33147
          CIP

Llewellyn Worldwide does not participate in, endorse, or have any authority or responsibility concerning private business transactions
between our authors and the public.

All mail addressed to the author is forwarded but the publisher cannot, unless specifically instructed by the author, give out an address or
phone number.

Llewellyn Publications
A Division of Llewellyn Worldwide, Ltd.
P.O. Box 64383, St. Paul, MN 55164-0383
www.llewellyn.com

Printed in the United States of America

Llewellyn's Sourcebook Series

Llewellyn's "Sourcebooks" are designed to be *resource files for esoteric technicians.*

For some readers, it may at first seem strange to apply the word "technology" to the concept of esotericism. Technology is basically how-to knowledge, and esotericism (by whatever name) is *True Sacred Living.* We publish many practical books that teach the reader "how to" in many areas of the esoteric sciences. These are the techniques, the practical programming, the procedures to follow in working toward a particular accomplishment, the *modus operandi.*

But the *technician of the Sacred* needs more than the knowledge of the method of operation. He or she also has to have basic information about the materials that will be utilized, or about the beings that will be invoked, or the tools to be used. And this information must be organized and presented from a sound, esoteric foundation.

Sourcebooks may be presented in the form of dictionaries, encylopedias, anthologies, or new editions of classical works. Always, we produce these to actually meet the needs of the esoteric practitioner and student. They bring to the reader *what* he or she needs to know in order to apply the *how-to* knowledge gained from text and guide books.

A sourcebook is the distillation of factual knowledge from dozens of books and sources (sometimes veritable libraries) compounded with the practical experience of the author. No one can do an adequate job of gathering such factual knowledge unless they are themselves expert in the field represented.

As publishers, we seek to provide the student with three out of the four vital elements essential to the sacred life: theoretical knowledge, practical knowledge, and factual knowledge. The fourth element can only come as the student brings these together, and gains experiential knowledge. These four kinds of knowledge then become the *pillars of wisdom.*

Other Books by Donald Tyson

Rune Magic, 1988
The Truth About Ritual Magic, 1989
The Truth About Runes, 1989
How to Make and Use a Magic Mirror, 1990
Ritual Magic, 1991
The Messenger, 1993
Tetragrammaton, 1995
New Millennium Magic, 1996 (Originally published as *The New Magus, 1988)*
Scrying for Beginners, 1997
The Tortuous Serpent (fiction), 1997
Enochian Magic for Beginners, 1997

Cards and Kits

Rune Magic Deck, 1988
Power of the Runes Kit, 1989

Forthcoming

Sexual Alchemy, 2000

Dedication

To my mother,
Ida Tyson
for her unfailing support.

Acknowledgements

I wish to sincerely thank all those authors and publishers who have allowed me to use quotations from works still under copyright. These have made the notes far more lively and useful than would otherwise have been the case. Acknowledgement is due for extracts from:

The Odyssey of Homer translated by Richmond Lattimore. Copyright ©1965 by Richmond Lattimore. Reprinted by permission of Harper Collins Publishers Inc.

The Iliad of Homer translated by Richmond Lattimore. Copyright ©1951 by The University of Chicago. Reprinted by permission of the University of Chicago Press.

Kabbalah by Gershom Scholem. Copyright ©1974 by Keter Publishing House Jerusalem Ltd. Reprinted by permission of Keter Publishing House.

The White Goddess by Robert Graves. Copyright ©1948 and renewal copyright ©1975 by Robert Graves. Reprinted by permission of Farrar, Straus and Giroux, Inc.

Pharsalia by Lucan, translated by Robert Graves. Copyright ©1961 by Robert Graves. Reprinted by permission of A. P. Watt Ltd. on behalf of the Executors of the Estate of Robert Graves.

Ptolemy: Tetrabiblos translated by F. E. Robbins. Reprinted by permission of The Loeb Classical Library, Harvard University Press, 1940.

Mathematics Useful for Understanding Plato by Theon of Smyrna, translated by Robert and Deborah Lawlor. Copyright ©1978 by Wizards Bookshelf. Reprinted by permission of Wizards Bookshelf.

Shamanism: Archaic Techniques of Ecstacy by Mircea Eliade, translated by Willard R. Trask. Bollingen Series LXXVI. Copyright ©1964 by Princeton University Press. Reprinted by permission of Princeton University Press.

Eleusis and the Eleusinian Mysteries by George E. Mylonas. Copyright ©1961 by Princeton University Press. Reprinted by permission of Princeton University Press.

The Survival of the Pagan Gods: The Mythological Tradition and Its Place in Renaissance Humanism and Art by Jean Seznec, translated by Barbara F. Sessions. Bollingen Series XXXVIII. Copyright ©1953 by Princeton University Press. Reprinted by permission of Princeton University Press.

Contents

To the R...

by Donald Tyson

diting and annotating the *Three Books of Occult Philosophy* was a monumental task. It was necessary to reconstruct and redraw, or at least amend, every one of the tables and illustrations, often with no guide, since the errors in the English edition were transcribed from their Latin model. Modern works such as *The Magus* of Barrett were no help—these works simply carried on the same errors. Fortunately by examining the interior logic of the structures it was possible to correct them, perhaps the first time this has been done anywhere in the 500-year history of the work.

All the names of pharmacological herbs, magical stones, obscure or forgotten places and long dead authorities were traced down and verified, wherever this was possible. Some names are hopelessly corrupt, or found in works existing only in manuscript or in rare Latin or Greek copies. Sometimes there is not sufficient information given to determine which authority Agrippa means. Occasionally Agrippa refers to works that no longer exist, although it is difficult to be sure of these, as there are many manuscripts in European libraries virtually unknown even to scholars.

In compiling the notes I have first tried to quote the actual sources Agrippa himself had before him as he was writing; then I have favored classical works that were probably available to him; then works contemporary with Agrippa that give the flavor of his age; and last

modern works that contribute some useful bit of information.

To the best of my ability I have tracked down and given exact page references to those works quoted or alluded to in the text. Where Agrippa's quotations are obscure or incomplete, I have quoted the same work in the notes for purposes of comparison. It was my goal to put before the reader in this volume as much of the source material Agrippa drew upon as could be compressed into so small a space, and to refer accurately to those sources that could not, or need not, be quoted in the notes. My purpose in including such copious notes is that the serious reader may be able to consider the text in the context of its classical allusions without the vexing and time-consuming labor of researching the references.

Inevitably there have been omissions. It was not possible in the time and with the resources available to me to track down and verify every one of Agrippa's hundreds of sources. The reader may rest assured that it was not for lack of trying, and where a question arises in his mind, it probably arose beforehand in the mind of the editor, who found it impossible to answer.

There are so many classical, semimythical and historical figures referred to, it was deemed useful to collect them at the back of the book and give a short biography for each. I have tried in these biographical sketches to touch upon the matter for which Agrippa brings up their names. Likewise the many references to obscure places

...or
in the ancient wo...... if he
ined with reg...... g the so-called
located on...... ....ases.
believes ......ave been included to illu-
tried to.....topics Agrippa may only have
autho...
......pon, such as the Soul of the World,
.....lements, the humors, geomancy, the esoteric Hebrew doctrine of emanations, and so on.
In Appendix V the magic squares and seals,
along with the related sigils of their spirits, have
been explained and accurately represented,
again perhaps for the first time anywhere. The
use of these sigils is virtually universal in modern occultism, but always the errors were simply copied, because those who use and transmit
them do not know what they mean or how to
make them. This single appendix will justify
many times over the purchase of this book for
those seriously interested in Western magic.

Indeed, so many errors that have been
handed down in the Western occult tradition for
centuries are here corrected for the first time, no
true student of the Art can afford not to possess
this book. I make no boast in saying this—it is a
simple fact. These corrections are too many to

......on, but I have tried to point out the more
significant ones in the notes.

The editor makes no pretense of omni-
science. On many occasions I have keenly felt
my lack of Latin, Greek and Hebrew. Some of
my astrological analysis is conjectural since I
am by no means an expert on ancient astrology.
It is highly unlikely the information provided in
the notes and appendices is error free. I ask forgiveness for any mistakes that may have crept
in, mistakes which I regret at least as much as
the reader.

Despite the great labor of this work, I have
valued every hour of it, because it has given me
what I hope it will give the serious reader—the
equivalent to a graduate degree in Renaissance
magic. This, I suspect, was Agrippa's intention.
He leads the reader from one subject to another, through one classical authority after another, until a fund of knowledge is accumulated
that encompasses the entire scope of neoclassi-
cal and Hebraic occultism, both theoretical and
practical, as it was understood during the latter
Middle Ages. Agrippa knew he could never
compress the entire literature of magic into a
single volume, so he pointed the way. The
reader will derive inestimable profit in following his direction.

The Life of Agrippa

Henricus Cornelius Agrippa von Nettesheim was born on September 14, 1486, in the German city of Cologne. His family, the von Nettesheims, were minor nobility who had served the royal house of Austria for generations. When Agrippa was born his father was engaged in this service, and Agrippa himself mentions in his letters (epistle 18, bk. 6; epistle 21, bk. 7)* that as a boy he aspired to nothing higher than to assist the new German emperor Maximilian I, who had succeeded his father Emperor Frederick III in 1493, when Agrippa was seven.

The name Agrippa was uncommon in those times. There are two possible explanations for it. Aulus Gellius (*Noctes Atticae* 16.16) says that the word "agrippa" was coined by the Romans to signify a child born feet first and the difficulty experienced by the mother at such a birth. It was used this way by the Romans, and there is evidence that this usage was adopted in later times by European scholars and nobility who were anxious to display their classical learning. The name may have been given to the infant von Nettesheim to commemorate the manner of his birth.

The other possibility involves the city of Cologne, which arose on the site of the chief town of the Ubii called Oppidum (or Civitas Ubiorum). The wife of the Emperor Claudius,

Agrippina, was born here, and in the year 51 caused a Roman colony to be established in the town, which was named Colonia Agrippina, or Agrippinesis, in her honor. The inhabitants were called Agrippinenses. Nettesheim, or Nettersheim, was a small hamlet about 25 miles southwest of Cologne, but it was Cologne that served as residence for the family von Nettesheim when they were not actually present at the imperial court. Since it was the custom for names to indicate place of origin, Agrippa may have been given to stand for Cologne, the true family home.

Agrippa dropped the first and last parts of his name—I am almost inclined to say the German half—and in his writings refers to himself only as Cornelius Agrippa.

As a boy Agrippa showed a precocious intellect and became the talk of the town when he refused to speak anything but Latin. His talent for languages was assisted by an unusually retentive memory. It is likely that the studies of this son of a noble family destined for the imperial court were supervised, at least indirectly, by the Archbishop of Cologne.

He himself confides in a letter (epistle 23, bk. 1) that at a very early age he was possessed by curiosity concerning the mysteries. This interest in secret things may have been romantically heightened by the historical shadow of the great occult scholar and reputed master magician, Albertus Magnus (1193–1280), who taught philosophy, and was buried, at Cologne.

---

*All letter references are to volume 2 of the Latin *Opera* published at Lyons.

He writes to Theodoricus, Bishop of Cyrene, that one of the first books on magic he ever studied was Albertus' *Speculum*.

It would have been easy for a bold and wealthy youth to gain possession of the forbidden grimoires of magic in such a great trading and scholastic center.

On July 22, 1499, he enrolled in the faculty of Arts at the University of Cologne under Petrus Capitis de Dunnen, and on March 14, 1502, received his licentiate in Arts. His other formal degrees are regarded as uncertain but seem not improbable. Agrippa claimed to possess doctorates in canon and civil law, as well as medicine, but the exact times and places these were earned remains a matter for speculation.

Agrippa writes (epistle 21, bk. 7) that he served the Emperor Maximilian first as a secretary, then as a soldier. The events of the early period in his court life are obscure. He was the kind of youth likely to appeal to the intellectual and physically bold Maximilian. At the age of 20 he appears at the University of Paris, ostensibly as a student, but perhaps in reality as a diplomatic spy and instrument for the ever continuing intrigues of the Emperor. Agrippa's language skills, his quick wit, and his undoubted loyalty made him a perfect choice for such a mission.

While at Paris, Agrippa gathered around him, as he was often to do later in life, a group of scholars pursuing studies into the occult mysteries. It was among this band that the incredible scheme was hatched which was so influential to his later life. One of his fellow students, the Spaniard Juanetin de Gerona (or in the Latinized form, Ianotus Bascus de Charona) had been driven out of the district of Terragon by a local peasant revolt. It was decided that he would be returned to power in Terragon, and would out of gratitude ally himself with Maximilian I against his own king, Ferdinand of Spain, in effect becoming a traitor. The full details of the plot cannot be known, and only with difficulty imagined—the politics of the period were unbelievably convoluted. The following account of the adventure from Morley's *Life of Agrippa* is conjectural, and no later biographer has been able to fix the geography of the affair with certainty.

Agrippa wrote to a friend at court, who heartily encouraged the intrigue (epistle 4, bk. 1), but it is not clear whether the emperor himself knew of it. The heart of the scheme was a bold plan to seize the impregnable Black Fort (Fuerto Negro) which stood on a height overlooking the town of Tarragon. This was to be held until reinforcements arrived to quell the local Catalonian uprising. The fort could not be taken by a direct assault, but was to be seized through subterfuge by a small band led by Agrippa and others. Agrippa was the mastermind and central mover of this entire affair.

Just before the attempt, which took place in the summer of 1508, Agrippa had serious doubts about the worthiness of his fellow conspirators and the loyalty of the courtiers of Maximilian, who where all too ready to throw one of their own to the wolves of fortune at the least sign of weakness. More distressing perhaps to a young man of spotless honor were the methods to be employed: "But with a profligate conscience to wish to continue in such cruel devices, which after all have more in them of crime than of high daring, and for the sake of the rage of one ill-advised prince to expose ourselves to universal hatred, would be utterly impious and mad" (epistle 5, bk. 1).

How did Agrippa and his small band of conspirators seize this impregnable fortress, erected in the misty past by the Celts? It is tempting to speculate that magic was involved, since this was so much the center of Agrippa's intellectual life at the time. The taking of the fort probably shared at least one element in common with a stage illusion—once the trick is known, the onlooker tends to hold it in contempt for its simplicity. Kidnapping, bribery, lies—it is impossible to know the actions of the plan. Somehow Agrippa and his men gained complete command of Fuerto Negro.

Having captured the fort, it is not clear the conspirators had any idea of what to do with it. Agrippa was sent with a small force to garrison the house of Gerona at Villarodona, a small town in the province of Tarragon. Gerona himself left for Barcelona to gain assistance, but on the road was captured by the rebels. After many days waiting anxiously without word for his return, Agrippa was informed of his capture, and told that the house would soon be laid under siege. It was impossible to defend the house with so small a band against a large determined force. Agrippa prudently decided to abandon it, and moved to an old stone tower three miles away which was almost completely surrounded by water, and much easier to fortify.

Hardly was he well settled within the walls when the peasant army attacked it. But Agrippa had chosen well. The peasants settled doggedly in for a long siege, determined to capture "the German," as they called Agrippa, blaming his black arts for the massacre of the garrison of Fuerto Negro. Weeks passed. It was necessary to get a message out in order to make an escape across the marsh and lake that lay behind the tower, but this was impossible by ordinary means.

Agrippa hit upon the device of disguising the son of the keeper of the tower as a leper, and so effective was this ruse, the boy was able to leave the tower and return with an answer from the Archbishop of Tarragon, who was opposed to the rebel cause, without once being challenged. In the dark of night the beleaguered band descended the tower in the rear and waited until the morning of August 14, 1508, when at 9 o'clock two fishing boats carried them to safety across the lake.

To the peasants this escape, so daring and unexpected, must have appeared more than natural. It nurtured the legend of Agrippa's unholy power, which at that time was only beginning to take root.

A demoralized Agrippa seems to have washed his hands once and for all both of the still unresolved intrigue in Tarragon, and all political machinations in general. After a stay of nine or ten days in the safety of the abbey, on August 24, 1508, he set out to travel and see more of the world, while at the same time seeking news of his scattered associates. He was in no hurry to return to the court of Maximilian. Indeed, his opinion of court service never recovered from the disillusioning effect of the Tarragon enterprise.

He traveled first to Barcelona, then to Valantia where he met with the astrologer Camparatus Saracenus, a disciple of Zacutus. Selling his horses, he sailed to Italy, stopping at the Balearic Islands and Sardinia, then Naples. From Naples he took ship to France. All the way he continued to write letters and make inquiries about the fate of the members of his Paris circle. At Avignon he was forced to pause for a time to earn money, his travels having exhausted his financial resources. In a letter he expressed his wish to draw once again his companions from Paris around him: "Nothing now remains but that, after so many dangers, we insist upon a meeting of out brother combatants, and absolve ourselves from the oaths of our confederacy, that we may recover our old state of fellowship and have it unmolested" (epistle 9, bk. 1).

There can be little doubt that the Paris circle was more than just a political marriage of convenience. It was an occult brotherhood of young men drawn around Agrippa by his knowledge of, and enthusiasm for, the mysteries of magic and religion. Although the term "Rosicrucianism" has no meaning before its appearance in a pamphlet published in Cassel, Germany in 1614, Agrippa's group of aspirants might be looked upon as a prototype for this movement. Magic for Agrippa was the highest and most sacred of disciplines, capable of transforming the soul. He would certainly have communicated this belief to his followers, and would never have tolerated anything less than reverence toward the study of the magical arts.

This was a time of intense debate and study of the mysteries for Agrippa. Even when his friends could not be with him, they referred others with a similar interest as potential members of the brotherhood: "The bearer of these letters," writes one friend to Agrippa, "is a German, native of Nuremberg, but dwelling at Lyons; and he is a curious inquirer after hidden mysteries, a free man, restrained by no fetters, who, impelled by I know not what rumour concerning you, desires to sound your depths" (epistle 11, bk. 1).

When he was financially able Agrippa rode to Lyons, where his friends awaited him, and

continued his studies, which at this time probably centered on the learning of Hebrew and the
Kabbalah from the works of Johannes Reuchlin:
De verbo mirifico, published in Germany in
1494, and Reuchlin's Hebrew grammar and dictionary, published in 1506. Reuchlin had an
enormous influence at that time on such minds
as Erasmus and Luther. His writings set the
philosophical tone of the Reformation.

At the age of 23 Agrippa was reveling in the
first golden flush of his intellectual maturity. He
had already gathered the notes for his *Occult
Philosophy.* Filled to overflowing with the wisdom of Reuchlin, he decided to give a series of
lectures on the *Mirific Word* in the summer of
1509 at the University of Dole. The lectures
were delivered free of charge to the general public in honor of Princess Margaret, the daughter
of the emperor Maximilian I. She was then 29
years old, and had been appointed by her father
governor over the Netherlands, Burgundy and
the Charolais, making her mistress of Dole. The
princess was renowned for her patronage of
learning, and more importantly from Agrippa's
point of view, for her generosity towards the arts
and letters. Agrippa found it prudent to open the
lectures with a panegyric on Margaret herself. A
friend made certain that a copy of the tribute
found its way to Margaret's court.

Although Agrippa could not have known it,
this was the most promising and perhaps the happiest time of his life. His lectures met with universal acclaim. The university conferred upon
him a professorship of theology and voted him a
stipend. Men traveled from distant places merely
to converse with him about arcane subjects.

To cement the favor of Princess Margaret,
Agrippa wrote in 1509 *De nobilitate et præcel-
lentia fœminei sexus* (The nobility of the female
sex and the superiority of women over men).
This contains sentiments that would endear
Agrippa to the feminists of the present century:

> . . . the tyranny of men prevailing over
> divine right and the laws of nature, slays by
> law the liberty of women, abolishes it by
> use and custom, extinguishes it by educa-
> tion. For the woman, as soon as she is born,
> is from her earliest years detained at home

in idleness, and as if destitute of capacity
for higher occupations, is permitted to conceive of nothing beyond needle and thread.
Then when she has attained years of
puberty she is delivered over to the jealous
empire of a man, or shut up for ever in a
shop of vestals. The law also forbids her to
fill public offices. No prudence entitles her
to plead in open court. (Quoted by Morley
1856, 1:109)

Also in 1509 and early 1510 Agrippa wrote
the first draft of his *Three Books of Occult Philosophy,* which he sent off to be read and criticized by the Abbot Johannes Trithemius, then
abbot of Saint James at Wurtzburg. Formerly
abbot of the Benedictine monastery of Saint
Martin at Sponheim (or Spannheim), in October
of 1506 he had become head of the abbey of
Saint James at Wurtzburg. According to Henry
Morley, Agrippa became acquainted with
Trithemius there upon his return from Spain
(Morley 1:214).

Of the *Occult Philosophy* Frances A. Yates
writes: "It was dedicated to Trithemius, who was
undoubtedly an important influence on
Agrippa's studies." (Yates 1983, 38). Although I
have no way of proving it based on the information I have been able to collect concerning the
life of Agrippa, I believe this is an understate-
ment. The tone of the letters between the abbot
and Agrippa, the nature of Trithemius' own
writings, the fact that he left some of those writings to Agrippa after he died, the harmony that
existed between the minds of the two men, all
lead me to believe that Trithemius was
Agrippa's mystical master and teacher, particularly in the branch of magic dealing with spirit
evocation. It would not surprise me to learn that
the two had corresponded, and even met, long
before 1508, perhaps even when Agrippa was a
youth living in Cologne. When his early interest
in magic began to quicken it would have been
natural for him to seek out the acknowledged
master of his art at Spanheim. It must be stressed
that all this is only conjecture on my part.

It was about this time that Agrippa's fortunes were to take a serious turn for the worse.
Had he been less honest and noble of mind he
might have anticipated it. The chief of the Fran-

ciscan monks in Burgundy, named John Catilinet, was chosen to deliver the Lenten sermons
of 1510 before Princess Margaret at Ghent. He
took as his subject the lectures on Reuchlin
delivered at Dole, and attacked both the ideas
expressed and their enthusiastic young exponent as impious. Margaret was strongly Christian. Whatever good opinion she may have
formed at a distance about Agrippa was poisoned. In that century it was always dangerous
to champion the Jews before the conservative
Church, which still blamed them for the crucifixion of Christ.

Whether Margaret had read the panegyric
to her is uncertain—it was sent to her court, but
this does not mean she saw it. She had not yet
read Agrippa's treatise *On the Pre-eminence of
Women*, which would not be published until
1532. Its publication was delayed so long
because of the unfavorable opinion created in
Margaret's mind toward Agrippa by the Franciscan monk. Had she been able to read it, the
bold ideas it contained might have softened her
hostility, but this was not to be. Agrippa had
lost, at least for the present, the one patron he
had earnestly sought above all others.

Unwillingly he was compelled to turn away
from the path of a scholar and return once again
to that of a diplomat in the court of Maximilian.
Late in the summer or early in the autumn of
1510 he was sent as ambassador to the court of
Henry VIII in London. Agrippa lodged in the
town of Stepney, near London, at the house of
Dean Colet, Dean of Saint Paul's. Here, when
not distracted by court duties—which seem to
have consisted of masquing, tournament displays, wrestling, and other amusements—he
found a congenial spirit and engaged in a serious study of the Epistles of Saint Paul under the
guidance of the good Dean.

It was during this period, I believe, that
Agrippa began to temper his enthusiasm for
magic and occult studies with a growing fervor
for the truths of Christianity. He had never been
lacking in piety, but the glamour of magic had
made the virtues of his own faith seem pale by
comparison. Now, with the example of a genuine Christian, Dean Colet, constantly before

him, Agrippa began to reassess the teachings of
Christ. The passion of his nature provoked, at
least for a short time, a revulsion against the
pagan beliefs he had not long before regarded as
the most sacred. This ambivalence between
Christian and pagan teachings persisted
throughout the rest of his life.

During this visit to England he must have
traveled to Stonehenge, or some other neolithic
site, as he mentions "heaps of stones, which I
saw in England put together by an incredible
art." *(Occult Philosophy,* 2.1). At the house of
Dean Colet he wrote an *Expostulation* on the
condemnation of his *Exposition on the Mirific
Word,* addressing it to John Catilinet, presumably to little effect. It was not likely to engender
by its tone a forgiving frame of mind in the
Franciscan monk, as this brief extract shows:

> But you to whom I was utterly unknown,
> who were never present at one lecture, and
> never heard me elsewhere speaking pri-
> vately about these things—who never, so
> far as I know, have seen me—yet have
> dared to utter against me an unjust opinion,
> that had better been omitted, and might
> have been, and ought to have been, not
> only because it is most false, but also
> because it is not fit that a religious man
> should disseminate among most serious
> and sacred Christian congregations such
> calumnies and contumelies, and they alto-
> gether misbecome the divine office of a
> preacher. (Quoted by Morley 1:244)

There is some reason to believe that
Agrippa was on a secret mission while in England. He speaks of his "most secret purpose"
(Opera 2.596). This is not unlikely given the
constant intrigues of Maximilian. Morley speculates that it was Agrippa's task to sow the seeds
of distrust in the mind of King Henry against
Pope Julius II (Morley 1:229), but it seems to
me that Maximilian was not so naive as to
believe that Henry could be swayed by the
words of a young German diplomat in so serious
a matter—unless Maximilian expected Agrippa
to use black arts to move the mind of the king.

In 1511 Agrippa returned to Cologne. He
delivered a series of lectures called *Quodlibetal*
on various subjects of divinity at Cologne Uni-

versity, indicating that his heart was still bent on scholastic pursuits. About this time the fury of orthodox theologians against Reuchlin and the Jews was reaching its fanatical peak in Cologne. Jewish books were being gathered up and burned in wholesale lots. Agrippa would certainly have found much matter for lively debate.

It is therefore surprising that in the spring or early summer of 1511 he enters military service. It may be that honor compelled him to offer his sword. Or perhaps he had some other plan—he writes to a friend (epistle 30, bk. 1) about the possibility of securing for them both professorships at the Italian University of Pavia. For the present this remained an idle dream. It was Captain Agrippa's immediate task to convey 1000 gold pieces from Trent to the military camp of Maximilian at Verona. This he accomplished without incident.

Of his other military service in the Italian wars little is certain, save that Agrippa was a very unhappy soldier. He writes: "I was for several years by the Emperor's command, and by my calling, a soldier. I followed the camp of the Emperor and the [French] King: in many conflicts gave no sluggish help: before my face went death, and I followed, the minstrel of death, my right hand soaked in blood, my left dividing spoil: my belly was filled with prey, and the way of my feet was over corpses of the slain: so I was made forgetful of my innermost honour, and wrapped round fifteenfold in Tartarean shade" (epistle 19, bk. 2).

In 1511, or perhaps the year following, he received his knighthood in the field. It is not known what service or feat of arms drew this reward.

Wars at that time were seasonal affairs. In late summer of 1511 Agrippa was chosen to act as theologist at the Council of Pisa, convened by King Louis XII of France and Emperor Maximilian I of Germany, ostensibly to reform ecclesiastical abuses, but really to defy the authority of Pope Julius II. Agrippa was a natural choice to represent Germany since he was in Italy (not a popular travel destination for the German bishops in that war year) and well known as a skilled orator. Along with all the others who attended

the Council, he risked excommunication. He took advantage of the occasion to lecture on Plato at the University of Pisa. When the Council was moved to Milan, Agrippa returned to military service, not much discomfited by the order of excommunication declared against him and his fellow Council members.

The fortunes of Pope Julius brightened toward the end of 1511, and Maximilian found it expedient to abandon Louis and to throw in with Henry VIII, who was at the time preparing to invade France. Agrippa refused to leave the soldiers who had fought beside him so many months. He stayed in Italy with a small force of German soldiers and battled with the French against the Swiss and Venetian armies of the Pope at Pavia, waiting for a specific command from the emperor that he quit Italy before abandoning them. There was nothing traitorous in this decision. It was Maximilian who injured his honor, not Agrippa.

Around the first of July, 1512, Agrippa was taken prisoner near Pavia by the Swiss, along with a force of about 300 German soldiers. He obtained his freedom, perhaps with the help of his new patron, William Palaeologus, the Marquis of Monferrat. At the end of November he formally attached himself to the service of the marquis, which he could do since the goals of the marquis were then in harmony with those of Emperor Maximilian, and settled in Monferrat's chief town of Casale.

In February 1513, when the aged Julius II died, the new pope, Leo X, sent a letter to Agrippa through his secretary revoking his excommunication. Military demands upon Agrippa were sporadic. He had been made captain of a troop of soldiers under Maximilian Sforza, the new Duke of Milan, but there was little fighting. For the next two years he served his masters more in the capacity of diplomat than soldier.

In the summer of 1515, with the blessing of his patron Monferrat, Agrippa delivered a series of lectures on the *Pymander* of Hermes Trismegistus at the University of Pavia, of which the introductory oration alone has survived. According to Morley, these met with such applause that the university conferred upon him doctorates of divinity, law and medicine.

During this time in Pavia, Agrippa seems to have married his first wife, a native of the town. Morley, who confuses the first with the second wife of Agrippa, says that she was a native of Geneva wed by Agrippa on his journey from Italy to France in 1509, but Nauert, who presumably is in a position to know better, confidently states that the first wife of Agrippa, whom he does not name, was of a noble family of Pavia, and that the earliest mention of the marriage occurs in a letter dated November 24, 1515 (see epistle 48, bk. 1). Although not much is said of her, it is apparent that Agrippa loved her deeply.

His happiness at this stage in his life can only be imagined. Secure in a faithful patron, performing the work that he most loved, blessed with a loving wife and two children, a boy and a girl, with no immediate prospect of military service, it was a golden time, bittersweet in its briefness. Years later Agrippa would write of his wife:

> I give innumerable thanks to the omnipotent God, who has joined me to a wife after my heart; a maiden noble and well-mannered, young, beautiful, who lives so much in harmony with all my habits, that never has a word of scolding dropped between us, and wherein I count myself happiest of all, however our affairs change, in prosperity and adversity always alike kind to me, alike affable, constant; most just in mind and sound in counsel, always self-possessed. (Epistle 19, bk. 2)

Some men seem destined never to secure a lasting peace and security. In the same year Agrippa was winning fame for his Pavia lectures, Louis XII of France died. His successor, Francis I, invaded Milan. Once more Agrippa was forced against his will to put on the mantle of a soldier in defense of his new master, Maximilian Sforza. At the battle of Marignano, which took place September 14, 1515, the Swiss and Italian forces of Maximilian, Agrippa with them, were routed by the French and the Venetian reinforcements. Power in Pavia passed to the French. Agrippa found that he could no longer lecture at the university. His military pay ceased.

The state of Agrippa's mind is clearly demonstrated by this letter:

> Either for our impiety, or through the usual influence of the celestial bodies, or by the providence of God, who governs all, so great a plague of arms, or pestilence of soldiers, is everywhere raging, that one can scarcely live secure even in hollows of the mountains. Whither, I ask, in these suspected times, shall I betake myself with my wife and son and family, when home and household goods are gone from us at Pavia, and we have been despoiled of nearly all that we possess, except a few things that were rescued. My spirit is sore, and my heart is disturbed within me, because the enemy has persecuted my soul, and humbled my life to the dust. I have thought over my lost substance, the money spent, the stipend lost, our no income, the dearness of everything, and the future threatening worse evils than the present; and I have praised the dead rather than the living, nor have I found one to console me. But turning back upon myself I have reflected that wisdom is stronger than all, and have said, Lord what am I that thou shouldst be mindful of me, or that thou shouldst visit me with mercy? (Epistle 49, bk. 1)

To repay the Marquis of Monferrat for his continuing support during these dangerous shifting political times, Agrippa dedicated to him two works, the *Dialogue on Man* and the *Triple Way of Knowing God*. The first has not survived.

During 1516 he lived with his family at Casale under the patronage of the marquis while his friends made strenuous efforts on his behalf to find him a place and an income. To occupy his time he gave lectures in theology at the university of Turin. They may have centered on the epistles of Saint Paul, to which Agrippa devoted so much study during his stay in England. Finally in the summer of 1517 Agrippa joined the court of the Duke of Savoy, Charles III, called the Gentle, who was half-brother to Philibert, the late husband of Margaret of Austria. Although he had no training or experience in practical medicine, he served as court physician. Monferrat had close blood ties with the ducal house of Savoy. At this time Germany and France were at peace.

One cannot help thinking that given the crude state of medicine in the period, Agrippa with his practical German mind and vast knowledge of natural magic would have made a better physician than many trained up in the profession from childhood. In some respects he resembles his contemporary, Paracelsus. Impatient with accepted platitudes, he sought to wrest living truth from the past with ancient texts, and the future through experiment. But Agrippa had no love for leechcraft. It was necessity that drove him to represent himself as a healer.

One of his friends took a dim view of his new appointment and wrote to express his misgivings in terms that proved all too prophetic. Of Agrippa's position in the court of Savoy he says:

> I do not praise it; you will be offered little pay, and get it at the day of judgement. I have sent repeated letters to the governor of Grenoble, by the hand of his own nephew, and am hoping soon to get an answer; after which, if you permit me, I will arrange and settle everything. In the mean time, so manage with the Duke of Savoy as not to close your way to richer fortune. (Epistle 5, bk. 2)

Why did Agrippa not send word of his situation to his father, or return with his family to Cologne? Pride kept him from writing. Having gone to Italy to make his fortune, he could not bear to return a beaten man begging for charity. His friends and relatives at Cologne heard nothing from him during this time, and naturally assumed that he had been killed in the Italian wars.

Although Agrippa labored as physician for the Duke of Savoy through the summer and into the fall of 1517, he was not paid anything. The Duke had yet to fix upon an appropriate wage. It may be assumed that Agrippa gained his bread by treating patients on the side, and performing the work of a scholar, writing letters, drawing up legal documents, and so on. Toward the end of November the duke at last set a figure on Agrippa's services. It was so low, Agrippa not only declined to accept the office, but would

not touch the back pay for his months of service that was rightfully his.

Fortunately an opening had been found for him as orator and advocate in the German town of Metz. Fortified by this good news, Agrippa was at last able to reconcile his pride and his shame, and returned to Cologne with his family to assure his parents that he was prospering. To his surprise he discovered that they had been mourning his death at the hands of the French at Pavia.

After visiting with his family for several months he went with his wife and son to take up his official duties at Metz. His daughter, who would have been only an infant, is not mentioned, but certainly accompanied them. Upon arrival Agrippa presented himself before the magistrates of Metz. His brief speech to them, which extols the town of Metz and explains his own background, has been preserved. Also extant are three orations he later wrote while in his official position. These are workmanlike but prosaic documents.

No doubt Agrippa had more pleasure in writing a treatise *On Original Sin,* which he completed a few months after settling in Metz in 1518. He probably also wrote his short work *Of Geomancy* during his stay at Metz—at least, it was among his papers there. Around this time a friend, Theodoric, Bishop of Cyrene, wrote asking Agrippa to suggest a prescription against the plague. He responded with the brief tract *Securest Antidotes Against the Plague.* It shows that he would have made a good physician. The best protection, he says, is to leave the city until the plague is over. If you cannot leave, your residence and clothing should be purified with the heat and smoke of a blazing fire. It is good to wash the hands and face often in vinegar and rosewater, and to suffumigate the house with rue beaten in vinegar, inhaling the vapor and allowing it to pass over the whole body and clothes. Many of the other remedies he gives would be worthless, but these few, at least, make some sense.

Agrippa traveled from Metz to Cologne in 1518, probably to be at the bedside of his ailing father. When he returned to Metz he received a letter from his mother informing him of his father's death. He was deeply moved:

I grieve most vehemently, and find but a single solice for this grief, that we must yield to the divine ordinance; for I know that God bestows upon men gifts, not indeed always pleasant, very often even of adversity, yet always to assist us here, or in the heavenly fatherland. For God acts in accordance with His own nature, His own essence, which is wholly goodness; therefore He ordains nothing but what is good and salutary. Nevertheless such is my human nature, that I vehemently grieve, and the depths are stirred within me. (Epistle 19, bk. 2)

The death of his father, the most personal of deaths, may have impelled Agrippa down the path he had begun to follow while at the house of Dean Colet in England: the serious, single-minded study of theology. The subject occurs more frequently in his letters. In 1519 he began to take pleasure in dining with his friend Father Claudius Deodatus (Nauert gives the name as Claude Dieudonne) at the Celestine monastery, where he would enter into involved talks on the state of man before the Fall, the fall of angels, and like marvelous topics. He made no effort to conceal his admiration for Martin Luther, who was just then beginning to attract notice to his stand against Church corruption. Father Claudius frequently met with him to study the works of Erasmus and Faber d'Etaples.

For all his boldness, intelligence and eloquence, Agrippa had the innocence of a child. He seems to have had no suspicion that the threads he had been spinning all his life were conspiring together to knot a noose around his neck. Because he loved truth, he believed all other men would welcome it. Because he was honorable he expected honor from others. Because his own thoughts soared freely wherever they willed, he actually believed other men would thank him for revealing to them their intellectual servitude and ignorance.

All the subjects that had captivated Agrippa's soul from boyhood were forbidden by the Church. Magic, Greek philosophy, the Kabbalah of the Jews, Hermes Trismegistus—these were purest poison to the pope and his bishops. Now Agrippa opened his truth-seeking heart to embrace the early ideas of reformation! A reaction was inevitable.

A letter to Agrippa from his disciple Father Claudius reveals the clouds that were gathering:

Your conclusions I have copied with my own hand in stolen hours (for I am too much occupied, and get almost no leisure), nor have I ventured to depute this task to anybody, because our brothers are loutish and idiotic, persecuting enviously all who love good literature. They decry not a little Master Jacques Faber, also you and me; so that some of them have attacked me with no trifling insults. Therefore I have thought it best to hide your conclusions, lest their hatred become wilder. (Epistle 24, bk. 2)

The prior of the Celestine monastery, Claudius Salini, after interrogating Father Claudius Deodatus on his frequent and lengthy visits to Agrippa's house, became convinced that Agrippa was teaching heresy and forbade the monk from seeing him. Agrippa was a notable city official. There was little Salini could do against him directly. But the rumor mill was turning and blowing a foul breeze. It must be mentioned that Metz was not a reform-minded city. It had persecuted the Jews with great cruelty, and resisted the ideas of Luther with equal ferocity.

Agrippa had the poor judgment to get into a debate with one of the deacons of the town, Nicolas Roscius, concerning the views of Faber d'Etaples. Faber, a monk at that time 83 years old, had put forward the seemingly innocuous opinion that the legend about Saint Anne, mother of the Virgin Mary, which said that she had married three husbands, and borne three daughters named Mary, was untrue. His work *Upon Three and One* was the subject of the debate. Agrippa compounded his imprudence by agreeing offhandedly that their casual argument should be submitted to independent umpires to be judged.

Called away from Metz on business, when he returned Agrippa discovered that three priests had constituted themselves umpires in the dispute, which had taken on a life of its own, and were denouncing him from the pulpit in the most violent manner. Agrippa describes the antics of Prior Claudius Salini, who preached against him "with mad barkings and marvelous gesticulations, with outstretched fingers, with hands cast forward and suddenly snatched back again, with grinding of the teeth, foaming, spitting, stamping, leaping, cuffing up and down, with tearing at the scalp and gnawing at the nails" (from the prefatory letter to Agrippa's defense of Faber d'Etaples' work, quoted by Morley 2:45).

It was at this stage that Agrippa ceased to see Metz as the city of his future and began to wish fervently it was already the city of his past. Nothing came directly from the invective of the priests, but the seeds had been planted. When in September of 1519 Agrippa wrote to Faber d'Etaples praising his work, and sent him his defense of the doctrines of the elderly monk, Faber wrote back with the excellent advice: "In my opinion, he is happier who does not contend than he who does. Act, therefore, if possible, so prudently as neither to offend God nor your neighbour" (perhaps epistle 29, bk. 2— Morley is not clear in his references). In another letter Faber cautions Agrippa not to invite the same censure that has crashed about the ears of Reuchlin. But it was too late for Agrippa.

The philosophical climate of Metz may be gathered from scattered references in the letters. When a friend of Agrippa's came into conflict with the Church and left the city suddenly, Agrippa wrote: "I know, and do you firmly believe, that it is well with you if you are safe and free away from here. What else I wish you to know I doubt whether I can commit safely to a letter" (epistle 36, bk. 2). Agrippa asks his friend to procure for him a copy of Martin Luther's works. In another letter he writes: "I cleave to this town, fastened by I know not what nail: but so cleaving, that I cannot determine how to go or stay. I never was in any place from which I could depart more willingly than (with submission to you) from this city of Metz, the stepmother of all good scholarship and virtue" (epistle 33, bk. 2). He cautions a friend: "When I am gone, when they have me no longer at Metz to worry, they will worry you instead, my friend" (epistle 44, bk. 2).

At this critical time when Agrippa was under suspicion and attack from all official quarters, an event occurred that was to prove pivotal in his life. A peasant woman of the village of Vuoypy (Nauert spells it Woippy), to the northwest of Metz, whose mother had been burned as a witch, was herself accused of witchcraft. A group of peasants broke into her house, took her out by force, and locked her up in a crude prison. Eight accusers took her to Metz for trial. Here they were advised by the Inquisitor of Metz, Nicolas Savin, while the case was postponed for two days. To win the favor of the Inquisitor they gave him eggs, butter and cakes; the judge who was to hear the case received gold pieces.

Agrippa was horrified at the unorthodox nature of these proceedings. He came forward to defend the woman's legal rights but was accused by Savin of favoring a heretic (as yet no judgement had been passed) and turned out of the courtroom. Behind his back Savin caused the accusers to return the woman to the jail at Vuoypy. Here the judge, John Leonard, heard the case in concert with the Inquisitor, even though it was beyond his jurisdiction and such double trials were illegal. The husband of the accused was prevented from seeing her for fear that he might raise an objection or appeal.

Using the infamous *Malleus Maleficarum* of Heinrich Kramer and James Sprenger, first published around 1486, as his guide, Savin supervised the torture of the woman in an effort to extract a confession. So horrified were the magistrates and those appointed as questioners, they fled the scene, leaving the woman alone with the Inquisitor and the executioner. The torture was redoubled without witnesses. The accused was then beaten, deprived of food and water, and cast into a dungeon described as "filthy" even by the modest standards of the day.

It seemed certain she was doomed. Then a very strange thing happened that was almost supernatural. The corrupt judge Leonard fell sick, and on his deathbed his conscience was haunted by the torments of the innocent woman. He pleaded for her release and wrote to Savin his conviction that she was wholly innocent. Savin refused to give her up. Because the judge had bothered to appeal to him at all, he took it as proof that the case was within his jurisdiction.

Agrippa was determined that the woman should not be executed. In this he merely upheld his office and duty, even though he knew it would lead to his own downfall. But the driving force behind his defense was his reverence for truth. It was intolerable to him that a beast in human form such as Savin could make a mockery of all law, justice and legal process without retribution.

To the judge appointed to oversee the trial as a replacement for the deceased John Leonard, Agrippa sent this letter, which deserves to be reprinted here in full:

You have seen lately, most honourable man, from the acts themselves, those impious articles of a most iniquitous information by virtue of which brother Nicolas Savin, of the Dominican convent, Inquisitor of heretics, has fraudulently dragged into his slaughterhouse this innocent woman, contrary to Christian conscience, brotherly kindness, contrary to sacerdotal custom, the profession of his rule, the form of laws and canons: and has also, as a wicked man, wickedly and wrongfully exposed her to atrocious and enormous torments: whereby he has earned for himself a name of cruelty that will not die, as the lord official John Leonard, your predecessor now departed, himself testified upon his death-bed: and the lords of the chapter themselves know it with abhorrence. Among those articles of accusation one and the first is, that the mother of the said woman was burnt for witchcraft. I have excepted against this man as impertinent, intrusive, and incompetent to exercise in this case the judicial function; but lest you be led astray by false prophets who claim to be Christ, and are Antichrist, I pray your reverence to bear with a word of help, and only pay attention to a conversation lately held with me upon the position of this article, by the before-named bloodthirsty brother. For he asserted superciliously that the fact was in the highest degree decisive, and enough to warrant torture; and not unreasonably he asserted it according to the knowledge of his sect, which he produced presently out of the depths of the "Malleus Maleficarum" and the principles of peripatetic Theology, saying: "It must be so, because it is the custom with witches, from the very first, to sacrifice their infants to the demons, and besides that" (he said), "commonly, or often, their infants are the result of intercourse with incubi. Thus it happens that in their offspring, as with an hereditary taint, the evil sticks." O egregious sophism! Is it thus that in these days we theologise? Do figments like these move us to the torturing of harmless women? Is there no grace in baptism, no efficacy in the priests bidding: "Depart, unclean spirit, and give place to the Holy Ghost," if, because an impious parent has been sacrificed, the offspring must be given to the devil? Let any one who will, believe in this opinion, that incubi can produce offspring in the flesh. What is the fruit of this impossible position, if it be admitted, unless, according to the heresy of the Faustinians and Donatists, we get a greater evil as result? But to speak as one of the faithful, what matters it if one is the child of an incubus, what hurt is it to have been devoted as an infant to the devil? Are we not all from the nature of our humanity born one mass of sin, malediction, and eternal perdition, children of the devil, children of the Divine wrath, and heirs of damnation, until by the grace of baptism Satan is cast out, and we are made new creatures in Jesus Christ, from whom none can be separated, except by his own offence. You see now the worth of this position as a plea for judgement, at enmity with law, perilous to receive, scandalous to propound. Farewell, and either avoid or banish, this blaspheming brotherkin. Written this morning in the city of Metz. (Epistle 39, bk. 2)

So persistent, and so lucid, was Agrippa that the Inquisitor fell into discredit and was removed from the case. The accused woman received absolution from the vicar of the church of Metz. Her accusers were fined 100 franks for unjust accusation.

This was the end of Agrippa's career at Metz and he knew it. Bad enough that he had espoused positions considered heretical and defied the will of the Dominicans. Now he had made a mockery of their Inquisitor and shaken, if only for a brief time, his absolute authority that was based on terror. People avoided Agrippa in the streets, afraid to be seen in his company. Bowing to the inevitable, he resigned his office. Toward the end of January 1520, he returned with his wife and young son—his daughter had died and been buried at Metz—to Cologne, virtually driven from Metz by the wolves snapping at his heels.

Once more Agrippa enjoyed the relative security of his hereditary home, which his family shared with his mother and sister. The University of Cologne was not receptive to his opinions, but there were many in the city of a like mind. Echoes continued to reach him from Metz. A friend, Jehan Rogier, whom Agrippa usually refers to as Brennonius, wrote that the Inquisitor Savin had succeeded in having an old woman burned as a witch and had incited a full-blown witch craze. All over Metz and surrounding regions women were being rounded up. Eventually common sense prevailed and the women were set free. The peasant woman whose life Agrippa had saved, at the cost of his career, knew that Brennon was a friend of Agrippa's and continued to bring him frequent gifts of butter and eggs merely for this reason (epistle 53, bk. 2).

Brennon was to have visited Agrippa at Cologne around Easter of 1520, bringing with him a manuscript he had secured with the title *De variis admirandisque animae humanae naturis* (On the various and admirable nature of the human soul) by the unidentified author Marcus Damascenus. The visit was deferred, and it is not clear if Brennon ever went to Cologne, but he sent Agrippa the manuscript, which as late as 1523 Agrippa was still planning to edit. It is from this document that he makes reference to Damascenus in the *Occult Philosophy* (bk. 1, chs. 58 and 65). At this same time a portion of the writings of the Abbot Trithemius, who had recently died, came into Agrippa's hands, and he looked forward to discussing them with Brennon.

Early in 1521 Agrippa's wife died after suffering a lingering, painful illness. He was just at this time returning to Metz to clear up business that remained unfinished after his hasty departure from that city. Whether his wife accompanied him on this journey and died on the way, or whether Agrippa carried her corpse to Metz to be buried beside the body of their infant daughter, is unclear. In either case she was laid to rest in the Church of Saint Cross at Metz by the curate of the church, Agrippa's friend Jehan Rogier Brennonius.

With this tie broken, Agrippa took his son to Geneva to earn his living as a physician. Here he remained for almost two years. Geneva was a city where he could speak his thoughts openly. He followed with great interest the progress of Martin Luther. On September 20, 1522, he wrote to ask a friend to procure for him a copy of the attack upon Luther written by Henry VIII of England, along with another work, saying: "whatever may be their price, I will pay promptly to their bearer." This suggests both the fervor of his interest, and that he was at least not destitute.

All this while Agrippa continued to seek a position at the court of the Duke of Savoy, the door to which had once more been held open in invitation. He could not know that he was chasing a shadow. While waiting at Geneva he took a second wife, a 19-year-old Swiss girl of noble family but no wealth named Jana Loysa Tytia. Finally when Agrippa could no longer endure hanging in the air in Geneva waiting for a firm decision from the Duke of Savoy, he accepted the job of physician to the town of Friburg in October of 1522.

Aymon, his infant son by his second wife, he left with the Abbot Bonmont at Geneva, and journeyed with his wife to the Swiss town of Friburg early in 1523. Bonmont was godfather to Aymon, and supervised the early education of the boy. He also had ties to Friburg and helped make Agrippa's initial welcome a warm one. Bonmont wrote to Agrippa shortly after his arrival at Friburg : "As for our little son Aymon, I wish you to be under no anxiety about him, for he is to me as my own son, and no help or labour of mine shall be wanting to train the boy in the right way and make a man of him" (epistle 39, bk. 3).

Agrippa found happiness at Friburg. Here he was treated with respect as a scholar and progressive thinker, as he was generally throughout Switzerland. His duties consisted not only of medicine, but as an aid to the magistrates of the town, and he was often employed on political business.

As is so often the case in life, when he had no need of employment, offers began to come in. He turned down a place with the Duke of Bourbon; but when it was proposed to him that he become court physician to the Queen Mother of France, Louise of Savoy, he succumbed to temptation. The pay at Friburg was meager—what the good Swiss burgers lacked in coin they made up for in respect. But Agrippa could not ensure the future of his new family on compliments. He was now 38 years old. His wife had borne him two children and was pregnant with a third. Perhaps he had reached the pragmatic age when he could no longer turn aside from the prospect of financial security. In March or April of 1524 he reluctantly left Friburg and traveled to Lyons, France. By early May he was settled in Lyons with his second wife and two children.

The Queen Mother was a narrow-minded Catholic utterly opposed to the reforms of Martin Luther. She was also parsimonious and avaricious to the point of criminality. Just four years earlier she had embezzled 400,000 crowns intended to pay Swiss mercenaries, contributing to the expulsion of the French from Italy. Neither was she a woman to forgive a slight easily. All this Agrippa learned to his sorrow. But in the first months of his residency at Lyons he had hope before him.

Around this time he probably wrote his *Commentary* on the *Ars Brevis* of Raymond Lully. He was studying Lully, the Kabbalah and astrology, and soon drew a circle of literary friends around him while he waited at Lyons.

At the end of July 1525, Agrippa's wife gave birth to a third son, Agrippa's fourth. His only daughter by his second wife had already died in infancy. King Francis had been defeated by the Duke of Bourbon and imprisoned in Spain, making Louise the regent of France in his absence. Toward the end of August she traveled to Spain to visit her son, leaving Agrippa still at Lyons, grasping at the slippery promises of her courtiers.

Having time on his hands, he produced the treatise *De Sacramento Matrimonii Declamatio*, which was probably written as a private tribute to his first wife. In it he advocates marriage for love, and as an eternal bond:

> Whoever has taken to himself an only wife, let him cherish her with love inviolate and constant mindfulness to the last moment of life; let father, mother, children, brothers and sisters, give place to her: let the whole concourse of friends give place to the good-will established between man and wife. Truly, so should they; for father, mother, children, brothers, sisters, relations, and friends, are gifts of nature and of fortune; man and wife are a mystery of God. (quoted by Morley 2:89)

Perhaps hoping for some favor, Agrippa dedicated his treatise on marriage to the French king's sister, Margaret of Valois, who would soon be better known by her married name, Margaret of Navarre. She is remembered as the author of a collection of ribald tales called the *Heptameron,* which is still read today—a rare accomplishment for a French noblewoman of the 16th century. Anyone who has read the *Heptameron* will appreciate at once that its loose morality was completely at odds with Agrippa's strict precepts on marriage. She was more likely to regard his gift as an indirect censure of her way of life. In acknowledgement of the dedication she sent Agrippa the sum of 20 gold pieces, but never received him into her inner circle.

Years later the sentiments expressed in the treatise would induce the Queen of England, Catherine of Aragon, to ask Agrippa to come to England and defend her against the divorce being forced upon her by Henry VIII. However at this late time in his life Agrippa had given up putting his trust in queens, and had no desire to antagonize yet another king— he would decline her request.

Waiting at Lyons began to stretch his meager resources to their breaking point. He had been promised money, but could not wring it out of the Queen Mother's treasurer, Barguyn. A letter written to John Chapelain, one of the French king's physicians, asking that he plead Agrippa's case before Louise, reveals Agrippa's state of mind: "Go to her, fasten on her, seize her, ask her, conjure her, compel her, torment her: add prayers, entreaties, complaints, sighs, tears and whatever else there is by which people are stirred" (epistle 6, bk. 4). He is laughing at his distress, but there is a hysterical note to his laughter.

A more serious letter lays out clearly how unfortunate his position had become:

Your letter, written on the twenty-ninth of June, my dearest Chapelain, I received on the seventh of July, and learn from it that our friend Barguyn has referred the payment of my salary to one Antony Bullion, of Lyons. If Barguyn wished me well, as you write that he does, and desired my money to be paid to me, he would not have referred me to that Antony whom he knew to be absent from here, but either to Martin of Troyes, as was arranged, or to some other, either resident here or passing through the town. On the day that I received your letter I went with M. Aimar de Beaujolois, a judge, a polished man, and one of my best friends here, and had some trouble in meeting with Thomas Bullion, the brother of Antony; he did not altogether deny that he had orders to pay me, but said he was ordered to pay in these words: if he found that he could,—if there remained any money with him. At last he said he would refer again to his instructions, and that I should have an answer from him the next morning. On the next day, therefore, when we anxiously called many times upon the man, he hiding at home, feigned absence, until at a late hour of the night we departed, having made a very close acquaintance with his door. On the next day, however, the before-mentioned judge meets him, questions him on my behalf, and presses him: he replies that he will come over shortly to my house and settle with me about the stipend; and, with that falsehood, securing an escape, in the same hour he mounted his horse and rode away, as it was said, to join the court. You see how we are played with! Think of me fought against on every side by sorrows—by griefs, indeed, greater and more incessant than I care to write. There is no friend here to help me; all comfort me with empty words; and the court title, which should have brought me honour and profit, aggravates my hurt, by adding against me envy to contempt. Held in suspense by this continual hope, to this hour no messenger has told me whether to remain at this place or quit it; here, therefore, I live with my large family as a pilgrim in a caravansary, and that the most expensive of all towns, under a load of charges, subject to no little loss. You write that the Queen will some day comply with my request; but that she is always slow— slow also in your affairs. What if in the mean time I perish? Truly, so slow a fortune cannot save me, mighty goddess as she is. Perhaps you will say I should propitiate her with some sacrifice—a ram, or a bull, and those of the fattest—that her wings may grow, and she may fly to me the faster; but so extreme is my want of everything, that I could not find her a cake or a pinch of frankincense. (Epistle 25, bk. 4)

Agrippa did what odd labor he could come by to feed his family, while running up debts. A courtier asked him for an astrological prediction. This he sent, but left no doubt as to his own opinion of those who let the courses of the stars determine their actions:

Why do we trouble ourselves to know whether man's life and fortune depend on the stars? To God, who made them and the heavens, and who cannot err, neither do wrong, may we not leave these things,— content, since we are men, to attain what is within our compass, that is to say, human knowledge? But since we are also Christian and believe in Christ, let us trust to God our Father hours and moments which are in His hand. And if these things depend not on the stars, astrologers, indeed, run a vain course. But the race of man, so timorous, is readier to hear fables of ghosts and believe in things that are not, than in things that are. Therefore, too eager in their blindness, they hurry to learn secrets of the future, and that which is least possible (as the return of the deluge) they believe the most; so, also, what is least likely they believe most readily of the astrologers, as that the destinies of things are to be changed by planning from the judgements of astrology—a faith that, beyond doubt, serves to keep those practitioners from hunger. (Epistle 8, bk. 4)

In the summer of 1526 the Queen Mother herself requested an astrological prediction concerning the outcome of a war between her son,

Francis I, and the forces of Bourbon and Emperor Charles V, who had succeeded Maximilian in 1520. Agrippa could scarcely contain his disgust and self-loathing. Having swallowed his great pride and allowed the lackeys of the Queen to keep him lingering about on promises like a dog for two years without the least payment, Louise was now showing her true opinion of his worth. He was to be court astrologer. This was intolerable.

He wrote to his friend Chapelain:

I am in the right way to become a prophet, and obey my mistress; I wish I may predict her something pleasant, but what pleasant prophecies are you to get out of the furies and Hecate? All the mad prophets of antiquity foresaw nothing but murder, slaughter, war, and havoc, and I know not how mad people can foresee other than the works of a madman. I fear, then, that I shall prophesy in this way, unless some good Apollo, chasing off the furies, visit me with his light in beams of gold. But I will mount the tripod, prophesy, or guess, and send the result ere long to the Princess, using those astrological superstitions by which the Queen shows herself so greedy to be helped—using them, as you know, unwillingly, and compelled by her violent prayers. I have written, however, to the Seneschal that he should admonish her no longer to abuse my talent by condemning it to such unworthy craft, nor force me any more to stumble through this idle work, when I am able to be helpful to her with more profitable studies. (Epistle 29, bk. 4)

Agrippa's anger was understandable. He was in the maturity of his intellectual development, schooled in many arts and sciences, with a broad understanding of men and the world. Had Louise chosen to make him her advisor on affairs of state, she could hardly have found a more able counselor. Instead she wanted him to play the court fool and tell her exactly what she wished to hear, disregarding his own true judgment. Not only was Agrippa imprudent enough to let it be known that he considered the stars favorable to the cause of Bourbon, but he was even prognosticating, privately if not publicly, the demise of Louise's son. The following year his prediction

would become more specific. The French chronicler Claude Bellievre wrote that in May of 1527 Agrippa forecast from the heavens the death of Francis I within six months.

What Agrippa did not know was that for some time Louise had been intercepting and reading his letters to members of her court, letters that frequently contained none too flattering remarks about herself. He may have begun to suspect what would have been plain to a man of a less innocent mind, that the Queen Mother and her court were laughing at his predicament, and had no intention of ever fulfilling their promises.

In September Agrippa's wife suffered an attack of double tertian fever. She was pregnant at the time. Under this load of cares Agrippa completed his *Uncertainty and Vanity of Sciences*. He was also at work on a treatise about war engines called *Pyromachy*, as this extract from a letter shows:

I have been writing in these last days a volume of some size, which I have entitled "On the Uncertainty and Vanity of Sciences, and on the Excellence of the Word of God." If ever you see it, I think you will praise the plan, admire the treatment, and consider it not unworthy of his majesty [Francis I, King of France]: but I do not mean to dedicate it to that king, for the work has found one who is most desirous to become its patron, and most worthy so to be. But I am writing now on Pyromachy, and not so much writing as experimenting, and I have now at my house buildings and models of machines of war, invented by me, and constructed at no little cost; they are both useful and deadly, such as (I know) this age has not yet seen. . . ." (Epistle 41, bk. 4)

The construction of siege engines shows that Agrippa was still chasing the chimerical favor of kings and princes. *The Uncertainty and Vanity of Sciences* was eventually dedicated to a friend, Augustine Furnario, a citizen of Genoa. Whether this is the person intended in the letter is not certain, but likely. *Pyromachy* was intended as a gift for King Francis when, and if, he ever came to Lyons.

While out walking in Saint James Church on October 7, 1526, he fell into casual conversation with a stranger and told the man his expectation daily of payment from the royal treasurer. The man replied: "I serve in the office of Barguyn the treasurer, and as a friend I warn you not to be misled by any false suggestion, but to take thought for some better way of prospering. A very little while ago I saw your name struck off the pension-list" (epistle 5, bk. 4).

This revelation shook Agrippa like a bolt of lightning. At once he saw his own folly. He sheds his bitterness on Chapelain, the physician of King Francis:

> Hear what rules I have prescribed for myself if ever I am tempted to return to the court service: to make myself a proper courtier, I will flatter egregiously, be sparing of faith, profuse of speech, ambiguous in counsel, like the oracles of old; but I will pursue gain, and prefer my own advantage above all things: I will cultivate no friendship save for money's sake; I will be wise to myself, praise no man except through cunning, decry any man you please. I will thrust forth whom I can, that I may take what he is forced to leave, will place myself on half a dozen seats, and despise every one who offers me his hospitality but not his money, as a barren tree. I will have faith in no man's word, in no man's friendship; I will take all things ill and brood on vengeance; the Prince only I will watch and worship, but him I will flatter, I will agree with, I will infest, only through fear or greed of my own gain."
> (Epistle 53, bk. 4)

Early in May, 1527, Agrippa's wife gave birth to a fourth son, Agrippa's fifth. He finally asked permission to leave France with his family in July. He had given up all hope of receiving anything from Louise:

> Take care never to address to me again as Counsellor, or Queen's Physician. I detest this title. I condemn all hope it ever raised in me. I renounce all fealty that I ever swore to her. She never more shall be mistress of mine (for already she has ceased to be so), but I have resolved to think of her as some atrocious and perfidious Jezebel, if she thus heeds rather dishonest words than honest deeds. (Epistle 62, bk. 4)

The Queen Mother was not through laughing at her German physician and astrologer. It was December 6 before Agrippa was finally able to leave Lyons. He traveled to Paris, on route to Antwerp, but was delayed in Paris for six months seeking the necessary papers to leave France. At least he had one hope to cherish. There was a prospect of obtaining the patronage of Margaret of Austria, which he had sought in vain so many years earlier.

When his household goods were detained at Antwerp, Agrippa was forced to cross the border alone to gain their release, leaving his wife and family in Paris. His wife, pregnant yet again, fell sick. There was no money to procure medical help. A relation wrote Agrippa at Antwerp informing him of this latest trouble. Agrippa was at wit's end:

> Alas! What do you announce, my dearest cousin? My dearest wife labouring under so perilous a disease, and she with child, and I absent, who had scarcely been able at great risk of my life to depart alone, that at last I might find means to bring into safety her who is to me my only soul, my spirit, my wit, my salvation, my life? Ah me, how wretchedly this die has fallen! I am here now in wretched agony. My wife is at Paris, miserably perishing, and I cannot come near her with any solice; my children are in tears, the whole family mourn, and this sword passes through her soul. Oh that I only could bear the hurt and she be safe! What shall I do? Whither shall I turn? Whom shall I implore? Except yourself I have no one.
> (Epistle 55, bk. 5)

This was the low point of the present cycle. His wife recovered. On November 5, 1528, his family was able to make their way to Mechlin, where Agrippa joined them. They proceeded to Antwerp.

Antwerp was a happier climate than Lyons. Agrippa found friends there and was received into honorable families. He began to practice his trade of medicine, quickly gaining a renown that spread beyond the confines of the city. The royal court took notice. Margaret of Austria, favorably impressed by both Agrippa's skill and his wife's charms, appointed Agrippa to the post of Indiciary Councillor, or Councillor in the matter of the Archives, and Historiographer to the Emperor, in January of 1529. At the same time Agrippa obtained license to print and retain the copyright in his own works for six years.

The long delayed printing of the treatise *On the Nobility and Pre-eminence of Women* at last occurred along with some other minor works. Agrippa's wife gave birth to yet another son on March 13, her fifth son and Agrippa's sixth—but the family consisted of five boys, one son, probably the eldest by his first wife, having died while in France. Pupils were sent to Agrippa for instruction, so largely had his fame spread. One was Johann Wierus, citizen of Gravelines, who in his *De præstigiis dæmonum* was later to give a biographical sketch of Agrippa. It is significant that Wier, like most men who knew Agrippa intimately, spoke of him only in terms of highest respect and refuted the lies told against him.

In July 1529, Agrippa had both the leisure and the money to take up the practice of alchemy. He writes concerning a slow distillation that must be watched carefully in his laboratory (epistle 73, bk. 5). This interest was not new. In 1526 the curate of Saint Cross at Metz, Jehan Rogier Brennonius, had written concerning the doings of an alchemist he calls "our Tyrius," a clockmaker by profession, who "has discovered a sweet water in which every metal is easily dissolved by the heat of the sun" (epistle 27, bk. 4). It is only in Antwerp that Agrippa was able to seriously study this fascinating subject. This may have been when he attempted the manufacture of gold, with only middling success (see *Occult Philosophy*, bk. 1, ch. 14).

His happiness was shattered by the death of his second wife from plague on August 7, 1529. This struck him, if possible, even more deeply than the loss of his first wife:

> Ah, she is lost to me, and dead, but eternal glory covers her. She had been well for nearly a whole month, was in all things prosperous and joyous, fortune smiling on us from all sides, and already we were engaged in furnishing a new and larger house, against the days that were coming to us, when on the last St. Lawrence's day a violent pestilential fever attacked her, with abscess of the groin . . . woe is me, no remedies availed, and on the seventh day, which was the seventh of August, at about nine in the morning, with great difficulty, but a clear intellect, a soul firm towards God and an innocent conscience, while we stood round she rendered up her spirit, the plague pouring itself through the entire body in large blotches. (Epistle 81, bk. 5)

The plague raged through the city of Antwerp. Agrippa remained to treat the sick while the more timid local physicians fled to the countryside. After the pestilence began to abate the physicians of the city accused Agrippa of practicing medicine without the proper credentials and forced him to desist, depriving him of his main source of income. They were motivated, one suspects, more by shame at their own cowardice and jealousy of Agrippa's methods of treatment than concern for his patients.

The publication of Agrippa's works, so long in manuscript, began in earnest in 1530. In September he published his *Uncertainty and Vanity of Sciences*. He had previously printed, in accordance with his official position as historiographer, the *Historiette of the Recent Double Coronation of the Emperor at Bologna by Pope Clement VII*. His patron, Margaret of Austria, died at the end of 1530, at age 52, and Agrippa composed her funeral oration.

In February of 1531 the first edition of the *Occult Philosophy* issued from the press of John Graphæus of Antwerp, paid for, there is every reason to believe, out of Agrippa's own pocket. Although it bears the title *Agrippa's Three Books of Occult Philosophy*, and carries the index to the entire work, it ends at the close of the first book. The work is dedicated to Hermann, Archbishop of Cologne, who had earlier shown some kindness to Agrippa.

With the death of Margaret of Austria he was sorely in need of a patron. The publication of the *Uncertainty and Vanity of Sciences* had stirred the ire of courtiers, priests, and other high officials, all of whom it satirizes unmercifully. The further issuing of the *Occult Philoso-*

phy laid Agrippa open to accusations that he was a sorcerer. Before there had been suspicions—now there was, so his enemies believed, printed proof.

It will perhaps come as no surprise to those who have read this history down to this point that Agrippa's promised salary as official historiographer, along with the expenses he incurred fulfilling his duties, was never paid. No wonder princes were wealthy, since they never paid their bills! Although Margaret had ordered the treasurers to pay, they had delayed, and now she was dead. Agrippa petitioned the Emperor Charles V with such tenacity over the monies owed him, the emperor was on the point of having him executed to be rid of his nuisance. Two cardinals, pleading Agrippa's case, were able to sooth his royal irritation for the moment. The priests had been very active against Agrippa, something he only at this late date began to appreciate fully.

He had been living on borrowed money in expectation of his salary. Now that there was no salary, his creditors closed in around him. Most of his closest friends were far removed. In vain he asked the privy council of the Emperor either to give enough of the monies due him to pay off his creditors, or grant him an order of liberty so that he could earn money to pay them off by his own exertions. The council referred him to the emperor. For seven months he dogged the heels of Charles begging for money to maintain his family. "The Emperor had been made deaf to him, stood as a statue to his supplications; cared no more, he says, for his incessant cry than for the croaking of a thirsty frog" (Morley 2:272–3).

In June of 1531 Agrippa was thrown into jail in Brussels by one of his creditors. His friends soon secured his release, but it must have been a humiliating blow to the feelings of so proud a man. Some solace came with a written guarantee, affixed with the emperor's seal, of a small salary. Alas, this too was only a promise. Agrippa retired to a small house in Mechlin in December, 1531, which he could just barely afford on the promised, but not given, pension.

At Mechlin he took to wife a native of the town, says Johann Wierus. Agrippa himself says not a word about her. The reason is not difficult to discover. She was unfaithful. The French satirist Rabelais, with a stony Gallic heart, mocks Agrippa for his blindness to his young bride's infamy:

> Hard by here, in the Brown-wheat-Island, dwelleth Her Trippa; you know how by the Arts of Astrology, Geomancy, Chiromancy, Metopomancy, and others of a like stuff and nature, he foretelleth all things to come: Let us talk a little, and confer with him about your Business. Of that (answered Panurge) I know nothing: But of this much concerning him I am assured, that one day, and that not long since, whilst he was prating to the Great King, of Cœlestial, Sublime, and Transcendent Things, the Lackqueys and Footboys of the Court, upon the upper Steps of Stairs between two Doors, jumbled, one after another, as often as they listed, his Wife; who is passable fair, and a pretty snug Hussie. Thus he who seemed very clearly to see all Heavenly and Terrestrial Things without Spectacles, who discoursed boldly of Adventures past, with great confidence opened up present Cases and Accidents, and stoutly professed the presaging of all future Events and Contingencies, and was not able with all the Skill and Cunning that he had, to perceive the Bumbasting of his Wife, whom he reputed to be very chast; and hath not till this Hour, got Notice of any thing to the contrary (*Gargantua*, 3:25).

Three short years later he would divorce this woman at Bonn.

Forced to leave Mechlin because of an unfair tax from which the Emperor would not grant him exemption, he traveled in spring 1532 to Poppelsdoft at the invitation of the Archbishop of Cologne, who kindly requested that Agrippa stay for a time at his residence. At least Agrippa had chosen one dedication of his works wisely. The archbishop was pleased with the *Occult Philosophy*. Most in need of a patron, Agrippa had a single one remaining in the world who would not desert him. Meanwhile in Cologne the printing of the first edition of the complete three books of the *Occult Philosophy* was under way.

The publication of his writings had the same effect on his critics as a stick thrust up a nest of wasps. Attempts were made to prohibit the sale and reading of the *Uncertainty and Vanity of Sciences*. Agrippa himself was accused of impiety, which was at the time a capital crime, punishable by death. The Emperor Charles V demanded that he recant all the impeached opinions found by the monks of Louvain in his writings. Having received the accusations made against him, he prepared a defense in late January 1532 and delivered it to the Head of the Senate at Mechlin. Ten months passed and still his name had not been cleared. He declined the demand of the emperor that he publicly recant, saying: "For the Emperor cannot condemn one whom the law hath not judged . . ." His defense, the *Apology,* was printed in 1533.

Having weathered all manner of storms in his life, the scholar was philosophical about this latest assault:

> I am condemned—unheard-of tyranny— before defense is heard, and to this tyranny the Emperor is provoked by superstitious monks and sophists. I have carried my mind written on my face, and wish the Emperor to know that I can sell him neither smoke nor oil. But I have lived honestly, having no reason to blush for my own deeds, and little to blame in fortune, except that I was born into the service of ungrateful kings. My folly and impiety have been, I own, worthy of condemnation, in that, against the warning of the Scriptures, I have put my trust in princes. I wished to live as a philosopher in courts where art and literature are unhonoured, unrewarded. If I am not wise, surely it is herein that I am most foolish, that I have trusted my well-being into the power of another, and, anxious and uncertain of my future, rested hope on those whose deeds I find unequal to their promises. Truly I am ashamed now of my lack of wisdom. (*Querela super calumnia,* as quoted by Morley 2:301)

These thoughts, the summary of a turbulent life, appear in the last work ever written by Agrippa, his *Complaint Against the Calumny of the Monks and Schoolmen.* It was printed together with the *Apology* in 1533. Much of the fire is spent, the virulence softened, replaced by a clarity of vision and a quiet sadness.

When he applied for his pension, guaranteed by the royal seal, he was mocked. The officials of the Duke of Brabant said that since he had left his residence at Mechlin he had in effect given up his office, and was entitled to no money. It did no good for Agrippa to argue that he still maintained a house in the town, and that he was historiographer to Charles V, not the Duke of Brabant or the Count of Flanders. It did no good. The petty officials who controlled the purse knew well enough the emperor would not intercede on Agrippa's behalf.

In 1532 he moved both his family and his library to Bonn. There were still battles to be fought: The Dominican monks held up the release of the complete edition of the *Occult Philosophy.* One of their number, Conrad Colyn of Ulm, the Inquisitor of Cologne, denounced the books in the strongest terms. Happily the Archbishop of Cologne, to whom the books were dedicated, had power within his own sphere. Agrippa delivered a spirited defense of the work before the magistrates of Cologne, making the point that the books had been approved by the whole council of the emperor, and were to appear under imperial privilege. The books duly were printed in 1533.

It is worth considering briefly the circumstances that allowed the *Occult Philosophy* to appear before the world. The books were dedicated to Hermannus, Archbishop of Cologne, who had a firm friendship for their author and an admiration for the work itself. Hermann, Agrippa's last patron on earth, happened to be a reformer, at odds with the Church establishment. The work was published in Cologne under his power, and Cologne was also the hereditary city of Agrippa's family, allowing Agrippa to draw support from a variety of sources. Finally, Agrippa had the good fortune to possess imperial approval of the work, obtained under the favor of Margaret of Austria.

In the same year Agrippa's *Commentary* on the *Ars Brevis* of Raymond Lully was also printed at Cologne, along with the *Disputation Touching the Monogamy of Anne,* Agrippa's defense of the views of Faber d'Etaples, written in 1519.

The life of our wandering scholar was winding to a close. The summer of 1533 he spent in holiday with Hermannus at Wisbaden. The following year he was a resident at Bonn. In spring of 1535 he divorced his third wife at Bonn. The small amount of money given him by the archbishop enabled him to feed and clothe his boys, but little more. All the while the wrath of his enemies continued to beat against him unabated. Emperor Charles V, at the urging of the Dominicans, had sentenced him to death as a heretic. Agrippa was able to flee in time into France, where the emperor, without renouncing the death sentence, condemned him to exile.

As soon as he crossed into France, King Francis caused him to be cast into prison. Agrippa's friends were able to procure his release. He wandered for a few months, trying to make his way to Lyons where he could publish his letters, along with his collected works. No doubt he was still battling vainly to salvage his wrecked reputation, and wanted to lay the story of his life before the world. Before he reached Lyons he fell sick. He was received into the house of a M. Vachon, the Receiver-General of the Province of Dauphine, which stood in the Rue des Clercs in Grenoble. There, alone among strangers in a hostile land, beset on all sides by his enemies, at the untimely age of 49, he died. His corpse was laid to rest within a convent of Dominicans, his most hated enemies.

He must have known that his end was near and made arrangements for his manuscripts to be carried to Lyons and given into the hands of his publisher. Shortly after his death his collected works along with his letters were published at Lyons. These formed the first edition of the Latin *Opera* which is most often consulted today.

A spurious *Fourth Book of Occult Philosophy* was added after the original three, but Agrippa's faithful pupil, Johann Wierus, denounced it as an imposture:

> To these may very justly be added, a work lately published [1567], and ascribed to my late honoured host and preceptor, Henry Cornelius Agrippa, who has been dead more than forty years; whence I conclude it is unjustly ascribed to his manes, under the title of *The Fourth Book of the Occult Philosophy, or of Magical Ceremonies,* which pretends likewise to be a Key to the three former books of the *Occult Philosophy,* and all kinds of magical operations." *(De præstigiis dæmonum)*

Concerning the Lyons edition, Henry Morley says that the *Uncertainty and Vanity of Sciences* was extensively cut to appease the censors (Morley 2:317).

The preceding account of the life of Agrippa is drawn mainly from the two-volume biography by Henry Morley, *The Life of Henry Cornelius Agrippa,* published by Chapman and Hall, London, 1856. Morley, in turn, has derived almost all of his biographical material from a close reading of Agrippa's letters as they appear in the Latin *Opera* of Lyons. It is indeed fortunate that these letters have survived. Had they not, we would today know as little about Agrippa as we know about Shakespeare.

There is a second, scattered and unofficial account of Agrippa's life made up of the fables and slanders penned by credulous monks. For example, when Agrippa mentions in one of his letters (epistle 9, bk. 1) that he must stop at Avignon for a time in order to make some money before he can continue his journey to Lyons, this was interpreted to mean that he set up his alchemical apparatus and manufactured gold. It is true that Agrippa dabbled in alchemy. But he was probably more concerned with finding useful medicinal extracts than the philosopher's stone. He says himself in the *Occult Philosophy* (1:14) on the making of gold: "And we know how to do that, and have seen it done: but we could make no more gold, than the weight of it was, out of which we extracted the Spirit." This is hardly a prescription for getting rich.

It was also said by Martin Del Rio (in his *Disquisitionum magicarum libri sex,* first edition, Louvain, 1599–1600) and others that Agrippa paid his inn bills with bits of horn, casting a glamour over them so that they appeared to those who received them to be coins until Agrippa was safely away, at which time they changed back to their true appearance. But this fable is told of a number of magicians such as Faust and Simon Magus.

The most famous story is a variation on the tale of the sorcerer's apprentice. It was probably inspired, as Lynn Thorndike notes (*History of Magic*, 5:8:136, n. 35) by a remark of Wierus, who says that once as a young pupil of Agrippa he had copied several pages of his master's manuscript edition of the *Steganographia* of Trithemius without Agrippa's knowledge *(De præstigiis dæmonum*, 2:6). Del Rio, using this germ to inspire his fancy, relates these events:

This happened to Cornelius Agrippa at Louvain. He had a boarder who was too curious, and Agrippa having gone somewhere, had given the keys of his museum to the wife whom he afterwards divorced, forbidding her to allow any one to enter. This thoughtless youth did not omit, in season and out of season, to entreat the woman to give him the means of entering, until he gained his prayer. Having entered the museum, he fell upon a book of conjurations—read it. Hark! there is knocking at the door; he is disturbed; but he goes on with his reading; some one knocks again; and the unmannerly youth answering nothing to this, a demon enters, asks why is he called? What is it commanded him to do? Fear stifles the youth's voice, the demon his mouth, and so he pays the price of his unholy curiosity. In the mean time the chief magician returns home, sees the devils dancing over him, uses the accustomed arts, they come when called, explain how the thing happened, he orders the homicide spirit to enter the corpse, and to walk now and then in the market-place (where other students were accustomed frequently to meet), at length to quit the body. He walks three or four times, then falls; the demon that had stirred the dead limbs taking flight. It was long thought that this youth had been seized with sudden death, but signs of suffocation first begot suspicion, afterwards time divulged all.

Morley, who quotes this tale (2:314–5), says that Del Rio lifted it whole from an earlier work published in Latin, Italian, French and Spanish, which bore the title in French of *Theatre de la Nature*, in Italian of *Stroze Cicogna*, and in Spanish of *Valderama*.

Another fable that enjoyed wide commerce was that Agrippa kept a familiar demon always with him in the form of a black female dog. This familiar traveled far and wide in the twinkling of an eye and brought Agrippa news of all the happenings around the world, informing him of wars, plagues, floods and other significant events. This story, like the other, is founded upon a kernel of truth. Agrippa was inordinately fond of dogs and kept them with him wherever he went. Wierus says that when he knew Agrippa, his master had two dogs, a black male named Monsieur and a bitch named Mamselle. Agrippa was very affectionate towards Monsieur and used to pet and fondle him excessively, allowed the dog to remain beside his chair when he ate and even took the dog onto his bed at night. This was in the period after Agrippa had divorced his third wife in 1535. Probably he was very lonely.

Wierus writes: "And when Agrippa and I were eating or studying together, this dog always lay between us" *(De præstigiis dæmonum*, 2:5). Bodin, in his *Demonomanie*, twists this innocent remark, inferring that Agrippa and Wierus were homosexual lovers and that the dog, which he assumes wrongly to have been a bitch, lay between them in their bed *(De la Demonomanie des Sorciers*, 1580 edition, 219–20). From the *Elogia* of Jovius we learn that the collar of the dog was inscribed with magical characters.

The explanation for Agrippa's wide and timely knowledge of world events is obvious to anyone who examines the *Opera*. He was an incurable letter writer, corresponding with a wide range of educated and prominent men throughout Europe. There was hardly a better way to keep abreast of events in the early 16th century, when travel was slow and communications uncertain, than by writing letters.

His death was glossed by his enemies with the same scandalous lies. A priest named Thevet wrote:

At last, having betaken himself to Lyons, very wretched, and deprived of his faculties, he tried all the means that he could to live, waving, as dexterously as he could, the end of his stick, and yet gained so little, that he died in a miserable inn, disgraced and abhorred before all the world, which detested him as an accursed and execrable magician, because he always carried about with him as his companion a devil in the figure of a dog, from whose neck, when he felt death approaching, he removed the collar, figured all over with magical characters, and afterwards, being in a half-mad state, he drove it from him with these words: "Go, vile beast, by whom I am brought utterly to perdition." And afterwards this dog, which had been so familiar with him, and been his assiduous companion in his travels, was no more seen; because, after the command Agrippa gave him, he began to run towards the Saone, where he leapt in, and never came out thence, for which reason it is judged that he was drowned there. *(Portraits et Vies des Hommes Illustres,* Paris edition of 1584, 2:543)

The same man gives Agrippa this churlish epitaph, which is more of a condemnation of its composer than of its subject:

This tomb, scarcely the graces keep, but the black daughters of hell; not the muses, but the furies with snakes spread abroad. Alecto collects the ashes, mixes them with aconite, and gives the welcome offering to be devoured by the Stygian dog, who now cruelly pursues through the paths of Orcus, and snatches at that of which when alive he was the companion, and he leaps up at him. And he salutes the furies because he had known them all, and he addressed each by her own name. O wretched Arts, which afford only this convenience—that as a known guest he can approach the Stygian waters.

Long-winded and foolish though it is, the sentiments expressed in this epitaph sum up the public memory of Cornelius Agrippa. Which, then, is stronger—truth, or the lies of malicious fools? It is sad that despite the facts of his life being plain to all who seek them, this honorable and courageous man is still denigrated.

The brief biographical sketch given by Lynn Thorndike in his *History of Magic* deserves special mention because of its surprising malignity. He opens it:

Neither is Henry Cornelius Agrippa of Nettesheim himself to be reckoned of much weight in intellectual history nor is his book on occult philosophy so important a work in the history of magic and experimental science as one might think at first sight. He was not a person of solid learning, regular academic standing, and fixed position, but rather one of those wayward geniuses and intellectual vagabonds so common in the late fifteenth and early sixteenth centuries. *(History of Magic,* 5:8:127)

His chief objections to Agrippa appear to be that he was not a prominent faculty member of a major university, and that he practiced medicine without a license. How it is possible to say he lacked learning, when his mind was so far advanced above the stultified academic standards of his day, is difficult to understand. He may have lacked the dogmatism and cant acquired by a formal Church education, but he was hardly unlearned. Erasmus, with whom Agrippa corresponded, called him a "fiery genius" (Erasmus, *Epistles*, bk. 27). He criticized Agrippa for his lack of discretion in his choice of subjects and his "disturbed" style, but this is not a slur against his learning, which is not the same thing as education. Agrippa learned most of what he knew himself, from books, not teachers.

Regarding his lack of university tenure, Agrippa would have liked nothing better than to have remained permanently at Pavia. Political events rendered this absolutely impossible, to his great sorrow. As for his lack of a medical degree, what did such things mean at the beginning of the 16th century? The fact that people sought him out for remedies and advice suggests that he was at least as good a physician as the quacks who killed according to ancient prescription. During the plague at Antwerp he stayed inside the city healing those afflicted while his better accredited colleagues fled. Had he been less honest he might have grown rich in medicine, for which he obviously possessed a great natural talent.

What, then, can be said in memory of Cornelius Agrippa? He was a genius whose wide-ranging mind refused to be bound by dogma. All his life he courted Truth as a lover, and even in his darkest days he never ceased to worship her. His courage, both physical and intellectual, was steadfast in times of trial. Always he behaved with honor. If he had faults, these were a mind impatient with empty rules and meaningless forms, whose quickness and boldness sometimes outraced its discipline; and an innocence of heart that caused him to take the word of other men as it was given. At his death he had no reason for shame. He left after him a book that has endured 500 years.

On the *Occult Philosophy*

The first cohesive edition of the *Three Books of Occult Philosophy, or of Magic,* was written by Agrippa in the latter part of 1509 and the beginning of 1510. While the ink was barely dry he sent it off to the Abbot Trithemius for his approval. He had visited Trithemius at his monastery of Saint James at Wurtzburg in the spring of 1509 and the long discussions the two had held on occult matters were still fresh in his mind. The manuscript version read by Trithemius still exists (Würzburg, Universitätsbibliotek, MS. ch. q. 30).

The first published edition appeared at Antwerp (the work was also sold at Paris) from the press of John Graphæus in the month of February 1531, to be sold by him under the sign of the Lime Tree in the street Lombardenveste. It is unnumbered, paged only by the lettering of the sheets from A to V. The title is *Agrippa's Three Books of Occult Philosophy.* Although it contains the index to the complete three books, it breaks off abruptly at the end of Book One with this notice:

To the Reader

Candid reader, the author of this most divine work intended to bring to light also the second and third book, which are indeed promised to readers at the beginning of the work, but suddenly almost, and unexpectedly, the death of the sainted Margaret, as well as other cares, changed his course, and compelled him to desist from what he had begun. But it is not to be doubted that when he has understood this little book not to be scorned, and to be not wholly unwelcome to the learned, he will edit also the other two. At present receive this, and embrace with good will the most occult mysteries and secrets of the divinest things that are contained in it.

Farewell.

The work is prefixed with a copy of the imperial privilege, dated January 7, 1529, granting Agrippa six years copyright of the *Occult Philosophy* and other writings. It is dedicated to the Reverend Father in Christ, and most Illustrious Prince Hermann, Count of Wied, Archbishop of Cologne.

The first complete edition was published at Cologne in July 1533 without the name of its place or printer. The printer was Soter and Hetorpius, but it was not considered necessary to draw attention to this fact, because the book had encountered considerable resistance from the Inquisitor of Cologne, Conrad Colyn of Ulm. This battle to publish is detailed by Henry Morley in his *Life of Agrippa,* 2:305–10.

The English edition that is the text of the present work bears the title *Three Books of Occult Philosophy, Written by Cornelius Agrippa of Nettesheim, Counsellor to Charles the Fifth, Emperor of Germany and Judge of the Prerogative Court,* translated by J. F., London, 1651. Morley calls it "the best of the English translations," but adds that it "is not very complete, and contains numerous blunders" (Morley 1:114–5, footnote). That it contains errors is undeniable, but then, most of them are also contained in the edition included in the Latin *Opera* published at Lyons shortly after Agrippa's death, which seems to be the source used in the translation. As for being incomplete, it corresponds more or less with the text of the version in the *Opera*—I cannot speak for the edition of 1533, which I have not seen.

"J. F." are the initials of James Freake, according to the "List of Books Quoted" in the *Oxford English Dictionary,* Compact Edition, 2:4101 (old edition). His first name is mentioned, not in the list, but in entries under various words—because of the many obscure words in the *Occult Philosophy,* it is frequently cited by the *OED.* Despite my efforts, and much to my vexation, I have been able to locate no information concerning James Freake in other reference works.

Freake is also the author of the introduction to the 1650 edition of the *Divine Pymander of Hermes Mercurius Trismegistus,* translated from the Arabic by Doctor Everard, and printed by Robert White for Thos. Brewster and Greg. Moule of London (see bibliography). Freake signs this brief introduction, as he does his own translation of the *Occult Philosophy,* simply with the initials J.F.

It is this English translation (I have seen no others) that formed the text of Francis Barrett's *The Magus, or Celestial Intelligencer,* published at London, 1801. Barrett's book is made up of large blocks of plagiarized material from the *Occult Philosophy*, and the spurious *Fourth Book of Occult Philosophy.* It contains nothing original. In no place does Barrett acknowledge that his book was written by Cornelius Agrippa. Anyone coming upon *The Magus,* as I did years ago, without a knowledge of the *Occult Philosophy,* would be struck by the excellent things in it. All its excellencies are Agrippa's, although the plates of the *Occult Philosophy* have been elegantly redrawn, complete with their original errors. Barrett himself deserves nothing but contempt.

The Freake translation was also the basis for *The Philosophy of Natural Magic,* published in Chicago, 1913, by the occult publisher and literary pirate L. W. de Laurence. It consists of the first of the three books of the *Occult Philosophy* with a very brief and incomplete life of Agrippa drawn from Morley. The text has modernized spelling and some punctuation modifications, but is otherwise unchanged from the Freake text. It also contains a few (very few) footnotes, and a hodgepodge of occult trash appended to the end from a variety of sources. I mention it only because it was reprinted by University Books in 1974, and is the one text of the *Occult Philosophy,* incomplete though it is, which was relatively easy to obtain. As for de Laurence, he may have been a reincarnation of Francis Barrett.

Agrippa had a clear, well-ordered mind. The structure of the *Occult Philosophy* is quite logical, despite its tendency to jump from one topic to another, and to treat single subjects in several places. The larger structure follows the threefold division of the world established in the first sentence of the first chapter:

> Seeing there is a threefold world, elementary, celestial, and intellectual, and every inferior is governed by its superior, and receiveth the influence of the virtues thereof, so that the very original, and chief Worker of all doth by angels, the heavens, stars, elements, animals, plants, metals, and stones convey from himself the virtues of his omnipotency upon us, for whose service he made, and created all these things: wise men conceive it no way irrational that it should be possible for us to ascend by the same degrees through each world, to the same very original world itself, the Maker of all things, the First Cause, from whence all things are, and proceed; and also to enjoy not only these virtues, which are already in the more excellent kind of things, but also besides these, to draw new virtues from above.

Book one concerns magic in the natural or elementary world of stones, herbs, trees, metals, and so on; book two examines the Celestial or mathematical world, the influence of the heavens and numbers (the planets and stars, because they move according to strict mathematical and geometrical relationships, are considered part of mathematical magic); book three looks at the intellectual world of pagan gods, spirits, angels, devils, and the methods of ceremonial magic used to interact with these beings, as well as with God.

Agrippa's system of magic is an amalgam of Greek and Roman occultism drawn from classical sources such as Pliny the Elder, Ovid, Virgil, Apuleius, and of course Hermes Trismegistus, as well as later writers such as Ficino; and the medieval Jewish Kabbalah, derived from the writings of Reuchlin and Pico della Mirandola. Agrippa was perhaps the first to thoroughly blend and integrate these two occult streams, which until that time were separate (Neoplatonism had some influence on Jewish Kabbalists, but the Kabbalah none at all on the descendants of Neoplatonism).

Frances A. Yates asserts that Agrippa regarded himself as a Christian Kabbalist after the model of Pico della Mirandola, who was the first to introduce the Kabbalah to non-Jewish western scholars. Maintaining the supremacy of Christ, he follows Mirandola in substituting the name of Jesus (IHShVH) as the supreme name of power, displacing the name Jehovah (IHVH) of the Jewish Kabbalists.

About the purpose behind the *Occult Philosophy* she writes: "In fact, I believe Agrippa's aim is precisely that of providing the technical procedures for acquiring the more powerful and 'wonder-making' philosophy which Reuchlin had called for, a philosophy ostensibly Neoplatonic but including a mystical Hermetic-Cabalist core" (Yates 1985, 5: 46).

It is thus not accident or carelessness that causes elements of the Kabbalah to be scattered through all three of the books, but a deliberate effort to energize with practical formulae and procedures the classical philosophy, just then re-emerging into the light of the Renaissance; and also, as Yates perceives, to sanctify the mysticism of the pagans. The Kabbalah was to Agrippa the magic of God.

There was a common saying in Agrippa's time: "Learn Greek and turn heretic." This insularity and bigotry he seeks to overcome, firm in the faith that the wonders of the ancient world, so freshly unearthed and vital, can transcend the arid cant and dogmatism of the Catholic schoolmen. Yates comments: "Agrippa's occult philosophy is intended to be a very white magic. In fact it is really a religion, claiming access to the highest powers, and Christian since it accepts the name of Jesus as the chief of the wonder-working names" (ibid.).

The *Occult Philosophy* had an enormous influence on those seeking a mystical perception of truth through the Art of magic. It was the foremost repository of practical knowledge, giving a host of names, associations and uses of spirits, occult characters and alphabets, sigils, herbs, stones, symbols, colors, fumes, numbers, prayers, stars, beasts and other elements employed magically. The major occult theses of the classical world were set clearly forth, where often before they were only implied by examples. The methods of the mysterious Kabbalah of the Hebrews were explained in detail, all its secrets laid bare. In effect Agrippa had produced the magical encyclopedia of the Renaissance, the handy one-volume reference source to all questions of a practical nature concerning magic.

It would be difficult to exaggerate the influence the book has exerted down to the present day within the occult world. Those who denigrate it—Lynn Thorndike, for example, who calls it a "disappointing book"—are those who have neither respect for, nor knowledge of, the readers for whom it was written. *The Occult Philosophy* is a book about magic written for magicians. It is a comprehensive textbook of the Art. Among European occultists it has served as the single most important guide for the past five centuries.

Anyone who seriously looks at the methods of modern magic, at least as it is worked in English-speaking countries, will acknowledge that they are foremostly based upon the teachings of the Golden Dawn, a Victorian magical society, and the writings of the magician Aleister Crowley. Crowley was a member of the Golden Dawn as a young man, and his magical system is based upon Golden Dawn teachings with surprisingly few innovations. The Golden Dawn, in turn, used as its primary source for names of spirits, sigils, magic squares, and Kabbalistic methods the *Occult Philosophy,* or more properly speaking, Barrett's *Magus,* which is the *Occult Philosophy* in a butchered form. Thus a single thread joins the ceremonial magic of the present day, which is being worked by many thousands of people, with this magical encyclopedia of the Renaissance.

Note on the Text

An effort was made to preserve the texture and quality of the Freake translation wherever this did not interfere with the clarity of Agrippa's meaning.

The spelling has been modernized, but where there was a choice between a modern form and an older form still recognized in dictionaries, the older form has been favored. The spelling of names and places, when modified by peculiarities of the period or typographical errors, has been corrected; but when there is some doubt as to what person, place or thing is intended, or where an older but accepted form for a name is used, the original has generally been retained, and reference made to it in the notes at the end of the chapter.

The antique punctuation has largely been left intact. It has its own logic which will become familiar to the reader with use. Emendations were made where the system of punctuation established locally in a particular chapter was arbitrarily violated, where obvious mistakes or printing errors were committed, and where the punctuation actively interfered with the sense of the text.

Reluctantly I have dispensed with the haphazard capitalization and italics that pepper the Freake edition. Although personally I find them charming, they make a comprehension of the subject matter more difficult, and in some chapters this is difficult enough in itself. An exception has been made in the case of personal names, which retain their italics in the body of the text, though not in the quotations. Because there are so many names, the italics are really quite useful as a reference aid when scanning to locate a particular author quoted.

The greatest departure from the original text of the translation has been the inclusion of paragraph breaks. Agrippa uses no paragraphing. Freake paragraphs rarely—for example, chapter X of book II is more than nine pages long and consists of two paragraphs, the first less than a page, the second more than eight pages. Even when Freake does break the text, he often does so with no regard to the subject. Wherever possible I have retained the paragraphing of the original. The need to further break the text to rest the eye has made it possible to illuminate Agrippa's meaning through the logical and systematic grouping of categories and ideas.

Heinricus Cornelius Agrippa von Nettesheim

Three Books of

Occult Philosophy

written by
Henry Cornelius Agrippa
of
Nettesheim

Counsellor to Charles the Fifth,

Emperor of Germany:

AND

Judge of the Prerogative Court.

Translated out of the Latin into the
English Tongue by J. Freake

Edited and Annotated by
Donald Tyson

An Encomium on the Three Books
of Cornelius Agrippa, Knight
by
Eugenius Philalethes[1]

Great, glorious Pen-man! whom I
    should not name,

Lest I might Seem to measure Thee by Fame.
Nature's Apostle, and her Choice High Priest,
Her Mystical, and bright Evangelist.
How am I rapt when I contemplate Thee,
And wind myself above All that I see!
The Spirits of thy Lines infuse a Fire
Like the World's Soul,[2] which makes me thus
    aspire:
I am unbodied by thy Books, and Thee,
And in thy Papers find my Ecstasy.
Or if I please but to descend a strain,
Thy Elements[3] do screen my Soul again.
I can undress my Self by thy bright Glass,
And then resume the Inclosure, as I was.
Now I am Earth, and now a Star, and then
A Spirit; now a Star, and Earth again;
Or if I will but ramass all that be,
In the least moment I engross all Three.
I span the Heaven and Earth, and things above,
And which is more, join Natures with their
    Jove.
He Crowns my Soul with Fire, and there doth
    shine
But like the Rainbow in a Cloud of mine.
Yet there's a Law by which I discompose

The Ashes, and the Fire itself disclose,
But in his Emerald[4] still he doth appear;
They are but Grave-clothes which he scatters
    here.
Who sees this Fire without his Mask, His Eye
Must needs be swallowed by the Light, and die.

These are the Mysteries for which I wept,
Glorious Agrippa, where thy Language slept,
Where thy dark Texture made me wander far,
Whiles through that pathless Night, I traced the
    star,
But I have found those Mysteries for which
Thy Book was more than thrice-piled o'er with
    Pitch.
Now a new East beyond the stars I see
Where breaks the Day of thy Divinity:
Heaven states a Commerce here with Man, had
    He
But grateful Hands to take, and Eyes to see.

Hence you fond Schoolmen, that high truths
    deride,
And with no Arguments but Noise, and Pride;
You that damn all but what yourselves invent,
And yet find nothing by Experiment:
Your Fate is written by an Unseen Hand,
But his Three Books with the Three worlds[5]
    shall stand.

Notes—Encomium

1. *Eugenius Philalethes*—The pen name of Thomas Vaughan (see biographical note). This poem occurs in his mystical alchemical work *Anthroposophia Theomagica* (1650). Above the poem Vaughan says: "But shall I not be counted a conjurer, seeing I follow the principles of Cornelius Agrippa, that grand Archimagus, as the antichristian Jesuits call him? He indeed is my author, and next to God I owe all that I have unto him" *(Magical Writings of Thomas Vaughan,* ed. A. E. Waite [London: George Redway, 1888], 33).

2. *World's Soul*—see Appendix II.

3. *Thy Elements*—see Appendix III.

4. *his Emerald*—see Appendix I.

5. *Three worlds*—the natural, celestial, and intelligible.

The Life of Henry Cornelius Agrippa, Knight

Henry Cornelius Agrippa, descended from a noble family of Nettesheim in Belgia, Doctor of the Laws and Physic, Master of the Rolls, and Judge of the Spiritual Court, from his youth he applied his mind to learning, and by his happy wit obtained great knowledge of all arts and sciences; afterwards also he followed the army of the princes, and for his valor was created knight in the field.

And when he was by these means famous for learning and arms about 1530, he gave his mind to writing, and composed Three Books of Occult Philosophy; afterward an invective or cynical declamation of the Uncertainty and Vanity of All Things in which he teacheth that there is no certainty in anything, but in the solid words of God, and that, to lie hid in the eminency of God's word. He also wrote an History of the Double Coronation of the Emperor *Charles,* and also of the Excellency of the Feminine Sex, and of the Apparitions of Spirits; but seeing that he published commentaries on the Ars Brevis of *Raymundus Lully,* and was very much addicted to occult philosophy and astrology, there were those who thought that he enjoyed commerce with devils, whom notwithstanding he confuted in his published Apology, and showed, that he kept himself within the bounds of art.

In 1538 he wrote many learned orations, which manifest all the excellency of all wit; but especially ten: the first on *Plato's* Banquet, uttered in the Academy of Tricina containing the praise of love; the second on *Hermes Trismegistus,* and of the power and wisdom of God; the third for one who was to receive his degree of Doctor; the fourth for the Lords of Metz, when he was chosen their advocate, syndic and orator; the fifth to the senate of Luxemburg, for the Lords of Metz; the sixth to salute the Prince and Bishop thereof, written for the Lords of Metz; the seventh to salute a noble man, written likewise for the Lords of Metz; the eight for a certain kinsman of his, a Carmelite, made Bachelor of Divinity, when he received his regency at Paris; the ninth for the son of *Christian,* King of Denmark, Norway, and Sweden, delivered at the coming of the Emperor; the tenth at the funeral of the Lady *Margaret,* Princess of Austria and Burgundy.

He wrote also a Dialogue Concerning Man, and a Declamation of a Disputable Opinion Concerning Original Sin to the Bishop of Cyrene; an Epistle to *Michael de Arando,* bishop of Saint Paul; a Complaint Upon a Calumny Not Proved, printed at Strasborg 1539.

And therefore by these monuments published, the name of Cornelius for his variety of learning was famous, not only amongst the Germans, but also other nations; for *Momus* himself carpeth at all amongst the gods; amongst the heros *Hercules* hunteth after monsters; amongst the devils *Pluto* the king of hell is angry with all the ghosts; amongst philosophers *Democritus* laugheth at all things, on the contrary *Heraclitus* weepeth at all things; *Pirrhias* is ignorant of all things, and *Aristotle* thinketh he knoweth all things; *Diogenes* condemneth all things; this *Agrippa* spareth none, he condemneth, knows, is ignorant, weeps, laughs, is angry, pursueth, carps at all things being himself a philosopher, demon, an hero, a god, and all things.

To the Reader

I do not doubt but the title of our book, Of Occult Philosophy, Or Of Magic, may by the rarity of it allure many to read it, amongst which, some of a crazy[1] judgement, and some that are perverse will come to hear what I can say, who by their rash ignorance may take the name of magic in the worse sense, and though scarce having seen the title, cry out that I teach forbidden arts, sow the seed of heresies, offend pious ears, and scandalize excellent wits; that I am a sorcerer, and superstitious, and devilish, who indeed am a magician.

To whom I answer that a magician doth not amongst learned men signify a sorcerer, or one that is superstitious, or devilish; but a wise man, a priest, a prophet; and that the sybils were magicianesses, and therefore prophesied most clearly of Christ;[2] and that magicians, as wise-men,[3] by the wonderful secrets the world, knew Christ the author of the world to be born, and came first of all to worship him; and that the name of magic was received by philosophers, commended by divines, and not unacceptable to the Gospel.

I believe that the supercilious censors will object against the sybils, holy magicians, and the Gospel itself sooner than receive the name of magic into favour; so conscientious are they, that neither *Apollo,* nor all the Muses, nor an angel from heaven can redeem me from their curse. Whom therefore I advise, that they read not our writings, nor understand them, nor remember them. For they are pernicious, and full of poison; the gate of Acheron[4] is in this book; it speaks stones, let them take heed that it beat not out their brains.

But you that come without prejudice to read it, if you have so much discretion of prudence as bees have in gathering honey, read securely, and believe that you shall receive no little profit, and much pleasure; but if you shall find any things that may not please you, let them alone, and make no use of them; for I do not approve of them, but declare them to you; but do not refuse other things, for they that look into the books of physicians, do together with antidotes and medicines, read also poisons. I confess that magic itself teacheth many superfluous things, and curious prodigies for ostentation; leave them as empty things, yet be not ignorant of their causes. But those things which are for the profit of man, for the turning away of evil events, for the destroying of sorceries, for the curing of diseases, for the exterminating of phantasms, for the preserving of life, honour, fortune, may be done without offense to God, or injury to religion, because they are, as profitable, so necessary.

But I have admonished you, that I have writ many things, rather narratively than affirmatively; for so it seemed needful that we should pass over fewer things following the judgements of Platonists, and other gentile philosophers when they did suggest an argument of writing to our purpose; therefore if any error have been committed, or anything hath been spoken more freely, pardon my youth; for I wrote this being scarce a young man, that I may excuse myself, and say, whilst I was a child, I spake as a child, I understood as a child, but being become a man, I retracted those things which I did being a boy, and in my book Of the Vanity and Uncertainty of Sciences[5] I did for the most part retract this book.

But here haply you may blame me again, saying, behold thou being a youth didst write and now being old hast retracted it; what therefore hast thou set forth? I confess whilst I was very young, I set upon the writing of these Books, but hoping that I should set them forth with corrections and enlargements, and for that cause I gave them to *Tritemius* a Neapolitanian abbot, formerly a Spanhemensian, a man very industrious after secret things. But it happened afterwards, that the work being intercepted, before I finished it, was carried about imperfect, and impolished, and did fly abroad in Italy, in France, in Germany through many men's hands, and some men, whether more impatiently, or imprudently, I know not, would have put it thus imperfect to the press, with which mischief I being affected, determined to set it forth myself, thinking that there might be less danger if these books came out of my hands with some amendments, than to come forth torn, and in fragments out of other men's hands. Moreover I thought it no crime if I should not suffer the testimony of my youth to perish.

Also we added some chapters, and we inserted many things, which did seem unfit to pass by, which the curious reader shall be able to understand by the inequality of the very phrase; for we were unwilling to begin the work anew, and to unravel all that we had done, but to correct it, and put some flourish upon it.

Wherefore now I pray thee, courteous reader, again, weigh not these things according to the present time of setting them forth, but pardon my curious youth, if thou shalt find anything in them that may displease thee.

Notes—To the Reader

1. *crazy*—Flawed.

2. *prophesied . . . of Christ*—See note 15, book I, chapter LX.

3. *wisemen*—Matthew 2:1–2.

4. *of Acheron*—a name of the land of the dead, derived from the River Acheron said to flow through the Underworld. The Etruscans worshiped Acheron and sacrificed to this god in order to deify the souls of their dead.

5. *Uncertainty of Sciences*—*De incertitudine et vanitate scientiarum,* etc., Antwerp, 1531.

To R.P.D. *John Tritemius,*
an abbot of Saint James in the suburbs of Herbipolis,
Henry Cornelius Agrippa of Nettesheym
sendeth greeting[1]

When I was of late (most reverend Father) for a while coversant with you in your Monastery of Herbipolis, we conferred together of divers things concerning chemistry, magic, and Cabalie, and of other things, which as yet lie hid in secret sciences, and arts; and then there was one great question amongst the rest, why magic, whereas it was accounted by all ancient phlosophers the chiefest science, and by the ancient wise men, and priests was always held in great veneration, came at last after the beginning of the Catholic Church to be always odious to, and suspected by the holy Fathers, and then exploded by divines, and condemned by sacred canons, and moreover by all laws and ordinances forbidden.

Now the cause, as I conceive is no other than this, viz. because by a certain fatal depravation of times, and men, many false philosophers crept in, and these under the name of magicians, heaping together through various sorts of errors and factions of false religions, many cursed superstitions and dangerous rites, and many wicked sacrileges, out of orthodox religion, even to the persecution of nature, and destruction of men, and injury of God, set forth very many wicked, and unlawful books, such as we see carried about in these days, to which they have by stealth prefixed the most honest name, and title of magic. They therefore by this sacred title of magic, hoped to gain credit to their cursed and detestable fooleries.

Hence it is that this name of magic, formerly honorable, is now in these days become most odious to good and honest men, and acounted a capital crime, if anyone dare profess himself to be a magician, either in doctrine or works, unless haply some certain old doting woman, dwelling in the country, would be believed to be skillful, and have a divine power, that (as saith *Apuleius*)[2] she can throw down the heaven, lift up the earth, harden fountains, wash away mountains, raise up ghosts, cast down gods, extinguish the stars, illuminate hell, or as *Virgil* sings,[3]

> She'll promise by her charms to cast
> great cares,
> Or ease the minds of men, and make the
> stars
> For to go back; and rivers to stand still,
> And raise the nightly ghosts even at her
> will,
> To make the earth to groan, and trees to
> fall
> From the mountains———

Hence those things, which *Lucan* relates of *Thessala*[4] that magicianess, and *Homer*[5] of the omnipotency of *Circe,* whereof many I confess are as well of a fallacious opinion, as superstitious diligence, and pernicious labor, as when they cannot come under a wicked art, yet they presume they may be able to cloak themselves under that venerable title of magic.

Since then these things are so, I wondered much, and was not less angry, that as yet there hath been no man, who did challenge this sublime and sacred discipline with the crime of impiety, or had delivered it purely, and sincerely to us, since I have seen of our modern writers *Roger Bacon, Robert* an English man,[6] *Peter Apponus,*[7] *Albertus* the Teutonich,[8] *Arnoldas de villa Nova, Anselme* the Parmensian,[9] *Picatrix* the Spaniard, *Cicclus Asculus*[10] of Florence, and many others, but writers of an obscure name, when they promised to treat of magic, to do nothing but irrational toys, and superstitions unworthy of honest men.

Hence my spirit was moved, and by reason partly of admiration, and partly of indignation, I was willing to play the philosopher, supposing that I should do no discommendable work, who have been always from my youth a curious, and undaunted searcher of wonderful effects, and operations full of mysteries; if I should recover that ancient magic the discipline of all wise men from the errors of impiety, purify and adorn it with its proper luster, and vindicate it from the injuries of its calumniators; which thing though I long deliberated of it in my mind, yet never durst as yet undertake, but after some conference betwixt us of these things at Herbipolis, your transcending knowledge, and learning, and your ardent adhortation put courage, and boldness into me.

There selecting the opinions of philosophers of known credit, and purging the introduction of the wicked (who dissembling, with a counterfeited knowledge did teach, that traditions of magicians must be learned from very reprobate books of darkness, as from institutions of wonderful operations) and removing all darkness, have at last composed three compendious books of magic, and titled them Of Occult Philosophy, being a title less offensive, which books I submit (you excelling in the knowledge of these things) to your correction and censure, that if I have wrote anything which may tend either to the contumely of nature, offending God, or injury of religion, you may condemn the error; but if the scandal of impiety be dissolved and purged, you may defend the tradition of truth; and that you would do so with these books, and magic itself, that nothing may be concealed which may be profitable, and nothing approved of which cannot but do hurt, by which means these three books having passed your examination with approbation, may at length be thought worthy to come forth with good success in public, and may not be afraid to come under the censure of posterity.

Farewell, and pardon these my bold undertakings.

Notes—To R.P.D. John Tritemius

1. *sendeth greeting*—This letter also appears as letter 23, bk. 1, in the Epistolarum of the Latin *Opera* of Agrippa's works (circa 1600), reprinted in facsimile in two volumes by Georg Olms Verlag, Hildesheim and New York, 1970, II:620–3.

2. *as saith Apuleius*—Socrates describes the witch Meroe to Apuleius:

> Verily shee is a Magitian, which hath power to rule the heavens, to bring downe the sky, to beare up the earth, to turne the waters into hills, and the hills into running waters, to lift up the terrestrial spirits into the aire, and to pull the gods out of the heavens, to extinguish the planets, and to lighten the deepe darkenesse of hell. (Apuleius, *The Golden Asse* ch. 4, trans. W. Adlington [1566] [London, ed. of 1639])

3. *Virgil sings*—This quotation is from the *Aeneid,* bk. 4, lines 487–91. It reminds me of this description in Ovid, spoken by Hypsipyle, the lover of the hero Jason, about her rival the witch Medea:

> but by her incantations has she influenced thee; and with her enchanted sickle does she reap the dreadful plants. She endeavours to draw down the struggling Moon from her chariot, and to envelope the horses of the Sun in darkness. She bridles the waves, and stops the winding rivers: she moves the woods and the firm rocks from their spot. Amid the tombs does she wander without her girdle, her locks all dishevelled, and certain bones does she collect from the warm piles. (Epistle VI: "Hypsipyle to Jason." In *The Heroides,* trans. H. T. Riley [London: George Bell and Sons, 1883], 56–7)

There is a remarkable similarity in the descriptions of the powers of witchcraft in Virgil, Apuleius, Ovid and Lucan—it may be presumed the latter three have drawn from Virgil.

4. *Thessala*—That is, Erichtho, a most potent witch of Thessaly. See Lucan's *Pharsalia* 6, c. line506.

5. *Homer*—see the *Odyssey* 10.

6. *Robert an English man*—Robertus Anglicus.

7. *Peter Apponus*—Petrus de Apono.

8. *Albertus the Teutonich*—Albertus Magnus.

9. *Anselme the Parmensian*—Georgio Anselmi.

10. *Cicclus Asculus*—Cecco d'Ascoli.

Johannes Trithemius

John Tritemius, abbot of Saint James of Herbipolis, formerly of Spanhemia, to his *Henry Cornelius Agrippa* of Nettesheym, health and love.[1]

Your work (nost renowned Agrippa) entitled Of Occult Philosophy, which you have sent by this bearer, to me to be examined, with how much pleasure I received it, no mortal tongue can ever express, nor the pen of any write; I wondered at your more than vulgar learning, that you being so young should penetrate into such secrets as have been hid from most learned men, and not only clearly, and truly, but also properly, and elegantly set them forth. Whence first I give you thanks for your good will to me, and if I shall ever be able, I shall return you thanks to the utmost of my power; your work, which no learned man can sufficiently commend, I approve of.

Now that you may proceed toward higher things, as you have begun, and not suffer such excellent parts of wit to be idle, I do with as much earnestness as I can advise, entreat, and beseech you, that you would exercise yourself in laboring after better things, and demonstrate the light of true wisdom to the ignorant, according as you yourself are divinely enlightened; neither let the consideration of idle vain fellows withdraw you from your purpose; I say of them, of whom it said, the wearied ox treads hard,

whereas no man, to the judgement of the wise, can be truly learned, who is sworn to the rudiments of one only faculty; but you hath God gifted with a large, and sublime wit, not that you should imitate oxen, but birds; neither think it sufficient that you stay about particulars, but bend your mind confidently to universals; for by so much the more learned anyone is thought, by how much fewer things he is ignorant of. Moreover your wit is fully apt to all things, and to be rationally employed, not in a few, or low things, but many, and sublimer.

Yet this one rule I advise you to observe, that you communicate vulgar secrets to vulgar friends, but higher and secret to higher, and secret friends only. Give hay to an ox, sugar to a parrot only; understand my meaning, lest you be trod under the oxen's feet, as oftentimes it falls out.

Farewell my happy friend, and if it lie in my power to serve you, command me, and according to your pleasure it shall without delay be done; also let our friendship increase daily; write often to me, and send me some of your labors I earnestly pray you. Again farewell.

From our Monastery at Peapolis, the 8. day of April, An. MDX.

Note—John Tritemius to his Henry Cornelius Agrippa

1. *health and love*—This letter appears as letter 24, bk. 1, the Epistolarum of the Latin *Opera* of Agrippa's works, 2:623–4.

To the reverend father in Christ, and most illustrious prince, *Hermannus*, Earl of Wyda, by the grace of God Archbishop of the holy Church of Colonia, Prince Elector of the Holy Roman Empire, and Chief Chancellor Through Italy, Duke of Westphalia, and Angaria, and descended of the legate of the holy Church of Rome, one of the Vicar General's court, *Henry Cornelius Agrippa* of Nettes-Heym, sendeth greeting.[1]

Such is the greatness of your renowned fame (most reverend and illustrious Prince), such is the greatness of your virtues, and splendor of learning, and frequent exercise of the best learning, and grave oration, with solid prudence, and elegant readiness of speaking, knowledge of many things, constant religion, and commendable conditions, with which you are endowed beyond the common custom of others; I say nothing of those ancient monuments to your eminent nobility, the treasures of your riches, both old, and new, the largeness of your dominion, the ornaments of the sacred dignities, with the excellency whereof you excel, together with the comely form, and strength of the body.

Though all these things be very great, yet I esteem you far greater than all these, for those your heroic, and super-illustrious virtues, by which you truly have caused, that by how much the more anyone is learned, and loves virtue, so much the more he may desire to insinuate himself into your favor, whence I also am resolved that your favor shall be obtained by me, but after the manner of the people of Parthia, i.e. not without a present, which custom of saluting princes, is indeed derived from the ages of the ancients, unto these very times, and still we see it observed. And when I see certain other very learned men to furnish you with fair, and great presents of their learning, lest I only should be a neglecter of your worship and reverence, I durst not apply myself with empty hands to your greatness.

Now being thoughtful, and looking about in my study to see what present I should bestow upon such an illustrious prince, behold! amongst such things as were closely laid up, the books Of Occult Philosophy, Or Of Magic, presently offered themselves, such as I attempted to write whilst I was very young, and now many years being past, as it were forgetting them, have neglected to perfect them; I presently made haste, as it were to pay my vows, to present them to your honor to complete them. Truly I was persuaded that I could give nothing more acceptable to you, than a new work of most ancient and abstruse learning; I say a work of my curious youth, but a doctrine of antiquity, by none I dare say hitherto attempted to be restored.

Yet my works are not wrote to you, because they are worthy of you, but that they might make a way open for me to gain your favor. I beseech you, if it may be, let them be excused by you. I shall be devotedly yours, if these studies of my youth shall by the authority of your greatness come into knowledge, envy being chased away by the power of your worthiness, there remain the memory of them to me, as the fruit of a good conscience, seeing many things in them seemed to me, being older, as most profitable, so most necessary to be known.

You have therefore the work, not only of my youth, but of my present age, for I have corrected many errata of the work of my youth, I have inserted many things in many places, and have added many things to many chapters, which may easily be perceived by the inequality of the style; and so shall you know that I shall all my life be devoted to your pleasure. Farewell most happy prince of happy Colonia.

From Mechlinia Anno M.D.XXXI. In the month of January.

Note—To Hermannus, Earl of Wyda

1. *sendeth greeting*—This letter also appears as letter 13, bk. 6 of the Epistolarum of the Latin *Opera*, 2:952–4.

Judicious Reader!

There is the outside, and the inside of philosophy; but the former without the latter is but an empty flourish; yet with this alone most are satisfied. To have a bare notion of a Deity, to apprehend some motions of the celestials, together with the common operations thereof, and to conceive of some terrestrial productions, is but what is superficial, and vulgar; but this is true, this is sublime, but occult philosophy; to understand the mysterious influences of the intellectual world upon the celestial, and of both upon the terrestrial; to know how to dispose, and fit ourselves so, as to be capable of receiving those superior operations, whereby we may be enabled to operate wonderful things, which indeed seem impossible, or at least unlawful, when as indeed they may be effected by a natural power, and without either offence to God, or violation of religion.

To defend kingdoms, to discover the secret counsels of men, to overcome enemies, to redeem captives, to increase riches, to procure the favor of men, to expel diseases, to preserve health, to prolong life, to renew youth, to foretell future events, to see and know things done many miles off, and such like as these, by virtue of superior influences, may seem things incredible; yet read but the ensuing treatise, and thou shalt see the possibility thereof confirmed both by reason, and example.

I speak now to the judicious, for as for the others, they neither know, nor believe, nor will know anything, but what is vulgar, nay they think, that beyond this there is scarce anything knowable; when as indeed there are profound mysteries in all beings, even from God in the highest heavens, to the devils in the lowest hell; yea in very numbers, names, letters, characters, gestures, time, place, and such like, all which are by this learned author profoundly discussed.

I cannot deny but in this his work there is much superstition, and vanity. But remember that the best gold must have the greatest allowance; consider the time of darkness, and of his youth, when, the place where, and the things which he hath discovered and wrote, and thou wilt rather admire his solidity, than condemn his vanity. Gold hath much blackness adhering to it as soon as it is taken out of the earth. Mysterious truths do not presently shine like rays of the Sun as soon as they are recovered from a long darkness, but are clouded with obscurity. Nay I will not say but this *Agrippa* might obscure these mysteries like an Hermetical philosopher, on purpose, that only the sons of art might understand them. He perhaps might mix chaff with his wheat, that quick sighted birds only might find it out, and not swine trample it underfoot.

From saying much as touching the excusing, or commending this author, I am already prevented; for at the beginning and ending of this book there are several epistles of his own and others, wherein he excuseth what may be expected against him; and of others to him sufficiently commending what is praiseworthy in him; to which may be added that honorable testimony given to him by the author[1] of that most witty, and sublime the Anthroposophia Theomagica, lately set forth. All that I shall say to persuade thee to read this book, is but to desire thee to cast thine eye upon the index of the chapters contained therein, which is at the end thereof:[2] and thou shalt therein see such variety of wonderful subjects, that at the sight thereof thou wilt be impatient til thou hast read them.

I shall crave leave now to speak one word for myself. If this my translation shall neither answer the worth of the author, or expectation of the reader; consider that the uncouthness of the author's style in many places, the manifold errata, as well literal, as those in respect of gramatical construction, may haply occasion some mistakes in this my translation. Yet notwithstanding, I hope I have, though without much elegancy (which indeed the matter would not bear) put it into as intelligible an English phrase as the original would afford. As for the terms of art, which are many, divers of them would not bear any English expression, therefore I have expressed them in Latinisms or Grecisms, according as I have found them. I hope an artist will be able to understand them; as for the errata, as I cursorily read over the book, I observe these as you see mentioned. If thou shalt meet with any more, as it is possible thou mayst, be thou candid, and impute them to the printer's mistake; for which, as also for taking in the best sense, what here I present thee withal, thou shalt forever oblige thy friend,

J.F.

Notes—Judicious Reader

1. *the author*—Thomas Vaughan.

2. *the end thereof*—Presumably Freake refers to the front end, since this is the location of the index in both the English and Latin versions.

To My Most Honorable, and no less learned Friend, *Robert Childe*, Doctor of Physic.

Sir! Great men decline, mighty men may fall, but an honest philosopher keeps his station forever. To yourself therefore I crave leave to present, what I know you are able to protect; not with the sword, but by reason; and not that only, but what by your acceptance you are able to give a lustre to. I see it is not in vain that you have compassed sea and land, for thereby you have made a proselyte, not of another, but of yourself, by being converted from the vulgar, and irrational incredulities to the rational embracing of the sublime, hermetical, and theomagical truths. You are skilled in the one as if *Hermes* had been your tutor; have insight in the other, as if *Agrippa* your master.

Many transmarine philosophers, which we only read, you have conversed with: many countries, rarities, and antiquities, which we have only heard of, and admire, you have seen. Nay you have not only heard of, but seen, not in maps, but in Rome itself the manners of Rome. There you have seen much ceremony, and little religion; and in the wilderness of New England, you have seen amongst some, much religion, and little ceremony; and amongst others, I mean the natives thereof, neither ceremony, nor religion, but what nature dictates to them. In this there is no small variety, and your observation not little. In your passage thither by sea, you have seen the wonders of God in the deep; and by land, you have seen the astonishing works of God in the unaccessible mountains. You have left no stone unturned, that the turning thereof might conduce to the discovery of what was occult, and worthy to be known.

It is part of my ambition to let the world know that I honor such as yourself, and my learned friend, and your experienced fellow traveler, Doctor Charlet, who have, like true philosophers neglected your worldly advantages to become masters of that which hath now rendered you both truly honorable. If I had as many languages as yourselves, the rhetorical and pathetical expressions thereof would fail to signify my estimation of, and affections towards you both.

Now sir! as in reference to this my translation, if your judgement shall find a deficiency therein, let your candor make a supply thereof. Let this treatise Of Occult Philosophy coming as a stranger amongst the English, be patronized by you, remembering that you yourself was once a stranger in the country of its nativity. This stranger I have dressed in an English garb; but if it be not according to the fashion, and therefore ungrateful to any, let your approbation make it the mode; you know strangers most commonly induce a fashion, especially if any once begin to approve of their habit. Your approbation is that which it will stand in need of, and which will render me,

SIR,
Most Obligedly yours,
J.F.

Pragmatic schoolmen, men made up of pride,
And railing arguments, who truth deride,
And scorn all else but what yourselves devise,
And think these high-learned tracts to be but lies,
Do not presume, unless with hallowed hand,
To touch these books who with the world shall stand;
They are indeed mysterious, rare and rich,
And far transcend the ordinary pitch.

Io. Booker

An index of all the chapters which are contained in this work.

Book II

Book III

Three Books of Occult Philosophy, or of Magic;

written by that Famous Man
Henry Cornelius Agrippa, Knight
And Doctor of both Laws, Counsellor to
Caesar's Sacred Majesty, and Judge of the
Prerogative Court.

BOOK I

CHAPTER 1

How magicians collect virtues from the threefold world, is declared in these three books.

Seeing there is a threefold world,[1] elementary, celestial, and intellectual, and every inferior is governed by its superior, and receiveth the influence of the virtues thereof, so that the very original, and chief Worker of all doth by angels, the heavens, stars, elements, animals, plants, metals, and stones convey from himself the virtues of his omnipotency upon us, for whose service he made, and created all these things: wise men conceive it no way irrational that it should be possible for us to ascend by the same degrees through each world, to the same very original world itself, the Maker of all things, and First Cause, from whence all things are, and proceed; and also to enjoy not only these virtues, which are already in the more excellent kind of things, but also besides these, to draw new virtues from above.

Hence it is that they seek after the virtues of the elementary world, through the help of physic, and natural philosophy in the various mixtions of natural things, then of the celestial world in the rays, and influences thereof, according to the rules of astrologers, and the doctrines of mathematicians, joining the celestial vertues to the former: moreover, they ratify and confirm all these with the powers of divers intelligencies, through the sacred ceremonies of religion.

The order and process of all these I shall endeavor to deliver in these three books: whereof the first contains natural magic, the second celestial, and the third ceremonial. But I know not whether it be an unpardonable presumption in me, that I, a man of so little judgement and learning should in my very youth so confidently set upon a business so difficult, so hard, and intricate as this is. Wherefore, whatsoever things have here already, and shall afterwards be said by me, I would not have anyone assent to them, nor shall I myself, any farther than they shall be approved of by the universal Church, and the congregation of the faithful.[2]

Notes—Chapter 1

1. *threefold world*—Agrippa divides the universe into the terrestrial, astrological and spiritual regions, each of which gives rise to its own branch of magic. This division echoes the threefold division of Plato:

> They [spirits] are the envoys and interpreters that ply between heaven and earth, flying upward with our worship and our prayers, and descending with the heavenly answers and commandments, and since they are between the two estates they weld

> both sides together and merge them into one great whole. They form the medium of the prophetic arts, of the priestly rites of sacrifice, initiation, and incantation, or divination and of sorcery, for the divine will not mingle directly with the human, and it is only through the mediation of the spirit world that man can have any intercourse, whether waking or sleeping, with the gods. And the man who is versed in

3

such matters is said to have spiritual powers, as opposed to the mechanical powers of the man who is expert in the more mundane arts. *(Symposium,* trans. M. Joyce. In *Collected Dialogues,* ed. Edith Hamilton and Huntington Cairns [Princeton University Press, 1973], 555)

Hermes Trismegistus divides the highest region, and separates the spirits into gods and souls, thereby arriving at a universe of four parts:

There are in the universe four regions, which are subject to law that cannot be transgressed, and to kingly presidency; namely heaven, the aether, the air, and the earth. Above, my son, in heaven, dwell gods, over whom, as over all else likewise, rules the Maker of the universe; in the aether dwell stars, over whom rules that great luminary, the Sun; in the air dwell souls, over whom rules the Moon; and upon earth dwell men, over whom rules he who is king for the time being; for the gods, my son, cause to be born at the right time a man that is worthy to govern upon earth. ("Aphrodite" excerpt 24. In *Hermetica,* trans. W. Scott [Boston: Shambhala, 1985], 1:495, 497.)

2. *of the faithful*—Agrippa knew he was walking a fine line between philosophy and witchcraft so far as the learned opinion of his day was concerned, and very much subject to the whim of the Church. See the guarded warning to this effect at the end of the letter from Trithemius to Agrippa, p. lvii.

CHAPTER II

What magic is, what are the parts thereof, and how the professors thereof must be qualified.

Magic is a faculty of wonderful virtue, full of most high mysteries, containing the most profound contemplation of most secret things, together with the nature, power, quality, substance, and virtues thereof, as also the knowledge of whole nature, and it doth instruct us concerning the differing, and agreement of things amongst themselves, whence it produceth its wonderful effects, by uniting the virtues of things through the application of them one to the other, and to their inferior suitable subjects, joining and knitting them together thoroughly by the powers, and virtues of the superior bodies.

This is the most perfect, and chief science, that sacred, and sublimer kind of philosophy, and lastly the most absolute perfection of all most excellent philosophy. For seeing that all regulative philosophy is divided into natural, mathematical, and theological: (Natural philosophy teacheth the nature of those things which are in the world, searching and enquiring into their causes, effects, times, places, fashions, events, their whole, and parts, also:

The number and the nature of those things,
Called elements, what Fire, Earth, Air forth
  brings:
From whence the heavens their beginnings
  had;
Whence tide, whence rainbow in. gay
  colours clad.
What makes the clouds that gathered are,
  and black,

To send forth lightnings, and a thundering
  crack;
What doth the nightly flames, and comets
  make;
What makes the Earth to swell, and then to
  quake:
What is the seed of metals, and of gold
What virtues, wealth, doth Nature's coffer
  hold.[1]

All these things doth natural philosophy, the viewer of nature contain, teaching us according to *Virgil's* muse:

————whence all things flow,
Whence mankind, beast, whence fire,
  whence rain, and snow,
Whence earthquakes are, why the whole
  ocean beats
Over his banks, and then again retreats:
Whence strength of herbs, whence courage,
  rage of brutes,
All kinds of stone, of creeping things, and
  fruits.[2]

But mathematical philosophy teacheth us to know the quantity of natural bodies, as extended into three dimensions, as also to conceive of the motion, and course of celestial bodies:

———— as in great haste,
What makes the golden stars to march so
  fast,
What makes the Moon sometimes to mask
  her face,
The Sun also, as if in some disgrace.[3]

And as *Virgil* sings:

5

How the Sun doth rule with twelve Zodiac
signs,
The orb that's measured round about with
lines,
It doth the heaven's starry way make known,
And strange eclipses of the Sun, and Moon,
Arcturus also, and the Stars of Rain,
The Seven Stars likewise, and Charles his
Wain,
Why winter Suns make towards the west
so fast;
What makes the nights so long ere they be
past?[4]

All which is understood by mathematical
philosophy.

————hence by the heavens we may
foreknow
the seasons all; times for to reap and sow,
And when 'tis fit to launch into the deep,
And when to war, and when in peace to
sleep,
And when to dig up trees, and them again
To set; that so they may bring forth amain.[5]

Now theological philosophy, or divinity,
teacheth what God is, what the mind, what an
intelligence, what an angel, what a devil, what
the soul, what religion, what sacred institutions, rites, temples, observations, and sacred
mysteries are: it instructs us also concerning
faith, miracles, the virtues of words and figures, the secret operations and mysteries of
seals, and as *Apuleius* saith, it teacheth us rightly to understand, and to be skilled in the ceremonial laws, the equity of holy things, and rule
of religions. But to recollect myself) these three
principal faculties magic comprehends, unites,
and actuates; deservedly therefore was it by the
ancients esteemed as the highest, and most
sacred philosophy.

It was, as we find, brought to light by most
sage authors, and most famous writers;
amongst which principally *Zamolxis* and
Zoroaster were so famous, that many believed
they were the inventors of this science. Their
track *Abbaris* the Hyperborean, *Charmondas,
Damigeron, Eudoxus, Hermippus* followed:
there were also other eminent, choice men, as
*Mercurius Tresmegistus, Porphyrius, Iambli-
cus, Plotinus, Proclus, Dardanus, Orpheus* the
Thracian, *Gog* the Grecian, *Germa* the Babylonian, *Apollonius* of Tyana. *Osthanes* also
wrote excellently in this art; whose books being
as it were lost, *Democritus* of Abdera[6] recovered, and set forth with his own commentaries.
Besides *Pythagoras, Empedocles, Democritus,
Plato,* and many other renowned philosophers
traveled far by sea to learn this art: and being
returned, published it with wonderful devoutness, esteeming of it as a great secret. Also it is
well known that *Pythagoras,* and *Plato* went to
the prophets of Memphis[7] to learn it, and traveled through almost all Syria, Egypt, Judea,
and the schools of the Chaldeans, that they
might not be ignorant of the most sacred
memorials, and records of magic, as also that
they might be furnished with divine things.

Whosoever therefore is desirous to study in
this faculty, if he be not skilled in natural philosophy, wherein are discovered the qualities of
things, and in which are found the occult properties of every being, and if he be not skillful in
the mathematics, and in the aspects, and figures
of the stars, upon which depends the sublime
virtue, and property of everything; and if he be
not learned in theology, wherein are manifested
those immaterial substances,[8] which dispense,
and minister all things, he cannot be possibly
able to understand the rationality of magic. For
there is no work that is done by mere magic, nor
any work that is merely magical, that doth not
comprehend these three faculties.

Notes—Chapter II

1. *coffer hold*—This quote is not from Virgil, but I
have been unable to locate its source.

2. *and fruits*—The second and third lines of this
quote are from the *Georgics* 2, lines 479–80. The
others I cannot identify.

3. *some disgrace*—Not Virgil, but again I cannot
place it.

4. *they be past*—A composite of *Georgics* 1, lines
231–2; *Georgics* 2., lines 477–8; and the *Aeneid* 1,
lines 744–6.

5. *forth amain*—*Georgics* 1, lines 252–6.

6. *Democritus of Abdera*—That is, pseudo-Democritus
the alchemist. See the biographical note on Ostanes.

7. *prophets of Memphis—*

This is also confirmed by the most learned of the Greeks (such as Solon, Thales, Plato, Eudoxus, Pythagoras, and as some say, even Lycurgus) going to Egypt and conversing with the priests; of whom they say Eudoxus was a hearer of Chonuphus of Memphis, Solon of Sonchis of Sais, and Pythagoras of Oenuphis of Heliopolis. Whereof the last named, being (as is probable) more than ordinarily admired by the men, and they also by him, imitated their symbolical and mysterious way of talking, obscuring his sentiments with dark riddles. (Plutarch *Isis and Osiris* 10, trans. William Baxter. In *Plutarch's Essays and Miscellanies,* ed. William W. Goodwin [London: Simpkin, Marshall, Hamilton, Kent and Co., 1874–8], 4:72)

8. *immaterial substances—*Specifically the aerial spirits referred to by Hermes, Augustine, Plato, and others.

CHAPTER III

Of the four elements,
their qualities, and mutual mixtions.

There are four elements,[1] and original grounds of all corporeal things, Fire, Earth, Water, Air, of which all elementated inferior bodies are compounded; not by way of heaping them up together, but by transmutation, and union; and when they are destroyed, they are resolved into elements. For there is none of the sensible elements that is pure, but they are more or less mixed, and apt to be changed one into the other: even as Earth becoming dirty, and being dissolved, becomes Water, and the same being made thick and hard, becomes Earth again; but being evaporated through heat, passeth into Air, and that being kindled, passeth into Fire, and this being extinguished, returns back again into Air, but being cooled again after its burning, becomes Earth, or stone, or sulphur, and this is manifested by lightning.[2]

Plato also was of that opinion, that Earth was wholly changeable, and that the rest of the elements are changed, as into this, so into one another successively.[3] But it is the opinion of the subtiler sort of philosophers, that Earth is not changed, but relented and mixed with other elements, which do not dissolve it, and that it returns back into itself again.

Now every one of the elements hath two special qualities, the former whereof it retains as proper to itself, in the other, as a mean, it agrees with that which comes next after it. For Fire is hot and dry, Earth dry and cold, the Water cold and moist, the Air moist and hot. And so after this manner the elements, according to two contrary qualities, are contrary one to the other, as Fire to Water, and Earth to Air.

Moreover, the elements are upon another account opposite one to the other: for some are heavy, as Earth and Water, and others are light, as Air and Fire. Wherefore the Stoics called the former passives, but the latter actives.

And yet once again *Plato* distinguisheth them after another manner,[4] and assigns to every one of them three qualities, viz. to the Fire brightness, thinness, and motion, but to the Earth darkness, thickness, and quietness. And according to these qualities the elements of Fire and Earth are contrary. But the other elements borrow their qualities from these, so that the Air receives two qualities of the Fire, thinness and motion; and one of the Earth, viz. darkness. In like manner Water receives two qualities of the Earth, darkness and thickness, and one of Fire, viz. motion. But Fire is twice more thin than Air, thrice more moveable, and four times more bright: and the Air is twice more bright, thrice more thin, and four times more moveable than Water. Wherefore Water is twice more bright than Earth, thrice more thin, and four times more moveable. As therefore the Fire is to the Air, so Air to the Water, and Water to the Earth; and again, as the Earth is to the Water, so the Water to the Air, and the Air to the Fire.

And this is the root and foundation of all bodies, natures, virtues, and wonderful works; and he which shall know these qualities of the elements, and their mixtions, shall easily bring to pass such things that are wonderful, and astonishing, and shall be perfect in magic.

Notes—Chapter III

1. *four elements*—See Appendix III.

2. *manifested lightning*—"Lightning and thunder are attended with a strong smell of sulphur, and the light produced by them is of a sulphureous complexion" (Pliny *Natural History* 35:50, trans. John Bostock and H. T. Riley [London: Henry G. Bohn, 1857], 6:293).

3. *one another successively*—Agrippa seems not to have read his Plato carefully:

> In the first place, we see that what we just now called water, by condensation, I suppose, becomes stone and earth, and this same element, when melted and dispersed, passes into vapor and air. Air, again, when inflamed becomes fire, and, again, fire, when condensed and extinguished, produces cloud and mist—and from these, when still more compressed, comes flowing water, and from water comes earth and stones once more—and thus generation appears to be transmitted from one to the other in a circle. *(Timaeus* 49c, trans. B. Jowett [Hamilton and Cairns])

But Plato goes on to say:

> Now it is time to explain what was before obscurely said. There was an error in imagining that all the four elements might be generated by and into one another; this, I say, was an erroneous supposition, for there are generated from the triangles which we have selected four kinds—three [fire, air and water] from the one which has the sides unequal, the fourth alone [earth] framed out of the isosceles triangle. Hence they cannot all be resolved into one another, a great number of small bodies being combined into a few large ones, or the converse. But three of them can be thus resolved and compounded, for they all spring from one. (ibid. 54c)

And farther on Plato is more specific:

> Earth, when meeting with fire and dissolved by its sharpness, whether the dissolution takes place in the fire itself or perhaps in some mass of air or water, is born hither and thither until its parts, meeting together and mutually harmonizing, again become earth, for they can never take any other form. (ibid. 56d)

4. *after another manner*—See Appendix III.

CHAPTER IV

Of a threefold consideration of the elements.

There are then, as we have said, four elements, without the perfect knowledge whereof we can effect nothing in magic. Now each of them is threefold,[1] that so the number of four may make up the number of twelve; and by passing by the number of seven into the number of ten, there may be a progress to the supreme Unity, upon which all virtue and wonderful operation depends.[2]

Of the first order[3] are the pure elements, which are neither compounded nor changed, nor admit of mixtion, but are incorruptible, and not of which, but through which the virtues of all natural things are brought forth into act. No man is able to declare their virtues, because they can do all things upon all things. He which is ignorant of these, shall never be able to bring to pass any wonderful matter.

Of the second order[4] are elements that are compounded, changeable, and impure, yet such as may by art be reduced to their pure simplicity, whose virtue, when they are thus reduced to their simplicity, doth above all things perfect all occult, and common operations of nature: and these are the foundation of the whole natural magic.

Of the third order[5] are those elements, which originally and of themselves are not elements, but are twice compounded, various, and changeable one into the other. They are the infallible medium, and therefore are called the middle nature, or soul of the middle nature: very few there are that understand the deep mysteries thereof. In them is, by means of certain numbers, degrees, and orders, the perfection of every effect in what thing soever, whether natural, celestial, or supercelestial; they are full of wonders, and mysteries, and are operative, as in magic natural, so divine: for from these, through them, proceed the bindings, loosings, and transmutations of all things, the knowing and foretelling of things to come, also the driving forth of evil, and the gaining of good spirits.

Let no man therefore, without these three sorts of elements, and the knowledge thereof, be confident that he is able to work anything in the occult sciences of magic, and nature. But whosoever shall know how to reduce those of one order, into those of another, impure into pure, compounded into simple, and shall know how to understand distinctly the nature, virtue, and power of them in number, degrees, and order, without dividing the substance, he shall easily attain to the knowledge, and perfect operation of all natural things, and celestial secrets.[6]

Noᴛes—Chapᴛer IV

1. *threefold*—Perhaps this refers to the Cardinal, Fixed, and Mutable qualities displayed in the signs of the Zodiac.

2. *depends*—These numbers would seem to refer to the seven planets, twelve Zodiac signs and ten Sephiroth. They may be manipulated in this way:

$$7 + 12 = 19 = 1 + 9 = 10 = 1 + 0 = 1$$

3. *first order*—Perhaps the prime single-digit numbers are implied; i.e., 2, 3, 5 and 7.

4. *second order*—Perhaps the compound single-digit numbers; i.e., 4, 6, 8 and 9.

5. *third order*—Perhaps numbers of more than one digit, which can be reduced to a single digit by magical, or Kabbalistic, addition. For example $12 = 1 + 2 = 3$. They are in this way reducible into one or the other of the first two sets, or into unity. It is upon the manipulation of Hebrew letters through their numerical values that much of magic is based.

6. *celestial secrets*—This chapter has the distinction of being the most obscure in the entire book. Thomas Vaughan, who virtually worshiped Agrippa ("hear the oracle of magick, the great and solemn Agrippa"), quotes it verbatim from the English edition, albeit with a couple of minor errors, in his own *Anima Magica Abscondita*. Vaughan goes on to quote a parallel passage from the writings of the Abbot Trithemius, which, although quite long, I feel compelled to give here because of the darkness of the question:

> "The first principle doth consist in that one substance through which, rather than from whom, is every potentiality of natural marvels developed into the actual. We have said 'through which,' because the Absolute which proceedeth out of unity is not compounded, neither hath it any vicissitude. Thereunto from the Triad, and from the Tetrad is an arcane progression to the Monad for the completion of the Decad, because thereby is the regression of number into unity, and, in like manner, the descent unto the Tetrad and the ascent unto the Monad. By this only can the Duad be completed. With joy and triumph is the Monad converted into the Triad. None who are ignorant of this principle which is after the principle of the Monad can attain unto the Triad, nor approach the most sacred Tetrad. Had they mastered all the books of the wise, were they perfectly conversant with the courses of the stars, with their virtues, powers, operations, and properties, did they keenly and clearly understand their types, signets, sigils, and their most secret things whatsoever, no performance of marvels could possibly follow these operations without the knowledge of this principle which cometh out of a principle, and returneth into a principle; whence all, without exception, which I have found experimenting in natural magic have either attained nothing or, after long and unproductive operations, have been driven into vain, trifling, and superstitious pursuits. Now the second principle, which is separated from the first in order and not in dignity, which alone existing doth create the Triad, is that which works wonders by the Duad. For in the one is the one and there is not the one; it is simple, yet in the Tetrad it is compounded, which being purified by fire cometh forth pure water, and reduced to its simplicity shall reveal unto the performer of arcane mysteries the completion of his labours. Here lieth the centre of all natural magic, whose circumference united unto itself doth display a circle, a vast line in the infinite. Its virtue is above all things purified, and it is less simple than all things, composed on the scale of the Tetrad. But the Pythagoric Tetrad supported by the Triad, the pure and purified in one, can, if order and grade be observed, most assuredly perform marvels and secrets of nature in respect of the Duad within the Triad. This is the Tetrad within the capacity whereof the Triad joined to the Duad, maketh all things one, and which worketh wonderfully. The Triad reduced to unity contains all things, *per aspectum,* in itself, and it doeth whatsoever it will. The third principle is by itself no principle, but between this and the Duad is the end of all science and mystic art, and the infallible centre of the mediating principle. It is no easier to blunder in the one than in the other for few flourish on earth who fundamentally comprehend its mysteries, both progressing by an eight-fold multiplication through the septenary into the triad, and remaining fixed. Therein is the consummation of the scale and series of Number. By this hath every philosopher, and every true Scrutator of natural secrets, attained unto admirable results; by this, reduced in the Triad unto a simple element, they suddenly performed

miraculous cures of diseases, and of all kinds of sickness in a purely natural manner, and the operations of natural and supernatural Magick attained results through the direction of the Tetrad. By this prediction of future events was truthfully performed, and no otherwise was the narrow entrance unto things kept secret wrested from Nature. By this only Medium was the secret of Nature laid bare unto Alchemists; without it no comprehension of the art can be acquired, nor the end of experiment discovered. Believe me, they do err, they do all err, who devoid of these three principles dream it possible for them to accomplish anything in the secret services of Nature." Thus far Trithemius, where for the better understanding of him, I must inform thee there is a two-fold Binarius, one of light and confusion; but peruse Agrippa seriously "Of the Scales of numbers," and thou mayst apprehend all, for our abbot borrowed this language from him, the perusal of whose books he had before he published anything in this nature of his own. (Vaughan *Anima Magica Abscondita*. In *The Magical Writings of Thomas Vaughan*, ed. A. E. Waite [London: George Redway, 1888], 58–60)

CHAPTER V

Of the wonderful natures of Fire, and Earth.

There are two things (saith *Hermes*)[1] viz. Fire and Earth, which are sufficient for the operation of all wonderful things: the former is active, the latter passive.

Fire (as saith *Dionysius*)[2] in all things, and through all things, comes and goes away bright, it is in all things bright, and at the same time occult, and unknown; when it is by itself (no other matter coming to it, in which it should manifest its proper action) it is boundless, and invisible, of itself sufficient for every action that is proper to it, moveable, yielding itself after a manner to all things that come next to it, renewing, guarding nature, enlightening, not comprehended by lights that are veiled over, clear, parted, leaping back, bending upwards, quick in motion, high, always raising motions, comprehending another, not comprehended itself, not standing in need of another, secretly increasing of itself, and manifesting its greatness to things that receive it. Active, powerful, invisibly present in all things at once; it will not be affronted or opposed, but as it were in a way of revenge, it will reduce on a sudden things into obedience to itself, incomprehensible, impalpable, not lessened, most rich in all dispensations of itself. Fire (as saith *Pliny*) is the boundless, and mischievous part of the nature of things, it being a question whether it destroys, or produceth most things.

Fire itself is one, and penetrates through all things (as say the Pythagorians) also spread abroad in the heavens, and shining: but in the infernal place straitened, dark, and tormenting, in the mid way it partakes of both. Fire therefore in itself is one, but in that which receives it, manifold, and in differing subjects it is distributed in a different manner, as *Cleanthes* witnesseth in *Cicero*. That fire then which we use is fetched out of other things. It is in stones, and is fetched out by the stroke of the steel: it is in earth, and makes that, after digging up, to smoke: it is in water, and heats springs, and wells: it is in the depth of the sea, and makes that, being tossed with winds, warm: it is in the air, and makes it (as we oftentimes see) to burn. And all animals, and living things whatsoever, and also all vegetables are preserved by heat: and everything that lives, lives by reason of the enclosed heat.

The properties of the Fire that is above, are heat, making all things fruitful, and light, giving life to all things. The properties of the infernal Fire are a parched heat, consuming all things, and darkness, making all things barren. The celestial, and bright Fire drives away spirits of darkness; also this our fire made with wood drives away the same, in as much as it hath an analogy with, and is the *vehiculum* of that superior light; as also of Him, who saith, I am the light of the world,[3] which is true Fire, the Father of Lights, from whom every good thing that is given comes; sending forth the light of his Fire, and communicating it first to the Sun, and the rest of the celestial bodies, and by these, as by mediating instruments conveying that light into our fire.

As therefore the spirits of darkness are stronger in the dark: so good spirits, which are angels of light, are augmented, not only by that light, which is divine, of the Sun, and celestial, but also by the light of our common fire. Hence it was that the first, and most wise institutors of religions, and ceremonies ordained, that prayers, singings, and all manner of divine worships whatsoever should not be performed without lighted candles, or torches. (Hence also was that significant saying of *Pythagoras:* do not speak of God without a light.)[4] And they commanded that for the driving away of wicked spirits, lights and fires should be kindled by the corpses of the dead, and that they should not be removed, until the expiations were after a holy manner performed, and they buried. And the great *Jehovah* himself in the old Law commanded that all his sacrifices should be offered with fire, and that fire should always be burning upon the altar,[5] which custom the priests of the altar did always observe, and keep amongst the Romans.

Now the basis, and foundation of all the elements, is the Earth, for that is the object, subject, and receptacle of all celestial rays, and influences; in it are contained the seeds, and seminal virtues of all things; and therefore it is said to be animal, vegetable, and mineral. It being made fruitful by the other elements, and the heavens, brings forth all things of itself; it receives the abundance of all things, and is, as it were the first fountain, from whence all things spring; it is the center, foundation, and mother of all things. Take as much of it as you please, separated, washed, depurated, subtilized, if you let it lie in the open air a little while, it will, being full, and abounding with heavenly virtues, of itself bring forth plants, worms, and other living things, also stones, and bright sparks of metals.[6] In it are great secrets, if at any time it shall be purified by the help of Fire, and reduced unto its simplicity by a convenient washing. It is the first matter of our creation, and the truest medicine that can restore, and preserve us.[7]

Notes—Chapter V

1. *saith Hermes*—

> Separate the Earth from the Fire, the subtle from the gross, gently and with care. Ascend from Earth to Heaven, and descend again to Earth, to unite the power of higher and lower things; thus you will obtain the glory of the whole World, and the shadows will leave you. *(Emerald Tablet* of Hermes Trismegistus) See Appendix I.

2. *saith Dionysius*—Dionysius the Areopagite, in the 15th chapter of his work, *Concerning the Celestial Hierarchy,* where fire is discussed at length.

3. *the world*—John 8:12.

4. *without a light*—"Speak not about Pythagoric concerns without light" (Iamblichus *Life of Pythagoras* ch. 18, trans. Thomas Taylor [1818] [London: John M. Watkins, 1926], 45). The same expression also occurs in ch. 23, p. 57. It is included in a list of things which should or should not be done that was spoken to initiates into the school of Pythagoras. Taylor mentions in a note that he has interpolated the words "Pythagoric concerns," which are not in the original.

5. *the altar*—Leviticus 6:12-3.

6. *sparks of metals*—The belief that some plants and animals, especially insects, were generated spontaneously in the earth without prior sexual union was universal in ancient times:

> Of these, all which are produced by union of animals of the same kind generate also after their kind, but all of which are not produced by animals, but from decaying matter, generate indeed but produce another kind, and the offspring is neither male nor female; such are some of the insects." (Aristotle *On the Generation of Animals* 1.1.715b, trans. A. Platt. In *The Basic Works,* ed. Richard McKeon [New York: Random House, 1941], 666)

Pliny repeats much of what Aristotle has to say:

> Many insects, however, are engendered in a different manner; and some more especially from dew. ... In the same manner, also, some animals are generated in the earth from rain, and some, again, in wood. ... Then, too, in dead carrion there are certain animals produced, and in the hair, too, of living men. ...

Other insects, again, are engendered from filth, acted upon by the rays of the sun—these fleas are called "petauristae," from the activity which they display in their hind legs. Others, again, are produced with wings, from the moist dust that is found lying in holes and corners. (Pliny 11.37–9 [Bostock and Riley, 3:39–40])

Belief in spontaneous generation was remarkably persistent. Although Redi proved in 1668 that maggots did not arise from rotten meat, the question was still up in the air when Goldsmith wrote his *Animated Nature* (1774):

> But later discoveries have taught us to be more cautious in making general conclusions, and have even induced many to doubt whether animal life may not be produced merely from putrefaction. (London:

Thomas Nelson, 1849, 97)

Of course, he was no authority. Doctor Johnson once said of Goldsmith, "If he can tell a horse from a cow, that is the extent of his knowledge of zoology."

In addition to plants and animals, metals were believed to grow in the ground, in exactly the same way that crystals actually do grow. Rock crystal, on the other hand, was thought to be ice formed under extremely cold temperatures that had caused it to petrify.

7. *preserve us*—The first matter, or *materia prima,* is an alchemical concept. Only when base materials are reduced to their original, pure state, prior to the corruption of impressions and passions, are they fit to receive the pattern of the divine spirit, which infuses them—or rather, it, since there is only one prime material—with healing virtue.

CHAPTER VI

Of the wonderful natures
of Water, Air, and winds.

The other two elements, viz. Water, and Air are not less efficacious than the former; neither is Nature wanting to work wonderful things in them.

There is so great a necessity of water, that without it no living thing can live. No herb, nor plant whatsoever, without the moistening of water can branch forth. In it is the seminary virtue of all things, especially of animals, whose seed is manifestly waterish. The seeds also of trees, and plants, although they are earthy, must notwithstanding of necessity be rotted in water, before they can be fruitful; whether they be imbibed with the moisture of the earth, or with dew, or rain, or any other water that is on purpose put to them.

For *Moses* writes, that only Earth, and Water bring forth a living soul.[1] But he ascribes a twofold production of things to Water, viz. of things swimming in the waters, and of things flying in the air above the earth.[2] And that those productions that are made in, and upon the earth, are partly attributed to the very water, the same scripture testifies, where it saith that the plants, and herbs did not grow because God had not caused it to rain upon the earth.[3]

Such is the efficacy of this element of Water, that spiritual regeneration cannot be done without it, as Christ himself testified to *Nicodemus*.[4] Very great also is the virtue of it in the religious worship of God, in expiations, and purifications; yea, the necessity of it is no less than that of Fire. Infinite are the benefits, and divers are the uses thereof, as being that by virtue of which all things subsist, are generated, nourished, and increased.

Thence it was that *Thales* of Miletus, and *Hesiod* concluded that Water was the beginning of all things, and said it was the first of all the elements, and the most potent, and that because it hath the mastery over all the rest.[5] For, as *Pliny* saith, waters swallow up the earth, extinguish flames, ascend on high, and by the stretching forth of the clouds, challenge the heaven for their own: the same falling down become the cause of all things that grow in the earth.[6] Very many are the wonders that are done by waters, according to the writings of *Pliny, Solinus,* and many other historians, of the wonderful virtue whereof, *Ovid* also makes mention in these verses:[7]

————horned Hammon's waters at high
   noon
Are cold; hot at sunrise, and setting Sun.
Wood, put in bubbling Athemas is fired,
The Moon then farthest from the Sun retired,
Ciconian streams congeal his guts to stone
That thereof drinks; and what therein is
   thrown.
Crathis, and Sybaris (from the mountains
   rolled)
Color the hair like amber, or pure gold.
Some fountains, of a more prodigious kind,
Not only change the body, but the mind.
Who hath not heard of obscene Salmacis?
Of the Aethiopian lake? for who of this
But only taste, their wits no longer keep,
Or forthward fall into a deadly sleep.

Who at Clitorius' fountain thirst remove,
Loath wine, and abstinent, mere water love.
With streams opposed to these Lincestus
flows:
They reel, as drunk, who drink too much of
those.
A lake in fair Arcadia stands, of old
Called Pheneus; suspected, as twofold:
Fear, and forebear to drink thereof by night:
By night unwholesome, wholesome by
daylight.

Josephus also makes relation of the wonderful nature of a certain river betwixt Arcea and Raphanea, cities of Syria: which runs with a full channel all the sabbath day, and then on a sudden ceaseth, as if the springs were stopped, and all the six days you may pass over it dryshod: but again on the seventh day (no man knowing the reason of it) the waters return again in abundance, as before. Wherefore the inhabitants thereabout called it the Sabbath Day River, because of the seventh day, which was holy to the Jews.[8]

The gospel also testifies of a sheep-pool, into which whosoever stepped first, after the water was troubled by the angel, was made whole of whatsoever disease he had.[9] The same virtue, and efficacy we read was in a spring of the Ionian nymphs, which was in the territories belonging to the town of Elis, at a village called Heraclea, near the river Citheron: which whosoever stepped into, being diseased, came forth whole, and cured of all his diseases.[10]

Pausanias also reports, that in Lyceus, a mountain of Arcadia, there was a spring called Agria, to which, as often as the dryness of the region threatened the destruction of fruits, *Jupiter's* priest of Lyceus went, and after the offering of sacrifices, devoutly praying to the waters of the spring, holding a bough of an oak in his hand, put it down to the bottom of the hallowed spring; then the waters being troubled, a vapour ascending from thence into the air was blown into clouds, with which being joined together, the whole heaven was overspread: which being a little after dissolved into rain, watered all the country most wholesomely.[11] Moreover *Ruffus* a physician of Ephesus, besides many other authors, wrote strange things

concerning the wonders of waters, which, for aught I know, are found in no other author.

It remains that I speak of the Air. This is a vital spirit, passing through all beings, giving life, and subsistence to all things, binding, moving, and filling all things. Hence it is that the Hebrew doctors reckon it not amongst the elements, but count it as a medium or glue, joining things together, and as the resounding spirit of the world's instrument.[12] It immediately receives into itself the influences of all celestial bodies, and then communicates them to the other elements, as also to all mixed bodies. Also it receives into itself, as if it were a divine looking glass, the species of all things, as well natural, as artificial, as also of all manner of speeches, and retains them; and carrying them with it, and entering into the bodies of men, and other animals, through their pores, makes an impression upon them, as well when they sleep, as when they be awake, and affords matter for divers strange dreams and divinations.

Hence they say it is, that a man passing by a place where a man was slain, or the carcass newly hid, is moved with fear and dread; because the air in that place being full of the dreadful species of manslaughter, doth, being breathed in, move and trouble the spirit of the man with the like species, whence it is that he comes to be afraid. For everything that makes a sudden impression, astonisheth nature.

Whence it is, that many philosophers were of opinion that Air is the cause of dreams, and of many other impressions of the mind, through the prolonging of images, or similitudes, or species (which are fallen from things, and speeches, multiplying in the very air) until they come to the senses, and then to the phantasy, and soul of him that receives them, which being freed from cares, and no way hindered, expecting to meet such kind of species, is informed by them. For the species of things, although of their own proper nature, they are carried to the senses of men, and other animals in general, may notwithstanding get some impression from the heaven, whilst they be in the Air, by reason of which, together with the aptness and disposition of him that receives them, they may be carried to the sense of one, rather than another.

And hence it is possible naturally, and far from all manner of superstition, no other spirit coming between, that a man should be able in a very little time to signify his mind unto another man, abiding at a very long and unknown distance from him, although he cannot precisely give an estimate of the time when it is, yet of necessity it must be within 24 hours; and I myself know how to do it, and have often done it. The same also in time past did the Abbot *Tritenius* both know and do.[13]

Also, when certain appearances, not only spiritual, but also natural do flow forth from things, that is to say, by a certain kind of flowings forth of bodies from bodies, and do gather strength in the Air, they offer, and show themselves to us as well through light as motion, as well to the sight as to other senses, and sometimes work wonderful things upon us, as *Plotinus* proves and teacheth. And we see how by the south wind the air is condensed into thin clouds, in which, as in a looking glass are reflected representations at a great distance of castles, mountains, horses, and men, and other things, which when the clouds are gone, presently vanish.

And *Aristotle* in his Meteors[14] shows, that a rainbow is conceived in a cloud of the air, as in a looking glass. And *Albertus* saith, that the effigies of bodies may by the strength of nature, in a moist air be easily represented, in the same manner as the representations of things are in things. And *Aristotle* tells of a man, to whom it happened by reason of the weakness of his sight, that the air that was near to him, became as it were a looking glass to him, and the optic beam did reflect back upon himself, and could not penetrate the air, so that whithersoever he went, he thought he saw his own image, with his face towards him, go before him.

In like manner, by the artificialness of some certain looking glasses, may be produced at a distance in the air, beside the looking glasses, what images we please; which when ignorant men see, they think they see the appearances of spirits, or souls; when indeed they are nothing else but semblances kin to themselves, and without life. And it is well known, if in a dark place where there is no light but by the coming in of a beam of the Sun somewhere through a little hole, a white paper, or plain looking glass be set up against the light, that there may be seen upon them, whatsoever things are done without, being shined upon by the Sun.

And there is another slight, or trick yet more wonderful. If anyone shall take images artificially painted, or written letters, and in a clear night set them against the beams of the full Moon, whose resemblances being multiplied in the Air, and caught upward, and reflected back together with the beams of the Moon, any other man that is privy to the thing, at a long distance sees, reads, and knows them in the very compass, and circle of the Moon, which art of declaring secrets is indeed very profitable for towns, and cities that are besieged, being a thing which *Pythagoras* long since did often do, and which is not unknown to some in these days, I will not except myself.

And all these, and many more, and greater than these are grounded in the very nature of the Air, and have their reasons, and causes declared in mathematics, and optics. And as these resemblances are reflected back to the sight, so also sometimes to the hearing, as is manifest in the echo. But there are more secret arts than these, and such whereby anyone may at a very remote distance hear, and understand what another speaks, or whispers softly.

There are also from the airy element winds. For they are nothing else, but air moved, and stirred up. Of these there are four that are principal, blowing from the four corners of the heaven, viz. Notus from the south, Boreas from the north, Zephyrus from the west, Eurus from the east, which *Pontanus* comprehending in these verses, saith,

> Cold Boreas from the top of 'lympus blows,
> And from the bottom cloudy Notus flows.
> From setting Phoebus fruitful Zeph'rus flies,
> And barren Eurus from the Sun's uprise.[15]

Notus is the southern wind, cloudy, moist, warm, and sickly, which *Hieronimus* calls the butler of the rains. *Ovid* describes it thus:[16]

Out flies South Wind, with dropping
wings, who shrouds
His fearful aspect in the pitchy clouds;
His white hair streams, his beard big-
swollen with showers;
Mists bind his brows; rain from his bosom
pours.

But Boreas is contrary to Notus, and is the northern wind, fierce, and roaring, and discussing clouds, makes the air serene, and binds the water with frost. Him doth *Ovid* thus bring in speaking of himself:[17]

Force me befits: with this thick clouds I
drive;
Toss the blue billows, knotty oaks up-rive;
Congeal soft snow, and beat the Earth with
hail:
When I my brethren in the air assail,
(For that's our field) we meet with such a
shock,
That thundering skies with our encounters
rock,
And cloud-struck lightning flashes from on
high,
When through the crannies of the Earth I fly,

And force her in her hollow caves, I make
The ghosts to tremble, and the ground to
quake.

And Zephyrus, which is the western wind, is most soft, blowing from the west with a pleasant gale, it is cold and moist, removing the effects of winter, bringing forth branches, and flowers. To this Eurus is contrary, which is the eastern wind, and is called Apeliotes, it is waterish, cloudy, and ravenous. Of these two *Ovid* sings thus:[18]

To Persis, and Sabea, Eurus flies;
Whose gums perfume the blushing morn's
uprise:
Next to the evening, and the coast that glows
With setting Phoebus, flowery Zeph'rus
blows:
In Scythia horrid Boreas holds his rain,
Beneath Boites, and the frozen Wain:
The land to this opposed doth Auster[19]
steep
With fruitful showers, and clouds which
ever weep.

Notes—Chapter VI

1. *living soul*—Genesis 1:21, 24.

2. *above the Earth*—Genesis 1:20.

3. *upon the Earth*—Genesis 2:5.

4. *to Nicodemus*—John 3:5.

5. *all the rest*—

They [Egyptian priests] believe also that the sun and moon do not go in chariots, but sail about the world perpetually in certain boats; hinting hereby at their feeding upon and springing first out of moisture. They are likewise of the opinion that Homer (as well as Thales) had been instructed by the Egyptians, which made him affirm water to be the spring and first origin of things; for that Oceanus is the same with Osiris, and Tethys with Isis, so named from τιτθη, *a nurse*, because she is the mother and nurse of all things. (Plutarch *Isis and Osiris* 34 [Goodwin, 4:94–5])

6. *in the earth*—

It is water that swallows up dry land, that extinguishes flame, that ascends aloft, and challenges possession of the very heavens: it is water that, spreading clouds as it does, far and wide, intercepts the vital air we breathe; and, through their collision, gives rise to thunders and lightnings, as the elements of the universe meet in conflict. What can there be more marvellous than waters suspended aloft in the heavens? And yet, as though it were not enough to reach so high an elevation as this, they sweep along with them whole shoals of fishes, and often stones as well, thus lading themselves with ponderous masses which belong to other elements, and bearing them on high. Falling upon the earth, these waters become the prime cause of all that is there produced ... (Pliny 31.1 [Bostock and Riley, 5.471])

For Pliny's discussion of the properties and uses of water, see the *Natural History* 2.65–68, 99–106, and 31.1–30.

7. *these verses*—*Metamorphoses* 15.3, c. line 308.

8. *to the Jews*—

He [Titus Caesar] then saw a river as he went along, of such a nature as deserves to be recorded in history; it runs in the middle between Arcea, belonging to Agrippa's kingdom, and Raphanea. It hath somewhat very peculiar in it; for when it runs, its current is strong, and has plenty of water; after which its springs fail for six days all together, and leave its channel dry, as any one may see; after which days it runs on the seventh day as it did before, and as though it had undergone no change at all: it hath also been observed to keep this order perpetually and exactly; whence it is that they call it the Sabbatic River,—that name being taken from the sacred seventh day among the Jews. (Josephus *Wars of the Jews* 7.5.1. In *The Works of Flavius Josephus,* trans. W. Whiston [London: George Routledge and Sons, n.d.], 665)

9. *disease he had*—John 5:2-4.

10. *all his diseases*—

The Elean village of Herakleia is six miles or so from Olympia on the banks of the river Kytheros; there is a water-spring that runs into the river with a sanctuary of the nymphs at the spring. These nymphs have the personal names of Kalliphaeia and Synallasis and Pegaia and Iasis, and their general title is the Ionides. If you wash in the spring you can be cured of all kinds of aches and pains; they say the nymphs are named after Ion son of Gargettos, who migrated here from Athens. (Pausanias *Guide to Greece* 6.22.7, trans. P. Levi [Middlesex: Penguin, 1971] 2:354–5)

11. *most wholesomely*—

Hagno's water-spring on Mount Lykaion has the same quality as the Danube of always producing the same volume of water in summer and winter alike. If a drought lasts a long time and the trees and the seeds in the ground are withering, then the priest of Lykaian Zeus prays to this water and sacrifices according to the holy law, dipping an oak-branch on to the surface but not into the depths of the spring; when he stirs the water, a vapour rises like a mist, and a little way off the mist becomes a cloud, collects other clouds, and

makes the rain drop on Arkadian land. (ibid. 8.38.3–4 [Levi 2:467])

12. *world's instrument*—"Water is silent, Fire is sibilant and Air derived from the Spirit is as the tongue of a balance standing between these contraries which are in equilibrium, reconciling and mediating between them" *(Sepher Yetzirah* 2.1, trans. W. Westcott [1887] [New York: Weiser, 1980] 18).

And the spark subsisted, and waited, until the pure air went forth which involved it around; and an ultimate extension having been made, He produced a certain hard skull [of Microprosopus] on four sides. And in that pure subtle air was the spark absorbed and comprehended and included therein. Dost thou not think therein? Truly it is hidden therein. And therefore is that skull expanded in its sides; and that air is the most concealed attribute of the Ancient of Days. (Von Rosenroth *Kabbalah Unveiled* ch. 27, sec. 538–41, trans. Mac-Gregor Mathers [1887] [London: Routledge and Kegan Paul, 1962], 178).

Thomas Vaughan, who had read Agrippa carefully, says of air:

This is no element, but a certain miraculous Hermaphrodite, the cement of two worlds, and a medley of extremes. It is Nature's common place, her index, where you may finde all that ever she did, or intends to do. This is the world's panegyrick, the excursions of both globes meet here, and I may call it the rendezvous. In this are innumerable magicall forms of men and beasts, fish and fowls, trees, herbs, and all creeping things. *(Anthroposophia Theomagica,* Waite 18)

13. *know and do*—Along with several similar casual references elsewhere in the text, this gives clear evidence that Agrippa's knowledge of magic was practical as well as theoretical and that Trithemius was at least his fellow student, if not his master, in the Art.

14 *Meteors*—*On Meteorology.*

15. *Sun's uprise*—A remarkably similar passage occurs in Ovid:

For at one moment, Eurus gathers strength from the glowing East, at another instant comes Zephyrus, sent from the evening West. At one time, the icy Boreas comes raging from the dry North; at another, the South wind wages battle with adverse front. *(Tristia* 1.2.27–30, trans. Henry T.

Riley [London: George Bell and Sons, 1881], 253.

16. *it thus*—Ovid *Metamorphoses* 1.8, c. line 262.

17. *of himself*—Ovid *Metamorphoses* 6.7, c. line 690.

18. *sings thus*—Ovid *Metamorphoses* 1.2, c. line 60.

19. *Auster*—A name for one of the south winds, which is now called Sirocco.

Salamander

from *Scrutinium Chymicum* (Frankfurt, 1687)

CHAPTER VII

Of the kinds of compounds, what relation they stand in to the elements, and what relation there is betwixt the elements themselves, and the soul, senses, and dispositions of men.

Next after the four simple elements follows the four kinds of perfect bodies compounded of them, and they are stones, metals, plants, and animals: and although unto the generation of each of these all the elements meet together in the composition, yet every one of them follows, and resembles one of the elements, which is most predominant.

For all stones are earthy, for they are naturally heavy, and descend, and so hardened with dryness, that they cannot be melted. But metals are waterish, and may be melted, which naturalists confess, and chemists find to be true, viz. that they are generated of a viscous water, or waterish argent vive.[1] Plants have such an affinity with the Air, that unless they be abroad in the open air, they do neither bud, nor increase. So also all animals:

Have in their natures a most fiery force,
And also spring from a celestial source.

And Fire is so natural to them, that that being extinguished they presently die.

And again every one of those kinds is distinguished within itself by reason of degrees of the elements. For amongst the stones they especially are called earthy that are dark, and more heavy; and those waterish, which are transparent, and are compacted of water, as crystal,[2] beryl,[3] and pearls[4] in the shells of fishes: and they are called airy, which swim upon the water, and are spongious, as the stones of a sponge,[5] the pumish stone,[6] and the stone sophus:[7] and they are called fiery, out of which fire is extracted, or which are resolved into fire, or which are produced of fire: as thunderbolts,[8] firestones,[9] and the stone asbestos.[10] Also amongst metals, lead and silver are earthy: quicksilver is waterish: copper, and tin are airy: and gold, and iron are fiery.

In plants also, the roots resemble the Earth, by reason of their thickness: and the leaves, Water, because of their juice: flowers, the Air, because of their subtilty, and the seeds the Fire, by reason of their multiplying spirit. Besides, they are called some hot, some cold, some moist, some dry, borrowing their names from the qualities of the elements.

Amongst animals also, some are in comparison of others earthy, and dwell in the bowels of the Earth, as worms and moles, and many other small creeping vermin: others are watery, as fishes: others airy, which cannot live out of the air: others also are fiery, living in the fire, as salamanders,[11] and crickets,[12] such as are of a fiery heat, as pigeons,[13] ostriches,[14] lions, and such as the wise man calls beasts breathing fire.[15] Besides, in animals the bones resemble the Earth, flesh the Air, the vital spirit the Fire, and the humours the Water. And these humours also partake of the elements, for yellow choler is instead of Fire, blood instead of Air, phlegm instead of Water, and black choler, or melancholy instead of Earth.[16]

And lastly, in the soul itself, according to *Austin*,[17] the understanding resembles Fire, reason the Air, imagination the Water, and the senses the Earth. And these senses also are divided amongst themselves by reason of the elements, for the sight is fiery; neither can it perceive without Fire, and light: the hearing is airy, for a sound is made by the striking of the Air: the smell, and taste resemble the Water, without the moisture of which there is neither smell, nor taste: and lastly the feeling is wholly earthy, and takes gross bodies for its object.

The actions also, and the operations of man are governed by the elements. The Earth signifies a slow, and firm motion: the Water signifies fearfulness, and sluggishness, and remissness in working: Air signifies cheerfulness, and an amiable disposition: but Fire a fierce, quick, and angry disposition.

The elements therefore are the first of all things, and all things are of, and according to them, and they are in all things, and diffuse their virtues through all things.

Notes—Chapter VII

1. *argent vive*—Latin: *argentum vivum*. Quicksilver, mercury.

2. *crystal*—Rock crystal, a variety of quartz, was thought in ancient times to be petrified ice.

> It is a diametrically opposite cause to this [heat] that produces crystal, a substance which assumes a concrete form from excessive congelation. At all events, crystal is only to be found in places where the winter snow freezes with the greatest intensity; and it is from the certainty that it is a kind of ice, that it has received the name [κρύσταλλος means both "rock crystal" and "ice"] which it bears in Greek. (Pliny 37.9 [Bostock and Riley, 6:394])

3. *beryl*—See note 3, chapter XXIV, book I.

4. *pearls*—

> The origin and production of the shell-fish is not very different from that of the shell of the oyster. When the genial [breeding] season of the year exercises its influence on the animal, it is said that, yawning, as it were, it opens its shell, and so receives a kind of dew, by means of which it becomes impregnated; and that at length it gives birth, after many struggles, to the burden of its shell, in the shape of pearls, which vary according to the quality of the dew. If this has been in a perfectly pure state when it flowed into the shell, then the pearl produced is white and brilliant, but if it was turbid, then the pearl is of a clouded colour also ... (Pliny 9.54 [Bostock and Riley, 2.431])

5. *sponge*—*Lapis Spongiae,* or sponge-stone. In ancient times sponges were thought to be plants that were prone to petrification. "The Spunge-Stone is made of the Matter of Spunges petrified." J. Pomet, *Complete History of Drugs,* trans. John Hill [London, 1712], bk. 1, p. 100. *Chambers' Cyclopedia Supplement* of 1753 describes the sponge-stone as a "tartarous incrustation." Elyot's *Dictionary* (1552 edition, enriched by T. Cooper) refers to *"Crystiolithi,* certayne stones, whiche growe in spunges, holsome against diseases of the bladder" (quoted in *Oxford English Dictionary* [hereafter cited as *OED*], s.v. "sponge" [def. 3]). Actually sponges are colonies of tiny animals, not plants, with skeletons usually (but not in all cases) made up in part by mineral material—silica, or carbonate of lime.

6. *pumish stone*—Pumice stone, a porous form of volcanic lava, usually obsidian, puffed like a sponge by steam and hot gasses. The Englishman John Evelyn scaled Vesuvius on February 7, 1645, and described the stones thrown up on the mountainside: "—some like pitch, others full of perfect brimstone, others metallic interspaced with innumerable pumices" *(John Evelyn's Diary* [abridged] [London: Folio Society, 1963], 64). Walter MacFarlane wrote in 1648 : "In this town ther ar aboundance of pumick stonis floating upon the water" *(Geographical Collections Relating to Scotland* [Scottish History Society, 1906–08], cited in *OED).*

7. *sophus*—Tophus, a general name for porous stones produced as sediments or incrustations, particularly a stony substance deposited by calcareous springs. See Pliny 36.48.

8. *thunderbolts*—This name is applied to several mineral substances supposed to have been formed or left by lightning strikes, including prehistoric stone implements, nodules of iron pyrites found in chalk, and meteorites. But Agrippa probably refers to

belemnite, the fossilized bone of a cephalopod similar to the cuttle-fish. It is found in fossel beds, and is a smooth, blue stone cylinder several inches long that tapers to a sharp point. Also called thunder-stone and elf-bolt. In fact, lightning actually can form a conical stone when it strikes and fuses fine sand into glass, called *ceraunia* ("thunder-stone"): see Pliny 37.51.

9. *fire-stones*—Stones for striking sparks to make fire. This name was applied to iron pyrites and flint—probably Agrippa means the latter.

10. *asbestos*—See note 19, ch. IX, bk. I.

11. *salamanders*—Pliny describes the salamander as:

> ... an animal like a lizard in shape, and with a body starred all over, never comes out except during heavy showers, and disappears the moment it becomes fine. This animal is so intensely cold as to extinguish fire by its contact, in the same way as ice does. It spits forth a milky matter from its mouth; and whatever part of the human body is touched with this, all the hair falls off, and the part assumes the appearance of leprosy. (Pliny 10.86 [Bostock and Riley, 2:545–6])

Elsewhere he expands on its poisonous powers:

> But of all venomous animals it is the salamander that is by far the most dangerous; for while other reptiles attack individuals only, and never kill many persons at a time ... the salamander is able to destroy whole nations at once, unless they take the proper precautions against it. For if this reptile happens to crawl up a tree, it infects all the fruit with its poison, and kills those who eat thereof by the chilling properties of its venom, which in its effects is in no way different from aconite. Nay, even more than this, if it only touches with its foot the wood upon which bread is baked, or if it happens to fall into a well, the same fatal effects will be sure to ensue. The saliva, too, of this reptile, if it comes in contact with any part of the body, the sole of the foot even, will cause the hair to fall off

> from the whole of the body. ... As to what the magicians say, that it is proof against fire, being, as they tell us, the only animal that has the property of extinguishing fire, if it had been true, it would have been made trial of at Rome long before this. (Pliny 29.23 [Bostock and Riley, 5:397–8])

As a natural extension of the fable of its deadly fire quenching cold, the salamander was said to live and breed in the heart of the hottest flames. In the folklore of the Middle Ages it was described as manlike in appearance. Paracelsus (1493–1541) was probably the first to ascribe the name to the class of elemental fire spirits, in his *Liber de nymphis, sylphis, pygmæis et salamandris et de cæteris spiritibus* (Book of nymphs, sylphs, pygmies, and salamanders and kindred beings).

12. *crickets*—Specifically *Acheta domestica,* the house cricket. In medieval times the cricket was confused with the salamander, probably due to its fondness for hearths and the heat of stoves and ovens: "The Crekette hyght Salamandra: for thys beest quenchyth fyre and lyueth in brennynge fyre" (John de Trevisa, *Bartholomeus [de Glanvilla] de proprietatibus rerum,* trans. 1398, cited in *OED* s.v. "cricket").

13. *pigeons*—It was an old medical practice to apply living pigeons to the soles of the feet of those gravely ill with fever. Samuel Pepys mentions this treatment given to Catherine of Braganza, wife of King Charles II, when she had spotted fever: "It seems she was so ill as to be shaved, and pidgeons put to her feet, and to have the extreme unction given her by the priests, who were so long about it that the doctors were angry" (*Diary of Samuel Pepys* October 19, 1663 (London: Everyman Library, 1906), 1:415.

14. *ostriches*—Ostriches were thought able to live without water and to digest iron. See Goldsmith's *Animated Nature, History of Birds,* bk. I, ch. IV (London: Nelson, 1849), 369.

15. *breathing fire*—Dragons.

16. *of earth*—See Appendix IV.

17. *Austin*—Saint Augustine.

How the elements are in the heavens, in stars, in devils, in angels, and lastly in God himself.

It is the unanimous consent of all Platonists, that as in the original, and exemplary world, all things are in all; so also in this corporeal world, all things are in all:[1] so also the elements are not only in these inferior bodies, but also in the heavens, in stars, in devils, in angels, and lastly in God, the maker, and original example of all things. Now in these inferior bodies, the elements are accompanied with much gross matter; but in the heavens the elements are with their natures, and virtues, viz. after a celestial, and more excellent manner, than in sublunary things. For the firmness of the celestial Earth is there without the grossness of Water: and the agility of the Air without running over its bounds; the heat of Fire without burning, only shining, and giving life to all things by its heat.

Amongst the stars also, some are fiery, as Mars and Sol: airy, as Jupiter, and Venus: watery, as Saturn, and Mercury: and earthy, such as inhabit the eighth orb,[2] and the Moon (which notwithstanding by many is accounted watery) seeing, as if it were Earth, it attracts to itself the celestial waters, with which being imbibed, it doth by reason of its nearness to us power out, and communicate to us. There are also amongst the signs, some fiery, some earthy, some airy, some watery: the elements rule them also in the heavens, distributing to them these four threefold considerations of every element, viz. the beginning, middle, and end: so Aries possesseth the beginning of Fire,

Leo the progress, and increase, and Sagittarius the end. Taurus the beginning of the Earth, Virgo the progress, Capricorn the end. Gemini the beginning of the Air, Libra the progress, Aquarius the end. Cancer the beginning of Water, Scorpius the middle, and Pisces the end.[3] Of the mixtions therefore of these planets, and signs, together with the elements are all bodies made.

Moreover devils also are upon this account distinguished the one from the other, so that some are called fiery, some earthy, some airy, and some watery. Hence also those four infernal rivers, fiery Phlegethon, airy Cocytus, watery Styx, earthy Acheron.[4] Also in the Gospel we read of hellfire,[5] and eternal fire, into which the cursed shall be commanded to go:[6] and in the Revelation we read of a lake of fire,[7] and *Isaiah* speaks of the damned, that the Lord will smite them with corrupt air.[8] And in Job, they shall skip from the waters of the snow to extremity of heat,[9] and in the same we read, that the Earth is dark, and covered with the darkness of death, and miserable darkness.[10]

Moreover also these elements are placed in the angels in heaven, and the blessed intelligences; there is in them a stability of their essence, which is an earthy virtue, in which is the steadfast seat of God; also their mercy, and piety is a watery cleansing virtue. Hence by the Psalmist they are called Waters, where he speaking of the heavens, saith, who rulest the Waters that are higher than the heavens;[11] also in them their subtle breath is Air, and their love is shining Fire: hence they are called in scripture the Wings of the Wind;[12] and in another place the Psalmist speaks of them: who makest angels thy spirits, and thy ministers a flaming fire.[13] Also according to orders of angels some are fiery, as Seraphim, and Authorities, and Powers: earthy as Cherubim: watery as Thrones, and Archangels: airy as Dominions, and Principalities.

Do we not also read of the original Maker of all things, that the Earth shall be opened and bring forth a Saviour?[14] Is it not spoken of the same, that he shall be a fountain of living Water, cleansing, and regenerating?[15] Is not the same Spirit breathing the breath of life: and the same according to *Moses'*,[16] and *Paul's*[17] testimony, a consuming Fire?

That elements therefore are to be found everywhere, and in all things after their manner, no man can deny. First in these inferior bodies feculent, and gross, and in celestials more pure, and clear; but in supercelestials living, and in all respects blessed. Elements therefore in the exemplary world are Ideas of things to be produced, in intelligences are distributed powers, in heavens are virtues, and in inferior bodies gross forms.

Notes—Chapter VIII

1. *all things are in all*—"Now, since there is nothing else besides the others and the one, and they must be in something, it follows at once that they must be in each other—the others in the one and the one in the others—or be nowhere at all" (Plato *Parmenides* 151a, trans. F. M. Cornford [Hamilton and Cairns, 943]).

"God contains all things, and there is nothing which is not in God, and nothing in which God is not. Nay, I would rather say, not that God *contains* all things, but that, to speak the full truth, God *is* all things" *(Corpus Hermeticum* 9.9 [Scott, 1:185]).

2. *eighth orb*—Probably refers to the Earth in this context, which is the eighth globular body, counting down from Saturn. Ordinarily the eighth sphere refers to the sphere of the Zodiac, eighth in order counting up from the Moon.

3. *the end*—This is somewhat misleading. Although the elemental trines of the zodiac are often written in this order, it does not display their parallel structure. This arrangement is more revealing:

	△	▽	△	▽
Beginning (Cardinal):	♈	♎	♋	♑
Middle (Fixed):	♌	♒	♏	♉
End (Mutable):	♐	♓	♊	♍

4. *earthy Acheron*—Homer mentions only the Styx in the *Iliad*, calling it the "fearful oath-river" (2.755, trans. Richmond Lattimore [University of Chicago Press, 1976], 96) because it was the ancient Greek custom to swear by its waters, and later the "steep-dripping Stygian water" (ibid. 8.369 [Lattimore, 192]), perhaps because the mythological Styx was linked with an actual stream that flowed in the form of a high waterfall near Nonacris in Arcadia (see Pausanias *Guide to Greece* 8.17.6). In the *Odyssey* all four rivers are placed firmly in hell: "There Pyriphlegethon and Kokytos, which is an off-break from the water of the Styx, flow into Acheron" (*Odyssey* 10.513–4, trans. Richmond Lattimore [New York: Harper and Row, 1977], 165). Milton presents the meanings of the Greek names of the rivers in his description of them:

Of four infernal Rivers that disgorge
Into the burning Lake thir baleful streams;
Abhorred *Styx* the flood of deadly hate,
Sad *Acheron* of sorrow, black and deep;
Cocytus nam'd of lamentation loud
Heard on the rueful stream; fierce *Phlegeton*
Whose waves of torrent fire inflame with
    rage.
(*Paradise Lost* 2.575–81. In *Milton: Complete Poems and Major Prose* [Indianapolis: Odyssey, 1975], 245–6.)

Dante mentions the four rivers together (*Inferno* canto 14, c. line 115). Spenser refers to them severally in the *Faerie Queene* (Acheron—bk. 1, canto 5, verse 33; Phlegeton—bk. 2, canto 6, v. 50; Cocytus—bk. 2, canto 7, v. 56; Styx—bk. 2, canto 8, v. 20).

5. *hellfire*—Matthew 5:22.

6. *commanded to*—Matthew 25:41.

7. *lake of fire*—Revelation 20:10.

8. *corrupt air*—Perhaps Isaiah 11:4.

9. *of heat*—Job 6:15–7.

10. *darkness*—Perhaps Job 24:16-7.

11. *the heavens*—Psalms 148:4.

12. *Wings of the Wind*—Psalms 18:10. This order of angels figures prominently in the second of the 48 evocations (known variously as Aethers, Airs, Calls and Keys) dictated by the Enochian spirits to the Elizabethan magician John Dee through his seer Edward Kelley during a seance that took place on the morning of April 25, 1584, in Cracow. See Meric. Casaubon's *True & Faithful Relation of What passed for many Yeers Between Dr. John Dee ... and Some Spirits* (London, 1659), p. 100.

13. *flaming fire*—Psalms 104:4.

14. *a Saviour*—Isaiah 45:8.

15. *regenerating*—John 4:14. See also Revelation 7:17.

16. *Moses'*—Deuteronomy 4:24.

17. *Paul's*—Hebrews 12:29.

CHAPTER IX

Of the virtues of things natural,
depending immediately upon elements.

Of the natural virtues of things, some are elementary, as to heat, to cool, to moisten, to dry; and they are called operations, or first qualities, and the second act: for these qualities only do wholly change the whole substance, which none of the other qualities can do.[1]

And some are in things compounded of elements, and these are more than first qualities, and such are those that are maturating,[2] digesting,[3] resolving,[4] mollifying,[5] hardening, restringing,[6] absterging,[7] corroding,[8] burning, opening, evaporating, strengthening, mitigating, conglutinating,[9] obstructing, expelling, retaining, attracting, repercussing,[10] stupifying,[11] bestowing,[12] lubrifying,[13] and many more. Elementary qualities do many things in a mixed body, which they cannot do in the elements themselves. And these operations are called secondary qualities, because they follow the nature, and proportion of the mixtion of the first virtues, as largely it is treated of in physic books. As maturation, which is the operation of natural heat, according to a certain proportion in the substance of the matter. Induration is the operation of cold; so also is congelation, and so of the rest.

And these operations sometimes act upon a certain member, as such which provoke urine, milk, the menstrua,[14] and they are called third qualities, which follow the second, as the second do the first. According therefore to these first, second, and third qualities many diseases are both cured, and caused.

Many things also there are artificially made, which men much wonder at; as is fire, which burns water, which they call the Greek Fire,[15] of which *Aristotle* teacheth many compositions in his particular treatise of this subject.[16] In like manner there is made a fire that is extinguished with oil, and is kindled with cold water, when it is sprinkled upon it;[17] and a fire which is kindled either with rain, wind, or the Sun; and there is made a fire, which is called burning water,[18] the confection whereof is well known, and it consumes nothing but itself: and also there are made fires that cannot be quenched, and incombustible oils, and perpetual lamps, which can be extinguished neither with wind, nor water, nor any other way; which seems utterly incredible, but that there had been such a most famous lamp, which once did shine in the temple of *Venus,* in which the stone asbestos did burn, which being once fired can never be extinguished.[19]

Also on the contrary, wood, or any other combustible matter may be so ordered, that it can receive no harm from the fire; and there are made certain confections, with which the hands being anointed, we may carry red hot iron in them, or put them into melted metal, or go with our whole bodies, being first anointed therewith, into the fire without any manner of harm, and such like things as these may be done.[20] There is also a kind of flax, which *Pliny* calls *asbestum,*[21] the Greeks ἄσβεϛον, which is not consumed by fire, of which *Anaxilaus* saith, that a tree compassed about with it, may be cut down with insensible blows, that cannot be heard.[22]

Notes—Chapter IX

1. *can do*—See Aristotle *On Generation and Corruption* 2.2.

2. *maturating*—Natural ripening through the operation of heat and motion.

3. *digesting*—Maturing with gentle heat.

4. *resolving*—Reducing into component elements, especially by decay.

5. *mollifying*—Softening, tenderizing.

6. *restringing*—Constipating, stopping, binding.

7. *absterging*—Cleansing, purging.

8. *corroding*—Gnawing away.

9. *conglutinating*—Cohering, especially healing together.

10. *repercussing*—Beating back, reflecting.

11. *stupifying*—Numbing, deadening.

12. *bestowing*—Storing up, depositing.

13. *lubrifying*—Lubricating.

14. *the menstrua*—Menstrual blood.

15. *Greek Fire*—Greek Fire was a compound substance used in naval warfare to burn the ships of the enemy, and in siege warfare—Lucan writes of "Greek fire from a siege catapult ..." (*Pharsalia* 6, c. line 195, trans. Robert Graves [London: Cassell, 1961], 109), which he elsewhere describes as "fire fixed to unctuous torches, and alive, beneath a covering of sulphur ..." (*Pharsalia* 3, c. line 681, trans. H. T. Riley [London: Henry G. Bohn, 1853], 123). It had the property of only burning more fiercely when doused with water, making it very difficult to extinguish. *The Book of Secrets* gives a recipe:

> Take quick Brimstone, lees of wine, *Sarcocollam* [a Persian gum-resin], *Piculam* [a little pitch], sodden salt, oil of stone [petroleum], and common oil, make them seethe well, and if any thing be put in it, it is kindled, whether it be Tree or Iron, and is not put out but by piss, vinegar or sand (Albertus Magnus [attrib.] *The Book of Secrets of Albertus Magnus,* ed. Michael R. Best and Frank H. Brightman [New York: Oxford University Press, 1974], 110 [hereafter cited as *Book of Secrets*]).

16. *this subject*—This treatise is mentioned in Aristotle's *Problems:* "This subject has been dealt with more clearly in dealing with Fire*"* (bk. 30, problem 1, sec. 954a), trans. E. S. Forster [Oxford: Clarendon Press, 1927], vol. 7. This lost work on *Fire* is unknown. The best known work on the subject of Greek Fire was the *Liber ignius* (Book of fires) of Marcus Græcus, with recipes dating from the beginning of the 13th century.

17. *sprinkled it*—"Take Lime which water hath not touched and put it with a weight equal to it of wax, and the half of it of the oil of Balm *[Cemmiphora opobalsamum]* and *Naphtha citrina,* with equal to it of Brimstone, and make a wick of it, and drop the water down like dew upon it and it shall be kindled, and drop down oil upon it, and it shall be put out" (Albertus Magnus [attrib.] "Marvels of the World" sec. 64. In *Book of Secrets* [Best and Brightman, 104] [hereafter cited as "Marvels of the World"]).

18. *burning water*—"Take black, thick, mighty and old wine, and in one quart of it thou shalt temper a little quick Lime and Brimstone, beaten into powder very small, and lees of good wine and common salt, white and gross; after thou shalt put it in a gourd, well clayed, and *de super posito alembico,* thou shalt distil burning water, which thou should keep in a glass" (ibid., sec. 76, 110). From this formula, burning water would seem to have been simple alcohol.

19. *be extinguished*—"The Arcadian asbestos, being once inflamed, will never be quenched" (Augustine *City of God* 21.5, trans. John Healey [1610] [London: J. M. Dent and Sons, 1957], 2:324). "If these be credible, then believe you also if you will (for one man has related both this and those), that there was a temple of Venus wherein there burned a lamp, which no wind or water could ever quench, so that it was called the inextinguishable lamp" (ibid., 6.325).

20. *may be done*—"A marvellous experience, which maketh men to go into the fire without hurt; or to bear fire or red hot Iron in their hand without hurt.— Take the juice of *Bismalva* [hollyhock] and the white of an egg, and the seed of an herb called *Psyllium [Plantago afra],* also *Pulicaria herba,* and break it into powder, and make a confection, and mix the juice of Radish with the white of the egg. Anoint thy body or hand with this confection, and let it be dried, and after anoint it again. After that thou may suffer boldly the fire without hurt" ("Marvels of the World" 75 [Best and Brightman, 109]). See also ibid. sec. 72, 107: "If thou wilt bear fire in thy hand, that it may not hurt thee."

21. *asbestum—Asbestinon*: ἀσβέστινον. Asbestos is a mineral that readily separates into hairlike fibers immune from the effects of common flame. For this reason it was called salamander's wool, down, hair, and when woven, salamander cloth. It makes an excellent lamp wick for a "perpetual" lamp—one constantly replenished with oil so that it does not go out—since such a wick does not need to be replaced, an operation necessitating the extinguishing of the lamp.

22. *cannot be heard*—

> There has been invented also a kind of linen which is incombustible by flame. It is generally known as "live" linen, and I have seen, before now, napkins that were made of it thrown into a blazing fire, in the room where the guests were at table, and after the stains were burnt out, come forth from the flames whiter and cleaner than they could possibly have been rendered by the aid of water. It is from this material that the corpse-cloths of monarchs are made, to ensure the separation of the ashes of the body from those of the pile. This substance grows in the deserts of India, scorched by the burning rays of the sun: here, where no rain is ever known to fall, and amid multitudes of deadly serpents, it becomes habituated to resist the action of fire. Rarely to be found, it presents considerable difficulties in weaving it into a tissue, in consequence of its shortness; its colour is naturally red, and it only becomes white through the agency of fire. By those who find it, it is sold at prices equal to those given for the finest pearls; by the Greeks it is called "asbestinon," a name which indicates its peculiar properties. Anaxilaus makes a statement to the effect that if a tree is surrounded with linen made of this substance, the noise of the blows given by the axe will be deadened thereby, and that the tree may be cut down without their being heard. For these qualities it is that this linen occupies the very highest rank among all the kinds that are known. (Pliny 19.4 [Bostock and Riley, 4:136–7])

CHAPTER X

Of the occult virtues of things.

There are also other virtues in things, which are not from any element, as to expel poison, to drive away the noxious vapours of minerals, to attract iron, or anything else; and this virtue is a sequel of the species, and form of this or that thing; whence also it being little in quantity, is of great efficacy; which is not granted to any elementary quality. For these virtues having much form, and little matter, can do very much; but an elementary virtue, because it hath more materiality, requires much matter for its acting.

And they are called occult qualities, because their causes lie hid, and man's intellect cannot in any way reach, and find them out. Wherefore philosophers have attained to the greatest part of them by long experience, rather than by the search of reason: for as in the stomach the meat is digested by heat, which we know; so it is changed by a certain hidden virtue which we know not: for truly it is not changed by heat, because it should rather be changed by the fireside, than in the stomach.

So there are in things, besides the elementary qualities which we know, other certain inbred virtues created by nature, which we admire, and are amazed at, being such as we know not, and indeed seldom or never have seen. As we read in *Ovid* of the phoenix, one only bird, which renews herself:[1]

All birds from others do derive their birth,
But yet one fowl there is in all the Earth,

Called by the Assyrians Phoenix, who the wain
Of age, repairs, and sows herself again.

And in another place:

Aegyptus came to see this wondrous sight:
And this rare bird is welcomed with delight.

Long since *Metreas* brought a very great wonderment upon the Greeks, and Romans concerning himself. He said that he nourished, and bred a beast that did devour itself. Hence many to this day are solicitous what this beast of *Matreas* should be. Who would not wonder that fishes should be digged out of the earth, of which *Aristotle, Theophrastus,* and *Polybius* the historian makes mention?[2] And these things which *Pausanias* wrote concerning the singing stones?[3] All these are effects of occult virtues.

So the ostrich[4] concocts cold, and most hard iron, and digests it into nourishment for his body; whose stomach they also report, cannot be hurt with red hot iron. So that little fish called echeneis[5] doth so curb the violence of the winds, and appease the rage of the sea, that, let the tempests be never so imperious, and raging, the sails also bearing a full gale, it doth notwithstanding by its mere touch stay the ships, and makes them stand still, that by no means they can be moved. So salamanders,[6] and crickets[7] live in the fire; although they seem sometimes to burn, yet they are not hurt. The like is said of a kind of bitumen, with which the weapons of the Amazons[8] were said to be smeared over, by which means they could be spoiled neither with sword nor fire; with which also the Gates of Caspia,[9] made of brass, are reported to be smeared over by *Alexander the Great*. We read also that *Noah's* ark was joined together with this bitumen, and that endured some thousands of years upon the mountains of Armenia.

There are many such kind of wonderful things, scarce credible, which notwithstanding are known by experience. Amongst which antiquity makes mention of satyrs,[10] which were animals, in shape half men, and half brutes, yet capable of speech, and reason; one whereof S. *Hierome* reporteth, spake once unto holy *Antonius* the Hermit, and condemned the error of the gentiles, in worshipping such poor creatures as they were, and desired him that he would pray unto the true God for him;[11] also he affirms that there was one of them showed openly alive, and afterwards sent to *Constantine* the Emperor.

Notes—Chapter X

1. *renews herself*—Ovid *Metamorphoses* 15.3, c. line 390.

2. *makes mention*—

> He [Theophrastus] says also, that in the vicinity of Heraclea and Cromna, and about the river Lycus, as well as in many parts of the Euxine, there is one kind of fish which frequents the waters near the banks of the rivers, and makes holes for itself, in which it lives, even when the water retires and the bed of the river is dry; for which reason these fishes have to be dug out of the ground, and only show by the movement of the body that they are still alive ... (Pliny 9.83 [Bostock and Riley, 2:471])

3. *singing stones*—

> Near this hearth is a stone on which they say Apollo put his harp . . . and if you hit this stone with a pebble it twangs like a struck harp-string. I was amazed by this, but still more amazed by the colossus of Egypt. In Egyptian Thebes, where you cross the Nile to the Reeds, as they call it, I saw a sounding statue of a seated figure. Most people call him Memnon . . . Kambyses cut it in half; the upper half from the head to the middle has been thrown away, but the rest is still enthrowned and cries out every day as the sun rises: the sound is very like the twang of a broken lyre-string or a broken harp-string." (Pausanias 1.42. 1–2 [Levi, 1:116–7])

4. *ostrich*—See note 14, ch. VII, bk. I.

5. *echeneis*—The remora, or sucking fish *(Echeneis remora),* was supposed to have the power of retarding, and even stopping, the progress of ships.

> There is a very small fish that is in the habit of living among the rocks, and is known as the echeneis. It is believed that when this has attached itself to the keel of a ship its progress is impeded, and that it is from this circumstance that it takes its name. For this reason, also, it has a disgraceful repute, as being employed in love philters, and for the purpose of retarding judgements and legal proceedings—evil properties, which are only compensated by a single merit that it possesses—it is good for staying fluxes of the womb in pregnant women, and preserves the foetus up to birth ... (Pliny 9.41 [Bostock and Riley, 2:412–3]).

Lucan speaks of "the sucking fish, that holds back the ship in the midst of the waves, while the eastern breeze stretches the rigging ..." *(Pharsalia* 6, line 674 [Riley, 240]). Ovid says: "There is, too, the little sucking-fish, wonderous to tell! a vast obstruction to ships" *(Halieuticon,* line 99. In *The Fasti, Tristia, Pontic Epistles, Ibis, and Halieuticon of Ovid,* trans. Henry T. Riley [London: George Bell and Sons, 1881]).

6. *salamanders*—See note 11, ch. VII, bk. I.

7. *crickets*—See note 12, ch. VII, bk. I.

8. *Amazons*—A nation of warrior women in Africa who burned off their right breasts to better draw the bow. The name was said by the Greeks to mean "deprived of a pap." There were no men in the nation. When a boy was born he was either killed or sent to live with his father in a neighboring state. Herodotus gives a long and entertaining description of Amazons transplanted by the Greeks to Scythia *(History* bk. 4).

Homer mentions them twice in the *Iliad,* calling them "men's equals" (3.189 [Lattimore, 105]), who "fight men in battle" (ibid. 6.186 [Lattimore, 158]). This is echoed by Virgil:

> Penthesilea [queen of the Amazons] raging in the fight leads the bands of Amazons armed with crescent shields, glowing with courage in the midst of thousands; her breast is exposed, she is girt with a golden belt, a female warrior, a maiden who dares to engage in battle with men. *(Aeneid* 1, c. line 490. In *Works of Virgil,* trans. Lonsdale and Lee [London: Macmillan, 1885], 92)

9. *Gates of Caspia*—*Caspiae Pylae* or *Caspiae Portae,* called the Iron Gates, stood at an unofficial dividing line between western and eastern Asia in the principal pass from Media into Parthia and Hyrcania through the Caspian mountains. This pass was so narrow only a single wagon could traverse it. Walls of stone overhung on either side and dripped salt water on the heads of those who filed through. At the narrowest point the Persians built iron gates (which perhaps were of bronze with iron bolts) and a guard house. The pass stood near the ancient city of Rhagae (present-day Teheran). There was another famous pass often called *Caspiae Portae,* but more correctly *Caucasiae Portae* or *Albaniae Portae,* which stood on the western side of the Caspian Sea south of Derbent in the southernmost extremity of the Caucasian wall, otherwise known as Alexander's Wall. It also had gates of iron, and was fortified.

10. *satyrs*—The *Satyri* are the woodland spirits, half beast and half man, of Greek mythology. They were represented as hairy and solid of frame, with flat noses, pointed ears and small horns growing from their foreheads, and were given the tail of either a goat or horse. They find no mention in Homer, but Hesiod calls them "the race of worthless Satyrs, unfit for work." Sensual by nature, they lusted after woodland nymphs and loved wine, dancing and music. The Romans identified satyrs with their own indigenous mythological *fauni,* and under the Romans satyrs acquired larger horns and goat's feet. The references to satyrs in the King James Bible (Isaiah 13:21 and 34:14) are translations of the Hebrew "hairy ones," and probably refer to a kind of Arabic demon.

11. *for him*—This refers to the meeting of Saint Antony with a satyr while on his journey to find Paul the Hermit. The satyr told the saint that he had been sent by his fellow satyrs to entreat his prayers and learn from him something about the saviour of the world. The story is related by Saint Jerome in his *Life of Paul, the First Hermit of Egypt.*

CHAPTER XI

How occult virtues are infused into the several kinds of things by Ideas, through the help of the Soul of the World, and rays of the stars: and what things abound most with this virtue.

Platonists say that all inferior bodies are exemplified by the superior Ideas. Now they define an Idea to be a form, above bodies, souls, minds, and to be but one, simple, pure, immutable, indivisible, incorporeal, and eternal: and that the nature of all Ideas is the same.[1]

Now they place Ideas in the first place in very goodness itself i.e. God, by way of cause;[2] and that they are distinguished amongst themselves by some relative considerations only, lest whatsoever is in the world, should be but one thing without any variety, and that they agree in essence, lest God should be a compound substance.

In the second place, they place them in the very intelligible itself i.e. in the Soul of the World,[3] differing the one from the other by absolute forms, so that all the Ideas in God indeed are but one form: but in the Soul of the World they are many. They are placed in the minds of all other things, whether they be joined to the body, or separated from the body, by a certain participation, and now by degrees are distinguished more, and more. They place them in nature, as certain small seed of forms infused by the Ideas, and lastly they place them in matter, as shadows.

Hereunto may be added, that in the Soul of the World there be as many seminal forms of things, as Ideas in the mind of God, by which forms she did in the heavens above the stars frame to herself shapes also, and stamped upon all these some properties; on these stars therefore, shapes, and properties, all virtues of inferior species, as also their properties do depend; so that every species hath its celestial shape, or figure that is suitable to it, from which also proceeds a wonderful power of operating, which proper gift it receives from its own Idea, through the seminal forms of the Soul of the World.

For Ideas are not only essential causes of every species, but are also the causes of every virtue, which is in the species: and this is that which many philosophers say, that the properties, which are in the nature of things (which virtues indeed are the operations of the Ideas) are moved by certain virtues, viz. such as have a certain, and sure foundation, not fortuitous, nor casual, but effacious, powerful, and sufficient, doing nothing in vain.

Now these virtues do not err in their actings, but by accident, viz. by reason of the impurity, or inequality of the matter: for upon this account there are found things of the same species, more, or less powerful, according to the purity, or indisposition of the matter; for all celestial influences may be hindered by the indisposition, and insufficiency of the matter. Whence it was a proverb amongst the Platonists, that celestial virtues were infused according to the desert of the matter: which also *Virgil* makes mention of, when he sings:

> Their natures fiery are, and from above,
> And from gross bodies freed, divinely
>   move.

Wherefore those things, in which there is less of the Idea of the matter i.e. such things which have a greater resemblance of things separated, have more powerful virtues in operation, being like to the operation of a separated Idea. We see then that the situation, and figure of celestials is the cause of all those excellent virtues, that are in inferior species.

Notes—Chapter XI

1. *is the same*—

"Does that absolute reality which we define in our discussions remain always constant and invariable, or not? Does absolute equality or beauty or any other independent entity which really exists ever admit to change of any kind? Or does each one of these uniform and independent entities remain always constant and invariable, never admitting any alteration in any respect or in any sense?"

"They must be constant and invariable, Socrates," said Cebes.

"Well, what about the concrete instances of beauty— such as men, horses, clothes, and so on—or of equality, or of any other members of a class corresponding to an absolute entity? Are they constant, or are they, on the contrary, scarcely ever in the same relation in any sense either to themselves or to one another?"

"With them, Socrates, it is just the opposite; they are never free from variation." *(Phaedo* 78d-e. trans. H. Tredennick [Hamilton and Cairns, 61–2]. See also the *Republic* 7.514–9b.)

2. *way of cause*—

This reality, then, that gives their truth to the objects of knowledge and the power of knowing to the knower, you must say is the idea of good, and you must conceive it as being the cause of knowledge, and of truth in so far as known. Yet fair as they both are, knowledge and truth, in supposing it to be something fairer still than these you will think rightly of it. But as for knowledge and truth, even as in our illustration it is right to deem light and vision sunlike, but never to think that they are the sun, so here it is right to consider these two their counterparts, as being like the good or boniform, but to think that either of them is the good is not right. Still higher honour belongs to the possession and habit of the good. (Plato *Republic* 6.508d–509a, trans. P. Shorey [Hamilton and Cairns, 744])

3. *Soul of the World*—See Appendix II.

Chapter XII

How it is that particular virtues are infused into particular individuals, even of the same species.

There are also in many individuals, or particular things, peculiar gifts, as wonderful as in the species, and these also are from the figure, and situation of celestial stars. For every individual, when it begins to be under a determined horoscope, and celestial constellation, contracts together with its essence a certain wonderful virtue both of doing, and suffering something that is remarkable, even besides that which it receives from its species, and this it doth partly by the influence of the heaven, and partly through that obedientialness of the matter of things to be generated, to the Soul of the World, which obedientialness indeed is such as that of our bodies to our souls.

For we perceive that there is this in us, that according to our conceptions of things, our bodies are moved, and that cheerfully,[1] as when we are afraid of, or fly from anything. So many times when the celestial souls conceive several things, then the matter is moved obedientially to it: also in nature there appear divers prodigies, by reason of the imagination of superior motions. So also they conceive, and imagine divers virtues, not only things natural, but also sometimes artificial, and this especially if the soul of the operator be inclined towards the same. Whence *Avicen*[2] saith, that whatsoever things are done here, must have been before in the motions, and conceptions of the stars, and orbs.

So in things, various effects, inclinations, and dispositions are occasioned not only from the matter variously disposed, as many suppose, but from a various influence, and divers form; not truly with a specific difference, but particular, and proper. And the degrees of these are variously distributed by the first cause of all things, God himself, who being unchangeable, distributes to everyone as he pleaseth, with whom notwithstanding second causes, angelical, and celestial cooperate, disposing of the corporeal matter, and other things that are committed to them. All virtues therefore are infused by God, through the Soul of the World, yet by a particular power of resemblances, and intelligences overruling them, and concourse of the rays, and aspects of the stars in a certain peculiar harmonious consent.

Notes—Chapter XII

1. *cheerfully*—Quickly.

2. *Avicen*—Avicenna.

CHAPTER XIII

Whence the occult virtues of things proceed.

It is well known to all, that there is a certain virtue in the loadstone, by which it attracts iron,[1] and that the diamond doth by its presence take away[2] that virtue of the loadstone: so also amber,[3] and jet[4] rubbed, and warmed draw a straw to them, and the stone asbestos being once fired is never, or scarce extinguished:[5] a carbuncle shines in the dark,[6] the stone aetites put above the young fruit of women, or plants, strengthens them, but being put under, causeth abortion;[7] the jasper stancheth blood;[8] the little fish echeneis[9] stops the ships; rhubarb expels choller;[10] the liver of the camelion burnt,[11] raiseth showers, and thunders. The stone heliotrophium[12] dazzles the sight, and makes him that wears it to be invisible, the stone lyncurius[13] takes away delusions from before the eyes, the perfume of the stone lypparis[14] calls forth all the beasts, the stone synochitis[15] brings up infernal ghosts, the stone anachitis[16] makes the images of the gods appear. The ennectis put under them that dream, causeth oracles.

There is a herb in Ethiopia, with which they report ponds, and lakes are dried up, and all things that are shut, to be opened; and we read of an herb called latace which the Persian kings give to their ambassadors, that whither soever they shall come, they shall abound with plenty of all things. There is also a Scythian herb,[17] with which being tasted, or at least held in the mouth, they report the Scythians will endure twelve days hunger, and thirst; and

Apuleius saith, that he was taught by an oracle that there were many kinds of herbs, and stones, with which men might prolong their lives forever, but that it was not lawful for men to understand the knowledge of those things, because, whereas they have but a short time to live, they study mischief with all their might, and attempt all manner of wickedness; if they should be sure of a very long time, they would not spare the gods themselves.

But from whence these virtues are, none of all these have showed, who have set forth huge volumes of the properties of things, not *Hermes,* not *Bochus,* not *Aaron,* not *Orpheus,* not *Theophrastus,* not *Thebith,* not *Zenothemis,* not *Zoroaster,* not *Evax,* not *Dioscorides,* not *Isaaick* the Jew, not *Zacharias* the Babylonian, not *Albertus,* not *Arnoldus;* and yet all these have confessed the same, that *Zacharias* wrote to *Mithridites,* that great power, and human destinies are couched in the virtues of stones, and herbs. But to know from whence these come, a higher speculation is required.

Alexander the Peripatetic not going any farther than his senses, and qualities, is of the opinion that these proceed from elements, and their qualities, which haply might be supposed to be true, if those were of the same species; but many of the operations of the stones agree neither in *genre,* nor *specie.* Therefore *Plato,* and his scholars attribute these virtues to Ideas, the formers of things. But *Avicen* reduceth these kinds of operations to intelligences, *Her-*

mes to the stars, *Albertus* to the specifical forms of things.

And although these authors seem to thwart one the other, yet none of them, if they be rightly understood, goes beside the truth: since all their sayings are the same in effect in most things. For God in the first place is the end, and beginning of all virtues, he gives the seal of the Ideas to his servants the intelligences; who as faithful officers sign all things entrusted to them with an ideal virtue, the heavens, and stars, as instruments, disposing the matter in the meanwhile for the receiving of those forms which reside in Divine Majesty (as saith *Plato* in Timæus)[18] and to be conveyed by stars; and the Giver of Forms distributes them by the ministry of his intelligences, which he hath set as rulers, and controllers over his works, to whom such a power is entrusted in things committed to them, that so all virtue of stones, herbs, metals, and all other things may come from the intelligences, the governors.

The form therefore, and virtue of things comes first from the Ideas, then from the ruling, and governing intelligences, then from the aspects of the heavens disposing, and lastly from the tempers of the elements disposed, answering the influences of the heavens, by which the elements themselves are ordered, or disposed. These kinds of operations therefore are performed in these inferior things by express forms, and in the heavens by disposing virtues, in intelligences by mediating rules, in the original cause by Ideas, and exemplary forms, all which must of necessity agree in the execution of the effect, and virtue of everything.

There is therefore a wonderful virtue, and operation in every herb, and stone, but greater in a star, beyond which, even from the governing intelligences everything receiveth, and obtains many things for itself, especially from the Supreme Cause, with whom all things do mutually, and exactly correspond, agreeing in an harmonious consent, as it were in hymns,

always praising the highest Maker of all things, as by the three children in the fiery furnace were all things called upon to praise God with singings: bless ye the Lord all things that grow upon the Earth, and all things which move in the waters, all fowls of the heavens, beasts, and cattle, together with the sons of men.[19]

There is therefore no other cause of the necessity of effects, than the connection of all things with the First Cause, and their correspondency with those divine patterns, and eternal Ideas, whence everything hath its determinate, and particular place in the exemplary world, from whence it lives, and receives its original being; and every virtue of herbs, stones, metals, animals, words and speeches, and all things that are of God, is placed there.

Now the First Cause, which is God, although he doth by intelligences, and the heavens work upon these inferior things, doth sometimes (these mediums being laid aside, or their officiating being suspended) work those things immediately by himself, which works then are called miracles: but whereas secondary causes, which *Plato,* and others call handmaids,[20] do by the command, and appointment of the First Cause, necessarily act, and are necessitated to produce their effects, if God shall notwithstanding according to his pleasure so discharge, and suspend them, that they shall wholly desist from the necessity of that command, and appointment; then they are called the greatest miracles of God.

So the fire in the Chaldeans' furnace did not burn the children; so also the Sun at the command of *Joshua*[21] went back from its course the space of one whole day; so also at the prayer of *Hezekiah*[22] it went back ten degrees, or hours. So when Christ was crucified the Sun was darkened,[23] though at full Moon: and the reasons of these operations can by no rational discourse, no magic, or occult, or profound science whatsoever be found out, or understood, but are to be learned, and inquired into by divine oracles only.

Notes—Chapter XIII

1. *attracts iron*—Loadstone is naturally magnetic.

> Upon quitting the marbles to pass on to the other more remarkable stones, who can for a moment doubt that the magnet will be the first to suggest itself? For what, in fact, is there endowed with more marvellous properties than this? or in which of her departments has Nature displayed a greater degree of waywardness? … Nature has here endowed stone with both sense and hands. What is there more stubborn than hard iron? Nature has, in this instance, bestowed upon it both feet and intelligence. It allows itself, in fact, to be attracted by the magnet, and, itself a metal which subdues all other elements, it precipitates itself toward the source of an influence at once mysterious and unseen. The moment the metal comes near it, it springs toward the magnet, and, as it clasps it, is held fast in the magnet's embraces. (Pliny 36.25 [Bostock and Riley, 6:355])

Lucretius elaborates on the notion that the loadstone works by creating a vacuum:

> In the first place, many atoms, or effluvia, must necessarily fly from off the stone, which, by their impact, disperse the air that is situated betwixt the stone and the iron. When this space is emptied, and a large void is made betwixt them, atoms of the iron, immediately darting forward, rush in a body into the vacuum; and the whole [iron] ring of necessity follows, and passes onward with its whole body. For no substance coheres and combines more closely,—having its primary-elements intimately involved,—than the cold and rough consistence of stout iron. *(On the Nature of Things* 6.998, trans. J S. Watson [London: George Bell and Sons, 1901], 287)

2. *take away*—"So great is the antipathy borne by this stone [diamond] to the magnet, that when placed near, it will not allow of its attracting iron; or if the magnet has already attracted the iron, it will seize the metal and drag it away from the other" (Pliny 37.15 [Bostock and Riley, 6:408]). "I have read furthermore of this stone [loadstone], that if you lay but a diamond near it, it will not draw iron at all, but puts it from it as soon as ever the diamond comes to touch it" (Augustine *City of God* 21.4 [Healey, 2:324]). This same power was ascribed to, of all things, garlic: "nor will the lodestone attract the iron if it is rubbed with garlic" (Ptolemy *Tetrabiblos* 1.3.13,

trans. F. E. Robbins [Cambridge: Harvard University Press, 1980], 27). All this lore is also to be found in the *Moralia* of Plutarch, *Platonicae quaestiones* 7.5. Needless to say, neither diamond nor garlic has the least effect on the loadstone.

3. *amber*—A golden, translucent fossil resin that burns with a pleasant odor, and sometimes contains insects. When rubbed it attracts straw and other such bits through static electricity. Pliny gives all the Greek lore of amber, saying that it was variously believed to have been formed from tears shed by trees or by birds or from the urine of lynxes, that it flows from the earth, that it is solidified brine, that it is the dew of sunbeams and that it exudes from warm mud, before he gives his own opinion:

> Amber is produced from a marrow discharged by trees belonging to the pine genus, like gum from the cherry, and resin from the ordinary pine. It is a liquid at first, which issues forth in considerable quantities, and is gradually hardened by heat or cold, or else by the action of the sea, when the rise of the tide carries off the fragments from the shores of these islands [in the Northern Ocean]. At all events, it is thrown up upon the coasts, in so light and voluble a form that in the shallows it has all the appearance of hanging suspended in the water. (Pliny 37.11 [Bostock and Riley, 6:401])

4. *jet*—Also called gagates. A hard, black form of coal capable of accepting a high polish. It was called black amber and often confused with amber ("It is of double colour; black, and of the colour of saffron" (*Book of Secrets* [Best and Brightman, 45]) because it shares with amber the power of attracting bits of straw when rubbed—a property mentioned by Albertus Magnus. Pliny says:

> It is black, smooth, light, and porous, differs but little from wood in appearance, is of a brittle texture, and emits a disagreeable odour when rubbed. Marks made upon pottery with this stone cannot be effaced. When burnt, it gives out a sulphureous smell; and it is a singular fact, that the application of water ignites it, while that of oil quenches it. The fumes of it, burnt, keep serpents at a distance, and dispel hysterical affections: they detect a tendency also to epilepsy, and act as a test of virginity. A decoction of this stone in wine is curative of tooth-ache; and, in combination with wax, it is good for scrofula. The magicians,

it is said, make use of gagates in the practice of what they call axinomancy [divination by placing jet on the red-hot blade of an ax]; and they assure us that it will be sure not to burn, if the thing is about to happen as the party desires. (Pliny 36.34 [Bostock and Riley, 6:361–2])

5. *scarce extinguished*—

If thou wilt make a fire continually unable to be quenched or put out—Take the stone which is called *Asbestos,* and it is of the colour of Iron, and there is found very much of it in Arabia. If this stone be kindled or inflamed, it may never be put out, or quenched, because it hath the nature of the first feathers of the Salamander, by reason of moisty fatness, which nourisheth the fire kindled in it. (*Book of Secrets* 2.10 [Best and Brightman, 30–1])

Albertus Magnus calls asbestos "salamander's down" *(Meteora* 4.3.17). See note 11, ch. VII, bk. I.

6. *in the dark*—The carbuncles of the ancient world were generally rubies and red garnets. Speaking of these "fiery red gemstones" Pliny says:

In the first rank among these [brilliant] stones is carbunculus, so called from its resemblance to fire; though in reality it is proof against the action of that element: hence it is that some persons call these stones "acaustoi" [incombustible]. ... In addition to this, each kind is subdivided into the male carbunculus and the female, the former of which is of a more striking brilliancy, the brightness of the latter being not so strong. In the male varieties too, we see some in which the fire is clearer than in others; while some, again, are of a darker hue, or else have their brilliancy more deeply seated, and shine with a more powerful lustre than others when viewed in the sun. ... According to Callistratus, the refulgence of this stone should be of a whitish hue, and, when placed upon a table, it should heighten by its lustre other stones placed near it that are clouded at the edge. (Pliny 37.25 [Bostock and Riley, 6:420–1])

From these references to its brilliance, the carbuncle became proverbial as a light-emitting stone. In the *Book of Secrets* directions are given for making an artificial carbuncle:

If thou wilt make a Carbuncle stone, or a thing shining in the night—Take very many of the little beasts shining by night

[glow worms and fireflies], and put them beaten small in a bottle of glass, and close it, and bury it in hot Horses' dung, and let it tarry fifteen days. Afterward thou shalt distil water of them *per alembicum,* which thou shalt put in a vessel of crystal or glass. It giveth so great clearness, that every man may read and write in a dark place, where it is. ("Marvels of the World" 79 [Best and Brightman, 111])

7. *causeth abortion*—The aetites, or eaglestone, is a hollow concretion containing crystals, or pebbles, or pellets of earth, that rattle when the geode is shaken. Pliny says that eagles build this stone into their nests. "This stone has the quality also, in a manner, of being pregnant, for when shaken, another stone is heard to rattle within, just as though it were enclosed in its womb; it has no medical properties, however, except immediately after it has been taken from the nest" (Pliny 10.4 [Bostock and Riley, 2:484]). Elsewhere he says:

Attached to pregnant women or to cattle, in the skins of animals that have been sacrificed, these stones act as a preventive of abortion, care being taken not to remove them till the moment of parturition; for otherwise procidence of the uterus is the result. If, on the other hand, they are not removed at the moment when parturition is about to ensue, that operation of Nature cannot be effected. (Pliny 36.39 [Bostock and Riley, 6:365])

The *Book of Secrets* says of the aetites: "It is profitable to women great with child; it letteth [stops] untimely birth" (2.41, p. 46). This is drawn from Albertus Magnus, who says of this stone that it mitigates the perils of childbirth. Lucan refers to "the stones that resound [explode] beneath the brooding bird" *(Pharsalia* 6, line 676 [Riley, 240]). Perhaps when cast into the fire, air and moisture in the hollow stone caused it to crack open, a kind of hatching, or birth.

8. *stancheth blood*—Jasper is an opaque quartz that may be red, yellow, brown or green. When red flecks of iron oxide occur in green jasper it is called bloodstone. It should not be confused with heliotrope, which is a translucent green chalcedony with crimson spots. It is easy to distinguish between them because jasper is always completely opaque. In ancient times the two stones were confounded together. In ancient Egypt red jasper was associated with the menstrual blood of Isis, and was "supposed to increase the milk in women who were suckling children, and to help pregnant women" (Budge 1968, 316). According to

medieval legend bloodstone was created at the crucifixion of Christ, when spatterings from his side,
where he was pierced by the spear of the Roman soldier, fell upon the ground.

> From this time onwards the stone seems to
> have been endowed with magical and
> divine powers in arresting hemorrhage
> from wounds, and was worn by Roman
> soldiers for this reason; among the natives
> of India it is customary to place the Blood-
> stone itself upon wounds and injuries after
> dipping it in cold water. (Thomas and
> Pavitt 1970 [1914], 138)

9. *echeneis*—See note 5, ch. X, bk. I.

10. *expels choler*—The dried root of the genus *Rheum*
was extensively used in medicine in the time of
Agrippa, the best variety being imported overland from
Tibet and China. It was called Turkey Rhubarb. Gerard
says: "The purgation which is made with Rubarb is
profitable and fit for all such as be troubled with
choler," adding "it purgeth forth cholericke and
naughty humors" (John Gerard, *The Herbal* [1633], bk.
2, ch. 83, sec. E, G [New York: Dover, 1975], 395).

11. *chameleon burnt*—The chameleon was the magical
beast of the air, as the salamander was of the fire,
because it was supposed to live on air. "It always holds
the head upright and the mouth open, and is the only
animal which receives nourishment neither by meat nor
drink, nor anything else, but from the air alone" (Pliny
8.51 [Bostock and Riley, 2:303]). "Democritus asserts
that if the head and neck of a chamaeleon are burnt in a
fire made with logs of oak, it will be productive of a
storm attended with rain and thunder; a result equally
produced by burning the liver upon the tiles of a house"
(Pliny 28.29 [Bostock and Riley, 5:316]).

12. *heliotrophium*—See note 8 above.

> Heliotropium is found in Aethiopia, Africa,
> and Cyprus: it is of a leek-green colour,
> streaked with blood-red veins. It has been
> thus named, from the circumstance that, if
> placed in a vessel of water and exposed to
> the full light of the sun, it changes to a
> reflected colour like that of blood; this
> being the case with the stone of Aethiopia
> more particularly. Out of the water, too, it
> reflects the figure of the sun like a mirror,
> and it discovers eclipses of that luminary
> by showing the moon passing over its disk.
> In the use of this stone, also, we have a
> most glaring illustration of the impudent
> effrontery of the adepts in magic, for they
> say that, if it is combined with the plant
> heliotropium and certain incantations are

then repeated over it, it will render the person invisible who carries it about him.
(Pliny 37.60 [Bostock and Riley, 6:450])

13. *lyncurius*—Lyncurium, or lynx water, a stone
thought to be formed from the urine of lynxes mixed
with a particular kind of earth.

> They assert, too, that it is a product of the
> urine of the lynx and of a kind of earth, the
> animal covering up the urine the moment it
> has voided it, from a jealousy that man
> should gain possession of it; a combination
> which hardens into stone. The colour of it,
> they inform us, like that of some kinds of
> amber, is of a fiery hue, and it admits, they
> say, of being engraved. They assert, too, that
> this substance attracts to itself not only
> leaves or straws, but thin plates of copper
> even or of iron; a story which Theophrastus
> even believes, on the faith of a certain Dio-
> cles. For my own part, I look upon the
> whole of these statements as untrue, and I
> do not believe that in our time there has ever
> been a precious stone seen with such a name
> as this. I regard, too, the assertions that have
> been made as to its medicinal properties, as
> equally false; to the effect that, taken in
> drink, it disperses urinary calculi, and that,
> taken in wine, or only looked at, it is cura-
> tive of jaundice. (Pliny 37.13 [Bostock and
> Riley, 6:404–5])

The *Book of Secrets*, citing Isidore of Seville, says it
is a stone taken from the head of the lynx, of a white
colour: "Also it taketh away a white spot or pearl
[cataract] in the eye" (*Book of Secrets* 2.49 [Best and
Brightman, 48–9]). It has been conjectured that lyncurium is brown tourmaline, which has electrical
properties similar to those described.

14. *lypparis*—Liparea. "… all that we find said about
liparea ['fat stone'] is, that employed in the form of a
fumigation, it allures all kinds of wild beasts" (Pliny
37.62 [Bostock and Riley, 6:453]). "This stone is
found in Libya, and all beasts run to it, as to their
defender. It letteth that neither dogs nor hunters may
hurt them" (*Book of Secrets* 2.33 [Best and Brightman,
42]). This is conjectured to be sulfur from the Lipari
Islands, a group of volcanic islands north of Sicily.

15. *synochitis*—"Anancitis ['stone of necessity'] is
used in hydromancy, they say, for summoning the
gods to make their appearance; and synochitis
['retaining stone'], for detaining the shades from
below when they have appeared" (Pliny 37.73
[Bostock and Riley, 6:461]). The stones are mentioned by St. Isidore, Bishop of Seville, in his *Ety-
mologiae* 16.15—see Evans 1976 [1922], 31.

16. *anachitis*—See note above.

17. *Scythian herb*—

> Entire nations, too, have been the discoverers of certain plants. The Scythae were the first to discover the plant known as "scythice," which grows in the vicinity of the Palus Maeotis. Among other properties, this plant is remarkably sweet, and extremely useful for the affection known as "asthma." It is also possessed of another great recommendation—so long as a person keeps it in his mouth, he will never experience hunger or thirst.
> The hippace, another plant that grows in Scythia, is possessed of similar properties: it owes its name to the circumstance that it produces the like effect upon horses. By the aid of these two plants, the Scythae, they say, are enabled to endure hunger and thirst, so long as twelve days even. (Pliny 25.43–4 [Bostock and Riley, 5:110–1])

Agrippa also mentions this herb in ch. LVIII, bk. I, where he calls it "herb of Sparta," perhaps because the Spartans were proverbial for their endurance. Riley conjectures that it is licorice. Hippace appears to have been a cheese made from mare's milk mentioned by Hippocrates *(Airs, Waters, Places* ch. 18), which Pliny mistook for a plant.

18. *in Timaeus*—

> After having made it he divided the whole mixture [of elements] into souls equal in number to the stars and assigned each soul to a star, and having there placed them as in a chariot he showed them the nature of the universe and declared to them the laws of destiny, according to which their first birth would be one and the same for all—

> no one should suffer a disadvantage at his hands. (Plato *Timaeus* 41d, trans. B. Jowett [Hamilton and Cairns, 1170])

> He who lived well during his appointed time was to return and dwell in his native star, and there he would have a blessed and congenial existence. But if he failed in attaining this, at the second birth he would pass into a woman, and if, when in that state of being, he did not desist from evil, he would continually be changed into some brute . . . (ibid., 42b, 1171)

> Now of the divine, he himself was the creator, but the creation of the mortal he committed to his offspring [the Intelligences]. And they, imitating him, received from him the immortal principle of the soul, and around this they proceeded to fashion a mortal body, and made it to be the vehicle of the soul, and constructed within the body a soul of another nature which was mortal, subject to terrible and irresistible affections . . . these they mingled with irrational sense and with all-daring love according to necessary laws, and so framed man. (ibid., 69c, -d, 1193)

19. *sons of men*—The Apocryphal *Song of the Three Holy Children*, verses 54–60.

20. *handmaids*—See the *Timaeus* 46c–e (Hamilton and Cairns, 1174).

21. *command of Joshua*—Joshua 10:12–3.

22. *prayer of Hezekiah*—II Kings 20:9–11.

23. *Sun was darkened*—Luke 23:44–5. A solar eclipse occurs only at the new moon and is not possible at full moon.

CHAPTER XIV

Of the Spirit of the World,
what it is, and how by way of medium
it unites occult virtues to their subjects.

Democritus, and *Orpheus*, and many Pythagoreans having most diligently searched into the virtues of celestial things, and natures of inferior things, said, that all things are full of God,[1] and not without cause: for there is nothing of such transcending virtues, which being destitute of divine assistance, is content with the nature of itself. Also they called those divine powers which are diffused in things, gods: which *Zoroaster* called divine allurements, *Synesius* symbolical inticements, others called them lives, and some also souls; saying, that the virtues of things did depend upon these; because it is the property of the soul to be from one matter extended into divers things, about which it operates: so is a man, who extends his intellect unto intelligible things, and his imagination unto imaginable things; and this is that which they understood, when they said, viz. that the soul of one thing went out, and went into another thing, altering it, and hindering the operations of it: as a diamond hinders[2] the operation of the loadstone, that it cannot attract iron.

Now seeing the soul is the first thing that is moveable, and as they say, is moved of itself; but the body, or the matter is of itself unable, and unfit for motion, and doth much degenerate from the soul, therefore they say there is need of a more excellent medium, viz. such a one that may be as it were no body, but as it were a soul, or as it were no soul, but as it were a body, viz. by which the soul may be joined to the body.

Now they conceive such a medium to be the Spirit of the World, viz. that which we call the quintessence:[3] because it is not from the four elements, but a certain fifth thing, having its being above, and besides them.

There is therefore such a kind of Spirit required to be, as it were the medium, whereby celestial souls are joined to gross bodies, and bestow upon them wonderful gifts. This Spirit is after the same manner in the body of the world, as ours is in the body of man. For as the powers of our soul are communicated to the members of the body by the spirit, so also the virtue of the Soul of the World[4] is diffused through all things by the quintessence: for there is nothing found in the whole world, that hath not a spark of the virtue thereof. Yet it is more, nay most of all infused into those things which have received, or taken in most of this Spirit: now this Spirit is received or taken in by the rays of the stars, so far forth as things render themselves conformable to them. By this Spirit therefore every occult property is conveyed into herbs, stones, metals, and animals, through the Sun, Moon, planets, and through stars higher than the planets.

Now this Spirit may be more advantageous to us, if anyone knew how to separate it from the elements: or at least to use those things chiefly, which do most abound with this Spirit. For these things, in which this Spirit is less drowned in a body, and less checked by matter, do more powerfully, and perfectly act, and also more readily

44

generate their like: for in it are all generative, and seminary virtues. For which cause the alchemists endeavour to separate this Spirit from gold, and silver; which being rightly separated, and extracted, if thou shalt afterward project upon any matter of the same kind i.e. any metal, presently will turn it into gold, or silver. And we know how to do that, and have seen it done: but we could make no more gold, than the weight of that was, out of which we extracted the Spirit. For seeing that is an extense form, and not intense, it cannot beyond its own bounds change an imperfect body into a perfect: which I deny not, but may be done by another way.[5]

Notes—Chapter XIV

1. *full of God*—"Certain thinkers say that soul is intermingled in the whole universe, and it is perhaps for this reason that Thales came to the opinion that all things are full of gods" (Aristotle *On the Soul* 1.5.411a. In *Basic Works,* trans. J. A. Smith [New York: Random House, 1941], 553).

> Of all the planets, of the moon, of years and months and all seasons, what other story shall we have to tell than just this same, that since soul, or souls, and those souls good with perfect goodness, have proved to be the cause of all, these souls we hold to be gods, whether they direct the universe by inhibiting bodies, like animated beings, or whatever their manner of their action? Will any man who shares this belief bear to hear it said that all things are not "full of gods?" (Plato *Laws* bk. 10, sec. 899b, trans. A. E. Taylor [Hamilton and Cairns, 1455])

2. *diamond hinders*—See note 2, ch. XIII, bk. I.

3. *quintessence*—The *quinta essentia,* or fifth essence, also known as aether, originated in Western philosophy with the Pythagoreans, who characterized it as more subtile and pure than fire and possessed of a circular motion. Supposedly it flew upward at creation, and from it the stars were formed, as Milton explains:

> Swift to thir several Quarters hasted then
> The cumbrous Elements, Earth, Flood, Air, Fire,
> And this Ethereal quintessence of Heav'n
> Flew upward, spirited with various forms,
> That roll'd orbicular, and turn'd to Stars
> *(Paradise Lost* bk. 3, ll. 714–8)

For in the whole range of time past, so far as our inherited records reach, no change appears to have taken place either in the whole scheme of the outermost heaven or in any of its proper parts. The common name, too, which has been handed down from our distant ancestors even to our own day, seems to show that they conceived of it in the fashion which we have been expressing. The same ideas, one must believe, recur in men's minds not once or twice but again and again. And so, implying that the primary body is something else beyond earth, fire, air, and water, they gave the highest place a name of its own, *aither,* derived from the fact that it "runs always" for an eternity of time. (Aristotle *On the Heavens* 1.3.270b, trans. J. L. Stocks [McKeon, 403])

4. *Soul of the World*—See Appendix II.

5. *by another way*—This is the Philosopher's Stone and Powder of Projection of alchemy. Edward Kelley is said to have purchased two small caskets in Wales from an innkeeper who had derived them from the rifled sepulchre of a bishop. In one was the White Powder, used for turning base metal into silver, and in the other shattered casket a small amount of the Red Powder, for turning base metal to gold. According to one account, he and John Dee made trial of the Red Powder and found that it could convert 272,230 times its own weight into gold. But "'they lost much gold in experiments before they knew the extent of its power'" *(The Alchemical Writings of Edward Kelly,* ed. A. E. Waite [1893] [New York: Weiser, 1976], p. xxii of the "Biographical Preface"). Waite is quoting Louis Figuier, *L'Alchimie et les Alchimistes,* Paris, 1860, 232 et seq.

CHAPTER XV

How we must find out, and examine the virtues of things by way of similitude.

It is now manifest that the occult properties in things are not from the nature of the elements, but infused from above, hid from our senses, and scarce at last known by our reason, which indeed come from the life, and the Spirit of the World,[1] through the rays of the stars: and can no otherwise but by experience, and conjecture be inquired into by us.

Wherefore, he that desires to enter upon this study, must consider, that everything moves, and turns itself to its like, and inclines that to itself with all its might, as well in property, viz. occult virtue, as in quality, viz. elementary virtue. Sometimes also in substance itself, as we see in salt, for whatsoever hath long stood with salt, becomes salt:[2] for every agent, when it hath begun to act, doth not attempt to make a thing inferior to itself, but as much as may be, like, and suitable to itself. Which also we manifestly see in sensible animals, in which the nutritive virtue doth not change the meat into an herb, or a plant, but turns it into sensible flesh.

In what things therefore there is an excess of any quality, or property, as heat, cold, boldness, fear, sadness, anger, love, hatred, or any other passion, or virtue; whether it be in them by nature, or sometimes also by art, or chance, as boldness in a harlot;[3] these things do very much move, and provoke to such a quality, passion, or virtue. So Fire moves to Fire, and Water moves to Water, and he that is bold moves to boldness.[4] And it is well known amongst physicians that brain helps the brain, and lungs, the lungs. So

also it is said, that the right eye of a frog helps the soreness of a man's right eye, and the left eye thereof, helps the soreness of his left eye, if they be hanged about his neck in a cloth of its natural colour: the like is reported of the eyes of a crab.[5] So the foot of a tortoise helps them that have the gout in their being applied thus, as foot to foot, hand to hand, right to right, left to left.

After this manner they say, that any animal that is barren causeth another to be barren;[6] and of the animal, especially the testicles, matrix, or urine. So they report that a woman shall not conceive, if she drink every month of the urine of a mule,[7] or anything steeped in it. If therefore we would obtain any property or virtue, let us seek for such animals, or such other things whatsoever, in which such a property is in a more eminent manner than in any other thing, and in these let us take that part in which such a property, or virtue is most vigorous: as if at any time we would promote love, let us seek some animal which is most loving, of which kind are pigeons, turtles,[8] sparrows, swallows, wagtails: and in these let us take those members, or parts, in which the venereal appetite is most vigorous, and such are the heart, testicles, matrix,[9] yard,[10] sperm, and menstrues.[11] And it must be done at that time when these animals have their affection most intense:[12] for then they do much provoke, and draw love.

In like manner to increase boldness, let us look for a lion, or a cock, and of these let us take the heart, eyes, or forehead. And so we must understand that which *Psellus* the Platonist saith, viz. that dogs, crows, and cocks conduce much to watchfulness: also the nightingale, and bat, and horn owl, and in these the heart, head, and eyes especially. Therefore it is said, if any shall carry the heart of a crow, or a bat about him, he shall not sleep till he cast it away from him. The same doth the head of a bat[13] dried, and bound to the right arm of him that is awake, for if it be put upon him when he is asleep, it is said that he shall not be awakened till it be taken off from him.

After the same manner doth a frog, and an owl make one talkative, and of these specially the tongue, and heart; so the tongue of a water frog[14] laid under the head, makes a man speak in his sleep, and the heart of a screech owl[15] laid upon the left breast of a woman that is asleep is said to make her utter all her secrets. The same also the heart of the horn owl is said to do, also the suet of a hare laid upon the breast of one that is asleep.

Upon the same account do animals that are long lived, conduce to long life; and whatsoever things have a power in themselves, to renew themselves, conduce to the renovation of our body, and restoring of youth, which physicians have often professed they know to be true; as is manifest of the viper, and snake.[16] And it is known that harts renew their old age by the eating of snakes.[17] After the same manner the phoenix[18] is renewed by a fire which she makes for herself; and the like virtue there is in a pelican, whose right foot being put under warm dung, after three months there is of that generated a pelican.[19] Therefore some physicians by some certain confections made of vipers, and hellebor, and the flesh of some such kind of animals do restore youth, and indeed do sometimes restore it so, as *Medea* restored old *Pileas*.[20] It is also believed that the blood of a bear, if it be sucked out of her wound, doth increase the strength of the body, because that animal is the strongest creature.[21]

Notes—Chapter XV

1. *Spirit of the World*—That is, the quintessence. See note 3, ch. XIV, bk. I.

2. *becomes salt*—"Also Avicenna said, when a thing standeth long in salt, it is salt, and if any thing stand in a stinking place, it is made stinking. And if any thing standeth with a bold man, it is made bold; if it standeth with a fearful man, it is made fearful" ("Marvels of the World" 2 [Best and Brightman, 74]).

3. *in a harlot*—". . . either after the whole kind, as boldness and victory is natural to a Lion, or *secundum individuum,* as boldness in a harlot, not by Man's kind, but *per individuum"* (ibid., sec. 3, 75).

4. *moves to boldness*—"Likewise in an harlot boldness is extreme. And therefore Philosophers say if any man put on a common harlot's smock, or look in the glass (or have it with him) in which she beholdeth herself, he goeth bold and unfearful" (ibid., sec. 14, 80).

5. *eyes of a crab*—the salve *Oculi Cancrorum,* or Crab's Eye Ointment, was used to heal ulcerous sores. Crab's Eye was the name for a concreation of carbonate of lime found in the stomachs of lobsters and crayfish. There seems to be a magical thread running from the eye of the crab through the zodiacal sign Cancer, the stone of that sign, the emerald, which was known in ancient times as a preserver of eyesight, down to the chalky contents in the stomach of crayfish.

6. *to be barren*—"And therefore Philosophers have written that the Mule, forasmuch as he is utterly barren of his property, and whosoever it be, maketh men and women barren, when some part of him is associated to women" ("Marvels of the World" 15 [Best and Brightman, 81]).

7. *urine of a mule*—Surely one of the more noxious methods of birth control.

8. *turtles*—Turtledoves.

9. *matrix*—Womb.

10. *yard*—Penis.

11. *menstrues*—Menstrual blood.

12. *most intense*—

Likewise they which will move love look what beast loveth most greatly, and specially in that hour in which it is most stirred up in love, because there is then greater strength in it in moving to love; they take a part of the beast, in which carnal appetite is stronger, as are the heart, the stones, and the mother or matrix.

And because the Swallow loveth greatly, as Philosophers saith, therefore they choose her greatly to stir up love.

Likewise the Dove and the Sparrow are holden to be of this kind, specially when they are delighted in love, or carnal appetite, for then they provoke and bring in love without resistance. ("Marvels of the World" 15–7 [Best and Brightman, 81]).

13. *head of a bat*—The inversion of the magical virtue of things when applied to opposite conditions is very common. "And Philosophers have invented that if any woman is barren, when there is put to her a thing that maketh a woman barren, that woman is not barren, but fruitful, and contrariwise" (ibid., sec. 30, 87).

14. *tongue of a water frog*—"Take a water Frog quick [alive], and take away her tongue, and put it again into the water, and put the tongue unto a part of the heart of the woman sleeping, which when she is asked, she shall say the truth" (ibid., sec. 56, 99–100). This charm is taken directly out of the *Kiranides:* "If he will know the secrets of woman, then must he cut the tongue out of the Frog alive, and turn the Frog away again, making certain characters upon the Frog's tongue, and so lay the same upon the panting of a woman's heart, and let him ask her what questions he will, she shall answer unto him all the truth, and reveal all the secret faults that ever she had committed" (ibid., 99, n. 56).

15. *heart of a screech owl*—"There be marvellous virtues of this fowl, for if the heart and right foot of it be put upon a man sleeping, he shall say anon to thee whatsoever thou shalt ask of him" (ibid., bk. 3, sec. 4, 52).

16. *viper, and snake*—Snakes shed their skin several times a year. The old dry skin makes them appear old, while the smooth new skin gives them a youthful look.

17. *eating of snakes*—"That deer are destructive to those reptiles [snakes] no one is ignorant; as also of the fact that they drag them from their holes when they find them, and so devour them" (Pliny 28.42 [Bostock and Riley, 5:329]).

18. *phoenix*—A fabulous bird in appearance like an eagle with gold and crimson plumage and a star on its brow. The only one of its race, it lives for 500 years on rare spices, then renews itself :

This bird, when it has completed the five ages of its life, with its talons and its crooked beak constructs for itself a nest in the branches of a holm-oak *[Quercus ilex],* or on the top of a quivering palm *[Phoenix dactylifera].* As soon as it has strewed in this cassia and ears of sweet spikenard and bruised cinnemon with yellow myrrh, it lays itself down on it, and finishes its life in the midst of odours. They say that thence, from the body of its parent, is reproduced a little Phoenix, which is destined to live as many years. When time has given it strength, and it is able to bear the weight, it lightens the branches of the lofty tree of the burden of the nest, and dutifully carries both its own cradle and the sepulchre of its parent; and having reached the city of Hyperion [Heliopolis in Egypt] through the yielding air, it lays it down before the sacred doors in the temple of Hyperion [Helios, the Sun]. (Ovid *Metamorphoses* 15.3, trans. H. T. Riley [London: George Bell and Sons, 1884], 532)

The body of the dead bird, wrapped in embalming spices, is then cremated on the altar. Its return to Egypt is heralded as a great and favorable omen. Almost certainly this bird is referred to in Psalms 103:5 under the name of the eagle. There are two main variations in the story of the regeneration of the phoenix. One states that the bird combusts itself by flapping its wings on the altar, and rises from its own ashes; the other less attractive variation is that the new phoenix first emerges from the decaying corpse of the old as a small white worm. For descriptions of the phoenix, see Herodotus *History* bk. 2; Pliny 10.2; Tacitus *Annals* 6.28; the beautiful poem of Claudius Claudianus, "The Phoenix"; and the short descriptive piece *The Phoenix,* attributed to Lactantius (Edinburgh: *Ante-Nicene Christian Library,* 1871, vol. 22).

19. *pelican*—"And the right foot of it [a pelican] under an hot thing, after three months shall be engendered quick, and shall move itself, of the humour and heat which the bird hath" *(Book of Secrets* 3.14 [Best and Brightman, 57]).

20. *old Pileas*—Agrippa errs. Medea tricked the daughters of Pelias into murdering their father with the false hope that he would be made young. It was Aeson, the aged father of the hero Jason, whom the sorceress restored to youth by infusing into his veins a potion:

There she boils roots cut up in the Hæmonian vallies, and seeds and flowers and acrid juices. She adds stones fetched from the most distant East, and sand, which the ebbing tide of the ocean has washed. She adds, too, hoar frost gathered at night by the light of the moon, and the ill-boding wings of a screech owl, together with its flesh; and the entrails of an ambiguous wolf, that was wont to change its appearance of a wild beast into that of a man. Nor is there wanting there the thin scaly slough of the Cinyphian water-snake, and the liver of the long-lived stag; to which, besides she adds the bill and head of a crow that had sustained an existence of nine ages. (Ovid *Metamorphoses* 7.2, c. line 260 [Riley, 234–5])

21. *strongest creature*—The proverbial strength of the bear is no doubt responsible for its employment by the witch Pariseta of Neuville, who in 1586 used it to heal Stephan Noach of an illness she had been accused of causing in him:

Then she took the sick man upon her shoulder and carried him into the garden, where she placed him upon an enormous bear which appeared there. Then the bear kept carrying him up and down and to and fro, all the time groaning as if it were being weighed down by too great a burden; but in reality it was the voice of the Demon, complaining because he was being forced against his nature to use his power for granting the man the great benefit of the restoration of his health. (Remy *Demonolatry* 3.3, trans. E. A. Ashwin [London: John Rodker, 1930], 149)

Remy adds: "It is in connection with this that we see tumblers and strolling jugglers always leading bears with them, upon which, for a fee, they place children in order, forsooth, that they may thereafter be more secure from the fear of hobgoblins and spectres" (ibid., 152).

CHAPTER XVI

How the operations of several virtues pass from one thing into another, and are communicated one to the other.

Thou must know, that so great is the power of natural things, that they not only work upon all things that are near them, by their virtue, but also besides this, they infuse into them a like power, through which by the same virtue they also work upon other things, as we see in the loadstone, which stone indeed doth not only draw iron rings, but also infuseth a virtue into the rings themselves,[1] whereby they can do the same, which *Austin*,[2] and *Albertus*[3] say they saw.

After this manner it is, as they say, that a common harlot, grounded in boldness, and impudence doth infect all that are near her, by this property, whereby they are made like herself. Therefore they say that if anyone shall put on the inward garment of an harlot, or shall have about him that looking glass, which she daily looks into, he shall thereby become bold,

confident, impudent, and wanton.[4] In like manner they say, that a cloth that was about a dead corpse hath received from thence the property of sadness, and melancholy: and that the halter[5] wherewith a man was hanged hath certain wonderful properties.

The like story tells *Pliny*, if any shall put a green lizard made blind,[6] together with iron, or gold rings into a glass vessel, putting under them some earth, and then shutting the vessel, and when it appears that the lizard hath received his sight, shall put him out of the glass, that those rings shall help sore eyes. The same may be done with rings, and a weasel,[7] whose eyes after they are with any kind of prick put out, it is certain are restored to sight again. Upon the same account rings are put for a certain time in the nest of sparrows, or swallows, which afterwards are used to procure love, and favor.

Notes—Chapter XVI

1. *rings themselves*—

We shall speak of the loadstone in its proper place, and of the sympathy which it has with iron. This is the only metal that acquires the properties of that stone, retaining them for a length of time, and attracting other iron, so that we may sometimes see a whole chain formed of these rings. The lower classes, in their ignorance, call this "live iron," and the wounds that are made by it are much more severe. (Pliny 34.42 [Bostock and

Riley, 6:209])

This stone does not simply attract the iron rings, just by themselves; it also imparts to the rings a force enabling them to do the same thing as the stone itself, that is, to attract another ring, so that sometimes a chain is formed, quite a long one, of iron rings, suspended from one another. For all of them, however, their power depends upon the loadstone. (Plato *Ion* 533d, trans. L. Cooper [Hamilton and Cairns, 220]

2. *Austin*—

> We know that the loadstone draws iron strangely: and surely when I observed it at first, it made me much aghast. For I beheld the stone draw up an iron ring, and then as if it had given its own power to the ring, the ring drew up another and made it hang fast by it, as it hung by the stone. So did a third by that, and a fourth by the third, and so until there was hung, as it were, a chain of rings which merely touched one another, without any interlinking. (Augustine *City of God* 21.4 [Healey, 2:323])

3. *Albertus*—Perhaps a reference to this passage in the *Book of Secrets:* "For although we know not a manifest reason wherefore the Loadstone draweth to it Iron, notwithstanding experience doth manifest it so, that no man may deny it" ("Marvels of the World" 20 [Best and Brightman, 82]).

4. *and wanton*—See notes 3 and 4, ch. XV, bk. I.

5. *halter*—

> And it is said, if a rope be taken, with which a thief is or hath been hanged up, and a little chaff, which a whirlwind lifted up in the air, and let them be put in a pot, and set among other pots, that pot shall break all the other pots.
>
> Also take thou a little of the aforesaid rope, and put it on the instrument with which the bread is put in the oven; when he that should put it in the oven, should put it in, he shall not be able to put it in, but it shall leap out. ("Marvels of the World" 50 [Best and Brightman, 97])

6. *lizard made blind*—

> Lizards, also, are employed in numerous ways as a remedy for diseases of the eyes. Some persons enclose a green lizard in a new earthen vessel, together with nine of the small stones known as "cinaedia," which are usually attached to the body for tumours in the groin. Upon each of these stones they make nine marks, and remove one from the vessel daily, taking care, when the ninth day is come, to let the lizard go, the stones being kept as a remedy for affections of the eyes. Others, again, blind a green lizard, and after putting some earth beneath it, enclose it in a glass vessel, with some small rings of solid iron or gold. When they find, by looking through the glass, that the lizard has recovered its sight, they set it at liberty, and keep the rings as a preservative against ophthalmia. (Pliny 29.38 [Bostock and Riley, 5:414–5])

7. *weasel*—"They say, too, that if the eyes of a weasel are extracted with a pointed instrument, its sight will return; the same use being made of it as of the lizards and rings above mentioned" (ibid., 415).

CHAPTER XVII

How by enmity and friendship the virtues of things are to be tried, and found out.

In the next place it is requisite that we consider that all things have a friendliness, and enmity[1] amongst themselves, and everything hath something that it fears and dreads, that is an enemy, and destructive to it; and on the contrary something that it rejoiceth, and delighteth in, and is strengthened by. So in the elements, Fire is an enemy to Water, and Air to Earth, but yet they agree amongst themselves.[2]

And again, in celestial bodies, Mercury, Jupiter, the Sun, and Moon are friends to Saturn; Mars, and Venus enemies to him: all the planets besides Mars are friends to Jupiter, also all besides Venus hate Mars: Jupiter, and Venus love the Sun; Mars, Mercury, and the Moon are enemies to him: all besides Saturn love Venus: Jupiter, Venus, and Saturn are friends to Mercury; the Sun, Moon, and Mars his enemies: Jupiter, Venus, Saturn are friends to the Moon; Mars and Mercury her enemies.

There is another kind of enmity amongst the stars, viz. when they have opposite houses;[3] as Saturn to the Sun and Moon, Jupiter to Mercury, Mars to Venus. And their enmity is stronger, whose exaltations[4] are opposite: as of Saturn, and the Sun; of Jupiter, and Mars; of Venus, and Mercury. But their friendship is the strongest, who agree in nature, quality, substance, and power; as Mars with the Sun, and Venus with the Moon, as Jupiter with Venus, as also their friendship whose exaltation is in the house of another,[5] as that of Saturn with Venus, of Jupiter with the Moon, of Mars with Saturn, of the Sun with Mars, of Venus with Jupiter, of the Moon with Venus.

And of what sort the friendships, and enmities of the superiors be, such are the inclinations of things subjected to them in these inferior. These dispositions therefore of friendship, and enmity are nothing else but certain inclinations of things of the one to another, desiring such, and such a thing if it be absent, and to move toward it, unless it be hindered, and to acquiesce in it when it is obtained, shunning the contrary, and dreading the approach of it, and not resting in, or being contented with it. *Heraclitus* therefore being guided by this opinion, professed that all things were made by enmity and friendship.[6]

Now the inclinations of friendship are such in vegetables and minerals, as is that attractive inclination, which the loadstone hath upon iron, and the emerald upon riches, and favour; the jasper upon the birth of anything, and the stone achates[7] upon eloquence; in like manner there is a kind of bituminous clay that draws fire,[8] and leaps into it, wheresoever it sees it: even so doth the root of the herb aproxis[9] draw fire from afar off. Also the same inclination there is betwixt the male palm, and female: whereof when the bough of one shall touch the bough of the other, they fold themselves into mutual embraces, neither doth the female bring forth fruit without the male.[10] And the almond tree, when she is alone is less fruitful.The vines love the elm, and the olive tree, and myrtle love one the other: also the olive tree, and fig tree.

Now in animals there is amity betwixt the blackbird, and thrush, betwixt the crow, and heron, betwixt peacocks, and pigeons, turtles, and parrots.[11] Whence *Sappho* writes to *Phaon:*[12]

> To birds unlike ofttimes joined are white doves;
> Also the bird that's green, black turtle loves.

Again, the whale, and the little fish[13] his guide are friendly.

Neither is this amity in animals only amongst themselves, but also with other things, as with metals, stones, and vegetables. So the cat delights in the herb nip,[14] by rubbing herself upon which she is said to conceive without a male; and there be mares in Cappadocia,[15] that expose themselves to the blast of the wind, and by the attraction thereof conceive. So frogs, toads, snakes, and all manner of creeping poisonous things delight in the plant called pasflower,[16] of whom, as the physicians say, if anyone eat, he shall die with laughing.

The tortoise also when he is hunted by the adder, eats origanum,[17] and is thereby strengthened: and the stork, when he hath ate snakes,[18] seeks for a remedy in origanum: and the weasel,[19] when he goes to fight with the basilisk, eats rue, whence we come to know that origanum, and rue[20] are effectual against poison. So in some animals there is an inbred skill, and medicinal art; for when the toad is wounded with a bite or poison of another animal, he is wont to go to rue, or sage, and rub the place wounded, and so escapes the danger of the poison.

So men have learned many excellent remedies of diseases, and virtues of things from brutes; so swallows have showed us that sallendine[21] is very medicinable for the sight, with which they cure the eyes of their young, and the pye when she is sick, puts a bay[22] leaf into her nest, and is recovered. In like manner, cranes, daws, partridges, blackbirds purge their nauseous stomachs[23] with the same, with which also crows allay the poison of the chameleon; and the lion, if he be feverish, is recovered by eating of an ape.[24] The lapwing being surfeited with eating of grapes, cures himself with southernwood;[25] so the harts have taught us that the herb dittany[26] is very good to draw out darts; for they being wounded with an arrow, cast it out by eating of this herb: the same do goats in Candy.

So hinds, a little before they bring forth, purge themselves with a certain herb called mountain osier.[27] Also they that are hurt with spiders, seek a remedy by eating of crabs:[28] swine also being hurt by snakes cure themselves by eating of them; and crows when they perceive they are poisoned with a kind of French poison, seek for cure in the oak; elephants, when they have swallowed a chamelion[29] help themselves with the wild olive. Bears being hurt with mandrakes, escape the danger by eating of pismires.[30] Geese, ducks, and such like watery fowl, cure themselves with the herb called wallsage. Pigeons, turtles, hens, with the herb called pellitory of the wall. Cranes with bulrushes.[31] Leopards cure themselves, being hurt with the herb called wolfsbane,[32] by man's dung:[33] boars with ivy, hinds with the herb called cinnara.[34]

Notes—Chapter XVII

1. *enmity*—

Now it is verified and put in all men's minds, that every natural kind, and that every particular or general nature, hath natural amity and enmity to some other. And every kind hath some horrible enemy, and destroying thing to be feared; likewise something rejoicing exceedingly, making glad, and agreeing by nature. ("Marvels of the World" 5 [Best and Brightman, 75–6]).

2. *amongst themselves*   Fire agrees with air, without which it could not burn; earth with water, without which it would not cohere. See Appendix III.

3. *opposite houses*—Planets are assigned certain zodiac signs, which they are said to rule. Each planet has two signs, while the Sun and Moon have one each:

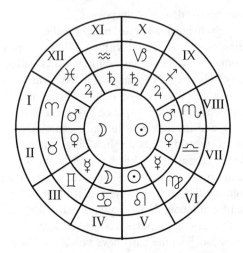

For a lucid explanation as to how this assignment arose, see Ptolemy *Tetrabiblos* 1.17. Each sign has its own house, comprising an arc of 30 degrees of the heavens. Thus when a planet is in its own sign, it may be spoken of as residing in the house that it rules. When a planet is in a sign opposite its own, located 180° away around the heavens, it is said to be in detriment. When a planet is in the sign it rules, its operation is strong and pure; when it is in the opposite sign, its operation is obstructed and troubled.

Planet	Rulership	Detriment
Sun	Leo	Aquarius
Moon	Cancer	Capricorn
Mercury	Virgo	Pisces
	Gemini	Sagittarius
Venus	Libra	Aries
	Taurus	Scorpio
Mars	Scorpio	Taurus
	Aries	Libra
Jupiter	Sagittarius	Gemini
	Pisces	Virgo
Saturn	Capricorn	Cancer
	Aquarius	Leo

4. *exaltations*—Each planet has a sign in which its action is most potent, called its exaltation, and a sign in which its action is weakest, opposite its exaltation, called its fall.

Planet	Exaltation	Fall
Saturn	Libra	Aries
Jupiter	Cancer	Capricorn
Mars	Capricorn	Cancer
Sun	Aries	Libra
Venus	Pisces	Virgo
Mercury	Virgo	Pisces
Moon	Taurus	Scorpio

5. *house of another*—Since Saturn is exalted in Libra, which is one of the signs ruled by Venus, these planets are friendly to each other; and so of the rest.

6. *enmity and friendship*—

As for the Grecians, their opinions are obvious and well known to every one; to wit, that they make the good part of the world to appertain to Jupiter Olympius, that they fable Harmonia to have been begotten by Venus and Mars, the one whereof is rough and quarrelsome, and the other sweet and generative. In the next place consider we the great agreement of the philosophers with these people. For Heraclitus doth in plain and naked terms call war the father, the king, and the lord of all things; and saith that Homer, when he first prayed,

Discord be damned from Gods and human race ... [*Iliad* 18.107],

little thought he was then cursing the origination of all things, they owing their rise to aversation and quarrel. (Plutarch *Isis and Osiris* 48 [Goodwin, 4:108])

7. *achates*—Agate, specifically ribbon agate, or banded chalcedony. "Take the stone which is called *Achates,* and it is black, and hath white veins" (*Book of Secrets* 2.12 [Best and Brightman, 32]). However there are many kinds of agate known to the ancients (see Pliny 37.54; ribbon agate is treated under "onyx" in ch. 24). The agate was not much esteemed by the Romans as jewelry, but was in high demand among the Persians and orientals, by whom "it was universally believed to confer eloquence" (Thomas and Pavitt [1914] 1970, 171).

8. *draws fire*—Naphtha, a natural liquid product of the earth that gives off a highly flammable invisible gas. "This naphtha, in other respects resembling bitumen, is so subject to take fire, that before it touches the flame it will kindle at the very light that surrounds it, and often inflame the intermediate air also" (Plutarch "Life of Alexander." In *Lives,* trans. J. Dryden [New York: Modern Library, n.d.], 827). See immediately following this quotation for a description of Alexander's unfortunate experiment with naphtha, in which he set one of his Greek soldiers on fire and very nearly killed him.

9. *aproxis*—"Pythagoras makes mention, too, of a plant called aproxis, the root of which takes fire at a distance, like naphtha ..." (Pliny 24.101 [Bostock and Riley, 5:63]). It is speculated that this may be white dittany *(Dictamnus albus).*

10. *without the male—*

In addition to the above particulars, it is asserted that in a forest of natural growth the female trees will become barren if they are deprived of the males, and that many female trees may be seen surrounding a single male with downcast heads and a foliage that seems to be bowing caressingly towards it; while the male tree, on the other hand, with leaves all bristling and erect, by its exhalations, and even the very sight of it and the dust from off it, fecundates the others: if the male tree, too, should happen to be cut down, the female trees, thus reduced to a state of widowhood, will at once become barren and unproductive. So well, indeed, is this sexual union between them understood, that it has been imagined even that fecundation may be ensured through the agency of man, by means of the blossoms and the down [pollen] gathered from off the male trees, and, indeed, sometimes by only sprinkling the dust from off them on the female trees. (Pliny 13.7 [Bostock and Riley, 3:172])

See also *Book of Secrets* (Best and Brightman, 83).

11. *turtles and parrots—*"On the other hand, there is a strict friendship existing between the peacock and the pigeon, the turtle-dove and the parrot, the blackbird and the turtle, the crow and the heron, all of which join in a common enmity against the fox. The harpe also, and the kite, unite against the triorchis" (Pliny 10.96 [Bostock and Riley, 2:552]).

12. *to Phaon—*Ovid *Heroides* epistle 15: "Sappho to Phaon," towards the beginning. Sappho was a poetess of Lesbos; Phaon was a beautiful youth with whom she was in love. When he deserted her and sailed to Sicily, she threw herself into the sea from Leucate, a promontory of Acarnania, in Epirus.

13. *little fish—*The pilot fish *(Naucrates ductor)* is about 12 inches long and was well known in ancient times for supposedly guiding ships into port. It also accompanies sharks and was thought to guide the shark to its food. The shark was often confused with the whale: "The shark so much resembles the whale in size, that some have injudiciously ranked it in the class of cetaceous fishes:" (Goldsmith 1849 [1774], bk. 2, ch. 2, 497).

14. *herb nip—*Catnip or catmint *(Nepeta cataria),* a type of mint. Also called nep. Gerard says of it: "Cats are very much delighted herewith; for the smel of it is so pleasant to them, that they rub themselves upon it, and wallow or tumble in it, and also feed on the branches and leaves very greedily" (Gerard [1633] 1975, bk. 2, ch. 226, 683).

15. *mares in Cappadocia—*

Love leads mares beyond Gargarus, and across the roaring Ascanius [in Cappadocia]; they pass the ridges of mountains, they swim across streams. And as soon as ever their kindled hearts have caught flame, in spring chiefly, for in spring warmth returns to the limbs, they all stand on high rocks with their faces turned to catch the Zephyr, and snuff the light breezes, and often without wedlock are impregnated by the wind. (Virgil *Georgics* 3, c. line 270. In *Works of Virgil,* trans. Lonsdale and Lee [London: Macmillan, 1885], 59)

16. *pas-flower—*Pass flower, called by Gerard pasque flower *(Anemone pulsatilla):* "They floure for the most part about Easter, which hath mooved mee to name it *Pasque Floure,* or Easter floure:" (Gerard [1633] 1975, bk. 2, ch. 79, 385). The purple anemone, a narcotic, acrid, poisonous plant with wide, bell-shaped, blue-purple flowers. Not to be confused with the passion flower *(Passiflora cærulea).*

17. *origanum—*Wild marjoram *(Origanum vulgare):* "Organy given in wine is a remedy against the bitings, and stingings of venomous beasts" (Gerard [1633] 1975, bk. 2, ch. 218, 667). "And they said that when the Snail is poisoned, it eateth the herb called Origanum, and is healed, and therefore they know that the herb called Origanum hath lain under poison" ("Marvels of the World" 29 [Best and Brightman, 87]).

18. *ate snakes—*"[It] is said of the Stork when she has eaten Snakes, she seeks for the same Herb Originum, and finds a Remedy" (Thomas Tryon, *The Way to Health* (1691), 562, quoted from *OED*, s.v. "origanum").

19. *weasel—*"Also it is said when the Weasel is poisoned of a Serpent it eateth Rue, and they know by this that Rue is contrary to the venom of Serpents" (Albertus Magnus [attrib.] "Marvels of the World" sec. 29. In *Book of Secrets* [Best and Brightman, 87]) This is from Pliny: "Employed in a similar manner, it is good for the stings of serpents; so much so, in fact, that weasels, when about to attack them, take the precaution first of protecting themselves by eating rue" (Pliny 20.51 [Bostock and Riley, 4:252]).

20. *rue—Ruta graveolens,* a perennial evergreen shrub with bitter, strong-scented leaves. Called "herb of grace" because it was used for sprinkling holy

water. "Rue bitter, a worthy gres, Mekyl of myth & vertu is" *Extracts from a Stockholm Medical MS.* (c. 1400), quoted from *OED*, s.v. "rue."

> *Dioscorides* writeth, that a twelve penny weight of the seed drunke in wine is a counterpoyson against deadly medicines or the poyson of Wolfs-bane, *Ixia,* Mush-roms, or Tode stooles, the biting of Ser-pents, stinging of Scorpions, spiders, bees, hornets, and wasps; and it is reported, that if a man be anointed with the iuyce of Rue these will not hurt him; and that the Ser-pent is driven away at the smell thereof when it is burned, insomuch that when the Weesell is to fight with the Serpent, she armeth her selfe by eating Rue against the might of the Serpent" (Gerard [1633] 1975, bk. 2, ch. 531, 1257).

21. *sallendine*—Greater celandine, or swallow-wort *(Chelidonium majus)*. "The swallow has shown us that the chelidonia is very serviceable to the sight, by the fact of its employing it for the cure of its young, when their eyes are affected" (Pliny 8.41 [Bostock and Riley, 2:292]). "It is by the aid of this plant that the swallow restores the sight of the young birds in the nest, and even, as some persons will have it, when the eyes have been plucked out" (Pliny 25.50 [Bostock and Riley, 5:114]). This belief arises from Dioscorides, who says that blindness in swallows is cured this way. The herb chelidonia was confused with the stone chelidonia, or swallow-stone, so called because it is "swallow-coloured." See Pliny 37.56 (Bostock and Riley, 6:446).

> Seeking with eager eyes that wonderous
>   stone, which the swallow
> Brings from the shore of the sea to restore
>   the sight of its fledglings;
>   (Longfellow, *Evangeline,* 1.1)

22. *bay*—Bay tree *(Laurus nobilis)*. It was into this tree that Daphne was changed by her father, the river Peneus, to escape the lust of Apollo (see Ovid *Meta-morphoses* bk. I, fable 12, c. line 548). The leaves of the bay are much used as a catalyst for other magical objects, about which they were wrapped : "If the foot of it [mole] be wrapped in the leaf of a Laurel tree, and be put in the mouth of a Horse, he will flee for fear" *(Book of Secrets* 3.18 [Best and Brightman, 59–60]). The bay and the laurel are the same.

23. *nauseous stomachs*—"Wood-pigeons, jackdaws, blackbirds, and partridges, purge themselves once a year by eating bay leaves ..." (Pliny 8.41 [Bostock and Riley, 2:294]).

24. *eating of an ape*—"The only malady to which the lion is subject, is loss of appetite; this, however, is cured by putting insults upon him, by means of the pranks of monkeys placed about him, a thing which rouses his anger; immediately he tastes their blood, he is relieved" (Pliny 8.19 [Bostock and Riley, 2:269]). "When they would denote a feverish man who cures himself, they depict a lion devouring an ape; for if, when in a fever, he devours an ape, he recovers." (Horapollo *Hieroglyphics* 2.76, trans. A. T. Cory [1840] [London: Chthonios Books, 1987], 133).

25. *southernwood*—*Artemisia abrotanum,* a decidu-ous shrub.

26. *ditany*—Dittany of Crete *(Origanum dictamnus,* or *Dictamnus creticus),* a hot sharp herb with cottony leaves and small red-purple flowers, long famed for its power of expelling darts. "Venus, distracted by her son's unmerited agony, plucks from Cretan Ida a stalk of dittany with downy leaves and feathery pur-ple bloom; well-known is the plant to the wild goats, when winged arrows chance to fix deep in their body" (Virgil *Aeneid* 12, c. line 460 [Lonsdale and Lee, 269]). Borrowing shamelessly from Virgil, Tasso writes:

> But the angel pure, that kept him, went and
>   sought
> Divine dictamnum, out of Ida wood,
>   This herb is rough, and bears a purple
>   flower,
>   And in his budding leaves lies all his
>   power.
>
> Kind nature first upon the craggy clift
> Bewrayed this herb unto the mountain
>   goat,
> That when her sides a cruel shaft hath rift,
> With it she shakes the reed out of her coat;
> *(Jerusalem Delivered* bk. 11, st. 72–3,
> trans. Edward Fairfax [1600] [New York:
> Collier and Son, 1901], 236)

"It is reported likewise that the wilde Goats and Deere in Candie when they be wounded with arrowes, do shake them out by eating of this plant, and heale their wounds" (Gerard [1633] 1975, bk. 2, ch. 281-D, 796). See also Pliny 8.41.

27. *mountain osier*—Water-willow *(Salix viminalis),* used for basket weaving.

28. *eating of crabs*—"The same animals [stags], too, when they happen to have been wounded by the pha-langium, a species of spider, or any insect of a simi-lar nature, cure themselves by eating crabs" (Pliny 8.41 [Bostock and Riley, 2:292]).

29. *swallowed a chamelion*—"When an elephant has happened to devour a chameleon, which is of the same colour with the herbage, it counteracts this poison by means of the wild olive" (Pliny 8.41 [Bostock and Riley, 2:294]).

30. *eating of pismires*—Pismires are ants. "Bears, when they have eaten of the fruit of the mandrake, lick up numbers of ants" (ibid).

31. *with bulrushes*—"... pigeons, turtle-doves, and poultry [purge themselves], with wall-pellitory, or helxine; ducks, geese, and other aquatic birds, with the plant sideritis or vervain; cranes, and birds of a similar nature, with the bulrush" (ibid). Wall-sage is a species of ironwort *(Sideritis)* said by Turner *(The Names of Herbs,* 1548) to be the *Sideritis prima* of Dioscorides. Pellitory of the wall *(Parietaria officinalis)* is a low, bushy plant with small leaves and greenish flowers that grows upon, or at the foot of, walls.

32 *wolfsbane*—From the Greek for "wolf-slayer," plants of the genus *Aconitum.* Turner distinguishes two kinds : (1) Yellow wolfsbane—a tall, handsome plant with large shining green leaves and beautiful yellow flowers in the shape of an enclosed bell *(Aconitum lycoctonum);* (2) Blue wolfsbane—better known as monkshood, a handsome plant with a tall stalk and large blue flowers in the shape of a helmet, for which reason it was also called helmet-flower *(Aconitum napellus).* Probably the latter is intended. Both are deadly poisons. See Hansen

(1983) who devotes an entire chapter to the lore of monkshood.

33. *man's dung*—

> The barbarous nations go to hunt the panther, provided with meat that has been rubbed with aconite, which is a poison. Immediately on eating it, compression of the throat overtakes them, from which circumstance it is, that the plant has received the name pardalianches ["pard-strangle"]. The animal, however, has found an antidote against this poison in human excrements; besides which, it is so eager to get at them, that the shepherds purposely suspend them in a vessel, placed so high, that the animal cannot reach them even by leaping, when it endeavours to get at them; accordingly, it continues to leap until it has quite exhausted itself, and at last expires: otherwise, it is so tenacious of life, that it will continue to fight long after its intestines have been dragged out of its body. (Pliny 8.41 [Bostock and Riley, 2:293–4])

34. *cinnara*—Garden artichoke *(Cynara scolymus),* so called, according to Gerard (bk. 2, ch. 479, 1154) because it grows well when planted in ashes: *cinis* = ashes. "The stag counteracts the effect of poisonous plants by eating the artichoke" (Pliny 8.41 [Bostock and Riley, 2:294]).

CHAPTER XVIII

Of the inclinations of enmities.

On the contrary there are inclinations of enmities, and they are as it were the odium, and anger, indignation, and a certain kind of obstinate contrariety of nature, so that anything shuns its contrary, and drives it away out of its presence. Such kind of inclinations hath rhubarb against choler,[1] treacle against poison,[2] the sapphire stone[3] against hot biles and feverish heats, and diseases of the eyes; the amethyst[4] against drunkenness, the jasper[5] against flux of blood, and offensive imaginations, the emerald,[6] and agnus castus[7] against lust, achates[8] against poison, peony[9] against the falling sickness, coral[10] against the ebullition of black choler, and pains of the stomach. The topaz[11] against spiritual heats, such as are covetousness, lust, and all manner of excesses of love.

The like inclination is there also of pismires against the herb origanus,[12] and the wing of a bat, and the heart of a lapwing, from the presence of which they fly. Also origanum is contrary to a certain poisonous fly, which cannot endure the Sun, and resists salamanders, and loaths cabbage with such a deadly hatred, that they destroy one the other: so cucumbers hate oil, and will run themselves into a ring lest they should touch it.

And it is said that the gall of a crow makes men afraid, and drives them away from where it is, as also certain other things; so a diamond doth disagree with the loadstone, that being set by it, it will not suffer iron to be drawn to it; and sheep fly from frog-parsley[13] as from some deadly thing: and that which is more wonderful, nature hath pictured the sign of this death in the livers of sheep, in which the very figure of frog-parsley being described, doth naturally appear; so goats do so hate garden basil,[14] as if there were nothing more pernicious.

And again, amongst animals, mice, and weasels[15] do disagree; whence it is said that mice will not touch cheese, if the brains of a weasel be put into the rennet,[16] and besides that the cheese will not corrupt with age. So a lizard is so contrary to scorpions, that it makes them afraid with its very sight, as also it puts them into a cold sweat, therefore they are killed with the oil of them, which oil also cures wounds made by scorpions. There is also an enmity betwixt scorpions, and mice;[17] wherefore if a mouse be applied to a prick or wound made by a scorpion, it cures it, as it is reported. There is also an enmity betwixt scorpions, and stalabors, asps, and wasps.

It is reported also that nothing is so much an enemy to snakes as crabs, and that if swine be hurt therewith they eat them, and are cured. The Sun also being in Cancer,[18] serpents are tormented. Also the scorpion, and crocodile[19] kill one the other; and if the bird ibis[20] doth but touch a crocodile with one of his feathers, he makes him immovable; the bird called bustard[21] flies away at the sight of a horse; and a hart runs away at the sight of a ram,[22] as also of a viper.[23] An elephant trembles at the hearing of the grunting of a hog,[24] so doth a lion at the sight of

58

a cock:[25] and panthers will not touch them that are anointed all over with the broth of a hen, especially if garlic hath been boiled in it.

There is also enmity betwixt foxes, and swans, bulls, and daws. Amongst birds also some are at a perpetual strife one with another, as also with other animals, as daws, and owls, the kite, and crows, the turtle,[26] and ringtail,[27] egepis,[28] and eagles, harts, and dragons. Also amongst water animals there is an enmity, as betwixt dolphins, and whirlpools,[29] mullets, and pikes, lampreys,[30] and congers:[31] also the fish called pourcontrel[32] makes the lobster so much afraid, that the lobster seeing the other but near him, is struck dead. The lobster, and conger tear one the other.

The civet cat is said to stand so in awe of the panther, that he hath no power to resist him, or touch his skin: and they say that if the skins of both of them be hanged up one against the other, the hairs of the panther's skin fall off.[33] And *Orus Apollo* saith[34] in his Hieroglyphics, if any one be girt about with the skin of the civet cat, that he may pass safely through the middle of his enemies, and not at all be afraid. Also the lamb is very much afraid of the wolf, and flies from him. And they say that if the tail, or skin, or head of a wolf be hanged upon the sheepcote, the sheep are much troubled, and cannot eat their meat for fear.

And *Pliny* makes mention of a bird called marlin, that breaks crows' eggs; whose young are annoyed by the fox that she also will pinch, and pull the fox's whelps, and the fox herself also: which when the crows see, they help the fox against her, as against a common enemy.[35] The little bird called a linnet living in thistles, hates asses, because they eat the flowers of thistles. Also there is such a bitter enmity betwixt the little bird called esalon, and the ass, that their blood will not mix together, and that at the braying of the ass both the eggs and young of the esalon perish.[36] There is also such a disagreement betwixt the olive tree and a harlot, that if she plant it, it will either be always unfruitful, or altogether wither.[37]

A lion fears nothing so much as fired torches,[38] and will be tamed by nothing so much as by these: and the wolf fears neither sword, nor spear, but a stone, by the throwing of which a wound being made, worms breed[39] in the wolf. A horse fears a camel, so that he cannot endure to see so much as his picture. An elephant when he rageth, is quieted by seeing of a cock. A snake is afraid of a man that is naked, but pursues a man that is clothed. A mad bull is tamed by being tied to a fig tree. Amber draws all things to it besides garden basil, and those things, which are smeared with oil, betwixt which there is a kind of a natural antipathy.

Notes—Chapter XVIII

1. *rhubarb against choler*—See note 10, ch. XIII, bk. I.

2. *treacle against poison*—Treacle was a medicinal salve said to be an antidote to serpent bites and other poisons.

> I should remark, however, that this preparation, it would appear, can only be made from the viper. Some persons, after cleaning the viper in the manner above described, boil down the fat, with one sextarius [pint] of olive oil, to one half. Of this preparation, when needed, three drops are added to some oil, with which mixture the body is rubbed, to repel the approach of all kinds of noxious animals. (Pliny 29.21 [Bostock and Riley, 5:396])

In later times snake fat gave way by a process of magical displacement to snake root.

3. *sapphire stone*—In ancient times this was the name applied generally to blue stones, and particularly to lapis lazuli, the stone described under this name by Pliny (37.38–39). *The Book of Secrets* says: "It maketh peace and concord; it maketh the mind pure and devout toward God; it strengtheneth the mind in good things, and maketh a man to cool from inward heat" (Albertus Magnus [attrib.] *Book of Secrets* bk. 2, sec. 45 [Best and Brightman, 48]). In the Middle Ages it was said to preserve the eyes from damage by smallpox if rubbed on them, and there was in the church of Old Saint Paul in London a sapphire given by Richard de Preston "'for the cure of infirmities in the eyes, of those thus afflicted who might resort to it'" (Thomas and Pavitt [1914] 1970, 156).

4. *amethyst*—A transparent purple variety of quartz. The name is from the Greek, meaning "without intoxication," and its most prevalent use was as an antidote to drunkenness, probably because its color matches that of the grape.

> The falsehoods of the magicians would persuade us that these stones are preventive of inebriety, and that it is from this that they have derived their name. They tell us also, that if we inscribe the names of the sun and moon upon this stone, and then wear it suspended from the neck, with some hair of the cynocephalus [baboon] and feathers of the swallow, it will act as a preservative against all noxious spells. It is said too, that worn in any manner, this stone will ensure access to the presence of kings; and that it will avert hail and the attacks of locusts, if a certain prayer is also repeated which they mention. (Pliny 37.40 [Bostock and Riley, 6:434])

5. *jasper*—See note 8, ch. XIII, bk. I.

6. *emerald*—Transparent green gemstone called by Pliny smaragdus, along with other green stones. It was held to promote constancy and domestic felicity, and in the presence of an unfaithful lover was believed to turn a brown color. (See Thomas and Pavitt [1914] 1970, 181-2.)

7. *agnus castus*—*Vitex agnus castus.* Called chaste tree and Abraham's balm. The name means "chaste lamb." Pliny says it is not very different from the willow, but has a more pleasant smell.

> The Greeks call it "lygos," or "agnos," from the fact that the matrons of Athens, during the Thesmophoria [festival honoring Demeter], a period when the strictest chastity is observed, are in the habit of strewing their beds with the leaves of this tree. ... From both [larger and smaller] trees also a liniment is prepared for the bites of spiders, but it is quite sufficient to rub the wounds with the leaves; and if a fumigation is made from them, or if they are spread beneath the bed, they will repel the attacks of all venomous creatures. They act also as an antaphrodisiac, and it is by this tendency in particular that they neutralize the venom of the phalangium [spider], the bite of which has an exciting effect upon the generative organs. (Pliny 24.38 [Bostock and Riley, 5:26–7])

Gerard says:

> Agnus Castus is a singular medicine and remedie for such as would willingly live chaste, for it withstandeth all uncleanness, or desire to the flesh, consuming and drying up the seed of generation, in what sort soever it be taken, whether in pouder onely, or the decoction drunke, or whether the leaves be carried about the body; for which cause it was called *Castus;* that is to say, chaste, cleane, and pure." (Gerard [1633] 1975, bk. 3, ch. 54-A, 1388)

8. *achates*—See note 7, ch. XVII, bk. I.

> In addition to the Moss or Tree Agate, the Greeks and Romans had great faith in the talismanic virtues of all other Agates, wearing them to avert sickness, regarding them particularly as an antidote to the bite of an Asp, if taken powdered in wine, or as an infallible cure for the sting of a Scorpion if tied over the wound. (Thomas and Pavitt [1914] 1970, 170)

9. *peony*—*Pæonia officinalis,* a tall plant with large round red or white flowers. The name derives from Paeon, physician to the gods of Olympus. Gerard says it is called "of some, *Lunaris,* or *Lunaria Pæonia:* because it cureth those that have the falling sicknesse, whom some men call *Lunaticos,* or Lunaticke" (Gerard [1633] 1975, bk. 2, ch. 380, 983).

10. *coral*—Coral was much favored in the treatment of children's diseases. It was worn or carried as a charm against whooping cough, teething problems, fits and cholic, and was powdered and drunk in water for stomach cramps. Gerard treats coral as a plant:

> Burned Corrall drieth more than when it is unburned, and being given to drinke in water, it helpeth the grippings of the belly, ... if the patient have an ague, then it is with better successe ministered in water, for the Corrall cooleth, and the water moistneth the body, by reason whereof it restraineth the burning heate in agues. (Gerard [1633] 1975, bk. 3, ch. 166-C, -D, 1578)

11. *topaz*—In modern times a golden transparent stone, Pliny uses this name for peridot, a soft greenish-yellow transparent stone mined in ancient times from St. John's Island, which lies 35 miles southeast of Ras Benas, Egypt.

> Juba says that there is an island in the Red Sea called "Topazos," at a distance of three hundred stadia from the main land; that it is surrounded by fogs, and is often sought by navigators in consequence; and that, owing to this, it received its present name, the word "topazin" meaning "to seek," in

the language of the Troglodytae. (Pliny 37.32 [Bostock and Riley, 6:427])

The belief that this stone has a moderating virtue seems to have arisen from an error in copying by Marbodus, who renders Pliny's *limam sentit* ("feels the file"; i.e., is relatively soft) into *lunam sentire putatur* ("is thought to feel the Moon"). Hence in *The Book of Secrets:* "It [topaz] is good also against ... lunatic passion or grief" (*Book of Secrets* 2 [Best and Brightman, 29]).

12. *origanus*—See note 16, ch. XVII, bk. I. "Ants, too, are killed by the odours of origanum, lime, or sulphur" (Pliny 10.90 [Bostock and Riley, 2:548]). "When they would symbolise the departure of ants, they engrave origanum. For if this plant be laid down over the spot from whence the ants issue forth, it causes them to desert it" (Horapollo 2.34 [Cory, 108]).

13. *frog-parsley*—This plant is not known. The *Oxford English Dictionary* speculates that it may be the same as fool's parsley *(Aethusa cynapium),* a European garden weed very like parsley in appearance with the poisonous qualities of hemlock. Or perhaps marsh parsley *(Apium graveolens),* an old name for smallage or wild celery, is intended. There was a kind of parsley called sheep's parsley, but unfortunately this also is unknown.

14. *garden basil—Ocymum basilicum,* also called sweet basil.

> Chrysippus has exclaimed as strongly, too, against ocimum as he has against parsley, declaring that it is prejudicial to the stomach and the free discharge of the urine, and is injurious to the sight; that it provokes insanity, too, and lethargy, as well as diseases of the liver; and that it is for this reason that goats refuse to touch it. Hence he comes to the conclusion, that the use of it ought to be avoided by man. ... Succeeding ages, again, have warmly defended this plant; it has been maintained, for instance, that goats do eat it, that the mind of no one who has eaten of it is at all affected, and, that mixed with wine, with the addition of a little vinegar, it is a cure for the stings of land scorpions, and the venom of those found in the sea. (Pliny 20.48 [Bostock and Riley, 4:249])

15. *mice, and weasels*—Of the weasel, Goldsmith says: "It makes war upon the rats and mice, with still greater success than the cat; for being more active and slender, it pursues them into their holes, and after a short resistance, destroys them" (Goldsmith [1774] 1849, bk. 4, ch. 3, 263).

16. *rennet*—The mass of curdled milk taken from the stomach of a sucking calf or other animal, used to cause milk to curdle in the making of cheese.

17. *Scorpions, and mice*—"And a mouse, put under the pricking of Scorpions, delivereth a man because she is contrary and feareth not him" ("Marvels of the World" 30 [Best and Brightman, 87]).

> Maupertuis put three scorpions and a mouse into the same vessel together, and they soon stung the little animal in different places. The mouse, thus assaulted, stood for some time upon the defensive, and at last killed them all, one after another. He tried this experiment, in order to see whether the mouse, after it had killed, would eat the scorpions; but the little quadruped seemed entirely satisfied with the victory, and even survived the severity of the wounds it had received. (Goldsmith [1774] 1849, bk. 1, ch. 9, 599)

18. *in Cancer*—The summer solstice, the longest day of the year when the Sun is highest in the sky, occurs while the Sun is in Cancer.

19. *scorpion, and crocodile*—"When they would symbolise one enemy engaging with another equal to himself, they depict a scorpion and a crocodile. For these kill one another" (Horapollo 2.35 [Cory, 109]).

20. *ibis*—The sacred, or Egyptian, ibis *(Ibis religiosa),* a bird about two and a half feet in length with white and black plumage and a long curved beak. The Egyptians held that it was the bird of Thoth, whom the Greeks called Hermes Trismegistus, and venerated it as the destroyer of serpents. Its plumage symbolized the light and dark faces of the Moon, with which the bird was linked (see Budge [1904] 1969, vol. 2, ch. 20, 375). Thoth was the Moon god in his capacity as regulator (ibid. 1:412–3), responsible for the creation of the Moon (ibid. 1:370). Since the crocodile was the beast of Set (ibid. 2:345), arch-foe of Isis and her protector, Thoth, it is not surprising the myth that ibis feathers frightened or killed crocodiles grew up. In this context, see the account given by Herodotus of the antagonism between ibises and flying serpents *(The History* 2, trans. George Rawlinson [1858] [New York: Tudor Publishing, 1947], 106). Agrippa's reference comes from Horapollo: "When they would denote a rapacious and inactive man, they portray a crocodile with the wing of an Ibis on his head; for if you touch him with the wing of an Ibis you will find him motionless" (Horapollo 2.81 [Cory, 136]).

21. *bustard*—Bird of the genus *Otis,* particularly the great bustard *(Otis tarda),* the largest European bird, weighing up to 30 pounds. It prefers running to flying, and feeds on frogs, mice, worms, turnip tops and other vegetation. "When they would symbolise a man that is weak and persecuted by a stronger, they delineate a bustard and a horse; for this bird flies away whenever it sees a horse" (ibid. 2.50 [Cory, 117]).

22. *of a ram*—"When they would symbolise a king that flees from folly and intemperance, they delineate an elephant and a ram; for he flies at the sight of a ram" (ibid. 2.85 [Cory 138]). "An elephant" has been rendered "a stag" by Trebatius in his Latin translation of 1515.

23. *of a viper*—"When they would symbolise a man that is quick in his movements, but who moves without prudence and consideration, they portray a stag and a viper; for she flees at the sight of the viper" (ibid. 2.87 [Cory, 139]).

24. *grunting of a hog*—"When they would symbolise a king that flees from a trifler, they depict an elephant with a hog; for he flees upon hearing the voice of the hog" (ibid. 2.86 [Cory, 138–9]).

25. *sight of a cock*—

> In the next place, there are many solar animals, such as lions and cocks, which participate according to their nature, of a certain solar divinity; whence it is wonderful how much inferiors yield to superiors in the same order, though they do not yield in magnitude and power. Hence it is said, that a cock is very much feared, and, as it were, reverenced by a lion; the reason of which we cannot assign from matter or sense, but from the contemplation alone of a supernal order. For thus we shall find that the presence of the solar virtue accords more with a cock than with a lion. This will be evident from considering that the cock, as it were, with certain hymns, applauds and calls to the rising sun, when he bends his course to us from the antipodes; and that solar angels sometimes appear in forms of this kind, who, though they are without shape, yet present themselves to us, who are connected with shape, in some sensible form. Sometimes, too, there are daemons with a leonine front, who when a cock is placed before them, unless they are of a solar order, suddenly disappear; and this because those natures which have an inferior rank in the same order always reverence their supe-

riors ... (Proclus *De sacrificio et magia,* a fragment preserved in the Latin translation of Ficinus [Venice, 1497], given in full by Thomas Taylor in his *Life of Pythagoras* [London: John M. Watkins, 1926], 72n, 214. See also *Marvels of the World* 14, 41 [Best and Brightman, 80, 92])

26. *turtle*—turtle dove *(Turtur communis).*

27. *ringtail*—Ringtail hawk, which is the female of the hen-harrier *(Circus cyaneus)* or blue hawk. It was thought to be a separate species until the beginning of the last century.

28. *egepis*—Egepy, a kind of vulture.

29. *whirlpools*—Or thirlepoll, an old name for a kind of whale. Perhaps the killer whale, which will eat other sea mammals when it can catch them.

30. *lampreys*—*Pteromyzon marinus,* a scaleless fish a little over a foot long shaped like an eel with a round mouth. It attaches itself by suction to a large fish, rasps a hole in its side, and lives on fluid and blood until its host dies.

31. *congers*—Conger eel *(Conger vulgaris),* which grows from six to ten feet in length. It is powerful and voracious.

32. *pourcontrel*—Octopus.

33. *skin fall off*—See note 15, ch. XXI, bk. I. "When they [ancient Egyptians] would symbolize a man overcome by his inferiors, they depict two skins, one of an hyæna, and the other of a panther; for if these two skins be placed together, the panther's shoots its hair, but the other does not" (Horapollo 2.70 [Cory, 129]). The hyena and the civet were sometimes confused together by writers of the Middle Ages.

34. *Orus Apollo saith*—"When they would denote a man who passes fearlessly through the evils which assail him, even until death, they delineate the skin of an hyæna; for if a man gird this skin about himself, and pass through any of his enemies, he shall be injured by none of them, but pass through fearlessly" (ibid. 2.72 [Cory, 130–1]).

35. *common enemy*—

> Aesalon is the name given to a small bird that breaks the eggs of the raven, and the young of which are anxiously sought by the fox; while in its turn it will peck at the young of the fox, and even the parent itself. As soon as the ravens espy this, they come

to its assistance, as though against a common enemy. The acanthis [gold-finch], too, lives among the brambles; hence it is that it also has an antipathy to the ass, because it devours the bramble blossoms. The aegithus [titmouse] and the anthus [yellow wagtail], too, are at such mortal enmity with each other, that it is the common belief that their blood will not mingle; and it is for this reason that they have the bad reputation of being employed in many magical incantations. (Pliny 10.95 [Bostock and Riley, 2:551–2])

36. *esalon perish*—

... the aegithus, so small a bird as it is, has an antipathy to the ass; for the latter, when scratching itself, rubs its body against the brambles, and so crushes the bird's nest; a thing of which it stands in such dread, that if it only hears the voice of the ass when it brays, it will throw its eggs out of the nest, and the young ones themselves will sometimes fall to the ground in their fright; hence it is that it will fly at the ass, and peck at its sores with its beak. (ibid., 551)

From the above two quotations it can be seen that Agrippa has derived his material from Pliny, but in a confused form. The aesalon is the marsh harrier *(Circus aeruginosus)*, also called the rustkite or moor buzzard, said to be the smallest type of buzzard. The name was also applied to the merlin *(Falco aesalon)*, one of the smallest, yet boldest, species of European falcon.

37 *altogether whither*—The olive was sacred among the Greeks to Pallas Athene, and was regarded as an emblem of chastity.

38. *fired torches*—

When they would denote a man calmed by fire even during anger, they portray lions and torches; for the lion dreads nothing so much as lighted torches and is tamed by nothing so readily as by them. (Horapollo 2.75 [Cory, 132–3])

39. *worms breed*—

When they would denote a man who is fearful lest accidents should happen unexpectedly to himself, they depict a wolf and a stone; for it fears neither iron, nor a stick, but a stone only; and indeed, if anyone throw a stone at him he will find him terrified: and wherever a wolf is struck by a stone maggots are engendered from the bruise. (ibid. 2.74 [Cory, 132])

CHAPTER XIX

How the virtues of things are to be tried and found out, which are in them specifically, or any one individual by way of special gift.

Moreover thou must consider that the virtues of things are in some things according to the species, as boldness, and courage in a lion, and cock,[1] fearfulness in a hare, or lamb, ravenousness in a wolf, treachery, and deceitfulness in a fox, flattery in a dog, covetousness in a crow, and daw, pride in a horse, anger in a tiger, and boar, sadness, and melancholy in a cat, lust in a sparrow,[2] and so of the rest. For the greatest part of natural virtues doth follow the species.

Yet some are in things individually; as there be some men which do so wonderfully abhor the sight of a cat,[3] that they cannot look upon her without quaking; which fear it is manifest is not in them as they are men. And *Avicen*

tells of a man that lived in his time, whom all poisonous things did shun, all of them dying, which did by chance bite him, he himself not being hurt; and *Albertus* reports that in a city of the Ubians he saw a wench which would catch spiders to eat them, and being much pleased with such a kind of meat, was wonderfully nourished therewith. So is boldness in a harlot, fearfulness in a thief.

And upon this account it is that philosophers say, that any particular thing that never was sick,[4] is good against any manner of sickness: therefore they say that a bone of a dead man, which never had a fever, being laid upon the patient, frees him of his quartan. There are also many singular virtues infused into particular things by celestial bodies, as we have showed before.

Notes—Chapter XIX

1. *lion, and cock*—"As the Lion is a beast unfearful, and hath a natural boldness, chiefly in his forehead and heart. ... Likewise there is great boldness in a Cock, in so much that Philosophers say that the Lion is astonished when he seeth him" ("Marvels of the World" 14 [Best and Brightman, 80]).

2. *lust in a sparrow*—"When they would symbolise a prolific man, they depict the house-sparrow, [for when the sparrow is driven to distraction by desire and an excess of seed, it mates with the female seven times in an hour, ejaculating all its seed at once]" (Horapollo 2.115 [Cory, 156]). The passage in brack-

ets has been translated from the Latin of the excessively prudish A. T. Cory.

3. *sight of a cat*—Agrippa was apparently familiar with phobias—in this particular case, ailourophobia—although the word "phobia" was not actually used until 1801.

4. *never was sick*—"And Philosophers say that some kind or singular, which never had sickness, is profitable to every sickness; and he that had never pain, helpeth and healeth a man from it" ("Marvels of the World" 45 [Best and Brightman, 94]).

CHAPTER XX

That natural virtues are in some things throughout their whole substance, and in other things in certain parts, and members.

Again thou must consider, that the virtues of things are in some things in the whole i.e. the whole substance of them, or in all their parts, as that little fish echeneis, which is said to stop a ship by its mere touch, this it doth not do according to any particular part, but according to the whole substance. So the civet cat hath this in its whole substance, that dogs by the very touch of his shadow hold their peace.[1] So salendine is good for the sight, not according to any one, but all its parts, not more in the root than in the leaves, and seeds; and so of the rest.

But some virtues are in things according to some parts of it, viz. only in the tongue, or eyes, or some other members, and parts; so in the eyes of a basilisk,[2] is a most violent power to kill men, as soon as they see them: the like power is there in the eyes of the civet cat,[3] which makes any animal that it hath looked upon, to stand still, to be amazed, and not able to move itself. The like virtue is there in the eyes of some wolves,[4] which if they see a man first, make him amazed, and so hoarse, that if he would cry out, he hath not the use of his voice. Of this *Virgil* makes mention,[5] when he sings:

Moeris is dumb, hath lost his voice, and why?
The wolf on Moeris first hath cast his eye.

So also there were some certain women in Scythia,[6] and amongst the Illyrians, and Triballians, who as often as they looked angrily upon any man, were said to slay him. Also we read of a certain people of Rhodes, called Telchines,[7] who corrupted all things with their sight, wherefore Jupiter drowned them. Therefore witches, when they would after this manner[8] work by witchcraft, use the eyes of such kind of animals in their waters for the eyes,[9] for the like effects.

In like manner do pismires fly from the heart of a lapwing, not from the head, foot, or eyes. So the gall of lizards being bruised in water is said to gather weasels together, not the tail or the head of it; and the gall of goats put into the earth in a brazen vessel, gathers frogs together; and a goat liver is an enemy to butterflies and all maggots, and dogs shun them that have the heart of a dog[10] about them, and foxes will not touch those poultry that have eaten of the liver of a fox.

So divers things have divers virtues dispersed variously through several parts, as they are from above infused into them according to the diversity of things to be received; as in a man's body the bones receive nothing but life, the eyes sight, the ears hearing. And there is in man's body a certain little bone,[11] which the Hebrews call LVZ, of the bigness of a pulse[12] that is husked, which is subject to no corruption, neither is it overcome with fire, but is always preserved unhurt, out of which, as they say, as a plant out of the seed, our animal bodies shall in the resurrection of the dead spring up. And these virtues are not cleared by reason, but by experience.

Notes—Chapter XX

1. *hold their peace*—For some reason that is not obvious, Freake has translated the Latin *hyaena,* the virtues of which Agrippa has correctly taken from Pliny, into the English "civet cat." Pliny says: "It is said also, that on coming in contact with its [the hyena's] shadow, dogs will lose their voice, and that, by certain magical influences, it can render any animal immoveable, round which it has walked three times " (Pliny 8.44 [Bostock and Riley, 2:296]).

2. *basilisk*—

There is the same power also in the serpent called the basilisk. It is produced in the province of Cyrene, being not more than twelve fingers in length. It has a white spot on the head, strongly resembling a sort of diadem. When it hisses, all the other serpents fly from it: and it does not advance its body, like the others, by a succession of folds, but moves along upright and erect upon the middle. It destroys all shrubs, not only by its contact, but those even that it has breathed upon; it burns up all the grass too, and breaks the stones, so tremendous is its noxious influence. It was formerly a general belief that if a man on horseback killed one of these animals with a spear, the poison would run up the weapon and kill, not only the rider, but the horse as well. (Pliny 8.33 [Bostock and Riley, 2:282])

Horapollo says of the ancient Egyptians:

But when they would represent Eternity differently, they delineate a serpent with its tail covered by the rest of its body: the Egyptians call this Ouraius [from the Coptic for "king"], which in the Greek language signifies Basilisk. (Horapollo 1.1 [Cory, 5–6])

It is clear that the basilisk is the king cobra, which raises the upper half of its body into the air, which has white markings on its hooded head, which hisses, which can shoot its venom some distance through the air by ejection and in this way blind its foes, and which was credited with the powers of fascination. In the Middle Ages the basilisk was even more mythologized:

And in the book *De Tyriaca* of Galen, it is said that the Serpent which is called *Regulus* in Latin, a Cocatrice in English, is somewhat white, upon whose head there be three hairs, and when any man seeth them he dieth soon. And when any man or any other living thing heareth his whistling, he

dieth. And every beast that eateth of it being dead, dieth also. ("Marvels of the World" 24 [Best and Brightman, 84–5])

If there is a distinction to be made between the basilisk and the cocatrice, which are always confused together by medieval writers, it is that the basilisk is a small serpent with a crown, or comb, on its head, whereas the cocatrice is a cock with the tail of a snake, hatched from a cock's egg by a serpent.

3. *eyes of the civet cat*—See note 1, above.

4. *eyes of some wolves*—"In Italy also it is believed that there is a noxious influence in the eye of a wolf; it is supposed that it will instantly take away the voice of a man, if it is the first to see him" (Pliny 8.34 [Bostock and Riley, 2:282–3]). Plato alludes to this ancient belief in the *Republic,* referring to the savage outburst of Thrasymachus: "And I, when I heard him, was dismayed, and looking upon him was filled with fear, and I believe that if I had not looked at him before he did at me I should have lost my voice" *(Republic* 1.336-d [Hamilton and Cairns, 586]). Theocritus makes a similar reference in his 14th Idyll regarding the silence of Cynisca: "Yet She said nothing, though I was there; how think you I like that? 'Won't you call a toast? You have seen the wolf!' said some one in jest, 'as the proverb goes,'" (Theocritus *Theocritus, Bion and Moschus,* trans. A. Lang [London: Macmillan, 1907], 72). Because of this belief the eye of the wolf was thought to possess magical potency: "And it is said, if the Wolf see a man and the man see him not, the man is astonished and feareth, and is hoarse. And therefore if any man beareth the eye of a Wolf, it helpeth to victory, to boldness, vanquishing, and fear in his adversary" ("Marvels of the World" 43 [Best and Brightman, 93]).

5. *Virgil makes mention*—Eclogue 9, lines 53–4.

6. *women in Scythia*—

Isogonus adds, that there are among the Triballi and the Illyrii, some persons of this description, who also have the power of fascination with the eyes, and can even kill those on whom they fix their gaze for any length of time, more especially if their look denotes anger; the age of puberty is said to be particularly obnoxious to the malign influence of such persons.

A still more remarkable circumstance is, the fact that these persons have two pupils in each eye. Apollonides says, that there are certain females of this description

Hyæna

from *The History of Four-footed Beasts and Serpents* by Edward Topsell (London, 1658)

Wolf

from *The History of Four-footed Beasts and Serpents* by Edward Topsell (London, 1658)

in Scythia, who are known as Bythiae, and Phylarchus states that a tribe of the Thibii in Pontus, and many other persons as well, have a double pupil in one eye, and in the other the figure of a horse. He also remarks, that the bodies of these persons will not sink in water, even though weighed down by their garments. (Pliny 7.2 [Bostock and Riley,2:126–7])

7. *Telchines*—Ovid refers to this people as "the Ialysian Telchines, whose eyes corrupting all things by the very looking upon them, Jupiter utterly hating, thrust beneath the waves of his brother [Neptune]" (Ovid *Metamorphoses* 7.3, c. line 365 [Riley, 239]). Ialysus was one of the three most ancient cities on the island of Rhodes. The Telchines were supposed to have migrated there from Crete. They were artistic and skillful in metalworking, to which Strabo attributes their reputation as magicians.

8. *after this manner*—By the evil eye, to which Horace alludes: "No one there files down my enjoyments with eye askance, nor poisons them with secret hate and venomous bite:" (Horace *Epistles* 1:14. In *Complete Works* [New York: Translation Publishing, 1961], 405–6). Apollonius of Rhodes describes the use of the evil eye by Medea to slay the bronze giant Talos:

> Medea went up on the deck. She covered both her cheeks with a fold of her purple mantle, and Jason led her by the hand as she passed across the benches. Then, with incantations, she invoked the Spirits of Death, the swift hounds of Hades who feed on souls and haunt the lower air to pounce on living men. She sank to her knees and called upon them, three times in song, three times with spoken prayers. She steeled herself with their malignity and bewitched the eyes of Talos with the evil in her own. She flung at him the full force of her malevolence, and in an ecstasy of rage

she plied him with images of death. (Apollonius Rhodius *The Voyage of Argo*, trans. E. V. Rieu [1959] [Harmondsworth: Penguin Books, 1985], 192)

Francis Bacon writes: "We see, likewise, the Scripture calleth envy an evil eye … [Proverbs 23:6, 28:22] so that still there seemeth to be acknowledged, in the act of envy, an ejaculation or irradiation of the eye" (Bacon *Essays* 9 [1597] [Philadelphia: Henry Altemus Company, n.d.]. There was more power of malice in the gaze when it was delivered from the corner of the eye ("That hoary cripple, with malicious eye/Askance …" [Browning *Childe Roland*, lines 2–3]), and when the victim was luxuriating in a glow of self-importance and well-being ("at such time, the spirits of the person envied do come forth most into the outward parts, and so meet the blow" [Bacon *Essays* 9, "Of Envy"]).

9. *waters for the eyes*—Collyriums, or eye washes. Witches were said to make a paste or lotion from the eyes of "eye-biting" animals to anoint their own eyes, and so increase their power of malice.

10. *heart of a dog*—"If any man bear a Dog's heart on his left side, all the Dogs shall hold their peace, and not bark at him" (*Book of Secrets* 3:22 [Best and Brightman, 61]).

11. *little bone*—This belief derives from the *Zohar*, the principal text of the Kabbalah. A. E Waite says: "Each man who is born into the world is provided with an imperishable bone in his present physical body, and it is from or on this that his organization will be built up anew at the time of the resurrection— it is like the rib taken from the side of Adam. The bone in question will be to the risen body that which the leaven is to the dough" (Waite 1975, 335).

12. *pulse*—Seed of a leguminous plant, in this case probably the lentil, the "least of all pulses" (R. Brown, *The Complete Farmer*, 1759, 86; quoted from *OED, s.v.* "pulse").

CHAPTER XXI

Of the virtues of things which are in them only in their lifetime, and such as remain in them even after their death.

Moreover we must know that there are some properties in things only whilst they live, and some that remain after their death. So the little fish echeneis stops the ships, and the basilisk, and catablepa[1] kill with their sight, when they are alive, but when they are dead do no such thing. So they say that in the colic, if a live duck be applied to the belly, it takes away the pain, and herself dies:[2] like to this is that which *Archytas* says. If you take a heart newly taken out of an animal, and whilst it is yet warm, and hang it upon one that hath a quartan fever,[3] it drives it away. So if anyone swallow the heart of a lapwing,[4] or a swallow,[5] or a weasel,[6] or a mole[7] whilst it is yet warm with natural heat, it shall be helpful to him for remembering, understanding, and foretelling.

Hence is this general rule, viz. that whatsoever things are taken out of animals, whether they be stones, any member, excrements, as hair, dung, nails, they must be taken from those animals, whilst they be yet living; and if it be possible, that so they may be alive afterwards. Whence they say, when you take the tongue of a frog, you must put the frog into the water again, and if you take the tooth of a wolf,[8] you must not kill the wolf; and so of the rest.

So writes *Democritus,* if anyone take out the tongue of a water frog, yet living, no other part of the body sticking to it, and she be let go into the water again, and lay it upon the place where the heart beats, of a woman, she shall answer truly whatsoever you ask her. Also they say, that if the eyes of a frog be before Sun rising bound to the sick party, and the frog be let go again blind into the water, they will drive away a tertian ague; as also that they will, being bound with the flesh of a nightingale in the skin of a hart, keep one always watchful without sleep.

Also the ray of the fork fish[9] being bound to the navel, is said to make a woman have an easier travail,[10] if it be taken from it alive, and that put into the sea again. So they say the right eye of a serpent being applied, doth help the watering of the eyes, if the serpent be let go alive. And there is a certain fish, or great serpent called myrus,[11] whose eye, if it be pulled out and bound to the forehead of the patient, is said to cure the inflammation of the eyes, and that the eye of the fish grows again, and that he is taken blind that did not let the fish go.

Also the teeth of all serpents, being taken out whilst they are alive, and hanged about the patient, are said to cure the quartan. So doth the tooth of a mole taken out whilst she is alive, being afterwards let go, cure the toothache: and dogs will not bark at those that have the tail of a weasel that is escaped. And *Democritus* relates that the tongue of a chamelion, if it be taken from her alive, doth conduce to a good success in trials, and is profitable for women that are in travail if it be about the outside of the house, for you must take heed that it be not brought into the house, because that would be most dangerous.

Moreover there be some properties that remain after death: and of these the Platonists say, that they are things in which the Idea[12] of the matter is less swallowed up; in these, even after death that which is immortal in them, doth not cease to work wonderful things. So in the herbs, and plants pulled asunder, and dried, that virtue is quick, and operative which was infused at first into them by the Idea.

Thence it is, that as the eagle all her lifetime doth overcome all other birds: so also her feathers after her death destroy, and consume the feathers[13] of all other birds. Upon the same account doth a lion's skin destroy all other skins: and the skin of the civet cat[14] destroys the skin of the panther: and the skin of a wolf corrodes the skin of a lamb: and some of these do not do it by way of a corporeal contract, but also sometimes by their very sound. So a drum made of the skin of a wolf, makes a drum made of a lambskin not to sound.[15] Also a drum made of the skin of the fish called rotchet,[16] drives away all creeping things, at what distance soever the sound of it is heard: and the strings of an instrument made of the guts of a wolf, and being strained upon a harp, or lute with strings made of sheep's guts, will make no harmony.

Noces—Chapter XXl

1. *catablepa*—

> Near this fountain [the spring Nigris in western Ethiopia], there is found a wild beast, which is called the catoblepas; an animal of moderate size, and in other respects sluggish in the movement of the rest of its limbs; its head is remarkably heavy, and it only carries it with the greatest difficulty, being always bent down towards the earth. Were it not for this circumstance it would prove the destruction of the human race; for all who behold its eyes, fall dead upon the spot. (Pliny 8.32 [Bostock and Riley, 2:281–2])

Perhaps the gnu is intended.

2. *herself dies*—"Another prescription mentioned for griping pains in the bowels is of a very marvellous nature: if a duck, they say, is applied to the abdomen, the malady will pass into the bird, and it will die" (Pliny 30.20 [Bostock and Riley, 5:442–3]).

3. *quartan fever*—The tertian and quartan agues are fevers characterized by violent shivering fits such as those of malaria. In quartan ague the paroxysm occurs every fourth day; in tertian ague, every third day. The first day of the cycle is counted the day of the previous attack—in quartan, one day sick, two days well, the next sick again; in tertian, one day sick, the next well, the next sick.

4. *lapwing*—"And if the heart, eye or brain of a Lapwing or Black Plover be hanged upon a man's neck, it is profitable against forgetfulness, and sharpeth man's understanding" ("Marvels of the World" 46 [Best and Brightman, 94]).

5. *swallow*—This same eloquence is conferred by the swallowstone, said to be "drawn out of the belly of Swallows" *(Book of Secrets* 2.23 [Best and Brightman, 37–8]). "Evax saith that this stone [the red stone, as opposed to the black stone] maketh a man eloquent, acceptable and pleasant" (ibid., 38).

6. *weasel*—"If the heart of this beast be eaten yet quaking it maketh a man to know things to come" (ibid. 3.12 [Best and Brightman, 56]).

7. *mole*—"If any man shall have this herb [swallowwort], with the heart of a Mole, he shall overcome all his enemies, and all matters in suit, and shall put away all debate" (ibid. 1.6 [Best and Brightman, 7]). Pliny says of the mole:

> There is no animal in the entrails of which they [the Magi] put such implicit faith, no animal, they think, better suited for the rites of religion; so much so, indeed, that if a person swallows the heart of a mole, fresh from the body and still palpitating, he will receive the gift of divination, they assure us, and a foreknowledge of future events. (Pliny 30.7 [Bostock and Riley, 5:429])

8. *tooth of a wolf*—A wolf tooth charm is mentioned in *The Book of Secrets* 1.3 (Best and Brightman, 4), but not the method of extracting the tooth—no doubt a tricky business.

9. *fork fish*—Thornback; the common ray, or skate *(Raia clavata),* distinguished by short, sharp spines on the back and tail. The ray is the tail.

10. *travail*—Labor.

11. *myrus*—Pliny says this is the male moray eel: "Aristotle calls the male, which impregnates the female, by the name of "zmyrus;" and says that there is a difference between them, the muraena being spotted and weakly, while the zmyrus is all of one colour and hardy, and has teeth which project beyond the mouth" (Pliny 9.39 [Bostock and Riley, 2:410]).

12. *Idea*—The ideal form, or archetype, eternal and perfect, upon which a class of derivative, imperfect things is based.

13. *consume the feathers*—"And Philosophers said that when the feathers of Eagles be put with the feathers of other fowls they burn and mortify them; for as he overcometh in his life all birds, and ruleth over them, so the feathers of Eagles are deadly to all feathers" ("Marvels of the World" 38 [Best and Brightman, 90–1).

14. *civet cat*—This should be the hyena.

15. *not to sound*—That the enmity between beasts continued after death was widely believed. "As the Sheep doth fear the Wolf, and it knoweth not only him alive, but also dead; ... For a skin of a Sheep is consumed of the skin of the Wolf; and a timbrel, tabor or drumslade made of the skin of a Wolf causeth [that] which is made of a Sheep's skin not to be heard, and so is it in all others" (ibid. 5 [Best and Brightman, 76])

16. *rotchet*—Rochet; the red gurnard *(Trigla cuculus or pini)*, a rose-colored edible fish about 16 inches in length with a large bony head and spines.

CHAPTER XXII

How inferior things are subjected to superior bodies, and how the bodies, the actions, and dispositions of men are ascribed to stars, and signs.

It is manifest that all things inferior are subject to the superior, and after a manner (as saith *Proclus*)[1] they are one in the other, viz. in inferior are superior, and in superior are inferior: so in the heaven are things terrestrial, but as in their cause, and in a celestial manner; and in the Earth are things celestial, but after a terrestrial manner, as in an effect.

So we say that there be here certain things which are solary, and certain which are lunary, in which the Sun, and Moon make a strong impression of their virtue. Whence it is that these kind of things receive more operations, and properties, like to those of the stars, and signs which they are under: so we know that solary things respect the heart, and head, by reason that Leo is the house of the Sun, and Aries the exaltation of the Sun:[2] so things under Mars are good for the head, and testicles, by reason of Aries, and Scorpio.[3] Hence they whose senses fail, and heads ache by reason of drunkenness, if they put their testicles into cold water,[4] or wash them with vinegar, find present help.

But in reference to these it is necessary to know how man's body is distributed to planets, and signs. Know therefore that according to the doctrine of the Arabians, the Sun rules over the brain, heart, the thigh, the marrow, the right eye, and the spirit; also the tongue, the mouth, and the rest of the organs of the senses, as well internal as external; also the hands, feet, legs, nerves, and the power of imagination. That Mercury rules over the spleen, stomach, blad-

der, womb, and right ear, as also the faculty of the common sense. That Saturn rules over the liver, and fleshy part of the stomach. That Jupiter over the belly, and navel, whence it is written by the ancients, that the effigy of a navel was laid up in the temple of *Jupiter Hammon*.[5] Also some attribute to him the ribs, breast, bowels, blood, arms, and the right hand, and left ear, and the powers natural. And some set Mars over the blood, and veins, and kidneys, the bag of the gall, the buttocks, the back, and motion of the sperm, and the irascible power. Again they set Venus over the kidneys, the testicles, the privities, the womb, the seed, and concupisible power; as also the flesh, fat, belly, breast, navel, and all such parts as serve to venereal acts, also the *ossacrum*,[6] the backbone, and loins; as also the head, mouth, with which they give a kiss, as a token of love. Now the Moon, although she may challenge the whole body, and every member thereof according to the variety of the signs: yet more particularly they ascribe to her the brain, lungs, marrow of the backbone, the stomach, the menstrues, and all other excrements, and the left eye, as also the power of increasing.[7] But *Hermes* saith, that there are seven holes[8] in the head of an animal, distributed to the seven planets, viz. the right ear to Saturn, the left to Jupiter, the right nostril to Mars, the left to Venus, the right eye to the Sun, the left to the Moon, and the mouth to Mercury.

The several signs also of the Zodiac take care of their members. So Aries governs the head, and face, Taurus the neck, Gemini the arms, and shoulders, Cancer the breast, lungs, stomach, and arms, Leo heart, stomach, liver, and back, Virgo the bowels, and bottom of the stomach, Libra the kidneys, thighs, and buttocks, Scorpius the genitals, the privaties, and womb, Sagittarius the thigh, and groins, Capricornus the knees, Aquarius the legs and shins, Pisces the feet. And as the triplicities[9] of these signs answer one the other, and agree in celestials, so also they agree in the members, which is sufficiently manifest by experience, because with the coldness of the feet, the belly, and breast are affected, which members answer the same triplicity; whence it is, if a medicine be applied to the one, it helps the other, as by the warming of the feet, the pain of the belly ceaseth.

Remember therefore this order, and know, that things which are under any one of the planets, have a certain particular aspect, or inclination to those members that are attributed to that planet, and especially to the houses, and exaltations thereof. For the rest of the dignities,[10] as those triplicities, and marks,[11] and face[12] are of little account in this; upon this account therefore peony, balm,[13] glove-gilliflowers,[14] citron peels,[15] sweet marjoram,[16] cinnamon,[17] saf-fron,[18] lignum aloes,[19] frankincense,[20] amber, musk,[21] and myrrh[22] help the head, and heart; by reason of Sol, Aries, and Leo: so doth ribwort,[23] the herb of Mars, help the head, and testicles by reason of Aries, and Scorpio: and so of the rest.

Also all things under Saturn conduce to sadness, and melancholy; those under Jupiter to mirth, and honour; those under Mars to boldness, contention, and anger; those under the Sun to glory, victory, and courage; those under Venus to love, lust, and concupiscence; those under Mercury to eloquence; those under the Moon to a common life.

Also all the actions, and dispositions of men are distributed according to the planets. For Saturn governs of men, monks, melancholy men, and hid treasures, and those things which are obtained with long journeys, and difficulty; but Jupiter, those that are religious, prelates, kings, and dukes, and such kind of gains that are got lawfully: Mars rules over barbers, surgeons, physicians, sergeants, executioners, butchers, all that make fires, bakers, soldiers, who are every where called martial men. Also do the other stars signify their office, as they are described in the books of astrologers.

Notes—Chapter XXII

1. *saith Proclus*—"Thus they [ancient priests] recognized things supreme in such as are subordinate, and the subordinate in the supreme: in the celestial regions, terrene properties subsisting in a causal and celestial manner; and in earth celestial properties, but according to a terrene condition" (Proclus *De sacrificio et magia,* frag. preserved in Latin translation of Marsilius Ficinus [Venice, 1497]. In Iamblichus *On the Mysteries,* trans. Thomas Taylor [1821] [London: Stuart and Watkins, 1968], 344).

2. *the Sun*—Leo rules the heart; Aries rules the head.

3. *and Scorpio*—Scorpio rules the organs of generation.

4. *cold water*—Scorpio is a Water sign.

5. *Jupiter Hammon*—Jupiter Ammon. Ammon was originally an Ethiopian or Libyan god, who was adopted by the Egyptians. He was represented as a ram, or a human figure with the head or horns of a ram, suggesting that he was at first a protector of the flocks. The Romans called him Jupiter Ammon, the Greeks Zeus Ammon, and the Hebrews simply Ammon. His main seats of worship were Meroe, Thebes, and the oasis of Siwah in the Libyan desert.

6. *ossacrum*—Bone in the lower back near the pelvis.

7. *power of increasing*—There is some overlap in these planetary attributions, which were probably compiled from several sources. For ancient systems, see "A Short Discourse of the Nature, and Qualities of the Seven Planets" in *The Book of Secrets* (Best and Brightman, 65–73); the *Tetrabiblos* of Ptolemy (3.12 [Robbins, 319, 321]); de Givry [1929] 1973, bk. 2, ch. 3, 242–3, which gives the assignments of Fludd, Gichtel and Belot; and Nasr 1978, pt. 1, ch. 4, 100–1, for the system of the Arabian encyclopedia, the *Rasa'il.*

8. *seven holes*—Correspondence between the orifices of the head and the planets also occurs in the *Sepher Yetzirah:*

> So now, behold the Stars of our World, the Planets which are seven; the Sun, Venus, Mercury, Moon, Saturn, Jupiter and Mars. The Seven are also the Seven Days of Creation; and the Seven Gateways of the Soul of Man—the two eyes, the two ears, the mouth, and the two nostrils." *(Sepher Yetzirah* 4.4, trans. W. Westcott [1887] [New York: Samuel Weiser, 1980], 23)

9. *triplicities*—The zodiac is divided into four groups of three signs, each group associated with one of the four elements:

Fire	Air	Water	Earth
Aries	Libra	Cancer	Capricorn
Leo	Aquarius	Scorpio	Taurus
Sagittarius	Gemini	Pisces	Virgo

10. *dignities*—Situations of planets in which their influence is heightened, either by their places in the zodiac or their aspects to other planets.

11. *marks*—A mark is one degree of the zodiac.

12. *face*—Division of five degrees of the zodiac. Ptolemy says: "The planets are said to be in their 'proper face' when an individual planet keeps to the sun or moon the same aspect which its house has to their houses;" *Tetrabiblos* 1.23 [Robbins, 111]).

13. *balm*—Balsam, a fragrant resinous product (resin mixed with oils) exuded naturally from trees of the genus *Balsamodendron.*

14 *glove-gilliflowers*—Clove gillyflower, or clove pink *(Dianthus caryophyllus),* a clove-scented pink flower.

15. *citron peels*—Lemon peel.

16. *sweet marjoram*—*Origanum majorana,* also called marjoram gentle, English marjoram, fine marjoram, and knotted marjoram.

17. *cinnamon*—The inner bark of the East Indian tree *Cinnamomum zeylanicum* dried in the form of aromatic yellow-brown rolls.

18. *saffron*—Orange-red powder made of the dried stigmas of the common crocus *(Crocus sativus).*

19. *lignum aloes*—Lignaloes, literally the "wood of the aloe," the fragrant wood, or resin, that is derived from two East Indian trees, genera *Aloexylon* and *Aquilaria.* It was also called agila wood, eagle wood, and agallochum. Not to be confused with the nauseating, bitter purgative of the same name, derived from the juice of plants of the genus *Aloe.*

20. *frankincense*—Olibanum. An aromatic gum-resin of the trees, genus *Boswellia,* burnt as incense. The name means "of high quality."

21. *musk*—Reddish-brown secretion of the musk deer *(Moschus moschatus)* used in perfume making because of its strong smell.

22. *myrrh*—Gum-resin of the tree *Balsamodendron myrrha* used in perfume and incense. It occurs in tears, grains, or lumps of yellow, red, or reddish-brown.

23. *ribwort*—Narrow-leaved plantain, or ribgrass *(Plantago lanceolata).* In *The Book of Secrets* it is called arnoglossus (i.e. lamb's tongue), because it was often planted in soil-poor meadows as fodder for sheep.

> The root of this herb is marvellous good against the pain of the head, because the sign of the Ram is supposed to be the house of the planet Mars, which is the head of the whole world. It is good also against evil customs of man's stones, and rotten and filthy boils, because his house is the sign *Scorpio,* [and] because a part of it holdeth *Sperma,* that is the seed, which cometh from the stones, whereof all living things be engendered, and formed. *(Book of Secrets* 1.24 [Best and Brightman, 20])

CHAPTER XXIII

How we shall know what stars natural things are under, and what things are under the Sun, which are called solary.

Now it is very hard to know, what star, or sign everything is under: yet it is known through the imitation of their rays, or motion, or figure of the superiors. Also some of them are known by their colours and odours, also some by the effects of their operations, answering to some stars.

So then solary things, or things under the power of the Sun are, amongst elements, the lucid flame; in the humours, the purer blood, and spirit of life; amongst tastes, that which is quick, mixed with sweetness. Amongst metals, gold by reason of its splendor, and its receiving that from the Sun which makes it cordial.

And amongst stones, they which resemble the rays of the Sun by their golden sparklings, as doth the glittering stone[1] aetites which hath power against the falling sickness, and poisons:[2] so also the stone, which is called the eye of the Sun,[3] being of a figure like to the apple of the eye, from the middle whereof shines forth a ray; it comforts the brain, and strengthens the sight: so the carbuncle which shines by night, hath a virtue against all airy, and vaporous poison: so the chrysolite[4] stone is of a light green colour, in which, when it is held against the Sun, there shines forth a golden star; and this comforts those parts that serve for breathing, and helps those that be asthmatical, and if it be bored through, and the hole filled with the mane of an ass, and bound to the left arm, it drives away idle imaginations, and melancholy fears, and puts away foolishness: so the stone called

iris,[5] which is like crystal in colour, being often found with six corners, when under some roof part of it is held against the rays of the Sun, and the other part is held in shadow, it gathers the rays of the Sun into itself, which, whilst it sends them forth, by way of reflection, makes a rainbow appear on the opposite wall.

Also the stone heliotropion,[6] green like the jasper, or emerald, beset with red specks, makes a man constant, renowned and famous, also it conduceth to long life; and the virtue of it indeed is most wonderful upon the beams of the Sun, which it is said to turn into blood i.e. to appear of the colour of blood, as if the Sun were eclipsed, viz. when it is joined to the juice of an herb of the same name, and be put into a vessel full of water: there is also another virtue of it more wonderful, and that is upon the eyes of men, whose sight it doth so dim, and dazzle, that it doth not suffer him that carries it to see it, and this it doth not do without the help of the herb of the said name, which also is called heliotropium,[7] i.e. following the Sun. These virtues doth *Albertus Magnus,* and *William of Paris* confirm in their writings.

The hyacinth[8] also hath a virtue from the Sun against poisons, and pestiferous vapours; it makes him that carries it to be safe, and acceptable; it conduceth also to riches, and wit, it strengthens the heart; being held in the mouth, it doth wonderfully cheer up the mind. Also there is the stone pyrophylus,[9] of a red mixture, which *Albertus Magnus* saith, *Aesculapius* makes mention of in one of his epistles unto *Octavius Augustus,* saying, that there is a certain poison so wonderful cold, which preserves the heart of man being taken out from burning, so that if for any time it be put into the fire, it is turned into a stone, and this is that stone which is called pyrophylus, from the fire. It hath a wonderful virtue against poison, and it makes him that carries it, to be renowned and dreadful to his enemies.

But above all, that stone is most solary, which *Apollonius* is reported to have found, and is called pantaura,[10] which draws other stones to it, as the loadstone doth iron, most powerful against all poisons; it is called by some pantherus, because it is spotted like the beast called the panther. It is therefore also called pantochras,[11] because it contains all colours. *Aaron* calls it evanthum. There are also other solary stones, as the topazius,[12] chrysopassus,[13] the rubine,[14] and balagius. So also is auripigmentum,[15] and things of a golden colour, and very lucid.

Amongst plants also and trees, those are solary, which turn towards the Sun, as the marigold, and those which fold in their leaves when the Sun is near upon setting, but when it riseth unfold their leaves by little and little. The lote-tree[16] also is solary, as is manifest by the figure of the fruit and leaves. So also peony, sallendine, balm, ginger, gentian,[17] dittany, and vervain,[18] which is of use in prophesying, and expiations, as also driving away evil spirits. The bay tree also is consecrated to *Phoebus,* so is the cedar, the palm tree, the ash, the ivy, the vine, and whatsoever repel poisons, and lightnings, and those things which never fear the extremities of the winter. Solary also are mint, mastic,[19] zedoary,[20] saffron, balsam, amber, musk, yellow honey, lignum aloes, cloves, cinnamon, calamus aromaticus,[21] pepper, frankincense, sweet marjoram, and libanotis,[22] which

Orpheus calls the sweet perfume of the Sun.

Amongst animals those are solary which are magnanimous, courageous, ambitious of victory, and renown: as the lion, king of beasts, the crocodile, the spotted wolf,[23] the ram, the boar, the bull, king of the herd, which was by the Egyptians at Heliopolis dedicated to the Sun, which they call Verites;[24] and an ox was consecrated to Apis in Memphi,[25] and in Herminthus a bull by the name of Pathis.[26] The wolf also was consecrated to *Apollo,* and *Latona.* Also the beast called baboon is solary, which twelve times in a day, viz. every hour barks, and in time of equinoctium pisseth twelve times every hour: the same also it doth in the night, whence the Egyptians did engrave him upon their fountains.[27]

Also amongst birds these are solary, the phoenix, being but one of that kind, and the eagle, the queen of birds, also the vulture, the swan, and those which sing at the rising Sun, and as it were calling upon it to rise, as the cock, crow, also the hawk,[28] which because in the divinity of the Egyptians it is an emblem of the spirit, and light, is by *Porphyrius* reckoned amongst the solary birds.

Moreover, all such things as have some resemblance of the works of the Sun, as worms[29] shining in the night, and the beetle,[30] which is a creature that lies under cow dung, also according to *Appious'*[31] interpretation, such whose eyes are changed according to the course of the Sun, are accounted solary, and those things which come of them.

And amongst fish, the sea calf[32] is chiefly solary, who doth resist lightning, also shellfish, and the fish called pulmo,[33] both which shine in the night, and the fish called stella[34] for his parching heat, and the fish called strombi,[35] that follow their king, and margari,[36] which also have a king, and being dried, are hardened into a stone of a golden colour.

Notes—Chapter XXIII

1. *glittering*—"Rattling" would be a better description—see note 7, ch. XIII, bk. I.

2. *and poisons*—"And as the men of Chaldea say, if poison be put in thy meat, if the aforesaid stone [aetites] be put in, it letteth that the meat may be swallowed down" *(Book of Secrets* 2.41 [Best and Brightman, 46]).

3. *eye of the Sun*—"Thus the sun-stone, by its golden rays, imitates those of the sun; but the stone called the eye of heaven, or of the sun, has a figure similar to the pupil of an eye, and a ray shines from the middle of the pupil" (Proclus *De sacrificio et magia* [Taylor, 345]). The first stone of Proclus would seem to be the "Solis gemma" of Pliny: "Solis Gemma is white, and like the luminary from which it takes its name, emits brilliant rays in a circular form" (Pliny 37.67 [Bostock and Riley, 6:456]). The second stone, referred to by Agrippa, sounds like tigereye, or perhaps a pale form of star sapphire, which Pliny seems to describe:

> Next among the white stones is "asteria," a gem which holds its high rank on account of a certain peculiarity in its nature, it having a light enclosed within, in the pupil of an eye as it were. This light, which has all the appearance of moving within the stone, it transmits according to the angle of inclination at which it is held; now in one direction, and now in another. When held facing the sun, it emits white rays like those of a star, and to this, in fact, it owes its name. (Pliny 37.47 [Bostock and Riley, 6:437])

4. *chrysolite*—Pale-green form of olivine. It is also called peridot. *Chryso* means "golden."

5. *iris*—A form of hexagonal quartz that can be used as a prism to split light into its spectrum. *Iris* is Greek for rainbow. "It takes its name 'iris' from the properties which it possesses; for, when struck by the rays of the sun in a covered spot, it projects upon the nearest walls the form and diversified colours of the rainbow; continually changing its tints, and exciting admiration by the great variety of colours which it presents" (Pliny 37.52 [Bostock and Riley, 6:439]).

6. *heliotropion*—See note 12, ch. XIII, bk. I.

7. *heliotrophium*—The herb *Heliotropium europæum.*

8. *hyacinth*—For Pliny, hyacinthus is the blue sapphire. In *The Book of Secrets* it has become a yellow, and thus solar, stone due to an error on the part of the Latin copyist, who changed the *blavus* (blue) of Albertus Magnus into *flavus* (yellow). "And it is written of this, in lectures of Philosophers, that it being borne on the finger, or neck, maketh strangers sure, and acceptable to their guests" *(Book of Secrets* 2.43 [Best and Brightman, 47]).

9. *pyrophylus*—

> It is asserted that the heart cannot be burnt of those persons who die of the cardiac disease; and the same is said of those who die by poison. At all events, there is still in existence an oration pronounced by Vitellius, in which he accuses Piso of this crime, and employs this alleged fact as one of his proofs, only asserting that the heart of Germanicus Caesar could not be burnt at the funeral pile, in consequence of his having been poisoned. (Pliny 11.71 [Bostock and Riley, 3:66–7])

10. *pantaura*—Iarchus, master of the Brahmans, tells Apollonius:

> As to the gem which attracts other stones to itself and holds them, there is no question about that, for you may examine it, and test all its wonderful properties. The largest of such gems is of the size of my thumb nail, and it is formed in cavities four cubits deep in the ground. It generates so much gas in forming that the ground swells up, and often cracks open. No one can find it by looking for it, for it conceals itself, if it is not scientifically extracted; and we Sages are the only ones who can successfully mine for the *pantarbe,* as it is called, and we do it by using both charms and spells. It turns night into day like a flame, for it is fiery and refulgent, and if looked at by daylight, it dazzles the eyes with ten thousand scintillations. Its light is due to an unspeakably powerful emanation, and it attracts everything in its vicinity. But why say, in its vicinity? For you may sink in rivers or the sea as large stones as you like, not close together but scattered far and wide at random, and if that gem be let down to them it will collect them all together by its inherent force, so that they will hang from it in a cluster like a swarm of bees. (Philostratus *Life and Times of Apollonius of Tyana* 3.46, trans. Charles P. Eells [Stanford University Press, 1923], 87–8.)

11. *pantochras*—"Panchrus ['of all colours'] is a stone which displays nearly every colour" (Pliny 37.66 [Bostock and Riley, 6:455]). Perhaps the opal.

12. *topazius*—Topaz, a golden yellow gemstone.

13. *chrysoprassus*—Chrysoprase, a light-green quartz, a variety of chalcedony.

14. *rubine*—Ruby.

15. *auripigmentum*—Orpiment, yellow arsenic, or king's yellow, a bright yellow sulfide of arsenic used as artist's pigment. "There is also one other method of procuring gold; by making it from orpiment, a mineral dug from the surface of the earth in Syria, and much used by painters. It is just the colour of gold, but brittle, like mirror-stone *[lapis specularis]*, in fact." (Pliny 33.22 [Bostock and Riley,6:104]). From what he says elsewhere (36.45) Pliny's "mirror-stone" appears to be a type of mica.

16. *lote-tree*—The fabled lotus tree, upon which flowers and fruits of the lotus were supposed to grow. Iamblichus says that the leaves and fruit, being round, represent "the motion of the intellect." One was seen by Mohammed in the seventh heaven, on the right hand of the throne of God, marking the boundary beyond which none dare pass. Under it worship the entire host of angels: "He also saw him another time, by the lote-tree beyond which there is no passing: near it is the garden of eternal abode. When the lote-tree covered that which it covered, his eyesight turned not aside, neither did it wander: and he really beheld some of the greatest signs of his Lord" *(Koran* 53, trans. Frederick Warne [London, 1887], 390).

17. *gentian*—Great felwort *(Gentiana lutea)*, a large plant with starlike yellow flowers set in rings or garlands at intervals on its upper stalk, which is of the thickness of a man's thumb. The root has a bitter taste and was used in medicine. "The root of Gentian given in pouder the quantitie of a dramme, with a little pepper and herbe Grace mixed therewith, is profitable for them that are bitten or stung with any manner of venomous beast or mad dog: or for any that hath taken poison" (Gerard [1633] 1975, bk. 2, ch. 105, 434).

18. *vervain—(Verbena officinalis)*. There are two kinds: upright vervain, called by Pliny the "male," which grows about a foot high, has leaves like oak but more deeply indented, and small blue or white flowers; creeping vervain, called by Pliny the "female," which lies upon the ground, has more leaves than the other, and small blue or purple flowers. The Romans called it the "sacred plant" *(hiera botane).* When official declaration of war was made, vervain was pulled from the soil of Rome and carried roots and earth to the land of the foe by a bearer, and when disasters such as plague struck the city, vervain was used in the *lectisternium* ceremony to restore the favor of the gods. It was also used by the Romans to cleanse the feast table of Jupiter and to purify their houses.

> The people in the Gallic provinces make use of them both for soothsaying purposes, and for the prediction of future events; but it is the magicians more particularly that give utterance to such ridiculous follies in reference to this plant. Persons, they tell us, if they rub themselves with it will be sure to gain the object of their desires; and they assure us that it keeps away fevers, conciliates friendship, and is a cure for every possible disease; they say, too, that it must be gathered about the rising of the Dog-star—but so as not to be shone upon by sun or moon—and that honey-combs and honey must be first presented to the earth by way of expiation. They tell us also that a circle must first be traced around it with iron; after which it must be taken up with the left hand, and raised aloft, care being taken to dry the leaves, stem, and root, separately in the shade. (Pliny 25.59 [Bostock and Riley, 5:121–2])

19. *mastic*—The gum-resin of an evergreen shrub *(Pistachia lentiscus)* that grows in the region of the eastern Mediterranean. The gum is tasteless and comes in the form of transparent yellow-green tears.

20. *zedoary*—Long zedoary, an aromatic East Indian root similar to ginger that comes from the *Curcuma zerumbet.* Yellow zedoary, or cassumunar, is from the *Zingiber casumunar;* round zedoary is from *Curcuma zedoaria.*

21. *calamus aromaticus*—Sweet calamus, an aromatic reed or grass. "Scented calamus also, which grows in Arabia, is common to both India and Syria, that which grows in the last country being superior to all the rest" (Pliny 12.48 [Bostock and Riley, 3:144]). The calamus of Pliny is not known with certainty, but may have been of the genus *Andropogon.* Agrippa probably refers to *Acorus calamus,* or sweet garden flag, which was early on substituted for the ancient herb (see Gerard [1633] 1975, bk. 1, ch. 45, 63).

22. *libanotis*—Probably rosemary *(Rosmarinus officinalis),* a shrub that smells like frankincense.

> Libanotis grows in a thin, crumbly soil, and is generally sown in spots exposed to

the falling dews; the root, which is just like that of olusatrum, has a smell in no way differing from that of frankincense; when a year old, it is extremely wholesome for the stomach; some persons give it the name of rosmarinum [rosemary]. (Pliny 19.62 [Bostock and Riley, 4:203])

23. *spotted wolf*—Lynx (see Pliny 8.28).

24. *Verites*—The bull worshiped at Heliopolis was called Mnevis by the Greeks.

25. *in Memphi*—A bull, not an ox, was worshiped at Memphis.

26. *Pathis*—A black bull was worshiped at Hermonthis, called by Macrobius "Bacchis" (or Bacis, or Basis, or Pacis).

27. *their fountains*—

> Again, to signify the two Equinoxes they depict a sitting Cynocephalus, for at the two equinoxes of the year it makes water twelve times in the day, once in each hour, and it does the same also during the two nights; wherefore not without reason do the Egyptians sculpture a sitting Cynocephalus on their Hydrologia (or waterclocks); and they cause the water to run from its member, because, as I said before, the animal thus indicates the twelve hours of the equinox. ... They also use this symbol, because it is the only animal that at the equinoxes utters its cries twelve times in the day, once in each hour." (Horapollo 1.16 [Cory, 36–8])

28. *hawk*—

> They symbolise by it [the hawk] God, because the bird is prolific and long-lived, or perhaps rather because it seems to be an image of the sun, being capable of looking more intently towards his rays than all other winged creatures: and hence physi-cians for the cure of the eyes use the herb hawkweed: hence also it is, that under the form of a Hawk they sometimes depict the sun as lord of vision. And they use it to denote height, because other birds, when they would soar on high, move themselves from side to side, being incapable of ascending vertically; but the hawk alone soars directly upward. (Horapollo 1.6 [Cory, 13–4])

29. *worms*—Glow-worms *(Lampyris noctiluca)*. The female of this insect species is wingless and emits a faint green light from her abdomen. The winged male does not glow.

30. *beetle*—The scarabæus, which lives on dung, specifically the first of three types described by Horapollo:

> Moreover there are three species of scarabæi, the first like a cat, and irradiated, which species they have consecrated to the sun from this similarity: for they say that the male cat changes the shape of the pupils of his eyes according to the course of the sun: for in the morning at the rising of the god, they are dilated, and in the middle of the day become round, and about sunset appear less brilliant: whence, also, the statue of the god in the city of the sun [Heliopolis] is of the form of a cat. (Horapollo 1.10 [Cory, 21–2])

31. *Appious'*—Apion.

32. *sea calf*—Seal.

33. *pulmo*—Jellyfish.

34. *stella*—Starfish.

35. *strombi*—Mollusk with a spiral shell.

36. *margari*—Pearl-fish, or oyster *(Meleagrina margaritifera)*.

CHAPTER XXIV

What things are lunary, or under the power of the Moon.

These things are lunary, amongst the elements, viz. the Earth, then the Water, as well that of the sea, as of the rivers, and all moist things, as the moisture of trees, and animals, especially they which are white, as the whites of eggs, fat, sweat, phlegm, and the superfluities of bodies. Amongst tastes, salt, and insipid: amongst metals, silver; amongst stones, crystal, the silver marcasite,[1] and all those stones that are white, and green. Also the stone selenites[2] i.e. lunary, shining from a white body, with a yellow brightness, imitating the motion of the Moon, having in it the figure of the Moon which daily increaseth, or decreaseth as doth the Moon. Also pearls, which are generated in shells of fishes from the droppings of water, also the beryl.[3]

Amongst plants and trees, these are lunary, as the selenotropion, which turns towards the Moon, as doth the heliotrophion towards the Sun, and the palm tree sends forth a bough at every rising of the Moon; hyssop[4] also, and rosemary, agnus castus, and the olive tree, are lunary. Also the herb chinosta,[5] which increaseth, and decreaseth with the Moon, viz. in substance, and number of leaves, not only in sap, and virtue, which indeed is in some sort common to all plants, except onions, which are under the influence of Mars, which have contrary properties; as amongst flying things the saturnine bird, called a quail, is a great enemy to the Moon and Sun.

Lunary animals are such as delight to be in man's company, and such as do naturally excel in love, or hatred, as all kinds of dogs: the chameleon also is lunary, which always assumes a colour according to the variety of the colour of the object: as the Moon changeth her nature according to the variety of the sign which it is found in. Lunary also are swine, hinds, goats, and all animals whatsoever, that observe, and imitate the motion of the Moon: as the baboon,[6] and panther,[7] which is said to have a spot upon her shoulder like the Moon, increasing into a roundness, and having horns that bend inwards. Cats also are lunary, whose eyes become greater or less, according to the course of the Moon: and those things which are of like nature, as menstruous blood, of which are made wonderful strange things by magicians; the civet cat[8] also changing her sex, being obnoxious to divers sorceries, and all animals that live in water as well as on land: as otters, and such as prey upon fish. Also all monstrous beasts, such as without any manifest seed are equivocally generated, as mice; which sometimes are generated by coition, sometimes of the putrefaction of the earth.

Amongst fowl, geese, ducks, didappers,[9] and all kind of watery fowl as prey upon fish, as the heron; and those that are equivocally produced, as wasps of the carcasses of horses,[10] bees of the putrefaction of cows, small flies of putrefied wine, and beetles of the flesh of asses; but most lunary of all is the two-horned beetle,[11] horned after the manner of a bull: which digs under cow dung, and there remains for the space of twenty-eight days, in which time the Moon measures the whole Zodiac, and in the twenty-ninth day, when it thinks there will be a conjunction of their brightness, it opens the dung and casts it into water, from whence then come beetles.

Amongst fish these are lunary, aelurus,[12] whose eyes are changed according to the course of the Moon, and whatsoever observe the motion of the Moon, as the tortoise, the echeneis, the crab, oysters, cockles,[13] and frogs.

Noτes—Chapτer XXIV

1. *silver marcasite*—Iron pyrites, or fool's gold, a very shiny cubic crystal used for jewelry and in ancient times the making of mirrors. The pale variety is called marcasite.

2. *selenites*—From the Greek σεληνη, moon. A form of gypsum, it is soft with a pearly luster.

> Selenitis [moonstone] is white and transparent, with a reflected colour like that of honey. It has a figure within it like that of the moon, and reflects the face of that luminary, if what we are told is true, according to its phases, day by day, whether on the wane or whether on the increase … (Pliny 37.67 [Bostock and Riley, 6:456]).

3. *beryl*—

> Beryls, it is thought, are of the same nature as the smaragdus [emerald], or at least closely analogous. … The most esteemed beryls are those which in colour resemble the pure green of the sea; the chrysoberyl being next in value, a stone of a somewhat paler colour, but approaching a golden tint. (Pliny 37.20 [Bostock and Riley, 6:414])

Beryls include emeralds, aquamarines, and gems of a clear or golden color.

4. *hyssop*—A small bushy aromatic herb *(Hyssopum officinalis)*. Not the biblical hyssop used by the Jews as an aspergillum, which is conjectured to have been the thorny caper *(Capparis spinosa)*. Gerard says the hyssop of the Greeks was "neerer to *Origanum*" (Gerard [1633] 1975, bk. 2, ch. 177, 580).

5. *chinosta*—?

6. *baboon*—

> And they symbolise the moon by it, because the animal has a kind of sympathy with it at its conjunction with the god. For at the exact instant of the conjunction of the moon with the sun, when the moon

becomes unilluminated, then the male Cynocephalus neither sees, nor eats, but is bowed down to the earth with grief, as if lamenting the ravishment of the moon: and the female also, in addition to its being unable to see, and being afflicted in the same manner as the male, [emits blood from her genitals]: hence even to this day cynocephali are brought up on the temples, in order that from them may be ascertained the exact instant of the conjunction of the sun and moon. (Horapollo 1.14 [Cory, 31–2])

7. *panther*—"It is said by some, that the panther has, on the shoulder, a spot which bears the form of the moon; and that, like it, it regularly increases to full, and then diminishes to a crescent" (Pliny 8.23 [Bostock and Riley, 2:274]).

8. *civet cat*—It is the hyena Pliny reports fabled to change its sex: "It is the vulgar notion, that the hyaena possesses in itself both sexes, being a male during one year, and a female the next, and that it becomes pregnant without the co-operation of the male; Aristotle, however *[Historia animalium* 6.32, *Generatione animalium* 3.6], denies this" (Pliny 8.44 [Bostock and Riley, 2:296]).

> If the door-posts are touched with this blood, the various arts of the magicians will be rendered of no effect; they will neither be able to summon the gods into their presence nor to converse with them, whatever the method to which they have recourse, whether lamps or basin, water or globe, or any other method. … The excrements or bones which have been voided by the animal at the moment when killed, are looked upon as counter-charms to magic spells. [Pliny 28.27 [Bostock and Riley, 5:313])

This long and remarkable chapter is entirely devoted to the virtues of the hyena.

9. *didappers*—*Podiceps minor*. Also called the dabchick; a small diving water fowl.

10. *carcasses of horses*—"When they would denote wasps, they depict a dead horse; for many wasps are generated from him when dead" (Horapollo 2.44 [Cory, 114]).

11. *two-horned beetle*—"The second species is the two horned and bull formed, which is consecrated to the moon; whence the children of the Egyptians say, that the bull in the heavens is the exaltation of this goddess" (Horapollo 1.10 [Cory, 22]). Of the scarabæus in general, Horapollo says:

> And they symbolize by this an only begotten, because the scarabaeus is a creature self-produced, being unconceived by a female; for the propagation of it is unique after this manner:—when the male is desirous of procreating, he takes dung of an ox, and shapes it into a spherical form like the world; he then rolls it from the hinder parts from east to west, looking himself towards the east, that he may impart to it the figure of the world, (for that is borne from east to west, while the course of the stars is from west to east): then, having dug a hole, the scarabaeus deposits this ball in the earth for the space of twenty-eight days, (for in so many days the moon passes through the twelve signs of the zodiac). By thus remaining under the moon, the race of scarabaei is endued with life; and upon the nine and twentieth day after having opened the ball, it casts it into water, for it is aware that upon that day the conjunction of the moon and sun takes place, as well as the generation of the world. From the ball thus opened in the water, the animals, that is the scarabaei, issue forth. (Horapollo 1.10 [Cory, 20–1])

12. *aelurus*—Sea-catfish, or seacat *(Aelurichthys marinus)*.

13. *oysters, cockles*—

> It is certain that the bodies of oysters and of whelks, and of shell-fish generally, are increased in size and again diminished by the influence of the moon. Certain accurate observers have found out, that the entrails of the field-mouse correspond in number to the moon's age, and that the very small animal, the ant, feels the power of this luminary, always resting from her labours at the change of the moon. (Pliny 2.41 [Bostock and Riley, 1:68])

CHAPTER XXV

What things are saturnine, or under the power of Saturn.

Saturnine things, amongst elements, are Earth, and also Water: amongst humours, black choler that is moist, as well natural, as adventitious, adust[1] choler is excepted. Amongst tastes, sour, tart, and dead. Amongst metals, lead, and gold, by reason of its weight, and the golden marcasite.[2] Amongst stones, the onyx,[3] the ziazaa,[4] the camonius,[5] the sapphire, the brown jasper, the chalcedon,[6] the loadstone, and all dark, weighty, earthy things.

Amongst plants, and trees the daffodil,[7] dragonwort,[8] rue, cummin,[9] hellebor,[10] the tree from whence benzoine[11] comes, mandrake,[12] opium, and those things which stupefy, and those things which are never sown, and never bear fruit, and those which bring forth berries of a dark colour, and black fruit, as the black fig tree, the pine tree, the cypress tree,[13] and a certain tree[14] used at burials, which never springs afresh with berries, rough, of a bitter taste, of a strong smell, of a black shadow, yielding a most sharp pitch, bearing a most unprofitable fruit, never dies with age, deadly, dedicated to *Pluto,* as is the herb pas-flower, with which they were wont anciently to strew the graves before they put the dead bodies into them, wherefore it was lawful to make their garlands at feasts with all herbs, and flowers besides pas-flower, because it was mournful, and not conducing to mirth.

Also all creeping animals, living apart, and solitary, nightly, sad, contemplative, dull, covetous, fearful, melancholy, that take much pains, slow, that feed grossly, and such as eat their young. Of these kinds therefore are the mole, the asses, the wolf, the hare, the mule, the cat, the camel, the bear, the hog, the ape, the dragon, the basilisk, the toad, all serpents, and creeping things, scorpions, pismires, and such things as proceed from putrefaction in the earth, in water, or in the ruins of houses, as mice, and many sorts of vermin.

Amongst birds those are saturnine, which have long necks, and harsh voices, as cranes, ostriches, and peacocks, which are dedicated to Saturn, and *Juno.* Also the screech owl, the horn owl, the bat, the lapwing, the crow, the quail, which is the most envious bird of all.

Amongst fishes, the eel,[15] living apart from all other fish; the lamprey, the dogfish,[16] which devours her young, also the tortoise, oysters, cockles, to which may be added sea sponges, and all such things as come of them.

Notes—Chapter XXV

1. *adust*—Dry, burning.

2. *golden marcasite*—Iron pyrites, or fool's gold.

3. *onyx*—Black onyx, a form of chalcedony, an opaque black or dark brown stone, usually with a white line running across it. Sometimes the line forms

Male mandrake

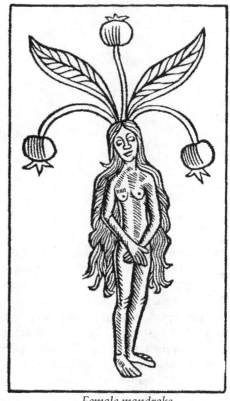

Female mandrake

from *Hortus Sanitatis* by Johannes de Cuba (Paris 1498)

a circle, and the stone is then called lynx-eye onyx. Connected astrologically with Capricorn and Saturn, it was used in rosaries and to avert the evil eye. "And it cometh from India, unto Araby, and if it be hanged upon the neck, or finger, it stirreth up anon sorrow or heaviness in a man, and terrors, and also debate" *(Book of Secrets* 2.4 [Best and Brightman, 27]).

4. *ziazaa*—"A black and white stone; it renders its possessor litigious, and causes terrible visions" (Spence [1920] 1968, 439).

5. *camonius*—In the Latin *Opera,* camoinus.

6. *chalcedon*—Chalcedony, a form of silica. "Take the stone which is called *Chalcedonius,* and it is pale, brown of colour, and somewhat dark" *(Book of Secrets* 2.22 [Best and Brightman, 36]).

7. *daffodil*—Affodill, or asphodel *(Asphodelus),* the white daffodil, as opposed to yellow daffodil *(Narcissus pseudo-Narcissus).*

8. *dragonwort*—Or dragons *(Dracunculus vulgaris);* the leaves and root protect against serpents.

9. *cummin*—*Cummin cyminum,* also called common, garden, or Roman cumin, a plant similar in appearance to fennel.

10. *hellebor*—Plants of the genus *Helleborus* or *Veratrum,* used in ancient times as a specific against madness. There are several kinds with various uses: (1) black hellebor *(Helleborus officinalis),* a species growing only in Greece; (2) green hellebor *(H. viridis),* also called bastard, or wild hellebor; (3) stinking hellebor *(H. fetidus),* also called fetid hellebor; (4) white hellebor *(Veratrum album);* (5) winter hellebor *(Eranthis hyemalis),* also called winter aconite. Used without qualification, black hellebor, or Christmas rose *(Helleborus niger),* is probably intended. Since *H. officinalis* was restricted to Greece, medieval and Renaissance writers substituted for it *H. niger.* Hellebor is poisonous. Pliny describes the gathering of black hellebor:

> This last plant, too, is gathered with more numerous ceremonies than the other: a circle is first traced around it with a sword, after which, the person about to cut it turns toward the East, and offers up a prayer,

entreating permission of the gods to do so. At the same time he observes whether an eagle is in sight—for mostly while the plant is being gathered that bird is near at hand—and if one should chance to fly close at hand, it is looked upon as a presage that he will die within the year. (Pliny 25.21 [Bostock and Riley, 5:97])

11. *benzoine*—A dry brittle aromatic resin extracted from the tree *Styrax benzoin,* which grows in Sumatra, Java, and surrounding countries. It was used as an incense and suffumation.

12. *mandrake*—*Mandragora officinalis.* Drake means dragon. Short, fleshy plant with lance-shaped leaves, said to imitate the human form because of its often forked root. Narcotic, emetic, and poisonous. It was thought to promote fertility in women (see Genesis 30:14–6). According to legend, when pulled from the earth the plant shrieks, and anyone hearing it dies, for which reason the plant is to be tied to a dog by a tether, and the dog sacrificed in its extraction. It was said of a sleepy man that he had eaten of mandrake, and mandrake was also called love apple, because of its supposed aphrodisiac qualities.

13. *cyprus*—Common cyprus *(Cupressus sempervirens),* a small evergreen said to be a funeral tree and dedicated to Pluto "because when once cut down it never grows again" (Brewer, 206, "cyprus").

14. *certain tree*—Perhaps the hemlock, which is a soporific and a poison; or possibly the yew, which has rough bark, is very long-lived and grows in graveyards.

15. *eel*—"When they would symbolise a man that is hostile to, and secluded from, all men, they depict an eel; for it is found associated with no other fishes" (Horapollo 2.103 [Cory, 149]).

16. *dogfish*—Large spotted dogfish *(Scyllium catulus),* a species of small shark, very ravenous.

CHAPTER XXVI

Ulhat things are under the power of Jupiter, and are called jovial.

Things under Jupiter, amongst elements, are the Air: amongst humors, blood, and the spirit of life, also all things which respect the increase, nourishment, and vegetation of the life. Amongst tastes such as are sweet, and pleasant. Amongst metals, tin, silver, and gold, by reason of their temperateness:[1] amongst stones, the hyacinth,[2] beryl, sapphire, the emerald, green jasper, and airy colours.

Amongst plants and trees, sea-green,[3] garden basil,[4] bugloss,[5] mace,[6] spike,[7] mints, mastic, elicampane,[8] the violet, darnel,[9] henbane,[10] the poplar tree, and those which are called lucky trees, as the oak, the tree aesculus,[11] which is like an oak, but much bigger, the holm tree,[12] the beech tree, the hazel tree, the service tree, the white fig tree, the pear tree, the apple tree, the vine, the plum tree, the ash, the dog tree,[13] and the olive tree, and also oil. Also all manner of corn, as barley, wheat, also raisins, licorice, sugar, and all

such things whose sweetness is manifest, and subtle, partaking somewhat of an astringent, and sharp taste, as are nuts, almonds, pineapples, filberts, pistake[14] nuts, roots of peony, mirabolaus,[15] rhubarb, and manna,[16] *Orpheus* adds storax.[17]

Amongst animals, such as have some stateliness, and wisdom in them, and those which are mild, well trained up, and of good dispositions, as the hart, elephant, and those which are gentle, as the sheep, and lambs.

Amongst birds, those that are of a temperate complexion, as hens, together with the yolk of their eggs. Also the partridge, the pheasant, the swallow,[18] the pelican,[19] the cuckoo,[20] the stork,[21] birds given to a kind of devotion which are emblems of gratitude. The eagle[22] is dedicated to Jupiter, she is the ensign of emperors, and an emblem of justice, and clemency.

Amongst fish; the dolphin, the fish called anchia,[23] the sheath fish,[24] by reason of his devoutness.

Notes—Chapter XXVI

1. *temperateness*—The ease with which they may be worked.

2. *hyacinth*—See note 8, ch. XXIII, bk. I.

3. *sea-green*—Or sengreen, the house leek *(Sempervivum tectorum)*, a herb with thick, succulent leaves and stem and pink flowers that grows on the tops of houses, and was often deliberately placed there to ward off lightning.

4. *basil*—See note 14, ch. XVIII, bk. I.

5. *bugloss*—In Pliny, Italian alkanet *(Anchusa italica)*: "To an account of the plantago may be annexed that of the buglosses, the leaf of which resembles an ox tongue. The main peculiarity of this plant is, that if put into wine, it promotes mirth and hilarity, whence it has obtained the additional name of 'euphrosynum' [plant that cheers]" (Pliny 25.40 [Bostock and Riley, 5:109]). Likely used by Agrippa

to signify viper's bugloss *(Echium vulgare)*, a very similar herb with long hairy leaves. "The root drunke with wine is good for those that be bitten with Serpents, and it keepeth such from being stung as have drunk of it before: the leaves and seeds do the same, as *Dioscorides* writes" (Gerard [1633] 1975, bk. 2, ch. 285–A, 803).

6. *mace*—The husk of nutmeg, used as a spice.

7. *spike*—French lavender *(Lavandula spica)*, from which a sweet-smelling oil is extracted.

8. *elicampane*—Horseheal *(Inula helenium)*, a herb with large yellow flowers and bitter aromatic leaves and root, used as a tonic and stimulant. Good against cholic. It was burned as a fragrant incense.

9. *darnel*—A kind of grass *(Lolium temulentum)* that grows as a weed among corn.

10. *henbane*—Narcotic plant *(Hyoscyamus niger)* used to deaden pain. It has dull yellow flowers that are streaked with purple and carry an unpleasant smell. *The Book of Secrets* calls it "the herb of the planet Jupiter," good against gout because "it worketh by virtue of those signs which have feet, and look upon the feet"—i.e., Pisces, which is ruled by Jupiter; also, "it is profitable against the griefs of the liver, and all his passions, because Jupiter holdeth the liver" *(Book of Secrets* 1.26 [Best and Brightman 21]).

11. *aesculus*—The chestnut oak *(Quercus sessiliflora)*, sacred to Jupiter (see Pliny 12.2 [Bostock and Riley, 3:102]).

12. *holm tree*—The holly *(Ilex aquifolium)*. It is very possible Agrippa intends the holm oak *(Quercus ilix)*, an evergreen oak native to southern Europe the foliage of which resembles that of the holly.

13. *dog tree*—Dogwood, or wild cornel *(Conus sanguinea)*.

14. *pistake*—Pistachio.

15. *mirabolaus*—Astringent, plum-like fruits of trees of the genus *Terminalia,* said to be sweet before they are ripe. They include belleric, from the *Terminalia bellerica* of India; chebule, from the *T. chebula* of Central Asia; also emblic, from *Emblica officinalis.* Gerard mentions six kinds that he calls "Indian plums" (Gerard [1633] 1975, bk. 3, ch. 128, 1500). They are not to be confused with the behen-nut tree *(Moringa oleifera),* a source of scented oil called "ben," described by Pliny (12.46 [Bostock and Riley, 3:142]).

16. *manna*—A sweet pale yellow or white granulated sap that drips from incisions made in the manna-ash tree *(Fraxinus ornus),* which grows in Sicily.

17. *storax*—Fragrant gum-resin, yellow or reddish-brown in color, extracted from the tree *Storax officinalis;* it also came in the form of clear, white tears, and was used for embalming in ancient times. In the Orphic hymn to Jupiter (14) and in the hymn to Thundering Jove (18), the direction reads: "The fumigation from storax" *(Hymns of Orpheus,* trans. Thomas Taylor [1787]. In *Thomas Taylor the Platonist: Selected Writings* [Princeton University Press, 1969], 230, 234).

18. *swallow*—"When they would signify that the whole of a parent's substance has been left to the sons, they depict a swallow. For she rolls herself in the mud, and builds a nest for her young, when she is herself about to die" (Horapollo 2.31 [Cory 107]).

19. *pelican*—The pelican was supposed to be able to revive her dead chicks with warm blood from her own breast. This myth appears in the bestiary of Physiologus (2nd-5th century AD), and is repeated in *The Book of Secrets* (3.14 [Best and Brightman 56]).

20. *cuckoo*—

> To represent gratitude, they delineate a cucupha, because this is the only one of dumb animals, which, after it has been brought up by its parents, repays their kindness to them when they are old. For it makes them a nest in the place where it was brought up by them, and trims their wings, and brings them food, till the parents acquire a new plumage, and are able to assist themselves: whence it is that the Cucupha is honoured by being placed as an ornament upon the sceptres of the gods. (Horapollo 1.55 [Cory 75–6])

21. *stork*—

> When they would denote a man fond of his father, they depict a stork; for after he has been brought up by his parents he departs not from them, but remains with them to the end of their life, taking upon himself the care of them." (Horapollo 2.58 [Cory 122])

22. *eagle*—

> Caius Marius, in his second consulship, assigned the eagle exclusively to the Roman legions. Before that period it had only held the first rank, there being four others as well, the wolf, the minotaur, the

horse, and the wild boar, each of which preceded a single division. Some few years before his time it had begun to be the custom to carry the eagle only into battle, the other standards being left behind in camp; Marius, however, abolished the rest of them entirely. Since then, it has been remarked that hardly ever has a Roman legion encamped for the winter, without a pair of eagles making their appearance at the spot. (Pliny 10.5 [Bostock and Riley, 2:485])

See also Pliny 10.6.

23. *anchia*—Perhaps the *anthias?*

These anthiae, it is said, when they see one of their number taken with a hook, cut the line with the serrated spines which they have on the back, the one that is held fast stretching it out as much as it can, to enable them to cut it. (Pliny 9.85 [Bostock and Riley, 2:474])

24. *sheath fish*—A large freshwater fish *(Silurus glanis)* found in the rivers of eastern Europe.

Chapter XXVII

What things are under the
power of Mars, and are called martial.

These things are martial, amongst elements, Fire, together with all adust, and sharp things: amongst humours, choler; also bitter tastes, tart, and burning the tongue, and causing tears: amongst metals, iron, and red brass;[1] and all fiery, red, and sulphurous things: amongst stones the diamond, loadstone, the bloodstone,[2] the jasper, the stone that consists of divers kinds,[3] the amethyst.

Amongst plants, and trees, hellebore, garlic, euphorbium,[4] cartabana,[5] armoniac,[6] radish, the laurel, wolfsbane,[7] scammony,[8] and all such as are poisonous, by reason of too much heat, and those which are beset round about with prickles, or by touching the skin, burn it, prick it, or make it swell, as cardis,[9] the nettle, crowfoot,[10] and such as being eaten cause tears, as onions, ascolonia,[11] leeks, mustard seed, and all thorny trees, and the dog tree, which is dedicated to Mars.

And all such animals as are warlike, ravenous, bold, and of clear fancy, as the horse, mule, goat, kid, wolf, libard,[12] the wild ass; serpents also, and dragons full of displeasure, and poison; also all such as are offensive to men, as gnats, flies, baboon, by reason of his anger.

All birds that are ravenous, devour flesh, break bones, as the eagle, the falcon, the hawk, the vulture; and those which are called the fatal birds, as the horn owl, the screech owl, kestrels,[13] kites, and such as are hungry, and ravenous, and such as make a noise in their swallowing, as crows, daws, and pie,[14] which above all the rest is dedicated to Mars.

And amongst fishes, the pike, the barbel,[15] the forkfish, the fish that hath horns like a

Notes—Chapter XXVII

1. *red brass*—As opposed to more common yellow brass. Red brass has a copper color.

2. *bloodstone*—The heliotrope.

3. *divers kinds*—This is the stone described in *The Book of Secrets* under the name gagatronica: "… and it is of divers colours. The ancient Philosophers say that it hath been proved in the prince Alcides [Hercules], which how long he did bear it, he had always victory. And it is a stone of divers colours, like the skin of a Kid" *(Book of Secrets* 2.24 [Best and Brightman, 38]). "Like the skin of a Kid" means mottled or

spotted. Perhaps a kind of agate; or perhaps opal.

4. *euphorbium*—Gum-resin of the herb euphorbia, also called spurge *(Euphorbia officinarum)*. Extremely acrid, it was used as an emetic and purge. The powdered resin causes violent and prolonged sneezing.

5. *cartabana*—?

6. *armoniac*—Gum-resin, called the "gum of Ammon" because it was obtained from a plant growing in Libya near the shrine of Jupiter Ammon. It has

a strong smell and bitter taste, and was used in emetics. The ammoniac of the ancients was probably obtained from the *Ferula tingitana* of North Africa. In more modern times the more potent *Dorema ammoniacum* went under this name.

7. *wolfsbane*—Poisonous plant *(Aconitum lycoctonum)* of the mountainous regions of western Europe, which bears a dull yellow flower. It contains the poison aconite and was closely linked with witches as an ingredient in their flying ointment.

8. *scammony*—Gum-resin extracted from the roots of the plant *Convolvulus scammonia,* which grows in Syria and Asia Minor. Used as a purgative.

9. *cardis*—Cardoon, or thistle.

10. *crowfoot*—A name applied to several species of *Ranunculus* or buttercup, said to raise blisters.

11. *ascolonia*—The scallion, or Welsh onion *(Allium fistulosum),* a bulbless variety much cultivated in Germany, the leafy tops of which are used in salads.

12. *libard*—Leopard.

13. *kestrels*—A small hawk *(Falco tinnunculus),* also called the stannel and windhover, the last because of its remarkable powers of sustaining itself motionless in the air.

14. *pie*—Magpie *(Pica caudata),* a noisy, aggressive bird that surrounds the opening of its nest with thorns and defends it forcefully. It was credited with the power of loosing bonds by means of a magic herb, perhaps mistletoe:

> Go into the wood, and look where the Pie hath her nest with her birds, and when thou

shalt be there, climb up the tree, and bind about the hole of it wheresoever thou wilt. For when she seeth thee, she goeth for a certain herb, which she will put to the binding, and it is broken anon and that herb falleth to the ground upon the cloth, which thou shouldst have put under the tree, and be thou present and take it. ("Marvels of the World" 55 [Best and Brightman, 99])

15. *barbel*—Large freshwater fish *(Barbus vulgaris)* with fleshy filaments, or barbs, hanging from its mouth.

16. *like a ram*—This is the *aries* or "sea ram" of Pliny:

> The sea-ram commits its ravages just like a wary robber; at one time it will lurk in the shadow of some large vessel that is lying out at sea, and wait for any one who may be tempted to swim; while at another, it will raise its head from the surface of the water, survey the fisherman's boats, and then slily swim towards them and sink them. (Pliny 9.67 [Bostock and Riley, 2:453])

Elsewhere he describes monsters left upon the shore during the reign of Tiberius (14–37 AD), among them "rams, which last, however, had only a white spot to represent horns" (Pliny 9.4 [Bostock and Riley, 2:364]). The most likely candidate seems to be the grampus, or killer whale *(Orca gladiator).*

17. *glaucus*—Or sea-stickling, a kind of fish that is said to swallow its young when they are threatened, then when the danger is past, release them. Pliny mentions the glaucus (9.25 and 32.54), but it is not known with certainty which species he intends.

CHAPTER XXVIII

What things are under the power of Venus, and are called venereal.

These things are under Venus, amongst elements, Air, and Water; amongst humours, phlegm, with blood, spirit, and seed; amongst tastes, those which are sweet, unctuous, and delectable; amongst metals, silver, and brass, both yellow, and red; amongst stones, the beryl, chrysolite, emerald, sapphire, green jasper, the corneola,[1] the stone aetites, the lazul[2] stone, coral, and all of a fair, various, white, and green colour.

Amongst plants and trees the vervain, violet,[3] maidenhair,[4] valerian,[5] which by the Arabian is called phu; also thyme,[6] the gum ladanum,[7] ambergris,[8] musk, sanders,[9] coriander,[10] and all sweet perfumes, and delightful, and sweet fruits, as sweet pears, figs, pomegranates,[11] which the poets say was, in Cyprus, first sown by *Venus.* Also the rose of Lucifer was dedicated to her, also the myrtle tree of Hesperus.[12]

Moreover all luxurious, delicious animals, and of a strong love, as dogs, conies,[13] stinking[14] sheep, and goats, both female, and male, which generates sooner than any other animal, for they say that he couples after the seventh day[15] of his being brought forth; also the bull for his disdain,[16] and the calf for his wantonness.

Amongst birds the swan,[17] the wagtail,[18] the swallow, the pelican, the burgander,[19] which are very loving to their young. Also the crow, the pigeon,[20] which is dedicated to Venus, and the turtle,[21] one whereof was commanded to be offered at the purification, after bringing forth.[22] The sparrow also was dedicated to Venus, which was commanded in the Law to be used in the purification, after the leprosy,[23] a martial disease, than which nothing was of more force to resist it. Also the Egyptians called the eagle Venus, because she is prone to venery, for after she hath been trod thirteen times in a day, if the male call her, she runs to him again.[24]

Amongst fishes, these are venereal, the lustful pilchards, the lecherous gilthead,[25] the whiting[26] for her love to her young, the crab fighting for his mate, and tithymallus[27] for its fragrant, and sweet smell.

Notes—Chapter XXVIII

1. *corneola*—Cornelian, a variety of chalcedony that might be red, yellow or blue in color, frequently with two or more colors combined in one stone. Pliny extols it as a seal because when engraved as a signet, sealing wax would not stick to its surface (Pliny 37.23 [Bostock and Riley, 6:418]).

2. *lazul*—Lapis lazuli, an opaque stone of deep blue or blue-green, often with golden flecks (iron pyrites). The unspotted stone is more highly valued.

3. *violet*—*Viola odorata,* flower of innocence. "I would give you some violets, but they withered all when my father died" *(Hamlet,* act 4, sc. 5, lines 183–4).

4. *maidenhair*—A fern *(Adiantum capillus-veneris)*, at one time called Venus-hair. It has hairlike stalks and very fine fronds.

5. *valerian*—A plant *(Valeriana officinalis)* with small flesh-colored flowers and a fleshy root from which is extracted a mild narcotic. It has intoxicating power over cats.

6. *thyme*—Wild thyme *(Thymus)* has purple flowers and was used as a stimulant and for its pleasing fragrance.

7. *ladanum*—Gum-resin extracted from the cistus, or rock rose *(Cistaceae)*, a flowering plant. It was used as a stimulant and in perfumes.

8. *ambergris*—Literally "gray amber"; the vomit of the sperm whale, used in perfume making because its smell, though unpleasant, is extremely powerful. It was found floating on the surface of the sea.

9. *sanders*—Sandalwood, the sweet-smelling wood of the sandalwood tree *(Santalum album)*. It was sawn into dust and burned in temples as incense.

10. *coriander*—*Coriandrum sativum*. The round, ripe fruit of this small branching plant has an agreeable smell.

11. *pomegranates*—Fruit of a small tree *(Punica granatum)*. It is the size of an orange and has a tough golden rind, inside of which are many seeds covered in sweet red pulp, like a cluster of red berries. When Adonis was killed by a wild boar, Venus created a flower in memory of her lover:

> … she sprinkles his blood with odoriferous nectar, which, touched by it, effervesces, just as the transparent bubbles are wont to rise in rainy weather. Nor was there a pause longer than a full hour, when a flower sprang up from the blood, of the same colour with it, such as the pomegranates are wont to bear, which conceal their seeds beneath their tough rind. (Ovid *Metamorphoses* 10.10, c. line 732 [Riley, 376–7]).

12. *Hesperus*—The plants sacred to Venus were the rose and the myrtle. The planet Venus, depending on its position relative to the Sun, can be both a morning and evening star. When it follows the Sun and is an evening star in the western sky, it is called Hesperus (of the west); when it precedes the Sun and appears before sunrise in the east, it is called Lucifer (light bringing).

13. *conies*—Rabbits.

14. *stinking*—Perhaps in rut.

15. *the seventh day*—"To denote the member of a prolific man, they depict a goat, and not a bull: [for the bull cannot serve a cow before he is a year old, but the goat mounts the female seven days after birth, ejaculating a sterile and empty sperm. Yet nevertheless it matures before all other animals.]" (Horapollo 1.48 [Cory, 68–9]). Again, for reasons of misplaced delicacy, the translator chose to give the passage in brackets in Latin.

16. *for his disdain*—"And the bull is always assumed as a symbol of temperance, because it never approaches the cow after conception" (Horapollo 2.78 [Cory, 134]).

17. *swan*—The mother swan swims with her unfledged young on her back.

18. *wagtail*—A small bird of the genus *Motacilla*, so called because it constantly wags its tail.

19. *burgander*—The cheldrake, or burrow duck *(Tadorna vulpanser)*, a bird like a goose that lives in holes by the seashore.

20. *pigeon*—

> Next to the partridge, it is the pigeon that similar [maternal] tendencies are to be seen in the same respect: but then, chastity is especially observed by it, and promiscuous intercourse is a thing quite unknown. Although inhabiting a domicile in common with others, they will none of them violate the laws of conjugal fidelity: not one will desert its nest, unless it is either widower or widow. … They both of them manifest an equal degree of affection for their offspring; indeed, it is not unfrequently that this is a ground for correction, in consequence of the female being too slow in going to her young. When the female is sitting, the male renders her every attention that can in any way tend to her solace and comfort. (Pliny 10.52 [Bostock and Riley, 2:517–8]).

21. *turtle*—Turtledove.

22. *after bringing forth*—Leviticus 12:6.

23. *after the leprosy*—Leviticus 14:4–7.

24. *runs to him again*—"For this reason they have consecrated the hawk to the sun; for, like the sun, it completes the number thirty in its conjunctions with the female (Horapollo 1.8 [Cory, 17]). Cory's Greek text is corrupt, and should read 13, not 30. There are 13 New Moons in the year, when the Sun and Moon are in conjunction.

25. *gilthead*—This name now refers to the genus *Chrysophrys*, but once meant the dolphin: "… it is by

sailors called the dolphin, and gives chase to the flying fish" (Goldsmith [1774] 1849, bk. 3, sec. I-3, 510).

26. *whiting*—A small fish *(Merlangus)* with pearly white flesh. In England "whiting mop" was a term of endearment for a girl, and "whiting's eye" meant an amorous look.

27. *tithymallus*—Name used in Pliny to refer to sea spurge *(Euphorbia polygonifolia)*. Spurge has a milky white juice with poisonous or narcotic qualities. It was used as a purgative and to remove warts.

CHAPTER XXIX

What things are under the power of Mercury, and are called mercurial.

Things under Mercury are these; amongst elements, Water, although it moves all things indistinctly; amongst humours, those especially which are mixed, as also the animal spirit; amongst tastes those that are various, strange, and mixed; amongst metals, quicksilver, tin, the silver marcasite; amongst stones, the emerald, achates, red marble, topaz, and those which are of divers colours, and various figures naturally, and those that are artificial, as glass, and those which have a colour mixed with yellow, and green.

Amongst plants, and trees, the hazel, five-leaved grass,[1] the herb mercury,[2] fumatory,[3] pimpernel,[4] marjoram, parsley, and such as have shorter and less leaves, being compounded of mixed natures, and divers colours.

Animals also, that are of quick sense, ingenious, strong, inconstant, swift, and such as become easily acquainted with men, as dogs, apes, foxes, weasels, the hart, and mule; and all animals that are of both sexes, and those which can change their sex, as the hare, civet cat, and such like.

Amongst birds, those which are naturally witty, melodious, and inconstant, as the linnet, nightingale, blackbird, thrush, lark, the gnat-sapper,[5] the bird calandra,[6] the parrot, the pie, the bird ibis, the bird porphyrio,[7] the black beetle with one horn.[8]

And amongst fish, the fish called trochius,[9] which goes into himself, also pourcontrel for deceitfulness, and changeableness,[10] and the forkfish for its industry; the mullet also that shakes off the bait on the hook with his tail.

Notes—Chapter XXIX

1. *five-leaved grass*—Cinquefoil, or pentaphyllon *(Potentilla reptans)*. It was used to repel witches.

2. *herb mercury*—Dog's mercury, or wild mercury, a poisonous plant *(Mercurialis perennis)*, historically confused with allgood, good henry, or false mercury *(Chenopodium bonus-henricus)*, a pot herb.

3. *fumatory*—Medicinal herb *(Fumaria officinalis)* that grows as a weed.

4. *pimpernel*—Burnet saxifrage *(Pimpinella saxifraga)*. The powder of this plant was said to close wounds, for which reason it was called selfheal.

5. *gnat-sapper*—Gnat-snapper; probably *Tringa canutus,* a kind of sandpiper.

6. *calandra*—Calander *(Alanda calandra),* a kind of lark.

7. *porphyrio*—A kind of water hen *(Porphyrio caeruleus)* with deep blue plumage and scarlet bill and legs.

8. *beetle with one horn*—"... the third species [of scarabæus] is the one horned and Ibis formed, which they regard as consecrated to Hermes in like manner as the bird Ibis" (Horapollo 1.10 [Cory, 22]). The

horn of the beetle resembles the long, curved beak of the ibis.

9. *trochius*—Trochus a gastropod mollusk with a conical shell.

10. *changeableness*—The octopus is able to change its color to blend in with its surroundings.

CHAPTER XXX

That the whole sublunary world, and those things which are in it, are distributed to planets.

Moreover whatsoever is found in the whole world is made according to the governments of the planets, and accordingly receives its virtue. So in Fire the enlivening light thereof is under the government of the Sun, the heat of it under Mars; in the Earth, the various superficies thereof under the Moon, and Mercury, and the starry heaven,[1] the whole mass of it under Saturn; but in the middle elements,[2] Air is under Jupiter, and Water the Moon, but being mixed are under Mercury, and Venus.

In like manner natural active causes observe the Sun, the matter the Moon, the fruitfulness of active causes Jupiter, the fruitfulness of the matter, Venus, the sudden effecting of anything, Mars, and Mercury, that for his vehemency, this for his dexterity, and manifold virtue: but the permanent continuation of all things is ascribed to Saturn.

Also amongst vegetables, everything that bears fruit is from Jupiter, and everything that bears flowers is from Venus, all seed, and bark is from Mercury, and all roots from Saturn, and all wood from Mars, and leaves from the Moon. Wherefore all that bring forth fruit, and not flowers, are of Saturn and Jupiter, but they that bring forth flowers, and seed, and not fruit, are of Venus, and Mercury; these which are brought forth of their own accord without seed, are of the Moon, and Saturn; all beauty is from Venus, all strength from Mars, and every planet rules, and disposeth that which is like to it.

Also in stones, their weight, clamminess, sliptickness[3] is of Saturn, their use, and temperament of Jupiter, their hardness from Mars, their life from the Sun, their beauty and fairness from Venus, their occult virtue from Mercury, their common use from the Moon.

Notes—Chapter XXX

1. *starry heaven*—The surface of the earth is ruled by the sphere of the fixed stars, or zodiac, through the angles of the rays made by planets, signs and houses with specific places on the earth.

2. *middle elements*—The order of the elements is Fire, Air, Water and Earth, making Air and Water the middle elements. See Appendix III.

3. *sliptickness*—Slipperiness.

CHAPTER XXXI

How provinces, and kingdoms are distributed to planets.

Moreover the whole orb of the Earth is distributed by kingdoms and provinces[1] to the planets, and signs: for Macedonia, Thracia, Illyria, India, Arriana, Gordiana (many of which countries are in the lesser Asia) are under Saturn with Capricorn; but with Aquarius, under him are the Sauromatian country, Oxiana, Sogdiana, Arabia, Phazania, Media, Ethiopia, which countries for the most part belong to the more inward Asia.

Under Jupiter with Sagittarius are Tuscana, Celtica, Spain, and Happy Arabia: under him with Pisces are Lycia, Lydia, Cilicia, Phamphylia, Paphlagonia, Nasamonia, and Libya.

Mars with Aries governs Britany, France, Germany, Bastarnia, the lower parts of Syria, Idumea, and Judea: with Scorpio, he rules Syria, Comagena, Cappadocia, Metagonium, Mauritania, and Getulia.

The Sun with Leo governs Italy, Apulia, Sicilia, Phenicia, Chaldea, and the Orchenians.

Venus with Taurus governs the Isles Cyclades, the seas of Little Asia, Cyprus, Parthia, Media, Persia: but with Libra she commands the people of the island Bractia, of Caspia, of Seres, of Thebais, of Oasis, and of Troglodys.

Mercury with Gemini, rules Hircania, Armenia, Mantiana, Cyrenaica, Marmarica, and the Lower Egypt: but with Virgo, Greece, Achaia, Creta, Babylon, Mesopotamia, Assyria, and Ela, whence they of that place are in Scripture called Elamites.

The Moon with Cancer governs Bithivia, Phrygia, Colchica, Numidia, Africa, Carthage, and all Carchedonia.

These we have in this manner gathered from *Ptolemy's* opinion,[2] to which according to the writings of other astrologers many more may be added. But he which knows how to compare these divisions of provinces according to the divisions of the stars, with the ministry of the ruling intelligences, and blessings[3] of the tribes of Israel, the lots[4] of the apostles, and typical seals of the sacred Scripture, shall be able to obtain great and prophetical oracles concerning every religion, of things to come.

Notes—Chapter XXXI

1. *kingdoms and provinces*—For notes on individual geographical entities, see the Geographical Dictionary, pp. 837-850.

2. *Ptolemy's opinion*—The foregoing list has been taken from Ptolemy's *Tetrabiblos* 2.3.

3. *blessings*—Genesis 49. See also Joshua 21.

4. *lots*—Perhaps refers to the selection by lot of Matthias (Acts 1:26), but more likely to some division of nations under the apostles.

CHAPTER XXXII

What things are under the signs, the fixed stars, and their images.

The like consideration is be be had in all things concerning the figures of the fixed stars: so they will have the terrestrial ram to be under the rule of the celestial Aries: and the terrestrial bull, and ox to be under the celestial Taurus. So also that Cancer should rule over crabs, and Leo over lions, Virgo over virgins, and Scorpio over scorpions, Capricorn over goats, Sagittarius over horses, and Pisces over fishes. Also the celestial Ursa[1] over bears, Hydra[2] over serpents, and the Dogstar[3] over dogs, and so of the rest.

Now *Apuleius* distributes certain and peculiar herbs to the signs, and planets, viz. to Aries the herb sange,[4] to Taurus vervain that grows straight, to Gemini vervain that grows bending, to Cancer comfrey,[5] to Leo sowbread,[6] to Virgo calamint,[7] to Libra mugwort,[8] to Scorpio scorpion grass,[9] to Sagittarius pimpernel, to Capricorn the dock,[10] to Aquarius dragonwort,[11] to Pisces hartwort.[12] And to the planets these, viz. to Saturn sengreen,[13] to Jupiter agrimony,[14] to Mars sulphurwort,[15] to the Sun marigold, to Venus woundwort,[16] to Mercury mullein,[17] to the Moon peony.

But *Hermes,* whom *Albertus* follows, distributes to the planets these, viz. to Saturn the daffodil,[18] to Jupiter henbane, to Mars ribwort, to the Sun knotgrass,[19] to Venus vervain, to Mercury cinquefoil, to the Moon goosefoot.[20] We also know by experience that asparagus is under Aries, and garden basil under Scorpio; for of the shavings of ramshorn sowed, comes forth asparagus, and garden basil rubbed betwixt two stones, produceth scorpions.

Moreover I will according to the doctrine of *Hermes,* and *Thebit* reckon up some of the more eminent stars, whereof the first is called the Head of Algol,[21] and amongst stones rules over the diamond, amongst plants, black hellebore, and mugwort.

The second are the Pleiades,[22] or Seven Stars, which amongst stones, rule over crystal, and the stone diodocus;[23] amongst plants, the herb diacedon,[24] and frankincense, and fennil;[25] and amongst metals, quicksilver.

The third is the star Aldeboran,[26] which hath under it, amongst stones, the carbuncle, and ruby; amongst plants, the milky thistle,[27] and matry-silva.[28]

The fourth is called the Goat Star,[29] which rules, amongst stones, the sapphire; amongst plants, horehound,[30] mint, mugwort, and mandrake.

The fifth is called the Great Dog Star, which amongst stones, rules over the beryl; amongst plants, savin,[31] mugwort, and dragonwort; and amongst animals the tongue of a snake.

The sixth is called the Lesser Dog Star,[32] and amongst stones, rules over achates; amongst plants the flowers of marigold, and pennyroyal.[33]

The seventh is called the Heart of the Lion,[34] which amongst stones, rules over the granite;[35] amongst plants, sallendine, mugwort, and mastic.

The eighth is the Tail of the Lesser Bear,[36] which amongst stones, rules over the loadstone; amongst herbs, succory,[37] whose leaves, and flowers turn towards the north, also mugwort, and the flowers of periwinkle;[38] and amongst animals the tooth of a wolf.

The ninth is called the Wing of the Crow,[39] under which, amongst stones, are such stones as are of the colour of the black onyx stone; amongst plants the burr,[40] quadraginus,[41] henbane, and comfrey; and amongst animals the tongue of a frog.

The tenth is called Spica,[42] which hath under it, amongst stones, the emerald; amongst plants, sage,[43] trifoil,[44] periwinkle, mugwort, and mandrake.

The eleventh is called Alchamech,[45] which amongst stones, rules over the jasper; amongst plants the plantain.[46]

The twelfth is called Elpheia,[47] under this, amongst stones, is the topaz; amongst plants, rosemary, trifoil, and ivy.

The thirteenth is called the Heart of the Scorpion,[48] under which, amongst stones, is the sardonius,[49] and amethyst; amongst plants long aristolochy,[50] and saffron.

The fourteenth is the Falling Vulture,[51] under which, amongst stones, is the chrysolite; amongst plants succory, and fumitory.

The fifteenth is the Tail of Capricorn,[52] under which, amongst stones, is the chalcedon; amongst plants, marjoram, mugwort, and nip, and the root of mandrake.

Moreover this we must know, that every stone, or plant, or animal, or any other thing is not governed by one star alone, but many of them receive influence, not separated, but conjoined, from many stars. So amongst stones, the chalcedony is under Saturn, and Mercury, together with the Tail of Scorpion,[53] and Capricorn. The sapphire under Jupiter, Saturn, and the star Alhajoth;[54] tutia[55] is under Jupiter, and the Sun, and Moon; the emerald under Jupiter, Venus, and Mercury, and the star Spica. The amethyst, as saith *Hermes,* is under Mars, Jupiter, and the Heart of the Scorpion. The jasper which is of divers kinds is under Mars, Jupiter, and the star Alchamech; the chrysolite is under the Sun, Venus, and Mercury, as also under the star which is called the Falling Vulture; the topaz under the Sun, and the star Elpheia; the diamond under Mars, and the Head of Algol.

In like manner amongst vegetables the herb dragon is under Saturn, and the celestial Dragon;[56] mastic, and mints, are under Jupiter, and the Sun; but mastic is also under the Heart of the Lion, and mint under the Goat Star; hellebore is dedicated to Mars, and the Head of Algol; moss, and sanders, to the Sun, and Venus; coriander to Venus, and Saturn.

Amongst animals, the sea calf is under the Sun, and Jupiter; the fox, and ape under Saturn, and Mercury; and domestical dogs under Mercury, and the Moon.

And thus we have showed more things in these inferiors, by their superiors.

Notes—Chapter XXXII

1. *Ursa*—The northern constellation Ursa Major, the Great Bear, better known today as the Big Dipper.

2. *Hydra*—The southern constellation Hydra, the Water Serpent.

3. *Dogstar*—Sirius, in the southern constellation Canis Major. It is the brightest star in the heavens.

4. *sange*—Sanguinaria, or blood root *(Sanguinaria canadensis),* a bright red root supposed by the ancients to staunch blood.

5. *comfrey*—A wound-herb *(Symphytum officinale)* with white or purple bell-shaped flowers.

6. *sowbread*—*Cyclamen europaeum,* the root of which was used as a purge.

7. *calamint*—An aromatic herb *(Calamintha officinalis)* said to be good against snakebite.

8. *mugwort*—*Artemisia vulgaris,* also called motherwort because it was used as an aid in childbirth.

9. *scorpion grass*—Of the genus *Myosotis;* forget-me-not or mouse-ear.

10. *dock*—A large plant *(Rumex obtusifolius)* often mistaken for rhubarb. Its juice was said to counteract stinging nettle.

11. *dragonwort*—See note 8, ch. XXV, bk. I.

12. *hartwort*—Heartwort *(Aristolochia clemantitis),* also called birthwort.

13. *sengreen*—See note 3, ch. XXVI, bk. I.

14. *agrimony*—*Agrimonia eupatoria,* also called liverwort.

15. *sulphurwort*—*Peucedanum officinale,* also called hog's fennel.

16. *woundwort*—In the Latin *Opera,* "*Veneri panace siue callitrichu.*" Of English, or common, maidenhair *(Asplenium trichomanes),* Gerard says, "*Apuleius in his 51 chapter maketh it all one with Callitrichon:*" (Gerard [1633] 1975, bk. 2, ch. 474, 1146). Woundwort was a general name for herbs that healed wounds. In ancient times three main types of woundwort, or *panaces,* were recognized, each named after its mythical discoverer. Conjecturally identified, these are: Hercules' woundwort *(Origanum heracleoticum),* Asclepius' woundwort *(Ferula galbaniflua)* and Chiron's woundwort *(Inula helenium).* See Pliny 25.11–3 (Bostock and Riley, 5:89–90).

17. *mullein*—Common, or great torch, mullein *(Verbascum thapsus),* a tall plant with woolly leaves and yellow flowers.

18. *daffodil*—White daffodil, or affodill. See note 7, ch. XXV, bk. I.

19. *knotgrass*—*Polygonum aviculare.* "This herb taketh the name of the Sun, for it engendereth greatly, and so this herb worketh many ways. Other hath called this herb *Alchone,* which is the house of the Sun" *(Book of Secrets* 1.22 [Best and Brightman, 19]).

20. *goosefoot*—Of the genus *Chenopodium,* so called because of the shape of the leaves.

21. *Head of Algol*—Algol means literally "the ghoul," a bright, variable star in the northern constellation Perseus. It has the reputation of being the most evil of all the stars. See note 3, ch. XXXI, bk. II.

22. *Pleiades*—Group of seven stars in the northern constellation Taurus, said to represent the seven daughters of Atlas and Pleione. Only six stars are now visible, and the seventh is called the "lost Pleiad." See note 4, ch. XXXI, bk. II.

23. *diodocus*—"Diadochos ['substitute'] is a stone that resembles beryl" (Pliny 37.57 [Bostock and Riley, 6:447]).

24. *diacedon*—Perhaps diaxylon, or camel's thorn *(Alhagi maurorum),* a thorny perfume-scented plant that is supposed to smell indescribably sweet when a rainbow forms over it. See Pliny 12.52 (Bostock and Riley, 3:146), also 24.69 (Bostock and Riley, 5:45).

25. *fennil*—A plant *(Faeniculum vulgare)* with yellow flowers that grows three to four feet high, and is allied to dill.

26. *Aldeboran*—Aldebaran, the name for the Sun in Arabian mythology. A bright red star in the constellation Taurus, called the Bull's Eye.

27. *milky thistle*—Milk thistle *(Carduus marianus),* a European plant that grows four to six feet tall and has milky veins running through its leaves. It is also called lady's thistle.

28. *matry-silva*—Mother of the wood, or woodruff *(Asperula odorata).*

29. *Goat Star*—Capella, in the northern constellation Auriga.

30. *horehound*—Common, or white, hoarhound *(Marrubium vulgare),* a bitter herb used in treating cough, the womb and the liver. It derives its name from the white cottony down that covers its stem and leaves, resembling hoarfrost.

31. *savin*—A small, bushy evergreen shrub *(Juniperus sabina)* with purple berries. It is poisonous. The dried tops of the herb were used to procure abortions, kill intestinal worms, and relieve asthma. Also spelled savine.

32. *Lesser Dog Star*—Procyon, in the southern constellation Canis Minor.

33. *pennyroyal*—A species of mint *(Mentha pulegium).*

34. *Heart of the Lion*—Cor Leonis, or Regulus, a star in the northern constellation Leo.

35. *granite*—Garnet, meaning "seed," from the resemblance of this gem to the seeds of pomegranate. A silicate that comes in a variety of colors, the most prized being a deep transparent red.

36. *Tail of the Lesser Bear*—Polaris, the North Star, which marks the tail of Ursa Minor.

37. *succory*—A plant *(Cichorium intybus)* with blue flowers, a carrot-like root and milky juice that grows from two to five feet tall. The juice poured into the ear or nostril on the opposite side of the head is sup-

posed to cure the pain of toothache. Pounded and placed in a poultice under the left nipple, it supposedly eased heartache. Also called chicory.

38. *periwinkle*—There are two kinds: greater periwinkle *(Vinca major)* and lesser periwinkle *(Vinca minor)*. An evergreen trailing sub-shrub with blue, or in *V. minor* sometimes white, flowers. It Italy it was called *fiore di morte* (flower of death) because those about to be executed were garlanded with it; and it was wrapped around dead infants. But Culpeper says the herbs are under Venus, and that "the leaves eaten by man and wife together cause love between them."

39. *Wing of the Crow*—Gienah, from the Arabic *Al Janah al Ghurab al Aiman,* "the Right Wing of the Raven"; however this star is marked on modern charts in the left wing of the southern constellation Corvus. The star in the right wing is called Algorab.

40. *burr*—Probably refers to the flowerhead of burdock *(Arctium lappa)*.

41. *quadraginus*—Perhaps the lent-lily, or yellow daffodil *(Narcissus pseudo-narcissus)*.

42. *Spica*—Latin for "ear of grain," a bright star in the constellation Virgo, which straddles the equator.

43. *sage*—A semi-shrub *(Salvia officinalis)* that grows about two feet high with oblong whitish-gray leaves and purple flowers. In ancient times it was said to help the memory.

44. *trifoil*—Trefoil, or clover *(Trifolium),* a name applied to small cultivated plants with triple leaves. Red clover *(T. pratense)* was reputed to repel witches, and was worn for this purpose as a charm.

45. *Alchamech*—Arcturus, in the northern constellation Boötes. The name given by Agrippa is a corruption of the Arabic *Al Simak al Ramih,* "the Lofty Lance-bearer."

46. *plantain*—Greater plantaini, or waybread *(Plantago major)*.

47. *Elpheia*—Alphecca, from the Arabic *Al Fakkah,* "the Dish," a star in the northern constellation Corona Borealis.

48. *Heart of the Scorpion*—Antares in the southern constellation Scorpio. The name means "like Ares (Mars)," after the red color of this star.

49. *sardonius*—Sardonyx, a variety of onyx, or layered chalcedony. The most prized have a white opaque layer of chalcedony on a flesh-colored transparent layer of sard (Greek: "flesh"). Cameos were cut in the white layer with the pink for a ground and were much prized by the Romans. It was generally a lucky stone, diminishing pain, giving self-control, conjugal happiness and success in legal affairs.

50. *long aristolochy*—Long aristolochia *(Aristolochia longa),* not to be confused with round aristolochia *(A. rotunda)*. Both are native to southern Europe and are often treated together. A herbaceous shrub used as an aid in childbirth. The name comes from the Greek for "well born."

51. *Falling Vulture*—The star Vega in the northern constellation Lyra. In ancient times the constellation itself was called the Swooping or Falling Vulture.

52. *Tail of Capricorn*—Deneb Algedi, from the Arabic *Al Dhanab al Jady,* "the Tail of the Goat." The star Delta Capricorni in the southern constellation Capricorn. It is also sometimes called Scheddi.

53. *Tail of Scorpion*—Shaula (Lambda Scorpii), from the Arabic *Al Shaulah,* "the Sting"; but according to Al Biruni, from *Mushalah,* "raised"; i.e., the sting raised to strike. It was, not surprisingly, regarded as an unlucky star. Located in the southern constellation Scorpio.

54. *Alhajoth*—From the Arabic *Al Ayyuk.* Capella, the Goat.

55. *tutia*—Tutty, an oxide of zinc that forms in flakes, or flowers, on the inside of the furnace flues where brass is smelted. It was made into an astringent ointment or lotion for treating wounds and clearing the eyes of rheum. The whiter oxide was distinguished by the name pomphorlyx, while the grayer was called tutty.

56. *celestial Dragon*—The northern constellation Draco.

CHAPTER XXXIII

Of the seals, and characters of natural things.

All stars have their peculiar natures, properties, and conditions, the seals and characters whereof they produce through their rays even in these inferior things, viz. in elements, in stones, in plants, in animals, and their members, whence everything receives from an harmonious disposition, and from its star shining upon it, some particular seal, or character stamped upon it, which is the significator of that star, or harmony, containing in it a peculiar virtue differing from other virtues of the same matter, both generically, specifically, and numerically.

Everything therefore hath its character pressed upon it by its star for some peculiar effect, especially by that star which doth principally govern it: and these characters contain, and retain in them the peculiar natures, virtues, and roots of their stars, and produce the like operations upon other things, on which they are reflected, and stir up, and help the influences of their stars, whether they be planets, or fixed stars, and figures, and celestial signs, viz. as oft as they shall be made in a fit matter, and in their due, and accustomed times.

Which ancient wise men considering, such as laboured much in the finding out of the occult properties of figures, seals, marks, characters, such as Nature herself did describe by the rays of the stars, in these inferior bodies, some in stones, some in plants, and joints, and knots of boughs, and some in divers members of animals. For the bay tree, the lote-tree, the marigold are solary plants, and in their roots, and knots being cut off, show the characters of the Sun, so also in the bone, and shoulder blades in animals: whence there arose a spatulary kind of divining i.e. by the shoulder blades; and in stones, and stony things the characters, and images of celestial things are often found.

But seeing that in so great a diversity of things there is not a traditional knowledge, only in a few things, which human understanding is able to reach: therefore leaving those things which are to be found out in plants, and stones, and other things, as also, in the members of divers animals, we shall limit ourselves to man's nature only, which seeing it is the completest image of the whole universe, containing in itself the whole heavenly harmony, will without all doubt abundantly afford us the seals, and characters of all the stars, and celestial influences, and those as the more efficacious, which are less differing from the celestial nature.

But as the number of the stars is known to God alone, so also their effects, and seals upon these inferior things: wherefore no human intellect is able to attain to the knowledge of them. Whence very few of those things became known to us, which the ancient philosophers, and chiromancers[1] attained to, partly by reason, and partly by experience, and there be many things yet lie hid in the treasury of nature.

We shall here in this place note some few seals, and characters of the planets, such as the ancient chiromancers knew in the hands of

THERE FOLLOW THE FIGURES OF DIVINE LETTERS.

The letters, or characters of *Saturn:*

The letters, or characters of *Jupiter:*

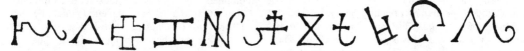

The letters, or characters of *Mars:*

The letters, or characters of the *Sun:*

The letters, or characters of *Venus:*

The letters, or characters of *Mercury:*

The letters, or characters of the *Moon:*

men.[2] These doth *Julian* call sacred, and divine letters, seeing that by them according to the holy Scripture is the life of men writ in their hands.[3] And there are in all nations, and languages, always the same, and like to them, and permanent; to which were added, and found out afterwards many more, as by the ancient, so by latter chiromancers. And they that would know them must have recourse to their volumes. It is sufficient here to show from whence the characters of nature have their original, and in what things they are to be inquired after.

Notes—Chapter XXXIII

1. *chiromancers*—From the Greek for "hand divination"; those who divine by reading the lines and other features of the hand. Chiromancy dates back to at least 3000 BC, when it was practiced in China. The most ancient classical writers refer to it—several allusions are made to palm reading by Homer, for example. Early writers on the subject include Melampus of Alexandria, Palemon, Adamantius, Aristotle, Hippocrates, Galen and Paulus Ægineta. A list of 98 works on this subject written before 1700 has been compiled, although, as with most received lore, they show little variation. Special mention might be made of *Die Kunst Ciromantia,* published at Augsburg in 1470, which may have been known by Agrippa.

2. *hands of men*—The lines in the palm may be broken down into a small number of basic elements, of which the Comte de Saint-Germain, in his *Practice of Palmistry* (1897), gives 16, as shown below.

3. *in their hands*—Proverbs 3:16. See also Job 37:7.

DOTS OR SPOTS	CIRCLES	ISLANDS	SQUARES
ANGLES	TRIANGLES	CROSSES	GRILLS
STARS	SIGN OF JUPITER	SIGN OF SATURN	SIGN OF THE SUN
SIGN OF MERCURY	SIGN OF MARS	SIGN OF THE MOON	SIGN OF VENUS

Table of 16 Signs

CHAPTER XXXIV

How by natural things, and their virtues we may draw forth, and attract the influences, and virtues of celestial bodies.

Now if thou desirest to receive virtue from any part of the world, or from any star, thou shalt (those things being used which belong to this star) come under its peculiar influence, as wood is fit to receive flame, by reason of sulphur, pitch, and oil. Nevertheless when thou dost to any one species of things, or individual, rightly apply many things, which are things of the same subject scattered amongst themselves, conformable to the same Idea, and star, presently by this matter so opportunely fitted, a singular gift is infused by the Idea, by means of the Soul of the World.

I say opportunely fitted, viz. under a harmony like to the harmony, which did infuse a certain virtue into the matter. For although things have some virtues, such as we speak of, yet those virtues do so lie hid that there is seldom any effect produced by them: but as in a grain of mustard seed bruised, the sharpness which lay hid is stirred up: and as the heat of the fire doth make letters apparently seen, which before could

not be read, that were writ with the juice of an onion or milk:[1] and letters wrote upon a stone with the fat of a goat, and altogether unperceived, when the stone is put into vinegar, appear and show themselves. And as a blow with a stick stirs up the madness of a dog, which before lay asleep, so doth the celestial harmony disclose virtues lying in the water, stirs them up, strengtheneth them, and makes them manifest, and as I may so say, produceth that into act, which before was only in power, when things are rightly exposed to it in a celestial season.

As for example; if thou dost desire to attract virtue from the Sun, and to seek those things that are solary, amongst vegetables, plants, metals, stones, and animals, these things are to be used, and taken chiefly, which in a solary order are higher. For these are more available: so thou shalt draw a singular gift from the Sun through the beams thereof, being seasonably received together, and through the Spirit of the World.

Notes—Chapter XXXIV

1. *onion or milk*—Milk is one of the oldest and simplest kinds of invisible ink. A formula containing it is given in *The Book of Secrets:* "To write letters or bills, which be not read but in the night. Take the gall of a Snail or milk of a Sow, and put it to the fire, or with water of a worm shining late" ("Marvels of the World" 49 [Best and Brightman, 96]). The "worm shining late" is the glowworm (*Lampyris noctiluca*).

CHAPTER XXXV

Of the mixtions of natural things one with another, and their benefit.

It is most evident, that in the inferior nature all the powers of superior bodies are not found comprehended in any one thing, but are dispersed through many kinds of things amongst us: as there are many solary things, whereof every one doth not contain all the virtues of the Sun: but some have some properties from the Sun, and others othersome. Wherefore it is sometimes necessary that there be mixtions in operations, that if a hundred or a thousand virtues of the Sun were dispersed through so many plants, animals, and the like, we may gather all these together, and bring them into one form, in which we shall see all the said virtues, being united, contained.[1]

Now there is a twofold virtue in commixtion, one, viz. which was first planted in its parts, and is celestial, the other is obtained by a certain, and artificial mixtion of things mixed amongst themselves, and of the mixtions of them according to certain proportions, such as agree with the heaven under a certain constellation; and this virtue descends by a certain likeness, and aptness that is in things amongst themselves towards their superiors, and as much as the following do by degrees correspond with them that go before, where the patient is fitly applied to its agent.

So from a certain composition of herbs, vapours, and such like, made according to natural philosophy, and astronomy, there results a certain common form, endowed with many gifts of the stars: as in the honey of bees, that which is gathered out of the juice of innumerable flowers, and brought into one form, contains the virtue of all, by a kind of divine, and admirable art of the bees. Yet this is not to be less wondered at which *Eudoxus Giudius* reports of an artificial kind of honey, which a certain nation of giants in Libya[2] knew how to make out of flowers, and that very good, and not far inferior to that of the bees.

For every mixtion, which consists of many several things, is then most perfect, when it is so firmly compacted on all parts, that it becomes one, is everywhere firm to itself, and can hardly be dissipated: as we sometimes see stones, and divers bodies to be by a certain natural power conglutinated, and united, that they seem to be wholly one thing: as we see two trees by grafting to become one, also oysters with stones by a certain occult virtue of nature, and there have been seen some animals which have been turned into stones,[3] and so united with the substance of the stone, that they seem to make one body, and that also homogeneous. So the tree ebony[4] is one while wood, and another while stone.

When therefore anyone makes a mixtion of many matters under the celestial influences, then the variety of celestial actions on one hand, and of natural powers on the other hand, being joined together doth indeed cause wonderful things, by ointments, by collyries, by fumes, and such like, which viz. are read in the book of *Chiramis, Archyta, Democritus,* and *Hermes,* who is named *Alchorat,*[5] and of many others.

Notes—Chapter XXXV

1. *being united, contained*—Agrippa's contemporary Paracelsus (1493–1541), the German mystical philosopher and physician, was less enthusiastic about the virtue of mixtures:

> The art of prescribing medicine lies in nature, which compounds them herself. If she has put into gold what belongs to gold, she has done likewise with violets ... Therefore understand me correctly: the virtue that is inherent in each thing is homogeneous and simple, it is not split into two, three, four, or five, but is an undivided whole ... The art of prescribing medicines consists in extracting and not in compounding, it consists in the discovery of that which is concealed in things, and not in compounding various things and piecing them together. (Paracelsus *Selected Writings,* trans. N. Guterman [Princeton University Press, 1973], 90)

2. *giants in Libya*—Libya is supposed to have been the birthplace of Antaeus, the giant who wrestled Hercules:

> Earth, not as yet barren, after the Giants being born, conceived a dreadful offspring in the Libyan caves. Nor to the Earth was Typhon so just a ground of pride, or Tityus and the fierce Briareus; and she spared the heavens, in that she did not bring forth Antaeus in the Phlegraen fields. By this privilege as well did the Earth redouble the strength so vast of her offspring, in that, when they touched their parent, the limbs now exhausted were vigorous again with renewed strength. This cavern was his abode; they report that under the lofty rock he lay concealed, and had caught lions for his food. For his sleep no skins of wild beasts were wont to afford a bed, no wood a couch, and lying on the bare earth he recovered his strength. (Lucan *Pharsalia* 4, c. line 593 ff. [Riley, 154])

3. *turned into stones*—Fossils.

4. *ebony*—Ebony *(Diospyros ebenum)* is the heartwood of a large tree native to Sri Lanka, very dense and hard, the best being a uniform black. Ebony is so hard, in fact, that it has many of the qualities of a mineral.

5. *Alchorat*—*The Book of Alchorath,* a collection of wonders, is attributed to Hermes in *The Book of Secrets,* where reference is made to "the book of *Alchorath,* of Mercury" (Best and Brightman, 54) and "Hermes in the book of *Alchorath"* (ibid., 57). Alchorat = *Arpocrationis,* i.e. Harpocration, or perhaps Hippocrates (see *Book of Secrets* [Best and Brightman, introduction, xli]).

CHAPTER XXXVI

Of the union of mixed things, and the introduction of a more noble form, and the senses of life.

oreover we must know, that by how much the more noble the form of anything is, by so much the more prone, and apt it is to receive, and powerful to act. Then the virtues of things do then become wonderful, viz. when they are put to matters that are mixed, and prepared in fit seasons, to make them alive, by procuring life for them from the stars, as also a sensible soul, as a more noble form. For there is so great a power in prepared matters which we see do then receive life, when a perfect mixtion of qualities seems to break the former contrarity. For so much the more perfect life things receive, by how much their temper is more remote from contrarity.

Now the heaven, as a prevalent cause doth from the beginning of everything to be generated by the concoction, and perfect digestion of the matter, together with life, bestows celestial influences, and wonderful gifts, according to the capacity that is in that life, and sensible soul to receive more noble, and sublime virtues. For the celestial virtue doth otherwise lie asleep, as sulphur kept from flame, but in living bodies it doth always burn, as kindled sulphur, then by its vapour it fills all the places that are next to it; so certain wonderful works are wrought, such as are read in the book of *Nemith,* which is titled a Book of the Laws of Pluto, because such kind of monstrous generations are not produced according to the laws of nature.

For we know that of worms are generated gnats; of a horse wasps; of a calf, and ox bees; of a crab, his legs being taken off, and he buried in the ground, a scorpion; of a duck dried into powder, and put into water, are generated frogs, but if it be baked in a pie, and cut into pieces, and put into a moist place under the ground, toads are generated of it; of the herb garden basil bruised betwixt two stones, are generated scorpions; and of the hairs of a menstruous woman put under dung, are bred serpents; and the hair of a horse tail put into water, receiveth life, and is turned into a pernicious worm. And there is an art wherewith by a hen sitting upon eggs may be generated a form like to a man,[1] which I have seen and know how to make, which magicians say hath in it wonderful virtues, and this they call the true mandrake.

You must therefore know which, and what kind of matters are either of nature, or art, begun, or perfected, or compounded of more things, and what celestial influences they are able to receive. For a congruity of natural things is sufficient for the receiving of influence from celestial; because when nothing doth hinder the celestials to send forth their lights upon inferiors, they suffer no matter to be destitute of their virtue. Wherefore as much matter as is perfect, and pure, is not unfit to receive the celestial influence. For that is the binding and continuity of the matter to the Soul of the World, which doth daily flow in upon things natural, and all things which nature hath prepared, that it is impossible that a prepared matter should not receive life, or a more noble form.

Homunculus

Notes—Chapter XXXVI

1. *form like a man*—A homunculus, or "little man." This magical being is most closely associated with Paracelsus, who expounded on its manufacture. Certain "spagyric" (a word coined by him, meaning hermetic, or alchemic) substances are shut in a glass vessel, then placed in the gentle warmth of horse manure for 40 days, at the end of which period some- thing living will stir inside the glass, like a man but transparent and without a body. He is fed each day on the arcanum of human blood for a span of 40 weeks while remaining in the womb of the dunghill. A perfectly proportioned living child emerges, smaller than one conceived in the normal way, and requiring greater care in the bringing up.

CHAPTER XXXVII

How by some certain natural, and artificial preparations we may attract certain celestial, and vital gifts.

Platonists, together with *Hermes,* say, and *Jarchus Brachmanus* and the mecubals[1] of the Hebrews confess, that all sublunary things are subject to generation, and corruption, and that also there are the same things in the celestial world, but after a celestial manner, as also in the intellectual world, but in a far more perfect, and better fashion, and manner, but in the most perfect manner of all in the exemplary. And after this course, that every inferior should in its kind answer its superior, and through this the Supreme itself, and receive from heaven that celestial power that they call the quintessence, or the Spirit of the World, or the middle nature, and from the intellectual world a spiritual and enlivening virtue transcending all qualities whatsoever, and lastly from the exemplary or original world, through the mediation of the other, according to their degree receive the original power of the whole perfection.

Hence everything may be aptly reduced from these inferiors to the stars, from the stars to their intelligences, and from thence to the First Cause itself; from the series, and order whereof whole magic, and all occult philosophy flows: for every day some natural thing is drawn by art, and some divine thing drawn by nature, which the Egyptians seeing, called Nature a magicianess, i.e. the very magical power itself, in the attracting of like by like, and of suitable things by suitable.

Now such kind of attractions by the mutual correspondency of things amongst themselves, of superiors with inferiors, the Grecians called συμπάθεια:[2] so the Earth agrees with cold Water, the Water with moist Air, the Air with Fire, the Fire with the Water in heaven; neither is Fire mixed with Water, but by Air, nor the Air with the Earth, but by Water.[3] So neither is the soul united to the body, but by the spirit, nor the understanding to the spirit but by the soul.

So we see when Nature hath framed the body of the infant, by this very preparative she presently fetcheth the spirit from the universe. This spirit is the instrument to obtain of God the understanding, and mind in the soul, and body, as in wood the dryness is fitted to receive oil, and the oil being imbibed is food for the fire, the fire is the vehiculum of light.

By these examples you see how by some certain natural, and artificial preparations, we are in a capacity to receive certain celestial gifts from above. For stones, and metals have a correspondency with herbs, herbs with animals, animals with the heavens, the heavens with intelligences, and those with divine properties, and attributes, and with God himself, after whose image, and likeness all things are created.

Now the first image of God is the world; of the world, man; of man, beasts; of beasts, the zeophyton[4] i.e. half animal, and half plant; of zeophyton, plants; of plants, metals; of metals, stones. And again in things spiritual, the plant agrees with a brute in vegetation,[5] a brute with a man in sense, man with an angel in understand-

110

ing, an angel with God in immortality. Divinity is annexed to the mind, the mind to the intellect, the intellect to the intention, the intention to the imagination, the imagination to the senses, the senses at last to things.

For this is the band, and continuity of nature, that all superior virtue doth flow through every inferior with a long, and continued series, dispersing its rays even to the very last things; and inferiors through their superiors, come to the very Supreme of all. For so inferiors are successively joined to their superiors, that there proceeds an influence from their head, the First Cause, as a certain string stretched out, to the lowermost things of all, of which string if one end be touched, the whole doth presently shake, and such a touch doth sound to the other end, and at the motion of the inferior, the superior also is moved, to which the other doth answer, as strings in a lute well tuned.

Notes—Chapter XXXVII

1. *mecubals*—Mecubalists, those versed in Jewish tradition.

2. συμπαθεια—*Sympatheia:* sympathy.

3. *but by Water*—See Appendix III.

4. *zeophyton*—Zoophytes.

5. *vegetation*—Growth.

CHAPTER XXXVIII

How we may draw not only celestial, and vital, but also certain intellectual and divine gifts from above.

Magicians teach that celestial gifts may through inferiors being conformable to superiors be drawn down by opportune influences of the heaven; and so also by these celestial, the celestial angels, as they are servants of the stars, may be procured and conveyed to us. *Jamblichus, Proclus,* and *Synesius,* with the whole school of Platonists confirm, that not only celestial, and vital, but also certain intellectual, angelical, and divine gifts may be received from above by some certain matters, having a natural power of divinity i.e. which have a natural correspondency with the superiors, being rightly received, and opportunely gathered together according to the rules of natural philosophy, and astronomy: and *Mercurius Trismegistus* writes,[1] that an image rightly made of certain proper things, appropriated to any one certain angel, will presently be animated by that angel. Of the same also *Austin* makes mention[2] in his eighth book De Civitate Dei.

For this is the harmony of the world, that things supercelestial be drawn down by the celestial, and supernatural by natural, because there is one operative virtue that is diffused through all kinds of things; by which virtue indeed, as manifest things are produced out of occult causes, so a magician doth make use of things manifest, to draw forth things that are occult, viz. through the rays of the stars, through fumes, lights, sounds, and natural things, which are agreeable to celestial: in which, besides corporeal qualities, there is a kind of reason, sense, and harmony, and incorporeal, and divine measures, and orders.

So we read that the ancients were wont often to receive some divine, and wonderful thing by certain natural things: so the stone that is bred in the apple of the eye of a civet[3] cat, held under the tongue of a man, is said to make him to divine, or prophesy: the same is selenites, the Moon stone reported to do: so they say that the images of gods may be called up by the stone called anchitis, and that the ghosts of the dead may be, being called up, kept up by the stone synochitis.

The like doth the herb aglauphotis[4] do, which is called marmorites, growing upon the marbles of Arabia, as saith *Pliny,* and the which magicians use. Also there is a herb called rheangelida,[5] which magicians drinking of, can prophesy. Moreover there are some herbs by which the dead are raised to life; whence *Xanthus* the historian tells, that with a certain herb called balus,[6] a young dragon being killed, was made alive again, also that by the same a certain man of Tillum, whom a dragon killed, was restored to life: and *Juba* reports,[7] that in Arabia a certain man was by a certain herb restored to life. But whether or no any such things can be done indeed upon man by the virtue of herbs, or any other natural thing, we shall discourse in the following chapter.

Now it is certain, and manifest that such things can be done upon other animals. So if flies, that are drowned, be put into warm ashes, they revive. And bees being drowned, do in like manner recover life in the juice of the herb nip; and eels being dead for want of water, if with their whole bodies they be put under mud in vinegar, and the blood of a vulture being put to them, will all of them in a few days recover life. They say that if the fish echeneis be cut into pieces, and cast into the sea, the parts will within a little time come together, and live. Also we know that the pelican doth restore her young to life, being killed, with her own blood.

Notes—Chapter XXXVIII

1. *Mercurius Trismegistus writes—*

Our ancestors went far astray from the truth about the gods; they had no belief in them, and gave no heed to worship and religion. But afterwards, they invented the art of making gods out of some material substance suited for the purpose. And to this invention they added a supernatural force whereby the images might have power to work good or hurt, and combined it with the material substance; that is to say, being unable to make souls, they invoked the souls of daemons, and implanted them in the statues by means of certain holy and sacred words. … They are induced [into the statues], Asclepius, by means of herbs and stones and scents which have in them something divine. And would you know why frequent sacrifices are offered to do them pleasure, with hymns and praises and concord of sweet sounds that imitate heaven's harmony? These things are done to the end that, gladdened by oft-repeated worship, the heavenly beings who have been enticed into the images may continue through long ages to acquiesce in the companionship of men. *(Asclepius III* 37, 38a. In Scott [1924] 1985, 1:359, 361)

2. *Austin makes mention—*

But Trismegistus says that the high God made some gods, and men made others. These words, as I write them, might be understood of images, because they are the works of men. But he calls visible and palpable images the bodies of the gods, wherein are spirits that have power to hurt or please such as give them divine honours. So then, to combine such an invisible spirit by art with a visible image of some certain substance, which it must use as the soul does the body, this is to make a god, says he, and this wonderful power of making gods is in the hands of man. (Augustine *City of God* 8.23 [Healey, 2:245–6])

3. *of a civet*—Again, it is the hyena, not the civet, to which this virtue is ascribed by Pliny: "Hyaenia [hyena stone] is derived from the eyes of the hyena, it is said, the animal being hunted to obtain it; pleaced beneath the tongue, if we believe the story, it will enable a person to prophesy the future" (Pliny 37.60 [Bostock and Riley, 6:451]).

4. *aglauphotis*—

According to him [Democritus], the plant aglaophotis ["bright light"], which owes its name to the admiration in which its beauteous tints are held by man, is found growing among the marble quarries of Arabia, on the side of Persia, a circumstance which has given it the additional name of "marmaritis." By means of this plant, he says, the Magi can summon the deities into their presence when they please. (Pliny 24.102 [Bostock and Riley, 5:64])

It has been conjectured that this herb is peony *(Paeonia officinalis).*

5. *rheangelida*—Theangelida. "The theangelis, he [Democritus] says, grows upon Mount Lebanus in Syria, upon the chain of mountains called Dicte in Crete, and at Babylon and Susa in Persia. An infusion of it in drink, imparts powers of divination to the Magi" (ibid., 65–6). This herb is unknown. The name means "messenger from god."

6. *balus*—Balis. "Xanthus, the author of some historical works, tells us, in the first of them, that a young dragon was restored to life by its parent through the agency of a plant to which he gives the name of 'ballis,' and that one Tylon, who had been killed by a dragon, was restored to life and health by similar means" (Pliny 25.5 [Bostock and Riley, 5:82]). Balis is conjectured to be squirting cucumber *(Momordica elaterium).*

7. *Juba reports*—"Juba too assures us that in Arabia a man was resuscitated by the agency of a certain plant" (ibid.).

CHAPTER XXXIX

That we may by some certain matters of the world stir up the gods of the world, and their ministering spirits.

No man is ignorant that evil spirits, by evil, and prophane arts may be raised up, as *Psellus* saith sorcerers are wont to do, whom most detestable, and abominable filthiness did follow, and accompany, such as were in times past in the sacrifices of *Priapus,*[1] and in the worship of the idol which was called *Panor,* to whom they did sacrifice with their privy members uncovered. Neither to these is that unlike (if it be true, and not a fable) which is read concerning the detestable heresy of old Church-men,[2] and like to these are manifest in witches and mischievous women,[3] which wickedness the foolish dotage of women is subject to fall into. By these, and such as these evil spirits are raised. As a wicked spirit spake once to *John,* of one *Cynops* a sorcerer; all the power, saith he, of Satan dwells there, and he is entered into a confederacy with all the principalities together, and likewise we, with him, and *Cynops* obeys us, and we again obey him.

Again, on the contrary side, no man is ignorant that supercelestial angels or spirits may be gained by us through good works, a pure mind, secret prayers, devout humiliation, and the like. Let no man therefore doubt that in like manner by some certain matters of the world, the gods of the world may be raised by us, or at least the ministering spirits, or servants of these gods, and as *Mercurius* saith, the airy spirits,[4] not supercelestial, much less higher.

So we read that the ancient priests made statues, and images, foretelling things to come, and infused into them the spirits of the stars, which were not kept there by constraint in some certain matters, but rejoicing in them, viz. as acknowledging such kinds of matter to be suitable to them, they do always, and willingly abide in them, and speak, and do wonderful things by them: no otherwise than evil spirits are wont to do, when they possess men's bodies.

Notes—Chapter XXXIX

1. *Priapus*—The ugly son of Dionysus and Aphrodite, he was the god of fertility in crops and domestic animals. Credited with prophetic powers, he was worshiped with the sacrifice of first fruits of gardens, vineyards, and fields, and with milk, honey and cakes, rams, asses, and fishes. Ovid calls him "ruddy Priapus, the deity and guardian of the gardens ..." *(Fasti* 1, line 415, trans. Henry T. Riley [London: George Bell and Sons, 1881], 28).

2. *old Church-men*—The Knights Templars, whose secret order was founded by the Burgundian Hugues de Payns, and the French knight Godeffroi de St. Omer, for the purpose of guarding pilgrims on the road to the Holy Land. Baldwin I, King of Jerusalem, gave them a portion of his palace next to the mosque that was reputed to have been part of the temple of Solomon. The Order quickly grew in wealth and influence. By the middle of the 12th century it had groups all over Europe. Because of its unique posi-

Priapus

tion it was able to amass an immense fortune trading between East and West. This attracted the avarice of Philip IV of France, and when his supporter Pope Clement V gained the papacy, the Templars were denounced as heretics. A man named Esquian de Horian was brought forward to reveal the horrible secrets of the Order, which supposedly included spitting and trampling on the cross, eating roast babies (an old favorite with denouncers), and worshiping a graven image named Baphomet. God was renounced thrice with the words *Je reney Deu.* No doubt some part of some of the stories was true. A strange cross fertilization had taken place between East and West in the sealed vaults of the Templars, resulting in the resurrection of some modified form of gnosticism. One theory is that God was renounced in a mystery play, in which the initiate played a sinner soon to be converted to Christianity. But the real motives for the persecution were fear and greed. Public proceedings were begun at Paris in the spring of 1316. Philip seized the treasure of the French Templars and

became as a result fabulously rich. The Order was suppressed everywhere, though not with the same severity as in France, and ceased to exist, at least officially.

3. *mischievous women*—Witches were widely reported to keep demon lovers, and even to cohabit with Satan himself. On this matter the *Malleus Malificarum* asserts:

> All witchcraft comes from carnal lust, which is in women insatiable. See Proverbs XXX: There are three things that are never satisfied, yea, a forth thing which says not, It is enough; that is, the mouth of the womb. Wherefore for the sake of fulfilling their lusts they consort even with devils. (Kramer and Sprenger *Malleus Malificarum* 1.6, trans. M. Summers [1928] [New York: Dover, 1971], 47)

Women were supposed not only to be driven by

Witch with Demon Lover

from *Von den Unholden oder Hexen* by Ulrich Molitor (Constanz, 1489)

Baphomet

from *Dogme et Rituel de la Haute Magie* by Eliphas Levi (Paris, 1855–6)

uncontrollable lust, but also to be inherently malicious, and to have the minds of children:

> Others again have propounded other reasons why there are more superstitious women found than men. And the first is, that they are more credulous [ibid. 43]. ... The second reason is, that women are naturally more impressionable, and more ready to receive the influences of a disembodied spirit; [ibid. 44]. ... The third reason is that they have slippery tongues, ... Terence says: Women are intellectually like children. ... But the natural reason is that she is more carnal than a man [ibid. 45], ... Women have also weak memories [ibid. 46]. ... et al. ad nauseam.

The *Malleus* is one of the few truly evil books that have ever been written. Agrippa was thoroughly familiar with this German work, published in 1486, and fought against it when he defended the accused witch at Metz.

4. *airy spirits*—"I say that there are daemons who dwell with us here on earth, and others who dwell above us in the lower air, and others again, whose abode is in the purest part of the air, where no mist or cloud can be, and where no disturbance is caused by the motion of any of the heavenly bodies" *(Asclepius 33b* [Scott, 1:369, 371]).

CHAPTER XL

Of bindings, what sort they are of, and in what ways they are wont to be done.

We have spoken concerning the virtues, and wonderful efficacy of natural things. It remains now that we understand a thing of great wonderment: and it is a binding of men into love, or hatred, sickness or health, and such like. Also the binding of thieves, and robbers, that they cannot steal[1] in any place; the binding of merchants, that they cannot buy, or sell in any place; the binding of an army, that they cannot pass over any bound; the binding of ships, that no winds, though never so strong, shall be able to carry them out of the haven. Also the binding of a mill, that it can by no force whatsoever be turned round: the binding of a cistern, or fountain, that the water cannot be drawn up out of them: the binding of the ground, that it cannot bring forth fruit: the binding of any place, that nothing can be built upon it: the binding of fire, that though it be never so strong, can burn no combustible thing that is put to it. Also the bindings of lightnings, and tempests, that they shall do no hurt. Also the binding of dogs, that they cannot bark. Also the binding of birds, and wild beasts, that they shall not be able to fly, or run away. And such like as these, which are scarce credible; yet often known by experience.

Now there are such kind of bindings as these made by sorceries, collyries, unguents, love potions, by binding to, and hanging up of things, by rings, by charms, by strong imaginations, and passions, by images, and characters, by enchantments, and imprecations, by lights, by sound, by numbers, by words, and names, invocations, sacrifices, by swearing, conjuring, consecrations, devotions, and by divers superstitions, and observations, and such like.

Notes—Chapter XL

1. *cannot steal*—Thieves can be bound not to steal by anointing the threshold of the door and other points of possible entrance to a house with an unguent made from the gall of a black cat, grease from a white fowl and the blood of a screech owl, concocted during the dog days of summer—that period when the Greater Dog Star, Sirius, rises and sets with the Sun. Its calculation has varied greatly through history, but in more modern times it is figured as the 40 days between July 3 and August 11. That guardian of the threshold, the dog, was said to be strongly affected during this period, and often to run mad.

It was far more common for bindings to be made in support of theft than in restraint of it. There are five charms in *The Book of Secrets* (Best and Brightman, 9, 52, 54, 56, 61) to prevent the barking of dogs. It is difficult to imagine any other use for such bindings than to aid in housebreaking at night.

Along the same lines is the Hand of Glory, a magical device formed of the severed hand of a gibbeted felon. The best description of its powers occurs in the once popular, but now almost forgotten, *Ingoldsby Legends:*

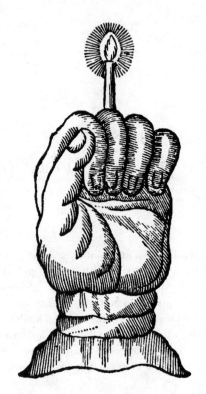

Hand of Glory

from *Secrets merveilleux de la magie naturelle et cabalistique du Petit Albert* (Cologne, 1722)

Now open lock   To the Dead Man's knock!
Fly bolt, and bar, and band!—
Nor move, nor swerve   Joint, muscle, or
    nerve,
At the spell of the Dead Man's hand!
Sleep all who sleep!—Wake all who
    wake!—
But be as the Dead for the Dead Man's sake!

In the *Petit Albert* there are detailed instructions for making the Hand. Either the left or right will do, but it must be from a gibbeted criminal, and wrapped about in a portion of his, or her, winding sheet, in which it is pressed to force out all the blood. Then the hand is pickled in an earthen pot for 15 days and heated, either by the Sun or in a furnace, to extract the fat, which is mixed with virgin wax and sesame (!) to make a candle. This taper is fixed in the grasp, or atop the fingers, of the hand; or in an alternate version, five candles are made and one is set on the tip of each extended finger. All this must be done during the dog days, under the influence of Sirius. When the candle (or candles) is lighted, a house can be robbed in relative security. See Waite (1911) 1961, 310–3.

CHAPTER XLI

Of sorceries, and their power.

The force of sorceries is reported to be so great, that they are believed to be able to subvert, consume, and change all inferior things, according to *Virgil's* muse:[1]

Moeris for me these herbs in Pontus chose,
And curious drugs, for there great plenty grows;
I many times, with these, have Moeris spied
Changed to a wolf, and in the woods to hide:
From sepulchres would souls departed charm,
And corn bear standing from another's farm.

Also in another place,[2] concerning the companions of *Ulysses*, whom:

The cruel goddess Circe there invests
With fierce aspects, and changed to savage beasts.

And a little after:[3]

When love from Picus Circe could not gain
Him with her charming wand, and hellish bane
Changed to a bird, and spots his speckled wings
With sundry colours—

Now there are some kind of these sorceries mentioned by *Lucan* concerning that sorceress *Thessala*,[4] calling up ghosts, where he saith:[5]

Here all nature's products unfortunate;
Foam of mad dogs, which waters fear and hate;

Guts of the lynx; hyena's knot inbred;
The marrow of a hart with serpents fed
Were not wanting; no not the sea lamprey
Which stops the ships; nor yet the dragon's eye.

And such as *Apuleius* tells[6] of concerning *Pamphila,* that sorceress, endeavouring to procure love; to whom *Fotis* a certain maid brought the hairs of a goat (cut off from a bag or bottle made with the skin thereof) instead of *Baeotius* a young man's hairs: now she (saith he) being out of her wits for the young man, goeth up to the tiled roof, and in the upper part thereof makes a great hole open to all the oriental, and other aspects, and most fit for these her arts, and there privately worships, having before furnished her mournful house with suitable furniture, with all kinds of spices, with plates of iron with strange words engraved upon them, with sterns of ships that were cast away, and much lamented, and with divers members of buried carcasses cast abroad: here noses, and fingers, there the fleshy nails of those that were hanged, and in another place the blood of them that were murdered, and their skulls mangled with the teeth of wild beasts; then she offers sacrifices (their enchanted entrails lying panting) and sprinkles them with divers kinds of liquors; sometimes with fountain water, sometimes with cow's milk, sometimes with mountain honey, and mead: then she ties those hairs into knots, and lays them on the fire, with divers odours to be burnt, then presently with an irresistible

121

power of magic, and blind force of the gods, the bodies of those whose hairs did smoke, and crash, assume the spirit of a man, and feel, and hear, and walk, and come whither the stink of their hair led them, and instead of *Baeotius* the young man, come skipping, and leaping with joy, and love into the house.

Austin also reports, that he heard of some women sorceresses, that were so versed in these kinds of arts, that by giving cheese to men they could presently turn them into working cattle,[7] and the work being done, restore them into men again.

Notes—Chapter XLI

1. *Virgil's muse*—Virgil *Eclogues* 8, lines 95–9.

2. *another place*—

> Here was distinctly heard the angry roars of lions, as they struggled against their bounds, and moaned in the depth of the night, and bristly boars and bears were ramping in their cages, and the forms of huge wolves were howling: all these transformed from human shape the cruel goddess had, by magic herbs, clothed with the faces and bodies of wild beasts. *(Aeneid* 7, c. line 18 [Lonsdale and Lee, 178])

There is no mention here of the crew of Ulysses, but they are referred to in Eclogue 8: "Circe by song transformed Ulysses' crew ..." *(Eclogues* 8, c. line 69 [Lonsdale and Lee, 26]). See also Homer *Odyssey* bk. 10.

3. *little after*—The *Aeneid* 7, line 189–91. Scorned by Picus, Circe turned him into a woodpecker. Ovid has described this scene:

> Then twice did she turn herself to the West, and twice to the East; thrice did she touch the youth with her wand; three charms did she repeat. He fled; wondering that he sped more swiftly than usual, he beheld wings on his body; and indignant that he was added suddenly as a strange bird to the Latin woods, he struck the wild oaks with his hard beak, and in his anger, inflicted wounds on the long branches. *(Metamorphoses* 14, c. line 386 [Riley, 497–8])

4. *Thessala*—That is, the Thessalian witch Erichtho.

5. *where he saith*—

> Then in the first place does she fill his breast, opened by fresh wounds, with reeking blood, and she bathes his marrow with gore, and plentifully supplies venom from the moon. Here is mingled whatever, by a monstrous generation, nature has produced. Not the foam of dogs to which water is an object of dread, not the entrails of the lynx, not the excrescence of the direful hyaena is wanting, and the marrow of the stag that has fed upon serpents; not the sucking fish, that holds back the ship in the midst of the waves, while the eastern breeze stretches the rigging; the eyes of dragons, too, and the stones that resound, warmed beneath the brooding bird; not the winged serpent of the Arabians, and the viper produced in the Red Sea, the guardian of the precious shell; or the slough of the horned serpent, of Libya that still survives; or the ashes of the Phoenix, laid upon the eastern altar.
>
> With this, after she has mingled abominations, vile, and possessing no names, she added leaves steeped in accursed spells, and herbs upon which, when shooting up, her direful mouth had spat, and whatever poisons she herself gave unto the world ... (Lucan *Pharsalia* 6, c. line 668 ff. [Riley, 239–40])

See a remarkably similar passage in Ovid's *Metamorphoses* 7, line 270.

6. *Apuleius tells*—The *Golden Ass* 15.

7. *working cattle*—

> For when I was in Italy, I heard such a report there, how certain women of one place there would but give one a little drug in cheese, and presently he became an ass, and so they made him carry their necessaries whither they would; and having done, they restored him to his proper shape; yet had he his human reason still, as Apuleius had while he was an ass, as himself writes in his book of *The Golden Ass;* be it a lie or a truth that he writes. (Augustine *City of God* 18.18 [Healey, 2:192])

CHAPTER XLII

Of the wonderful virtues of some kinds of sorceries.

Now I will show you what some of the sorceries are, that by the example of these there may be a way opened for the consideration of the whole subject of them.

Of these therefore the first is menstruous blood, which, how much power it hath in sorcery, we will now consider; for, as they say, if it comes over new wine, it makes it sour, and if it doth but touch the vine it spoils it forever, and by its very touch it makes all plants, and trees barren, and they that be newly set, to die; it burns up all the herbs in the garden, and makes fruit fall off from the trees,[1] it darkens the brightness of a looking glass,[2] dulls the edges of knives, and razors, dims the beauty of ivory, and it makes iron presently rusty, it makes brass rust, and smell very strong:[3] it makes dogs mad, if they do but taste of it, and if they being thus mad shall bite anyone, that wound is incurable:[4] it kills whole hives of bees, and drives them from the hives that are but touched with it:[5] it makes linen black that are boiled:[6] it makes mares cast their foal[7] if they do but touch it, and makes women miscarry if they be but smeared with it: it makes asses barren as long as they eat of the corn that hath been touched with it.

The ashes of menstruous clothes, if they be cast upon purple garments that are to be washed, change the colour of them, and takes away colours from flowers.[10] They say that it drives away tertian and quartan agues, if it be put into the wool of a black ram, and tied up in a silver bracelet, as also if the soles of the patients' feet be anointed therewith, and especially if it be done by the woman herself, the patients not knowing of it; moreover it cures the fits of the falling sickness. But most especially it cures them that are afraid of water, or drink, after they are bitten with a mad dog, if only a menstruous cloth be put under the cup.[11] Besides, they report, that if menstruous women shall walk naked about the standing corn, they make all cankers, worms, beetles, flies, and all hurtful things fall off from the corn: but they must take heed that they do it before Sun rising, or else they will make the corn to wither.[12] Also they say that they are able to expel hail, tempests, and lightnings,[13] more of which *Pliny* makes mention of.

Know this, that they are a greater poison if they happen in the decrease of the Moon, and yet much greater, if they happen betwixt the decrease, and change of the Moon: but if they happen in the eclipse of the Moon or Sun, they are an incurable poison.[14] But they are of greatest force of all, when they happen in the first years, even in the years of virginity,[15] for if they do but touch the posts of the house[16] there can no mischief take effect in it.

Also they say that the threads of any garment touched therewith cannot be burnt, and if they be cast into the fire, it will spread no farther.[17] Also it is said that the root of peony being given with castor, and smeared over with a menstruous cloth, cureth the falling sickness. More-

123

over if the stomach of a hart be burnt or roasted, and to it be put a perfuming made with a menstruous cloth, it will make crossbows useless for the killing of any game. The hairs of a menstruous women put under dung breed serpents: and if they be burnt, will drive away serpents[18] with their smell. So great a poisonous force is in them, that they are poison to poisonous creatures.

There is also hippomanes,[19] which amongst sorceries is not the least taken notice of, and it is a little venomous piece of flesh as big as a fig, and black, which is in the forehead of a colt newly foaled, which unless the mare herself doth presently eat, she will never after love her foal, or let it suck. And for this cause they say there is a most wonderful power in it to procure love, if it be powdered, and drank in a cup with the blood of him that is in love. There is also another sorcery, which is called by the same name, viz. hippomanes, viz. a venomous humour,[20] issuing out of the share of a mare what time she desires a horse, of which *Virgil* makes mention,[21] when he sings:

> Hence comes that poison which the shepherds call
> Hippomanes, and from mares' groins doth fall,
> The woeful bane of cruel stepdames use
> And with a charm 'mongst powerful drugs infuse.

Of this doth *Juvenal*[22] the satirist make mention:

> Hippomanes, poisons that boiled are, and charms
> Are given to sons-in-law, with such like harms.

Apollonius also in his Argonantics makes mention of the herb of *Prometheus*,[23] which he saith groweth from corrupt blood dropping upon the earth, whilst the vulture was gnawing upon the liver of *Prometheus* upon the hill Caucasus. The flower of this herb, he saith, is like saffron, having a double stalk hanging out, one farther than another the length of a cubit; the root under the earth, as flesh newly cut, sends forth a blackish juice as it were of a beech, with which, saith

he, if anyone shall after he hath performed his devotion to *Proserpina*,[24] smear over his body, he cannot be hurt either with sword, or fire. Also *Saxo Grammaticus* writes, that there was a certain man called *Froton*, who had a garment, which when he had put on he could not be hurt with the point or edge of any weapon.

The civet cat also abounds with sorceries: for, as *Pliny* reports,[25] the posts of a door being touched with her blood, the arts of jugglers, and sorcerers are so invalid, that the gods cannot be called up, and will by no means be persuaded to talk with them. Also that they that are anointed with the ashes of the ankle bone of her left foot, being decocted with the blood of a weasel, shall become odious to all. The same also is done with the eye, being decocted. Also it is said that the straight gut is administered against the injustice, and corruption of princes, and great men in power, and for success of petitions, and to conduce to ending of suits, and controversies, if anyone hath never so little of it about him; and that if it be bound unto the left arm, it is such a present charm, that if any man do but look upon a woman, it will make her follow him presently; and that the skin of her forehead doth withstand bewitchings.

They say also that the blood of a basilisk,[26] which they call the blood of Saturn, hath such great force in sorcery, that it procures for him that carries it about him, good success of his petitions, from great men in power, and of his prayers from God, and also remedies of diseases, and grant of any privilege.

They say also that a tick,[27] if it be pulled out of the left ear of a dog, and if be it altogether black, hath great virtue in the prognostic of life, for if the sick party shall answer him that brought it in, and who standing at his feet, shall ask of him concerning his disease, there is certain hope of life, and that he shall die, if he make no answer. They say also, that a stone that is bit with a mad dog[28] hath power to cause discord, if it be put in drink, and that he shall not be barked at by dogs, that puts the tongue of a dog[29] in his shoe under his great toe, especially if the herb of the same name, viz. houndstongue be joined with it. And that a membrane of the secondines of a dog[30] doth the same; and that dogs will shun him that hath a dog's heart.

And *Pliny* reports that there is a red toad[31] that lives in briars, and brambles, and is full of sorceries, and doth wonderful things: for the little bone which is in his left side, being cast into cold water, makes it presently very hot, by which also the rage of dogs is restrained, and their love is procured, if it be put in drink; and if it be bound to anyone, it stirreth up lust. On the contrary, the little bone which is on the right side, makes hot water cold, and that it can never be hot again, unless that be taken out, also it is said to cure quartans if it be bound to the sick in a snake's skin, as also all other fevers, and restrain love, and lust. And that the spleen, and heart is an effectual remedy against the poisons of the said toad. Thus much *Pliny* writes.

Also it is said that the sword, with which a man is slain, hath wonderful power in sorceries: for if the snaffle of the bridle, or spurs be made of it, they say that with these any horse, though never so wild, may be tamed, and gentled: and that if a horse should be shod with shoes made with it, he would be most swift and fleet, and never, though never so hard rode, tire. But yet they will that some characters, and names should be written upon it. They say also, if any man shall dip a sword, wherewith men were beheaded, in wine; and the sick drink thereof, he shall be cured of his quartan.

They say also that a cup of liquor being made with the brains of a bear,[32] and drank out of the skull, shall make him that drinks of it, be as fierce, and as raging as a bear, and think himself to be changed into a bear, and judge all things he sees to be bears, and so continue in that madness, until the force of that draught shall be dissolved, no other distemper being all the while perceived in him.

Notes—Chapter XLII

1. *from the trees*—

> It would indeed be a difficult matter to find anything which is productive of more marvellous effects than the menstrual discharge. On the approach of a woman in this state, must [new wine] will become sour, seeds which are touched by her become sterile, grafts wither away, garden plants are parched up, and the fruit will fall from the tree beneath which she sits. (Pliny 7.13 [Bostock and Riley, 2:151])

2. *looking glass*—"Her very look, even, will dim the brightness of mirrors ..." (ibid.). "Bithus of Dyrrhachium informs us that a mirror, which has been tarnished by the gaze of a menstruous female, will recover its brightness if the same woman looks steadily upon the back of it ..." (Pliny 28.23 [Bostock and Riley, 5:306]).

3. *smell strong*—"Her very look, even, will ... blunt the edge of steel, and take away the polish from ivory. ... brass and iron will instantly become rusty, and emit an offensive odour" (Pliny 7.13 [Bostock and Riley, 2:151–2]). "I have to state, in addition ... that the edge of a razor will become blunted, and that copper vessels will contract a fetid smell and become covered in verdigrease, on coming in contact with her" (Pliny 28.23 [Bostock and Riley, 5:305]).

4. *wound is incurable*—"... dogs which have tasted of the matter so discharged are seized with madness, and their bite is venomous and incurable" (Pliny 7.13 [Bostock and Riley, 2:152]).

5. *touched with it*—"... bees, it is a well known fact, will forsake their hives if touched by a menstruous woman ..." (Pliny 28.23 [Bostock and Riley, 5:305]).

6. *are boiled*—"... linen boiled in the cauldron will turn black ... on coming in contact with her" (ibid.). Linen was boiled for cleaning.

7. *cast their foal*—

> A mare big with foal, if touched by a woman in this state, will be sure to miscarry; nay, even more than this, at the very sight of a woman, though seen at a distance even, should she happen to be menstruating for the first time after the loss of her virginity, or for the first time, while in a state of virginity" (ibid.).

8. *makes women miscarry*—"Indeed so pernicious are its properties, that women themselves, the source from which it is derived, are far from being proof against its effects; a pregnant woman, for instance, if touched with it, or indeed if she so much as steps over it, will be liable to miscarry" (ibid.).

9. *makes asses barren*—

Lais and Elephantis have given statements quite at variance, on the subject of abortives; they mention the efficacy for that purpose of charcoal of cabbage root, myrtle root, or tamarisk root, quenched in the menstrual discharge; they say that she-asses will be barren for as many years as they have eaten barley-corn steeped in this fluid; and they have enumerated various other monstrous and irreconcilable properties, the one telling us, for instance, that fruitfulness may be ensured by the very same methods, which, according to the statement of the other, are productive of barrenness; to all which stories it is the best plan to refuse credit altogether. (Pliny 28.23 [Bostock and Riley, 5:305–6])

10. *colours from flowers*—"At this period also, the lustre of purple is tarnished by the touch of a woman: so much more baneful is her influence at this time than at any other" (ibid., 304). The time referred to is menstruation during eclipse or conjunction of the Sun and Moon. See the second quotation in note 17 below.

11. *under the cup*—

According to Lais and Salpe, the bite of a mad dog, as well as tertian and quartan fevers, may be cured by putting some menstruous blood in the wool of a black ram and enclosing it in a silver bracelet; and we learn from Diotimus of Thebes that the smallest portion will suffice of any kind of cloth that has been stained therewith, a thread even, if inserted and worn as a bracelet. The midwife Sotira informs us that the most effective cure for tertian and quartan fevers is to rub the soles of the patient's feet therewith, the result being still more successful if the operation is performed by the woman herself, without the patient being aware of it; she says, too, that this is an excellent method for reviving persons when attacked with epilepsy.

Icatidas the physician pledges his word that quartan fever may be cured by sexual intercourse, provided the woman is just beginning to menstruate. It is universally agreed, too, that when a person has been bitten by a dog and manifests a dread of water and of all kinds of drink, it will be quite sufficient to put under his cup a strip of cloth that has been dipped in this fluid; the result being that the hydrophobia will immediately disappear. (ibid., 306–7)

12. *corn to wither*—

At any other time, also, if a woman strips herself naked while she is menstruating, and walks round a field of wheat, the caterpillars, worms, beetles and other vermin, will fall from off the ears of corn. Metrodorus of Scepsos tells us that this discovery was first made in Cappadocia; and that, in consequence of such multitudes of cantharides [Spanish fly] being found to breed there, it is the practice for women to walk through the middle of the fields with their garments tucked up above the thighs. In other places, again, it is the usage for women to go barefoot, with the hair dishevelled and the girdle loose; due precaution must be taken, however, that this is not done at sun-rise, for if so, the crop will wither and dry up. Young vines, too, it is said, are injured irremediably by the touch of a woman in this state; and both rue and ivy, plants possessed of highly medicinal virtues, will die instantly upon being touched by her. (ibid., 304–5)

13. *tempests, and lightnings*—

For, in the first place, hailstorms, they say, whirlwinds, and lightning even will be scared by a woman uncovering her body while her monthly courses are upon her. The same, too, with all other kinds of tempestuous weather; and out at sea, a storm may be lulled by a woman uncovering her body merely, even though not menstruating at the time. (ibid., 304)

14. *incurable poison*—"If the menstrual discharge coincides with an eclipse of the moon or sun, the evils resulting from it are irremediable; and no less so, when it happens while the moon is in conjunction with the sun; the congress with a woman at such a period being noxious, and attended with fatal effects to the man" (ibid., 304).

15. *years of virginity*—"… the nature of the discharge is most virulent in females whose virginity has been destroyed solely by the lapse of time" (ibid., 307).

16. *posts of the house*—"Another thing universally acknowledged and one which I am ready to believe with the greatest pleasure, is the fact, that if the door-posts are only touched with the menstruous fluid all spells of the magicians will be neutralized" (ibid.).

17. *spread no farther*—This refers to two rather obscure passages in Pliny that have been translated by Riley:

In addition to this, the bitumen which is found at certain periods of the year, floating on the lake of Judaea, known as Asphaltites, a substance which is peculiarly tenacious, and adheres to everything that it touches, can only be divided into separate pieces by means of a thread which has been dipped in this virulent matter." (Pliny 7.13 [Bostock and Riley, 2:152])

And also:

The bitumen that is found in Judaea, will yield to nothing but the menstrual discharge; its tenacity being overcome, as already stated, by the agency of a thread from a garment which has been brought in contact with this fluid. Fire itself even, an element which triumphs over every other substance, is unable to conquer this; for if reduced to ashes and then sprinkled upon garments when about to be scoured, it will change their purple tint, and tarnish the brightness of the colours. (Pliny 28.23 [Bostock and Riley, 5:305])

Pliny means that a thread from a cloth stained with menstrual blood can be used to cut bitumen without sticking to it. The same fable appears in Tacitus *(History* 5.6), who calls it "the account of old authors." Agrippa seems to interpret these passages to mean that burning pitch, which is very difficult to extinguish, can be put out by a menstruous thread. He seems to have attached the words "Fire itself even, an element which triumphs over every other substance, is unable to conquer this" to the preceding sentence.

18. *drive away serpents*—"The smell of a woman's hair, burnt, will drive away serpents ..." (Pliny 28.20 [Bostock and Riley, 5:302]).

19. *hippomanes*—

The horse is born with a poisonous substance on its forehead, known as hippomanes, and used in love philtres; it is the size of a fig, and of a black colour; the mother devours it immediately on the birth of the foal, and until she has done so, she will not suckle it. When this substance can be rescued from the mother, it has the property of rendering the animal quite frantic by the smell. (Pliny 8.66 [Bostock and Riley, 2:321])

"... the love-charm is sought for that is torn away from the forehead of a colt at its birth, and seized before the dam can take it" (Virgil *Aeneid* 4, c. line 516 [Londale and Lee, 138]).

"And not only do noxious potions avail; or when they [witches] withdraw the pledges swelling with its

juices from the forehead of the mother [horse] about to show her affection" (Lucan *Pharsalia* 6, line 454 [Riley, 230].

20. *venomous humour*—"The hippomanes has been distinguished under two species; the one a liquor distilling from a mare, during the time of her heat" *(Gentleman's Magazine* 26:170, 1756, quoted from *OED,* "hippomanes."

21. *Virgil makes mention*—"Hence at last a slimy substance distills from their sides, which the shepherds call by a true name Hippomanes, gathered often by malicious step-mothers, who mix with it herbs and baneful charms" *(Georgics* 3, c. line 282 [Lonsdale and Lee, 59]).

22. *Juvenal*—"Shall I speak of the love-philters, the incantations, the poison mingled with the food and given to the step-son?" *(Satires* 6.8, trans. L. Evans [New York: Hinds, Noble and Eldridge, n.d.], 44). A little after this passage Juvenal says: "Yet even this [love potion from Thessaly] is endurable, if you do not go running mad as well, like that uncle of Nero for whom his Caesonia infused the whole forehead of a foal new dropped" (ibid. 6.39 [Evans, 64]). He is referring to Caligula, about whom Suetonius makes more explicit reference: "It is for certain thought that poisoned he was with a potion given unto him by his wife Caesonia, which indeed was a love medicine, but such a one as cracked his wits and enraged him" ("Gaius Caesar Caligula" 50. In *History of the Twelve Caesars,* trans. P. Holland [1606] [London: George Routledge, n.d.], 215).

23. *herb of Prometheus*—

This salve was named after Prometheus. A man had only to smear it on his body, after propitiating the only begotten Maiden with a midnight offering, to become invulnerable by sword or fire and for that day to surpass himself in strength and daring. It first appeared in a plant that sprang from the blood-like ichor of Prometheus in his torment, which the flesh-eating eagle had dropped on the spurs of Caucasus. The flowers, which grew on twin stalks a cubit high, were of the colour of Corycian saffron, while the root looked like flesh that had just been cut, and the juice like the dark sap of a mountain oak. (Apollonius of Rhodes *Voyage of Argo* 3, c. line 845 [Rieu, 132–3])

24. *Proserpina*—The Roman form of the Greek Persephone, goddess of the underworld and spouse of Pluto (Greek: Hades).

25. *Pliny reports*—All these things are related of the hyena, not the civet, in Pliny 28.27 [Bostock and Riley, 5:309–14].

26. *blood of a basilisk*—

As to the basilisk, a creature which the very serpents fly from, which kills by its odour even, and which proves fatal to man by only looking upon him, its blood has been marvellously extolled by the magicians. This blood is thick and adhesive, like pitch, which it resembles also in colour: dissolved in water, they say, it becomes of a brighter red than that of cinnabar. They attribute to it also the property of ensuring success to petitions preferred to potentates, and to prayers even offered to the gods; and they regard it as a remedy for various diseases, and as an amulet preservative against all noxious spells. Some give it the name of "Saturn's blood." (Pliny 29.19 [Bostock and Riley, 5:394])

It seems to me that this was a dried ink used to draft petitions and write charms. Perhaps bloods in general were used magically in this way.

27. *tick*—

According to these authorities [the Magi], a tick from a dog's left ear, worn as an amulet, will allay all kinds of pains. They presage, too, from it on matters of life and death; for if the patient, they say, gives an answer to a person who has a tick about him, and, standing at the foot of the bed, asks how he is, it is an infallible sign that he will survive; while, on the other hand, if he makes no answer, he will be sure to die. They add, also, theat the dog from whose left ear the tick is taken, must be entirely black. (Pliny 30.24 [Bostock and Riley, 5:449])

28. *mad*—Perhaps this superstition has its origin in this passage from Pliny: "These marvellous properties of the poison will occasion the less surprise, when we remember that, 'a stone bitten by a dog' has become a proverbial expression for discord and variance" (Pliny 29.32 [Bostock and Riley, 5:406]).

29. *tongue of a dog*—"Dogs will fly from any one who has a dog's heart about him, and they will never bark at a person who carries a dog's tongue in his shoe, beneath the great toe ..." (ibid., 405). This same charm occurs in *The Book of Secrets,* but the tongue of a dog has been magically transmuted into hound's tongue *(Cynoglossum officinale)*: "And if thou shalt have the aforenamed herb under thy foremost toe, all the Dogs shall keep silence, and shall not have power to bark" *(Book of Secrets* 1.9 [Best and Brightman, 9]). Agrippa has combined the two.

3O. *secondines of a dog*—"A dog will not bark at a person who has any part of the secondines [afterbirth] of a bitch about him ..." (Pliny 30.53 [Bostock and Riley, 5:469]).

31. *red toad*—For all these wonders of the creature Pliny calls a "bramble-toad," see Pliny 32.18 [Bostock and Riley, 6:22–3].

32. *brains of a bear*—"The people of Spain have a belief, that there is some kind of magical poison in the brain of the bear, and therefore burn the heads of those that have been killed in their public games; for it is averred, that the brain, when mixed with drink, produces in man the rage of the bear" (Pliny 8.54 [Bostock and Riley, 2:307]). This appears to be the vestige of some bear cult similar to that of northern Europe, where warriors believed they could transform themselves into bears. They were called *berserkir,* dressed in bear skins, and were subject to fits of violent rage. These might be voluntary or involuntary.

No sword would wound them, no fire could burn them, a club alone could destroy them, by breaking their bones, or crushing in their skulls. Their eyes glared as though a flame burned in the sockets, they ground their teeth, and frothed at the mouth; they gnawed at their shield rims, and are said to have sometimes bitten them through, and as they rushed into conflict they yelped as dogs or howled as wolves. (Baring-Gould [1865] 1973, 40). Baring-Gould is drawing from Saxo Grammaticus, bk. 7.

CHAPTER XLIII

Of perfumes, or suffumigations, their manner, and power.

Some suffumigations also, or perfumings, that are proper to the stars, are of great force for the opportune receiving of celestial gifts under the rays of the stars, in as much as they do strongly work upon the Air, and breath. For our breath is very much changed by such kind of vapours, if both vapours be of another like: the Air also being through the said vapours easily moved, or affected with the qualities of inferiors, or celestials, daily, and quickly penetrating our breast, and vitals, doth wonderfully reduce us to the like qualities; wherefore suffumigations are wont to be used by them that are about to soothsay, for to affect their fancy, which indeed being appropriated to any certain deities, do fit us to receive divine inspiration: so they say that fumes made with linseed,[1] and fleabane seed,[2] and roots of violets, and parsley, doth make one to foresee things to come, and doth conduce to prophesying.

Let no man wonder how great things suffumigations can do in the Air, especially when he shall with *Porphyrius* consider, that by certain vapours exhaling from proper suffumigations, airy spirits are presently raised, as also thunderings, and lightnings, and such like things. As the liver of a chamelion[3] being burnt on the top of the house, doth, as it is manifest, raise showers, and lightnings. In like manner the head, and throat, if they be burnt with oaken wood, cause storms, and lightnings.

There are also suffumigations under opportune influences of stars, that make the images of spirits forthwith appear in the air, or elsewhere. So they say, that if of coriander, smallage, henbane, and hemlock[4] be made a fume, that spirits will presently come together; hence they are called the spirits' herbs. Also it is said that a fume made of the root of the reedy herb sagapen,[5] with the juice of hemlock, and henbane, and the herb tapus barbatus,[6] red sanders,[7] and black poppy,[8] makes spirits and strange shapes appear: and if smallage be added to them, chaseth away spirits from any place, and destroys their visions. In like manner a fume made of calamint, peony, mints, and palma christi,[9] drives away all evil spirits, and vain imaginations.

Moreover it is said that by certain fumes certain animals are gathered together, and put to flight, as *Pliny* mentions concerning the stone liparis,[10] that with the fume thereof all beasts are called out; so the bones in the upper part of the throat of a hart, being burnt, gather all the serpents together, but the horn of the hart[11] being burnt doth with its fume chase them all away. The same doth a fume of the feathers of peacocks. Also the lungs of an ass being burnt, puts all poisonous things to flight; the fume of the burnt hoof of a horse drives away mice, the same doth the hoof of a mule, with which also if it be the hoof of the left foot, flies are driven away; and they say, if a house, or any place be smoked with the gall of a cuttlefish,[12] made into a confection with red storax,[13] roses, and lignum-aloes, and if then there be some sea water, or blood cast into that place, the whole house will seem to be full of water, or blood; and if some earth of plowed ground be cast there, the Earth will seem to quake.

Now such kinds of vapours we must conceive do infect any body, and infuse a virtue into it which doth continue long, even as any contagious, or poisonous vapour of the pestilence, being kept for two years in the wall of a house, infects the inhabitants, and as the contagion of pestilence, or leprosy lying hid in a garment, doth long after infect him that wears it. Therefore were certain suffumigations used to images, rings, and such like instruments of magic, and hid treasures, and as *Porphyrius* saith, very effectually.

So they say, if anyone shall hide gold, or silver, or any other precious thing, the Moon being in conjunction with the Sun, and shall fume the place with coriander, saffron, henbane, smallage, and black poppy, of each a like quantity, bruised together, and tempered with the juice of hemlock, that which is so hid shall never be found, or taken away, and that spirits shall continually keep it: and if anyone shall endeavour to take it away, he shall be hurt by them, and shall fall into a phrensy. And *Hermes* saith, that there is nothing like the fume of spermaceti[14] for the raising of spirits: wherefore if a fume be made of that, and lignum-aloes, pepperwort,[15] musk, saffron, red storax, tempered together, with the blood of a lapwing, it will quickly gather airy spirits together, and if it be used about the graves of the dead, it gathers together spirits, and the ghosts of the dead.

So, as often as we direct any work to the Sun, we must make suffumigations with solary things, if to the Moon, with lunary things, and so of the rest. And we must know, that as there is a contrariety and enmity in stars, and spirits, so also in suffumigations unto the same. So there is a contrarity betwixt lignum-aloes, and sulphur, frankincense, and quicksilver, and spirits that are raised by the fume of lignum-aloes, are allayed by the burning of sulphur. As *Proclus*[16] gives an example in a spirit, which was wont to appear in the form of a lion, but by the setting of a cock before it, vanished away, because there is a contrarity betwixt a cock, and a lion; and so the like consideration, and practice is to be observed concerning such like things.

Notes—Chapter XLIII

1. *linseed*—Seed of flax *(Linum usitatissimum)* used to make linseed oil.

2. *fleabane seed*—Fleabane *(Pulicaria dysenterica)* is a plant growing in wet places, just over a foot high, with yellow flowers that smell of soap. It was said to repel fleas and was used to treat dysentery. The Latin *Opera* gives "psyllii," or psyllium, which is a different plant *(Plantago afra)* with a similar power over fleas. *The Book of Secrets* treats the two as one ("Marvels of the World" 75 [Best and Brightman, 109]), but Turner distinguishes them and calls the latter herb fleawort.

3 *liver of a chamelion*—See note 11, ch. XIII, bk. I.

4. *hemlock*—Common hemlock *(Conium maculatum)*, a large plant from two to seven feet tall with small white flowers, finely divided leaves, and a smooth stem spotted with purple. A powerful poison, it was reputedly used in the execution of the Greek philosopher Socrates. It was sacred to Hecate and an ingredient in the flying ointment of witches.

Medieval monks and nuns may have used it to reduce sexual desire by smearing its juice on their genitals.

5. *sagapen*—Sagapenum, or giant fennel *(Ferula persica)*, a plant native to southern Europe. The gum resin, called gum sagapenum, came in fine tears, transparent with a yellow exterior, and was used to treat head cold.

6. *tapus barbatus*—Tapsus barbatus, the great mullein *(Verbascum thapsus)*. The poet Lucan mentions this herb in a fumigation against serpents:

> And these [Psylli], then following the Roman standards, as soon as the general [Cato] ordered the tents to be pitched, in the first place, purged the sands which the compass of the trenches enclosed, with charms and words that put the snakes to flight. A fire made with drugs surrounds the extremity of the camp. Here does wallwort crackle, and foreign galbanum steam, and tamarisk rejoicing in no foliage, and

eastern costus, and pungent all-heal, and Thessalian centaury; and sulphur-wort resounds in the flames, and the thapsus of Eryx. Larch-trees, too, they burn, and the southern-wood, with its smoke stifling to serpents, and the horns of stags bred afar. *(Pharsalia* 9, c. line 911 [Riley, 375])

Eryx is an island just off Sicily.

7. *red sanders*—Red sandalwood, or rubywood *(Pterocarpus santalinus),* used in dying cloth and as an astringent and tonic. It is a tree about 60 feet tall that grows in India and Sri Lanka. The heartwood is deep red, veined, and so heavy that it sinks in water, but has no appreciable scent.

8. *black poppy*—A variety of the opium poppy *(Papaver somniferum)* distinguished by its purple flowers and dark seeds, which when pressed yield an edible oil *(Oleum papaveris).* The milky juice is strongly narcotic, the source of opium.

9. *palma christi*—Also called palmchrist, because its leaves are like the human hand: the castor oil plant *(Ricinus communis).*

10. *liparis*—See note 14, ch. XIII, bk. I.

11. *horn of the hart*—"The fumes of their horns, while burning, will drive away serpents, as already stated [8.50]; but the bones, it is said, of the upper part of a stag's throat, if burnt upon a fire, will bring those reptiles together" (Pliny 28.42 [Bostock and Riley, 5:329]). The magical rationale of this last, is that since the hart eats snakes (though of course it does not), the bones of its throat is where they will naturally accrue.

12. *cuttlefish*—A sea mollusk *(Sepia officinalis)* about two feet long, similar to the squid, with ten arms. It ejects black ink when in danger, and has a hard inner shell that was used by goldsmiths for casting precious metals and as a polishing powder. The powdered bone was also taken internally for excess stomach acid. Also called the ink fish.

13. *red storax*—Name applied to storax-in-the-lump, as opposed to storax-in-the-tear.

14. *spermaceti*—A fatty white substance found in the head of the sperm whale, once commonly applied to treat bruises.

15. *pepperwort*—Species of cress *(Lepidium latifolium),* sometimes called dittany, although Turner says this is an error. It is almost like pepper in taste, and grows in wet places near the sea.

16. *Proclus*—See note 25, ch. XVIII, bk. I.

CHAPTER XLIV

The compositions of some fumes appropriated to the planets.

We make a suffumigation for the Sun in this manner, viz. of saffron, ambergris, musk, lignum-aloes, lignum-balsam,[1] the fruit of the laurel,[2] cloves, myrrh, and frankincense, all which being bruised, and mixed in such a proportion as may make a sweet odour, must be incorporated with the brain of an eagle, or the blood of a white cock, after the manner of pills, or trochisks.[3]

For the Moon we make a suffumigation of the head of a frog dried, the eyes of a bull, the seed of white poppy,[4] frankincense, and camphor,[5] which must be incorporated with menstruous blood, or the blood of a goose.

For Saturn take the seed of black poppy, of henbane, the root of mandrake, the loadstone, and myrrh, and make them up with the brain of a cat, or the blood of a bat.

For Jupiter take the seed of ash,[6] lignum-aloes, storax, the gum benjamin,[7] the lazule stone, the tops of the feathers of a peacock, and incorporate them with the blood of a stork, or a swallow, or the brain of a hart.

For Mars take euphorbium, bdellium,[8] gum armoniac, the roots of both hellebores, the loadstone, and a little sulphur, and incorporate them all with the brain of a hart, the blood of a man, and the blood of a black cat.

For Venus take musk, ambergris, lignum-aloes, red roses, and red coral, and make them up with the brain of sparrows, and the blood of pigeons.

For Mercury take mastic, frankincense, cloves, and the herb cinquefoil, and the stone achates, and incorporate them all with the brain of a fox, or weasel, and the blood of a pie.

Besides, to Saturn are appropriated for fumes all odoriferous roots, as pepperwort root, etc. and the frankincense tree:[9] to Jupiter odoriferous fruits, as nutmegs, cloves: to Mars all odoriferous wood, as sanders, cypress, lignum-balsam, and lignum-aloes: to the Sun, all gums, frankincense, mastic, benjamin, storax, laudanum,[10] ambergris, and musk: to Venus flowers, as roses, violets, saffron, and such like: to Mercury all the peels of wood and fruit, as cinnamon, lignum-cassia,[11] mace, citron peel, and bayberries, and whatsoever seeds are odoriferous: to the Moon the leaves of all vegetables, as the leaf Indum,[12] the leaves of the myrtle,[13] and bay tree.

Know also, that according to the opinion of the magicians, in every good matter, as love, goodwill, and the like, there must be a good fume, odoriferous, and precious; and in every evil matter, as hatred, anger, misery, and the like, there must be a stinking fume, that is of no worth.

The twelve signs also of the Zodiac have their proper fumes, as Aries hath myrrh; Taurus, pepperwort; Gemini, mastic; Cancer, camphor; Leo, frankincense; Virgo, sanders; Libra, galbanum;[14] Scorpio, opoponax;[15] Sagittarius, lignum-aloes; Capricornus, benjamin; Aquarius, euphorbium; Pisces, red storax.

But *Hermes* describes the most powerful fume to be, viz. that which is compounded of the seven aromatics, according to the powers of the seven planets, for it receives from Saturn, pepperwort, from Jupiter, nutmeg, from Mars, lignum-aloes, from the Sun, mastic, from Venus, saffron, from Mercury, cinnamon, and from the Moon, the myrtle.

Noτes—Chapτer XLIV

1. *lignum-balsam*—probably the wood of *Liquadambar orientalis,* which grows in the eastern Mediterranean, from which liquid storax is supposed to have been extracted. But perhaps the wood of the tree from which the balm of Gilead was extracted, thought to be *Balsamodendron gileadense,* a small tree growing in Arabia and Abyssinia; or by some, the tree *Commiphora opobalsamum.*

2. *fruit of the laurel*—The sweet bay tree *(Laurus nobilis)* bears a bluish-black oval berry half an inch long that is bitter and astringent, but agreeably aromatic.

3. *trochisks*—A medicated lozenge or tablet.

4. *white poppy*—Variety of the opium poppy with light-colored seeds, as opposed to the black poppy, the seeds of which are dark. There is no narcotic in the seeds, which are harvested and pressed for their edible oil.

5. *camphor*—A white, solid, strong-smelling essential oil extract of the camphor laurel *(Camphora officinarum),* a large tree growing in China, Japan, and Formosa. Camphor is flammable, burning with a white smoke, lighter than water, and highly noxious to insects. It was thought to diminish sexual desire.

6. *seed of ash*—Seed of the *Fraxinus excelsior,* called an "ash key" because of its peculiar winged shape.

7. *gum benjamin*—Gum benzoin, extracted from the benjamin tree *(Styrax benzoin).* Called the "frankincense of Jawa" (i.e., Sumatra) by Ibn Batuta around 1350. A dry, brittle resinous substance with a fragrant odor and aromatic taste.

8. *bdellium*—Gum resin similar to myrrh, but weaker and more acrid, with a pungent taste and agreeable odor. It was extracted from the *Balsamodendron roxburghii* in India and the *B. africanum* in Senegal. Egyptian bdellium comes from the doom palm *(Hyphaene thebaica).* "Bidellium is … a blacke tre moost lyke to the Oliue and the gumme therof is bryght and bytter" (Trevisa *Bartholomeus de Proprietatibus Rerum* [1398], quoted from *OED,* "bdellium").

9. *frankincense tree*—The frankincense of the Hebrews, Greeks and Romans is believed to be olibanum, of the tree *Boswellia serrata,* a large timber tree with pinnate leaves and small pink flowers that grows in India.

10. *laudanum*—Gum laudanum is not to be confused with the laudanum of Paracelsus, which was a medical preparation containing, among other things, opium. The name now refers to the alcoholic tincture of opium, but this was unknown in Agrippa's time.

11. *Lignum-cassia*—Cassia bark, or China cinnamon, an inferior kind of cinnamon that is thicker, coarser and less delicate in flavor than true cinnamon. It comes from the *Cinnamomum cassia,* a tree native to China.

12. *leaf Indum*—Indian leaf, an aromatic leaf of the species *Cinnamomum malabathrum* of the East Indies. Also called Malabar leaf.

13. *myrtle*—The common myrtle *(Myrtus communis)* is a shrub native to southern Europe with shiny evergreen leaves and sweet-scented flowers. It was sacred to Venus and an emblem of love.

14. *galbanum*—Gum resin of the *Ferula galbaniflua* of Iran. It occurs in irregular lumps of light brown, yellowish, or greenish yellow, and occasionally tears, and has a musky odor and bitter taste. Moses mentions it (Exodus 30:34) as a sweet spice used for perfume for the tabernacle, employing the word *chelbenah,* translated "galbanum" in the English Bible.

15. *opoponax*—Fetid gum resin from the root of *Opoponax chironium,* a plant like a parsnip with yellow flowers, native to southern Europe. Obtained by pricking the root, the gum is yellow outside and white within. It was held in high regard as an antispasmodic by the ancients, and was described by Hippocrates, Theophrastus and Dioscorides.

CHAPTER XLV

Of collyries, unctions, love medicines, and their virtues.

oreover collyries,[1] and unguents[2] conveying the virtues of things natural, and celestial to our spirit, can multiply, transmute, transfigure, and transform it accordingly, as also transpose those virtues which are in them into it, that so it cannot act only upon its own body, but also upon that which is near it, and affect that by visible rays, charms, and by touching it, with some like quality. For because our spirit is the subtle, pure, lucid, airy, and unctuous vapour of the blood; it is therefore fit to make collyries of the like vapours, which are more suitable to our spirit in substance, for then by reason of their likeness, they do the more stir up, attract, and transform the spirit. The like virtues have certain ointments, and other confections.

Hence by the touch sometimes sickness, poisonings, and love is induced; some things, as the hands, or garments being annointed: also by kisses, some things being held in the mouth, love is induced, as in *Virgil* we read that *Venus* prays *Cupid:*[3]

> That when glad Dido hugs him in her lap
> At royal feasts, crowned with the cheering grape,
> When she embracing, shall sweet kisses give,
> Inspire hid flame, with deadly bane deceive,
> He would———

Now the sight, because it perceives more purely, and clearly than the other senses, and fastening in us the marks of things more acutely, and deeply, doth most of all, and before others agree with the phantastic spirit, as is apparent in dreams, when things seen do more often present themselves to us than things heard, or any thing coming under the other senses.

Therefore when collyries transform visual spirits, that spirit doth easily affect the imagination, which indeed being affected with divers species, and forms, transmits the same by the same spirit unto the outward sense of sight, by which occasion there is caused in it a perception of such species, and forms in that manner; as if it were moved by external objects, that there seem to be seen terrible images, and spirits, and such like: so there are made collyries,[4] making us forthwith to see the images of spirits in the air, or elsewhere, as I know how to make of the gall of a man, and the eyes of a black cat, and of some other things. The like is made also of the blood of a lapwing, of a bat, and of a goat, and they say, if a smooth shining piece of steel[5] be smeared over with the juice of mugwort, and made to fume, it will make invocated spirits to be seen in it.

So also there are some suffumigations, or unctions, which make men speak in their sleep, to walk, and to do those things which are done by men that are awake, and sometimes to do those things, which men that are awake cannot, or dare not do. Some there are that make us to hear horrid, or delectable sounds, and such like. And this is the cause why maniacal, and melancholy men believe they see, and hear those things without, which their imagination doth only fancy within, hence they fear things not to be feared, and fall into wonderful, and most false suspicions, and fly when none pursueth them, are angry, and contend, nobody being present, and fear where no fear is.

Such like passions also can magical confections induce, by suffumigations, by collyries, by unguents, by potions, by poisons, by lamps, and lights, by looking glasses, by images, enchantments, charms, sounds, and music. Also by divers rites, observations, ceremonies, religions, and superstitions; all which shall be handled in their places.

And not only by these kind of arts, passions, apparitions, and images are induced, but also things themselves, which are really changed, and transfigured into divers forms, as the poet[6] relates of *Proteus*,[7] *Periclimenus*,[8] *Achelous*,[9] and *Merra*,[10] the daughter of *Erisichthon:* so also *Circe*[11] changed the companions of *Ulysses,* and of old in the sacrifices of *Jupiter Lycaeus*,[12] the men that tasted of the inwards of the sacrifices, were turned into wolves, which *Pliny* saith, befell a certain man called *Demarchus*.[13] The same opinion was *Austin* of: for he saith, whilst he was in Italy, he heard of some women that by giving sorceries in cheese to travelers, turned them into working cattle, and when they had done such work as they would have them, turned them into men again, and that this befell a certain Father called *Prestantius*.[14] The Scriptures themselves testify that Pharaoh's sorcerers turned their rods into serpents,[15] and water into blood,[16] and did such like things.

Notes—Chapter XLV

1. *collyries*—Salve, drops, or other treatment applied to the eyes.

2. *unguents*—Ointment rubbed on the body.

3. *Venus prays Cupid*—Following the request of his mother, Venus, Cupid puts on the appearance of Ascanius, the son of Aeneas, to cause Queen Dido to fall in love with Aeneas. He "breathes secret fire" filled with "love's poison" into her when they kiss, but there is no suggestion that he is holding anything in his mouth at the time. See the *Aeneid* 1, c. line 695.

4. *are made collyries*—Such a collyrium is described in *The Book of Secrets:* "If thou wilt see that other men can not. Take of the gall of a male Cat, and the fat of a Hen all white, and mix them together, and anoint thy eyes, and thou shalt see it that others can not see" ("Marvels of the World" 53 [Best and Brightman, 98]).

5. *piece of steel*—Agrippa does not say, but this would likely be the blade of a sword, anointed and heated in an open flame, acting as a magic mirror to reflect the spirits which are present, but invisible to the naked eye. Evil spirits like to conceal themselves from their evocator so that when he or she steps out of the magic circle, they can work mischief.

6. *the Poet*—Applied to Ovid.

7. *Proteus*—

There are some whose privilege it is to pass into many shapes, as thou, Proteus, inhabitant of the sea that embraces the earth. The people have seen thee one while a young man, and again a lion; at one time thou wast a furious boar, at another a serpent, which they dreaded to touch; and sometimes, horns rendered thee a bull. Ofttimes thou mightest be seen as a stone; often, too, as a tree. Sometimes imitating the appearance of flowing water, thou wast a river; sometimes fire, the very contrary of water. (Ovid *Metamorphoses* 8.6, c. line 730 [Riley, 292–3])

8. *Periclimenus*—

… but the death of Periclymenus is wonderful; to whom Neptune, … had granted to be able to assume whatever shapes he might choose, and again, when assumed, to lay them aside. He, after he had in vain been turned into all other shapes, was turned into the form of the bird that is wont to carry the lightnings in his crooked talons [eagle] … The Tirynthian hero [Hercules] aims at him his bow, too unerringly, and hits him … (ibid. 12.5, c. line 554 [Riley, 435])

9. *Achelous*—He wrestled with Hercules, first in his own form, then as a serpent, and lastly as a bull,

Werewolf

from *Die Emeis* by Johann Geiler von Kaysersberg (Strassburg, 1517)

whereupon Hercules tore out one of his horns and defeated him (ibid. 9.1, c. line 20 [Riley 301–3]).

10. *Merra*—As punishment for cutting down a sacred oak, her father, Erisicthon, is cursed with insatiable hunger, to appease which he sells his daughter into slavery. She appeals to Neptune, who gives her the power to transform herself, and so escapes in the form of a man. Her father sells her again and again, but each time she escapes, "sometimes as a mare, sometimes as a bird, now as a cow, now as a stag ..." (ibid. 8.7, c. line 870 [Riley, 298]).

11. *Circe*—Ibid. 14.5, c. line 276 [Riley, 493].

12. *Jupiter Lycaeus*—For the sacrilege of attempting to trick Jupiter into consuming human flesh, Lycaon, king of Arcadia, is transformed into a wolf: "His garments are changed into hair, his arms into legs; he becomes a wolf, and he still retains vestiges of his ancient form. His hoariness is still the same, the same violence appears in his features; his eyes are bright as before; he is still the same image of ferocity." (ibid. 1.7, c. line 234 [Riley, 17]).

Kekrops first named Zeus the Supreme, and decided to offer him no slaughtered sacrifices but to incinerate on the altar those local honey-cakes the Athenians

today still call oatmeals, but Lykaon brought a human child to the altar of Lykaian Zeus, slaughtered it and poured its blood on the altar, and they say at that sacrifice he was suddenly turned into a wolf. (Pausanias *Guide to Greece* 8.2.3 [Levi, 2:372])

For example, they say that after Lykaon someone was always turned into a wolf at the sacrifice of Lykaian Zeus, but not for his whole life, because if he kept off human meat when he was a wolf he turned back into a man after nine years, though if he tasted man he stayed a wild beast for ever. (ibid. sec. 6 [Levi, 2:373])

13. *Demarchus*—

Euanthes [or Evanthes], a Grecian author of no mean reputation, informs us that the Arcadians assert that a member of the family of one Anthus is chosen by lot, and then taken to a certain lake in that district, where, after suspending his clothes on an oak, he swims across the water and goes away into the desert, where he is changed into a wolf and associates with other animals of the same species for a space of nine years. If he has kept himself from beholding a man during the whole of that time, he returns to the same lake, and, after swimming across it, resumes his original form, only with the addition of nine years in age to his former appearance. To this Fabius adds, that he takes his former clothes as well. ... So too, Agriopas [or Apollas], who wrote the Olympionics [Olympic victors], informs us that Demaenetus, the Parrhesian, during a sacrifice of human victims, which the Arcadians were offering up to the Lucaean Jupiter, tasted the entrails of a boy who had been slaughtered; upon which he was turned into a wolf, but, ten years afterwards, was restored to his original shape and his calling of an athlete, and returned victorious in the pugilistic contests at the Olympic games. (Pliny 8.34 [Bostock and Riley, 2:283–4])

Such transformations were not confined to Arcadia. Of werewolves Herodotus writes:

It seems that those people are conjurers; for both the Scythians and the Greeks who dwell in Scythia say, that every Neurian once a year becomes a wolf for a few days, at the end of which time he is restored to his proper shape. *(History* bk. 4 [Rawlinson, 236])

14. *Prestantius—*

For one Prestantius told me that his father took that drug in cheese at his own house, whereupon he lay in such a sleep that no man could awake him: and after a few days he awoke of himself and told all he had suffered in his dreams in the meanwhile; how he had been turned into a horse and carried the soldier's victuals about in a sack. This had truly happened as he recorded it, yet seemed it but a dream unto him. (Augustine *City of God* 18.18 [Healey 2:192])

15. *rods into serpents—*Exodus 7:12.

16. *water into blood—*Exodus 7:22.

CHAPTER XLVI

Of natural alligations, and suspensions.

When the Soul of the World, by its virtue doth make all things that are naturally generated, or artificially made, fruitful, by infusing into them celestial properties for the working of some wonderful effects, then things themselves not only applied by suffumigations, or collyries, or ointments, or potions, or any other such like way, but also when they being conveniently wrapped up, are bound to, or hanged about the neck, or any other way applied, although by never so easy a contact, do impress their virtue upon us.

By these alligations[1] therefore, suspensions,[2] wrappings up, applications, and contacts the accidents[3] of the body, and mind are changed into sickness, health, boldness, fear, sadness, and joy, and the like: they render them that carry them gracious or terrible, acceptable, or rejected, honoured and beloved, or hateful and abominable.

Now these kind of passions are conceived to be by the abovesaid, infused no otherwise, than is manifest in the grafting of trees, where the vital virtue is sent, and communicated from the trunk to the twig grafted into it, by way of contact and alligation; so in the female palm tree, when she comes near to the male, her boughs bend to the male, and are bowed: which the gardeners seeing, bind ropes from the male to the female, which becomes straight again, as if it had by this continuation of the rope received the virtue of the male. In like manner we see, that the crampfish[4] being touched afar off with a long pole, doth presently stupify the hand of him that toucheth it. And if any shall touch the sea hare[5] with his hand or stick, doth presently run out of his wits. Also if the fish called stella, as they say, be fastened with the blood of a fox and a brass nail to a gate, evil medicines can do no hurt. Also it is said, that if a woman take a needle and beray it with dung, and then wrap it up in earth, in which the carcass of a man was buried, and shall carry it about her in a cloth which was used at the funeral, that no man shall be able to lie with her[6] as long as she hath it about her. Now by these examples we see, how by certain alligations of certain things, as also suspensions, or by a simple contact, or the continuation of any thread, we may be able to receive some virtues thereby.

It is necessary that we know the certain rule of alligation, and suspension, and the manner which the Art requires, viz. that they be done under a certain, and suitable constellation, and that they be done with wire, or silken threads, with hair, or sinews of certain animals.[7] And things that are to be wrapped up must be done in the leaves of herbs, or the skins of animals, or fine cloths, and the like, according to the suitableness of things: as if you would procure the solary virtue of anything, this being wrapped up in bay leaves, or the skin of a lion, hang it about thy neck with a golden thread, or a silken thread of a yellow colour, whilst the Sun rules in the heaven: so thou shalt be endued with the solary virtue of anything. But if thou dost desire the virtue of any saturnine thing, thou shalt in like manner take that thing whilst Saturn reigns, and wrap it up in the skin of an ass, or in a cloth used at a funeral, especially if thou desirest it for sadness, and with a black thread hang it about thy neck. In like manner we must conceive of the rest.

Notes—Chapter XLVI

1. *alligations*—Physical conjunction or contact.

2. *suspensions*—Things hung; in this case, on the body.

3. *accidents*—Causal appearances or effects; phenomena.

4. *crampfish*—Electric ray, or torpedo *(Torpedo vulgaris)*, a kind of ray that grows up to 100 pounds in weight and has the ability to send forth an electrical shock when touched. It is common to the Mediterranean and is also known as the cramp ray and numb-fish.

5. *sea hare*—A mollusk *(Aplysia depilans)* with four tentacles and an oval body. Pliny called this *lepus marinus,* probably because of the resemblance of two skinny lobes on the mollusk to the ears of a hare, and thought it was venomous. This belief has no foundation.

6. *lie with her*—Perhaps the smell had more to do with the effectiveness of this charm than any occult virtue.

7. *certain animals*—These are all magical conductors.

CHAPTER XLVII

Of rings, and their compositions.

Rings also, which were always much esteemed of by the ancients, when they are opportunely made, do in like manner impress their virtue upon us, in as much as they do affect the spirit of him that carries them with gladness or sadness, and render him courteous, or terrible, bold, or fearful, amiable, or hateful; in as much also as they do fortify us against sickness, poisons, enemies, evil spirits, and all manner of hurtful things, or at least will not suffer us to be kept under them.

Now the manner of making these kinds of rings, is this, viz. when any star ascends fortunately, with the fortunate aspect, or conjunction of the Moon, we must take a stone, and herb that is under that star, and make a ring of the metal that is suitable to this star, and in it fasten the stone, putting the herb, or root under it; not omitting the inscriptions of images, names, and characters, as also the proper suffumigations, but we shall speak more of these in another place, when we shall treat of images, and characters.

So we read in *Philostratus* that *Jarchus*, a wise prince of the Indians bestowed seven rings made after this manner, marked with the virtues, and names of the seven planets to *Apol-*

lonius, of which he wore every day one, distinguishing them according to the names of the days,[1] by the benefit of which he lived above one hundred and thirty years, as also always retained the beauty of his youth.

In like manner *Moses* the lawgiver, and ruler of the Hebrews, being skilled in the Egyptian magic, is said by *Josephus* to have made rings of love and oblivion. There was also, as saith *Aristotle*, amongst the Cireneans a ring of *Battus*, which could procure love and honour. We read also that *Eudamus* a certain philosopher made rings against the bites of serpents, bewitchings, and evil spirits. The same doth *Josephus* relate of *Solomon*.[2]

Also we read in *Plato* that *Gygus*,[3] King of Lydia had a ring of wonderful, and strange virtues, the seal of which, when he turned toward the palm of his hand, nobody could see him, but he could see all things: by the opportunity of which ring he ravished the Queen, and slew the King his master, and killed whomsoever he thought stood in his way, and in these villainies nobody could see him, and at length by the benefit of this ring he became king of Lydia.

Notes—Chapter XLVII

1. *names of the days*—"Damis also says that Iarchus gave to Apollonius seven rings, engraved respectively with the names of the seven planets, and that Apollo- nius used to wear each of them on its own day of the week" (Philostratus *Life and Times of Apollonius of Tyana* 3.41 [Eells, 86]).

Gnostic Ring

from *Rings for the Finger* by George Frederick Kunz (Philadelphia, 1917)

2. *of Solomon*—

I have seen a certain man of my own country whose name was Eleazar, releasing
people that were demoniacal in the presence of Vespasian, and his sons, and his
captains, and the whole multitude of his
soldiers. The manner of the cure was
this:—He put a ring that had a root of one
of those sorts mentioned by Solomon to the
nostrils of the demoniac, after which he
drew out the demon through his nostrils;
and when the man fell down immediately,
he abjured him to return into him no more,
making still mention of Solomon, and
reciting the incantations which he composed. And when Eleazar would persuade
and demonstrate to the spectators that he
had such a power, he set a little way off a
cup or basin full of water, and commanded
the demon as he went out of the man to
overturn it, and thereby to let the spectators
know that he had left the man; and when
this was done, the skill and wisdom of
Solomon was shown very manifestly …
(Josephus *Antiquities of the Jews* 8.2.5
[Whiston, 194])

3. *Gygus*—Gyges.

They relate that he was a shepherd in the
service of the ruler at that time of Lydia,
and that after a great deluge of rain and an
earthquake the ground opened and a chasm
appeared in the place where he was pastur-
ing, and they say that he saw and wondered
and went down into the chasm. And the
story goes that he beheld other marvels
there and a hollow bronze horse with little
doors, and that he peeped in and saw a
corpse within, as it seemed, of more than
mortal stature, and that there was nothing
else but a gold ring on its hand, which he
took off, and so went forth. And when the
shepherds held their customary assembly
to make their monthly report to the king
about the flocks, he also attended, wearing
the ring. So as he sat there it chanced that
he turned the collet of the ring toward himself, toward the inner part of his hand, and
when this took place they say that he
became invisible to those who sat by him
and they spoke of him as absent, and that
he was amazed, and again fumbling with
the ring turned the collet outward and so

Ring of Gyges

became visible. On noting this he experimented with the ring to see if it possessed this virtue, and he found the result to be that when he turned the collet inward he became invisible, and when outward visible, and becoming aware of this, he immediately managed things so that he became one of the messengers who went up to the king, and on coming there he seduced the king's wife and with her aid set upon the king and slew him and possessed his kingdom. (Plato *Republic* 2.359d–360b [Hamilton and Cairns, 607])

CHAPTER XLVIII

Of the virtue of places, and what places are suitable to every star.

There be wonderful virtues of places accompanying them, either from things there placed, or the influences of the stars, or any other way. For as *Pliny* relates of a cuckoo,[1] in what place anyone doth first hear him, if his right foot be marked about, and that footstep digged up, there will no fleas be bred in that place where it is scattered. So they say that the dust of the track of a snake[2] being gathered up, and scattered amongst bees, makes them return to their hives. So also that the dust, in which a mule[3] hath rolled himself, being cast upon the body, doth mitigate the heats of love, and that the dust wherein a hawk[4] hath rolled herself, if it be bound to the body in a bright red cloth, cures the quartan.

So doth the stone taken out of the nest of a swallow,[5] as they say, presently relieve those that have the falling sickness, and being bound to the party, continually preserve them, especially if it be rolled in the blood, or heart of a swallow. And it is reported, that if anyone having cut a vein, and being fasting, shall go over a place where anyone lately fell with the fit of a falling sickness, that he shall fall into the same disease. And *Pliny* reports, that to fasten an iron nail[6] in that place where he that fell with a fit of the falling sickness first pitched his head, will free him from his disease.

So they say that an herb growing upon the head[7] of any image, being gathered, and bound up in some part of one's garment with a red thread, shall presently allay the headache; and that any herb gathered out of the brooks or rivers before Sun rising, that nobody see him that gathers it, shall cure the tertian, if it be bound to the left arm, the sick party not knowing what is done.

But amongst places that are appropriated to the stars, all stinking places, dark, underground, religious, and mournful places, as churchyards, tombs, and houses not inhabited by men, and old, tottering, obscure, dreadful houses, and solitary dens, caves, and pits, also fishponds, standing pools, fens, and such like are appropriated to Saturn.

Unto Jupiter are ascribed all privileged places, consistories[8] of noble men, tribunals, chairs, places for exercises, schools, and all beautiful, and clean places, scattered, or sprinkled with divers odours.

To Mars, fiery, and bloody places, furnaces, bakehouses, shambles, places of execution, and places where there have been great battles fought, and slaughters made, and the like.

To the Sun, light places, the serene air, kings' palaces, and princes' courts, pulpits, theaters, thrones, and all kingly, and magnificent places.

To Venus, pleasant fountains, green meadows, flourishing gardens, garnished beds, stews[9] (and according to *Orpheus)* the sea, the seashore, baths, dancing places, and all places belonging to women.

To Mercury, shops, schools, warehouses, an exchange for merchants, and the like.

To the Moon, wildernesses, woods, rocks, hills, mountains, forests, fountains, waters, rivers, seas, seashores, ships, groves, highways, and granaries for corn, and such like.

Upon this account they that endeavor to procure love, are wont to bury for a certain time the instruments of their art, whether they be rings, images, looking glasses, or any other, to hide them in a stewhouse, because in that place they will contract some venereal faculty, no otherwise than things that stand in stinking places, become stinking, and those in an aromatical place, become aromatical, and of a sweet savour.

The four corners of the Earth also pertain to this matter. Hence they that are to gather a saturnine, martial, or jovial herb, must look towards the east, or south, partly because they desire to be oriental[10] from the Sun, and partly, because their principal houses, viz. Aquarius, Scorpius, Sagittarius are southern signs, so also are Capricornus, and Pisces. But they that will gather a venereal, mercurial, or lunary herb, must look towards the west, because they delight to be western, or else they must look northward, because their principal houses, viz. Taurus, Gemini, Cancer, Virgo are northern signs. So in any solary work we must look toward the east, or south, but rather towards the solary body, and light.

Notes—Chapter XLVIII

1. *of a cuckoo*—"There is another marvellous fact also mentioned, with reference to the cuckoo: if, upon the spot where a person hears this bird for the first time, he traces round the space occupied by his right foot and then digs up the earth, it will effectually prevent fleas from breeding, wherever it is thrown" (Pliny 30.25 [Bostock and Riley, 5:450]).

2. *track of a snake*—"The dust gathered from the track of a snake, sprinkled among bees, will make them return to the hive" (Pliny 30.53 [Bostock and Riley, 5:469–70]).

3. *a mule*—"The dust in which a she-mule has wallowed, sprinkled upon the body, will allay the flames of desire" (ibid., 469).

4. *a hawk*—"… the dust, for instance, in which a hawk has bathed itself, tied up in a linen cloth, with a red thread, and attached to the body [is good against quartans] …" (Pliny 30.30 [Bostock and Riley, 5:453–4]).

5. *nest of a swallow*—"Nay, even more than this, a small stone taken from a swallow's nest will relieve the patient the moment it is applied, they say; worn, too, as an amulet, it will always act as a preservative against the malady"(Pliny 30.27 [Bostock and Riley, 5:451–2]).

6. *iron nail*—"To thrust an iron nail into the spot where a person's head lay at the moment he was seized with a fit of epilepsy, is said to have the effect of curing him of that disease" (Pliny 28.17 [Bostock and Riley, 5:299]).

7. *upon the head*—Cicero mentions this herb as an evil omen: "Many other signs, at this time, announced to the Spartans the calamities of the battle of Leuctra; for, at Delphi, on the head of the statue of Lysander, who was the most famous of the Lacedaemonians, there suddenly appeared a garland of wild prickly herbs" *(De divinatione* 1.34. In *The Treatises of M. T. Cicero,* trans. C. D. Yonge [London: Bell and Daldy, 1872], 176). He goes on to say that such plants grow from seeds deposited by birds (2.32).

8. *consistories*—Council chambers.

9 *stews*—Brothels. Ancient bath houses, called "stews," were often used for prostitution.

10. *oriental*—"To be Orientall is no other thing than to rise before the Sun" (W. Lilly, *Christian Astrology* (1647), ch. 19, p. 114, quoted from *OED,* "oriental"). Thus the herb is to be gathered at the moment of sunrise.

CHAPTER XLIX

Of light, colours, candles, and lamps, and to what stars, houses, and elements several colours are ascribed.

Light also is a quality that partakes much of form, and is a simple act, and a representation of the understanding: it is first diffused from the mind of God into all things, but in God the Father, the father of light, it is the first true light; then in the Son a beautiful overflowing brightness; and in the Holy Ghost a burning brightness, exceeding all intelligences, yea, as *Dionysius* saith, of Seraphims.[1]

In angels therefore it is a shining intelligence diffused, an abundant joy beyond all bounds of reason, yet received in divers degrees, according to the nature of the intelligence that receives it. Then it descends into celestial bodies, where it becomes a store of life, and an effectual propagation, even a visible splendor. In the fire, a certain natural liveliness infused into it by the heavens. And lastly in men, it is a clear discourse of reason, and knowledge of divine things, and the whole rational faculty: but this is manifold, either by reason of the disposition of the body, as the Peripatetics will have it, or which is more true, by reason of the good pleasure of him that bestows it, who gives it to everyone as he pleaseth.

From thence it passeth to the fancy, yet above the sense, but only imaginable, and thence to the sense, but especially to that of the eyes; in them it becomes a visible clearness, and is extended to other perspicuous[2] bodies, in which it becomes a colour, and shining beauty, but in dark bodies it is a certain beneficial and generative virtue, and penetrates, to the very center, where the beams of it being collected into a narrow place, it becomes a dark heat, tormenting, and scorching, so that all things perceive the vigour of the light according to their capacity, all which joining to itself with an enlivening heat, and passing through all things, doth convey its qualities, and virtues through all things.

Therefore magicians forbid the urine of a sick man[3] to be sprinkled in the shadow of a sick man, or to be uncovered against the Sun or the Moon, because the rays of the light penetrating, bringing suddenly with it the noxious qualities of the sick bodies, convey them into the opposite body, and affect that with a quality of the same kind. This is the reason why enchanters have a care to cover their enchantments with their shadow. So the civet cat[4] makes all dogs dumb with the very touch of her shadow.

Also there are made artificially some lights, by lamps, torches, candles, and such like, of some certain things, and liquors opportunely chosen, according to the rule of the stars, and composed amongst themselves according to their congruity, which when they be lighted, and shine alone, are wont to produce some wonderful, and celestial effects, which men many times wonder at, as *Pliny* reports out of *Anaxilaus,* of a poison of mares[5] after copulation, which being lighted in torches, doth monstrously represent a sight of horse heads: the like may be done of asses, and flies, which being tempered with wax and lighted, make a strange sight of flies: and the skin of a serpent lighted in a lamp, makes serpents appear.

And they say when grapes are in their flower, if anyone shall bind a vial to them full of oil, and shall let it alone till they be ripe, and then the oil be lighted in a lamp, it makes grapes to be seen. And so in other fruits. If centory[6] be mixed with honey, and the blood of a lapwing, and be put in a lamp, they that stand about will seem a great deal bigger than they are wont: and if it be lighted in a clear night, the stars will seem to be scattered the one from the other.[7] Such force also is in the ink of the cuttlefish, that it being put into a lamp, makes blackamoors[8] appear. It is also reported, that a candle made of some certain saturnine things, if being lighted, it be extinguished in the mouth of a man newly dead, will afterwards, as oft as it shines alone, bring great sadness, and fear upon them that stand about it. Of such like torches, lamps, doth *Hermes* speak more of, also *Plato,* and *Chyrannides,* and of the latter writers *Albertus* in a certain treatise[9] of this particular thing.

Colours also are a kind of lights, which being mixed with things, are wont to expose them to those stars, to which they are agreeable. And we shall afterwards speak of some colours, which are the lights of the planets, by which even the natures of fixed stars themselves are understood, which also may be applied to the flames of lamps, and candles. But in this place we shall relate how the colours of inferior mixed things are distributed to divers planets.

For all colours, black, lucid, earthy, leaden, brown, have relation to Saturn. Sapphire, and airy colours, and those which are always green, clear, purple, darkish, golden, mixed with silver, belong to Jupiter. Red colours, and burning, fiery, flaming, violet, purple, bloody, and iron colours, resemble Mars. Golden, saffron, purple, and bright colours, resemble the Sun. But all white, fair, curious, green, ruddy, betwixt saffron, and purple, resemble Venus, Mercury, and the Moon.

Moreover amongst the houses of the heaven,[10] the first, and seventh hath white colour: the second, and twelfth green: the third, and eleventh saffron: the fourth, and the tenth red: the fifth, and ninth honey colour: the sixth and eighth, black.

The elements[11] also have their colours, by which natural philosophers judge of the complexion and property of their nature; for an earthy colour, caused of coldness, and dryness is brown, and black, and manifests black choler, and a saturnine nature; the blue tending toward whiteness, doth denote phlegm: for cold makes white, moisture and dryness makes black: reddish colour shows blood, but fiery, flaming, burning hot, show choler, which by reason of its subtilty, and aptness to mix with others, doth cause divers colours more: for if it be mixed with blood, and blood be most predominant, it makes a florid red; if choler predominate, it makes a reddish colour; if there be an equal mixtion, it makes a sad red. But if adust choler be mixed with blood, it makes a hempen colour, and red, if blood predominate, and somewhat red if choler prevail; but if it be mixed with a melancholy humour, it makes a black colour, but with melancholy, and phlegm together, in an equal proportion, it makes a hempen colour: if phlegm abound, a mud colour, if melancholy, a bluish; but if it be mixed with phlegm alone, in an equal proportion, it makes a citrine colour; if unequally, a pale, or palish.

Now all colours are more prevalent, when they be in silk, or in metals, or in perspicuous substances, or precious stones; and in those things which resemble celestial bodies in colour, especially in living things.

Notes—Chapter XLIX

1. *Seraphims*—The highest of the angelic orders.

2. *perspicuous*—Transparent or translucent.

3. *urine of a sick man*—

The adepts in magic expressly forbid a person, when about to make water, to uncover the body in the face of the sun or moon, or to sprinkle with his urine the shadow of any object whatsoever. Hesiod [*Works and Days* line 727] gives a precept, recommending persons to make water against an object standing full before them, that no divinity may be offended by their nakedness being uncovered" (Pliny 28.19 [Bostock and Riley, 5:301]).

4. *civet cat*—That is, the hyena.

5. *poison of mares*—"Anaxilaus assures us that if the liquid which exudes from a mare when covered, is ignited on the wick of a lamp, it will give out a most marvellous representation of horses' heads; and the same with reference to the she-ass" (Pliny 28.49 [Bostock and Riley, 5:339–40]). This is the second type of hippomanes—see note 20, ch. XLII, bk. I.

6. *centory*—Centaury, named after Chiron the centaur, who is said to have discovered its medicinal properties. The ancients recognized two species, greater and lesser centaury, thought to be, respectively, yellow centaury *(Chlora perfoliata)* and common centaury *(Erythraea centaurea)*. Probably common centaury is the herb intended by Agrippa.

7. *one from the other*—

> Witches [i.e. Magi] say this herb hath a marvellous virtue, for if it be joined with the blood of a female Lapwing, or Black Plover, and be put with oil in a lamp, all they that compass it about shall believe themselves to be witches, so that one shall believe of another that his head is in heaven and his feet in the earth. And if the aforesaid thing be put in the fire when the stars shine it shall appear that the stars run one against another, and fight." *(Book of Secrets* 1.13 [Best and Brightman, 13])

8. *blackamoors*—A light for causing men to appear to have black faces is given in "Marvels of the World" 63 (Best and Brightman, 103). It does not call for cuttlefish ink, however.

9. *certain treatise*—Probably refers to the "Marvels of the World," a work appended to *The Book of Secrets*, which was attributed to Albertus Magnus.

10. *houses of heaven*—The assignment of colors to the houses of the zodiac shows a bilateral symmetry around the Aries-Libra axis. This structure is based on the system of commanding and obeying signs in astrology (see note 8, ch. L, bk. II).

11. *elements*—These colors refer to skin complexions, based on the direct relationship between the elements and the bodily humors—see Appendix IV.

△ Fire: Choler (hot-dry)
🜁 Air: Blood (hot-moist)
▽ Water: Phlegm (cold-moist)
🜃 Earth: Melancholy (cold-dry)

Adust choler seems to be what Burton refers to as a diseased humor, an aberrant form of choler proper. The attributions have been codified below. "P" indicates the humor that is predominant.

🜃 —brown-black
▽ —blue-white
△ —dull red
🜁 —fiery yellow
adust △ —dull yellow

△ + 🜁 (P)—florid red
△ (P) + 🜁—reddish
△ + 🜁—sad red

adust △ + 🜁—hempen
adust △ + 🜁 (P)—red
adust △ (P) + 🜁—somewhat red
adust △ + 🜃—black
adust △ + 🜃 + ▽—hempen
adust △ + 🜃 + ▽ (P)—mud
adust △ + 🜃 (P) + ▽—bluish
adust △ + ▽—citrine
adust △ + ▽ (unequally)—pale, or palish

CHAPTER L

Of fascination, and the art thereof.

Fascination is a binding, which comes from the spirit of the witch, through the eyes of him that is bewitched, entering to his heart.

Now the instrument of fascination is the spirit, viz. a certain pure, lucid, subtle vapour, generated of the purer blood, by the heat of the heart. This doth always send forth through the eyes, rays like to itself; those rays being sent forth, do carry with them a spiritual vapour, and that vapour a blood, as it appears in blear, and red eyes, whose rays being sent forth to the eyes of him that is opposite, and looks upon them, carries the vapour of the corrupt blood, together with itself, by the contagion of which, it doth infect the eyes of the beholder with the like disease.

So the eye being opened, and intent upon anyone with a strong imagination, doth dart its beams, which are the vehiculum of the spirit into the eyes of him that is opposite to him, which tender spirit strikes the eyes of him that is bewitched, being stirred up from the heart of him that strikes, and possesseth the breast of him that is stricken, wounds his heart, and infects his spirit. Whence *Apuleius* saith,[1] thy eyes sliding down through my eyes, into mine inward breast, stirs up a most vehement burning in my marrow.

Know therefore that men are then most bewitched, when with often beholding they direct the edge of their sight[2] to the edge of their sight that bewitch them, and when their eyes are reciprocally intent one upon the other, and when rays are joined to rays, and lights to lights, for then the spirit of the one is joined to the spirit of the other, and fixeth its sparks: so are strong ligations[3] made, and so most vehement loves are inflamed with the only rays of the eyes, even with a certain sudden looking on, as if it were with a dart, or stroke penetrating the whole body, whence then the spirit, and amorous blood being thus wounded, are carried forth upon the lover, and enchanter, no otherwise than the blood, and spirit of the vengeance of him that is slain, are upon him that slays him. Whence *Lucretius* sang[4] concerning those amorous bewitchings:

> The body smitten is, but yet the mind
> Is wounded with the darts of Cupid blind.
> All parts do sympathize in the wound, but know
> The blood appears in that which had the blow.

So great is the power of fascination, especially when the vapours of the eyes are subservient to the affection. Therefore witches use collyries, ointments, alligations, and such like, to affect, and corroborate the spirit this or that manner. To procure love, they use venereal collyries, as hyppomanes, the blood of doves, or sparrows, and such like. To induce fear, they use martial collyries, as of the eyes of wolves, the civet cat, and the like. To procure misery or sickness, they use saturnine, and so of the rest.

Notes—Chapter L

1. *Apuleius saith*—"I am so stricken and subdued with thy shining eyes, ruddy cheekes, glittering haire, sweet cosses, and lilly white paps, that I neither have minde to goe home, nor to depart hence, but esteeme the pleasure which I shall have with thee this night, above all the joyes of the world" (Apuleius *The Golden Asse* ch. 15 [Adlington])

2. *edge of their sight*—The corner of the eye.

3. *ligations*—Bindings.

4. *Lucretius sang*—*On the Nature of Things* bk. 4, c. line 1042 ff. Lucretius is making the analogy that even as the blood flows toward the weapon, and the foe, that drew it forth in battle, so does the heart leap toward the individual who wounds it in love.

CHAPTER LI

Of certain observations, producing wonderful virtues.

They say that certain acts, and observations[1] have a certain power of natural things, that they believe diseases may be expelled, or brought thus, and thus. So they say that quartans may be driven away if the parings of the nails of the sick be bound to the neck of a live eel in a linen clout, and she be let go into the water. And *Pliny* saith, that the paring of the sick man's nails[2] of his feet, and hands being mixed with wax, cure the quartan, tertian, and quotidian ague,[3] and if they be before Sun rising fastened to another man's gate, will cure such like diseases. In like manner let all the parings of the nails be put into pismires' caves,[4] and they say that that which begun to draw the nails first must be taken, and bound to the neck, and by this means will the disease be removed.

They say that by wood stricken with lightning,[5] and cast behind the back with one's hands, any disease may be cured, and in quartans a piece of a nail from a gibbet, wrapt up in wool, and hanged about the neck, cures them; also a rope doth the like, that is taken from a gallows, and hid under ground, that the Sun cannot reach it.[6] Also the throat of him that hath a hard swelling, or imposthume, being touched with the hand of him that died by an immature death,[7] is cured thereby.

Also they say, that a woman is presently eased of her hard travail, if anyone shall put into the bed, where the woman in travail is, a stone, or dart, with which either of these animals, viz.

a man, a boar, or a bear were at one blow killed. The same also, as they say, doth a spear that is pulled out of the body of a man, if it shall not first touch the ground; also they say that arrows pulled out of the body of man, if they have not touched the Earth, and be put under anyone lying down, will procure love; also they say that the falling sickness is cured by meat made of the flesh of a wild beast, slain in the same manner as a man is slain.[8]

Also they say that a man's eyes that are washed three times with the water wherein he hath washed his feet,[9] shall never be sore or blear. It is said that some do cure diseases of the groin with thread taken out of the weaver's loom, being tied in nine, or seven knots, the name of some widow being named at every knot.[10] Also the spleen of cattle extended upon pained spleens, cures them, if he that applies it, saith that he is applying a medicine to the spleen to cure, and ease it: after this, they say, the patient must be shut into a sleeping room, the door being sealed up with a ring, and some verse repeated over nineteen times.[11]

The urine of a green lizard[12] cures the same disease, if it be hanged up in a pot before the patient's bedchamber, so that he may, as he comes in and out, touch it with his hand. Also a lizard killed[13] in the urine of a calf, as they say, restrains his lust that put it in: but he that shall put his own urine into a dog's urine,[14] is said to be made thereby dull to venerous acts, and to feel a benumbedness in his loins. They say, that if one's own urine be dropped upon the foot[15] in the morning, it is a remedy against all evil medicines.

And a little frog climbing up a tree, if anyone shall spit in his mouth, and then let him escape, is said to cure the cough.[16] It is a wonderful thing, but easy to experience, what *Pliny* speaks of, if anyone shall be sorry for any blow that he hath given another afar off, or nigh at hand, if he shall presently spit into the middle of that hand with which he gave the blow, the party that was smitten shall presently be freed from pain. This hath been approved of in a four-footed beast that hath been sorely hurt. Some there are that aggravate the blow before they give it.[17] In like manner spittle carried in the hand, or to spit in the shoe of the right foot before it be put on, is good when anyone passeth through a dangerous place.[18]

They say that wolves will not come to a field, if one of them be taken, and the blood let by little and little out of his legs, being unbroken, with a knife, and sprinkled about the outsides of the field, and he himself be buried in that place, from which he was first drawn.[19] The Methanenses, citizens of Trezenium, accounted it as a present remedy for preserving of vines from the wrong of the southern wind, having always found it by most certain experience; if whilst the wind blows, a white cock should be pulled to pieces in the middle by two men, both which keeping their part, must walk round the vineyard, and both meeting in the place from whence they began their circuit, must in that place bury the pieces of the cock. They say also that if anyone shall hold a viper over a vapour with a staff, he shall prophesy, and that the staff wherewith a snake was beaten is good against diseases of breeding women. These things *Pliny* recites.

It is said also in gathering of roots and herbs, we must draw three circles round about them first with a sword, then dig them up, taking heed in the mean time of a contrary wind. Also they say, that if anyone shall measure a dead man with a rope, first from the elbow to the biggest finger, then from the shoulder to the same finger, and afterwards from the head to the feet, making thrice those mensurations, if anyone afterward shall be measured with the same rope, in the same manner, he shall not prosper, but be unfortunate, and fall into misery, and sadness.

And *Albertus* out of *Chyrannis* saith, that if any woman hath enchanted thee to love her, take the sheet she lies in, and piss through her hood,[20] and her right sleeve, out of doors, and the enchantment will be quitted. And *Pliny* saith, that to sit by women great with child, or when a medicine is given to any one of them, the fingers being joined together like the teeth of a comb,[21] is a charm. This was known by experience in *Alcumena* breeding *Hercules:* and so much the worse, if that be done about one, or both knees.

Also to sit cross-legged,[22] is sorcery, therefore it was forbidden to be done in the counsels of princes, and rulers, as a thing which hindered all acts. And it is said, if anyone standing before the door call the man by his name, that is lying with a woman, and he answer, if then he fasten a knife, or needle on the door, and break it, the edge being downward, he that is in the bed with the woman cannot couple with her as long as those things shall be there.

Notes—Chapter LI

1. *observations*—Observances.

2. *sick man's nails*—

I will give an example of one of the most reasonable of their prescriptions—Take the parings of the toe-nails and finger-nails of a sick person, and mix them up with wax, the party saying that he is seeking a remedy for the tertian, quartan, or quotidian fever, as the case may be; then stick this wax, before sunrise, upon the door of another person—such is the prescription they give for these diseases! What deceitful persons they must be if there is no truth in it! And how criminal, if they really do transfer diseases from one person to another! Some of them, again, whose practices are of a less guilty nature, recommend that the parings of all the finger-nails should be thrown at the entrance of ant-holes, the first ant to be taken which attempts to draw one into the hole; this, they say, must be attached to the neck of the patient, and he will experience a speedy cure. (Pliny 28.23 [Bostock and Riley, 5:307]).

3. *quotidian*—An ague that recurs daily.

4. *pismires' caves*—Ant hills.

5. *wood stricken with lightning*—"To bite off a piece from wood that has been struck by lightning, the hands held behind the back, and then to apply it to the tooth, is a sure remedy, they say, for toothache" (Pliny 28.11 [Bostock and Riley, 5:293]).

6. *Sun cannot reach it*—"So, too, in cases of quartan fever, they take a fragment of a nail from a cross, or else a piece of a halter that has been used for crucifixion, and, after wrapping it in wool, attach it to the patient's neck; taking care, the moment he has recovered, to conceal it in some hole to which the light of the sun cannot penetrate" (ibid.).

7. *immature death*—

Scrofula, imposthumes of the parotid glands, and throat diseases, they say, may be cured by the contact of the hand of a person who has been carried off by an early death; indeed there are some who assert that any dead body will produce the same effect, provided it is of the same sex as the patient, and that the part affected is touched with the back of the left hand. (ibid., 292–3)

8. *man is slain*—

It is said, that if a person takes a stone or other missile which has slain three living creatures, a man, a boar, and a bear, at three blows, and throws it over the roof of a house in which there is a pregnant woman, her delivery, however difficult, will be instantly accelerated thereby. In such a case, too, a successful result will be rendered all the more probable, if a light infantry lance is used, which has been drawn from a man's body without touching the earth; indeed, if it is brought into the house it will be productive of a similar result. In the same way, too, we find it stated in the writings of Orpheus and Archelaüs, that arrows, drawn from a human body without being allowed to touch the ground, and placed beneath the bed, will have all the effect of a philtre; and, what is even more than this, that it is a cure for

epilepsy if the patient eats the flesh of a wild beast killed with an iron weapon with which a human being has been slain. (Pliny 28.6 [Bostock and Riley, 5:288])

9. *washed his feet*—"We are assured, too, that if persons, when washing their feet, touch the eyes three times with the water, they will never be subject to ophthalmia or other diseases of the eyes" (Pliny 28.10 [Bostock and Riley, 5:292]).

10. *every knot*—"For the cure of inguinal tumours, some persons take the thrum of an old web, and after tying seven or nine knots in it, mentioning at each knot the name of some widow woman or other, attach it to the part affected" (Pliny 28.12 [Bostock and Riley, 5:294]).

11. *nineteen times*—

According to the prescriptions given by the magicians, a fresh sheep's milt [spleen] is the best application for pains in the spleen, the person who applies it uttering these words: "This I do for the cure of the spleen." This done, it is enjoined that the milt should be covered up with mortar in the wall of the patient's sleeping-room, and sealed with a ring, a charm being repeated thrice nine times. (Pliny 30.17 [Bostock and Riley, 5:439–40])

Marcus Empiricus says that the charm to be repeated 27 times is the same one already mentioned by Pliny. See also the remedy for the spleen involving a calf's spleen (Pliny 28.57 [Bostock and Riley, 5:345]).

12. *green lizard*—"A green lizard has a remedial effect, suspended alive in an earthen vessel, at the entrance of the sleeping-room of the patient, who, every time he enters or leaves it, must take care to touch it with his hand ..." (Pliny 30.17 [Bostock and Riley, 5:440]). For the same cure against the quartan, see Pliny 30.30 [Bostock and Riley, 5:456]. This is a transference charm. The touch conveys the disease to the lizard, who dies in the pot, supposedly from troubles of the spleen but in reality from starvation and want of water.

13. *lizard killed*—"A lizard drowned in a man's urine has the effect of an antaphrodisiac upon the person whose urine it is; for this animal is to be reckoned among the philtres, the magicians say" (Pliny 30.49 [Bostock and Riley, 5:467]).

14. *dog's urine*—"If a man makes water upon a dog's urine, he will become disinclined to copulate, they say" (ibid., 468).

15. *upon the foot*—"Osthanes maintains that every one who drops some urine upon his foot in the morning will be proof against all noxious medicaments" (Pliny 28.19 [Bostock and Riley, 5:301]).

16. *cure the cough*—The disease is thus magically transferred to the frog, who carries it away with him. Frazer records the actual use of this cure:

> In Cheshire the ailment known as aphtha or thrush, which affects the mouth or throat of infants, is not uncommonly treated in much the same manner [as spitting in a frog's mouth to cure the toothache]. A young frog is held for a few moments with its head inside the mouth of the sufferer, whom it is supposed to relieve by taking the malady to itself. "I assure you," said an old woman who had often superintended such a cure, "we used to hear the poor frog whooping and coughing, mortal bad, for days after; it would have made your heart ache to hear the poor creature coughing as it did about the garden." (J. G. Frazer, *The Golden Bough*, ch. 55, sec. 4 [New York: Macmillan, 1951, abridged edition], 631)

17. *they give it*—

> What we are going to say is marvellous, but it may easily be tested by experiment: if a person repents of a blow given to another, either by hand or with a missile, he has nothing to do but to spit at once into the palm of the hand which has inflicted the blow, and all feelings of resentment will be instantly alleviated in the person struck. This, too, is often verified in the case of a beast of burden, when brought on its haunches with blows; for upon this remedy being adopted, the animal will immediately step out and mend its pace. Some persons, however, before making an effort, spit into the hand in the manner above stated, in order to make the blow more heavy. (Pliny 28.7 [Bostock and Riley, 5:289])

18. *dangerous place*—"Among the counter-charms too, are reckoned, the practice of spitting into the urine the moment it is voided, of spitting into the shoe of the right foot before putting it on, and of spitting while a person is passing a place in which he has incurred any kind of peril" (ibid., 290).

19. *first drawn*—"Wolves will never approach a field, if, after one has been caught and its legs broken and throat cut, the blood is dropped little by little along the boundaries of the field, and the body buried on the spot from which it was first dragged" (Pliny 28.81 [Bostock and Riley, 5:367]).

20. *piss through her hood*—The book *Kiranides*, referred to in *The Book of Secrets*: "… I myself, Albert, have found the truth in many things, and I suppose the truth to be in some part of the book of *Kiranides* …" (*Book of Secrets* 1.1 (Best and Brightman, 3). However this charm does not occur in the Oxford edition of *The Book of Secrets*. Perhaps it appears in a different version of the text, or in the works of Albertus Magnus proper.

21. *teeth of a comb*—

> To sit by a pregnant woman, or by a person to whom any remedy is being administered, with the fingers of one hand inserted between those of the other, acts as a magic spell; a discovery that was made, it is said, when Alcmena was delivered of Hercules. If the fingers are thus joined, clasping one or both knees, or if the ham of one leg is first put upon the knee of the other, and then changed about, the omen is of still worse signification. Hence it is, that in councils held by generals and persons in authority, our ancestors forbade these postures, as being an impediment to all business. (Pliny 28.17 [Bostock and Riley, 5:298])

See also Ovid's *Metamorphoses*, bk. 9, line 299.

22. *sit cross-legged*—See note above.

CHAPTER LII

Of the countenance, and gesture, the habit, and figure of the body, and what stars any of these do answer; whence physiognomy, and metoposcopy, and chiromancy, arts of divination, have their grounds.

The countenance, gesture, the motion, setting,[1] and figure of the body, being accidental to us, conduce to the receiving of celestial gifts, and expose us to the superior bodies, and produce certain effects in us, no otherwise than in hellebore, which when thou gatherest, if thou pullest the leaf upward, it draws the humours upward, and causeth vomiting; if downward, it causeth purging, by drawing the humour downward.

How much also the countenance, gesture, do affect the sight, imagination, and animal spirit, no man is ignorant. So they that couple for generation, for the most part are wont to make an impression on the children that are then begotten, of that countenance which they themselves then form, or imagine:[2] so a mild, and cheerful countenance of a prince in the city, makes the people joyful: but fierce, and sad, terrifies them: so the gesture, and countenance of anyone lamenting, doth easily move to pity: so the shape of an amiable person, doth easily excite to love.

Thou must know that such like gestures, and figures, as harmonies of the body do expose it no otherwise to the celestials, than odours, and the spirit of a medicine, and internal passions do the soul. For as medicines, and passions of the mind are by certain dispositions of the heaven increased, so also the gesture, and motion of the body do get an efficacy by certain influences of the heavens.

For there are gestures resembling Saturn, which are melancholy, and sad, as are beating of the breast, striking of the head: also such as are religious, as the bowing of the knee, and a fixed look downward, as of one praying, also weeping, and such like, as are used by an austere, and saturnine man, such an one as the Satirist[3] describes, saying:

> With hanged down head, with eyes fixed to
> the ground,
> His raging words bites in, and muttering
> sound
> He doth express with pouting lips———

A cheerful, and honest countenance, a worshipful gesture, clapping of the hands, as of one rejoicing, and praising; also the bending of the knee, with the head lifted up, as of one that is worshipping, are ascribed to Jupiter. A sour, fierce, cruel, angry, rough countenance, and gesture, are ascribed to Mars. Solary are honourable, and courageous gestures, and countenances: also walking abroad, bending of the knee, as of one honouring a king with one knee. Venereal, are dances, embraces, laughters, amiable, and cheerful countenances. Mercurial are inconstant, quick, variable, and such like gestures, and countenances. Lunary are such as are moveable, poisonful, and childish, and the like.

And as we have spoke of gestures, so also are the shapes of men distinct. For Saturn bespeaks a man to be of a black, and yellowish colour, lean, crooked, of a rough skin, great veins, hairy all over his body, little eyes, of a frowning forehead, of a thin beard, great lips, eyes intent upon the ground, of a heavy gait, striking his feet together as he walks, crafty, witty, a seducer, and murderous.

Jupiter signifies a man to be of a pale colour, darkish red, a handsome body, good stature, bold, of great eyes, not black altogether, large pupils, short nostrils, not equal,[4] great teeth before, curled hair, of good disposition, and manners.

Mars makes a man red, of a red hair, round face, yellowish eyes, of a terrible, and sharp looks, bold, jocund, proud, crafty.

The Sun makes a man of a tawny colour, betwixt yellow and black, dashed with red, of a short stature, yet of a handsome body, without much hair, and curled, of yellow eyes, wise, faithful, desirous of praise.

Venus signifies a man to be tending towards blackness, but more white, with mixture of red, of a handsome body, a fair, and round face, fair hair, fair eyes, the blackness whereof is more intense,[5] of good manners, and honest love, also kind, patient, and jocund.

Mercury signifies a man not much white, or black,[6] of a long face, high forehead, fair eyes, not black, to have a straight, and long nose, thin beard, long fingers, to be ingenious, a subtile inquisitor, turncoat, and subject to many fortunes.

The Moon signifies a man to be in colour white, mixed with a little red, of a fair stature, round face, with some marks in it, eyes not fully black, frowning forehead, also kind, gentle, sociable.

The signs also, and faces of signs have their figures, and shapes, which he that would know, must seek them out in books of astrology. Lastly, upon these figures, and gestures, physiognomy,[7] and metoposcopy,[8] arts of divination do depend: also chiromancy, foretelling future events, not as causes, but as signs through like effects, caused by the same cause.[9]

And although these divers kinds of divinations may seem to be done by inferior, and weak signs, yet the judgements of them are not to be slighted, or condemned, when prognostication is made by them, not out of superstition, but by reason of the harmonical correspondency of all the parts of the body. Whosoever therefore doth the more exactly imitate the celestial bodies, either in nature, study, action, motion, gesture, countenance, passions of the mind, and opportunity of the season, is so much the more like to the heavenly bodies, and can receive larger gifts from them.

Notes—Chapter LII

1. *setting*—Probably the posture.

2. *or imagine*—

These strong features of resemblance proceed, no doubt, from the imagination of the parents, over which we may reasonably believe that many casual circumstances have a very powerful influence; such, for instance, as the action of the eyes, the ears, or the memory, or impressions received at the moment of conception. A thought even, momentarily passing through the mind of either of the parents, may be supposed to produce a resemblance to one of them separately, or else to the two combined. Hence it is that the varieties are much more numerous in the appearance of man than in that of other animals; seeing that, in the former, the rapidity of ideas, the quickness of the perception, and the varied powers of the intellect, tend to impress upon the features peculiar and diversified marks; while in the case of the other animals, the mind is immovable, and just the same in each and all individuals of the same species. (Pliny 7.10 [Bostock and Riley, 2:146])

3. *Satirist*—Presumably Juvenal, although I cannot locate this passage in his writings.

4. *not equal*—A crooked nose, probably one that is pug or turned up at the end.

5. *more intense*—The black of the pupil stands out the more because of the paleness of the iris.

6. *white, or black*—Neither very white of skin, nor very dark of hair or eyes.

7. *physiognomy*—Divination by the lines and structure of the face.

8. *metoposcopy*—Divination by the lines and shape of the forehead.

9. *the same cause*—The lines of the hand or face do not cause the foretold events to occur, but reflect the circumstances in which those events arise, and are themselves the result of the same supernal cause that shapes fortune.

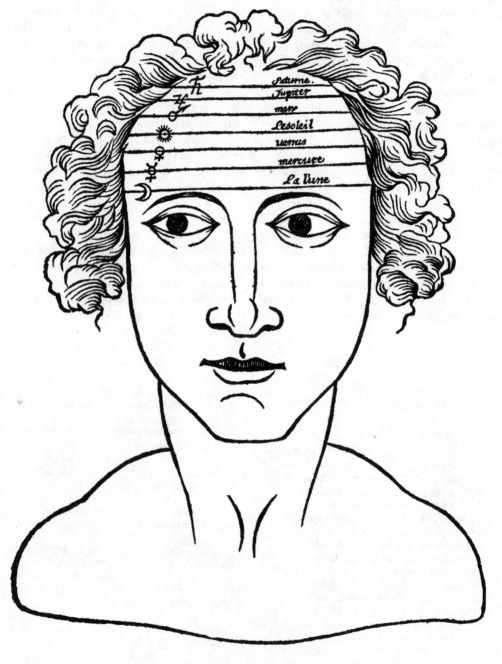

Metoposcopy

from *Metoposcopia* by Jerome Cardan (Paris, 1658)

CHAPTER LIII

Of divination, and its kinds.

There are some other kinds of divinations depending upon natural causes, which are known to everyone in his art, and experience, to be in divers things; by which physicians, husbandmen, shepherds, mariners, and every one of these out of probable signs do prognosticate. Many of these kinds *Aristotle* makes mention of in his Book of Times.[1]

Amongst which auguria,[2] and auspicia[3] are the chiefest, which were in former time in such esteem amongst the Romans, that they would do nothing that did belong to private or public business, without the counsel of the augurs: *Cicero* also in his Book of Divinations largely declares, that the people of Tuscia would do nothing without this art.[4]

Now there are divers kinds of auspicias: for some are called pedestria[5] i.e. which are taken from four-footed beasts: some are called auguria,[6] which are taken from birds: some are celestial,[7] which are taken from thunderings, and lightnings: some are called caduca[8] i.e. when any fell in the temple, or elsewhere: some were sacred, which were taken from sacrifices. Some of these were called piacula,[9] and sad auspicia, as when a sacrifice escaped from the altar, or being smitten made a bellowing, or fell upon another part of his body than he should. To these is added exauguration,[10] viz. when the rod fell out of the hand of the augur, with which it was the custom to view, and take notice of the auspicium.

Michael Scotus makes mention of twelve kinds of augurias, viz. six on the right hand, the names of which he saith are fernova, fervertus, confert, emponenthem, sonnasarnova, sonnasarvetus: and the other six on the left hand, the names of which are, confernova, confervetus, viaram, herrenam, scassarnova, scassarvetus.

Then expounding their names, he saith, fernova is an augurium; when thou goest out of thy house for to do any business, and in going thou seest a man, or a bird going, or flying, so that either of them set himself before thee upon thy left hand, that is a good signification, in reference to thy business.

Fervetus is an augurium; when thou shalt go out of thy house for to do any business, and in going thou findest or seest a bird, or a man resting himself before thee on the left side of thee, that is an ill sign in reference to thy business.

Viaram is an augurium; when a man or a bird in his journey, or flying passeth before thee, coming from the right side of thee, and bending toward the left, goeth out of thy sight, that is a good sign concerning thy business.

Confernova is an augurium; when thou dost first find a man, or a bird going, or flying, and then he rests himself before thee on thy right side, thou seeing of it, that is a good sign concerning thy business.

Confervetus is an augurium; when first thou findest, or seest a man, or a bird bending from thy right side, it is an ill sign concerning thy business.

Scimasarnova is an augurium; when a man, or a bird comes behind thee, and outgoeth thee, but before he comes at thee, he rests, thou seeing of him on thy right side, it is to thee a good sign.

Scimasarvetus is an augurium; when thou seest a man, or a bird behind thee, but before he comes to thee he rests in that place, thou seeing of it, it is a good sign.

Scassarvetus is when thou seest a man, or a bird passing by thee, and resting in a place on thy left side, it is an evil sign to thee.

Emponenthem is when a man, or a bird coming from thy left side, and passing to thy right, goeth out of thy sight without resting, it is a good sign.

Hartena is an augurium; if a man or a bird coming from thy right hand, passing behind thy back to thy left, and thou shalt see him resting anywhere, this is an evil sign. Thus much *Scotus*.[11]

The ancients did also prognosticate from sneezings, of which *Homer*[12] in the seventeenth book of his Odes, makes mention, because they thought they proceeded from a sacred place, viz. the head, in which the intellect is vigorous, and operative. Whence also whatsoever speech came into the breast, or mind of a man rising in the morning unawares, is said to be some presage, and an augurium.

Notes—Chapter LIII

1. *book of times*—Perhaps a spurious work attributed to Aristotle. I find no mention of it.

2. *auguria*—Auguries, a specific kind of divination practiced by the College of Augurs at Rome, whose duty it was to read the portents relating to public undertakings. Originally there were three, but by the time of Julius Caesar their number had swelled to sixteen, and Augustus Caesar was given the power to elect as many as he pleased.

There were five official types of augury: (1) *ex coelo* (from the sky): thunder, lightning, meteors, comets, and other heavenly phenomena; (2) *ex avibus* (from birds), which fell into two classes: (a) *alites,* the flight of birds, specifically the eagle and vulture; (b) *oscines,* the voice of birds, specifically the owl, crow, raven and hen; (3) *ex tripudiis* (from feeding of birds): whether or not a bird, usually a fowl, dropped a kernel while eating, this being a favorable omen; (4) *ex quadrupedibus* (from animals): the motions and sounds of four-footed beasts and reptiles; (5) *ex diris* (from warnings): any chance incident that might forebode disaster.

These five types of augury were divided by the ancients into two classes: (1) *auspicia impetrativa,* signs asked for as a guide; and (2) *auspicia oblativa,* signs occurring of themselves. The duties of the College of Augurs were chiefly concerned with the first class. All official acts were sanctioned by favorable auguries, or delayed until the portents were more auspicious.

3. *auspicia*—Auguries were originally called auspices, from *auspex* (observer of birds). When the term *auspex* fell out of use and was replaced by

augur, auspicium was retained as the scientific term for the observation of signs. Not only augurs but chief magistrates of Rome might hold auspices, but auguries were the sole province of augurs. Generally the terms are used interchangably.

4. *without this art*—This statement seems to derive from this passage:

> In the first place, the founder of this city, Romulus, is said not only to have founded the city in obedience to the auspices, but also to have been himself an augur of the highest reputation. After him the other kings also had recourse to soothsayers; and after the kings were driven out, no public business was ever transacted, either at home or in war, without reference to the auspices. And as there appeared to be great power and usefulness in the system of the soothsayers *(haruspices),* in reference to the people's succeeding in their objects, and consulting the Gods, and arriving at an understanding of the meaning of prodigies and averting evil omens, they introduced the whole of their science from Etruria, to prevent the appearance of allowing any kind of divination to be neglected. (Cicero *De divinatione* 1.2 [Yonge, 142–3])

Further, he says:

> … nor will I be persuaded to think, either that all Etruria is mad on the subject of the entrails of victims, or that the same nation is all wrong about lightnings, or that it

interprets prodigies fallaciously ..." (ibid. 1.18 [Yonge, 160])

The people of Tuscia, or Etruria, were proverbial for their powers of divination.

> The mode in which the gods were wor-
> shipped was prescribed in certain sacred
> books, said to have been written by Tages
> [god of the Etruscans]. These books con-
> tained the "Etruscan Disciplina" and gave
> minute directions respecting the whole of
> ceremonial worship. They were studied in
> the schools of the Lucumones, to which the
> Romans also were accustomed to send
> some of their noblest youths for instruc-
> tion, since it was from the Etruscans that
> the Romans borrowed most of their arts of
> divination. (W. Smith, *Classical Diction-
> ary* [New York: Harper and Brothers,
> 1862], 292)

5. *pedestria—Ex quadrupedibus.*

6. *auguria—Ex avibus.*

7. *celestial—Ex coelo.*

8. *caduca*—From the Latin *caducus* (that falls, that has fallen, etc.), a form of *auspicia oblativa.*

9. *piacula—Piacularia auspicia* is mentioned by Pompeius Festus, a Roman grammarian of the 4th century, in his Latin dictionary *Sexti Pompeii Festi de verborum significatione.*

10. *exauguration*—The staff of the augur was a symbol of his office. Called a *lituus,* it was free from
knots and crooked at the top. With it the augur
marked out the *templum,* or consecrated space, upon
the sky and the Earth, where the augury of the animal
entering was to be read. This was done on the night
before the event in the presence of a magistrate, at
midnight. Entry of an animal from the east was favorable, from the west unfavorable. The Roman augurs
looked to the south, the Greek augurs to the north;
therefore the left was lucky in Rome, the right lucky
in Greece.

11. *Thus much Scotus*—These six pairs of auguria are
taken directly from Michael Scot's *Physiognomia,* ch.
57, where, however, only 11 are described, *confert*
being omitted. *Scimasarvetus* is the same as *sonnasarvetus,* and *scimasarnova* the same as *sonnasarnova.* The exposition of *confert* has been left out
of both Agrippa's Latin *Opera* and the English translation. *Scassarnova* appears in the Latin edition, but not
in the English. However, because of the gap caused by
its omission from the English edition, the translator has
made an error, and put the exposition that rightly
belongs to *scassarnova* (which comes directly after *scimasarvetus* in the Latin text) with *scimasarvetus,* while
the exposition of *scimasarvetus* given in the Latin text
is omitted from the English entirely. I have attempted
to give below the definitions of the two terms as they
should appear, based on the *Opera:*

> Scimasarvetus is an augurium; when thou
> seest a man or bird behind thee, resting in a
> place on thy right side, it is an evil sign.

> Scassarnova is when thou seest a man, or a
> bird behind thee, but before he comes to
> thee he rests in that place, thou seeing of it,
> it is a good sign.

The description of the auguries is taken almost verbatim from ch. 57 of Michael Scot's *Physiognomia,* a
popular work that was published at least 19 times
between 1477 and 1669.

12. *Homer*—When Apollo seizes the infant Hermes in
an effort to learn where Hermes has hidden his stolen
cattle, Hermes sneezes, causing Apollo to drop him:

> Thus then he spake, and Phoebus Apollo
> took up and carried the boy, but then the
> brave slayer of Argus, taking counsel, as he
> was lifted up in his arms, sent forth an
> augury into his hands, a sad report from his
> belly, an impudent messenger. And
> quickly after it he sneezed. But Apollo
> heard it, and cast glorious Mercury from
> his hands upon the ground. (*Homeric
> Hymns* 2, "To Hermes" c. line 294. In *The
> Odyssey of Homer, with the Hymns, Epi-
> grams, and Battle of the Frogs and Mice,*
> trans. Theodore Alois Buckley [New York:
> Harper and Brothers, 1872], 377–8)

CHAPTER LIV

Of divers certain animals, and other things which have a signification in augurias.

All the auspicia which first happen in the beginning of any enterprise are to be taken notice of: as if in the beginning of thy work thou shalt perceive that rats have gnawn[1] thy garments, desist from thy undertakings; if going forth thou shalt stumble at the threshold,[2] on in the way thou shalt dash thy foot against anything, forbear thy journey; if any ill omen happen in the beginning of thy business, put off thy undertakings, lest thy intentions be wholly frustrated, or accomplished to no purpose; but expect and wait for a fortunate hour for the dispatching of thy affairs with a better omen.

We see that many animals are, by a natural power inbred in them, prophetical. Doth not the cock, by his crowing[3] diligently tell you the hours of the night, and morning, and with his wings spread forth chase away the lion; and many birds with their singing, and chattering, and flies by their sharp pricking foretell rain, and dolphins by their often leaping above the water, forerun tempests?

It would be too long to relate all the presages, which the Phrygians, Cilicians, Arabians, Umbrians, Tuscians, and other people, which follow the augurias, learned by birds. These they have proved by many experiments, and examples. For in all things the oracles of things to come are hid: but those are the chiefest which omenal birds shall foretell. These are those which the poets relate were turned from men into birds.

Therefore what the daw[4] declares, harken, and mark, observing her setting as she sits, and her manner of flying, whether on the right hand, or left, whether clamorous, or silent, whether she goes before, or follows after, whether she waits for the approach of him that passeth by, or flies from him, and which way she goes; all these things must be diligently observed. *Orus Apollo* saith[5] in his Hieroglyphics, daws that are twins signify marriage, because this animal brings forth two eggs, out of which male, and female must be brought forth: but if (which seldom happens) two males be generated, or two females, the males will not couple with any other females, nor females with any other males, but will always live without a mate; and solitary. Therefore they that meet a single daw, divine thereby that they shall live a single life. The same also doth a black hen pigeon[6] betoken; for after the death of her mate, she always lives single.

Thou shalt as carefully observe crows,[7] which are as significant as daws, yea, and in greater matters. It was *Epictetus* the Stoic philosopher's judgement, who was a sage author, that if a crow did croak over against anyone, it did betoken some evil, either to his body, fortune, honour, wife, or children. Then thou shalt take heed to swans,[8] who foreknow the secrets of the waters, for their cheerfulness doth presage happy events not only for mariners, but all other travelers, unless they be overcome by the coming over of a stronger, as of an eagle,[9] who by the most potent majesty of her sovereignty makes null the predictions of all other birds, if she speaks to the contrary; for she flies higher than all other birds, and is of more acute sight, and is never excluded from the secrets of *Jupiter:* she portends advancement, and victory, but by blood; because she drinks no water but blood.

An eagle flying over the Locrensians, fighting against the Crotoniensians, gave them victory. An eagle setting herself unawares upon the target[10] of *Hiero,* going forth to the first war, betokened that he should be king. Two eagles sitting all day upon the house at the birth of *Alexander* of Macedonia, did portend to him an omen of two kingdoms, viz. Asia, and Europe. An eagle also taking off the hat of *Lucias Tarquinius Priscus,*[11] son to *Demarathus* the Corinthian (flying from home by reason of some discord, and being come into Hetraria,[12] and going to Rome) and then flying high with it, and afterwards putting it upon his head again, did portend to him the kingdom of the Romans.

Vultures[13] also signify difficulty, hardness, ravenousness, which was verified in the beginning of building of cities. Also they foretell the places of slaughter, coming seven days before hand; and because they have most respect to that place where the greatest slaughter shall be, as if they gaped after the greatest number of the slain; therefore the ancient kings were wont to send out spies to take notice what place the vultures had most respect to.

The phoenix promiseth singular good success, which being seen anew, Rome was built very auspiciously. The pelican, because she hazards herself for her young, signifies that a man should out of the zeal of his love undergo much hardship. The painted bird gave the name to the city of Pictavia, and foreshowed the lenity of that people by its colour, and voice. The heron is an augurium of hard things. The stork is a bird of concord, and makes concord. Cranes[14] give us notice of the treachery of enemies. The bird cacupha betokens gratitude, for she alone doth express love to her dam, being spent with old age. On the contrary, hippopotamus[15] that kills his dam, doth betoken ingratitude for good turn, also injustice. The bird origis[16] is most envious, and betokens envy.

Amongst the smaller birds, the pie is talkative, and foretells guests. The bird albanellus flying by anyone, if from the left to the right, betokens cheerfulness of entertainment, if contrarywise, betokens the contrary. The screech owl[17] is always unlucky, so also is the horn owl,[18] who because she goes to her young by night unawares, as death comes unawares, is therefore said to foretell death:[19] yet sometimes, because she is not blind in the dark of the night, doth betoken diligence,[20] and watchfulness, which she made good, when she sat upon the spear of *Hiero.* *Dido,*[21] when she sees the unlucky owl, pitied *Aeneas,* whence the poet sang:[22]

> The owl sitting on top of the house alone,
> Sends forth her sad complaint with mournful tone.

And in another place:[23]

> The slothful owl by mortals is esteemed
> A fatal omen————

The same bird sang in the Capitol when the Roman affairs were low at Numantia, and when Fregelia was pulled down for a conspiracy made against the Romans. *Almadel* saith, that owls, and night-ravens, when they turn aside to strange countries, or houses, betoken the death of the men of that country, and those houses; for those birds are delighted with dead carcasses, and perceive them beforehand. For men that are dying have a near affinity with dead carcasses. The hawk also is a foreteller of contention, as *Naso* sings:[24]

> We hate the hawk, because that arms amongst
> She always lives————

Lelius the ambassador of *Pompey* was slain in Spain amongst the purveyors,[25] which misfortune, a hawk flying over his head, is said to foretell. And *Almadel* saith, that these kind of birds fighting amongst themselves, signify the change of a kingdom; but if birds of another kind shall fight with them, and are never seen to come together again, it portends a new condition, and state of that country.

Also little birds by their coming to, or departing from, foreshow that a family shall be enlarged, or lessened, and their flight, by how much the more serene it is, by so much the more laudable. Whence *Melampus* the augur conjectured at the slaughter of the Greeks by the flight of little birds, when he saith, thou seest that no bird taketh his flight in fair weather. Swallows, because when they are dying they provide a place of safety for their young, do portend a great patrimony, or legacy after the death of friends.

A bat[26] meeting anyone running away, signifies an evasion: for although she have no wings, yet she flies. A sparrow is a bad omen to one that runs away, for she flies from the hawk, and makes haste to the owl,[27] where she is in as great danger: yet in love she is fortunate, for being stirred up with lust, couples seven times in an hour. Bees[28] are a good omen to kings, for they signify an obsequious people. Flies[29] signify importunity, and impudency, because being oftentimes driven away, they do yet continually return.

Also domestic birds are not without some augurias, for cocks by their crowing promote hope, and the journey of him that is undertaking it. Moreover *Livia* the mother of *Tiberius,* when she was great with him, took a hen egg and hatched it in her bosom,[30] and at length came forth a cock chick with a great comb, which the augurs interpreted that the child that should be born of her should be king. And *Cicero* writes[31] that at Thebais cocks, by their crowing all night, did presage that the Baeotians would obtain victory against the Lacedaemonians, and the reason is according to the augurs' interpretations, because that bird when he is beaten is silent, but when he himself hath overcome, crows.

In like manner also omens of events are taken from beasts. For the meeting of a weasel is ominous, also meeting of a hare is an ill omen to a traveler, unless she be taken. A mule[32] also is bad, because barren. A hog is pernicious, for such is his nature, and therefore signifies pernicious men. A horse betokens quarrelings, and

fightings: whence *Anchises* seeing of white horses, cries out in *Virgil:*[33]

> War thou bearest, O land of our reception,
> With war are horses armed, yea threaten
> war.

But when they are joined together in a chariot, because they draw with an equal yoke, they signify that peace is to be hoped for.

An ass is an unprofitable creature, yet did *Marius* good,[34] who when he was pronounced enemy to his country, saw an ass disdaining provender that was offered to him, and running to the water, by which augury, he supposing he saw a way of safety showed to him, entreated the aid of his friends, that they would convey him to the sea; which being granted, he was set into a little ship, and so escaped the threats of *Sulla* the conqueror. If the foal of an ass meet anyone going to an augury, he signifies labour, patience, and hinderances.

A wolf meeting anyone is a good sign, the effect whereof was seen in *Hiero* of Sicilia, from whom a wolf snatching away a book whilst he was at school, confirmed to him the success of the kingdom: but yet the wolf makes him speechless whom he sees first. A wolf rent in pieces a watchman of *P. Africanus* and *C. Fulvius* at Minturn, when the Roman army was overtaken by the fugitives in Sicilia.[35] Also he signifies perfedious men, such as you can give no credit to: which was known in the progeny of Romans. For the faith which they long since sucked from their mother the wolf,[36] and kept to themselves from the beginning, as by a certain law of nature, passed over to their posterity.

To meet a lion, seeing she is amongst animals the strongest, and striking terror into all the rest, is good. But for a woman to meet a lioness, is bad,[37] because she hinders conception, for a lioness brings forth but once.

To meet sheep, and goats is good. It is read also in the Ostentarian[38] of the Tuscians, if this animal shall wear any unusual colour, it portends to the emperor plenty of all things, together with much happiness. Whence *Virgil*[39] to *Pollio* sings thus:

But in the meadows rams shall scarlet bear,
And changing, sometimes golden fleeces
  wear.

It is good also to meet oxen treading out corn, but better to meet them plowing, which although breaking the way hinder thy journey, yet by the favour of their auspicium will recompence thee again. A dog in a journey is fortunate, because *Cyrus* being cast into the woods was nourished by a dog[40] till he came to the kingdom, which also the angel, companion of *Tobit*[41] did not scorn as a companion. The castor,[42] because he bites off his testicles, and leaves them to the hunters, is an ill omen, and portends that a man will injure himself.

Also amongst small animals, mice signify danger. For the same day that they did gnaw gold in the Capitol, both the consuls[43] were intercepted by *Hannibal* by way of ambush near Tarentum. The locust making a stand in any place, or burning the place, hinders one from their wishes, and is an ill omen; on the contrary the grasshoppers promote a journey, and foretell a good event of things. The spider weaving a line downwards, is said to signify hope of money to come. Also the pismires, because they know how to provide for themselves, and to prepare safe nests for themselves, portend security, and riches, a great army. Hence, when the pismires had devoured a tame dragon[44] of *Tiberius Caesar,* it was advised, that he should take heed of the tumult of a multitude.

If a snake meet thee, take heed of an ill-tongued enemy; for this animal hath no other power but in his mouth.[45] A snake creeping into *Tiberius* his palace, portended his fall. Two snakes[46] were found in the bed of *Sempronius Gracchus,* wherefore a soothsayer told him, if he would let the male, or the female escape, either he or his wife would shortly die; he preferring the life of his wife, killed the male, and let the female escape, and within a few days he died. So a viper[47] signifies lewd women, and wicked children; and an eel[48] signifies a man displeased with everybody: for she lives apart from all other fishes, nor is ever found in the company of any.

But amongst all auspicias and omens, there is none more effectual, and potent than man, none that doth signify the truth more clearly. Thou shalt therefore diligently note, and observe the condition of the man that meeteth thee, his age, profession, station, gesture, motion, exercise, complexion, habit, name, words, speech, and all such like things. For seeing there are in all other animals so many discoveries of presages, without all question these are more efficacious, and clear, which are infused into man's soul; which *Tully*[49] himself testifies, saying, that there is a certain auspicium naturally in men's souls of their eternity, for the knowing of all the courses, and causes of things.

In the foundation of the city of Rome the head of a man[50] was found with his whole face, which did presage the greatness of the Empire, and gave the name to the mountain of the Capitol. The Brutian soldiers[51] fighting against *Octavius,* and *M. Antonius,* found an Ethiopian in the gate of their castle; whom though they did slay as a presage of ill success, yet they were unfortunate in the battle, and *Brutus,* and *Cassius,* both generals, were slain. Meeting of monks is commonly accounted an ill omen, and so much the rather, if it be early in the morning, because these kind of men live for the most by the sudden death of men, as vultures do by slaughters.

Notes—Chapter LIV

1. *rats have gnawn*—Cicero mocks the portent of mice gnawing:

> We are, however, so silly and inconsiderate, that if mice, which are always at work, happen to gnaw anything, we immediately regard it as a prodigy. So because, a little before the Marsian war, the mice gnawed

the shields at Lanuvium, the soothsayers declared it to be a most important prodigy; as if it could make any difference whether mice, who day and night are gnawing something, had gnawed bucklers or sieves. (Cicero *De divinatione* 2.27 [Yonge, 224])

2. *dash foot*—"There is something in omens; just now, when she was preparing to go, Nape stopped short, having struck her foot against the threshold" (Ovid *Amores* 1.12. In *The Heroides, The Amours, The Art of Love, The Remedy of Love, and Minor Works,* trans. Henry T. Riley [London: George Bell and Sons, 1883], 291). For other instances of the same superstition in Ovid, see *The Metamorphoses* 10.8, c. line 352, and *The Heroides* 13, line 88.

3. *by his crowing*—"As, then, this animal is so much inclined to crow of its own accord, what made it occur to Callisthenes to assert that the Gods had given the cocks a signal to crow; since either nature or chance might have done it?" (Cicero *De divinatione* 2.26 [Yonge, 223])

4. *daw*—The jackdaw (*Corvus monedula*) is a small bird like a crow with a reputation for foolishness and thievery. Arne was transformed into a jackdaw because she betrayed her own city to its enemies for gold. See Ovid *Metamorphoses* 7.4, line 466 (Riley, 246).

5. *Orus Apollo saith*—

When they would denote Ares and Aphrodite (Horus and Athor) otherwise, they depict two crows as a man and a woman; because this bird lays two eggs, from which a male and female ought to be produced, and ([except] when it produces two males or two females, which, however, rarely happens), the males mate with the females, and hold no intercourse with any other crow, neither does the female with any other crow, till death; but those that are widowed pass their lives in solitude. And hence, when men meet with a single crow, they look upon it as an omen, as having met with a widowed creature ..." (Horapollo *Hieroglyphics* 1.8 [Cory 17–8])

The translation of the name of this bird is not certain. "To denote marriage, they again depict two crows, on account of what has been mentioned" (ibid. 1.9 [Cory 19]).

6. *black hen pigeon*—"When they would symbolise a woman who remains a widow till death, they depict a black dove; for this bird has no connection with another mate from the time that it is widowed" (ibid. 2.32 [Cory 107]). A dove is a type of pigeon. The two daughters of Anius were changed into doves by Bacchus to free them from Agamemnon, who forced them to use their magic to feed the Greek fleet. See Ovid *Metamorphoses* 13.5, line 673 (Riley, 464).

7. *crows*—The virgin Coronis was transformed into a crow by Minerva to escape the lust of Neptune (ibid. 2.8, c. line 580 [Riley, 69]). Virgil mentions the direful portent of the crow: "Indeed, had not a crow on my left hand warned me from a hollow ilex-tree by some means to break off the new-begun dispute, neither I, your Moeris, nor Menalcas himself would be living" (Virgil *Eclogues* 9, line 14 [Lonsdale and Lee, 27]).

8. *swans*—Venus draws a happy augury from swans to encourage Aeneas:

Behold those twelve swans in joyful line, whom just now Jove's bird [eagle] stooping from the region of the sky threw into confusion in the open firmament, but now they seem in a long extended row either to be choosing, or having chosen to be gazing downwards on their ground. As they returning sport with flapping wings, and gird the pole with their circling flock, and give forth their song; even so your ships, and youthful comrades either are safe in the port, or are just entering its mouth with full sail. (Virgil *Aeneid* 1, c. line 392 [Lonsdale and Lee, 90])

Cycnus, the king of Liguria, was transformed into a swan by his mourning over the death of Phaeton, killed by the thunderbolt of Zeus. See Ovid *Metamorphoses* 2.4, c. line 372 (Riley, 61).

9. *eagle*—"And they use it [eagle] to denote excellence, because it appears to excel all birds—and for blood, because they say that this animal does not drink water, but blood—and for victory, because it shows itself capable of overcoming every winged creature ..." (Horapollo *Hieroglyphics* 1.6 [Cory, 14]).

10. *target*—A small round shield.

11. *Lucias Tarquinius Priscus*—

The pair [Tarquinius and his wife] had reached Janiculum [a hill then outside of Rome] and were sitting together in their carriage, when an eagle dropped gently down and snatched off the cap which Lucumo [i.e. Tarquinius] was wearing. Up went the bird with a great clangour of wings until, a moment later, it swooped down again and, as if it had been sent by heaven for that very purpose, neatly replaced the cap on Lucumo's head, and then vanished into the blue." (Livy *Early History of Rome* 1.34, trans. Aubrey de Selincourt [1960] [Harmondsworth: Penguin Books, 1982], 73.

12. *Hetraria*—Etruria.

13. *vultures*—"Umbricius, the most skillful among the aruspices of our time, says that the vulture lays thirteen eggs, and that with one of these eggs it purifies the others and its nest, and then throws it away: he states also that they hover about for three days, over the spot where carcasses are about to be found" (Pliny 10.7 [Bostock and Riley, 2:486–7]).

14. *cranes*—"When they would symbolise a man that guards himself from the plots of his enemies, they depict a crane on the watch; for these birds guard themselves by watching in turns during the whole night" (Horapollo *Hieroglyphics* 2.94 [Cory, 143]).

15. *hippopotamus*—

> To symbolise an unjust and ungrateful man, they depict two claws of an hippopotamus turned downwards. For this animal when arrived at its prime of life contends in fight against his father, to try which is the stronger of the two, and should the father give way he assigns him a place of residence, permitting him to live, and consorts himself with his own mother; but if his father should not permit him to hold intercourse with his mother, he kills him, being the stronger and more vigorous of the two. (ibid. 1.56 [Cory, 76–7]

16. *origis*—

> To denote impurity, they delineate an oryx (a species of wild goat), because when the moon rises, this animal looks intently towards the goddess and raises an outcry, and that, neither to praise nor welcome her; and of this the proof is most evident, for it scrapes up the earth with its fore legs, and fixes its eyes in the earth, as if indignant and unwilling to behold the rising of the goddess. And it acts in the same manner at the rising of (the divine star) the sun. (ibid. 1.49 [Cory 69–70])

In the editions of the *Hieroglyphics* of Mercer (1548) and Caussin (1631), quail (ὄρτυγα) is given instead of oryx (ὄρυγα), which accounts for Agrippa calling this a bird—presumably he used the same manuscript version as his source.

17. *screech owl*—*Strix flammea*, also called the barn owl.

> Large are their heads, fixed is their gaze, for plunder are their beaks adapted; on their wings is a greyish colour, crooked talons are on their claws. By night they fly,

and they seek the children unprotected by the nurse, and pollute their bodies, dragged from their cradles. With their beaks they are said to tear the entrails of the sucklings, and they have their maws distended with the blood which they have swallowed. "Stirges," are they called; and the origin of the name is, the fact, that they are wont to screech in the dismal night. (Ovid *Fasti* 6, lines 133–40 [Riley, 216])

18. *horn owl*—Horned owl *(Asio otus* or *Otus vulgaris),* so called because of the long tufts of feathers, like horns, on its head.

19. *foretell death*—"A night raven signifies death; for it suddenly pounces upon the young of the crows by night, as death suddenly overtakes men" (Horapollo *Hieroglyphics* 2.25 [Cory 103–4]). The very soft feathers of the owl allow it to approach its prey without alerting it by the rustle of its wings.

20. *betoken diligence*—The owl is the symbol of learning, and of the goddess Athena. This unlikely correspondence is said to have arisen from the abundance of owls dwelling in Athens during ancient times, by an association of the name of the goddess with the name of the city. Hence the old proverb "to carry owls to Athens," which has been replaced by one with an identical meaning: "to carry coals to Newcastle"; that is, to take something where it already abounds.

21. *Dido*—Also called Elissa, the reputed founder and queen of the city of Carthage.

22. *poet sang*—Queen Dido contemplates suicide:

> Hence she plainly seemed to hear the solemn speech and summons of her lord [i.e. her dead husband] when gloomy night was mistress of the world; and oft she heard the solitary owl on her high station give forth the sad sepulchral strain, and prolong her lingering lamentable cry; and moreover many a prediction of ancient prophets affrights her with its awful warning. (Virgil *Aeneid* 4, c. line 462 [Lonsdale and Lee, 137])

For a similar description of the owl, see the *Georgics* 1, c. line 402.

23. *another place*—I do not find this in Virgil, but in Ovid: "He [Ascalaphus] becomes an obscene bird, the foreboder of approaching woe, a lazy owl, a direful omen to mortals" (Ovid *Metamorphoses* 5.5, c. line 549 [Riley, 181]).

24. *as Naso sings*—"We dislike the hawk, because it is always living in warfare; the wolves too, that are

wont to rush upon the startled flocks" (Ovid *Ars Amatoria* 2, c. line 148 [Riley, 412]).

25. *purveyors*—Those who supplied the Roman army with provisions.

26. *bat*—"When they would symbolise a man who is weak and audacious, they portray a bat, for she flies though destitute of feathers" (Horapollo *Hieroglyphics* 2.52 [Cory, 118].

27. *haste to the owl*—"When they would denote a man who flees for refuge to his patron, and receives no assistance, they depict a sparrow and an owl; for the sparrow when pursued betakes itself to the owl, and being near it is seized" (ibid. 2.51 [Cory, 117]).

28. *bees*—"To denote a people obedient to their king, they depict a bee, for this is the only one of all creatures which has a king whom the rest of the tribe of bees obey, as men serve their king" (ibid. 1.62 [Cory, 82]).

29. *flies*—"To denote impudence, they represent a fly, for this, though perpetually driven away, nevertheless returns"(ibid. 1.51 [Cory, 72]).

30. *In her bosom*—

Julia Augusta [i.e. Livia] when pregnant in her early youth of Tiberius Caesar, by Nero, was particularly desirous that her offspring should be a son, and accordingly employed the following mode of divination, which was then much in use among young women: she carried an egg in her bosom, taking care, whenever she was obliged to put it down, to give it to her nurse to warm in her own, that there might be no interruption in the heat: it is stated that the result promised by this mode of augury was not falsified. (Pliny 10.76 [Bostock and Riley, 2:535–6])

For Livia whiles she went with child of him [Tiberius], among many and sundry experiments which she made, and signs that she observed (and all to know whether she should bring forth a man-child or no), took closely an egg from under a hen that was sitting, and kept it warm sometime in her own, otherwhiles in her woman's hands by turns one after another, so long until there was hatched a cock-chicken with a notable comb upon the head. (Suetonius, "Tiberius Nero Caesar" sec. 14. In *History of Twelve Caesars,* trans. Philemon Holland [1606] [London: George Routledge and Sons, n.d.], 141)

31. Cicero writes—

And at the same period, at Lebadia, where divine rites were being performed in honour of Trophonius, all the cocks in the neighbourhood began to crow so incessantly as never to leave off at all; and the Boeotian augurs affirmed that this was a sign of victory to the Thebans, because these birds crow only on occasions of victory, and maintain silence in case of defeat. (Cicero *De divinatione* 1.34 [Yonge, 176])

32. *mule*—"When they would symbolise a barren woman, they delineate a mule; for this animal is barren, [because its uterus is not straight]" (Horapollo *Hieroglyphics* 2.62 [Cory, 113]). The passage in brackets is given in Latin by Cory lest the sensibilities of Victorian maids be offended.

33. *in Virgil*—"'Tis war, thou stranger-land, that thou dost offer; for war are horses armed, and this herd threatens war. And yet, for all that, these steeds at times will often submit to the chariot, and underneath the yoke in concord bear the bit. So there is hope of peace'" (Virgil *Aeneid* 3, lines 539–42 [Lonsdale and Lee, 124]. In the Latin *Opera* lines 539–40 of the passage above are provided, but in the Freake translation only line 540 appears. I have supplied the missing line to the text.

34. *did Marius good*—

When he was brought to Fannia's house, as soon as the gate was opened, an ass came running out to drink at a spring hard by, and giving a bold and encouraging look, first stood still before him, then brayed aloud and pranced by him. From which Marius drew his conclusion, and said, that the fates designed his safety, rather by sea than land, because the ass neglected his dry fodder, and turned from it to the water. (Plutarch, "Caius Marius." In *Lives of the Noble Grecians and Romans,* trans. John Dryden [New York: Modern Library, (1864) n.d.], 518–9)

35. *fugitives in Sicilia*—The servile, or slave, revolt of 134–132 BC was brought about by the vast number of slaves used in agriculture in Sicily and the cruelty with which they were handled. It was led by Eunus, a native of Apamea in Syria, who was credited by his followers with the power of prophecy and dream interpretation, and the ability to breathe fire. Proclaimed king by the slaves, he defeated the efforts of the consuls C. Fulvius Flaccus and L. Calpurnius Piso Frugi to crush him, but was captured by the consul P. Rupilius and thrown into prison at Margantia, where he died.

36. *mother the wolf*—Romulus and Remus, the mythical brothers supposed to have been the founders of the city of Rome, as infants were suckled by a wolf in the wilderness.

37. *meet a lioness*—"When they would symbolise a woman that has brought forth once, they depict a lioness; for she never conceives twice" (Horapollo *Hieroglyphics* 2.82 [Cory, 136]).

38. *Ostentarian*—Latin *ostentum* (portent, prodigy, wonder), the book of auguries used by the people of Etruria, supposedly given to them by Tages. See note 4, ch. LIII, bk. I.

39. *whence Virgil*—In the consulship of Pollio (40 BC) a wondrous child is to be born (perhaps the son of Octavianus, lately married to Scribania) who will herald the dawn of a new age of peace:

> The soil shall not feel the hoe, nor the vineyard the pruninghook; also the stout ploughman shall now unloose his oxen from the yoke; the wool shall not learn to counterfeit various hues; but of himself the ram in the meadows shall now begin to change the whiteness of his fleece for sweetly-blushing crimson, and for saffron dye; scarlet of its own accord shall dress the browsing lambs." (Virgil *Eclogues* 4, c. line 40 [Lonsdale and Lee, 18–9])

40. *nourished by a dog*—See the biographical note.

41. *Tobit*—Apocryphal book of Tobit, 5:16.

42. *castor*—"When they would symbolise a man injured by self inflictions, they delineate a beaver; for when pursued he tears out his own testicles, and casts them as spoil to his pursuers" (Horapollo *Hieroglyphics* 2.65 [Cory, 126]). "The beavers of the Euxine [Black Sea], when they are closely pressed by danger, themselves cut off the same [sexual] part, as they know that it is for this that they are pursued. This substance is called castoreum by the physicians" (Pliny 8.47 [Bostock and Riley, 2:297]).

43. *both the consuls*—The consuls M. Claudius Marcellus V and T. Quinctius (Pennus Capitolinus) Crispinus were both defeated by Hannibal near Venusia in 208 BC, the eleventh year of the Second Punic War.

44. *tame dragon*—"Among other delights he took great pleasure in a serpent dragon, which when, according to his usual manner, he would have fed with his own hand and found eaten by pismires [ants], he was warned thereupon to beware the vio-

lence of a multitude" (Suetonius, "Tiberius Nero Caesar" 72. In *History of Twelve Caesars* [Holland, 176–7]). Holland adds the note: "A creeping dragon. Which implieth that there be others winged, or at leastwise supposed to fly, in the common opinion of men; for the attribute *Serpens* signifieth creeping. Now, because all of them use most to do, the general name of dragons goeth under serpents" (ibid., p. 60 of the notes). *Draco* was used to designate the python. Pliny says, "The dragon is a serpent destitute of venom" (Pliny 29.20 [Bostock and Riley, 5:395]). All of the large constrictor snakes kill by squeezing their prey so that it cannot breathe and suffocates to death. None have venom. The boa and anaconda are confined to the New World, but the reticulate python of southeast Asia is one of the largest, if not the largest, of all snakes. Specimens have been found well over 30 feet in length. The African rock python grows up to 25 feet in length.

45. *in his mouth*—"To represent the mouth they depict a serpent, because the serpent is powerful in no other of its members except the mouth alone" (Horapollo *Hieroglyphics* 1.45 [Cory, 66]).

46. *two snakes*—Cicero recounts this story of the two snakes and raises the logical point : "But I marvel, if the release of the female snake caused the death of Tiberius Gracchus, and that of the male was to be fatal to Cornelia, why he let either of them escape" (Cicero *De divinatione* 2.29 [Yonge, 225]). See also 1.18 (Yonge, 160–1).

47. *a viper*—

> When they would symbolise a woman that hates her own husband, and designs his death, and is complaisant only during intercourse, they delineate a viper; for when in connection with the male, she places his mouth in her mouth, and after they have disjoined, she bites the head of the male and kills him. (Horapollo *Hieroglyphics* 2.59 [Cory, 123])

> When they would denote children plotting against their mothers, they delineate a viper; for the viper is not brought forth in the [usual manner], but disengages itself by gnawing through the belly of its mother. (ibid. 2.60 [Cory, 123–4]).

48. *eel*—"When they would symbolise a man that is hostile to, and secluded from, all men, they depict an eel; for it is found associating with no other fishes" (ibid. 2.103 [Cory, 149]).

49. *which Tully*—"For there is a certain power and nature, which, by means of indications which have

been observed a long time, and also by some instinct and divine inspiration, pronounces a judgement on future events" (Cicero *De divinatione* 1.6 [Yonge, 147]).

50. *head of a man*—

While they were digging on the Tarpeian Hill for the foundations of a temple, a human head was found; upon which deputies were sent to Olenus Calenus, the most celebrated diviner of Etruria. He, foreseeing the glory and success which attached to such a presage as this, attempted, by putting a question to them, to transfer the benefit of it to his own nation. First describing, on the [Etrurian] ground before him, the outline of a temple with his staff—"Is it so, Romans, as you say?" said he; "here then must be the temple of Jupiter, all good and all powerful; it is here that we have found the head"—and the

constant asseveration of the Annals is, that the destiny of the Roman empire would have been assuredly transferred to Etruria, had not the deputies, forewarned by the son of the diviner, made answer—"No, not here exactly, but at Rome, we say, the head was found." (Pliny 28.4 [Bostock and Riley, 5:280–1])

51. *Brutian soldiers*—Soldiers under the command of Marcus Junius Brutus, who together with those under C. Cassius Longinus opposed the forces of C. Julius Caesar Octavianus (later known as Augustus) and those of Marcus Antonius in Macedonia in 42 BC. There were two engagements. In the first Cassius was defeated by Anthony, while Brutus, who commanded the other wing of the army, was victorious over Octavius. Thinking Brutus had also lost in the confusion of battle, Cassius had his own freedman put him to death. In the second engagement Brutus was defeated. He fell on the sword of his friend, Strato, and so took his own life.

CHAPTER LV

How auspicias are verified by the light of natural instinct, and of some rules of finding of it out.

uspicia and auguria, which foretell things to come by animals, and birds, *Orpheus*[1] the divine himself (as we read) did teach and show first of all, which afterwards were had in great esteem with all nations. Now they are verified by the light of natural instinct, as if from this, some lights of divination may descend upon four-footed beasts, winged, and other animals, by which they are able to presage to us of the events of things: which *Virgil*[2] seems to be sensible of, when he sings:

> Nor think I heaven on them such knowl-
> edge states,
> Nor that their prudence is above the fates.

Now this instinct of nature, as saith *William of Paris,* is more sublime than all human apprehension, and very near, and most like to prophecy. By this instinct there is a certain wonderful light of divination in some animals naturally, as it manifestly appears in some dogs, who know by this instinct thieves, and men that are hid, unknown both to themselves, and men, and find them out, and apprehend them, falling upon them with a full mouth.[3] By the like instinct vultures foresee future slaughters in battles, and gather together into places where they shall be, as if they foresaw the flesh of dead carcasses. By the same instinct partridges know their dam, which they never saw, and leave the partridge which stole away her dam's eggs, and sat upon them.

By the same instinct also certain hurtful and terrible things are perceived (the soul of the men being altogether ignorant of them) whence terror, and horror seizeth much upon men when they think nothing of these things. So a thief lying hid in any house, although nobody knows, or thinks of his being there strikes fear, and terror, and a troublesomeness of mind into the inhabitants of that house, although haply not of all, because the brightness of this instinct is not in all men; yet of some of them. So a harlot being hid in some very large house, is sometimes perceived to be there by some one that is altogether ignorant of her being there. It is mentioned in histories that *Heraiscus* a certain Egyptian, a man of a divine nature, could discern unclean women, not only by his eyes, but by their voice, being heard afar off, and thereupon did fall into a most grievous headache.

William of Paris also makes mention of a certain woman in his time, that by the same instinct perceived a man whom she loved, coming two miles off.[4] Also he relates that in his time was a certain stork convicted of unchastity by the smell of the male, who being judged guilty by a multitude of storks whom the male gathered together, discovering to them the fault of his mate, was, her feathers being first pulled off, torn in pieces by them. He also makes mention of a certain horse,[5] who not knowing his dam, and leaping of her, when afterwards he understood what he had done, bit off his own stones by way of revenge upon himself for his incest. The same doth *Varro, Aristotle,* and *Pliny* relate concerning horses.

And *Pliny* makes mention of a certain serpent,[6] called the asp, that did such a like thing, for she coming to a certain man's table in Egypt, was there daily fed, and she having brought forth some young, by one of which a son of her host's was killed, after she knew of it, killed that young one, and would never return to that house anymore.

Now by these examples you see, how the lights of presage may descend upon some animals, as signs, or marks of things, and are set in their gesture, motion, voice, flying, going, meat, colour, and such like. For according to the doctrine of the Platonists, there is a certain power put into inferior things, by which for the most part they agree with the superiors; whence also the tacit consents of animals seem to agree with divine bodies, and their bodies, and affections to be affected with their powers, by the name of which they are ascribed to the deities.

We must consider therefore what animals are saturnine, what are jovial, and what martial, and so of the rest, and according to their properties to draw forth their presages: so those birds which resemble Saturn, and Mars, are all of them called terrible, and deadly, as the screech owl, the hawlet,[7] and others which we have mentioned before, also the horn owl, because she is a saturnal solitary bird, also nightly, and is reputed to be most unfortunately ominous, of which the poet saith:

> The ugly owl which no bird well resents,
> Foretells misfortunes, and most sad events.

But the swan is a delicious bird, venereal, and dedicated to *Phoebus,* and is said to be most happy in her presages, especially in the auspicias of mariners, because she is never drowned in water, whence *Ovid* sings:

> Most happy is the cheerful, singing swan
> In her presages———

There are also some birds that presage with their mouth, and singing, as the crow, pie, daw, whence *Virgil:*[8]

> ———this did foreshow
> Oft from the hollow holm that ominous crow.

Now the birds that portend future things by their flying are, viz. buzzards,[9] the bone-breakers,[10] eagles, vultures, cranes, swans, and the like: for they are to be considered in their flying, whether they fly slowly, or swiftly, whether to the right hand, or to the left, how many fly together: upon this account if cranes[11] fly apace, they signify a tempest: when slowly, fair weather. Also when two eagles fly together, they are said to portend evil, because that is a number of confusion. In like manner thou shalt enquire into the reason of the rest, as this is showed of number. Moreover it belongs to an artist to observe a similitude in these conjectures, as in *Virgil,*[12] *Venus* dissembling, teacheth her son *Aeneas* in these verses:

> ———all this is not for naught,
> Else me in vain my parents augury taught,
> Lo! twice six swans in a glad company
> Jove's bird pursued through the ethereal sky
> In heaven's broad tracks: now earth in a
>   long train
> They seem to take, or taken to disdain;
> As they return with sounding wings, they
>   sport,
> And heaven surrounding in a long consort.
> Just so, I say, thy friends and fleet have
>   gained
> The port, or with full sails the bay obtained.

Most wonderful is that kind of auguring of theirs, who hear, and understand the speeches of animals, in which as amongst the ancients, *Melampus,* and *Tiresias,* and *Thales,* and *Apollonius* the Tyanean, who as we read, excelled, and whom they report had excellent skill in the language of birds: of whom *Philostratus,* and *Porphyrius* speak, saying, that of old when *Apollonius* sat in company amongst his friends, seeing sparrows sitting upon a tree, and one sparrow coming from elsewhere unto them, making a great chattering and noise, and then flying away, all the rest following him, he said to his companions, that that sparrow told the rest that an ass being burdened with wheat fell down in a hole near the city, and that the wheat was scattered upon the ground: many being much moved with these words, went to see, and so it was, as *Apollonius* said,[13] at which they much wondered.

Also *Porphyrius* the Platonist in his third book of Sacrifices,[14] saith, that there was a swallow: for it was certain, because every voice of any animal is significative of some passion of its soul, as joy, sadness, or anger, or the like, which voices it is not so wonderful a thing should be understood by men conversant about them.

But *Democritus* himself declared this art, as saith *Pliny*,[15] by naming the birds, of whose blood mixed together was produced a serpent, of which whosoever did eat, should understand the voices of birds. And *Hermes* saith, if anyone shall go forth to catch birds on a certain day of the Kalends[16] of November, and shall boil the first bird which he catcheth, with the heart of a fox, that all that shall eat of this bird, shall understand the voices of birds, and all other animals. Also the Arabians say, that they can understand the meaning of brutes, who shall eat the heart, and liver of dragons.[17] *Proclus* also the Platonist believed, and wrote, that the heart of a mole conduceth to presages.

There were also divinations and auspicias which were taken from the inwards of sacrifices, the inventor whereof was *Tages*,[19] of whom *Lucan* sang:[20]

And if the inwards have no credit gained,
And if this art by Tages was but feigned.

The Roman religion thought that the liver was the head of the inwards.[21] Hence the soothsayers inquiring after future things in the inwards, did first look into the liver, in which were two heads, whereof the one was called the head for the city, the other for the enemy; and the head of this, or another part being compared together, they pronounced victory, as we read in *Lucan,* that the inwards did signify the slaughter of *Pompey's* men, and the victory of *Caesar's,* according to these verses:[22]

In the inwards all defects are ominous.
One part, and branch of the entrails doth increase,

Another part is weak, and flagging lies,
Beats, and moves with quick pulse the arteries.

Then the bowels being finished, they search the heart. Now if there were a sacrifice found without an heart, or a head was wanting in the liver, these were deadly presages, and were called piacularia.[23] Also if a sacrifice fled from the altar, or being smitten, made a lowing, or fell upon any part of his body than he ought to do, it was the like ominous.

We read that when *Julius Caesar* upon a day went forth to procession with his purple robe, and sitting in a golden chair, and sacrificing, there was twice a heart wanting;[24] and when *C. Marius* was sacrificing at Utica, there was wanting a liver.[25] Also when *Caius* the prince, and *M. Marcellus, C. Claudius,* and *L. Petellius Coss* were offering sacrifices, that the liver was consumed away suddenly: and not long after, one of them died of a disease, another was slain by men of Lyguria, the entrails foretelling so much: which was thought to be done by the power of the gods, or help of the Devil: hence it was accounted a thing of great concernment amongst the ancients as oft as anything unusual was found in the inwards: as when *Sulla* was sacrificing at Laurentum, the figure of a crown appeared[26] in the head of the liver: which *Posthumius* the soothsayer interpreted to portend a victory with a kingdom, and therefore advised that *Sulla* should eat those entrails himself.

The colour also of the inwards is to be considered. Of these *Lucan* made mention:[27]

Struck at the colour prophets were with fear,
For with foul spots pale entrails tinged were.
Both black, and blue, with specks of sprinkled blood
They were————

There was in times past such a venerable esteem of these arts, that the most potent, and wise men sought after them, yea the senate, and kings did nothing without the counsel of the augurs. But all these in these days, partly by the negligence of men, and partly by the authority of the Fathers,[28] are abolished.

Notes—Chapter LV

1. *Orpheus*—Horace calls Orpheus the interpreter of the gods, and Philostratus says that his head was preserved after death at Lesbos to give oracles.

2. *Virgil*—

> ... 'tis their [ravens] delight now that the rain is over to revisit their little progeny, and beloved nestlings; not that I can believe that they have from heaven any inspiration, or from fate a further foresight of things to come; but when the weather and changeful moisture of the sky alter the course of nature, and the god of the air with the damp winds condenses what just now was rare, and anon rarefies what was dense, the images of their minds are turned, and their breasts conceive impulses other than what they felt, while the wind chased the clouds ... (Virgil *Georgics* 1, c. line 415 [Lonsdale and Lee, 40]

3. *full mouth*—That is, barking.

4. *two miles off*—An early description of what is now known as an extrasensory monition of approach.

5. *certain horse*—"Another horse, upon the bandage being removed from his eyes, found that he had covered his mother, upon which he threw himself down a precipice, and was killed. We learn, also, that for a similar cause, a groom was torn to pieces, in the territory of Reate" (Pliny 8.64 [Bostock and Riley, 2:318]).

6. *certain serpent*—Pliny relates this story and credits it to Phylarchus, a Greek writer. See Pliny 10.96 [Bostock and Riley, 2:552].

7. *hawlet*—That is, howlet, or owlet, a young or little owl. The *Oxford English Dictionary* does not attach a species to this term, but obviously one is intended—probably *Carine noctua,* the little owl represented on coins and sculptures as the bird of Pallas Athene and the town of Athens.

8. *whence Virgil*—See note 7, ch. LIV, bk. I.

9. *buzzards*—The common buzzard *(Buteo vulgaris)* was regarded as an inferior kind of hawk, little valued because its weak beak and talons and lack of courage made it useless for falconry. Of it Pliny says:

> "... the triorchis also, so called from the number of its testicles, and to which Phemonoe has assigned the first rank in augury. This last is by the Romans known as the 'buteo;' indeed there is a family that

has taken its surname from it, from the circumstance of this bird having given a favourable omen by settling upon the ship of one of them when he held a command" (Pliny 10.9 [Bostock and Riley, 2:487]).

10. *bone-breakers*—Osprey *(Pandion haliaetus).* Pliny in describing the kinds of eagles says: "Some writers add to the above a seventh kind, which they call the 'bearded' eagle; the Tuscans, however, call it the ossifrage [*ossifraga:* bone-breaker]" (Pliny 10.3 [Bostock and Riley, 2:484]). It is conjectured that the bird originally referred to was the lammergeyer, or bearded vulture *(Gypaetus barbatus),* which breaks bones open by dropping them from a great height, but in the late 16th century the name bone-breaker was transferred by English and French writers to the sea eagle, or osprey.

11. *cranes*—Pliny says that when cranes "make for the interior" or fly inland, it foretells a storm, but "Cranes when they fly aloft in silence announce fine weather ..." (Pliny 18.87 [Bostock and Riley, 4:124]).

12. *in Virgil*—See note 8, ch. LIV, bk. I,

13. *Apollonius said*—

> The sparrows were sitting quietly in the trees roundabout, when another sparrow flew to them and piped up as if inviting the others to do something, and as soon as they heard him all the birds began to chirp, and took wing and flew away. Apollonius knew why they had flown away, but made no comment on it, and went on with his subject; then seeing his audience all looking after the birds, and that some superstitious persons among them were drawing presages of evil from the sparrows leaving, he gave them this explanation: "A boy who was carrying grain in a trough fell down, and after picking up the spilled grain very carelessly, he went away, leaving a good deal of it scattered in the road. That first sparrow found it, and came to invite these others to be his guests at that unexpected treat." Many of his hearers ran way to investigate, while Apollonius went on with his discourse about community of goods to those who remained. (Philostratus *Life and Times of Apollonius of Tyana* 4.3 [Eells, 93])

14. *book of Sacrifices*—De abstinentia (On abstinence from animal food), one of the few extant works of Porphyry, which was translated into English by Thomas Taylor in 1823.

15. *saith Pliny*—"... as also what Democritus says, when he gives the names of certain birds, by the mixture of whose blood a serpent is produced, the person who eats of which will be able to understand the language of birds ..." (Pliny 10.70 [Bostock and Riley, 2:530]). "Democritus, he has given some monstrous preparations from snakes, by the aid of which the language of birds, he says, may be understood" (Pliny 29.22 [Bostock and Riley, 5:397]).

16. *Kalends*—Calends, the first day of any month in the Roman calendar; therefore November first.

17. *liver of dragons*—"Even to this day it is peculiar to Arabs that they harken to the voices of birds as foretelling future events like oracles, and they interpret animals, because as some say they eat the liver of dragons, or as others say, the heart" (Philostratus *Life and Times of Apollonius of Tyana* 1.20 [Eells, 21]).

18 *heart of a mole*—"The heart of a mole is subservient to divination" (Proclus *De sacrificio et magia*, frag. preserved by Ficinus and given in its entirety in Iamblichus *Life of Pythagoras*, trans. Thomas Taylor [1818] [London: John M. Watkins,. 1926], 213–8). Taylor also gives this fragment at the end of his translation of *On the Mysteries*. See also note 7, ch. XXI, bk. I.

19. *Tages*—

They tell us that as a labourer one day was ploughing in a field in the territory of Tarquinium, and his ploughshare made a deeper furrow than usual, all of a sudden there sprang out of this furrow a certain Tages, who, as it is recorded in the books of the Etrurians, possessed the visage of a child, but the prudence of a sage. When the labourer was surprised at seeing him, and in his astonishment made a great outcry, a number of people assembled round him, and before long all the Etrurians came together at the spot. Tages then discoursed in the presence of an immense crowd, who treasured up his words with the greatest care, and afterwards committed them to writing. The information they derived from this Tages was the foundation of the science of the soothsayers, and was subsequently improved by the accession of many new facts, all of which confirmed the same principles. (Cicero *De divinatione* 2.23 [Yonge, 220–1]).

An Etruscan soothsayer who examined the entrails was called a *haruspex,* and the practice itself is haruspicy.

20. *Lucan sang*—Spoken by Arruns, the dean of soothsayers, upon seeing the unhappy double, or two-lobed, liver in a sacrifice: "May the Gods grant a prosperous result to what has been seen, and may there be no truth in the entrails; but rather may Tages, the founder of the art, have fondly invented all these things!" (Lucan *Pharsalia* 1, line 636 [Riley, 42]).

21. *head of the inwards*—"The liver is on the right side: in this part is situate what has been called the 'head of the entrails,' and it is subject to considerable variations" (Pliny 11.73 [Bostock and Riley, 3:67–8]).

22. *these verses*—"...and, shocking sign! that which has appeared with impunity in no entrails, lo! he [Arruns] sees growing upon the head of the entrails [liver] the mass of another head—a part hangs weak and flabby, a part throbs and with a rapid pulsation incessantly moves the veins" (Lucan *Pharsalia* 1, line 626 [Riley, 41]).

23. *piacularia*—See note 9, ch. LIII, bk. I.

24. *twice a heart wanting*—

The first day that the Dictator Caesar appeared in public, clothed in purple, and sitting on a seat of gold, the heart was twice found wanting when he sacrificed. From this circumstance has risen a great question among those who discuss matters connected with divination—whether it was possible for the victim to have lived without that organ, or whether it had lost it at the very moment of its death. (Pliny 11.71 [Bostock and Riley, 3:66]).

... on that very day on which [Caesar] first sat on the golden throne and went forth clad in a purple robe, when he was sacrificing, no heart was found in the intestines of the fat ox. ... He was himself surprised at the novelty of the phenomenon; on which Spurinna [soothsayer who cried "Beware the Ides of March"] observed that he had reason to fear that he would lose both sense and life, since both of these proceed from the heart. The next day the liver of the victim was found defective in the upper extremity. (Cicero *De divinatione* 1.52 [Yonge, 193–4]).

As Caesar was sacrificing, the victim's heart was missing, a very bad omen, because no living creature can subsist without a heart. (Plutarch "Caesar." In *Lives* [Dryden, 890])

25. *wanting a liver*—

No liver at all was found in a victim which was sacrificed by M. Marcellus, about the period when he was killed in battle against Hannibal; while in a victim which was slain on the following day, a double liver was found. It was wanting, also, in a victim sacrificed by C. Marius, at Utica, and in one which was offered by the Emperor Gaius [Caligula] upon the calends of January, on the occasion of his entering the year of the consulship in which he was slain: the same thing happened, also, to his successor, Claudius, in the month in which he was cut off by poison. (Pliny 11.73 [Bostock and Riley, 3:68])

26. *crown appeared*—Relying on Sulla's own testimony in his *Memoirs,* Plutarch writes: "For when he was sacrificing at his first landing near Tarentum, the victim's liver showed the figure of a crown of laurel with two fillets hanging from it" (Plutarch "Sylla." In *Lives* [Dryden, 566]).

Posthumius is mentioned by Plutarch in connection with a sacrifice that took place at Nola (east of modern Naples) some time prior to the one noticed above: "As he [Sulla] was sacrificing, Postumius the soothsayer, having inspected the entrails, stretched forth both hands over Sylla, required to be bound and kept in custody till the battle was over, as willing, if they had not speedy and complete success, to suffer the utmost punishment" (ibid. 552).

Cicero makes still another reference to this pair:

> For when Sylla was in the territory of Nola, and was sacrificing in front of his tent, a serpent suddenly glided out from beneath the altar; and when, upon this, the soothsayer Posthumius exhorted him to give orders for the immediate march on the army, Sylla obeyed the injunction, and entirely defeated the Samnites, who lay before Nola, and took possession of their richly-provided camp. (Cicero *De divinatione* 1.33 [Yonge, 175])

27. *Lucan made mention*—"The very colour alarmed the prophet; for a pervading lividness streaked with spots of blood the pallid vitals, tinted with foul spots and gorged with congealed blood. He perceives the liver reeking with corruption, and beholds the veins threatening on the enemy's side" (Lucan *Pharsalia* 1, line 620 [Riley, 41]).

28. *Fathers*—The early leaders and writers of the Christian Church.

CHAPTER LVI

Of the soothsayings of flashes, and lightnings, and how monstrous, and prodigious things are to be interpreted.

Now the soothsayings of flashes, and lightnings, and of wonders, and how monstrous and prodigious things are to be interpreted, the prophets, and priests of Hetruscus[1] have taught the art. For they have ordained sixteen regions[2] of the heavens, and have ascribed gods to every one of them; and besides eleven kinds[3] of lightnings, and nine gods, which should dart them forth, by showing rules for the understanding the signification of them. But as often as monstrous, prodigious, and wondrous things happen, they do presage, as is most certain, some great matter.

Now their interpreter must be some excellent conjecturer of similitudes, as also some curious searcher, and of them who at that time are employed about the affairs of princes, and provinces. For the celestials take such care only for princes, peoples, and provinces, that before the rest they might be prefigured, and admonished, by stars, by constellations, by wonders, and by prodigies. Now if the same thing, or the like hath been seen in former ages, we must consider that very thing, and what happened after that, and according to these, to foretell the same, or the like, because the same signs are for the same things, and the like for like.

So prodigies have come before the birth, and death of many eminent men and kings; as *Cicero* makes mention of *Midas* a boy, into whose mouth, whilst he was sleeping, the pismire put corns of wheat,[4] which was an omen of great riches. So bees sat upon the mouth of *Plato*[5]

when he was sleeping in the cradle, by which was foretold the sweetness of his speech. *Hecuba,* when she was bringing forth *Paris,* saw a burning torch,[6] which should set on fire Troy, and all Asia. There appeared unto the mother of *Phalaris*[7] the image of Mercury pouring forth blood upon the earth, with which the whole house was overflowed. The mother of *Dionysius*[8] dreamed she brought forth a satyr, which prodigious dreams the event that followed made good.

The wife of *Tarquinius Priscus* seeing a flame lick the head of *Servius Tullius,*[9] foretold that he should have the kingdom. In like manner after Troy was taken, *Aeneas* disputing with *Anchises* his father concerning a flight, there appeared a flame licking the crown of *Ascanius* his head,[10] and doing of him no hurt: which thing, seeing it did portend the kingdom to *Ascanius,* persuaded him to depart, for monstrous prodigies did forerun great and imminent destruction.

So we read in *Pliny,* that *M. Attilius,* and *C. Portius* being consuls, it rained milk, and blood,[11] which did presage that a very great pestilence should the next year overspread Rome. Also in Lucania it rained spongious iron,[12] and in the year before *Marcus Crassus* was slain in Parthia; with which also all the soldiers of Lucania, being a very numerous army, were slain. Also *L. Paulus,* and *C. Marcellus* being consuls, it rained wool[13] about the castle of Corisanum, near which place a year after *T. Annius* was slain by *Milus.* Also in the wars of Denmark, the noise of arms,[14] and sound of a trumpet was heard in the air. And *Livy* concerning the Macedonian wars, saith, in the year when *Hannibal* died it rained blood for two days. Also concerning the second Punic war, he saith, that water mixed with blood came down from heaven like rain, at that time when *Hannibal* did spoil Italy. A little before the destruction of Leuctra the Lacedemonians heard a noise of arms in the temple of *Hercules*,[15] and at the same time in the temple of *Hercules,* the doors that were shut with bars, opened themselves, and the arms that were hanged on the wall, were found on the ground.

The like events may be prognosticated of other like things, as oftentimes in times past something hath been foretold of them. But concerning these also, the judgements of the celestial influences must not be neglected, of which we shall more largely treat in the following chapters.

Notes—Chapter LVI

1. *Hetruscus*—Etruria.

2. *sixteen regions*—

In relation to this object [lightning] the Etrurians have divided the heavens into sixteen parts. The first great division is from north to east; the second to the south; the third to the west; and the fourth occupies what remains from west to north. Each of these has been subdivided into four parts, of which the eight on the east have been called the left, and those on the west the right divisions. Those which extend from the west to the north have been considered the most unpropitious. It becomes therefore very important to ascertain from what quarter the thunder proceeds, and in what direction it falls. It is considered a very favourable omen when it returns into the eastern division. But it prognosticates the greatest felicity when the thunder proceeds from the first-mentioned part of the heavens and falls back into it; it was an omen of this kind which, as we have heard, was given to Sylla the Dictator. The remaining quarters of the heavens are less propitious, and also less to be dreaded. (Pliny 2.55 [Bostock and Riley, 1:85])

See also the story about Attus Navius in Cicero *De divinatione* 1.17.

3. *eleven kinds*—

The Tuscan books inform us, that there are nine Gods who discharge thunderstorms, that there are eleven different kinds of them, and that three of them are darted out by Jupiter. Of these the Romans retain only two, ascribing the diurnal kind of Jupiter, and the nocturnal to Summanus ... (Pliny 2.53 [Bostock and Riley, 1:82])

4. *corns of wheat*—"When Midas, who became king of Phrygia, was yet an infant, some ants crammed some grains of wheat into his mouth while he was sleeping" (Cicero *De divinatione* 1.36 [Yonge, 177]).

5. *mouth of Plato*—"While Plato was an infant in his cradle, a swarm of bees settled on his lips during his slumbers; and the diviners answered that he would become extremely eloquent ..." (ibid.).

6. *burning torch*—Cicero quotes an unidentified poet:

Queen Hecuba dream'd—an ominous
    dream of fate—
That she did bear no human child of flesh,
But a fierce blazing torch.
(Cicero *De divinatione* 1.21 [Yonge, 163])

7. *mother of Phalaris*—

Heraclides of Pontus, an intelligent man, who was one of Plato's disciples and followers, writes that the mother of Phalaris fancied that she saw in a dream the statues of the gods whom Phalaris had consecrated in his house. Among them it appeared to her that Mercury held a cup in his right hand, from which he poured blood, which as soon as it touched the earth gushed forth like a fresh fountain, and filled the house with streaming gore. (Cicero *De divinatione* 1.23 [Yonge, 164])

8. *mother of Dionysius*—

The mother of Dionysius—of that Dionysius, I mean, who was the tyrant of Syracuse, as it is recorded by Philistus, a man of learning and diligence, and who was a contemporary of the tyrant—when she was pregnant with this very Dionysius, dreamt that she had become the mother of a little Satyr. (Cicero *De divinatione* 1.20 [Yonge, 162])

Satyrs are servants of the god Dionysus.

9. *head of Servius Tullius*—"And all our histories relate that the head of Servius Tullius while sleeping appeared to be on fire, which was a sign of the extra-ordinary events which followed" (Cicero *De divinatione* 1.53 [Yonge, 194]).

"... when Servius Tullius, while a child, was sleeping, flame darted out from his head ..." (Pliny 2.111 [Bostock and Riley, 1:143]).

> They relate, that the head of a boy, called Servius Tullius, as he lay fast asleep, blazed with fire in the sight of many persons. That by the very great noise made at so miraculous a phenomenon, the royal family was awakened; and when one of the servants was bringing water to extinguish the flame, that he was kept back by the queen, and after the confusion was over, that she forbad the boy to be disturbed till he should awake of his own accord. As soon as he awoke the flame disappeared. (Livy *The History of Rome* 1.39, trans. D. Spillan and Cyrus Edmonds [New York: Noble and Eidridge, n.d.], 52–3)

10. *Ascanius his head*—"... a light crest of fire seems to shed a gleam from the crown of the head of Iulus [i.e. Ascanius], and, with harmless touch, to lick his wavy locks and play about his temples" (Virgil *Aeneid* 2, c. line 682 [Lonsdale and Lee, 111]).

11. *milk, and blood*—"Besides these, we learn from certain monuments, that from the lower part of the atmosphere it rained milk and blood, in the consulship of M. Acilius and C. Porcius [114 BC], and frequently at other times" (Pliny 2.57 [Bostock and Riley, 1:87]).

12. *spongious iron*—

> It also rained iron among the Lucanians, the year before Crassus was slain by the Parthians [53 BC], as well as all the Lucanian soldiers, of whom there was a great number in this army. The substance which fell had very much the appearance of sponge; the augurs warned the people against wounds that might come from above. (ibid., 87–8)

13. *rained wool*—"In the consulship of L. Paulus and C. Marcellus it rained wool, round the castle of Carissanum, near which place, a year after, T. Annius Milo was killed" (ibid., 88).

14. *noise of arms*—"We have heard, that during the war with the Cimbri, the rattling of arms and the sound of trumpets were heard through the sky, and that the same thing has frequently happened before and since" (Pliny 2.58 [Bostock and Riley, 1:88]).

15. *temple of Hercules*—

> "How many intimations were given to the Lacedaemonians a short time before the disaster of Leuctra, when arms rattled in the temple of Hercules, and his statue streamed with profuse sweat! At the same time, at Thebes (as Callisthenes relates), the folding-doors in the temple of Hercules, which were closed with bars, opened of their own accord, and the armour which was suspended on the walls was found fallen to the ground." (Cicero *De divinatione* 1.34 [Yonge, 176])

CHAPTER LVII

Of geomancy, hydromancy, aeromancy, pyromancy, four divinations of elements.

Moreover the elements themselves teach us fatal events; whence those four famous kinds of divinations, geomancy, hydromancy, aeromancy, and pyromancy, have got their names, of which that sorceress in *Lucan* seems to boast herself, when she saith:[1]

> The earth, the air, the chaos, and the sky,
> The seas, the fields, the rocks, and moun-
>   tains high
> Foretell the truth————

The first therefore is geomancy, which foreshoweth future things by the motions of the Earth, as also the noise, the swelling, the trembling, the chops, the pits, and exhalation, and other impressions, the art of which *Almadel* the Arabian sets forth. But there is another kind of geomancy, which divines by points written upon the earth, by a certain power in the fall of it, which is not of present speculation; but of that we shall speak hereafter.[2]

Now hydromancy doth perform its presages by the impressions of water, their ebbing and flowing, their increases and depressions, their tempests, and colours, and the like; to which also are added visions, which are made in the waters. By a kind of divination found by the Persians,[3] as *Varro* reports, a boy saw in the water the effigies of *Mercury*, which foretold in an hundred and fifty verses all the event of *Mithridates* his war. We read also that *Numa Pompilius* practised hydromancy; for in the water he called up the gods, and learned of them things to come; which art also *Pythagoras,* a long time after *Numa* practiced.

There was of old a kind of hydromancy, had in great esteem amongst the Assyrians, and it was called lecanomancy, from a skin full of water, upon which they put plates of gold, and silver, and precious stones, written upon with certain images, names, and characters. To this may be referred that art, by which lead, and wax being melted, and cast into the water,[5] do express manifest marks of images, what we desire to know. There were also in former years fountains that did foretell things to come, as the Father's Fountain at Achaia, and that which was called the Water of *Juno* in Epidaurus; but of these more in the following chapters, where we shall speak of oracles.[6]

Hither also may be referred the divination of fishes, of which kind there was use made by the Lycians in a certain place, which was called Dina, near the sea, in a wood dedicated to *Apollo,* made hollow in the dry sand, into which, he that went to consult of future things, let down roasted meat, and presently that place was filled with waters, and a great multitude of fish, and of strange shapes, unknown to men, did appear, by the forms of which the prophet foretold what should come to pass. These things doth *Atheneus* more at large relate out of *Polycharmus,* in the history of the Lycians.

After the same manner doth aeromancy divine by airy impressions, by the blowing of the winds, by rainbows, by circles about the Moon and stars, by mists, and clouds, and by imaginations in clouds, and visions in the air.

So also pyromancy divines by fiery impressions, and by stars with long tails,[7] by fiery colours, by visions, and imaginations in the fire. So the wife of *Cicero*[8] foretold that he would be consul the next year, because when a certain man after the sacrifice was ended, would look in the ashes, there suddenly broke forth a flame. Of this kind are those that *Pliny* speaks of,[9] that terrene, pale, and buzzing fires presage tempests, circles about the snuffs of candles[10] betoken rain; if the flame fly turning, and winding, it portends wind. Also torches when they strike the fire before them, and are not kindled: also when a coal sticks to pots taken off from the fire, and when the fire casts off the ashes, and sparkles, or when ashes are hard grown together on the hearth, and when a coal is very bright.

To these is added capnomancy,[11] so called from smoke, because it searcheth into the flame, and smoke, and thin colours, sounds, and motions, when they are carried upright, or on one side, or round, which we read in these verses in *Statius:*

Let piety be bound, and on the altar laid,
Let us implore the gods for divine aid.
She makes acute, red, towering flames, and bright,
Increased by the air, the middle being white;
And then she makes the flames without all bound,
For to wind in and out, and to run round,
Like to a serpent————

Also in the Aethnean caves, and fields of the nymphs in Apollonia, auguries were taken from fires, and flames; joyful, if they did receive what was cast into them, and sad, if they did reject them. But of these we shall speak in the following chapters, amongst the answers of the oracles.[12]

Notes—Chapter LVII

1. *when she saith*—Erichtho, speaking to Sextus Pompey, says: "But if thou art content to learn the events beforehand, paths easy and manifold will lie open to the truth; earth, and sky, and Chaos, and seas, and plains, and the rocks of Rhodope, will converse with us" (Lucan *Pharsalia* 6, line 615 [Riley, 237]).

2. *speak hereafter*—See Appendix VIII.

3. *the Persians*—Of hydromancy, Augustine says: "Which kind of divination, says Varro *[De cultu deorum]*, came from Persia and was used by Numa, and afterwards by Pythagoras" (*City of God* 7.35, [Healey I:224]).

4. *Numa Pompilius*—"So that Numa's taking nymph Egeria to his wife was (as Varro says) nothing but his use of water in hydromancy. For so actions are wont to be spiced with falsehood and turned into fables. So by this hydromancy did this curious king learn his religious laws that he gave the Romans, and which the priests have in their books …" (ibid.).

5. *cast into the water*—Small amounts of molten material are quickly dropped into a vessel of water, where they solidify almost at once. The divination is derived from the curious shapes assumed by the hardened masses.

6. *speak of oracles*—See notes 14 and 15, ch. XLVIII, bk. III.

7. *stars with long tails*—Comets, regarding divination by which Pliny says: "It is thought important to notice towards what part it darts its beams, or from what star it receives its influence, what it resembles, and in what places it shines." (Pliny 2.23 [Bostock and Riley, 1:57]). In ancient astrology there was an elaborate classification of comets according to their shapes, after which they were named; for example, "long-haired stars" when the tail was up, "bearded stars" when the tail was down, "javelin stars" when the tail was long and narrow, "dagger stars" when it was short and sloped to a point, and so on. For a listing of some of these, see Pliny 2.22 (Bostock and Riley, 1:55–6). Ptolemy also mentions them briefly in the *Tetrabiblos* 2.9, but more briefly than Pliny. For a complete account, consult Hephaestion of Thebes.

8. *wife of Cicero*—Terentia, Cicero's first wife. Cicero was consul in 63 BC. It is curious he makes no use of this story in *De divinatione* (44 BC). Perhaps his divorce from Terentia in 45 BC, coupled with his

divorce from Publilia, his second wife, in that same year, had turned his mind away from domestic reminiscences.

9. Pliny speaks of—

> Next to these are the prognostics that are derived from fire kindled upon the earth. If the flames are pallid, and emit a murmuring noise, they are considered to presage stormy weather; and fungi upon the burning wick of the lamp are a sign of rain. If the flame is spiral and flickering, it is an indication of wind, and the same is the case when the lamp goes out of itself, or is lighted with difficulty. So, too, if the snuff hangs down, and sparks gather upon it, or if the burning coals adhere to vessels taken from off the fire, or if the fire, when covered up, sends out hot embers or emits sparks, or if the cinders gather into a mass upon the hearth, or the coals burn bright and glowing. (Pliny 18.84 [Bostock and Riley, 4:122])

10. *snuffs of candles*—"And behold when Pamphiles did see the candle standing on the table, she said, Verily wee shall have much raine to morrow. Which when her husband did heare, he demanded of her by what reason she knew it? Mary (quoth shee) the light on the table sheweth the same" (Apuleius *The Golden Asse* ch. 10 [Adlington]).

11. *capnomancy*—When the smoke rose lightly in a vertical column from the sacrifice on the altar it was a good sign, but if the smoke hung low it was bad. Another kind of capnomancy concerned the smoke from poppy or jasmine seeds. Smoke of the sacrifice was also inhaled to produce an exalted state.

12. *of the oracles*—All these forms of divination are described in a short work which the editors of the Latin *Opera* thought fit to afix as a kind of appendix to the *Occult Philosophy*. It bears the title *De speciebus magiae ceremonialis, quam goetiam uocant, epitome per Georgiu Pictorium Villinganum, doctorem medicum, nuperrime conscripta*. Six of the appended works on magic in the first volume of the *Opera* were gathered together and translated into English in 1655 by Robert Turner under the misleading title *Agrippa His Fourth Book of Occult Philosophy*—misleading because this is only one of the six tracts, and Agrippa did not even write it—but the *De speciebus* seems for some reason to have been overlooked.

CHAPTER LVIII

Of the reviving of the dead, and of sleeping, and wanting victuals many years together.

The Arabian philosophers agree, that some men may elevate themselves above the powers of their body, and above their sensitive powers; and those being surmounted, receive into themselves by the perfection of the heavens, and intelligences, a divine vigour. Seeing therefore all the souls of men are perpetual, and also all the spirits obey the perfect souls; magicians think that perfect men may by the powers of their soul repair their dying bodies with other inferior souls newly separated, and inspire them again; as a weasel that is killed, is made alive again by the breath, and cry of his dam; and lions make alive their dead whelps[1] by breathing upon them.

And because, as they say, all like things being applied to their like, are made of the same natures; and every patient, and thing that receives into itself the act of any agent, is endowed with the nature of that agent, and made connatural: hence they think, that to this vivication, or making alive, some herbs, and magical confections, such as they say are made of the ashes of the phoenix,[2] and the cast skin of a snake do much conduce, which indeed to many seems fabulous, and to some impossible, unless it could be accounted approved of by an historical faith.

For we read of some that have been drowned in water, others cast into the fire, and put upon the fire, others slain in war, others otherwise tried, and after a few days were alive again, as *Pliny* testifies[3] of *Aviola,* a man per-

taining to the consul, of *L. Lamia, Calius Tubero, Corfidius,*[4] *Gabienus,*[5] and many others. Also we read that *Aesop* the tale maker, *Tindoreus,*[6] *Hercules,*[7] and *Palicy*[8] the sons of *Jupiter* and *Thalia,* being dead, were raised to life again; also that many were by physicians, and magicians raised from death again, as the historians relate of *Aesculapius;*[9] and we have above mentioned out of *Juba,* and *Xanthus,* and *Philostratus* concerning *Tillo,* and a certain Arabian, and *Apollonius*[10] the Tyanean.

Also we read that *Glaucus,*[11] a certain man that was dead,whom they say, beyond all expectation, the physicians coming to see it, the herb dragonwort restored to life. Some say that he revived by the putting into his body a medicine made of honey, whence the proverb, *Glaucus* was raised from death by taking in honey into his body.

Apuleius also relating the manner of these kinds of restorings to life, saith of *Zachla*[12] the Egyptian prophet: the prophet being thus favourable, lays a certain herb upon the mouth of the body of a young man being dead, and another upon his breast, then turning towards the east, or rising of the propitious Sun, praying silently (a great assembly of people striving to see it) in the first place heaved up his breast, then makes a beating in his veins, then his body to be filled with breath, after which the carcass ariseth, and the young man speaks.

If these things are true, the dying souls must, sometimes lying hid in their bodies, be

181

oppressed with vehement ecstasies, and be freed from all bodily action: so that the life, sense, motion, forsake the body, but so, that the man is not yet truly dead, but lies astonied,[13] and as it were dead for a certain time. And this is often found, that in times of pestilence many that are carried for dead to the graves to be buried, revive again. The same also hath often befallen women, by reason of fits of the mother.[14]

And Rabbi *Moises*[15] out of the book of *Galen,* which *Patriarcha* translated, makes mention of a man, who was suffocated for six days, and did neither eat, nor drink, and his arteries became hard. And it is said in the same book, that a certain man by being filled with water, lost the pulse of his whole body, so that his heart was not perceived to move, and he lay like a dead man. Also it is said that a man by reason of a fall from an high place, or great noise, or long staying under the water, may fall into a swoon, which may continue forty-eight hours, and so he lie as if he were dead, with his face being very green.

And in the same place there is mention made of a man that buried a man that seemed to be dead seventy-two hours after his seeming decease, and so killed him, because he buried him alive, and there are given signs whereby it may be known who are alive; although they seem to be dead, and indeed will die, unless there be some means used to recover them, as phlebotomy, or some other cure. And these are such as very seldom happen. This is the manner, by which we understand magicians, and physicians do raise dead men to life, as they that were tried by the stinging of serpents, were by the nation of the Marsi, and the Psilli[16] restored to life.

Now we may conceive that such kind of ecstasies may continue a long time, although a man be not truly dead, as it is in dormice, and crocodiles, and many other serpents,[17] which sleep all winter, and are in such a dead sleep, that they can scarce be awakened with fire. And I have often seen a dormouse dissected, and continue immovable, as if she were dead, until she was boiled, and then presently in boiling water the dissected members did show life.

Also, although it be hard to be believed, we read in some approved historians, that some men have slept for many years together, and in the time of sleep, until they awaked, there was no alteration in them, as to make them seem older: the same doth *Pliny* testify of a certain boy, whom he saith, being wearied with heat, and his journey, slept fifty-seven years in a cave. We read also that *Epimenides Gnosius*[18] slept fifty-seven years in a cave. Hence the proverb arose, to outsleep *Epimenides*. M. *Damascenis* tells, that in his time a certain countryman being wearied in Germany, slept for the space of a whole autumn, and the winter following, under a heap of hay, until the summer, when the hay began to be eaten up, then he was found awakened as a man half dead, and out of his wits.

Ecclesiastical histories confirm this opinion concerning the Seven Sleepers,[19] whom they say slept 196 years. There was in Norvegia[20] a cave in a high seashore, where, as *Paulus Diaconus,* and *Methodius* the martyr write, seven men lay sleeping a long time without any corruption, and the people that went in to disturb them were contracted, or drawn together, so that after a while being forewarned by that punishment, they durst not hurt them.

Now *Xenocrates,* a man of no mean repute amongst philosophers was of opinion, that this long sleeping was appointed by God as a punishment for some certain sins. But *Marcus Damascenus* proves it by many reasons to be possible, and natural, neither doth he think it irrational, that some should without meat, and drink, and voiding excrements, without consuming, or corruption, sleep many months. And this may befall a man by reason of some poisonous potion, or sleepy disease, or such like causes, for certain days, months, or years, according to the intention, or remission of the power of the medicine, or of the passions of their mind.

And physicians say that there are some antidotes, of which they that take too great a potion, shall be able to endure hunger a long time, as *Elias*[21] in former time being fed with a certain food by an angel, walked, and fasted in the strength of that meat, forty days. And *John*

Bocatius makes mention of a man in his time, in Venice, who would every year fast forty days without any meat. But that was a greater wonder, that there was a woman in lower Germany at the same time, who took no food till the thirteenth year of her age, which to us may seem incredible, by that he lately confirmed it; as also he tells of a miracle of our age, that of his brother *Nicolaus Stone,* an Helvetian by nation, who lived twenty years in the wilderness without meat, till he died. That also is wonderful which *Theophrastus* mentions concerning a certain man, called *Philinus,* who used no meat, or drink, besides milk. And there are grave authors who describe a certain herb of Sparta, with which they say the Scythians can endure twelve days hunger, without meat or drink, if they do but taste it, or hold it in their mouth.

Notes—Chapter LVIII

1. *dead whelps*—Certain animals, notably the lion and the bear, were believed to give birth to small, shapeless lumps of flesh. "After the birth, these animals warm their young by licking them, and thereby give them their proper shape" (Pliny 10.83 [Bostock and Riley, 2:542]). Significantly, in reference to this comment about the weasel and the lion by Agrippa, Pliny says: "Aristotle then informs us ... The young ones, when first born, are shapeless and extremely small in flesh, being no larger than a weasel ..." (Pliny 8.17 [Bostock and Riley, 2:265–6]).

2. *ashes of the phoenix*—

> ... among the very first remedies mentioned, we find those said to be derived from the ashes and nest of the phoenix, as though, forsooth, its existence were a well ascertained fact, and not altogether a fable. And then besides, it would be a mere mockery to describe remedies that can only return to us once in a thousand years. (Pliny 29.9 [Bostock and Riley, 5:382])

3. *Pliny testifies*—

> Aviola, a man of consular rank, came to life again when on the funeral pile; but, by reason of the violence of the flames, no assistance could be rendered him, in consequence of which he was burnt alive. The same thing is said to have happened to L. Lamia, a man of praetorian rank. Messala, Rufus, and many other authors, inform us, that C. Aelius Tubero, who had filled the office of praetor, was also rescued from the funeral pile. (Pliny 7.53 [Bostock and Riley, 2:210])

4. *Corfidius*—"Varro informs us. ... that Corfidius, who had married his maternal aunt, came to life again, after the funeral had been all arranged, and that he afterwards attended the funeral of the person who had so arranged his own" (ibid., 212).

5. *Gabienus*—

> In the Sicilian war, Gabienus, the bravest of all Caesar's naval commanders, was taken prisoner by Sextus Pompeius, who ordered his throat to be cut; after which, his head almost severed from his body, he lay the whole of the day upon the seashore. Towards evening, with groans and entreaties, he begged the crowds of people who had assembled, that they would prevail upon Pompeius to come to him, or else send one of his most confidential friends, as he had just returned from the shades below, and had some important news to communicate. Pompeius accordingly sent several of his friends, to whom Gabienus stated that the good cause and virtuous partisans of Pompeius were well pleasing to the infernal deities, and that the event would shortly prove such as he wished: that he had been ordered to announce to this effect, and that, as a proof of its truthfulness, he himself should expire the very moment he had fulfilled his commission; and his death actually did take place. (ibid., 213)

6. *Tindoreus*—"... Aesculapius was struck by lightning for presuming to raise Tyndareus to life" (Pliny 29.1 [Bostock and Riley, 5:370]). Hippolytus was also raised from the dead by Aesculapius.

7. *Hercules*—Poisoned by the trick of Nessus the centaur, the hero built his funeral pyre and ascended it.

> And as when a serpent revived, by throwing off old age with his slough, is wont to be instinct with fresh life, and to glisten in his new-made scales; so, when the Tirynthian hero has put off his mortal limbs, he

flourishes in his more aethereal part, and begins to appear more majestic, and to become venerable in his august dignity. (Ovid *Metamorphoses* 9.2, c. line 266 [Riley, 311])

8. *Palici*—The Palici, two sons born from the union of Zeus with the nymph Thalea. Fearing the wrath of Hera, the nymph prayed that she might be swallowed up by the Earth. In due time the Earth split apart and sent forth twin boys who were worshipped in Sicily, where the event is said to have occurred. Their name derives—according to ancient writers—from the Greek for "to come again," that is, to be reborn. Two sulfurous pools, supposedly the places where the twins emerged, were named after them.

9. *Aesculapius*—The god of healing, son of Apollo and Coronis. Ovid says that in a fit of jealous rage the god killed his pregnant lover. "Yet ... he did not suffer his own offspring to sink into the same ashes; but he snatched the child from the flames and from the womb of his mother, and carried him into the cave of the two-formed Chiron" (Ovid *Metamorphoses* 2.9, c. line 620 [Riley, 71]). Chiron the centaur taught the child Aesculapius the art of medicine. His symbol was the serpent "creeping and sliding on the knotted staff" (Apuleius *The Golden Asse* 2), his chief place of worship Epidaurus in Argolis, from which seat the god was carried in the form of a serpent to save Rome from a plague in 293 BC, as related by Ovid (*Metamorphoses* 15.7 [Riley, 544–8]).

10. *Apollonius*—

A marriageable maiden had died, to all appearance, and her betrothed was following her bier, lamenting their uncompleted nuptials, as is the custom, and all the city was mourning with him, for the girl was of consular family. Apollonius happening upon this mournful sight, said: "Set down the bier, and I will put an end to your tears for the maiden!" He asked at the same time what her name was, and many supposed that he intended to deliver the customary funeral oration, in order to increase their grief; but by merely touching the body, and murmuring a few words over her, he woke the girl from her seeming death, and she found her voice at once, and returned to her father's house, like Alcestis when called back to life by Hercules. (Philostratus *Life and Times of Apollonius of Tyana* 4.45 [Eells, 119])

11. *Glaucus*—One of the sons of King Minos of Crete. When a child, he fell into a barrel of honey and died. The soothsayer Polyidus was charged with restoring the boy to life and shut into a vault alone with the corpse. A snake came and he killed it. Soon another snake came and placed an herb on the first snake, whereupon it came to life. Polyidus covered the body of Glaucus with the same herb, and the boy revived. It may be assumed that the second serpent was Aesculapius. Ovid refers to the story of Glaucus when he relates how Aesculapius restored the life of Hippolytus, son of Theseus:

Forthwith he brings out the herbs from his ivory casket; they had formerly benefited the manes of Glaucus: 'twas at that time when the augur stooped to the examination of herbs, and the snake experienced the benefit of the remedy that was given by a snake. Thrice did he touch his breast; thrice did he repeat the healing charms; the other raised from the ground his head, as it lay there. (Ovid *Fasti* 6, lines 749–54 [Riley, 243])

For the story of Glaucus, see Apollodorus 3.3.1 [Cambridge: Harvard University Press], 1:311.

12. *Zachla*—That is, Zachlas.

Whereat this Prophet was mooved, and tooke a certaine herbe and layd it three times upon the mouth of the dead, and he took another and laid it upon his breast in like sort. Thus when he had done hee turned himselfe into the East, and made certaine Orisons unto the Sunne, which caused all the people to marvell greatly, and to looke for this strange miracle that should happen. Then I pressed in amongst them nigh unto the biere, and got upon a stone to see this mysterie, and behold incontinently the dead body began to receive spirit, his principall veines did moove, his life came again, and he held up his head and spake ... (Apuleius *The Golden Asse* ch. 11 [Adlington])

13. *astonied*—Benumbed, paralyzed.

14. *fits of the mother*—Hysteria was thought in ancient times to arise from the "mother," or womb.

15. *Rabbi Moises*—Maimonides. The reference is to either his work on *Poisons* or the *Aphorisms,* both of which are said to draw heavily on Galen. Probably the *Aphorisms,* which is filled with marvelous anecdotes.

16. *Marsi, and the Psilli*—

Crates of Pergamum relates, that there formerly existed in the vicinity of Parium, in the Hellespont, a race of men whom he calls Ophiogenes, and that by their touch they were able to cure those who had been stung by serpents, extracting the poison by the mere imposition of the hand. Varro tells us, that there are still a few individuals in that district, whose saliva effectually cures the stings of serpents. The same, too, was the case with the tribe of the Psylli, in Africa, according to the account of Agatharchides; there people received their name from Psyllus, one of their kings, whose tomb is in existence, in the district of the Greater Syrtes. In the bodies of these people there was by nature a certain kind of poison, which was fatal to serpents, and the odour of which overpowered them with torpor: with them it was a custom to expose children immediately after their birth to the fiercest serpents, and in this manner to make proof of the fidelity of their wives, the serpents not being repelled by such children as were the offspring of adultery. ... The Marsi, in Italy, are still in possession of the same power, for which, it is said, they are indebted to their origin from the son of Circe [Agrius, son of Odysseus], from whom they acquired it as a natural quality. (Pliny 7.2 [Bostock and Riley, 2:125–6])

17. *other serpents*—Pliny mentions hibernation in bears (8.54 [Bostock and Riley, 2:306]), mice (8.55 [Bostock and Riley, 2:308]) and snakes (8.59 [Bostock and Riley, 2:311]).

18. *Epimenides Gnosius*—Agrippa makes two separate references to a single passage in Pliny:

> It is told of Epimenides of Cnossus, that when he was a boy, being fatigued by heat and walking, he fell asleep in a cave, where he slept for fifty-seven years; and that when he awoke, as though it had been the following day, he was much astonished at the changes which he saw in the appearance of every thing around him: after this, old age, it is said, came upon him in an equal number of days with the years he had slept, but his life was prolonged to his hundred and fifty-seventh year. (Pliny 7.53 [Bostock and Riley, 2:211])

19. *Seven Sleepers*—The legend of the Seven Sleepers was first recorded by Gregory of Tours late in the 6th century in his work *De Gloria Martyrum*. He is said to have translated it from the Syriac language. As the story goes, in the time of the persecutions against the Christians by the emperor Decius (249–251), seven young noblemen of Ephesus fled into a cave on Mount Coelian. They were walled in with stones and left to die. During the reign of Theodosius in the year 447 the stones were removed for building material and the seven, who had slept all this time, awoke. Imagining only hours to have passed and feeling hungry, they sent one of their number, Jamblichus, into the city to buy food. When he tried to pay the baker with a coin two centuries old, he was questioned before a judge and finally led the officials of the town to the cave, where the truth became known. Theodosius himself hastened to speak with these prodigies, but as soon as he had done so, the seven died (or according to another version, fell back asleep). Their bodies were supposed to have been placed in a stone coffin and taken to Marseilles. According to Al-Biruni's *Chronology* the bodies of seven monks were exhibited in a cave in the 9th century as the Seven Sleepers. The story is related at length in Gibbon's *Decline and Fall of the Roman Empire*, ch. 33, and with colorful additions such as a faithful guard dog in the *Koran*, sura 18.

20. *Norvegia*—Norway.

21. *Elias*—Elijah. See I Kings 19:5–8.

CHAPTER LIX

Of divination by dreams.

There is also a certain kind of divination by dreams, confirmed by the traditions of philosophers, the authorities of divines, the examples of histories, and daily experience. A dream I call here, not vain dreams, or idle imaginations: for those are vain, and have no divination in them, but arise from the remains of watchings, and disturbance of the body. For as the mind is taken up about, and wearied with cares, it suggests itself to him that is asleep. I call that a dream here, which is caused by the celestial influences in the phantastic spirit, mind, or body, being all well disposed.

The rule of interpreting this is found amongst astrologers, in that part which is wrote concerning questions; but yet that is not sufficient, because these kind of dreams come by use to divers men after a divers manner, according to the divers quality, and dispositions of the phantastic spirit: wherefore there cannot be given one common rule to all for the interpretation of dreams.

But according to the opinion of *Synesius*, seeing there are the same accidents to things, and like befall like; so he which hath often fallen upon the same visible thing, hath assigned to himself the same opinion, passion, fortune, action, event, and as *Aristotle* saith, the memory is confirmed by sense, and by keeping in memory the same thing knowledge is obtained, as also by the knowledge of many experiences, by little, and little, arts and sciences are obtained. After the same account you must conceive of dreams. Whence *Synesius* commands that everyone should observe his dreams, and their events, and such like rules, viz. to commit to memory all things that are seen, and accidents that befall, as well in sleep, as watching, and with a diligent observation consider with himself the rules by which these are to be examined, for by this means shall a diviner be able by little, and little to interpret his dreams, if so be nothing slip out of his memory.

Now dreams are more efficacious, when the Moon overruns that sign, which was in the ninth number[1] of the nativity, or revolution of that year,[2] or in the ninth sign from the sign of perfection.[3] For it is a most true, and certain divination, neither doth it proceed from nature or human arts, but from purified minds, by divine inspiration. Now we shall discuss, and examine that which belongs to prophesyings, and oracles.

Notes—Chapter LIX

1. *ninth number*—There are 12 astrological signs in the zodiac. The sign of nativity, or birth, is the one through which the Sun is passing at the time of birth. Following the circle of the zodiac counterclockwise will reveal the ninth sign from the birth sign. For example, if the nativity occurs on April 2, the birth sign is Aries, and the ninth sign following is Capricorn. Since the Moon makes a circle of the sky in a

period of approximately 28 days, it will successively pass through each sign every lunar month, taking a little over two days to do so.

2. *that year*—Year of birth.

3. *sign of perfection*—When the Moon is full she is said to be perfected, in the sense of having reached maturity. Therefore the sign of perfection would be the zodiac sign in which the Moon is full that particular lunar cycle. The ninth sign is obtained by counting counterclockwise from this sign.

CHAPTER LX

Of madness, and divinations which are made when men are awake, and of the power of a melancholy humour, by which spirits are sometimes induced into men's bodies.

It happens also sometimes, that not only they that are asleep, but also they that are watchful do with a kind of instigation of mind, divine, which divination *Aristotle* calls ravishment or a kind of madness, and teacheth that it proceeds from a melancholy humour, saying in his treatise Of Divination:[1] melancholy men, by reason of their earnestness, do far better conjecture, and quickly conceive a habit, and most easily receive an impression of the celestials. And in his Problems[2] saith, that the sibyls[3] and the Bacchides,[4] and *Niceratus* the Syracusan, and *Amon,*[5] were by their natural melancholy complexion prophets, and poets.

The cause therefore of this madness, if it be anything within the body, is a melancholy humour, not that which they call black choler, which is so obstinate, and terrible a thing, that the violence of it is said by physicians, and natural philosophers, besides madness, which it doth induce, also to entice evil spirits to seize upon men's bodies. Therefore we understand a melancholy humour here, to be a natural, and white choler.

For this, when it is stirred up, burns, and stirs up a madness conducing to knowledge, and divination, especially if it be helped by any celestial influx, especially of Saturn, who seeing he is cold, and dry, as is a melancholy humour, hath his influence upon it, increaseth, and preserveth it. Besides, seeing he is the author of secret contemplation, and estranged from all public affairs, and the highest of all the planets, doth always as he withcall his mind from outward businesses, so also makes it ascend higher, and bestows upon him the knowledge, and passages of future things.

And this is *Aristotle's* meaning[6] in his book of Problems. By melancholy, saith he, some men are made as it were divine, foretelling things to come, and some men are made poets. He saith also, that all men that were excellent in any science, were for the most part melancholy. *Democritus,*[7] and *Plato*[8] attest the same, saying, that there were some melancholy men, that had such excellent wits, that they were thought, and seemed to be rather divine than human.

So also there have been many melancholy men at first rude, ignorant, and untractable, as they say, *Hesiod,*[9] *Ion,*[10] *Tynnichus Calcinenses,*[11] *Homer,* and *Lucretius*[12] were, who on a sudden were taken with a madness, and became poets, and prophesied wonderful, and divine things, which they themselves scarce understood. Whence divine *Plato* in Ion saith, many prophets, after the violence of their madness was abated, do not well understand what they wrote, yet treated accurately of each art in their madness, as all artists by reading of them judge.

So great also they say the power of melancholy is of, that by its force, celestial spirits also are sometimes drawn into men's bodies, by whose presence, and instinct, antiquity testifies men have been made drunk, and spake most wonderful things. And that they think happens under a threefold difference, according to a threefold apprehension of the soul, viz. imaginative, rational, and mental.

They say therefore, when the mind is forced with a melancholy humour, nothing moderating the power of the body, and passing beyond the bounds of the members, is wholly carried into imagination, and doth suddenly become a seat for inferior spirits, by whom it oftentimes receives wonderful ways, and forms of manual arts. So we see that any most ignorant man doth presently become an excellent painter, or contriver of buildings, and to become a master in any such art. But when these kinds of spirits portend to us future things, then they show those things which belong to the disturbing of the elements, and changes of times, as rain, tempests, inundations, earthquakes, great mortality, famine, slaughter, and the like. As we read in *Aulus Gelius,* that *Cornelius Patarus*[13] his priest did at that time, when *Caesar,* and *Pompey* were to fight in Thessalia,[14] being taken with a madness, foretell the time, order, and issue of the battle.

But when the mind is turned wholly into reason, it becomes a receptacle for middle spirits. Hence it obtains the knowledge, and understanding of natural, and human things. So we see that a man sometimes doth on a sudden become a philosopher, physician, or an excellent orator, and foretells mutations of kingdoms, and restitutions of ages, and such things as belong to them, as the sibyl did to the Romans.

But when the mind is wholly elevated into the understanding, then it becomes a receptacle of sublime spirits, and learns of them the secrets of divine things, as the Law of God, the orders of the angels, and such things as belong to the knowledge of things eternal, and salvation of souls. It foretells things which are appointed by God's special predestination, as future prodigies, or miracles, the prophet to come, the changing of the Law. So the sibyls prophesied of Christ[15] a long time before his coming. So *Virgil* understanding that Christ was at hand, and remembering what the sibyl *Cumea*[16] had said, sang thus to *Pollio:*

> Last times are come, Cumaea's prophecy
> Now from high heaven springs a new
>   progeny,

And time's great order now again is born,
The Maid returns, Saturnian realms return.

And a little after[17] intimating that original sin shall be of no effect, saith:

> If any prints of our old vice remained,
> By thee they're void, and fear shall leave
>   the land;
> He a god's life shall take, with gods shall see
> Mixed heros, and himself their object be,
> Rule with paternal power the appeased Earth
> He shall————

Then he adds,[18] that thence the fall of the serpent, and the poison of the tree of death, or the knowledge of good and evil, shall be nulled, saying:

> ————the serpent shall
> And the deceitful herb of venom fall.

Yet he intimates[19] that some sparks of original sin shall remain, when he saith:

> Some steps of ancient fraud shall yet be
>   found.

And at last with a most great hyperbole cries out to this child, as the offspring of God, adoring of him in these words:[20]

> Dear race of gods, great stock of Jupiter,
> Behold! the world shakes on its ponder-
>   ous axe,
> See earth, and heavens immense, and the
>   ocean tracts,
> How all things at the approaching age
>   rejoice!
> Oh! that my life would last so long, and
>   voice,
> As would suffice thy actions to rehearse.

There are also some prognostics, which are in the middle, betwixt natural, and supernatural divination, as in those who are near to death, and being weakened with old age, so sometimes foresee things to come, because as saith *Plato,*[21] by how much the more men are less hindered by their sense, so much the more accurately they understand, and because they are nearer to the place whither they must go, and their bonds being as it were a little loosed, seeing they are no more subject to the body, easily perceive the light of divine revelation.

Notes—Chapter LX

1. *treatise Of Divination*—

With regard to the fact that some persons who are liable to derangement have this foresight, its explanation is that normal mental movements do not impede [the alien movements], but are beaten off by the latter. Therefore it is that they have an especially keen perception of the alien movements. (Aristotle *De divinatione per somnum* [Prophesying by dreams] 2.464a. In *Basic Works,* 629)

Earlier in the same chapter Aristotle says:

... the power of foreseeing the future and of having vivid dreams is found in persons of inferior type, which implies that God does not send the dreams; but merely that all those whose physical temperment is, as it were, garrulous and excitable, see sights of all descriptions; for, inasmuch as they experience many movements of every kind, they just chance to have visions resembling objective facts ... (ibid., 628)

Aristotle thinks that those who become ecstatic or furious through some disease, especially melancholy persons, possess a divine gift of presentiment in their minds. (Cicero *De divinatione* 1.37 [Yonge, 179])

2. *in his Problems*—

Many too, if this heat approaches the region of the intellect, are affected by diseases of frenzy and possession; and this is the origin of Sibyls and soothsayers and all inspired persons, when they are affected not by disease but by natural temperament. Maracus, the Syracusan, was actually a better poet when he was out of his mind. (Aristotle *Problems* 30.1.954a, lines 35–40 [Forster, vol. 7])

3. *sibyls*—Women with the power of prophecy. There were generally considered to be ten, distinguished by their places of residence: (1) Cumaean, (2) Babylonian, (3) Libyan, (4) Delphian (an elder and a younger), (5) Cimmerian, (6) Erythraean (an elder and a younger), (7) Samian, (8) Hellespontian, (9) Phrygian and (10) Tiburtine.

4. *Bacchides*—The priestesses of Bacchus, who with wine and dancing worked themselves into a frenzy at the festivals of the god. It was these women who tore Orpheus into pieces. As they worshiped they cried out: "Evoë, Bacche ! O Iacche! Io, Bacche! Evoë sabae!" For this reason Bacchus was sometimes called Bromius, from the Greek for "to shout." The famous "Evie, Evoë" of the Bacchae is said to derive from a saying of Jupiter to Bacchus when Bacchus killed a giant: "Well done, son" (εὐ ὑιέ). See Ovid *Metamorphoses* 4.1 and footnote 5 (Riley, 119); also the *Ars amatoria* 1 [Riley, 400, 94n].

5. *Amon*—The oracle of Zeus Ammon in Egypt.

6. *Aristotle's meaning*—"Now black bile, which is naturally cold ... when it is overheated, it produces cheerfulness accompanied by song, and frenzy ..." (Aristotle *Problems* 30.1.945a, [Forster, vol. 7]). See note 2, above.

7. *Democritus*—

Hippocrates relates at large in his Epistle to Damagetus, wherein he doth express, how coming to visit him one day, he found Democritus in his garden at Abdera, in the suburbs, under a shady bower, with a book on his knees, busy at his study, sometimes writing, sometimes walking. The subject of his book was melancholy and madness; about him lay the carcasses of many several beasts, newly by him cut up and anatomized; not that he did contemn God's creatures, as he told Hippocrates, but to find out the seat of this *atra bilis* [black bile], or melancholy, whence it proceeds, and how it was engendered in men's bodies, to the intent he might better cure it in himself, and by his writings and observations teach others how to prevent and avoid it. (Burton *Anatomy of Melancholy* [London: J. M. Dent and Sons, 1961 (1621)], 1:19–20)

8. *Plato*—

... the epic poets, all the good ones, have their excellence, not from art, but are inspired, possessed, and thus they utter all these admirable poems. So is it also with the good lyric poets; as the worshipping Corybantes [priests of Cybele in Phrygia] are not in their senses when they dance, so the lyric poets are not in their senses when they make these lovely lyric poems. No, when once they launch into harmony and rhythm, they are seized with the Bacchic transport, and are possessed. (Plato *Ion* 534a [Hamilton and Cairns, 220])

9. *Hesiod*—By his own assertion, Hesiod was an inspired poet without training:

> The Muses once taught Hesiod to sing
> Sweet songs, while he was shepherding his
>   lambs
> On holy Helicon;
>
> (Hesiod *Theogony* c. line 20. In *Hesiod and Theogonis,* trans. Dorothea Wender [Harmondsworth: Penguin Books, 1973], 23)

10. *Ion*—

> But the majority are possessed and held by Homer, and, Ion, you are one of these, and are possessed by Homer. And whenever anyone chants the work of any other poet, you fall asleep, and haven't a thing to say, but when anyone gives tongue to a strain of this one, you are awake at once, your spirit dances, and you have much to say, but by dispensation from above and by divine possession. (Plato *Ion* 536b [Hamilton and Cairns, 222])

11. *Tynnichus Calcinenses*—Tynnichus Chalcidensis, or Tynnichus of Chalcis.

> He never composed a single poem worth recalling, save the song of praise which everyone repeats, wellnigh the finest of all lyrical poems, and absolutely what he called it, an "Invention of the Muses." By this example above all, it seems to me, the god would show us, lest we doubt, that these lovely poems are not of man or human workmanship, but are divine and from the gods, and that the poets are nothing but interpreters of the gods, each one possessed by the divinity to whom he is in bondage. And to prove this, the deity on purpose sang the loveliest of all lyrics through the most miserable poet. (Plato *Ion* 534d–e [Hamilton and Cairns, 220–1])

12. *Lucretius*—See biographical note.

13. *Cornelius Patarus*—

> An augur [Gaius Cornelius], if there is implicit credit to be given to those who relate it, sitting on the Euganean hill, where the steaming Aponus arises from the earth, and the waters of Timavus of Antenor are dispersed in various channels, exclaimed:—"The critical day is come, a combat most momentous is being waged, the impious arms of Pompey and of Caesar are meeting." (Lucan *Pharsalia* 7. line 192 [Riley, 259])

14. *fight in Thessalia*—Caesar and Pompey met in battle in Thessaly on the plains of Pharsalus the 9th of August in the year 48 BC. The outcome was utter defeat for Pompey.

15. *prophesied of Christ*—The Christian version of the Sibylline prophecies are monkish forgeries. The monks reckoned 12 sibyls: (1) Libyan—"The day shall come when men shall see the King of all living things." (2) Samian—"The Rich One shall be born of a pure virgin." (3) Cumana—"Jesus Christ shall come from heaven and live and reign in poverty on earth." (4) Cumae—"God shall be born of a pure virgin, and hold converse with sinners." (5) Erythraea—"Jesus Christ, Son of God, the Saviour." (6) Persian—"Satan shall be overcome by a true Prophet." (7) Tiburtine—"The Highest shall descend from heaven, and a virgin be shown in the valleys of the deserts." (8) Delphic—"The Prophet born of the virgin shall be crowned with thorns." (9) Phrygian—"Our Lord shall rise again." (10) European—"A virgin and her Son shall flee into Egypt." (11) Agrippina—"Jesus Christ shall be outraged and scourged." (12) Hellespontic—"Jesus Christ shall suffer shame upon the cross." Agrippina perhaps refers to Agrippinensis (modern Cologne). See Brewer 1870.

16. *sibyl Cumea*—"Now has come the latest age of the Cumaean hymn; the mighty line of cycles begins its round anew. Now too the maiden Astraea returns, the reign of Saturn returns ..." (Virgil *Eclogues* 4, lines 4–7 [Lonsdale and Lee, 18]).

17. *little after*—"... under your auspices, whatever traces of our nation's guilt remain shall be effaced, and release the earth from everlasting dread. He shall receive the life of the gods, and see heros mingled with gods, and shall himself be seen by them, and with his father's virtues shall rule a reconciled world" (ibid., lines 13–7).

18. *Then he adds*—"The serpent too shall perish, and the treacherous poison-plant shall perish ..." (ibid., line 24).

19. *Yet he intimates*—"Yet a few traces of ancient guile shall still be left behind ..." (ibid., line 31).

20. *in these words*—

> Begin to assume, I pray, your sovereign honours, (the time will soon arrive,) dear offspring of the gods, majestic child of Jove! See the world nodding with its ponderous vault, and lands, and plains of sea, and deep heaven! See how all things exult in the age that is to come! O may there be left me the latest portion of a life so long, and breath so much, as shall suffice to sing your deeds! (ibid., lines 49–54 [Lonsdale and Lee, 19])

21. *as saith Plato*—

Surely the soul can best reflect when it is free of all distractions such as hearing or sight or pain or pleasure of any kind—that is, when it ignores the body and becomes as far as possible independent, avoiding all physical contacts and associations as much as it can in its search for reality. ... We are in fact convinced that if we are ever to have pure knowledge of anything, we must get rid of the body and contemplate things by themselves with the soul by itself. (Plato *Phaedo* 65c, 66d [Hamilton and Cairns, 48–9])

CHAPTER LXI

Of the forming of man, of the external senses, and also of the inward, and the mind: of the threefold appetite of the soul, and passions of the will.

It is the opinion of some divines, that God did not immediately create the body of man, but by the assistance of the heavenly spirits compounded and framed him; which opinion *Alcinous,* and *Plato* favour; thinking that God is the chief creator of the whole world, of the spirits both good and bad, and therefore immortalized them: but that all kinds of mortal animals were made at the command of God;[1] for if he should have created them, they must have been immortal.

The spirits therefore mixing Earth, Fire, Air, and Water[2] together, made of them all, put together, one body, which they subjected to the service of the soul, assigning in it several provinces to each power thereof, to the meaner of them, mean and low places: as to anger the midriff, to lust the womb, but to the more noble senses the head,[3] as the tower of the whole body, and then the manifold organs of speech. They divide the sense into external, and internal.

The external are divided into five, known to everyone, to which there are allotted five organs, or subjects, as it were foundations; being so ordered, that they which are placed in the more eminent part of the body, have a greater degree of purity. For the eyes placed in the uppermost place, are the most pure, and have an affinity with the nature of Fire, and light: then the ears have the second order of place, and purity, and are compared to the Air: the nostrils have the third order, and have a middle nature betwixt the Air, and the Water:

then the organ of tasting, which is grosser and most like to the nature of Water: last of all, the touching is diffused through the whole body, and is compared to the grossness of Earth.

The more pure senses are those which perceive their objects farthest off, as seeing, and hearing, then the smelling, then the taste, which doth not perceive but those that are nigh. But the touch perceives both ways, for it perceives bodies nigh; and as sight discerns by the medium of the air, so the touch perceives by the medium of a stock or pole, bodies hard, soft, and moist. Now the touch only is common to all animals. For it is most certain that man hath this sense, and in this, and taste he excels all other animals, but in the other three he is excelled by some animals, as by a dog, who hears, sees, and smells more accurately than man; and the lynx, and eagles see more acutely than all other animals, and man.

Now the interior senses are, according to *Averrois,* divided into four, whereof the first is called common sense, because it doth first collect, and perfect all the representations which are drawn in by the outward senses. The second is the imaginative power, whose office is, seeing it represents nothing, to retain those representations which are received by the former senses, and to present them to the third faculty of inward sense, which is the phantasy, or power of judging, whose work is also to perceive, and judge by the representations received, what or what kind of thing that is of which the representations are, and to commit those things which are thus discerned, and adjudged, to the memory to be kept.[4]

For the virtues thereof in general, are discourse, dispositions, persecutions, and flights, and stirrings up to action: but in particular, the understanding of intellectuals, virtues, the manner of discipline, counsel, election. And this is that which shows us future things by dreams: whence the fancy is sometimes named the phantastical intellect.[5] For it is the last impression of the understanding; which, as saith *Iamblicus,* is belonging to all the powers of the mind, and forms all figures, resemblances of species, and operations, and things seen, and sends forth the impressions of other powers unto others: and those things which appear by sense, it stirs up into an opinion, but those things which appear by the intellect, in the second place it offers to opinion, but of itself it receives images from all, and by its property, doth properly assign them, according to their assimilation, forms all the actions of the soul, and accommodates the external to the internal, and impresses the body with its impression.

Now these senses have their organs in the head, for the common sense, and imagination take up the two former cells of the brain, although *Aristotle* placeth the organ of the common sense in the heart,[6] but the cogitative power possesseth the highest, and middle part of the head; and lastly, the memory the hindmost part thereof.

Moreover, the organs of voice, and speech are many, as the inward muscles of the breast betwixt the ribs, the breasts, the lungs, the arteries, the windpipe, the bowing of the tongue, and all those parts and muscles that serve for breathing. But the proper organ of speech is the mouth, in which are framed words, and speeches, the tongue, the teeth, the lips, the palate, etc.

Above the sensible soul, which expresseth its powers by the organs of the body, the incorporeal mind possesseth the highest place, and it hath a double nature, the one, which inquireth into the causes, properties, and progress of those things which are contained in the order of nature, and is content in the contemplation of the truth, which is therefore called the contemplative intellect. The other is a power of the mind, which discerning by consulting what things are to be done, and what things to be shunned is wholly taken up in consultation, and action, and is therefore called the active intellect.

This order of powers therefore nature ordained in man, that by the external senses we might know corporeal things, by the internal the representations of bodies, as also things abstracted by the mind and intellect, which are neither bodies, nor anything like them.

And according to this threefold order of the powers of the soul, there are three appetites in the soul: the first is natural, which is an inclination of nature into its end, as of a stone downward, which is in all stones: another is animal, which the sense follows, and it is divided into irascible, and concupiscible: the third is intellective, which is called the will, differing from the sensitive in this, the sensitive is of itself, of these things, which may be presented to the senses, desiring nothing unless in some manner comprehended. But the will, although it be of itself, of all things that are possible, yet because it is free by its essence, it may be also of things that are impossible, as it was in the Devil, desiring himself to be equal with God, and therefore is altered and depraved with pleasure and continual anguish, whilst it assents to the inferior powers.

Whence from its depraved appetite there arise four passions in it, with which in like manner the body is affected sometimes. Wherefore the first is called oblectation,[7] which is a certain quietness or assentation of the mind or will, because it obeys, and not willingly consents to that pleasantness which the senses hold forth; which is therefore defined to be an inclination of the mind to an effeminate pleasure. The second is called effusion, which is a remission of, or dissolution of the power, viz. when beyond the oblectation the whole power of the mind, and intension of the present good is melted, and diffuseth itself to enjoy it. The third in vaunting, and loftiness, thinking itself to have attained to some great good, in the enjoyment of which it prides itself, and glorieth. The fourth and the last is envy, or a certain kind of pleasure or delight at another man's harm, without any advantage to itself. It is said to be without any

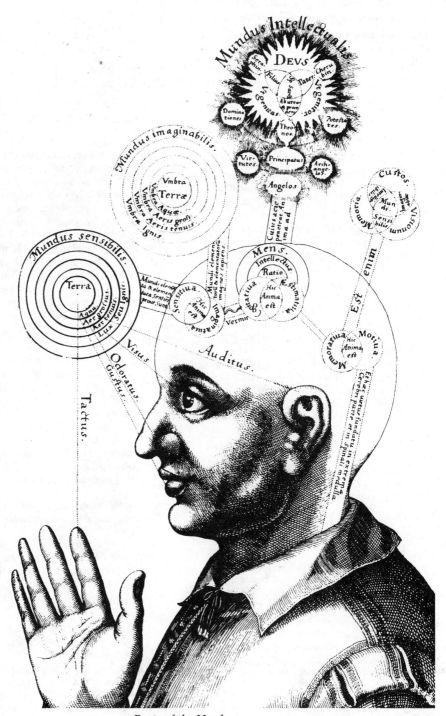

Parts of the Head

·from *Tomus secundus de supernaturali, naturali, praeternaturali et contranaturali microcosmi historia*
by Robert Fludd (Oppenheim, 1619)

advantage to itself, because if anyone should for his own profit rejoice at another man's harm, this would rather be out of love to himself, than out of ill will to another.

And these four passions arising from a depraved appetite of pleasure, the grief or per-plexity itself doth also beget so many contrary passions, as horror, sadness, fear, and sorrow at another's good, without his own hurt, which we call envy, i.e. sadness at another's prosper-ity, as pity is a certain kind of sadness at another's misery.

Notes—Chapter LXI

1. *command of God*—

Gods, children of gods, who are my works and of whom I am the artificer and father, my creations are indissoluble, if so I will. All that is bound may be undone, but only an evil being would wish to undo that which is harmonious and happy. Wherefore, since ye are but creatures, ye are not altogether immortal and indissoluble, but ye shall cer-tainly not be dissolved, nor be liable to the fate of death, having in my will a greater and mightier bond than those with which ye were bound at the time of your birth. And now listen to my instructions. Three tribes of mortal beings remain to be created—without them the universe will be incom-plete, for it will not contain every kind of animal which it ought to contain, if it is to be perfect. On the other hand, if they were created by me and received life at my hands, they would be on an equality with the gods. In order then that they may be mortal, and that this universe may be truly universal, do ye, according to your natures, betake yourselves to the formation of ani-mals, imitating the power which was shown by me in creating you. The part of them worthy of the name immortal, which is called divine and is the guiding principle of those who are willing to follow justice and you—of that divine part I will myself sow the seed, and having made a beginning, I will hand the work over to you. And do ye then interweave the mortal with the immor-tal and make and beget living creatures, and give them food and make them grow, and receive them again in death. (Plato *Timaeus* 4l [Hamilton and Cairns, 1170)

2. *Earth, Fire, Air, and Water*—

When the creator had made all these ordi-nances he remained in his own accustomed nature, and his children heard and were obedient to their father's word, and receiv-ing from him the immortal principle of a mortal creature, in imitation of their own creator they borrowed portions of fire and earth and water and air from the world, which were hereafter to be restored—these they took and welded them together, not with the indissoluble chains by which they were themselves bound, but with little pegs too small to be visible, making up out of all the four elements each separate body, and fastening the courses of the immortal soul in a body which was in a state of perpetual influx and efflux. (ibid. 42e–43a [Hamilton and Cairns, 1171])

3. *the head*—

First, then, the gods, imitating the spherical shape of the universe, enclosed the two divine courses in a spherical body, that, namely, which we now term the head, being the most divine part of us and the lord of all that is in us; to this the gods, when they put together the body, gave all the other mem-bers to be servants, considering that it must partake of every sort of motion. (ibid. 44d [Hamilton and Cairns, 1173])

4. *memory to be kept*—See Aristotle *De anima* 3.3–8, on perceiving, discriminating and thinking.

5. *phantastical intellect*—"As sight is the most high-ly developed sense, the name phantasia (imagina-tion) has been formed from phaso (light) because it is not possible to see without light" (Aristotle *De anima* 3.3 [McKeon, 549]).

6. *in the heart*—

Again, as the sensory faculty, the motor fac-ulty, and the nutritive faculty are all lodged in one and the same part of the body ... it is the heart which in sanguineous animals constitutes this central part, and in bloodless animals it is that which takes the place of a heart. (Aristotle *De partibus animalium* [Parts of animals] 2.1.647a [McKeon, 661])

7. *oblectation*—Delight, pleasure, enjoyment.

CHAPTER LXII

Of the passions of the mind, their original, difference, and kinds.

The passions of the mind are nothing else but certain motions or inclinations proceeding from the apprehension of anything, as of good or evil, convenient or inconvenient. Now these kind of apprehensions are of three sorts, viz. sensual, rational, and intellectual.

And according to these three, are three sorts of passions in the soul; for when they follow the sensitive apprehension, then they respect a temporal good or evil, under the notion of profitable, or unprofitable, delightful and offensive, and are called natural, or animal passions. When they follow the rational apprehension, and so respect good or bad, under the notions of virtue or vice, praise or disgrace, profitable or unprofitable, honest or dishonest, they are called rational, or voluntary passions. When they follow the intellectual apprehension, and respect good or bad, under the notion of just or unjust, true or false, they are called intellectual passions, or synderesis.[1]

Now the subject of the passions of the soul, is the concupitive power of the soul, and is divided into concupiscible, and irascible,[2] and both respect good and bad, but under a different notion.

For when the concupiscible power respects good, and evil absolutely; love or lust, or on the contrary, hatred is caused: when it respects good, as absent, so desire is caused; or evil, as absent, or at hand, and so is caused horror, flying from, or loathing: or if it respect good, as present, then there is caused delight, mirth, or pleasure; but if evil, as present, then sadness, anxiety, grief.

But the irascible power respects good or bad, under the notion of some difficulty; to obtain the one, or avoid the other, and this sometimes with confidence: and so there is caused hope or boldness; but when with diffidency, then despair, and fear. But when that irascible power riseth into revenge, and this be only about some evil past, as it were of injury or hurt offered, there is caused anger.

And so we find eleven passions[3] in the mind, which are love, hatred; desire, horror; joy, grief; hope, despair; boldness, fear; and anger.

Notes—Chapter LXII

1. *synderesis*—"Sinderesis is a naturall power of the soule sette in the hyghest parte therof, mouynge and sterrynge it to good & abhorrynge euyll" (Saint-German, *Fyrst dyaloge in Englisshe betwyxt a doctoure of dyvnyte and a student in the laws of Englande* (1531), quoted from *OED*. An archaic form of the word synteresis: prick of conscience that moves right actions.

2. *concupiscible, and irascible*—"The sensitive appetite is one generic power, and is called sensuality; but it is divided into two powers, which are species of the sensitive appetite—the irascible and the concupiscible" (Thomas Aquinas *Summa theologica* 81.2. In *Introduction to Saint Thomas Aquinas,* ed. Anton C. Pegis [New York: Random House, 1948], 356).

3. *eleven passions*—

Perturbations and passions which trouble the phantasy, though they dwell between the confines of sense and reason, yet they rather follow sense than reason, because they are drowned in corporeal organs of sense. They are commonly reduced into two inclinations, irascible and concupiscible. The Thomists [disciples of Aquinas] subdivide them into eleven, six in the coveting, and five in the invading. Aristotle reduceth all to pleasure and pain, Plato to love and hatred, Vives to good and bad. If good, it is present, and then we absolutely joy and love; or to come, and then we desire and hope for it. If evil, we absolutely hate it; if present, it is sorrow; if to come, fear. These four passions [joy, desire; sorrow, fear] Bernard compares to the wheels of a chariot, by which we are carried in this world. All other passions are subordinate unto these four, or six, as some will: love, joy, desire, hatred, sorrow, fear; the rest, as anger, envy, emulation, pride, jealousy, anxiety, mercy, discontent, despair, ambition, avarice, etc., are reducible unto the first; and if they be immoderate, they consume the spirits, and melancholy is especially caused by them. (Burton *Anatomy of Melancholy* 1.2.3.3, 1:258)

CHAPTER LXIII

How the passions of the mind change the proper body, by changing the accidents, and moving the spirit.

The phantasy, or imaginative power hath a ruling power over the passions of the soul, when they follow the sensual apprehension. For this doth of its own power, according to the diversity of the passions, first of all change the proper body with a sensible transmutation, by changing the accidents in the body, and by moving the spirit upward or downward, inward or outward, and by producing divers qualities in the members.

So in joy, the spirits are driven outward, in fear, drawn back, in bashfulness, are moved to the brain. So in joy, the heart is dilated outward, by little, and little, in sadness, is constringed by little, and little inward. After the same manner in anger or fear, but suddenly. Again anger, or desire of revenge produceth heat, redness, a bitter taste, and aloofness. Fear induceth cold, trembling of the heart, speechlessness, and paleness. Sadness causeth sweat, and a bluish-whiteness. Pity, which is a kind of sadness, doth often ill affect the body of him that takes pity, that it seems to be the body of another man affected. Also it is manifest, that amongst some lovers there is such a strong tie of love, that what the one suffers, the other suffers. Anxiety induceth dryness, and blackness. And how great heats love stirs up in the liver, and pulse, physicians know, discerning by that kind of judgement the name of her that is beloved, in an heroic passion.[1] So *Naustratus* knew that *Antiochus* was taken with the love of *Stratonica*.[2]

It is also manifest that such like passions, when they are most vehement, may cause death.

And this is manifest to all men, that with too much joy, sadness, love, hatred, men many times die, and are sometimes freed from a disease. So we read, that *Sophocles,* and *Dionysius* the Sicilian tyrant, did both die suddenly at the news of a tragical victory. So a certain woman seeing her son returning from the Canensian battle, died suddenly.[3] Now what sadness can do, is known to all. We know that dogs oftentimes die with sadness[4] for the death of their masters. Sometimes also by reason of these like passions, long diseases follow, and are sometimes cured.

So also some men looking from an high place,[5] by reason of great fear, tremble, are dim-sighted, and weakened, and sometimes lose their senses. So fears, and falling sickness, sometimes follow sobbing. Sometimes wonderful effects are produced, as in the son of *Croesus,* whom his mother brought forth dumb, yet a vehement fear, and ardent affection made him speak, which naturally he could never do. So with a sudden fall oftentimes life, sense, motion on a sudden leave the members, and presently again are sometimes returned.

And how much vehement anger, joined with great audacity, can do, *Alexander the Great* shows, who being circumvented with a battle in India, was seen to send forth from himself lightning and fire.[6] The father of *Theodoricus*[7] is said to have sent forth out of his body, sparks of fire; so that sparkling flames did leap out with a noise. And such like things sometimes appear in beasts, as in *Tiberius* his horse, which is said to send forth a flame out of his mouth.

Notes—Chapter LXIII

1. *heroic passion*—For the physiological effects of the passions, see their individual treatment in Burton's *Anatomy of Melancholy* 1.2.3.4–14.

2. *love of Stratonica*—Stratonice was wife of the Syrian king Seleucus I (312–280 BC) and stepmother to his son Antiochus, who conceived a secret passion for his father's young bride but from shame kept it hidden, and began to pine away with love-sickness. The court physician Erasistratus knew from the symptoms of the disease that love was its cause, and observing the young man when he was with his stepmother soon divined its object. He convinced Seleucus to give Stratonice in wedlock to his son as the only way to preserve Antiochus' life, which the old king did out of affection for his child. The story is related in Plutarch's *Life of Demetrius*. Julian the Apostate in his *Misopogon* says that Antiochus waited for the death of his father before marrying Stratonice.

3. *died suddenly*—

> Besides Chilo, who has been already mentioned [Pliny 7.32 {Bostock and Riley, 2:178–9}], Sophocles and Dionysius the tyrant of Sicily, both of them, died of joy, on learning that they had obtained the prize for tragedy. After the defeat at Cannae, a mother died of joy, on seeing that her son had returned in safety, she having heard a false report of his death. (Pliny 7.54 [Bostock and Riley, 2:213–4])

4. *die with sadness*—"Jason, the Lycian, having been slain, his dog refused to take food, and died of famine" (Pliny 8.61 [Bostock and Riley, 2:312–3]).

5. *an high place*—Altophobia.

6. *lightning and fire*—

> But at a siege of a town of the Mallians, who have the repute of being the bravest people of India, he [Alexander] ran in great danger of his life. For having beaten off the defendants with showers of arrows, he was the first man who mounted the wall by a scaling-ladder, which, as soon as he was up, broke and left him almost alone, exposed to the darts which the barbarians threw at him in great numbers from below. In this distress, turning himself as well as he could, he leaped down in the midst of his enemies, and had the good fortune to land upon his feet. The brightness and clattering of his armour when he came to the ground made the barbarians think they saw rays of light, or some bright phantom playing before his body, which frightened them so at first that they ran away and dispersed. (Plutarch "Alexander." In *Lives* [Dryden, 846])

7. *father of Theodoricus*—Probably Theudemir, father of Theodoric the Great, king of the Ostrogoths (?454–526). Many legends grew up around the life and exploits of Theodoric under the name Dietrich of Bern: for example, Theodoric was said to emit flaming breath when angry. The Byzantine historians made the mistake of calling Walamir, who was Theodoric's uncle, his father.

CHAPTER LXIV

How the passions of the mind change the body by way of imitation from some resemblance; also of the transforming, and translating of men, and what force the imaginative power hath not only over the body, but the soul.

The foresaid passions sometimes alter the body by way of imitation, by reason of the virtue which the likeness of the thing hath to change it, which power the vehement imagination moves, as in setting the teeth on edge at the sight or hearing of something, or because we see or imagine another to eat sharp or sour things: so he which sees another gape,[1] gapes also; and some when they hear anyone name sour things, their tongue waxeth tart. Also the seeing of any filthy thing causeth nauseousness. Many at the sight of man's blood fall into a swoon. Some when they see bitter meat given to any, perceive a bitter spittle in their mouth. And *William of Paris* saith, that he saw a man, that at the sight of a medicine,[2] went to stool as oft as he pleased; when as neither the substance of the medicine, nor the odour, nor the taste of it came to him: but only a kind of resemblance was apprehended by him.

Upon this account some that are in a dream think they burn, and are in a fire, and are fearfully tormented, as if they did truly burn, whenas the substance of the fire is not near them, but only a resemblance apprehended by their imagination. And sometimes men's bodies are transformed, and transfigured, and also transported, and this ofttimes when they are in a dream, and sometimes when they are awake. So *Cyprus*[3] after he was chosen king of Italy, did very much wonder at, and meditate upon the fight, and victory of bulls, and in the thought thereof did sleep

a whole night, but in the morning was found horned, no otherwise than by the vegetative power being stirred up by a vehement imagination, elevating corniferous[4] humours into his head, and producing horns.

For a vehement cogitation, whilst it vehemently moves the species, pictures out the figure of the thing thought on, which they represent in their blood, and the blood impresseth from itself, on the members that are nourished by it, as upon those of the same body, so upon those of another's. As the imagination of a woman with child impresseth the mark of the thing longed for upon her infant, and the imagination of a man bit with a mad dog, impresseth upon his urine the image of dogs. So men may grow grey on a sudden. And some by the dream of one night, have grown up from boys into perfect men. Hitherto may be referred those many scars of King *Dagobertus,* and marks of *Franciscus,* which they received, the one whilst he was afraid of correction, the other whilst he did wonderfully meditate upon the wounds of Christ.[5]

So, many are transported from place to place, passing over rivers, fires, and unpassable places, viz. when the species of any vehement desire, or fear, or boldness are impressed upon their spirits, and being mixed with vapours, do move the organ of the touch in their original, together with phantasy, which is the original of local motion. Whence they stir up the members, and organs of motion to motion and are moved without any mistake unto the imagined place, not out of sight, but from the interior phantasy. So great a power is there of the soul upon the body, that which way soever that imagines, and dreams that it goes, thither doth it lead the body.

We read many other examples by which the power of the soul upon the body is wonderfully explained, as is that which *Avicen* describes of a certain man, who when he pleased could affect his body with the palsy. They report of *Gallus Vibius*, that he did fall into madness, not casually, but on purpose: for whilst he did imitate mad men, he assimilated their madness to himself, and became mad indeed.

And *Austin* makes mention of some men who would move their ears at their pleasure, and some that would move the crown of their head to their forehead, and could draw it back again when they pleased: and of another that could sweat at his pleasure. And it is well known, that some can weep at their pleasure, and pour forth abundance of tears: and that there are some that can bring up what they have swallowed, when they please, as out of a bag, by degrees. And we see that in these days there are many who can so imitate, and express the voices of birds, cattle, dogs, and some men, that they can scarce at all be discerned.

Also *Pliny* relates by divers examples, that women have been turned into men.[6] *Pontanus* testifieth that in his time a certain woman called *Caietava,* and another called *Aemilia,* who, many years after they were married, were changed into men.

Now how much imagination can do upon the soul, no man is ignorant: for it is nearer to the substance of the soul than the sense is; wherefore it acts more upon the soul than the sense doth. So women by certain strong imaginations, dreams, and suggestions brought in by certain magical arts do oftentimes bind them into most strong loving of anyone. So they say that *Medea* only by a dream burnt in love towards *Jason.*[7]

So the soul sometimes is by a vehement imagination, or speculation altogether abstracted from the body,[8] as *Celsus* relates of a certain presbyter, who as oft as he pleased, could make himself senseless, and lie like a dead man, that when anyone pricked, or burned him, he felt no pain, but lay without any motion or breathing, yet he could, as he said, hear men's voices as it were afar off, if they cried out aloud. But of these abstractions we shall discourse more fully in the following chapters.

Notes—Chapter LXIV

1. *gape*—Yawn.

2. *a medicine*—Laxative.

3. *Cyprus*—Genucius Cippus, praetor of Rome, either going out of the city or about to return into it, discovered horns upon his head. Alarmed by this prodigy, he consulted a soothsayer, who predicted that if he entered Rome once again, he would surely become king. Cippus had a horror of kings, as did all good Romans, the title being synonymous in their minds with tyranny. As Ovid says: "He retreated backwards, and turning his stern visage away from the walk of the City, he exclaimed, 'Far, O far away may the Gods drive such omens! Much more righteously shall I pass my life in exile, than if the Capitol were to see me a king'" (Ovid *Metamorphoses* 15.6, c. line 565 [Riley, 539]). So struck were the citizens of Rome by his noble sacrifice, they erected a horned bronze statue over the gate through which he had made his last exit, and named the gate Porta

Raudusculana (Latin: *raudus* = brass). This strange story is told by Valerius Maximus. Pliny considered it no more than a fable.

4. *corniferous*—Horn producing.

5. *wounds of Christ*—

For straightaway in the hands and feet of S. Francis began to appear the marks of the nails, in such wise as he had seen them in the body of Jesu Christ, the Crucified, the which had shown Himself to him in the likeness of a seraph: and thus his hands and feet appeared to be pierced through the middle with nails, and the heads of them were in the palms of his hands and the soles of his feet outside the flesh, and their points came out on the back of his hands and feet, so that they seemed bent back and rivetted in such fashion that under the bend and rivetting, which all stood out above the flesh, might easily be put a finger of the hand, as in a ring: and the heads of the nails were round and black. Likewise in the right side appeared an image of a wound made by a lance, unhealed, and red and bleeding, the which afterwards ofttimes dropped blood from the sacred breast of S. Francis, and stained with blood his tunic and his hose. (Anon. *Little Flowers of S. Francis of Assisi,* trans. T. W. Arnold [London: Chatto and Windus, 1908], 186–7)

6. *turned into men—*

The change of females into males is undoubtedly no fable. We find it stated in the Annals, that, in the consulship of P. Licinius Crassus and C. Cassius Longinus [171 BC], a girl, who was living at Casinum with her parents, was changed into a boy; and that, by the command of the Aruspices, he was conveyed away to a desert island. Licinius Muscianus informs us, that he once saw at Argos a person whose name was then Arescon, though he had been formerly called Arescusa: that this person had been married to a man, but that, shortly after, a beard and marks of virility made

their appearance, upon which he took to himself a wife. He had also seen a boy at Smyrna, to whom the very same thing had happened. I myself saw in Africa one L. Cossicius, a citizen of Thysdris, who had been changed into a man the very day on which he was married to a husband. (Pliny 7.3 [Bostock and Riley, 2:138])

It is difficult to believe that Pliny would not have guessed that this last was merely a case of sexual impersonation discovered in the marriage bed—we may suspect that the husband's shock was considerable. Very likely all the cases may be explained in a similar way.

7. *love toward Jason—*When the hero Jason sailed to Colchis to obtain the Golden Fleece, the goddess Hera convinced Aphrodite to send Cupid to Earth, so that he might shoot one of his arrows into Medea's heart and cause her to love Jason, thereby insuring his safety through the power of her sorcery: "Her heart smouldered with pain and as he passed from sight her soul crept out of her, as in a dream, and fluttered in his steps" (Apollonius Rhodius *The Voyage of Argo* 3, c. line 448 [Rieu, 121]).

8. *from the body—*See notes 5, 6 and 7, ch. L, bk. III.

CHAPTER LXV

How the passions of the mind can work out of themselves upon another's body.

The passions of the soul which follow the phantasy, when they are most vehement, cannot only change their own body, but also can transcend so, as to work upon another body, so that some wonderful impressions are thence produced in elements, and extrinsical things, and also can so take away, or bring some diseases of the mind or body. For the passions of the soul are the chiefest cause of the temperament of its proper body. So the soul being strongly elevated, and inflamed with a strong imagination, sends forth health or sickness, not only in its proper body, but also in other bodies.

So *Avicen* is of the opinion, that a camel may fall by the imagination of anyone. So he which is bitten with a mad dog presently falls into a madness, and there appear in his urine the shapes of dogs. So the longing of a woman with child doth act upon another's body, when it signs the infant in the womb with the mark of the thing longed for. So many monstrous generations proceed from monstrous imaginations of women with child, as *Marcus Damascenus* reports was at Petra Sancta, a town situated upon the territories of Pisa, viz. a wench that was presented to *Charles* King of Bohemia, who was rough and hairy all over her body, like a wild beast, whom her mother, affected with a religious kind of horror upon the picture of *John Baptist,* which was by her bed in time of conception, afterwards brought forth after this fashion.

And this we see is not only in men, but also is done amongst brute creatures. So we read that *Jacob* the patriarch, with his speckled rods set in the watering places, did discolour the sheep of *Laban*.[1] So the imaginative powers of peacocks, and other birds, whilst they be coupling, impress a colour upon their wings. Whence we produce white peacocks,[2] by hanging round the places where they couple, with white clothes.

Now by these examples it appears how the affection of the phantasy, when it vehemently intends itself, doth not only affect its own proper body, but also another's. So also the desire of witches to hurt,[3] doth bewitch men most perniciously with steadfast looks. To these things *Avicen, Aristotle, Algazel,* and *Galen* assent. For it is manifest that a body may most easily be affected with the vapour of another's diseased body, which we plainly see in the plague, and leprosy. Again, in the vapours of the eyes there is so great a power, that they can bewitch and infect any that are near them, as the cockatrice, or basilisk, killing men with their looks. And certain women in Scythia, amongst the Illyrians, and Triballi, killed whomsoever they looked angry upon.

Therefore let no man wonder that the body, and soul of one may in like manner be affected with the mind of another, seeing the mind is far more powerful, strong, fervent, and more prevalent by its motion than vapours exhaling out of bodies; neither are there wanting mediums, by which it should work, neither is another's body less subjected to another's mind, than to another's body. Upon this account they say, that a man by his affection, and habit only, may act upon another.

Therefore philosophers advise that the society of evil, and mischievous men be shunned, for their soul being full of noxious rays, infects them that are near with a hurtful contagion. On the contrary, they advise that the society of good, and fortunate men be endeavoured after, because by their nearness they do us much good. For as the smell of assafetida,[4] or musk, so of bad something of bad, of good something of good, is derived upon them that are nigh, and sometimes continues a long time.

Now then, if the foresaid passions have so great a power in the phantasy, they have certainly a greater power in the reason, in as much as the reason is more excellent than the phantasy; and lastly, they have much greater power in the mind; for this, when it is fixed upon God for any good with its whole intention, doth oftentimes affect another's body as well as its own with some divine gift. By this means we read that many miracles were done by *Apollonius, Pythagoras, Empedocles, Philolaus,* and many prophets, and holy men of our religion.

But of these more fully in the following chapters, where we shall discourse of religion.

Notes—Chapter LXV

1. *sheep of Laban*—Genesis 30:37-9.

2 *white peacocks*—Pure white peacocks, in which even the eye spots on the tail are very faint, occasionally hatch, and these are valued as curiosities.

3. *witches to hurt*—"And there are witches who can bewitch their judges by a mere look or glance from their eyes" (Kramer and Sprenger *Malleus Maleficarum* 2.12 [Summers, 139]). See also 3.15 (Summers, 228).

4. *assafetida*—Gum resin extruded from the cut root of the *Narthex ferula,* an umbelliferous plant that grows in Afghanistan and Iran. It dries into tears but was more usually sold in the form of lumps, and was used medicinally as an antispasmodic and stimulant. Its smell is powerful and unpleasant, pervading the body and occurring in the breath, saliva and urine. Because it much resembles garlic, it was used to flavor food. Some think it is the same as the juice of the silphion, mentioned by Discorides and highly esteemed among Greek physicians.

CHAPTER LXVI

That the passions of the mind are helped by a celestial season, and how necessary the constancy of the mind is in every work.

The passions of the mind are much helped, and are helpful, and become most powerful by virtue of the heaven, as they agree with the heaven, either by any natural agreement, or voluntary election. For, as saith *Ptolomeus,* he which chooseth that which is the better, seems to differ nothing from him who hath this of nature. It conduceth therefore very much for the receiving the benefit of the heavens, in any work, if we shall by the heaven make ourselves suitable to it in our thoughts, affections, imaginations, elections, deliberations, contemplations, and the like.

For such like passions do vehemently stir up our spirit to their likeness, and suddenly expose us, and ours to the superior significators of such like passions; and also by reason of their dignity, and nearness to the superiors, do much more partake of the celestials, than any material things. For our mind can through imaginations, or reason by a kind of imitation, be so conformed to any star, as suddenly to be filled with the virtues of that star, as if it were a proper receptacle of the influence thereof.

Now the contemplating mind, as it withdraws itself from all sense, imagination, nature, and deliberation, and calls itself back to things separated, unless it exposeth itself to Saturn,[1] is not of present consideration, or inquiry. For our mind doth effect divers things by faith, which is a firm adhesion, a fixed intension, and vehe-

ment application of the worker, or receiver, to him that cooperates in anything, and gives power to the work which we intend to do. So that there is made as it were in us the image of the virtue to be received, and the thing to be done in us, or by us.

We must therefore in every work, and application of things, affect vehemently, imagine, hope, and believe strongly, for that will be a great help. And it is verified amongst physicians that a strong belief,[2] and an undoubted hope, and love towards the physician, and medicine, conduce much to health, yea more sometimes than the medicine itself. For the same that the efficacy, and virtue of the medicine works, the same doth the strong imagination of the physician work, being able to change the qualities in the body of the sick, especially when the patient placeth much confidence in the physician, by that means disposing himself for the receiving the virtue of the physician, and physic.

Therefore he that works in magic, must be of a constant belief, be credulous, and not at all doubt of the obtaining the effect. For as a firm, and strong belief doth work wonderful things, although it be in false works, so distrust and doubting doth dissipate, and break the virtue of the mind of the worker, which is the medium betwixt both extremes, whence it happens, that he is frustrated of the desired influence of the superiors, which could not be joined, and united to our labours without a firm, and solid virtue of our mind.

Notes—Chapter LXVI

1. *to Saturn*—The contemplating mind would be appropriate to draw down the influence of Saturn, but inappropriate for the other planets. Saturn presides over a deep and brooding thoughtfulness. "As if Saturn be predominant in his nativity, and cause melancholy in his temperment, then he shall be very austere, sullen, churlish, black of colour, profound in his cogitations, full of cares, miseries, and discontents, sad and fearful, always silent, solitary ..." (Burton *Anatomy of Melancholy* 1.3.1.3, 1:397).

2. *strong belief*—

> ... although another man's imagination hath little force upon me, yet mine own

much alters the body and either hinders or furthers a remedy in its working. As this is cleare in many diseases, so especially in Hypocondriack Melancholy, called the shame of Physicians, because rarely cured; wherein the non-effecting of the cure depends upon the prejudiced imaginations of the Patient, who despairs of help ... (Michael Maier *Laws of the Fraternity of the Rosie Crosse* [1618, trans. 1656] [Los Angeles: Philosophical Research Society, 1976], 55)

CHAPTER LXVII

How man's mind may be joined with the mind, and intelligences of the celestials, and together with them impress certain wonderful virtues upon inferior things.

The philosophers, especially the Arabians,[1] say, that man's mind, when it is most intent upon any work, through its passion, and effects, is joined with the mind of the stars, and intelligences, and being so joined is the cause that some wonderful virtue be infused into our works, and things; and this, as because there is in it an apprehension, and power of all things, so because all things have a natural obedience to it, and of necessity an efficacy, and more to that which desires them with a strong desire.

And according to this is verified the art of characters, images, enchantments, and some speeches,[2] and many other wonderful experiments to everything which the mind affects. By this means whatsoever the mind of him that is in vehement love affects, hath an efficacy to cause love, and whatsoever the mind of him that strongly hates, dictates, hath an efficacy to hurt, and destroy. The like is in other things, which the mind affects with a strong desire.

For all those things which the mind acts, and dictates by characters, figures, words, speeches, gestures, and the like, help the appetite of the soul,[3] and acquire certain wonderful virtues, as from the soul of the operator, in that hour when such a like appetite doth invade it, so from the opportunity, and celestial influence, moving the mind in that manner. For our mind, when it is carried upon the great excess of any passion, or virtue, oftentimes presently takes of itself a strong, better, and more convenient hour, or opportunity. Which *Thomas Aquinas*[4] in his third book Against the Gentiles, confesseth. So many wonderful virtues both cause, and follow certain admirable operations by great affections, in those things which the soul doth dictate in that hour to them.

But know, that such kind of things[5] confer nothing, or very little but to the author of them, and to him which is inclined to them, as if he were the author of them. And this is the manner by which their efficacy is found out. And it is a general rule in them, that every mind that is more excellent in its desire, and affection, makes such like things more fit for itself, as also efficacious to that which it desires. Everyone therefore that is willing to work in magic, must know the virtue, measure, order, and degree of

Notes—Chapter LXVII

1. *the Arabians*—

We must observe, however, that Avicenna also *(Metaph.* X) holds that the movements of the heavenly bodies are the causes of our

choice, not merely by being the occasion thereof, but even as a *per se* cause. For he holds the heavenly bodies to be animate: and, since the heaven's movement proceeds from its soul, and is the movement of a body, it follows that just as forasmuch as it is a body's movement, it must have the power to transform bodies, so forasmuch as it comes from a soul, it must have the power to make impressions on our soul; wherefore the heavenly movement is the cause of our acts of will and choice. The position of Albumasar would seem to come to the same as expounded in the First Book of his *Introductorium*. (Aquinas *Summa contra gentiles* 3.87 [London: Burns, Oats and Washbourne, 1928], 3:2:16)

After stating the Arab position, that the soul of the heavens acts on man's soul through the movement of the heavens, Aquinas goes on to dispute it, arguing that the soul of the heavens, if there is one, acting through the body of the heavens, has only the power to act upon the human body by stirring passions, but that the will of man is free to either acquiesce or contend with these passions as it chooses. However, he admits that those who are able to control their passions are in the minority:

It is evident, however, and we know by experience, that such occasions whether exterior or interior are not necessarily cause of choice: since man can use his reason to reject or obey them. But those who follow their natural bent are in the majority, and few, the wise alone to wit, are those who avoid the occasions of ill-doing and who follow not the impulse of nature. Hence Ptolemy says *(Centiloq.* 8, 7, 1) that *the soul of the wise man assists the work of the stars* ..." (ibid. 3.85, p. 11)

2. *some speeches*—Incantations.

3. *appetite of the soul*—The will.

Now of all the parts of man, the intellect is the highest mover; for it moves the appetite, by proposing its object to it; and the intellective appetite or will, moves the sensitive appetites, namely the irascible and concupiscible, so that we do not obey the concupiscence, unless the will command; and the sensitive appetite, the will consenting, moves the body. Therefore the end of the intellect is the end of all human actions. (ibid. 3.25, 3:1:59)

4. *Thomas Aquinas*—

Since then man, as to his body, is subordinate to the heavenly bodies; as to his intellect, to the angels; and as to his will, to God: it is possible for something to happen beside the intention of man, which is nevertheless according to the order of the heavenly bodies, or the influence of the angels or even of God. And although God's action alone has a direct bearing on man's choice, nevertheless the angel's action has a certain bearing on man's choice by way of persuasion; and the action of a heavenly body by way of disposition, insomuch as the corporeal impressions of heavenly bodies on our bodies dispose us to choose in certain ways. Accordingly when, through the influence of higher causes, in the aforesaid manner, a man is led to choose such things as turn to his profit without his being aware of the utility by his own reason; and besides this, his understanding is enlightened from the light of intellectual substances to the effect of doing those same things; and through the divine operation his will is inclined so as to choose that which is profitable to him, without knowing why it is so; he is said to be *fortunate* ..." (ibid. 3.92, 3:2:26–7)

5. *such kind of things*—Talismans, seals, amulets, and so on.

CHAPTER LXVIII

How our mind can change, and bind inferior things to that which it desires.

There is also a certain virtue in the minds of men, of changing, attracting, hindering, and binding to that which they desire, and all things obey them, when they are carried into a great excess of any passion or virtue, so as to exceed those things which they bind. For the superior binds that which is inferior, and converts it to itself, and the inferior is by the same reason converted to the superior, or is otherwise affected, and wrought upon. By this reason, things that receive a superior degree of any star, bind, or attract, or hinder things which have an inferior, according as they agree, or disagree amongst themselves.[1]

Whence a lion is afraid of a cock, because the presence of the solary virtue is more agreeable to a cock than to lion:[2] so a loadstone draws iron, because in order it hath a superior degree of the Celestial Bear. So the diamond hinders the loadstone, because in the order of Mars it is superior than it.

In like manner any man when he is opportunely exposed to the celestial influences, as by the affections of his mind, so by the due application of natural things, if he become stronger in solary virtue, binds and draws the inferior into admiration, and obedience; in order of the Moon to servitude or infirmities; in a saturnal order to quietness or sadness; in order of Jupiter to worship; in order of Mars to fear, and discord; in order of Venus to love, and joy; in a mercurial order to persuasion, and obsequiousness, and the like.

Now the ground of such a kind of binding is the very vehement, and boundless affection of the souls, with the concourse of the celestial order. But the dissolutions, or hinderances of such a like binding, are made by a contrary effect, and that more excellent or strong, for as the greater excess of the mind binds, so also it looseth, and hindereth. And lastly, when thou fearest Venus, oppose Saturn. When Saturn or Mars, oppose Venus or Jupiter: for astrologers say, that these are most at enmity, and contrary the one to the other i.e. causing contrary effects in these inferior bodies; for in the heaven, where there is nothing wanting, where all things are governed with love, there can in no wise be hatred, or enmity.

Notes—Chapter LXVIII

1. *amongst themselves*—All this is based on the fragment from Proclus called *De sacrificio et magia* (see note 1, ch. XXII, bk. I). Agrippa draws heavily on this fragment for his magical theory.

2. *a lion*—Again, Proclus. See note 25, ch. XVIII, bk. I.

CHAPTER LXIX

Of speech, and the virtue of words.

It being showed that there is a great power in the affections of the soul, you must know moreover, that there is no less virtue in words, and the names of things, but greatest of all in speeches, and motions, by which we chiefly differ from brutes, and are called rational, not from reason, which is taken for that part of the soul, which contains the affections, which *Galen* saith, is also common to brutes, although in a less degree; but we are called rational from that reason which is according to the voice understood in words, and speech, which is called declarative reason,[1] by which part we do chiefly excel all other animals. For λόγος in Greek signifies, reason, speech, and a word.

Now a word is twofold, viz. internal, and uttered. An internal word is a conception of the mind, and motion of the soul, which is made without a voice. As in dreams we seem to speak, and dispute with ourselves, and whilst we are awake we run over a whole speech silently. But an uttered word hath a certain act in the voice, and properties of locution, and is brought forth with the breath of a man, with opening of his mouth, and with the speech of his tongue, in which nature hath coupled the corporeal voice, and speech to the mind, and understanding, making that a declarer, and interpreter of the conception of our intellect to the hearers. And of this we now speak.

Words therefore are the fittest medium betwixt the speaker and the hearer, carrying with them not only the conception of the mind, but also the virtue of the speaker with a certain efficacy unto the hearers, and this oftentimes with so great a power, that oftentimes they change not only the hearers, but also other bodies,[2] and things that have no life. Now those words are of greater efficacy than others, which represent greater things, as intellectual, celestial, and supernatural, as more expressly, so more mysteriously. Also those that come from a more worthy tongue, or from any of a more holy order:[3] for these, as it were certain signs, and representations, receive a power of celestial, and supercelestial things, as from the virtue of things explained, of which they are the vehicula,[4] so from a power put into them by the virtue of the speaker.

Notes—Chapter LXIX

1. *declarative reason—*

That perceiving and practical thinking are not identical is therefore obvious; for the former is universal in the animal world, the latter is found in only a small division of it. Further, speculative thinking is also distinct from perceiving—I mean that in which we find rightness and wrongness—rightness in prudence, knowledge, true opinion, wrongness in their opposites; for perception of the special objects of sense is always free from error, and is found in all animals, while it is possible to think falsely as well as truly, and thought is found only where there is discourse of reason as well as sensibility. (Aristotle *De anima* 3.3 [McKeon, 586–7])

2. *other bodies*—On the question of the occult power of words, Pliny writes:

> Thus, for instance, it is a general belief that without a certain form of prayer it would be useless to immolate a victim, and that, with such an informality, the gods would be consulted to little purpose. And then besides, there are different forms of address to the deities, one form for entreating, another form for averting their ire, and another for commendation. ... At the present day, too, it is a general belief, that our Vestal virgins have the power, by uttering a certain prayer, to arrest the flight of runaway slaves, and to rivet them to the spot, provided they have not gone beyond the precincts of the City. If then these opinions be once received as truth, and if it be admitted that the gods do listen to certain prayers, or are influenced by set forms of words, we are bound to conclude in the affirmative upon the whole question. Our ancestors, no doubt, always entertained such a belief, and have even assured us, a thing by far the most difficult of all, that it is possible by such means to bring down lightning from heaven, as already mentioned [2.54] on a more appropriate occasion. (Pliny 28.3 [Bostock and Riley, 5:279–80])

3. *more holy order*—

> For because the Gods have shown that the whole dialect of sacred nations, such as those of the Egyptians and Assyrians, is adapted to sacred concerns; on this account we ought to think it necessary that our conference with the Gods should be in a language allied to them. Because likewise, such a mode of speech is the first and most ancient. And especially because those who first learned the names of the Gods, having mingled them with their own proper tongue, delivered them to us, that we might always preserve immoveable the sacred law of tradition, in a language peculiar and adapted to them. For if any other thing pertains to the Gods, it is evident that the eternal and immutable must be allied to them. (Iamblichus *On the Mysteries* 6.4 [Taylor, 293–4])

> For if names subsisted through compact it would be of no consequence whether some were used instead of others. But if they are suspended from the nature of things, those names which are more adapted to it will also be more dear to the Gods. From this, therefore, it is evident that the language of sacred nations is very reasonably preferred to that of other men. (ibid. 6.5 [Taylor, 294])

4. *vehicula*—Vehicles, used here in the sense of media of expression or utterance, and also in the sense of the form in which something spiritual is embodied or manifested.

Chapter LXX

Of the virtue of proper names.

That proper names of things are very necessary in magical operations, almost all men testify: for the natural power of things proceeds first from the objects to the senses, and then from these to the imagination, and from this to the mind, in which it is first conceived, and then is expressed by voices, and words. The Platonists therefore[1] say, that in this very voice, or word, or name framed, with its articles, that the power of the thing as it were some kind of life, lies under the form of the signification. First conceived in the mind as it were through certain seeds of things, then by voices or words, as a birth brought forth, and lastly kept in writings.

Hence magicians say, that proper names of things are certain rays of things, everywhere present at all times, keeping the power of things, as the essence of the thing signified, rules, and is discerned in them, and know the things by them, as by proper, and living images. For as the great Operator doth produce divers species, and particular things by the influences of the heavens, and by the elements, together with the virtues of planets; so according to the properties of the influences proper names result to things, and are put upon them by him who numbers the multitude of the stars, calling them all by their names,[2] of which names Christ in another place speaks, saying, Your names are written in heaven.[3]

Adam therefore that gave the first names to things, knowing the influences of the heavens, and properties of all things, gave them all names according to their natures, as it is written in Genesis,[4] where God brought all things that he had created before *Adam,* that he should name them, and as he named anything, so the name of it was, which names indeed contain in them wonderful powers of the things signified.

Every voice therefore that is significative, first of all signifies by the influence of the celestial harmony; secondly, by the imposition of man, although oftentimes otherwise by this, than by that. But when both significations meet in any voice or name, which are put upon them by the said harmony or men, then that name is with a double virtue,[5] viz. natural, and arbitrary, made most efficacious to act, as oft as it shall be uttered in due place, and time, and seriously with an intention exercised upon the matter rightly disposed, and that can naturally be acted upon by it.

So we read in *Philostratus,* that when a maid at Rome died the same day she was married, and was presented to *Apollonius,* he accurately inquired into her name, which being known, he pronounced some occult thing, by which she revived. It was an observation amongst the Romans in their holy rites, that when they did besiege any city, they did diligently inquire into the proper, and true name of it, and the name of that god, under whose protection it was, which being known, they did then with some verse call forth the gods that were the protectors of that city, and did curse the inhabitants of that city, so at length their gods being absent, did overcome them, as *Virgil* sings:[6]

————that kept this realm, our gods
Their altars have forsook, and blest abodes.

Now the verse with which the gods were called out, and the enemies were cursed, when the city was assaulted round about, let him that would know, find it out in *Livy*,[7] and *Macrobius*;[8] but also many of these *Serenus Samonicus* in his book of secret things makes mention of.

Notes—Chapter LXX

1. *Platonists therefore*—Plato's dialogue *Cratylus* is entirely concerned with the nature of names. In it Socrates (Plato's alter ego) puts forward the notion in the abstract that a name may embody a thing:

> *Socrates:* Again, is there not an essence of each thing, just as there is a colour, or sound? And is there not an essence of colour and sound as well as of anything else which may be said to have an essence?
> *Hermogenes:* I should think so.
> *Socrates:* Well, and if anyone could express the essence of each thing in letters and syllables, would he not express the nature of each thing?
> (Plato *Cratylus* 423e [Hamilton and Cairns, 458])

However he goes on to argue that in fallible human language names and essences do not necessarily agree.

2. *their names*—This is the view Plato puts into the mouth of Cratylus, which is disputed by Socrates:

> *Cratylus:* I believe, Socrates, the true account of the matter to be that a power more than human gave things their first names, and that the names which are thus given are necessarily their true names.
> (ibid. 438c [Hamilton and Cairns, 472])

3. *written in heaven*—Luke 10:20.

4. *written in Genesis*—Genesis 2:19.

5. *double virtue*—Proclus in his *Commentary on Plato's Timaeus* distinguishes between two kinds of names, those given by the gods and those contrived by men: "For as the knowledge of the Gods is different from that of partial souls, thus also the names of the one are different from those of the other; since divine names unfold the whole essence of the thing named, but those of men only partially come into contact with them" (Iamblichus *On the Mysteries* [Taylor 290–2n]). On this subject see Homer *Iliad* 14, line 291, and 20, line 74, which lines are discussed by Plato in the *Cratylus* 392a.

6. *Virgil sings*—

> "Warriors, hearts in vain most valiant, if you have a determined desire to follow one of desperate daring, you see what is the state of our fortunes; the gods by whom this realm stood fast, have all departed from it, and left the sanctuaries and shrines; haste to succour a city that is set on fire; let us die, and rush into the thickest of the fight. To despair of being saved by any means is the only means of safety for the vanquished." (Virgil *Aeneid* 2, c. line 350 [Lonsdale and Lee, 104])

7. *in Livy*—The Roman dictator Camillus (396 BC) in the encampment beneath the walls of besieged Veii just prior to the Roman assault on that city:

> "Pythian Apollo," he prayed, "led by you and inspired by your holy breath, I go forward to the destruction of Veii, and I vow to you a tenth part of the spoils. Queen Juno, to you too I pray, that you may leave this town where now you dwell and follow our victorious arms into our City of Rome, your future home, which will receive you in a temple worthy of your greatness." (Livy *Early History of Rome* 5.20 [de Selincourt, 364])

8. *Macrobius*—Nicolas Remy quotes in full the curse used by the Romans against their enemies, which occurs in the *Saturnalia* of Macrobius, 3.9:

> "O Father Dis, O Shades of Jupiter, or by whatever other name it is right to invoke you, fill full of panic, fear and terror all that city and army which I have in my mind; and whosoever bears arms or weapons against our legions and army, do you confound those armies, those enemies, those men and their cities and lands, and all who live in the lands and cities of this place and district: take from them the light of heaven: curse and execrate the enemy's army, his cities and his lands with the strongest curse

ever pronounced against an enemy. By the faith of my office I give and consecrate them to you on behalf of the Roman People and our armies and legions. If you will perform this according to my wishes, intention and understanding, then whosoever accomplishes this vow, let it be done aright. With three black sheep I beseech thee,O Jupiter."

As he invokes the Earth, he touches the ground with his hands. As he invokes Jupiter, he raises his hands to Heaven. And as he takes his vow, he places his hands upon his breast. (Remy *Demonolatry* 2.9, trans. E. A. Ashwin [London: John Rodker, 1930 (1595)], 124)

CHAPTER LXXI

Of many words joined together, as in sentences, and verses, and of the virtues, and astrictions of charms.

B esides the virtues of words, and names, there is also a greater virtue found in sentences, from the truth contained in them, which hath a very great power of impressing, changing, binding, and establishing, so that being used it doth shine the more, and being resisted is more confirmed, and consolidated; which virtue is not in simple words, but in sentences, by which anything is affirmed, or denied, of which sort are verses, enchantments,[1] imprecations,[2] deprecations,[3] orations,[4] invocations,[5] obtestations,[6] adjurations,[7] conjurations,[8] and such like.

Therefore in composing verses, and orations, for the attracting the virtue of any star, or deity, you must diligently consider what virtues any star contains, as also what effects, and operations, and to infer them in verses, by praising, extolling, amplifying, and setting forth those things which such a kind of star is wont to cause by way of its influence, and by vilifying, and dispraising those things which it is wont to destroy, and hinder, and by supplicating, and begging for that which we desire to get, and by condemning, and detesting that which we would have destroyed, and hindered: and after the same manner to make an elegant oration, and duly distinct by articles, with competent numbers, and proportions.

Moreover magicians command that we call upon, and pray by the names of the same star, or name, to them to whom such a verse belongs, by their wonderful things, or miracles, by their courses, and ways in their sphere, by their light, by the dignity of their kingdom, by the beauty, and brightness that is in it, by their strong, and powerful virtues, and by such like as these. As *Psyche* in *Apuleius*[9] prays to *Ceres,* saying, I beseech thee by thy fruitful right hand, I intreat thee by the joyful ceremonies of harvests, by the quiet silence of thy chests, by the winged chariots of dragons thy servants, by the furrows of the Sicilian earth, the devouring wagon, the clammy earth, by the place of going down into cellars at the light nuptials of *Proserpina,* and returns at the light inventions of her daughter, and other things which are concealed in her temple in the city Eleusis in Attica.

Besides, with the divers sorts of the names of the stars, they command us to call upon them by the names of the intelligences, ruling over the stars themselves, of which we shall speak more at large in their proper place. They that desire further examples of these, let them search into the hymns of *Orpheus,* than which nothing is more efficacious in natural magic, if they together with their circumstances, which wise men know, be used according to a due harmony, with all attention.

But to return to our purpose. Such like verses being aptly, and duly made according to the rule of the stars, and being full of signification, and meaning, and opportunely pronounced with vehement affection, as according to the number, proportion of their articles, so according to the form resulting from the articles, and by the violence of imagination, do confer a very great power in the enchanter, and sometimes transfer it upon the thing enchanted, to bind, and direct it to the same purpose for which the affections, and speeches of the enchanter are intended.

Now the instrument[10] of the enchanters is a most pure harmonical spirit, warm, breathing, living, bringing with it motion, affection and signification, composed of its parts, endued with sense, and conceived by reason. By the quality therefore of this spirit, and by the celestial similitude thereof, besides those things which have already been spoken of, verses also from the opportunity of time receive from above most excellent virtues, and indeed more sublime, and efficacious than spirits, and vapours exhaling out of the vegetable life, out of herbs, roots, gums, aromatical things, and fumes, and such like. And therefore magicians enchanting things, are wont to blow, and breathe upon[11] them the words of the verse, or to breathe in the virtue with the spirit, that so the whole virtue of the soul be directed to the thing enchanted, being disposed for the receiving the said virtue.

And here it is to be noted, that every oration, writing, and words, as they induce accustomed motions by their accustomed numbers, and proportions, and form, so also besides their usual order, being pronounced, or wrote backwards,[12] move unto unusual effects.

Notes—Chapter LXXI

1. *enchantments*—Incantations; formulae of words spoken or sung for a magical effect.

2. *imprecations*—Prayers for invoking a deity or spirit.

3. *deprecations*—Prayers for averting evil.

4. *orations*—Prayers of supplication to God.

5. *invocations*—Callings upon the presence or power of deities or spirits.

6. *obtestations*—Chargings or beseechings by sacred names in which God or other spiritual agencies are called to witness.

7. *adjurations*—Retractions and renouncings of oaths or pacts.

8. *conjurations*—Constraining and compelling of spirits by oaths.

9. *Psyche in Apuleius*—

> O great and holy Goddesse, I pray thee by thy plenteous and liberall right hand, by the joyfull ceremonies of thy harvest, by the secrets of thy Sacrifice, by the flying chariots of thy dragons, by the tillage of the ground of Sicilie, which thou hast invented, by the marriage of Proserpin, by the diligent inquisition of thy daughter and by the other secrets which are within the temple of Eleusis in the land of Athens ..." (Apuleius *The Golden Asse* ch. 22 [Adlington])

10. *instrument*—The articulated breath.

11. *breathe*—This is why gamblers blow upon dice for luck, and why shamans chant over the sick in such a way that their breath touches the patient.

12. *wrote backwards*—Writing or speaking magical words backwards inverts their effects.

CHAPTER LXXII

Of the wonderful power of enchantments.

They say that the power of enchantments, and verses is so great, that it is believed they are able to subvert almost all nature, as saith *Apuleius,*[1] that with a magical whispering, swift rivers are turned back, the slow sea is bound, the winds are breathed out with one accord, the Sun is stopped, the Moon is clarified, the stars are pulled out, the day is kept back, the night is prolonged. And of these sings *Lucan:*[2]

> The courses of all things did cease, the night
> Prolonged was, 'twas long before 'twas
>   light;
> Astonied was the headlong world, all this
> Was by the hearing of a verse————

And a little before:[3]

> Thessalian verse did into his heart so flow,
> That it did make a greater heat of love.

And elsewhere:[4]

> No dregs of poison being by him drunk,
> His wits decayed enchanted————

Also *Virgil* in *Damon:*[5]

> Charms can command the Moon down
>   from the sky,
> Circe's charms changed Ulysses' company.
> A cold snake being charmed, burst in the
>   meads.

And in another place:[6]

Charms bear corn standing from another's
  farm.

And *Ovid* in his book *sine titulo,*[7] saith:

> With charms doth withering Ceres die,
> Dried are the fountains all,
> Acorns from oaks, enchanted grapes,
> And apples from trees fall.

If these things were not true, there would not be such strict penal statutes made against them, that should enchant fruit. And *Tibullus* saith[8] of a certain enchantress:

> Her with charms drawing stars from
>   heaven, I
> And turning the course of rivers, did espy,
> She parts the earth, and ghosts from sep-
>   ulchers
> Draws up, and fetcheth bones away from
>   the fires
> And at her pleasure scatters clouds in the air,
> And makes it snow in summer hot, and fair.

Of all which that enchantress seems to boast herself in *Ovid,*[9] when she saith:

> ————at will, I make swift streams retire
> To their fountains, whilst their banks
>   admire;
> Seas toss, and smooth; clear clouds, with
>   clouds deform,
> With spells, and charms I break the
>   viper's jaw,
> Cleave solid rocks, oaks from their sea-
>   sures draw,

Whole woods remove, the airy mountains
    shake,
Earth for to groan, and ghosts from graves
    awake,
And thee O Moon I draw————

Moreover all poets sing, and philosophers do not deny, that by verses many wonderful things may be done, as corn to be removed, lightnings to be commanded, diseases cured, and such like. For *Cato* himself in Country Affairs used some enchantments against the diseases of beasts, which as yet are extant in his writings. Also *Josephus* testifies[10] that *Solomon* was skilled in those kind of enchantments. Also *Celsus Africanus* reports,[11] according to the Egyptian doctrine, that man's body, according to the number of the faces[12] of the Zodiac signs, was taken care of by so many, viz. thirty-six spirits, whereof each undertake, and defend their proper part, whose names they call with a peculiar voice, which being called upon, restore to health with their enchantments the diseased parts of the body.

Notes—Chapter LXXII

1. *saith Apuleius*—

Verily this tale is as true, as if a man would say that by sorcery and inchantment the floods might be inforced to run against their course, the seas to be immovable, the aire to lacke the blowing of windes, the Sunne to be restrayned from his naturall race, the Moone to purge his skimme upon herbes and trees to serve for sorceries: the starres to be pulled from heaven, the day to be darkned, and the darke night to continue still. (Apuleius *The Golden Asse* ch. 1 [Adlington])

Lucan adds further light on this practice of purging the Moon:

There, too [in Thessaly], for the first time were the stars brought down from the headlong sky; and serene Phoebe, beset by the dire influences of their words, grew pale and burned with dusky and earthy fires, not otherwise than if the earth hindered her from the reflection of her brother, and interposed its shade between the celestial flames; and arrested by spells, she endures labours so great, until, more nigh, she sends her foam upon the herbs situate beneath. (Lucan *Pharsalia* 6, line 499 [Riley, 232–3])

2. *sings Lucan*—"The courses of things are stayed, and, retarded by lengthened night, the day stops short. The sky obeys not the laws of nature; and on hearing the spells the headlong world is benumbed; Jupiter, too, urging them on, is astounded that the poles of heaven do not go on, impelled by the rapid axles" (ibid., line 461 [Riley, 231]). Concerning the calling of night, Lucan elsewhere writes: "… the shades of night redoubled by her [Erichtho's] art, wrapped as to her direful head in a turbid cloud, she wanders amid the bodies of the slain, exposed, sepulchres being denied" (ibid., line 624 [Riley, 237]). And later: "The heavens wearing the aspect of light, until they [Erichtho and Sextus Pompey] brought their footsteps safe within the tents, the night, commanded to withhold the day, afforded its dense shades." (ibid., line 828 [Riley, 248]).

3. *little before*—"Through the charms of the Thessalian witches a love not induced by the Fates has entered into hardened hearts; and stern old men have burned with illicit flames" (Lucan *Pharsalia* 6, line 451 [Riley, 230]).

4. *and elsewhere*—"The mind, polluted by no corruption of imbibed poison, perishes by force of spells" (ibid., line 457 [Riley, 230]).

5. *Virgil in Damon*—"Song has even power to draw the moon from heaven; Circe by song transformed Ulysses' crew; by song the clammy snake is burst asunder in the meadows" (Virgil *Eclogues* 8, c. line 67 [Lonsdale and Lee, 26]). Damon is a singing shepherd mentioned in this Eclogue, but in fact it is the shepherd Alphesiboeus who sings these lines.

6. *another place*—"… oft have I seen him [Moeris] call up spirits from the deep of the grave, and draw sown corn away to other fields" (ibid., c. line 100).

7. *his book sine titulo*—*Amores* 3.7, lines 31–4.

8. *Tibullus saith*—

I have seen her draw down the stars from heaven; she turns the course of the swift lightning by her incantations; she cleaves the earth, brings out the Manes from the sepulchres, and calls down the bones from the still smouldering pile. Now she makes the infernal hosts swarm round her with her magic screamings, and now she bids them be gone, sprinkling them with milk. When she pleases, she sweeps away the clouds from the sombre sky; when she pleases, she calls down the snow in summer by a word from her mouth. She is said to possess alone all the evil herbs known to Medea, alone to have brought the fierce dogs of Hecate under subjection. This witch has composed for me chants by which you may deceive all eyes. (Tibullus *Elegies* 1.2. In *Poems of Catullus and Tibullus,* trans. W. K. Kelly [London: George Bell and Sons, 1884], 111)

9. *in Ovid*—the speaker is Medea:

"O Night, most faithful to these my mysteries, and ye golden Stars, who with the Moon, succeed the fires of the day, and thou, three-faced Hecate, who comest conscious of my design, and ye charms and arts of the enchanters, and thou, too, Earth, that does furnish the enchanters with powerful herbs; ye breezes, too, and winds, mountains, rivers, and lakes, and all ye Deities of the groves, and all ye Gods of night, attend here; through whose aid, whenever I will, the rivers run back from their astonished banks to their sources, and by my charms I calm the troubled sea, and rouse it when calm; I dispense the clouds, and I bring clouds upon the Earth; I both allay the winds, and I raise them; and I break the jaws of serpents with my words and my spells; I move, too, the solid rocks, and the oaks torn up with their own native earth, and the forests as well; I command the mountains, too, to quake, and the Earth to groan, and the ghosts to come forth from their tombs. Thee, too, O Moon, do I draw down, although the Temesaean brass relieves thy pangs. By my spells, also, the chariot of my grandsire is rendered pale; Aurora, too, is pale through my enchantments." (Ovid *Metamorphoses* 7.2, c. line 193 [Riley, 231–2])

10. *Josephus testifies—*

God also enabled him [Solomon] to learn that skill which expels demons, which is a science useful and sanative to men. He composed such incantations also by which distempers are alleviated. And he left behind him the manner of using exorcisms, by which they drive away demons, so that they never return, and this method of cure is of great force unto this day ..." (Josephus *Antiquities of the Jews* 7.2.5 [Whiston, 194])

11. *Celsus Africanus reports—*

Celsus goes on to say: "Let any one inquire of the Egyptians, and he will find that everything, even to the most insignificant, is committed to the care of a certain demon. The body of man is divided into thirty-six parts, and as many powers of the air are appointed to the care of it, each having charge of a different part, although others make the number much larger. All these demons have in the language of that country distinct names; as Chnoumen, Chnachoumen, Cnat, Sicat, Biou, Erou, Erebiou, Ramanor, Reianoor, and other such Egyptian names. Moreover, they call upon them, and are cured of diseases of particular parts of the body." (Origen *Against Celsus* 8.58. In *The Ante-Nicene Fathers* [Buffalo: Christian Literature Publishing Company, 1885], 4:661)

See Budge 1904, 2:19, sec. 14, where are given the Egyptian names of the decans, their images, and their equivalent Greek names. A description of the spirits of the decans occurs in the grimoire *Picatrix*. For example, the three decans of Aries are "a huge dark man with red eyes, holding a sword and clad in a white garment," "a woman clad in green and lacking one leg" and "a man holding a golden sphere and dressed in red" (McIntosh 1985, 84, quoted from Yates 1964, 53). Agrippa was familiar with the *Picatrix*.

12. *faces*—Decans.

CHAPTER LXXIII

Of the virtue of writing, and of making imprecations, and inscriptions.

The use of words and speech, is to express the inwards of the mind, and from thence to draw forth the secrets of the thoughts, and to declare the will of the speaker. Now writing is the last expression of the mind, and is the number of speech and voice, as also the collection, state, end, continuing, and iteration, making a habit, which is not perfected with the act of one's voice. And whatsoever is in the mind, in voice, in word, in oration, and in speech, the whole, and all of this is in writing also. And as nothing which is conceived in the mind is not expressed by voice, so nothing which is expressed is not also written.

And therefore magicians command, that in every work, there be imprecations, and inscriptions made, by which the operator may express his affection: that if he gather an herb, or a stone, he declare for what use he doth it; if he make a picture, he say, and write to what end he maketh it; which imprecations, and inscriptions,

Albertus also in his book called Speculum,[1] doth not disallow, without which all our works would never be brought into effect; seeing a disposition doth not cause an effect, but the act of the disposition.[2] We find also that the same kind of precepts was in use amongst the ancients, as *Virgil* testifies, when he sings:[3]

> ————I walk around
> First with these threads, in number which
>   three are,
> 'Bout the altars thrice I shall thy image bear.

And a little after:[4]

> Knots, Amaryllis, tie! of colours three
> Then say, these bonds I knit, for Venus be.

And in the same place:[5]

> As with one fire this clay doth harder prove,
> The wax more soft; so Daphnis with our
>   love.

Notes—Chapter LXXIII

1. *Speculum—Speculum astronomiae*, a work attributed to Albertus Magnus. For a discussion on the authenticity of this work, see the article by Lynn Thorndike in the *Speculum* 30 (1955), 413–33.

2. *act of the disposition*—A very important point in practical magic. It is not the chance conjunction of things that releases power, but their deliberate joining by a willful act.

3. *Virgil testifies*—

First these three threads of three hues each distinct around you I entwine, and thrice around these altars draw your image; in an unequal number heaven delights. Draw Daphnis from the city home, draw Daphnis home, my song. Amaryllis, in three knots three colours weave; weave them, Amaryllis, pray, and

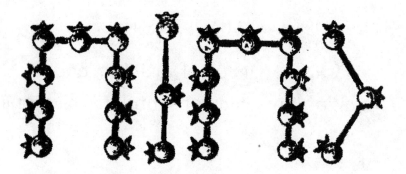

Tetragrammaton Written in Stars

from *Dogme et Rituel de la Haute Magie* by Eliphas Levi (Paris, 1855–6)

say these words; "Venus' bands I weave." Draw Daphnis from the city home, draw Daphnis home, my song. As this clay hardens, and as this wax melts in one and the self-same fire, even so let Daphnis melt with love for me, to others' love be hard. (Virgil *Eclogues* 8, c. line 70 [Lonsdale and Lee, 26])

4. *little after*—See note 3, above.

5. *same place*—See note 3, above.

CHAPTER LXXIV

Of the proportion, correspondency, reduction of letters to the celestial signs, and planets, according to various tongues, with a table showing this.

God gave to man a mind, and speech, which (as saith *Mercurius Trismegistus*)[1] are thought to be a gift of the same virtue, power, and immortality. The omnipotent God hath by his providence divided the speech of men into divers languages; which languages have according to their diversity received divers, and proper characters of writing, consisting in their certain order, number, and figure, not so disposed, and formed by hap, or chance, nor by the weak judgement of man, but from above, whereby they agree with the celestial, and divine bodies, and virtues. But before all notes of languages, the writing of the Hebrews is of all the most sacred in the figures of characters, points of vowels, and tops of accents, as consisting in matter, form, and spirit.

The position of the stars being first made in the seat of God, which is heaven, after the figure of them[2] (as the masters of the Hebrews testify) are most fully formed the letters of the celestial mysteries, as by their figure, form, and signification, so by the numbers signified by them, as also by their various harmony of their conjunction. Whence the more curious mecubals of the Hebrews do undertake by the figure of their letters, the forms of characters, and their signature, simpleness, composition, separation, crookedness, directness, defect, abounding, greatness, littleness, crowning, opening, shutting, order, transmutation, joining together, revolution of letters, and of points, and tops,[3] and by the supputation of numbers by the letters of things signified to explain all things, how they proceed from the First Cause, and are again to be reduced into the same.[4]

Moreover they divide the letters of their Hebrew alphabet, viz. into twelve simple, seven double, and three mothers, which they say signify as characters of things, the twelve signs, seven planets, and three elements, viz. Fire, Water, and Earth, for they account Air no element, but as the glue, and spirit of the elements.[5] To these also they appoint points, and tops: as therefore by the aspects of planets, and signs, together with the elements, the working spirit, and truth all things have been, and are brought forth, so by these characters of letters, and points, signifying those things that are brought forth, the names of all things are appointed, as certain signs, and vehicula of things explained carrying with them everywhere their essence, and virtues.

The profound meanings, and signs are inherent in those characters, and figures of them, as also numbers, place, order, and revolution; so that *Origenes*[6] therefore thought that those names being translated into another idiom, do not retain their proper virtue. For only original names, which are rightly imposed, because they signify naturally, have a natural activity: it is not so with them which signify at pleasure, which have no activity, as they are signifying, but as they are certain natural things in themselves.

223

Now if there be any original, whose words have a natural signification, it is manifest that this is the Hebrew, the order of which he that shall profoundly, and radically observe, and shall know to resolve proportionably the letters thereof, shall have a rule exactly to find out any idiom. There are therefore two and twenty letters which are the foundation of the world, and of creatures that are, and are named in it, and every saying, and every creature are of them, and by their revolutions receive their name, being, and virtue.

He therefore that will find them out, must by each joining together of the letters so long examine them, until the voice of God is manifest, and the framing of the most sacred letters be opened and discovered. For hence voices and words have efficacy in magical works: because that in which nature first exerciseth magical efficacy, is the voice of God. But these are of more deep speculation, than to be handled in this book.

But to return to the division of the letters. Of these, amongst the Hebrews, are three mothers,[7] viz. אוי, seven double,[8] viz. בגדכפרת; the other twelve,[9] viz. הזחטלמנסעצקש are simple. The same rule is amongst the Chaldeans; and by the imitation of these also the letters of other tongues are distributed to signs, planets, and elements, after their order.

For the vowels in the Greek tongue, viz. A E H I O Υ Ω answer to the seven planets, B Γ Δ Z K Λ M N Π P Σ T are attributed to the twelve signs of the Zodiac, the other five Θ Ξ Φ X Ψ represent the four elements and the Spirit of the World. Amongst the Latin there is the same signification of them: for the five vowels A E I O U, and J and V consonants, are ascribed to the seven planets; but the consonants B C D F G L M N P R S T are answerable to the twelve signs. The rest, viz. K Q X Z make four elements. H the aspiration represents the Spirit of the World. Y because it is a Greek, and not a Latin character, and serving only to Greek words, follows the nature of its idiom.[10]

But this you must not be ignorant of, that it is observed by all wise men, that the Hebrew letters are the most efficacious of all, because they have the greatest similitude with celestials, and the world, and that the letters of the other tongues have not so great an efficacy, because they are more distant from them. Now the dispositions of these, the following table[11] will explain.

Also all the letters have double numbers of their order, viz. extended, which simply express of what number the letters are, according to their order: and collected, which recollect with themselves the numbers of all the preceding letters.[12] Also they have integral numbers,[13] which result from the names of letters, according to their various manners of numbering. The virtues of which numbers, he that shall know, shall be able in every tongue to draw forth wonderful mysteries by their letters, as also to tell what things have been past, and foretell things to come.

There are also other mysterious joinings of letters with numbers: but we shall abundantly discourse of all these in the following books: wherefore we will now put an end to this first book.

Notes—Chapter LXXIV

1. *saith Mercurius Trismegistus*—

There are two gifts which God has bestowed on man alone, and on no other mortal creature. These two are mind and speech; and the gift of mind and speech is equivalent to that of immortality. If a man uses these two gifts rightly, he will differ in nothing from the immortals; or rather, he will differ from them only in this, that he is embodied upon earth; and when he quits the body, mind and speech will be his guides, and by them he will be brought into the troop of the gods and the souls that have attained to bliss. *(Poimandres* 12(i).12 [Scott, 1:231])

2. *figure of them*—The shape of the Hebrew letters is based on the constellations. See note 2, ch. LI, bk. II.

3. *points, and tops*—The Hebrew alphabet contains no vowels. The letters are pointed, that is, distinguished by certain small marks, to indicate their pronunciation.

Astrological Signs	Hebrew Letters	Chiromantic Signs	Greek Letters	Latin Letters
♈	ה		B	B
♉	ז		Γ	C
♊	ח		Δ	D
♋	ט		Z	F
♌	ל		K	G
♍	מ		Λ	L
♎	נ		M	M
♏	ס		N	N
♐	ע		Π	P
♑	צ		P	R
♒	ק		Σ	S
♓	ש		T	T
♄	ב		A	A
♃	ג		E	E
♂	ד		H	I
☉	כ		I	O
♀	פ		O	U
☿	ר		Υ	J consonant
☽	ת		Ω	V consonant
Earth	א		Θ	K
Water	ו		Ξ	Q
Air			Φ	X
Fire	׳		X	Z
Spirit			Ψ	H

4. *into the same*—Mystical meaning is derived from seemingly mundane words by applying certain techniques of the practical Kabbalah that are described in Appendix VII.

5. *of the elements*—

> First; the Spirit of the God of the living; Blessed and more than blessed by the Living God of ages. The Voice, the Spirit, and the Word, these are the Holy Spirit. Second; from the Spirit He produced Air, and formed in it twenty-two sounds—the letters; three are mothers, seven are double, and twelve are simple; but the Spirit is first and above these. Third; from the Air He formed the Waters, and from the formless and void made mire and clay, and designed surfaces upon them, and hewed recesses in them, and formed the strong material foundation. Fourth; from the Water He formed Fire and made for Himself a Throne of Glory with Auphanim, Seraphim and Kerubim, as his ministering angels; and with these three he completed his dwelling, as it is written, "Who maketh his angels spirits and his ministers a flaming fire." *(Sepher Yetzirah* 1 [Westcott, 16–7])

Perhaps Agrippa has confounded the first emanation of Spirit with the second emanation of Air. *The Book of Formation,* quoted above, was first published in Latin by William Postel in 1552, and it is difficult to know whether Agrippa had access to a manuscript copy in Hebrew or Latin.

6. *Origenes*—

> And while still on the subject of names, we have to mention that those who are skilled in the use of incantations, relate that the utterance of the same incantation in its proper language can accomplish what the spell professes to do; but when translated into any other tongue, it is observed to become inefficacious and feeble. And thus it is not the things signified, but the qualities and peculiarities of words, which possess a certain power for this or that purpose. (Origen *Against Celsus* 1.25. In *The Ante-Nicene Fathers,* 4:406–7)

7. *three mothers*—See the table of the Hebrew alphabet in Appendix VII. The three mothers of Agrippa do not agree with the *Sepher Yetzirah*:

> The Three Mothers are Aleph, Mem and Shin, they are Air, Water and Fire. Water is silent, Fire is sibilant, and Air derived from the Spirit is as the tongue of a balance

> standing between these contraries which are in equilibrium, reconciling and mediating between them. *(Sepher Yetzirah* 2.1 [Westcott, 18])

See also ch. 3 of *Sepher Yetzirah*.

8. *seven double*—

> The Seven double letters, Beth, Gimel, Daleth, Kaph, Peh, Resh and Tau have each two sounds associated with them. They are referred to Life, Peace, Wisdom, Riches, Grace, Fertility and Power. The two sounds of each letter are the hard and the soft—the aspirated and the softened. They are called Double, because each letter presents a contrast or permutation; thus Life and Death; Peace and War; Wisdom and Folly; Riches and Poverty; Grace and Indignation; Fertility and Solitude; Power and Servitude." *(Sepher Yetzirah* 4.1 [Westcott, 22])

There is much dispute over the correct agreement between the seven double letters and the planets. If we may assume that the order of planets given in ch. 4, sec. 4 of the *Sepher Yetzirah* is parallel to the order of letters (by no means a safe assumption), this arrangement results: Beth—Sun; Gimel—Venus; Daleth—Mercury; Kaph—Luna; Peh—Saturn; Resh—Jupiter; Tau—Mars. Presumably this was the reasoning followed by Kircher, who made this assignment (see note 40 to ch. 4, *Sepher Yetzirah* [Westcott, 46]). It should be noted that the planets are presented in *Sepher Yetzirah* in their ancient order according to apparent speed of motion across the heavens—Saturn, Jupiter, Mars, Sun, Venus, Mercury, Moon—but that this list is broken into two parts in order to set the Sun at the head. If the original order of the planets were restored, it is possible a hidden attribution of the planets to the seven double letters would emerge: Beth—Moon; Gimel—Mercury; Daleth—Venus; Kaph—Sun; Peh—Mars; Resh—Jupiter; Tau—Saturn.

9. *other twelve*—The 12 simple, or single, letters of Agrippa do not agree with those given in the *Sepher Yetzirah*:

> The Twelve Simple Letters are Heh, Vau, Zain, Cheth, Teth, Yod, Lamed, Nun, Samech, Oin [Ayin], Tzaddi and Qoph; they are the foundations of these twelve properties: Sight, Hearing, Smell, Speech, Taste, Sexual Love, Work, Movement, Anger, Mirth, Imagination and Sleep. These Twelve are also allotted to the directions in space: North-east, South-east, the East above, the East below, the North

above, the North below, the South-west, the North-west, the West above, the West below, the South above, and the South below; these diverge to infinity, and are as the arms of the Universe. *(Sepher Yetzirah 5.1 [Westcott, 25])*

The assignment of the 12 simple letters to the signs of the zodiac is not explicitly given in *Sepher Yetzirah*, but most authorities have allotted the letters in their natural order, beginning with Heh for Aries, Vau for Taurus, and so on. This is the modern practice.

10. *its idiom*—Y is not included in the list of Latin letters.

11. *following table*—I have corrected the errors in the table, and to avoid confusion have taken the liberty of rendering the last Latin vowel, given by Agrippa in the form V, into the modern form U; and also changed the first consonant I, into J.

12. *preceding letters*—The extended number would seem to be the position of the letter in the alphabet—for example, Daleth would have the extended number 4; the collected number would seem to be the sum of the extended number of that letter and of the letters preceding it—for example, Daleth would have the collected number $1 + 2 + 3 + 4 = 10$.

13. *integral numbers*—Any Hebrew letter can be written out at length. Yod, which has a value of 10, can be written Yod-Vau-Daleth for a numerical value of $10 + 6 + 4 = 20$.

To the Most Honorable Lord, Most Illustrious Prince, *Hermannus of Wyda,* Prince Elector, Duke of Westphalia, and Angaria, Lord and Arch-prelate of Colonia, and Paderbornia, his most gracious Master, *Henry Cornelius Agrippa* of Nettes-heym wisheth health.

Behold now (most illustrious Prince, and most honourable Prelate!) the rest of the books of Occult Philosophy, or Magic, which I promised your worthiness that I would put forth when I published the first of them: but the sudden, and almost unexpected death of holy *Margaret of Austria* my princess coming upon it, hindered me then from the endeavoring to put it forth.

Then the wickedness of some pulpit sycophants, and of some school sophisters incessantly raging against me for a declamation I put forth concerning the Vanity of Things,[1] and the Excellency of the Word of God, and contending against me continually with bitter hatred, envy, malice, and calumnies, hindered me from putting it forth; whereof some very proudly, with a full mouth, and loud voice aspersed me with impiety in the temple amongst a promiscuous people. Others with corner whisperings from house to house, street by street, did fill the ears of the ignorant with my infamy: others in public, and private assemblies did instigate prelates, princes, and Caesar himself[2] against me.

Hence I began to be at a stand, whether I should put forth the rest of the book or no. Whilst I did doubt that I should by this means expose myself to greater calumnies, and as it were cast myself out of the smoke into the fire, a certain rude fear seized upon me, lest by putting them forth I should seem more offensive than officious to you, and expose Your Highness to the envy of malicious carpers, and tongues of detractors.

Whilst these things troubled me with a various desperation, the quickness of your understanding, exact discretion, uprightness of judgement, religion without superstition, and other most known virtues in you, your authority, and integrity beyond exception, which can easily check, and bridle the tongues of slanderers, removed my doubting, and enforced me to set upon that again more boldly, which I had almost left off by reason of despair.

Therefore (most illustrious Prince) take in good part this second book of Occult Philosophy, in which we show the mysteries of the celestial magic, all things being opened, and manifested, which experienced antiquity makes relation of, and which came to my knowledge, that the secrets of celestial magic (hitherto neglected, and not fully apprehended by men of latter times) may with your protection be by me, after the showing of natural virtues, proposed to them that are studious, and curious of these secrets: by which let him that shall be profited and receive benefit, give you the thanks, who have been the occasion of this edition, and setting of it at liberty to be seen abroad.[3]

FAREWELL

229

Notes—To Hermannus of Wyda

1. *vanity of things*—*De incertitudine et vanitate scientiarum.*

2. *Caesar himself*—Emperor Charles V.

3. *seen abroad*—Hermannus of Wyda was in rebellion against the authority of the Church and a Protestant reformer, the ideal patron to champion Agrippa in the name of freethinking and protect him from the wrath of the conservative clergy. See his biographical note.

The Second Book of
Occult Philosophy,
or Magic;

written by
Henry Cornelius Agrippa.

BOOK II

CHAPTER 1

Of the necessity of mathematical learning, and of the many wonderful works which are done by mathematical arts only.

The doctrines of mathematics are so necessary to, and have such an affinity with magic, that they that do profess it without them, are quite out of the way, and labour in vain, and shall in no wise obtain their desired effect. For whatsoever things are, and are done in these inferior natural virtues, are all done, and governed by number, weight, measure, harmony, motion, and light. And all things which we see in these inferiors, have root, and foundation in them.

Yet nevertheless without natural virtues, of mathematical doctrines only works like to naturals can be produced, as *Plato* saith,[1] a thing not partaking of truth or divinity, but certain images kin to them, as bodies going, or speaking, which yet want the animal faculty, such as were those which amongst the ancients were called *Dedalus* his images,[2] and αυτόματα,[3] of which *Aristotle* makes mention, viz. the three-footed images[4] of *Vulcan*,[5] and *Dedalus,* moving themselves, which *Homer* saith[6] came out of their own accord to exercise, and which we read, moved themselves at the feast of *Hiarba* the philosophical exerciser: as also that golden statues performed the offices of cup-bearers, and carvers to the guests. Also we read of the statues of *Mercury,*[7] which did speak, and the wooden dove of *Arthita,* which did fly, and the miracles of *Boethius,* which *Cassiodorus* made mention of, viz. *Diomedes* in brass, sounding a trumpet, and a brazen snake hissing, and pictures of birds singing most sweetly.

Of this kind are those miracles of images which proceed from geometry, and optics, of which we made some mention in the first book, where we spoke of the element of Air.[8] So there are made glasses, some concave, others of the form of a column, making the representations of things in the air seem like shadows at a distance: of which sort *Apollonius,* and *Vitellius* in their books De Perspectiva, and Speculis, taught the making, and the use.[9]

And we read that *Magnus Pompeius* brought a certain glass[10] amongst the spoils from the East, to Rome, in which were seen armies of armed men. And there are made certain transparent glasses, which being dipped in some certain juices of herbs, and irradiated with an artificial light, fill the whole air round about with visions.[11] And I know how to make reciprocal glasses, in which the Sun shining, all things which were illustrated by the rays thereof are apparently seen many miles off.

Hence a magician, expert in natural philosophy, and mathematics, and knowing the middle sciences consisting of both these, arithmatic, music, geometry, optics, astronomy, and such sciences that are of weights, measures, proportions, articles, and joints, knowing also mechanical arts resulting from these, may without any wonder, if he excel other men in art, and wit, do many wonderful things, which the most prudent, and wise men may much admire.

Are there not some relics extant of the ancients' works, viz. *Hercules',*[12] and *Alexan-*

der's pillars, the Gate of Caspia made of brass, and shut with iron beams, that it could by no wit or art, be broken? And the pyramis[13] of *Julius Caesar* erected at Rome near the hill Vaticanus, and mountains built by art[14] in the middle of the sea, and towers, and heaps of stones,[15] such as I saw in England put together by an incredible art.

And we read in faithful histories that in former times rocks have been cut off, and valleys made, and mountains made into a plain, rocks have been digged through, promontories have been opened in the sea, the bowels of the Earth made hollow, rivers divided,[16] seas joined to seas,[17] the seas restrained, the bottom of the sea been searched, pools exhausted, fens dried up, new islands made,[18] and again restored to the continent,[19] all which, although they may seem to be against nature, yet we read have been done, and we see some relics of them remaining till this day, which the vulgar say were the works of the Devil, seeing the arts, and artificers thereof have been dead out of all memory, neither are there any that care to understand, or search into them.

Therefore they seeing any wonderful sight, do impute it to the Devil, as his work, or think it is a miracle, which indeed is a work of natural, or mathematical philosophy. As if anyone should be ignorant of the virtue of the loadstone, and should see heavy iron drawn upwards, or hanged in the air (as we read the iron image of *Mercury* did long since at Treveris hang up in the middle of the temple by loadstones,[20] this verse attesting the same:

The iron white rod bearer flies in the air.

The like to which we read was done concerning the image of the Sun at Rome, in the temple of *Serapis)*[21] would not such an ignorant man, I say, presently say it is the work of the Devil? But if he shall know the virtue of the loadstone to the iron, and shall make trial of it, he presently ceaseth to wonder, and doth no more scruple it to be the work of nature.

But here it is convenient that you know, that as by natural virtues we collect natural virtues, so by abstracted, mathematical, and celestial, we receive celestial virtues, as motion, life, sense, speech, soothsaying, and divination, even in matter less disposed, as that which is not made by nature, but only by art. And so images that speak, and foretell things to come, are said to be made, as *William of Paris* relates of a brazen head[22] made under the rising of Saturn,[23] which they say spake with a man's voice.

But he that will choose a disposed matter, and most fit to receive, and a most powerful agent, shall undoubtedly produce more powerful effects. For it is a general opinion of the Pythagoreans, that as mathematical things are more formal than natural, so also they are more efficacious: as they have less dependence in their being, so also in their operation. But amongst all mathematical things, numbers, as they have more of form in them, so also are more efficacious, to which not only heathen philosophers, but also Hebrew, and Christian divines do attribute virtue, and efficacy, as well to effect what is good, as what is bad.

Notes—Chapter 1

1. *Plato saith*—See note 8, ch. LXIII, bk. III.

2. *Dedalus his images*—About the wooden statues scattered throughout ancient Greece, called *daidala,* Plato says: "Your statements, Euthyphro, look like the work of Daedalus, founder of my line. If I had made them, and they were my positions, no doubt you would poke fun at me, and say that, being in his line, the figures I construct in words run off, as did his statues, and will not stay where they are put" *(Euthyphro* 11c [Hamilton and

Cairns, 180]). And in another place he makes a similar reference:

> *Socrates:* It is because you have not observed the statues of Daedalus. Perhaps you don't have them in your country.
> *Meno:* What makes you say that?
> *Socrates:* They too, if no one ties them down, run away and escape. If tied, they stay where they are put.
> *(Meno* 97d [Hamilton and Cairns, 381])

On the *daidala,* see the biographical note on Daedalus.

3. αυτόματα—Automata: contrivances that move by themselves.

4. *three-footed images*—Tripods, ornamental vessels often presented as prizes or votive offerings. They were taken as plunder in war and served almost as monetary units.

5. *Vulcan*—Roman fire god and artificer, who is bound up and confused with the Greek god Hephaestos. In classical times they were treated as the same deity. He was the son of Zeus and Hera, or of Hera alone, lame in one foot but strong and hardy with a handsome bearded face and powerful arms. The homes of the gods and all their magical possessions and beautiful jewelry were made by Hephaestos, who despite his skill was constantly mocked because of his infirmity: "But among the blessed immortals uncontrollable laughter/went up as they saw Hephaistos bustling about the palace" (Homer *Iliad* 1, lines 599–600 [Lattimore, 75]). In Homer the god is characterized both as a cunning craftsman *(Odyssey* 8, lines 272–81 [Lattimore, 128)] and as the lord of heat and flame *(Iliad* 21, lines 342–76 [Lattimore, 427–8]).

6. *Homer saith*—Of the 20 serving tripods fashioned by the smith of the gods, Hephaestos, Homer writes: "And he had set golden wheels underneath the base of each one/so that of their own motion they could wheel into the immortal/gathering, and return to his house: a wonder to look at" *(Iliad* 18, lines 375–8 [Lattimore, 385]). Homer also writes of the mechanical attendants that helped the lame god to walk: "These are golden, and in appearance like living young women./There is intelligence in their hearts, and there is speech in them/and strength, and from the immortal gods they have learned how to do things" (ibid., lines 418–20 [Lattimore, 386]).

7. *statues of Mercury*—See note 11, ch. LII, bk. III.

8. *element of Air*—See ch. VI, bk. I.

9. *and the use*—A method of projecting images with concave and plane mirrors was known from ancient times, and is described by Roger Bacon in his *De speculis.*

10. *certain glass*—Pompey must have obtained this mirror in his pursuit of the fleeing army of Mithradates in 65 BC, or during the subsequent two-year eastern campaign in Syria and Palestine. Or can it possibly have been a crude telescope?

11. *with visions*—This sounds very much like a slide projector, which presumably cast the shadows of substances clinging to the glass upon the wall.

12. *Hercules'*—The pillars of Hercules are the two great rocks that stand on opposite sides of the entrance to the Mediterranean Sea. According to myth, they were once together, but Hercules tore them apart in order to get to Cadiz.

13. *pyramis*—Pyrame, or obelisk, a large single block of stone carved in the shape of a four-sided pillar with a pyramidal top sheathed in reflective metal. The Roman emperors admired those in Egypt and stole many to erect in Rome.

14. *mountains built by art*—Perhaps such legends took their origin from coral atolls, which can be very symmetrical; or volcanic uprisings, which appear with relative suddenness.

15. *heaps of stones*—Stonehenge, or some similar site.

16. *rivers divided*—The prodigies in the preceding list appear to derive from Plato's description of the great building works of Atlantis, in his *Critias.*

17. *seas joined to seas*—The Egyptians constructed a canal between the Mediterranean and the Red Sea:

> Pasammetichus left a son called Necos, who succeeded him upon the throne. This prince was the first to attempt the construction of the canal to the Red Sea—a work completed afterwards by Darius the Persian—the length of which is four day's journey, and the width such as to admit of two triremes being rowed along it abreast. (Herodotus *History* 2 [Rawlinson, 137]).

18. *new islands made*—Perhaps this refers to the artificial Lake of Moeris: "It is manifestly an artificial excavation, for nearly in the center there stand two pyramids, rising to the height of fifty fathoms above the surface of the water, and extending as far beneath, crowned each of them with a colossal statue sitting upon a throne" (ibid., 134).

19. *restored to the continent*—The island of Pharos was joined to the Egyptian city of Alexandria by an artificial dyke called the Heptastadium.

20. *temple by loadstones*—

> So then, if human art can effect such rare conclusions, that such as know them not would think them divine effects—as when an iron image was hung in a certain temple so strangely that the ignorant would have

verily believed they had seen a work of God's immediate power, yet it hung so just because it was between two loadstones, whereof one was placed in the roof of the temple, and the other in the floor, without touching anything at all ..." (Augustine *City of God* 21.6 [Healey, 2:326])

The architect Timochares began to erect a vaulted roof of loadstone, in the Temple of Arsinoë [wife and sister of King Ptolemy II of Egypt], at Alexandria, in order that the iron statue of that princess might have the appearance of hanging suspended in the air: his death, however, and that of King Ptolemaeus, who had ordered this monument to be erected in honour of his sister, prevented the completion of the project. (Pliny 34.42 [Bostock and Riley, 6:209])

It is just as likely that work stopped when Timochares began to realize the enormity of the technical difficulties involved in such a feat of engineering, and that the scale he planned was effectively impossible. The Latin poet Claudius Claudianus, who lived in the beginning of the fourth century, mentions a temple that held a statue of Venus made of loadstone, and another of Mars, of iron. During marriage ceremonies these were allowed to come together. If the two statues were suspended on wires, and gently swung together so that they clung, this is feasible.

21. *Serapis*—The Ptolomaic form of Osiris, said to be a combination of the names Apis and Osiris: "But the greatest part of the priests do say that Osiris and Apis are both of them but one complex being, while they tell us in their sacred commentaries and sermons that we are to look upon the Apis as the beautiful image of the soul of Osiris" (Plutarch *Isis and Osiris* 29 [Goodwin, 4:90]). Serapis was linked with the Sun, as Isis was with the Moon, and was regarded as

the "male counterpart of Isis" (Budge 1904, 2:20:349). Their worship was introduced into Rome in the time of Sulla (81–79 BC), and despite resistance from both the senate, and later the Emperor Augustus, soon took firm hold.

22. *brazen head*—Tales of oracular heads of brass were popular. Brewer (1870) enumerates five, the most notable being that of Albertus Magnus, which took 30 years to make and was shattered by his disciple, Thomas Aquinas, who is also supposed to have smashed his master's automatic doorman. Also famous is that of Roger Bacon:

> With seven years tossing nigromantic charms,
> Poring upon dark Hecat's principles,
> I have framed out a monstrous head of brass,
> That, by the enchanting forces of the devil,
> Shall tell out strange and uncouth aphorisms,
> And girt fair England with a wall of brass.
> (Robert Green *Friar Bacon and Friar Bungay*, sc. 11, lines 17–22. In *Elizabethan Plays*, ed. Arthur H. Nethercot, Charles R. Baskervill, and Virgil B. Heitzel [New York: Holt, Rinehart and Winston, 1971])

According to Lewis Spence, it was revealed in 1818 that in the imperial museum of Vienna had been discovered several heads of Baphomet, the god of the Knights Templars: "These heads represent the divinity of the gnostics, named *Mêtê*, or Wisdom. For a long time there was preserved at Marseilles one of these gilded heads, seized in a retreat of the Templars when the latter were pursued by the law" (Spence 1920, 203).

23. *rising of Saturn*—The head of Baphomet was supposed to possess a beard and the horns of a goat, or by other accounts to be a goat's head (ibid., 63–4). Saturn, who is depicted as an ancient bearded man, rules in the zodiac sign of Capricorn, the Goat.

CHAPTER II

Of numbers, and of their power, and virtue.

Severinus Boethius saith,[1] that all things which were first made by the nature of things in its first age, seem to be formed by the proportion of numbers, for this was the principal pattern in the mind of the Creator. Hence is borrowed the number of the elements, hence the courses of times, hence the motion of the stars, and the revolution of the heaven, and the state of all things subsist by the uniting together of numbers. Numbers therefore are endowed with great and sublime virtues.

For it is no wonder, seeing there are so many, and so great occult virtues in natural things, although of manifest operations, that there should be in numbers much greater, and more occult, and also more wonderful, and efficacious, for as much as they are more formal, more perfect, and naturally in the celestials, not mixed with separated substances; and lastly, having the greatest, and most simple commixtion with the Ideas in the mind of God, from which they receive their proper, and most efficacious virtues: wherefore also they are of more force, and conduce most to the obtaining of spiritual, and divine gifts, as in natural things, elementary qualities are powerful in the transmuting of any elementary thing.

Again, all things that are, and are made, subsist by, and receive their virtue from numbers. For time consists of number, and all motion, and action, and all things which are subject to time, and motion.[2] Harmony also, and voices have their power by, and consist of numbers, and their proportions, and the proportions arising from numbers, do by lines, and points make characters, and figures: and these are proper to magical operations, the middle which is betwixt both being appropriated by declining to the extremes, as in the use of letters.[3]

And lastly, all species of natural things, and of those things which are above nature, are joined together by certain numbers: which *Pythagoras* seeing,[4] saith, that number is that by which all things consist, and distributes each virtue to each number. And *Proclus* saith, number hath always a being: yet there is one in voice, another in the proportion of them, another in the soul, and reason, and another in divine things. But *Themistius,* and *Boethius,* and *Averrois* the Babylonian, together with *Plato,* do so extol numbers, that they think no man can be a true philosopher without them.

Now they speak of a rational, and formal number, not of a material, sensible, or vocal, the number of merchants[5] buying, and selling, of which the Pythagoreans, and Platonists, and our *Austin* make no reckoning, but apply it to the proportion resulting from it, which number they call natural, rational, and formal, from which great mysteries flow, as well in natural, as divine, and heavenly things. By it is there a way made for the searching out, and understanding of all things knowable. By it the next access to natural prophesying is had: and the Abbot *Joachim* proceeded no other way in his prophecies, but by formal numbers.

Notes—Chapter 11

1. *Boethius saith*—See Boethius *Consolation of Philosophy* 3.9, the substance of which comes from Plato *Timaeus* 29–42.

2. *time, and motion*—"Time is the number of the motion of the celestial bodies" (Proclus *On Motion* 2. In Taylor [1831] 1976, 86).

3. *use of letters*—Agrippa seems to be saying that letters derive their efficacy from the numerical harmony of the voice and the numerical geometry of their written symbols.

4. *Pythagoras seeing*—

> But the Pythagoreans have said in the same way that there are two principles, but added this much, which is peculiar to them, that they thought that finitude and infinity were not attributes of certain other things, e.g. of fire or earth or anything else of this kind, but that infinity itself and unity itself were the substance of the things of which they are predicated. This is why number was the substance of all things. (Aristotle *Metaphysica* 1.5.987a [McKeon, 700])

Also Aristotle says:

> ... since, then, all other things seemed in their whole nature to be modeled on numbers, and numbers seemed to be the first things in the whole of nature, they supposed the elements of numbers to be the elements of all things, and the whole heaven to be a musical scale and a number. (ibid. 985b [McKeon, 698])

The two principles of the Pythagoreans were limit and the unlimited, which they identified, respectively, with odd and even numbers.

5. *number of merchants*—

> It is befitting, then, Glaucon, that this branch of learning should be prescribed by our law and that we should induce those who are to share the highest functions of state to enter upon the study of calculation and take hold of it, not as amateurs, but to follow it up until they attain to the contemplation of the nature of number, by pure thought, not for the purpose of buying and selling, as if they were preparing to be merchants and hucksters, but for the uses of war and for facilitating the conversion of the soul itself from the world of generation to essence and truth. (Plato *Republic* 7.525c [Hamilton and Cairns, 757–8])

CHAPTER III

How great virtues numbers have, as well in natural things, as in supernatural.

That there lies wonderful efficacy, and virtue in numbers, as well to good as to bad, not only most eminent philosophers do unanimously teach, but also Catholic doctors, and especially *Hierom, Austin, Origen, Ambrose, Gregory of Nazianzen, Athanasius, Basilius, Hilarius, Rabanus, Bede,* and many more confirm. Hence *Hilarius* in his Commentaries upon the psalms, testifies that the seventy elders,[1] according to the efficacy of numbers, brought the psalms into order. *Rabanus* also, a famous doctor, composed an excellent book of the virtues of numbers.

But now how great virtues numbers have in nature, is manifest in the herb which is called cinquefoil, i.e. five-leaved grass; for this resists poisons by virtue of the number of five; also drives away devils, conduceth to expiation;[2] and one leaf of it taken twice in a day in wine, cures the fever of one day: three the tertian fever: four the quartan.[3] In like manner four grains of the seed of turnisole[4] being drunk, cures the quartan, but three the tertian. In like manner vervain[5] is said to cure fevers, being drunk in wine, if in tertians it be cut from the third joint, in quartans from the fourth. A serpent, if he be once struck with a spear, dieth, if twice, recovers strength. These and many such as these are read, and testified in divers authors.

We must know now whence these are done, which certainly have a cause, which is a various proportion of various numbers amongst themselves. There is also a wonderful experiment of the number of seven, that every seventh male,[6] born without a female coming betwixt, hath power to cure the King's Evil by his touch alone, or word. Also every seventh daughter that is born, is said wonderfully to help forward the birth of children: neither is the natural number here considered, but the formal consideration that is in the number.

And let that which we spake before, be always be kept in mind, viz. that these powers are not in vocal, or numbers of merchants buying, and selling, but in rational, formal, and natural; these are distinct mysteries of God, and nature. But he that knows how to join together the vocal numbers, and natural with divine, and order them into the same harmony, shall be able to work and know wonderful things by numbers; the Pythagorians profess that they can prognosticate many things by the numbers of names,[7] in which truly, unless there did lie a great mystery, *John* had not said in the Revelation,[8] he which hath understanding, let him compute the number of the name of the beast, which is the number of a man, and this is the most famous manner of computing amongst the Hebrews, and Cabalists, as we shall show afterwards.

But this you must know, that simple numbers signify divine things: numbers of ten; celestial: numbers of an hundred; terrestrial: numbers of a thousand; those things that shall be in a future age. Besides, seeing the parts of the mind are according to an arithmetical mediocrity, by reason of the identity, or equality of excess, coupled together: but the body, whose parts differ in their greatness, is according to a geometrical mediocrity, compounded: but an animal consists of both, viz. soul and body, according to that mediocrity, which is suitable to harmony: hence it is that numbers do work very much upon the soul, figures upon the body, and harmony upon the whole animal.

Notes—Chapter III

1. *seventy elders*—Numbers 11:16.

2. *expiation*—The averting of evil.

3. *four the quartan*—

> It is reported, that foure branches [of cinquefoil] hereof cureth quartaine agues, three tertians, and one branch quotidians: which things are most vaine and frivolous, as likewise many other such like, which are not only found in *Dioscorides,* but also in other Authors, which we willingly withstand. (Gerard 1633, 2:382–H:992)

4. *turnisole*—Small, or female, turnsole *(Crozophora tinctoria).* Also called *heliotrophium minus* according to Gerard, not because it turns to face the Sun, but because it flowers at the summer solstice. It is a small trailing plant with little gray and yellow flowers irregularly placed. Not to be confused with great turnsole *(Heliotrophius eurpoaeum).*

5. *vervain*—

> It [vervain] is reported to be of singular force against the Tertian and Quartane Fevers: but you must observe mother *Bombies* rules, to take iust so many knots or sprigs, and no more, lest it fall out so that it do you no good, if you catch no harm by it. Many odde old wives fables are written of Vervaine tending to witchcraft and sorcerie, which you may read elsewhere, for I am not willing to trouble your eares with reporting such trifles, as honest eares abhorre to heare. (Gerard 1633, 2:246–C:718–9)

Mother Bombie is the John Doe of witches. Gerard seems to have been a little frightened of the whole subject of magic.

6. *seventh male*—The power of healing is also said to reside in the seventh son of a seventh son.

7. *numbers of names*—

> ... of the discoveries made by Pythagoras, one of the most unerring, is the fact, that in the name given to infants, an odd number of vowels is portentous of lameness, loss of eyesight, or similar accidents, on the right [male] side of the body, and an even number of vowels of the like infirmities on the left [female]." (Pliny 28.6 [Bostock and Riley 5:287–8])

8. *In the Revelation*—Revelation 13:18.

CHAPTER IV

Of unity, and the scale thereof.

Now let us treat particularly of numbers themselves: and because number is nothing else but a repetition of unity, let us first consider unity itself. For unity doth most simply go through every number, and is the common measure, fountain, and original of all numbers, contains every number joined together in itself entirely, the beginner of every multitude, always the same, and unchangable: whence also being multiplied into itself, produceth nothing but itself: it is indivisible, void of all parts: but if it seem at any time to be divided, it is not cut, but indeed multiplied into unities: yet none of these unities is greater or lesser than the whole unity, as a part is less than the whole: it is not therefore multiplied into parts, but into itself.[1]

Therefore some called it concord, some piety, and some friendship, which is so knit, that it cannot be cut into parts. But *Martianus,* according to the opinion of *Aristotle,* saith, it is named *Cupid,*[2] because it is made one alone, and will always bewail itself, and beyond itself it hath nothing, but being void of all haughtiness, or coupling, turns its proper heats into itself.

It is therefore the one beginning, and end of all things, neither hath it any beginning, or end itself: nothing is before one, nothing is after one, and beyond it is nothing, and all things which are, desire that one, because all things proceeded from one, and that all things may be the same, it is necessary that they partake of that one: and as all things proceeded of one into many things, so all things endeavour to return to that one, from which they proceeded; it is necessary that they should put off multitude.

One therefore is referred to the high God, who seeing he is one, and innumerable, yet creates innumerable things of himself, and contains them within himself. There is therefore one God, one world of the one God, one Sun of the one world, also one phoenix in the world, one king amongst bees,[3] one leader amongst flocks of cattle, one ruler amongst herds of beasts, and cranes follow one,[4] and many other animals honour unity; amongst the members of the body there is one principal by which all the rest are guided, whether it be the head, or (as some will) the heart. There is one element overcoming, and penetrating all things, viz. Fire.

There is one thing[5] created of God, the subject of all wondering, which is on Earth, or in heaven; it is actually animal, vegetable, and mineral, everywhere found, known by few, called by none by its proper name, but covered with figures, and riddles, without which neither alchemy, nor natural magic, can attain to their complete end, or perfection.

From one man, *Adam,* all men proceed, from that one all become mortal, from that one *Jesus* Christ they are regenerated: and as saith *Paul,*[6] one Lord, one faith, one baptism, one God, and Father of all, one mediator betwixt God and man, one most high Creator, who is over all, by all, and in us all. For there is one Father, God, from whence all, and we in him: one Lord *Jesus* Christ, by whom all, and we by him: one God Holy Ghost, into whom all, and we into him.

The Scale of Unity

In the Exemplary World	' Yod	One divine essence, the fountain of all virtues, and power, whose name is expressed with one most simple letter
In the Intellectual World	The Soul of the World	One supreme intellect, the first creature, the fountain of lives
In the Celestial World	The Sun	One king of stars, the fountain of life
In the Elemental World	The Philosopher's Stone	One subject, and instrument of all virtues, natural, and supernatural
In the Lesser World	The Heart	One first living, and last dying
In the Infernal World	Lucifer	One price of rebellion, of angels, and Darkness

Notes—Chapter IV

1. *into itself*—Any one thing, divided, produces several single things, each one thing in itself. And the oneness of a thing cannot be greater or less than the oneness of any other thing.

2. *Cupid*—The Roman Eros, who according to Hesiod was the third born:

> Chaos was first of all, but next appeared
> Broad-bosomed Earth, sure standing place
>   for all
> The gods who live on snowy Olympus'
>   peak,
> And misty Tartarus, in a recess
> Of broad-pathed earth, and Love, most
>   beautiful
> Of all the deathless gods. He makes men
>   weak,
> He overpowers the clever mind, and tames
> The spirit in the breasts of men and gods.
> (Hesiod *Theogony* [Wender, 27])

3. *king amongst bees*—The ancients entertained the mistaken notion that the single oversized bee in each hive was its king, whereas it is in fact female, and the queen. See Virgil's description of the warfare between two rival "kings" in his *Georgics* 4, c. line 67.

4. *cranes follow one*—"These birds agree by common consent at what moment they shall set out, fly aloft to look out afar, select a leader for them to follow, and have sentinels duly posted in the rear, which relieve each other by turns, utter loud cries, and with their voice keep the whole flight in proper array" (Pliny 10.30 [Bostock and Riley, 501]).

5. *one thing*—The mysterious *Azoth* of philosophers—a word coined by hermetic alchemists from the first and last letters of the Latin, Greek and Hebrew alphabets to signify the hidden essence that pervades the universe. Paracelsus is represented with the word—minus the first letter—inscribed on the pommel of his sword in a woodcut from 1567 (see next page).

6. *saith Paul*—I Corinthians 12:4–13.

Paracelsus, showing the last four letters of Azoth on the pommel of his sword.

from *Astronomica et astrologica opuscula* by Theophrastus Paracelsus (Cologne, 1567)

CHAPTER V

Of the number of two, and the scale thereof.

The first number is of two, because it is the first multitude, it can be measured by no number besides unity alone, the common measure of all numbers: it is not compounded of numbers, but of one unity only; neither is it called a number uncompounded, but more properly not compounded: the number of three is called the first number uncompounded: but the number of two is the first branch of unity, and the first procreation.[1]

Hence it is called generation, and *Juno*,[2] and an imaginable corporation,[3] the proof of the first motion, the first form of parity: the number of the first equality, extremity, and distance betwixt, and therefore of peculiar equity, and the proper act thereof, because it consists of two equally poised:[4] and it is called the number of science, and memory, and of light, and the number of man, who is called another, and the lesser, world:[5] it is also called the number of charity, and mutual love, of marriage, and society, as it is said by the Lord, two shall be one flesh.[6]

And *Solomon* saith:[7] it is better that two be together than one, for they have a benefit by their mutual society: if one shall fall, he shall be supported by the other. Woe to him that is alone, because when he falls he hath not another to help him: and if two sleep together, they shall warm one the other; how shall one be hot alone? And if any prevail against him, two resist him.

And it is called the number of wedlock and sex; for there are two sexes, masculine and feminine: and two doves[8] bring forth two eggs, out of the first of which is hatched the male, out of the second the female. It is also called the middle, that is capable, that is good and bad, partaking, and the beginning, of division, of multitude, and distinction, and signifies matter.

This is also sometimes the number of discord, and confusion, of misfortune, and uncleanness, whence Saint *Hierom* against *Jovianus*[9] saith, that therefore it was not spoken in the second day of the creation of the world, and God said, that it was good, because the number of two is evil.[10] Hence also it was that God commanded that all unclean animals should go into the ark by couples:[11] because as I said, the number of two, is a number of uncleanness, and it is most unhappy in their soothsayings, especially if those things, from whence the soothsaying is taken, be saturnal, or martial, for these two are accounted by the astrologers unfortunate. It is also reported, that the number of two doth cause apparitions of ghosts, and fearful goblins, and bring mischiefs of evil spirits to them that travel by night.

Pythagoras (as *Eusebius* reports)[12] said, that unity was God, and a good intellect; and that duality was a devil, and an evil intellect, in which is a material multitude: wherefore the Pythagoreans say, that two is not a number, but a certain confusion of unities. And *Plutarch* writes,[13] that the Pythagoreans called unity *Apollo,* and two, strife, and boldness; and three, justice, which is the highest perfection, and is not without many mysteries.

245

Hence there were two tables[14] of the Law in Sina, two cherubins[15] looking to the propitiatory in *Moses,* two olives[16] dropping oil in *Zachariah,* two natures in Christ, divine and human; hence *Moses* saw two appearances of God, viz. his face, and backparts,[17] also two tes- taments, two commands of love,[18] two first dig- nities,[19] two first people, two kinds of spirits, good and bad, two intellectual creatures, an angel and soul, two great lights,[20] two solsticia,[21] two equinoctials,[22] two poles, two elements pro- ducing a living soul, viz. Earth, and Water.[23]

Notes—Chapter V

1. *first procreation—*

> Some among the numbers are called absolute prime or incomposite numbers; ... They are the only indivisible numbers; thus none of the numbers other than unity (monad) can divide 3 in such a way that 3 could result from their multiplication. Indeed one times 3 is 3. Likewise, one times 5 is 5, one times 7 is 7, and one times 11 is 11. ... Also, only odd numbers can be prime and incomposite. Indeed the even numbers are not prime or incomposite; it is not only unity which measures them, but other numbers also. For example, the dyad measures 4 because 2 times 2 makes 4; 2 and 3 measure 6 because 2 times 3 and 3 times 2 make 6. All the other even numbers with the exception of 2 are likewise mea- sured by numbers greater than the unit. The number 2 is the only one among the even numbers which is similar to the odd num- bers in having only unity for its measure. Indeed one times two is two. Because of this it is said that the number two has the nature of the odd numbers because it has the same property as the odd. (Theon of Smyrna *Mathematics Useful for Under- standing Plato* 1.6, trans. R. and D. Lawlor from 1892 French edition of J. Dupuis [San Diego: Wizards Bookshelf, 1979], 15–6) [hereafter cited as Theon]

2. *Juno*—The Roman form of Hera, wife of Zeus and second only to him among the Olympians.

3. *corporation*—Embodiment.

4. *equally poised*—"The first increase, the first change from unity is made by the doubling of unity which becomes 2, in which are seen matter and all that is perceptible, the generation of motion, multipli- cation and addition, composition and the relationship of one thing to another" (ibid. 2.41 [Lawlor, 66]).

5. *lesser, world*—Microcosm.

6. *one flesh*—Genesis 2:24.

7. *Solomon saith*—Ecclesiastes 4:8–12.

8. *two doves*—Perhaps a reference to Horapollo's *Hieroglyphics,* 1.8, although the birds referred to here are crows, or ravens, not doves.

9. *against Jovianus*—*Adversum Jovinianum libri II,* written by Jerome in 393 at Bethlehem to denounce the supposed revival of gnostic ideas by Jovinianus.

10. *two is evil*—Genesis 1:6–8. Concerning the sec- ond day, the great Jewish commentator Rashi writes:

> And why was the expression "that it was good" not said on the second day? Because the work of creating the waters was not completed until the third day; for He had only begun it on the second; and a thing that is not completed is not at its perfection and at its best; on the third day however, when the work of creating the waters was completed and He began and completed another work of creation, the expression "that it was good" was there repeated two times. Once for the completion of the work of the second day and the other for the completion of the work of that third day. (*The Pentateuch and Rashi's Commentary* 1, *Genesis* [Brooklyn, NJ: S. S. and R. Publishing, 1949], 6)

11. *by couples*—Genesis 7:9.

12. *Eusebius reports*—In *Praeparatio evangelica,* a collection of classical quotations and pagan beliefs in fifteen books.

13. *Plutarch writes*—"They likewise called the unit Apollo; the number two, contention and audacious- ness; and the number three, justice, for, wronging and being wronged being two extremes caused by deficiency and excess, justice came by equality in the middle" (Plutarch *Isis and Osiris* 76, trans. William Baxter [Goodwin 4:133]. The ancients incorrectly

The Scale of the Number of Two

In the Exemplary World	יָהּ Yah	The names of God expressed with two Letters
	אֵל El	
In the Intellectual World	An Angel	The Soul	Two Intelligible Substances
In the Celestial World	The Sun	The Moon	Two Great Lights
In the Elementary World	The Earth	The Water	Two Elements Producing a Living Soul
In the Lesser World	The Heart	The Brain	Two Principal Seats of the Soul
In the Infernal World	Behemoth	Leviathan	Two Chiefs of the Devils
	Weeping	Gnashing of Teeth	Two things which Christ threatens to the Damned

derived the name Apollo from a Greek word meaning "one." See Plutarch's *The E at Delphi* 9 (Goodwin 4:486–7).

14. *two tables*—Exodus 31:18.

15. *two cherubins*—Exodus 25:18.

16. *two olives*—Zechariah 4:11–2.

17. *face, and backparts*—Exodus 33:11, 33:23.

18. *two commands of love*—Matthew 5:43–4.

19. *two first dignities*—First principles, namely heaven and Earth. See Genesis 1:1.

20. *two great lights*—Sun and Moon.

21. *two solsticia*—The summer and winter solstices.

22. *two equinoctials*—The spring and fall equinoxes.

23. *Earth, and Water*—Genesis 2:6–7. About this passage Rashi says: "He caused the deep to rise and the clouds to water and soak the earth and Adam was created. Like the baker who puts water in the dough, then kneads the dough, so here 'and He watered' then 'He formed' man" *(The Pentateuch and Rashi's Commentary* 1:20).

In the same vein Thomas Vaughan writes:

> I am now to speak of Water. This is the first element we read of in Scripture, the most ancient of principles and the Mother of all things among visibles. Without the mediation of this, the Earth can receive no blessing at all, for moysture is the proper cause of mixture and fusion. (Vaughan *Anthroposophia Theomagica.* In Waite 1888, 17)

CHAPTER VI

OF the number of three, and the scale thereof.

The number of three is an incompounded number,[1] a holy number,[2] a number of perfection, a most powerful number. For there are three persons in God, there are three theological virtues[3] in religion. Hence it is that this number conduceth to the ceremonies of God, and religion, that by the solemnity of which, prayers, and sacrifices are thrice repeated. Whence *Virgil* sings:[4]

Odd numbers to the god delightful are.

And the Pythagoreans use it in their significations, and purifications, whence in *Virgil:*[5]

The same did cleanse, and wash with
    water pure
Thrice his companions————

And it is most fit in bindings, or ligations, hence that of *Virgil:*[6]

————I walk around
First with these threads, which three, and
    several are,
'Bout the altar thrice I shall thy image bear.

And a little after:[7]

Knots, Amaryllis, tie of colours three,
Then say, these bonds I knit, for Venus be.

And we read of *Medea:*[8]

She spake three words, which caused sweet
    sleep at will,
The troubled sea, the raging waves stand
    still.

And in *Pliny* it was the custom in every medicine to spit[9] with three deprecations, and hence to be cured.

The number of three is perfected with three augmentations,[10] long, broad, and deep, beyond which there is no progression of dimension, whence the first number[11] is called square. Hence it is said that to a body that hath three measures, and to a square number, nothing can be added. Wherefore *Aristotle*[12] in the beginning of his speeches concerning heaven, calls it as it were a law, according to which all things are disposed. For corporeal, and spiritual things consist of three things, viz. beginning, middle, and end. By three (as *Tresmegistus* saith)[13] the world is perfected: harmony, necessity, and order i.e. concurrence of causes, which many call fate, and the execution of them to the fruit, or increase, and a due distribution of the increase.

The whole measure of time is concluded in three, viz. past, present, to come; all magnitude is contained in three, line, superficies,[14] and body; every body consists of three intervals, length, breadth, thickness. Harmony contains three consents in time, diapason,[15] hemiolion,[16] diatessaron.[17] There are three kinds of souls, vegetative, sensitive, and intellectual. And as saith the prophet,[18] God orders the world by number, weight, and measure, and the number of three is deputed to the ideal forms thereof, as the number two is to the procreating matter, and unity to God the maker of it.

Magicians do constitute three princes of the world, *Oromasis,*[19] *Mitris,*[20] *Araminis*[21] i.e. God, the Mind, and the Spirit. By the three square or solid,[22] the three numbers of nine of things produced are distributed, viz. of the supercelestial into nine orders of intelligences: of celestial into nine orbs: of inferiors into nine kinds of generable, and corruptible things. Lastly in this ternal orb,[23] viz. twenty-seven, all musical proportions are included, as *Plato,*[24] and *Proclus,* do at large discourse. And the number of three hath in a harmony of five, the grace of the first voice.[25]

Also in intelligences there are three hierarchies[26] of angelical spirits. There are three powers of intellectual creatures, memory, mind, and will. There are three orders of the blessed, viz. of Martyrs, Confessors, and Innocents. There are three quaternions of celestial signs,[27] viz. of Fixed, Moveable, and Common, as also of houses,[28] viz. Centers, Succeeding, and Falling. There are also three faces and heads[29] in every sign, and three lords of each triplicity.[30]

There are three Fortunes[31] amongst the planets. Three Graces[32] amongst the goddesses. Three Ladies of Destiny[33] amongst the infernal crew. Three Judges.[34] Three Furies.[35] Three-headed *Cerberus.*[36] We read also of a thrice-double *Hecate.*[37] Three mouths of the virgin *Diana.* Three persons in the supersubstantial divinity. Three times, of nature, law, and grace. Three theological virtues, faith, hope, and charity. *Jonas* was three days in the whale's belly;[38] and so many was Christ in the grave.[39]

Noꞇes—Chapꞇer VI

1. *incompounded number*—Prime number. See note 1, ch. V, bk. II.

2. *holy number*—"This is the third time; I hope good luck lies in odd numbers. … They say there is divinity in odd numbers, either in nativity, chance or death" (Shakespeare *Merry Wives of Windsor* act 5, sc. 1, lines 2–5).

3. *theological virtues*—I Corinthians 13:13.

4 *Virgil sings*—See note 3, ch. LXXIII, bk. I.

5. *whence in Virgil*—"He [Aeneas] too thrice bore to his comrades all around clear water, sprinkling them with light dew from the branch of a fruitful olive, and purified the warriors, and spoke the farewell words" (Virgil *Aeneid* 6, c. line 230 [Lonsdale and Lee, 164]).

6. *that of Virgil*—See note 3, ch. LXXIII, bk. I.

7. *a little after*—Ibid.

8. *read of Medea*—

> After he has sprinkled him [the dragon] with herbs of Lethaean juice, and has thrice repeated words that cause placid slumbers, which would even calm the boisterous ocean, and which would stop

the rapid rivers, sleep creeps upon the eyes that were strangers to it, and the hero, the son of Aeson, gains the gold …" (Ovid *Metamorphoses* 7.1, c. line 152 [Riley, 227–8])

As can be seen from the quotation, it is Jason who speaks thrice and puts the dragon to sleep, not Medea. Agrippa has confused this quote with the description of the same scene in the *Argonautica* of Apollonius Rhodius, bk. 4, c. line 156, where it is indeed Medea who charms the dragon.

9. *to spit*—

> We ask pardon of the gods, for spitting in the lap, for entertaining some too presumptuous hope or expectation. On the same principle, it is the practice in all cases where medicine is employed, to spit three times on the ground, and to conjure the malady as often; the object being to aid the operation of the remedy employed. It is usual, too, to mark a boil, when it first makes its appearance, three times with fasting spittle. (Pliny 28.7 [Bostock and Riley, 5:289])

The saliva of someone who fasted was considered more potent.

10. *augmentations*—Three dimensions of space: length, breadth and height.

The Scale of the Number of Three

In the Original World	The Father	שׁדּי Shaddai The Son	The Holy Ghost	The name of God with three letters
In the Intellectual World	Supreme	Middle	Lowest of all	Three Hierarchies of Angels
	Innocents	Martyrs	Confessors	Three Degrees of the Blessed
In the Celestial World	Movable	Fixed	Common	Three Quaternions of Signs
	Corners	Succeeding	Falling	Three Quaternions of Houses
	Of the Day	Noctournal	Partaking .	Three Lords of the Triplicities
In the Elementary World	Simple	Compounded	Thrice-Compounded	Three Degrees of Elements
In the Lesser World	The head, in which the intellect grows, answering to the Intellectual World	The breast, where is the heart, the seat of life, answering to the Celestial World	The belly, where the faculty of generation is, and the genital members, answering the Elemental World	Three Parts, answering the Three-fold World
In the Infernal World	Alecto	Megera	Ctesiphone	Three Infernal Furies
	Minos	Aeacus	Rhadamancus	Three Infernal Judges
	Wicked	Apostates	Infidels	Three Degrees of the Damned

11. *first number*—The Pythagoreans considered three the first true number:

> The all-perfect multitude of forms, therefore, they obscurely signified through the duad; but they indicated the first formal principles by the monad and duad, as not being numbers; and also by the first triad and tetrad, as being the first numbers, the one being odd, the other even ... (Thomas Taylor, *Theoretic Arithmetic,* as quoted by him in his translation of Iamblichus' *Life of Pythagoras,* 219)

12. *Wherefore Aristotle*—

> A magnitude if divisible one way is a line, if two ways a surface, and if three a body. Beyond these there is no other magnitude, because the three dimensions are all that there are, and that which is divisible in three directions is divisible in all. For, as the Pythagoreans say, the world and all that is in it is determined by the number three, since beginning and middle and end give the number of an "all," and the number they give is the triad. And so, having taken these three from nature as (so to speak) laws of it, we make further use of the number three in the worship of the Gods. Further, we use the terms in practice in this way. Of two things, or men, we say "both," but not "all:" three is the first number to which the term "all" has been appropriated. And in this, as we have said, we do but follow the lead which nature gives. (Aristotle *De caelo* [On the heavens] 1.1.268a [McKeon, 398])

13. *Tresmegistus saith*—See Appendix I, lines 12–3 of the Emerald Tablet.

14. *superficies*—Surface.

15. *diapason*—The interval of an octave in music.

16. *hemiolion*—The perfect fifth interval.

17. *diatessaron*—The interval of a fourth.

18. *the Prophet*—Isaiah 40:12.

19. *Oromasis*—A corruption of Ormazd (Ahura Mazda), the ancient Persian god of creation, corresponding in the Zoroastrian trinity to the Father.

20. *Mitris*—Corruption of Mithra, the second person of the trinity of Zoroaster, the eternal intellect and architect of the world.

21. *Araminis*—Corruption of Ahriman (Angra Mainyu), the third of the Zoroastrian trinity, corresponding to Psyche, the mundane soul.

22. *square or solid*—Three square is 3 × 3; three solid is 3 × 3 × 3. "The composite numbers which are the product of two numbers are called *planar,* they are considered as having two dimensions, length and width. Those which are the product of three numbers are called *solids* since they possess the third dimension" (Theon 1.7 [Lawlor, 16]).

23. *ternal orb*—Threefold orb; i.e., 3 × 3 × 3.

24. *as Plato*—

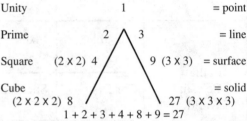

Unity	1		= point
Prime	2	3	= line
Square	(2 × 2) 4	9 (3 × 3)	= surface
Cube	(2 × 2 × 2) 8	27 (3 × 3 × 3)	= solid

$$1 + 2 + 3 + 4 + 8 + 9 = 27$$

The Pythagoreans formed a tetractys based on multiplication of odd and even numbers united in unity, the sum of which was 27. This, together with the tetractys of addition (1 + 2 + 3 + 4 = 10) symbolized the musical, geometric and arithmetic ratios upon which the universe is based. See Plato's *Timaeus* 34–6; also Theon 2.38; also the note to page 80 in Thomas Taylor's translation of Iamblichus' *Life of Pythagoras,* 235–9.

25. *first voice*—According to the Pythagoreans, man is a full chord in the greater harmony of the world, consisting of a fundamental or tonic, its major third, its just fifth and its octave.

26. *three hierarchies*—The nine choirs of angels are divided into three groups of three, as is indicated in the chart accompanying ch. VII, bk. II.

27. *celestial signs*—

Common = (Cardinal)	Aries	Cancer	Libra	Capricorn
Fixed =	Taurus	Leo	Scorpio	Aquarius
Movable = (Mutable)	Gemini	Virgo	Sagittarius	Pisces

28. *also of houses*—

Centers (Angular) =	I	IV	VII	X
Succeeding (Succedent) =	II	V	VIII	XI
Falling (Cadent) =	III	VI	IX	XII

29. *heads*—In modern astrology, a face is a division

of five degrees of arc in a zodiac sign. Each sign has six faces. Agrippa uses the term to signify a decan, or division of ten degrees. Each sign has three decans. By heads he may perhaps refer to the lords of the decans, the 36 spirits that originated with the Egyptians and that are described in the *Picatrix*.

30. *triplicity*—A triplicity is a set of three zodiac signs associated with an element:

Fire—	Aries	Leo	Sagittarius
Air—	Libra	Aquarius	Gemini
Water—	Cancer	Scorpio	Pisces
Earth—	Capricorn	Taurus	Virgo

31. *three Fortunes*—Sun, Jupiter and Venus.

32. *three Graces*—Daughters of Zeus and Eurynome (or by some, of Dionysus and Aphrodite), Euphrosyne, Aglaia and Thalia. Their office is to bestow civility, courtesy, elegance and felicity of manner.

33. *Ladies of Destiny*—The Fates were daughters of Themis (Law) and were figured as three old women present at the birth of every child. Lachesis assigns the individual his or her lot; Clotho spins the thread of life; Atropos cuts with her "abhorred shears" that thread. They are equivalent to the Norns of Norse mythology, and pop up in such varied places as Shakespeare's *Macbeth* and the fairy tale "Sleeping Beauty."

34. *three Judges*—Aeacus, Minos and Rhadamanthys, who formed the tribunal of Hades that judged the souls of the dead. Minos, son of Zeus and Europa, and former king of Crete, was supreme judge; Rhadamanthys, his brother, former king of the Cyclades, tried Asians; Aeacus, son of Zeus and Aegina, who had been selected for his post by the gods, tried Europeans.

35. *three Furies*—Alecto, Tisiphone and Megaera, three terrifying goddesses with serpent tresses who punished with their secret stings those who otherwise escaped justice. Also called the Erinnyes (the angry ones) and euphemistically the Eumenides (the kindly ones). They sprang from Gaea (Earth) and the dripping blood of castrated Uranus (the sky).

36. *Cerberus*—Three-headed dog with a serpent tail and a mane of serpents who guards the gate of hell.

37. *thrice-double Hecate*—The Greeks called Hecate *Triceps* and *Triformis* in her Moon goddess role, giving her three heads: that of a lion, a dog and a mare. The three goddess-forms of Hecate were Phoebe (Moon) in heaven, Diana on Earth, and Proserpine in hell. Robert Graves says:

> As Goddess of the Underworld she was concerned with Birth, Procreation and Death. As Goddess of the Earth she was concerned with the three seasons of Spring, Summer and Winter: she animated trees and plants and ruled all living creatures. As Goddess of the Sky she was the Moon, in her three phases of New Moon, Full Moon, and Waning Moon. This explains why she was so often enlarged to an ennead. (Graves [1948] 1973, 386)

Her sacred animal was the dog, her sacred place the crossroads, where her statues were erected.

38. *whale's belly*—Jonah 1:17.

39. *Christ in the grave*—Luke 24:21.

CHAPTER VII

Of the number of four, and the scale thereof.

The Pythagoreans call the number of four tetractys,[1] and prefer it before all the virtues of numbers, because it is the foundation, and root of all other numbers; whence also all foundations, as well in artificial things, as natural, and divine, are four square,[2] as we shall show afterwards: and it signifies solidity, which also is demonstrated by a four square figure.[3] For the number four is the first four square plain, which consists of two proportions, whereof the first is of one to two, the latter of two to four,[4] and it proceeds by a double procession and proportion, viz. of one to one, and of two to two, beginning at a unity, and ending at a quaternity: which proportions differ in this, that according to arithematic, they are unequal to one the other: but according to geometry are equal.[5]

Therefore a four square is ascribed to God the Father, and also contains the mystery of the whole Trinity: for by its single proportion, viz. by the first of one to one,[6] the unity of the paternal substance is signified, from which proceeds one Son, equal to him; by the next procession, also simple, viz. of two to two,[7] is signified by the second procession the Holy Ghost from both, that the Son be equal to the Father by the first procession; and the Holy Ghost be equal to both by the second procession.

Hence that superexcellent, and great name[8] of the divine trinity of God is written with four letters, viz. *Yod, He,* and *Vau; He,* where it is the aspiration *He,* signifies the proceeding of the spirit from both: for *He* being duplicated, terminates both syllables, and the whole name, but is pronounced *Jove,* as some will, whence that *Jovis*[9] of the heathen, which the ancients did picture with four ears, whence the number four is the fountain, and head of the whole divinity.

And the Pythagoreans call it the perpetual fountain of nature:[10] for there are four degrees in the scale of nature, viz. to be, to live, to be sensible, to understand. There are four motions in nature, viz. ascendent, descendent, going forward, circular. There are four corners[11] in the heaven, viz. rising, falling, the middle of the heaven, and the bottom of it. There are four elements under heaven, viz. Fire, Air, Water, and Earth; according to these there are four triplicities[12] in heaven: there are four first qualities under the heaven, viz. cold, heat, dryness, and moistness, from these are the four humours, blood, phlegm, choler, melancholy. Also the year is divided into four parts, which are spring, summer, autumn, and winter; also the wind is divided into eastern, western, northern, and southern. There are also four rivers of Paradise,[13] and so many infernal.

Also the number four makes up all knowledge: first it fills up every simple progress of numbers with four terms, viz. with one, two, three, and four, constituting[14] the number ten. It fills up every difference of numbers, the first even, and containing the first odd in it.[15] It hath in music diatessaron, the grace of the fourth voice. Also it contains the instrument of four strings,[16] and a Pythagorean diagram,[17] whereby are found out first of all musical tunes, and all harmony of music. For double, treble, fourtimes double, one and half, one and a third part, a concord of all, a double concord of all, of five, of four, and all consonancy is limited within the bounds of the number four.

It doth also contain the whole of mathematics in four terms, viz. point, line, superficies, and profundity. It comprehends all nature in four terms, viz. substance, quality, quantity, and motion. Also all natural philosophy, in which are the seminary virtues of nature, the natural springing, the growing form, and the compositum. Also metaphysic is comprehended in four bounds, viz. being, essence, virtue, and action. Moral philosophy is comprehended with four virtues, viz. prudence, justice, fortitude, temperence. It hath also the power of justice; hence a fourfold law: of providence, from God; fatal, from the Soul of the World; of nature, from heaven; of prudence, from man. There are also four judiciary powers in all things being, viz. the intellect, discipline, opinion, and sense.

It hath also great power in all mysteries. Hence the Pythagoreans did ratify the number four with an oath, as if it were the chiefest ground whereon their faith was grounded, and their belief might be confirmed. Hence it was called the Pythagoreans' oath,[18] which is expressed in these verses:

I with pure mind by the number four do
    swear;
That's holy, and the fountain of nature
Eternal, parent of the mind————

Also there are four rivers of Paradise; four Gospels received from four Evangelists[19] throughout the whole Church. The Hebrews received the chiefest name of God[20] written with four letters. Also the Egyptians, Arabians, Persians, Magicians, Mahometans, Grecians, Tuscans, Latins, write the name of God with only four letters, viz. thus: *Thet,*[21] *Alla,*[22] *Sire,*[23] *Orsi, Abdi,* Θεός,[24] *Esar,*[25] *Deus.* Hence the Lacedemonians were wont to paint *Jupiter* with four wings. Hence also in *Orpheus* his divinity,[26] it is said that *Neptune's* chariots are drawn with four horses.[27] There are also four kinds of divine furies,[28] proceeding from several deities, viz. from the Muses, *Dionysus, Apollo,* and *Venus.*

Also the prophet *Ezekiel* saw four beasts[29] by the river Chobar, and four Cherubims[30] in four wheels. Also in Daniel,[31] four great beasts did ascend from the sea, and four winds did fight. And in the Revelations four beasts were full of eyes,[32] before, and behind, standing round about the throne of God: and four angels,[33] to whom was given power to hurt the Earth, and the sea, did stand upon the four corners of the Earth, holding the four winds, that they should not blow upon the Earth, nor upon the sea, nor upon any tree.

Notes—Chapter VII

1. *tetractys*—Greek word meaning four. The tetractys is usually represented graphically by a triangular arrangement of ten dots:

$$
\begin{array}{c}
* \\
* \quad * \\
* \quad * \quad * \\
* \quad * \quad * \quad *
\end{array}
$$

It is formed from the addition $1 + 2 + 3 + 4 = 10$. "The importance of the quarternary obtained by addition (that is to say $1, + 2, + 3, + 4$) is great in music because all the consonances are found in it. But it is not only for this reason that all Pythagoreans hold it in highest esteem: it is also because it seems to outline the entire nature of the universe" (Theon 2.38 [Lawlor, 62]). See

the figure at the end of ch. XIII, bk. II for the tetractys formed from the Tetragrammaton.

2. *four square*—Four is the first square number (2×2).

3. *four square figure*—That is, the square.

4. *two to four*—$1 : 2 : 4$ is the double proportion referred to, where 1 stands for the point, 2 for the line, and 4 for the plane.

5. *geometry are equal*—

In particular, the arithmetic mean is the one in which the mean term is greater than

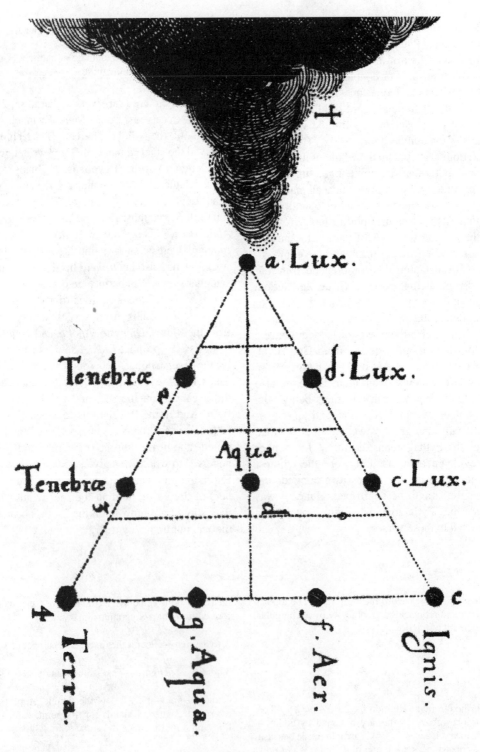

The Tetractys

from *Philosophia sacra et vere Christiana Seu Meterorologia Cosmica* by Robert Fludd (Frankfurt, 1626)

The Scale of the Number of Four

In the Original World, whence the Law of Providence	יהוה				The name of God with four letters
In the Intellectual World, whence the Fatal Law	Seraphim Cherubim Thrones	Domina-tions Powers Virtues	Principal-ities Archangels Angels	Innocents Martyrs Confessors	Four triplicities of intelligible hierarchies
	מיכאל Michael	רפאל Raphael	גבריאל Gabriel	אוריאל Uriel	Four angels ruling over the corners of the world
	שרף Seraph	כרוב Cherub	תרשיש Tharsis	אריאל Ariel	Four rulers of the elements
	The lion	The eagle	Man	A calf	Four consecrated animals
	Dan Asher Naphtali	Judah Issachar Zebulun	Manasseh Benjamin Ephraim	Reuben Simeon Gad	Four triplicities of the tribes of Israel
	Matthias Peter Jacob the Elder	Simon Bartholo-mew Matthew	John Philip James the Younger	Thaddeus Andrew Thomas	Four triplicities of the apostles
	Mark	John	Matthew	Luke	Four Evangelists

The Scale of the Number of Four (cont'd.)

	Aries Leo Sagittarius	Gemini Libra Aquarius	Cancer Scorpius Pisces	Taurus Virgo Capricornus	Four triplicities of signs
In the Celestial World, where is the Law of Nature	Mars, and the Sun	Jupiter, and Venus	Saturn, and Mercury	The fixed stars, and the Moon	The stars, and planets related to the elements
	Light	Diaphan-ousness	Agility	Solidity	Four qualities of the celestial elements
In the Elementary World, where the Law of Generation and Corruption is	אש Fire	רוח Air	מים Water	עפר Earth	Four elements
	Heat	Moisture	Cold	Dryness	Four qualities
	Summer	Spring	Winter	Autumn	Four seasons
	The East	The West	The North	The South	Four corners of the world
	Animals	Plants	Metals	Stones	Four perfect kinds of mixed bodies
	Walking	Flying	Swimming	Creeping	Four kinds of animals
	Seeds	Flowers	Leaves	Roots	What answer the elements, in plants
	Gold, and Iron	Copper, and Tin	Quick-silver	Lead, and Silver	What, in metals
	Bright, and burning	Light, and transparent	Clear, and congealed	Heavy, and dark	What, in stones

The Scale of the Number of Four (cont'd.)

	The Mind	The Spirit	The Soul	The Body	Four elements of Man
	Intellect	Reason	Phantasy	Sense	Four powers of the soul
	Faith	Science	Opinion	Experience	Four judiciary powers
	Justice	Temperance	Prudence	Fortitude	Four moral virtues
In the Lesser World, viz. Man, from whom is the Law of Prudence	Sight	Hearing	Taste, and smell	Touch	The senses answering to the elements
	Spirit	Flesh	Humours	Bones	Four elements of man's body
	Animal	Vital	Generative	Natural	A fourfold spirit
	Choler	Blood	Phlegm	Melancholy	Four humours
	Violence	Nimble-ness	Dullness	Slowness	Four manners of complexion
In the Infernal World, where is the Law of Wrath, and Punishment	סאמל Samael	אזאזל Azazel	עזאל Azael	מהזאל Mahazael	Four Princes of Devils, offensive in the elements
	Phlegethon	Cocytus	Styx	Acheron	Four infernal rivers
	Oriens	Paymon	Egyn	Amaymon	Four Princes of Spirits, upon the four angles of the world

one extreme and is less than the other by the same number, as in the proportion 3, 2, 1. In fact, the number 2 is greater than 1 by one unit and is less than 3 by one unit. ... The geometric mean, also called the proportion proper, is the one in which the mean term is greater than one extreme and is less than the other by a multiple or superpartial ratio (of the first term to the second or of the second to the third), as in the proportion 1, 2, 4. Four is indeed the double of 2, and 2 is the double of the unit, and likewise, the difference 2 – 1 is 1, and the difference 4 – 2 is 2. These numbers, compared with one another, are thus in double ratio. (Theon 2.55–6 [Lawlor, 76])

6. *one to one*—1 : 2, where 2 is 1 more than 1.

7. *two to two*—2 : 4, where 4 is 2 more than 2.

8. *great name*—Tetragrammaton, specifically the Hebrew written form יהוה.

9. *Jovis*—Jove, the Roman Zeus, father of the gods.

10. *fountain of nature*—See the Pythagorean oath, note 18 below.

11. *four corners*—Respectively, the positions of the sun at sunrise, sunset, noon, and midnight.

12. *four triplicities*—See table at end of chapter.

13. *four rivers of Paradise*—Pison, Gihon, Hiddekel, and Euphrates. See Genesis 2:10–4.

14. *constituting*—By addition. See note 1 above.

15. *odd in it*—See note 11, ch. VI, bk. II.

16. *four strings*—The cithara, a kind of simple harp originally strung with four strings, to the accompaniment of which was sung the "tetrachordal chant," as Euclid calls it.

17. *Pythagorean diagram*—

Tthe quaternary, 1, 2, 3, 4, includes all the consonances, since it contains those of the fourth, the fifth, the octave, the octave and fifth, and the double octave, which are sesquitertian, sesquialter, double, triple and quadruple ratios (that is to say, 4/3, 3/2, 2, 3 and 4)" (Theon 2.12a [Lawlor, 39]).

18. *Pythagoreans' oath*—"I swear it by the one who in our hearts engraved the sacred Tetrad, symbol immense and pure, Source of Nature and model of the Gods" *(Golden Verses of Pythagoras,* trans. Fabre d' Olivet [1813] [New York:Weiser, 1975], 7 and 112). Theon gives the formula: "I swear by the one who has bestowed the tetraktys to the coming generations, source of eternal nature, into our souls" (Theon 2.38[Lawlor, 62]). Notice that in these versions, the oath is taken on the bestower of the tetractys, whereas in the version of Agrippa, the oath is placed on the tetractys itself. D'Olivet, Theon, and indeed Thomas Taylor held the opinion that the oath refers to Pythagoras when it speaks of the bestower, but I am not so certain this is so.

19. *four Evangelists*—Matthew, Mark, Luke and John.

20. *chiefest name of God*—יהוה.

21. *Thet*—Perhaps Tet is intended, a symbol in the shape of a pillar representing the tree in which the body of Osiris had been concealed by Isis. The setting up of the tet as Busiris was a ceremonial reconstruction of the severed members of Osiris, and in Busiris, Osiris was called Tet (Budge 1904, 2:139). However, in the Latin *Opera* the form Theut is given, so Theutus, or Thoth, seems more likely.

22. *Alla*—Allah.

23. *Sire*—Sire, or Soru, from the Persian *kohr,* signifying the Sun. The title was assumed by the founder of the Persian empire, Cyrus, whose real name was Kobad.

24. $\Theta\epsilon\grave{o}\varsigma$—$\Theta\epsilon\acute{o}\varsigma$: ThEOS.

25. *Esar*—Aesar, a collective name for the Etruscan gods, as it was (Aesir) for the Norse gods.

26. *Orpheus his divinity*—The earliest account of the Greek gods is given by Hesiod in his *Theogony* around the 8th century BC. From about the 6th century BC to the time of Christ a separate set of myths grew up within the Orphic mystery religion. This was never as popular as that of Hesiod.

27. *four horses*—The horse was sacred to Neptune (Poseidon), and horse races were held in his honor. In the Orphic hymn to Neptune mention is made of the horses of the god, but they are not numbered: "Thee I invoke, whose steeds the foam divide" *(Hymns of Orpheus* 16, trans. Thomas Taylor. In *Thomas Taylor the Platonist: Selected Writings,* ed. Kathleen Raine and George Mills Harper [Princeton: Princeton University Press, 1969], 232). However, the chariot of the sun is drawn by four horses: "With sounding whip four fiery steeds you guide ..." (ibid. 7 [Taylor,

219]. Also the chariot of Pluto has four steeds: "Drawn in a four-yok'd car with loosen'd reins ..." (ibid. 17 [Taylor, 233]).

28. *divine furies*—The divine inspired madness of the Muses was various forms of artistic expression; of Dionysus the murderous fury of the Bacchiadae; of Apollo the power of true prophecy; of Venus unbridled lust.

29. *four beasts*—Ezekiel 1:10.

30. *four Cherubims*—Ezekiel 1:21.

31. *in Daniel*—Daniel 7:2–7.

32. *full of eyes*—Revelation 4:6–7.

33. *four angels*—Revelation 7:1.

CHAPTER VIII

Of the number five, and the scale thereof.

The number five is of no small force, for it consists of the first even, and the first odd, as of a female, and male: for an odd number is the male, and the even the female. Whence arithmeticians call that the Father, and this the Mother.[1] Therefore the number five is of no small perfection, or virtue, which proceeds from the mixtion of these numbers: it is also the just middle of the universal number, viz. ten. For if you divide the number ten, there will be nine and one, or eight and two, or seven and three, or six and four, and every collection makes the number ten, and the exact middle always is the number five, and it's equidistant; and therefore it is called by the Pythagoreans the number of wedlock,[2] as also of justice,[3] because it divides the number ten in an even scale.

There be five senses in man, sight, hearing, smelling, tasting, and touching: five powers in the soul, vegetative, sensitive, concupiscible, irascible, rational: five fingers of the hand: five wandering planets in the heavens, according to which there are fivefold terms[4] in every sign. In elements there are five kinds of mixed bodies, viz. stones, metals, plants, plant-animals, animals; and so many kinds of animals, as men, four-footed beasts, creeping, swimming, flying. And there are five kinds by which all things are made of God, viz. essence, the same,[5] another,[6] sense, motion.

The swallow brings forth but five young, which she feeds with equity, beginning with the eldest, and so the rest, according to their age.

Also this number hath great power in expiations: for in holy things it drives away devils. In natural things, it expels poisons. It is also called the number of fortunateness, and favour, and it is the seal of the Holy Ghost, and a bond that binds all things, and the number of the cross,[7] yea eminent with the principal wounds[8] of Christ, whereof he vouchsafed to keep the scars in his glorified body. The heathen philosophers did dedicate it as sacred to *Mercury*,[9] esteeming the virtue of it to be so much more excellent than the number four, by how much a living thing is more excellent than a thing without life.[10]

For in this number the father *Noah* found favour with God, and was preserved in the flood of waters.[11] In the virtue of this number *Abraham*,[12] being an hundred years old, begat a son of *Sarah*, being ninety years old, and a barren woman, and past child bearing, and grew up to be a great people.

Hence in time of grace the name of divine omnipotency is called upon with five letters. For in time of nature the name of God was called upon with three letters, שׁדי *Sadai*:[13] in time of the Law, the ineffable name of God was expressed with four letters, יהוה, instead of which the Hebrews express אדני *Adonai*: in time of grace the ineffable name of God was with five letters, יהשוה, *Ihesu*,[14] which is called upon with no less mystery than that of three letters, ישׁו.[15]

The Scale of the Number of Five

In the Exemplary World	אליון Elion / אלהים Elohim					The names of God with five letters
	יהשוה Jhesuh					The name of Christ with five letters
In the Intellectual World	Spirits of the first hierarchy, called Gods, or the Sons of God	Spirits of the second hierarchy, called Intelligences	Spirits of the third hierarchy, called Angels which are sent	Souls of celestial bodies	Heroes, or Blessed Souls	Five Intelligible Substances
In the Celestial World	Saturn	Jupiter	Mars	Venus	Mercury	Five wandering stars, lords of the terms
In the Elementary World	Water	Air	Fire	Earth	A mixed body	Five kinds of corruptible things
	Animal	Plant	Metal	Stone	Plant-animal	Fives kinds of mixed bodies
In the Lesser World	Taste	Hearing	Seeing	Touching	Smelling	Five senses
In the Infernal World	Deadly bitterness	Horrible howling	Terrible darkness	Unquenchable heat	A piercing stink	Five corporeal elements

Notes—Chapter VIII

1. *this the Mother*—Masculine 3 and feminine 2.

2. *number of wedlock*—Theon says that 6 is the number of wedlock, because it is a perfect number, equal to the sum of its parts (1 + 2 + 3 = 6), explaining: "This is why it is called that of marriage, because the task of marriage produces children similar to their parents" (Theon 2.45 [Lawlor, 67–8]). Since 5 is produced by the addition of 2 and 3, while 6 is produced by the multiplication of 2 and 3, it seems to me that 5 might be called the number of love, or union, whereas 6 is the number of generation, because multiplication yields more than the sum of its parts.

3. *of justice*—

> The Pythagoreans call the pentad providence and justice, because it equalizes things unequal, justice being a medium between excess and defect, just as 5 is the middle of the numbers that are equally distant from it on both sides as far as the decad, some of which it surpasses, and by others is surpassed, as may be seen in the following arrangement:

> | | | |
> |---|---|---|
> | 1. | 4. | 7. |
> | 2. | 5. | 8. |
> | 3. | 6. | 9. |

> For here, as in the middle of the beam of a balance, 5 does not depart from the line of the equilibrium, while one scale is raised, and the other is depressed. (Thomas Taylor, *Theoretic Arithmetic,* 194, quoted by Taylor in his note [pp. 240–1] to p. 98 of his translation of Iamblichus' *Life of Pythagoras*)

A virtually identical explanation of five as the number of justice occurs in Theon 2.44 (Lawlor, 67).

4. *fivefold terms*—Astrological terms are unequal divisions of the 30-degree arc of each sign of the zodiac into five parts, which are assigned to the planets Mercury, Venus, Mars, Jupiter and Saturn in varying orders. Ptolemy gives the Egyptian, the Chaldean, and his own system (which he pretends he has discovered in an ancient manuscript) of terms in the *Tetrabiblos* 20 and 21. Terms are not much used in modern astrology.

5. *the same*—Similarity.

6. *another*—Difference.

7. *number of the cross*—One for each of the four arms and one for the point of intersection.

8. *principal wounds*—Principal, because the sixth, caused by the thorns of Christ's crown, is not included.

9. *sacred to Mercury*—Meursius in his *Denarius Pythagoricus,* which is based on the *Theological Arithmetic* of Nicomachus the Pythagorean and other Platonic philosophers, says that four is the number of Mercury. See Thomas Taylor's introduction to the *Hymns of Orpheus* (Raine and Harper, 202).

10. *thing without life*—Four signified the four inert elements, therefore the fifth number must be something beyond, something spiritual.

11. *flood of waters*—There were five in Noah's family. See Genesis 7:13.

12. *number Abraham*—This may refer to the breaking of bread between Abraham, his wife, and the three angels of God (Genesis 18:6), or to God's use of the name El Shaddi (אלשדי), a name of five letters, to describe himself when he proclaims the coming birth of Isaac (Genesis 17:1), or to God's changing of Abram's name (אברם) to Abraham (אברהם), increasing it to five letters by the addition of He (ה), the fifth letter of the Hebrew alphabet (Genesis 17:5).

13. *Sadai*—Now more commonly rendered Shaddi.

14. *Ihesu*—Usually rendered into English as Yeheshuah.

15. ישׁו—Jesu.

CHAPTER IX

Of the number six, and the scale thereof.

Six is the number of perfection, because it is the most perfect in nature, in the whole course of numbers, from one to ten, and it alone is so perfect, that in the collection of its parts it results the same, neither wanting, nor abounding. For if the parts thereof, viz. the middle, the third, and sixth part, which are three, two, one, be gathered together, they perfectly fill up the whole body of six, which perfection all other numbers want:[1] hence by the Pythagoreans it is said to be altogether applied to generation, and marriage,[2] and is called the scale of the world.

For the world is made of the number six, neither doth it abound, or is defective. Hence that is, because the world was finished by God the sixth day. For the sixth day[3] God saw all the things which he had made, and they were very good. Therefore the heaven, and the Earth, and all the host thereof were finished.

It is also called the number of man, because the sixth day man was created:[4] and it is also the number of our redemption, for the sixth day Christ suffered[5] for our redemption: whence there is a great affinity betwixt the number six and the cross, labour, and servitude: hence it is commanded in the Law, that in six days the work[6] is to be done, six days manna[7] is to be gathered, six years the ground[8] was to be sown, and that the Hebrew servant[9] should serve his master six years; six days the glory of the Lord appeared upon Mount Sinai,[10] covering it with a cloud: the Cherubims had six wings;[11] six circles in the firmament, arctic, antarctic, two tropics,[12] equinoctial,[13] and ecliptical;[14] six wandering planets, Saturn, Jupiter, Mars, Venus, Mercury, the Moon, running through the latitude of the Zodiac, on both sides of the ecliptic.

There are six substantial qualities in the elements,[15] viz. sharpness, thinness, motion, and the contrary to these, dullness, thickness, rest. There are six differences of position, upwards, downwards, before, behind, on the right side, on the left side. There are six natural offices, without which nothing can be, viz. magnitude, colour, figure, interval, standing, motion. Also a solid figure of any foursquare thing hath six superficies.[16] There are six tones of all harmony, viz. five tones, and two halftones, which make one tone, which is the sixth.

Notes—Chapter IX

1. *all other numbers want*—"That sacrifices also should be made to Venus on the sixth day, because this number is the first that partakes of every number, and, when divided in every possible way, receives the power of the numbers subtracted and of those that remain" (Iamblichus *Life of Pythagoras* 28 [Taylor, 81]). Commenting on this dictate of Pythagoras, Taylor says:

> Because 6 consists of 1, 2 and 3, the two

The Scale of the Number Six

							Names of Six Letters
In the Exemplary World		אל גבר El Gebor	אלהים Elohim				
In the Intelligible World	Seraphim	Cherubim	Thrones	Dominations	Powers	Virtues	Six orders of angels, which are not sent to inferiors
In the Celestial World	Saturn	Jupiter	Mars	Venus	Mercury	The Moon	Six planets wandering through the latitude of the Zodiac from the Ecliptic
In the Elemental World	Rest	Thinness	Sharpness	Dullness	Thickness	Motion	Six substantifical qualities of elements
In the Lesser World	Intellect	Memory	Sense	Motion	Life	Essence	Six degress of men
In the Infernal World	Acteus	Magalesius	Ormenus	Lycus	Nicon	Mimon	Six devils, the authors of all calamities

first of which are the principles of all number, and also because 2 and 3 are the first even and odd, which are the sources of all the species of numbers; the number 6 may be said to partake of every number. In what Iamblichus afterwards adds, I suppose he alludes to 6 being a perfect number and therefore equal to all its parts. (ibid., 240)

2. *and marriage*—See note 2, ch. VIII, bk. II.

3. *sixth day*—Genesis 1:31.

4. *man was created*—Genesis 1:27.

5. *Christ suffered*—Mark 15:42, Luke 23:54, John 19:31.

6. *the work*—Exodus 20:9.

7. *manna*—Exodus 16:5.

8. *the ground*—Exodus 23:10.

9. *Hebrew servant*—Exodus 21:2.

10. *upon Mount Sinai*—Exodus 24:16.

11. *six wings*—Revelation 4:8.

12. *two tropics*—Tropic of Cancer; Tropic of Capricorn.

13. *equinoctial*—The equator.

14. *ecliptical*—The plane passing through the center of the Earth and defined by the apparent orbit of the Sun. The ecliptic.

15. *in the elements*—See Plato's *Timaeus* 61d–63d; also Appendix III.

16. *six superficies*—A cube has six sides.

17. *six tones*—On the five tones expressed in the quarternary, see note 17, ch. VII, bk. II. The fourth interval is composed of two tones and an excess, or remainder (leimma); the fifth, of three tones and a leimma. On this remainder Theon writes :

> The half-tone is not designated as such because it is the half of the tone in the way that the half-cubit is the half division of the cubit as maintained by Aristoxenes; but because it is a musical interval less than the tone, in the same manner that we call certain letters demi-vowels, not because half of a sound is indicated, but because it does not completely compose the sound itself. It can actually be demonstrated that the tone, considered in the sesquioctave ratio (9/8), cannot be divided into two equal parts, any more than can any other sesquipartial, since 9 is not divisible by 2. (Theon 2.8 [Lawlor, 36])

For Theon's proof, see 2.16, where he adds: "With regard to the ideal tone, one might conceive that it could be divided into two equal parts" (Lawlor, 47).

CHAPTER X

Of the number seven, and the scale thereof.

The number seven is of various, and manifold power, for it consists of one, and six, or of two, and five, or of three, and four, and it hath a unity, as it were the coupling together of two threes: whence if we consider the several parts thereof, and the joining together of them, without doubt we shall confess that it is as well by the joining together of the parts thereof, as by its fullness apart, most full of all majesty.

And the Pythagoreans call it the vehiculum of man's life, which it doth not receive from its parts so, as it perfects by its proper right of the whole, for it contains body, and soul, for the body consists of four elements, and is endowed with four qualities: also the number three respects the soul, by reason of its threefold power, viz. rational, irascible, and concupiscible. The number seven therefore, because it consists of three, and four, joins the soul to the body, and the virtue of this number relates to the generation of men, and it causeth man to be received, formed, brought forth, nourished, live, and indeed altogether subsist.

For when the genital seed is received in the womb of the woman, if it remain there seven hours after the effusion of it, it is certain that it will abide there for good: then the first seven days it is coagulated, and is fit to receive the shape of a man: then it produceth mature infants, which are called infants of the seventh month, i.e. because they are born the seventh month.[1] After the birth, the seventh hour tries whether it will live or no: for that which shall bear the breath of the air after that hour is conceived will live.

After seven days it casts off the relics of the navel. After twice seven days its sight begins to move after the light. In the third seventh it turns its eyes, and whole face freely.

After seven months it breeds teeth:[2] after the second seventh month it sits without fear of falling: after the third seventh month it begins to speak: after the fourth seventh month it stands strongly, and walks: after the fifth seventh month it begins to refrain from sucking its nurse.

After seven years its first teeth fall, and new are bred fitter for harder meat, and its speech is perfected: after the second seventh year boys wax ripe,[3] and then is a beginning of generation: at the third seventh year they grow to be men in stature, and begin to be hairy,[4] and become able, and strong for generation: at the fourth seventh year they begin to barnish,[5] and cease to grow taller:[6] in the fifth seventh year they attain to the perfection of their strength: the sixth seventh year they keep their strength: the seventh seventh year they attain to their utmost discretion, and wisdom, and the perfect age of men. But when they come to the tenth seventh year, where the number seven is taken for a complete number, then they come to the common term of life, the prophet saying,[7] our age is seventy years.

The utmost height of man's body is seven feet. There are also seven degrees in the body, which complete the dimension of its altitude from the bottom to the top, viz. marrow, bone, nerve, vein, artery, flesh, skin. There are seven, which by the Greeks are called black members,[8] the tongue, the heart, the lungs, the liver, the spleen, and two kidneys. There are also seven principal parts of the body, the head, the breast, the hands, the feet, and the privy members.

It is manifest concerning breath, and meat, that without drawing of the breath the life doth not endure above seven hours: and they that are starved with famine, live not above seven days.[9] The veins also, and arteries (as physicians say) are moved by the seventh number. Also judgements in diseases[10] are made with greater manifestation upon the seventh days, which physicians call critical, i.e. judicial.

Also of seven portions God creates the soul, as divine *Plato* witnesseth in Timaeus.[11] The soul also receives the body by seven degrees. All difference of voices proceeds to the seventh degree, after which there is the same revolution.[12] Again, there are seven modulations[13] of the voices, diatonus, semiditonus, diatessaron, diapente with a tone, diapente with a halftone, and diapason.

There is also in celestials a most potent power of the number seven. For seeing there are four corners of the heaven diametrically looking one towards the other, which indeed is accounted a most full, and powerful aspect,[14] and consists of the number seven. For it is made from the seventh sign,[15] and makes a cross,[16] the most powerful figure of all, of which we shall speak in its due place. But this you must not be ignorant of, that the number seven hath a great communion with the cross.

By the same radiation, and number the solstice is distant from winter, and the winter equinoctium from the summer, all which are done by seven signs.[17] There are also seven circles[18] in the heaven, according to the longitudes of the axel tree.[19] There are seven stars about the Arctic Pole, greater, and lesser, called Charles' Wain,[20] also seven stars called the Pleiades, and seven planets, according to those seven days, constituting a week.

The Moon is the seventh of the planets and next to us, observing this number more than the rest, this number dispensing the motion, and light thereof. For in twenty-eight days it runs round the compass of the whole Zodiac, which number of days, the number seven, with its seven terms, viz. from one to seven, doth make, and fill up, as much as the several numbers, by adding to the antecedents, and makes four times seven days, in which the Moon runs through, and about all the longitude, and latitude of the Zodiac by measuring, and measuring again:[21] with the like seven of days it dispenseth its light, by changing it; for the first seven days unto the middle as it were of the divided world, it increaseth; the second seven days it fills its whole orb with light; the third by discreasing is again contracted into a divided orb; but after the fourth seven days, it is renewed with the last diminution of its light,[22] and by the same seven of days it disposeth the increase, and decrease of the sea, for in the first seven of the increase of the Moon, it is by little lessened; in the second by degrees increased: but the third is like the first, and the fourth doth the same as the second.[23]

It is also applied to Saturn, which ascending from the lower, is the seventh planet, which betokens rest, to which the seventh day[24] is ascribed, which signifies the seven thousandth, wherein (as *John* witnesseth)[25] the dragon, which is the Devil, and Satan, being bound, men shall be quiet, and lead a peaceable life.

Moreover the Pythagoreans call seven the number of virginity, because the first is that which is neither generated, or generates,[26] neither can it be divided into two equal parts, so as to be generated of another number repeated, or being doubled to bring forth any other number of itself, which is contained within the bounds of the number ten, which is manifestly the first bound of numbers, and therefore they dedicate the number seven to *Pallas*.[27]

It hath also in religion most potent signs of its esteem, and it is called the number of an oath. Hence amongst the Hebrews to swear is called septenare[28] i.e. to protect by seven. So *Abraham,* when he made a covenant with *Abimelech,* appointed seven ewe lambs[29] for a testimony. It is also called the number of blessedness, or of rest, whence that:

O thrice, and four times blessed!

viz. in soul, and body. The seventh day the Creator rested[30] from his work, wherefore this day was by *Moses* called the Sabbath[31] i.e. the day of rest; hence it was that Christ rested the seventh day in the grave.[32] Also this number hath a great communion with the cross, as is above showed, as also with Christ. For in Christ is all our blessedness, rest, and felicity.

Besides, it is most convenient in purifications. Whence *Apuleius* saith,[33] and I put myself forthwith into the bath of the sea, to be purified, and put my head seven times under the waves. And the leprous person that was to be cleansed, was sprinkled seven times with the blood of a sparrow:[34] and *Elisha* the prophet, as it is written in the Second Book of the Kings, saith unto the leprous person; go and wash thyself seven times in Jordan, and thy flesh shall be made whole, and thou shalt be cleansed, and it follows a little after, and he washed himself seven times in Jordan, according to the prophet's saying, and he was cleansed.[35]

Also it is a number of repentance, and remission: hence was ordained the seventh year's repentance for every sin, according to the opinion of the wise man, saying, and upon every sinner sevenfold:[36] also the seventh year there were granted remissions, and after full seven years there was given a full remission, as is read in Leviticus.[37] And Christ with seven petitions[38] finished his speech of our satisfaction: hence also it is called the number of liberty, because the seventh year the Hebrew servant[39] did challenge liberty for himself. It is also most suitable to divine praises. Whence the prophet saith, seven times a day do I praise thee, because of thy righteous judgements.[40]

It is moreover called the number of revenge, as saith the Scripture, and *Cain* shall be revenged sevenfold.[41] And the psalmist saith, render unto our neighbours sevenfold into their bosom, their reproach.[42] Hence there are seven wickednesses,[43] as saith *Solomon,* and seven wickeder spirits[44] taken, are read of in the Gospel. It signifies also the time of the present circle,[45] because it is finished in the space of seven days.

Also it is consecrated to the Holy Ghost, which the prophet *Isaiah* describes to be sevenfold,[46] according to his gifts,viz. the spirit of wisdom, and understanding, the spirit of counsel, and strength, the spirit of knowledge, and holiness, and the spirit of the fear of the Lord, which we read in Zechariah to be the seven eyes of God.[47]

There are also seven angels, spirits standing in the presence of God, as is read in Tobias,[48] and in Revelation;[49] seven lamps[50] did burn before the throne of God, and seven golden candlesticks,[51] and in the middle thereof was one like to the Son of Man, and he had in his right hand seven stars.[52] Also there were seven spirits before the throne of God, and seven angels stood before the throne, and there were given to them seven trumpets.[53] And he saw a lamb having seven horns, and seven eyes,[54] and he saw the book sealed with seven seals,[55] and when the seventh seal was opened, there was made silence in heaven.[56]

Now by all what hath been said, it is apparent that the number seven, amongst the other numbers, may deservedly be said to be most full of all efficacy. Moreover, the number seven hath great conformity with the number twelve; for as three and four makes seven, so thrice four make twelve, which are the numbers of the celestial planets, and signs, resulting from the same root, and by the number four of the nature of inferior things.

There is also in sacred writ a very great observance of this number, before all others, and many, and very great are the mysteries thereof; many we have decreed to reckon up here, repeating them out of holy writ, by which it will easily appear, that the number seven doth signify a certain fullness of sacred mysteries.

For we read in Genesis, that the seventh was the day of the rest of the Lord;[57] and *Enoch,* a pious, holy man, was the seventh from *Adam,*[58] and that there was another seventh man from Adam, a wicked man, by name *Lamech,*[59] that had two wives; and that the sin of *Cain*[60] should be abolished the seventh generation: as it is written, *Cain* shall be punished sevenfold: and he that shall slay *Cain,* shall be revenged sevenfold, to which the master of the History[61] collects, that there were seven sins of *Cain.* Also of all clean beasts seven,[62] and seven were brought into the ark, as also of fowls: and after seven days the Lord rained upon the Earth, and upon the seventh day the fountains of the deep[63] were broken up, and the waters covered the Earth. Also *Abraham* gave to *Abimelech* seven ewe lambs:[64] and *Jacob* served seven years for *Leah,* and seven more for *Rachael:*[65] and seven days the people of Israel bewailed the death of *Jacob.*[66] Moreover, we read in the same place, of seven kine, and seven ears of corn, seven years of plenty, and seven years of scarcity.[67]

And in Exodus, the sabbath of sabbaths,[68] the holy rest to the Lord, is commanded to be on the seventh day. Also on the seventh day *Moses* ceased to pray.[69] On the seventh day there shall be a solemnity of the Lord:[70] the seventh year the servant shall go out free:[71] seven days let the calf, and the lamb be without its dam:[72] the seventh year let the ground that hath been sown six years, be at rest:[73] the seventh day shall be a holy sabbath, and a rest: the seventh day, because it is the Sabbath, shall be called holy.[74]

In Leviticus the seventh day[75] also shall be more observed, and be more holy: and the first day of the seventh month shall be a sabbath of memorial.[76] Seven days shall the sacrifices be offered to the Lord,[77] seven days shall the holy days of the Lord be celebrated, seven days in a year everlastingly in the generations.[78] In the seventh month you shall celebrate feasts, and shall dwell in the tabernacles seven days:[79] seven times he shall sprinkle himself before the Lord, that hath dipped his finger in blood:[80] he that is cleansed from the leprosy, shall dip seven times in the blood of a sparrow:[81] seven days shall she be washed with running water, that is menstruous:[82] seven times he shall dip his finger in the blood of a bullock:[83] seven times I will smite you for your sins.[84]

In Deuteronomy seven people possessed the land of promise.[85] There is also read of a seventh year of remission,[86] and seven candles[87] set up on the south side of the candlesticks.

And in Numbers it is read, that the sons of Israel offered up seven ewe lambs[88] without spot, and that seven days they did eat unleavened bread,[89] and that sin was expiated with seven lambs and a goat,[90] and that the seventh day was celebrated, and holy,[91] and the first day[92] of the seventh month was observed, and kept holy, and the seventh month of the feast of tabernacles,[93] and seven calves[94] were offered on the seventh day, and *Baalam*[95] erected seven altars;[95] seven days *Mary* the sister of *Aaron* went forth leprous[96] out of the camp, seven days he that touched a dead carcass[97] was unclean.

And in Joshua seven priests carried the ark of the covenant before the host, and seven days they went round the cities, and seven trumpets were carried by the seven priests, and on the seventh day the seven priests sounded the trumpets.[98]

And in the book of Judges, *Abessa*[99] reigned in Israel seven years, *Sampson*[100] kept his nuptials seven days and the seventh day he put forth a riddle to his wife, he was bound with seven green withes,[101] seven locks of his head were shaved off,[102] seven years were the children of Israel oppressed by the king of Maden.[103]

And in the books of the Kings, *Elias* prayed seven times, and at the seventh time, behold a little cloud!:[104] seven days the children of Israel pitched over against the Syrians, and in the seventh day the battle was joined:[105] seven years famine was threatened to *David* for the people's murmuring;[106] and seven times the child sneezed, that was raised by *Elisha;*[107] and seven men were crucified[108] together in the days of the first harvest. *Naaman* was made clean with seven washings by *Elisha;*[109] the seventh month *Golias* was slain.[110]

And in Hester we read, that the King of Persia had seven eunuchs:[111] and in Tobias seven men were coupled with *Sara*[112] the daughter of *Raguel:* and in Daniel *Nebuchadnezzar's* furnace was heated seven times hotter[113] than it was used to be, and seven lions[114] were in the den, and the seventh day came *Nebuchadnezzar.*

In the book of Job there is made mention of seven sons of *Job,*[115] and seven days and nights

Job's friends[116] sat with him on the earth; and in the same place, in seven troubles[117] no evil shall touch thee.

In Ezra we read of *Artaxerxes* his seven counsellors:[118] and in the same place the trumpet sounded:[119] the seventh month of the feast of tabernacles were in *Ezra's* time,[120] whilst the children of Israel were in the cities: and on the first day of the seventh month *Esdras* read the Law[121] to the people.

And in the Psalms *David* praised the Lord[122] seven times in a day: silver is tried seven times;[123] and he renders to our neighbours sevenfold into their bosoms.[124]

And *Solomon* saith, that wisdom hath hewn herself seven pillars;[125] seven men[126] that can render a reason, seven abominations[127] which the Lord abhors, seven abominations in the heart of an enemy,[128] seven overseers, seven eyes beholding.

Isaiah numbers up seven gifts of the Holy Ghost,[129] and seven women shall take hold on a man.[130]

And in Jeremiah, she that hath born seven,[131] languisheth, she hath given up the ghost.

In Ezekiel, the prophet continued sad for seven days.[132]

In Zechariah seven lamps,[133] and seven pipes to those seven lamps, and seven eyes running to and fro throughout the whole Earth,[134] and seven eyes upon one stone,[135] and the fast of the seven days is turned into joy.[136]

And in Micah, seven shepherds[137] are raised against the Assyrians.

Also in the Gospel we read of seven blessednesses,[138] and seven virtues,[139] to which seven vices[140] are opposed; seven petitions[141] of the Lord's prayer, seven words of Christ[142] upon the cross, seven words of the blessed *Virgin Mary,*[143] seven loaves[144] distributed by the Lord, seven baskets[145] of fragments, seven brothers[146] having one wife, seven disciples[147] of the Lord that were fishers, seven waterpots[148] in Cana of Galilee, seven woes[149] which the Lord threatens to the hypocrites, seven devils[150] cast out of the unclean woman, and seven wickeder devils[151] taken in after that which was

cast out. Also seven years Christ was fled into Egypt;[152] and the seventh hour the fever left the governor's son.[153]

And in the Canonical Epistles, *James* describes seven degrees of wisdom,[154] and *Peter* seven degrees of virtues.[155]

And in the Acts are reckoned seven deacons,[156] and seven disciples[157] chosen by the apostles.

Also in the Revelations there are many mysteries of this number: for there we read of seven candlesticks,[158] seven stars,[159] seven crowns,[160] seven churches,[161] seven spirits before the throne,[162] seven rivers of Egypt,[163] seven seals,[164] seven marks,[165] seven horns, seven eyes,[166] seven spirits of God,[167] seven angels with seven trumpets,[168] seven horns of the dragon,[169] seven heads of the dragon, who had seven diadems:[170] also seven plagues,[171] and seven vials,[172] which were given to one of the seven angels,[173] seven heads of the scarlet beast,[174] seven mountains,[175] and seven kings[176] sitting upon them, and seven thunders[177] uttered their voices.

Moreover this number hath much power, as in natural, so in sacred, ceremonial, and also in other things: therefore the seven days are related hither, also the seven planets, the seven stars called Pleiades, the seven ages of the world,[178] the seven changes of man,[179] the seven liberal arts,[180] and so many mechanic, and so many forbidden, seven colours,[181] seven metals,[182] seven holes in the head of a man,[183] seven pair of nerves,[184] seven mountains[185] in the city of Rome, seven Roman kings,[186] seven civil wars, seven wise men in the time of *Jeremiah* the prophet, and seven wise men of Greece.[187] Also Rome did burn seven days by *Nero.*[188] By seven kings were slain ten thousand martyrs.

There were Seven Sleepers, seven principal churches of Rome, and so many monasteries did *Gregory* build: so many sons Saint *Felicity* brought forth: there were seven electors of the Empire[189] appointed, and seven solemn acts in crowning the Emperor;[190] the laws in the Testament require seven witnesses,[191] there are seven civil punishments, and seven canonical, and seven canonical hours,[192] the priest makes seven obeisances in the mass; seven sacraments, and seven orders of the clergy,[193] and a boy of seven years may be ordained by the lesser, and may obtain a benefice *fine cura*.[194]

There are seven penitential psalms,[195] and seven commands of the second table,[196] and seven hours were *Adam* and *Eve* in Paradise, and there were seven men foretold by an angel before they were born, viz. *Ismael, Isaac, Sampson, Jeremiah, John Baptist, James* the brother of the Lord, and Christ *Jesus*.

Lastly, this number is most potent of all, as in good, so evil; of this *Livy*,[197] the most ancient poet sang:

The seventh light is come, and then all
  things
To absolve the father of all light begins,
The seventh's of all things original,
The first seventh, seventh seven we call
Perfect, with wandering stars the heaven's
  'volved,
And with as many circles is round rolled.

Notes—Chapter X

1. *seventh month*—"It is also in the seventh month that the foetus can be born living" (Theon 2.46 [Lawlor, 69]).

2. *breeds teeth*—"Children develop teeth starting from the seventh month after birth, and fully produce their teeth in seven years …" (ibid.). See also Pliny 7.15 (Bostock and Riley, 2:153).

3. *boys wax ripe*—"… the semen and puberty make their appearance at the age of fourteen …" (Theon 2.46 [Lawlor, 69]).

4. *to be hairy*—"… it is in the third period, i.e. at the age of twenty-one, that the beard begins to grow. It is then also that a man acquires his full height …" (ibid.).

5. *barnish*—Burnish: to grow stout.

6. *cease to grow taller*—"… it is only in the fourth period, i.e. at twenty-eight, that he acquires his stoutness" (ibid.).

7. *prophet saying*—David in Psalms 90:10.

8. *black members*—"There are seven viscera, the tongue, the heart, the lungs, the liver, the spleen and the two kidneys" (Theon 2.46 [Lawlor, 69]).

9. *above seven*—It is perhaps unnecessary to add that these estimates of endurance are wildly inaccurate. Seven minutes without air would kill most people, and it has, unfortunately, been demonstrated through experience that man can live more than a month without food, though not without water, which is required after a week or so.

10. *judgements in diseases*—"Seven days are needed to diagnose illness, and in all periodic fevers, even in three and four-day fevers, the seventh day is always the most serious" (ibid.).

11. *in Timaeus*—

And he proceeded to divide after this manner. First of all, he took away one part of the whole [1], and then he separated a second part which was double the first [2], and then he took away a third part which was half as much again as the second and three times as much as the first [3], and then he took a fourth part which was twice as much as the second [4], and a fifth part which was three times the third [9], and a sixth part which was eight times the first [8], and a seventh part which was twenty-seven times the first [27]. (Plato *Timaeus* 35b [Hamilton and Cairns, 1165)

12. *same revolution*—In music, every eighth note is repeated, forming the octave, which is the same tone separated by a ratio 2:1.

13. *seven modulations*—Ditone: major third; semiditone: imperfect third; diatessaron: fourth; diapente: fifth; diapason: octave.

14. *powerful aspect*—Called in astrology the aspect of opposition, when two planets or significant points are 180 degrees apart, resulting in maximum tension and polarization between them.

15. *seventh sign*—"From one solstice of the sun to the other there are seven months, and the planets are seven in number. Similarly seven months are counted from one equinox to the other" (Theon 2.46 [Lawlor, 69]). Bear in mind that the ancients began to count from the first element in a series, whereas we begin on the second. By modern reckoning there are only six signs between equinoxes and solstices.

The Scale of the Number Seven

World	Description	Saturn	Jupiter	Mars	Sun	Venus	Mercury	Moon
In the Original World	The name of God with seven letters	Ararita אראריתא — Asher Eheieh אשר אהיה						
In the Intelligible World	Seven angels which stand in the presence of God	Zaphkiel צפקיאל	Zadkiel צדקיאל	Camael כמאל	Raphael רפאל	Haniel האניאל	Michael מיכאל	Gabriel גבריאל
In the Celestial World	Seven planets	Saturn שבתאי	Jupiter צדק	Mars מאדים	The Sun שמש	Venus נוגה	Mercury כוכב	The Moon לבנה
	Seven birds of the planets	Lapwing	Eagle	Vulture	Swan	Dove	Stork	Owl
	Seven fish of the planets	Cuttlefish	Dolphin	Pike	Seacalf	Thymallus	Mullet	Seacat
In the Elementary World	Seven animals of the planets	Mole	Hart	Wolf	Lion	Goat	Ape	Cat
	Seven metals of the planets	Lead	Tin	Iron	Gold	Copper	Quicksilver	Silver
	Seven stones of the planets	Onyx	Sapphire	Diamond	Carbuncle	Emerald	Achates	Crystal

The Scale of the Number Seven (cont'd.)

In the Lesser World	Right foot	Head	Right hand	Heart	Privy members	Left hand	Left foot	Seven integral members distributed to the planets
	Right ear	Left ear	Right nostril	Right eye	Left nostril	Mouth	Left eye	Seven holes of the head distributed to the planets
In the Infernal World[198]	רדום Hell	צלמות The gates of death	דצלמות The shadow of death	באראשית The pit of destruction	טיטהיון The clay of death	אבדון Perdition	שאול The depth of the Earth	Seven habitations of infernals; which Rabbi Joseph of Castilia the Cabalist describes in the Garden of Nuts

16. *makes a cross*—The Grand Cross of astrology is formed when four planets or significant points such as the nodes of the Moon are at 90 degrees to each other, and is the constellation of maximum tension.

17. *seven signs*—Agrippa seems to be echoing Theon here (see note 15 above), but the wording is far from clear, and perhaps might better read: "By the same radiation, and number the summer solstice is distant from the winter, and the autumnal equinoctium from the spring, all which are done by seven signs."

18. *seven circles*—Since Agrippa speaks of longitude, he is presumably referring to the house circles of astrology, which define the houses of the zodiac. There are six of these that go round the Earth north to south, intersecting at the poles. It is not clear to me how Agrippa gets seven circles, unless it is through the same system of counting whereby he gets seven signs in 180 degrees (see note 15 above).

19. *axel tree*—Axis of the Earth, which in ancient times was considered to be the axis of the universe.

20. *Charles' Wain*—The constellation Ursa Major, which is formed of seven bright stars.

21. *measuring again*—$1 + 2 + 3 + 4 + 5 + 6 + 7 = 28$. The Moon crosses the plane of the ecliptic twice every revolution about the Earth. These intersections are called the nodes of the Moon. For 14 days the Moon is above the ecliptic, and for 14 days below it.

22. *of its light*—"The month is composed of four weeks (*four* times *seven* days); in the first week the moon appears divided in two; in the second it becomes full, in the third it is again divided, and in the fourth, it returns to meet the sun in order to begin a new month and to increase during the following week" (Theon 2.46 [Lawlor, 68]).

23. *same as the second*—The tides are highest during the full and new Moon because in these phases the Moon and Sun are aligned and their tidal forces compounded; during the waxing and waning phases, the Sun and Moon war against each other, and the tidal effect of the Sun cancels out a portion of the tidal effect of the Moon.

24. *seventh day*—Saturday is the Jewish sabbath.

25. *John witnesseth*—Revelation 20.

26. *generated, or generates*—

Among the numbers contained in the decad, some create and some are created, for example 4 multiplied by 2 creates 8, and is created by 2. Others are created but do not create, like 6 which is the product of 2 and 3, but which does not create any of the numbers in the decad. Others create but are not created, such as 3 and 5 which are not created by any combination of numbers, but which create: 3 produces 9, and multiplied by 2 produces 6, and 5 multiplied by 2 produces 10.

Seven is the only number which, multiplied by another number, creates none of the numbers in the decad, and which is not produced by the multiplication of any number. (Theon 2.46 [Lawlor, 68])

27. *Pallas*—

Another number of the decad, the number seven, is endowed with a remarkable property: it is the only one which does not give birth to any number contained in the decad and which is not born out of any of them, which fact moved the Pythagoreans to give it the name Athena, because this goddess was not born out of a mother and gave birth to none. (ibid.)

Pallas Athene sprang from the brow of Zeus asexually, and remained a virgin.

28. *septenare*—The Hebrew *saba,* from the root SBAa (שבע), "seven," one of two kinds of oath taken by Jews, the other being the *alah* (curse), which invokes the curse of God should the oath be violated.

29. *seven ewe lambs*—Genesis 21:29–31.

30. *Creator rested*—Genesis 2:2.

31. *called the Sabbath*—Exodus 20:8–11.

32. *in the grave*—Matthew 28:1.

33. *Apuleius saith*—"... I plunged my selfe seven times into the water of the Sea, which number of seven is conveniable and agreeable to holy and divine things, as the worthy and sage Philosopher Pythagoras hath declared" (Apuleius *The Golden Asse* 47).

34. *blood of a sparrow*—Leviticus 14:7. In the Bible the type of bird is not specified, but Rashi says: "Since plagues come from evil talk, which is the act of babbling words, consequently there were required for his purification birds which babble continually with chirping sounds" (Rashi 1949, 3:129).

35. *he was cleansed*—2 Kings 5:10–4.

36. *every sinner sevenfold*—the wiseman is Solomon. See Proverbs 6:31.

37. *in Leviticus*—Leviticus 25. Full seven years is 7 x 7.

38. *seven petitions*—Matthew 6:9–13.

39. *Hebrew servant*—See note 9, ch. IX, bk. II.

40. *righteous judgements*—Psalms 119:164.

41. *revenged sevenfold*—Genesis 4:15.

42. *their reproach*—Psalms 79:12.

43. *seven wickednesses*—Proverbs 6:16–9.

44. *wickeder spirits*—Matthew 12:45.

45. *present circle*—Week.

46. *to be sevenfold*—Isaiah 11:2. Presumably the holiness of the Spirit is indicated in the biblical phrase "of the Lord."

47. *seven of God*—Zechariah 4:10.

48. *in Tobias*—Apocryphal book of Tobit 12:15.

49. *in Revelation*—Revelation 8:2.

50. *seven lamps*—Revelation 4:5.

51. *golden candlesticks*—Revelation 1:12.

52. *seven stars*—Revelation 1:16.

53. *seven trumpets*—See note 49 above.

54. *seven eyes*—Revelation 5:6.

55. *seven seals*—Revelation 5:1.

56. *silence in heaven*—Revelation 8:1.

57. *rest of the Lord*—See note 30 above.

58. *seventh from Adam*—Genesis 5:24. Enoch was the sixth generation by modern reckoning.

59. *by name Lamech*—Genesis 4:19. Lamech was descended from Cain.

60. *sin of Cain*—Genesis 4:24.

61. *master of the History*—Perhaps this refers to Josephus *Antiquities of the Jews* 1.2.2.

62. *clean beasts seven*—Genesis 7:2–3.

63. *fountains of the deep*—Genesis 7:10–1.

64. *seven ewe lambs*—See note 29 above.

65. *for Rachael*—Genesis 29:18–28.

66. *death of Jacob*—Genesis 50:10.

67. *seven years of scarcity*—Genesis 41.

68. *sabbath of sabbaths*—The root of sabbath is SBTh (שבת), meaning "rest." Thus "the sabbath of rest"—Exodus 31:15 and 35:2—where שבתון indicates intensity, a great sabbath or solemn sabbath.

69. *Moses ceased to pray*—Exodus 24:16.

70. *solemnity of the Lord*—Exodus 31:15.

71. *go out free*—See note 9, ch. IX, bk. II.

72. *without its dam*—Exodus 22:30.

73. *be at rest*—Exodus 23:11.

74. *called holy*—See note 68 above.

75. *the seventh day*—Leviticus 23:8.

76. *sabbath of memorial*—Leviticus 23:24.

77. *offered to the Lord*—Leviticus 23:36.

78. *in the generations*—Leviticus 23:41.

79. *tabernacles seven days*—Leviticus 23:42.

80. *finger in blood*—Leviticus 4:6.

81. *blood of a sparrow*—See note 34 above.

82. *menstruous*—Leviticus 15:19, in the context of 15:13.

83. *blood of a bullock*—See note 80 above.

84. *for your sins*—Leviticus 26:18.

85. *land of promise*—Perhaps Deuteronomy 27:3, with reference to Joshua 18:6.

86. *year of remission*—Deuteronomy 15:1.

87. *seven candles*—This would seem to refer to Numbers 8:2.

88. *seven ewe lambs*—Numbers 28:11. But there is no mention here of ewes; in fact, Rashi says the lambs are male (Rashi 1949, 4:300). Agrippa may have been misled by Genesis 21:29, where the seven lambs are indeed ewes.

89. *unleavened bread*—Numbers 28:17.

90. *lambs and a goat*—Numbers 28:21–2.

91. *celebrated, and holy*—Numbers 28:25.

92. *first day*—Numbers 29:1.

93. *feast of tabernacles*—Numbers 29:12.

94. *seven calves*—Numbers 29:32. Young bullocks. See 29:17.

95. *seven altars*—Numbers 23:1.

96. *went forth leprous*—Miriam, in Numbers 12:14.

97. *dead carcass*—Numbers 19:11.

98. *sounded the trumpets*—Joshua 6:3–4.

99. *Abessa*—Abiezer, the clan of Gideon, which drove out Midian after Midian had ruled Israel seven years. See Judges 6:1, 11, 34. Agrippa's reference is confused.

100. *Sampson*—Judges 14:12, 17.

101. *seven green withes*—A withe is a green, flexible sapling used for binding or plaiting; willow wands. See Judges 16:8.

102. *shaved off*—Judges 16:19.

103. *king of Maden*—Midian. See note 99 above.

104. *little cloud*—I Kings 18:44.

105. *battle was joined*—I Kings 20:29.

106. *people's murmuring*—probably II Kings 8:1.

107. *raised by Elisha*—II Kings 4:35.

108. *seven men were crucified*—II Samuel 21:9.

109. *seven washings by Elisha*—II Kings 5:14.

110. *Golias was slain*—Gedaliah. II Kings 25:25.

111. *seven eunuchs*—Esther 1:10.

112. *coupled with Sara*—Tobit 3:8.

113. *seven times hotter*—Daniel 3:19.

114. *seven lions*—Daniel was cast into the den of lions by Darius (Daniel 6:16). The reference is to Daniel 14:31, 39. See the Knox translation—this chapter is not included in King James.

115. *seven sons of Job*—Job 1:2.

116. *Job's friends*—Job 2:13.

117. *seven troubles*—Job 5:19.

118. *seven counsellors*—Ezra 7:14.

119. *trumpet sounded*—Ezra 3:10; see also Nehemiah 12:35.

120. *Ezra's time*—Ezra 3:1, 4.

121. *read the Law*—Nehemiah 13:1.

122. *praised the Lord*—See note 40 above.

123. *tried seven times*—Psalms 12:6.

124. *into their bosoms*—Psalms 79:12.

125. *seven pillars*—Proverbs 9:1.

126. *seven men*—Proverbs 26:16.

127. *seven abominations*—See note 43 above.

128. *heart of an enemy*—Proverbs 26:25.

129. *Holy Ghost*—See note 46 above.

130. *hold on a man*—Isaiah 4:1.

131. *hath born seven*—Jeremiah 15:9.

132. *sad for seven days*—Ezekiel 3:15.

133. *seven lamps*—Zechariah 4:2.

134. *whole Earth*—See note 47 above.

135. *one stone*—Zechariah 3:9.

136. *turned into joy*—Zechariah 8:19.

137. *seven shepherds*—Micah 5:5.

138. *seven blessednesses*—Matthew 5: 3–11. But I count nine.

139. *seven virtues*—Matthew 19:18–21.

140. *seven vices*—Matthew 15:19.

141. *seven petitions*—See note 38 above.

142. *seven words of Christ*—Luke 23:46.

143. *Virgin Mary*—Perhaps John 2:5.

144. *seven loaves*—Matthew 15:36.

145. *seven baskets*—Matthew 15:37.

146. *seven brothers*—Matthew 22:25–6.

147. *seven disciples*—John 21:2.

148. *seven waterpots*—John 2:6. The pots were six.

149. *seven woes*—Matthew 23:13–29.

150. *seven devils*—Luke 8:2.

151. *seven wickeder devils*—See note 44 above.

152. *fled into Egypt*—Matthew 2:14–5.

153. *governor's son*—John 4:52.

154. *seven degrees of wisdom*—James 3:17.

155. *seven degrees of virtues*—II Peter 1:5–7.

156. *seven decons*—Acts 20:4.

157. *seven disciples*—Perhaps Acts 20:4.

158. *seven candlesticks*—See note 51 above.

159. *seven stars*—See note 52 above.

160. *seven crowns*—Revelation 12:3.

161. *seven churches*—Revelation 1:11.

162. *before the throne*—Revelation 1:4.

163. *seven rivers of Egypt*—Isaiah 11:15, not Revelation.

164. *seven seals*—See note 55 above.

165. *seven marks*—Perhaps Revelation 13:16.

166. *seven eyes*——See note 54 above.

167. *seven spirits of God*—See note 49 above.

168. *seven trumpets*—See note 53 above.

169. *horns of the dragon*—Revelation 12:3. But the horns are ten. Perhaps Agrippa has confused this passage with Revelation 5:6.

170. *seven diadems*—See note 160 above.

171. *seven plagues*—Revelation 15:1.

172. *seven vials*—Revelation 15:7.

173. *seven angels*—Revelation 17:1.

174. *scarlet beast*—Revelation 17:3.

175. *seven mountains*—Revelation 17:9.

176. *seven kings*—Revelation 17:10.

177. *seven thunders*—Revelation 10:4.

178. *seven ages of the world*—Hesiod gives five ages: (1) golden, (2) silver, (3) bronze, (4) heroic and (5) iron. Ovid omits the fourth age, perhaps because it offended his sense of poetic symmetry. Lucretius names three, which are the ones that have come down to modern times: (1) stone, (2) bronze, and (3) iron. The division of seven ages originated with Nennius, a Welsh historian who lived at the end of the 8th century, and wrote the *Historia Britanum*. They are: (1) Adam to Noah, (2) Noah to Abraham, (3) Abraham to David, (4) David to Daniel, (5) Daniel to John the Baptist, (6) John the Baptist to Judgement Day, (7) Second coming of Christ. On this subject, see Graves [1948] 1973, 266–8.

179. *seven changes of man*—

> His acts bring seven ages. At first the infant,
> Mewling and puking in the nurse's arms.
> And then the whining school-boy, with his satchel,
> And shining morning face, creeping like snail
> Unwillingly to school. And then the lover,
> Sighing like furnace, with a woeful ballad
> Made to his mistress' eyebrow. Then a soldier,
> Full of strange oaths, and bearded like a pard,
> Jealous in honour, sudden and quick in quarrel,
> Seeking the bubble reputation
> Even in the cannon's mouth. And then the justice,
> In fair round belly with good capon lin'd,
> With eyes severe, and beard of formal cut,
> Full of wise saws and modern instances;
> And so he plays his part. The sixth age shifts
> Into the lean and slipper'd pantaloon,
> With spectacles on nose and pouch on side,
> His youthful hose well sav'd, a world too wide
> For his shrunk shank; and his big manly voice,
> Turning again toward childish treble, pipes
> And whistles in his sound. Last scene of all,
> That ends this strange eventful history,
> Is second childishness and mere oblivion,
> Sans teeth, sans eyes, sans taste, sans everything.
> (Shakespeare *As You Like It* act 2, sc. 7, lines 143–66)

180. *seven liberal arts*—Descended from the nine *disciplinae* of Varro, the seven liberal arts were recognized by Augustine and Martianus Capella. In the Middle Ages they were divided into a *Trivium* of grammar, logic and rhetoric and a *Quadrivium* of music, arithmetic, geometry and astronomy.

181. *seven colours*—Black, white, red, green, yellow, blue, purple.

182. *seven metals*—See table at end of chapter.

183. *head of man*—See table at end of chapter.

184. *seven pairs of nerves*—The nerves were fixed at seven by Celsus in his *De Medicina,* written early in the first century. Actually there are 12 recognized pairs.

185. *seven mountains*—Rome is built on seven hills: (1) Mons Palatinus, (2) Mons Capitolinus, (3) Mons Quirinalis, (4) Mons Caelius, (5) Mons Aventinus, (6) Mons Viminalis, (7) Mons Esquilinus. Hence it was named Urbs Septicollis.

186. *seven Roman kings*—(1) Romulus (753–716 BC), (2) Numa Pompilius (716–673 BC), (3) Tullus Hostilius (673–641 BC), (4) Ancus Marcius (640–616 BC), (5) L. Tarquinius Priscus (616–578 BC), (6) Survius Tullius (578–534 BC), (7) L. Tarquinius Superbus (534–510 BC).

187. *wise men of Greece*—(1) Solon of Athens, (2) Chilo of Sparta, (3) Thales of Miletos, (4) Bias of Priene, (5) Cleobulos of Lindos, (6) Pittacos of Mitylene, (7) Periander of Corinth.

188. *seven days by Nero*—"For six days and seven nights together raged he [Nero] in this wise, making havoc of all and driving the common people to take up their inns and shroud themselves the while about the tombs and monuments of the dead" (Suetonius "Nero Claudius Caesar" 38. In *History of the Twelve Caesars* [Holland, 290]).

189. *electors of the Empire*—Seven German princes who held the office of electing the German emperor under the authority of the pope from the 13th to 19th centuries. They possessed considerable power in Agrippa's time. When the Holy Roman Empire was dissolved in 1806, the electors ceased to exist.

190. *crowning the Emperor*—Prior to Maximilian I (until 1440) the coronation of the German emperor was performed at Rome by the pope. The future emperor was met at the silver doors of St. Peter's, where the first prayer was recited. He was then led inside where a second prayer was spoken. He went to the confessio of St. Peter and was anointed on the right arm and between the shoulders. Ascending the high altar, the pope delivered to him a naked sword, which he flourished and sheathed. The pope then delivered the scepter. The crown was placed on the emperor's head by the pontiff. The ceremony concluded with a coronation mass said by the pope.

191. *seven witnesses*—Genesis 21:30.

192. *canonical hours*—See note 47, ch. XVIII, bk. III.

193. *orders of the clergy*—These were divided into Major (bishop, priest and deacon [with subdeacon]) and Minor (doorkeeper, reader, exorcist and acolyte). This ordering was established at the beginning of the third century.

194. *fine cura*—Literally, "at the end of care." A benifice is an ecclesiastical living. This circumstance occurred to the Venerable Bede (see biographical note).

195. *penitential psalms*—Psalms 6, 32, 38, 51, 102, 130 and 143 of the King James version; 6, 31, 37, 50, 101, 129 and 142 of the Vulgate. They are used ceremonially; for example, in the consecration of altars.

196. *second table*—There is a myth that three commandments were on one of the stone tablets Moses brought down from Mount Sinai, and seven on the other. See the plate at the start of *The Sixth and Seventh Books of Moses* published by de Laurence, Chicago.

197. *Livy*—Livius Andronicus. See biographical note.

198. *the infernal world*—Many of these Hebrew spellings appear to be printer's errors dating back to the original Latin edition. Since that time, they have been faithfully copied by imitators, including Francis Barrett in *The Magus* (1801), who corrupted them even further. Some effort at restoration was made by either MacGregor Mathers or Aleister Crowley in the 19th century; their version at least has the advantage of being actual Hebrew words:

Valley of Hinnom, Gehenna (Joshua 15:8)   גי הנם
  (Hell fire [Matthew 5:22]   γέεννα)
Gates of death (Psalms 9:13)   שַׁעֲרֵי־מָוֶת
Shadow of death (Psalms 23:4)   צַל־מָוֶת
Pit of destruction (Psalms 55:23)   בְּאֵר שַׁחַת
Miry clay (Psalms 40:2)   טִיט הַיָּוֵן
Destruction (Psalms 88:11)   אֲבַדּוֹן
Grave, hell (Psalms 9:17)   שְׁאוֹל

Most of these expressions occur more than once in the Bible, some of them (e.g, שְׁאוֹל) many times. Some (e.g., טִיט הַיָּוֵן) occur only once. I have simply cited the first appearance in Psalms, if there is one.

CHAPTER XI

OF the numbeR of eight, and the scale theReof.

The Pythagoreans call eight the number of justice, and fullness: first, because it is first of all divided into numbers equally even, viz. into four, and that division is by the same reason made into twice two, viz. by twice two twice; and by reason of this equality of division,[1] it took to itself the name of Justice, but the other[2] received the name, viz. of Fullness, by reason of the contexture of the corporeal solidity, since the first makes a solid body.

Hence the custom of *Orpheus,* swearing by eight deities,[3] if at any time he would beseech divine justice, whose names are these: Fire, Water, Earth, the Heaven, Moon, Sun, Phanes, the Night. There are also only eight visible spheres[4] of the heavens: also by it the property of corporeal nature is signified, which *Orpheus* comprehends in eight of his sea songs.[5]

This is also called the covenant of circumcision, which was commanded to be done by the Jews the eight day.[6] There were also in the old Law eight ornaments of the priest,[7] viz. a breastplate, a coat, a girdle, a miter, a robe, an ephod, a girdle of the ephod, a golden plate; hither belongs the number to eternity,[8] and the end of the world, because it follows the number seven, which is the mystery of time:[9] hence also the number of blessedness; for Christ teacheth so many degrees of blessedness, as you may see in Matthew:[10] it is also called the number of safety, and conservation, for there were so many souls of the sons of *Jesse,*[11] from which *David* was the eighth. Also *Zacharias,* the father of *John,* received his speech the eighth day.[12]

They say this number was dedicated to *Dionysus,*[12] because he was born the eighth month, in everlasting memory whereof, Naxos the island was dedicated to him, which obtained this prerogative, that only the women of Naxos should safely bring forth in the eighth month, and their children should live, whereas the children of the eighth month in other nations die, and their mothers then bringing forth are in manifest danger.

Notes—ChapteR XI

1. *equality of division*—2 × 4.

2. *the other*—2 × 2 × 2.

3. *eight deities*—

Some people say that there are eight principle gods in the universe, and this is also found in the oaths of Orpheus:

"By the creators of things forever immortal: fire and water, earth and heaven, the moon and the sun, the great torch and the black night." (Theon 2.47 [Lawlor, 69])

See the *Hymns of Orpheus*: 2, "To Night"; 3, "To Heaven"; 4, "To Fire"; 5, "To Protogonus" (i.e. Phanes); 7, "To the Sun"; 8, "To the Moon"; 21, "To the Sea, or Tethys"; 25, "To the Earth."

4. *eight visible spheres*—Seven spheres of the planets and the eighth of the zodiac. The ninth was God and invisible. "Timotheus also relates the proverb 'eight is all,' because the spheres of the world which turn around the earth are eight in number" (Theon 2.47 [Lawlor, 69–70]).

5. *his sea songs*—In the Orphic hymn "To Ocean" the sea was venerated as "the greatest purifier of the gods" and was called by Pythagoras, according to Porphyry, "a tear of Saturn" because, as Thomas Taylor says, Saturn represents pure intellect (Taylor 1875, 108). The Orphic hymns most closely connected with the sea are: 16, "To Neptune"; 21, "To the Sea, or Tethys"; 22, "To Nereus"; 23, "To the Nereids"; 24, "To Proteus"; 73, "To Leucothea"; 74, "To Palaemon"; 82, "To Ocean." Agrippa may be referring to other hymns.

6. *the eight day*—Genesis 17:12.

7. *ornaments of the priest*—Exodus 28:4, 8, 36.

8. *number to eternity*—Eight on its side forms the lemniscate (∞), symbol of eternity.

9. *mystery of time*—Because seven neither arises nor gives rise to other numbers (see note 26, ch. X, bk. II); therefore it neither begins nor ends.

10. *in Matthew*—See note 138, ch. X, bk. II.

11. *sons of Jesse*—I Samuel 16:10–3.

12. *the eighth day*—Luke 1:59–64.

13. *to Dionysus*—Dionysus was the son of Zeus and the Theban princess Semele. In love with Semele, Zeus made the intemperate promise that he would do whatever thing she demanded. At the jealous prompting of Hera, Semele asked to see Zeus in all his splendor. Zeus could not refuse since he had sworn an oath by the River Styx, and when he lifted the veil off his face Semele was consumed by his burning fire, but Zeus snatched the growing fetus out of her womb and put it safely into his thigh, where he brought it to term.

The Scale of the Number Eight

	Eight entries								The names of God with eight letters
In the Original World	אלוה ודעת יהוה ודעת Eloha Vedaath Jehovah Vedaath								The names of God with eight letters
In the Intelligible World	Joy	A kingdom	Grace	The vision of God	Victory	Power	Incorruption	Inheritance	Eight rewards of the blessed
In the Celestial World	The heaven of the Moon	The heaven of Mercury	The heaven of Venus	The heaven of the Sun	The heaven of Mars	The heaven of Jupiter	The heaven of Saturn	The starry heaven	Eight visible heavens
In the Elementary World	The coldness of the earth	The dryness of the fire	The moisture of the water	The heat of the air	The heat of the fire	The moisture of the air	The coldness of the water	The dryness of the earth	Eight particular qualities
In the Lesser World	Mourners	Poor in spirit	Merciful	Pure in heart	They which are persecuted for righteousness' sake	The meek	That hunger and thirst after righteousness	The peace-makers	Eight kinds of blessed men
In the Infernal World	Anguish	Tribulation	Indignation	Darkness	The wrath of God	Judgement	Death	Prison	Eight rewards of the damned

CHAPTER XII

Of the number of nine, and the scale thereof.

The number nine is dedicated to the Muses, by the help of the order of the celestial spheres, and divine spirits: hence there are nine movable spheres, and according to those there are nine Muses,[1] viz. *Calliope, Urania, Polymnia, Terpsichore, Clio, Melpomene, Erato, Euterpe, Thalia,* which nine Muses indeed are appropriated to the nine spheres, so that the first resembles the supreme sphere, which they call primum mobile, and so descending by degrees, according to the written order, unto the last, which resembles the sphere of the Moon, so, viz. *Calliope* is appropriated to the primum mobile, *Urania* to the starry heaven, *Polymnia* to Saturn, *Terpsichore* to Jupiter, *Cleo* to Mars, *Melpomene* to the Sun, *Erato* to Venus, *Euterpe* to Mercury, *Thalia* to the Moon.

There are also nine orders of blessed angels, viz. Seraphim, Cherubim, Thrones, Dominations, Powers, Virtues, Principalities, Archangels, Angels, which *Ezekiel* figures out of nine stones,[2] which are the sapphire, emerald, carbuncle, beryl, onyx, chrysolite, jasper, topaz, sardis: this number hath also a great, and occult mystery of the cross: for the ninth hour our Lord *Jesus* Christ breathed out his spirit.[3] And in nine days the ancients buried their dead,[4] and in so many years they say *Minea* received laws from *Jupiter* in a cave;[5] whence this number was most especially taken notice of by *Homer,* when laws were to be given, or answers were to be given, or the sword was like to rage. The astrologers also take notice of the number nine in the ages of men, no otherwise than they do of seven, which they call climaterical years, which are eminent for some remarkable change.

Yet sometimes it signifies imperfectness, and incompleteness, because it doth not attain to the perfection of the number ten, but is less by one, without which it is deficient, as *Austin* interprets it out of the ten lepers:[6] neither is the longitude of nine cubits of *Og,*[7] king of Balan, who is a type of the Devil, without a mystery.

Notes—Chapter XII

1. *nine Muses*—Calliope, epic poetry; Urania, astronomy; Polyhymnia, sacred poetry; Terpsichore, choral dance and song; Clio, history; Melpomene, tragedy; Erato, love poetry; Euterpe, lyric poetry; Thalia, comedy.

2. *nine stones*—Ezekiel 28:13.

3. *his spirit*—Matthew 27:46. This exclamation of Christ is in the King James Bible nine words.

4. *buried their dead*—This is derived from Homer, and pertains to the myth of Niobe, whose sons and daughters were slain by the gods to punish her for her pride and vanity: "Nine days long they lay in their blood; nor was there anyone/to bury them, for the son of Kronos made stones out of/the people; but the tenth day the Uranian gods buried them" *(Iliad* 24, lines 610–2 [Lattimore, 491]). The same myth is related with poetic coloring by Ovid in the *Metamorphosis*

The Scale of the Number Nine

World	Seraphim	Cherubim	Thrones	Dominations	Powers	Virtues	Principalities	Archangels	Angels	Description
In the Original World	יהוה צבאות Jehovah Sabaoth / יהוה צדקנו Jehovah Zidkenu / אלהים גבור Elohim Gibor[8]									The names of God with nine letters
In the Intelligible World	Seraphim	Cherubim	Thrones	Dominations	Powers	Virtues	Principalities	Archangels	Angels	Nine quires of angels
	Metattron	Ophaniel[9]	Zaphkiel	Zadkiel	Camael	Raphael	Haniel	Michael	Gabriel	Nine angels ruling the heavens
In the Celestial World	Primum mobile	Starry heaven	Sphere of Saturn	Sphere of Jupiter	Sphere of Mars	Sphere of the Sun	Sphere of Venus	Sphere of Mercury	Sphere of the Moon	Nine movable spheres
In the Elementary World	Sapphire	Emerald	Carbuncle	Beryl	Onyx	Chrysolite	Jasper	Topaz	Sardis	Nine stones representing the nine quires of angels
In the Lesser World	Memory	Cogitative	Imaginative	Common sense	Hearing	Seeing	Smelling	Tasting	Touching	Nine senses inward, and outward together
In the Infernal World	False spirits	Lying spirits	Vessels of iniquity	Avengers of wickedness	Jugglers	Airy powers	Furies, sowing mischiefs	Sifters, or Tryers	Tempters, or Ensnarers	Nine orders of devils

6.2. Ovid makes the sons and daughters each seven in number. It seems probable that the nine days echo some ancient burial custom or mystery of religion.

5. *Jupiter in a cave*—Homer speaks of: "Knossos, the great city, the place where Minos/was king for nine-year periods, and conversed with great Zeus" *(Odyssey* 19, lines 178–9 [Lattimore, 286]).

6. *ten lepers*—Luke 17:12–9.

7. *nine cubits of Og*—Deuteronomy 3:11.

8. *Gibor*—Agrippa gives the Hebrew for Gibor as GIBR (גיבר), which disagrees with the modern spelling GBVR (גבור).

9. *Ophaniel*—The name of this angel should probably be Jophiel. However, it occurs in this form in both the English and Latin editions.

CHAPTER XIII

Of the number ten, and the scale thereof.

The number ten is called every number, or an universal number, complete, signifying the full course of life: for beyond that we cannot number, but by replication; and it either implies all numbers within itself, or explains them by itself, and its own, by multiplying them:[1] wherefore it is accounted to be of a manifold religion, and power, and is applied to the purging of souls. Hence the ancients called ceremonies denary,[2] because they that were to be expiated, and to offer sacrifices, were to abstain from some certain things for ten days. Whence amongst the Egyptians it was the custom for him that would sacrifice to *Io*,[3] to fast ten days before, which *Apuleius* testifies of himself, saying, it was commanded that I should for the space of ten days refrain all meat, and be fasting.[4]

There are ten sanguine parts of man, the menstrues, the sperm, the plasmatic spirit,[5] the mass,[6] the humours, the organical body, the vegetative part, the sensitive part, reason, and the mind. There are also ten simple integral parts constituting man, the bone, cartilage, nerve, fiber, ligament, artery, vein, membrane, flesh, skin. There are also ten parts of which a man consists intrinsically, the spirit, the brain, the lungs, the heart, the liver, the gall, the spleen, the kidneys, the testicles, the matrix.

There were ten curtains in the temple,[7] ten strings in the psaltery,[8] ten musical instruments with which the psalms were sung, the names of which were: neza, on which their odes were sung; nablum, the same as organs; mizmor, on which the psalms; sit, on which the canticles; tehila, on which orations; beracha, on which benedictions; halel, on which praises; hodaia, on which thanks; asre, on which the felicity of anyone; hallelujah,[9] on which the praises of God only, and contemplations. There were also ten singers of psalms, viz. *Adam, Abraham, Melchisedech, Moses, Asaph, David, Solomon,* and three sons of *Chora;*[10] there are also ten commandments; and the tenth day[11] after the ascension of Christ the Holy Ghost came down. This lastly is the number in which *Jacob* wrestling with the angel all night overcame, and at the rising of the Sun was blessed, and called by the name of *Israel*.[12] In this number *Joshua* overcame thirty-one kings,[13] and *David* overcame *Goliath*,[14] and the Philistines, and *Daniel* escaped the danger of the lions.[15]

This number also is as circular as unity, because being heaped together,[16] returns into a unity, from whence it had its beginning, and it is the end, and perfection of all numbers, and the beginning of tens. As the number ten flows back into a unity, from whence it proceeded, so everything that is flowing is returned back to that from which it had the beginning of its flux. So water returns to the sea, from whence it had its beginning, the body returns to the earth, from whence it was taken; time returns into eternity, from whence it flowed, the spirit shall return to God that gave it; and lastly, every creature returns to nothing, from whence it was created,

287

The Scale of

	יהיהיהויהי The name of Jehovah with ten letters collected			ואו הא The name of Jehovah of	
In the Original World	אהיה Eheie	י יהוה Iod Jehovah	יהוה אלהים Jehovah Elohim	אל El	אלהים גיבר Elohim Gibor
	כתר Kether	חכמה Hochmah	בינה Binah	חסד Hesed	גבורה Geburah
In the Intelligible World	Seraphim	Cherubim	Thrones	Dominations	Powers
	Haioth ha-Kados	Ophanim	Aralim	Hasmallim	Seraphim
	Metattron	Jophiel	Zaphkiel	Zadkiel	Camael
In the Celestial World	Rashith ha-Gallalim Primum mobile	Masloth Sphere of the Zodiac	Sabbathi Sphere of Saturn	Zedeck Sphere of Jupiter	Madim Sphere of Mars
In the Elementary World	Dove	Leopard	Dragon	Eagle	Horse
In the Lesser World	Spirit	Brain	Spleen	Liver	Gall
In the Infernal World	False gods	Lying spirits	Vessels of iniquity	Revengers of wickedness	Jugglers

the Number Ten

יוד הא ten letters extended		אלהים צבאות The name Elohim Sabaoth			The names of God with ten letters
אליה Eloha	יהוה צבאות Jehovah Sabaoth	אלהים צבאות Elohim Sabaoth	שדי Shaddai	אדנ מלך Adonai Malekh	Ten names of God
תפארת Tiphereth	נצח Netzach	הוד Hod	יסוד Iesod	מלכות Malchuth	Ten Sephiroth
Virtues	Principal- ities	Archangels	Angels	Blessed Souls	Ten orders of the blessed according to Dionysius
Malachim	Elohim	BeniElohim	Cherubim	Issim	Ten orders of the blessed according to the traditions of men
Raphael	Haniel	Michael	Gabriel	The soul of Messiah	Ten angels ruling
Shemes Sphere of the Sun	Noga Sphere of Venus	Cochab Sphere of Mercury	Levanah Sphere of the Moon	Holom Jesodoth Sphere of the Elements	Ten spheres of the world
Lion	Man	Serpent	Bull	Lamb	Ten animals consecrated to the gods
Heart	Kidneys	Lungs	Genitals	Matrix	Ten parts intrinsical of man
Airy powers	Furies, the seminaries of evil	Sifters, or Tryers	Tempters, or Ensnarers	Wicked souls bearing rule	Ten orders of the damned

neither is it supported but by the word of God, in whom all things are hid; and all things with the number ten, and by the number ten, make a round, as saith *Proclus,* taking their beginning from God, and ending in him.

God therefore that First Unity, or One Thing, before he communicated himself to inferiors, diffused himself into the first of numbers, viz. the number three,[17] then into the number ten, as into ten Ideas, and measures of making all numbers, and all things, which the Hebrews call ten attributes,[18] and account ten divine names; for which cause there cannot be a further number. Hence all tens have some divine thing in them, and in the Law are required of

God as his own,[19] together with the first fruits,[20] as the original of things, and beginning of numbers, and every tenth is as the end given to him, who is the beginning, and end of all things.

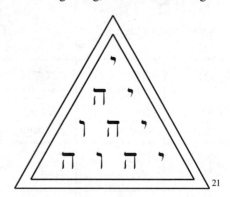

Notes—Chapter XIII

1. *multiplying them*—"The decad completes the series of numbers, containing in itself the nature of both even and odd, of that which is in motion and that which is still, of good and evil" (Theon 2.49 [Lawlor, 70]).

2. *denary*—Of the number ten.

3. *Io*—In Greek mythology, Io was daughter of Inachus and Zeus, who changed her into a heifer to conceal her from jealous Hera. In revenge Hera caused Io to be tormented by a gadfly until she swam across the Ionian Sea to Egypt and escaped. She was represented as a woman with a cow's head, and confused with Hathor.

4. *be fasting*—Apuleius was ordered by the high priest of Isis "to fast by the space of ten continuall daies, without eating of any beast, or drinking any wine" *(The Golden Asse* ch. 48 [Adlington]).

5. *plasmatic spirit*—The spirit that shapes or moulds.

6. *the mass*—The whole quantity of blood or fluid in the body.

7. *the temple*—Exodus 26:1.

8. *psaltery*—A musical instrument like a dulcimer or santir, said to have ten strings. See Psalms 33:2, and the Knox translation (Psalms 32:2), where it is more clearly described as "a harp of ten strings."

9. *hallelujah*—Not an instrument, but an exclamation of praise to God: Hebrew *halelu* (הללו) from *halal,* "to shine," plus *yah* (ה), a shortened form of Jehovah.

10. *sons of Chora*—Korah rebelled against Moses and was killed by God (Numbers 16:32), but his children were spared (Numbers 26:11). Their descendants formed one of the Levite choirs, and are mentioned in the titles of almost a dozen psalms (for example, Psalms 44–9) as the "sons of Korah."

11. *tenth day*—Acts 2:4.

12. *name of Israel*—Genesis 32:24–8. Rashi says that the same number of hours the sun hastened to set for Jacob's sake at Beersheba (Genesis 28:11) it now hastened to shine (Genesis 32:31), but he does not specify the number of hours (Rashi 1949, 1:332–3). At Beersheba Jacob promised a tenth part of his wealth to God (Genesis 28:22).

13. *thirty-one kings*—Joshua 4:19.

14. *overcame Goliath*—I Samuel 17:17–8.

15. *the lions*—Perhaps the number of hours Daniel was supposed, by one version of the story, to have spent in the lion's den. See Daniel 6:16–9, where, however, the number of hours is not specified.

16. *heaped together*—1 + 0 = 1; also 1 + 2 + 3 + 4 + 5 + 6 + 7 + 8 + 9 + 10 = 55, and 5 + 5 = 10, and 1 + 0 = 1.

17. *number three*—"The number 2 added to unity produces 3, which is the first number having a beginning, a middle and an end. This is why this number is the first to which the name *multitude* applies, for all the numbers less than this are not called multitude

Name of Jehovah of Ten Letters Collected

From *The Magus* by Francis Barrett (London, 1801)

(or many) but one or one and other; while three is called multitude" (Theon 2.42 [Lawlor, 66]). See notes 11 and 12, ch. VI, bk. II.

18. *ten attributes*—The Kabbalistic Sephiroth, from Hebrew for "sapphire" (ספיר), not as is so often stated, from the Hebrew *saphar* (ספר), "to number." These are described as spherical vessels which contain the emanations from the Ain Soph (אין סוף), the Limitless. They are listed in the table at the end of the chapter. See also Appendix VI.

19. *as his own*—The tithe. See Genesis 28:22 and Numbers 18:21.

20. *first fruits*—Exodus 13:2 and 23:19.

21. illustration—In this diagram the letters of Tetragrammaton are written so as to form the tetractys of Pythagoras. These same letters, written side to side, make up the name of "Jehovah with ten letters collected" that appears in the table at the end of the chapter. In the *Opera* this diagram is correctly given; however, in the English edition of 1651 it is so grossly distorted as to be unrecognizable, and represents quite a challenge for those who solve it, as I did, before seeing the corrected version. Francis Barrett has copied this distorted version from the English edition and put it into his *Magus* (1801), apparently without the least idea of what it signifies.

CHAPTER XIV

Of the number eleven, and the number twelve, with a double scale of the number twelve Cabalistical, and Orphical.

The number eleven as it exceeds the number ten, which is the number of the commandments, so it falls short of the number twelve, which is of grace and perfection, therefore it is called the number of sins, and the penitent. Hence in the tabernacle there were commanded to be made eleven coats of hair[1] which is the habit of those that are penetent, and lament for their sins, whence this number hath no communion with divine or celestial things, nor any attraction, or scale tending to things above: neither hath it any reward; but yet sometimes it receives a gratuitous favour from God, as he which was called the eleventh hour[2] to the vineyard of the lord, received the same reward as those who had born the burden, and heat of the day.

Now the number twelve is divine, and that whereby the celestials are measured; it is also the number of the signs in the Zodiac over which there are twelve angels[3] as chiefs, supported by the irrigation of the great name of God.[4] In twelve years also Jupiter perfects his course,[5] and the Moon daily runs through twelve degrees. There are also twelve chief joints in the body of man, viz. in hands, elbows, shoulders, thighs, knees, and vertebrae of the feet.

There is also a great power of the number twelve in divine mysteries. God chose twelve families[6] of Israel, and set over them twelve princes;[7] so many stones[8] were placed in the midst of Jordan, and God commanded that so many should be set on the breast of the priest;[9] twelve lions did bear the brazen sea[10] that was made by *Solomon:* there were so many fountains in Helim,[11] and so many spies[12] sent to the land of promise, and so many apostles of Christ[13] set over the twelve tribes, and twelve thousand people were set apart and chosen,[14] the Queen of Heaven crowned with twelve stars,[15] and in the Gospel twelve baskets[16] of the fragments were taken up, and twelve angels[17] are set over the twelve gates of the city, and twelve stones[18] of the heavenly Jerusalem.

In inferior things many breeding things proceed after this number; so the hare and cony[19] being most fruitful, bring forth twelve times in the year, and the camel is so many months in breeding, and the peacock brings forth twelve eggs.[20]

Notes—Chapter XIV

1. *coats of hair*—Actually "curtains of goat's hair" (Exodus 26:7). Camel-hair mantles, called *'adderet*, were worn by the prophets as a kind of badge of office: see Zechariah 13:4.

2. *eleventh hour*—Matthew 20:9.

3. *twelve angels*—See table at end of chapter.

4. *great name of God*—The twelve permutations of Tetragrammaton, which are listed in the table.

5. *his course*—The cycle of Jupiter is 11 years, 315 days.

6. *twelve families*—Genesis 49:28.

7. *twelve princes*—Numbers 1:5–16.

8. *stones*—Joshua 4:5.

9. *breast of the priest*—Exodus 28:15–20.

10. *brazen sea*—Actually oxen. I Kings 7:25.

11. *fountains in Helim*—Elim. See Numbers 33:9.

12. *spies*—Numbers 13:4–15.

13. *apostles of Christ*—Matthew 10:2–6.

14. *chosen*—Perhaps the 12,000 of each tribe in Revelation 7:5–8.

15. *twelve stars*—Revelation 12:1.

16. *twelve baskets*—Matthew 14:20.

17. *twelve angels*—Revelation 21:12.

18. *heavenly Jerusalem*—Revelation 21:19–20.

19. *cony*—Rabbit.

20. *twelve eggs*—"The peahen seldom lays above five or six eggs in this climate before she sits. Aristotle describes her as laying twelve ..." (Goldsmith [1774] 1849, 3:3:396).

> The pea-hen produces at three years [months?] old. In the first year she will lay one or two eggs, in the next four or five, and in the remaining years twelve, but never beyond that number. She lays for two or three days at intervals, and will produce three broods in the year, if care is taken to put the eggs under a common hen. (Pliny 10.79 [Bostock and Riley, 2:538])

The Scale of the

	הקדוש ברוך הוא אב בן דריה הקדש					
In the Original World	יהוה	יההו	יוהה	הודי	הויה	הדיו
In the Intelligible World	Seraphim	Cherubim	Thrones	Dominations	Powers	Virtues
	Malchidiel	Asmodel	Ambriel	Muriel	Verchiel	Hamelial
	Dan	Reuben	Judah	Manasseh	Asher	Simeon
	Malachi	Haggai	Zechariah	Amos	Hosea	Micah
	Matthias	Thaddeus	Simon	John	Peter	Andrew
In the Celestial World	Aries	Taurus	Gemini	Cancer	Leo	Virgo
	March	April	May	June	July	August
In the Elemental World	Sage	Upright Vervain	Bending Vervain	Comfrey	Lady's Seal	Calamint
	Sardonius	Cornelian	Topaz	Calcedony	Jasper	Emerald
In the Lesser World	The head	The neck	The arms	The breast	The heart	The belly
In the Infernal World	False gods	Lying spirits	Vessels of iniquity	Revengers of wickedness	Jugglers	Airy powers

Number Twelve

Holy Blessed He Father, Son, Holy Ghost						The names of God with twelve letters
וְהָיָה	וְהָיִי	וִיהָֿה	הָיְדָו	הָיוֹה	הֹהֵוִי	The great name returned back into twelve banners[21]
Principal-ities	Arch-angels	Angels	Innocents	Martyrs	Confessors	Twelve orders of the blessed spirits
Zuriel	Barbiel	Adnachiel[22]	Hanael	Gabiel[23]	Barchiel	Twelve angels ruling over the signs
Issachar	Benjamin	Naphtali	Gad	Zebulun	Ephraim	Twelve tribes
Jonah	Obadiah	Zephaniah	Nahum	Habakkuk	Joel	Twelve prophets
Bartholo-mew	Philip	James the elder	Thomas	Matthew	James the younger	Twelve apostles
Libra	Scorpius	Sagittarius	Capricorn	Aquarius	Pisces	Twelve signs of the Zodiac
September	October	November	December	January	February	Twelve months
Scorpion grass	Mugwort	Pimpernel	Dock	Dragon-wort	Aris-tolochy	Twelve plants
Beryl	Amethyst	Hyacinth	Chryso-prasus	Crystal	Sapphire	Twelve stones
The kidneys	The genitals	The hams	The knees	The legs	The feet	Twelve principal members
Furies, the sowers of evils	Sifters, or Tryers	Tempters, or Ensnarers	Witches	Apostates	Infidels	Twelve degrees of the damned, and of devils

The Orphic Scale of the

In the Intelligible World	Pallas	Venus	Phoebus	Mercury	Jupiter	Ceres
In the Celestial World	Aries	Taurus	Gemini	Cancer	Leo	Virgo
	March	April	May	June	July	August
In the Elementary World	Owl	Dove	Cock	Ibis	Eagle	Sparrow
	She-goat	He-goat	Bull	Dog	Hart	Sow
	Olive tree	Myrtle tree	Laurel	Hazel	Aesculus	Apple tree
In the Lesser World	The head	The neck	The arms	The breast	The heart	The belly

Number Twelve

Vulcan	Mars	Diana	Vesta	Juno	Neptune	Twelve deities
Libra	Scorpius	Sagittarius	Capricorn	Aquarius	Pisces	Twelve signs of the Zodiac
September	October	November	December	January	February	Twelve months
Goose	Pie	Daw	Heron	Peacock	Swan	Twelve consecrated birds
Ass	Wolf	Hind	Lion	Sheep	Horse	Twelve consecrated beasts
Box tree	Dog tree	Palm tree	Pine tree	Ramthorn	Elm tree	Twelve consecrated trees
The kidneys	The genitals	The hams	The knees	The legs	The feet	Twelve members of man distributed to the signs

Notes—Chapter XIV (cont'd.)

21. *twelve banners*—In the English edition, this order of the names is shown: (1) יהוה, (2) יההו, (3) יוהה, (4) הוהי, (5) היוה, (6) ההיו, (7) וההי*, (8) ריהה*, (9) והיה*, (10) היהו, (11) היוה, (12) ההוי. The Latin *Opera* gives this order: (1) יהוה, (2) וההי, (3) יוהה, (4) הוהי, (5) היוה, (6) ההיו, (7) והיה, (8) ויהה*, (9) וההי*, (10) היהו, (11) היוה, (12) ההוי. Both are obviously incorrect, based on the numerical structure of the sequence. I have given the corrected order in the table. For a numerical breakdown of the 12 names, as well as my assignment of them to the signs of the Zodiac based upon the elemental trines, see my book *The New Magus* (1988) 1:17:169–71.

22. *Adnachniel*—Perhaps this should be Advachiel. See note 13, ch. XXIV, bk. III.

23. *Gabiel*—The Latin *Opera* gives Gabriel, but perhaps should give Cambiel. See note 13, ch. XXIV, bk. III.

CHAPTER XV

Of the numbers which are above twelve, and of their powers and virtues.

The other numbers also which are above twelve, are endowed with many, and various effects, the virtues whereof you must understand by their original, and parts, as they are made of a various gathering together of simple numbers, or manner of multiplication. Sometimes as their significations arise from the lessening, or exceeding of another going before, especially more perfect, so they contain of themselves the signs of certain divine mysteries.

So you see the third number above ten shows the mysteries of Christ's appearing to the gentiles, for the thirteenth day after his birth a star was a guide to the wise men.[1]

The fourteenth day doth typify Christ, who the fourteenth day of the first month was sacrificed for us; upon which day the children of Israel were commanded by the Lord to celebrate the passover.[2] This number *Matthew* doth so carefully observe, that he passed over some generations, that he might everywhere observe this number in the generations of Christ.[3]

The fifteenth number is a token of spiritual ascensions, therefore the song of degrees is applied to that in fifteen psalms.[4] Also fifteen years were added to the life of King *Hezekiah:*[5] and the fifteenth day of the seventh month was observed, and kept holy.[6]

The number sixteen, the Pythagoreans call the number of felicity. It also comprehends all the prophets of the Old Testament, and the apostles, and Evangelists of the New.

The number eighteen, and twenty, divines interpret to be unhappy, for in the former, Israel served *Eglon,* king of Moab;[7] and in the other *Jacob* served,[8] and *Joseph* was sold.[9] And lastly, amongst creatures that have many feet, there is none that hath above twenty feet.[10]

The twenty-two signifies the fullness of wisdom, and so many are the characters of the Hebrew letters, and so many books doth the Old Testament contain.

To the number twenty-eight, the favour of the Moon is designed, for the motion thereof[11] is distant from the course of other stars, and as it were alone is completed the twenty-eighth day, when it returns to the same point of the Zodiac from whence it came: hence twenty-eight mansions of the Moon, having singular virtue, and influence, are numbered in the heavens.

The number thirty is memorable for many mysteries. Our Lord *Jesus* Christ was baptized[12] the thirtieth year of his age, and began to do miracles, and to teach the kingdom of God. Also *John Baptist* was thirty years old when he began to preach in the wilderness,[13] and to prepare the ways of the Lord. Also *Ezekiel* at the same age began to prophesy;[14] and *Joseph* was brought out of prison[15] on the thirtieth year of his age, and received the government of Egypt from Pharaoh.

The number thirty-two, the Hebrew doctors ascribe to wisdom, and so many paths of wisdom are described by *Abraham.*[16] But the Pythagoreans call this the number of justice, because it is always divisible into two parts, even unto unity.[17]

The number forty, the ancients did honour with great observation, concerning which they did celebrate the feast Tessarosten.[18] It is said that it doth conduce to the account of birth, for in so many days the seed is fitted, and transformed in the womb, until it be by its due, and harmonical proportions brought unto a perfect organical body, being disposed to receive a rational soul. And so many days they say women be, after they have brought forth, before all things are settled within them, and they are purified,[19] and so many days infants refrain from smiling, are infirm, and live with a great deal of hazard. This also is in religion a number of expiation, and penitency, and signifying great mysteries. For in the time of the deluge the Lord rained forty days[20] and nights upon the Earth: the children of Israel lived forty years[21] in the wilderness: forty days the destruction of Nineveh[22] was put off. The same number was accounted as holy in the fasts of the saints: for Moses,[23] Elias,[24] and Christ[25] fasted forty days. Christ was carried forty weeks in the womb of a virgin: Christ tarried forty days after his birth at Bethlehem before he was presented in the temple: he preached forty months publicly: he lay forty hours dead in the sepulchre: the fortieth day[26] after his resurrection he ascended into heaven, all which divines say, were not done without some occult property, and mystery of this number.

The number fifty signifies remission of sins, of servitudes, and also liberty. According to the Law, on the fiftieth year they did remit debts, and everyone did return to his own possessions. Hence by the year of Jubilee,[27] and by the psalm of repentance[28] it shows a sign of indulgency, and repentance. The Law also, and the Holy Ghost are declared in the same: for the fiftieth day[29] after Israel's going forth out of Egypt, the Law was given to Moses in Mount Sinai: the fiftieth day after the resurrection, the Holy Ghost came[30] down upon the apostles in Mount Sion; whence also it is called the number of grace, and attributed to the Holy Ghost.

The number sixty was holy to the Egyptians, for it is proper to the crocodile, that as she in sixty days brings forth sixty eggs,[31] and so many days sits on them, so she is said also to live so many years, and to have so many teeth, and so many days every year to rest solitary without any meat.

The number seventy hath also its mysteries, for so many years the fire of the sacrifice in the Babylonian captivity lay under the water, and was alive, so many years Jeremiah foretold the destruction of the temple,[32] and so many years the Babylonian captivity[33] endured, and in so many years the desolation of Jerusalem[34] was finished. Also there were seventy palms[35] in the place where the children of Israel pitched their tents. The Fathers went down to Egypt with seventy souls.[36] Also seventy kings with their fingers and toes cut off did gather meat under the table of Adonibezeck;[37] seventy sons came forth of the loins of Joas, seventy men, all sons of Jero;[38] seventy weights[39] of silver were given to Abimelech, and so many men Abimelech slew upon one stone;[40] Abdon had seventy sons, and nephews, who rode upon seventy foals of asses;[41] Solomon had seventy thousand men[42] which carried burdens. Seventy sons of King Ahab were beheaded in Samaria; seventy years, according to the Psalmist, are the age of man.[43] Lamech shall be avenged seventy-seven fold;[44] thou shalt forgive thy brother if he offend against thee, seventy-seven times.[45]

Also the number seventy-two was famous for so many languages, for so many elders of the synagogue,[46] for so many interpreters of the Old Testament, for so many disciples of Christ:[47] it hath also a great communion with the number twelve; hence in the heavens, every sign being divided into six parts,[48] there result seventy-two fives, over which so many angels bear rule; and so many are the names of God;[49] and every five is set over one idiom with such efficacy, that the astrologers, and physiognomists can know from thence from what idiom everyone ariseth. Answerable to these are so many manifest joints in man's body, whereof in every finger and toe there are three, which together with the twelve principal reckoned before in the number twelve make up seventy-two.[50]

The number a hundred in which the sheep that was found,[51] was placed, which also passeth from the left hand to the right, is found holy: and because it consists of tens it shows a complete perfection.

But the complement of all numbers is a thousand, which is the foursquare measure[52] of the number ten, signifying a complete, and absolute perfection.

There are also two numbers[53] especially celebrated by *Plato* in his Republic and not disallowed by *Aristotle* in his Politics, by which great mutations in cities are foretold: these are the square of twelve, and the foursquare measure thereof, viz. the forty-four above a hundred, and seven hundred twenty-eight above a thousand, which number is fatal: to which when any city, or commonwealth hath attained, it shall afterward with a complete foursquare measure decline: but in squares it undergoeth a change, but for the better, if it be governed with prudent discipline, and then it shall not with fate, but imprudency fall.[54]

And let thus much suffice for numbers in particular.

Notes—Chapter XV

1. *wise men*—Matthew 2:2. Herod asks the wise men what time the star appeared (Matthew 2:7), but the time is not stated.

2. *the passover*—Symbolically appropriate, as the 14th day of the first Jewish month was the Passover, when the paschal lamb was slaughtered and eaten (Exodus 12:2–7). The last supper took place a day earlier so as not to conflict with the rules of the sabbath, after the custom of the Pharisees, although it was the Passover feast.

3. *generations of Christ*—Matthew 1:17.

4. *fifteen psalms*—Psalms 120–134.

5. *King Hezekiah*—II Kings 20:6.

6. *kept holy*—Leviticus 23:34.

7. *Eglon, king of Moab*—Judges 3:14.

8. *Jacob served*—Genesis 31:41.

9. *Joseph was sold*—Genesis 37:28.

10. *above twenty feet*—The centipede has 21 pairs of legs, but the last pair is enlarged and might have been discounted by Agrippa's source. Presumably he was not aware of the millipede, or did not consider it to have feet.

11. *motion thereof*—The Moon is distinguished from the other planets by the rapidity of its motion and by its marked rise and fall across the plane of the ecliptic, which is defined by the apparent revolution of the Sun around the Earth. The limits of this deviation mark the boundaries of the zodiac, a band that extends nine degrees above and nine degrees below the ecliptic.

12. *Christ was baptized*—Luke 3:23.

13. *in the wilderness*—John the Baptist was born six months before Christ. See Luke 1:36.

14. *began to prophesy*—Ezekiel 1:1.

15. *out of prison*—Genesis 41:46.

16. *described by Abraham*—"The Thirty-two Paths of Wisdom" is a Kabbalistic tract appended to the *Sepher Yetzirah*. The paths referred to are the 10 Sephiroth and the 22 Hebrew letters, usually represented in a single glyph as a tree with 10 fruit and 22 branches. Abraham was the reputed author of the *Sepher Yetzirah:* "And after that our father Abraham had perceived and understood, and had taken down and engraved all these things, the Lord most high revealed Himself, and called him His beloved" *(Sepher Yetzirah* 6.4 [Westcott, 33]). Westcott says in his introduction to this work: "The old title has, as an addition, the words 'The Letters of our Father Abraham' or 'ascribed to the patriarch Abraham,' and it is spoken of as such by many medieval authorities …" (ibid., 13).

17. *even unto unity*—32, 16, 8, 4, 2, 1.

18. *feast Tessarosten*—From the Greek *tessarakonta* (forty).

19. *they are purified*—The period of purification for a woman following the eighth day circumcision of her son was 33 days, after which a sacrifice was offered at the door of the tabernacle. See Leviticus 12:2–6.

20. *rained forty days*—Genesis 7:12.

21. *lived forty years*—Deuteronomy 8:2.

22. *destruction of Nineveh*—Jonah 3:4.

23. *Moses*—Exodus 34:28.

24. *Elias*—I Kings 19:8.

25. *Christ*—Matthew 4:2.

26. *fortieth day*—Acts 1:3.

27. *year of Jubilee*—Leviticus 25:10.

28. *psalm of repentance*—Psalm 50 of the Vulgate, but 51 of King James.

29. *fiftieth*—Presumably calculated from Exodus 19:1, 16.

30. *Holy Ghost came*—Calculated from Acts 1:3, 12 and 2:1.

31. *sixty eggs*—Aristotle *(History of Animals* 5) says that the crocodile brings forth 60 eggs and sits on them 60 days.

32. *destruction of the temple*—Jeremiah 7:14.

33. *Babylonian captivity*—Jeremiah 25:11.

34. *desolation of Jerusalem*—Jeremiah 25:18.

35. *seventy palms*—Exodus 15:27.

36. *seventy souls*—Genesis 46:27, which seems to disagree with Acts 7:14.

37. *Adonibezeck*—Adoni-bezek. Judges 1:7.

38. *sons of Jero*—Jerubbaal. Judges 9:2.

39. *seventy weights*—Judges 9:4.

40. *upon one stone*—Judges 9:5.

41. *foals of asses*—Judges 12:14.

42. *seventy thousand men*—I Kings 5:15.

43. *age of man*—See note 7, ch. X, bk. II.

44. *avenged seventy-seven fold*—Genesis 4:24.

45. *seventy-seven times*—Matthew 18:22. Actually Christ says "seventy times seven."

46. *elders of the synagogue*—Numbers 11:16. There are said to be 70 elders.

47. *disciples of Christ*—Luke 10:1. The disciples are 70 in number.

48. *six parts*—In astronomy each five-degree division of the zodiacal signs is linked with a specific physiognomy, making a total of 72 distinct faces, as they are now called.

49. *names of God*—The Schemhamphoras, a set of 72 names of God formed kabbalistically from Exodus 14:19–21. See Appendix VII.

50. *make seventy-two*—It need hardly be pointed out that the thumb and big toe have only two joints, leaving Agrippa four joints shy of a pleasing example.

51. *sheep that was found*—Luke 15:4.

52. *foursquare measure*—Ten cubed: 10 x 10 x 10.

53. *two numbers*—Twelve squared (12 x 12 = 144) and cubed (12 x 12 x 12 = 1728).

54. *imprudency fall*—

> Hard in truth it is for a state thus constituted to be shaken and disturbed, but since for everything that has come into being destruction is appointed, not even such a fabric as this will abide for all time, but it shall surely be dissolved, and this is the manner of its dissolution. Not only for plants that grow from the earth but also for animals that live upon it there is a cycle of bearing and barrenness for soul and body as often as the revolutions of their orbs come full circle, in brief courses for the short-lived and oppositely for the opposite. ... Now for divine begettings there is a period comprehended by a perfect number, and for mortal by the first in which augmentations dominating and dominated when they have attained to three distances and four limits of the assimilating and the dissimilating, the waxing and the waning, render all things conversable and commensurable with one another, whereof a basal four thirds wedded to the pempad yields to harmonies at the third augmentation, the one the product of equal factors taken one hundred times, the other of equal length one way but oblong—one dimension of a hundred numbers determined by the rational diameters of the pempad lacking one in each case, or of the irrational lacking two; the other dimension of a hundred cubes of the triad. (Plato Republic 8.546 [Hamilton and Cairns, 775.])

Pempad is Greek for "a body of five."

CHAPTER XVI

Of the notes of numbers, placed in certain gesturings.

I have often read in books of magicians, and their works, and experiments, certain wonderful, and as they seemed to me ridiculous gesturings,[1] and I did think they were certain occult agreements of the devils, by reason of which I did reject them: but after I did more seriously examine the matter, then I did presently understand that they were not the compacts of devils; but that there lay in them the reason of numbers, by which the ancients did by the various bending forward, and backward, their hands, and fingers, represent numbers, by whose gesturings the magicians did silently signify words unknown by sound, various with numbers, yet of great virtue, by their fingers joined together, and sometimes changed, and did with sacred silence worship the gods that rule over the world.

The rites whereof *Martianus* also makes mention of in his Arithmetic,[2] saying, the fingers of the virgin were moved all manner of ways, who after she went in, did by expressing seven hundred and seventeen numbers with her bended fingers call upon *Jupiter*.

But that these things may be better understood, I shall bring something out of the sayings of *Beda* who saith, when thou sayest one, bend in the little finger on thy left hand, and set it in the middle of the palm; when thou sayest two, place the next finger to the little finger in the same place; when three, the middle finger after the same manner; when four, thou shalt lift up thy little finger; when five, the next to it after the same manner; when six, the middle, that finger alone which is called the ring finger, being fixed on the middle of the palm;[3] when thou sayest seven, thou shalt put only thy little finger above the root[4] of thy palm, the rest in the meantime being lifted up; and by it when thou sayest eight, thy ring finger; when thou sayest nine, thou shalt set thy middle finger contrary[5] to them.

When thou sayest ten, thou shall set the nail of thy forefinger on the middle joint of thy thumb. When thou sayest twenty, thou shalt put the top of thy middle finger close betwixt the joints of thy thumb, and forefinger. When thou sayest thirty, thou shalt join the nail of thy thumb, and forefinger lightly together. When thou sayest forty, thou shalt bring the inside of thy thumb to the outside of thy forefinger, both being lifted up. When thou sayest fifty, thou shalt bend thy thumb with the outward joint, like to the Greek gamma,[8] to the palm. When thou sayest sixty, compass about thy thumb being bended as before, with thy forefinger bowed over it. When thou sayest seventy, thou shalt supply thy forefinger being bowed about as before, with thy thumb stretched at length, the nail thereof being lifted up beyond the middle joint of thy forefinger. When thou sayest eighty, thou shalt supply thy forefinger bowed about as before, with thy thumb stretched forth at length, the nail thereof being set upon the middle joint of the forefinger. When thou sayest ninety, thou shall set the nail of thy forefinger bent into the root of thy thumb stretched out. Thus much for the left hand.

Now thou shalt make 100 on thy right hand, as thou didst ten on thy left; and 200 on thy right, as thou didst twenty on thy left; 2000 on thy right, as thou didst two on thy left, and so to 9000. Moreover when thou sayest 10,000 thou shalt put thy left hand upward on thy breast, thy fingers only being lifted towards heaven.[9] When thou sayest 20,000 thou shalt put the same spread forth[10] upon thy breast. When thou sayest 30,000 thou shalt put thy thumb on the same hand downwards,[11] on the cartilage of the middle of thy breast. When thou sayest 40,000 thou shalt lay the same upright,[12] and stretched forth on thy navel. When thou sayest 50,000 thou shalt lay thy thumb of the same hand downward on thy navel.[13] When thou sayest 60,000 thou shalt hold thy left thigh with the same, being downwards. When thou sayest 70,000 the same thou shalt put upon thy thumb upright.[14] When thou sayest 80,000 thou shalt put the same downward on thy thigh.[15] When thou sayest 90,000 thou shalt hold thy loins with the same, thy thumb being turned downwards.[16] But when thou sayest 100,000 or 200,000 and so unto 900,000 thou shalt in the same order as we have spoken, fill them up on the right part of thy body. But when thou sayest 1,000,000 thou shall join both thy hands together, and clasp thy fingers one within the other.[17]

Let these suffice which have been observed out of *Beda;* thou shalt find more of these in Brother *Luke* of Saint Sepulchers, in his great Arithmetic.[18]

Notes—Chapter XVI

1. *ridiculous gesturings*—In Eastern occultism ritual gestures are termed *mudra,* and often focus upon the hands as expressing in miniature the posture of the whole body. These hand gestures are numerous in early Christian art. See Ward [1928] 1969 for many examples.

2. *his Arithmetic*—Martianus Minneus Felix Capella, *Satyricon* bk. 7. See his biographical note.

3. *middle of the palm*—That is, lift up the middle and set down the ring finger.

4. *above the root*—Perhaps this means to hold the tip of the finger in the air over the place where it joins the palm. See the quotation in note 17 below.

5. *contrary*—together with *(compono).*

6. *middle joint*—This probably means the inside of the first joint, as the second joint is occupied in forming 90. "Joint" here may mean segment, as opposed to the modern meaning, hinge.

7. *thumb, and forefinger*—That is, press the end segments of the thumb, forefinger and middle finger together.

8. Greek gamma—Γ.

9. *towards heaven*—Lay the left hand flat on the breast diagonally with the fingers and thumb together, pointing upward.

10. *spread forth*—Spread the thumb away from the fingers.

11. *downwards*—Tuck the thumb out of sight under the palm.

12. *same upright*—Lay the palm flat on the navel with the thumb separated and pointing upward.

13. *on thy navel*—Tuck the thumb under the palm.

14. *thumb upright*—That is, lay the left hand flat on the thigh with the thumb separated from the fingers.

15. *on thy thigh*—Tuck the thumb under the palm.

16. *turned downwards*—Probably means to simply lay the hand over the groin, fingers and thumb together, since there is no need to distinguish the gesture in this position.

17. *within the other*—This fascinating and practical system of counting on the fingers was also described by Nicholaus Rhabda of Smyrna in the 8th century:

> The left hand was held up flat with the fingers together. The units from 1 to 9 were expressed by various positions of the third, fourth and fifth fingers alone, one or more of these being either closed on the palm or simply bent at the middle joint, according to the number meant. The thumb and index finger were thus left free to express the

tens by a variety of relative positions, *e.g.* for 30 their points were brought together and stretched forward; for 50 the thumb was bent like the Greek Γ and brought against the ball of the index. The same set of signs if executed with the thumb and index of the right hand meant hundreds instead of tens, and the unit signs if performed on the right hand meant thousands. *(Encyclopædia Britannica* 1910, 19:866)

18. *Arithmetic*—The *Summa de arithmetica geometria proportioni et proportionalita* (1494) of Lucas Paciolus. See biographical note.

CHAPTER XVII

Of the various notes of numbers observed amongst the Romans.

The notes of numbers are made divers ways in divers nations. The Romans did figure them by these following notes, which *Valerius Probus* describes concerning the ancient letters, and which are still in use,[1] viz:

One	Five	Ten	Fifty
I	V	X	L

A hundred	Two hundred	Five hundred
C	ꟼ, CC	D

A thousand	Five thousand
M, S, Ī, CXꟼ	Iꟼꟼ, ICC, V̄

Ten thousand
CCIꟼꟼ, CMꟼ, ꟼMC, IMI, X̄

Fifty thousand
Iꟼꟼꟼ, Dꟼꟼ, L̄

A hundred thousand
CCCIꟼꟼꟼ, 木 , 木 , CM, C̄

Two hundred thousand
ꟼ, C̄C̄

Five hundred thousand   A thousand thousand
DM, ꟼꟼ, D̄   CMꟼ, Cꟼꟼ, M̄, S̄

There are also other notes of numbers nowadays used amongst arithmeticians, and calculators, which according to the order of numbers are made after this matter: 1, 2, 3, 4, 5, 6, 7, 8, 9, to which is added a note of privation signed with the mark 0 which although it signify no number, yet makes others to signify either tens, or hundreds, or thousands, as is well known to arithmeticians.

Also there are some that mark the number ten with a line downward, and another made cross it; and five by that line which toucheth the other, but doth not go cross it, and a unity by that which is put by itself, as you may see in this example: ⊤ signifies ten, ⊤̄ signifies ten and five, ꜧ signifies sixteen, ꜧı ten and seven; and the round O being put by itself signifies a hundred; but being joined to others, signifies so many hundreds as the numbers are to which it is put, so thus, OO or thus IIO signifies two hundred, thus OOO or thus IIIO three hundred, ⊦° five hundred, ⊤̊ ten hundred or a thousand. And these notes are commonly seen added in magical characters.

Notes—Chapter XVII

1. *still in use*—The Roman system of numerals is not based on letters, as is commonly assumed, but on an older system of simple symbols. The vertical stroke (I) indicates one. The circle divided horizontally (⊖)

306

shows one hundred, and when divided vertically (ⓓ), one thousand. This is often represented in old prints as CIꓷ, and from this division arose the Roman D, signifying half the circle, or 500. The Roman L, equaling 50, is half a hundred and at one time was written ⊥ or ⊥ . Likewise the Roman V, with a value of five, is half the Roman X, or ten. In fact, X is not a true Roman letter. Notice that in the system described at the end of the chapter, the cross also represents ten. The S on its side is formed of two linked Cs, and is equivalent to 200. The horizontal bar signifies 1000, the letter or letters under it, its multiplier. Thus ⲱ equals 200,000. Also, each time a C is added, the value of the symbols is increased by a factor of ten. Thus, Iꓷ or D equals 500, while Iꓷꓷ equals 50,000. The standing S suggests the two linked halves of the circle symbol divided vertically, that is ꓷ plus D, or 500 plus 500. The � multiplies the value by 1000—Iꓷ or D equals 500, but ꝯꓷ equals 500,000. Regarding the two curious symbols, each stroke may indicate a factor of ten (10 x 10 x 10 x 10 x 10), with the crossbar of the second figure standing for two separate strokes.

CHAPTER XVIII

Of the various notes or figures of the Grecians.

The Grecians use the alphabetical letters for their notes of numbers, and that three ways; first by every element according to the series of the alphabet signifying the number of its place. For in the order of which any number doth possess the place of the alphabet, it represents the number thereof, as here you may see:

1	2	3	4	5	6	7	8	9	10	11	12
A	B	Γ	Δ	E	Z	H	Θ	I	K	Λ	M

13	14	15	16	17	18	19	20	21	22	23	24
N	Ξ	O	Π	P	Σ	T	Υ	Φ	X	Ψ	Ω

And this is the first order of numbers amongst the Greeks.

Secondly, the Greeks divide the whole alphabet into three classes, whereof the first beginning from alpha, is of unities. The second beginning from iota is of tens. The third beginning from rho is of hundreds; and this order by the latter of the Greeks is instituted after the imitation of the Hebrews.[1] Now because their alphabet wants by that rule, three letters, it is necessary to add to them three figures,[2] and to interlace them with the letters, by which, viz. they explain the sixth, the ninetieth, and the nine hundredth, as is manifest in the following classes:[3]

1	2	3	4	5	6	7	8	9
A	B	Γ	Δ	E	ς	Z	H	Θ

10	20	30	40	50	60	70	80	90
I	K	Λ	M	N	Ξ	O	Π	ϙ

100	200	300	400	500	600	700	800	900
P	Σ	T	Υ	Φ	X	Ψ	Ω	ϡ

Now if to any of these letters there be subscribed the stroke of an acute tone,[4] then it signifies so many thousands, as in these examples:

1000	10,000	100,000
,A	,I	,P

After the third manner,[5] the Greeks use only six letters in signifying their numbers, viz. I for an unity, Π for the number five, because it is the head of the word πέντε[6] i.e. five, Δ for the number ten, from δέκα,[7] H for a hundred from ἑκατόν,[8] X for a thousand, from the word χίλια,[9] M for ten thousand, from μύρια.[10] From which six letters joined in number after their manner unto four, or to other numbers, they make other numbers, besides Π which is not multiplied, nor joined to itself, but always signifies the fives of others,[11] as appears in the following examples:

1	2	3	4	5	6	7	8	9
I	II	III	IIII	Π	ΠI	ΠII	ΠIII	ΠIIII

10	11	12	13	14	15	16	20	21
Δ	ΔI	ΔII	ΔIII	ΔIIII	ΔΠ	ΔΠI	ΔΔ	ΔΔI

50	60	100	200	500	1000	5000	10,000	50,000
⟨Δ|	⟨Δ|Δ	H	HH	⟨H|	X	⟨X|	M	⟨M|

Noces—Chapcer XVlll

1. *imitation of the Hebrews*—The first Greek use of this numbering system occurs on coins from the reign of Ptolemy II of Egypt in the 3rd century BC, whereas the first use on Jewish coins is from the time of the Hasmoneans in the 2nd century BC. This evidence contradicts Agrippa's assertion.

2. *three figures*—Added were two old Phoenician letters not used in writing (ϛ or Ϝ, and Ϙ), called *digamma* and *koppa,* and the early form of the letter San (ϡ), called in modern times *sampi.*

3. *following classes*—I have shown the numbers in this chapter in Greek print letters, but numbers might be written with either print or script letters.

4. *acute tone*—That is, written with an acute accent mark at the lower left corner.

5. *third manner*—This system is actually older than the previous one and was called Herodian after the grammarian who described it around 200 AD. It is said to date back to the time of Solon (7th century BC).

6. πέντε—Pente.

7. δέκα—Deka.

8. ἑκατόν—Hekaton.

9. χίλια—Chilia.

10. μύρια—Myria.

11. *fives of others*—A letter-number placed in *pi* (Π) is multiplied to five times its value.

CHAPTER XIX

Of the notes of the Hebrews, and Chaldeans, and certain other notes of magicians.

The Hebrew letters also have marks of numbers, but far more excellently than any other languages, since the greatest mysteries lie in Hebrew letters, as is handled concerning these in that part of Cabaly[1] which they call Notaricon.[2]

Now the principal Hebrew letters are in number twenty-two, whereof five have divers other certain figures in the end of a word, which therefore they call the five ending letters, which being added to them aforesaid make twenty-seven, which being divided into three degrees,[3] signifies the unities, which are the first degree; tens which are in the second; and hundreds which are in the third degree. Now every one of them if they be marked with a great character, signifies so many thousands, as here:

3000	2000	1000
ג	ב	א

Now the classes of the Hebrew numbers are these:

9	8	7	6	5	4	3	2	1
ט	ח	ז	ו	ה	ד	ג	ב	א

90	80	70	60	50	40	30	20	10
צ	פ	ע	ס	נ	מ	ל	כ	י

900	800	700	600	500	400	300	200	100
ץ	ף	ן	ם	ך	ת	ש	ר	ק

Now there are some which do not use those final letters, but instead of them write thus:

1000	900	800	700	600	500
א	קתת	תת	שת	רת	קת

And by those simple figures by the joining them together they describe all other compound numbers, as eleven, twelve, a hundred and ten, a hundred and eleven, by adding to the number ten, those which are of unities; and in like manner to the rest after their manner; yet they describe the fifteenth number not by ten and five, but by nine and six, viz. thus טו, and that out of honour to the divine name יה,[4] which imports fifteen, lest it should happen that the sacred name should be attributed to prophane things.

Also the Egyptians, Aethiopians, Chaldeans, and Arabians, have their marks of numbers, which also oftentimes happen amongst magical characters. He therefore that would know them, must seek them, of them that are skillful of these letters. For the Chaldeans mark the numbers with the letters of their alphabet after the manner of the Hebrews. We have set down their alphabet in the end of the first book.[5]

Moreover I found in two most ancient books of astrologers, and magicians, certain most elegant marks of numbers, which I thought good to set down in this place; now they were in both volumes such:

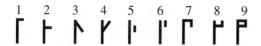

Now by these marks turned to the left hand are made tens, after this manner:

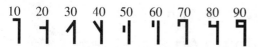

    And by those marks which are turned downwards on the right hand, are made hundreds; on the left thousands, viz. thus:

100 200 300 400 500 600 700 800 900

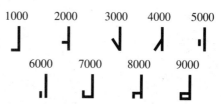

And by the composition, and mixture of these marks other mixed and compounded numbers also are most elegantly made, as you may perceive by these few:

| 1510 | 1511 | 1471 | 1486 | 2421 |

According to the example of which we must proceed in other compound numbers; and so much suffice for the marks of numbers.

Notes—Chapter XIX

1. *Cabaly*—Kabbalah.

2. *Notaricon*—See Appendix VII.

3. *three degrees*—See the table of the Hebrew alphabet in Appendix VII.

4. יי׳—Jah, one half of the Tetragrammaton (יהוה), usually rendered into English Jehovah.

5. *first book*—See ch. LXXIV, bk. I.

CHAPTER XX

What numbers are attributed
to letters; and of divining by the same.

The Pythagoreans say *(Aristotle,* and *Ptolemy* are of opinion) that the very elements of letters have some certain divine numbers, by which collected from proper names of things, we may draw conjectures concerning occult things to come. Whence they call this kind of divination arithmancy,[1] because, viz. it is done by numbers, as *Terentianus* hath made mention of it in these verses:[2]

> Names are, they say, made of but letters few,
> Unfortunate, of many, do foreshow
> Success; so Hector did Patroclus slay,
> So Hector to Achilles was a prey.

Also *Pliny* saith,[3] that there was added to what *Pythagoras* invented, an uneven number of vowels of imposed names, which did betoken lameness, or want of eyes, and such like misfortunes, if they be assigned to the right side parts; but an even number of them of the left. And *Alexandrinus*[4] the philosopher taught, how that by the number of letters we may find out the ruling stars of anyone that is born, and whether the husband or wife shall die first, and know the prosperous, or unhappy events of the rest of our works. His traditions which were not disallowed by *Ptolemy*[5] the astrologer we shall here add, and put under.

But those numbers which are deputed to each letter, we have above showed in the Greek, and Hebrew letters, the alphabet being divided into three classes, whereof the first is of unities, the second of tens, the third of hundreds. And seeing in the Roman alphabet there are wanting four to make up the number of twenty-seven characters, their places are supplied with I, and V, simple consonants, as in the names of *John,* and *Valentine,* and *hi* and *hu,* aspirate consonants, as in *Hierom,* and *Huilhelme,* although the Germans for *hu* the asperate use a double vv;[6] the true Italians, and French in their vulgar speech put G joined with U instead thereof, writing thus, *Vuilhelmus,* and *Guilhelmus.*

1	2	3	4	5	6	7	8	9
A	B	C	D	E	F	G	H	I

10	20	30	40	50	60	70	80	90
K	L	M	N	O	P	Q	R	S

100	200	300	400	500	600	700	800	900
T	V	X	Y	Z	I	V	HI	HV

But if thou desirest to know the ruling star of anyone that is born, compute his name,[7] and of both his parents, through each letter according to the number above written, and divide the sum of the whole being gathered together by nine, subtracting it as often as thou canst; and if there remain a unity, or four, both signify the Sun; if two or seven, both signify the Moon; but three, Jupiter; five, Mercury; six, Venus; eight, Saturn; nine, Mars;[8] and the reasons thereof are showed elsewhere.

In like manner if thou desirest to know the horoscope[9] of anyone that is born, compute his name, and of his mother, and father, and divide the whole collected together by twelve; if there remain a unity, it signifies the Lion; if *Juno's* deuce, Aquarius; if the Vestal[10] three, Capricorn; if four, Sagittarius; if five, Cancer; if *Venus'* six, Taurus; if Palladian[11] seven, Aries; if *Vulcan's* eight, Libra; if *Mars* his nine, Scorpio; if ten, Virgo; if eleven, Pisces; if *Phoebus'* twelve, they represent Geminos; and the reasons of them are given elsewhere.

And let no man wonder that by the numbers of names many things may be prognosticated, seeing (the Pythagorean philosophers, and Hebrew Cabalists testifying the same) in those numbers lie certain occult mysteries understood by few: for the Most High created all things by number, measure, and weight,[12] from whence the truth of letters, and names had its original, which were not instituted casually, but by a certain rule (although unknown to us). Hence *John* in the Revelation saith, let him which hath understanding compute the number of the name of the beast, which is the number of a man.[13]

Yet these are not to be understood of those names, which a disagreeing difference of nations, and divers rites of nations according to the causes of places, or education have put upon men;[14] but those which were inspired into everyone at his birth, by the very heaven with the conjunction of stars, and those which the Hebrew mecubals, and wise men of Egypt long since taught to draw from the generation of everyone.

Notes—Chapter XX

1. *arithmancy*—Numerology.

2. *these verses* —Perhaps Spence has this passage in mind when he writes: "The Greeks examined the number and value of the letters in the names of two combatants, and predicted that he whose name contained most letters, or letters of the greatest value, would be the victor" (Spence [1920] 1968, 36).

3. *Pliny saith*—See note 7, ch. III, bk. II.

4. *Alexandrinus*—Perhaps Alexander of Aphrodisias. See biographical note.

5. *Ptolemy*—Ptolemy seems to disdain celestial numerology when he writes: "What, however, admits of prediction we shall investigate, not by means of lots and numbers, of which no reasonable explanation can be given, but merely through the science of the aspects of the stars ..." (*Tetrabiblos* 3.3 [Robbins, 237]). But presumably Agrippa is referring to one of the apocryphal works attributed to Ptolemy— perhaps *On the Apparitions of the Fixed Stars and a Collection of Prognostics.*

6. *double vv*—W.

7. *compute his name*—Agrippa does not specify if only the given names or the given and family names are to be used. However, in modern numerology, both given and family names are calculated together.

8. *Mars*—If nine divides evenly into the sum of the letter values of the names, it signifies Mars.

9. *horoscope*—The sign on the ascendant.

10. *Vestal*—The word comes from Vesta, the Roman form of the Greek Hestia, goddess of fire, whose sacred flame was tended by virgin priestesses, which cult Livy says originated in Alba, and was carried to Rome by Numa: "The priestesses were paid out of public funds to enable them to devote their whole time to the temple service, and were invested with special sanctity by the imposition of virginity" (Livy *Early History of Rome* [de Selincourt, 55]). Vestals were originally elected by the king from girls between six and ten years of age who had living parents, were free from physical and mental defects, and were children of freeborn residents in Italy. They served a term of 30 years, after which they were free to marry. At first four, their number was increased to six by either Tarquin I or Servius Tullius, and very late in their history a seventh was added. On the Vestals, see Plutarch's *Lives:* "Numa Pompilius."

11. *Palladian*—The Palladium was the most sacred of the seven objects guarded by the Vestal Virgins upon which the security of Rome was thought to depend. It was kept hidden from profane eyes, but consisted of a crude early statue of Pallas Athene said to have been carried to Rome from fallen Troy by Aeneas. It is represented on a coin struck by Antoninus Pius in honour of his wife, Faustina.

12. *number, measure, and weight*—See note 18, ch. VI, bk. II.

13. *number of a man*—See Revelation 13:18. The long accepted theory is that the Beast refers to the Roman emperor Nero. Caesar Nero written in Greek is NERON KESAR, which translated into Hebrew letters yields:

$$
\begin{array}{rl}
\text{N (נ)} & = 50 \\
\text{R (ר)} & = 200 \\
\text{O (ו)} & = 6 \\
\text{N (נ)} & = 50 \\
\text{K (ק)} & = 100 \\
\text{S (ס)} & = 60 \\
\text{R (ר)} & = \underline{200} \\
& 666
\end{array}
$$

This is the traditionally accepted solution. The classical scholar Robert Graves raises the objection that the Qoph, or Koph (ק) should more properly be a Kaph (כ) = 20, which would reduce the sum to 586. He offers an ingenious alternate solution based on the acronym D.C.L.X.V.I., Roman numerals which add up to 666 and which he makes stand for the words *Domitius Caesar Legatos Xti Violenter Interfecit* (Domitius Caesar basely killed the envoys of Christ). Domitius was Nero's original name. See Graves [1948] 1973, 345–6.

14. *put upon men*—Those names that have suffered translation from one language to another, or have arisen from the place of residence, or have been conferred as honorary titles, are not subject to numerical examination.

CHAPTER XXI

What numbers are consecrated to the gods, and which are ascribed, and to what elements.

Moreover the Pythagoreans have dedicated to the elements, and deities of heaven sacred numbers; for to the Air, they have assigned the number eight, and to Fire five, to the Earth six, to the Water twelve.

Besides, unity[1] is ascribed to the Sun, which is the only king of the stars, in which God put his tabernacle; and that this also is of *Jupiter,* doth the causative power of his ideal and intellectual species testify, who is the head, and the father of the gods, as unity is the beginning, and parent of numbers.

The number two[2] is ascribed to the Moon, which is the second great light, and figures out the Soul of the World, and is called *Juno,* because betwixt that and unity there is the first conjunction, and near fellowship; it is also ascribed to Saturn, and Mars, two unfortunate planets with the astrologers.

So the number three[3] is ascribed to Jupiter, the Sun, and Venus, viz. three fortunate planets, and is deputed to *Vesta, Hecate,* and *Diana;* hence they say:[4]

> Threefold is Hecate, three mouths Diana
> The virgin hath————

The number three therefore is dedicated to this virgin whom they say to be powerful in heaven, and in hell.[5]

The number four[6] is of the Sun, which by that number constitutes the corners of the heav-

ens, and distinguisheth seasons: it is also ascribed to *Cyllenius,* because he alone is called the foursquare god.[7]

The number five[8] consisting of the first even, and the first odd, as of female, and male, both sexes,[9] is assigned to Mercury; it is also attributed to the celestial world, which beyond the four elements is itself under another form, the fifth.[10]

The number six,[11] which consists of two threes, as a commixtion[12] of both sexes, is by the Pythagoreans ascribed to generation, and marriage, and belongs to Venus, and *Juno.*

The number seven[13] is of rest, and belongs to Saturn; the same also doth dispense the motion, and light of the Moon, and therefore is called by the name of *Tritonia* the Virgin,[14] because it begets nothing. It is assigned to *Minerva,*[15] because it proceeds of nothing; also to *Pallas* the Virago,[16] because it consists of numbers, as of males, and females. This also *Plutarch* ascribes[17] to *Apollo.*

The number eight,[18] by reason it contains the mystery of justice, is ascribed to Jupiter; it is also dedicated to *Vulcan,* for of the first motion, and number two, which is *Juno* drawn twice into itself, it consists; it is also attributed to *Cybele*[19] the mother of the gods, to whom every foursquare[20] is attributed. *Plutarch* assigns it to *Bacchus,* or *Dionysus,* who is said to be born the eighth month: others, because infants of the eighth month do not live, have attributed it to Saturn, and the three Ladies of Destiny.

315

The number nine[21] belongs to the Moon, the utmost receptacle[22] of all celestial influences, and virtues, as also it is dedicated to the nine Muses, as also to *Mars,* from whom is the end[23] of all things.

The number ten[24] is circular,[25] and belongs to the Sun, after the same manner as unity; also it is attributed to *Janus,*[26] because it is the end of the first order, and from whence begins the second unity; it is also ascribed to the world.

In like manner the number twelve, because the Sun going round twelve signs, distributes the year into twelve months, is attributed to the world, the heaven, and the Sun.

The number eleven, because it is semicircular,[27] is attributed to the Moon, and also deputed to *Neptune.*

Notes—Chapter XXI

1. *unity*—The monad was called by the Orphic and Pythagorean philosophers the Sun, Jupiter, Love, Proteus and Vesta.

2. *two*—The duad was named Phanes, Nature, Justice, Rhea, Diana, Cupid, Venus, Fate and Death.

3. *three*—The triad was called Juno, Latonia, Thetis, Hecate, Diana, Pluto, Tritogena and Minerva.

4. *hence*—The same reference occurs in ch. VI, bk. II.

5. *heaven, and in hell*—See note 37, ch. VI, bk. II.

6. *four*—The tetrad was called Hercules, Vulcan, Mercury, Bacchus, Bassarius, Pan, Harmony, Justice, the Two Mothered and the Key Keeper of Nature.

7. *foursquare*—Hermes was born on Mount Cyllene, hence his designation Cyllenius; he was called foursquare because his statues, which decorated gardens, consisted of an oblong block of stone with a square base surmounted by a carved head, or head and torso.

8. *five*—The pentad was named Nature, Pallas, Immortal, Providence, Nemesis, Venus and Justice.

9. *both sexes*—Female 2 plus male 3.

10. *the fifth*—Quintessence.

11. *six*—The hexad was named Venus, Health, the World, the Far Darting, Persaea, Triform and Amphitrite.

12. *commixtion*—2 × 3.

13. *seven*—The heptad was called Fortune, Minerva and Mars.

14. *Tritonia the Virgin*—In one story the goddess Athene was the daughter of Poseidon and Lake Tritonis, for which reason she was called Tritogenia (born of Triton). By a Cretan account that attempts to explain this epithet and reconcile it with the more common notion that the goddess sprang from the forehead of Zeus, Zeus is said to have struck his head against a cloud in which Athene lay hidden, knocking her out near the stream Triton.

15. *Minerva*—The Roman version of Athene.

16. *Pallas the Virago*—A virago is a manlike or heroic woman, which describes Athene, the warrior goddess. In this capacity she slew the giant Pallas and made from his skin the fabled aegis. Less poetically, her epithet Pallas is conjectured to derive from the Greek for "to strike," or possibly "girl."

17. *Plutarch ascribes*—

> It is not meet too eagerly to oppose these young men about these things, except by saying that every one of the numbers will afford you, if you desire to praise it, no small subject of commendations. And what need is there to speak of others? For the septener, sacred to Apollo, will take up a day's time, before one can in words run through all its powers. (Plutarch, "The E at Delphi." In *Moralia* 17 [Kippax, 4:493])

18. *eight*—The ogdoad was named Rhea, Love, Neptune and Law.

19. *Cybele*—Originally a Phrygian goddess of caverns and the Earth, when she became established in Greece she was merged with Rhea. The Romans called her the Great Mother because as wife of Cronus, she was mother to all the Olympic gods. She wore a square turreted crown in the shape of a city fortification, gaining her the title *Mater Turrita.* Another of her symbols was the whip decorated with knuckle bones with which her frenzied worshippers,

the Corybantes, would lash themselves to the beating of drums, the piping of flutes and the clashing of cymbals. These were the lunatics Apuleius describes:

> The day following I saw there a great number of persons apparelled in divers colours, having painted faces, mitres on their heads, vestiments coloured like saffron, Surplesses of silke, and on their feet yellow shooes, who attired the goddesse in a robe of Purple, and put her upon my backe. Then they went forth with their armes naked to their shoulders, bearing with them great swords and mightie axes, and dancing like mad persons. ... They made a thousand gestures with their feete and their hands, they would bite themselves, finally, every one tooke out his weapon and wounded his armes in divers places.
>
> Amongst whom there was one more mad then the rest ... therewithall he tooke a whip, and scourged his owne body, that the bloud issued out aboundantly, which thing caused me greatly to feare, to see such wounds and effusion of bloud, least the same goddesse desiring so much the bloud of men, should likewise desire the bloud of an Asse. *(The Golden Asse* 36)

20. *every foursquare*—Every cube number; in this case, 2 x 2 x 2.

21. *nine*—the ennead was named Ocean, Prometheus, Vulcan, Poean (Apollo), Juno and Proserpine.

22. *utmost receptacle*—Because the Moon is the celestial body nearest the Earth, she is the final intermediary between God and the Earth.

23. *the end*—Death, brought by Mars.

24. *ten*—The decad was named Heaven, the Sun, Unwearied, Fate, Phanes and Necessity. For all these designations of the ten numbers, see the introduction of Thomas Taylor to his translation of the *Hymns of Orpheus,* where he draws from the *Denarius Pythagoricus* of Meursius.

25. *circular*—Because it returns into unity. See note 16, ch. XIII, bk. II.

26. *Janus*—One of the few completely Roman deities, this god with two faces presided over doorways and ruled comings and goings. He was originally one of the Numina—the nebulous Powers that were the early deities of Rome—and was called the god of good beginnings.

27. *semicircular*—The Greeks knew π by the fraction 22/7, which is the ratio—roughly—of the diameter of a circle to its circumference. Perhaps this is why 11 (half of 22) is called semicircular: "... for the circumference of the circle equals three times the diameter plus a seventh part of this diameter. If the diameter is seven, the circumference is 22" (Theon 3.3 [Lawlor, 85]).

CHAPTER XXII

Of the tables of the planets, their virtues, forms, and what divine names, intelligences, and spirits are set over them.

It is affirmed by magicians, that there are certain tables of numbers distributed to the seven planets, which they call the sacred tables of the planets, endowed with many, and very great virtues of the heavens, in as much as they represent that divine order of celestial numbers, impressed upon celestials by the Ideas of the Divine Mind, by means of the Soul of the World, and the sweet harmony of those celestial rays, signifying according to the proportion of effigies,[1] supercelestial intelligencies, which can no other way be expressed, than by the marks of numbers, and characters.

For material numbers, and figures can do nothing in the mysteries of hid things, but representatively by formal numbers, and figures, as they are governed, and informed by intelligences, and divine numerations, which unite the extremes of the matter, and spirit to the will of the elevated soul, receiving through great affection, by the celestial power of the operator, a power from God, applied through the Soul of the Universe, and observations of celestial constellations, to a matter fit for a form, the mediums being disposed by the skill, and industry of magicians; but let us hasten to explain the tables severally.

The first of them is assigned to Saturn, and consists of a square of three, containing the particular numbers of nine, and in every line three every way, and through each diameter[2] making fifteen. Now the whole sum of numbers is forty-five. Over this are of divine names set such names as fill up the numbers with an intelli-

gency to what is good, with a spirit to what is bad,[3] and out of the same numbers is drawn the seal, or character of Saturn, and of the spirits thereof, such as we shall beneath ascribe to its table. They say that this table being with a fortunate Saturn[4] engraven on a plate of lead, doth help to bring forth, or birth, and to make a man safe, and powerful, and to cause success of petitions with princes, and powers: but if it be done with an unfortunate Saturn, that it hinders buildings, plantings, and the like, and casts a man from honours, and dignities, and causes discords, and quarrelings, and disperses an army.

The second is called the table of Jupiter, which consists of a quarternian drawn into itself,[5] containing sixteen particular numbers, and in every line, and diameter four, making thirty-four. Now the sum of all is 136. And there are over it divine names with an intelligence to good, with a spirit to bad, and out of it is drawn the character of Jupiter, and the spirits thereof. They say that if it be impressed upon a silver plate with Jupiter being powerful, and ruling, it conduceth to gain and riches, favour and love, peace and concord, and to appease enemies, to confirm honours, dignities, and counsels; and dissolve enchantments, if it be engraven on a coral.

The third table belongs to Mars, which is made of a square of five containing twenty-five numbers, and of these in every side and diameter five, which makes sixty-five, and the sum of all is 325. And there are over it divine names with an intelligence to good, with a spirit to bad, and out of it is drawn the character of Mars, and of his spirits. These with Mars being fortunate, being engraven on an iron plate, or sword, makes a man potent in war, and judgements, and petitions, and terrible to his enemies, and victorious against them; and if engraven upon the stonc corncola,[6] it stops blood, and the mestrues; but if it be engraven with Mars being unfortunate, on a plate of red brass it hinders buildings, casts down the powerful from dignities, honours, and riches, and causeth discord, strife, and hatred of men, and beasts, chaseth away bees, pigeons, and fish, and hinders mills, and renders them unfortunate that go forth to hunting, or fighting, and causeth barrenness in men and women, and other animals, and strikes a terror in all enemies, and compels them to submit.

The fourth table is of the Sun, and is made of a square of six, and contains thirty-six numbers, whereof six in every side, and diameter produce 111, and the sum of all is 666. There are over it divine names with an intelligency to what is good, and spirit to what is evil, and out of it are drawn characters of the Sun, and of the spirits thereof. This being engraven on a golden plate with the Sun being fortunate, renders him that wears it to be renowned, amiable, acceptable, potent in all his works, and equals a man to kings, and princes, elevating him to high fortunes, enabling to do whatsoever he pleaseth: but with an unfortunate Sun, it makes a tyrant, and a man to be proud, ambitious, unsatisfiable, and to have an ill ending.

The fifth table is of Venus, consisting of a square of seven drawn into itself, viz. of forty-nine numbers, whereof seven on each side and diameter make 175, and the sum of all is 1225. And there are over it divine names with an intelligency to good, and spirit to evil; and there is drawn out of it the character of Venus, and of the spirits thereof. This being engraven on a silver plate, Venus being fortunate, procureth concord, endeth strife, procureth the love of women, conduceth to conception, is good against barrenness, causeth ability for generation, dissolves enchantments, and causeth peace between men, and women, and maketh all kind of animals and cattle fruitful; and being put into a dove house, causeth an increase of pigeons. It conduceth to the cure of all melancholy distempers, and causeth joyfulness; and being carried about travelers makes them fortunate. But if it be formed upon brass with an unfortunate Venus, it causeth contrary things to all that hath been above said.

The sixth table is of Mercury, resulting from the square of eight drawn into itself, containing sixty-four numbers, whereof eight on every side and by both diameters make 260, and the sum of all 2080. And over it are set divine names with an intelligency to what is good, with a spirit to what is evil, and from it is drawn a character of Mercury, and of the spirits thereof; and if it be with Mercury being fortunate engraven upon silver, or tin, or yellow brass, or be writ upon virgin parchment,[7] it renders the bearer thereof grateful, and fortunate to do what he pleaseth: it bringeth gain, and prevents poverty, conduceth to memory, understanding, and divination, and to the understanding of occult things by dreams: and if it be an unfortunate Mercury, doth all things contrary to these.

The seventh table is of the Moon, of a square of nine multiplied into itself, having eighty-one numbers, in every side and diameter nine, producing 369, and the sum of all is 3321. And there are over it divine names with an intelligency to what is good, and a spirit to what is bad. And of it are drawn the characters of the Moon, and of the spirits thereof. This fortunate Moon being engraven on silver, renders the bearer thereof grateful, amiable, pleasant, cheerful, honoured, removing all malice, and ill will. It causeth security in a journey, increase of riches, and health of body, drives away enemies and other evil things from what place thou pleaseth; and if it be an unfortunate Moon engraven in a plate of lead, wherever it shall be buried, it makes that place unfortunate, and the inhabitants thereabouts, as also ships, rivers, fountains, mills, and it makes every man unfortunate, against whom it shall be directly done, making him fly from his country, and that place of his abode where it shall be buried, and it hinders physicians, and orators, and all men whatsoever in their office, against whom it shall be made.

Now how the seals, and characters of the stars,[8] and spirits are drawn from these tables, the wise searcher, and he which shall understand the verifying of these tables, shall easily find out.[9]

Divine names answering
to the numbers of Saturn.

3	Ab	אב
9	Hod	הד
15	Jah	יה
15	Hod	הוד
45	Jehovah extended	יוד הא ואו הא

The Intelligence of Saturn.

| 45 | Agiel | אגיאל |

The Spirit of Saturn.

| 45 | Zazel | זאזל |

Divine names answering
to the numbers of Jupiter.

4	Aba[10]	אבא
16	—	הוה
16	—	אהי
34	El Ab	אלאב

The Intelligence of Jupiter.

| 136 | Johphiel | יהפיאל |

The Spirit of Jupiter.

| 136 | Hismael | הסמאל |

Divine names answering
to the numbers of Mars.

5	He, the letter of the holy name.	ה
25	—	יהי
65	Adonai	אדני

The Intelligence of Mars.

| 325 | Graphiel | גראפיאל |

The Spirit of Mars.

| 325 | Barzabel[11] | ברצבאל |

Divine names answering
to the numbers of the Sun.

6	Vau, the letter of the holy name.	ו
6	He extended, the letter of the holy name.	הא
36	Eloh	אלה

The Intelligence of the Sun.

| 111 | Nachiel | נכיאל |

The Spirit of the Sun.

| 666 | Sorath | סורת |

Divine names answering
to the numbers of Venus.

| 7 | — | אהא |

The Intelligence of Venus.

| 49 | Hagiel | הגיאל |

The Spirit of Venus.

| 175[12] | Kedemel | קדמאל |

The Intelligences of Venus.

| 1225[13] | Bne Seraphim | בני שרפים |

Divine names answering
to the numbers of Mercury.

8	Asboga,[14] eight extended.	אזבוגה
64	Din	דין
64	Doni	דני

The Intelligence of Mercury.

| 260 | Tiriel | טיריאל |

The Spirit of Mercury.

| 2080 | Taphthartharath | תפתרתרת |

Divine names answering
to the numbers the Moon.

| 9 | Hod | הד |
| 81 | Elim | אלים |

The Spirit of the Moon.

| 369 | Hasmodai | חשמודאי |

The Spirit of the Spirits of the Moon.

| 3321 | Schedbarschemoth Schartathan | שדברשהמעת שרתתן |

The Intelligency of the Intelligence of the Moon.

| 3321 | Malcha betharsithim hed beruah schehakim | מלכא בתרשיתים עד ברוח שחקים |

SATURN

The table of Saturn in his Compass

4	9	2
3	5	7
8	1	6

In Hebrew notes

ד	ט	ב
ג	ה	ז
ח	א	ו

The Seals or Characters

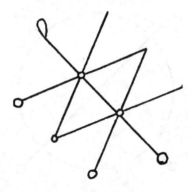

Of Saturn

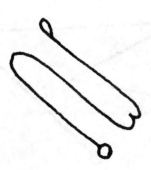

Of the Intelligence of Saturn

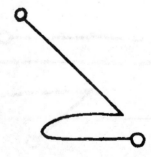

Of the Spirit of Saturn

JUPITER

The table of Jupiter in his Compass

4	14	15	1
9	7	6	12
5	11	10	8
16	2	3	13

In Hebrew notes

ד	יד	טו	א
ט	ז	ו	יב
ה	יא	י	ח
יו	ב	ג	יג

The Seals or Characters

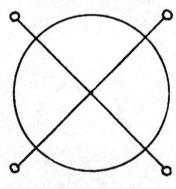

Of Jupiter

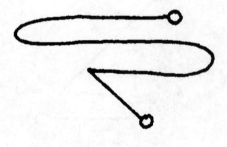

Of the Intelligence of Jupiter

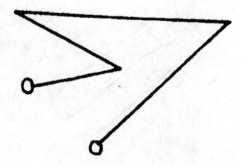

Of the Spirit of Jupiter

MARS

The table of Mars in his Compass

11	24	7	20	3
4	12	25	8	16
17	5	13	21	9
10	18	1	14	22
23	6	19	2	15

In Hebrew notes

יא	כד	ז	כ	ג
ד	יב	כה	ח	יו
יז	ה	יג	כא	ט
י	יח	א	יד	כב
כג	ו	יט	ב	יה

The Seals or Characters

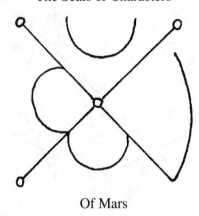

Of Mars

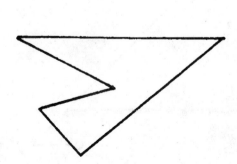

Of the Intelligence of Mars

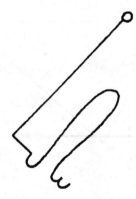

Of the Spirit of Mars

SOL

The table of the Sun in his Compass

In Hebrew notes

6	32	3	34	35	1
7	11	27	28	8	30
19	14	16	15	23	24
18	20	22	21	17	13
25	29	10	9	26	12
36	5	33	4	2	31

ו	לב	ג	לד	לה	א
ז	יא	כז	כח	ח	ל
יט	יד	יו	יה	כג	כד
יח	כ	כב	כא	יז	יג
כה	כט	י	ט	כו	יב
לו	ה	לג	ד	ב	לא

The Seals or Characters

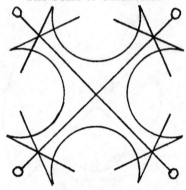

Of the Sun

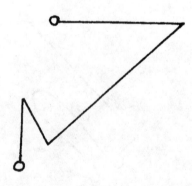

Of the Intelligence of the Sun

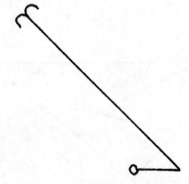

Of the Spirit of the Sun

VENUS

The table of Venus in her Compass

22	47	16	41	10	35	4
5	23	48	17	42	11	29
30	6	24	49	18	36	12
13	31	7	25	43	19	37
38	14	32	1	26	44	20
21	39	8	33	2	27	45
46	15	40	9	34	3	28

In Hebrew notes

כב	מז	יו	מא	י	לה	ד
ה	כג	מח	יז	מב	יא	כט
ל	ו	כד	מט	יח	לו	יב
יג	לא	ז	כה	מג	יט	לז
לח	יד	לב	א	כו	מד	כ
כא	לט	ח	לג	ב	כז	מה
מו	יה	מ	ט	לד	ג	כח

The Seals or Characters

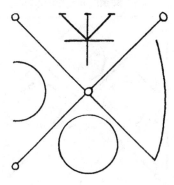

Of Venus

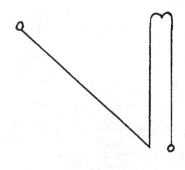

Of the Intelligence
of Venus

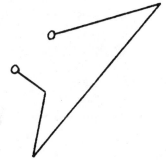

Of the Spirit of
Venus

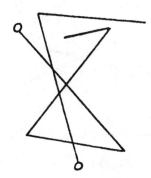

Of the Intelligences
of Venus

MERCURY

The table of Mercury in his Compass

8	58	59	5	4	62	63	1
49	15	14	52	53	11	10	56
41	23	22	44	45	19	18	48
32	34	35	29	28	38	39	25
40	26	27	37	36	30	31	33
17	47	46	20	21	43	42	24
9	55	54	12	13	51	50	16
64	2	3	61	60	6	7	57

In Hebrew notes

ח	נח	נט	ה	ד	סג	סב	א
מט	יה	יד	נב	נג	יא	י	נו
מא	כג	כב	מד	מה	יט	יח	מח
לב	לד	לה	כט	כח	לח	לט	כה
מ	כו	כז	לז	לו	ל	לא	לג
יז	מז	מו	כ	כא	מג	מב	כד
ט	נה	נד	יב	יג	נא	נ	יו
סד	ב	ג	סא	ס	ו	ז	נז

The Seals or Characters

Of Mercury

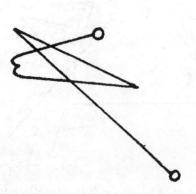

Of the Intelligence of Mercury

Of the Spirit of Mercury

LUNA

The table of the Moon in her Compass

37	78	29	70	21	62	13	54	5
6	38	79	30	71	22	63	14	46
47	7	39	80	31	72	23	55	15
16	48	8	40	81	32	64	24	56
57	17	49	9	41	73	33	65	25
26	58	18	50	1	42	74	34	66
67	27	59	10	51	2	43	75	35
36	68	19	60	11	52	3	44	76
77	28	69	20	61	12	53	4	45

In Hebrew notes

לז	עח	כט	ע	כא	סב	יג	נד	ה
ו	לח	עט	ל	עא	כב	סג	יד	מו
מז	ז	לט	פ	לא	עב	כג	נה	יה
יו	מח	ח	מ	פא	לב	סד	כד	נו
נז	יז	מט	ט	מא	עג	לג	סה	כה
כו	נח	יח	נ	א	מב	עד	לד	סו
סז	כז	נט	י	נא	ב	מג	עה	לה
לו	סח	יט	ס	יא	נב	ג	מד	עו
עז	כח	סט	כ	סא	יב	נג	ד	מה

The Seals or Characters

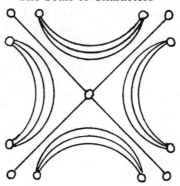

Of the Moon

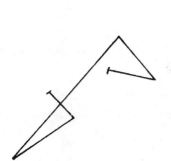

Of the Spirit
of the Moon

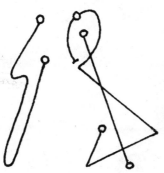

Of the Spirit of
the Spirits of the Moon

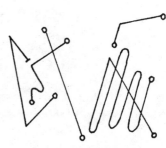

Of the Intelligence
of the Intelligences
of the Moon

Notes—Chapter XXII

1. *effigies*—Sigils.

2. *diameter*—Diagonal.

3. *what is bad*—Agrippa uses the term intelligence to denote a benevolent supernatural being, and spirit to denote a malevolent supernatural being.

4. *fortunate Saturn*—At the time when Saturn occupies a favorable position in the heavens astrologically, causing its influence to be benign.

5. *drawn into itself*—4 x 4.

6. *stone corneola*—Cornelian, the stone favored by Pliny for seal rings, is said to cause concord, to still angry passions, to drive away evil thoughts, and to render harmless witchcrafts and the evil eye. The description applied to it here belongs with coral, about which Gerard says: "It [coral] is a soveraigne remedy to drie, to stop, and stay all issues of bloud whatsoever in man or woman" (Gerard 1633, 3:166:1578). Since coral is the stone of Mars because of its red color and power over blood, it is certain that an error has been made by Agrippa or one of his early copyists, and cornelian should rightly be placed with Jupiter, while coral should appear with Mars.

7. *virgin parchment*—

Genuine Virgin Parchment is necessary in many Magical Operations and should be properly prepared and consecrated. There are two kinds, one called Virgin, the other Unborn. Virgin parchment is that which is taken from an Animal which hath not attained the age of generation, whether it be ram, or kid, or other animal.

Unborn parchment is taken from an animal which hath been taken before its time from the uterus of its mother. (*The Greater Key of Solomon* 2.17, trans. S. L. MacGregor Mathers [Chicago: De Laurence Company, 1914 {1889}], 114)

8. *stars*—Planets.

9. *easily find out*—See Appendix V.

10. *Aba*—This divine name of Jupiter is spelled "Abab" in the English edition and "Abba" in the Latin *Opera*.

11. *Barzabel*—For some inexplicable reason this name appears as ברצאבאל in both English and Latin editions. The Aleph (א) in the middle is superfluous.

12. *175*—Incorrectly given as "157" in both English and Latin editions.

13. *1225*—Incorrectly given as "1252" in both editions, but strangely enough the divine name accurately corresponds to this faulty number. See Appendix V for the numerical breakdown of the name.

14. *Asboga*—The Hebrew version of this name appears with only five letters in both English and Latin editions, whereas it should have six—it is explained at the end of Appendix V.

Talismans

From *The Magus* by Francis Barrett (London, 1801)

Chapter XXIII

Of geometrical figures and bodies, by what virtue they are powerful in magic, and which are agreeable to each element, and the heaven.

Geometrical figures also arising from numbers, are conceived to be of no less power.

Of these first of all, a circle doth answer to unity, and the number ten; for unity is the center, and circumference of all things; and the number ten being heaped together returns into a unity from whence it had its beginning, being the end, and complement of all numbers. A circle is called an infinite line in which there is no *terminus a quo* nor *terminus ad quem*,[1] whose beginning and end is in every point, whence also a circular motion is called infinite, not according to time but according to place; hence a circular being the largest[2] and perfectest of all is judged to be most fit for bindings and conjurations; whence they who adjure evil spirits are wont to environ themselves about with a circle.[3]

A pentangle[4] also, as with the virtue of the number five hath a very great command over evil spirits, so by its lineature, by which it hath within five obtuse angles, and without five acutes,[5] five double triangles[6] by which it is surrounded. The interior pentangle contains in it great mysteries, which also is to be inquired after, and understood of the other figures, viz. triangle, quadrangle, sexangle, septangle, octangle, and the rest, of which many, as they are made of many and divers insections,[7] obtain divers significations and virtues according to the divers manner of drawing, and proportions of lines, and numbers.

The Egyptians, and Arabians confirmed that the figure of the cross hath very great power, and that is the most firm receptacle of all celestial powers, and intelligences, because it is the rightest figure of all, containing four right angles, and it is the first description of the superficies, having longitude and latitude:[8] and they said it is inspired with the fortitude of the celestials, because their fortitude results by the straightness of angles and rays: and stars are then most potent when they possess four corners in the figure of the heaven, and make a cross,[9] by the projection of their rays mutually. It hath moreover (as we showed before) a very great correspondency with the numbers 5, 7, 9, most potent numbers. It was also reckoned by the Egyptian priests, from the beginning of religion amongst sacred letters, signifying amongst them allegorically the life of future salvation.[10] It was also impressed on the picture of *Serapis*, and was had in great veneration amongst the Greeks. But what here belongs to religion we shall discuss elsewhere.

This is to be observed, whatsoever wonderful thing figures work when we write them in papers, plates, or images, they do not do it but by the virtue acquired from sublimer figures, by a certain affection which natural aptitude or resemblance procures, in as much as they are exactly configured to them, as from an opposite wall the echo is caused, and in a hollow glass[11] the collection of the solary rays, which afterward reflecting upon an opposite body, either wood, or any combustible thing, doth forthwith burn it: or as an harp causeth a resounding in another harp, which is no otherwise but because a suitable and like figure is set before it, or as two strings on a harp being touched with an equal distance of time, and modulated to the same intention, when one is touched the other shakes also:[12] also the figures, of which we have spoken, and what characters soever concern the virtues of the celestial figures as they shall be opportunely impressed upon things, those ruling, or be rightly framed, as one figure is of affinity with, and doth express another. And as these are spoken of figures, so also they are to be understood of geometrical bodies, which are a sphere, a tetrahedron, hexahedron, octahedron, icosahedron, dodecahedron, and such like.

Neither must we pass over what figures *Pythagoras* and his followers *Timaeus, Locrus,*

and *Plato* assigned to the elements[13] and heavens: for first of all they assigned to the Earth a four square, and a square of eight solid angles, and of twenty-four planes,[14] and six bases in form of a dice: to the Fire, a pyramis of four triangular bases, and of so many solid angles, and of twelve planes: to the Air octahedron, of eight triangular bases, and six solid angles, and twenty-four planes: and lastly, to Water they have assigned icosahedron twenty bases, twelve solid angles: to the heaven they have assigned dodecahedron of twelve five-cornered bases, and twenty solid angles, and sixty planes.

Now he which knows the powers, relations, and properties of these figures and bodies, shall be able to work many wonderful things in natural and mathematical magic, especially in glasses. And I know how to make by them wonderful things, in which anyone might see whatsoever he pleased at a long distance.[15]

Notes—Chapter XXIII

1. *terminus ad quem*—Terminus a quo is scholastic Latin for "term from which," thus the starting point; *terminus ad quem* means "term to which," thus the end point.

2. *largest*—A circle of a given circumference comprehends a larger area than any other plane figure with the same perimeter.

3. *with a circle*—In ritual evocation, where evil or dangerous spirits are called forth into the world, the magician stands within a protective circle. This acts as a magical barrier and bars the entry of the spirit or its influence.

4. *pentangle*—Pentagram:

5. *five acutes*—The five obtuse angles are those within the open center of the pentagram; the acute angles are those within the points.

6. *double triangles*—"Double" is used in the sense of correspondence or correlation, and indicates that the five surrounding triangles are all alike.

7. *insections*—Divisions or indentations.

8. *longitude and latitude*—A plane is described by two dimensions, length and breadth.

9. *make a cross*—See note 16, ch.X, bk. II.

10. *future salvation*—The ankh is an Egyptian hieroglyphic symbol signifying life and resurrection:

11. *glass*—That is, a concave mirror. This method of starting fires was used by the Vestal virgins to ritually rekindle the flame of Vesta, as fire brought down directly from the Sun was considered more primal, and thus more holy, than fire generated in common ways. Of the perpetual fire of Vesta, Plutarch writes:

> … it was esteemed an impiety to light it from common sparks or flame, or from anything but the pure and unpolluted rays

of the sun, which they usually effect by concave mirrors, of a figure formed by the revolution of an isosceles rectangular triangle, all the lines from the circumference of which meeting in the centre, by holding it in the light of the sun they can collect and concentrate all its rays at this one point of convergence; where the air will now become rarefied, and any light, dry, combustible matter will kindle as soon as applied, under the effect of the rays, which here acquired the substance and active force of fire. (Plutarch "Numa Pompilius." In *Lives* [Dryden, 82])

12. *other shakes also*—This phenomenon is called sympathetic vibration.

13. *to the elements*—See Appendix III.

14. *twenty-four planes*—Twenty-four plane angles.

15. *at a distance*—This sounds very much like the telescope. The exact time and place of its invention is in considerable dispute. It is evident that Roger Bacon, who died at the end of the 13th century, at least knew the theory of the telescope:

> Glasses [mirrors] or diaphanous bodies [lenses] may be so formed that the most remote objects may appear just at hand, and the contrary, so that we may read the smallest letters at an incredible distance, and may number things, though never so small, and may make the stars [planets] also appear as near as we please. (Bacon *Epistola ad Parisiensem*)

Giambattista della Porte, writing not long after Agrippa, says: "If you do but know how to join the two (vis. the concave and the convex glasses) rightly together, you will see both remote and near objects larger than they otherwise appear, and withal very distinct" *(Magia Naturalis, 1558)*.

CHAPTER XXIV

Of musical harmony,
of the force and power thereof.

Musical harmony also is not destitute of the gifts of the stars; for it is a most powerful imaginer of all things, which whilst it follows opportunely the celestial bodies, doth wonderfully allure the celestial influence, and doth change the affections, intentions, gestures, motions, actions and dispositions of all the hearers, and doth quietly allure them to its own properties, as to gladness, lamentation, to boldness, or rest, and the like; also it allures beasts, serpents, birds, dolphins to the hearing of its pleasant tunes.

So birds are allured with pipes, and harts[1] are caught by the same. Fish in the lake of Alexandria[2] are delighted with a noise. Music hath caused friendship betwixt men and dolphins.[3] The sound of the harp doth lead up and down the Hyperborean[4] swans. Melodious voices tame the Indian elephants: and the very elements delight in music. The Hulesian fountain[5] otherwise calm and quiet, if the trumpet sound, riseth up rejoicing, and swells over its banks. There are in Lydia those which they call the Nymphs' Islands,[6] which at the sound of a trumpet forthwith come into the middle of the sea, and turning round lead a dance, and then are returned to the shores; *M. Varro* testifies that he saw them.

And there are more wonderful things than these. For in the shore of Attica the sea sounds like a harp. A certain stone of Megaris[7] makes a sound like a harp every time the string of a harp

is struck; so great is the power of music, that it appeaseth the mind, raiseth the spirit, stirreth up soldiers to fight, and refresheth the weary, calls back them that are desperate, refresheth travelers. And the Arabians say, that camels carrying burdens are refreshed by the singing of their leaders. In like manner, they that carry great burdens, sing, and are thereby strengthened and refreshed: for singing causeth delight and strength, pacifieth enemies, moderates the rage of madmen, chaseth away vain imaginations.[8]

Hence it is that *Democritus* and *Theophrastus* affirm that some diseases of the body, and mind may thus be cured, or caused.[9] So we read that *Therpander,* and *Arion* of Lesbos cured the Lesbians, and Ionians by music; and *Ismenia*[10] of Thebes cured divers of very great diseases by music; moreover *Orpheus, Amphion, David, Pythagoras, Empedocles,*[11] *Asclepiades, Timotheus,* were wont to do many wonderful things by sounds: sometimes they did stir up dull spirits by familiar sounds; sometimes they did restrain wanton, furious, angry spirits by more grave tones. So *David* with a harp moderated *Saul* in a rage.[12] So *Pythagoras* recalled a luxurious young man from immoderate lust.[13] So *Timotheus* stirred up King *Alexander* to a rage, and again repressed him.[14]

Saxo the Grammarian, in his History of the Danes, tells of a certain musician, who boasted that he could by his music make everyone that heard it mad; and when he was constrained by the king's command to perform the same, he endeavoured to work several ways upon the affections; and first, by a tone of musical gravity filled the hearers with a kind of sadness and unsensibleness; then by a more lively sound he made them rejoice, and dance; and lastly, he by a more earnest music, reduced them to fury and madness.

We read also, that they in Apulia that were touched with a kind of dangerous spider,[15] were astonished until they heard a certain sound, at the hearing of which everyone riseth up and danceth. And it is believed *(Gellius* being witness) that they that are pained with the sciatica,[16] are eased at the sound of a pipe. Also *Theophrastus* reports, that the sound of a flute cures the biting of spiders, and *Democritus* himself confesseth that the consort of pipers, hath been a cure for very many diseases.

Notes—Chapter XXIV

1. *harts*—Of the musical proclivity of deer, Pliny says: "They are soothed by the shepherd's pipe and his song ..."(Pliny 8.50 [Bostock and Riley, 2:300]).

2. *lake of Alexandria*—Mareotis, which lay just behind the city. A canal ran from Eunostos, one of the two harbors of Alexandria, into the lake. It may be to this that Pliny refers when he writes "Fish have neither organs of hearing, nor yet the exterior orifice. And yet, it is quite certain that they do hear; for it is a well-known fact, that in some fish-ponds they are in the habit of being assembled to be fed by the clapping of the hands" (Pliny 10.89 [Bostock and Riley, 2:547]

3. *dolphins*—"The dolphin is an animal not only friendly to man, but a lover of music as well; he is charmed by melodious concerts, and more especially by the notes of the water-organ" (Pliny 9.8 [Bostock and Riley, 2:371–2]).

4. *Hyperborean*—Familiarly applied to the most northerly of anything. In legend Hyperborea was a land "beyond the north wind" inhabited by a blessed people that enjoyed perpetual sunshine, free from disease, hunger, toil, care and war. The Hyperboreans worshipped Apollo, who had visited them for a year shortly after his birth, and were a cheerful race delighting in song and dance. At first Hyperborea was probably the land of northern Thessaly, but as knowledge of geography grew, it was pushed north, becoming identified with western Europe and the Celtae, and later with the region on the shores of the fabled Hyperboreus Oceanus, beyond the mythical Grypes and Arimaspi, who were reputed to dwell north of the Scythians.

5. *Hulesian*—Perhaps located in the Halesian plain in the Troad (land surrounding Troy), which has hot salt springs.

6. *Nymphs' Islands*—"There are some small islands in the Nymphaeus [in Illyria], called the Dancers, because, when choruses are sung, they are moved by the motions of those who beat time" (Pliny 2.96 [Bostock and Riley, 1:123]).

7. *Megaris*—See note 3, ch. X, bk. I.

8. *vain imaginations*—

> And is it not for this reason, Glaucon, said I, that education in music is most sovereign, because more than anything else rhythm and harmony find their way to the inmost soul and take strongest hold upon it, bringing with them and imparting grace, if one is rightly trained, and otherwise the contrary? And further, because omissions and the failure of beauty in things badly made or grown would be most quickly perceived by one who was properly educated in music, and so, feeling distaste rightly, he would praise beautiful things and take delight in them and receive them into his soul to foster its growth and become himself beautiful and good. (Plato *Republic* 3.401d [Hamilton and Cairns, 646])

> And harmony, which has motions akin to the revolutions of our souls, is not regarded by the intelligent votary of the Muses as given by them with a view to irrational pleasure, which is deemed to be the purpose of it in our day, but as meant to correct any discord which may have arisen in the courses of the soul, and to be our ally in bringing her into harmony and agreement with herself, and rhythm too was given by them for the same reason, on account of the irregular and graceless ways which prevail among mankind generally, and to help us against them. (Plato *Timaeus* 47d [Hamilton and Cairns, 1175])

9. *cured, or caused*—The Cretan musician Thaletas was invited to Sparta during a pestilence around 620 BC, which he is supposed to have ended.

10. *Ismenia*—Apollo was called Ismenius by virtue of having one of his temples located beside the Ismenus River, which rose in Mount Cithaeron and flowed through Thebes. According to legend the boy Ismenus was struck by an arrow of Apollo and leaped into the river, giving it his name.

11. *Empedocles*—

> When a certain youth also rushed with a drawn sword on Anchitus, the host of Empedocles, because, being a judge, he had publicly condemned his father to death, and would have slain him as a homicide, Empedocles changed the intention of the youth, by singing to his lyre that verse of Homer,
>
> Nepenthe, without gall, o'er every ill
> Oblivion spreads; *[Odyssey* 4, lines 793–4]
>
> and thus snatched his host Anchitus from death, and the youth from his crime of homicide. (Iamblichus *Life of Pythagoras* 25 [Taylor, 60–1])

12. *Saul in a rage*—I Samuel 16:23.

13. *immoderate lust*—

> Among the deeds of Pythagoras likewise, it is said, that once through the spondaic song of a piper, he extinguished the rage of a Tauromenian lad, who had been feasting by night, and intended to burn the vestibule of his mistress, in consequence of seeing her coming from the house of a rival. For the lad was inflamed and excited [to this rash attempt] by a Phrygian song; which however Pythagoras most rapidly suppressed. But Pythagoras, as he was astronomizing, happened to meet with the Phrygian piper at an unseasonable time of night, and persuaded him to change his Phrygian for a spondaic song; through which the fury of the lad being immediately repressed, he returned home in an orderly manner, though a little before this, he could not be in the least restrained, nor would in short, bear any admonition; and even stupidly insulted Pythagoras when he met him. (Iamblichus *Life of Pythagoras* 25 [Taylor, 60])

14. *repressed him*—Timotheus was a flute player of Thebes. Once when he was performing before Alexander the Great an Orthian Nome to Athene, Alexander leapt from his seat and seized the musician by the arms. This was the germ for the well known poem of Dryden, *Alexander's Feast,* which is based on a passage in Plutarch's *Life of Alexander,* where, however, Timotheus is not mentioned by name. Dryden gives the musician a lyre, perhaps confusing him with Timotheus of Miletus (see biographical note).

15. *dangerous spider*—The bite of the tarantula *(Lycosa tarantula,* formerly called *Tarantula apuliae),* a large venomous wolf spider that was found in abundance in the town of Tarentum in the Italian region of Apulia, was thought to be the cause of tarantism, an hysterical malady characterized by a wild impulse to dance. Tarantism was said to be similar to St Vitus' dance, and was epidemic in Apulia from the 15th to the 17th century. The tarantella, a peasant dance of southern Italy popular since the 15th century, is supposed to cure tarantism if those bitten by the spider dance it until they drop from exhaustion. It may be that there never was a disease as such, and that all the dancing originated as a folk remedy against the bite of the spider.

16. *sciatica*—A disease characterized by neuralgic pain in the hip.

CHAPTER XXV

Of sound, and harmony, and whence their wonderfulness in operation.

oreover we shall not deny, that there is in sounds a virtue to receive the heavenly gifts; if with *Pythagoras* and *Plato* we thought the heavens to consist by an harmonical composition, and to rule and cause all things by harmonical tones and motions.[1]

Singing can do more than the sound of an instrument, in as much as it arising by an harmonical consent, from the conceit of the mind, and imperious affection of the phantasy[2] and heart, easily penetrateth by motion, with the refracted and well tempered air, the aerious spirit of the hearer, which is the bond of soul and body; and transferring the affection and mind of the singer with it, it moveth the affection of the hearer by his affection, and the hearer's phantasy by his phantasy, and mind by his mind, and striketh the mind, and striketh the heart, and pierceth even to the inwards of the soul, and by little and little, infuseth even dispositions: moreover it moveth and stoppeth the members and humours of the body.

From hence in moving the affections harmony conferreth so much, that not only natural, but also artificial and vocal harmony doth yield a certain power both to the souls and bodies: but it is necessary that all consorts[3] proceed from fit foundations, both in stringed instruments, in pipes, and vocal singings, if you would have them agree well together: for no man can make the roaring of lions, the lowing of oxen, the neighing of horses, the braying of asses, the grunting of

hogs to be harmonious: neither can the strings made of sheep's and wolf's guts, be brought to any agreement, because their foundations are dissonant; but the many and divers voices of men agree together, because they have one foundation in the species or kind: so many birds agree, because they have one nigh genus or kind, and a resemblance from above; also artificial instruments agree with natural voices, because the similitude that is betwixt them, is either true and manifest, or hath a certain analogy.

But every harmony is either of sounds or voices. Sound is a breath, voice is sound and animate breath; speech is a breath pronounced with sound, and a voice signifying something: the spirit of which proceedeth out of the mouth with sound and voice; *Chalcidius* saith, that a voice is sent forth out of the inward cavity of the breast and heart, by the assistance of the spirit. By which, together with the tongue, forming, and striking the narrow passages of the mouth, and by the other vocal organs, are delivered articulate sounds; the elements of speech, by which interpreter the secret motions of the mind are laid open: but *Lactantius* saith,[4] that the nature of the voice is very obscure, and cannot be comprehended how it is made, or what it is.

To conclude, all music consisteth in voice, in sound, and hearing: sound without air cannot be audible, which though it be necessary for hearing, yet, as air, it is not of itself audible, nor to be perceived by any sense, unless by accident; for the sight seeth it not, unless it be coloured, nor the ears unless sounding, nor the smell unless odoriferous, nor the taste unless it be sapid, nor the touch unless it be cold or hot, and so forth: therefore though sound cannot be made without air, yet is not sound of the nature of air, nor air of the nature of sound, but air is the body of the life of our sensitive spirit, and is not of the nature of any sensible object, but of a more sim- ple and higher virtue; but it is meet that the sensitive soul should vivify the air joined to it; and in the vivified air, which is joined to the spirit, perceive the species of objects put forth into act, and this is done in the living air, but in a subtile and diaphanous the visible species, in an ordinary air the audible, in a more gross air the species of other senses are perceived.

Notes—Chapter XXV

1. *tones and motions—*

> But for all this, my most honored friends, methinks you have forgot the chiefest thing of all, and that which renders music most majestic. For Pythagoras, Archytas, Plato, and many others of the ancient philosophers, were of opinion, that there could be no motion of the world or rolling of the spheres without the assistance of music, since the Supreme Deity created all things harmoniously. (Plutarch *On Music* 44, trans. John Philips [Goodwin, 1:134])

> And the spindle [of the universe] turned on the knees of Necessity, and up above on each of the rims of the circles a Siren stood, borne around in its revolution and uttering one sound, one note, and from all the eight there was the concord of a single harmony. And there were three others who sat round about at equal intervals, each one on her throne, the Fates, daughters of Necessity, clad in white vestments with fil- leted heads, Lachesis, and Clotho, and Atropos, who sang in unison with the music of the Sirens, Lachesis singing the things that were, Clotho the things that are, and Atropos the things that are to be. (Plato *Republic* 10.617b-c [Hamilton and Cairns, 841])

"'The seven spheres give the seven sounds of the lyre/and produce a harmony (that is to say, an octave), because of the intervals which separate them from one another'" (Alexander of Aetolia, quoted by Theon 3.15 [Lawlor, 92]).

2. *phantasy—*Imagination.

3. *consorts—*The harmonious combination of voices or instruments.

4. *Lactantius saith—*

> But what account can we give of the voice? Grammarians, indeed, and philoso- phers, define the voice to be air struck by the breath; from which words [*verba,* pre- sumed to be from *verbero:* to strike] derive their name: which is plainly false. For the voice is not produced outside of the mouth, but within, and therefore that opinion is more probable, that the breath, being com- pressed, when it has struck against the obstacle presented by the throat, forces out the sound of the voice: ... Now, whether this is true, God, who is the designer, may see. For the voice appears to arise not from the mouth, but from the innermost breast. In fine, even when the mouth is closed, a sound such as is possible is emitted from the nostrils. Moreover, also, the voice is not affected by the greatest breath with which we gasp, but with a light and not compressed breath, as often as we wish. It has not therefore been comprehended in what manner it takes place, or what it is altogether. (Lactantius *De opificio dei sive de formatione hominis* [On the workman- ship of God, or the formation of man] 15. In *The Writings,* trans. William Fletcher, in *Ante-Nicene Christian Library* [Edin- burgh: T. and T. Clark, 1871], 22:82)

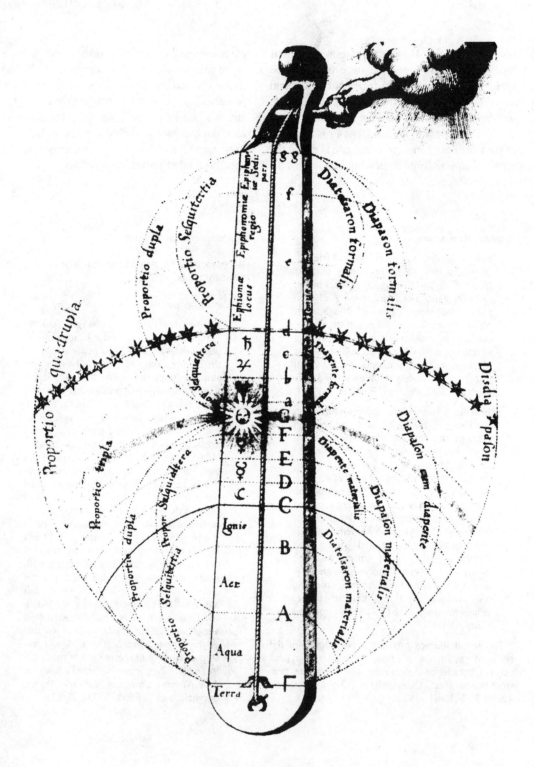

Harmony of the World

From *Utriusque cosmi maioris scilicet et minoris metaphysica, physica atque technica historia*
by Robert Fludd (Oppenheim, 1617)

CHAPTER XXVI

Concerning the agreement of them with the celestial bodies, and what harmony and sound is correspondent of every star.

But understand now, that of the seven planets, Saturn, Mars, and the Moon have more of the voice than of the harmony. Saturn hath sad, hoarse, heavy, and slow words, and sounds, as it were pressed to the center; but Mars, rough, sharp, threatening, great, and wrathful words; the Moon observeth a mean betwixt these two.

But Jupiter, Sol, Venus and Mercury, do possess harmonies; yet Jupiter hath grave, constant, fixed, sweet, merry, and pleasant consorts; Sol venerable, settled, pure and sweet, with a certain grace; but Venus lascivious, luxurious, delicate, voluptuous, dissolute and fluent; Mercury hath harmonies more remiss, and various, merry and pleasant, with a certain boldness: but the tone of particulars, and proportionated consorts obeyeth the nine Muses. Jupiter hath the grace of the octave, and also the quinte,[1] viz. the diapason[2] with the diapente:[3] Sol obtains the melody of the octave voice, viz. diapason; in like manner by fifteen tones, a disdiapason:[4] Venus keepeth the grace of the quinte or diapente: Mercury hath diatessaron;[5] viz. the grace of the quarte.[6]

Moreover the ancients being content with four strings,[7] as with the number of elements, accounted Mercury the author of them, as *Nicomachus* reports, and by their bass strings would resemble the Earth; by their parhypas[8] or middle the Water; by their note *diezeugmenon,* or hyperboleon[9] the Fire; by the paranete[10] or synemmenon, or treble, the Air; but afterwards *Terpander* the Lesbian finding out the seventh string, equaled them to the number of the planets.

Moreover, they that followed the number of the elements, did affirm, that the four kinds of music do agree to them, and also to the four humours, and did think the Dorian music to be consonant to the Water and phlegm, the Phrygian to choler and Fire, the Lydian to blood and Air, the mixed-Lydian to melancholy and Earth: others respecting the number and virtue of the heavens, have attributed the Dorian to the Sun, the Phrygian to Mars, the Lydian to Jupiter, the mixed-Lydian to Saturn, the hypo-Phrygian to Mercury, the hypo-Lydian to Venus, the hypo-Dorian to the Moon, the hypo-mixed-Lydian to the fixed stars.[11]

Moreover they refer these modes of music to the Muses, and the strings to the heavens, but not in that order as we have declared concerning the nine Muses, amongst our numbers and celestial souls; for they say *Thalia* hath no harmony, therefore ascribe her to silence, and the Earth; but *Cleo* with the Moon move after the hypo-Dorian manner, the string proslambanomenos[12] or Air. *Calliope* and Mercury possess the hypo-Phrygian manner, and the chord hypate-hypaton, or B-Mi. *Terpsichore* with Venus the hypo-Lydian manner, and parahypote, hypaton; and for *Melpomene* and the Dorian manner with licanos, hypaton, or D-Sol-Re are applied to the Sun. *Erato* with Mars keep the Phrygian fashion, and the hypatemise, or E-La-Mi. *Euterpe,* and the Lydian music, and pachyparemeson agree with Jupiter; *Polymnia* and Saturn keep the mixed-Lydian manner, and lichanos meson D-Sol-Re. To *Urania* and the fixed stars the hypo-mixed-Lydian music, and the string mese, or A-Le-Mi-Re are ascribed,[13] as we read them expressed in these verses:

Silent Thalia we to the Earth compare,
For she by music never doth ensnare;
After the hypo-Dorian Clio sings,
Persephone likewise doth strike the bass strings;
Calliope also doth chord second touch,
Using the Phrygian; Mercury as much:
Terpsichore strikes the third, and that rare,
The Lydian music makes so Venus fair.
Melpomene, and Titan do with a grace
The Dorian music use in the fourth place.
The fifth ascribed is to Mars the god
Of war, and Erato after the rare mode
Of the Phrygians, Euterpe doth also love
The Lydian, and sixth string; and so doth Jove.
Saturn the seventh doth use with Polymny,
And causeth the mixed-Lydian melody.
Urania also doth the eighth create,
And music hypo-Lydian elevate.

Moreover there are some who find out the harmony of the heavens by their distance one from another. For that space which is betwixt the Earth and the Moon, viz. an hundred and twenty-six thousand Italian miles,[14] maketh the interval of a tone; but from the Moon to Mercury being half that space, maketh half a tone; and so much from Mercury to Venus maketh another half tone; but from thence to the Sun, as it were a threefold tone and a half, and makes diapente; but from the Moon to the Sun, maketh a twofold diatessaron with a half; again from the Sun to Mars is the same space as from the Earth to the Moon, making a tone; from thence to Jupiter half of the same making half a tone; so much likewise from Jupiter to Saturn, constituting an half tone; from whence to the starry firmaments is also the space of an half tone.[15]

Therefore there is from the Sun to the fixed stars a diatessaron distance of two tones and an half, but from the Earth a perfect diapason of six perfect tones; moreover also from the proportion of the motions of the planets amongst themselves, and with the eighth sphere, resulteth the sweetest harmony of all; for the proportion of the motions of Saturn to Jupiter's motion, is twofold and an half; of Jupiter to Mars, a sixfold proportion; of Mars to the Sun, Venus and Mercury, which in a manner finisheth their course in the same time, is a double proportion; their motions to the Moon have a twelvefold proportion; but Saturn's proportion to the starry sphere is a thousand and two hundred, if it be true which *Ptolomy* saith, viz. that the heaven is moved contrary to the primum mobile in an hundred years, one degree.[16]

Therefore the proper motion[17] of the Moon being more swift, maketh a more acute sound than the starry firmament, which is the slowest of all, and therefore causeth the most base sound; but by the violent motion[18] of the primum mobile, is the most swift, and acute sound of all; but the violent motion of the Moon is most slow and heavy, which proportion and reciprocation of motions yields a most pleasant harmony; from hence there are not any songs, sounds, or musical instruments more powerful in moving man's affections, or introducing magical impressions, than those which are composed of numbers, measures, and proportions, after the example of the heavens.

Also the harmony of the elements is drawn forth from their bases, and angles,[19] of the which we have spoken before; for betwixt Fire and Air, there is a double proportion in the bases, and one and an half in solid angles, again in planes, a double; there ariseth hence an harmony of a double diapason, and a diapente. Betwixt the Air and Water, the proportion in their bases is double, and one and an half;[20] hence diapason, and diapente; but in their angles double; hence again diapason. But betwixt Water and Earth the proportion in the bases is threefold and a third part more; from hence ariseth diapason-diapente, diatessaron; but in the angles one and an half, again constituting diapente. To conclude, betwixt Earth and Fire, in the bases the proportion is one and an half, making diapente; but in the angles, double, causing diapason: but betwixt Fire and Water, Air and Earth, there is scarce any consonancy, because they have a perfect contrariety in their qualities, but they are united by the intermediate element.[21]

Nores—Chaprer XXVI

1. *quinte*—Fifth.

2. *diapason*—Octave.

3. *diapente*—Fifth.

4. *disdiapason*—Double octave, or fifteenth.

5. *diatessaron*—Fourth.

6. *quarte*—Fourth.

7. *four strings*—The cithara originally had four strings. Terpander increased this number to seven, and Timotheus to eleven. See their biographical notes.

8. *parhypas*—Parhypate, the lowest note but one in either of the lowest two tetrachords (see note 12 below); the sound of the string next to the bass string.

9. *hyperboleon*—In Greek music the hyperboles were the highest tones of the scale; the highest string on the four-string cithara.

10. *paranate*—Greek: "neighbor of the *nete*," the *nete* being the highest string; therefore the second highest string.

11. *fixed stars*—The ancient Greeks used six modes, which are musical scales of differing pitches corresponding more or less to the modern keys. There were the Dorian, Phrygian, Lydian, mixo-Lydian, Ionic and Aeolian. They were assigned moral values by philosophers. For example, the "soft and convivial modes" are "certain Ionian and also Lydian modes that are called lax." The "dirgelike modes" which are the "mixed Lydian [mixo-Lydian]" and the "tense or higher Lydian [hypo-Lydian]" are "useless even to women who are to make the best of themselves, let alone to men." On the other hand the "Dorian and the Phrygian" are those that "would fittingly imitate the utterances and the accents of a brave man who is engaged in warfare or any enforced business" and "for such a man engaged in works of peace, not enforced but voluntary ..." (Plato *Republic* 3.398e–399b [Hamilton and Cairns, 643–4]). Departure from these established modes was resisted as an anti-intellectual pandering to the mass appetite for pleasure. The names of the Greek modes were preserved in the system of church music known as plainsong, or plain chant (Gregorian chants), established in the 6th century by Gregory the Great, although these differed completely from the Greek. Others were added for a total of 14, of which two—the 11th

and 12th—are never used because they are impractical. Agrippa would have been familiar with this system:

Authentic Modes	Plagal Modes
1. Dorian	2. Hypodorian
3. Phrygian	4. Hypophrygian
5. Lydian	6. Hypolydian
7. Mixolydian	8. Hypomixolydian
9. Aeolian	10. Hypoaeolian
11. Locrian	12. Hypolocrian
13. Ionian	14. Hypoionian

12. *proslambanomenos*—The Greek scale consisted of two octaves made from four tetrachords (derived from the four-string cithara). The first and second tetrachords shared a common string, as did the third and fourth, resulting in 14 sounds. To complete the double octave a 15th string, called the proslambanomenos, was added to the bottom of the scale, one tone below the lowest of the hypates:

Strings	Tetrachord
1. Nete	
2. Paranete or diatone	1st Tetrachord
3. Trite	(hyperboles)
4. Nete of the disjuncts	
5. Paranete or diatone	2nd Tetrachord
6. Trite	(disjuncts)
7. Paramese	
8. Mese	
9. Lichanos or diatone	3rd Tetrachord
10. Parhypate	(meses)
11. Hypate	
12. Hyperhypatate or diatone	
13. Parhypate	4th Tetrachord
14. Hypate	(hypates)
15. Proslambanomenos	

13. *are ascribed*—

Planet	Muse	String	Mode
Earth	Thalia	Silence	—
Moon	Clio	Proslamba-nomenos	Hypodorian
Mercury	Calliope	Hypate-Hypaton (B. Mi.)	Hypo-phrygian
Venus	Terpsichore	Parahypate-Hypaton	Hypolydian
Sun	Melpomene	Licanos-Hypaton (D. Sol. Re.)	Dorian
Mars	Erato	Hypatemise (E. La. Mi.)	Phrygian
Jupiter	Euterpe	Pachy-paremeson	Lydian

Planet	Muse	String	Mode
Saturn	Polymnia	Lichanos-Meson (D. Sol. Re.)	Mixo-lydian
Zodiac	Urania	Mese (A. La. Mi. Re.)	Hypomixo-lydian

The strings described are those in the table of note 12, from the bottom, comprising the lower two tetrachords, those of the hypates and the meses. Seven syllables, called the solfeggio, designate the seven notes of the scale: *ut* (or *do*), *re, mi, fa, sol, la,* and *si.* They come from an ancient monkish hymn to John the Baptist, in which the first syllable of each line was sung one degree higher than the first syllable of the line that preceded it. The first person to use these syllables was Guido of Arezzo in the 11th century.

14. *Italian miles*—An Italian mile was almost the same as a Roman mile, the Italian mile being 1/100th longer. A Roman mile equaled 0.9193 of an English mile. Therefore 126,000 Italian miles would be roughly 116,000 English miles. This is not even close to the true distance between the Earth and the Moon, which is around 240,000 miles.

15. *an half tone*—This same arrangement is given in this verse by Alexander of Aetolia:

The earth at the center gives the low sound
  of the hypate;
the starry sphere gives the conjunct nete;
the sun placed in the middle of the errant
  stars gives the mese;
the crystal sphere gives the fourth in relation to it;
Saturn is lower by a half-tone;
Jupiter diverges as much from Saturn as
  from the terrible Mars;
the sun, joy of mortals, is one tone below;
Venus differs from the dazzling sun by a
  trihemitone;
Hermes continues with a half-tone lower
  than Venus;
then comes the moon which gives to nature
  such varying hue;
and finally, the earth at the centre gives the
  fifth with respect to the sun . . .
(Theon 3.15 [Lawlor, 92])

Pythagoras, employing the terms that are used in music, sometimes names the distance between the Earth and the Moon a tone; from her to Mercury he supposes to be half this space, and about the same from him to Venus. From her to the Sun is a tone and a half; from the Sun to Mars is a tone, the same as from the Earth to the Moon; from

him there is half a tone to Jupiter, from Jupiter to Saturn also half a tone, and thence a tone and a half to the zodiac. Hence there are seven tones, which he terms the diapason harmony, meaning the whole compass of the notes. In this, Saturn is said to move in the Doric time, Jupiter in the Phrygian, and so forth of the rest; but this is a refinement rather amusing than useful. (Pliny 2.20 [Bostock and Riley, 1:52–3])

A trihemitone is three semitones, which is what Agrippa means by "a threefold tone." Codified, the arrangement is:

Zodiac, giving the nete		
Saturn	} half tone	
Jupiter	} half tone	} fourth
Mars	} half tone	
Sun, giving the mese	} tone	
Venus	} trihemitone	
Mercury	} half tone	} fourth
Moon	} half tone	
Earth, giving the hypate	} tone	

16. *one degree*—The phenomenon referred to here is the precession of the equinoxes. Because the axis of the Earth wobbles, the equinoctial points—location of the Sun when day and night are equal—move slowly around the ecliptic from east to west; that is, contrary to the usual order of the zodiac signs. The complete revolution of the equinoxes takes about 25,000 years. This is called a Platonic Year. To cross each sign takes 2,120 years, a Platonic Month. Since there are 30 degrees in each sign, the actual period of passage through each degree is roughly 71 years.

17. *proper motion*—Proper motion is the true motion of a planet, as opposed to its apparent motion as observed from Earth. The ancient astronomers based their opinions on the theory of solid crystal spheres nestled one inside the other with the Earth at the center. Later there was the elaboration of smaller spheres circling larger spheres. Consequently there arose confusion over what was the true motion of a planet and what was only its seeming motion. Planetary motion was divided into: (1) *Forward motion*—the apparent motion of a planet through the zodiac from east to west; (2) *Contrary motion*—the apparent motion of a planet through the zodiac from west to east. Plato thought this to be proper, or true, motion, but Adrastus believed it a seeming motion; (3) *Station*—the apparent motionlessness of a planet; (4) *Retrograde motion*—the apparent return of a planet from its station in a direction opposite its former motion, a backtracking. See Theon 3.17–21 (Lawlor 96).

18. *violent motion*—The rapid, or violent, motion of the stars results from the rotation of the Earth on its

axis. The stars complete the apparent revolution about the Earth in approximately 23 hours, 56 minutes—a sidereal or stellar day. The planets pursue this violent motion of stars, but each night lag a little farther behind, until eventually they come full circle against the stellar backdrop. The Moon is the greatest laggard, completing its circuit in just over 27 days, which means that it must fall behind the stars approximately 13 degrees each night.

19. *bases and angles*—

Elements	Solids	Bases	Solid Angles	Plane Angles
Fire	Tetrahedron	4	4	12
Earth	Hexahedron	6	8	24
Air	Octahedron	8	6	24
Spirit	Dodecahedron	12	20	60
Water	Icosahedron	20	12	60

Fire and Air	4:8	4:6	12:24
Air and Water	8:20	6:12	24:60
Water and Earth	20:6	12:8	60:24
Earth and Fire	6:4	8:4	24:12
Fire and Water	4:20	4:12	12:60
Air and Earth	8:6	6:8	24:24

Consonances	Ratios
Diatessaron (4th)	4:3 (Sesquitertian)
Diapente (5th)	3:2 (Sesqualter)
Diapason (octave)	2:1 (Double)
Diapason-diapente (octave + 5th = 12th)	3:1 (Triple)
Disdiapason (double octave = 15th)	4:1 (Quadruple)

20. *and one and an half*—Actually it is double and one half.

21. *intermediary element*—Air is between Fire and Water; Water is between Air and Earth. See Appendix III.

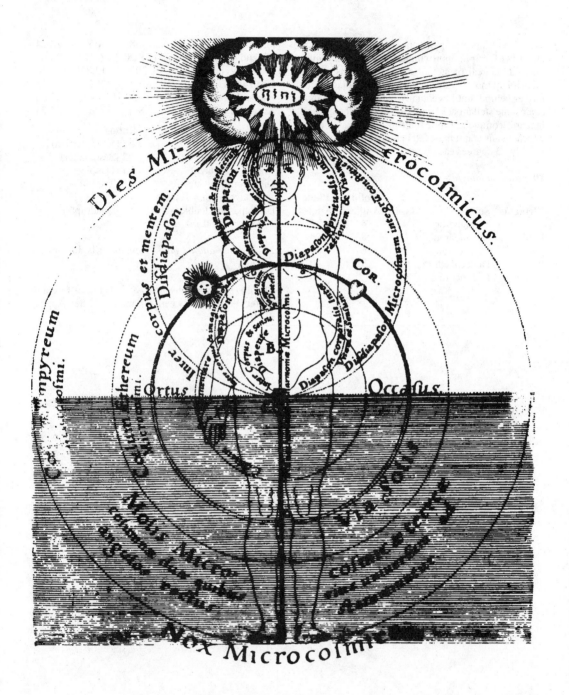

Harmony of Man

From *Tomus secundus de supernaturali, naturali, praeternaturali et contranaturali microcosmi historia*
by Robert Fludd (Oppenheim, 1619)

CHAPTER XXVII

Of the proportion, measure, and harmony of man's body.

Seeing man is the most beautiful and perfectest work of God, and his image, and also the lesser world; therefore he by a more perfect composition, and sweet harmony, and more sublime dignity doth contain and maintain in himself all numbers, measures, weights, motions, elements, and all other things which are of his composition; and in him as it were in the supreme workmanship, all things obtain a certain high condition, beyond the ordinary consonancy which they have in other compounds.

From hence all the ancients in time past did number by their fingers,[1] and showed all numbers by them; and they seem to prove that from the very joints of man's body all numbers, measures, proportions, and harmonies were invented; hence according to this measure of the body, they framed, and contrived their temples, palaces, houses, theaters; also their ships, engines, and every kind of artifice, and every part and member of their edifices, and buildings, as columns, chapiters[2] of pillars, bases, buttresses, feet of pillars, and all of this kind.

Moreover God himself taught *Noah*[3] to build the ark according to the measure of man's body, and he made the whole fabric of the world proportionable to man's body; from hence it is called the great world, man's body the less; therefore some who have written of the microcosm, or of man, measure the body by six feet, a foot by ten degrees, every degree by five minutes; from hence are numbered sixty degrees, which make three hundred minutes, to the which are compared so many geometrical cubits, by which *Moses* describes[4] the ark; for as the body of man is in length three hundred minutes, in breadth fifty, in height thirty; so the length of the ark was three hundred cubits, the breadth fifty, and the height thirty; that the proportion of the length to the breadth be sixfold, to the height tenfold, and the proportion of the breadth to the height about two thirds.

In like manner the measures of all the members are proportionate, and consonant both to the parts of the world, and measures of the Archetype, and so agreeing, that there is no member in man which hath not correspondence with some sign, star, intelligence, divine name, sometimes in God himself the Archetype.

But the whole measure of the body may be turned, and proceeding from roundness, is known to tend to it again:[5]

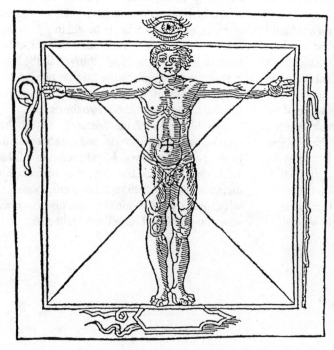

Also the four square measure is the most proportionated body; for, if a man be placed upright with his feet together, and his arms stretched forth, he will make a quadrature equilateral, whose center is in the bottom of his belly:[6]

But if on the same center a circle be made by the crown of the head, the arms being let fall so far, till the end of the fingers touch the circumference of that circle, and the feet spread abroad in the same circumference, as much as the fingers' ends are distant from the top of the head; then they divide that circle, which was drawn from the center of the lower belly, into five equal parts, and do constitute a perfect pentagon; and the heels of the feet having reference to the navel, make a triangle of equal sides:[7]

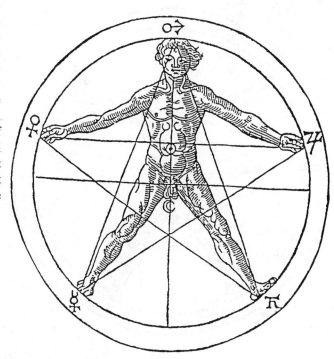

But if the heels being unmoved, the feet be stretched forth on both sides to the right and left, and the hands lifted up to the line of the head, then the ends of the fingers and toes do make a square of equal sides, whose center is on the navel, in the girdling of the body:[8]

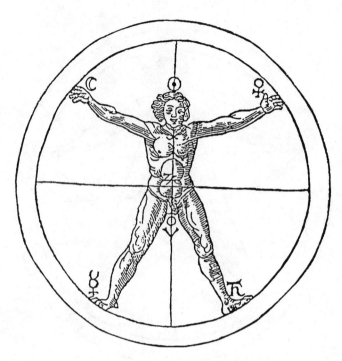

But if the hands be thus elevated, and the feet and thighs extended in this manner, by the which a man is made shorter by the fourteenth part of his upright stature, then the distance of his feet having reference to the lower belly, they will make an equilateral triangle; and the center being placed in his navel, a circle being brought about, will touch the ends of the fingers and toes:[9]

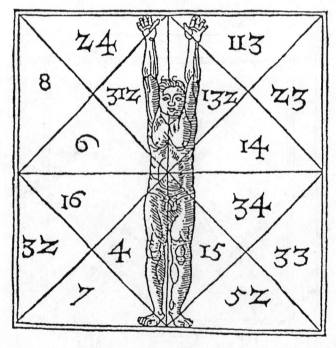

But if the hands be lifted up as high as can be, above the head, then the elbow will be equal to the crown of the head, and if then the feet being put together, a man stand thus, he may be put into an equilateral square brought by the extremities of the hands and feet: the center of this square is the navel, which is the middle betwixt the top of the head and the knees:[10]

Now let us proceed to particular measures. The compass of a man under the armpits contains the middle of his length,[11] whose middle is the bottom of his breast: and from thence upward to the middle of his breast betwixt both dugs,[12] and from the middle of his breast unto the crown of his head, on every side the fourth part; also from the bottom of his breast to the bottom of the knees, and from thence to the bottom of the ankles the fourth part of man. The same is the latitude[13] of his shoulder blades from one extreme to the other: the same is the length from the elbow to the end of the longest finger, and therefore this is called a cubit. Hence four cubits make the length of man, and one cubit the breadth which is in the shoulder blades, but that which is in the compass, one foot;[14] now six handbreadths make a cubit, four a foot, and four fingers' breadths make a handbreadth, and the whole length of man is of twenty-four handbreadths, of six foot, of ninety-six fingers' breadths.

From the bottom of his breast to the top of his breast,[15] is the sixth part of his length, from the top of his breast to the top of his forehead, and lowermost root of his hairs, the seventh part of his length; of a strong, and well set body, a foot is the sixth part of the length, but of a tall the seventh. Neither can (as *Varro,* and *Gellius* testify) the tallness of man's body exceed seven feet. Lastly the diameter of his compass[16] is the same measure as is from the hand, being shut unto the inward bending of the elbow, and as that which is from the breast to both dugs,[17] upward to the upward lip, or downward to the navel; and as that which is from the ends of the bones[18] of the uppermost part of the breast compassing the gullet; and as that which is from the sole of the foot to the end of the calf of the leg, and from thence to the middle whirlbone of the knee. All these measures are coequal, and make the seventh part of the whole height.

The head of a man from the bottom of the chin to the crown of his head is the eighth part of his length, as also from the elbow to the end of the shoulder blade: so great is the diameter of the compass of a tall man. The compass of the head drawn by the top of the forehead, and the bottom of the hinder part of the head, make the fifth part of his whole length; so much also doth the breadth of the breast.

Nine face breadths make a square, well set man, and ten a tall man. The length of man therefore being divided into nine parts, the face from the top of the forehead to the bottom of the chin is one; then from the bottom of the throat, or the top of the breast unto the top of the stomach is another; from thence to the navel is a third; from thence to the bottom of the thigh,[19] a fourth; from thence the hip to the top of the calf of the leg, makes two; from thence to the joint of the foot the legs make two more; all which are eight parts. Moreover the space from the top of the forehead to the crown of the head, and that which is from the chin to the top of the breast, and that which is from the joint of the foot to the sole of the foot, I say these three spaces joined together make the ninth part. In breadth the breast hath two parts, and both arms seven.[20]

But that body which ten face breadths make is the most exactly proportioned. Therefore the first part of this is from the crown of the head to the bottom of the nose; from thence to the top of the breast, the second; and then to the top of the stomach the third; and from thence to the navel, the fourth; from thence to the privy members, the fifth, where is the middle of the length of man; from whence to the soles of his feet are five other parts, which being joined to the former, make ten whole, by which every body is measured by a most proportioned measure.

For the face of a man from the bottom of his chin, to the top of his forehead, and bottom of the hair is the tenth part. The hand of a man from the shutting,[21] to the end of the longest finger is also one part; also betwixt the middle[22] of both dugs is one part, and from both to the top of the gullet is an equilateral triangle. The latitude of the lower part of the forehead from one ear to the other is another part; the latitude of the whole breast, viz. from the top of the breast to the joints of the shoulder blades, is on both sides[23] one part, which makes two.

The compass of the head crosswise[24] from the distance of the eyebrows by the top of the forehead unto the bottom of the hinder part of the head, where the hair ends, hath also two parts; from the shoulders on the outside unto the coupling together of the joints of the hand, and on the inside from the armpits unto the beginning of the palm of the hand, and of the fingers,[25] are three parts. The compass of the head by the middle of the forehead hath three parts; the compass of the girdling place hath four parts in a well set man, but in a thin body three parts and a half, or as much as is from the top of the breast to the bottom of the belly. The compass of the breast by the armpit to the back hath five parts, viz. as much as half the whole length. From the crown of the head, to the knurls of the gullet[26] is the thirteenth part of the whole altitude. The arms being stretched upward, the elbow is even to the crown of the head.

But now let us see how equal the other commensurations are to one the other. As much as the distance is from the chin to the top of the breast, so great is the latitude of the mouth;[27] as much as is the distance betwixt the top of the breast, to the navel, so great is the compass of the mouth;[28] as much as the distance is from the chin to the crown of the head, so great is the latitude of the girdling place;[29] as is the distance from the top of the nose to the bottom, such is the distance betwixt the chin and the throat. Also the cavity of the eyes from the place betwixt the eyebrows unto the inward corners, and the extension of the bottom of the nose, and the distance from the bottom of the nose to the end of the upper lip; I say these three are equals amongst themselves; and as much as from the top of the nail of the forefinger to the lowermost joint[30] thereof.

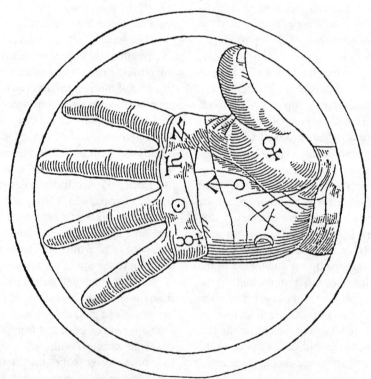

And from thence where the hand is joined to the arm on the outside,[31] and in the inside from the top of the nail of the middle finger unto the lowermost joint,[32] and from thence to the shutting of the hand;[33] I say all these parts are equal amongst themselves. The greater joint of the forefinger equals the height of the forehead; the other two to the top of the nail equal the nose, from the top to the bottom; the first and the greater joint of the middle finger equals the space which is betwixt the end of the nose to the end of the chin; and the second joint of the middle finger is as much as the distance from the bottom of the chin to the top of the lower lip; but the third as from the mouth to the end of the nose; but the whole hand as much as the whole face. The greater joint of the thumb is as much as the wideness of the mouth, and as the distance betwixt the bottom of the chin, and the top of the lower lip; but the lesser joint is as much as the distance betwixt the top of the lower lip and the end of the nose; the nails are half as much as those joints which they call the nail joints.

The distance betwixt the middle of the eyebrows to the outward corners of the eyes is as much as betwixt those corners and the ears. The height of the forehead, the length of the nose, and the wideness of the mouth are equal. Also the breadth of the hand, and foot are the same. The distance betwixt the lower part of the ankle to the top of the foot is the same as that betwixt the top of the foot and the end of the nails.[34] The distance from the top of the forehead to the place betwixt the eyes, and from that to the end of the nose, and from thence to the end of the chin is the same. The eyebrows joined together are as much as the circle of the eyes, and the half circle of the ears equals the wideness of the mouth: whence the circles of the eyes, ears, and mouth opened are equal. The breadth of the nose is as much as the length of the eye; hence the eyes have two parts of that space which is betwixt both extremities of the eyes; a third part the nose that is betwixt takes up.

From the crown of the head to the knees the navel is the middle; from the top of the breast to the end of the nose the knurl of the throat makes the middle; from the crown of the head to the bottom of the chin, the eyes are the middle; from the space betwixt the eyes to the bottom of the chin, the end of the nose is the middle; from the end of the nose to the bottom of the chin, the end of the lower lip is the middle; a third part of the same distance is the upper lip.

Moreover all these measures are through manifold proportions, and harmonical consents consonant one to the other; for the thumb is to the wrist in a circular measure in a double proportion and half; for it contains it twice and a half, as five is to two; but the proportion of the

same[35] to the brawn of the arm near the shoulder is triple; the greatness of the leg is to that of the arm, a proportion half as much again, as of three to two; and the same proportion is of the neck to the leg, as of that to the arm.[36] The proportion of the thigh is triple to the arm; the proportion of the whole body to the trunk,[37] is eight and a half; from the trunk or breast to the legs, and from thence to the soles of the feet,[38] a third and a half; from the neck to the navel, and to the end of the trunk a double.[39] The latitude of them[40] to the latitude of the thigh, is half so much again; of the head to the neck triple, of the head to the knee triple, the same to the leg. The length of the forehead betwixt the temples[41] is fourfold to the height thereof.

These are those measures which are everywhere found;[42] by which the members of man's body according to length, breadth, height, and circumference thereof agree amongst themselves, and also with the celestials themselves: all which measures are divided by manifold proportions either upon them that divide, or are mixed, from whence there results a manifold harmony. For a double proportion makes thrice a diapason; four times double, twice a diapason and diapente.[43]

After the same manner are elements, qualities, complexions, and humours proportioned. For these weights of humours and complexions are assigned to a sound and well composed man, viz. the eight weights of blood, of phlegm four, of choler two, of melancholy one, that on both sides there be by order a double proportion;[44] but of the first to the third, and of the second to the fourth, a four times double[45] proportion; but of the first to the last an eightfold.[46]

Dioscorides saith, that the heart of a man in the first year hath the weight of two drams,[47] in the second year four, and so proportionably in the fiftieth year to have the weight of a hundred drams, from which time the decreases are again reckoned to an equilibrium, which, the course being ended, may return to the same limit, and not exceed the space of life by the decay of that member: by which account of a hundred years, he circumscribed the life of man. And this saith *Pliny*[48] was the heresy of the Egyptians.

The motions also of the members of men's bodies answer to the celestial motions, and every man hath in himself the motion of his heart, which answers to the motion of the Sun,[49] and being diffused through the arteries into the whole body, signifies to us by a most sure rule, years, months, days, hours, and minutes. Moreover, there is a certain nerve found by the anatomists about the node of the neck, which being touched doth so move all the members of the body, that every one of them move according to its proper motion; by which like touch *Aristotle* thinks the members of the world are moved by God. And there are two veins in the neck, which being held hard presently the man's strength fails, and his senses are taken away until they be loosened.

Therefore the eternal Maker of the world when he was to put the soul into the body, as into its habitation, first made a fit lodging worthy to receive it, and endows the most excellent soul with a most beautiful body, which then the soul knowing its own divinity, frames and adorns for its own habitation. Hence the people of Aethiopia, which were governed by the wisdom of Gymnosophists, as *Aristotle* witnesseth, did make them kings not those which were most strong, and wealthy, but those only which were most proper and beautiful; for they conceived that the gallantry of the mind did depend upon the excellency of the body.

Which many philosophers, as well ancient as modern, considering, such as searched into the secrets of causes hid in the very majesty of nature, were bold to assert, that there was no fault of, and no disproportion in the body, which the vice and intemperance of the mind did not follow, because it is certain that they do increase, thrive, and operate by the help one of the other.[50]

Notes—Chapter XXVII

1. *by their fingers*—See ch. XVI, bk. II.

2. *chapiters*—Capitals.

3. *Noah*—Genesis 6:14–6.

4. *Moses describes*—Moses was the supposed author of the book of Genesis.

5. *tend to it again*—In the first illustration, the cubic stone indicates the Earth, as does the great circle itself. On the belly of the figure is a medieval builder's tool for finding plumb—a mason's symbol. The pentagrams around the hands are pointing downward, which in the occultism of the 19th century is a symbol of Satanism; however, Agrippa would not have made this distinction between the upright and inverted pentagram. The cross through the great circle suggests the cardinal points. The small circle atop the head may stand for the Sun.

6. *of his belly*—In the second illustration, the center of the figure is the groin. The cross on the navel marks the other center used in the preceding illustration. On the border is the serpent and knobbed stick of Aesculapius, god of physicians, and above the figure, the eye of God.

7. *of equal sides*—In the third illustration, the Moon is set over the lower groin center, the Sun over the upper solar plexus center. The five planets are arrayed about the perimeter in order of their quickness of apparent motion clockwise: Mercury, Venus, Mars, Jupiter, Saturn.

8. *of the body*—In the fourth illustration, the symbols around the border are the zodiac signs beginning with Aries at the head and running counterclockwise.

9. *fingers, and toes*—In the fifth illustration, the most masculine planets—Sun, Jupiter, Mars—are spread along the axis of the body; the fully feminine planets—Moon, Venus—are over the hands, and the somewhat feminine planets—Mercury, Saturn—on the feet.

10. *and the knees*—In the sixth illustration, I must confess that I have not been able to determine the numerological significance of the 16 numbers around the figure, though I am sure the explanation is quite simple.

11. *middle of his length*—The circumference around the upper chest is half the height.

12. *both dugs*—Both nipples.

13. *latitude*—Width.

14. *the compass, one foot*—Perhaps the depth through the chest at the level of the nipples.

15. *top of his breast*—From the solar plexus to the top of the shoulders.

16. *diameter of his compass*—Diameter of the circumference of the breast.

17. *breast to both dugs*—The distance between the level of the nipples and the upper lip, and down to the navel.

18. *ends of the bones*—The distance between the ends of the collarbones.

19. *bottom of the thigh*—The end of the buttocks.

20. *both arms seven*—That is, in the ninefold division of the distance between the fingertips of the outspread arms.

21. *the shutting*—The length of the hand from the fingertips to the heel.

22. *betwixt the middle*—Distance between the nipples.

23. *on both sides*—The distance from the spine to the ends of the shoulders.

24. *head crosswise*—That is, the measure from the middle of the eyebrows over the top of the head down to the hairline at the nape of the neck.

25. *of the fingers*—From the shoulder to the wrist, or from the armpit to the root of the fingers.

26. *knurls of the gullet*—The Adam's apple.

27. *latitude of the mouth*—Width.

28. *compass of the mouth*—This must refer to the circumference of the head at the level of the mouth and hairline.

29. *girdling place*—Width of the waist.

30. *lowermost joint*—Agrippa means the segments of the fingers when he speaks of joints; thus, probably from the tip of the nail to the middle knuckle of the forefinger.

31. *on the outside*—From the large knuckle to the wrist on the back of the hand.

32. *lowermost joint*—The place where the finger joins the palm.

33. *shutting of the hand*—Probably the place on the heel of the palm where the tips of the fingers touch when closed.

34. *end of the nails*—From the heel through the ankle to the instep, and from the instep to the tip of the big toe.

35. *of the same*—That is, the wrist to the upper arm.

36. *to the arm*—Perhaps as the middle of the forearm is to the middle of the shank, so the middle of the shank is to the neck.

37. *to the trunk*—It is not clear to me what is meant here; perhaps the distance from the navel to the groin compared with the height of the body.

38. *soles of the feet*—From the top of the breast to groin is one third the entire height; from the groin to the soles of the feet one half.

39. *trunk a double*—From the pit of the throat to the navel is twice from the navel to the groin.

40. *latitude of them*—Distance across, or width, of the waist.

41. *betwixt the temples*—Measured across.

42. *everywhere found*—These measures and proportions of the human body are very similar to the list compiled by the Italian artist and inventer Leonard da Vinci (see *The Notebooks of Leonardo da Vinci*, ed. Edward MacCurdy [New York: George Braziller, 1955], 7:206–14). Since Agrippa spent so much time in Italy between 1511 and 1517, when Leonardo was in his early 60s and still very active, it is not impossible that the two corresponded or even met. However, the link, if there is one, appears to be the book *Summa de arithmetica geometria proportioni et proportionalita* by the mathematician Lucas Paciolus (see his biographical note), who was a close friend of da Vinci. Agrippa mentions this work at the end of ch. XVI, bk. II, referring to its author as "Brother Luke of Saint Sepulchers."

43. *and diapente*—A double proportion (2:1) yields a diapason, or octave; four times double (4:1) yields a disdiapason or double octave.

44. *double proportion*—Blood and phlegm (8:4), and choler and melancholy (2:1).

45. *four times double*—Blood and choler (8:2), and phlegm and melancholy (4:1).

46. *eightfold*—Blood and melancholy (8:1).

47. *two drams*—A dram is 60 grains, or about 1/8th of an ounce.

48. *saith Pliny*—

It is said that the heart increases every year in man, and that two drachmae in weight are added yearly up to the fiftieth year, after which period it decreases yearly in a similar ratio; and that it is for this reason that men do not live beyond their hundredth year, the heart then failing them: this is the notion entertained by the Egyptians, whose custom it is to embalm the bodies of the dead, and so preserve them. (Pliny 11.70 [Bostock and Riley, 3:65–6])

49. *motion of the Sun*—That is, the heart keeps time by its beats even as the Sun does by its motion.

50. *one of the other*—It was this pernicious belief that led to so many ugly old women being executed for witchcraft and, by an opposite logic, necessitated the physical perfection of the Vestal Virgins of Rome and the students of the Kabbalah among the Jews.

CHAPTER XXVIII

Of the composition and harmony of the human soul.

As the consonancy of the body consists of a due measure and proportion of the members: so the consonancy of the mind of a due temperment, and proportion of its virtues and operations which are concupiscible, irascible, and reason, which are so proportioned together. For reason to concupiscence hath the proportion diapason;[1] but to anger diatessaron:[2] and irascible to concupiscible hath the proportion diapente.[3] When therefore the best proportioned soul is joined to the best proportioned body, it is manifest that such a man also hath received a most happy lot in the distribution of gifts, for as much as the soul agrees with the body in the disposition of naturals,[4] which agreement indeed is most hid, yet after some manner shadowed to us by the wise.

But to hasten to the harmony of the soul, we must inquire into it by those mediums by which is passeth to us, i.e. by celestial bodies, and spheres; knowing therefore what are the powers of the soul to which the planets answer, we shall by those things which have been spoken of before, the more easily know their agreements amongst themselves. For the Moon governs the powers of increasing and decreasing; the phantasy and wits depends on Mercury; the concupiscible virtue on Venus; the vital on the Sun; the irascible on Mars; the natural on Jupiter;[5] the receptive on Saturn.[6]

But the will as the primum mobile, and the guide of all these powers at pleasure, being joined with the superior intellect, is always tending to good; which intellect indeed doth always show a pathway to the will, as a candle to the eye; but it moves not itself, but is the mistress of her own operation, whence it is called free will; and although it always tends to good, as an object suitable to itself: yet sometimes being blinded with error, the animal power forcing it, it chooseth evil, believing it to be good. Therefore free will is defined to be a faculty of the intellect, and will whereby good is chosen by the help of grace; and evil, that not assisting. Grace therefore, which divines call charity, or infused love is in the will, as a first mover; which being absent, the whole consent[7] falls into dissonancy.

Moreover the soul answers to the earth by sense, to the water by imagination, to the air by reason, to the heaven by the intellect,[8] and the soul goes out into an harmony of them, according as these are tempered in a mortal body.

The wise ancients therefore knowing that the harmonious dispositions of bodies and souls are divers, according to the diversity of the complexions of men, did not in vain use musical sounds and singings, as to confirm the health of the body, and restore it being lost, so to bring the mind to wholesome manners, until they make a man suitable to the celestial harmony, and make him wholly celestial. Moreover, there is nothing more efficacious to drive away evil spirits than musical harmony (for they being fallen from that celestial harmony, cannot endure any true consent, as being an enemy to them, but fly from it) as *David* by his harp appeased *Saul*,[9] being troubled with an evil spirit. Hence by the ancient prophets and Fathers, who knew these harmonical mysteries, singing and musical sounds were brought into sacred services.

Notes—Chapter XXVlll

1. *diapason*—2:1.

2. *diatessaron*—4:3.

3. *diapente*—3:2.

4. *naturals*—Human qualities received at birth.

5. *natural on Jupiter*—The inherent virtues—artistic ability, athletic aptitude, personal power—depend on Jupiter.

6. *receptive on Saturn*—The acquired virtues, and the ability to learn, depend on Saturn.

7. *consent*—Consonance.

8. *the intellect*—The moral sphere of the mind, which is higher than reason, the logical sphere.

9. *appeased Saul*—See note 12, ch. XXIV, bk. II.

CHAPTER XXIX

Of the observation of celestials, necessary in every magical work.

Every natural virtue doth work things far more wonderful when it is not only compounded of a natural proportion, but also is informed by a choice observation of the celestials opportune to this (viz. when the celestial power is most strong to that effect which we desire, and also helped by many celestials) by subjecting inferiors to the celestials, as proper females to be made fruitful by their males. Also in every work there are to be observed the situation, motion, and aspect of the stars and planets, in signs and degrees, and how all these stand in reference to the length and latitude of the climate; for by this are varied the qualities of the angles, which the rays of celestial bodies upon the figure of the thing describe, according to which celestial virtues are infused. So when thou art working anything which belongs to any planet, thou must place it in its dignities, fortunate and powerful, and ruling in the day, hour, and in the figure of the heaven.

Neither shalt thou expect the signification of the work to be powerful, but also thou must observe the Moon opportunely directed to this; for thou shalt do nothing without the assistance of the Moon: and if thou hast more patterns of thy work, observe them all being most powerful, and looking upon one the other with a friendly aspect:[1] and if thou canst not have such aspects, it will be convenient at least that thou take them angular.[2] But thou shalt take the Moon, either when she looks upon both, or is joined to one, and looks upon the other; or when she passeth from the conjunction, or aspect of one to the conjunction, or aspect of the other: for that I conceive must in no wise be omitted; also thou shalt in every work observe Mercury; for he is a messenger betwixt the higher gods, and infernal gods; when he goeth to the good he increaseth their goodness; when to the bad, hath influence upon their wickedness.

We call it an unfortunate sign, or planet, when it is by the aspect of Saturn or Mars, especially opposite, or quadrant;[3] for these are aspects of enmity; but a conjunction, or a trine, or sextile aspect are of friendship; betwixt these there is a greater conjunction: but yet if thou dost already behold it through a trine, and the planet be received, it is accounted as already conjoined. Now all planets are afraid of the conjunction of the Sun, rejoicing in the trine, and sextile aspect thereof.

Notes—Chapter XXIX

1. *friendly aspect*—The major aspects of astrology are:

Conjunction ($\conjunction$), when planets are together. This causes them to act in unison, though not necessarily in harmony.

Opposition ($\opposition$), when planets are separated by 180 degrees of arc. This is the aspect of maximum tension, tending to a polarization of their powers.

Square ($\square$), when planets are separated by 90

357

degrees. This aspect liberates energy and moves events.

Semisquare (∠), when planets are separated by 45 degrees. This is the aspect of minor tension.

Trine (△), when planets are separated by 120 degrees. This aspect is of harmonious but non-dynamic relationships and equal communication.

Sextile (⚹), when planets are separated by 60 degrees. This aspect conduces to balanced under-standing.

Semisextile (⋎), when planets are separated by 30 degrees. This is an aspect of minor or partially harmonious relationships.

Conjunction, trine, sextile and semisextile have historically been considered favorable; opposition, square and semisquare unfavorable. But the effect of an aspect may more properly be said to depend upon the response of the individual.

2. *take them angular*—The angles, or corners, of the heavens are the ascendent, midheaven *(Medium Coeli),* descendent, and lower midheaven *(Immum Coeli),* respectively the eastern horizon, the highest point in the sky, the western horizon, and the lowest point on the opposite side of the Earth. Historically the planets in the angles were considered the strongest. The angular houses (see note 28, ch. VI, bk. II) give power and initiate new actions. House I affects the individual, House IV the home, House VII the partner, and House X the worldly life. The angular signs at the ascendent and midheaven affect the psyche—the first, the awakening self-consciousness, or personality; the second, the established self-con-sciousness, or ego. The descendent and lower mid-heaven signs complement their opposites.

3. *opposite, or quadrant*—Opposition, or square. See above.

CHAPTER XXX

When planets are of most powerful influence.

Now we shall have the planets powerful when they are ruling in a house,[1] or in exaltation,[2] or triplicity,[3] or term,[4] or face[5] without combustion[6] of what is direct in the figure of the heavens, viz. when they are in angles,[7] especially of the rising, or tenth, or in houses presently succeeding,[8] or in their delights.[9] But we must take heed that they be not in the bounds or under the dominion of Saturn or Mars, lest they be in dark degrees, in pits, or vacuities.[10]

Thou shalt observe that the angles of the ascendent, and tenth, and seventh be fortunate,[11] as also the lord of the ascendent[12] and place of the Sun and Moon, and the place of part of the Fortune,[13] and the lord thereof,[14] the lord of the foregoing conjunction and prevention:[15] but that they of the malignant planet fall unfortunate,[16] unless haply they be significators of thy work, or can be any way advantageous to thee; or if in thy revolution or birth, they had the predominancy; for then they are not at all to be depressed.

Now we shall have the Moon powerful if she be in her house,[17] or exaltation, or triplicity, or face, and in degree convenient for the desired work, and if it hath a mansion of these twenty and eight suitable to itself and the work; let her not be in the way burnt up,[18] nor slow in course;[19] let her not be in the eclipse, or burnt by the Sun, unless she be in unity with the Sun;[20] let her not descend in the southern latitude, when she goeth out of burning,[21] neither let her be opposite to the Sun,[22] nor deprived of light;[23] let her not be hindered by Mars or Saturn.

I will not here discourse any longer of these, seeing these, and many more necessary things are sufficiently handled in the volumes of astrologers.

Notes—Chapter XXX

1. *ruling in a house*—See note 3, ch. XVII, bk. I.

2. *exaltation*—See note 4, ch. XVII, bk. I.

3. *triplicity*—The rulers of the triplicities are those planets that govern the action of the four elemental trines of the zodiac signs (see note 3, ch. VIII, bk. I). One planet is assigned to govern the trine by day and another by night, the planets most in harmony with the nature of the trine being selected for these roles. For example, the Fire triplicity is Aries-Leo-Sagittarius. The Sun, which rules Leo, is the governor of these signs by day, while Jupiter, which rules Sagittarius, is the governor by night. Mars, which rules Aries, is not used because it is of the lunar sect, and so discordant with the other planets, both of the solar sect. Since there are seven planets but eight governors, the final unassigned planet,.Mars, is given to the last trine, Water, both day and night. Venus is appointed co-ruler by day and the Moon by night because this watery trine is feminine. The triplicities are given by Ptolemy in his *Tetrabiblos* 1.18 (Robbins, 83–7). For convenience I have tabulated them below:

Triplicity	Day	Night
Fire (♈, ♌, ♐)	☉	♃
Earth (♉, ♍, ♑)	♀	☽
Air (♊, ♎, ♒)	♄	☿
Water (♋, ♏, ♓)	♂, ♀	♂, ☽

4. *term*—See note 4, ch. VIII, bk. II.

5. *face*—There are three faces in each sign, each face ten degrees. In ancient times the faces were assigned to the planets in their Ptolemaic order:

		Face	
Sign	**1st**	**2nd**	**3rd**
♈	♂	☉	♀
♉	☿	☽	♄
♊	♃	♂	☉
♋	♀	☿	☽
♌	♄	♃	♂
♍	☉	♀	☿
♎	☽	♄	♃
♏	♂	☉	♀
♐	☿	☽	♄
♑	♃	♂	☉
♒	♀	☿	☽
♓	♄	♃	♂

The faces are distinguished by Agrippa from the decans, which have a different system by which planets are assigned to rule them (see note 3, ch. XXXVI, bk. II). In other respects the decans and faces, as Agrippa uses the term, seem indistinguishable. See also note 12, ch. XXII, bk. I.

6. *combustion*—A planet within three degrees of the Sun's longitude is said to be combust, because the power of the Sun overwhelms its operation.

7. *in angles*—See note 2, ch. XXIX, bk. II.

A planet was said to be *essentially* dignified when in its own sign, exaltation, triplicity, term or face: and was said to be *accidentally* dignified when in the mid-heaven, ascendant, 7th, 4th, 11th, 9th, 2nd or 5th house. A planet is *accidentally strong* when swift and direct in motion, and near its greatest distance from the Sun; a superior planet (♂, ♃, ♄), when oriental of the Sun; an inferior planet (☽, ☿, ♀), when occidental.

A planet is *essentially weak* when it is in fall or detriment. It is *accidentally weak* when in the 12th, 8th or 6th house, retrograde or very slow in motion, within 8 degrees, 30 minutes of the Sun: a superior planet, when occidental of the Sun; an inferior, when oriental.

Although a planet was held to be weak when within 8 degrees, 30 minutes of the Sun, it was said to be strong when within 17 minutes, or in exact conjunction with the Sun—'in cazimi' as the ancients term it. (Pearce 1970 [1879], 436)

8. *succeeding*—Ptolemy says planets are most powerful "when they are in mid-heaven or approaching it, and second when they are exactly on the horizon or in the succedent place ..." *(Tetrabiblos* 1.24 [Robbins, 117]). The succedent is in this case the house immediately following—the one on the left of the house in question. On the relative power of the houses as given by Ptolemy, see note 5, ch. XXVI, bk. III.

9. *delights*—According to Ptolemy, planets "rejoice" when they are contained in a sign of the zodiac which "even though the containing signs have no familiarity with the stars themselves, nevertheless they have it with the stars of the same sect ..." (ibid. 1.23 [Robbins, 113]). The sect of the Sun contains, in addition to the Sun, the planets Jupiter and Saturn; the sect of the Moon contains the Moon, Venus and Mars. Mercury belongs to both sects according to its position—when it is seen as a morning star (in the east) it is in the sect of the Sun; when seen as an evening star (in the west) it belongs to the sect of the Moon. For example, Venus would be said to rejoice in Aries, because Aries is ruled by Mars, and Mars is in the sect of the Moon. If planets find themselves in signs under the dominion of planets of the opposite sect, "a great part of their proper power is paralysed, because the temperament which arises from the dissimilarity of the signs produces a different and adulterated nature" (ibid.).

10. *pits, or vacuities*—That is, the powers of a planet should not be used when the planet is in a sign ruled by Saturn or Mars, or when the planet falls within the orb, or bounds, of Saturn or Mars—conjunction with these bodies. The orbs of the planets are their circles of greatest influence: Saturn—10 degrees; Jupiter—12 degrees; Mars—7 degrees, 30 minutes; Sun—17 degrees; Venus—8 degrees; Mercury 7 degrees, 30 minutes; Moon—12 degrees, 30 minutes. There is a wide variance of opinion as to the extent of the orbs. The influence of Saturn and Mars is generally considered to be malefic. Ptolemy calls them "the two destructive stars." *(Tetrabiblos* 1.7 [Robbins, 43]

11. *fortunate*—That is, insure that there are fortunate planets in a harmonious arrangement in the first (ascendent), tenth (midheaven) and seventh (descendent) houses of the zodiac.

12. *lord of the ascendent*—This is the planet ruling the sign on the ascendent. The house which the planet

occupied was held to be very important, particularly if the house was at one of the angles, or near midheaven.

13. *part of the Fortune*—The Part, or Lot, of Fortune is a hypothetical point the position of which determines the material acquisitions of an individual or other subject of inquiry. "What the subject's material acquisitions will be is to be gained from the so-called 'Lot of Fortune;' ... For when the planets which govern the Lot of Fortune are in power, they make the subjects rich, particularly when they chance to have the proper testimony of the luminaries ..." (ibid. 4.2 [Robbins, 373, 375]). On the method of determining this point, Ptolemy says:

> Take as the Lot of Fortune always the amount of the number of degrees, both by night and by day, which is the distance from the sun to the moon [in the order of the following signs], and which extends to an equal distance from the horoscope [i.e. the Ascendant] in the order of the following signs, in order that, whatever relation and aspect the sun bears to the horoscope, the moon also may bear to the Lot of Fortune, and that it may be as it were a lunar horoscope. (ibid. 3.10 [Robbins, 275, 277])

What the Greeks knew as the "order of the following signs" is what is today regarded as their natural order—counterclockwise from Aries to Taurus to Gemini, and so on. Pierce describes the calculation of the Lot of Fortune more concisely: "The Part of Fortune is that point of the heavens in which the Moon would be if the Sun were exactly rising" (Pierce 1970 [1879], 438).

14. *Lord thereof*—Whatever planet rules the sign on which the Lot of Fortune falls.

15. *prevention*—See note 10 above.

16. *fall unfortunate*—That is, Mars and Saturn should be in a position that minimizes their potency.

17. *her house*—The house of Cancer, the fourth house, named the Lower Midheaven.

18. *burnt up*—Combust. See note 6 above.

19. *slow in course*—On the apparent motion of the planets generally, Theon comments: "They do not cover the same distance in space in the same amount of time; they go faster when they appear larger because of their lesser distance from Earth, and they go less fast when they appear smaller because of their greater distance" (Theon 3.12 [Lawlor, 90]).

About the Moon specifically, Pliny writes: "After remaining for two days in conjunction with the sun, on the thirtieth day she again very slowly emerges to pursue her accustomed course ..." (Pliny 2.6 [Bostock and Riley, 1:32])

20. *unity with the Sun*—See note 7 above.

21. *out of burning*—Let the Moon not set on the western horizon below the plane of the ecliptic while under the proximate influence of the Sun.

22. *opposite to the Sun*—In opposition, when the Moon is full.

23. *deprived of light*—Perhaps by lunar eclipse, when the shadow of the Earth falls upon the face of the Moon and makes it dull red or black; but if the eclipse referred to in the text above is a lunar eclipse, this must refer to the new Moon.

CHAPTER XXXI

Of the observation of the fixed stars, and of their natures.

There is the like consideration to be had in all things concerning the fixed stars. Know this, that all the fixed stars are of the signification and nature of the seven planets; but some are of the nature of one planet, and some of two: hence as often as any planet is joined with any of the fixed stars of its own nature, the signification of that star is made more powerful, and the nature of the planet augmented: but if it be a star of two natures, the nature of that which shall be the stronger with it shall overcome in signification; as for example, if it be of the nature of Mars and Venus; if Mars shall be the stronger with it, the nature of Mars shall overcome; but if Venus, the nature of Venus shall overcome.

Now the natures of fixed stars are discovered by their colours,[1] as they agree with certain planets, and are ascribed to them. Now the colours of the planets are these: of Saturn, blue and leaden, and shining with this; of Jupiter, citrine near to a paleness, and clear with this; of Mars, red and fiery; of the Sun, yellow, and when it riseth red, afterward glittering; of Venus, white and shining, white with the morning and reddish in the evening; of Mercury, glittering; of the Moon, fair.

Know also that of the fixed stars by how much the greater and the brighter and apparent they are, so much the greater and stronger is the signification; such are these stars which are called by the astrologers of the first, and second magnitude.

I will tell thee some of these which are more potent to this faculty, as are viz. the Navel of Andromeda[2] in two and twentieth degree of Aries, of the nature of Venus, and Mercury; some call it jovial, and saturnine.

The Head of Algol[3] in the eighteenth degree of Taurus, of the nature of Saturn, and Jupiter. The Pleiades[4] are also in the two and twentieth degree, a lunary star by nature, and by complexion martial.

Also in the third degree of Gemini is Aldeboram,[5] of the nature of Mars, and complexion of Venus: but *Hermes* placeth this in the twenty-fifth degree of Aries. The Goat Star[6] is in the thirteenth degree of the said Gemini, of the nature of Jupiter, and Saturn.

The Greater Dog Star[7] is in the seventh degree of Cancer, and Venereal: the Lesser Dog Star[8] is in the seventeenth degree of the same, and is of the nature of Mercury, and complexion of Mars.

The King's Star,[9] which is called the Heart of the Lion, is in the one and twentieth degree of Leo, and of the nature of Jupiter, and Mars.

The Tail of the Greater Bear[10] is in the nineteenth degree of Virgo, and is venereal, and lunary.

The star which is called the Right Wing of the Crow[11] is in the seventh degree of Libra, and in the thirteenth degree of the same is the Left Wing[12] of the same, and both of the nature of Saturn, and Mars. The star called Spica[13] is in the sixteenth degree of the same, and is venereal, and mercurial. In the seventeenth degree of the same is Alchameth,[14] of the nature of Mars, and Jupiter; but of this when the Sun's aspect is full towards it, of that when on the contrary.

Elepheia[15] is in the fourth degree of Scorpio, of the nature of Venus, and Mars.

The Heart of the Scorpion[16] is in the third degree of Sagittarius, of the nature of Mars, and Jupiter.

The Falling Vulture[17] is in the seventh degree of Capricorn, temperate, mercurial, and venereal.

The Tail of Capricorn[18] is in the sixteenth degree of Aquarius, of the nature of Saturn, and Mercury.

The star called the Shoulder of the Horse[19] is in the third degree of Pisces, of the nature of Jupiter, and Mars.

And it shall be a general rule for thee to expect the proper gifts of the stars whilst they rule, to be prevented of them, they being unfortunate, and opposite, as is above showed. For celestial bodies, in as much as they are affected fortunately, or unfortunately, so much do they affect us, our works, and those things which we use, fortunately, or unhappily. And although many effects proceed from the fixed stars, yet they are attributed to the planets, as because being more near to us, and more distinct and known, so because they execute whatsoever the superior stars communicate to them.[20]

Notes—Chapter XXXI

1. *their colours—*

Each of the planets has its peculiar colour; Saturn is white, Jupiter brilliant, Mars fiery, Lucifer [Venus in the east] is glowing, Vesper [Venus in the west] refulgent, Mercury sparkling, the Moon mild; the Sun, when he rises, is blazing, afterwards he becomes radiating. The appearance of the stars, which are fixed in the firmament, is also affected by these causes. (Pliny 2.16 [Bostock and Riley, 1:50])

2. *Navel of Andromeda—*Mirach, a yellow star said to be fortunate in honors and matrimony.

3. *Head of Algol—*Algol is a white variable star that brightens and dims, making it very conspicuous in the northern heavens. The Arabs called it the Blinking Demon. The Hebrews named it Satan's Head and Lilith, after the demon lover of Adam. The Chinese called it the Piled-up Corpses. It was everywhere regarded as violent, dangerous, and highly unlucky. Al Sufi described it as a red star, and this occasional redness was observed by an astronomer named Schmidt at Athens in 1841.

4. *Pleiades—*This small cluster of stars, called the Seven Sisters, ranges in color from silvery white, to a lucid white tending to violet, to an intense white. It was connected with rain showers and the time of planting and was regarded as a portent of blindness and accidents to the sight.

5. *Aldeboram—*Aldebaran, of a pale rose colour, was a fortunate star that foretold wealth and honor.

6. *Goat Star—*Capella is white, and signified wealth, civic honor, and military renown. Ptolemy described it as a red star, perhaps due to a peculiarity in his color vision.

7. *Greater Dog Star—*Sirius, the brightest star in the heavens, is a binary noted in ancient times for its scintillation and rapid color changes, ranging from brilliant blue-white to yellow, and even perhaps to red if old accounts are to be believed. It was in earliest ages considered to be an evil star, the bringer of plagues, fevers, drought, and death, by virtue of its connection with the heat of the dog days of summer, and was propitiated with sacrifice and worship. In more recent centuries it was thought to foretell wealth and renown.

8. *Lesser Dog Star—*Procyon is a binary star yellowish white in color that was said to portend wealth, fame and good fortune.

9. *King's Star—*Regulus, or Cor Leonis, is flushed white in color and was said to confer a royal destiny of riches and power upon those born under its influence.

10. *Tail of the Greater Bear—*Alkaid is a brilliant white star reputed to shine down on the fall of princes and the overthrow of empires.

11. *Right Wing of the Crow—*Gienah, the brightest star of the constellation Corvus, called the Right Wing, though it is located on modern star charts in the *left* wing—perhaps it depends on whether one visualizes the Raven from above or below.

12. *Left Wing*—Algorab, a pale yellow star located on modern charts in the *right* wing of Corvus—but see note above.

13. *Spica*—Of a brilliant flushed white color, this star was identified with Virgo and presided over the harvest.

14. *Alchameth*—Arcturus (see note 45, ch. XXXII, bk. I), a bright golden yellow star said to bring storms upon the Earth, but riches and honors to those born under it. Ptolemy describes it as golden red.

15. *Elepheia*—Alphecca (see note 47, ch. XXXII, bk. I), a brilliant white star said by astrologers, along with the other stars of the constellation Corona Borealis, to conduce to fertility and a gentle, loving nature.

16. *Heart of the Scorpion*—Antares, a bright star of a fiery red color closely associated for this reason with Mars. It was one of the four Royal Stars of the ancient Persians (3000 BC), who called it the Guardian of the Heavens.

17. *Falling Vulture*—Vega, a bright star of pale sapphire colour, and good omen.

18. *Tail of Capricorn*—Deneb Algedi, a star of average brightness (magnitude 3.1) and few occult associations. See note 52, ch. XXXII,.bk. I.

19. *Shoulder of the Horse*—Menkib (β Pegasi), from the Arab *Mankib al Faras,* an irregular variable star with a considerable range of brightness that is of a deep yellow color. It is more commonly called Scheat, from the Arab *Al Sa'id,* the Upper Part of the Arm, or possibly from *Sa'd,* Lucky. This name was also applied to Markab (α Pegasi), which has richer occult associations, portending danger to life from cuts, stabs, or fire; however, this is a white star, which seems a less appropriate color to the mingled natures of Jupiter and Mars.

20. *communicate to them*—The zodiacal longitudes of the fixed stars given by Agrippa are eight or nine degrees behind their present positions, due to the precession of the equinoxes. The positions were correct some 240 years before the writing of the *Occult Philosophy,* which strongly suggests that Agrippa made use of the Alphonsine Tables, astrological tables compiled in 1253 in Toledo. See note 12, ch. XXVII, bk. III. I am indebted to David Godwin for these astrological calculations.

CHAPTER XXXII

Of the Sun, and Moon, and their magical considerations.

The Sun, and Moon have obtained the administration or ruling of the heavens, and all bodies under the heavens. The Sun is the lord of all elementary virtues; and the Moon by virtue of the Sun is the mistress of generation, increase, or decrease. Hence *Albumasar* saith, that by the Sun and Moon life is infused into all things, which therefore *Orpheus* calls the enlivening eyes of the heaven.[1]

The Sun giveth light to all things of itself, and gives it plentifully to all things not only in the heaven and air, but Earth and deep: whatsoever good we have, as *Jamblichus* saith, we have it from the Sun alone, or from it through other things. *Heraclitus* calls the Sun the fountain of celestial light; and many of the Platonists placed the Soul of the World chiefly in the Sun, as that which filling the whole globe of the Sun doth send forth its rays on all sides as it were a spirit through all things, distributing life, sense and motion to the very universe.

Hence the ancient naturalists called the Sun the very heart of heaven; and the Chaldeans put it as the middle of the planets. The Egyptians also placed it in the middle of the world, viz. betwixt the two fives of the world, i.e. above the Sun they place five planets, and under the Sun, the Moon and four elements. For it is amongst the other stars the image and statue of the great Prince of both worlds, viz. terrestrial, and celestial; the true light, and the most exact image of God himself; whose essence resembles the Father, light the Son, heat the Holy Ghost. So that the Platonists have nothing to hold forth the Divine Essence more manifestly by, than this. So great is the consonancy of it to God, that *Plato* calls it the conspicuous son of God, and *Iamblicus* calls it the divine image of divine intelligence. And our *Dionysius* calls it the perspicuous statue of God.

It sits as king in the middle of other planets, excelling all in light, greatness, fairness, enlightening all, distributing virtue to them to dispose inferior bodies, and regulating and disposing of their motions, so that from thence their motions are called daily, or nightly, southern, or northern, oriential, or occidental, direct, or retrograde;[2] and as it doth by its light drive away all the darkness of the night, so also all powers of darkness, which we read of in Job;[3] as soon as morning appears, they think of the shadow of death: and the Psalmist[4] speaking of the lion's whelps seeking leave of God to devour, saith, the Sun is risen, and they are gathered together, and shall be placed in their dens; which being put to flight, it follows, man shall go forth to his labour.

The Sun therefore as it possesseth the middle region of the world, and as the heart is in animals to the whole body, so the Sun is over the heaven, and the world, ruling over the whole universe, and those things which are in it, the very author of seasons, from whence day and year, cold and heat, and all other qualities of seasons;[5] and as saith *Ptolemy*,[6] when it comes unto the place of any star, it stirs up the power thereof which it hath in the air. So as with Mars, heat; with Saturn, cold; and it disposeth even the very spirit and mind of man; from hence it is said by *Homer,* and approved by *Aristotle,* that there are in the mind such like motions, as the Sun the prince and moderator of the planets every day bringeth to us.

But the Moon, the nighest to the Earth, the receptacle of all the heavenly influences, by the swiftness of her course is joined to the Sun, and the other planets and stars, every month, and being made as it were the wife of all the stars, is the most fruitful of the stars, and receiving the beams and influences of all the other planets and stars as a conception, bringing them forth to the inferior world as being next to itself; for all the stars have influence on it, being the last receiver,[7] which afterwards communicateth the influences of all the superiors to these inferiors, and pours them forth on the Earth; and it more manifestly disposeth these inferiors than the others, and its motion is more sensible by the familiarity and propinquity which it hath with us; and as a medium betwixt both superiors and inferiors, communicateth them to them all.

Therefore her motion is to be observed before the others, as the parent of all concep-tions, which it diversely issueth forth in these inferiors, according to the divers complexion, motion, situation, and different aspects to the planets and other stars; and though it receiveth powers from all the stars, yet especially from the Sun; as oft as it is in conjunction with the same, it is replenished with vivifying virtue, and according to the aspect thereof it borroweth its complexion; for in the first quarter, as the Peri-patetics deliver, it is hot and moist; in the sec-ond, hot and dry; in the third, cold and dry; in the fourth, cold and moist.[8]

And although it is the lowest of the stars, yet it bringeth forth all the conceptions of the superiors; for from it in the heavenly bodies beginneth that series of things which *Plato* cal-leth the Golden Chain,[9] by the which every thing and cause being linked one to another, do depend on the superior, even until it may be brought to the Supreme Cause of all, from which all things depend; from hence it is, that without the Moon intermediating, we cannot at any time attract the power of the superiors.

Therefore *Thebit* adviseth us, for the taking of the virtue of any star, to take the stone and herb of that planet, when the Moon doth either fortunately get under, or hath a good aspect on, that star.

Notes—Chapter XXXII

1. *of the heaven*—In an Orphic hymn to Jove pre-served by Proclus, where the god is described as the universe, occurs the line: "His eyes, the sun, and moon with borrow'd ray ..." (*Hymns of Orpheus,* Introduction, in *Thomas Taylor the Platonist: Selected Writings,* 178). In the Orphic hymn "To the Sun," is written "Hear golden Titan, whose eternal eye/With broad survey, illumines all the sky ..." (ibid., hymn 7, p. 218). This echoes Homer, who refers to the Sun as: "... a dreaded god,/Helios, who sees all things and listens to all things" (*Odyssey* 12, lines 322–3, [Lattimore, 193], also bk. 11, line 109 [Lattimore, 171]).

2. *direct, or retrograde*—See note 17, ch. XXVI, bk. II.

3. *in Job*—Job 24:17. See also 17:12. There is a per-vasive darkness motif running throughout the book of Job.

4. *Psalmist*—Psalms 104:21–3.

5. *qualities of seasons*—

The sun is carried along in the midst of these [planets], a body of great size and power, the ruler, not only of the seasons and of the different climates, but also of the stars themselves and of the heavens. When we consider his operations, we must regard him as the life, or rather the mind of the universe, the chief regulator and the God of nature; he also lends his light to the other stars. He is most illustrious and excellent, beholding all things and hearing all things, which, I perceive, is ascribed to him exclu-sively by the prince of poets, Homer. (Pliny 2.4 [Bostock and Riley, 1:20])

For the sun, together with the ambient [the atmosphere], is always in some way affecting everything on the earth, not only by the changes that accompany the seasons of the year to bring about the generation of animals, the production of plants, the flowing of waters, and the changes of bodies, but also by its daily revolutions, furnishing heat, moisture, dryness, and cold in regular order and in correspondence with its positions relative to the zenith. (Ptolemy *Tetrabiblos* 1.2 [Robbins, 7])

6. *saith Ptolemy*—"Now, mark you, likewise, according to their aspects to the sun, the moon and three of the planets [Saturn, Jupiter and Mars] experience increase and decrease in their own powers" (ibid. 1.8 [Robbins, 45]). Elsewhere Ptolemy says: "… the sun and Mercury, however, they [the ancients] thought to have both powers [beneficent and malevolent], because they have a common nature, and to join their influences with those of the other planets, with whichever of them they are associated" (ibid. 1.5 [Robbins, 39]). The magnifying power of the sun is most pronounced in the phenomenon of cazimi (see note 7, ch. XXX, bk. II).

7. *last receiver*—

The moon, too, as the heavenly body nearest the earth, bestows her effluence most abundantly upon mundane things, for most of them, animate or inanimate, are sympathetic to her and change in company with her; the rivers increase and diminish their streams with her light, the seas turn their own tides with her rising and setting, and plants and animals in whole or in some part wax and wane with her. (ibid. 1.2 [Robbins, 7])

See Deuteronomy 33:14.

8. *cold and moist*—"For in its waxing from new moon to first quarter the moon is more productive of moisture; in its passage from first quarter to full, of heat; from full to last quarter, of dryness, and from last quarter to occultation, of cold" (ibid. 1.8 [Robbins, 45]).

9. *Golden Chain*—This image originates with Homer, who makes Zeus boast:

Let down out of the sky a cord of gold; lay
    hold of it
all you who are gods and all who are god-
    desses, yet not
even so can you drag down Zeus from the
    sky to the ground, not
Zeus the high lord of counsel, though you
    try until you grow weary.
Yet whenever I might strongly be minded
    to pull you,
I could drag you up, earth and all and sea
    and all with you,
then fetch the golden rope about the horn
    of Olympos
and make it fast, so that all once more
    should dangle in mid air.
    (*Iliad* 8, lines 19–26 [Lattimore, 182–3])

Probably Agrippa is referring to the "spindle of Necessity" of Plato, which "extended from above throughout the heaven and the Earth, a straight light like a pillar, most nearly resembling a rainbow, but brighter and purer" (Plato *Republic* 10.616b [Hamilton and Cairns, 840]). Plato's chain is a chain of reincarnating souls, which, however, he does not specifically embody in this metaphor (see *Republic* 10.619–20). He makes a somewhat humorous allusion to the Golden Chain when he compares the chain of poets depending from the Muse to a chain of magnetized rings hanging from a loadstone (*Ion* 533d–534a). The Golden Chain inevitably calls to mind the ladder of Jacob, upon which angels constantly ascended and descended (Genesis 28:12).

CHAPTER XXXIII

Of the twenty-eight mansions of the Moon, and their virtues.

And seeing the Moon measureth the whole Zodiac in the space of twenty-eight days; hence it is, that the wise-men of the Indians[1] and ancient astrologians have granted twenty-eight mansions to the Moon,[2] which being fixed in the eighth sphere, do enjoy (as *Alpharus* saith) divers names and properties from the divers signs and stars which are contained in them, through which while the Moon wandereth, it obtaineth other and other powers and virtues; but every one of these mansions according to the opinion of *Abraham,* containeth twelve degrees, and one and fifty minutes, and almost twenty-six seconds, whose names and also their beginnings in the Zodiac[3] of the eighth sphere are these.

The first is called Alnath, that is the Horns of Aries; his beginning is from the head of Aries of the eighth sphere; it causeth discords, and journeys.

The second is called Allothaim or Albochan, that is the Belly of Aries, and his beginning is from the twelfth degree of the same sign, fifty-one minutes, twenty-two seconds complete; it conduceth to the finding of treasures, and to the retaining of captives.

The third is called Achaomazon or Athoray, that is, Showering or Pleiades; his beginning is from the twenty-five degrees of Aries complete forty-two minutes, and fifty-one seconds; it is profitable to sailors, huntsmen, and alchemists.

The fourth mansion is called Aldebaram or Aldelamen, that is the Eye or Head of Taurus; his beginning is from the eighth degree of Taurus, thirty-four minutes, and seventeen seconds of the same Taurus being excluded; it causeth the destruction and hinderances of buildings, fountains, wells, of gold mines, the flight of creeping things, and begetteth discord.

The fifth is called Alchatay or Albachay; the beginning of it is after the twenty-one degree of Taurus twenty-five minutes, forty seconds; it helpeth to the return from a journey, to the instruction of scholars, it confirmeth edifices, it giveth health and good will.

The sixth is called Alhanna or Alchaya, that is the Little Star of Great Light; his beginning is after the fourth degree of Gemini, seventeen minutes, and nine seconds; it conduceth to hunting, and besieging of towns, and revenge of princes, it destroyeth harvests and fruits and hindereth the operation of the physician.

The seventh is called Aldimiach or Alarzach, that is the Arm of Gemini, and beginneth from the seventeenth degree of Gemini, eight minutes and thirty-four seconds, and lasteth even to the end of the sign; it conferreth gain and friendship, it's profitable to lovers, it feareth flies, destroyeth magisteries.

And so is one quarter of the heaven compleated in these seven mansions; and in the like order and number of degrees, minutes and seconds, the remaining mansions in every quarter have their several beginnings; namely so, that in the first sign of this quarter three mansions take their beginnings, in the other two signs two Mansions in each.

Therefore the seven following mansions begin from Cancer, whose names are Alnaza or Anatrachya, that is Misty or Cloudy, viz. the eighth Mansion; it causeth love, friendship, and society of fellow travelers, it driveth away mice and afflicteth captives, confirming their imprisonment.

After this is the ninth called Archaam or Arcaph, that is the Eye of the Lion; it hindereth harvests and travelers, and putteth discord between men.

The tenth is called Algelioche or Albgebh, that is the Neck or Forehead of Leo; it strengtheneth buildings, yieldeth love, benevolence and help against enemies.

The eleventh is called Azobra or Arduf, that is the Hair of the Lion's Head; it is good for voyages, and gain by merchandise, and for redemption of captives.

The twelfth is called Alzarpha or Azarpha, that is the Tail of Leo; it giveth prosperity to harvests, and plantations, but hindereth seamen, but it is good for the bettering of servants, captives and companions.

The thirteenth is named Alhaire, that is Dog Stars, or the Wings of Virgo; it is prevalent for benevolence, gain, voyages, harvests, and freedom of captives.

The fourteenth is called Achureth or Arimet, by others Azimeth or Alhumech or Alcheymech, that is the Spike of Virgo, or Flying Spike; it causeth the love of married folk, it cureth the sick, it's profitable to sailors, but it hindereth journeys by land; and in these the second quarter of heaven is completed.

The other seven follow, the first of which beginneth in the head of Libra, viz. the fifteenth Mansion, and his name is Agrapha or Algarpha, that is, Covered, or Covered Flying; it's profitable for the extracting of treasures, for digging of pits, it helpeth forward divorce, discord, and the destruction of houses and enemies, and hindereth travelers.

The sixteenth is called Azubene or Ahubene, that is, the Horns of Scorpio; it hindereth journeys and wedlock, harvests and merchandise, it prevaileth for redemption of captives.

The seventeenth is called Alchil, that is, the Crown of Scorpio; it bettereth a bad fortune, maketh love durable, strengtheneth buildings, and helpeth seamen.

The eighteenth is called Alchas or Altob, that is the Heart of Scorpio; it causeth discord, sedition, conspiracy against princes and mighty ones, and revenge from enemies, but it freeth captives and helpeth edifices.

The nineteenth is called Allatha or Achala, by others Hycula or Axala, that is the Tail of Scorpio; it helpeth in the besieging of cities and taking of towns, and in the driving of men from their places, and for the destruction of seamen, and perdition of captives.

The twentieth is called Abnahaya, that is a Beam; it helpeth for the taming of wild beasts, for the strengthening of prisons, it destroyeth the wealth of societies, it compelleth a man to come to a certain place.

The one and twentieth is called Abeda or Albeldach, which is a Defeat; it is good for harvests, gain, buildings and travelers, and causeth divorce; and in this is the third quarter of heaven completed.

There remaineth the seven last Mansions completing the last quarter of heaven; the first of which being in order to the two and twentieth, beginning from the head of Capricorn, called Sadahacha or Zodeboluch or Zandeldena, that is a Pastor; it promoteth the flight of servants and captives, that they may escape, and helpeth in the curing of diseases.

The three and twentieth is called Zabadola or Zobrach, that is Swallowing; it maketh for divorce, liberty of captives and the health of the sick.

The twenty-fourth is called Sadabath or Chadezoad, that is the Star of Fortune; it is prevalent for the benevolence of married folk, for the victory of soldiers, it hurteth the execution of government, and hindereth that it may not be exercised.

The twenty-fifth is called Sadalabra or Sadalachia, that is a Butterfly, or a Spreading Forth; it helpeth besieging and revenge, it destroyeth enemies, maketh divorce, confirmeth prisons and buildings, hasteneth messengers, it conduceth to spells against copulation, and so bindeth every member of man, that it cannot perform his duty.

The twenty-sixth is called Alpharg or Phragol Mocaden, that is the First Drawing; it maketh for the union and love of men, for the health of captives, it destroyeth prisons and buildings.

The twenty-seventh is called Alcharya or Alhalgalmoad, that is the Second Drawing; it increaseth harvests, revenues, gain, it healeth infirmities, but hindereth buildings, prolongeth prisons, causeth danger to seamen, and helpeth

to infer mischiefs on whom you shall please.

The twenty-eighth and last is called Albotham or Alchalcy, that is Pisces; it increaseth harvests and merchandise, it secureth travelers through dangerous places, it maketh for the joy of married couples, but it strengtheneth prisons, and causeth loss of treasures.

And in these twenty-eight mansions do lie hid many secrets of the wisdom of the ancients, by the which they wrought wonders on all things which are under the circle of the Moon; and they attributed to every mansion his resemblances, images, and seals, and his president intelligences, and they did work by the virtue of them after diverse manners.

Notes—Chapter XXXIII

1. *Indians*—The moon is much more prominent in Hindu astrology then in the astrology of the West.

2. *Mansions of the Moon*—From the Arabic *Al Manazil al Kamr* (Resting Places of the Moon), *manzil* signifying the noonday rest of a camel rider in the desert. The mansions are perhaps the most ancient division of the heavens, older even than the zodiac. They are found in India, China, Arabia, Babylonia, Egypt, Persia, and other sites of early civilization. The Indians recognize 27 mansions, the Arabs 28. This difference of opinion arises because the revolution of the Moon about the Earth takes 27.3 days. Until the time of Christ the list of mansions began with the Pleiades at the beginning of Taurus, but after this time it was shifted to the stars in the beginning of Aries due to the precession of the equinoxes, these stars having been associated with the 27th Mansion of the earlier series. Three of the names from the Chinese and Arabic series are the same, at least suggesting the possibility of a common origin lost in time. With typical syncretic zeal the Arabs associated the mansions with the letters of the Arabic alphabet (the

first mansion being silent) and with the essential divisions of the universe. The mansions were named after the bright star that occupied each—or perhaps the stars were named for the mansions.

3. *beginnings in the Zodiac*—When the seven divisions of the first quarter of the zodiac are translated into seconds of arc, it will easily be seen that they are by no means regular:

1st Mansion:	46,282"
2nd	46,289"
3rd	46,286"
4th	46,283"
5th	46,289"
6th	46,285"
7th	46,286"

Total: 324,000" = 90 degrees

The measure that Agrippa gives from Abraham (12°51'26", or 46,286") is in fact very close to the 28th part of the Zodiac: 360° X 3600" = 1,296,000" ÷ 28 = 46,285.7". And Agrippa says "almost twenty-six seconds," indicating that he knew the exact measure.

CHAPTER XXXIV

Of the true motion of the heavenly bodies to be observed in the eighth sphere, and of the ground of planetary hours.

Whosoever will work according to the celestial opportunity, ought to observe both or one of them, namely the motion of the stars, or their times; I say their motions, when they are in their dignities or dejections, either essential or accidental;[1] but I call their times, days and hours distributed to their dominions. Concerning all these, it is abundantly taught in the books of astrologers; but in this place two things especially are to be considered and observed by us.

One, that we observe the motions and ascensions and windings of stars,[2] even as they are in truth in the eighth sphere, through the neglect of which it happeneth that many err in fabricating the celestial images, and are defrauded of their desired effect.

The other thing we ought to observe, is about the times of choosing the planetary hours; for almost all astrologers divide all that space of time from the Sun rising to setting into twelve equal parts, and call them the twelve hours of the day; then the time which followeth from the setting to the rising, in like manner being divided into twelve equal parts, they call the

twelve hours of the night, and then distribute each of those hours to every one of the planets according to the order of their successions, giving always the first hour of the day to the lord of that day, then to every one by order, even to the end of twenty-four hours.[3]

And in this distribution the magicians agree with them; but in the partition of the hours some do dissent, saying that the space of the rising and setting is not to be divided into equal parts, and that those hours are not therefore called unequal because the diurnal are unequal to the nocturnal, but because both the diurnal and nocturnal are even unequal amongst themselves.[4]

Therefore the partition of unequal or planetary hours hath a different reason of their measure observed by magicians, which is of this sort; for as in artificial hours, which are always equal to themselves, the ascensions of fifteen degrees[5] in the equinoctial[6] constituteth an artificial hour: so also in planetary hours the ascensions of fifteen degrees in the ecliptic constituteth an unequal or planetary hour, whose measure we ought to inquire and find out by the tables of the oblique ascensions of every region.

Notes—Chapter XXXIV

1. *essential or accidental*—See note 7, ch. XXX, bk. II.

2. *windings of the stars*—Because of the tilt of the Earth's axis, the stars and the planets seem to describe

paths that wind around the Earth like the windings of a ball of string as the Earth progresses in its orbit.

3. *twenty-four hours*—For convenience the planetary hours have been tabulated on the following page.

Planetary Hours

DAY	Sun.	Mon.	Tues.	Wed.	Thurs.	Fri.	Sat.
1	☉	☽	♂	☿	♃	♀	♄
2	♀	♄	☉	☽	♂	☿	♃
3	☿	♃	♀	♄	☉	☽	♂
4	☽	♂	☿	♃	♀	♄	☉
5	♄	☉	☽	♂	☿	♃	♀
6	♃	♀	♄	☉	☽	♂	☿
7	♂	☿	♃	♀	♄	☉	☽
8	☉	☽	♂	☿	♃	♀	♄
9	♀	♄	☉	☽	♂	☿	♃
10	☿	♃	♀	♄	☉	☽	♂
11	☽	♂	☿	♃	♀	♄	☉
12	♄	☉	☽	♂	☿	♃	♀

NIGHT	Sun.	Mon.	Tues.	Wed.	Thurs.	Fri.	Sat.
1	♃	♀	♄	☉	☽	♂	☿
2	♂	☿	♃	♀	♄	☉	☽
3	☉	☽	♂	☿	♃	♀	♄
4	♀	♄	☉	☽	♂	☿	♃
5	☿	♃	♀	♄	☉	☽	♂
6	☽	♂	☿	♃	♀	♄	☉
7	♄	☉	☽	♂	☿	♃	♀
8	♃	♀	♄	☉	☽	♂	☿
9	♂	☿	♃	♀	♄	☉	☽
10	☉	☽	♂	☿	♃	♀	♄
11	♀	♄	☉	☽	♂	☿	♃
12	☿	♃	♀	♄	☉	☽	♂

Notes—Chapter XXXIV (cont'd.)

4. *unequal amongst themselves*—This is due to the angle between the plane of the ecliptic and the plane of the equator, or equinoctial, which results from the tilt of the axis of the Earth. Half the signs of the zodiac—Cancer, Leo, Virgo, Libra, Scorpio, Sagittarius—take more than two hours to rise. These are called the signs of long ascension. The other half of the zodiac—Capricorn, Aquarius, Pisces, Aries, Taurus, Gemini—take less than two hours to ascend. These signs are called the signs of short ascension. This unequal division of times is reflected in the unequal house systems of Campanus (13th century), Regiomontanus (15th century) and Placidus (17th century).

5. *fifteen degrees*—Because 360° ÷ 24 = 15°.

6. *equinoctial*—The celestial equator. When the sun is on this circle, or plane, day and night are of exactly equal length. This is termed the equinox, and on these two days of the year the artificial clock hours are of the same duration as the planetary hours.

CHAPTER XXXV

How some artificial things as images, seals, and such like may obtain some virtue from the celestial bodies.

So great is the extent, power and efficacy of the celestial bodies, that not only natural things, but also artificial when they are rightly exposed to those above, do presently suffer by that most potent agent, and obtain a wonderful life, which oftentimes gives them an admirable celestial virtue; which thing Saint *Thomas Aquinas* that holy doctor, thus confirmeth in his book De Fato, when he saith, that even garments, buildings and other artificial works whatsoever, do receive a certain qualification from the stars.

So the magicians affirm that not only by the mixture and application of natural things, but also in images, seals, rings, glasses,[1] and some other instruments, being opportunely framed under a certain constellation, some celestial illustration may be taken, and some wonderful thing may be received; for the beams of the celestial bodies being animated, living, sensual, and bringing along with them admirable gifts, and a most violent power, do, even in a moment, and at the first touch, imprint wonderful powers in the images, though their matter be less capable.[2]

Yet they bestow more powerful virtues on the images, if they be framed not of any, but of a certain matter, namely whose natural, and also special virtue is agreeable with the work, and the figure of the image is like to the celestial; for such an image, both in regard of the matter naturally congruous to the operation and celestial influence, and also for its figure being like to the heavenly one, is best prepared to receive the operations and powers of the celestial bodies and figures, and instantly receiveth the heavenly gift into itself; then it constantly worketh on another thing, and other things do yield obedience to it.

Hence saith *Ptolemy* in Centiloquio,[3] that inferior things do obey the celestial, and not only them, but also even their images; even as earthly scorpions obey not only the celestial Scorpion, but also his image, if it shall be opportunely figured under his ascent and dominion.

Notes—Chapter XXXV

1. *glasses*—Magic mirrors, which were used for scrying and to communicate with spirits. The most ancient of these is the surface of a liquid such as water, or oil, or ink. See Pausanias *(Guide to Greece* 7.21.5) for the use of a mirror in divination.

2. *less capable*—Though the matter upon which the images are formed is less susceptible to influence.

3. *Centiloquio*—The *Centiloquium,* a work consisting of 100 aphorisms on astrology attributed to Ptolemy. It is also sometimes called the *Fructus librorum suorum.*

Egyptian Zodiac

From *The Gods of the Egyptians* by E. A. Wallis Budge (London, 1904)

CHAPTER XXXVI

Of the images of the Zodiac, what virtues they being engraven, receive from the stars.

But the celestial images, according to whose likeness images of this kind are framed, are very many in the heavens: some visible and conspicuous, others only imaginable, conceived and set down by Egyptians, Indians and Chaldeans; and their parts are so ordered, that even the figures of some of them are distinguished from others: for this reason they place in the Zodiac circle twelve general[1] images, according to the number of the signs.

Of these they constituting Aries, Leo and Sagittary for the fiery and oriental triplicity, do report that it's[2] profitable against fevers, palsy, dropsy, gout, and all cold and phlegmatic infirmities, and that it makes him who carrieth it to be acceptable, eloquent, ingenious and honorable, because they are the houses of Mars, Sol and Jupiter. They made also the image of a lion against melancholy phantasies, the dropsy, plague, fevers, and to expel diseases, at the hour of the Sun, the first degree of the sign of Leo ascending, which is the face and decanate[3] of Jupiter; but against the stone, and diseases of the reins, and against the hurts of beasts, they made the same image when Sol in the heart of the Lion obtained the midst of heaven.[4] And again, because Gemini, Libra and Aquarius do constitute the aerial and occidental triplicity, and are the houses of Mercury, Venus and Saturn, they are said to put to flight diseases, to conduce to friendship and concord, to prevail against melancholy, and to cause health; and

they report that Aquarius especially freeth from the quartan.

Also, that Cancer, Scorpio and Pisces, because they constitute the watery and northern triplicity, do prevail against hot and dry fevers; also against the hectic,[5] and all choleric passions; but Scorpio, because amongst the members it respecteth the privy parts, doth provoke to lust: but these did frame it for this purpose, his third face ascending, which belongeth to Venus; and they made the same against serpents and scorpions, poisons, and evil spirits, his second face ascending, which is the face of the Sun,[6] and decanate of Jupiter; and they report that it maketh him who carrieth it, wise, of a good colour;[7] and they report that the image of Cancer is most efficacious against serpents, and poisons, when Sol and Luna are in conjunction in it, and ascend in the first and third face; for this is the face of Venus, and the decanate of Luna; but the second face of Luna, the decanate of Jupiter: they report also that serpents are tormented when the Sun is in Cancer.

Also, that Taurus, Virgo and Capricorn, because they constitute the earthly and southern triplicity, do cure hot infirmities, and prevail against the synocal fever;[8] it maketh those that carry it grateful, acceptable, eloquent, devout and religious, because they are the houses of Venus, Mercury and Saturn: Capricorn also is reported to keep men in safety, and also places in security, because it is the exaltation of Mars.

Notes—Chapter XXXVI

1. *general*—Universally accepted and recognized.

2. *it's*—That is, the image so constituted.

3. *decanate*—The decans are divisions of the signs of the zodiac into three portions, each comprising ten degrees. In this sense they are the same as the faces, as Agrippa uses this term. The first decan in each sign is strongly of the nature of the sign, and is ruled by the ruling planet of the sign. The second decan is ruled by the ruling planet of the next sign in the elemental triplicity to which the sign belongs. The third decan is ruled by the ruling planet of the third sign of the same elemental triplicity. The following table shows the decans and the planets that rule them.

Sign	1st	2nd	3rd
♈	♂	☉	♃
♉	♀	☿	♄
♊	☿	♀	♄
♋	☽	♂	♃
♌	☉	♃	♂

Sign	1st	2nd	3rd
♍	☿	♄	♀
♎	♀	♄	☿
♏	♂	♃	☽
♐	♃	♂	☉
♑	♄	♀	☿
♒	♄	☿	♀
♓	♃	☽	♂

4. *midst of heaven*—That is, when the Sun in the middle decan of Leo was in the tenth house, midheaven.

5. *hectic*—Consumptive fever, or tuberculosis. It is characterized by flushed cheeks and a hot, dry skin.

6. *face of the Sun*—See table, note 5, ch. XXX, bk. II.

7. *colour*—Flushed with health.

8. *synocal fever*—A continuing fever accompanied by inflammation.

CHAPTER XXXVII

Of the images of the faces, and of those images which are without the Zodiac.

There are besides in the Zodiac thirty-six images,[1] according to the number of the faces, of the which (as *Porphyry* saith) *Teucer* the Babylonian long since wrote, who was a most ancient mathematician, after whom the Arabians also wrote of these things.

Therefore it is said, that in the first face of Aries, ascendeth the image of a black man, standing and clothed in a white garment, girdled about, of a great body, with reddish eyes, and great strength, and like one that is angry; and this image signifieth and causeth boldness, fortitude, loftiness, and shamelessness: in the second face ascendeth a form of a woman, outwardly clothed with a red garment, and under it a white, spreading abroad over her feet, and this image causeth nobleness, height of a kingdom, and greatness of dominion: in the third face ariseth the figure of a white man, pale, with reddish hair, and clothed with a red garment, who carrying on the one hand a golden bracelet, and holding forth a wooden staff, is restless, and like one in wrath, because he cannot perform the good he would. This image bestoweth wit, meekness, joy and beauty.

In the first face of Taurus ascendeth a naked man, an archer, harvester or husbandman, and goeth forth to sow, plough, build, people and divide the Earth, according to the rules of geometry: in the second face ascendeth a naked man, holding in his hand a key; it giveth power, nobility, and dominion over people: in the third face, ascendeth a man in whose hand is a serpent, and a dart, and is the image of necessity and profit, and also of misery and slavery.

In the first face of Gemini ascendeth a man in whose hand is a rod, and he is, as it were, serving another; it granteth wisdom, and the knowledge of numbers and arts in which there is no profit: in the second face ascendeth a man in whose hand is a pipe, and another being bowed down, digging the earth; and they signify infamous and dishonest agility, as that of jesters and jugglers; it also signifies labours and painful searchings: in the third, ascendeth a man seeking for arms, and a fool holding in the right hand a bird, and in his left a pipe; and they are the significations of forgetfulness, wrath, boldness, jests, scurrilities, and unprofitable words.

In the first face of Cancer ascendeth the form of a young virgin, adorned with fine clothes, and having a crown on her head; it giveth acuteness of senses, subtilty of wit, and the love of men: in the second place ascendeth a man clothed in comely apparel, or a man and woman sitting at the table and playing; it bestoweth riches, mirth, gladness, and the love of women: in the third face ascendeth a man, a hunter with his lance and horn, bringing out dogs for to hunt; the signification of this is the contention of men, the pursuing of those who fly, the hunting and possessing of things by arms and brawlings.

In the first face of Leo ascendeth a man riding on a lion; it signifieth boldness, violence, cruelty, wickedness, lust and labours to be sustained: in the second ascendeth an image with hands lifted up, and a man on whose head is a crown; he hath the appearance of an angry man, and one that threateneth, having in his right hand a sword drawn out of the scabbard, and in his left a buckler; it hath signification upon hidden contentions, and unknown victories, and upon base men, and upon the occasions of quarrels and battles: in the third face ascendeth a young man in whose hand is a whip, and a man very sad, and of an ill aspect; they signify love and society, and the loss of one's right for avoiding strife.

In the first face of Virgo ascendeth the figure of a good maid, and a man casting seeds; it signifieth getting of wealth, ordering of diet, plowing, sowing, and peopling: in the second face ascendeth a black man clothed with a skin, and a man having a bush of hair, holding a bag; they signify gain, scraping together of wealth and covetousness: in the third face ascendeth a white woman and deaf, or an old man leaning on a staff; the signification of this is to show weakness, infirmity, loss of members, destruction of trees, and depopulation of lands.

In the first face of Libra ascendeth the form of an angry man, in whose hand is a pipe, and the form of a man reading in a book; the operation of this is in justifying and helping the miserable and weak against the powerful and wicked: in the second face ascend two men furious and wrathful, and a man in a comely garment, sitting in a chair; and the signification of these is to show indignation against the evil, and quietness and security of life with plenty of good things: in the third face ascendeth a violent man holding a bow, and before him a naked man, and also another man holding bread in one hand, and a cup of wine in the other; the signification of these is to show wicked lusts, singings, sports and gluttony.

In the first face of Scorpio ascendeth a woman of good face and habit, and two men striking her; the operations of these are for comeliness, beauty, and for strifes, treacheries, deceits, detractations, and perditions: in the second face ascendeth a man naked, and a woman naked, and a man sitting on the earth, and before him two dogs biting one another; and their operation is for impudence, deceit, and false dealing, and for to send mischief and strife amongst men: in the third face ascendeth a man bowed downward upon his knees, and a woman striking him with a staff; and it is the signification of drunkenness, fornication, wrath, violence, and strife.

In the first face of Sagittarius ascendeth the form of a man armed with a coat of mail, and holding a naked sword in his hand; the operation of this is for boldness, malice, and liberty: in the second face ascendeth a woman weeping, and covered with clothes; the operation of this is for sadness and fear of his own body: in the third face ascendeth a man like in colour to gold, or an idle man playing with a staff; and the signification of this is in following our own wills, and obstinacy in them, and in activeness for evil things, contentions, and horrible matters.

In the first face of Capricorn ascendeth the form of a woman, and a man carrying full bags; and the signification of these is for to go forth and to rejoice, to gain and to lose with weakness and baseness: in the second face ascendeth two women and a man looking towards a bird flying in the air; and the signification of these is for the requiring of those things which cannot be done, and for the searching after those things which cannot be known: in the third face ascendeth a woman chaste in body, and wise in her work, and a banker gathering his money together on the table; the signification of this is to govern in prudence, in covetousness of money, and in avarice.

In the first face of Aquarius ascendeth the form of a prudent man, and of a woman spinning; and the signification of these is in the thought and labour for gain, in poverty and baseness: in the second face ascendeth the form of a man with a long beard; and the signification of this belongeth to the understanding, meekness, modesty, liberty and good manners: in the third face ascendeth a black and angry man; and the signification of this is in expressing insolence, and impudence.

In the first face of Pisces ascendeth a man carrying burdens on his shoulder, and well clothed; it hath his signification in journeys, change of place, and in carefulness of getting wealth and clothes: in the second face ascendeth a woman of a good countenance, and well adorned; and the signification is to desire and put one's self on or about high and great matters: in the third face ascendeth a man naked, or a youth, and nigh him a beautiful maid, whose head is adorned with flowers; and it hath his signification for rest, idleness, delight, fornication, and for embracing of women. And thus far concerning the images of faces.

Besides these, there are as yet three hundred and sixty images in the Zodiac, according to the number of the degrees, whose forms *Petrus de Abano* hath described.[2]

Without the Zodiac there are also general figures, which *Hyginius* and *Aratus* describe for us, and very many particular ones, according to the number of faces and degrees, existing therein, of all which to speak it would be too long; but of these the more principal are accounted, Pegasus,[3] which prevaileth against the diseases of horses, and preserveth horsemen in battle: then is Andromache,[4] which begetteth love betwixt husband and wife, so that it is said

even to reconcile adulterers: Cassiopeia[5] restoreth weak bodies, and strengtheneth the members: Serpentarius[6] chaseth away poisons, and cureth the bitings of venomous beasts: Hercules[7] giveth victory in war: the Dragon[8] with both the Bears[9] maketh a man crafty, ingenious, valiant, acceptable to the gods and men: Hydra[10] conferreth wisdom and riches, and resisteth poisons: Centaurus[11] bestoweth health and long old age: Ara[12] conserveth chastity, and maketh one acceptable to the gods: Cetus[13] maketh one amiable, prudent, happy both by sea and land, and helps him to recover his lost goods: the Ship[14] affordeth security in the waters: the Hare[15] prevaileth against deceits and madness: the Dog[16] cureth the dropsy, resisteth the plague, and also preserveth from beasts, and fierce creatures: Orion[17] granteth victory: the Eagle[18] giveth new honours, and preserveth the old: the Swan[19] freeth from the palsy and the quartan: Perseus[20] freeth from envy and witchcrafts, and preserveth from lightnings and tempests: the Hart[21] preserveth phrenetical and mad people. And thus much may suffice to have been spoken.

Notes—Chapter XXXVII

1. *thirty-six images*—Described in the *Picatrix,* a popular medieval grimoire.

2. *Abano hath described*—Peter of Abano speaks of the astronomical images of the 360 degrees of the heavens in his *Conciliator,* written around 1303. Johannes Angelus reprinted Peter's *Astrolabium planum* at Venice in 1488 under the title *Opus astrolabii plani in tabulis: a Iohanne Angeli,* and included in this work the section from Abano describing the 360 spirits, leading some to attribute these spirits incorrectly to Johannes Angelus.

3. *Pegasus*—Northern constellation of the winged horse.

4. *Andromache*—Northern constellation Andromeda, the mythical daughter of Cepheus and Cassiopeia, who was bound to a rock as a sacrifice to a sea monster but was rescued by the hero Perseus.

5. *Cassiopeia*—Northern constellation representing the seated figure of the mother of Andromeda. She

raised the ire of Neptune by boasting that she was more beautiful than the Nereids. Neptune sent a sea monster against the kingdom, which could only be appeased by the sacrifice of Andromeda.

6. *Serpentarius*—Serpens, a constellation representing a serpent.

7. *Hercules*—Northern constellation representing the hero on one knee drawing a bow, his foot resting on the head of Draco.

8. *the Dragon*—Northern constellation Draco, which wraps around Ursa Minor and terminates near Ursa Major.

9. *the Bears*—Ursa Minor (Little Bear) and Ursa Major (Great Bear), better known as the Little and Big Dippers.

10. *Hydra*—An extended southern constellation representing the sea serpent of Lake Lerna in Argolis

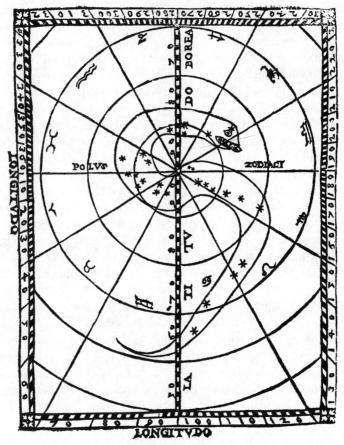

Constellation Draco

from *Theatrum Mundi* by Giovanni Paolo Gallucci (Venice, 1588)

that was slain by Hercules as one of his 12 labors.

11. *Centaurus*—Southern constellation representing a centaur, a mythical beast half horse and half man. Centaurs were known for their long lifespan.

12. *Ara*—Small southern constellation representing an altar.

13. *Cetus*—Mostly southern constellation representing a whale.

14. *the Ship*—The Argo Navis, the ship in which Jason sailed after the golden fleece. This southern constellation was so large, it has been broken into four parts: Carina (the Keel), Puppis (the Stern), Vela (the Sails) and Pyxis (the Mariner's Compass).

15. *the Hare*—Southern constellation Lepus.

16. *the Dog*—Southern constellation Canis Major, which contains Sirius, the Dog Star.

17. *Orion*—The hunter, a giant slain by Artemis and set in the sky.

18. *the Eagle*—Northern constellation Aquila.

19. *the Swan*—Northern constellation Cygnus.

20. *Perseus*—Northern constellation representing the hero.

21. *the Hart*—The Deer was an Egyptian constellation shown by Petosiris, which corresponded roughly to Cassiopeia. It is no longer recognized. It was called Cerva (the Roe) by the German astronomer Johann Bayer (1572–1625), who described it in his *Uranometria* (1603) and placed it north of Pisces.

CHAPTER XXXVIII

Of the images of Saturn.

But now, what images they did attribute to the planets, although of these things very large volumes have been written by the ancient wise men, so that there is no need to declare them here, notwithstanding I will recite a few of them.

For they made, from the operations of Saturn, Saturn ascending, in a stone which is called the loadstone, the image of a man having the countenance of an hart, and camel's feet and sitting upon a chair or dragon,[1] holding in his right hand a scythe, in his left hand a dart; which image they did hope would be profitable for prolongation of life; for *Albumasar* in his book Sadar, proveth that Saturn conduceth to the prolongation of life: where also he telleth that certain regions of India being subject to Saturn, there men are of a very long life, and die not unless by extreme old age.

They made also another image of Saturn for length of days in a sapphire, at the hour of Saturn, Saturn ascending or fortunately constituted, whose figure was an old man setting upon an high chair, having his hands lifted up above his head, and in them holding a fish or sickle, and under his feet a bunch of grapes,[2] his head covered with a black or dusky-coloured cloth, and all his garments black or dark coloured: they also make this same image against the stone[3] and diseases of the kidneys, viz. in the hour of Saturn, Saturn ascending with the third face of Aquarius.

They made also from the operations of Saturn, an image for the increasing in power, Saturn ascending in Capricorn; the form of which was an old man leaning on a staff, having in his hand a crooked sickle, and clothed in black.[4]

They also made an image of melted copper, Saturn ascending in his rising, viz. in the first degree of Aries, or which is more true in the first degree of Capricorn, which image they affirm to speak with a man's voice.[5]

They made also out of the operations of Saturn, and also Mercury, an image of cast metal, like a beautiful man, which they promised would foretell things to come, and made it on the day of Mercury, on the third hour of Saturn, the sign of Gemini ascending, being the house of Mercury, signifying prophets, Saturn and Mercury being in conjunction in Aquarius in the ninth place of heaven, which is also called God;[6] moreover let Saturn have a trine aspect on the ascendent, and the Moon in like manner, and the Sun have an aspect on the place of conjunction. Venus obtaining some angle may be powerful and occidental; let Mars be combust by the Sun, but let it not have an aspect on Saturn and Mercury; for they said, that the splendour of the powers of these stars was diffused upon this image, and it did speak with men, and declare those things which are profitable for them.

Notes—Chapter XXXVIII

1. *chair or dragon*—"'The form of Saturn, in the opinion of the learned Picatrix, is that of a man seated on a throne, having a crow's head and the feet of a camel.'" *(Picatrix,* quoted by Seznec [1940] 1972, 1:2:55).

2. *bunch of graces*—

The Latin manuscripts of Picatrix contain variants capable of producing wholly different images: thus the figure of Saturn "according to the learned Mercury," is that of a man having under his feet, as is said in some texts, "similem unius lagori id est racam"; in others, "aliquid simile racemo." In the first case, a lizard must be placed beneath Saturn's feet; in the second, a bunch of grapes. (Seznec [1940] 1972, 2:1:182)

3. *the stone*—Kidney stone, and perhaps gallstone as well. "Cutting for the stone" was one of the least pleasant aspects of medieval life, as there was no such thing as anesthetic. John Evelyn describes what must have been a typical operation:

The manner of its removal was thus: the sick creature was stripped to his shirt, and bound, arms and thighs, to a high chair. Two men held his shoulders down. Then the surgeon probed with a crooked instrument till he hit on the stone. Next, without stirring the probe—which had a small channel in it for the edge of the lancet to run in—and without wounding any other part, he made an incision of about an inch in length through the scrotum. Then he put his forefingers in to get the stone as near the orifice of the wound as he could and, with another instrument like a crane's neck, he pulled it out with incredible torture to the patient—especially at his raking so unmercifully up and down the bladder with a third instrument, in order to find any other stones that may possibly be left behind: the effusion of blood is great. *(John Evelyn's Diary,* May 3, 1650 [London: Folio Society, 1963], 77).

Needless to say, any magical way of avoiding the operation would be sought with great eagerness—Evelyn's own brother died rather than allowing himself to be cut.

4. *clothed in black*—See illustration 64 in Seznec ([1940] 1972), where this image is represented in a manuscript from the Vatican Library.

5. *man's voice*—This sounds very much like yet another oracular brazen head, which was usually associated with Saturn. See notes 22 and 23, ch. I, bk. II.

6. *called God*—The houses of the zodiac bore ancient names, which were:

I Horoscope	VII Occident
II Gate of Hades	VIII Beginning of Death
III Goddess (☽)	IX God (☉)
V Lower Midheaven	X Midheaven
V Good Fortune	XI Good Daemon
VI Bad Fortune	XII Bad Daemon

CHAPTER XXXIX

Of the images of Jupiter.

From the operations of Jupiter they made for prolongation of life, an image, in the hour of Jupiter, Jupiter being in his exaltation fortunately ascending, in a clear and white stone, whose figure was a man crowned, clothed with garments of a saffron colour, riding upon an eagle or dragon, having in his right hand a dart, about as it were to strike it into the head of the same eagle or dragon.[1]

They made also another image of Jupiter at the same convenient season, in a white and clear stone, especially in crystal, and it was a naked man crowned, having both his hands joined together and lifted up, as it were deprecating something, sitting in a four-footed chair, which is carried by four winged boys;[2] and they affirm that this image increaseth felicity, riches, honour, and confereth benevolence and prosperity, and freeth from enemies.

They made also another image of Jupiter for a religious and glorious life, and advancement of fortune; whose figure was a man having the head of a lion, or a ram,[3] and eagle's feet, clothed in saffron-coloured clothes, and he was called the son of Jupiter.

Notes—Chapter XXXIX

1. *eagle or dragon*—See Seznec 1972 [1940], illustration 71, which depicts this Jupiter.

2. *four winged*—see Seznec 1972 [1940], illustration 12. This image is from the *Picatrix*. Seznec points out that it originated from the figure of Zeus described by Pausanias *(Guide to Greece* 5.11.1–2).

3. *lion, or a ram*—Perhaps derived from Zeus Ammon, or even from Mithra.

Figures of the Planets

From *Secrets merveilleux de la magie naturelle et cabalistique de Petit Albert* (Cologne, 1722)

CHAPTER XL

Of the images of Mars.

From the operations of Mars they made an image in the hour of Mars, Mars ascending in the second face of Aries, in a martial stone, especially in a diamond;[1] the form of which was a man armed, riding upon a lion, having in his right hand a naked sword erected, carrying in his left hand the head of a man; they report, that an image of this kind rendereth a man powerful in good and evil, so that he shall be feared of all; and whosoever carryeth it they give him the power of enchantment, so that he shall terrify men by his looks when he is angry, and stupify them.

They made another image of Mars for the obtaining of boldness, courage, and good fortune in wars, and contentions, the form of which was a soldier armed and crowned, girt with a sword, carrying in his right hand a long lance; and they made this at the hour of Mars, the first face of Scorpio ascending with it.

Note—Chapter XL

1. *in a diamond*—Diamond was the stone of Mars because of its hardness. It is difficult to imagine how a diamond might be carved in ancient times. The gem makers used scribes tipped with diamond dust to carve and drill other stones, but using diamond to carve diamond, even with modern machines, is a laborious business.

CHAPTER XLI

Of the images of the Sun.

From the operations of the Sun, they made an image at the hour of the Sun, the first face of Leo ascending with the Sun, the form of which was a king crowned, sitting in a chair, having a raven in his bosom, and under his feet a globe; he is clothed in saffron-coloured clothes; they report that this image rendereth men invincible, and honorable, and helps to bring their businesses to a good end, and to drive away vain dreams; also to be prevalent against fevers, and the plague; and they made it in a balanite stone,[1] or a rubin,[2] at the hour of the Sun, when it in his exaltation fortunately ascendeth.

They made another image of the Sun in a diamond, at the hour of the Sun, it ascending in his exaltation; the figure of which was a women crowned with the gesture of one dancing and laughing, standing in a chariot drawn with four horses, having in her right hand a looking glass, or buckler, in the left a staff, leaning on her breast, carrying a flame of fire on her head; they report that this image rendereth a man fortunate and rich, and beloved of all; and they made this image on a corneol[3] stone at the hour of the Sun, ascending in the first face of Leo, against lunatic passions which proceed from the combustion[4] of the Moon.

Note—Chapter XLI

1. *balanite*—

Of balanites ["acorn stone"] there are two kinds, the one of a greenish hue, and the other like Corinthian bronze in appearance; the former comes from Coptos, and the latter from Troglodytica. They are both of them intersected by a flame-like vein, which runs through the middle. (Pliny 37.55 [Bostock and Riley, 6:443])

The *Chambers Cyclopædia Supplement* of 1753 offers the conjecture that this stone may be the same as *lapis judaicus*, or Jewstone, which in turn is of two kinds: the fossil spine of a large sea urchin found in Syria that was used medicinally, particularly against kidney stones, and marcasite, which is iron pyrites of a silver color.

2. *rubin*—Ruby.

3. *corneol*—Cornelian.

4. *combustion*—See note 6, ch. XXX, bk. II.

CHAPTER XLII

Of the images of Venus.

From the operations of Venus they made an image, which was available for favour and benevolence, at the very hour it ascended into Pisces, the form of which was the image of a woman having the head of a bird, and feet of an eagle, holding a dart in her hand.

They made another image of Venus for to get the love of women, in the lapis lazulus,[1] at the hour of Venus, Venus ascending in Taurus, the figure of which was a naked maid with her hair spread abroad, having a looking glass in her hand, and a chain tied about her neck, and nigh her a handsome young man, holding her with his left hand by the chain, but with his right hand making up her hair, and they both look lovingly on one another, and about them is a little winged boy[2] holding a sword or a dart.

They made another image of Venus, the first face of Taurus or Libra or Pisces ascending with Venus, the figure of which was a little maid with her hair spread abroad, clothed in long and white garments, holding a laurel,[3] apple,[4] or flowers in her right hand, in her left a comb. It's reported to make men pleasant, jocund, strong, cheerful, and to give beauty.

Notes—Chapter XLII

1. *lapis lazulus*—Lapis lazuli.

2. *winged boy*—Cupid, son of Venus.

3. *laurel*—A laurel wreath was given as a crown to the victor in the Pythian games in ancient Greece. It is a symbol of victory, and by extension peace.

4. *apple*—Symbol of erotic love, the apple, along with other red fruits, was once thought to be an aphrodisiac.

CHAPTER XLIII

Of the images of Mercury.

From the operations of Mercury, they made an image at the hour of Mercury, Mercury ascending in Gemini, the form of which was an handsome young man, bearded, having in his left hand a rod in which a serpent is tied about,[1] in his right carrying a dart,[2] having his feet winged; they report that this image conferreth knowledge, eloquence, diligence in merchandising and gain; moreover to beget peace and concord, and to cure fevers.

They made another image of Mercury, Mercury ascending in Virgo, for good will, wit and memory; the form of which was a man sitting upon a chair, or riding on a peacock, having eagle's feet, and on his head a crest, and in his left hand holding a cock or fire.

Notes—Chapter XLIII

1. *serpent is tied about*—The caduceus, which has become the modern symbol of medicine.

2. *a dart*—Perhaps this should be a flute. See Seznec [1940] 1972, illustrations 82 and 83.

CHAPTER XLIV

Of the images of the Moon.

From the operations of the Moon, they made an image for travelers against weariness, at the hour of the Moon, the Moon ascending in its exaltation; the figure of which was a man leaning on a staff, having a bird on his head, and a flourishing tree before him.

They made another image of the Moon for the increase of the fruits of the Earth, and against poisons, and infirmities of children, at the hour of the Moon, it ascending in the first face of Cancer, the figure of which was a woman cornuted,[1] riding on a bull, or a dragon with seven heads,[2] or a crab;[3] and she hath in her right hand a dart, in her left a looking glass, clothed in white or green, and having on her head two serpents with horns twined together, and to each arm a serpent twined about,[4] and to each foot one in like manner.

And thus much spoken concerning the figures of the planets, may suffice.

Notes—Chapter XLIV

1. *cornuted*—Horned.

2. *dragon with seven heads*—See Revelation 12:3 and 17:3.

3. *a crab*—The moon rules Cancer, the Crab.

4. *serpent twined about*—A familiar symbol of the goddess Ishtar, who is closely connected with the Moon.

CHAPTER XLV

Of the images of
the Head and Tail of the Dragon of the Moon.

They made also the image of the Head and Tail of the Dragon of the Moon,[1] namely betwixt an arial and fiery circle, the likeness of a serpent, with the head of an hawk tied about them, after the manner of the great letter Theta,[2] and they made it when Jupiter with the Head obtained the midst[3] of heaven, which image they affirm to avail much for the success of petitions, and would signify by this image 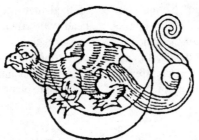 a good and fortunate genius, which they would represent by this image of the serpent.

For the Egyptians and Phenitians[4] do extol this creature above all others, and say it is a divine creature and hath a divine nature; for in this is a more acute spirit, and a greater fire than in any other, which thing is manifested both by his swift motion without feet, hands or any other instruments, and also that it often reneweth his age with his skin, and becometh young again.[5]

But they made the image of the Tail like as when the Moon was eclipsed, in the Tail, or ill affected by Saturn or Mars, and they made it to introduce anguish, infirmity and misfortune; and they called it the evil genius. Such an image a certain Hebrew had included in a golden belt full of jewels, which *Blanche* the daughter of the Duke of *Bourbon* (either willingly or ignorantly) bestowed on her husband *Peter* King of Spain, the first of that name, with which when he was girt, he seemed to himself to be compassed about with a serpent; and afterwards finding the magical virtue in the girdle, for this cause he forsook his wife.[6]

Notes—Chapter XLV

1. *dragon of the Moon*—The Moon's nodes are the points in space where the paths of the Moon and Sun intersect—not the Moon or Sun at these points, but the places where their circles cross. When the Moon is rising from below to above the ecliptic, or plane of the Sun, the point of intersection is called the ascending node, or Caput Draconis (Head of the Dragon); when the Moon is passing from above to below the ecliptic, the point is called the descending node, or Cauda Draconis (Tail of the Dragon). These points are not fixed, but move in a circle about the zodiac, forming different aspects with the planets and other significant astrological points. They are always located 180 degrees apart from each other.

2. *Theta*—The Greek print letter: Θ, as opposed to the script letter: θ.

3. *the midst*—Midheaven.

4. *Phenitians*—Phoenicians.

5. *becometh young again—*

> I am the serpent Sata whose years are infinite. I lie down dead. I am born daily. I am the serpent Sa-en-ta, the dweller in the uttermost parts of the earth. I lie down in death. I am born, I become new, I renew my youth every day" *(The Book of the Dead* 87, "Of Changing into the Serpent Sata," trans. E. A. Wallis Budge [New York: University Books, 1970 {1913}] 544–5).

Horapollo says of the Egyptians:

> When they would represent the universe, they delineate a serpent bespeckled with variegated scales, devouring its own tail; by the scales intimating the stars in the universe. The animal is also extremely heavy, as is the earth, and extremely slippery, like the water: moreover, it every year puts off its old age with its skin, as in the universe the annual period effects a corresponding change, and becomes renovated. And the making use of its own body for food implies, that all things whatsoever, that are generated by divine providence in the world, undergo a corruption into it again. (Horapollo *Hieroglyphics* 1.2 [Cory, 7–8])

6. *forsook his wife*—See biographical note for Peter the Cruel.

CHAPTER XLVI

Of the images of the mansions of the Moon.

They made also images for every mansion of the Moon.

In the first for the destruction of someone, they made in an iron ring the image of a black man in a garment made of hair, and girdled round, casting a small lance with his right hand; they sealed this in black wax, and perfumed it with liquid storax,[1] and wished some evil to come.

In the second, against the wrath of the prince, and for reconciliation with him, they sealed in white wax and mastic, the image of a king crowned, and perfumed it with lignum aloes.

In the third, they made an image in a silver ring, whose table[2] was square, the figure of which was a woman well clothed, sitting in a chair, her right hand being lifted up on her head; they sealed it and perfumed it with musk, camphire and calamus aromaticus.[3] They affirmed that this giveth happy fortune and every good thing.

In the fourth, for revenge, separation, enmity and ill will, they sealed in red wax the image of a soldier sitting on an horse, holding a serpent in his right hand; they perfumed it with red myrrh, and storax.

In the fifth, for the favour of kings and officers, and good entertainment, they sealed in silver the head of a man, and perfumed it with sanders.

In the sixth, for to procure love betwixt two, they sealed in white wax two images embracing one another, and perfumed them with lignum aloes and amber.

In the seventh, for to obtain every good thing, they sealed in silver the image of a man well clothed, holding up his hands to heaven as it were praying and supplicating, and perfumed it with good odours.

In the eighth, for victory in war, they made a seal of tin, being an image of an eagle having the face of a man, and perfumed it with brimstone.[4]

In the ninth, to cause infirmities, they made a seal of lead, being the image of a man wanting his privy parts, shutting his eyes with his hands; and they perfumed it with rosin of the pine.

In the tenth, to facilitate child-bearing, and to cure the sick, they made a seal of gold, being the head of a lion, and perfumed it with amber.

In the eleventh, for fear, reverence and worship, they made a seal of a plate of gold, being the image of a man riding on a lion, holding the ear thereof in his left hand, and in his right, holding forth a bracelet of gold, and they perfumed it with good odours and saffron.

In the twelfth, for the separation of lovers, they made a seal of black lead, being the image of a dragon fighting with a man, and they perfumed it with the hairs of a lion, and assafetida.[5]

In the thirteenth, for the agreement of married couples, and for the dissolving of the charms against copulation, they made a seal of the images of both, of the man in red wax, of the woman in white, and caused them to embrace one another, perfuming it with lignum aloes and amber.

In the fourteenth, for divorce and separation of the man from the woman, they made a seal of red copper, being the image of a dog biting his tail, and they perfumed it with the hair of a black dog, and black cat.

In the fifteenth, for to obtain friendship and good will, they made the image of a man sitting, and inditing of letters, and perfumed it with frankincense and nutmegs.

In the sixteenth, for to gain much merchandising, they made a seal of silver, being the image of a man sitting upon a chair, holding a balance in his hand, and they perfumed it with well smelling spices.

In the seventeenth, against thieves and robbers, they sealed with an iron seal the image of an ape, and perfumed it with the hair of an ape.

In the eighteenth, against fevers and pains of the belly, they made a seal of copper, being the image of a snake holding his tail above his head, and they perfumed it with hartshorn,[6] and reported the same seal to put to flight serpents,[7] and all venomous creatures from the place where it is buried.

In the nineteenth for facilitating birth and provoking the menstrues, they made a seal of copper, being the image of a woman holding her hands upon her face; and they perfumed it with liquid storax.

In the twentieth, for hunting, they made a seal of tin, being the image of Sagittary, half a man and half an horse, and they perfumed it with the head of a wolf.[8]

In the twenty-one for the destruction of somebody, they made the image of a man with a double countenance,[9] before and behind, and they perfumed it with brimstone and jet, and did put it in a box of brass, and with it brimstone and jet, and the hair of him whom they would hurt.

In the two and twentieth, for the security of runaways,[10] they made a seal of iron, being the image of a man with wings on his feet, bearing an helmet on his head,[11] and they perfumed it with argent vive.[12]

In the three and twentieth, for destruction and wasting, they made a seal of iron, being the image of a cat, having a dog's head, and they perfumed it with the hairs of a dog's head, and buried it in the place where they did pretend to hurt.

In the four and twentieth, for the multiplying of herds of cattle, they took the horn of a ram, bull, or goat, or of that sort of cattle which they would increase, and sealed in it burning with an iron seal,[13] the image of a woman giving suck to her son, and they hanged it on the neck of that cattle who was the leader of the flock, or they sealed it in[14] his horn.

In the five and twentieth, for the preservation of trees and harvests, they sealed in the wood of a figure, the image of a man planting, and they perfumed it with the flowers of the fig tree, and did hang it on the tree.

In the six and twentieth, for love and favour, they sealed in white wax and mastic the image of a woman washing and combing her hairs,[15] and they perfumed it with things smelling very well.

In the seven and twentieth, for to destroy fountains, pits,[16] medicinal waters and baths, they made of red earth the image of a man winged, holding in his hand an empty vessel, and perforated, and the image being burnt, they did put in the vessel assafetida and liquid storax, and they did overwhelm and bury it in the pond or fountain which they would destroy.

In the eight and twentieth, for to gather fishes together, they made a seal of copper, being the image of a fish, and they perfumed it with the skin of a sea fish, and did cast it into the water, wheresoever they would have the fish to gather together.

Moreover together with the foresaid images, they did write down also the names of the spirits and their characters, and did invoke and pray for those things which they pretended to obtain.

Notes—Chapter XLVI

1. *liquid storax*—There are two kinds of storax, a gum that was stored and sold in hollow reeds, called storax-calamite, and a liquid resin, of which Gerard says: "... there floweth from some of these trees a certain gummie liquor, which never groweth naturally hard, but remaineth alwaies thinne, which is

called liquid Styrax, or Storax" (Gerard [1633] 1975, 3:143:1526. See also note 17, ch. XXVI, bk. I.

2. *table*—The wider flat part of a ring, called the bezel.

3. *calamus aromaticus*—Sweet calamus *(Calamus aromaticus)*, also called sweet rush, conjectured to be the sweet-scented lemon grass *(Andropogon schaenanthus)* of Malabar.

4. *brimstone*—Sulphur.

5. *assafetida*—Asafoetida.

6. *hartshorn*—The antlers of the *Cervus elaphus* were much used in medicinal and other ways, being a prime source of ammonia. It was the custom to rasp them to powder and treat the powder either by burning or boiling in water to produce artist's sable black pigment, hartshorn jelly, salt of hartshorn (smelling salts), hartshorn tea and hartshorn drops.

7. *put to flight serpents*—Deer were the proverbial enemies of serpents, and the fume of burning hartshorn was for this reason thought to drive snakes away.

8. *head of a wolf*—The wolf had power over the horse. Pliny says: "Indeed, so powerful is the influence of this animal, in addition to what we have already stated [8.34], that if a horse only treads in its track, it will be struck with torpor in consequence" (Pliny 28.44 [Bostock and Riley, 5:331–2]).

9. *double countenance*—Janus, the Roman god who presided over comings and goings.

10. *security of runaways*—To secure (catch, or keep) runaway slaves.

11. *helmet on his head*—This is a description of Mercury.

12. *argent vive*—Quicksilver, or mercury.

13. *burning with an iron seal*—That is, they heated the iron seal and branded its image into the horn.

14. *sealed it in*—Burned it into.

15. *combing her hairs*—Venus.

16. *pits*—Wells.

CHAPTER XLVII

Of the images of the fixed Behenian[1] stars.

But now for the operations of the fixed stars, according to *Hermes'* opinion.

Under the Head of Algol, they made an image whose figure was the head of a man with a bloody neck; they report that it bestoweth good success to petitions, and maketh him who carrieth it bold and magnanimous, and preserveth the members of the body sound: also it helpeth against witchcraft, and reflecteth evil endeavours and wicked incantations upon our adversaries.

Under the constellation of Pleiades, they made the image of a little virgin, or the figure of a lamp; it's reported to increase the light of the eyes, to assemble spirits, to raise winds, to reveal secret and hidden things.

Under Aldebora,[2] they made an image after the likeness of God, or of a flying man; it giveth riches and honour.

Under the Goat[3] they made an image, the figure of which was, as it were, a man willing to make himself merry with musical instruments; it maketh him who carrieth it acceptable, honoured and exalted before kings and princes; and helpeth the pain of the teeth.

Under the Greater Dog Star,[4] they made the image of an hound and a little virgin; it bestoweth honour and good will, and the favour of men, and aerial spirits, and giveth power to pacify and reconcile kings, princes, and other men.

Under the Lesser Dog Star[5] they made the image of a cock, or of three little maids; it conferreth the favour of the gods, of spirits, and men; it giveth power against witchcrafts, and preserveth health.

Under the Heart of Leo,[6] they made the image of a lion or cat, or the figure of an honourable person sitting in a chair; it rendereth a man temperate, appeaseth wrath, and giveth favour.

Under the Tail of Ursa Major[7] they made the image of a pensive man, or of a bull, or the figure of a calf; it availeth against incantations, and maketh him who carrieth it secure in his travels.

Under the Wing of Corvus,[8] they made the image of a raven, or snake, or of a black man clothed in black;[9] this maketh a man choleric, bold, courageous, full of thoughts, a backbiter, and causeth naughty dreams; also it giveth the power of driving away evil spirits, and of gathering them together; it is profitable against the malice of men, devils and winds.

Under the Spike[10] they made the image of a bird, or of a man laden with merchandise; it conferreth riches, and maketh one overcome contentions, it taketh away scarcity and mischief.

Under Alchameth[11] they made the image of an horse or wolf, or the figure of a man dancing; it is good against fevers, it astringeth and retaineth the blood.

Under Elphrya,[12] they made the image of an hen, or of a man crowned and advanced; it bestoweth the good will and love of men, and giveth chastity.

Under the Heart of Scorpio[13] they made the image of a man armed, and with a coat of mail, or the figure of a scorpion; it giveth understanding and memory, it maketh a good colour, and aideth against evil spirits, and driveth them away, and bindeth them.

Under the Vulture,[14] they made the image of a vulture or hen, or of a traveler; it maketh a man magnanimous and proud, it giveth power over devils and beasts.

Under the Tail of Capricorn[15] they made the image of an hart, or goat, or of an angry man; it bestoweth prosperity, and increaseth wrath.

These are the images of some of the fixed stars which they command to be engraven on their stones under them.[16]

Notes—Chapter XLVII

1. *Behenian*—"Behen" is from the Arabic: *bahman*—a kind of root. The old herbalists adopted it without knowing its attribution (see Gerard [1633] 1975, 679), so its meaning was never clearly fixed. Agrippa uses the term as a synonym for Arabian.

2. *Aldebora*—Aldebaran.

3. *the Goat*—Capella.

4. *Greater Dog Star*—Sirius.

5. *Lesser Dog Star*—Procyon.

6. *Heart of Leo*—Regulus.

7. *Tail of Ursa Major*—Alkaid.

8. *Wing of Corvus*—Gienah.

9. *black man clothed in black*—It should not always be assumed that when reference is made to a black man, a Negro is intended. For medieval Europeans, oftentimes a black man is a Caucasian with swarthy skin, or with black hair and dark eyes, dressed in black clothing. This is clear from the excerpts of witch trials quoted by Margaret Murray (1921, 2:2), which describe the Lord of the Witches. Black signified evil and hidden works.

10. *the Spike*—Spica.

11. *Alchameth*—Arcturus.

12. *Elphrya*—Alphecca.

13. *Heart of Scorpio*—Antares.

14. *the Vulture*—Vega.

15. *Tail of Capricorn*—Deneb Algedi.

16. *under them*—See ch. XXXII, bk. I, and ch. XXXI, bk. II, for references to the fixed stars.

CHAPTER XLVIII

Of geomantical figures, which are the middle betwixt images and characters.

There are moreover certain other figures, framed by the number and situation of the stars, and ascribed both to the elements, and also to the planets and signs, which are called geomantical,[1] because that geomantical diviners do reduce the points of their lots projected, by the excess of parity or imparity,[2] into those figures; and they also being engraven or imprinted under the dominion of their planets and signs, do conceive the virtue and power of images; and these figures are as a middle betwixt images and characters.[3]

But whosoever desireth exactly to know the natures, qualities, proprieties, conditions, significations, and nativities of these figures, let him read the volumes of geomancy;[4] but they are in number sixteen, whose names and figures are these [see next page]:

Notes—Chapter XLVIII

1. *geomantical*—On geomantic divination, see Appendix VIII.

2. *parity or imparity*—By whether there is an even or odd number of dots.

3. *images and characters*—Between pictures and letters.

4. *volumes of geomancy*—In Robert Turner's 1655 English translation of Agrippa's *Of Geomancy* there is bound up a work called *Astronomical Geomancy* by Gerard Cremonensis, which is one of the magical works appended to the Latin *Opera*.

Geomantic Figures

Figure	Name	Element	Planet	Sign
• • • •	Way Journey	Water	☽	♌
• • • • • • • •	People Congregation	Water	☽	♑
• • • • • • •	Conjunction An Assembling	Air	☿	♍
• • • • • • •	A Prison Bound	Earth	♄	♓
• • • • • •	Great Fortune Greater Aid Safeguard Entering	Earth	☉	♒
• • • • • •	Lesser Fortune Lesser Aid Safeguard Going Out	Fire	☉	♉
• • • • • •	Obtaining Comprehending Within	Air	♃	♈
• • • • • •	Loss Comprehending Without	Fire	♀	♎
• • • • • •	Joy; Laughing; Healthy; Bearded	Air	♃	♉
• • • • • •	Sadness Damned Cross	Earth	♄	♏
• • • • •	A Girl Beautiful	Water	♀	♎
• • • • •	A Boy Yellow Beardless	Fire	♂	♈

Geomantic Figures (cont'd.)

Figure	Name	Element	Planet	Sign
∴∴ (White/Fair)	White Fair	Water	☿	♋
∴∴ (Reddish/Red)	Reddish Red	Fire	♂	♊
∴ (The Head)	The Head The Threshold Entering The Upper Threshold	Earth	☊	♍
∴ (The Tail)	The Tail The Threshold Going Out The Lower Threshold	Fire	☋	♐

Of images, the figure whereof is not after the likeness of any celestial figure, but after the likeness of that which the mind of the worker desires.

There remains as yet another manner of images not according to the similitude of celestial figures, but according to the similitude of that which the mind of the worker desires, of whose they are the effigies, and representation: so to procure love we make images embracing one the other; to discord, striking one the other; to bring misery, or destruction, as damage to a man, or house, or city, or anything else, we make images distorted, broken in members and parts, after the likeness and figure of that thing which we would destroy or damnify.

And magicians advise us that in casting or engraving images we would write upon it the name of the effect; and this on the back when evil, as destruction; on the belly when good, as love. Moreover in the forehead of the image[1] let be written the name of the species or individuum which the image represents, or for whom or against whom it is made. Also on the breast let the name of the sign or face ascending, and lord thereof be written; also the names and characters of its angels. Moreover in making the image they advise that prayer for the effect for which it is made, be used. All of which *Albertus Magnus* in his Speculo[2] affirms.

Now they use the images being made diversely according to the virtues thereof: sometimes they hang them or bind them to the body; sometimes they bury them under the earth, or a river; sometimes they hang them in a chimney over the smoke,[3] or upon a tree that they be moved by the wind; sometimes with the head upward and sometimes downward; sometimes they put them into hot water, or into the fire. For they say as the workers of the images do affect the image itself, so doth it bring the like passions upon those to whom it was ascribed, as the mind of the operator hath dictated it. As we read that *Nectanabus* the magician made images of ships with wax after that manner and art, that when he drowned those images in water, that the ships of his enemies were in like manner drowned in the sea, and hazarded.[4]

Now that part of astrology which is writ concerning elections[5] teacheth us that the constellations also are to be observed for the making of images, and such like.

Notes—Chapter XLIX

1. *forehead of the image*—See Revelation 7:3 and 13:16.

2. *Speculo*—*Speculum astronomiae*, a work attributed to Albertus Magnus.

3. *over the smoke*—The practice of sticking magical charms up the chimney seems to have been common, although there was no clear consensus as to why this was done. Elworthy discusses several instances where animal hearts and other objects were discov-

ered inside chimneys in the south of England:

> Some of the old people declared it to have been a custom when a pig died from the "overlooking" of a witch to have its heart stuck full of pins and white thorns, and to put it up the chimney, in the belief that as the heart dried and withered so would that of the malignant person who had "ill wisht" the pig. As long as that lasted no witch could have power over the pigs belonging to that house. (Elworthy [1895] 1971, ch. 2, n. 79, p. 53)

The above gives two reasons, not one, as to why the charm was put in the chimney, and a third is later suggested: "… to prevent the descent of witches down the chimney" (ibid., 55). However, charms were also put up the chimney by witches to work evil. Elworthy recounts the case of a farm boy with a pain in his foot, who discovered that his employers had concealed a poppet in this place to work against him. "''Twas a mommet thing, and he knowd 'twas a-made vor he.' He saw that the feet of the little figure were stuck full of pins and thorns!" (ibid., n. 80, p. 55). Onions found in chimneys are wrapped with paper upon which is written the name of the victim, the paper being held in place by the pins, and in the chimney of a woman who had borne children to a lover who later cast her over was discovered a model of a man's erect penis stuck full of pins (ibid.).

4. *hazarded*—

> If the enemy came against him by sea, instead of sending out his sailors to fight them, he retired into a certain chamber, and having brought forth a bowl which he kept for the purpose, he filled it with water, and then, having made wax figures of the ships and men of the enemy, and also of his own men and ships, he set them upon the water in the bowl, his men on one side, and those of the enemy on the other. He then came out, and having put on the cloak of an Egyptian prophet and taken an ebony rod in his hand, he returned into the chamber, and uttering words of power he invoked the gods who help men to work magic, and the winds, and the subterranean demons,

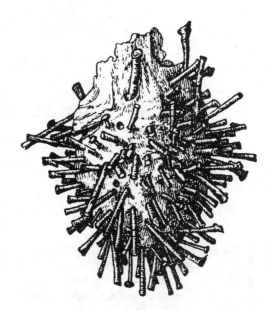

Heart of a Pig Stuck
with Pins and White Thorns

From *The Evil Eye* by Frederick Elworthy
(London, 1895)

which straightaway came to his aid. By their means the figures of the men in wax sprang into life and began to fight, and the ships of wax began to move about likewise; but the figures which represented his own men vanquished those which represented the enemy, and as the figures of the ships and men of the hostile fleet sank through the water to the bottom of the bowl, even so did the real ships and men sink through the waves to the bottom of the sea. (Budge [1901] 1971, ch. 3, 92)

See also the biographical note on Nectanebus.

5. *elections*—The choosing of an astrologically suitable time for any action, such as Christening a child, launching a ship, or opening a public building. Elections are adhered to even today with fanatical zeal in the East.

CHAPTER L

Of certain celestial observations and the practice of some images.

I will now show thee the observation of celestial bodies which are required for the practice of some of these kind of images.

So to make anyone fortunate, we make an image in which these are fortunate, viz. the significator of the life[1] thereof, the givers of life,[2] the signs, and planets. Moreover let the ascendent, the middle of the heaven, and the lords thereof be fortunate: also the place of the Sun, and place of the Moon; Part of Fortune, and lord of conjunction or prevention[3] made before their nativity, by depressing the malignant planets. But if we will make an image to procure misery, we must do contrariwise, and those which we place here fortunate, must there be unfortunate, by raising malignant stars.

In like manner must we do to make any place, region, city, or house fortunate. Also for destroying or prejudicing any of the foresaid, let there be made an image under the ascension of that man whom thou wouldst destroy, and prejudice, and thou shall make unfortunate,[4] the lord of the house of his life, the lord of the ascending, and the Moon, the lord of the house of the Moon, and the lord of the house of the lord ascending, and the tenth house, and the lord thereof. Now for the fitting of any place, place Fortunes[5] in the ascendent thereof; and in the first, and tenth, and second, and eighth house, thou shall make the lord of the ascendent, and the lord of the house of the Moon fortunate.

But to chase away certain animals from certain places, that they may not be generated, or abide there, let there be an image made under the ascension of that animal, which thou wouldst chase away, and after the likeness thereof; as if thou wouldst chase away scorpions from any place, let an image of the scorpion be made, the sign of Scorpio ascending with the Moon, and thou shalt make unfortunate the ascendent, and lord thereof, and the lord of the house of Mars; and thou shall make unfortunate the lord of the ascendent in the eighth house, and let them be joined with an aspect malignant, opposite, or quadrant: and let there be writ upon the image the name of the ascendent, of the lord thereof, and of the Moon, and of the lord of the day, and of the lord of the hour. And let there be a pit made in the middle of the place, from which thou wouldst drive them; and let there be carried into it, some of the earth taken out of the four corners of the same place, and let the image be buried there with the head downward, with saying, this is the burying of the scorpions, that they may not come into this place, and so of the rest.

So for gain let there be made an image under the ascendent of the nativity[6] of the man, or under the ascension of that place to which thou wouldst appoint the gain; and thou shalt make the lord of the second house, which is in the house of substance to be joined with the lord of the ascendent in the trine or sextile, and let there be a reception amongst them; thou shall make fortunate the eleventh and the lord thereof, and the eighth; and if thou canst, put part of the Fortune in the ascendent, or second; and let the image be buried in that place, or carried from that place, to which thou wouldst appoint the gain.

Also for concord, and love, let there be an image made in the day of Jupiter under the ascendent of the nativity of him whom thou wouldst have be beloved, make fortunate the ascendent, and the tenth, and hide the evil from the ascendent; and thou must have the lord of the tenth, and the planets of the eleventh fortune, joined to the lord of the ascendent, from the trine or sextile with reception;[7] then make another image for him whom thou wouldst stir up to love; consider if he be a friend, or companion of him whom thou wouldst have be beloved; and if so, let there be an image made under the ascension of the eleventh house from the ascendent of the first image; but if the party be a wife, or a husband, let it be made under the ascension of the seventh; if a brother, or a sister, or a cousin, let it be made under the ascension of the third, and so of the like; and put the significator of the ascendent of the second image, joined to the significator of the ascendent of the first image; and let there be betwixt them a reception, and let the rest be fortunate, as in the first image; afterwards join both images together into a mutual embracing, or put the face of the second image to the back of the first image, and let them be wrapped up in silk, and cast away or spoiled.

Also for success of petitions, and for the obtaining of a thing denied, or taken, or possessed by another, let there be an image made under the ascendent of him who petitions for the thing; and cause that the lord of the second be joined with the lord of the ascendent from a trine, or sextile, and let there be a reception betwixt them, and if it can be, let the lord of the second be in the obeying signs, and the lord of the ascendent in the ruling,[8] make fortunate the ascendent, and the lord thereof, and take heed that the lord of the ascendent be not retrograde or combust, or falling, or in the house of opposition, i.e. in the seventh from his own house; let him not be hindered by the malignant, let him be strong, and in an angle; thou shalt make fortunate the ascendent, and the lord of the second, and the Moon; and make another image for him

that is petitioned to, and begin it under the ascendent belonging to him, as if he be a king or a prince, begin it under the ascendent of the tenth house from the ascendent of the first image; if he be a father under the fourth; if a son under fifth; and so of the like; and put the significator of the second image, joined with the lord of the ascendent of the first image, from a trine or sextile, and let him receive it, and put them both strong, and fortunate without any let; make all evil fall from them. Thou shall make fortunate the tenth, and the fourth if thou canst, or any of them; and when the second image shall be perfected, join it with the first, face to face, and wrap them in clean linen, and bury them in the middle of his house who is the petitioner under a fortunate significator, the Fortune being strong, and let the face of the first image be toward the north, or rather toward that place where the thing petitioned for doth abide; or if it happen that the petitioner goeth forward towards him with whom the thing petitioned for is, let him bring the images with him as far as he goes.

And let there be made an image of dreams, which being put under the head of him that sleeps, makes him dream true dreams concerning anything that he hath formerly deliberated of: and let the figure of that be the figure of a man sleeping in the bosom of an angel, which thou shall make in the Lion[9] ascending, the Sun keeping the ninth house in Aries; thou shalt write upon the breast of the man the name of the effect desired, and in the hand of the angel the name of the intelligence of the Sun. Let the same image be made in Virgo ascending, Mercury being fortunate in Aries in the ninth house,[10] or Gemini ascending in Mercury being fortunate, and keeping the ninth house in Aquarius; and let it be received from Saturn with a fortunate aspect, and let the name of the Spirit of Mercury be writ upon it. Let also the same be made in Libra ascending, Venus being received from Mercury in Gemini in the ninth house, by writing upon it the angel of Venus. Besides also let the same image be made in Aquarius ascending, Saturn fortunately possessing the ninth house in his exaltation, which is in Libra, and let there be writ upon it the angel of

Saturn; moreover let it be made in Cancer ascending, the Moon being received by Jupiter and Venus in Pisces,[11] and being fortunately placed in the ninth house, and let there be writ upon it the spirit of the Moon.

There are also made rings of dreams of wonderful efficacy; and there are rings of the Sun, and Saturn, and the constellation of them is when the Sun or Saturn ascend in their exaltations[12] in the ninth house, and in that sign, which was the ninth house of nativity; and let there be writ upon the rings the name of the spirit of the Sun, or Saturn.

Let this which hath been spoken suffice concerning images, for now thou mayst find out more of this nature of thyself. But know this,

that such images work nothing, unless they be so vivified that either a natural, or celestial, or heroical,[13] or animastical,[14] or demoniacal, or angelical virtue be in them, or assistant to them.

But who can give a soul to an image, or make a stone to live, or metal, or wood, or wax? And who can raise out of stones children unto *Abraham?*[15] Certainly this arcanum doth not enter into an artist of a stiff neck: neither can he give those things which hath them not. Nobody hath them but he who doth (the elements being restrained, nature being overcome, the heavens being overpowered) transcend the progress of angels, and comes to the very Archetype itself, of which being then made a cooperator may do all things, as we shall speak afterwards.

Notes—Chapter L

1. *significator of the life*—The significator is what Ptolemy calls the prorogator, which the Greeks also called the *apheta,* and which the Persians knew as the *hyleg.* It is a planet or part of the heavens which in a nativity becomes the moderator and significator of life. According to Ptolemy a life may be likened to an arc on the wheel of the zodiac which begins from its particular place of departure with more or less momentum, depending on its prorogative place and the stars that rule the prorogation, travels around the zodiac never more than one quarter of the way, and is stopped by various destructive placements of the planets. The number of degrees traversed by this arc, converted into degrees of right ascension, gives the number of years of life. See the *Tetrabiblos* 3.10 (Robbins, 271–307).

2. *givers of life*—Of the planets ruling the length of life in relation to the prorogator, Ptolemy says: "The beneficent stars add and the maleficent subtract. Mercury, again, is reckoned with the group to which he bears an aspect. The number of the addition or subtraction is calculated by means of the location in degrees in each case" (ibid., 281). The beneficent planets are the Moon, Jupiter and Venus. Saturn and Mars are maleficent. The Sun and Mercury have a common nature, and join their influence to the planets with which they are associated.

3. *prevention*—

However, it must not be thought that these places always inevitably destroy, but only when they are afflicted. For they are pre-

vented both if they fall within the term of a beneficent planet and if one of the beneficent planets projects its ray from quartile, trine, or opposition either upon the destructive degree itself or upon the parts that follow it, in the case of Jupiter not more than 12°, and in the case of Venus not over 8° ... (ibid., 285)

4. *make unfortunate*—When Agrippa speaks of "making fortunate" and "making unfortunate," he means the choice of a time to manufacture the image when either a fortunate or unfortunate astrological arrangement exists with reference to the work at hand and the place it is accomplished. No one can "make" the planets unfortunate but must wait for them to become so.

5. *Fortunes*—Jupiter is the Greater Fortune; Venus is the Lesser Fortune. Together they are referred to as the Fortunes.

6. *nativity*—When the nativity, or moment and place of birth, is not known, the ascendent must be established by natural correspondence.

7. *reception*—When two planets are each in the sign that the other rules, they are said to be in mutual reception: for example, Venus in Aries and Mars in Libra.

8. *in the ruling*—

Similarly the names "commanding" and "obeying" are applied to the divisions of the zodiac which are disposed at an equal distance from the same equinoctial sign, whichever it may be, because they ascend in equal periods of time and are on equal parallels. Of these the ones in the summer hemisphere are called "commanding" and those in the winter hemisphere are called "obedient" because the sun makes the day longer than the night when he is in the summer hemisphere, and shorter in the winter. (Ptolemy *Tetrabiblos* 1.14 (Robbins, 75, 77).

Thus the pairs of commanding and obeying signs are, excluding the equinoctials Aries-Libra:

Commanding	Obeying
Taurus	Pisces
Gemini	Aquarius
Cancer	Capricorn
Leo	Sagittarius
Virgo	Scorpio

9. *the Lion*—Leo, ascending in the first house with the Sun in Aries in the ninth house.

10. *Ninth house*—If Virgo were ascending, Taurus would be in the ninth house.

11. *Venus in Pisces*—That is, Jupiter in Cancer and the moon in Pisces, with Venus also in Pisces.

12. *in their exaltations*—Perhaps when the sign of exaltation of either the Sun (Aries) or Saturn (Cancer) is in the ascendent with the corresponding planet in the ninth house.

13. *heroical*—Exalted above the ordinary human level, especially applied to men who have achieved a semi-godlike status, such as Perseus.

14. *animastical*—Having to do with the soul; spiritual. Agrippa (ch. 34, bk. III) equates the anamastic-heroic order with the Ashim (or Ishim) of the Kabbalah, the "Flaming Ones" (see Psalms 104:4).

15. *children unto Abraham*—Genesis 28:11-8. Perhaps this is a veiled reference to the golem legend. The golem was a slave formed out of clay and infused with spirit by magic to protect the Jews from their Christian persecutors. Although the golem of Rabbi Loew was created too late (1580) to be known to Agrippa, it had its origin in the Talmud: "Rava created a man; he sent him to Rabbi Zera, who spoke to him; when he did not reply, Rabbi Zera told him: 'You are a creation of magic; return to your dust'"(Patai 1980, 239).

CHAPTER LI

Of characters which are made after the rule and imitation of celestials, and how with the table thereof they are deduced out of geomantical figures.

haracters also have their community from the rays of the celestials cast together according to a certain number by a certain peculiar property, which celestials as in divers strokes of their rays falling several ways amongst themselves produced divers virtues: so also characters being variously protracted, according to the various concourse of those rays quickly obtain divers operations, and also more efficacious many times than the properties of natural commixtions.

Now the true characters of the heavens is the writing of angels, which amongst the Hebrews is called the writing Malachim,[1] by which all things are described and signified in the heaven[2] for every knowing man to read. But of these hereafter.

But now they make characters of geomantical figures, binding together the points of each variously, and attributing them according to the manner of their figurings, to those planets and signs of which they were made, the making of which the following table will show:[3]

Geomantic Characters

The Characters of the Moon

From the Way:

From the People:

The Characters of Mercury

From Conjunction:

From White:

The Characters of Venus

From Loosing:

Geomantic Characters (cont'd.)

The Characters of Venus (cont'd.)

From Girl:

The Characters of the Sun

From a Greater Fortune:

From a Lesser Fortune:

The Characters of Mars

From Red:

From a Boy:

The Characters of Jupiter

From Obtaining:

From Joyfulness:

The Characters of Saturn

From a Prison:

From Sadness:

The Characters of the Dragon

From the Head:

From the Tail:

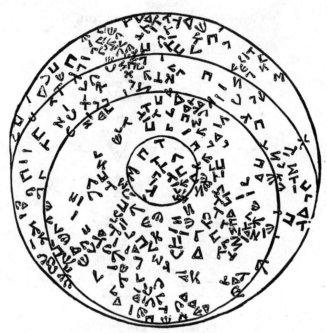

Writing in the Stars

from *Curiosites innouies* by Jacques Gaffarel (1637)

Notes—Chapter LI

1. *Malachim*—The Malachim are the angelic order of the sixth Sephirah, Tiphareth. The book of Malachi was an anonymous work, the title for which was derived from verse 3:1, where the Hebrew for "my messenger" was converted into a proper name. In verse 3:16 it is written: "Then they that feared the Lord spake often one to another: and the Lord harkened, and heard it, and a book of remembrance was written before him for them that feared the Lord, and that thought upon his name." The Hebrew for *maliku* signifies "king"—i. e. god. There is reference made to this celestial alphabet in the *Greater Key of Solomon:* "Come ye, then, by the virtue of these Names by the which we exorcise ye; ANAI, ÆCHHAD, TRANSIN, EMETH, CHAIA, IONA, PROFA, TITACHE, BEN ANI, BRIAH, THEIT; all which names are written in Heaven in the characters of Malachim, that is to say, the tongue of the Angels" (*Greater Key of Solomon* 1.7 [Mathers, 33]). Mathers adds the note: "The Mystic Alphabet known as the 'writing of Malachim' is formed from the positions of the Stars in the heavens, by drawing imaginary lines from one star to another so as to obtain the shapes of the characters of this Alphabet" (ibid.).

2. *in the heaven*—The accompanying illustration makes clear exactly what Agrippa means. It is from a work by Jacopo Gaffarelli, also known as James Gaffarelli and Jacques Gaffarel (?1601–1681) who was Cardinal Richelieu's librarian and was sent by him on a book-buying expedition to Venice. He appears to have been a Kabbalist, and wrote two works: (1) *Unheard-of Curiosities Concerning the Talismanic Sculpture of the Persians, and Horoscope of the Patriarchs, and the Reading of the Stars* (1637), written in French, from which this illustration is taken, and (2) a quarto volume in Latin defending the Kabbalah. He also appears to have been a plagiarist, as he had a new title page printed for a *History of the Conquest of Constantinople* by Girolamo Gaspare (1532–1600) and made a gift of it to Richeleau, claiming it as his own.

3. *table will show*—Many of the geomantic figures were defective and have been here corrected. The most glaring error, which also occurs in the Latin *Opera,* was the depiction of all the characters for Puer upside down. In addition to righting these and reordering them to parallel the figures for Puella, I have righted the third figure for Tristitia, also inverted in both the English and Latin editions, corrected the second figure of Laetitia and the third figure of Albus, defective in both editions, and the third figure of Acquisitio, defective only in the English.

CHAPTER LII

Of characters which are drawn from things themselves by a certain likeness.

We have spoken above of a certain manner of images made not after the likeness of celestial images, but according to the emulation of that which the mind of the operator doth desire. In like manner also it is to be understood of characters; for such like characters are nothing else than images ill dearticulated; yet having a certain probable similitude with the celestial images, or with that which the mind of the operator desires, whether that be from the whole image, or from certain marks thereof expressing the whole image.

As the characters of Aries and Taurus we make thus from their horns, ♈, ♉; of Gemini from embracing, ♊; of Cancer from a progress and regress,[1] ♋; of Leo, Scorpio, and Capricorn from their tails, ♌, ♏, ♑; of Virgo from Spike,[2] ♍, ♍; of Libra from a balance, ♎; of Sagittarius from a dart, ♐; of Aquarius from waters, ♒; and of Pisces from fishes, ♓.

In like manner the character of Saturn is made from a sickle, ♄, ♄; of Jupiter from a scepter, ♃, ♃; of Mars from a bolt, ♂; of the Sun from roundness and a golden brightness, ☉, ☉; of Venus from a looking glass,[3] ♀; of Mercury from a wand, ☿, ☿; of the Moon from her horns of increasing and decreasing, ☾.

Besides, of these, according to the mixtions of signs and stars, and natures, are made also mixed characters, as of a fiery triplicity ♈♌♐; of earthly ♉♍♑; of airy ♊♎♒; of watery ♋♏♓.

Also according to the hundred and twenty conjunctions[4] of planets, result so many compound characters of various figures; as of Saturn and Jupiter, viz. thus, ♃♄, ♃♄, or thus ♃♄; or thus of Saturn and Mars, ♂♄ or thus ♂♄; of Jupiter and Mars, ♃♂ or thus ♃♂; of Saturn, Jupiter and Mars, ♃♄♂ or thus ♃♄♂. And as these are exemplified by two and three, so also of the rest, and of more may they be framed.

After the same manner may the characters of other celestial images ascending in any face or degree of signs, be compendiously drawn after the likeness of the images, as in these which are made according to the way of imitation of that which the mind of the operator desires, as to love, the figures be mixed together embracing and obeying one the other; but to hatred, on the contrary, turning away the one from the other, contending, unequal, loosed.[5]

But now we will here set down those characters which *Hermes* assigned[6] to the fixed stars, and Behenii, and they are these:

Characters of the Fixed Stars

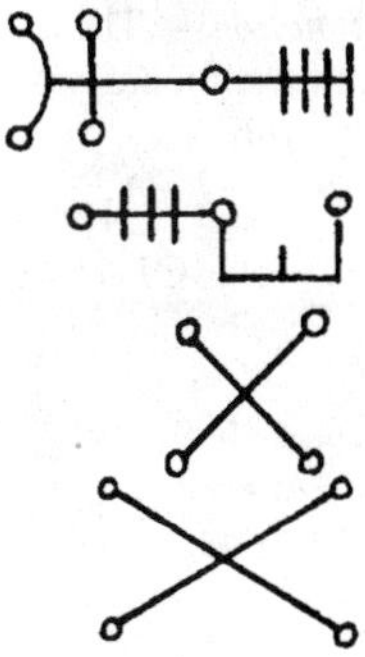

The Head of Algol

The Pleiades

Aldaboram

The Goat Star

Characters of the Fixed Stars (cont'd)

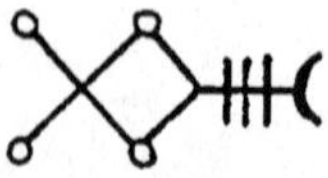
The Greater Dog Star

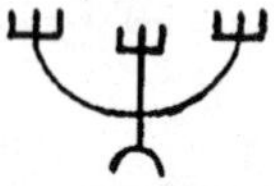
The Lesser Dog Star

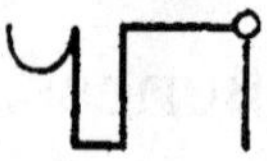
The Heart of the Lion

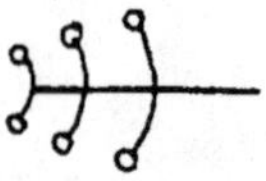
The Tail of the Bear

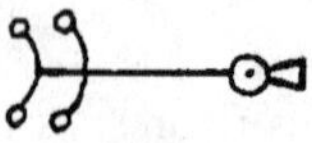
The Wing of the Crow

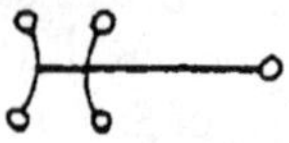
Spica

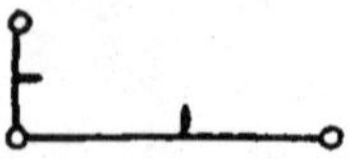
Alcameth

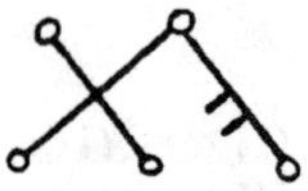
Elpheia

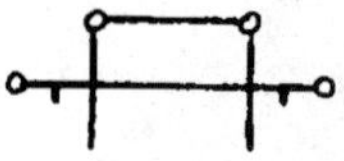
The Heart of the Scorpion

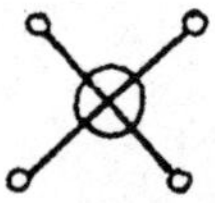
The Vulture Falling

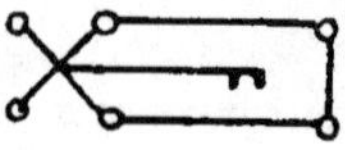
The Tail of Capricorn

Notes—Chapter LII

1. *progress and regress*—Cancer has come to be symbolized ♋, which is usually said to express the two claws of a crab, or two opposite swirls. An older way of representing the sign is 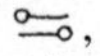, which suggests opposite motions. This is appropriate for a sign that falls on the summer solstice, when the Sun reaches its highest point in the heavens, then begins to decline once again.

2. *Spike*—The star Spica in the constellation Virgo. The resemblance between the symbol for Virgo and that for Spica is the cross, present in both. The Latin word *spica* means "ear of corn," and Virgo is associated with the Greek corn goddess Demeter and the Roman Ceres.

3. *looking glass*—In the English edition this symbol is upside down.

4. *hundred and twenty conjunctions*—These hypothetical (some will never occur) conjunctions of the planets can be tabulated in this way:

21	+ 35	+ 35	+ 21	+ 7	+ 1 = 120
☉☽	☉☽☿	☉☽☿♀	☉☽☿♀♂	☉☽☿♀♂♃	☉☽☿♀♂♃♄
☉☿	☉☽♀	☉☽☿♂	☉☽☿♀♃	☉☽☿♀♂♄	
☉♀	☉☽♂	☉☽☿♃	☉☽☿♀♄	☉☽☿♀♃♄	
☉♂	☉☽♃	☉☽☿♄	☉☽☿♂♃	☉☽☿♂♃♄	
☉♃	☉☽♄	☉☽♀♂	☉☽☿♂♄	☉☽♀♂♃♄	
☉♄	☉☿♀	☉☽♀♃	☉☽☿♃♄	☉☿♀♂♃♄	
☽☿	☉☿♂	☉☽♀♄	☉☽♀♂♃	☽☿♀♂♃♄	
☽♀	☉☿♃	☉☽♂♃	☉☽♀♂♄		

☽♂	☉☿♄	☉☽♂♄	☉☽♀♃♄
☽♃	☉♀♂	☉☽♃♄	☉☽♂♃♄
☽♄	☉♀♃	☉☿♀♂	☉☿♀♂♃
☿♀	☉♀♄	☉☿♀♃	☉☿♀♂♄
☿♂	☉♂♃	☉☿♀♄	☉☿♀♃♄
☿♃	☉♂♄	☉☿♂♃	☉☿♂♃♄
☿♄	☉♃♄	☉☿♂♄	☉♀♂♃♄
♀♂	☽☿♀	☉☿♃♄	☽☿♀♂♃
♀♃	☽☿♂	☉♀♂♃	☽☿♀♂♄
♀♄	☽☿♃	☉♀♂♄	☽☿♀♃♄
♂♃	☽☿♄	☉♀♃♄	☽☿♂♃♄
♂♄	☽♀♂	☉♂♃♄	☽♀♂♃♄
♃♄	☽♀♃	☽☿♀♂	☿♀♂♃♄
	☽♀♄	☽☿♀♃	
	☽♂♃	☽☿♀♄	
	☽♂♄	☽☿♂♃	
	☽♃♄	☽☿♂♄	
	☿♀♂	☽☿♃♄	
	☿♀♃	☽♀♂♃	
	☿♀♄	☽♀♂♄	
	☿♂♃	☽♀♃♄	
	☿♂♄	☽♂♃♄	
	☿♃♄	☿♀♂♃	
	♀♂♃	☿♀♂♄	
	♀♂♄	☿♀♃♄	
	♀♃♄	☿♂♃♄	
	♂♃♄	♀♂♃♄	

5. *unequal, loosed*—On these principles are formed the characters of good and evil spirits given in pseudo-Agrippa's *Fourth Book of Occult Philosophy*.

6. *Hermes assigned*—Although Agrippa assigns these characters to Hermes, the same set of stars and characters occurs in a 15th-century manuscript called the *Book of Enoch* (Bodleian ms. e. Meseo 52, folios 44–7) in the Bodleian Library at Oxford, and also in the early 14th-century British Museum manuscript Harley 1612, folios 15–18 v. The manuscripts are in Latin. A French translation of a similar work is Trinity College, Cambridge, 1313, folios 11–25 v. In the Bodleian manuscript the information is arranged in five columns, which give 15 stars and their related stones, herbs, characters and virtues. Referring to the British Museum manuscript, Joan Evans says: "The exactitude of its astrology, the presence of such linguistic forms as *Gergonsa* and the difference between this treatise and the usual Western lapidary of engraved stones, makes it seem not improbable that it is derived from a Spanish source" (Evans [1922] 1976, 109). In a footnote she adds: "It is the source of the treatise of Abdul Hassan Isabet ben Cora, familiar in Western MSS. as Thebit *de Imaginibus* (e.g. B. M. Royal 12, C. xviii, fol. 10 v)" (ibid.). Below are the characters from the Bodleian manuscript (see Evans [1922] 1976, Appendix G) for comparison with those of Agrippa, along with their names in the manuscript and the names assigned to them in the English Agrippa. It will be at once apparent that Agrippa has omitted (perhaps deliberately) portions of some of the characters.

Star Characters from Book of Enoch

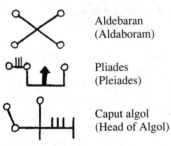

Aldebaran
(Aldaboram)

Pliades
(Pleiades)

Caput algol
(Head of Algol)

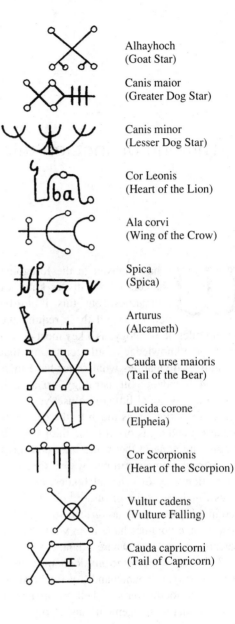

Alhayhoch
(Goat Star)

Canis maior
(Greater Dog Star)

Canis minor
(Lesser Dog Star)

Cor Leonis
(Heart of the Lion)

Ala corvi
(Wing of the Crow)

Spica
(Spica)

Arturus
(Alcameth)

Cauda urse maioris
(Tail of the Bear)

Lucida corone
(Elpheia)

Cor Scorpionis
(Heart of the Scorpion)

Vultur cadens
(Vulture Falling)

Cauda capricorni
(Tail of Capricorn)

CHAPTER LIII

That no divination without astrology is perfect.

We have spoken in the foregoing chapters of the divers kinds of divinations: but this is to be noted, that all these require the use and rules of astrology, as a key most necessary for the knowledge of all secrets; and that all kinds of divinations whatsoever have their root and foundation in astrology, so as that without it they are of little or no use; yet astrological divination, in as much as the celestials are causes and signs of all those things which are, and are done in these inferiors, doth give most certain demonstrations by the situation, and motion only of celestial bodies, of those things which are occult or future;[1] of which we shall in this place speak no further, since of this science huge volumes have been wrote by the ancients, and are everywhere extant.

Therefore whether the physiognomists look upon the body, or countenance, or forehead, or hand, or the soothsayer searcheth by dreams or auspicia,[2] that the judgement may be right, the figure of heaven is also to be inquired into. From the judgements whereof, together with conjectures of similitudes and signs, are produced true opinions of the significators.

Also, if any prodigy shall appear, the figure of the heaven is to be erected; also such things are to be inquired after, which have gone before in the revolutions of years from great conjunctions, and eclipses: then also the nativities, beginnings, enthronizations,[3] foundations, and revolutions, perfections, directions of princes, nations, kingdoms, cities, when these shall appear, and upon what place of the celestial figure these fell; that by all these at length we may come to a rational and probable signification of these things. After the same manner, but with less labour, we must proceed in the exposition of dreams.

Moreover, they that being distempered[4] foretell future things, do it not but as they are instigated by the stars, or inferior instruments of these, whence their predictions must at length be imputed to the celestials, as we read in *Lucan* the old prophet *Tuscus:*[5]

> The lightning's motion, and the veins which are
> Fibrous, and warm, and motion of a fair
> Plume wandering in the air, being taught———

After the city was viewed,[6] the sacrifice slain, the inspection into the entrails did at length by the dispositions of the celestial stars pronounce judgement.[7]

Also geomancy itself, the most accurate of divinations, which divines by points of the earth,[8] or any other superfices, or by a fall,[9] or any other power inscribed, doth first reduce them to celestial figures, viz. to those sixteen which we above named, making judgement after an astrological manner, by the properties and observations thereof: and hither are referred all natural divinations by lots whatsoever, the power whereof can be from nowhere else than from the heaven, and from the mind of them that work them.

For whatsoever is moved, caused or produced in these inferiors, must of necessity imitate the motions, and influences of the superiors, to which, as to its roots, causes, and signs it is reduced, the judgement whereof is showed by astrological rules. Hence dice,[10]

tetrahedron, hexahedron, octahedron, dodecahedron, icosahedron, being made by certain numbers, signs and stars at opportune times, under the influences of the celestials, and being inscribed, obtain a wonderful virtue of divining, and foretelling by their castings, such as those dice Preneste[11] had, in which we read the destinies of the Romans were contained.

Notes—Chapter LIII

1. *occult or future*—

> But all things come to pass according to Providence, and there is no place destitute of Providence. Now Providence is the sovereign design of the God who rules over the heavens; and that sovereign design has under it two subordinate powers, namely, Necessity and Destiny. Necessity is the firm and unalterable decision of Providence, and Destiny is subservient to Providence in accordance with Necessity. And the stars are subservient to Destiny. For no man can either escape from Destiny, or guard himself from the terribleness of the stars. For the stars are the instruments of Destiny; it is in accordance with Destiny that they bring all things to pass for the world of nature and for men. *(Stobaei Hermetica,* excerpt 12. In Scott [1924] 1985, 1:435)

The original text is very broken. I have taken the liberty of incorporating Scott's footnotes into the body of the text.

2. *auspicia*—Specifically, signs or tokens by the flight of birds. See note 3, ch. LIII, bk. I. The term is used here in its broader sense.

3. *enthronizations*—The induction of a king, bishop, pope, duke, and so on, into office; the seating upon a throne.

4. *distempered*—Rapt in ecstasy, or frenzied.

5. *old prophet Tuscus*—

> By reason of these things it seemed good that, according to the ancient usage, the Etrurian prophets should be summoned. Of whom, Aruns, the one most stricken in years, inhabited the walls of deserted Luca, well-skilled in the movements of lightnings, and the throbbing veins in the

entrails, and the warnings of the wing hovering in the air. (Lucan *Pharsalia* 1, line 583 [Riley, 37–8])

6. *city was viewed*—Arruns ordered the citizens of Rome to circumambulate the city in a ceremony of purification (ibid., c. line 592).

7. *pronounce judgement*—Agrippa is referring to Lucan's placement of the prediction of the astrologer Nigidius Figulus after the description of the official inspection of the entrails by Arruns, implying that it placed a final seal on the foretellings of disaster that was to visit Rome:

> Why have the Constellations forsaken their courses, and why in obscurity are they borne along throughout the universe? Why thus intensely shines the side of the sword-girt Orion? The frenzy of arms is threatening; and the might of the sword shall confound all right by force; and for many a year shall this madness prevail. And what avails it to ask an end from the Gods of heaven? That peace comes with a tyrant alone. Prolong, Rome, the continuous series of thy woes; protract for a length of time thy calamities, only now free during civil war. (ibid., line 663 [Riley, 43])

It is Figulus who explicitly predicts war from this figure of the heavens, whereas Arruns is ambiguous and refuses to commit himself on the basis of his reading of the entrails.

8. *points of the earth*—Holes poked in the earth. See Appendix VIII.

9. *by a fall*—Fall of dice or other lots, or patterns made by cast pebbles or other objects.

10. *dice*—Dice have probably been placed at the beginning of this list or regular bodies because there are commonly two of them—thus, 2, 4, 6, 8, 12, 20 (see note 19, ch. XXVI, bk. II). However, since dice

are cubic, the cube is referred to twice, unless Agrippa is implying a nonregular hexahedron, one with six equilateral triangles. But this does not seem likely. It is possible that by dice *(tesserae)* Agrippa means tablets or lots with two faces. This would make better sense.

11. *Preneste*—

We read in the records of the Praenestines, that Numerius Suffucius, a man of high reputation and rank, had often been commanded by dreams (which at last became very threatening) to cut a flint-stone in two, at a particular spot. Being extremely alarmed at the vision, he began to act in obedience to it, in spite of the derision of his fellow-citizens; and he had no sooner divided the stone, than he found therein certain lots, engraved in ancient characters on oak. ... At the same time and place in which the Temple of Fortune is now situated, they report that honey flowed out of an olive. Upon this the augurs declared that the lots there instituted would be held in the highest honour; and, at their command,

a chest was forthwith made out of this same olive-tree, and therein these lots are kept by which the oracles of Fortune are still delivered. But how can there be the least degree of sure and certain information in lots like these, which, under Fortune's direction, are shuffled and drawn by the hands of a child? How were the lots conveyed to this particular spot, and who cut and carved the oak of which they are composed? ... It is only the antiquity and beauty of the Temple of Fortune that any longer preserves the Praenestine lots from contempt even among the vulgar. For what magistrate, or man of any reputation, ever resorts to them now? And in all other places they are wholly disregarded. (Cicero *De Divinatione* 2.41 [Yonge, 235–6])

The lots were plates of oak upon which words were carved. They were taken out of their special case, shuffled, and drawn by a child, who watched and waited for the nodding of the head of the statue of Fortuna, which was in the form of a woman with two suckling infants held to her breasts. See the geographical note on Praeneste.

CHAPTER LIV

Of lottery, when, and whence the virtue of divining is incident to it.

hatsoever divinations and predictions of human events are made by lottery, must of necessity, besides the lot, have some sublime occult cause; which indeed shall not be a cause by accident, such as *Aristotle* describes fortune to be.[1] For in the series of causes, seeing according to the Platonists, a cause by accident can never be the prime and sufficient cause, we must look higher, and find out a cause which may know and intend the effect.[2] Now this we must not place in corporeal nature, but in immaterial, and incorporeal substances which indeed administer the lot, and dispense the signification of the truth, as in men's souls, or separated spirits, or in celestial intelligences, or in God himself.

Now that there is in man's soul a sufficient power and virtue to direct such kind of lots, it is hence manifest, because there is in our soul a divine virtue, and similitude, and apprehension, and power of all things; and as we said in the first book,[3] all things have a natural obedience to it, and of necessity have a motion and efficacy to that which the soul desires with a strong desire; and all the virtues and operations of natural and artificial things, obey it when it is carried forth into the excess of desire, and then all lots of what kind soever are assisting to the appetite of such a mind, and acquire to themselves wonderful virtues of presages, as from that, so from the celestial opportunity in that hour in which the excess of such a like appetite doth most of all exceed[4] in it.

And this is that ground and foundation of all astrological questions, wherefore the mind being elevated into the excess of any desire, taketh of itself an hour and opportunity most convenient and efficacious, on which the figure of the heaven being made, the astrologer may then judge in it, and plainly know concerning that which anyone desires, and is inquisitive to know.

But now because lots are not directed always by man's mind, but also, as we said before, by the help of other spirits; nor is the mind of a prophet always disposed to that excess of passion as we spoke of: hence amongst the ancients, it was a custom to premise before the casting of the lot, some sacred performances, in which they called upon divine intelligences and spirits for to direct the lot aright.

Whatsoever kind of presage therefore these kind of lots portend, must of necessity not be by chance or fortune, but from a spiritual cause, by virtue whereof the phantasy,[5] or hand of him that cast the lot is moved, whether that power proceed from the soul of the operator through the great excess of his affection, or from a celestial influence, and opportunity, or from a certain deity or spirit assisting, or moving from on high, whether these lots are placed in casting of cockals,[6] or throwing of dice, or in the meeting of verses,[7] such as were formerly the lot of *Homer* and *Virgil,* of which, we read in *Aetlius* of Sparta, *Hadrianus* long since made inquiry, and which we read befell *Trajanus* the Emperor:[8]

415

What's he far off graced with the olive
   bough
Presenting offerings? His white chin we
   know,
A Roman king, whose laws first settled
   Rome,
And from small Cures a poor soil, shall
   come
To great command————

By which verses he did not in vain become to
have hopes of enjoying the Empire. Also
amongst Hebrews, and even amongst us Christians (some divines not disapproving of it) lots
are taken out of verses of Psalms.[9]

There are also more, and other kinds of
lots, as are human lots, which had no divination
in them amongst the ancients, and are observed
by us in choosing of magistrates,[10] to prevent
envy, of which also *Cicero* against *Verres*[11]
makes mention: but they are not of our purpose:
but those which are divine, and sacred lots,
respecting oracles, and religion, of which we
shall discourse in the following book: only thus
far I would advise you, that how much presag-
ing, divining or soothsaying soever lots are
found to have, they have them not as they are
lots, but by reason of a virtue of a higher operation joined to them.

Notes—Chapter LIV

1. *fortune to be*—See the *Metaphysica* 5.30, and all
of bk. 6, for Aristotle's examination of chance.

2. *intend the effect*—

   The lover of intellect and knowledge ought
   to explore causes of intelligent nature first
   of all, and, secondly, of those things
   which, being moved by others, are compelled to move others. And this is what we
   too must do. Both kinds of causes should
   be acknowledged by us, but a distinction
   should be made between those which are
   endowed with mind and are the workers of
   things fair and good, and those which are
   deprived of intelligence and always produce chance effects without order or
   design. (Plato *Timaeus* 46e [Hamilton and
   Cairns, 1174])

3. *in the first book*—See ch. LXVII, bk. I.

4. *exceed*—Abound.

5. *phantasy*—Imagination.

6. *cockals*—The astragalus or "knuckle-bone," usually of a sheep, marked on four sides and cast like
dice. The Greeks and Romans had two games: *ludus
talorum,* or cockal; and *ludus tessararum,* or dice.
"What now is a lot? Much the same as the game of
mora, or dice [or knuckle-bones], in which luck and
fortune are all in all, and reason and skill avail nothing" (Cicero *De Divinatione* 2.41 (Yonge, 235]). The
Latin reads *quod talos jacere, quod tesseras,* which
is inadequately translated as "dice." Morra, or mora,

is a game in which one player tries to guess the number of fingers displayed by another player.

7. *meeting of verses*—Rhapsodomancy, where the
book of some poet is opened and a verse read at random as an oracle.

8. *Trajanus the Emperor*—The quote is from Virgil's
Aeneid, bk. 6, c. line 808. It refers to Numa, the second king of Rome. Because Trajan was prematurely
gray, he accepted the verse as a personal omen of
greatness. The Cures, or Sabines, mentioned in the
quote, were noted for simplicity and austerity.

9. *verses of Psalms*—There is a form of divination
known as bibliomancy; however (according to Spence
1920), it was a way of discovering witches, whereby
an accused person was weighed against the great
church Bible. If lighter than the book, he or she was
deemed innocent—a practice that harks back to the
weighing of the heart of the dead by the Egyptians.

10. *choosing of magistrates*—

   Then there is a seventh kind of rule by the
   favour of heaven and fortune, as we say.
   We bring our men to a casting of lots, and
   call it the most equitable of arrangements
   that he who has the chance of the lot
   should rule, and he who misses it retire
   into the ranks of subjects. (Plato *Laws*
   3.690c [Hamilton and Cairns, 1285])

11. *against Verres*—*Divinatio in Q. Caecilium* in
De Oratore of Cicero. See the biographical note on
Verres.

CHAPTER LV

Of the Soul of the World, and of the celestials, according to the traditions of the poets, and philosophers.

It is necessary that the heaven and celestial bodies, seeing they have a power, influence, and manifest operation upon these inferiors, should be animated: seeing an operation cannot proceed from a mere body.[1] All famous poets, and philosophers affirm therefore that the world and all celestial bodies must have a soul, and that also intelligent:[2] hence *Marcus Manillius* in his Astronomy to *Augustus*[3] sings:

> The great corporeal world, which doth appear
> In divers forms, of air, earth, sea, and fire,
> A divine soul doth rule, a deity
> Doth wisely govern————

Also *Lucan:*[4]

> The Earth that's weighed in the air's sustained
> By great Jove————

And *Boetius:*[5]

> Thou dost join to the world a soul, that moves
> All things of threefold nature, and diffuse
> It through the members of the same, and this

Into two orbs of motion rounded is
Being divided, and for to return
Into itself makes haste————

And *Virgil*[6] most full of all philosophy, sings thus:

> And first the heaven, Earth, and liquid plain,
> The Moon's bright globe, and stars Titanian
> A spirit fed within, spread through the whole
> And with the huge heap mixed infused a soul;
> Hence man, and beasts, and birds derive their strain,
> And monsters floating in the marbled main;
> These seeds have fiery vigor, and a birth
> Of heavenly race, but clogged with heavy earth.

For what do these verses seem to mean, than that the world should not only have a spirit soul, but also to partake of the Divine Mind, and that the original, virtue, and vigour of all inferior things do depend on the Soul of the World? This do all Platonists, Pythagoreans, *Orpheus, Trismegistus, Aristotle, Theophrastus, Avicen, Algazeles,* and all Peripatetics confess, and confirm.

Notes—Chapter LV

1. *mere body*—See Aquinas *Summa contra gentiles* 3.87.

2. *that also intelligent*—

Now when the creator had framed the soul

according to his will, he framed within her the corporeal universe, and brought the two together and united them centre to centre. The soul, interfused everywhere from the centre to the circumference of

417

heaven, of which also she is the external envelopment, herself turning in herself, began a divine beginning of never-ceasing and rational life enduring throughout all time. (Plato *Timaeus* 36e [Hamilton and Cairns, 1166])

3. *Astronomy to Augustus*—*Astronomica* of Manilius, an astrological poem in five books, now lost. See biographical note.

4. *also Lucan*—"Perhaps a large portion of the entire Jove, pervading the earth by him to be swayed, which sustains the globe poised in the empty air, passes forth through the Cirrhaean caves, and is attracted, in unison with the aethereal Thunderer" (Lucan *Pharsalia* 5, lines 93–6 [Riley, 169–70]). Lucan is speaking of the vapors arising from the cave at Delphi which intoxicated the Pythoness.

5. *Boetius*—Boetius *Consolation of Philosophy* 3.9.

6. *Virgil*—*Aeneid* 6, c. line724.

CHAPTER LVI

The same is confirmed by reason.

The world, the heavens, the stars, and the elements have a soul, with which they cause a soul in these inferior and mixed bodies. They have also as we said in the former book,[1] a spirit, which by the mediating of the soul is united to the body: for as the world is a certain whole body, the parts whereof are the bodies of all living creatures, and by how much the whole is more perfect and noble than the parts, by so much more perfect, and noble is the body of the world than the bodies of each living thing.

It would be absurd, that all imperfect bodies and parts of the world, and every base animal, as flies, and worms should be worthy of life, and have a life and soul, and the whole entire world a most perfect, whole, and most noble body, should have neither life, nor soul;[2] it is no less absurd, that heavens, stars, elements, which give to all things life, and soul most largely, should themselves be without life, and soul; and that every plant, or tree should be of a more noble condition than the heaven, stars, and elements, which are naturally the cause of them.

And what living man can deny that earth, and water live, which of themselves generate, vivify, nourish, and increase innumerable trees, plants, and living creatures? As most manifestly appears in things that breed of their own accord,[3] and in those which have no corporeal seed. Neither could elements generate and nourish such kind of living creatures, if they themselves were without life or soul.

But some haply may say, that such kind of living creatures are not generated by the soul of the earth, or water, but by the influences of celestial souls; these the Platonists answer,[4] that an accident cannot beget a substance, unless haply as an instrument it be subjected to the next substance, because an instrument removed from an artificer is not moved to the effect of the art; so also those celestial influences, seeing they are certain accidents being removed far from vital substances, or from the life itself, cannot generate a vital substance in these inferiors.

And *Mercurius* in his book which he calls De Communi, saith, all that is in the world is moved either by increase, or decrease.[5] Now what moves must needs have life; and seeing that all things move, even the Earth, especially with a generative and alterative motion, they must themselves live. And if any doubt that the heavens live, saith *Theophrastus,* he is not to be accounted a philosopher; and he which denies the heaven to be animated, so that the mover thereof is not the form thereof, destroys the foundation of all philosophy; the world therefore lives, hath a soul, and sense; for it gives life to plants, which are not produced of seed; and it gives sense to animals, which are not generated by coition.

Notes—Chapter LVI

1. *former book*—See ch. XIV, bk. I.

2. *soul*—The notion that the world is a single living being with a soul received a new impetus recently by the admission of science that not only has the Earth formed life, but life has formed the Earth, adapting the atmosphere and climate to suit its needs. The world is the way it is not by accident, but because living things have made it so.

3. *own accord*—A reference to spontaneous generation. See note 6, ch. V, bk. I.

4. *Platonists answer*—See note 2, ch. LIV, bk. II.

5. *increase, or decrease*—"For in the case of everything which comes into being, the coming-to-be must be followed by destruction. For that which comes into being ... increases; and in the case of everything which increases, the increase is followed by destruction" *(Stobaei Hermetica* 20 [Scott 1985 {1924}, 1:451). "Dissoluble bodies increase and diminish ..." (ibid. 11, 431). However in seeming direct contradiction to the conclusion Agrippa draws, it is explicitly stated: "Moreover, the forces work not only in bodies that have souls in them, but also in soulless bodies, such as logs and stones and the like, increasing their bulk and bringing them to maturity, corrupting, dissolving, rotting and crumbling them, and carrying on in them all processes of that sort that it is possible for soulless bodies to undergo" (ibid. 3, 397).

CHAPTER LVII

That the Soul of the World, and the celestial souls are rational, and partake of divine understanding.

That the above named souls have reason, is apparent hence; for whereas the universal works of the foresaid souls do with a certain perpetual order conspire amongst themselves, it is necessary that they be governed not by chance but by reason; by which reason they do direct, and bring all their operations to a certainty. For it is necessary that the earth should have the reason of terrane things, and water of watery things; and so in the rest; by which reason each in their time, place, and order are generated, and being hurt are repaired.

Therefore philosophers do not think the Soul of the Earth[1] to be as it were the soul of some contemptible body, but to be rational and also intelligent, yea and to be a deity. Besides it would be absurd, seeing we have reasons of our works, that celestial souls, and the Soul of the Universe should not have reasons of theirs. But if (as saith *Plato*)[2] the world be made by very goodness itself, as well as it could be made, it is certainly endowed with not only life, sense, and reason, but also understanding. For the perfection of a body is its soul, and that body is more perfect which hath a more perfect soul.

It is necessary therefore, seeing celestial bodies are most perfect, that they have also most perfect minds. They partake therefore of an intellect, and a mind; which the Platonists also prove by the perseverance of their order, and tenor, because motion is of its nature free, it may easily swerve, and wander now one way, now another, unless it were ruled by an intellect and a mind, and that also by a perfect mind foreseeing from the beginning the best way, and chief end. Which perfect mind indeed, because it is most powerful in the soul, as is the Soul of the World, and as are the souls of celestial bodies, and of elements, without all doubt doth most orderly, and perfectly govern the work allotted to it. For bodies do not resist a most powerful soul, and a perfect mind doth not change its counsel.

The Soul of the World therefore is a certain only thing, filling all things, bestowing all things, binding, and knitting together all things, that it might make one frame of the world, and that it might be as it were one instrument making of many strings, but one sound, sounding from three kinds of creatures, intellectual, celestial, and incorruptible, with one only breath and life.

Notes—Chapter LVII

1. *Soul of the Earth*—See Appendix II.

2. saith Plato—

Let me tell you then why the creator made this world of generation. He was good, and the good can never have any jealousy of anything. And being free from jealousy, he desired that all things should be as like

421

himself as they could be. This is in the truest sense the origin of creation and of the world, as we shall do well in believing on the testimony of wise men. God desired that all things should be good and nothing bad, so far as this was attainable. Wherefore also finding the whole visible sphere not at rest, but moving in an irregular and disorderly fashion, out of disorder he brought order, considering that this was in every way better than the other. Now the deeds of the best could never be or have been other than the fairest, and the creator, reflecting on the things which are by nature visible, found that no unintelligent creature taken as a whole could ever be fairer than the intelligent taken as a whole, and again that intelligence could not be present in anything which was devoid of soul. For which reason, when he was forming the universe, he put intelligence in soul, and soul in body, that he might be the creator of a work which was by nature fairest and best. On this wise, using the language of probability, we may say that the world came into being—a living creature truly endowed with soul and intelligence by the providence of God. (Plato *Timaeus* 29e–30b [Hamilton and Cairns, 1162–3])

CHAPTER LVIII

Of the names of the celestials, and their rule over this inferior world, viz. man.

The names of celestial souls are very many, and divers according to their manifold power and virtue upon these inferior things, from whence they have received divers names, which the ancients in their hymns and prayers made use of.

Concerning which you must observe, that every one of these souls according to *Orpheus'* divinity,[1] is said to have a double virtue; the one placed in knowing, the other in vivifying, and governing its body. Upon this account in the celestial spheres, *Orpheus* calls the former virtue *Bacchus,* the other a Muse. Hence he is not inebriated by any *Bacchus,* who hath not first been coupled to his Muse. Therefore nine *Bacchuses* are designated about the nine Muses.

Hence in the ninth sphere *Orpheus* puts *Bacchus Cribonius,* and the Muse *Calliope;* in the starry heaven, *Picionius,* and *Urania;* in the sphere of Saturn, *Amphietus,* and *Polyphymnia;* in the sphere of Jupiter, *Sabasius,* and *Terpsichore;* in the sphere of Mars, *Bassarius,* and *Clio;* in the sphere of the Sun, *Trietericus,* and *Melpemene;* in the sphere of Venus, *Lysius,* and *Erato;* in the sphere of Mercury, *Silenus,* and *Euterpe;* in the sphere of the Moon, *Bacchus Lyeus,* and the Muse *Thalia.*

Also in the spheres of the elements, he names the souls after this manner: in the Fire he puts the Planet, and the Morning; in the Air, Lightning, *Jupiter,* and *Juno;* in Water, the Ocean, and *Thetys;* in the Earth, *Pluto,* and *Proserpina.*

But the Soul of the World, or Universe, magicians call the *Jupiter* of the World; and the Mind of the World, *Apollo;* and the Nature of the World, *Minerva.* Besides in the fire they put *Vulcan,* in the water *Neptune,* and they did name them by divers names.

Also in the stars of the Zodiac the Pythagoreans did put twelve particular gods or souls placed in the hearts of those stars, and thence governing the whole star, viz. in the heart of Aries is placed a particular *Pallas,* in the heart of Taurus a particular *Venus,* of Gemini a particular *Phebus,* of Cancer *Mercury,* of Leo *Jupiter,* of Virgo *Ceres,* of Libra *Vulcan,* of Scorpio *Mars,* of Sagittarius *Diana,* of Capricorn *Vesta,* of Aquarius a particular *Juno,* in the heart of Pisces a particular *Neptune.* This did *Manilius* sing forth in these verses:

> Pallas doth rule the Ram, Venus the Bull,
> Phebus the Twins and Mercury doth rule
> The Cancer, and the Lion guides doth Jove,
> Ceres doth Virgo, Vulcan Libra move.
> For Scorpion Mars; for Sagittarius fair
> Diana cares; for Capricorn doth care
> Vesta; Aquarius Juno doth protect;
> And Neptune Pisces————

And most ancient *Orpheus* writing to *Museus,* reckons up more deities of the heavens than these, signifying their names, respects, and duties, calling them all in proper songs.[2] Let no one therefore think that they are the names of evil deceiving spirits; but of natural, and divine virtues, distributed to the world by the true God, for the service, and profit of man, who knew how to use them.

And antiquity itself hath ascribed to each of these deities the several members of man; as the ear to memory, which *Virgil* also dedicates to *Phebus,* saying, *Cynthius* pulls my ear,[3] and admonisheth me. So the right hand being a token of fortitude, and by which an oath is made, *Numa Pompilius,* as saith *Livy,* hath dedicated to faith:[4] the fingers are under the tuition of *Minerva,* and the knees given to mercifulness; hence they that beg pardon bend them. Some dedicate the navel to *Venus* as the place of luxury; some who refer all the members to it as the center, say it is dedicated to *Jupiter.* Hence in the Temple of *Jupiter Hammon* the effigy of a navel is celebrated.[5]

Many other things the ancients did observe, ascribing every little member and joint to their deities, which if they be rightly understood, and the true deities ruling over them known, would not at all swerve from their duty, seeing also sacred writ testifies that all our members are governed by the superior virtues, of which we shall speak more largely in the following book; and not members only, but every exercise of men is distributed to its deity, as hunting to *Diana,* wars to *Pallas,* husbandry to *Ceres,* of which thus speaks *Apollo* in his Oracles in *Porphyry:*[6]

Pallas loves wars, woods to Diana fair
Ascribed are, to Juno humid air,
To Ceres corn, and fruits; to Osiris
The water, also humours waterish.

Noꞇes—Chapꞇer LVIII

1. *Orpheus' divinity*—In his *Hymns of Orpheus* Thomas Taylor quotes a passage from the *Theologia Platonica de immortalitate animae* by Marsilio Ficino, published around 1482, in which Ficino has quoted from an unknown Orphic source. Regrettably Ficino does not bother to identify this source book. Since Agrippa has obviously consulted either Ficino, or his source, in this chapter, it is worth giving the quote from Ficino in full as translated by Taylor:

"Those who profess the Orphic theology consider a two-fold power in souls and in the celestial orbs: the one consisting in knowledge, the other in vivifying and governing the orb with which that power is connected. Thus in the orb of the earth, they call the nostic power Pluto, the other Proserpine. In water, the former power Ocean, and the latter Thetis. In air, that thundering Jove, and this Juno. In fire, that Phanes, and this Aurora. In the soul of the lunar sphere, they call the nostic power Licniton Bacchus, the other Thalia. In the sphere of Mercury, that Bacchus Silenus, this Euterpe. In the orb of Venus, that Lysius Bacchus, this Erato. In the sphere of the sun, that Trietericus Bacchus, this Melpomene. In the orb of Mars, that Bassareus Bacchus, this Clio. In the sphere of Jove, that Sebazius, this Terpsichore. In the orb of Saturn, that Amphietus, this Polymnia. In the eighth sphere, that Pericionius, this Urania. But in the soul of the

world, the nostic power, Bacchus Eribromus, but the animating power Calliope. From all which the Orphic theologers infer, that the particular epithets of Bacchus are compared with those of the Muses, on this account, that we may understand the powers of the Muses as intoxicating with the nectar of divine knowledge; and may consider the nine Muses, and nine Bacchuses, as revolving round one Apollo, that is about the splendor of one invisible Sun." (*Thomas Taylor the Platonist: Selected Writings* [Raine and Harper, 203–4)

For a discussion of this passage, see Mead 1965 (1896), 92–6. Mead rightly points out that the doctrine of interdependent male-female pairs of intellect and power is the Hindu Tantric doctrine of Shiva-Shakti under another name. Briefly, all power to manifest and change lies in the female aspect, while the male aspect is pure mind and as such, completely impotent in the world. On this subject the books of Sir John Woodroffe (Arthur Avalon) are not merely useful, but are absolutely necessary, particularly his *Sakti and Sakta,* and his translation of the *Principles of Tantra.* These repay a thousandfold a careful reading.

2. *proper songs*—A reference to the *Orphic Hymns,* which are addressed by Orpheus to Museus.

3. *Cynthius pulls my ear*—"When I would sing of kings and battles, Phoebus plucked me by the ear,

and warned me thus: "'Tis a shepherd's business, Tityrus, to feed fat sheep, to sing a thindrawn lay'" (Virgil *Eclogues* 6, c. line 3 [Lonsdale and Lee, 21]). Hyacinthus was said to have been a beautiful youth beloved by Apollo who was killed by the god when his carelessly thrown discus struck the boy in the forehead. In fact he was an older, pre-Greek god whose worship and festival (the Hyakinthia) was almost completely taken over by Apollo. Pausanias says: "… the tomb of Hyakinthos is in Amyklia under Apollo's statue" *(Guide to Greece* 3.1.3 [Levi, 2:10]). This is a succinct, though unintentional, history of the two gods in Greece.

4. *dedicated to faith—*

> He [Numa] instituted an annual ceremony dedicated to Troth-keeping, with priests whose duty was to drive in a covered wagon drawn by a pair of horses to the place of celebration and there perform their rites with hands swathed to the fingers, signifying that troth must be religiously preserved and that she dwelt inviolable in a man's right hand. (Livy *The Early History of Rome* 1.21 [de Selincourt, 56])

5. *navel is celebrated*—Pausanias describes such a "navel" stone of Saturn: "Going on upwards from this memorial [of Neoptolemos] you come to a stone, not very large; they pour oil on it every day and at every festival they offer unspun wool. There is an opinion that this stone was given to Kronos instead of his child, and that Kronos vomited it up again" *(Guide to Greece* 10.24.5 [Levi 1:468]). The worship of small, rounded, polished oracular stones is very widespread. See Genesis 28:11–8.

6. *Oracles in Porphyry*—The work referred to is *De philosophia ex oraculis haurienda,* in which Porphyry defends the oracles of various gods and which is preserved in fragments in the *Praeparatio evangelica* of Eusebius.

Of the seven governors of the world, the planets, and of their various names serving to magical speeches.

oreover they did call those seven governors of the world (as *Hermes* calls them)[1] Saturn, Jupiter, Mars, the Sun, Venus, Mercury, and the Moon, by many names, and epithets,[2] viz. calling Saturn *Coelius*,[3] scythe-bearer, the father of the gods, the lord of the time, the high lord, the great, the wise, the intelligent, ingenious, revolutor of a long space, an old man of great profundity, the author of secret contemplation, impressing, or depressing great thoughts in the hearts of men, destroying and preserving all things, overturning force and power, and constituting a keeper of secret things, and a shower of them, causing the loss, and finding of the author of life and death.

So Jupiter is called as it were a helping father, the king of heaven, magnanimous, thundering, lightning, unconquored, high and mighty, great and mighty, good, fortunate, sweet, mild, of good will, honest, pure, walking well, and in honour, the lord of joy and of judgements, wise, true, the shower of truth, the judge of all things, excelling all in goodness, the lord of riches, and wisdom.

Mars is called *Mavors*,[4] powerful in war, bloody, powerful in arms, a sword bearer, magnanimous, bold, untamed, generous, lightning, of great power and furious haste, against whom none can defend himself if he resist him, who destroys the strong, and powerful, and deposeth kings from their thrones, the lord of heat and power, the lord of fiery heat, and of the planet

of blood; who inflames the hearts of contenders, and gives them boldness.

The Sun is called *Phoebus*,[5] *Diespiter*,[6] *Apollo, Titan*,[7] *Pean*,[8] *Phanes*,[9] *Horus, Osiris*, as it is in that oracle:[10]

The Sun, Osiris, Dionysus gay,
Apollo, Horus, king ruling the day
Who changeth times, who giveth winds
 and rain,
The king of stars, and the immortal flame.

He is called also *Arcitenens*,[11] burning, fiery, golden, flaming, radiating, of a fiery hair, of a golden hair, the eye of the world, *Lucifer*,[12] seeing all things, ruling all things, the creator of light, the king of stars, the great lord, good, fortunate, honest, pure, prudent, intelligent, wise, shining over the whole world, governing, and vivifying all bodies that have a soul, the prince of the world keeping all the stars under himself, the light of all the stars, darkening, burning, overcoming their virtue by his approach, yet by his light and splendour giving light and splendour to all things: in the night he is called *Dionysus*, but in the day *Apollo*,[13] as if driving away evil things. Therefore the Athenians called him *Alexicacon*,[14] and *Homer, Vlion*,[15] i.e. the driver away of evil things. He is also called *Phoebus* from his beauty and brightness, and *Vulcan* from his fiery violence, because the force thereof consists of many fires. He is also called the Sun, because he contains the light of all the stars: hence he is called by the Assyrians אדאד, Adad,[16] which signifies *only,* and by the Hebrews שמש, Schemesch,[17] which signifies *proper.*

Venus is called the lady,[18] nourishing, beautiful, white, fair, pleasing, powerful, the fruitful lady of love and beauty, the progeny of ages, the first parent of men, who in the beginning of all things joined diversity of sexes together with a growing love, and with an eternal offspring propagates kinds of men and animals, the queen of all delights, the lady of rejoicing, friendly, sociable, pitiful, taking all things in good part, always bountiful to mortals, affording the tender affection of a mother to the conditions of them in misery, the safeguard of mankind, letting no moment of time pass without doing good, overcoming all things by her power, humbling the high to the low, the strong to the weak, the noble to the vile, rectifying, and equaling all things: and she is called *Aphrodite,* because in every sex, she is found to be of every mind:[19] and she is called *Lucifera,* i.e. bringing light, bringing the years of the Sun to light; and she is called *Hesperus,*[20] when she follows the Sun, and *Phosperus,*[21] because she leads through all things though never so hard.

Mercury is called the son of *Jupiter,* the crier of the gods, the interpreter of gods, *Stilbon,*[22] the serpent-bearer, the rod-bearer, winged on his feet, eloquent, bringer of gain, wise, rational, robust, stout, powerful in good and evil, the notary of the Sun, the messenger of *Jupiter,* the messenger betwixt the supernal and infernal gods, male with males, female with females,[23] most fruitful in both sexes; and *Lucan* calls him the arbitrator of the gods. He is also called *Hermes,* i.e. interpreter, bringing to light all obscurity, and opening those things which are most secret.

The Moon is called *Phebe,*[24] *Diana, Lucina,*[25] *Proserpina, Hecate,* menstruous, of a half form, giving light in the night, wandering, silent, having two horns, a preserver, a nightwalker, horn bearer, the queen of heaven, the chiefest of the deities, the first of the heavenly gods and goddesses, the queen of spirits, the mistress of all the elements, whom the stars answer, seasons return, elements serve; at whose nod lightnings breathe forth, seeds bud, plants increase, the initial parent of fruit, the sister of *Phoebus,*[26] light and shining, carrying light from one planet to another, enlightening all powers by its light, restraining the various passings of the stars, dispensing various lights by the circuits of the Sun, the lady of great beauty, the mistress of rain and waters, the giver of riches, the nurse of mankind, the governor of all states, kind, merciful, protecting men by sea and land, mitigating all tempests of fortune, dispensing with fate, nourishing all things growing on the Earth, wandering into divers woods, restraining the rage of goblins,[27] shutting the openings of the Earth, dispensing the light of the heaven, the wholesome rivers of the sea, and the deplored silence of the infernals, by its nods: ruling the world, treading hell under her feet; of whose majesty the birds hasting in the air are afraid, the wild beasts straggling in the mountains, serpents lying hid in the ground, fishes swimming in the sea.

But of these and the like names of stars and planets, and their epithets, surnames, and callings upon, he that will know more, and make more curious inquiry, must betake himself to the Hymns of *Orpheus,* which he that truly understands, hath attained to a great understanding of natural magic.

<h2 style="text-align:center">Notes—Chapter LIX</h2>

1. *Hermes calls them*—"And the first Mind—that Mind which is Life and Light,—being bisexual, gave birth to another Mind, a Maker of things; and this second Mind made out of fire and air seven Administrators, who encompass with their orbits the world perceived by sense; and their administration is called Destiny" *(Corpus Hermeticum* 1.9 [Scott, 1:119]).

2. *epithets*—The surnames, or epithets, given to the classical gods are very many in number. Their purpose was to distinguish particular functions. To take examples from the Hermetic writings:

The Ruler of Heaven, or of whatsoever is included under the name "Heaven," is Zeus

Hypatos [Highest]; for life is given to all beings by Zeus through the medium of Heaven. … The Ruler of the air is the subordinate distributor of life; to him belongs the region between heaven and earth; we call him Zeus Neatos [Lowest]. … Earth and sea are ruled by Zeus Chthonios [Of the Underworld]; he it is that supplies nutriment to all mortal beings that have soul, and to all trees that bear fruit; and it is by his power that the fruits of the earth are produced.

And there are other gods beside, whose powers and operations are distributed through all things that exist. *(Asclepius* 3.19b, 27c [Scott, 1:325])

3. *Coelius*—Coelius means heavenly, and was a name given to Uranus, father of Cronos, or Saturn, who personified the night sky.

4. *Mavors*—Mars is a contraction of Mavors.

5. *Phoebus*—Phoebus means shining (or bright, or pure).

6. *Diespiter*—From *Diovis pater,* or Father of Heaven, a name applied to Jupiter.

7. *Titan*—This name is sometimes applied to the descendants of the Titans, especially Helios (Sun) and Selene (Moon).

8. *Pean*—Paeon, a name for Apollo.

9. *Phanes*—Phanes (the Manifestor) is God as the ideal cause of things, "Bright Space Son of Dark Space" (Mead [1896] 1965, 7:108]). About this god, Lactantius writes: "Orpheus tells us that Phanes is the father of all the Gods, for their sake he created the heaven with forethought for his children, in order that they might have a habitation and a common seat—'he founded for the immortals an imperishable mansion'" (ibid., 110–11).

10. *that oracle*—Quoted by Eusebius in his *Praeparatio evangelica.*

11. *Arcitenens*—From the Latin *arcitenent:* which bears or shoots with a bow. Apollo is Lord of the Silver Bow, the Far-Shooting, the Archer.

12. *Lucifer*—Bringer of Light, or Light-bearer, a title usually assigned to Venus as the Morning Star.

13. *in the day Apollo*—There is a mystic link between Dionysus and Apollo that is expressed in the Orphic myth that while the boy Dionysus was staring captivated into a mirror, the Titans tore him

to pieces, then boiled and roasted his parts. Smelling the savour and realizing what had occurred, Zeus hurled his thunderbolt at the Titans and consumed them in fire. He gave the parts of Dionysus to Apollo to bury. Dionysus emerged from the earth reconstituted and restored to life. Commenting on this fable, Olympiodorus in his commentary on the *Phaedo* of Plato says:

> For Dionysus or Bacchus because his image was formed in a mirror, pursued it, and thus became distributed into everything. But Apollo collected him and brought him up; being a deity of purification, and the true saviour of Dionysus; and on this account he is styled in the sacred hymns, Dionusites. (Taylor 1875, 2:137)

On this same subject, see Mead 1965 (1896), 7:118–20.

14. *Alexicacon*—Alexicacus (Averter of Evil), a surname applied particularly to Zeus, Apollo and Hercules.

15. *Vlion*—Perhaps Helios "who brings joy to mortals" is referred to. See the *Odyssey,* bk. 12, lines 269, 279 (Lattimore, 192).

16. *Adad*—An Elamite god called In-Shushinak (He of Susa), local god of Susa, the chief city of Elam, but also called the Sovereign of the Gods, the Master of Heaven and Earth, and the Maker of the Universe. He is generally identified with Adad, the Assyro-Babylonian god of lightning and tempest who controlled the rains. Adad also had the power of revealing the future and was known as Lord of Foresight. The name of the god occurs as a personal name in I Kings 11:17.

17. *Schemesch*—Hebrew for "sun." The word occurs in its masculine and feminine forms in Psalms 104:19 and Genesis 15:17.

18. *the lady*—The Lady of Paphos, because Old Paphos, on the western coast of Cyprus, was the chief seat of the worship of Aphrodite, who is said to have landed there after her birth amid the waves of the sea. See Lucan *Pharsalia* 8, c. line 457.

19. *of every mind*—It is not clear to me what is meant by this statement, unless it is intended to indicate that Aphrodite presides over all forms of love. As Aphrodite Urania she is goddess of pure and ideal love; as Aphrodite Genetrix she is goddess of married love; and as Aphrodite Porne she is goddess of prostitution. There was a bearded Aphrodite of Cyprus called Aphroditos that embodied both male and female characteristics in one image.

20. *Hesperus*—Venus is called Hesperus, Vesperugo, Vesper, Noctifer or Nocturnus when the planet appears in the western sky after sunset.

21. *Phosperus*—Phosphorus, another name for Venus as the Morning Star, when it appears in the eastern sky before sunrise.

22. *Stilbon*—From the Greek: στιλβειν *(stilbein),* to flash or glitter. Applied to Mercury because the planet glitters or twinkles in the sky.

23. *female with females*—This refers to the sects of the Sun (male-day) and the Moon (female-night) described by Ptolemy, who says: "… the tradition has consequently been handed down that the moon and Venus are nocturnal, the sun and Jupiter diurnal, and Mercury common as before, diurnal when it is a morning star and nocturnal as an evening star" *(Tetrabiblos* 1.7 [Robbins, 43]). Saturn and Mars are contrarily assigned to the sects of the Sun and Moon, respectively.

24. *Phebe*—Artemis Phoebe, goddess of the Moon; the feminine of Phoebus (Sun).

25. *Lucina*—"Goddess that brings to light," the Roman version of the Greek goddess Ilithyia. She presides over the birth of children. The name Lucina is attached as a surname to Juno and Diana.

26. *Phoebus*—Mene, another name for Selene, was sister to Helios. See also note 24 above.

27. *goblins*—A mischievous familiar spirit with a fondness for children, horses, and (according to Keightley [1880] 1978), young women. The name is from the medieval Latin *cobalus.* It first occurs in the *Historia ecclesiastica* of Orderic Vitalis (1142), who in describing the demon that St. Taurin drove from a temple of Diana, says, *"Hunc vulgus Gobelinum appellat."* Keightley says the goblin "is evidently the same as the Kobold," a German spirit. (Keightley [1880] 1978, 476). Freake uses the term "goblins" to translate the Latin *larvae,* which were the ghosts of wicked men risen from the grave to wander at night and torment the living. Larvae were distinguished by the Romans from the *lares,* who were the ghosts of good men. This translation of larvae into goblins is misleading—"ghosts" would have been a better translation.

CHAPTER LX

That human imprecations do naturally impress their powers upon external things; and how man's mind through each degree of dependencies ascends into the intelligible world, and becomes like to the more sublime spirits, and intelligences.

The celestial souls send forth their virtues to the celestial bodies, which then transmit them to this sensible world. For the virtues of the terrene orb proceed from no other cause than celestial. Hence the magician that will work by them, useth a cunning invocation of the superiors, with mysterious words,[1] and a certain kind of ingenious speech, drawing the one to the other, yet by a natural force through a certain mutual agreement betwixt them, whereby things follow of their own accord, or sometimes are drawn unwillingly.

Hence saith *Aristotle* in the sixth book of his Mystical Philosophy,[2] that when anyone by binding or bewitching doth call upon the Sun or other stars, praying them to be helpful to the work desired, the Sun and other stars do not hear his words, but are moved after a certain manner by a certain conjunction, and mutual series, whereby the parts of the world are mutually subordinate the one to the other, and have a mutual consent, by reason of their great union: as in man's body one member is moved by perceiving the motion of another, and in a harp one string is moved at the motion of another. So when anyone moves any part of the world, other parts are moved by the perceiving the motion of that. The knowledge therefore of the dependency of things following one the other, is the foundation of all wonderful operation, which is necessarily required to the exercising the power of attracting superior virtues.

Now the words of men are certain natural things; and because the parts of the world mutually draw one the other, therefore a magician invocating by words, works by powers fitted to nature, by leading some by the love of one to the other, or drawing others by reason of the following of one after the other, or by repelling by reason of the enmity of one to the other, from the contrary, and difference of things, and multitude of virtues; which although they are contrary, and different, yet perfect one part; sometimes also he compels things by way of authority, by the celestial virtue, because he is not a stranger to the heaven.

A man therefore, if he receives the impression of any ligation,[3] or fascination, doth not receive it according to the rational soul, but sensual, and if he suffers in any part, suffers according to the animal part. For they cannot draw a knowing and intelligent man by reason, but by receiving that impression and force by sense, in as much as the animal spirit of man is by the influence of the celestials, and cooperation of the things of the world, affected beyond his former and natural disposition.

As the son moves the father to labour, although unwilling, for to keep and maintain him, although he be wearied; and the desire to rule is moved to anger and other labours, for to get the dominion; and the indigency of nature, and fear of poverty, moves a man to desire riches; and the ornaments, and beauty of women is an incitement to concupiscence; and

women is an incitement to concupiscence; and the harmony of a wise musician moves his hearers with various passions, whereof some do voluntarily follow the consonancy of art, others conform themselves by gesture,[4] although unwillingly, because their sense is captivated, their reason not being intent to these things.

But these kinds of fascinations and ligations the vulgar doth neither admire, nor detest, by reason of their usualness: but they admire other natural things, because they are ignorant of them, and are not accustomed to them. Hence they fall into errors, thinking those things to be above nature, or contrary to nature, which indeed are by nature, and according to nature.

We must know therefore that every superior moves its next inferior, in its degree, and order, not only in bodies, but also in spirits. So the universal soul moves the particular soul; and the rational acts upon the sensual, and that upon the vegetable; and every part of the world acts upon another, and every part is apt to be moved by another; and every part of this inferior world suffers from the heavens according to their nature, and aptitude, as one part of the animal body suffers[5] from another. And the superior intellectual world moves all things below itself, and after a manner contains all the same beings from the first to the last, which are in the inferior world.

Celestial bodies therefore move the body of the elementary world, compounded, generable, sensible, from the circumference to the center, by superior, perpetual, and spiritual essences, depending on the primary intellect, which is the acting intellect; but upon the virtue put in by the word of God,[6] which word the wise Chaldeans of Babylon call the cause of causes, because from it are produced all beings, the acting intellect which is the second from it depends; and that by reason of the union of this word with the First Author, from whom all things being are truly produced. The word therefore is the image of God, the acting intellect the image of the word; the soul is the image of this intellect; and our word is the image of the soul, by which it acts upon natural things naturally, because nature is the work thereof.

And every one of those perfects his subse-

quent, as a father his son,[7] and none of the latter exists without the former. For they are depending amongst themselves, by a kind of ordinate dependency, so that when the latter is corrupted, it is returned into that which was next before it, until it come to the heavens, then unto the universal soul, and lastly unto the acting intellect, by which all other creatures exist, and which itself exists in the principal author, which is the creating word of God, to which at length all things are returned.

Our soul therefore, if it will work any wonderful thing in these inferiors, must have respect to their beginning, that it may be strengthened, and illustrated by that, and receive power of acting through each degree from the very First Author. Therefore we must be more diligent in contemplating the souls of the stars than their bodies, and the supercelestial, and intellectual world, than the celestial corporeal, because that is more noble, although also this be excellent, and the way to that; and without which medium the influence of the superior cannot be attained to.[8]

As for example, the Sun is the king of the stars, most full of light, but receives it from the intelligible world above all other stars, because the soul thereof is more capable of intelligible splendour. Wherefore he that desires to attract the influence of the Sun, must contemplate upon the Sun, not only by the speculation of the exterior light, but also of the interior. And this no man can do unless he return to the soul of the Sun, and become like to it,[9] and comprehend the intelligible light thereof with an intellectual sight, as the sensible light with a corporeal eye.

For this man shall be filled with the light thereof; and the light thereof which is an undertype impressed by the supernal orb it receives into itself, with the illustration whereof his intellect being endowed and truly like to it, and being assisted by it shall at length attain to that supreme brightness, and to all forms that partake thereof. And when he hath received the light of the supreme degree, then his soul shall come to perfection, and be made like to the spirits of the Sun, and shall attain to the virtues, and illustrations of the supernatural virtue, and shall enjoy the power of them, if he hath obtained

"The Sun is the king of the stars, most full of light . . ."

In the first place therefore we must implore assistance from the First Author, and praying not only with mouth but a religious gesture and supplicant soul, also abundantly, incessantly, and sincerely, that he would enlighten our mind, and remove darkness growing upon our souls by reason of our bodies.

Notes—Chapter LX

1. *mysterious words*—The barbarous names of evocation that occur in the grimoires of magic. For the most part they consist of names of gods copied from foreign languages so many times that they have become hopelessly corrupt. Yet in their very obscurity lies a curious attraction. Being themselves without meaning, meaning can be projected into them. See note 6, ch. XI, bk. III. "Change not the barbarous Names of Evocation for there are sacred Names in every language which are given by God, having in the Sacred Rites a Power Ineffable" (*The Chaldean Oracles of Zoroaster,* Westcott [1895] 1983, 57). The "oracle" quoted comes from a collection made by Psellus, and was translated by Thomas Taylor. In the context of this quotation, consider the statement in the prologue to the apocryphal book of Ecclesiasticus: "For the same things uttered in Hebrew, and translated into another tongue, have not the same force in them: and not only these things, but the law itself, and the prophets, and the rest of the books, have no small difference, when they are spoken in their own language" (*Apocrypha,* Oxford, 131).

2. *Mystical Philosophy*—One of the many works on magic wrongly attributed to Aristotle.

3. *ligation*—Binding of the will.

4. *conform themselves by gesture*—Tap their toe, and the like.

5. *suffers*—Is acted upon.

6. *word of God*—See John 1:1.

7. *father his son*—

> But from the Light there came forth a holy Word, which took its stand upon the watery substance; and methought this Word was the voice of the Light [see Genesis 7:2–3]. … "That Light," he [Poimandres] said, "is I, even Mind, the first God, who was before the watery substance which appeared out of the darkness; and the Word, which came forth from the Light is son of God." "How so?" said I. "Learn my meaning," said he, "by looking at what you yourself have in you; for in you too, the word is son, and the mind is father of the word. They are not separate from one the other; for life is the union of word and mind." (*Corpus Hermeticum* 1.5a–6 [Scott, 1:117])

See also John 1:14.

8. *attained to*—Agrippa is saying not to confuse the material stars and planets with the supernatural realities they shadow, but at the same time do not despise them, because they are a necessary medium by which the reality is grasped.

9. *like to it*—This is a vital magical truth: to know anything, you must become that thing; you can know nothing beyond yourself, but you are everything.

To the Most Renowned and Illustrious Prince,
Hermannus of Wyda,
Prince Elector, Duke of Westphalia, and Angaria, Lord Arch-Bishop of Colonia, and Paderborne, his most gracious Lord, Henry Cornelius Agrippa of Nettes-heim.

I t is a very excellent opinion of the ancient magicians (most illustrious Prince) that we ought to labour in nothing more in this life, than that we degenerate not from the excellency of the mind, by which we come nearest to God and put on the divine nature: lest at any time our mind waxing dull by vain idleness, should decline to the frailty of our earthly body and vices of the flesh: so we should lose it, as it were cast down by the dark precipices of perverse lusts. Wherefore we ought so to order our mind, that it by itself being mindful of its own dignity and excellency, should always both think, do and operate something worthy of itself.

But the knowledge of the divine science, doth only and very powerfully perform this for us. When we by the remembrance of its majesty being always busied in divine studies do every moment contemplate divine things, by a sage and diligent inquisition, and by all the degrees of the creatures ascending even to the Archetype himself, do draw from him the infallible virtue of all things, which those that neglect, trusting only to natural and worldly things, are wont often to be confounded by divers errors and fallicies, and very oft to be deceived by evil spirits; but the understanding of divine things purgeth the mind from errors, and rendereth it divine, giveth infallible power to our works, and driveth far the deceits and obstacles of all evil spirits, and together subjects them to our commands.

Yea, it compels even good angels and all the powers of the world unto our service, viz. the virtue of our works being drawn from the Archetype himself, to whom when we ascend, all creatures necessarily obey us, and all the quire of heaven do follow us; for (as *Homer* saith) none of the gods durst remain in their seats, *Jove* being moved; and then presently he ruleth (as saith *Aristophanes)* by one of the gods, whose right it is to execute his commands, who then out of his duty doth manage our petitions according to our desire.

Seeing therefore (most illustrious Prince) you have a divine and immortal soul given you, which seeing the goodness of the divine providence, a well disposed fate, and the bounty of nature have in such manner gifted, that by the acuteness of your understanding, and perfectness of senses you are able to view, search, contemplate, discern and pierce through the pleasant theaters of natural things, the sublime house of the heavens, and the most difficult passages of divine things: I being bound to you by the band of these your great virtues am so far a debtor as to communicate without envy by the true account of all opinions, those mysteries of divine and ceremonial magic which I have truly learned, and not to hide the knowledge of those things, whatsoever concerning these matters the Isiaci[1] those old priests of the Egyptians, and Chaldeans the ancient prophets of the Babylonians, the Cabalists the divine magicians of the Hebrews, also the Orpheans, Pythagoreans and Platonists the profoundest philosophers of Greece, further what the Bragmanni[2] of the

Indians, the Gymnosophists[2] of Ethiopia, and the uncorrupted theologians of our religion have delivered, and by what force of words, power of seals, by what charms of benedictions and imprecations, and by what virtue of observations they in old time wrought so stupendous and wonderful prodigies, intimating to you in this third book of Occult Philosophy and exposing to the light those things which have been buried in the dust of antiquity and involved in the obscurity of oblivion, as in Cymmerian darkness[4] even to this day.

We present therefore now to you, a complete and perfect work in these Three Books of Occult Philosophy Or Magic, which we have perfected with diligent care, and very great labour and pains both of mind and body; and though it be untrimmed in respect of words, yet it's most elaborate truly in respect of the matter: wherefore I desire this one favour, that you would not expect the grace of an oration, or the elegancy of speech in these books, which we long since wrote in our youth when our speech was as yet rough, and our language rude; and now we have respect, not to the style of an oration, but only to the series or order of sentences; we have studied the less elegancy of speech, abundance of matter succeeding in the place thereof; and we suppose we have sufficiently satisfied our duty, if we shall to the utmost of our power perform those things we have promised to declare concerning the secrets of magic, and have freed our conscience from a due debt.

But seeing without doubt, many scoffing sophisters will conspire against me, especially of those who boast themselves to be allied to God, and fully replenished with divinity, and presume to censure the leaves of the Sibyls,[5] and will undertake to judge and condemn to the fire these our works even before they have read or rightly understood anything of them (because such lettuce agrees not with their lips, and such sweet ointment with their nose, and also by reason of that spark of hatred long since conceived against me, and scarce containing itself under the ashes); therefore (most illustrious Prince and wise Prelate) we further submit this work ascribed by me to the merits of your virtue, and now made yours, to your censure, and commend it to your protection, that, if the base and perfidious sophisters[6] would defame it, by the gross madness of their envy and malice, you would by the perspicacity of your discretion and candor of judgement, happily protect and defend it.

Farewell and prosper.

Notes—To Hermannus of Wyda

1. *Isiaci*—Priests of Isis (Latin: *isiacus*).

2. *Bragmanni*—A Bragman, or Brahman, is a member of the priest cast of India.

3. *Gymnosophists*—A sect of ancient Hindu ascetic philosophers who owned no possessions and went naked, or nearly naked, in the world. They were first described to the Greeks in reports of the companions of Alexander the Great on his campaign into India. Later the name became extended to cover similar sects, such as the one described in the sixth book of the *Life of Apollonius of Tyana* as dwelling at the very confines of Ethiopia along the Nile. It is to this latter group that Agrippa refers.

4. *Cymmerian darkness*—"The proverbial expression of *Cimmerian darkness* was originally borrowed from the description of Homer (in the eleventh book of the *Odyssey,*) which he applies to a remote and fabulous country on the shores of the ocean" (Gibbon [1776–88] 1830, 31:505, n. "t").

> There lie the community and city of Kimmerian people,
> hidden in fog and cloud, nor does Helios, the radiant
> sun, ever break through the dark, to illuminate them with his shining,
> neither when he climbs up into the starry heaven,
> nor when he wheels to return again from heaven to earth,
> but always a glum night is spread over wretched mortals.
> (Homer *Odyssey* 11, lines 14–9 [Lattimore, 168])

5. *leaves of the Sibyls*—According to Varro, the Sibylline prophecies were written in Greek on palm leaves.

6. *perfidious sophisters*—"I tell you then that the men of after times will be misled by cunning sophists, and will be turned away from the pure and holy teachings of true philosophy" *(Asclepius* 1.14a [Scott, 1:311]).

The Third and Last Book of Magic, or Occult Philosophy;

written by
Henry Cornelius Agrippa.

BOOK III

CHAPTER 1

Of the necessity, power, and profit of religion.

Now it is time to turn our pen to higher matters, and to that part of magic which teacheth us to know and presently understand the rules of religion, and how we ought to obtain the truth by divine religion, and how rightly to prepare our mind and spirit, by which only we can comprehend the truth; for it is a common opinion of the magicians, that unless the mind and spirit be in good case, the body cannot be in good health: but then a man to be truly sound when body and soul are so coupled, and agree together, that the firmness of the mind and spirit be not inferior to the powers of the body.

But a firm and stout mind (saith *Hermes*)[1] can we not otherwise obtain, than by integrity of life, by piety, and last of all, by divine religion: for holy religion purgeth the mind, and maketh it divine, it helpeth nature, and strengtheneth natural powers, as a physician helpeth the health of the body, and a husbandman the strength of the earth. Whosoever therefore, religion being laid aside, do confide only in natural things, are wont very oft to be deceived by evil spirits; but from the knowledge of religion, the contempt and cure of vices ariseth, and a safeguard against evil spirits.

To conclude, nothing is more pleasant and acceptable to God, than a man perfectly pious, and truly religious, who so far excelleth other men, as he himself is distant from the immortal gods; therefore we ought, being first purged,[2] to offer and commend ourselves to divine piety and religion; and then our senses being asleep, with a quiet mind to expect that divine ambrosian nectar (nectar I say, which *Zachary*[3] the prophet calleth wine making maids merry), praising and adoring that supercelestial *Bacchus,* the chiefest ruler of the gods and priests, the author of regeneration, whom the old poets sang was twice born,[4] from whom rivers most divine flow into our hearts.

Notes—Chapter 1

1. *saith Hermes*—

But when the mind has entered a pious soul, it leads that soul to the light of knowledge; and such a soul is never weary of praising and blessing God, and doing all manner of good to all men by word and deed, in imitation of its Father. Therefore, my son, when you are giving thanks to God, you must pray that the mind assigned to you may be a good mind. *(Corpus Hermeticum* 10.21–22a [Scott, 1:203])

Those souls then of which mind takes command are illuminated by its light, and it counteracts their prepossessions; for as a good physician inflicts pain on the body, burning or cutting it, when disease has taken possession of it, even so mind inflicts pain on the soul, ridding it of pleasure, from which spring all the soul's diseases. (ibid. 12(i).3 [Scott, 1:225])

2. *first purged*—A ritual cleansing, in which a washing of the soul is expressed in a washing of the body, was regarded as absolutely necessary before any magical act for a holy purpose. For this reason it is explicitly stated in the chapter devoted to ritual cleansing in the *Key of Solomon:* "The Bath is necessary for all Magical and Necromantic Arts" *(The Greater Key of Solomon* 2.5 [Mathers, 93]).

3. *Zachary*—Zechariah 9:17.

4. *twice born*—Dionysus was born twice, once prematurely from his dead mother Semele, who had dared to gaze upon the full glory of Zeus and had been consumed by it; and again from the thigh of Zeus, where his divine father had placed him for safekeeping until he came full term. Thus Dionysus was called *Dithyrambus*. The OED gives no explanation for the origin of this term, but since *di* (δι) in Greek means "two," and *thyra* (θυρα) means "door," surely it refers to the issuing from the doors of two different wombs, the first belonging to Semele and the second to Zeus. "Dithyrambus" was also the name of the hymn sung in honour of Bacchus.

CHAPTER II

Of concealing of those things which are secret in religion.

hosoever therefore thou art that now desirest to study this science, keep silent and constantly conceal within the secret closets of your religious breast, so holy a determination; for (as *Mercury* saith)[1] to publish to the knowledge of many a speech thoroughly filled with so great majesty of the deity, is a sign of an irreligious spirit; and divine *Plato* commanded,[2] that holy and secret mysteries should not be divulged to the people; *Pythagoras* also,[3] and *Porphyrius* consecrated their followers to a religious silence; *Orpheus* also, with a certain terrible authority of religion did exact an oath of silence from those he did initiate to the ceremonies of holy things: whence in the verses concerning the holy word he sings:[4]

> You, that admirers are of virtue, stay,
> Consider well what I to you shall say.
> But you, that sacred laws contemn, pro-
>   phane,
> Away from hence, return no more again!
> But thou O Museus whose mind is high,
> Observe my words, and read them with
>   thine eye,
> And them within thy sacred breast repone,
> And in thy journey, think of God alone
> The author of all things, that cannot die,
> Of whom we shall now treat————

So in *Virgil* we read of the Sibyl:[5]

> The goddess comes, hence, hence, all ye
>   prophane,
> The prophet cries, and from her grove
>   refrain.

Hence also in celebrating the holy mysteries of *Ceres Eleusine,* they only were admitted to be initiated, the crier[6] proclaiming the prophane and vulgar to depart; and in Esdras[7] we read this precept concerning the Cabalistical secret of the Hebrews, declared in these verses, thou shalt deliver those books to the wise men of the people, whose hearts thou knowest can comprehend them, and keep those secrets.

Therefore the religious volumes of the Egyptians and those belonging to the secrets of their ceremonies, were made of consecrated paper;[8] in these they did write down letters which might not easily be known, which they call holy. *Macrobius, Marcellinus* and others say, they were called hieroglyphics,[9] lest perchance the writings of this kind should be known to the prophane, which also *Apuleius* testifies[10] in these words, saying, the sacrifice being ended, from a secret retired closet he bringeth forth certain books noted with obscure letters, affording compendious words of the conceived speech, partly by the figures of beasts of this kind, partly by figures full of knots, and crooked in manner of a wheel and set thick, twining about like vine tendrils, the reading thereby being defended from the curiosity of the prophane.

Therefore we shall be worthy scholars of this science, if we be silent, and hide those things which are secret in religion, for the promise of silence (as saith *Tertullian)* is due to religion; but they which do otherwise, are in very great danger, whence *Apuleius* saith[11] concerning secrets of holy writs: I would tell it you, if it were lawful to tell it; you should know it, if it were lawful to hear it; but both ears and tongue would contract the same guilt of rash curiosity.

So we read *Theodorus*[12] the tragical poet, when he would have referred some things of the mysteries of the Jews' Scripture to a certain fable, was deprived of sight. *Theopompus* also who began to translate something out of the divine Law into the Greek tongue, was presently troubled in mind and spirit, whence afterwards earnestly desiring God, wherefore this had happened to him, received an answer in a dream, because he had basely polluted divine things, by setting them forth in public. One *Numenius* also being very curious of hidden things, incurred the displeasure of the divine powers, because he interpreted the holy mysteries of the goddess *Eleusina* and published them, for he dreamed that the goddess of Eleusis stood in a whore's habit before the brothel house, which when he wondered at, they wrathfully answered, that they were by him violently drawn from their modesty and prostituted everywhere to all comers, by which he was admonished, that the ceremonies of the gods ought not to be divulged.

Therefore it hath always been the great care of the ancients to wrap up the mysteries of God and nature, and hide them with divers enigmas, which law the Indians, Brachmans, Aethopians, Persians, and Egyptians also observed; hence *Mercurius, Orpheus,* and all the ancient poets and philosophers, *Pythagoras, Socrates, Plato, Aristoxenus, Ammonius,* kept them inviolably. Hence *Plotinus* and *Origenes* and the other disciples of *Ammonius* (as *Porphyry* relates[13] in his book of the education and discipline of *Plotinus*) swore, never to set forth the decrees of their master. And because *Plotinus* brake his oath made to *Ammonius,* and published his mysteries, for the punishment of his transgression, he was consumed (as they say) by the horrible disease of lice.

Christ also himself, while he lived on Earth, spoke after that manner and fashion that only the more intimate disciples should understand the mystery of the word of God, but the other should perceive the parables only:[14] commanding moreover that holy things should not be given to dogs, nor pearls cast to swine:[15] therefore the prophet saith, I have hid thy words in my heart, that I might not sin against thee.[16] Therefore it is not fit that those secrets which are amongst a few wise men, and communicated by mouth only,[17] should be publicly written.

Wherefore you will pardon me, if I pass over in silence many and the chiefest secret mysteries of ceremonial magic. I suppose I shall do enough, if I open those things which are necessary to be known, and you by the reading of this book go not away altogether empty of these mysteries; but on that condition let these things be communicated to you, on which *Dionysius*[18] bound *Timothy,*[19] that they which perceive these secrets, would not expose them to the unworthy, but gather them together amongst wise men, and keep them with that reverence that is due to them.

Furthermore I would also warn you in this beginning, that even as the divine powers detest public things and prophane, and love secrecy: so every magical experiment fleeth the public, seeks to be hid, is strengthened by silence, but is destroyed by publication, neither doth any complete effect follow after; all these things suffer loss, when they are poured into prating and incredulous minds; therefore it behoveth a magical operator, if he would get fruit from this art, to be secret, and to manifest to none, neither his work nor place, nor time, neither his desire nor will, unless either to a master, or partner, or companion, who also ought to be faithful, believing, silent, and dignified by nature and education: seeing that even the prating of a companion, his incredulity and unworthiness hindereth and disturbeth the effect in every operation.

Notes—Chapter 11

1. *Mercury saith*—There are five reasons for silence, or circumspection, concerning holy doctrine given by Hermes. The first, referred to by Agrippa, is that sharing holy matters with profane minds pollutes them:

> "You may call Ammon; but summon no one else, lest a discourse which treats of the holiest of themes, and breathes the deepest reverence, should be prophaned by the entrance and presence of a throng of listeners." ... Then Ammon also entered the sanctuary; and the place was made holy by the pious awe of the four men, and was filled with God's presence. And the hearers listened in fitting silence ... *(Asclepius* prologue 1b [Scott, 1:287, 289])

The second reason for silence is that profane minds cannot grasp holy doctrine, mock those who preach it, and are incited by it to a greater evil:

> But avoid converse with the many. Not that I wish you to grudge a benefit to others; my reason for this warning is rather that the many will think you one to be laughed at if you speak to them as I have spoken to you. Like welcomes like; but men that are unlike are never friends. ... Moreover, my teaching has a certain property which is particular to it; it urges on bad men to worse wickedness. ... You must therefore beware of talking to them, in order that, being in ignorance, they may be less wicked. *(Stobaei Hermetica* 11.4–5 [Scott, 1:433, 435])

The third reason for silence is that it allows the divine enlightenment of the doctrine to occur: "And now, my son, speak not, but keep a solemn silence; so will the mercy come down on us from God" *(Corpus Hermeticum* 13.8a [Scott, 1:245]).

The fourth reason for silence is simply the futility of attempting to express the inexpressible: "For there is, my son, a secret doctrine, full of holy wisdom, concerning Him who alone is lord of all and preconceived God, whom to declare is beyond the power of man" *(Fragments* 12 [Scott, 1:537]).

The fifth reason for silence involves a proscription against translation of the doctrines into other languages because the words themselves are holy and embody power:

> Translation will greatly distort the sense of the writings, and cause much obscurity. Expressed in our native language, the teaching conveys its meaning clearly; for the very quality of the sounds [text missing]; and when the Egyptian words are spoken, the force of the things signified works in them" *(Corpus Hermeticum* 16.1b–2 [Scott, 1:263, 265]).

2. *Plato commanded*—

> But the best way would be to bury them [the Mysteries] in silence, and if there were some necessity for relating them, only a very small audience should be admitted under pledge of secrecy and after sacrificing, not a pig, but some huge and unprocurable victim, to the end that as few as possible should have heard these tales. (Plato *Republic* 2.378a [Hamilton and Cairns, 624-5]).

3. *Pythagoras also*—On this subject Clemens Alexandrinus writes: "They say that Hipparchus, the Pythagorean, being guilty of writing the tenents of Pythagoras in plain language, was expelled from the school, and a pillar raised for him as if he had been dead" *(Stromateis* 5.9. In *Ante-Nicene Christian Library,* vol. 12).

Pythagoras enforced not only a silence concerning the secrets of his fraternity but a period of general silence to be endured by all disciples: "Pythagoras enjoined young men five years' silence, which he called *echemychia,* abstinence from all speech, or holding of the tongue" (Plutarch *On Curiosity* 9, trans. Philemon Holland. In *Plutarch's Moralia: Twenty Essays* [London: J. M. Dent and Sons, n.d.], 143).

4. *holy word he sings*—This Orphic hymn is quoted by Thomas Taylor in the appendix to his *Eleusinian and Bacchic Mysteries* (Taylor 1875, 166). Agrippa seems to have taken his Latin version of the hymn from the translation of Marsilio Ficino. (See Charles G. Nauert's *Agrippa and the Crisis of Renaissance Thought* [University of Illinois Press, 1965], 137, n. 72].)

5. *of the Sibyl*—Virgil *Aeneid* 6, c. line 260.

6. *the crier*—One of the officials who conducted the Greater Mysteries of Demeter at Eleusis (as opposed to the Lesser Mysteries, held at Agrae) was titled the Crier, or Keryx (as Xenophon called him), but more properly the *Hierokeryx,* whose duty it was to read the proclamation, or *prorrhesis,* at the opening of the ceremonies and enforce silence upon the initiates.

> Exactly what was stated in the proclamation we cannot know, but its sense can be pieced together from a variety of sources.

"Everyone who has clean hands and intelligible speech," meaning Greek of course, "he who is pure from all pollution and whose soul is conscious of no evil and who has lived well and justly," the proclamation seems to have stated, could proceed with the initiation; the rest should abstain. (Mylonas 1974, 247)

The sources Mylonas has used to reconstruct the proclamation are cited in footnote 116 on the same page. See also pp. 224–29 for an interesting discussion concerning the secrecy of the rites. One of the Homeric hymns refers to the mysteries of Demeter as: "... her sacred rites ... which it is in no wise lawful either to neglect, or to inquire into, or mention, for a mighty reverence of the gods restrains the voice" (*Homeric Hymns* 32, "To Ceres," c. line 480, trans. Buckley. In *The Odyssey of Homer, with the Hymns, Epigrams, and Battle of the Frogs and Mice* [New York: Harper & Brothers, 1872], 425).

7. *in Esdras*—The apocryphal Second Book of Esdras 12:37–8.

8. *consecrated paper*—Papyrus, which was not well known in medieval times. It was even strange to Nicholas Flammel (?1330–1417), who by his own account learned the secret of alchemy from an ancient grimoire that fell into his hands "for the sum of two florins, a guilded Book, very old and large. It was not of Paper, nor of Parchment, as other Books be, but was only made of delicate rinds (as it seemed unto me) of tender young trees" (Flammel [1624, 1889] 1980, 6).

9. *hieroglyphics*—

Now those who are instructed by the Egyptians, first of all learn that system of Egyptian writing, which is called the Epistolographic [or enchorial]; secondly, the Hieratic, which is used by the sacred scribes; thirdly and lastly, the Hieroglyphic. Of this [last] one kind expresses its own meaning *by the first elements [alphabetically];* but the other kind is *symbolical.* Of the symbolical, one sort directly conveys its meaning by *imitation;* another sort is written as it were *metaphorically;* while the remaining sort speaks *allegorically* as it were by means of aenigmas. (Clemens Alexandrinus *Stromateis* 5. In Horapollo *Hieroglyphics,* appendix [Cory, 169–70]).

Pythagoras travelled also among the Egyptians; and in Egypt he lived with the priests, and learned from them the wisdom and language of the Egyptians, and the three kinds of writings, viz. the *epistolographic,* the *hieroglyphic,* and the *symbolic,* the one conveying its meaning directly by imitation, the other allegorically, by means of aenigmas. (Porphyry *The Life of Pythagoras.* In Horapollo *Hieroglyphics,* appendix [Cory, 171]).

10. *Apuleius testifies*—"... partly written with unknown characters, and partly painted with figures of beasts declaring briefly every sentence, with tops and tailes, turning in fashion of a wheele, which were strange and impossible to be read of the prophane people" (Apuleius *Golden Asse* ch. 48 [Adlington]).

12. *Theodorus*—

We hear of another man, Theodoras, who tried to make fun of a Hierophant [of the Greek Mysteries] by asking him: "Explain to me, Eurykleides, who are those who are impious in the eyes of the gods?" Eurykleides replied, "Those who expose the secrets to the uninitiated." Theodoras countered, "You are an impious man, you also, since you give explanations to a person who is not initiated." For this sacrilege Theodoras was saved from being brought before the Areopagas only through the intervention of Demetrios of Phaleron. (Mylonas 1974, 225–6)

According to Amphikrates *(Famous Men)* Theodoras was condemned to drink hemlock (ibid., n. 8). The story referred to by Agrippa is apparently some corruption of the above.

13. *Porphyry relates*—

Erennius, Origen and Plotinus had made a compact not to disclose any of the doctrines which Ammonius had revealed to them. Plotinus kept faith, and in all his intercourse with his associates divulged nothing of Ammonius' system. But the compact was broken, first by Erennius and then by Origen, following suit: Origen, it is true, put in writing nothing but the treatise *On the Spirit-Beings,* and in Galienus' reign that entitled *The King the Sole Creator.* Plotinus himself remained a long time without writing, but he began to base his Conferences on what he had gathered from his studies under Ammonius. (Porphyry *On the Life of Plotinus and the Arrangement of His Work* 3, trans. Stephen Mackenna. In *Plotinus: The Ethical Treatises* [London: Philip Lee Warner, 1917], 1:3–4)

Porphyry does not link the disease and death of Plotinus to this betrayal of the agreement of silence. Agrippa has apparently consulted the more highly colored account of the death of Plotinus that appears in Firmicus Maternus:

> First his limbs became stiff and his blood became sluggish and congealed. Little by little his eyesight lost its sharpness and his vision failed. Soon after, a malignant infection under his whole skin burst forth. Polluted blood weakened his limbs and his whole body. Every hour and every day small parts of his inner organs were dissolved and carried away by the creeping sickness. A part of his body might be in good condition one moment and the next deformed by the festering disease. *(Ancient Astrology Theory and Practice (Matheseos libri VIII)* 1.7.20, trans. Jean Rhys Bram [Park Ridge, NJ: Noyes Press, 1975], 23)

14. *parables only*—Matthew 13:10–4.

15. *pearls cast to swine*—Matthew 7:6.

16. *sin against thee*—Psalms 119:11.

17. *by mouth only*—Secret doctrine was transmitted orally from master to disciple, literally whispered in the ear. On the Kabbalah, Christian Ginsburg says:

> It is for this reason that it is called *Kabbalah* (קבלה from קבל *to receive)* which primarily denotes *reception* and then *a doctrine received by oral tradition.* The Kabbalah is also called by some *Secret Wisdom* (חכמה סתרה), because it was only handed down by tradition through the initiated, and is indicated in the Hebrew Scriptures by signs which are hidden and unintelligible to those who have not been instructed in its mysteries. (Ginsburg [1863–4] 1970, 86)

Speaking about what he calls "the archaic periods of the world's history," Isaac Myer says:

> Teacher and pupil, stood more in the relation of father and son, and master and servant, as in the case to-day between the *Guru* or Brahminical master and his scholar. ... Thus the orally traditional in religion, philosophy, science and art, the real, inner, intelligible to the intellect, spirituality of the whole; was taught and faithfully handed down and preserved, among the initiates and intellectual workers; and to all the ignorant and uncultivated, the higher spirituality remained unaccessible and closed. (Myer [1888] 1974, 176–7)

18. *Dionysius*—Pseudo-Dionysius, author of *Concerning the Celestial Hierarchy.*

19. *Timothy*—Since pseudo-Dionysius was supposed to have been the disciple of Paul (Acts 17:34), the Timothy referred to was supposedly the companion of the apostle named in the First and Second Epistle of Paul to Timothy.

CHAPTER III

What dignification is required, that one may be a true magician and a worker of miracles.

About the beginning of the first book of this work, we have spoken what manner of person a magician ought to be;[1] but now we will declare a mystical and secret manner, necessary for everyone who desireth to practice this art, which is both the beginning, perfection, and key of all magical operations, and it is the dignifying[2] of men to this so sublime virtue and power; for this faculty requireth in man a wonderful dignification, for that the understanding which is in us the highest faculty of the soul, is the only worker of wonders, which when it is overwhelmed by too much commerce with the flesh, and busied about the sensible soul of the body, is not worthy of the command of divine substances; therefore many prosecute[3] this art in vain.

Therefore it is meet that we who endeavour to attain to so great a height should especially meditate of two things: first, how we should leave carnal affections, frail sense, and material passions; secondly, by what way and means we may ascend to an intellect pure and conjoined with the powers of the gods, without which we shall never happily ascend to the scrutiny of secret things, and to the power of wonderful workings, or miracles: for in these dignification consists wholly, which nature, desert, and a certain religious art do make up.

Natural dignity is the best disposition of the body and its organs, not obscuring the soul with any grossness, and being without all distemper, and this proceedeth from the situation, motion,

light, and influence of the celestial bodies and spirits which are conversant in the generation of everyone, as are those whose Ninth house is fortunate by Saturn, Sol, and Mercury; Mars also in the Ninth house commandeth the spirits; but concerning these things we have largely treated in the books of the stars: but whoso is not such a one, it is necessary that he recompense the defect of nature by education, and the best ordering and prosperous use of natural things until he become complete in all intrinsical and extrinsical perfections.

Hence so great care is taken in the Law of *Moses* concerning the priest,[4] that he be not polluted by a dead carcass, or by a woman a widow, or menstruous, that he be free from leprosy, flux of blood, burstness,[5] and be perfect in all his members, not blind, nor lame, nor crook-backed, or with an ill-favoured nose. And *Apuleius* saith in his Apology,[6] that the youth to be initiated to divination by magic spells,[7] ought to be chosen sound without sickness, ingenious, comely, perfect in his members, of a quick spirit, eloquent in speech, that in him the divine power might be conversant as in the good houses; that the mind of the youth having quickly attained experience, may be restored to its divinity.

But the meritorious dignity is perfected by two things; namely learning and practice. The end of learning is to know the truth; it is meet therefore, as is spoken in the beginning of the first book, that he be learned and skillful in those three faculties; then all impediments being removed, wholly to apply his soul to contemplation and to convert itself into itself;[8] for there is even in our own selves the apprehension and power of all things; but we are prohibited, so as that we little enjoy these things, by passions opposing us even from our birth, and vain imaginations and immoderate affections, which being expelled, the divine knowledge and power presently take place; but the religious operation obtains no less efficacy which ofttimes of itself alone is sufficiently powerful for us to obtain this deifying virtue, so great is the virtue of holy duties rightly exhibited and performed, that though they be not understood, yet piously and perfectly observed, and with a firm faith believed, that they have no less efficacy than to adorn us with a divine power.[9]

But what dignity is acquired by the art of religion, is perfected by certain religious ceremonies, expiations, consecrations, and holy rites proceeding from him whose spirit the public religion hath consecrated, who hath power of imposition of hands, and of initiating with sacramental power,[10] by which the character of the divine virtue and power is stamped on us which they call the divine consent, by which a man supported with the divine nature, and made as it were a companion of the angels beareth the ingrafted power of God; and this rite is referred to the ecclesiastical mysteries.

If therefore now thou shalt be a man perfect in the sacred understanding of religion, and piously and most constantly meditatest on it, and without doubting believest, and art such an one on whom the authority of holy rites and nature hath conferred dignity above others, and one, whom the divine powers contemn not, thou shalt be able by praying, consecrating, sacrificing, invocating, to attract spiritual and celestial powers, and to imprint them on those things thou pleasest, and by it to vivify every magical work; but whosoever beyond the authority of his office, without the merit of sanctity and learning, beyond the dignity of nature and education, shall presume to work anything in magic, shall work in vain, and deceive both himself and those that believe on him, and with danger incur the displeasure of the divine powers.

Notes—Chapter III

1. *magician ought to be*—See ch. II, bk. I.

2. *dignifying*—The word is used in the sense of purifying and exalting, with allusion to the astrological dignification of a planet, where a planet's power of working is increased by its position or aspects.

3. *prosecute*—Seek to attain or bring about.

4. *concerning the priest*—Leviticus 21. See also 15:19 and 22:2–8.

5. *burstness*—Rupture, or hernia. See Leviticus 21:20. Perhaps inguinal hernia.

6. *his Apology*—*Apologia,* also known as *De magia liber,* the defense against a charge of sorcery Apuleius delivered at Sabrata in 173 AD before Claudius Maximus, proconsul of Africa. It is extant.

7. *divination by magic spells*—See note 4 to the chapter "Of Goetia and Necromancy," which Freake has appended to the text. It forms chapter 45 of Agrippa's *De incertitudine et vanitate scientiarum.*

8. *convert itself into itself*—Turn inward.

9. *divine power*—This is an important point. The action of ritual is to some extent automatic; it need not be understood to cause an effect upon its practitioner.

10. *sacramental power*—Magical initiation is specific and concrete, designed to accomplish some change. It is best exemplified in the Tibetan *angkur:*

> The main idea that we attach to initiation is the revelation of a secret doctrine, admission to the knowledge of certain mysteries, whereas the angkur is, above all, the transmission of a power, a force, by a kind of psychic process. The object in view is to communicate to the initiate the capacity to perform some particular act or to practise certain exercises which tend to develop various physical or intellectual faculties. (David-Neel [1931] 1959, 43)

CHAPTER IV

Of the two helps of
ceremonial magic, religion and superstition.

.

There are two things, which rule every operation of ceremonial magic, namely religion and superstition.

This religion is a continual contemplation of divine things, and by good works an uniting oneself with God and the divine powers, by which in a reverent family, a service, and a santification of worship worthy of them is performed, and also the ceremonies of divine worship are rightly exercised; religion therefore is a certain discipline of external holy things and ceremonies by the which as it were by certain signs we are admonished of internal and spiritual things, which is so deeply implanted in us by nature, that we more differ from other creatures by this than rationality.[1]

Whosoever therefore neglects religion (as we have spoken before) and confides only in the strength of natural things, are very often deceived by the evil spirits; therefore they who are more religiously and holily instructed, neither set a tree nor plant their vineyard, nor undertake any mean work without divine invocation, as the Doctor of the Nations commands in Colossians,[2] saying, whatsoever you shall do in word or deed, do all in the name of the Lord *Jesus* Christ giving thanks to him, and to God the Father by him.

Therefore to superadd the powers of religion to physical and mathematical virtues is so far from a fault, that not to join them, is an heinous sin: hence in Libro Senatorum saith Rabbi *Henina,* he that enjoyeth any of the creatures without divine benediction, is supposed both by God and the Church to have used it as taken by theft and robbery, of whom it is written by *Solomon,* he that takes away any things violently from father and mother, is a destroyer;[3] but God is our Father, and the Church our Mother, as it is written, is not he thy father who possesseth thee?[4] And elsewhere, hear my son the discipline of thy father, and despise not the law of thy mother.[5]

Nothing more displeaseth God, than to be neglected and contemned; nothing pleaseth him more, than to be renowned and adored. Hence he hath permitted no creature of the world to be without religion. All do worship God, pray (as *Proclus* saith), frame hymns to the leaders of their order; but some things truly after a natural, others after a sensible, others a rational, others an intellectual manner, and all things in their manner, according to the Song of the Three Children,[6] bless the Lord: but the rites and ceremonies of religion, in respect of the diversity of times and places, are divers.

Every religion hath something of good, because it is directed to God his creator: and although God allows the Christian religion only, yet other worships which are undertaken for his sake, he doth not altogether reject, and leaveth them not unrewarded, if not with an eternal, yet with a temporal reward, or at least doth punish them less; but he hateth, thundereth against and utterly destroys prophane persons and altogether irreligious as his enemies, for their impiety is greater than the others who follow a false and erroneous religion: for there is no religion (saith *Lactantius)* so erroneous, which hath not somewhat of wisdom in it, by which they may obtain pardon, who have kept the chiefest duty of man, if not in deed, yet in intention: but no man can of himself attain to the true religion, unless he be taught it of God.

All worship therefore, which is different from the true religion, is superstition; in like manner also that which giveth divine worship, either to whom it ought not, or in that manner which it ought not. Therefore we must especially take heed lest at any time, by some perverse worship of superstition, we be envious to the Almighty God, and to the holy powers under him; for this would be not only wicked, but an act most unworthy of philosophers; superstition therefore although it be far different from the true religion, yet it is not all and wholly rejected, because in many things it is even tolerated, and observed by the chief rulers of religion.

But I call that superstition especially, which is a certain resemblance of religion, which for as much as it imitates whatsoever is in religion, as miracles, sacraments, rites, observations and such like, from whence it gets no small power, and also obtains no less strength by the credulity of the operator; for how much a constant credulity can do, we have spoken in the first book, and is manifestly known to the vulgar. Therefore superstition requireth credulity, as religion faith, seeing constant credulity can do so great things, as even to work miracles in opinions and false operations.

Whosoever therefore in his religion, though false, yet believeth most strongly that it is true, and elevates his spirit by reason of this his credulity, until it be assimilated to those spirits who are the chief leaders of that religion, may work those things which nature and reason discern not; but incredulity and diffidence doth weaken every work not only in superstition, but also in true religion, and enervates the desired effect even of the most strong experiments.

But how superstition imitateth religion, these examples declare; namely when worms and locusts are excommunicated, that they hurt not the fruits; when bells and images are baptised, and such like.

But because the old magicians and those who were the authors of this art amongst the ancients, have been Chaldeans, Egyptians, Assyrians, Persians and Arabians, all whose religion was perverse and polluted idolatry, we must very much take heed, lest we should permit their errors to war against the grounds of the Catholic religion; for this was blasphemous, and subject to the curse.[7]

And I also should be a blasphemer, if I did not admonish you of these things, in this science; wheresoever therefore you shall find these things written by us, know that those things are only related out of other authors, and not put down by us for truth, but for a probable conjecture which is allied to truth, and an instruction for imitation in those things which are true.[8]

Therefore we ought from their errors to collect the truth, which work truly requireth a profound understanding, perfect piety, and painful and laborious diligence, and also wisdom which knoweth out of every evil to extract good, and to fit oblique things unto the right use of those things which it governeth, as concerning this *Augustine* gives us an example of a carpenter to whom oblique and complicate things are no less necessary and convenient than the straight.

Notes—Chapter IV

1. *than rationality—*

Therefore the chief good of man is in religion only; for the other things, even those which are supposed to be peculiar to man, are found in the other animals also. For when they discern and distinguish their own voices by particular marks among themselves, they seem to converse: they also appear to have a kind of smile, when with soothed ears, and contracted mouth, and with eyes relaxed to sportiveness, they fawn upon man, or upon their own mates and young. Do they not give a greeting which bears some resemblance to natural love and indulgence? Again, those creatures which look forward to the future and lay up for themselves food, plainly have foresight. Indications of reason are also found in many of them. ... It is therefore uncertain whether those things which are given to man are common with other living creatures: they are certainly without religion. I indeed thus judge, that reason is given to all animals, but to the dumb creatures only for the protection of life, to man also for its prolongation. And because reason itself is perfect in man, it is named wisdom, which renders man distinguished in this respect, that to him alone it is given to comprehend divine things. (Lactantius *Divine Institutions* 3.10 *[Ante-Nicene Christian Library* 21:158])

2. *in Colossians*—Colossians 3:17. The Doctor of the Nations is Paul.

3. *is a destroyer*—Proverbs 28:24.

4. *who possesseth thee*—Deuteronomy 32:6.

5. *law of thy mother*—Proverbs 1:8.

6. *Song of the Three Children*—The Apocryphal Song of the Three Holy Children 29–68.

7. *subject to the curse*—God placed a curse on man in the Garden of Eden because Adam ate the apple (Genesis 3:17). Christ took that curse upon himself when he was crucified, and redeemed those who follow him (Galatians 3:13), but not the rest of mankind (Matthew 25:41). Therefore a lapsed Christian reassumes the mantle of original sin.

8. *things which are true*—This paragraph was included largely to forestall the attacks Agrippa knew would be launched against him by his orthodox critics.

CHAPTER V

Of the three guides of religion, which bring us to the path of truth.

There are three guides which bring us even to the paths of truth and which rule all our religion, in which it wholly consisteth, namely love, hope and faith.

For love is the chariot of the soul, the most excellent of all things, descending from the intelligences above even to the most inferior things. It congregates and converts our mind into the divine beauty, preserves us also in all our works, gives us events according to our wishes, administereth power to our supplications: as we read in *Homer, Apollo* heard *Chrysons'* prayers because he was his very great friend:[1] and some read of *Mary Magdalene* in the Gospel, many sins were forgiven her, because she loved much.[2]

But hope immoveably hanging on those things it desireth, when it is certain and not wavering, nourisheth the mind and perfecteth it.

But faith the superior virtue of all, not grounded on human fictions, but divine revelations wholly, pierceth all things through the whole world, for seeing it descends from above from the first light, and remains nearest to it, is far more noble and excellent than the arts, sciences and beliefs arising from inferior things: this being darted into our intellect by reflection from the first light.

To conclude, by faith man is made somewhat the same with the superior powers and enjoyeth the same power with them: hence *Proclus* saith, as belief which is a credulity, is below science: so belief which is a true faith, is supersubstantially above all science and understanding, conjoining us immediately to God; for faith is the root of all miracles, by which alone (as the Platonists testify) we approach to God, and obtain the divine power and protection.

So we read that *Danial* escaped the mouths of the lions, because he believed on his God.[3] So to the woman with the bloody issue saith Christ, thy faith hath made thee whole;[4] and of the blind man desiring sight, he required faith, saying, do you believe that I can open your eyes?[5] So *Pallas* in *Homer* comforteth *Achilles* with these words, I am come to pacify your wrath, if you will believe.[6]

Therefore *Linus* the poet[7] sings all things are to be believed, because all things are easy to God; nothing is impossible to him, therefore nothing incredible; therefore we believing those things which belong to religion, do obtain the virtue of them; but when we shall fail in our faith, we shall do nothing worthy admiration, but of punishment; as we have an example of this in Luke,[8] in these words, therefore certain of the vagabond Jews, exorcists, took upon them to call over them which had evil spirits in the name of the Lord Jesus, saying, we adjure you by *Jesus* whom *Paul* preacheth; and the evil spirit answered and said, *Jesus* I know, and *Paul* I know, but who art thou? And the man in whom the evil spirit was, leapt on them, and overcame them, so that they fled out of the house naked and wounded.

Notes—Chapter V

1. *very great friend*—Chryses, a priest of Apollo, went to Agamemnon to beg for the release of his daughter, Chryseis, who had been captured by the Greeks and given to Agamemnon. Agamemnon refused. Chryses prayed to his god for vengeance:

> So he spoke in prayer, and Phoibos Apollo heard him,
> and strode down along the pinnacles of Olympos angered
> in his heart, carrying across his shoulders the bow and the hooded
> quiver; and the shafts clashed on the shoulders of the god walking
> angrily. He came as night comes down and knelt then
> apart and opposite the ships and let go an arrow.
> Terrible was the clash that rose from the bow of silver.
> First he went after the mules and the circling hounds, then let go
> a tearing arrow against the men themselves and struck them.
> The corpse fires burned everywhere and did not stop burning.
>
> (Homer *Iliad* 1, lines 43–52 [Lattimore, 60])

2. *she loved much*—Luke 7:47. Traditionally the sinful woman who anoints Christ's feet is supposed to be Mary Magdalen. However, she is not named, and there is no evidence as to her identity.

3. *believed on his God*—Daniel 6:23.

4. *made thee whole*—Matthew 9:22.

5. *open your eyes*—Matthew 9:28–9.

6. *if you will believe*—Caught in the torrent of a river, Achilles is reassured by the gods Poseidon and Athene: "Do not be afraid, son of Peleus, nor be so anxious,/such are we two of the gods who stand beside you to help you,/by the consent of Zeus, myself and Pallas Athene. ... But we also have close counsel to give you, if you will believe us" (Homer *Iliad* 21, lines 288–93 [Lattimore, 426]).

7. *Linus the poet*—In the time of the grammarians of Alexandria, Linus was credited as the author of apocryphal works describing the exploits of Dionysus. See his biographical note.

8. *in Luke*—Actually in the Acts of the Apostles 19:13–6. Agrippa may have confused these verses in his mind with Luke 9:49.

CHAPTER VI

How by these guides the soul of man ascendeth up into the divine nature, and is made a worker of miracles.

Therefore our mind being pure and divine, inflamed with a religious love, adorned with hope, directed by faith, placed in the height and top of the human soul, doth attract the truth, and suddenly comprehend it, and beholdeth all the stations,[1] grounds, causes and sciences of things both natural and immortal in the divine truth itself, as it were in a certain glass[2] of eternity.

Hence it comes to pass that we, though natural, know those things which are above nature, and understand all things below, and as it were by divine oracles receive the knowledge not only of those things which are, but also of those that are past and to come, presently, and many years hence; moreover not only in sciences, arts and oracles the understanding challengeth[3] to itself this divine virtue, but also receiveth this miraculous power in certain things by command to be changed.[4]

Hence it comes to pass that though we are framed a natural body, yet we sometimes predominate over nature, and cause such wonderful, sudden and difficult operations, as that evil spirits obey us, the stars are disordered, the heavenly powers compelled, the elements made obedient; so devout men and those elevated by these theological virtues, command the elements, drive away fogs, raise the winds, cause rain, cure diseases, raise the dead, all which things to have been done amongst divers nations, poets and historians do sing and relate: and that these things may be done, all the famousest philosophers, and theologians do confirm; so the prophets, apostles, and the rest, were famous by the wonderful power of God.

Therefore we must know, that as by the influx of the first agent, is produced oftentimes something without the cooperation of the middle causes, so also by the work of religion alone, may something be done without the application of natural and celestial virtues; but no man can work by pure religion alone, unless he be made totally intellectual:[5] but whosoever, without the mixture of other powers, worketh by religion alone, if he shall persevere long in the work, is swallowed up by the divine power and cannot live long: but whosoever shall attempt this and not be purified, doth bring upon himself judgement, and is delivered to the Evil Spirit, to be devoured.

Notes—Chapter VI

1. *stations*—Places, or positions, perhaps with allusion to the stations of the cross, a series of 14 positions representing the passion of Christ which were used for devotional exercises.

2. *glass*—Mirror.

3. *challengeth*—Claims, or summons.

4. *to be changed*—In other words, the mind not only receives understanding, but also the power to act and cause change.

5. *totally intellectual*—Free from attachment, in the Buddhist sense; liberated not only from desires of the flesh, but from emotional attachments and all other aspects of karma (action-reaction).

CHAPTER VII

That the knowledge of the true God is necessary for a magician, and what the old magicians and philosophers have thought concerning God.

Seeing that the being and operation of all things, depend on the most high God, Creator of all things, from thence also on the other divine powers, to whom also is granted a power of fashioning and creating, not principally indeed, but instrumentally by virtue of the First Creator (for the beginning of everything is the First Cause, but what is produced by the second causes, is much more produced by the First, which is the producer of the second causes, which therefore we call secondary gods), it is necessary therefore that every magician know that very God, which is the First Cause, and Creator of all things; and also the other gods, or divine powers (which we call the second causes), and not to be ignorant, with what adoration, reverence, holy rites conformable to the condition of everyone, they are to be worshipped.

Whosoever therefore invocates the gods, and doth not confer on them their due honour, nor rightly distribute to them what belongs to them, shall neither enjoy their presence, nor any successful effect from them. As in harmony, if one string be broken, the whole music jars, and sometimes incurs the hazard of punishment, as it is written of the Assyrians, whom *Salmanasar* planted in Samaria,[1] because they knew not the customs of the god of the land, the Lord did send lions amongst them, who slew them, because they were ignorant of the rights of the god of the land.

Now therefore let us see, what the old magicians and philosophers thought concerning God; for we read that *Nicocreonte,* a tyrant of Cyprus, long since asking, who was the greatest god, the Serapian oracle[2] answered him, that he was to be accounted the greatest god, whose head was the heavens, the seas his belly, the Earth his feet, his ears placed in the sky, his eyes the light of the glorious Sun. Not much unlike to this, *Orpheus* sang[3] in these verses:

> The heaven's Jove's royal palace, he's king,
> Fountain, virtue and God of everything;
> He is omnipotent, and in his breast
> Earth, water, fire and air do take their rest.
> Both night and day, true wisdom with
>   sweet love,
> Are all contained in this vast bulk of Jove.
> His neck and glorious head if you would see,
> Behold the heavens high, and majesty;
> The glorious rays of stars do represent
> His golden locks, and head's adornment.

And elsewhere:[4]

> Bright Phoebus and the Moon, are the two
>   eyes
> Of this great Jove by which all things he
>   spies;
> His head which predicts all, is placed in
>   the sky,
> From which no noise can whisper secretly.
> It pierceth all; his body vast extends,
> Both far and wide, and knows no bounds
>   nor ends.
> The spacious air's his breast, his wings the
>   wind,
> By which he flies far swifter than the mind.
> His belly is our mother Earth, who swells

457

Into huge mountains, whom the ocean fills
And circles; his feet are the rocks and stones
Which of this globe are the foundations.
This Jove, under the earth conceals all
      things,
And from the depth into the light them
      brings.

Therefore they thought the whole world to be *Jupiter*,[5] and truly he hath produced the Soul of this world, which containeth the world in itself. Hence *Sophocles* saith, in truth there is but one only God, who hath made this heaven and this spacious Earth; and *Euripides* saith, behold the Most High, who everywhere embraceth in his arms, the immensurable heaven and Earth; believe that he is *Jupiter*, account him God; and *Ennius* the poet sings:

Behold this bright sublime shining, whom all
Call Jove————

Therefore the whole world is *Jupiter*, as *Porphyry* saith, a creature made of all creatures, and a God constituted of all gods; but *Jupiter* is, so far as we can understand, from whence all things are produced, creating all things by his wisdom. Hence *Orpheus* sings concerning the holy Word:[6]

There is one God, who all things hath
      created,
Preserves, and over all is elevated.
He only by our mind is comprehended,
And to poor mortals he ne'er ill intended.
Besides whom, there no other is————

And a little after:[7]

      He himself is the beginning, middle and end,

As the ancient prophets have taught us, to whom God long since delivered these things in two tables; and he calleth him in the same verse the only great Creator, and immortal.

Zoroastes likewise in his Sacred History[8] of the Persians defineth God thus, God is the first of all those things which suffer neither decay nor corruption, unbegot, never dying, without parts, and most like himself, the author and promoter of all good things, the father of all, most bountiful and wise, the sacred light of justice, the absolute perfection of nature, the contriver, and wisdom thereof.[9]

Apuleius also describes him to be a king, the cause, foundation and original beginning of all nature, the supreme begetter of spirits, eternal, the preserver of living creatures, a father with propagation, not to be comprehended by time, place or any other circumstance, and therefore imaginable to a few, utterable to none.

From hence therefore *Euripedes* commanded the highest God to be called *Jupiter*, through whose head *Orpheus* sang all things came into this light, but the other powers he supposeth to be subservient, viz. which are without God, and separated from him, and are by the philosophers called the ministers or angels of God, and separated intelligences; therefore they say religious worship to be due to this most high *Jupiter* and to him only, but to the other divine powers not to be due unless for his sake.

Notes—Chapter VII

1. *in Samaria*—Shalmaneser. See II Kings 17:24–5.

2. *Serapian oracle*—The main seat of worship of the god Serapis (Osiris-Apis) was Alexandria in Egypt, where the original statue of the god had been brought by Ptolemy Soter and housed in the first Serapeum (place where Serapis was worshipped). In Graeco-Roman times the places of worship of Osiris (i.e. Serapis) were 42, one for each of the nomes of Egypt, and the cult of the god had spread throughout the ancient world. The god was ministered to by a priesthood of ascetic Egypt-

ian holy men who probably followed the regimen of the Pythagorean brotherhood—celibacy, vegetarianism, communal property. Serapis first spoke to Ptolemy in a dream, and Cicero mentions a dream oracle of Serapis: "Can Esculapius, or Serapis, by a dream, best proscribe to us the way to obtain a cure for weak health?" *(De divinatione* 2.59 [Yonge, 252]).

3. *Orpheus sang*—This hymn is given by Thomas Taylor in the introductory Dissertation, sec. 2, of his *Hymns of Orpheus.*

4. *And elsewhere*—See note 3 above. This quote is from the same hymn.

5. *world to be Jupiter*—Proclus in his *Commentary on Plato's Parmenides* 3.22 writes:

> Orpheus says that after swallowing Phanes, all things were generated in Zeus; for all things were manifested primally and unitedly in the former, but secondarily and partibly in the Demiurgus, the cause of the Mundane Order. For in him are the sun and the moon, and the heaven itself and the elements, and "All-pleasing Love," and all things being simply one, "were massed in the belly of Zeus."

And in the *Commentary on Plato's Cratylus*, he comments:

> Orpheus hands down the tradition that he [Zeus] created the whole of the celestial creation, and made the sun and moon and all the starry gods, and created the elements below the moon. (quoted by Mead [1896] 1965, 133–4)

6. *the holy Word*—

> He is the One, self-proceeding; and from
>   him all things proceed,
> And in them he himself exerts his activity;
>   no mortal
> Beholds Him, but he beholds all.
>   (Taylor 1875, 166)

7. *a little after*—

> Zeus, the mighty thunderer, is first; Zeus is
>   last;
> Zeus is the head, Zeus the middle of all
>   things;
> From Zeus were all things produced. (ibid.)

8. *Sacred History*—The sacred books of Zoroaster are collected in the *Zend-Avesta,* or more properly *Avesta, Zend* (interpretation) being the accompanying translation and commentary. The history of these books is very long and interesting. Pausanius mentions them in describing a Persian priest of Lydia:

> A magician comes into the building and piles up some dry wood on the altar: and

first he puts a crown on his head and then he chants the cult-title of some god in barbarous words quite incomprehensible to any Greek, reading what he chants out of a scroll, and it is absolutely certain the wood will take fire and strong, clear flame will break out. *(Guide to Greece* 5.27.6 [Levi, 2:280])

The 10th century Arabian historian Masudi describes the books:

> Zartusht gave to the Persians the book called Avesta. It consisted of twenty-one parts, each containing 200 leaves. This book, in the writing which Zartusht invented and which the Magi called the writing of religion, was written on 12,000 cowhides, bound together by golden bands. Its language was the Old Persian, which now no one understands. *(Encyclopædia Britannica,* 11th ed., 28:968)

The *Arda-Viraf-Nama* blamed Alexander the Great for burning these hides at Persepolis.

9. *wisdom thereof*—

> But God is He having the head of the Hawk. The same is the first, incorruptible, eternal, unbegotten, indivisible, dissimilar: the dispenser of all good; indestructible; the best of the good, the Wisest of the wise; He is the Father of Equity and Justice, self-taught, physical, perfect, and wise—He who inspires the Sacred Philosophy. (Eusebius *Praeparatio evangelica* 1.10. In Westcott [1895] 1983, 33)

Of this oracle Westcott comments:

> This Oracle does not appear in either of the ancient collections, nor in the group of oracles given by any of the medieval occultists. Cory [Isaac Preston Cory, *Ancient Fragments,* London, 1828] seems to have been the first to discover it in the voluminous writings of Eusebius, who attributes the authorship to the Persian Zoroaster. (ibid.)

I cannot help thinking that this must be very close to what was chanted by the Persian priest mentioned in note 8 above.

CHAPTER VIII

What the ancient philosophers have thought concerning the divine Trinity.

*A*ustine and *Porphyry* testify, that the Platonists held three persons in God,[1] the first of which, they call the Father of the world; the second they call the Son and the First Mind, (and so he is named by *Macrobius*); the third, the Spirit or Soul of the World, which *Virgil* also from *Plato's* opinion calleth a spirit, when he sings:[2]

Within the spirit nourisheth, the mind
Diffused through the whole doth in its kind
The lump both act, and agitate————

Plotinus[3] and *Philo* deliver, that the Son of God, viz. the First Mind or divine intellect floweth from God the Father, even as a word from the speaker, or as light from light;[4] from hence it is that he is called both the Word and Speech, and splendour of God the Father; for the divine mind by itself, with one only and uninterrupted act understandeth the chiefest good without any vicissitude, or mediate knowledge; he generateth in himself an issue and Son, who is the full intelligence, complete image of himself, and the perfect pattern of the world, whom our *John*[5] and *Mercurius*[6] name the Word or Speech; *Plato*,[7] the Son of God the Father; *Orpheus*,[8] *Pallas* born from *Jupiter's* brain, that is, Wisdom.

This is the most absolute image of God the Father, yet by a certain relation, or some intrinsical absolute thing, as it were begot and distinguished from the Father, who saith in Ecclesiasticus,[9] I have proceeded from the mouth of the Most High, I am the first begot before all creatures: *Jamblichus* testifieth this Son to be one and the same God with the Father in essence, namely calling God, both the Father and Son of himself.

Also *Mercurius Trismegistus* in Asclepius mentioneth the Son of God in divers places; for he saith my God and Father begat a Mind, a work divers from himself; and elsewhere, Unity begets Unity, and reflecteth his flagrant love on himself;[10] and in Pimander (where he seemeth to prophesy of the covenant of grace to come, and of the mystery of regeneration) saith, the author of regeneration is the Son of God,[11] the man by the will of the one only God, and also that God is most replenished with the fruitfulness of both sexes.[12]

In like manner the Indian philosophers affirm, the world to be an animal,[13] partly masculine, and partly feminine; and *Orpheus* also calleth nature or the *Jove* of this world, both the male and female[14] thereof, and that the gods partake of both sexes. Hence it is, that in his Hymns he thus salutes *Minerva,* you are indeed both man and woman;[15] and *Apuleius* in his Book of the World,[16] out of the divinity of *Orpheus* produceth this verse of *Jupiter:*

Jove is both male and female, immortal.

And *Virgil* speaking of *Venus* saith:

I descend, and the God guiding————

460

And elsewhere, understanding *Juno* or *Alecto,* he saith:

> Neither was God absent from her praying.

And *Tibullus* sings:[17]

> I who prophaned have the deities
> Of Venus great———————

And it is reported that the people of Cacenia[18] wonderfully adored the god Moon.

From this complete intelligence of supreme fecundity his love is produced, binding the intelligence with the mind. And by so much the more, by how much it is infinitely more intimate to itself, than other offsprings to their parents. This is the third person, viz. the Holy Spirit. *Jamblichus* also brings the oracles of the Chaldeans placing a fatherly power in God,[19] and an emanation of the intellect from the Father, and a fiery love proceeding from Father and Son, and the same to be God.

Hence we read in *Plutarch,* that the gentiles described God to be an intellectual and fiery spirit, having no form, but transforming himself into whatsoever he pleaseth, equalizing himself to all things; and we read in Deuteronomy,[20] our God is a consuming fire; of whom also *Zoroastes* saith, all things were begot of fire alone;[21] so also *Heraclitus* the Ephesian teacheth; hence divine *Plato* hath placed God's habitation in fire,[22] namely understanding, the unspeakable splendour of God in himself, and love about himself.

And we read in *Homer,*[23] the heavens to be the kingdom of *Jupiter,* when he sings:

> Jove darkening clouds and reigning in the
> sky,

And the same elsewhere:[24]

> The lot of Jove the heaven is in the air,
> He sits———————

But aether is derived according to the Greek grammer from *aetho,* which signifies to burn, and *aer spiritus quasi aethaer,* that is, a burning spirit.

And therefore *Orpheus* calleth the heaven *Pyripnon,* that is a fiery breathing place; therefore the Father, Son, and the aimable Spirit, which is also fiery, are by the divines called three persons; whom *Orpheus* also in his adurations invocateth with these words, heaven I admire thee, thou wise work of the great God; I adjure thee, O thou Word of the Father, which he first spake when he established the whole world by his wisdom.[25]

Hesiod[26] also confesseth the same things under the names of *Jupiter, Minerva* and *Bule* in his Theogony, declaring the twofold birth of *Jupiter* in these words: the first Daughter called *Tritonia* with grey eyes, having equal power with the Father, and prudent *Bule,*[27] that is Counsel, which *Orpheus* in the forenamed verses pronounceth plurally, because of his twofold emanation, for he proceedeth both from *Jupiter* and *Minerva.*

And *Austin* himself in his fourth book[28] De Civit Dei doth testify that *Porphyry* the Platonist placed three persons in God; the first he calls the Father of the universe, the second, the First Mind (and *Macrobius* the Son), the third the Soul of the World, which *Virgil*[29] according to *Plato's* opinion, calleth a spirit, saying:

> The spirit within maintains———————

Therefore it is God, as *Paul* saith,[30] from whom, in whom, by whom are all things: for from the Father as from a fountain flow all things;[31] but in the Son as in a pool all things are placed in their Ideas; and by the Holy Ghost are all things manifested, and everything distributed to his proper degrees.

Notes—Chapter VIII

1. *three persons in God—*

> For we have said that there are three principles consequent to each other: viz., *father, power* and *paternal intellect. But these in reality are neither one nor three nor one and at the same time three.* But it is necessary that we should explain these by names and conceptions of this kind, through our penury in what is adapted to their nature, or rather through our desire of expressing something proper on the occasion. For as we denominate this triad *one,* and *many,* and *all,* and *father, power,* and *paternal intellect,* and again *bound, infinite* and *mixed* [after Plato]—so likewise we call it a *monad,* and the *indefinite duad,* and a *triad* [after Pythagoras], and a paternal nature composed from both of these. (Damascius, as quoted by Mead [1896] 1965, 67)

For an exhaustive treatment of the threefold divisions of deity, see this text, particularly ch. 5.

2. *when he sings—*"First the sky, and earth, and watery plains, and the sun's bright sphere, and Titan's star, a Spirit feeds within; and a Mind, instilled throughout the limbs, gives energy to the whole mass, and mingles with the mighty body" (Virgil *Aeneid* 6, c. line 724 [Lonsdale and Lee, 174]).

3. *Plotinus—*

> Given this immobility in the Supreme, it can neither have yielded assent nor uttered decree nor stirred in any way towards the existence of a secondary. What happened then? What are we to conceive as rising in the neighbourhood of that immobility? It must be a circumradiation—produced from the Supreme but from the Supreme unaltering—and may be compared to the brilliant light encircling the sun and ceaselessly generated from the unchanging substance. (Plotinus *Enneads* 5.1.6, trans. Stephen Mackenna [London and Boston: The Medici Society, 1926], 4:8])

> The author of the causing principle, of the divine mind, is to him [Plato] the Good, that which transcends the Intellectual-Principle and transcends Being: often too he uses the term "The Idea" to indicate Being and the Divine Mind. Thus Plato knows the order of generation—from the Good, the Intellectual-Principle; from the Intellectual-Principle, the Soul. (ibid. 5.1.8 [Mackenna, 4:12])

4. *light from light—*On this subject may be quoted the oracle extracted from Proclus: "When the Monad is extended, the Dyad is generated" *(Chaldean Oracles of Zoroaster* 26 [Westcott, 38]).

5. *John—*John 5:7.

6. *Mercurius—*"For I deem it impossible that he who is the maker of the universe in all its greatness, the Father or Master of all things, can be named by a single name, though it be made up of ever so many others; I hold that he is nameless, or rather, that all names are names of him" *(Asclepius* 3.20a [Scott, 1:333]).

7. *Plato—*Perhaps this refers to a reference in one of the letters: "... the god who is ruler of all things present and to come, and is rightful father of the ruling active principle ..." (Plato, Letter 6.323d [Hamilton and Cairns, 1604).

8. *Orpheus—*

> From thy great father's fount supremely bright,
> Like fire resounding, leaping into light.
> ("Hymn to Minerva." In Taylor 1875, 155)

About Pallas Athene, Proclus says: "Orpheus says that Zeus brought her forth from his head—'shining forth in full panoply, a brazen flower to see'" *(Commentary on the Timaeus* 1.51. In Mead [1896] 1965, 143).

9. *Ecclesiasticus—*The Apocryphal Ecclesiasticus 24:3, 9.

10. *love on himself—*I cannot find exact correspondences to these references in Scott's *Asclepius.* However, on this same subject is written:

> When the Master, the Maker of all things, whom by usage we name God, had made him who is second [Cosmos], a god visible and sensible;—and I call him "sensible," not because he perceives things by sense, ... but because he can be perceived by sense and sight;—when, I say, God had made this being, his first and one and only creation, and when he saw that the being he had made was beautiful, and wholly filled with all things good, he rejoiced in him, and loved him dearly, as being his own offspring. *(Asclepius* 1.8 [Scott, 1:299, 301])

11. *Son of God—*

> *Tat:* Tell me this too; who is the ministrant by whom the consummation of the

Rebirth is brought to pass?

Hermes: Some man who is a son of God, working in subordination to God's will.

Tat: And what manner of man is he that is brought into being by the Rebirth?

Hermes: He that is born by that birth is another; he is a god, and son of God. He is the All, and is in all; for he has no part in corporeal substance; he partakes of the substance of things intelligible, being wholly composed of Powers of God. *(Corpus Hermeticum* 13.2 [Scott, 1:239, 241])

12. *fruitfulness of both sexes*—Agrippa seems to refer to a passage in the *Asclepius:* "He, filled with all the fecundity of both sexes in one, and ever teeming with his own goodness, unceasingly brings into being all that he has willed to generate; and all that he wills is good" *(Asclepius* 3.20b [Scott, 1:333].

13. *an animal*—Plato also describes the world as an animal:

But let us suppose the world to be the very image of that whole of which all other animals both individually and in their tribes are portions. For the original of the universe contains in itself all intelligible beings, just as this world comprehends us and all other visible creatures. For the deity, intending to make this world like the fairest and most perfect of intelligible beings, framed one visible animal comprehending within itself all other animals of a kindred nature. *(Timaeus* 30c–d [Hamilton and Cairns, 1163]).

Since the world is solitary, yet gives rise to all living things by generation, it follows that it must be bisexual.

14. *male and female*—"For Zeus were all things produced. He is male and female ..." (Orphic hymn in appendix to Taylor 1875, 166).

15. *man and woman*—

Shield-bearing goddess, hear, to whom belong
A manly mind, and power to tame the strong!
(Orphic hymn to Minerva in Taylor 1875, 155)

16. *Book of the World*—*De mundo liber,* a translation of the Greek work Περὶ κόσμου, which at one time was wrongly ascribed to Aristotle.

17. *Tibullus sings*—"Have I outraged the divinity of great Venus by any words of mine, and do I now suf-

fer the penalty due to my impious tongue? Am I charged with having assailed the abodes of the gods, and torn the garlands from their sacred shrines?" (Tibullus *Elegies* 1.5. trans. Walter K. Kelly [London: George Bell and Sons, 1884], 119).

18. *Cacenia*—In the Latin *Opera* this is spelled Carenus. I do not know which city is intended, but might guess either Carana in Armenia Magna (Erzurum, Turkey), or Karanis in Egypt, which lay just northeast of Lake Moeris; probably the latter.

19. *fatherly power in God*—God is frequently referred to in the *Chaldean Oracles of Zoroaster* as Father, Intellect, and Fire, but there is no explicit mention of the son of God. Some of the titles given to God in translation in the *Oracles* are: "Mind of the Father" (Westcott, 40), "Paternal Intellect" (41), "Paternal Principle" (35), "Father of Gods and Men" (37), "Paternal Fountain" (40), "brilliant Fire" (37) and "a heat animating all things" (36). The fire of God, otherwise known as the "Father begotten Light" (44) is linked to the fire of soul: "Who first sprang from Mind, clothing the one Fire with the other Fire, binding them together, that he might mingle the fountainous craters while preserving unsullied the brilliance of His own Fire" (Westcott, 37).

20. *Deuteronomy*—Actually Hebrews 12:29. Agrippa may be confusing this verse with Deuteronomy 32:22.

21. *of fire alone*—"All things have issued from that one Fire" (An oracle recorded by Psellus. In *Chaldean Oracles of Zoroaster* [Westcott, 36]).

22. *habitation in fire*—"Of the heavenly and divine [gods], he created the greater part out of fire, that they might be the brightest of all things and fairest to behold ..." (Plato *Timaeus* 40a [Hamilton and Cairns, 1169])

23. *in Homer*—From the prayer of Agamemnon: "Zeus, exalted and mightiest, sky-dwelling in the dark mist ..." *(Iliad* 2, line 412 [Lattimore, 87]).

24. *elsewhere*—Perhaps "Zeus son of Kronos who sits on high, the sky-dwelling ..." (Homer *Iliad* 4, line 166 [Lattimore, 117]).

25. *his wisdom*—This does not seem to refer to the Orphic hymn "To Heaven."

26. *Hesiod*—"First a girl, Tritogeneia, the grey-eyed,/ Equal in spirit and intelligence/ To Zeus her father ..." *(Theogony* c. line 896 [Wender, 52])

27. *prudent Bule*—Athene was called *Boulaia* (counselor-goddess). The Greek Βουλαîος means "of or in the council."

28. *fourth book*—Actually the tenth book:

> For he [Porphyry] speaks of God the Father and God the Son, called in Greek the Father's intellect: but of the Spirit not a word, at least not a plain one, though what he means by a mean between the two I cannot tell. For if he follow Plotinus in his discourse of the three prime essences [Ennead 5, Tractate 1], and would have this third the soul's nature, he should not have put it as the mean between the Father and the Son. For Plotinus puts it after the Father's intellect; but Porphyry, in calling it the mean, interposes it between them. (Augustine *City of God* 10.23 [Healey, 1:296])

29. *which Virgil*—See note 2 above.

30. *Paul saith*—Romans 11:36.

31. *fountain flow all things*—The metaphor of the fountain occurs a number of times in the *Chaldean Oracles:* "The Mind of the Father whirled forth in re-echoing roar, comprehending by invincible Will Ideas omniform; which flying forth from that one fountain issued; for the Father alike was the Will and the End" *(Chaldean Oracles of Zoroaster* 39 [Westcott, 40]).

CHAPTER IX

What the true and most orthodox faith is concerning God and the most holy Trinity.

The Catholic doctors and faithful people of God have decreed, that we ought thus to believe and profess that there is one only true God, increate,[1] infinite, omnipotent, eternal, Father, Son and Holy Ghost, three persons, coeternal and coequal, of one most simple essence, substance and nature. This is the Catholic faith, this is the orthodox religion, this is the Christian truth, that we worship one God in trinity, and trinity in unity, neither confounding the persons, nor dividing the substance.[2]

The Father begat the Son from all eternity and gave him his substance, and nevertheless retained it himself. The Son also by being begot, received the substance of the Father, but assumed not the proper person of the Father; for the Father translated it not into the Son; for they are both of one and the same substance, but of divers persons. This Son also although he be coeternal with the Father, and begot of the substance of the Father before the world, yet notwithstanding was born into the world out of the substance of a virgin, and his name was called *Jesus,* perfect God, perfect man, of a reasonable soul and human flesh, who in all things was man, sin excepted.

Therefore it is necessary, that we believe, that our Lord *Jesus* Christ the Son of God, is God and man, one person, two natures; God begot before the world without a mother, man born into the world without a father, from a pure virgin, both before and after his birth; he suffered on the cross, and died, but on the cross restored life, and destroyed death by his death; he was buried and descended into hell, but brought forth the souls of the Fathers from hell, and rose again by his own power; the third day he ascended into the heavens, and sent his spirit the comforter, and shall come to judge the quick and the dead; and at his coming all men shall rise again in their flesh, and shall give an account of their works.

This is the true faith, concerning which if any man doubt, and not firmly believe, he is far from the hope of eternal life and salvation.[3]

Notes—Chapter IX

1. *increate*—Uncreated.

2. *nor dividing the substance*—

The philosophers speak freely, never fearing to offend religious ears in those incomprehensible mysteries; but we must regulate our words, that we produce no impious error by our freedom of speech concerning these matters. Wherefore when we speak of God, we neither talk of two principles, nor three, any more than we say there are two Gods or three, though when we speak of the Father, the Son, or the Holy Ghost, we say

465

that each of these is God. Nor say we with the Sabellian heretics, that He that is the Father is the Son, and He that is the Holy Ghost is the Father and the Son, but the Father is the Son's Father, and the Son the Father's Son, and the Holy Spirit both the Father's and the Son's, but neither Father nor Son. (Augustine *City of God* 10.23 [Healey, 1:296])

3. *life and salvation*—One detects in this very dry recitation of the points of orthodoxy a veiled irony in Agrippa. It was necessary for him to make such a statement of faith in order to insure the survival of his book. In the social climate of his day, men were afraid not only to write, but even to think freely.

CHAPTER X

Of divine emanations, which the Hebrews call numerations, others attributes; the gentiles gods and deities; and of the ten Sephiroth and ten most sacred names of God which rule them, and the interpretation of them.

God himself, though he be Trinity in persons, yet is but one only simple essence; notwithstanding we doubt not but that there are in him many divine powers, which as beams flow from him,[1] which the philosophers of the gentiles call gods, the Hebrew masters numerations, we name attributes.

As wisdom which *Orpheus* calls *Pallas;* understanding, which he *Mercury;* the conception of the form, which he *Saturn;* the productive power, which he *Neptune;* the secret nature of things, which he *Juno;* love, which he *Venus;* pure life, which he the Sun, or *Apollo.* The matter of the whole world, he calleth *Pan;* the Soul, as it engendereth things below, contemplateth things above, and retracteth itself into itself, he honoured with three names, viz. *Maris, Neptune* and *Ocean,* and more of this kind, of which he sings elsewhere:

Pluto and Jupiter, and Phoebus, are one:
But why do we speak twice? God's one
alone.

And of the same *Valerius Soranus* sang:

Omnipotent Jove, the god and king of kings,
The father of the gods, one, yet all things.

Therefore the most prudent theologians of the gentiles did worship the one God, under divers names and powers, yea divers sexes; whom, as *Pliny* saith,[2] frail and weak mortality

hath digested unto more, being mindful of his one frailty, that every man might worship that portion which he especially wanteth; so those who had need of faith invocated *Jupiter;* they that wanted providence, *Apollo;* wisdom, *Minerva;* and so as they wanted other things, they invocated other powers. Hence arose that great variety of deities, by reason of the many and divers distribution of graces; but God is one, from whom all things.

Therefore *Apuleius* in his book De Mundo,[3] to *Faustin* saith, whereas there is but one God and one power, yet he is named by divers names, for the multitude of species, by whose variety he is made of many shapes; and *Marcus Varro* in his book Of the Worship of God, saith, as all souls are reduced to the one Soul of the World, or Universe, so are all the gods referred to *Jupiter,* who is the same God, worshipped under divers names.[4]

Therefore it is meet to know the sensible proprieties, and perfectly to intellectualize them by the way of more secret analogy; whosoever understandeth truly the Hymns of *Orpheus* and the old magicians, shall find that they differ not from the Cabalistical secrets and orthodox traditions; for whom *Orpheus* calls Curetes[5] and unpolluted gods, *Dionysius*[6] names Powers; the Cabalists appropriate them to the numeration Pahad,[7] that is to the divine fear: so that which is En Soph[8] in the Cabala, *Orpheus* calleth Night;[9] and *Typhon*[10] is the same with *Orpheus,* as *Zamael*[11] in the Cabala.[12]

But the mecubals of the Hebrews, the most learned in divine things, have received the ten principal names of God, as certain divine powers, or as it were members of God, which by ten numerations which they call Sephiroth,[13] as it were vestiments, instruments or examplars of the Archetype, have an influence on all things created, through the high things, even to the lowest, yet by a certain order; for first and immediately they have influence on the nine orders of angels, and quire of Blessed Souls, and by them into the celestial spheres, planets and men, by the which Sephiroth everything then receiveth power and virtue.

The first of these is the name *Eheia,*[14] the name of the divine essence; his numeration is called Cether,[15] which is interpreted a Crown or Diadem, and signifieth the most simple essence of the Divinity, and it is called That Which the Eye Seeth Not, and is attributed to God the Father, and hath his influence by the order of Seraphinus,[16] or as the Hebrews call them *Haioth Hacadosch,*[17] that is Creatures of Holiness, and then by the primum mobile, bestows the gift of being to all things, filling the whole universe both through the circumference and center, whose particular intelligence is called *Metattron,*[18] that is, the Prince of Faces, whose duty it is to bring others to the face of the Prince; and by him the Lord spake to *Moses.*[19]

The second name is *Iod* or *Tetragrammaton* joined with *Iod;*[20] his numeration is Hochma,[21] that is Wisdom, and signifies the Divinity full of Ideas, and the first begotten, and is attributed to the Son, and hath his influence by the order of Cherubins,[22] or that the Hebrews call *Orphanim,*[23] that is, Forms or Wheels; and from thence into the starry heaven,[24] where he fabricateth so many figures as he hath Ideas in himself, and distinguisheth the very chaos of the creatures, by a particular intelligence called *Raziel,*[25] who was the ruler of *Adam.*[26]

The third name is called *Tetragrammaton Elohim;* his numeration is named Prina,[27] viz. Providence and Understanding, and signifies remission, quietness, the Jubilee,[28] penitential conversion, a great trumpet, redemption of the world, and the life of the world to come; it is attributed to the Holy Spirit,[29] and hath his influence by the order of the Thrones, or which the Hebrews call *Aralim,* that is Great Angels Mighty and Strong, and from thence by the sphere of Saturn administereth form to the unsettled matter, whose particular intelligence is *Zaphchiel,*[30] the ruler of *Noah,*[31] and another intelligence named *Iophiel,*[32] the ruler of *Sem.*[33]

And these are three supreme and highest numerations, as it were seats of the divine persons, by whose commands all things are made, but are executed by the other seven, which are therefore called the numerations framing.

Therefore the fourth name is *El* whose numeration is Hesed,[34] which is Clemency or Goodness, and signifieth grace, mercy, piety, magnificence, the scepter and the right hand, and hath his influx by the order of the Dominations,[35] which the Hebrews call *Hasmalim,*[36] and so through the sphere of Jupiter fashioning the images of bodies, bestowing clemency and pacifying justice on all; his particular intelligence is *Zadkiel*[37] the ruler of *Abraham.*[38]

The fifth name is *Elohim Gibor,* that is the Mighty God, punishing the sins of the wicked; and his numeration is called Geburach,[39] which is to say, Power, Gravity, Fortitude, Security, Judgement, punishing by slaughter and war; and it is applied to the tribunal of God, the girdle, the sword and left hand of God; it is also called Pachad, which is Fear,[40] and hath his influence through the order of Powers, which the Hebrews call *Seraphim,*[41] and from thence through the sphere of Mars, to whom belongs fortitude, war, affliction, it draweth forth the elements; and his particular intelligence is *Camael,*[42] the ruler of *Samson.*

The sixth name is *Eloha,*[43] or a name of four letters, joined with *Vaudahat;*[44] his numeration is Tiphereth, that is Apparel, Beauty, Glory, Pleasure, and signifieth the Tree of Life,[45] and hath his influence through the order of Virtues, which the Hebrews call *Malachim,*[46] that is Angels, into the sphere of the Sun, giving brightness and life to it, and from thence producing metals; his particular intelligence is *Raphael,* who was the ruler of *Isaac* and *Toby* the younger,[47] and the angel *Peliel,* ruler of *Jacob.*

The seventh name is *Tetragrammaton Sabaoth*,[48] or *Adonai Sabaoth*, that is the God of Hosts; and his numeration is Nezah,[49] that is Triumph and Victory; the right column[50] is applied to it, and it signifies the eternity and justice of a revenging God; it hath his influence through the order of Principalities, whom the Hebrews call *Elohim*, that is Gods, into the sphere of Venus, gives zeal and love of righteousness, and produceth vegetables; his intelligence is *Haniel* and the angel *Cerviel*, the ruler of *David*.

The eighth is called also *Elohim Sabaoth*,[51] which is also interpreted the God of Hosts, not of war and justice, but of piety and agreement; for this name signifieth both, and precedeth his army; the numeration of this is called Hod, which is interpreted both Praise, Confession, Honour and Famousness; the left column is attributed to it; it hath his influence through the order of the Archangels, which the Hebrews call *Ben Elohim*,[52] that is the Sons of God, into the sphere of Mercury, and gives elegancy and consonancy of speech and produceth living creatures; his intelligence is *Michael*, who was the ruler of *Solomon*.

The ninth name is called *Sadai*,[53] that is Omnipotent, satisfying all, and *Elhai*,[54] which is the Living God; his numeration is Iesod,[55] that is Foundation, and signifieth a good understanding, a covenant, redemption and rest, and hath his influence through the order of Angels, whom the Hebrews name *Cherubim*, into the sphere of the Moon, causing the increase and decrease of all things, and taketh care of the genii,[56] the keepers of men, and distributeth them; his intelligence is *Gabriel*, who was the keeper of *Joseph, Joshua* and *Daniel*.

The tenth name is *Adonai Melech*,[57] that is Lord and King; his numeration is Malchuth,[58] that is Kingdom and Empire, and signifieth a church, temple of God, and a gate, and hath his influence through the order of Animastic, viz. of Blessed Souls, which by the Hebrews is called *Issim*,[59] that is Nobles, Lords and Princes; they are inferior to the hierarchies, and have their influence on the sons of men, and give knowledge and the wonderful understanding of things, also industry and prophecy; and the soul of *Messiah*[60] is president amongst them, or (as others say) the intelligence *Metattron*,[61] which is called the First Creature, or the Soul of the World, and was the ruler of *Moses*.

Notes—Chapter X

1. *flow from him*—"And thence a Fiery Whirlwind drawing down the brilliance of the flashing flame, penetrating the abysses of the Universe; for from thence downwards do extend their wonderous rays" *(Chaldean Oracles of Zoroaster* 24 [Westcott, 38]).

2. *Pliny saith*—

> To believe that there are a number of Gods, derived from the virtues and vices of man, as Chastity, Concord, Understanding, Hope, Honour, Clemency, and Fidelity; or, according to the opinion of Democritus, that there are only two, Punishment and Reward, indicates still greater folly. Human nature, weak and frail as it is, mindful of its own infirmity, has made these divisions, so that every one might have recourse to that which he supposed himself to stand more particularly in need of. Hence we find different names employed by different nations; the inferior deities are arranged in classes, and dis-

eases and plagues are deified, in consequence of our anxious wish to propitiate them. (Pliny 2.5 [Bostock and Riley, 1:20–1])

3. *De Mundo*—See note 16, ch. VIII, bk. III.

4. *divers names*—

> Our author [Varro] has said that the true gods are but parts of the world's soul, and the soul itself: ... So Varro says plainly that God is the world's soul, and this soul is God. ... Therefore if Jove be a god, and the king of gods, they cannot make any but him to be the world, because he must reign over the rest, as over his own parts. To this purpose Varro in his book of the worship of the gods [*De cultu deorum*], which he published separate from these other [*Antiquitatium libri*], set down a distich of Valerius Soranus' making: it is this:

High Jove, kings' king, and parent
   general
To all the gods: God only, and God
   all.

These verses Varro expounds, and calling
the giver of seed the male, and the receiver
the female, accounts Jove the world, that
both gives all seed itself, and receives it
unto itself. And therefore Soranus (says he)
calls Jove *progenitor, genetrixque,* father
and mother, "full parent general, to all,"
etc., and by the same reason is it that he
was called one and all: for the world is one,
and all things are in that one. (Augustine
City of God 7.9 [Healey, 1:204],

I have omitted the original Latin of the verse by
Soranus.

5. *Curetes*—

Plato, following Orpheus, calls the inflexi-
ble and undefiled triad of the intellectual
Gods Curetic, as is evident from what the
Athenian guest says in the Laws, celebrating the armed sports of the Curetes, and
their rhythmical dance. For Orpheus represents the Curetes, who are three, as the
guards of Jupiter. (Proclus *Theology of
Plato* 5.3. In Mead [1896] 1965, 74)

6. *Dionysius*—Pseudo-Dionysius. The Powers are
the angels of the fifth sphere of Mars. See table, ch.
XII, bk. II.

7. *Pahad*—Pachad (פחד), or Fear, one of the names
of the fifth Sephirah, or Emanation, from the godhead. See Appendix VI.

8. *En Soph*—Ain Soph (אין סוף), the Limitless. See
Appendix VI.

9. *Night*—

Night, parent goddess, source of sweet
   repose,
From whom at first both Gods and men
   arose,
(*Hymns of Orpheus* 2 [Taylor, *Selected
Writings,* 213])

10. *Typhon*—A flaming monster with a hundred heads
who rose up from his mother the Earth to challenge the
gods. Zeus cast thunderbolts into his heart and turned
his strength to ashes, burying him under Mount Aetna,
where his rumblings are still occasionally heard.

11. *Zamael*—The dark angel Samael, the serpent of
Genesis, who according to ancient Jewish legend

engendered a child by Eve before she lay with Adam.
One version says this child was Cain. See Waite
[1929] 1975, 7:3:286 and n. 5, same page.

12. *in the Cabala*—

The names of the gods, of whom Orpheus
sings, are not the titles of deceiving demons
but the designations of divine virtues. Just as
the Psalms of David are admirably designed
for the "work" of the Kabalah, so are the
Hymns of Orpheus for natural magic. The
number of the Hymns of Orpheus is the
same as the number by which the three-fold
deity created the aeon, numerated under the
form of the Pythagorean quarternary. He
who does not know perfectly how to intellectualize sensible properties by the method
of occult analogy, will never arrive at the
real meaning of the Hymns of Orpheus. The
Curetes of Orpheus are the same as the powers of Dionysius. The Orphic Typhon is the
same as the Zamael of the Kabalah. The
Night of Orpheus is the En Suph of the
Kabalah ... (Pico della Mirandola. In Mead
[1896] 1965, 36)

Waite calls Mirandola "the first true Christian student
of the Kabbalah" (Waite [1929] 1975, 443).

13. *Sephiroth*—See note 18, ch. XIII, bk. II.

14. *Eheia*—Eheieh (אהיה).

15. *Cether*—Kether (כתר).

16. *Seraphinus*—Seraphim, the highest Christian
order of angels given by pseudo-Dionysius. See Isaiah 6:1–7.

17. *Haioth Hacadosch*—Chaioth ha-Qadesh
(חיות הקדש), Holy Living Creatures.

18. *Metattron*—Metatron (מטטרון), the highest
angel, also called the Angel of the Presence and the
World Prince, who according to the *Zohar* guarded
the temple of Solomon and was the flaming sword
that barred the gates of Eden. It is Metatron who will
take charge of souls at the Resurrection.

19. *spoke to Moses*—This refers to Exodus 23:20–3,
about which verses Rashi remarks: "And our Rabbis
have said: 'This (angel) is Mattatron whose name is
like the name of his Master,' (i.e.,) Mattatron has the
numerical value of the Almighty (314)" (Rashi 1949,
2:278). Rashi refers to the numerical equivalency of
the sums of the letters in the name of the angel Metatron (מטטרון = 50 + 6 + 200 + 9 + 9 + 40 = 314)
and the name of God Shaddai (שדי = 10 + 4 + 300 =

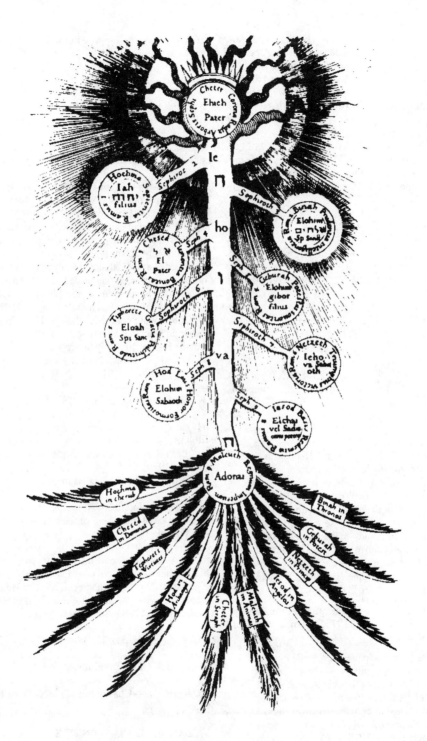

Inverted Tree of the Sephiroth

From *Tomi secundi tractatus secundus: de praenaturali utriusque mundi historia*
by Robert Fludd (Frankfurt, 1621)

314). In the *Siphra di zenioutha* (Book of conceal-ment), perhaps the oldest book of the *Zohar,* occurs this passage: "... the finger of God was the messen-ger (מטטרון) or guide to Moses, and showed him all the land of Israel" (In Ginsburg [1863], 1970, 109, n. 11). By tradition Metatron was the cloud that covered the Tabernacle.

20. *joined with Iod*—See the table at the end of ch. XIII. bk. II. Yod Jehovah (י יהוה) differs from the names, or combined name, usually associated with Chokmah in modern occultism, which is Jah or Yah (יה) or Jah Jehovah (יה יהוה).

21. *Hochma*—Chokmah (חכמה).

22. *Cherubins*—Cherubim. See table, ch. XII, bk. II.

23. *Orphanim*—Auphanim (אופנים), or Wheels.

24. *starry heaven*—The sphere of the zodiac, or eighth sphere. The zodiac is a great wheel.

25. *Raziel*—רזיאל, sometimes given as Ratziel.

26. *ruler of Adam*—See Genesis 5:1. Speaking of this biblical verse on the Book of the Generations of Adam, Waite says:

> It is supposed by the ZOHAR to signify that there was a Secret and Supreme Book, the source of all, including the Hebrew let-ters—presumably in that form under which they are manifested below. It expounded the Holy Mystery of Wisdom and the effi-ciency resident in the Divine Name of sev-enty-two letters. It was sent down from heaven by the hands of the angel Raziel and Adam was entrusted therewith. Raziel is said to be the angel of the secret regions and chief of Supreme Mysteries. (Waite [1929] 1975, 1:1:16)

The *Sepher Raziel* is a medieval grimoire falsely (according to Waite [1929] 1975, 519, n. 2) ascribed to Eleazer of Worms.

> With its long catalogues of angelic names, its talismans and philtres, its double seal of Solomon, its mystical or occult alphabetical symbols, its figures for the government of evil spirits, and its conjurations by means of Divine Names, this work constitutes one of the storehouses of Medieval Magic, besides being broadly representative of the Practi-cal Kabbalah at large. (ibid.)

Waite also refers to "a legend of an old MIDRASH called the BOOK OF RAZIEL ..." (Waite [1929] 1975,

16, n. 5) that was supposed to have been the precur-sor to the *Sepher Raziel.*

27. *Prina*—Binah (בינה).

28. *Jubilee*—"And IVBL, *Yobel,* 'jubilee,' is H, *He* (the first *He* of the Tetragrammaton); and *He* is the spirit rushing forth over all ..." (Mathers [1887] 1962, 1:5:42:107). Jubilee was a time of restitution, remis-sion and release. See Leviticus 25:9.

29. *Spirit*—The Shekinah, which Waite describes as "the principle of Divine Motherhood—that is, the fem-inine side of Divinity ..." (Waite [1929] 1975, 8:1:369). It is not clear from the texts of the Kabbalah whether the Shekinah can be completely identified with the Holy Spirit, is completely distinct, or should be regarded as the exhaler of Holy Spirit in the form of breath. However, in one place in the *Zohar* is written: "The Holy Spirit—this is the Shekinah with which Ester [Ester 5:1] clothed herself." (Waite [1929] 1975, 8:1:368). Waite concludes that the Holy Spirit of the *Zohar* and the Shekinah of the *Zohar* are the same, but that the Kabbalistic Holy Spirit is not identical with the Christian Holy Spirit, although there are many similar-ities. See Waite [1929] 1975, 362–9.

30. *Zaphchiel*—Tzaphkiel (צפקיאל).

31. *ruler of Noah*—In the *Zohar* the ark of Noah is Elohim. "It is said that Noah walked with Elohim ... But Elohim is the Celestial Bride, who is Shekinah" (Waite [1929] 1975, 7:4:292–3). Therefore the angel of Elohim and the Shekinah is the angel set over Noah.

32. *Iophiel*—Jophiel (יהפיאל), is said to be the intelligence of the sphere of the zodiac in the table to ch. XIII, bk. II.

33. *Sem*—Shem, one of the sons of Noah, who with his brother Japheth covered his father's nakedness (Genesis 9:23), which had been seen by Ham. In the Hebrew original of the bible the "God of Shem" is Elohim (אלהי שם). See Genesis 9:26.

34. *Hesed*—Chesed (חסד).

35. *Dominations*—Dominions.

36. *Hasmalim*—Chasmalim (חשמלים), or Brilliant Ones.

37. *Zadkiel*—Tzadkiel (צדקיאל).

38. *Abraham*—The patriarchs are variously assigned to the ten Sephiroth. Here is the arrangement given by Ginsburg, which does not agree with that of Agrippa:

When thus fulfilling the commandments the pious not only enjoy a prelibation of that sublime light which shines in heaven, and which will serve them as a garment when they enter into the other world and appear before the Holy Ones (Sohar, ii, 299b), but become on earth already the habitation of the Sephiroth, and each saint has that Sephira incarnate in him which corresponds to the virtue he most culti- vates, or to the feature most predominant in his character. Among the patriarchs, therefore, who were the most exalted in piety, we find that LOVE, the fourth Sephira, was incarnate in Abraham; RIGOUR, the fifth Sephira, in Isaac; MILDNESS, the sixth Sephira, in Jacob; FIRMNESS, the seventh Sephira, in Moses; SPLENDOUR, the eighth Sephira, in Aaron; FOUNDATION, the ninth Sephira, in Joseph; and KINGDOM, the tenth Sephira, was incarnate in David. (Ginsburg [1863] 1970, 1:122)

39. *Geburach*—Geburah (גבורה), or Severity.

40. *Fear*—See note 7 above. Another name for this Sephirah is Din (דין), or Justice.

41. *Seraphim*—Fiery Serpents.

42. *Camael*—Khamael (כמאל).

43. *Eloha*—Aloah (אלוה).

44. *Vaudahat*—va Daath (ודעת).

45. *Tree of Life*—Genesis 2:9 and 3:22. For the par- ticular Kabbalistic meaning of this term, see Appen- dix VI.

46. *Malachim*—Kings.

47. *Toby the younger*—See the Apocryphal book of Tobit 1:1.

48. *Tetragrammaton Sabaoth*—That is, IHVH Tzabaoth (יהוה צבאות).

49. *Nezah*—Netzach (נצח).

50. *right column*—The Kabbalistic Tree of Life is divided into three pillars: the Pillar of Mercy (right side), Pillar of Severity (left side), and the Middle Pillar of Mildness. See Appendix VI.

51. *Elohim Sabaoth*—Elohim Tzabaoth (אלהים צבאות).

52. *Ben Elohim*—Beni Elohim (בני אלהים).

53. *Sadai*—Shaddai (שדי), the Almighty.

54. *Elhai*—El Chai (אל חי), the Mighty Living One.

55. *Iesod*—Yesod (יסוד).

56. *genii*—Tutelary spirits presiding over the affairs of individuals or over localities or institutions. They were spirits of the lower air:

> I say that there are daemons who dwell with us here on earth, and others who dwell above us in the lower air, and others again whose abode is in the purest part of the air, where no mist or cloud can be, and where no disturbance is caused by the motion of any of the heavenly bodies. (*Asclepius* 3.33b [Scott, 1:369, 371])

The sphere of the Moon was the great divider between heavenly and earthly things: "... note how the Moon, as she goes her round, divides the immortals from the mortals" (*Corpus Hermeticum* 11(ii).7 [Scott, 213]). To the Moon was assigned governance of all lower spirits: "... in the air dwell souls, over whom rules the Moon ..." (*Stobaei Hermetica* 24.1 [Scott, 497].

57. *Adonai Melech*—Adonai Melekh (אדני מלך).

58. *Malchuth*—Malkuth (מלכות).

59. *Issim*—Ashim (אשים), the Souls of Fire.

60. *Messiah*—Literally "the anointed one," the sav- iour of the Jews, promised in the prophetic books. See Daniel 9:25 and Isaiah 9:6.

61. *Metattron*—It is interesting that Metatron is the angel of the first and the tenth Sephirah. In this con- text it might be worth noting that there are two Meta- trons—the highest heavenly angel created with, or even before, the creation of the world; and the angel that Enoch is transformed into after his ascent into heaven. The first rivals God in his glory, while the second is very much a servant, the scribe who records the deeds of men. There are also two ways of writing the name Metatron, with six (מטטרון) and with seven (מיטטרון) letters. The seven-letter form is the oldest, occurring almost always in the earliest manu- scripts. The seven-letter Metatron is the supreme emanation of the Shekinah, whereas the six-letter Metatron is the transformed Enoch. Often San- dalphon is given as the angel of Malkuth, but San- dalphon is more properly the angel who presides over the planet Earth, as opposed to Uriel, the angel of ele- mental Earth. See Knight [1965] 1980, 1:16:32:199.

CHAPTER XI

Of the divine names, and their power and virtue.

God himself though he be only one in essence, yet hath divers names, which expound not his divers essences or deities, but certain properties flowing from him, by which names he doth pour down, as it were by certain conduits, on us and all his creatures many benefits and divers gifts.

Ten of these names we have above described, which also *Hierom* reckoneth up to *Marcella.*[1] *Dionysius* reckoneth up forty-five names of God and Christ.[2] The mecubals of the Hebrews from a certain text of Exodus,[3] derive seventy-two names, both of the angels and of God,[4] which they call the name of seventy-two letters, and *Schemhamphores,*[5] that is, the Expository; but others proceeding further, out of all places of the Scripture do infer so many names of God as the number of those names is: but what they signify is altogether unknown to us.

From these therefore, besides those which we have reckoned up before, is the name of the divine essence, *Eheia*[6] אהיה, which *Plato* translates ὤν;[7] from hence they call God τὸ ὄν,[8] others ὁῶν,[9] that is the Being. *Hua*[10] הוא, is another name revealed to *Esay,*[11] signifying the abyss of the Godhead, which the Greeks translate ταυτὸν,[12] the Same, the Latins *Ipse,* Himself. *Esch*[13] אש, is another name received from *Moses,* which soundeth Fire, and the name of God *Na*[14] נא, is to be invocated in purturbations and troubles. There is also the name *Iah*[15] יה, and the name *Elion*[16] עליון, and the name *Macom*[17] מקום, the name *Caphu* כפו, the

name *Innon* ינון, and the name *Emeth*[18] אמת, which is interpreted Truth, and is the seal of God; and there are two other names, *Zur*[19] צור, and *Aben*[20] אבן, both of them signify a solid work, and one of them express the Father with the Son.

And many more names have we placed above in the scale of numbers; and many names of God and the angels are extracted out of the holy Scriptures by the Cabalistical calculation, Notarian and Gimetrian[21] arts, where many words retracted by certain of their letters make up one name, or one name dispersed by each of its letters signifieth or rendereth more.

Sometimes they are gathered from the heads of words, as the name *Agla*[22] אגלא, from this verse of the holy Scripture

אתה גביר לעולם אדני,

that is the mighty God forever; in like manner the name *Iaia* יאי, from this verse

יהוה אלהינו יהוה אחד,

that is God our God is one God; in like manner the name *Iava*[23] יאו, from this verse

יהי אור ויהי אור,

that is let there be light, and there was light; in like manner the name *Ararita*[24] אראריתא, from this verse

אחד ראש אחדותי ראש ייחודו
תמורתו אחד,

that is one principle of his unity, one beginning of his individuality, his vicissitude is one thing; and this name *Hacaba* הקבא, is extracted from this verse

הקדוש ברוך הוא,

474

the holy and the blessed one; in like manner this name *Jesu* יש״ו, is found in the heads of these two verses, viz.

יכיא של והולו,

that is, until the *Messiah* shall come, and the other verse

ינון שמי וית,

that is, his name abides till the end; thus also is the name *Amen* אמן, extracted from this verse

אדני מלך נאמן,

that is, the Lord the faithful King.

Sometimes these names are extracted from the end of words, as the same name *Amen*, from this verse

לא כן הרשעים,

that is, the wicked not so,[25] but the letters are transposed; so by the final letters of this verse

לי מה שמו מה,

that is, to me what? or what is his name? is found the name Tetragrammaton.

In all these a letter is put for a word, and a letter extracted from a word, either from the beginning, end, or where you please; and sometimes these names are extracted from all the letters, one by one, even as those seventy-two names of God are extracted from those three verses of Exodus[26] beginning from these three words ויט, ויבא, ויסע, the first and last verses being written from the right to the left, but the middle contrarywise from the left to the right, as we shall show hereafter.

And so sometimes a word is extracted from a word, or a name from a name, by the transposition of letters, as *Messia* משיה, from *Ismah* ישמה; and *Michael* מיכאל, from מלאכי, *Malachi*. But sometimes by changing of the alphabet, which the Cabalists call Ziruph[27] צירוף, so from the name Tetragrammaton יהוה, are drawn forth מצפצ, *Maz Paz,*[28] כוזו, *Kuzu;*[29] sometimes also by reason of the equality of numbers, names are changed, as *Metattron* מטטרון, for *Sadai* שדי, for both of them make three hundred and fourteen;[30] so *Iiai* ייא, and *El* אל, are equal in number, for both make thirty-one.[31]

And these are the hidden secrets concerning which it is most difficult to judge, and to deliver a perfect science; neither can they be understood and taught in any other language except the Hebrew; but seeing the names of God (as *Plato* saith in Cratylus)[32] are highly esteemed of the barbarians, who had them from God, without the which we can by no means perceive the true words and names by which God is called, therefore concerning these we can say no more, but those things which God out of his goodness hath revealed to us; for they are the mysteries and conveyances of God's omnipotency, not from men, nor yet from angels, but instituted and firmly established by the most high God, after a certain manner, with an immovable number and figure of characters, and breathe forth the harmony of the Godhead, being consecrated by the divine assistance.

Therefore the creatures above fear them, those below tremble at them, the angels reverence, the devils are affrighted, every creature doth honour, and every religion adore them; the religious observation whereof, and devout invocation with fear and trembling, doth yield us great virtue, and even deifies the union, and gives a power to work wonderful things above nature.

Therefore we may not for any reason whatsoever change them; therefore *Origen* commandeth that they be kept without corruption in their own characters;[33] and *Zoroastes* also forbiddeth the changing of barbarous and old words;[34] for as *Plato* saith in Cratylus, all divine words or names have proceeded either from the gods first, or from antiquity, whose beginning is hardly known, or from the barbarians:[35] *Jamblicus* in like manner adviseth, that they may not be translated out of their own language into another; for, saith he, they keep not the same force being translated into another tongue.[36]

Therefore these names of God are the most fit and powerful means of reconciling and uniting man with God, as we read in Exodus,[37] in every place in which mention is made of my name, I will be with thee, and bless thee; and in the book of Numbers,[38] the Lord saith, I will put my name upon the sons of Israel and I will bless them.

Therefore divine *Plato* in Cratylus, and in Philebus[39] commandeth to reverence the names of God more than the images or statues of the gods: for there is a more express image and power of God, reserved in the faculty of the mind, especially if it be inspired from above, than in the works of men's hands.

Therefore sacred words have not their power in magical operations, from themselves, as they are words, but from the occult divine powers working by them in the minds of those who by faith adhere to them; by which words the secret power of God as it were through conduit pipes, is transmitted into them, who have ears purged by faith, and by most pure conversation and invocation of the divine names are made the habitation of God, and capable of these divine influences.

Whosoever therefore useth rightly these words or names of God with that purity of mind, in that manner and order, as they were delivered, shall both obtain and do many wonderful things, as we read of *Medea*:[40]

> Most pleasant sleep she caused, words thrice she spake,
> The seas appeased, and soon their fury brake.

Which the ancient doctors of the Hebrews have especially observed, who were wont to do many wonderful things by words; the Pythagoreans also have showed, how to cure very wonderfully the diseases both of body and mind, with certain words;[41] we read also, that *Orpheus,* being one of the Argonauts diverted a most fierce storm[42] by certain words; in like manner that *Apollonius,* by certain words whispered, raised up a dead maid at Rome;[43] and *Philostratus* reporteth that some did by certain words call up *Achilles'* ghost.[44]

And *Pausanias* relates,[45] that in Lydia in the cities of Hero-Cesarea and Hypepis, were two temples consecrated to the goddess whom they called *Persica*,[46] in both of which when divine service was ended, a certain magician, after he had laid dry wood upon the altar, and in his native language had sang hymns, and pronounced certain barbarous words, out of a book which he held in his hand, presently the dry wood, no fire being put to it, was seen to be kindled, and burn most clearly.

Also *Serenus Samonicus* delivereth amongst the precepts of physic, that if this name *Abracadabra*[47] be written, as is here expressed, viz. diminishing letter after letter backward, from the last to the first, it will cure the hemitritaean fever or any other, if the sheet of paper or parchment be hanged about the neck, and the disease will by little and little decline and pass away:

a	b	r	a	c	a	d	a	b	r	a
a	b	r	a	c	a	d	a	b	r	
a	b	r	a	c	a	d	a	b		
a	b	r	a	c	a	d	a			
a	b	r	a	c	a	d				
a	b	r	a	c	a					
a	b	r	a	c						
a	b	r	a							
a	b	r								
a	b									
a										

But Rabbi *Hama* in his Book of Speculation delivereth a sacred seal more efficacious against any diseases of man, or any griefs whatsoever, in whose foreside are the four squared names of God, so subordinated to one another in a square, that from the highest to the lowest those most holy names or seals of the Godhead do arise, whose intention is inscribed in the circumferential circle, but on the backside is inscribed the seven-lettered name *Araritha,* and his interpretation is written about, viz. the verse from which it is extracted, even as you see it here described [see facing page]:[48]

But all must be done in most pure gold, or virgin parchment, pure, clean and unspotted, also with ink made for this purpose, of the smoke[49] of consecrated wax lights, or incense, and holy water; the actor must be purified and cleansed by sacrifice, and have an infallible hope, a constant faith, and his mind lifted up to the most high God, if he would surely obtain this divine power.

The former part

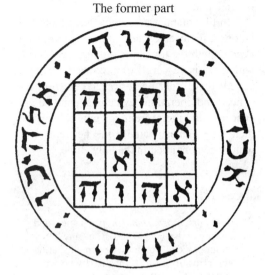

The hinder part

In the fore part

In the hinder part

Neither let any distrust or wonder, that sacred words, applied outwardly can do very much, seeing by them the Almighty God made the heavens and the Earth; and further, by experience it is found, as saith *Rab Costa Ben Luca,* that many things not having physical virtues do very much; as for example, the finger of an abortive child hanged on the neck of a woman hindereth conception, so long as it remaineth there.

Moreover that in divers sacred words and names of God, there is great and divine power, which worketh miracles, *Zoroastes, Orpheus, Jamblicus, Synesius, Alchindus,* and all the famous philosophers testify; and *Artephius,* both a magician and philosopher, hath written a peculiar book concerning the virtue of words and characters. *Origen* not inferior to the famousest philosophers, doth maintain against *Celsus,* that there doth lie hid wonderful virtue in certain divine names,[51] and in the book of Judges the Lord saith, my name which is *Pele* פלא, signifieth with us, a worker of miracles, or causing wonders.[52]

But the true name of God is known neither to men nor to angels, but to God alone, neither shall it be manifested (as holy Scriptures testify) before the will of God be fulfilled; notwithstanding God hath other names amongst the angels, others amongst us men; for there is no

In like manner against the affrightments and mischief of evil spirits and men, and what dangers soever, either of journey, waters, enemies, arms, in the manner as is above said, these characters on the one side בוווו, and these on the backside צמרכד, which are the beginnings and ends of the five first verses of Genesis, and representation of the creation of the world; and by this ligature[50] they say that a man shall be free from all mischiefs, if so be that he firmly believeth in God the creator of all things:

name of God amongst us (as *Moses* the Egyptian[53] saith) which is not taken from his works, and signifieth with participation, besides the name Tetragrammaton, which is holy, signifying the substance of the Creator in a pure signification, in which no other thing is partaker with God the Creator; therefore it is called the separated name, which is written and not read,[54] neither is it expressed by us, but named, and signifieth the second supernal idiom, which is of God, and perhaps of angels.

In like manner the angels have their name amongst themselves, and in their idiom, which *Paul* calleth the tongue of angels,[55] concerning which we have very little knowledge with us, but all their other names are taken from their offices and operations, which have not so great efficacy; and therefore magicians call them by their true names, namely the heavenly ones, which are contained in the holy Bible.

Notes—Chapter XI

1. *to Marcella*—It was at the house of Marcella in Rome between 382 and 385 AD that Saint Jerome instructed a number of wealthy widows and maidens in the scriptures, teaching them Hebrew and preaching the virtues of monastic life. See his biographical note.

2. *of God and Christ*—Pseudo-Dionysius the Areopagite, in his work *Concerning Divine Names.*

3. *text of Exodus*—Exodus 14:19–21. See Appendix VII.

4. *angels and of God*—The verses can be written in two ways to produce two sets of 72 names:

> Now, if these three verses be written at length one above another, the first from right to left, the second from left to right, and the third from right to left (or, as the Greeks would say, *boustrophedon), they will give 72 columns of three letters each. Then each column will be a word of three letters, and as there are 72 columns, there will be 72 words of three letters, each of which will be the 72 names of the Deity alluded to in the text [of the *Zohar*]. And these are called the Schemahamphorasch, or the divided name. By writing the verses all from right to left, instead of *boustrophedon,* &c., there will be other sets of 72 names obtainable. (Mathers [1887] 1962, 170n)

5. *Schemhamphores*—

> It is well known that all the names of God occurring in Scripture are derived from His actions, except one, namely, the Tetragrammaton, which consists of the letters *yod, hé, vau* and *hé.* This name is applied exclusively to God, and is on that account called *Shem ha-meforash,* "The nomen proprium." ... Every other name of God is a derivative; only the Tetragrammaton is a

real *nomen proprium* [proper name], and must not be considered from any other point of view. You must beware of sharing the error of those [Kabbalists] who write amulets *(kameot).* Whatever you hear from them, or read in their works, especially in reference to the names which they form by combination, is utterly senseless; they call these combinations *shemot* (names) and believe that their pronunciation demands sanctification and purification, and that by using them they are enabled to work miracles. Rational persons ought not to listen to such men, nor in any way believe their assertions. No other name is called *shem ha-meforash* except the Tetragrammaton, which is written, but is not pronounced according to its letters." (Moses Maimonides *The Guide for the Perplexed* 1.61, trans. M. Friedlander [New York: Dover Publications, [1904] 1956], 89, 91)

Maimonides was an Aristotelian, which explains his antagonistic attitude toward the Kabbalah.

6. *Eheia*—Eheieh. See Exodus 3:14. The full name Eheieh Asher Eheieh (אהיה אשר אהיה), translated in the Bible "I am that I am," is said by MacGregor Mathers to be better rendered "Existence is existence" or "I am He who is" (Mathers [1887] 1962, 17). Mathers probably gets this from Maimonides:

> Then God taught Moses how to teach them [the Israelites], and how to establish amongst them the belief in the existence of Himself, namely, by saying *Ehyeh asher Ehyeh,* a name derived from the verb *hayah* in the sense of "existing," for the verb *hayah* denotes "to be," and in Hebrew no difference is made between the verbs "to be" and "to exist."*(Guide for the Perplexed* 1.63 [Friedlander], 94])

The translators of Rashi's *Commentary* have rendered this in a different tense: "I will be what I will be" (Rashi 1949, 2:23).

7. ὤν—ὄν (being). See Plato *Cratylus* 421a (Hamilton and Cairns, 456).

8. τοὄν—"Hence being."

9. ὅως—ὄον or ὄν (that; what; which).

10. *Hua*— "He" or in the Latin rendering "himself." See Isaiah 43:10 and 48:12; also 7:14 for the second meaning. It is sometimes used emphatically with reference to God (Deuteronomy 32:39). According to Gesenius (1890, 218) it should not be regarded as a divine name.

However, it is written in the *Zohar:*

> 204. And since in Him beginning and end exist not, hence He [the Ancient One] is not called AThH, *Atah,* Thou; seeing that He is concealed and not revealed. But HVA, *Hoa,* He, is He called.
>   205. But in that aspect wherein the beginning is found, the name AThH, *Atah,* Thou, hath place, and the name AB, *Ab,* Father. For it is written, Isa. lxiii. 16: "Since *Atah,* Thou, art *Ab,* our Father."
>   206. In the teaching of the school of Rav Yeyeva the Elder, the universal rule is that Microprosopus be called AThH, *Atah,* Thou; but that the most Holy Ancient One, who is concealed, be called HVA, *Hoa,* He; and also with reason. *(Lesser Holy Assembly* 7.204–6 [Mathers {1887} 1962, 279])

About this name MacGregor Mathers writes:

> Himself, HVA, *Hoa,* whom we can only symbolize by this pronoun; HE, Who is the Absolute; HE, Who is beyond us; that awful and unknowable Crown, Who hath said, I AM; in Whom is neither past nor future, He Who is the ETERNAL PRESENT. Therefore is HE, *Hoa,* the Father, known of none save the Son, IHVH, and him to whom the Son will reveal Him. For none can see *Hoa* and live, for they would be absorbed in Him. (Mathers [1887] 1962, 156n)

11. *Esay*—Isaiah.

12. ταυτόν—ταὐτόν, "the same." In Latin it is sometimes translated "himself."

13. *Esch*—Fire. Used to signify the fire of God, literally when referring to lightning (I Kings 18:38) and figuratively for God's wrath (Deuteronomy 32:22). It also means fire more generally.

14. *Na*—Translated in the Bible "I pray thee," or "now," used in the form of a submissive request or entreaty (Genesis 24:2), or by those who deliberate in their own minds and, in effect, ask their own permission (Exodus 3:3). It occurs in the courteous address to superiors (Genesis 18:3).

15. *Iah*—Yah (יה). Used in the Bible as an abbreviated form of IHVH in such phrases as "praise ye Jehovah!" (Psalms 104:35). "With that word [Yah] it is said; 'Elohim formed the worlds.' See Ya'lkut ha-Zohar on; 'Forming the Worlds'" (Myer [1888] 1974, 319).

16. *Elion*—Supreme, or Most High (Genesis 14:18; Psalms 7:17).

17. *Macom*—A place, or habitation, sometimes used for the place of God (Genesis 33:21).

18. *Emeth*—Truth. Used in the Bible for truth in general (Genesis 42:16) and also the truth of God (Psalms 25:5, 26:3). In the *Zohar* this word stands for an aspect of the beard of Microprosopus: "The word AMTh, *Emeth,* Truth, therefore dependeth from the Ancient One ..." (*Greater Holy Assembly* 35.852 [Mathers {1887} 1962, 217]). "When He [Microprosopus] shineth in the light of the Ancient of Days [Macroprosopus], then is He called 'abundant in Mercy,' and when another of the other forms is considered, in that form is He called 'and in truth,' for this is the light of His countenance" (ibid. 36.866 [Mathers {1887} 1962, 218–9]).

19. *Zur*—A rock, specifically applied to God as the refuge of Israel (Isaiah 30:29; Deuteronomy 32: 37).

20. *Aben*—A rock, specifically the rock of Israel, Jehovah (Genesis 49:24). *Aben,* אבן, contains the two Hebrew words *ab,* אב (father) and *ben,* בן (son).

21. *Notarian and Gimetrian*—Notaricon and Gematria: see Appendix VII.

22. *Agla*—The sentiment "Thou art mighty forever, O Lord!" is common in the Old Testament, particularly the psalms (see Psalms 92:8), but I have not been able to locate the source of its Hebrew verse.

23. *Iava*—Genesis 1:3.

24. *Ararita*—The Hebrew of this verse in both the Latin and English texts is faulty. I have tried to correct these errors, which most authorities simply copy.

25. *the wicked not so*—Psalms 1:4.

26. *three verses of Exodus*—See note 3 above.

27. *Ziruph*—See Appendix VII.

28. *Maz Paz*—By the permutation known as ATH-BASH. See Appendix VII.

29. *Kuzu*—I have not been able to extract this name from the tables of Ziruph. Perhaps the Right Table of Commutations is intended.

30. *three hundred and fourteen*—See note 19, ch. X, bk. III.

31. *both make thirty-one*—Iiai = I + I + A + I = 10 + 10 + 1 + 10 = 31; El = A + L = 1 + 30 = 31.

32. *Plato saith in Cratylus*—

> Yes, indeed, Hermogenes, and there is one excellent principle which, as men of sense, we must acknowledge—that of the gods we know nothing, either of their natures or of the names which they give themselves, but we are sure that the names by which they call themselves, whatever they may be, are true. And this is the best of all principles, and the next best is to say, as in prayers, that we will call them by any sort or kind of names or patronymics which they like, because we do not know of any other. *(Cratylus* 400d–e [Hamilton and Cairns, 438])

This seems to be one of the passages Agrippa alludes to (see also note 35 below), but as in other places, he interprets Plato to suit his own purposes. Socrates, Plato's alter ego, is being ironic as he speaks the above, and is arguing *against* the assertion of Cratylus, who holds an opinion in harmony with Agrippa's: "I believe, Socrates, the true account of the matter to be that a power more than human gave things their first names, and that the names which are thus given are necessarily their true names" (ibid. 438c [Hamilton and Cairns, 472]).

33. *their own characters*—

> If, then, we shall be able to establish ... the nature of powerful names, some of which are used by the learned amongst the Egyptians, or by the Magi among the Persians, and by the Indian philosophers called Brahmans, or by the Samanaeans, and others in different countries; and shall be able to make out that the so-called magic is not, as the followers of Epicurus and Aristotle

> suppose, an altogether uncertain thing, but is, as those skilled in it prove, a consistent system, having words which are known to exceedingly few; then we say that the name Sabaoth and Adonai, and the other names treated with so much reverence among the Hebrews, are not applicable to any ordinary created things, but belong to a secret theology which refers to the Framer of all things. These names, accordingly, when pronounced with that attendant train of circumstances which is appropriate to their nature, are possessed of great power; and other names, again, current in the Egyptian tongue, are efficacious against certain demons who can only do certain things; and other names in the Persian language have corresponding power over other spirits; and so on in every individual nation, for different purposes. (Origen *Against Celsus* 1.24 [*Ante-Nicene Fathers*, 4:406)

> And while still on the subject of names, we have to mention that those who are skilled in the use of incantations, relate that the utterance of the same incantation in its proper language can accomplish what the spell professes to do; but when translated into any other tongue, it is observed to become inefficacious and feeble. (ibid. 25 [*Ante-Nicene Fathers*, 4:406–7)

See also all of ch. 45, bk. 5 of this work by Origen.

34. *barbarous and old words*—See note 1, ch. LX, bk. II.

35. *from the barbarians*—Again Agrippa twists, or does not grasp, Plato's meaning:

> That objects should be imitated in letters and syllables and so find expression, may appear ridiculous, Hermogenes, but it cannot be avoided—there is no better principle to which we can look for the truth of first names. Deprived of this, we must have recourse to divine help, like the tragic poets, who in any perplexity have their gods waiting in the air, and must get out of our difficulty in like fashion, by saying that "the gods gave the first names, and therefore they are right." This will be the best contrivance, or perhaps that other notion may be even better still, of deriving them from some barbarous people, for the barbarians are older than we are, or we may say that antiquity has cast a veil over them, which is the same sort of excuse as the last,

for all these are not reasons but only ingenious excuses for having no reasons concerning the truth of words. (Plato *Cratylus* 425d–e [Hamilton and Cairns, 460])

36. *another tongue—*

For if names subsisted through compact it would be of no consequence whether some were used instead of others. But if they are suspended from the nature of things, those names which are more adapted to it will also be more dear to the Gods. From this, therefore, it is evident that the language of sacred nations is very reasonably preferred to that of other men. To which may be added, that names do not entirely preserve the same meaning when translated into another language; but there are certain idioms in each nation which cannot be signified by language to another nation. And, in the next place, though it should be possible to translate them, yet they no longer preserve the same power when translated. Barbarous names, likewise, have much emphasis, great conciseness, and participate of less ambiguity, variety, and multitude. Hence, on all these accounts, they are adapted to more excellent natures. (Iamblichus *On the Mysteries* 7.5 [Taylor, 294–5])

37. *in Exodus*—Exodus 20:24.

38. *book of Numbers*—Numbers 6:27.

39. *in Philebus*—"For myself, Protarchus, in the matter of naming the gods I am always more fearful than you would think a man could be; nothing indeed makes me so afraid" (Plato *Philebus* 12c [Hamilton and Cairns, 1088]). Agrippa derives his reference from Origen *Against Celsus* 1.25.

40. *we read of Medea*—See note 8, ch. VI, bk. II.

41. *certain words*—"Some diseases also they cured by incantations. Pythagoras, however, thought that music greatly contributed to health, if it was used in a proper manner. The Pythagoreans likewise employed select sentences of Homer and Hesiod for the amendment of souls" (Iamblichus *Life of Pythagoras* 29 [Taylor, 88]). See also ch. 25. In the present context it may be useful to give an extract from Proclus translated by Taylor: "Pythagoras, being asked what was the wisest of things, said it was number; and being asked what was the next in wisdom, said, he who gave names to things. ... Pythagoras therefore said, that it was not the business of any casual person to

fabricate names, but of one looking to intellect and the nature of things" (ibid. 18 [Taylor, 43–4n].

42. *most fierce storm*—Perhaps this refers to Apollonius Rhodius *Argonautica* 1, c. line 1036, where Orpheus instructs the young warriors to dance in their armour while Jason sacrifices and prays to divert the storm winds.

43. *dead maid at Rome*—Philostratus *Life of Apollonius of Tyana* 4.45; also Eusebius *Against the Life of Apollonius of Tyana Written by Philostratus* 26. See note 10, ch. LVIII, bk. I.

44. *Achilles' ghost*—Apollonius tells his disciples:

"To bring about my meeting with Achilles I did not dig a trench like Ulysses, nor did I evoke his ghost by shedding the blood of lambs, but I offered those prayers by which the Indian Sages say they invoke departed heroes, and then I said: 'O, Achilles, the vulgar herd say that you are dead, but I do not at all agree with that opinion, nor does Pythagoras, the source of my philosophy. If we are right, appear to us. My eyes will be of great service to you, if you use them as witnesses that you still live!' Thereupon the earth about the mound quivered slightly, and out came a youth about five cubits high, clad in a Thessalian mantle." (Philostratus *Life and Times of Apollonius of Tyana* 4.16 [Eells, 99])

45. *Pausanias relates*—See note 8, ch. VII, bk. III.

46. *Persica*—"Hierocaesarea went back to a higher antiquity, and spoke of having a Persian Diana, whose fame was consecrated in the reign of Cyrus" (Tacitus *Annals* 3.62. In *Complete Works*, trans. Alfred John Church and William Jackson Brodribb [New York: Random House {Modern Library}, 1942], 136).

47. *Abracadabra*—Perhaps no other magical formula is so well known. Budge treats it at length in his *Amulets and Talismans*, ch. 8. He is not satisfied that Serenus himself invented the word, saying:

... it seems to me that the formula is based upon something which is much older, and that in any case the idea of it is derived from an older source. Many attempts have been made to find a meaning for the formula, but the explanation put forward by Bischoff in his "Kabbalah" (1903) is the most likely to be correct. He derives the formula from the Chaldee words אַבְרָא

כְּדָבְרָא i.e. ABBÂDÂ KÉ DÂBRÂ, which seem to be addressed to the fever and to mean something like "perish like the word." (Budge [1930] 1968, 8:220–1)

The attraction of this charm continues into modern times. The well known magician Aleister Crowley attached considerable importance to the word, but altered it to suit his preconceptions into ABRA-HADABRA, the "word of the Aeon" by which the union of human and solar consciousness would occur: "It represents the Great Work complete, and it is therefore an archetype of all lesser magical operations" (Crowley [1929] 1976, 42). According to Kenneth Grant, the reason for the change in spelling was Crowley's belief that he had discovered the true esoteric name of the god Hod, which is the Chaldean for Set. See Grant 1976, 3:59.

48. *here described*—On the front of the amulet the names of God are, from top to bottom: IHVH, ADNI, YIAI and AHIH. Around the edge is written: IHVH ALHIKV IHVH AKD: "IHVH Our God is IHVH One." Concerning the words on the back, see note 24 above, and the part of the text to which it refers. The dots indicate that each letter stands for a word.

49. *of the smoke*—The ink is made from the soot deposited by the smoke.

50. *ligature*—A charm tied to the body.

51. *certain divine names*—See note 33 above.

52. *causing wonders*—Judges 13:18. "Why askest thou thus after my name seeing it is a secret?" Name = PLA: something wonderful or admirable, a miracle of God.

53. *Moses the Egyptian*—See note 5 above.

54. *written and not read*—

We were commanded that, in the sacerdotal blessing, the name of the Lord should

be pronounced as it is written in the form of the Tetragrammaton, the *shem hameforash*. It was not known to every one how the name was to be pronounced, what vowels were to be given to each consonant, and whether some of the letters capable of reduplication should receive a dagesh. Wise men successively transmitted the pronunciation of the name; it occurred only once in seven years that the pronunciation was communicated to a distinguished disciple. I must however, add that the statement "The wise men communicated the Tetragrammaton to their children and their disciples once in seven years," does not only refer to the pronunciation but also to its meaning, because of which the Tetragrammaton was made a *nomen proprium* of God, and which includes certain metaphysical principles. (Maimonides *Guide for the Perplexed* 1.62 [Friedlander, 91])

He adds: "There is a tradition, that with the death of Simeon the Just, his brother priests discontinued the pronunciation of the Tetragrammaton in the blessing …" (ibid., 92).

This zeal not to defile the most holy name of God has led to the loss of its true pronunciation. When a Jew reads scripture and encounters the name IHVH, he pronounces it "Adonai" (ADNI).

… therefore He (YHVH) is only named with the name of the She'kheen-ah אֲדֹנָי *Adonai i.e.,* Lord: therefore the Rabbins say (of the name YHVH); Not as I am written *(i.e.,* YHVH) am I read. In this world My Name is written YHVH and read Adonoi, but in the world to come, the same will be read as it is written, so that Mercy (represented by YHVH) shall be from all sides. (Myer [1888] 1974, 18:341)

Myer is quoting the *Zohar.*

55. *tongue of angels*—I Corinthians 13:1.

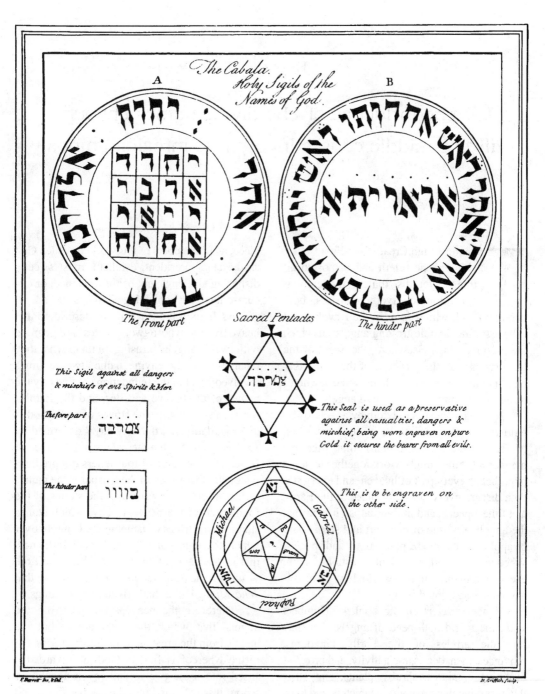

Kabbalistic Names of God

from *The Magus* by Francis Barrett (London, 1801)

CHAPTER XII

Of the influence of the divine names through all the middle causes into these inferior things.

The most high Creator and First Cause, although he ruleth and disposeth all things, yet distributeth the care of execution to divers ministers, both good and bad, which *John* in the Revelations[1] calls assisting, and destroying angels: of which the prophet[2] sings elsewhere, the angel of the Lord remains in the presence of them that fear him, that he may preserve them; and elsewhere[3] he describes immissions[4] by evil angels.

Now whatsoever God doth by angels, as by ministers, the same doth he by heavens, stars, but as it were by instruments, that after this manner all things might work together to serve him, that as every part of heaven, and every star doth discern every corner or place of the Earth, and time, species and individual: so it is fit that the angelical virtue of that part and star should be applied to them, viz. place, time, and species. Whence *Austin* in his Book of Questions,[5] saith, every visible thing in this world, hath an angelical power appointed for it.

Hence *Origen*[6] on the book of Numbers saith, the world hath need of angels, that may rule the armies of the Earth, kingdoms, provinces, men, beasts, the nativity, and progress of living creatures, shrubs, plants, and other things, giving them that virtue which is said to be in them, from an occult propriety; much more need is there of angels that may rule holy works, virtues and men, as they who always see the face of the most high Father, and can guide men in the right path, and also even the least thing to this place, as fit members of this world in which God as the chief president, dwelleth, most sweetly disposing all things, not being contained, or circumscribed, but containing all things.

As *John* in the Revelations describeth that heavenly city, whose twelve gates[7] are guarded with twelve angels, infusing on them what they receive from the divine name, twelve times revolved;[8] and in the foundations of that city the names of the twelve apostles, and the Lamb;[9] for as in the Law, in the stones of the ephod,[10] and foundations of the holy city[11] described by *Ezekiel,* were written the names of the tribes of Israel, and the name of four letters did predominate over them;[12] so in the Gospel,[13] the names of the apostles are written in the stones of the foundation of the heavenly city, which stones stand for the tribes of Israel in the Church, over which the name of the Lamb hath influence, that is, the name of *Jesus,*[14] in which is all the virtue of the four lettered name; seeing that *Jehovah* the Father hath given him all things.

Therefore the heavens receive from the angels, that which they dart down; but the angels from the great name of God and *Jesu,* the virtue whereof is first in God, afterward diffused into these twelve and seven angels, by whom it is extended into the twelve signs, and into the seven planets, and consequently into all the other ministers and instruments of God, penetrating even to the very depths.

Hence Christ saith, whatsoever you shall ask the Father in my name, he will give you;[15]

and after his resurrection saith, in my name they shall cast out devils,[16] and do as followeth; so that the name of four letters is no further necessary, the whole virtue thereof being translated into the name of *Jesus,* in which only miracles are done; neither is there any other (as *Peter* saith)[17] under heaven given unto men, by which they can be saved, but that.

But let us not think, that by naming *Jesus* prophanely, as the name of a certain man, we can do miracles by virtue of it: but we must invocate it in the holy Spirit, with a pure mind and a fervent spirit, that we may obtain those things which are promised us in him; especially knowledge going before, without which there is no hearing of us, according to that of the prophet, I will hear him because he hath known my name.[18]

Hence at this time no favour can be drawn from the heavens, unless the authority, favour and consent of the name *Jesu* intervene; hence the Hebrews and Cabalists most skillful in the divine names, can work nothing after Christ by those old names, as their fathers have done long since; and now it is by experience confirmed, that no devil nor power of hell, which vex and trouble men, can resist this name, but will they,

nill they,[19] bow the knee and obey, when the name *Jesu* by a due pronunciation is proposed to them to be worshipped.

And they fear not only the name but also the cross, the seal thereof;[20] and not only the knees of earthly, heavenly, and hellish creatures are bowed, but also insensible things do reverence it, and all tremble at his beck, when from a faithful heart and a true mouth the name *Jesus* is pronounced, and pure hands imprint the salutiferous sign of the cross.

Neither truly doth Christ say in vain to his disciples, in my name they shall cast out devils, etc. unless there were a certain virtue expressed in that name over devils and sick folk, serpents, and persons, and tongues, and so forth, seeing the power which this name hath, is both from the virtue of God the institutor, and also from the virtue of him who is expressed by this name, and from a power implanted in the very word.

Hence is it that seeing every creature feareth and reverenceth the name of him who hath made it, sometimes even wicked and ungodly men, if so be they believe the invocation of divine names of this kind, do bind devils, and operate certain other great things.

Notes—Chapter XII

1. *in the Revelations*—Revelation 7:2, 15 and elsewhere.

2. *the prophet*—Psalms 34:7. In this context, see Psalms 91:9–12.

3. *and elsewhere*—Psalms 78:49.

4. *immissions*—Insertions or injections into something.

5. *Book of Questions*—Perhaps *De doctrina Christiana* of Augustine.

6. *Origen*—

And what is so pleasant, what is so magnificent as the work of the sun or moon by whom the world is illuminated? Yet there is work in the world itself too for angels who are over beasts and for angels who preside over earthly armies. There is work for angels who preside over the nativity of

animals, of seedlings, of plantations, and many other growths. And again there is work for angels who preside over holy works, who teach the comprehension of eternal light and the knowledge of God's secrets and the science of divine things. (Origen *Fourteenth Homily on Numbers,* trans. Rufinus. In Thorndike 1929, 1:454)

… nor are we to suppose that it is the result of accident that a particular office is assigned to a particular angel: as to Raphael, e.g., the work of curing and healing; to Gabriel, the conduct of wars; to Machael, the duty of attending to the prayers and supplications of mortals. For we are not to imagine that they obtained these offices otherwise than by their own merits, and by the zeal and excellent qualities which they severally displayed before the world was formed; so that afterwards, in the order of archangels, this or that office was assigned to each one, while others deserved to be enrolled in the order of angels, and to act under this or that archangel, or that leader or head of an order. (Origen *De principiis* 1.8 [*Ante-Nicene Fathers* 4:264–5])

7. *twelve gates*—Revelation 21:12.

8. *twelve times revolved*—The twelve permutations of Tetragrammaton. See the table accompanying ch. XIV, bk. II.

9. *and the Lamb*—Revelation 21:14.

10. *stones of the ephod*—Exodus 28:29.

11. *holy city*—Ezekiel 48:31.

12. *predominate over them*—"… the name of the city from that day shall be, The Lord (יהוה) is there." Ezekiel 48:35.

13. *in the Gospel*—Matthew 19:28.

14. *name of Jesus*—Ginsburg, referring to the Christian Kabbalistic work *De verbo mirifico* (Basle, 1494) by the German mystic John Reuchlin, says: "The name Jesus in Hebrew י"ה"ש"ו"ה ... yields the name יהוה *Jehovah;* and the ש which in the language of the Kabbalah is the symbol of fire or light. ... This mysterious name therefore contains a whole revelation, inasmuch as it shows us that Jesus is God himself, the Light or the *Logos"* (Ginsburg [1863] 1970, 3:5:211). Agrippa was familiar with this work by Reuchlin.

15. *he will give you*—John 15:16.

16. *cast out devils*—Luke 16:17.

17. *as Peter saith*—Acts 4:12.

18. *known my name*—Psalms 91:14.

19. *will they, nill they*—Willy-nilly.

20. *seal thereof*—The sign of the cross made with the hand.

CHAPTER XIII

Of the members of God, and of their influence on our members.

We read in divers places of the holy Scripture, of divers members of God, and ornaments; but by the members of God, are understood manifold powers, most simply abiding in God himself, distinguished amongst themselves by the sacred names of God; but the garments of God and ornaments, are as it were certain ways and relations, or emanations, or conduit pipes, by the which he diffuseth himself; the hems of which as oft as our mind shall touch, so often the divine power of some member goeth forth, even as *Jesus* cried out, concerning the woman with the bloody issue, somebody hath touched me, for I perceive virtue to go forth from me.[1]

These members therefore in God are like to ours, but the Ideas and exemplars[2] of our members, to the which if we rightly conform our members, then being translated into the same image, we are made the true sons of God, and like to God, doing and working the works of God.

Therefore concerning the members of God, many things are drawn forth out of the Scriptures; for we read of his head in the Canticles;[3] thy head as carmel, and the locks of thy head as the purple of a king; but this carmel signifieth not the mountain in the seacoast of Syria, but a little creature, which engendereth the purple.[4] Also of his eyes, eyelids and ears, we read in the Psalms, the eyes of the Lord on the just, and his ears to their prayers,[5] his eyes look towards the poor,[6] and his eyelids inquire after the sons of men:[7] also of his mouth, taste, throat, lips, and teeth, we read in Esay, thou hast not inquired at my mouth;[8] and in the Canticles, thy throat as the best wine for my beloved, that goeth down sweetly, causing the lips of those that are asleep to speak;[9] there are also nostrils, by the which (as we often find in the Law) he smelleth the sacrifices for a sweet odour.[10]

He hath shoulders, arms, hands, and fingers, of the which we read in Esay: the government is laid upon his shoulders;[11] to whom is the arm of the Lord[12] revealed? And the Kingly Prophet singeth, thy hands O Lord[13] have made me and fashioned me, and I will behold the heavens, the work of thy fingers.[14] He hath also a right and left hand; hence the Psalmist saith, the Lord saith to my Lord, sit at my right hand:[15] and of the left we read, in the Gospel, on which the damned shall be placed at the last day.[16]

Further we read of the heart, breast, back, and backparts of God; as in the book of Kings, that God found *David* a man according to his own heart;[17] we read also in the Gospel, his breast upon which the disciple sleeping[18] conceived divine mysteries; and the Psalmist describeth his back, in the paleness of gold; and he himself saith in Jeremiah, I will show my back and not my face in the day of their perdition,[19] and he saith to *Moses,* thou shalt see my backparts;[20] of his feet the Psalmist also saith, darkness under his feet,[21] and in Genesis he is said to walk to the south.[22]

In like manner also we read of the garments, and ornaments of God, as with the Psalmist, the Lord hath reigned, he hath put on beauty, clothed with light as with a garment;[23] and elsewhere, thou hast put on comeliness and beauty;[24] the abyss as a garment and his clothing;[25] and in Ezekiel, the Lord speaketh, saying, I spread my garment over thee and covered thy nakedness.[26]

Moreover also we read of the rod, staff, sword and buckler of God, as in the Psalmist, thy rod and thy staff,[27] they have comforted me; his truth hath compassed thee about as with a shield;[28] and in Deuteronomy we read of the sword of his glory.[29]

And very many of this sort the sacred word declares to us; from which members and divine ornaments, there is no doubt, but that our members and all things about us, and all our works, are both ruled, directed, preserved, governed, and also censured, as the Prophet saith, he hath put my foot upon a rock,[30] and directed my goings; and elsewhere he saith, blessed be the Lord my God, who teacheth my hand to war, and my fingers to fight;[31] and of his mouth he saith, the Lord hath put a new song into my mouth;[32] and elsewhere our Saviour saith, I will give you a mouth and wisdom;[33] and of the hair he saith, an hair of your head shall not perish;[34] and in another place, the hairs of your head are numbered.[35]

For the Almighty God seeing he would have us to be his images and like to himself, hath framed members, limbs, and figures after many ways laid open in us, according to the similitude of his hidden virtues, as it were signs keeping the same order and proportion to them.

Whence the mecubals of the Hebrews say, that if a man capable of the divine influence do make any member of his body clean and free from filthiness, then it becometh the *habitale*[36] and proper seat of the secret limb of God, and of the virtue to the which the same name is ascribed: so that if that member want anything, the name being invoked, whence it dependeth, it is presently heard effectually, according to that, I will hear him, because he hath known my name;[37] and these are the great and hidden mysteries, concerning which it is not lawful to publish more.

Notes—Chapter XIII

1. *go forth from me*—Mark 5:30.

2. *Ideas and exemplars*—Ideals and archetypes.

3. *in the Canticles*—Song of Solomon 7:5.

4. *engendereth the purple*—Kermes is a red pigment which was anciently obtained from the pregnant female of the insect *Coccus ilicis,* found in southern Europe and northern Africa clinging to a species of evergreen oak like red berries. At the beginning of the 16th century it began to be supplanted by cochineal, a similar pigment made from the insect females of *Coccus cacti,* imported from Mexico and Peru by the Spanish. The name carmine (from kermes) was applied to both. Agrippa is of course referring to the Old World product. What the ancients called purple, we would call red.

5. *to their prayers*—Psalms 34:15.

6. *towards the poor*—Perhaps Psalms 10:8.

7. *sons of men*—Psalms 11:4.

8. *inquired at my mouth*—Isaiah 30:2.

9. *asleep to speak*—Song of Solomon 7: 9.

10. *sweet odour*—Genesis 8:21.

11. *upon his shoulders*—Isaiah 9:6.

12. *arm of the Lord*—Isaiah 53:1.

13. *hands O Lord*—Psalms 8:6.

14. *work of thy fingers*—Psalms 8:3.

15. *my right hand*—Psalms 110:1.

16. *the last day*—Matthew 25:33, 41.

17. *his own heart*—I Samuel 13:14.

18. *disciple sleeping*—John 13:25 and 21:20.

19. *their perdition*—Jeremiah 18:17.

20. *see my backparts*—Exodus 33:23.

21. *under his feet*—Psalms 18:9.

22. *walk to the south*—Genesis 3:8. Of this passage Rashi says: "In that direction [interpreting רוח as 'direction' instead of 'wind'] [towards] which the sun comes, and that is, the west. For towards evening the sun is in the west ..." (Rashi 1949, 1:30). The brackets are those of the editors of the *Commentary*.

23. *with a garment*—Psalms 91:1.

24. *comeliness and beauty*—Perhaps Psalms 104:1.

25. *his clothing*—Psalms 104:6.

26. *thy nakedness*—Ezekiel 15:8.

27. *rod and staff*—Psalms 23:4.

28. *with a shield*—Psalms 5:12.

29. *sword of his glory*—Deuteronomy 33:29. See Psalms 45:3.

30. *foot upon a rock*—Psalms 40:2.

31. *fingers to fight*—Psalms 144:1.

32. *into my mouth*—Psalms 40:3.

33. *mouth and wisdom*—Luke 21:15.

34. *shall not perish*—Luke 21:18.

35. *are numbered*—Matthew 10:30.

36. *habitale*—Habitation. The word habitation was used to describe the Jewish tabernacle.

37. *hath known my name*—See note 18, ch. XII, bk. III.

CHAPTER XIV

Of the gods of the gentiles, and the souls of the celestial bodies, and what places were consecrated in times past, and to what deities.

The philosophers have maintained, as we have showed before, that the heavens and stars are divine animals, and their souls intellectual, participating of the divine mind; and they aver, that some separated substances are superior, others inferior to them, as it were governing and serving, which they call intelligences and angels; moreover *Plato* himself affirmed, that celestial souls[1] are not confined to their bodies, as our souls to our bodies, but to be, where they will, and also that they rejoice in the vision of God, and without any labour or pains do rule and move their bodies, and together in moving them do easily govern these inferior things.

Therefore they often called the souls of this kind, gods, and appointed divine honours for them, and dedicated prayers and sacrifices to them, and did worship them with divine worship; and these are the gods to the which all people are attributed, concerning which *Moses* commanded in Deuteronomy,[2] saying, lest perchance your eyes being lifted up to heaven, thou shouldest see the Sun, the Moon, and all the stars of heaven, and being turned back shouldest adore and worship them, to which all the nations are subjected, which are under the heaven; but the Lord *Jehovah* hath taken and brought you forth from the furnace of Egypt, that thou shouldest be an hereditary people to himself; and in the same book, chapter 17,[3] he calleth the Sun, Moon and stars gods.

And the doctors of the Hebrews upon that place of Genesis[4] where it is said, that *Abraham* gave gifts to the sons of the concubines, viz. *Shemoth, Steltoma,* that is strange names, but left *Isaac* heir of all that he possessed, say, that the sons of the concubines were not in the blessing of *Abraham* given to *Jehovah* the most high Creator, but to strange gods and deities,[5] but that *Isaac* and his seed were given to the omnipotent *Jehovah,* and in no part to any strange deities; therefore they are upbraided in Deuteronomy, because they served strange gods and worshipped them they knew not, and to whom they were not given.

And also *Joshua Nave,* after that the people were brought into the land of promise, their enemies overcome, and the lots of the possessions of Israel distributed, give the people leave to choose that God whom they would worship, saying, leave is given you this day to choose whom you will especially serve, whether the gods which your fathers served in Mesopotamia, or the gods of the Amorites, whose land you inhabit; but the people answered, we will serve the Lord *Jehovah,* and he shall be our God; *Joshua* said to them, ye cannot do it, for the Lord *Jehovah* is holy, strong, and jealous; but the people persevering to serve *Jehovah,* he saith to them, ye are witnesses yourselves that ye have chosen for yourselves the Lord, to serve him; take away therefore strange gods out of the midst of you, and incline your hearts to the Lord God of Israel; and he erected a great stone saying, this stone shall be for a witness, lest perhaps afterwards ye will deny and lie to the Lord your God.[6]

Therefore the other gods, to which the other nations were given, were the Sun, Moon, twelve signs, and other celestial bodies, and divine fabrics, yet not as they were bodies, but as the soul adhereth to them, and the whole militia of heaven, which *Jeremy* calls the Queen of Heaven,[7] that is the power by which the heaven is governed, viz. the Soul of the World, of which *Jeremy* saith, the sons gather sticks, and part thereof maketh a fire, and the women mingle oil, that they might make a cake for the Queen of Heaven: neither was the worship of doulia to this Queen and other celestial souls prohibited them, but of latria only,[8] which they that gave, are reproved of the Lord.

But the name of these souls or gods, we have declared; but to what regions, people, and cities they were ascribed as proper and tutelar, *Origen,*[9] *Tertullian,*[10] *Apuleius,*[11] *Diodorus,*[12] and very many other historians, partly relate to us.

Therefore all people worshipped their gods with their proper ceremonies: the Beotians, *Amphiarus;*[13] the Africans, *Mopsus;*[14] the Egyptians, *Osiris* and *Isis;* the Ethiopians who inhabit Meroe, *Jupiter* and *Bacchus;* the Arabians, *Bacchus* and *Venus;* the Scythians, *Minerva;* the Naucratians, *Serapis;* the Syrians, *Atargates;*[15] the Arabians, *Diaphares;* the Africans, *Celestus;*[16] the Nornians, *Tibelenus.*[17]

In Italy also by the free cities' consecration, *Delventius* was the god of the Crustumensians, *Viridianus* of the Narvensians, *Aucharia*[18] of the Aesculans, *Nursia*[19] of the Volsians, *Valentia* of the Otriculans, *Nortia*[20] of the Sutrinians, *Curis*[21] of the Phaliscians; these especially were famous.

The Latians did adore with the highest worship, *Mars;* the Egyptians, *Isis;* the Moors, *Iuba;*[22] the Macedonians, *Cabrius;*[23] the Chartheginians, *Uranus;* the Latins, *Faunus;* the Romans, *Quirinus;*[24] the Sabines, *Sangus;*[25] the Athenians, *Minerva;* Samos, *Juno;* Paphos, *Venus;* Lemnos, *Vulcan;* Naxos, *Bacchus;* Delphos, *Apollo.*

And as *Ovid* singeth in his Fasti:[26]

Athens do Pallas; Crete, Dian' implore.
The island Lemnos, Vulcan doth adore.
The Spartans, Juno————

The Carthaginians and Leucadians did worship *Saturn;* Crete, Pyreus, Homole, Ida, Elis and Libya, *Jupiter,* where was his oracle;[27] Epirus, Latium, Gnidus, Lycia, Pisa, Macedonia, *Mars;* the Thermodonians, Scythians, and Thracia, the Sun.

The Scythians did worship only one god, sacrificing an horse[28] to him; the same also the Heliopolitans, and Assyrians did worship; and under the name of *Apollo,* the Rhodians, Hyperboreans and Milesians; and the mountains Parnassus, Phaselus, Cynthus, Soracte,[29] were holy to him, and the islands Delos, Claros, Tenedos and Mallois, a place in the Isle Lesbos, and the Grynean grove or town, besides the cities Patara, Chrysa, Tarapnas, Cyrrha, Delphos, Arrephina, Entrosi, Tegyra; also Thebes, the island Naxos, Nise a city of Arabia, Callichoros a river of Paphlagonia, were consecrated to him under the name of *Bacchus* and *Dionysus;* also Parnassus and Cytheros mountains of Boeotia, in which every second year by course, the feasts Bacchanalia[30] were kept; also the Thamaritans a people neighbours to the Hircanians did worship *Bacchus* with their own ceremonies.

The Assyrians first of all introduced the worship of *Venus;* then the Paphians in Cyprus, the Phoenicians, and Cythereans, whom (as *Ageus* reports) the Athenians followed: amongst the Lacedaemonians, *Venus Armatha*[31] was worshipped; at Delphos, *Venus Epitybia;*[32] she was also adored of the Coans; and in Amathus an island of the Aegean Sea, and in Memphi a city of Egypt, and in Gnido[33] and Sicilia, and the Idalian grove, and the city Hypepa, and Erice a mountain of Sicilia, and in Calidonia, Cyrene and Samos; and no deity of the old gods (*Aristotle* being witness) is reported to have been worshipped with greater ceremonies, and in more places.

The French did especially worship *Mercury,* calling him *Teutates;*[34] so also the Arcadians, Hermopolites, Egyptians and Memphites.

The Scythians about Mount Taurus, did worship the Moon under the name of *Diana;* and in Ephesus, she had a most stately temple;[35] and in Mycena after the death of *Thoantes,* king of Taurica, her image being stolen away by *Iphigenia* and *Orestes,*[36] she was worshipped nigh

Aricia.[37] The rite of ceremonies being changed, she was worshipped likewise by the Magnesians a people of Thessalia, and in Pisa a city of Achaia,[38] and in Tybur, and the Aventinum a Roman hill, and in Perga a city of Pamphila, and in Agras in the kingdom of Attica; and the Catenian people are reported to have worshipped the Moon under the masculine sex.[39]

There were also other places consecrated to other deities, as to *Pallas,* who is called *Minerva,* were consecrated Athens, the mountains Pyreus, Aracynthus, the river Tritones, and Alcomeneum a city of Boeotia, and Neo one of the islands of the Cyclades.

The holy places of *Ceres* are Eleusis, Attica, Enna, and Catana, cities of Sicilia, and Mount Aetna.

The chief worship to *Vulcan* was in the island of Lemnos, and in Imbres an island of Thracia, and Therasia an island consecrated to *Vulcan,* and also Sicilia.

Vesta was the goddess of the Trojans, whom runaway *Aeneas* carried into Italy,[40] and to her are given the Phrygians, Idea and Dindymus mountains of Phrygia, and Reatum a city of Umbria; also the mountain Berecynthus, and Pessinuntium a city of Phrygia.

The cities Carthage, Prosenna, Argos and Mycena, worshipped *Juno.*

Also the island Samos, and the people of Phaliscia, Orchestus a city of Boeotia, and Tenatus a promontory of Laconia, were consecrated to *Neptune,* and the Trezenian nation and city were under the protection of *Neptune.*

Of this sort therefore were the gods of the nations, which did rule and govern them, which *Moses* himself in Deuteronomy[41] calleth gods of the Earth, to the which all nations were attributed, not signifying others than the heavenly stars, and their souls.

Notes—Chapter XIV

1. *celestial souls*—See Plato's *Laws,* bk. 10, particularly secs. 898–9.

2. *in Deuteronomy*—Deuteronomy 4:19–20.

3. *same book, chapter 17*—Deuteronomy 17:3.

4. *of Genesis*—Genesis 25:6.

5. *gods and deities*—Rashi alludes to this tradition somewhat obliquely: "(This verse) [Gen. 25:6] is written incompletely (the names of the concubines are not mentioned), for there was only one concubine, she was Hagar, the same as Keturah. ... Our Rabbis explained: The name of unclean (evil) powers he handed over to them" (Rashi 1949, 1:235).

6. *Lord your God*—Joshua 24:15–27.

7. *Queen of Heaven*—Jeremiah 7:18. See also 44:17–26. This unnamed goddess is conjectured to be the Mesopotamian Ishtar, mother goddess of fertility, love and war, whose cult was popular in Judah during the Assyrian vassalage of 7th century BC.

8. *latria only*—Dulia and latria are words adopted by the Roman Catholics: latria expresses that supreme reverence and adoration which is offered to God alone; dulia that secondary reverence and adoration which is offered to saints. Latria is the reverence of a *latris* or hired servant, while dulia is the reverence of a *doulos* or slave.

9. *Origen*—See Origen *Against Celsus* 2.55 and 3.34.

10. *Tertullian*—See Tertullian *Ad nationes* 2.8.

11. *Apuleius*—See Apuleius *De magia.*

12. *Diodorus*—See Diodorus *Bibliotheca historica* bks. 1–5.

13. *Amphiarus*—Amphiaraus, a Greek hero recognized as a god after his death. He was the son of Oicles and Hypermnestra, and was descended on his father's side from the seer Melampus. One of the Argonauts, he also took part in the siege of Thebes. While fleeing away from that city in his chariot, pursued by Periclymenus, the earth opened and swallowed him. Zeus raised him to the rank of god.

> The Oropians were the first to believe Amphiaraos was a god, but since then all Greece has come to think of him as one. ... Oropos has a temple of Amphiaraos and a white stone statue. ... The Oropians have a spring called Amphiaraos's spring near the

shrine; they never sacrifice anything to it and never use it for the rites of purifying or for holy water, but when a disease has been healed for a man by oracular prescriptions, they have a custom of dropping silver and gold coins into the spring, because this is where they say Amphiaraos rose up as a god. ... I think Amphiaraos was particularly good as an arbiter of dreams; obviously, since he was recognized as a god for having instituted oracular dreaming. (Pausanias *Guide to Greece* 1.34.2–3 [Levi, 1:97–9])

14. *Mopsus*—Greek hero and seer, the son of Ampyx by the nymph Chloris. Out of deference to his prophetic gift he was called a son of Apollo by Himantis. Along with Amphiaraus he was one of the Calydonian hunters who pursued the giant boar of Artemis, and one of the crew of the *Argos* who sought the golden fleece. While on this voyage he died in Libya from the bite of a serpent and was buried there. In after times he was worshipped as an oracular hero. He is not to be confused with another seer of the same name who was the son of the Cretan seer Rhacius and Manto, the daughter of Tiresias.

15. *Atargates*—Atargatis is a Syrian "fish-goddess," the wife of Baal, who had many functions. She was ancestor of the royal house, founder of social and religious customs, and fertility goddess. In the last role she represented the life-giving powers of water and earth. She was known to the Greeks as Derketo and Dea Syria (or Deasura). Apuleius describes her cult in *The Golden Ass*, ch. 36. Lucian wrote a treatise *De dea Syria* (On the Syrian goddess) describing her temples and priests. Legends link her with the astrological Pisces. She is variously said to have been transformed into a fish, hatched from an egg found by fish, and saved by fish from the wrath of Typhon. Regarding this last version, see Ovid *Fasti* 2, c. line 470. She is also mentioned in the apocryphal II Maccabees 12:26.

16. *Celestus*—Coelestis. See note 10 above.

17. *Tibelenus*—Tiberinus, one of the mythical kings of Alba. According to Livy, he drowned while trying to cross the Albula, and his name was given to the river, which became known as the Tiberis, or Tiber (*History of Rome* 1.3). The spirit of the king became the guardian of the river.

18. *Aucharia*—Or Ancharia (see note 10 above). The old Roman goddess Angerona (or Angeronia). The ancients said she relieved pain and sorrow, and cured *angina* (quinsy); or that she was the protecting goddess of Rome whose name was the sacred name of the city. Modern authorities hold her to have been similar to the goddesses Ops, Acca Larentia and Dea Dia. She may have been goddess of the new year, as her festival, called Angeronalia (or Divalia), was celebrated on December 21. In Faesulae (Fiesole, near Florence), where her altar has been discovered, she was worshipped under the name Ancharia.

19. *Nursia*—Nortia. See note 10 above. Nortia (or Nurtia) was an Etruscan goddess worshiped at Volsinii (Bolsena, located on the Italian lake of the same name). She is chiefly remembered because each year a nail was driven into the wall of her temple as a form of primitive calendar—perhaps originally begun as a magical practice for averting plague or some other evil. See Livy *History* 7.3.7. This practice also took place in the temple of Jupiter Optimus Maximus in Rome.

20. *Nortia*—See note 19 above.

21. *Curis*—Juno Curis, or Curitis, or Quiritis, was a goddess especially worshipped in Falerii (or Falerium) in Etruria, which was about 32 miles north of Rome at present-day Civita Castellana. The name comes from *curia*, a division of the Roman people made up of an association of families *(gentes)* that formed a political and religious unit. All ten *curiae* performed ceremonies *(sacra)* to Juno Curis. Tertullian speaks of a "Father Curis of Falisci, in honour of whom, too, Juno got her surname" (see note 10 above). Presumably there was a Jupiter Curis.

22. *Iuba*—Juba II was given divine honors after his death. See biographical note.

23. *Cabrius*—Cabeiros, one of the Cabiri, mystical Greek divinities that occur in various places in the ancient world. Originally there were two, an older identified with Hephaestus and a younger identified with Hermes. When their cult was united with that of Demeter and Kore, their number increased to four. The goddess Cabeiro, who is said by ancient writers to be the wife of Hephaestus, is identical with Demeter—Demeter was called Kabeiria in Thebes. Also in Thebes was found a depiction of a god called Cabeiros who resembles Dionysus. The chief seat of the worship of the Cabeiri was the island of Samothrace (now Samothraki) off the coast of Thrace near Macedonia. Philip of Macedon and his wife were initiated into the mysteries of the Cabeiri here.

24. *Quirinus*—A Sabine word *(quiris: spear)* used as a surname of Romulus and Augustus when they had been raised to the ranks of divinities, and of the gods Mars and Janus. The festival in honour of the translation to heaven of divine Romulus was called Quirinalia. The god Quirinus was similar to Mars, and was

worshipped in earliest times at Rome on the Quirinal Hill, where according to tradition a group of Sabines had come to settle.

25. *Sangus*—Semo Sancus, also called Dius Fidius, was a god of light and oaths worshipped by the Sabines, Umbrians and Romans. He has been identified with the Italian Hercules, but this is questionable. The sanctuary of the god on the Quirinal Hill had a hole in the roof, because he could only be invoked beneath an open sky. An inscription on an altar in a second chapel located on an island in the Tiber led the early Christian Fathers Justin Martyr, Tertullian and Eusebius to wrongly identify the god with Simon Magus, whom they inferred was worshipped in Rome.

"... when you install in your Pantheon Simon Magus, giving him a statue and the title of Holy God ..." (Tertullian *Apology* 13 [*Ante-Nicene Fathers*, 3:29]).

> There was a Samaritan, Simon, a native of the village called Gitto, who in the reign of Claudius Caesar, and in your royal city of Rome, did mighty acts of magic, by virtue of the art of the devils operating in him. He was considered a god, and as a god was honored by you with a statue, which statue was erected on the river Tiber, between the two bridges, and bore the inscription, in the language of Rome:
>
> "Simoni Deo Sancto,"
> "To Simon the holy God."

(Justin Martyr *First Apology* 26. In *Ante-Nicene Christian Library* [Edinburgh: T. and T. Clark, 1867], 2:29)

26. *in his Fasti*—

> The people of Cecrops [Athenians] venerate Pallas; Crete, the land of Minos, Diana; the land of Hypsipyle [Lemnos], adores Vulcan; Sparta, and Mycenae the Pelopian city, Juno; the district of Maenalus [Arcadia], the pine-wreathed head of Faunus. Mars was a deserving object of worship to Larium ... (Ovid *Fasti* 3, lines 81–5 [Riley, 89–90])

27. *where was his oracle*—The oracle of Jupiter Ammon was in the oasis of Ammonium (now Siwa).

28. *horse*—Herodotus gives this account of the religion of the Scythians:

> They worship only the following gods, namely, Vesta, whom they reverence beyond all the rest, Jupiter, and Tellus, whom they consider to be the wife of Jupiter; and after these Apollo, Celestial Venus, Hercules, and Mars. These gods are worshipped by the whole nation: the Royal Scythians offer sacrifice likewise to Neptune. (*History* 4 [Rawlinson, 221–2])

He mentions horse sacrifice only with regard to funeral observances for a king: "Fifty of the best of the late king's attendants are taken, all native Scythians ... and strangled, with fifty of the most beautiful horses" (ibid., 225–6).

29. *Soracte*—The whole mountain was sacred to Apollo. On the festival of the god his worshippers walked over burning embers. "'Highest of the gods to me, Apollo, guardian of holy Soracte, whom first we honour, for whom is fed the blaze of pines piled up, whose votaries we, passing through the fire in the strength of our piety, press the soles of our feet on many a burning coal ...'" (Virgil *Aeneid* 11, c. line 785 [Lonsdale and Lee, 258]). I might mention in this context that the supposed sacrifice by pagans of their children to fire, referred to so often in the Bible, was only an initiatory rite of fire walking.

30. *Bacchanalia*—The festival of Dionysus (Bacchus), which seems to have consisted of a prolonged orgy. Plato says: "I have seen such reveling before now in your Attica on the 'wagons,' and at Tarentum, a settlement of our own, I beheld the whole city in its cups at the feast of Dionysus ..." (*Laws* 1:637b, [Hamilton and Cairns, 1237]). The custom was introduced into Rome through Etruria. In the beginning the festivals were secret, attended by women only, held three days a year in the grove of Simila (see Ovid *Fasti* 6, lines 503–17). Men were later admitted, and the festivals spread to such an extent that in 186 BC a decree was issued banning them throughout Italy, except in special circumstances. Even so, they continued for many years after.

31. *Venus Armatha*—*Armata* means "furnished with weapons." Pausanias mentions a temple of Armed Venus in Lakonia: "Not far from here you will come to a hill, not very high, on which there is an ancient temple and an armed cult-statue of Aphrodite" (*Guide to Greece* 3.15.10 [Levi, 2:53]). It is not surprising the warlike Spartans would worship a warrior Venus.

32. *Venus Epitybia*—Aphrodite Epitymbia (Aphrodite of the Tomb), equivalent to Venus Libitina (*libitinarii*: undertakers), a goddess of the dead. Plutarch mentions a statue of Aphrodite Epitymbia at Delphi to which the spirits of the dead were summoned (*Roman Questions* 23). He explains the seeming incongruity of the goddess of love presiding over

the tomb by saying that one and the same deity rules both birth and death, and that the goddess points out the truth that death is not to be feared, but should be desired—a sentiment in keeping with the Roman passion for suicide. Other similar unlikely epithets for Aphrodite are Gravedigger, Goddess of the Depths, and the Dark One.

33. *Gnido*—The most famous statue of Aphrodite in the ancient world was housed in a temple at Gnidus (Cnidus). It was the work of Praxiteles, and was imitated on the coins of the town and much copied. A reproduction resides in the Vatican.

34. *Teutates*—Lucan mentions this obscure god in passing: "... the whole of long-haired Gaul ... by whom the relentless Teutates is appeased by direful bloodshed, and Hesus, dreadful with his merciless altars; and the shrine of Taranis, not more humane than that of Scythian Diana" *(Pharsalia* 1, lines 443–6 [Riley, 29]). Riley mentions in his notes that Teutas or Teutates was identified with Mercury, Hesus or Esus with Mars, and Taranis with Jupiter by Roman writers. Teutates was worshipped with human sacrifice: "The Gauls used to appease Hesus and Teutas with human blood" (Lactantius *Divine Institutes* 1.21 [*Ante-Nicene Christian Library,* 21:48]). Charles Anthon states that some derived the name Teutates from two British words, *deu-tatt,* signifying God (see *A Classical Dictionary* [New York: Harper and Brothers, 1843], 1301). He describes Teutates as the "genius of commerce" and says "he was regarded as the inventory of all arts and the protector of routes" (ibid., 534). It is difficult not to notice the similarity between the names of the Egyptian god Thoth and the Gallic Teutas, particularly since both are associated with art, commerce, travel, and Roman Mercury.

35. *most stately temple*—In a plain to the northwest of the city of Ephesus, beyond its walls, stood the temple of Artemis, which had been built in the 6th century BC, but burned down on the night Alexander the Great was born (October 13–14, 356 BC). The Ionian city states jointly rebuilt it to such a splendor that it came to be regarded as one of the wonders of the world.

36. *Iphigenia and Orestes*—Having offended Artemis by killing one of her stags and boasting of the deed, Agamemnon was compelled to offer his daughter, Iphigenia, for sacrifice in order to gain a fair wind so that his navy could sail against Troy. At the last moment Artemis snatched the girl from the altar and carried her in a cloud to Tauris, where Iphi-

genia became a priestess of the goddess. When her brother, Orestes, came to Tauris to steal the sacred image of Artemis Thoantea that had fallen from heaven, Iphigenia helped him, and eventually carried the statue to the Attic town of Brauron near Marathon, where she died. The Lacedaemonians maintained that Iphigenia brought the statue to Sparta, where the goddess was worshipped under the name Artemis Orthia. In early times human sacrifices were offered to Iphigenia in both Attica and Sparta, and in later times youths were scourged in Sparta at the festival of Artemis Orthia.

37. *Aricia*—Near the town of Aricia was a grove and temple of Diana (Artemis) Aricina. The priest here was always a runaway slave, and was obliged to fight for his place any other slave who broke off a bough from a certain sacred tree in challenge. The combat was to the death.

38. *Pisa a city of Achaia*—Pisa was in Elis, not Achaea.

39. *the masculine sex*—This refers to the bearded Aphrodite of Cyprus, which was called Aphroditos by Aristophanes, according to Macrobius who mentions the goddess in his *Saturnalia* 3.8.2. Philochorus in his *Atthis* (referred to by Macrobius) identifies this male-female god with the Moon, and says that at its sacrifices men and women exchanged clothing. Aphroditos is the same as the later god Hermaphroditus, whose name means "Aphroditos in the form of a herm"—a statue shaped as a quadrangular pillar surmounted by a head or bust. In later mythology Hermaphroditus came to be regarded as the son of Hermes and Aphrodite.

40. *carried into Italy*—Aeneas was supposed to have carried the eternal fire of Hestia (Vesta) along with the Penates with him when he fled the sack of Troy. "Forth am I borne an exile into the deep, with my comrades, and son, and Penates, and great gods" (Virgil *Aeneid* 3, c. line 11 [Lonsdale and Lee, 114]). The Penates were household gods of the Romans belonging to private families or to the state. Vesta was one of the Penates. They were kept in the central part of the house, and a fire was maintained in their honor on the hearth. At each meal libations were poured onto the hearth or upon the table as sacrifices to the Penates. When a Roman was absent for any length of time, he greeted the household gods on his return as he would any other member of his family.

41. *Deuteronomy*—Deuteronomy 13:7.

CHAPTER XV

What our theologians think concerning the celestial souls.

That the heavens and the heavenly bodies are animated with certain divine souls, is not only the opinion of poets and philosophers, but also the assertion of the sacred Scriptures, and of the Catholics; for Ecclesiastes also describeth the soul of heaven,[1] and *Jerome* upon the same expressly confesseth it: in like manner *Origen* in his book of Principles,[2] seemeth to think that celestial bodies are animated, because they are said to receive commands from God, which is only agreeable to a reasonable nature; for it is written, I have enjoined a command on all the stars; moreover *Job* seemeth to have fully granted, that the stars are not free from the stain of sin; for there we read, the stars also are not clean in his sight; which cannot verily be referred to the brightness of their bodies.

Moreover that the celestial bodies are animated, even *Eusebius* the Pamphilian thought, and also *Austin* in his Enchiridion;[3] but of the latter writers *Albertus Magnus*[4] in his book of Four Coequals, and *Thomas Aquinas*[5] in his book of Spiritual Creatures, and *John Scot* upon the second of the Sentences;[6] to these the most learned Cardinal *Nicholas Cusaus* may be added.

Moreover *Aureolus*[7] himself in a strong disputation doth convince these things; who moreover thinketh it not strange, that the heavenly bodies are worshipped with the worship of doulia, and that their suffrages and helps are implored; to whom also *Thomas*[8] himself consenteth, unless the occasion of idolatry should hinder this rite; moreover *Plotinus* maintaineth that they know our wishes, and hear them.[9]

But if anyone would contradict these, and account them sacrilegious tenets, let him hear *Austin* in his Enchiridion, and in his book of Retractions,[10] and *Thomas* in the second book Against the Gentiles,[11] and in his Quodlibets,[12] and *Scotus* upon the Sentences,[13] and *Gulielmus Parisiensis* in his Sum of the Universe, who unanimously answer, that to say the heavenly bodies are animated or inanimated, nothing belongeth to the Catholic faith.[14]

Therefore although it seemeth to many ridiculous, that the souls themselves be placed in the spheres and stars, and as it were the gods of the nations, every one doth govern his regions, cities, tribes, people, nations and tongues, yet it will not seem strange to those who rightly understand it.

Notes—Chapter XV

1. *soul of heaven*—Perhaps Ecclesiasticus 24:5.

2. *Book of Principles*—

We think, then, that they [the stars] may be designated as living beings, for this reason,

that they are said to receive commandments from God, which is ordinarily the case only with rational beings. "I have given a commandment to all the stars," says the Lord [Isaiah 45:12]. What, now,

496

are these commandments? Those, namely, that each star, in its order and course, should bestow upon the world the amount of splendour which has been entrusted to it. … Yet if the stars are living and rational beings, there will undoubtedly appear among them both an advance and a falling back. For the language of Job "the stars are not clean in His sight" [Job 25:5], seems to me to convey some such idea. (Origen *De principiis* 1.7 [*Ante-Nicene Fathers*, 4:263])

3. *his Enchiridion*—Augustine considers the nature of the stars in several places—*Enchiridion* 1.58; *City of God* 13.16; *De genesi ad litteram* 2.18; and in the letters between himself and Orosius. When Orosius brings up the opinion of Origen that the Sun, Moon and stars are rational,

> Augustine in his reply states that we can see that the sun, moon and stars are celestial bodies, but not that they are animated. He agrees firmly with Paul that there are Seats, Dominions, Principalities, and Powers in the heavens, "but I do not know what they are or what the difference is between them." On the whole Augustine is inclined to regard this state of ignorance as a blissful one. He is somewhat troubled by the verses in the Book of Job [Job 25:4–5—see note 2 above] … Augustine evades this difficulty by questioning whether this passage is to be received as of divine authority, since it is uttered by one of Job's comforters and not by Job himself, of whom alone it is said that he had not sinned with his lips against God. (Thorndike, *History of Magic and Experimental Science*, 1:22:520–1)

4. *Albertus Magnus*—Albertus expressly denies the notion that the stars are animals, in the commonly accepted sense of the word, but regards them as instruments of the First Intelligence:

> The first mover moves the first heaven and through it the other spheres included within it. Whether every other heaven has its own celestial intelligence to move it is a question upon which Albert is somewhat obscure. Others certainly thought so. He mentions, for instance, the opinion of certain Arabs that floods are due to the imagination of the intelligence which moves the sphere of the moon, and concedes that there is some truth in it. (ibid., 2:59:581–2)

Thorndike is describing *De causis et proprietatibus*

elementorum et planetarum, where Albertus "subdivides the heavenly substance into three elements composing respectively the sun, the moon and stars, and the sky apart from the celestial bodies" (ibid. 581).

5. *Thomas Aquinas*—Aquinas, in his *De substantiis separatis,* agrees that angels move the stars. "He also frequently affirms, both in the course of his chief works and in briefer answers to special inquiries that God rules inferior through superior creatures and earthly bodies by the stars" (ibid., 2:60:609).

6. *second of the Sentences*—Duns Scotus *Opus Oxoniense,* a commentary on the *Sententiae* (Four Books of Sentences) of Peter Lombard. Agrippa is referring to the commentary on the second book of the *Sententiae.*

7. *Aureolus*—Perhaps Aurelius Augustinus, or Saint Augustine, in his letters to his Spanish disciple Orosius, referred to in note 3 above.

8. *Thomas*—Thomas Aquinas.

9. *and hear them*—

> Similarly with regard to prayers; there is no question of a will that grants; the powers that answer to incantations do not act by will. … some influence falls from the being addressed upon the practitioner—or upon someone else—but the being itself, sun or star, perceives nothing at all. The prayer is answered by the mere fact that part and other part are wrought to one tone like a musical string which, plucked at one end, vibrates at the other also. (Plotinus *Enneads* 4.4.40–1 [Mackenna, 3:96–7])

10. *Book of Retractions*—*Retractationum libri.*

11. *Against the Gentiles*—*Summa contra gentiles.*

12. *Quodlibets*—*XII Quodlibeta disputata.*

13. *upon the Sentences*—See note 6 above.

14. *the Catholic faith*—

> William states that Plato and Aristotle, Boethius, Hermes Trismegistus, and Avicenna, all believed the stars to be divine animals whose souls were as superior to ours, as their celestial bodies are. … But he leaves Christians free, if they will, to believe with the Aristotelians and many Italian philosophers that the superior world is either one or many animals, that the

heavens are either animated or rational. In this he sees no peril to the Faith. ... But he declares that "it is manifest that human souls are nobler than those which they put in heavenly bodies." (Thorndike, *History of Magic and Experimental Science*, 2:52:366–7)

CHAPTER XVI

Of intelligences and spirits, and of the threefold kind of them, and of their divers names, and of infernal and subterraneal spirits.

Now consequently we must discourse of intelligences, spirits and angels. An intelligence is an intelligible substance, free from all gross and putrifying mass of a body, immortal, insensible, assisting all, having influence over all; and the nature of all intelligences, spirits and angels is the same.

But I call angels here, not those whom we usually call devils, but spirits so called from the propriety of the word,[1] as it were, knowing, understanding and wise. But of these according to the tradition of the magicians, there are three kinds, the first of which they call supercelestial, and minds altogether separated from a body, and as it were intellectual spheres, worshipping the one only God, as it were their most firm and stable unity or center; wherefore they even call them gods, by reason of a certain participation of the divinity; for they are always full of God, and overwhelmed with the divine nectar. These are only about God, and rule not the bodies of the world, neither are they fitted for the government of inferior things, but infuse the light received from God unto the inferior orders, and distribute everyone's duty to all of them.

The celestial intelligences do next follow these in the second order, which they call worldly angels, viz. being appointed besides the divine worship for the spheres of the world, and for the government of every heaven and star, whence they are divided into so many orders, as there are heavens in the world, and as there are

stars[2] in the heavens: and they called those saturnine, who rule the heaven of Saturn and Saturn himself; others jovial, who rule the heaven of Jupiter and Jupiter himself; and in like manner they name divers angels, as well for the name, as the virtue of the other stars.

And because the old astrologers did maintain fifty-five motions,[3] therefore they invented so many intelligences or angels; they placed also in the starry heaven, angels, who might rule the signs, triplicities, decans, quinaries, degrees and stars; for although the school of the Peripatetics assign one only intelligence to each of the orbs of the stars: yet seeing every star and small part of the heaven hath its proper and different power and influence, it is necessary that it also have his ruling intelligence, which may confer power and operate.

Therefore they have established twelve princes of the angels, which rule the twelve signs of the Zodiac, and thirty-six which may rule the so many decans, and seventy-two, which may rule the so many quinaries of heaven, and the tongues of men and the nations, and four which may rule the triplicities and elements, and seven governors of the whole world, according to the seven planets.

And they have given to all of them names, and seals, which they call characters, and used them in their invocations, incantations, and carvings, describing them in the instruments of their operations, images, plates, glasses, rings, papers, wax lights and such like; and if at any time they did operate for the Sun, they did invocate by the name of the Sun, and by the names of solar angels, and so of the rest.

Thirdly they established angels as ministers[4] for the disposing of those things which are below, which *Origen* calleth certain invisible powers[5] to the which those things which are on Earth, are committed to be disposed of. For sometimes they being visible to none do direct our journeys and all our businesses, are oft present at battles, and by secret helps do give the desired successes to their friends, for they are said, that at their pleasures they can procure prosperity, and inflict adversity.

In like manner they distribute these into more orders, so as some are fiery, some watery, some aerial, some terrestrial; which four species of angels are computed according to the four powers of the celestial souls, viz. the mind, reason, imagination, and the vivifying and moving nature; hence the fiery follow the mind of the celestial souls, whence they concur to the contemplation of more sublime things, but the aerial follow the reason, and favour the rational faculty, and after a certain manner separate it from the sensitive and vegetative; therefore it serveth for an active life, as the fiery for a contemplative; but the watery following the imagination, serve for a voluptuous life; the earthly following nature, favour vegetable nature.

Moreover they distinguish also this kind of angels into saturnine and jovial, according to the names of the stars, and the heavens; further, some are oriental,[6] some occidental,[7] some meridional,[8] some septentrional.[9]

Moreover there is no part of the world destitute of the proper assistance of these angels, not because they are there alone, but because they reign there especially, for they are everywhere, although some especially operate and have their influence in this place, some elsewhere; neither truly are these things to be understood, as though they were subject to the influences of the stars, but as they have correspondence with the heaven above the world, from whence especially all things are directed, and to the which all things ought to be conformable.

Whence as these angels are appointed for divers stars, so also for divers places and times, not that they are limited by time or place, neither by the bodies which they are appointed to govern, but because the order of wisdom hath so decreed; therefore they favour more, and patronize those bodies, places, times, stars; so they have called some diurnal, some nocturnal, other meridional;[10] in like manner some are called woodmen, some mountaineers, some fieldmen, some domestics.

Hence the gods of the woods, country gods, satyrs, familiars,[11] fairies of the fountains, fairies of the woods, nymphs of the sea, the Naiades,[12] Neriades,[13] Dryades,[14] Pierides,[15] Hamadryades,[16] Potumides,[17] Hinnides, Agapte, Pales,[18] Pareades, Dodonae,[19] Feniliae,[20] Lavernae,[21] Pareae, Muses, Aonides,[22] Castalides,[23] Heliconides,[24] Pegasides,[25] Meonides,[26] Phebiades,[27] Camenae,[28] the Graces,[29] the Genii,[30] hobgoblins[31] and such like; whence they call them vulgar superiors, some the demigods and goddesses.

Some of these are so familiar and acquainted with men, that they are even affected with human perturbations, by whose instruction *Plato* thinketh that men do oftentimes wonderful things, even as by the instruction of men, some beasts which are most nigh unto us, as apes, dogs, elephants, do often strange things above their species.[32]

And they who have written the Chronicles of the Danes and Norwegians, do testify, that spirits of divers kinds in those regions are subject to men's commands; moreover some of these to be corporeal and mortal, whose bodies are begotten and die, yet to be long lived,[33] is the opinion of the Egyptians and Platonists, and especially approved by *Proclus. Plutarch*[34] also and *Demetrius*[35] the philosopher, and *Aemilianus*[36] the rhetorician affirm the same.

Therefore of these spirits of the third kind, as the opinion of the Platonists is; they report that there are so many legions, as there are stars in the heaven, and so many spirits in every legion, as in heaven itself stars, but there are (as *Athanasius* delivereth) who think, that the true number of the good spirits, is according to the number of men, ninety-nine parts, according to the parable of the hundred sheep;[37] others think only nine parts, according to the parable of the ten groats;[38] others suppose the number of the angels equal with men, because it is written, he hath appointed the bounds of the people according to the number of the angels of God.

And concerning their number many have written many things, but the latter theologians, following the Master of the Sentences,[39] *Austin,* and *Gregory,* easily resolve themselves, saying, that the number of the good angels transcendeth human capacity; to the which on the contrary, innumerable unclean spirits do correspond, there being so many in the inferior world, as pure spirits in the superior, and some divines affirm that they have received this by revelations.

Under these they place a kind of spirits, subterrany or obscure, which the Platonists call angels that failed, revengers of wickedness, and ungodliness, according to the decree of the divine justice, and they call them evil angels and wicked spirits, because they oft annoy and hurt even of their own accords; of these also they reckon more legions, and in like manner distinguishing them according to the names of the stars and elements, and parts of the world, they do place over them kings, princes and rulers and the names of them.

Of these, four most mischievous kings do rule over the others, according to the four parts of the world; under these many more princes of legions govern, and also many of private offices. Hence the wicked Gorgons,[40] the Furies.[41] Hence *Tisiphone, Alecto, Megera, Cerberus.*[42]

They of this kind of spirits, *Porphyry* saith, inhabit a place nigh to the Earth, yea within the Earth itself; there is no mischief, which they dare not commit; they have altogether a violent and hurtful custom, therefore they very much plot and endeavour violent and sudden mischiefs; and when they make incursions, sometimes they are wont to lie hid, but sometimes to offer open violence, and are very much delighted in all things done wickedly and contentiously.[43]

Notes—Chapter XVI

1. *propriety of the word*—The word "intelligent," from the Latin *intelligere:* to see into, perceive, understand.

2. *stars*—Planets.

3. *fifty-five motions*—Aristotle distinguishes 55 spheres upon which the planets and stars move, in his *De caelo* (On the heavens).

4. *angels as ministers*—Hebrews 1:14.

For we indeed acknowledge that angels are "ministering spirits," and we say that "they are sent forth to minister for them who shall be heirs of salvation;" and that they ascend, bearing the supplications of men, to the purest of the heavenly places in the universe, or even to supercelestial regions purer still; and that they come down from these, conveying to each one, according to his deserts, something enjoined by God to be conferred by them upon those who are to be the recipients of His benefits. Having thus learned to call these beings "angels" [i.e., messengers] from their employments, we find that because they are divine they are sometimes termed "god" in the sacred Scriptures, but not so that we are commanded to honour and worship in place of God those who minister to us, and bear to us His blessings. (Origen *Against Celsus* 5.4 [*Ante-Nicene Fathers,* 4:544])

5. *invisible powers*—

We indeed also maintain with regard not only to the fruits of the earth, but to every flowing stream and every breath of air, that the ground brings forth those things which are said to grow up naturally,—that the water springs in fountains, and refreshes the earth with running streams,—that the air is kept pure, and supports the life of those who breathe it, only in consequence of the agency and control of certain beings whom we may call invisible husbandmen and guardians; but we deny that those invisible agents are demons. (ibid. 8.31 [*Ante-Nicene Fathers,* 4:650–1])

6. *oriental*—Eastern.

7. *occidental*—Western.

8. *meridional*—Southern.

9. *septentrional*—Northern.

10. *meridional*—Here used to refer to midday, or noon.

11. *familiars*—Familiar spirits are mentioned a number of times in the Old Testament and seem to have been connected with divination. Saul sought out the witch of Endor because of her familiar spirit (I Samuel 28:7). The punishment for having such a spirit was death (Leviticus 20:27). God specifically prohibits seeking out those with familiar spirits (Leviticus 19:31). On this last verse Rashi gives the interesting commentary: "A prohibition against a בעל אוב and a ידעוני. A בעל אוב is a wizard who (appears to) speak from his armpits, and a ידעוני is one who places the bone of an animal, the name of which is Yiddo'a, into his mouth and the bone (appears to) speak" (Rashi 1949, 3:196).

12. *Naiades*—Nymphs of streams, ponds and fresh waters.

13. *Neriades*—Nereids, the fifty sea nymphs who were the daughters of Nereus and Doris.

14. *Dryades*—Dryads, wood nymphs.

15. *Pierides*—A surname of the Muses derived from Pieria, a region on the southeast coast of Macedonia, where they were first worshipped among the Thracians. According to legend Pierus, King of Emathia in Macedonia, had nine beautiful daughters called the Pierides who dared to challenge the Muses in a poetry contest. For punishment they were turned into magpies, and the Muses kept their name.

16. *Hamadryades*—Tree nymphs who lived and died with the tree they inhabited, and were thus mortal, though long in years.

17. *Potumides*—Potameides, river nymphs.

18. *Pales*—Roman god of shepherds and their flocks. The festival of the deity, called Parilia, or Palilia, was celebrated April 21, the supposed birth date of the city of Rome. It is uncertain whether the god was male or female, as it is referred to by ancient writers under both sexes (Ovid says female; Varro says male). This has led to the conjecture that there were two gods, a male Pales similar to Pan, and a female Pales associated with Vesta. For a description of the Palilia. see Ovid *Fasti* 4, lines 721–82.

19. *Dodonae*—Dodonides, a class of nymphs specific to Dodona and its oak trees. Zeus Dodonaios was worshipped at Dodona, the second most celebrated oracle in the ancient world, after Delphi. In earliest times the oracle was received by the rustling leaves of an oak, or grove of oaks, sacred to Zeus, and interpreted by his priests, the Selloi. See Homer *Iliad* 16, lines 333–5; Pausanias *Guide to Greece* 10.12.5.

20. *Feniliae*—Perhaps nymphs of the grasses, or fields. The Latin *fenilia* means "a place where hay is kept."

21. *Lavernae*—Laverna was the Roman goddess of thieves and imposters. She had a sacred grove on the Via Salaria, and an altar near the Porta Lavernalis. Presumably her nymphs would be located in the grove.

22. *Aonides*—A name for the Muses deriving from Aonia, the region of Boeotia that contained Mount Helicon and the fountain Aganippe, both of which the Muses were known to frequent. In the *Metamorphoses* of Ovid, one Muse refers to herself and her sisters as "we of Aonia" *(Metamorphoses* 5.2, line 333 [Riley, 169]).

23. *Castalides*—Name of the Muses that comes from the fountain Castalia on Mount Parnassus. The fountain was also sacred to Apollo, and its name was said to derive from Castalia, daughter of Achelous, who cast herself into the fountain to escape the rape of Apollo. The Pythia, Apollo's oracle, bathed in its waters.

24. *Heliconides*—The Muses were called Heliconiades, or Heliconides, by the Roman poets after Mount Helicon. See note 22 above.

25. *Pegasides*—Pegasus was supposed to have created the fountain Hippocrene on Mount Helicon with a kick of his hoof. Thus the fountain was called *Pegasis* (sprung from Pegasus), and the Muses received the name Pegasides, because they lived in the fountain.

26. *Meonides*—Perhaps Maenades, the Bacchantes, frenzied women who worshipped Dionysus. They were also called Thyiades, Clodones and Mimallones.

27. *Phebiades*—Perhaps the Muses, after Phoebus, another name for Apollo, with whom they are so closely associated.

28. *Camenae*—Also called Casmenae, and Carmenae, prophetic water nymphs of ancient Italy. The most important was Carmenta (or Carmentis) who

was worshipped in her temple at the foot of the Capitoline Hill, and at her altars near the Porta Carmentalis, in Rome. Juvenal connects them with a spring and sacred grove near the Porta Capena in the south wall of the old city of Rome:

> Here, where Numa used to make assignations with his nocturnal mistress [Egeria, one of the Camenae, who instructed the king in forming his religious laws] the grove of the once-hallowed fountain and the temples are in our days let out to Jews, whose whole furniture is a basket and bundle of hay. For every single tree is bid to pay a rent to the people, and the Camenae having been ejected, the wood is one mass of beggars. (Juvenal *Satires* 3, c. line 12, trans. Lewis Evans [New York: Hinds, Noble and Eldredge, n.d.], 15)

29. *Graces*—The *Gratiae* of the Romans, called *Charites* by the Greeks, after Charis wife of Hephaestus, the personification of grace and beauty (see Homer *Iliad* 18, lines 382–3). They were three in number, and bore the names Euphrosyne, Aglaia and Thalia.

30. *genii*—Plural of genius, a protecting spirit of the Romans. The Greeks called them daemons. Hesiod says there are 30,000 of them on Earth, that they are invisible, and that they are the souls of good men from the Golden Age. (See Plato *Cratylus* 397e–398c.) The Romans viewed them as the generators or producers of life who accompanied each man as a second higher self. The idea is very similar to that of guardian angels. Gregory Thaumaturgus speaks of his genius in his address to Origen:

> ... if I may seek to discourse of aught beyond this, and, in particular, of any of those beings who are not seen, but yet are more godlike, and who have a special care for men, it shall be addressed to that being who, by some momentous decision, had me allotted to him from my boyhood to rule, and rear, and train,—I mean that holy angel of God who fed me from my youth, as says the saint dear to God, meaning thereby his own particular one [see Genesis 48:15–6]. ... But we, in addition to the homage we offer to the Common Ruler of all men, acknowledge and praise that being, whosoever he is, who has been the wonderful guide of our childhood, who in all other matters has been in time past my beneficent tutor and guardian. (*Oration and Panegyric Addressed to Origen* 4 [*Ante-Nicene Fathers,* 6:24])

31. *hobgoblins*—In the Latin *Opera, lemures* is given. The lemures were ghosts, the spirits or specters of the dead. Sometimes they were divided into two classes: *lares,* the ghosts of good men, and *larvae,* the ghosts of evil men. Usually this distinction was not made. The Romans celebrated the festival of Lemuralia (or Lemuria) to propitiate these spirits.

32. *above their species*—

> Cronus was of course aware that, as we have explained, no human being is competent to wield an irresponsible control over mankind without becoming swollen with pride and unrighteousness. Being alive to this he gave our communities as their kings and magistrates, not men but spirits, beings of diviner and superior kind, just as we still do the same with our flocks of sheep and herds of other domesticated animals. We do not set oxen to manage oxen, or goats to manage goats; we, their betters in kind, act as their masters ourselves. Well, the god, in his kindness to man, did the same; he set over us this superior race of spirits who took charge of us with no less ease to themselves than convenience to us, providing us with peace and mercy, sound law and unscanted justice, and endowing the families of mankind with internal concord and happiness. (Plato *Laws* 4.713c–d [Hamilton and Cairns, 1304–5])

33. *long lived*—Referring to a passage near the end of the second book of the *De nuptiis Philologiae et Mercurii et de septem artibus liberalibus* (The nuptials of Philology and Mercury and the seven liberal arts) by Martianus Capella, Thorndike says: "Finally the earth itself is inhabited by a long-lived race of dwellers in woods and groves, in fountains and lakes and streams, called Pans, Fawns, satyrs, Silvani, nymphs, and other names. They finally die as men do, but possess great power of foresight and of inflicting injury" (Thorndike, 1:546).

34. *Plutarch*—

> And moreover, Hesiod imagines that the Daemons themselves, after certain revolutions of time, do at length die. For, introducing a Nymph speaking, he marks the time wherein they expire:

> Nine ages of men in their flower doth live
> The railing crow; four times the stags surmount
> The life of crows; to ravens doth Nature give
> A threefold age of stags, by true account;
> One phoenix lives as long as ravens nine.

But you, fair Nymphs, as the daughters
verily
Of mighty Jove and Nature divine,
The phoenix years tenfold do multiply.

Now those which do not well understand what the poet means by this word γενεά (age) do cause this computation of time to amount to a great number of years. For the word means a year; so that the total sum makes but 9720 years, which is the space of the age of Daemons. And there are several mathematicians who make it shorter than this. Pindar himself does not make it longer when he says, Destiny has given Nymphs an equal life with trees; and therefore they are called Hamadryades, because they spring up and die with oaks. (Plutarch *Obsolescence of Oracles* 11, trans. Robert Midgley [Goodwin, 4:15])

35. *Demetrius*—Demetrius of Tarsus, a grammarian who is one of the speakers in Plutarch's dialogue, the *Obsolescence of Oracles*. See note 34 above.

36. *Ameilianus*—Orator of the 1st century who is mentioned by Plutarch in his *Obsolescence of Oracles*, ch. 17. Agrippa has merely plucked the names Demetrius and Ameilianus out of Plutarch to impress the reader, not for any good reason.

37. *hundred sheep*—Luke 15:4.

38. *ten groats*—Luke 15:8.

39. *Master of the Sentences*—Peter Lombard. See his biographical note.

40. *Gorgons*—Originally there was only Gorgo, a terrifying shade of Hades mentioned by Homer in the *Odyssey* 11, line 633. In the *Iliad* the aegis of Athene is said to contain the head of Gorgo:

And across her shoulders she threw the
betasselled, terrible
aegis, all about which Terror hangs like a
garland,
and Hatred is there, and Battle Strength,
and heart-freezing Onslaught
and thereon is set the head of the grim
gigantic Gorgon,
a thing of fear and horror, portent of Zeus
of the aegis.
(Homer *Iliad* 5, lines 738–42 [Lattimore,
148])

Hesiod speaks of three Gorgons named Stheno, Euryale, and Medusa, the daughters of Phorcys and Ceto, from which they derive the name Phorcydes.

They lived in the far west in the Ocean, had serpents for hair, wings, brazen claws and enormous teeth. Medusa alone was mortal. Everyone who looked at her face was turned to stone. After Perseus killed her, Athene placed her head in the center of her shield (or breastplate).

41. *Furies*—The Eumenides, or more anciently the Erinyes, of the Greeks (Roman Furiae, or Dirae) were avenging goddesses who punished crimes. *Erinyes* means "angry goddesses" or "goddesses who persecute the criminal." The later title *Eumenides* is a euphemism meaning "soothed goddesses," and was a way to avoid inadvertently naming, and thereby evoking, them. They are described as black, winged figures with serpent-infested hair and bleeding eyes, who visit unease and misfortune upon the heads of those who have been cursed for their crimes. Hesiod says they were born from the drops of blood that fell from the castrated Uranus onto the body of the goddess Gaea (Earth). Their names are Tisiphone, Alecto and Megaera.

42. *Cerberus*—The dog-monster who stood guard at the gate of Hades, where the ferryman Charon landed the shades on the far side of Styx. Homer mentions "the dog" in both the *Iliad* (8, line 368) and the *Odyssey* (11, lines 623 and 625) but does not actually name him. Hesiod describes him with fifty heads, and says he is the offspring of Typhaon and Echidna. In later writers he is three-headed with a serpent tail and serpents twining about his neck: "These are the realms huge Cerberus makes ring with the barking of his threefold jaws, reposing his enormous bulk in the cave that fronts the ferry" (Virgil *Aeneid* 6, lines 417–8 [Lonsdale and Lee, 167]). See also the *Georgics* 4, c. line 470.

43. *wickedly and contentiously*—

In the most holy of the mysteries, before the God appears, certain terrestrial daemons present themselves, and fights which disturb those that are to be initiated, tear them away from undefiled goods, and call forth their attention to matter. Hence the Gods exhort us not to look at these, till we are fortified by the powers which the mysteries confer. For thus they speak: It is not proper for you to behold them till your body is initiated. And on this account the oracles (i.e. the Chaldaeans) add, that such daemons, alluring souls, seduce them from the mysteries. (Proclus *Commentary on the First Alcibiades of Plato,* trans. Thomas Taylor. In Proclus *An Apology for the Fables of Homer* 1, n. 8 [*Thomas Taylor the Platonist: Selected Writings,* 461])

CHAPTER XVII

Of these according to the opinion of the theologians.

But our theologians, together with *Diony-sius,* maintain the three distinctions of angels, everyone of which they divide into three orders; they call these hierarchies, those quires, whom *Proclus* also distinguisheth by the number nine.

They place therefore in the superior hierarchy, Seraphim, Cherubim, and Thrones, as it were supercelestial angels contemplating the order of the divine providence; the first in the goodness of God; the second in the essence of God, as the form; the third in the wisdom.

In the middle hierarchy they place the Dominations, Virtues, and Powers, as it were worldly angels concurring to the government of the world; the first of these command that which the other execute; the second are ministers to the heavens and sometimes conspire to the working of miracles; the third drive away those things which seem to be able to disturb the divine law.

But in the inferior hierarchy they place the Principalities, Archangels, and Angels, whom also *Jamblicus* reckoneth up,[1] these as ministering spirits descend to take care of inferior things; the first of these take care of public things, princes and magistrates, provinces and kingdoms, every one those that belong to themselves; when we read in *Daniel,*[2] but the prince of the kingdom of Persia withstood me twenty-one days; and *Jesus* the son of *Sirach* testifieth,[3] that for every nation a ruling angel is appointed; which also *Moses* by his song in Deuteronomy[4] seemeth to show forth, saying, when the Most

High divided the nations, he appointed them bounds according to the number of the angels of God. The second are present at sacred duties, and direct the divine worship about every man, and offer up the prayers and sacrifices of men before the gods. The third dispose every smaller matter, and to each thing each one is a preserver. There are also of these, who afford virtue to the least plants and stones and to all inferior things; to whom many things are common with God, many with men, and they are mediating ministers.

But *Athanasius,* besides Thrones, Cherubins, and Seraphins, who are next to God, and magnify him uncessantly with hymns and continual praises, praying for our salvation, nameth the other orders, which by a common name he calleth the militia of heaven.

The first of these is the Doctrinal order, of the which he was, who spake to *Daniel,* saying, come, that I may teach thee what shall come to thy people in the last days.[5]

Then there is the Tutelar order, of the which we read also in Daniel, behold, *Michael* one of the princes cometh to my help;[6] and there, in that time shall rise up *Michael* a great prince, who standeth for the sons of thy people;[7] of this order was that *Raphael* also, who carried forth and brought back *Tobiah* the younger.[8]

After this is the Procuratory order, of the which mention is made in Job, where we read, if the angel shall speak for him, he will entreat the Lord, and the Lord will be pleased with him;[9]

and of the same order is expounded also that which is written in the sixteenth chapter of Ecclesiasticus, about the end, the works of the Lord have been made by his appointment from the beginning, and he hath distributed their portions from the time they have been made, he hath adorned their works forever, they have not hungered, nor been wearied, and have not desisted from their works, none of them shall oppress his neighbour even forever.[10]

The Ministerial order followeth, of the which *Paul* to the Hebrews saith, are they not all ministering spirits, sent forth for them who shall be heirs of salvation?[11]

After these is the Auxiliary order, of the which we read in Esay, the angels of the Lord went forth and slew in the tent of the Assyrians 185 thousands.[12]

The Receptory order of souls followeth this, of which we read in Luke, the soul of *Lazarus* was carried by angels into the bosom of *Abraham*,[13] and there we are taught, that we should make to ourselves friends of the unrighteous *Mammon,* that we may be received into eternal tabernacles.[14]

Moreover, there is the order of the Assistants, of the which we read in Zachary, these are the two sons of the oil of splendour, who assist the ruler of the whole Earth.[15]

But the theologians of the Hebrews do otherwise number and call these orders.[16]

For in the highest place are those which they call Haioth Hacadosh[17] חיות הקדש,

that is, Creatures of Sanctity, or by the which God אהיה giveth the gift of being.

In the second place succeed Ophanim[18] אופנים, that is Forms or Wheels, by the which God יהוה distinguisheth the chaos.

In the third place are Aralim[19] אראלים, great, strong, and mighty angels, by the which *Jehova Elohim* pronounced, or *Jehova* joined with *He* היהוה, administereth form to the liquid matter.

In the fourth place are Hasmalim[20] חשמלים, by which El לא God framed the effigies of bodies.

The fifth order is Seraphim[21] שרפים, by the which God *Elohim Gibor* אלהים גיבר draweth forth the elements.

The sixth is Malachim[22] מלאכים, that is of Angels, by the which God *Eloha* אליה produceth metals.

The seventh Elohim אלהים, that is the Gods, by the which God *Jehovah Sabaoth* יהוה צבאות produceth vegetables.

The eighth Beni Elohim[23] בני אלהים, that is the Sons of God, by the which God *Elohim Sabaoth* אלהים צבאות procreateth animals.

The ninth and lowest Cherubim[24] כרובים, by the which God *Sadai* שדי createth mankind.

Under these is the order anamasticus[25] called Issim[26] אישים, that is Nobles, Strong Men, or Blessed, by the which God *Adonai* אדני bestoweth prophecy.[27]

Notes—Chapter XVII

1. *Jamblicus reckoneth*—

And, in short, all these genera exhibit their proper orders; viz. the aerial genera exhibit aerial fire; the terrestrial a terrestrial and blacker fire; and the celestial a more splendid fire. But in these three boundaries all the genera are distributed according to a triple order of beginning, middle, and end. And the Gods, indeed, exhibit the supreme and most pure causes of this triple order. But the genera of angels depend on those of archangels. The genera of daemons appear to be subservient to those of angels;

and in a similar manner to these, the genera of heros are ministrant. They are not, however, subservient to angels in the same way as daemons. Again, the genera of archons, whether they preside over the world or over matter, exhibit the order which is adapted to them. But all the genera of souls present themselves to the view as the last of more excellent natures. (Iamblichus *On the Mysteries* 2.7 [Taylor, 98–9])

2. *in Daniel*—Daniel 10:13.

3. *Sirach testifieth*—Ecclesiasticus 17:17.

4. *in Deuteronomy*—Deuteronomy 32:8. However, Agrippa's interpretation of this verse is questionable—perhaps he links it to Deuteronomy 4:19.

5. *in the last days*—Daniel 10:14.

6. *to my help*—Daniel 10:13.

7. *sons of thy people*—Daniel 12:1.

8. *Tobiah the younger*—Tobit 5:4, 16 and 11:4.

9. *pleased with him*—Job 33:23. The meaning of this verse is clearer in the Knox translation than in the King James.

10. *even forever*—Ecclesiasticus 16:26–8.

11. *heirs of salvation*—Hebrews 1:14.

12. *185 thousands*—Isaiah 37:36.

13. *bosom of Abraham*—Luke 16:22.

14. *eternal tabernacles*—Luke 16:9.

15. *the whole Earth*—Zechariah 4:14.

16. *these orders*—

> The Holy, Blessed be He! affixed to the Throne legions to serve it, (the Ten Angelic Hosts, the Ye'tzeeratic World.) These are; Malakheem, Areleem, 'Häy-yôth, Ophaneem, Hash-maleem, E'leem, Eloheem, Benai Eloheem, Isheem and Serapheem. And for the service of these, the Holy, Blessed be He! made Samä-el and his legions, who are as it were, the clouds to be used to come down upon the earth. (*Zohar* 2.43a. In Myer [1888] 1974, 17:329)

17. *Haioth Hacadosch*—Chaioth ha-Qadesh. See Ezekiel 1:5–14. See also Appendix VI here and in the following notes.

18. *Ophanim*—Auphanim. See Ezekiel 1:15–20.

19. *Aralim*—See Ezekiel 1:26.

20. *Hasmalim*—Chashmalim. See Ezekiel 1:27.

21. *Seraphim*—See Isaiah 6:6.

22. *Malachim*—Melakim, usually derived from the Hebrew מלך (king), plural מלכים (see Ezra 4:13). But surely it is derived from מלאך, MLAK (a messenger of God); i.e., an angel (see Exodus 23:20 and 33:2).

23. *Beni Elohim*—See Genesis 6:4.

24. *Cherubim*—Kerubim.

25. *anamasticus*—*Dii animalie,* gods who were originally men; in other words, heros.

26. *Issim*—Ashim (Valorous Men; Men of God). See Isaiah 53:3 in the Hebrew for this plural form of איש (a man). It is used with reference to angels in Judges 13:6, 8. MacGregor Mathers' use of the form אשים, AShIM, from the root אש (fire) seems to be an error (see Mathers [1887] 1962, 26). Along with his other error, mentioned in note 22 above, it has gained universal acceptance in modern popular occultism. Mathers borrows most of his material on the names of the Sephiroth directly from Ginsburg's *Kabbalah* [1863] 1970 (see the table in this latter text, p. 93).

27. *bestoweth prophecy*—See Judges 13:8, where this form of divine name is used and where the angel of the Lord gives prophecy.

Apollyon

from *The Magus* by Francis Barrett (London, 1801)

CHAPTER XVIII

Of the orders of evil spirits, and of their fall, and divers natures.

There are some of the school of the theologians, who distribute the evil spirits into nine degrees,[1] as contrary to the nine orders of the angels.

Therefore the first of these are those which are called False Gods, who usurping the name of God, would be worshipped for gods, and require sacrifices and adorations, as that Devil, who saith to Christ, if thou wilt fall down and worship me, I will give thee all these things, showing him all the kingdoms of the world;[2] and the prince of these is he who said, I will ascend above the height of the clouds, and will be like to the Most High;[3] who is therefore called *Beelzebub*,[4] that is, an old god.

In the second place follow the Spirits of Lies, of which sort was he who went forth, and was a lying spirit in the mouth of the prophets of Achab;[5] and the prince of these is the serpent *Pytho*;[6] from whence *Apollo* is called *Pythius*,[7] and that woman a witch in *Samuel*,[8] and the other in the Gospel,[9] who had *Pytho* in their belly.[10] Therefore this kind of devils joineth himself to the oracles, and deludeth men by divinations, and predictions, so that he may deceive.

In the third order are the Vessels of Iniquity, which are also called the Vessels of Wrath; these are the inventors of evil things and of all wicked arts, as in *Plato*, that devil *Theutus*[11] who taught cards and dice; for all wickedness, malice and deformity proceedeth from these; of the which in Genesis, in the benedictions of *Simeon* and *Levi, Jacob* saith, Vessels of Iniquity[12] are in their habitations; into their counsel let not my soul come; whom the Psalmist calleth Vessels of Death,[13] *Esay* Vessels of Fury,[14] and *Jeremy* Vessels of Wrath,[15] *Ezekiel* Vessels of Destroying and Slaying;[16] and their prince is *Belial*,[17] which is interpreted without a yoke or disobedient, a prevaricator and an apostate, of whom *Paul* to the Corenthians saith, what agreement hath Christ with *Belial?*[18]

Fourthly follow the Revengers of Evil, and their prince is *Asmodeus*,[19] viz. causing judgement.

After these in the fifth place come the Deluders, who imitate miracles, and serve wicked conjurers and witches, and seduce the people by their miracles, as the serpent seduced *Eve*,[20] and their prince is *Satan,* of whom is written in the Revelations, that he seduced the whole world, doing great signs, and causing fire to descend from heaven in the sight of men, seducing the inhabitants of the Earth, by reason of the signs, which are given him to do.[21]

Sixthly the Aerial Powers offer themselves; they join themselves to thundering and lightnings, corrupting the air, causing pestilences and other evils; in the number of which, are the four angels, of whom the Revelation speaketh, to whom it is given to hurt the earth and sea, holding the four winds, from the four corners of the Earth;[22] and their prince is called *Meririm;*[23] he is the meridian devil, a boiling spirit, a devil raging in the south, whom *Paul* to the Ephesians calleth the prince of the power of this air, and the spirit which worketh in the children of disobedience.[24]

The seventh mansion the Furies possess, which are powers of evil, discords, war and devastations, whose prince in the Revelations[25] is called in Greek *Apollyon,* in Hebrew *Abaddon,*[26] that is destroying and wasting.

In the eighth place are the Accusers, or the Inquisitors, whose prince is *Astarath,*[27] that is, a searcher out: in the Greek language he is called *Diabolos,*[28] that is an accuser, or calumniator, which in the Revelations is called the accuser of the brethren, accusing them night and day before the face of our God.[29]

Moreover the Tempters and Ensnarers have the last place, one of which is present with every man, which we therefore call the evil genius, and their prince is *Mammon,*[30] which is interpreted covetousness.

But all unanimously maintain that evil spirits do wander up and down in this inferior world, enraged against all, whom they therefore call devils, of whom *Austine* in his first book of the incarnation of the word to *Januarius,* saith: concerning the devils and his angels contrary to virtues, the Ecclesiastical preaching hath taught, that there are such things; but what they are and how they are, he hath not clear enough expounded: yet there is this opinion amongst most, that this Devil was an angel, and being made an apostate,[31] persuaded very many of the angels to decline with himself, who even unto this day are called his angels: Greece notwithstanding thinketh not that all these are damned, nor that they are all purposefully evil, but that from the creation of the world, the dispensation of things is ordained by this means, that the tormenting of sinful souls is made over to them.

The other theologians[32] say that not any devil was created evil, but that they were driven and cast forth of heaven, from the orders of good angels for their pride, whose fall not only our and the Hebrew theologians, but also the Assyrians, Arabians, Egyptians, and Greeks do confirm by their tenets; *Pherecydes* the Syrian describeth the fall of the devils, and that *Ophis,*[33] that is the devilish serpent, was the head of that rebelling army; *Trismegistus* sings the same fall in his Pymander,[34] and *Homer* under the name of *Ararus,*[35] in his verses; and *Plutarch* in his speech Of Usury,[36] signifieth, that *Empedocles* knew that the fall of the devils was after this manner: the devils also themselves often confess their fall.

They therefore being cast forth into this valley of misery, some that are nigh to us wander up and down in this obscure air, others inhabit lakes, rivers and seas, others the earth, and terrify earthly things, and invade those who dig wells and metals, cause the gapings of the earth, strike together the foundations of mountains, and vex not only men, but also other creatures.

Some being content with laughter and delusion only, do contrive rather to weary men, than to hurt them, some heightening themselves to the length of a giant's body, and again shrinking themselves up to the smallness of the pygmy's, and changing themselves into divers forms, do disturb men with vain fear: others study lies and blasphemies, as we read of one in the first book of Kings, saying, I will go forth and be a lying spirit in the mouth of all the prophets of *Achab:*[37] but the worst sort of devils are those, who lay wait and overthrow passengers in their journeys, and rejoice in wars and effusion of blood, and afflict men with most cruel stripes: we read of such in Matthew, for fear of whom no man durst pass that way.[38]

Moreover the Scripture reckoneth up nocturnal, diurnal, and meridional devils, and describeth other spirits of wickedness by divers names, as we read in Esay[39] of satyrs, screech owls, sirens, storks, owls; and in the Psalms[40] of apes, basilisks, lions, dragons; and in the Gospel we read of scorpions[41] and *Mammon*[42] and the prince of this world[43] and rulers of darkness, of all which *Beelzebub* is the prince, whom Scripture calleth the prince of wickedness.[44]

Porphyry saith, their prince is *Serapis,* who is also called *Pluto* by the Greeks, and also *Cerberus* is chief amongst them, that three-headed dog: viz. because he is conversant in three elements, Air, Water and Earth, a most pernicious devil; whence also *Proserpina,* who can do very much in these three elements, is their princess, which she testifies of herself in her answers, in these verses:

> Of threefold nature I Lucina fair,
> The daughter am, sent from above the air;
> The golden Phoebe am, and with heads trine,
> Whom many forms do change, and the trine sign
> Which I bear with forms of earth, fire, and air,
> I for black mastiffs of the earth do care.

Origen's opinion[45] concerning the devils is: the spirits who act of their own free will, left the service of God with their prince the Devil; if they begin to repent a little, are clothed with human flesh; that further by this repentance, after the resurrection, by the same means by the which they came into the flesh, they might at the last return to the vision of God, being then also freed from etherial and aerial bodies, and then all knees are to be bowed to God, of celestial, terrestrial, and infernal things, that God may be all in all.

Moreover Saint *Iraneus* approveth the opinion of *Justine Martyr,* who hath said, *Satan never durst speak blasphemy against God, before that the Lord came on the Earth, because* that he knew not as yet his condemnation; but there are many of the devils who are fallen, who hope for their salvation.[46]

Very many think by the history of *Paul* the Hermit, written by *Jerome,* and reverenced by the Church with canonical hours,[47] also by the legend of *Brandan,* they are so taught; and even by this argument they maintain that their prayers are heard; that we read in the Gospels, that Christ heard the prayers of the devils, and granted that they should enter into the herd of swine;[48] to these also agreeth the 71 psalm, according to our supputation, but according to the supputation of the Hebrews the 72, where we read, the Ethiopians shall fall before him, and his enemies lick the dust;[49] there it is read according to the Hebrew text, they that inhabit the desert, shall bend their knees before him, that is, the airy spirits[50] shall adore him, as the Cabalists affirm, and his enemies shall lick the dust, which they understand of *Zazel,*[51] and his army: of which we read in Genesis, dust shall thou eat all the days of thy life,[52] and elsewhere the Prophet saith, because the dust of the Earth is his bread;[53] hence the Cabalists think, that even some devils shall be saved, which opinion also it is manifest that *Origen* was of.

Notes—Chapter XVIII

1. *nine degrees*—The consensus in ancient times seems to be for a threefold division of fallen angels, or evil spirits. One of the ninety-three visions of Saint Francisca (1384–1440) concerns the hierarchy of hell. She says that one third of the fallen angels took up residence in the air where they cause storms and disease, another third dwell on the Earth and lure souls to damnation, while the third part inhabit hell.

> Lucifer, she tells us, is the monarch of all the hells, but he rules in chains of iron, and is supreme in misery as well as in power. Under him are three princes, each absolute in his own department. The first of these is Asmodëus, once a cherub, but now holding the "principality" of carnal sins. The next is Mammon, the demon of avarice who holds the "throne" of this world. The third is Beëlzebub, who holds the "dominion" of idolaters. These three powers and Lucifer never leave their prisons, except under special permission from God; but they have legions and legions of subordinates on earth who are responsible to them. (Brewer 1901, 352)

On the same subject the *Zohar* says:

> "Come, See! In these evil species are *three* degrees, one above the other. The upper degree of these *three* hang in the air, the lowest degree of them, are these which laugh at people and trouble them in their dreams, because they are impudent like dogs [see *Chaldean Oracles* 75]. And there is a higher degree upon them which are from the Above and the Below [a middle degree], which make known to man things which are sometimes true and sometimes not true, and those things which are true they happen in the future." (Myer [1888] 1974, 20:435)

2. *kingdoms of the world*—Matthew 4:8.

3. *the Most High*—Isaiah 14:14.

4. *Beelzebub*—In the Old Testament, the god of the Philistine city of Ekron (II Kings 1:2). In the New Testament the Pharisees ascribed the ability of Jesus to cast out devils to the power of this arch-demon (Matthew 12:24). The name *beelzeboub* in the Vulgate is usually translated "Lord of the Flies," but in the best Greek manuscripts it is written *beelzeboul,* "Lord of the Earth," which seems to be the correct rendering.

5. *prophets of Achab*—Ahab. See I Kings 22:22.

6. *serpent Pytho*—The Latin *pytho* means the familiar spirit possessing a soothsayer that gives prophecy. The name Python came to be applied to the soothsayer.

7. *Pythius*—Apollo killed the Python, a great serpent monster born from the mud that covered the Earth after the deluge, which lived in the caves on Mount Parnassus. In memory of his victory the god instituted the Pythian games and was himself called Apollo Pythius.

8. *witch in Samuel*—I Samuel 28:7.

9. *in the Gospel*—Acts 16:16.

10. *Pytho in their belly*—See note 11, ch. XVI, bk. III. Ventriloquism, in the original use of the word, means "speaking from the belly," for which reason those possessed by prophetic spirits were known as ventriloquists. By ancient accounts the voice of the spirit seemed to come from deep in the abdomen or "armpit" and was base and guttural. This is a genuine phenomenon unaffected by culture or time (see Isaiah 29:4). Oesterreich writes:

> The second characteristic which reveals change of personality is closely related to the first: it is the voice. At the moment when the countenance alters, a more or less changed voice issues from the mouth of the person in the fit. The new intonation also corresponds to the character of the new individuality manifesting itself in the organism and is conditioned by it. In particular the top register of the voice is displaced; the feminine voice is transformed into a bass one, for in all the cases of possession which it has hitherto been my lot to know the new individuality was a man. (Oesterreich [1921] 1974, 1:2:19–20)

Perhaps this masculine quality of voice was in part the source of the belief expressed by Crysostom

in his *Homilies on the First Epistle to the Corinthians* 29.12.1, regarding the oracle at Delphi:

> Of this priestess, the Pythoness, it is now said that she sat with parted thighs on the tripod of Apollo and the evil spirit entered her from below passing through her genital organs and plunged her into a state of frenzy, so that she began with loosened hair to foam and rage like one drunken. (In Oesterreich [1921] 1974, 2:9:315)

11. *Theutus*—Thoth.

> The story is that in the region of Naucratis in Egypt there dwelt one of the old gods of the country, the god to whom the bird called Ibis is sacred, his own name being Theuth. He it was that invented number and calculation, geometry and astronomy, not to speak of draughts and dice, and above all writing. (Plato *Phaedrus* 274c [Hamilton and Cairns, 520])

As in other places, it may be conjectured Agrippa did not understand his own reference, as he is unlikely to have knowingly spoken in so disparaging a way of the Egyptian Hermes.

12. *Vessels of Iniquity*—Genesis 49:5, which in King James reads "instruments of cruelty."

13. *Vessels of Death*—Psalms 7:13.

14. *Vessels of Fury*—Perhaps Isaiah 51:20.

15. *Vessels of Wrath*—I do not find this in Jeremiah but in Romans 9:22.

16. *Destroying and Slaying*—see Ezekiel 9.

17. *Belial*—A demon of the New Testament (II Corinthians 6:15), from the Greek *beliar,* which is a corruption of the Hebrew בליעל, meaning "what is useless, of no fruit," and by extension "wickedness, a wicked man, a destroyer." The word is not used in the Old Testament as a proper name. "Sons of *belial"* signifies sons of wickedness (Judges 19:22).

18. *Christ with Belial*—II Corinthians 6:15.

19. *Asmodeus*—The Destroyer, the demon who killed the seven husbands of Sarah in the Apocryphal Book of Tobit (3:8). It was driven away to Upper Egypt by the burning fume from the heart and liver of a fish, and bound there by the power of the angel Raphael (8:2–3). In Jewish folklore Asmodeus has the distinction of being able to outwit King Solomon himself.

Belial Dancing Before Solomon

from *Das Buch Belial* by Jacobus de Teramo (Ausgburg, 1473)

Asmodeus

from *Dictionnaire infernal* by Collin de Plancy (Paris, 1863)

Mammon

from *The Magus* by Francis Barrett
(London, 1801)

By tricking the king into removing the magic ring he used to control devils, Asmodeus sat upon the throne for 40 years while Solomon wandered through his own kingdom as a beggar. For this reason he was called "king of the demons." The story is told of his birth that King David had an emission of seed while coupling with the succubus demon Igrat in his sleep, and Igrat bore Adad, king of Edom. When asked his name, he answered *"Sh'mi Ad, Ad sh'm,"* that is, "My name is Ad, Ad is my name." Hence he was called Ashm'dai, or Ashmodai (Asmodeus), king of the demons. See Patai 1980, 457 and 459. It is believed the name is actually a corruption of Aeshma-Daeva (covetous demon), one of a group of seven principle demons in Persian mythology.

20. *serpent seduced Eve*—Genesis 3:13.

21. *given him to do*—Revelation 13:13–4.

22. *corners of the Earth*—Revelation 7:1–2.

23. *Meririm*—Perhaps from the Hebrew כמרירים, KMRIRIM, occurring in Job 3:5 as the "blackness of the day," an eclipse or obscuration of the Sun, which was an evil omen. Ancient interpreters regarded the K as a prefix to the substantive MRIRIM and read the

meaning to be "the greatest bitternesses (calamities) which could befall a day." See Gesenius 1890, 402.

24. *children of disobedience*—Ephesians 2:2.

25. *in the Revelations*—Revelation 9:11.

26. *Abaddon*—Hebrew: אבדון, ABDON (destruction). See Job 28:22. It was used as the name for a region of Gehenna in later rabbinical writings, after such usages as occur in Proverbs 15:11 and 27:20. In the New Testament it is the name of the angel of the abyss, and occurs only in Revelation 9:11.

27. *Astarath*—Astaroth, עשתרת, AShThRTh. In Greek, Astarte, a form of the Babylonian goddess Ishtar. Since she is the female counterpart of Baal (Judges 2:13) and is said to have been depicted with horns by Lucian and Herodian, she is supposed to have been a Moon goddess. She is called the goddess of the Zidonians (I Kings 11:5) and was worshipped by Solomon, who had married "many strange women" (I Kings 11:1), among them some Zidonians, who influenced his religious practices in his old age. In the medieval grimoires Astaroth is metamorphosed into a male demon: "He is a Mighty, Strong Duke and appeareth in the Form of an hurtful Angel riding on an Infernal Beast like a Dragon, and carrying in his right hand a Viper" *(Goetia* [demon number 29]. In *Lemegeton, or The Lesser Key of Solomon,* British Museum ms. Sloane 2731). The *Goetia* was transcribed from this manuscript and published by MacGregor Mathers.

28. *Diabolos*—Διαβολος, the Slanderer; the Devil.

29. *face of our God*—Revelation 12:10.

30. *Mammon*—From *mamôna,* the Aramaic word for "riches." It occurs only in the New Testament, where it is almost personified (Luke 16:13). The personification was completed in the 14th–16th centuries, when Mammon became the demon of covetousness.

31. *an apostate*—

In this manner, then, did that being once exist as light before he went astray, and fell to this place, and had his glory turned into dust, which is peculiarly the mark of the wicked, as the prophet also says; whence, too, he was called the prince of this world, i.e., of an earthly habitation: for he exercised power over those who were obedient to his wickedness, since "the whole of this world"—for I term this place of earth, world—"lieth in the wicked one," [I John 5:19] and in this apostate. That he is an apostate, i.e., a fugitive, even the Lord in

Ophis

from *The Magus* by Francis Barrett
(London, 1801)

the book of Job says, "Thou wilt take with a hook the apostate dragon," [Job 41:1] i.e., a fugitive. (Origen *De principiis* 1.5 [*Ante-Nicene Fathers*, 4:259])

32. *other theologians*—Origen is the prime exponent of the doctrine of universal free will, which necessitates the possibility of the redemption of devils, as well as the corruption of angels:

If then they are called opposing powers [the fallen angels], and are said to have been once without stain, while spotless purity exists in the essential being of none save the Father, Son, and Holy Spirit, but is an accidental quality in every created thing; and since that which is accidental may also fall away, and since these opposite powers once were spotless, and were once among those which still remain unstained, it is evident from all this that no one is pure either by essence or nature, and that no one was by nature polluted. (ibid. [*Ante-Nicene Fathers*, 4:259–60])

And the same view is to be entertained of those opposing influences which have given themselves up to such places and offices, that they derive the property by which they are made "principalities," or "powers," or rulers of the darkness of the world, or spirits of wickedness, or malignant spirits, or unclean demons, not from their essential nature, nor from their being so created, but have obtained these degrees in evil in proportion to their conduct, and the progress which they made in wickedness. (ibid. 1.8 [*Ante-Nicene Fathers*, 4:266])

33. *Ophis*—ὄφις, a serpent. Ophion, one of the first Titans, ruled over Olympus with his queen, Eurynome, until dethroned by Saturn and Rhea:

And Fabl'd how the Serpent, whom they call'd
Ophion with *Eyrynome,* the wide-
Encroaching *Eve* perhaps, had first the rule
Of high Olympus, thence by Saturn driv'n
    (Milton *Paradise Lost* 10, lines 581–3)

34. *in his Pymander*—There is no specific mention of the fall of the angels in the version of the *Pymander* given by Scott. Mention is made of troops of avenging demons which are marshalled under the seven planets: "By means of storms and hurricanes and fiery blasts, and corruptions of the air, and earthquakes, and famines also and wars, they punish men's impiety" *(Corpus Hermeticum* 16.10b [Scott, 1:269). Also referred to is a single "avenging demon," the office of which is more pithily set forth in the 1650 Everard translation than in Scott:

> For there is no part of the World void of the Devil, which entering in privately, sowed the seed of his own *proper* operation, and the mind did make pregnant, or did bring forth that which was sown, *Adulteries, Murders, Striking of Parents, Sacrileges, Impieties, Stranglings,* throwing down headlong, and all other things which are the work of Evil *Demons.* (Everard [1650, 1884] 1978, 13:14:88)

It is, however, made clear that souls migrate both up and down the order of being according to their worth, moving from men to demons on the way up, or into birds on the way down. The implication is that demons have free will either to elevate or degrade themselves. (See *Corpus Hermeticum* 10.7–8 [Scott, 1:191, 193].)

35. *Araraus*—This reference is obscure to me. Araros was the son of Aristophanes, and a Greek playwright. The Latin *Opera* spells this name *Atarus*. Perhaps an oblique reference to the casting of Hephaistos down from heaven by the wrathful Zeus (see the *Iliad* 1, lines 590–4).

36. *speech of Usury*—

> Nor is there any means for these debtors to make their escape into those fair pastures and meadows which once they enjoyed, but they wander about, like those Daemons mentioned by Empedocles to have been driven out of heaven by the offended Gods
>
> By the sky's force they're thrust into the main,
> Which to the earth soon spews them back again.
> Thence to bright Titan's orb [the sun] they're forced to fly,
> And Titan soon remits them to the sky.
>
> (Plutarch *De vitando aere alieno* [That we ought not to borrow] 7, trans. R. Smith [Goodwin, 5:420–1])

Empedocles is of course describing the passage of the damned souls through the four elements,

respectively Water, Earth, Fire and Air. The same quotation occurs in Plutarch's *Isis and Osiris* 26 (Goodwin, 4:87), with the additional line: "Received by each in turn, by all abhorred."

Elsewhere in the *Moralia* Plutarch quotes this related passage from another, or the same, lost work of Empedocles:

> This old decree of fate unchanged stands,—
> Whoso with horrid crimes defiles his hands,
> To long-lived Daemons this commission's given
> To chase him many ages out of heaven.
> Into this sad condition I am hurled,
> Banished from God to wander through the world,—
> (Plutarch *De exilio* [On exile] 17, trans. John Patrick [Goodwin 3:34])

37. *prophets of Achab*—See note 5 above.

38. *durst pass that way*—Matthew 8:28.

39. *read in Esay*—Isaiah 13:21–2; 34:11, 14–5.

40. *in the Psalms*—Psalms 91:13.

41. *of scorpions*—Luke 10:19.

42. *Mammon*—Luke 16:9. See note 30 above.

43. *prince of this world*—John 12:31; 14:30; 16:11.

44. *prince of wickedness*—See note 4 above.

45. *Origen's opinion*—These matters are more or less found in Origen's *De principiis* 1.6. However, Agrippa draws inferences that are flatly contradicted by Origen. On the question of whether demons who repent are clothed in human flesh, Origen asserts: "From which, I think, this will appear to follow as an inference, that every rational nature may, in passing from one order to another, go through each to all, and advance from all to each ...," but of demons specifically he says:

> It is to be borne in mind, however, that certain beings who fell away from that one beginning of which we have spoken, have sunk to such a depth of unworthiness and wickedness as to be deemed altogether undeserving of that training and instruction by which the human race, while in the flesh, are trained and instructed with the assistance of the heavenly powers ... *(De principiis* 1.6 [Ante-Nicene Fathers, 4:261]

On the question of whether they will be freed from ethereal and aerial bodies, Origen says:

And if any one imagine that at the end material, i.e., bodily, nature will be entirely destroyed, he cannot in any respect meet my view, how beings so numerous and powerful are able to live and to exist without bodies, since this is an attribute of the divine nature alone—i.e., of the Father, Son, and Holy Spirit—to exist without any material substance, and without partaking in any degree of a bodily adjunct. Another, perhaps, may say that in the end every bodily substance will be so pure and refined as to be like the aether, and of a celestial purity and cleanness. How things will be, however, is known with certainty to God alone, and to those who are His friends through Christ and the Holy Spirit. (ibid., 262)

46. *for their salvation*—

Before the advent of the Lord, Satan never ventured to blaspheme God, inasmuch as he was not yet sure of his own damnation, since that was announced concerning him by the prophets only in parables and allegories. But after the advent of the Lord, learning plainly from the discourses of Christ and His apostles that eternal fire was prepared for him who voluntarily departed from God, and for all who, without repentance, persevere in apostasy, then, by means of a man of this sort, he, as if already condemned, blasphemes that God who inflicts judgement upon him, and imputes the sin of his apostasy to his Maker, instead of his own will and predilection. (frag. from a lost work of Justine Martyr, preserved by Irenaeus in *Against the Heresies* 5.26 [*Ante-Nicene Christian Library*, 2:355–6])

47. *canonical hours*—The seven times a day when sacred offices may be performed in the Roman

Church: matins (12 AM), prime (6 AM), tierce (9 AM), sext (12 PM), nones (3 PM), vespers (6 PM) and compline (9 PM). See Psalms 119:164.

48. *herd of swine*—Matthew 8:31.

49. *lick the dust*—Psalms 72:9 in King James.

50. *airy spirits*—Satan is "prince of the power of the air" (Ephesians 2:2) and dwells in the desert, which is why Christ was tempted in the desert (Matthew 4:1).

51. *Zazel*—Azazel, who in the *Zohar* is one of the angels cast down from heaven who sin with the daughters of men, and who teach men sorceries. This is also stated in the Book of Enoch:

> What power was in them [men] that they were able to bring them [the stars] down? They would not have been able to bring them down but for 'UZZA, 'AZZA and 'AZZIEL who taught them sorceries whereby they brought them down and made use of them. *(Hebrew Book of Enoch by Rabbi Ishmael ben Elisha* 5.9, trans. Hugo Odeburg [Cambridge University Press, 1928], 16).

The Apocryphal Book of Enoch says:

> And Azâzêl taught men to make swords, and knives, and shields, and breastplates, and made known to them the metals (of the earth) and the art of working them, and bracelets, and ornaments, and the use of antimony, and the beautifying of the eyelids, and all kinds of costly stones, and all colouring tinctures. (Enoch 8:1 [Charles 1913, 2:192])

52. *days of thy life*—Genesis 3:14.

53. *Earth is his bread*—Isaiah 65:25.

CHAPTER XIX

Of the bodies of the devils.

Concerning the bodies of angels, there is a great dissension betwixt the late divines, and philosophers; for *Thomas* affirms that all angels are incorporeal, even evil angels, yet that they do assume bodies sometimes, which after a while they put off again; *Dionysius* in Divine Names[1] strongly affirms that angels are incorporeal.

Yet *Austin* upon Genesis[2] delivers his opinion, that angels are said to be airy, and fiery animals: because they have the nature of aerial bodies, neither can they be dissolved by death, because the element which is more active than passive is predominant in them; the same seem to affirm, that all angels in the beginning of their creation had aerial bodies, being formed of the more pure, and superior part of the air, being more fit to act than to suffer; and that those bodies were after the confirmation preserved in good angels, but changed in the evil in their fall, into the quality of more thick air, that they might be tormented in the fire.

Moreover *Magnus Basilius*[3] doth attribute bodies not only to devils, but also to pure angels, as certain thin, aerial, pure spirits; to which *Gregory Nazianzen* doth agree. *Apuleius* was of opinion, that all angels had not bodies; for in the book Of the Demon of Socrates,[4] he saith, that there is a more propitious kind of spirits, which being always free from corporeal bonds, are procured by certain prayers.

But *Psellus* the Platonist, and *Christianus* do think that the nature of spirits is not without a body; but yet not that the body of angels, and devils are the same; for that is without matter; but the bodies of devils are in a manner material, as shadows, and subject to passion, that they being struck are pained, and may be burnt in the fire, into conspicuous ashes, which as is recorded, was done in Tuscia.[5] And although it be a spiritual body, yet it is most sensible, and being touched, suffers; and although it be cut asunder, yet comes together again, as air and water, but yet in the mean time is much pained. Hence it is that they fear the edge of the sword, and any weapon.

Hence in *Virgil* the Sibyl saith to *Aeneas:*[6]

Do thou go on thy way and draw thy sword.

Upon which *Servius* saith that she would have *Aeneas* have his sword consecrated.

Orpheus also describes the kinds of demoniacal bodies; there is indeed one body, which only abides the fire, but being seen, doth not suffer, which *Orpheus* calls fiery, and celestial[7] demons: the other is contemperated with the mixtion of fire, and air, whence they are called etherial, and aerial; to which if any waterish thing was added, there arose a third kind, whence they are called watery, which sometimes are seen: to which if any earthiness be added, this is not very thick; they are called terrene demons, and they are more conspicuous, and sensible.

Now the bodies of sublime demons are nourished of the most pure etherial element, and are not rashly to be seen of any, unless they be sent from God; being weaved of such bright threads, and so small, that they transmit all the rays of our sight by their fineness, and reverberate them with splendour, and deceive by their subtlety; of which *Calcidius* saith, etherial, and aerial demons, because their bodies have not so much fire as that they are conspicuous, nor yet so much earth that the solidity of them resists the touch, and their whole composure being made up of the clearness of the sky, and moisture of the air, hath joined together an indissoluble superficies.[8]

The other demons are neither so appearable, nor invisible, being sometimes conspicuous are turned into divers figures, and put upon themselves bodies like shadows, of bloodless images, drawing the filthiness of a gross body, and they have too much communion with the world (which the ancients did call the wicked soul) and by reason of their affinity with earth, and water, are also taken with terrene pleasures, and lust; of which sort are hobgoblins, and incubi, and succubi,[9] of which number it is no absurd conjecture to think that *Melusina*[10] was.

Yet there is none of the demons (as *Marcus* supposeth)[11] is to be supposed male or female, seeing this difference of sex belongs to compounds, but the bodies of demons are simple, neither can any of the demons turn themselves into all shapes at their pleasure; but to the fiery, and aiery it is easy so to do, viz. to change themselves into what shapes their imagination conceives: now subterraneal and dark demons, because their nature being concluded in the straits of a thick and unactive body, cannot make the diversity of shapes, as others can.

But the watery, and such as dwell upon the moist superficies of the Earth, are by reason of the moistness of the element, for the most part like to women; of such kind are the fairies of the rivers, and nymphs of the woods: but those which inhabit dry places, being of drier bodies, show themselves in form of men, as satyrs, or onosceli[12] with ass's legs, or fauni, and incubi, of which he saith, he learned by experience there were many, and that some of them oftentimes did desire, and made compacts with women to lie with them: and that there were some demons, which the French call dusii,[13] that did continually attempt this way of lust.

Notes—Chapter XIX

1. *in Divine Names*—*Concerning Divine Names* by pseudo-Dionysius, Ch. 4.

2. *Genesis*—*De Genesi ad litteram* by Saint Augustine.

3. *Magnus Basilius*—Basil the Great. See biographical note.

4. *demon of Socrates*—*De deo Socratis* by Apuleius. According to Thorndike, Apuleius has a good deal to say in this treatise about the substance forming the bodies of demons. "Their native element is the air, which Apuleius thought extended as far as the moon. … But their bodies are very light and like clouds, a point peculiar to themselves" (Thorndike, 1:240).

5. *Tuscia*—Etruria.

6. *saith to Aeneas*—" 'Away, I pray you, away, ye uninitiated,' the prophetess exclaims aloud, 'and withdraw from all the grove; and do you enter on the path, and quickly draw your sword from its sheath; now you need courage, Aeneas, now resolve of soul' " (Virgil *Aeneid* 6, c. line 260 [Lonsdale and Lee, 164]).

7. *celestial*—A kind of clear tenuous fire was thought to abide above the level of the air.

8. *indissoluable superficies*—An indestructible body.

9. *incubi, and succubi*—An incubus (*incubo,* night-mare, from *incubare,* to lie upon, weigh down, brood) is a demon who has sexual intercourse with women in the form of a man during sleep. As the Latin root suggests, it was linked with the oppression and difficulty of breathing that often accompany nightmares, and is in fact caused by the substance of spirits interacting with the human body. A succubus (*succuba,* strumpet) is a demon who has intercourse with men in the form of a woman, also during sleep. This belief is very ancient.

Though, indeed, the wise Egyptians do not plausibly make the distinction, that it may be possible for a divine spirit so to apply itself to the nature of a woman, as to inbreed in her the first beginnings of generation, while on the other side they conclude it impossible for the male kind to have any intercourse or mixture by the body with any divinity, not considering, however, that what takes place on the one side must also take place on the other; intermixture, by force of terms, is reciprocal. (Plutarch "Numa Pompilius." In *Lives* [Dryden, 77])

The offspring of such unions, among them Merlin and the future Antichrist, are called *Adamitici,* "and they say that in their infancy such children cry day and night, and are heavy but emaciated, and yet can suck five nurses dry. ... Others, on the other hand, claim superhuman powers for such children, and assert that they possess some attributes of divinity ..." (Remy [1595] 1930, 1:7:20).

10. *Melusina*—A water nymph of the fountain of Lusignan in Poitou who married Raymond of Poitiers and became the legendary ancestress and tutelary spirit of his descendants. According to Jean d'Arras in his *Chronique de la Princesse,* written around 1387, she made Raymond promise never to look upon her on a Saturday, when she reverted from the form of a woman back to that of a nymph with fishy attributes. Naturally he broke his word, and she fled. But whenever danger threatened one of his descendants, she uttered a shriek as a warning.

11. *Marcus supposeth*—Marcus the Valentinian. Agrippa is quoting his statement from the writings of Psellus.

12. *onosceli*—Onocentaurs, which are beings like a centaur, but with the lower body of an ass instead of a horse.

13. *dusii*—

And seeing it is so general a report, and so many aver it either from their own experience or from others, that are of indubitable honesty and credit, that the silvans and fawns, commonly called incubi, have often injured women, desiring and acting carnally with them, and that certain devils whom the Gauls call *dusii* do continually practise this uncleanness, and tempt others to it, which is affirmed by such persons, and with such confidence that it were impudence to deny it ..." (Augustine *City of God* 15.23 [Healey, 2:90])

An alternate plural of the name is "Dusiens."

CHAPTER XX

Of the annoyance of evil spirits, and the preservation we have by good spirits.

It is the common opinion of divines, that all evil spirits are of that nature, that they hate God as well as men; therefore divine providence hath set over us more pure spirits, with whom he hath entrusted us, as with shepherds and governors, that they should daily help us, and drive away evil spirits from us, and curb, and restrain them, that they should not hurt us as much as they would; as is read in Tobia, that *Raphael* did apprehend the demon called *Asmodeus,* and bound him in the wilderness of the Upper Egypt.[1] Of these *Hesiod* saith,[2] there are 30,000 of *Jupiter's* immortal spirits living on the Earth, which are the keepers of mortal men, who that they might observe justice and merciful deeds, having clothed themselves with air, go everywhere on the Earth.

For there is no prince, nor potentate could be safe, nor any woman continue uncorrupted, no man in this valley of ignorance could come to the end appointed to him by God, if good spirits did not secure us; or if evil spirits should be permitted to satisfy the wills of men; as therefore amongst the good spirits there is a proper keeper or protector deputed to everyone, corroborating the spirit of the man to good; so of evil spirits there is sent forth an enemy ruling over the flesh, and desire thereof; and the good spirit fights for us as a preserver against the enemy, and flesh.

Now man betwixt these contenders is the middle, and left in the hand of his own counsel, to whom he will give victory; we cannot therefore accuse angels, if they do not bring the nations entrusted to them, to the knowledge of the true God, to true piety, and suffer them to fall into errors and perverse worship: but it is to be imputed to themselves, who have of their own accord declined from the right path, adhering to the spirits of errors, giving victory to the Devil; for it is in the hand of man to adhere to whom he please, and overcome whom he will, by whom, if once the enemy the Devil be overcome, he is made his servant, and being overcome, cannot fight anymore with another, as a wasp that hath lost his sting: to which opinion *Origen* assents in his book Periarchon,[3] concluding, that the saints fighting against evil spirits, and overcoming, do lessen their army, neither can he that is overcome by any, molest any more.

As therefore there is given to every man a good spirit, so also there is given to every man an evil diabolical spirit, whereof each seeks an union with our spirit, and endeavours to attract it to itself, and to be mixed with it, as wine with water;[4] the good indeed, through all good works conformable to itself, change us into angels, by uniting us, as it is writ of *John Baptist* in Malachi: behold I send mine angel before thy face:[5] of which transmutation, and union it is writ elsewhere; he which adheres to God is made one spirit with him.[6] An evil spirit also by evil works studies to make us conformable to itself, and to unite, as Christ saith of *Judas,* have not I chosen twelve, and one of you is a devil?[7]

And this is that which *Hermes* saith, when a spirit hath influence upon the soul of man, he scatters the seed[8] of his own notion, whence such a soul being sown with seeds, and full of fury, brings forth thence wonderful things, and whatsoever are the offices of spirits: for when a good spirit hath influence upon a holy soul, it doth exalt it to the light of wisdom; but an evil spirit being transfused into a wicked soul, doth stir it up to theft, to manslaughter, to lusts, and whatsoever are the offices of evil spirits.

Good spirits (as saith *Jamblicus*) purge the souls most perfectly; and some bestow upon us other good things; they being present do give health to the body, virtue to the soul, security to the soul, what is mortal in us they take away, cherish heat, and make it more efficacious to life, and by an harmony do always infuse light into an intelligible mind.[9]

But whether there be many keepers of a man, or one alone, theologians differ amongst themselves; we think there are more, the Prophet saying, he hath given his angels a charge concerning thee, that they should keep thee in all thy ways:[10] which as saith *Hierome,* is to be understood of any man, as well as of Christ.

All men therefore are governed by the ministry of divers angels, and are brought to any degree of virtue, deserts, and dignity, who behave themselves worthy of them; but they which carry themselves unworthy of them are deposed, and thrust down, as well by evil spirits, as good spirits, unto the lowest degree of misery, as their evil merits shall require: but they that are attributed to the sublimer angels, are preferred before other men, for angels having the care of them, exalt them, and subject others to them by a certain occult power; which although neither of them perceive, yet he that is subjected, feels a certain yoke of presidency, of which he cannot easily acquit himself, yea he fears and reverenceth that power, which the superior angels make to flow upon superiors, and with a certain terror bring the inferiors into a fear of presidency.

This did *Homer* seem to be sensible of, when he saith, that the Muses begot of *Jupiter,* did always as inseparable companions assist the kings begot of *Jupiter,* who by them were made venerable, and magnificent. So we read that *M. Antonius*[11] being formerly joined in singular friendship with *Octavus Augustus,*[12] were wont always to play together. But when as always *Augustus* went away conqueror, that a certain magician counselled *M. Antonius* thus, O *Antony,* what dost thou do with that young man? Shun and avoid him, for although thou art elder than he, and art more skillful than he, and art better descended than he, and hast endured the wars of more emperors, yet thy genius doth much dread the genius of this young man, and thy fortune flatter his fortune; unless thou shalt shun him, it seemeth wholly to decline to him.

Is not the prince like other men? How should other men fear, and reverence him, unless a divine terror should exalt him, and striking a fear into others, depress them, that they should reverence him as a prince? Wherefore we must endeavour, that being purified by doing well, and following sublime things, and choosing opportune times, and seasons, we be entrusted or committed to a degree of sublimer, and more potent angels, who taking care of us, we may deservedly be preferred before others.

Notes—Chapter XX

1. *the Upper Egypt*—Tobit 8:3.

2. *Hesiod saith*—

Three times ten thousand watchers-over-men,
Immortal, roam the fertile earth for Zeus.
Clothed in a mist, they visit every land
And keep a watch on law-suits and on crimes.
(Hesiod *Works and Days* c. line 252
[Wender, 66])

3. *Periarchon*—Περὶ Ἀρχῶν *(Peri Archon)* is the original Greek title of the work more commonly known under its Latin title, *De principiis.*

4. *wine with water*—

That certain thoughts are suggested to men's hearts either by good or evil angels, is shown both by the angel that accompanied Tobias [Tobit 5:4–6], and by the language of the prophet, where he says, "And the angel who spoke in me answered" [Zechariah 1:14]. The book of the Shepherd [Shepherd of Hermas 6:2] declares the same, saying that each individual is attended by two angels; that whenever good thoughts arise in our hearts, they are suggested by the good angel; but when of a contrary kind, they are the instigation of the evil angel. ... We are not, however, to imagine that any other result follows from what is suggested to our heart, whether good or bad, save a (mental) commotion only, and an incitement instigating us either to good or evil. For it is quite within our reach, when a malignant power has begun to incite us to evil, to cast away from us the wicked suggestions, and to resist the vile inducements, and to do nothing that is at all deserving of blame. And, on the other hand, it is possible, when a divine power calls us to better things, not to obey the call; our freedom of will being preserved to us in either case. (Origen *De principiis* 3.2 [*Ante-Nicene Fathers,* 4:332])

5. *before thy face*—Malachi 3:1.

6. *one spirit with him*—I Corinthians 6:17.

7. *is a devil*—John 6:70.

8. *scatters the seed*—"And besides this, my son, you must know that there is yet another sort of work which the Decans do; they sow upon the earth the seed of certain forces, some salutary and others pernicious, which the many call daemons" *(Stobaei Hermetica* 6.11 [Scott, 1:415]).

9. *intelligible mind*—

> But the presence of the Gods, indeed, imparts to us health of body, virtue of soul, purity of intellect, and in one word elevates every thing in us to its proper principle. And that, indeed, in us which is cold and destructive it annihilates; that which is hot it increases, and renders more powerful and predominant; and causes all things to accord with soul and intellect. It also emits a light, accompanied with intelligible harmony, and exhibits that which is not body as body to the eyes of the soul, through those of the body. (Iamblichus *On the Mysteries* 2.6 [Taylor, 95–6])

10. *all thy ways*—Psalms 91:11.

11. *M. Antonius*—Mark Anthony.

12. *Octavus Augustus*—Octavius Augustus. In 30 BC Anthony committed suicide with Cleopatra in Alexandria to avoid being captured by the approaching army of Augustus.

CHAPTER XXI

Of obeying a proper genius, and of the searching out the nature thereof.

As every region in the celestials hath a certain star, and celestial image which hath influence upon it before others: so also in super-celestials doth it obtain a certain intelligence set over it, and guarding it, with infinite other ministering spirits of its order, all which are called by a common name, the Sons of *Elohim Sabaoth* בני אלהים שבאות, i.e. Sons of the God of Hosts.[1]

Hence as often as the Most High doth deliberate of war, or slaughter, or the desolation of any kingdom, or subduing of any people in these inferiors, then no otherwise, when these shall come upon the Earth, there proceeds a conflict of these spirits above, as it is written in Isaiah,[2] the Lord of Hosts shall visit the army of the high, in the heavens; and the kings of the Earth, in the Earth; of which conflicts of spirits and presidents, we read also in Daniel,[3] viz. of the prince of the kingdom of the Persians, of the prince of the Grecians, of the prince of the people of Israel; and of their conflict amongst themselves, of which also *Homer*[4] seemed formerly to be sensible of, when he sang:

Great was the rumour in the court above
When that the gods war mutually did
   move:
When Phoebus did to Neptune battle give,
Pallas with Mars the god of war did strive,
Diana did withstand in hostile way
Juno, and Latona did for to slay
Mercury attempt————

Nevertheless seeing there be in every region spirits of all sorts, yet they are more powerful there which are of the same order with the president of that region. So in the solary region, the solary spirits are most potent; in the lunary, lunary, and so of the rest. And hence it is that various events of our affairs offer themselves, and follow us in places and provinces, being more fortunate in one place more than another, where viz. the demon our Genius shall receive more power, or we shall there obtain a more powerful demon of the same order. So solary men, if they shall travel into a solary region, or province, shall be made there far more fortunate, because there they shall have more powerful, and more advantageous conductors or Genii, by the present aid of whom they shall be brought beyond expectation, and their own power, to happy events.

Hence it is that the choice of a place, region, or time doth much conduce to the happiness of life where anyone shall dwell, and frequent, according to the nature and instinct of his own Genius. Sometimes also the change of the name doth conduce to the same, for whereas the properties of names being the significators of things themselves, do as it were in a glass declare the conditions of their forms; thence it comes to pass, that names being changed, the things oftentimes are changed. Hence the sacred writ doth not without cause bring in God, whilst he was blessing *Abram,* and *Jacob,* changing their names, calling the one *Abraham,*[5] and the other *Israel.*[6]

Now the ancient philosophers teach us to know the nature of the Genius of every man, by stars, their influx, and aspects, which are potent in the nativity of anyone; but with instructions so divers, and differing amongst themselves, that it is much difficult to understand the mysteries of the heavens by their directions.

For *Porphyry*[7] seeks the Genius of the star, which is the lady of the nativity:[8] but *Maternus*[9] either from thence, or from the planets, which had then most dignities, or from that into whose house the Moon was to enter after that, which at the birth of the man it doth retain. But the Chaldeans inquire after the Genius, either from the Sun above, or from the Moon. But others, and many Hebrews, think it is to be inquired after from some corner of the heaven, or from all

of them. Others seek a good Genius from the eleventh house, which therefore they call a Good Demon; but an evil Genius from the sixth, which therefore they call an Evil Demon.[10]

But seeing the inquisition of these is laborious, and most occult, we shall far more easily inquire into the nature of our Genius from ourselves, observing those things which the instinct of nature doth dictate to, and the heaven inclines us to[11] from our infancy, being distracted with no contagion; or those things which the mind, the soul being freed from vain cares, and sinister affections, and impediments being removed, doth suggest to us: these without all doubt are the persuasions of a Genius which is given to everyone from their birth, leading, and persuading us to that whither the star thereof inclines us to.

Notes—Chapter XXI

1. *God of Hosts*—In the hierarchy of the Kabbalah the ninth Sephirah, Hod, carries the associated name of God, Elohim Sabaoth, אלהים צבאות, ALHIM TzBAOTh (God of Hosts), and the order of angels Beni Elohim, בני אלהים, BNI ALHIM (Sons of God). See Appendix VI.

2. *written in Isaiah*—Isaiah 24:21. This verse simply mentions the Lord (יהוה, IHVH), but elsewhere in many places in Isaiah the title Lord of Hosts (יהוה צבאות, IHVH TzBAOTh) is used; for example, Isaiah 19:4.

3. *in Daniel*—Daniel 10:20-1.

4. *Homer*—

> ... such was the crash that sounded as the
> gods came driving together
> in wrath. For now over against the lord
> Poseidon
> Phoibos Apollo took his stand with his
> feathered arrows,
> and against Enyalios the goddess grey-
> eyed Athene.
> Against Hera stood the lady of clamour, of
> the golden distaff,
> of the showering arrows, Artemis, sister of
> the far striker.
> Opposite Leto stood the strong one, gener-
> ous Hermes
> and against Hephaistos stood the great
> deep-eddying river

> who is called Xanthos by the gods, but by
> mortals Skamandros.
> (Homer *Iliad* 20, line 66 [Lattimore, 406])

5. *one Abraham*—Genesis 17:5.

6. *other Israel*—Genesis 32:28.

7. *Porphyry*—Probably refers to the commentary by Porphyry on the *Tetrabiblos* of Ptolemy.

8. *lady of the nativity*—Perhaps the Moon when she is hyleg, and ruler of the nativity.

9. *Maternus*—

> Some have said that the ruler of the chart is the planet which is located in favorable houses of the chart, in his own house or his own terms. But others have figured from the Sun and Moon, arguing that the ruler of the chart is the one in whose terms the Sun and Moon are found, that is, the Sun in the daytime and the Moon at night. There is some point to this theory. Others say that the ruler of the chart is the ruler of the exaltation of the Moon. Still others maintain that the ruler is the one whose sign the Moon enters after she has left the one in which she is found at the birth. (Firmicus Maternus *Matheseos libri VIII* 4.19.2, trans. J. R. Bram. In *Ancient Astrology* [Park Ridge, NJ: Noyes Press, 1975], 138)

10. *Evil Demon*—See note 6, ch. XXXVIII, bk. II.

11. *heaven inclines us to—*

For if it is possible to discover the lord of the geniture, the daemon imparted by him will be known; but if this knowledge is unattainable, we shall be ignorant of the lord of the geniture according to this hypothesis, and yet, nevertheless, he will have an existence, and also the daemon imparted by him. What therefore hinders, but that the discovery of him may be diffi- cult through prediction from the nativity, and yet through sacred divination, or theurgy, there may be a great abundance of scientific knowledge on this subject? In short, the daemon is not alone imparted by the lord of the geniture, but there are many other principles of it more universal than this. And farther still, a method of this kind introduces a certain artificial and human disquisition concerning the particular dae- mon. (Iamblichus *On the Mysteries* 9.5 [Taylor, 320])

CHAPTER XXII

That there is a threefold keeper of man, and from whence each of them proceed.

Every man hath a threefold good demon,[1] as a proper keeper, or preserver, the one whereof is holy, another of the nativity, and the other of profession.

The holy demon is one, according to the doctrine of the Egyptians, assigned to the rational soul, not from the stars or planets, but from a supernatural cause, from God himself, the president of demons, being universal, above nature: this doth direct the life of the soul, and doth always put good thoughts into the mind, being always active in illuminating us, although we do not always take notice of it; but when we are purified, and live peaceably, then it is perceived by us, then it doth as it were speak with us, and communicates its voice to us, being before silent, and studieth daily to bring us to a sacred perfection.[2]

Also by the aid of this demon we may avoid the malignity of a fate, which being religiously worshipped by us in honesty, and sanctity, as we know was done by *Socrates;*[3] the Pythagoreans think we may be much helped by it, as by dreams, and signs, by diverting evil things, and carefully procuring good things. Wherefore the Pythagoreans were wont with one consent to pray to *Jupiter,* that he would either preserve them from evil, or show them by what demon it should be done.

Now the demon of the nativity, which is called the Genius, doth here descend from the disposition of the world, and from the circuits of the stars, which were powerful in his nativity. Hence there be some that think, when the soul is coming down into the body, it doth out of the quire of the demons naturally choose a preserver to itself, nor only choose this guide to itself, but hath that willing to defend it. This being the executor, and keeper of the life, doth help it to the body, and takes care of it, being communicated to the body, and helps a man to that very office, to which the celestials have deputed him, being born.[4] Whosoever therefore have received a fortunate Genius, are made thereby virtuous in their works, efficacious, strong, and prosperous. Wherefore they are called by the philosophers fortunate, or luckily born.

Now the demon of profession is given by the stars, to which such a profession, or sect, which any man hath professed, is subjected, which the soul, when it began to make choice in this body, and to take upon itself dispositions, doth secretly desire. This demon is changed, the profession being changed; then according to the dignity of the profession, we have demons of our profession more excellent and sublime, which successively take care of man, which procures a keeper of profession, as he proceeds from virtue to virtue.

When therefore a profession agrees with our nature, there is present with us a demon of our profession like unto us, and suitable to our Genius, and our life is made more peaceable, happy, and prosperous: but when we undertake a profession unlike, or contrary to our Genius, our life is made laborious, and troubled with disagreeable patrons. So it falls out that some profit more in any science, art, or office, in a little time, and with little pains, when another takes much pains, and studies hard, and all in vain.

And although no science, art, or virtue be to be contemned, yet that thou mayst live prosperously, carry on thy affairs happily; in the first place know thy good Genius, and thy nature, and what good the celestial disposition promiseth thee, and God the distributor of all these, who distributes to each as he pleaseth, and follow the beginnings of these, profess these, be conversant in that virtue to which the Most High Distributor doth elevate, and lead thee, who made *Abraham*[5] excel in justice and clemency, *Isaac*[6] with fear, *Jacob*[7] with strength, *Moses*[8] with meekness and miracles, *Joshua*[9] in war, *Phinias*[10] in zeal, *David*[11] in religion and victory, *Solomon*[12] in knowledge and fame, *Peter*[13] in faith, *John*[14] in charity, *Jacob*[15] in devotion, *Thomas*[16] in prudence, *Magdalen*[17] in contemplation, *Martha*[18] in officiousness.

Therefore in what virtue thou thinkest thou canst most easily be a proficient in, use diligence to attain to the height thereof, that thou mayest excel in one, when in many thou canst not: but in the rest endeavour to be as great a proficient as thou canst: but if thou shalt have the overseers of nature, and religion agreeable, thou shalt find a double progress of thy nature, and profession: but if they shall be disagreeing, follow the better, for thou shalt better perceive at some time a preserver of an excellent profession, than of nativity.

Notes—Chapter XXII

1. *threefold good demon*—Porphyry in his *Epistle to Anebo* mentions the popular opinion that there are three daemons, "that one daemon presides over the body, another over the soul, and another over the intellect" (Iamblichus *On the Mysteries* [Taylor, 15]). He adds: "I see likewise, that there is a twofold worship of the particular daemon; the one being the worship as of two, but the other as of three [daemons]" (ibid.). This notion Iamblichus refutes most definitely:

> You must not, therefore, distribute one daemon to the body, but another to the soul, and another to intellect: for it is absurd that the animal should be one, but the daemon that presides over it multiform. For every where the natures that govern are more simple than the natures that are governed. And it will be still more absurd if the many daemons that rule over the parts are not connascent, but separated from each other. (ibid. 9.7 [Taylor, 322–3])

2. *sacred perfection*—The communication with this holy daemon, or guardian angel, is the object of the ritual process described in such detail in the medieval grimoire *The Book of the Sacred Magic of Abramelin the Mage*.

3. *Socrates*—Socrates himself never speaks of his divine sign as a daemon. It is personified in this way by the writers who came after Plato. Describing it, Socrates says: "It began in my early childhood—a sort of voice which comes to me, and when it comes it always dissuades me from what I am proposing to do, and never urges me on" (Plato *Apology* 31d [Hamilton and Cairns, 17]). Referring to his intention to commit suicide, in accordance with the judgement of the state, he goes on:

> In the past the prophetic voice to which I have become accustomed has always been my constant companion, opposing me even in quite trivial things if I was going to take the wrong course. Now something has happened to me, as you can see, which might be thought and is commonly considered to be a supreme calamity; yet neither when I left home this morning, nor when I was taking my place here in the court, nor at any point in any part of my speech did the divine sign oppose me. In other discussions it has often checked me in the middle of a sentence, but this time it has never opposed me in any part of this business in anything that I have said or done. What do I suppose to be the explanation? I will tell you. I suspect that this thing that has happened to me is a blessing, and we are quite mistaken in supposing death to be an evil. (ibid. 40a–b [Hamilton and Cairns, 24])

Xenophone writes:

> Most people say that they are diverted from an object, or prompted to it, by birds, or by the people who meet them; but

Socrates spoke as he thought, for he said it was the divinity that was his monitor. He also told many of his friends to do certain things, and not to do others, intimating that the divinity had forewarned him; and advantage attended those who obeyed his suggestions, but repentance, those who disregarded them. *(Memorabilia of Socrates 1.1.4. In The Anabasis, or Expedition of Cyrus and the Memorabilia of Socrates,* trans. J. S. Watson [London: George Bell and Sons, 1875], 350.

4. *being born—*

This daemon, therefore, is established in the paradigm before the soul descends into generation; and when the soul has received him as its leader, the daemon immediately presides over the soul, giving completion to its lives, and binds it to body when it descends. He likewise governs the common animal of the soul, directs its peculiar life, and imparts to us the principles of all our thoughts and reasonings. We also perform such things as he suggests to our intellect, and he continues to govern us till, through sacerdotal theurgy, we obtain a God for the inspective guardian and leader of the soul. (Iamblichus *On the Mysteries* 9.6 [Taylor, 321])

5. *Abraham*—Genesis 13:9; 14:23; 18:23–32.

6. *Isaac*—Perhaps Genesis 26:7.

7. *Jacob*—Genesis 32:24–8.

8. *Moses*—Exodus 3:11; 4:2–7.

9. *Joshua*—Joshua 6:2.

10. *Phinias*—Numbers 25:11.

11. *David*—I Samuel 17:46.

12. *Solomon*—I Kings 3:12; 10:1.

13. *Peter*—Matthew 16:16–7.

14. *John*—John 20:25.

15. *Jacob*—Perhaps Hebrews 11:21.

16. *Thomas*—John 20:25.

17. *Magdalen*—John 20:11, unless Agrippa has confused Mary Magdalene with Mary the sister of Lazarus, in which case Luke 10:39 is intended.

18. Martha—Luke 10:40.

CHAPTER XXIII

Of the tongue of angels, and of their speaking amongst themselves, and with us.

We might doubt whether angels, or demons, since they be pure spirits, use any vocal speech, or tongue amongst themselves, or to us; but that *Paul* in some place saith,[1] if I speak with the tongue of men, or angels: but what their speech or tongue is, is much doubted by many.

For many think that if they use any idiom, it is Hebrew, because that was the first of all, and came from heaven, and was before the confusion of languages[2] in Babylon, in which the Law was given by God the Father, and the Gospel was preached by Christ the Son, and so many oracles were given to the prophets by the Holy Ghost: and seeing all tongues have, and do undergo various mutations, and corruptions, this alone doth always continue inviolated. Moreover an evident sign of this opinion is, that though each demon, and intelligence do use the speech of those nations, with whom they do inhabit, yet to them that understand it, they never speak in any idiom, but in this alone.

But now how angels speak it is hid from us, as they themselves are. Now to us that we may speak, a tongue is necessary with other instruments, as are the jaws, palate, lips, teeth, throat, lungs, the aspera arteria,[3] and muscles of the breast, which have the beginning of motion from the soul. But if any speak at a distance to another, he must use a louder voice; but if near, he whispers in his ear: and if he could be coupled to the hearer, a softer breath would suffice; for he would slide into the hearer without any noise, as an image in the eye, or glass. So souls going out of the body, so angels, so demons speak: and what man doth with a sensible voice, they do by impressing the conception of the speech in those to whom they speak, after a better manner than if they should express it by an audible voice.

So the Platonists say that *Socrates* perceived his Demon[4] by sense indeed, but not of this body, but by the sense of the etherial body concealed in this: after which manner *Avicen* believes the angels were wont to be seen, and heard by the prophets: that instrument, whatsoever the virtue be, by which one spirit makes known to another spirit what things are in his mind, is called by the apostle *Paul* the tongue of angels.

Yet oftentimes also they send forth an audible voice, as they that cried at the ascension of the Lord, ye men of Galilee, why stand ye there gazing into the heaven?[5] And in the old Law they spake with divers of the Fathers with a sensible voice, but this never but when they assumed bodies.

But with what senses those spirits and demons hear our invocations, and prayers, and see out ceremonies, we are altogether ignorant. For there is a spiritual body of demons everywhere sensible by nature, so that it toucheth, seeth, heareth, without any medium, and nothing can be an impediment to it: yet neither do they perceive after that manner as we do with different organs, but haply as sponges drink in water, so do they all sensible things with their body, or some other way unknown to us: neither are all animals endowned with those organs; for we know that many want ears, yet we know they perceive a sound, but after what manner we know not.[6]

Notes—Chapter XXIII

1. *some place saith*—I Corinthians 13:1.

2. *confusion of languages*—Genesis 11:6–7.

3. *aspera arteria*—Lain *arteria aspera,* the trachea or windpipe.

4. *perceived his Demon*—See note 3, ch. XXII, bk. III.

5. *into the heaven*—Acts 1:11.

6. *we know not*—The answer to this puzzle is that angels and demons perceive the world of men through the senses of men. It would be difficult to imagine how else they could be conceived to perceive it, since the human world is defined and shaped by human perceptions.

CHAPTER XXIV

Of the names of spirits,
and their various imposition; and
of the spirits that are set over the stars,
signs, corners of the heaven, and the elements.

any and divers are the names of good spirits, and bad: but their proper, and true names, as those of the stars, are known to God alone, who only numbers the multitude of stars, and calls them all by their names, whereof none can be known by us but by divine revelation, and very few are expressed to us in the sacred writ.

But the masters of the Hebrews think that the names of angels were imposed upon them by *Adam,* according to that which is written, the Lord brought all things which he had made unto *Adam,* that he should name them, and as he called anything, so the name of it was.[1] Hence the Hebrew mecubals think, together with magicians, that it is in the power of man to impose names upon spirits, but of such a man only who is dignified, and elevated to this virtue by some divine gift, or sacred authority.

But because a name that may express the nature of divinity, or the whole virtue of angelical essences cannot be made by any human voice, therefore names for the most part are put upon them from their works, signifying some certain office, or effect, which is required by the quire of spirits: which names then no otherwise than oblations, and sacrifices offered to the gods, obtain efficacy and virtue to draw any spiritual substance from above or beneath, for to make any desired effect.

I have seen and known some, writing on virgin parchment the name and seal of some spirit in the hour of the Moon: which when afterward he gave to be devoured by a water frog, and had muttered over some verse, the frog being let go into the water, rains and showers presently followed. I saw also the same man[2] inscribing the name of another spirit with the seal thereof in the hour of Mars, which was given to a crow, who being let go, after a verse muttered over, presently there followed from that corner of the heaven, whither he flew, lightnings, shakings, and horrible thunders, with thick clouds. Neither were those names of spirits of an unknown tongue, neither did they signify anything else but their offices.

Of this kind are the names of those angels, *Raziel,*[3] *Gabriel,*[4] *Michael,*[5] *Raphael,*[6] *Haniel,*[7] which is as much as the vision of God, the virtue of God, the strength of God, the medicine of God, the glory of God. In like manner in the offices of evil demons are read their names, a player, deceiver, a dreamer, fornicator, and many such like.

So we receive from many of the ancient Fathers of the Hebrews the names of angels set over the planets,[8] and signs: over Saturn, *Zaphkiel;* over Jupiter, *Zadkiel;* over Mars, *Camael;* over the Sun, *Raphael;* over Venus, *Haniel;* over Mercury, *Michael;* over the Moon, *Gabriel.* These are those seven spirits which always stand before the face of God,[9] to whom is entrusted the disposing of the whole celestial, and terrene kingdoms, which is under the Moon. For these (as say the more curious theologians) govern all things by a certain vicissitude of hours, days, and years, as the astrologers teach concerning the planets which they are set over; which therefore *Mercurius Trismegistus* calls the seven governors[10] of the world, who by the heavens, as by instruments, distribute the influences of all the stars and signs upon these inferiors.

Now there are some that do ascribe them to the stars, by names somewhat differing, saying, that over Saturn is set an intelligence called *Oriphiel;* over Jupiter, *Zachariel;* over Mars, *Zamael;* over the Sun, *Michael;* over Venus, *Anael;* over Mercury, *Raphael;* over the Moon, *Gabriel.* And every one of these governs the world 354 years, and four months; and the government begins from the intelligence of Saturn; afterward in order, the intelligences of Venus, Jupiter, Mercury, Mars, the Moon, the Sun reign, and then the government returns to the spirit of Saturn.[11] *Abbas Tritemius* writ to *Maximilian Caesar* a special treatise[12] concerning these, which he that will thoroughly examine, may from thence draw great knowledge of future times.

Over the twelve signs[13] are set these, viz. over Aries, *Malchidael;* over Taurus, *Asmodel;* over Gemini, *Ambriel;* over Cancer, *Muriel;* over Leo, *Verchiel;* over Virgo, *Hamaliel;* over Libra, *Zuriel;* over Scorpio, *Barbiel;* over Sagittarius, *Advachiel;* over Capricorn, *Hanael;* over Aquarius, *Cambiel;* over Pisces, *Barchiel.*

Of these spirits set over the planets, and signs, *John* made mention in the Revelation, speaking of the former in the beginning; and of the seven spirits[14] which are in the presence of the throne of God, which I find are set over the seven planets: the latter in the end of the book, where he describes the platform of the heavenly city, saying that in the twelve gates thereof were twelve angels.[15]

There are again twenty-eight angels, which rule in the twenty-eight mansions of the Moon, whose names in order are these: *Geniel, Enediel, Amixiel, Azariel, Gabiel, Dirachiel, Scheliel, Amnediel, Barbiel, Ardesiel, Neciel, Abdizuel, Jazeriel, Ergediel, Ataliel, Azeruel, Adriel, Egibiel, Amutiel, Kyriel, Bethnael,* *Geliel, Requiel, Abrinael, Aziel, Tagriel, Alheniel, Amnixiel.*

There are also four princes[16] of the angels, which are set over the four winds, and over the four parts of the world, whereof *Michael* is set over the eastern wind; *Raphael* over the western; *Gabriel* over the northern; *Nariel,* who by some is called *Uriel,* is over the southern.

There are also assigned to the elements[17] these, viz. to the Air, *Cherub;* to the Water, *Tharsis;* to the Earth, *Ariel;* to the Fire, *Seruph,* or according to *Philon, Nathaniel.*

Now every one of these spirits is a great prince, and hath much power and freedom in the dominion of his own planets, and signs, and in their times, years, months, days, and hours, and in their elements, and parts of the world, and winds. And every one of them rules over many legions.

And after the same manner amongst evil spirits,[18] there are four which as most potent kings are set over the rest, according to the four parts of the world, whose names are these, viz. *Urieus,* king of the east; *Amaymon,* king of the south; *Paymon,* king of the west; *Egin,* king of the north: which the Hebrew doctors perhaps call more rightly thus, *Samuel,*[19] *Azazel,*[20] *Azael,*[21] *Mahazuel,* under whom many other rule as princes of legions, and rulers;[22] also there are innumerable demons of private offices.

Moreover the ancient theologians of the Greeks reckon up six demons, which they call Telchines,[23] others Alastores;[24] which bearing ill will to men, taking up water out of the River Styx with their hand, sprinkle it upon the Earth, whence follow calamities, plagues, and famines; and these are said to be *Acteus, Megalezius, Ormenus, Lycus, Nicon, Mimon.*

But he which desires to know exactly the distinct names, offices, places, and times of angels, and evil demons, let him inquire into the book of Rabbi *Simon* of the Temples,[25] and in his Book of Lights,[26] and in his treatise of the Greatness of Stature;[27] and in the treatise of the Temples of Rabbi *Ishmael,*[28] and in almost all the commentaries of his Book of Formation;[29] and he shall find it written at large concerning them.

Notes—Chapter XXIV

1. *name of it was*—Genesis 2:19.

2. *same man*—This may have been the Abbot Trithemius, the magical master of Agrippa.

3. *Raziel*—

> Instantly, the Holy One, blessed be He, made Moses pass on from there, and he encountered Galetzur who is called Raziel. And why is his name Galetzur? Because he reveals *(m' galle)* the reasons of the Rock *(Tzur,* i.e., God). And he is called Raziel, because he hears behind the Curtain the secrets of God *(raze El),* that which has been decreed to come to pass, and he announces it in the world. It is said of Galetzur that he stands before the Throne and his wings are spread out to receive the breath of the mouths of the Beasts, and were it not so, all the Ministering Angels would be burnt by the breath from the mouth of the Beasts. And Galetzur has yet another task: he takes a kind of an iron pan which is of fire, and receives in it the fiery coals of the River Rigyon, and places it opposite the kings, and rulers, and princes of the world so that their splendor should succeed and their fear fall upon the world. *(Ma' ayan Hokhma* [Source of wisdom], a 12th-century Midrash quoted by Patai 1980, 404)

"When Adam was in the Garden of Eden, the Holy One, blessed be He, sent down to him a book by the hand of Raziel the holy angel, who is in charge of the supernal holy mysteries. And in it were inscribed supernal inscriptions and sacred wisdom" *(Zohar,* describing the *Book of Raziel,* as quoted by Patai 1980, 469).

4. *Gabriel*—There a division of opinion as to what the name means. Some authorities translate it "man of God," but others "strength of God" or "God is strong" or "God is my strength." Gabriel is usually mentioned in conjunction with Michael. Together they will subdue the "Prince of Power," Samael, and end the government of evil in heaven and Earth.

> The red colour is Gabriel. He is the one who destroyed Sodom, he is of the left side. He is appointed over all the judgements of the world from the left side, to be executed by the Angel of Death, who is the master of slaying the house of the king. And all of them carry out their tasks. The angel Gabriel has the task of taking the holy soul, and the Angel of Death has the task of taking the soul with the Evil Inclination. *(Sitre Tora* [Secrets of the Tora], quoted by Patai 1980, 440–1)

Elsewhere the *Zohar* says that at the birth of every man four angels descend on his right side and four on his left. On the right are Michael, Gabriel, Raphael, and Nuriel [Uriel]. These are ruled by Michael. On the left are the angels Sin, Destroyer, Anger, and Wrath. These are ruled by Gabriel. "On the side of Gabriel (which is the left side), there are also four faces which are punishing, that is, have the quality of stern judgement over the wicked. And they taunt the wicked, for, as we have established, it is permitted to taunt the wicked in this world" *(Zohar,* quoted by Patai 1980, 431). Notice that Gabriel is said to be both on the left and the right side—it is not uncommon in the Kabbalah for different angels to share the same name.

5. *Michael*—The name means "who is like God," the leader of the archangels. Along with Gabriel, the second in command, he is appointed over Israel. It is Michael who led the battle against Satan and the evil angels (Revelation 12:7). He rules over the right side, his face is white, and with Gabriel he slays false Messiahs.

6. *Raphael*—The name means "God heals." The healing angel who figures so prominently in the book of Tobit. He instructs Tobias to rub his father's eyes with the gall of a fish to cure his cataracts (Tobit 11:8). According to a story in the Midrash his name was originally Leviel, but because of his prudence in not contradicting the intention of God, was changed into Raphael: "Instantly He changed his name and called his name Raphael [God heals], and placed into his hands all kinds of remedies in the world" *(Konen* (He established), quoted by Patai 1980, 265).

7. *Haniel*—The name means "grace of God." This is the angel of Venus, allotted in the system of the Kabbalah to the seventh Sephirah, Netzach.

> On the sixth day [Friday] rules 'Anael. He is appointed on all manner of love. This ruler is in the likeness of a woman. She has in one hand a mirror in which she beholds herself and in the other a comb with which she is combing her hair. *(The Wisdom of the Chaldeans,* Hebrew manuscript of the 14th century or earlier, trans. M. Gaster [1900]. In *Three Works of Ancient Jewish Magic* [London:Chthonios Books, 1986], 2:16)

8. *set over the planets*—The angels set over the planets are:

♄	Zaphkiel	TzPQIAL	צפקיאל
♃	Zadkiel	TzDQIAL	צדקיאל
♂	Camael	KMAL	כמאל
☉	Raphael	RPhAL	רפאל
♀	Haniel	HANIAL	האניאל
☿	Michael	MIKAL	מיכאל
☽	Gabriel	GBRIAL	גבריאל

This same set of names is found, with minor variations, in *The Wisdom of the Chaldeans*. In his introduction to this work, Gaster mentions the same list of angels in a commentary on the *Sepher Yetzirah* by Jehuda ben Barzillai of Barcelona (12th century) and, with the exception of a single name, in the *Book of Raziel*. (See *Three Works of Ancient Jewish Magic*, 2:7–8.) A somewhat different arrangement of planetary angels is found in the *Heptameron,* a magical text attributed to Pietro d'Abano (1250–1316):

> ♄—Cassiel
> ♃—Sachiel
> ♂—Samael
> ☉—Michael
> ♀—Anael
> ☿—Raphael
> ☽—Gabriel

This list is taken from the *Conciliator* of Pietro d'Abano, written in 1303, but first published at Venice in 1471. Thorndike says that Peter derives this system from Averroes (1126–1198). (See Thorndike, 2:900.)

9. *face of God*—Revelation 4:5. The seven spirits who stand before the throne of God are described in the *Book of Enoch:*

> And these are the names of the holy angels who watch. Uriel, one of the holy angels, who is over the world and over Tartarus. Raphael, one of the holy angels, who is over the spirits of men. Raguel, one of the holy angels who takes vengeance on the world of the luminaries. Michael, one of the holy angels, to wit, he that is set over the best part of mankind and over chaos. Saraqâêl, one of the holy angels, who is set over the spirits, who sin in the spirit. Gabriel, one of the holy angels, who is over Paradise and the serpents and the Cherubim. Remiel, one of the holy angels, whom God set over those who rise. (Charles 1913, 2:201)

In the *Hebrew Book of Enoch* these angels are assigned the seven heavens:

> Seven (are the) princes, the great, beautiful, revered, wonderful and honoured ones who are appointed over the seven heavens.

… Mikael, the great prince, is appointed over the seventh heaven, the highest one, which is in the *'Araboth.* Gabriel, the prince of the host, is appointed over the sixth heaven which is in *Makon.* Shataqiel, prince of the host, is appointed over the fifth heaven which is in *Ma'on.* Shahaqiel, prince of the host, is appointed over the fourth heaven which is in *Zebul.* Badariel, prince of the host, is appointed over the third heaven which is in *Shehaqim.* Barakiel, prince of the host, is appointed over the second heaven which is in the height of *(Merom) Raqia'.* Pazriel, prince of the host, is appointed over the first heaven which is in *Wilon,* which is in *Shamayim.* (Odeburg 1928, 17:45–8)

10. *seven governors*—See note 1, ch. LIX, bk. II.

11. *spirit of Saturn*—This ordering follows the days of the week in reverse:

> ♄—Oriphiel (Saturday)
> ♀—Anael (Friday)
> ♃—Zachariel (Thursday)
> ☿—Raphael (Wednesday)
> ♂—Zamael (Tuesday)
> ☽—Gabriel (Monday)
> ☉—Michael (Sunday)

The relationship between the days of the week and the traditional ordering of the planets by their apparent rapidity of motion cannot be expressed more elegantly than by the symbol of the heptagram:

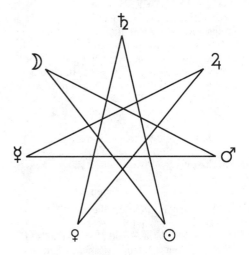

Moving in a circle around the points, beginning with Saturn, the order of the planets by their motions reveals itself, but tracing the interlocking line of the heptagram from point to point shows the attribution of the planets to the days of the week.

12. *special treatise*—Agrippa's second list of spirits of the planets is derived from *De septem secundeis, id est, intelligentiis, sive spiritibus orbes post deum moventibus,* a work written by his magical master, the Abbot Johannes Trithemius (1462–1516). In it Trithemius puts forward a system whereby the Platonic months—periods of around 2120 years during which each equinox progresses through a complete sign of the zodiac—are divided into six parts of 354 years and four months, and allotted to the angels in the order given in note 11 above. By the reckoning of Trithemius the Age of Gabriel ended in 1879. We are now living in the Age of Michael, which will continue until 2233. Trithemius purports to show how the different quality of each age reflects in its history—the "knowledge of future times" intimated by Agrippa.

13. *twelve signs*—

♈	Malchidael	MLKIDAL	מלכידאל
♉	Asmodel	ASMODAL	אסמודאל
♊	Ambriel	AMBRIAL	אמבריאל
♋	Muriel	MURIAL	מוריאל
♌	Verchiel	VRKIAL	ורכיאל
♍	Hamaliel	HMLIAL	המליאל
♎	Zuriel	ZURIAL	זוריאל
♏	Barbiel	BRBIAL	ברביאל
♐	Advachiel	ADVKIAL	אדוכיאל
♑	Hanael	HNAL	הנאל
≈	Cambiel	KAMBIAL	כאמביאל
♓	Barchiel	BRKIAL	ברכיאל

Malchidael can also be spelled Melchidael.

An alternate form of Cambiel is Cambriel, KAMBRIAL, כאמבריאל.

In the original text (both English and Latin) Agrippa gives the angel Barchiel for both Scorpio and Pisces. This would seem to be an error. Here I have taken the angel Barbiel from the table, ch. XIV, bk. II, and assigned it to Scorpio. In an otherwise identical list of zodiacal angels given in Regardie [1937–40] 1982, 1:174 and 3:44, the angel Amnitziel (אמניציאל) is assigned to Pisces.

14. *seven spirits*—See note 9 above.

15. *twelve angels*—Revelation 21:12.

16. *four princes*—See Revelation 7:1.

> "This first is Michael, the merciful and long-suffering: and the second, who is set over all the diseases and all the wounds of the children of men, is Raphael: and the third, who is set over all the powers, is Gabriel: and the fourth, who is set over the repentance unto hope of those who inherit eternal life, is named Phanuel." (*Book of Enoch* 40:9 [Charles 1913, 2:211–2])

17. *to the elements*—

Air	Cherub (Kerub)	KRUB	כרוב
Water	Tharsis	ThRShISh	תרשיש
Earth	Ariel	ARIAL	אריאל
Fire	Seruph (Seraph)	ShRP	שרף

These four names occur in the sixth of the seven pentacles of Jupiter given in the *Greater Key of Solomon,* where they are written in the form of a cross and surrounded by the biblical verse: "They pierced my hands and my feet, I may tell all my bones" (Psalms 22:16–7). It is more common in modern occultism to find Kerub assigned to Earth and Ariel assigned to Air.

18. *evil spirits*—These names occur in a variety of forms and places. It may be useful to give some comparisons:

Testament of Solomon (12th or 13th century):

East	South	West	North
Oriens	Amemon	Boul	Eltzen

Pseudomonarchia Daemonum by John Wierus (1515–1588):

East	South	West	North
Amaymon	Gerson	Goap	Zymymar

Livre des Esprits (late 15th or early 16th century):

East	South	West	North
Orient	Amoymon	Paymon	Cham

Grimoire of Pope Honorius III:

East	South	West	North
Magoa	Egym	Baymon	Amaymon

Grimoire of Pope Honorius III (variant edition):

East	South	West	North
Maymon	Egin	Paymon	Amaymon

19. *Samuel*—Samael, one of the three great princes of Gehenna, the storehouse in the north of the world that holds all the reserves of fire, frost, snow, hailstones, storm, darkness, and violent winds. It is the dwelling place of harmful demons and destructive spirits, and has three gates opening onto the Earth. Samael guards the third gate in the valley of Ben Hinnom opposite Zion and Jerusalem. He is the archfoe of the highest angel, Metatron, and is called Prince of the Accusers and the Evil Inclination (as opposed to Gabriel, the Good Inclination).

> "The sons of God were the sons of Cain. For when Samael mounted Eve, he injected filth into her, and she conceived and bare Cane. And his aspect was unlike that of the other humans, and all those who came from his side were called sons of God." (*Zohar.* In Patai 1980, 471)

He is mentioned in the *Hebrew Book of Enoch* by Metatron, who says: "Even Sammael, the Prince of the Accusers, who is greater than all the princes of kingdoms on high, feared and trembled before me" (14:2 [Odeberg 1928, 37]).

20. *Azazel*—See note 51, ch. XVIII, bk. III.

21. *Azael*—Or Asael, one of the "leaders of tens" of the 200 angels who lusted after the daughters of men and descended to Earth. (Apocryphal Book of Enoch 6.7-8).

22. *and rulers*—In the *Faustbook* published by Scheible (Stuttgart, 1849) is the separate treatise titled *Doctoris Johannis Fausti magiae naturalis et innatural*, Passau, 1505, which assigns these evil angels to the elements in this order:

> Samael—Fire
> Azazel—Air
> Azael—Water
> Mahazael—Earth

23. *Telchines*—The Telchines were a tribe or family said to have been descended from either Thalassa or Poseidon. They came from Crete to Cyprus, then migrated to Rhodes where they founded the towns of Camirus, Lindus and Ialysus. On their account Rhodes acquired the name Telchinis. When they saw with their divine arts that Rhodes was to be drowned in the sea, they fled in different directions. Lycus went to Lycia and built there the temple to Lycian Apollo. Apollo had previously been worshipped at Lindus, while Hera had received worship at Camirus and Ialysus. Despite their homage, Apollo was hostile to the Telchines. He transformed himself into a wolf and destroyed them. By a different story it was Zeus who overwhelmed the tribe in a flood, presumably at Rhodes. They were credited with inventing arts and crafts, such as metal working. They made the images of the gods, the sickle of Cronos and the trident of Poseidon. Strabo was of the opinion that the Telchines had existed historically as a tribe of highly skilled artists and craftsmen, and this skill was the reason they were known as magicians in later times. A parallel may be drawn with the Heruli, a Germanic tribe of skilled craftsmen proverbial as magicians. The Telchines acquired a very evil reputation as sorcerers whose glance and features were tainted and caused destruction. They could call down the hail, rain or snow, change their shape, and had the unpleasant habit of concocting a poison from the waters of the Styx mixed with sulfur to kill animals and plants.

24. *Alastores*—Alastor was the surname of Zeus in his guise as avenger of evil. By extension it was applied to any deity who avenges foul deeds.

25. *the Temples*—Perhaps the *Heikhalot de-R. Simeon B. Yohai*, the section of the *Zohar* that treats of the seven palaces in Eden and the "seven palaces of uncleanness" in hell, and angelology.

26. *Book of Lights*—Perhaps *Midrash Yehi Or*, a name applied to the *Zohar* by Israel al-Nakawa (died 1391) because the manuscript he possessed began with a commentary on the verse "Let there be light" (Genesis 1:3) (see Scholem 1977, 2:1:213). Spanish Kabbalists of the Middle Ages knew the *Zohar* under the titles *Midrash de-R. Simeon B. Yohai* and *Mekhilta de-R. Simeon B. Yohai*.

27. *Greatness of Stature*—Perhaps the *Idra Rabba* (Greater assembly), the section of the *Zohar* that treats of the form of Adam Kadmon.

28. *Rabbi Ishmael*—A. E. Waite speaks of a treatise called *Delineation of the Heavenly Temples*, criticized by Nahmanides (died c. 1270) under the title *Proportion of the Height*, and also called *Description of the Body of God*, which was attributed to a Rabbi Ishmael (Waite [1929] 1975, 91). The work purports to be a revelation from the archangel Metatron to Rabbi Ishmael (or Yeshmael) on the proportions and holy names attached to the members of the body of God.

29. *Book of Formation*—*Sepher Yetzirah*, upon which numerous commentaries were written. Its true authorship is unknown.

CHAPTER XXV

How the Hebrew mecubals drew forth the sacred names of angels out of the sacred writ, and of the seventy-two angels, which bear the name of God, with the tables of Ziruph, and the commutations of letters and numbers.

There are also other sacred names of good, and evil spirits deputed to each offices, of much greater efficacy than the former, which the Hebrew mecubals drew forth out of sacred writ, according to that art which they teach concerning them; as also certain names of God are drawn forth out of certain places.

The general rule of these is, that wheresoever anything of divine essence is expressed in the Scripture, from that place the name of God may rightly be gathered; but in what place soever in the Scripture the name of God is found expressed, there mark what office lies under that name. Wheresoever therefore the Scripture speaks of the office or work of any spirit, good, or bad, from thence the name of that spirit, whether good, or bad, may be gathered; this unalterable rule being observed, that of good spirits we receive the names of good spirits, of evil the names of evil.

And let us not confound black with white, nor day with night, nor light with darkness: which by these verses, as by an example, is manifest: let them be as dust before the face of the wind, and let the angel of the Lord scatter them; let their ways be darkness, and slippery, and let the angel of the Lord pursue them:[1]

יהיו כמץ לפני רוח ומלאך יהוה
דחה יהי דרכם חשך והלקלקת
ומלאך יהוה רדפם

In the 35 psalm with the Hebrews, but with us the 34, out of which the names of those angels are drawn, מידאל *Midael,* and מיראל *Mirael,* of the order of warriors.

So out of that verse, thou shalt set over him the wicked, and *Satan* shall stand at his right hand,[2] out of the psalm 109 with the Hebrews, but with the Latins the 108:

הפקד עליו רשע ושטן יעמד על ימינו

is extracted the name of the evil spirit *Schii* שיעי, which signifies a spirit that is a work of engines.

There is a certain text in Exodus[3] contained in three verses, whereof every one is writ with seventy-two letters, beginning thus: the first, Vajisa ויסע; the second, Vajabo ויבא; the third, Vajot ויט: which are extended into one line, viz. the first, and third from the left hand to the right; but the middle in a contrary order, beginning from the right to the left, is terminated on the left hand: then each of the three letters being subordinate the one to the other, make one name, which are seventy-two names, which the Hebrews call Schemhamphorae:[4] to which if the divine name *El* אל, or *Jah* יה, be added, they produce seventy-two trisyllable names of angels, whereof every one carries the great name of God, as it is written: my angel shall go before thee; observe him, for my name is in him.[5]

And these are those that are set over the seventy-two celestial quinaries, and so many nations, and tongues,[6] and joints of man's body, and cooperate with the seventy-two seniors[7] of the synagogue, and so many disciples of Christ:[8] and their names according to the extraction which the Cabalists make, are manifest in this following table, according to one manner which we have spoken of.

Now there are many other manner or ways of making Schemhamphorac out of those verses, as when all three are in a right order written one after the other from the right to the left, besides those which are extracted by the tables of Ziruph, and the tables of commutations, of which we made mention above. And because these tables serve for all names, as well divine, as angelical, we shall therefore subjoin them to this chapter.

Notes—Chapter XXV

1. *Lord pursue them*—Psalms 35:5–6.

2. *his right hand*—Psalms 109:6.

3. *text in Exodus*—Exodus 14:19–21.

4. *Schemhamphorae*—The Schemhamphoras.

5. *my name is in him*—Exodus 23:20–1.

6. *nations, and tongues*—Genesis 10. Seventy, not 72.

7. *seventy-two seniors*—Numbers 11:24. Seventy elders are mentioned, but if an equal number was selected from each tribe, they must total 72.

8. *disciples of Christ*—Luke 10:1. Again, 70 are mentioned, but 72 are intended.

These are the seventy-two angels, bearing the name of God, Schemhamphorae.

ו	ס	ע	מ	ל	ה	א	כ	ה	א	ל	ה	י	מ	ה	ה	ל	כ	ל	כ
ה	ל	י	ל	ה	ה	ל	כ	ז	י	א	ה	ו	ב	ר	ד	ק	א	ל
ו	י	ל	פ	ה	מ	ש	ה	ת	ד	י	ע	ל	ה	מ	ה	ל	ו	מ	י
יה	אל	אל	אל	יה	אל	יה	יה	אל	יה	אל	יה	יה	אל	אל	אל	אל	אל	יה	אל
Vehuiah	Ieliel	Sitael	Elemiah	Mehasiah	Lelahel	Akaiah	Cahethel	Haziel	Aladiah	Lauiah	Hahaiah	Ieiazel	Mebahel	Hariel	Hakamiah	Leviah	Caliel
ל	פ	נ	י	מ	ה	ה	ת	י	ש	א	ו	י	ל	י	ל	כ	מ
ו	ה	ל	י	ל	ה	ת	ר	א	ה	ר	כ	ח	ה	ו	ח	נ
ו	ל	ל	כ	ה	ה	א	ה	ה	ד	מ	ב	ר	ו	ח	ח	ד
יה	יה	אל	אל	אל	יה	יה	אל	יה	יה	אל	אל	יה	יה	אל	יה	אל
Leuuiah	Pahaliah	Nelkael	Ieiaiel	Melahel	Chahuiah	Nithhaiah	Haaiah	Ierathel	Seehiah	Reiiel	Omael	Lecabel	Vasariah	Iechuiah	Lehachiah	Kavakiah	Monadel
א	נ	ר	ח	י	ו	מ	י	ס	ר	ע	ע	מ	ו	ד	ה	א	נ	נ	נ
נ	א	ה	ה	ז	י	ה	ל	א	ש	ש	ה	י	ה	נ	ה	מ	נ	נ	י
י	מ	ר	ב	ה	כ	ה	ה	ל	ל	ה	ה	ו	מ	ש	מ	א	מ	א	ת
אל	יה	אל	אל	אל	יה	יה	יה	אל	יה	יה	אל	אל	אל	יה	יה	אל	אל	אל	אל
Aniel	Chaamiah	Rehael	Ihiazel	Hahahel	Mikael	Vevaliah	Ielahiah	Sealiah	Ariel	Asaliah	Mihael	Vehuel	Daniel	Hachasiah	Imamiah	Nanael	Nithael
מ	פ	נ	י	ה	מ	י	ו	ע	מ	ד	מ	א	ח	ר	י	ה	מ
ב	ו	מ	י	ר	צ	ה	ה	נ	ח	נ	ע	י	נ	א	ב	ו	ו
ה	י	ל	מ	ב	ר	ח	ה	י	ב	ק	א	ו	ה	ה	מ	י	מ
יה	אל	יה	אל	אל	אל	אל	אל	אל	אל	אל	יה	אל	יה	אל	יה	אל	יה
Mebahiah	Poiel	Nemamiah	Ieialel	Harachel	Mizrael	Umabel	Iahhel	Annauel	Mecheiel	Damabiah	Menkiel	Eiael	Chabuiah	Raehel	Iibamiah	Haiaiel	Mumiah

The Right Table of the Commutations.

ת	ש	ר	ק	צ	פ	ע	ס	נ	מ	ל	כ	י	ט	ח	ז	ו	ה	ד	ג	ב	א
א	ת	ש	ר	ק	צ	פ	ע	ס	נ	מ	ל	כ	י	ט	ח	ז	ו	ה	ד	ג	ב
ב	א	ת	ש	ר	ק	צ	פ	ע	ס	נ	מ	ל	כ	י	ט	ח	ז	ו	ה	ד	ג
ג	ב	א	ת	ש	ר	ק	צ	פ	ע	ס	נ	מ	ל	כ	י	ט	ח	ז	ו	ה	ד
ד	ג	ב	א	ת	ש	ר	ק	צ	פ	ע	ס	נ	מ	ל	כ	י	ט	ח	ז	ו	ה
ה	ד	ג	ב	א	ת	ש	ר	ק	צ	פ	ע	ס	נ	מ	ל	כ	י	ט	ח	ז	ו
ו	ה	ד	ג	ב	א	ת	ש	ר	ק	צ	פ	ע	ס	נ	מ	ל	כ	י	ט	ח	ז
ז	ו	ה	ד	ג	ב	א	ת	ש	ר	ק	צ	פ	ע	ס	נ	מ	ל	כ	י	ט	ח
ח	ז	ו	ה	ד	ג	ב	א	ת	ש	ר	ק	צ	פ	ע	ס	נ	מ	ל	כ	י	ט
ט	ח	ז	ו	ה	ד	ג	ב	א	ת	ש	ר	ק	צ	פ	ע	ס	נ	מ	ל	כ	י
י	ט	ח	ז	ו	ה	ד	ג	ב	א	ת	ש	ר	ק	צ	פ	ע	ס	נ	מ	ל	כ
כ	י	ט	ח	ז	ו	ה	ד	ג	ב	א	ת	ש	ר	ק	צ	פ	ע	ס	נ	מ	ל
ל	כ	י	ט	ח	ז	ו	ה	ד	ג	ב	א	ת	ש	ר	ק	צ	פ	ע	ס	נ	מ
מ	ל	כ	י	ט	ח	ז	ו	ה	ד	ג	ב	א	ת	ש	ר	ק	צ	פ	ע	ס	נ
נ	מ	ל	כ	י	ט	ח	ז	ו	ה	ד	ג	ב	א	ת	ש	ר	ק	צ	פ	ע	ס
ס	נ	מ	ל	כ	י	ט	ח	ז	ו	ה	ד	ג	ב	א	ת	ש	ר	ק	צ	פ	ע
ע	ס	נ	מ	ל	כ	י	ט	ח	ז	ו	ה	ד	ג	ב	א	ת	ש	ר	ק	צ	פ
פ	ע	ס	נ	מ	ל	כ	י	ט	ח	ז	ו	ה	ד	ג	ב	א	ת	ש	ר	ק	צ
צ	פ	ע	ס	נ	מ	ל	כ	י	ט	ח	ז	ו	ה	ד	ג	ב	א	ת	ש	ר	ק
ק	צ	פ	ע	ס	נ	מ	ל	כ	י	ט	ח	ז	ו	ה	ד	ג	ב	א	ת	ש	ר
ר	ק	צ	פ	ע	ס	נ	מ	ל	כ	י	ט	ח	ז	ו	ה	ד	ג	ב	א	ת	ש
ש	ר	ק	צ	פ	ע	ס	נ	מ	ל	כ	י	ט	ח	ז	ו	ה	ד	ג	ב	א	ת

The Averse Table of the Commutations.

א	ב	ג	ד	ה	ו	ז	ח	ט	י	כ	ל	מ	נ	ס	ע	פ	צ	ק	ר	ש	ת
ת	א	ב	ג	ד	ה	ו	ז	ח	ט	י	כ	ל	מ	נ	ס	ע	פ	צ	ק	ר	ש
ש	ת	א	ב	ג	ד	ה	ו	ז	ח	ט	י	כ	ל	מ	נ	ס	ע	פ	צ	ק	ר
ר	ש	ת	א	ב	ג	ד	ה	ו	ז	ח	ט	י	כ	ל	מ	נ	ס	ע	פ	צ	ק
ק	ר	ש	ת	א	ב	ג	ד	ה	ו	ז	ח	ט	י	כ	ל	מ	נ	ס	ע	פ	צ
צ	ק	ר	ש	ת	א	ב	ג	ד	ה	ו	ז	ח	ט	י	כ	ל	מ	נ	ס	ע	פ
פ	צ	ק	ר	ש	ת	א	ב	ג	ד	ה	ו	ז	ח	ט	י	כ	ל	מ	נ	ס	ע
ע	פ	צ	ק	ר	ש	ת	א	ב	ג	ד	ה	ו	ז	ח	ט	י	כ	ל	מ	נ	ס
ס	ע	פ	צ	ק	ר	ש	ת	א	ב	ג	ד	ה	ו	ז	ח	ט	י	כ	ל	מ	נ
נ	ס	ע	פ	צ	ק	ר	ש	ת	א	ב	ג	ד	ה	ו	ז	ח	ט	י	כ	ל	מ
מ	נ	ס	ע	פ	צ	ק	ר	ש	ת	א	ב	ג	ד	ה	ו	ז	ח	ט	י	כ	ל
ל	מ	נ	ס	ע	פ	צ	ק	ר	ש	ת	א	ב	ג	ד	ה	ו	ז	ח	ט	י	כ
כ	ל	מ	נ	ס	ע	פ	צ	ק	ר	ש	ת	א	ב	ג	ד	ה	ו	ז	ח	ט	י
י	כ	ל	מ	נ	ס	ע	פ	צ	ק	ר	ש	ת	א	ב	ג	ד	ה	ו	ז	ח	ט
ט	י	כ	ל	מ	נ	ס	ע	פ	צ	ק	ר	ש	ת	א	ב	ג	ד	ה	ו	ז	ח
ח	ט	י	כ	ל	מ	נ	ס	ע	פ	צ	ק	ר	ש	ת	א	ב	ג	ד	ה	ו	ז
ז	ח	ט	י	כ	ל	מ	נ	ס	ע	פ	צ	ק	ר	ש	ת	א	ב	ג	ד	ה	ו
ו	ז	ח	ט	י	כ	ל	מ	נ	ס	ע	פ	צ	ק	ר	ש	ת	א	ב	ג	ד	ה
ה	ו	ז	ח	ט	י	כ	ל	מ	נ	ס	ע	פ	צ	ק	ר	ש	ת	א	ב	ג	ד
ד	ה	ו	ז	ח	ט	י	כ	ל	מ	נ	ס	ע	פ	צ	ק	ר	ש	ת	א	ב	ג
ג	ד	ה	ו	ז	ח	ט	י	כ	ל	מ	נ	ס	ע	פ	צ	ק	ר	ש	ת	א	ב
ב	ג	ד	ה	ו	ז	ח	ט	י	כ	ל	מ	נ	ס	ע	פ	צ	ק	ר	ש	ת	א

Another Averse Table, Called the Irregular.

ת	ש	ר	ק	צ	פ	ע	ס	נ	מ	ל	כ	י	ט	ח	ז	ו	ה	ד	ג	ב	א
ש	ל	א	ת	ר	ק	צ	פ	ע	ס	נ	מ	כ	י	ט	ח	ז	ו	ה	ד	ג	ב
ר	מ	ב	א	ת	ש	ק	צ	פ	ע	ס	נ	ל	כ	י	ט	ח	ז	ו	ה	ד	ג
ק	ג	מ	ב	א	ת	ש	ר	צ	פ	ע	ס	נ	ל	כ	י	ט	ח	ז	ו	ה	ד
צ	נ	ד	ג	ב	א	ת	ש	ר	ק	פ	ע	ס	מ	ל	כ	י	ט	ח	ז	ו	ה
פ	ד	נ	ה	ג	ב	א	ת	ש	ר	ק	צ	ע	ס	מ	ל	כ	י	ט	ח	ז	ו
ע	ס	ה	ו	ד	ג	ב	א	ת	ש	ר	ק	צ	פ	נ	מ	ל	כ	י	ט	ח	ז
ס	ה	ע	ז	ו	ד	ג	ב	א	ת	ש	ר	ק	צ	פ	נ	מ	ל	כ	י	ט	ח
נ	ע	ו	ח	ז	ה	ד	ג	ב	א	ת	ש	ר	ק	צ	פ	ס	מ	ל	כ	י	ט
מ	ו	פ	שׁ	ח	ז	ה	ד	ג	ב	א	ת	טּ	ר	ק	צ	ע	ס	נ	ל	כ	י
ל	פ	ז	י	ט	ח	ו	ה	ד	ג	ב	א	ת	ש	ר	ק	צ	ע	ס	נ	מ	כ
כ	ז	צ	מ	י	ט	ח	ו	ה	ד	ג	ב	א	ת	ש	ר	ק	פ	ע	ס	נ	ל
י	צ	ח	נ	ל	כ	ט	ח	ז	ו	ה	ד	ג	ב	א	ת	ש	ר	ק	פ	ע	מ
ט	ח	ק	ס	מ	ל	כ	י	ז	ו	ה	ד	ג	ב	א	ת	ש	ר	ק	צ	פ	נ
ח	כּ	ט	ע	נ	מ	ל	ל	י	ז	ו	ה	ד	ג	ב	א	ת	ש	ר	צ	פ	ס
ז	ר	י	פ	ס	נ	מ	ל	כ	ט	ח	ו	ה	ד	ג	ב	א	ת	ש	ק	צ	ע
ו	י	סּ	צ	ע	ד	מ	ל	כ	י	ט	ח	ז	ה	ד	ג	ב	א	ת	ש	ק	פ
ה	ק	ש	כ	פ	ע	ס	נ	מ	ל	י	ט	ח	ז	ו	ד	ג	ב	א	ת	ר	צ
ד	טּ	ל	ר	כ	צ	פ	ע	ס	נ	מ	י	שׁ	ח	ז	ו	ה	ג	ב	א	ת	ק
ג	ח	כּ	ל	שׁ	סּ	י	פ	ק	ח	צ	ז	פ	ו	ע	ה	נ	ד	מ	ב	א	ר
ב	א	ת	טּ	ק	י	ר	כּ	ח	צ	ז	פ	ו	ע	ה	ס	נ	ד	ג	מ	ל	שׁ
א	ב	ג	ד	ה	ו	ז	ח	ט	י	כ	ל	מ	נ	ס	ע	פ	צ	ק	ר	שׁ	ת

The Table of the Combinations of Ziruph.

כמ	ין	טס	חע	זפ	וצ	הק	דר	גש	בת	אל
לם	כנ	יס	טע	חפ	זצ	וק	הר	דש	גת	אב
בם	לן	כס	יע	טפ	חצ	זק	ור	הש	דת	אג
מן	לס	כע	יפ	טצ	חק	זר	וש	הת	בג	אד
גן	מס	לע	כפ	יצ	טק	חר	זש	ות	בד	אה
גס	מע	לפ	כצ	יק	טר	חש	זת	גד	בה	או
דס	נע	מפ	לצ	כק	יר	טש	חת	גה	בו	אז
סע	נפ	מצ	לק	כר	יש	טת	דה	גו	בז	אח
הע	ספ	נצ	מק	לר	כש	ית	דו	גז	בח	אט
עפ	סצ	נק	מר	לש	כת	הו	דז	גח	בט	אי
ופ	עצ	סק	נר	מש	לת	הז	דח	גט	בי	אכ
פצ	עק	סר	נש	מת	וז	הח	דט	גי	בכ	אל
זצ	פק	ער	סש	נת	וח	הט	די	גכ	בל	אמ
צק	פר	עש	סת	זח	וט	הי	דכ	גל	במ	אן
חק	צר	פש	עת	זט	וי	הכ	דל	גמ	בנ	אס
קר	צש	פת	חט	זי	וכ	הל	דמ	גנ	בס	אע
טר	קש	צת	חי	זכ	ול	המ	דנ	גס	בע	אפ
רש	קת	טי	חכ	זל	ומ	הנ	דס	גע	בפ	אצ
יש	רת	טכ	חל	זמ	ון	הס	דע	גפ	בצ	אק
שת	יך	טל	חמ	זנ	וס	הע	דפ	גצ	בק	אר
כת	יל	טמ	חנ	זס	וע	הפ	דע	גק	בר	אש
כל	ים	טנ	חס	זע	ופ	הצ	דק	גר	בש	את

Another Table of Ziruph, Which Is Called the Rational.

אב	גת	דש	הר	וק	זצ	חפ	טע	יס	כנ	למ
אג	דב	הת	וש	זר	חק	טצ	יפ	כע	לס	מן
אד	הג	וב	זת	חש	טר	יק	כץ	לפ	מע	נס
אה	וד	זג	חב	טת	יש	כר	לק	מץ	נפ	סע
או	זה	חד	טג	יב	כת	לש	מר	נק	סץ	עפ
אז	חו	טה	יד	כג	לב	מת	נש	סר	עק	פץ
אח	טז	יו	כה	לד	מג	נב	סת	עש	פר	צק
אט	יח	כז	לו	מה	נד	סג	עב	פת	צש	קר
אי	כט	לח	מז	נו	סה	עד	פג	צב	קת	רש
אכ	לי	מט	נח	סז	עו	פה	צד	קג	רב	שת
אל	מכ	ני	סט	עח	פז	צו	קה	רד	שג	תב
אמ	נל	סכ	עי	פט	צח	קז	רו	שה	תד	בג
אנ	סמ	על	פכ	צי	קט	רח	שז	תו	בה	גד
אס	ענ	פמ	צל	קכ	רי	שט	תח	בז	גו	דה
אע	פס	צנ	קמ	רל	שכ	תי	בט	גח	דז	הו
אפ	צע	קס	רן	שמ	תל	בכ	גי	דט	הח	וז
אצ	קפ	רע	שס	תן	במ	גל	דכ	הי	וט	זח
אק	רצ	שפ	תע	בס	גן	דמ	הל	וכ	זי	חט
אר	שק	תצ	בפ	גע	דס	הן	ומ	זל	חכ	טי
אש	תר	בק	גץ	דפ	הע	וס	זן	המ	טל	יך
את	בש	גר	דק	הץ	ופ	זע	חס	טנ	ימ	כל
אב	גד	הו	זח	טי	כל	מן	סע	פץ	קר	שת

Tables of the Numerical Transpositions.

Ones

Tens

Hundreds

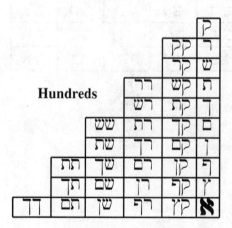

11-19

110-190

1100-1300

Key

5	10	10	10	10
ה	דו	גז	בח	אט
50	100	100	100	100
נ	מס	לע	כפ	יצ
500	1000	1000	1000	1000
ד	תם	שן	רף	קץ

CHAPTER XXVI

Of finding out of the names of spirits, and geniuses from the disposition of celestial bodies.

The ancient magicians did teach an art of finding out the name of a spirit to any desired effect, drawing it from the disposition of the heaven; as for example, any celestial harmony being proposed to thee for the making an image or ring, or any other work to be done under a certain constellation; if thou will find out the spirit that is the ruler of that work; the figure of the heaven being erected, cast forth letters in their number and order from the degree of the ascendent, according to the succession of signs through each degree by filling the whole circle of the heaven: then those letters which fall into the places of the stars the aid whereof thou wouldest use, being according to the number, and powers of those stars, marked without into number, and order, make the name of a good spirit: but if thou shalt do so from the beginning of a degree falling against the progress of the signs, the resulting spirit shall be evil.[1]

By this art some of the Hebrew and Chaldean masters teach that the nature, and name of any genius may be found out; as for example, the degree of the ascendent of any-one's nativity being known, and the other corners of the heaven being coequated, then let that which had the more dignities of planets in those four corners, which the Arabians call almutez,[2] be first observed amongst the rest: and according to that in the second place, that which shall be next to it in the number of dignities, and so by order the rest of them, which obtain any dig-

nity in the foresaid corners: this order being used, thou mayest know the true place, and degree of them in the heaven, beginning from the degree of the ascendent through each degree according to the order of signs to cast twenty-two of the letters of the Hebrews; then what letters shall fall into the places of the aforesaid stars, being marked, and disposed according to the order found out above in the stars, and rightly joined together according to the rules of the Hebrew tongue, make the name of a genius: to which, according to the custom, some mono-syllable name of divine omnipotency, viz. *El,* or *Iah* is subjoined. But if the casting of the letters be made from an angle of the falling, and against the succession of signs,[3] and the letters which shall fall in the nadir (that is, the opposite point) of the aforesaid stars, be after that order as we said, joined together, shall make the name of an evil genius.

But the Chaldeans proceed another way; for they take not the almutez of the corners, but the almutez of the eleventh house, and do in all things as hath been said. Now they find out an evil genius from the almutez of the angle of the twelfth house, which they call an Evil Spirit, casting from the degree of the falling against the progress of the signs.[4]

There are also the Arabians, and many others, and some Hebrews, who find out the name of a genius by the places of the five hylegians,[5] and making projection always from the beginning of Aries, and the letters being found out according to the order of hylegians with the astrologers, being reduced into a known order, and being joined together, make the name of a good Genius: but they draw the name of an evil Genius from the opposite hylegian places, projection being made from the last degree of Pisces against the order of signs.

But other some do not take the places of hylegians, but the places of almutez upon the five hylegians making projection from an horoscope, as abovesaid.

And these names being thus distributed according to the proportioned numbers to the starry account, compacted or joined, and changed letters, although unknown in sound and significative, we must of necessity confess may do more by the secret of the chiefest philosophy in a magical work, than significative names, whilst the mind being astonished at the obscurity of them, and deeply intent, firmly believing that something divine is under it, doth reverently pronounce these words, and names, although not understood, to the glory of God, captivating himself with a spiritual affection of piety, in the obedience of him.

Notes—Chapter XXVI

1. *shall be evil*—In other words, determine the degree of the ascendent, which is the degree just rising above the horizon, for any given magically significant moment, then place the Hebrew letters into the 360 degrees of the zodiac, one letter per degree, beginning with *aleph* in the ascendent degree and proceeding counterclockwise. The letters are begun anew after each cycle of the alphabet—for example, *beth* is placed in the 24th degree. Then choose in the same order, starting at the ascendent, those planets and astrological points that will be most fruitful in forming the qualities of the spirit, omitting discordant elements, and write down the letters, always maintaining the order. Some names will be more potent then others, depending on the astrological configuration at the moment of their making. For evil spirits the same process is followed, but the direction is clockwise. Vowels must be added to make the Hebrew names pronounceable.

2. *almutez*—Arabic: "the prevailing"; the prevailing or ruling planet in the horoscope; the strongest planet in a nativity, also called the Lord of Figure. The word is often corrupted in old texts into *almuten*. Agrippa seems to apply the term more broadly to the house with the greatest number of planetary dignities—planets which are so placed as to promote their vigorous action, most usually in their ruling sign, in exaltation, and in the angles.

3. *succession of signs*—That is, from the degree of the descendent sign on the western horizon, proceeding clockwise.

4. *progress of the signs*—It seems to me that Agrippa is saying that the names may be found by drawing a Grand Cross through either the angular (I, IV, VII and X), the succedent (II, V, VIII and XI), or the cadent (III, VI, IX and XII) houses, taking first that house of the four which has the greatest number of dignified planets, and beginning to letter the name in that house, counterclockwise for good spirits, clockwise for evil spirits, proceeding successively to the remaining three houses in the Cross in the order of their dignities. In all cases the degrees of the zodiac are lettered counterclockwise from the ascendent for good spirits and clockwise from the descendent for evil spirits. The Arabians derive both good and evil spirits from the angular houses by taking the degrees upon which the planets fall for the letters of good spirits and the degrees exactly opposite on the circle of the zodiac from those planets for the letters of evil spirits. The Chaldeans, on the other hand, find out good spirits from the succedent houses, and evil spirits from the cadent houses. The succedent house XI is in fact named the Good Daemon, while the cadent house XII is named the Evil Daemon.

5. *five hylegians*—The hyleg is the planet or part of heaven that forms the Prorogator of Life. There are five hylegical places. Ptolemy gives the order referred to by Agrippa:

> Among these there are to be preferred, with reference to power of domination, first those [degrees] which are in the midheaven [Xth house], then those in the orient [Ist house], then those in the sign succedent to the mid-heaven [XIth house], then those in the occident [VIIth house], then those in the sign rising before midheaven [IXth house]; for the whole region below the earth must, as is reasonable, be disregarded when a domination of such importance is concerned, except only those parts which in the ascendant itself are coming into the light. (*Tetrabiblos* 3.10 [Robbins, 273])

CHAPTER XXVII

Of the calculating art of such names by the tradition of Cabalists.

There is yet another art of these kinds of names, which they call calculatory, and it is made by the following tables, by entering with some sacred, divine, or angelical name, in the column of letters descending; by taking those letters which thou shalt find in the common angles[1] under their stars, and signs: which being reduced into order, the name of a good spirit is made of the nature of that star, or sign, under which thou didst enter: but if thou shalt enter in the column ascending, by taking the common angles above the stars, and signs marked in the lowest line, the name of an evil spirit is made.

And these are the names of spirits of any order, or heaven ministering; as of good, so of bad, which thou mayst after this manner multiply into nine names[2] of so many orders, in as much as thou mayst by entering with one name draw forth another of a spirit of a superior order out of the same, as well of a good, as bad one.

Yet the beginning of this calculation depends upon the names of God; for every word hath a virtue in magic, in as much as it depends on the word of God, and is thence framed. Therefore we must know that every angelical name must proceed from some primary name of God. Therefore angels are said to bear the name of God, according to that which is written, because my name is in him.[3]

Therefore that the names of good angels may be discerned from the names of bad, there is wont oftentimes to be added some name of divine omnipotency, as *El*,[4] or *On*[5] or *Jah*,[6] or *Jod*,[7] and to be pronounced together with it: and because *Jah* is a name of beneficence, and *Jod* the name of a deity, therefore these two names are put only to the names of angels; but the name *El*, because it imports power,[8] and virtue, is therefore added not only to good but bad spirits, for neither can evil spirits either subsist, or do anything without the virtue of *El*, God.

But we must know that common angles of the same star, and sign are to be taken, unless entrance be made with a mixed name, as are the names of Genii, and those of which it hath been spoken in the preceeding chapter, which are made of the dispositions of the heaven, according to the harmony of divers stars. For as often as the table is to be entered with these, the common angle is to be taken under the star, or sign of him that enters.[9]

There are moreover some that do extend[10] those tables, that they think also if there be an entrance with an extrance, with the name of a star, or office, or any desired effect, a demon whether good, or bad, serving to that office, or effect, may be drawn out. Upon the same account they that enter with the proper name of any person, believe that they can extract the names of the Genii, under that star which shall appear to be over such a person, as they shall by his physiognomy, or by the passions and inclinations of his mind, and by his profession, and fortune, know him to be martial, or saturnine, or solary, or of the nature of any other star.

And although such kind of primary names have none or little power by their signification, yet such kind of extracted names, and such as are derived from them, are of very great efficacy; as the rays of the Sun collected in a hollow glass,[11] do indeed most strongly burn, the Sun itself being scarce warm.

Now there is an order of letters in those tables under the stars, and signs, almost like that which is with the astrologers, of tens, elevens, twelves. Of this calculatory art *Alfonsus Cyprius*[12] once wrote, and I know not who else, and also fitted it to Latin characters; but because the letters of every tongue, as we showed in the first book, have in their number, order, and figure a celestial and divine original, I shall easily grant this calculation concerning the names of spirits to be made not only by Hebrew letters, but also by Chaldean, and Arabic, Egyptian, Greek, Latin, and any other, the tables being rightly made after the imitation of the precedents.

But here it is objected by many, that it falls out, that in these tables men of a different nature, and fortune, do oftentimes by reason of the sameness of name obtain the same Genius of the same name. We must know therefore that it must not be thought absurd that the same demon may be separated from any one soul, and the same be set over more. Besides, as divers men have many times the same name, so also spirits of divers offices and natures may be noted or marked by one name, by one and the same seal, or character, yet in a divers respect: for as the serpent doth sometimes typify Christ,[13] and sometimes the Devil,[14] so the same names, and the same seals may be applied sometimes to the order of a good demon, sometimes of a bad. Lastly, the very ardent intention of the invocator, by which our intellect is joined to the separated intelligences, causeth that we have sometimes one spirit, sometimes another, although called upon under the same name, made obsequious to us.

There follow the tables of the calculation of the names of spirits, good and bad, under the presidency of the seven planets, and under the order of the twelve militant signs.

Notes—Chapter XXVII

1. *common angles*—The column of squares under the planet or zodiac sign. Each angle, or square, is "common" in the sense that it relates both to the planet, or sign, and the letter being entered.

2. *nine names*—A name being entered and another extracted of the first, or lowest, hierarchy, that second name may in turn be entered to yield a name of the second hierarchy, and so on to the ninth hierarchy, each succeeding name being of greater occult potency.

3. *name is in him*—See note 5, ch. XXV, bk. III.

4. *El*—אֵל, AL, as in Gabriel.

5. *On*—ון, VN, as in Metatron.

6. *Jah*—יה, IH, as in Laviah.

7. *Jod*—י, I; or יד, ID; or יוד, YOD.

8. *imports power*—Yod means "hand" and by extension "power of the hand of God." El also means "power" or "might of God." The compound name Yod El, ID AL, יד אל (Job 27:11), "hand of God," is singularly potent, though it is little used in magic.

9. *him that enters*—In the name of a Genius, or daemon, where the letters are separately extracted from the heavens by the planets (see ch. XXVI, bk. III), the letters are entered into the table of planets under those same planets that presided over their formation. When the name is entered into the table of the signs, each letter is entered under the sign in which the planet that gave it birth resided at the time of its formation.

10. *extend*—Extend the use of.

11. *hollow glass*—Concave mirror.

12. *Alfonsus Cyprius*—Probably a reference to the Alphonsine Tables, astronomical tables made by Arab and Spanish astronomers which were collected under the order of Alphonso X, ruler of Castile, in 1253. They are also called the Toletan Tablets, after the city of Toledo, where they were adapted to be used. See Chaucer, "The Franklin's Tale," line 1273, in *The Canterbury Tales*.

13. *typify Christ*—John 3:14.

14. *sometimes the Devil*—Revelation 12:9.

Table of the Seven Planets

The entrance of the evil angels (left side) — The entrance of the good angels (right side)

	☽	☿	♀	☉	♂	♃	♄	The line of good
ת	ז	ו	ה	ד	ג	ב	א	א
ש	נ	מ	ל	כ	י	ט	ח	ב
ר	ש	ר	ק	צ	פ	ע	ס	ג
ק	ו	ה	ד	ג	ב	א	ת	ד
צ	מ	ל	כ	י	ט	ח	ז	ה
פ	ר	ק	צ	פ	ע	ס	נ	ו
ע	ה	ד	ג	ב	א	ת	ש	ז
ס	ל	כ	י	ט	ח	ז	ו	ח
נ	ק	צ	פ	ע	ס	נ	מ	ט
מ	ד	ג	ב	א	ת	ש	ר	י
ל	כ	י	ט	ח	ז	ו	ה	כ
כ	צ	פ	ע	ס	נ	מ	ל	ל
י	ג	ב	א	ת	ש	ר	ק	מ
ט	י	ט	ח	ז	ו	ה	ד	נ
ח	פ	ע	ס	נ	מ	ל	כ	ס
ז	ב	א	ת	ש	ר	ק	צ	ע
ו	ט	ח	ז	ו	ה	ד	ג	פ
ה	ע	ס	נ	מ	ל	כ	י	צ
ד	א	ת	ש	ר	ק	צ	פ	ק
ג	ח	ז	ו	ה	ד	ג	ב	ר
ב	ס	נ	מ	ל	כ	י	ט	ש
א	ת	ש	ר	ק	צ	פ	ע	ת
The line of evil	♄	♃	♂	☉	♀	☿	☽	

Table of the Twelve Signs

The entrance of the evil angels (left) — The entrance of the good angels (right)

	♓	♒	♑	♐	♏	♎	♍	♌	♋	♊	♉	♈	The line of good
ת	ל	כ	י	ט	ח	ז	ו	ה	ד	ג	ב	א	א
ש	א	ב	ג	ד	ה	ו	ז	ח	ט	י	כ	ל	ב
ר	ב	א	ת	ש	ר	ק	צ	פ	ע	ס	נ	מ	ג
ק	מ	נ	ס	ע	פ	צ	ק	ר	ש	ת	א	ב	ד
צ	נ	מ	ל	כ	י	ט	ח	ז	ו	ה	ד	ג	ה
פ	ג	ד	ה	ו	ז	ח	ט	י	כ	ל	מ	נ	ו
ע	ד	ג	ב	א	ת	ש	ר	ק	צ	פ	ע	ס	ז
ס	ס	ע	פ	צ	ק	ר	ש	ת	א	ב	ג	ד	ח
נ	ע	ס	נ	מ	ל	כ	י	ט	ח	ז	ו	ה	ט
מ	ה	ו	ז	ח	ט	י	כ	ל	מ	נ	ס	ע	י
ל	ו	ה	ד	ג	ב	א	ת	ש	ר	ק	צ	פ	כ
כ	פ	צ	ק	ר	ש	ת	א	ב	ג	ד	ה	ו	ל
י	צ	פ	ע	ס	נ	מ	ל	כ	י	ט	ח	ז	מ
ט	ז	ח	ט	י	כ	ל	מ	נ	ס	ע	פ	צ	נ
ח	ח	ז	ו	ה	ד	ג	ב	א	ת	ש	ר	ק	ס
ז	ק	ר	ש	ת	א	ב	ג	ד	ה	ו	ז	ח	ע
ו	ר	ק	צ	פ	ע	ס	נ	מ	ל	כ	י	ט	פ
ה	ט	י	כ	ל	מ	נ	ס	ע	פ	צ	ק	ר	צ
ד	י	ט	ח	ז	ו	ה	ד	ג	ב	א	ת	ש	ק
ג	ש	ת	א	ב	ג	ד	ה	ו	ז	ח	ט	י	ר
ב	ת	ש	ר	ק	צ	פ	ע	ס	נ	מ	ל	כ	ש
א	כ	ל	מ	נ	ס	ע	פ	צ	ק	ר	ש	ת	ת
The line of evil	♈	♉	♊	♋	♌	♍	♎	♏	♐	♑	♒	♓	

How sometimes names of spirits are taken from those things over which they are set.

I find yet another kind of names given to the spirits from those things, which they are set over, their names being as it were borrowed from the stars, or men, or places, or times, or such like things, the divine name being added at the end.

Thus, the spirit of Saturn is called *Sabathiel;* the spirit of Jupiter, *Zedekiel;* the spirit of Mars, *Madimiel;* the spirit of the Sun, *Semeliel,* or *Semeschia;* the spirit of Venus, *Nogahel;* the spirit of Mercury, *Cochabiah,* or *Cochabiel;* the spirit of the Moon, *Jareahel,* or *Levanael.*[1] In like manner also they call the spirits which are set over the signs by the names of the signs, in order from Aries: *Teletiel, Suriel, Tomimiel, Sattamiel, Ariel, Betuliel, Masniel, Acrabiel, Chesetiel, Gediel, Deliel, Dagymiel.*[2]

And if we call them from the Latin words: *Ariel, Tauriel, Geminiel, Cancriel, Leoniel, Virginiel, Libriel, Scorpiel, Sagittariel, Capriel, Aquariel, Pisciel;* and from the planets: *Saturniel, Joviel, Martiel, Soliah, Veneriel, Mercuriel, Lunael,* or *Lunaiah.*

Now because (as we said before) all spirits, as well good as bad, seek for a union with man, which oftentimes in some sort they obtain, we read that some men are called gods, and angels, and devils. So the names of them which are endowed with any singular excellency of virtue, or with some desperate wickedness have departed this life, have obtained a place amongst the names of good and bad demons, and are reckoned amongst them, whether we shall think that the souls of those men, or the Genii whether good or bad, are signified.

So we read in Esdras[3] that the name of the archangel *Jeremiel* was from *Jeremiah* the prophet. So *Zachariel* from *Zacharia;* and *Uriel* from *Uriah* the prophet, whom *Joachim* slew. In like manner *Samuel, Ezekiel, Daniel,* were the names of angels as well as prophets. *Phaniel*[4] is the name of an angel, and of the place where *Jacob* wrestled all night. *Ariel* is the name of an angel, and is the same as the Lion of God;[5] sometimes also it is the name of an evil demon,[6] and of a city which is thence called Ariopolis, where the idol *Ariel* was worshipped.

We find also in sacred writ that many names of evil demons had their rise from most wicked men, or from the habitations of wicked men; as the name *Astaroth,* which is the name of an evil demon, was formerly the name of the city of *Og,* king of Basan, in which dwelt giants;[7] in like manner Astaroth was formerly the city of the Amorrhei;[8] *Raphaim*[9] a valley, and Jeramiel the country of the Allophyli;[10] and also they were the names of idols, and evil demons; as *Remma*[11] was the statue of the idol of Damascus; *Chamos*[12] the idol of Moab; *Melchim*[13] the idol of the Amontae; *Bel*[14] the idol of Babylonians; *Adramelech*[15] the idol of the Assyrians; *Dagon*[16] the idol of the Allophyli.

And *Philo* makes mention of seven golden statues which the Amorrhei[17] had, which they called the Holy Nymphs, which being called upon did show to the Amorrhei every hour their works; and the names of them were the names of women, which were the wives of seven wicked men, which consecrated them after the flood, viz. *Chanaan, Phut, Selath, Nebroth, Abirion, Elath, Desuat,* and there were put upon them precious stones, engraven, and consecrated, one of which had a virtue to restore sight to the blind; neither could any fire burn these stones; and the books were consecrated with stones, which in like manner could not be burnt with fire, nor cut with iron, nor obliterated with water, until the angel of the Lord took them, and buried them in the bottom of the sea.

Moreover we know that *Nimbroth,*[18] *Chodorlaomor,*[19] *Balach,*[20] *Amalech,*[21] names of kings, have obtained the order of evil spirits.

Also giants are called with devils after a common name, *Enakim*[22] עֲנָקִים, because they did not partake of the image of God, i.e. they have not received the splendour of the spiritual intellect, but their reason hath multiplied evil kinds of frauds and sins. Therefore they are not reckoned of the species of man (as saith Rabbi *Moses* the Egyptian) but of the species of beasts, and devils, only that they have the shape of a man; and such (he saith) were the sons of *Adam,* which were pre-

decessors to *Seth* after *Abel;* of which the wise men of the Hebrews said, that *Adam* begat *Tochot*[23] תוכות, i.e. devils. But after that he had found favour in the eyes of God, he begot *Seth* after his own image, and likeness, i.e. who according to the image of God obtained a human perfection, which he that hath not, is not reckoned of the species of man, by reason of the pravities which are the cause of all evils and mischief.

It is also (as saith *Porphyry*) the opinion of magicians, that evil souls are turned into the nature of devils, and become as pernicious as they; which Christ confirmed, when he spake concerning *Judas Iscariot:* have not I chosen twelve, and one of you is a devil?[24] Which devils therefore they call adventitious,[25] because of men's souls, they are become devils. Whence the names of wicked men and devils are the same, whether by these we call their souls, or evil Genii which have taken upon them the names of wicked men, as if it were their persons.

Also *Behemoth,* and the *Leviathan*[26] signify beasts, and devils.

By these examples he that is inquisitive shall find out the names of good, as well as of evil spirits.

Notes—Chapter XXVIII

1. *or Levanael*—The spheres of the planets bear the following names in the Kabbalistic world of Assiah, the world of actions. The English titles that accompany the names in Hebrew are given by Mathers (1887), 27–8:

♄	Shabbathai (Rest)	ShBThAI	שבתאי
♃	Tzedek (Righteousness)	TzDQ	צדק
♂	Madim (Vehement Strength)	MDIM	מדים
☉	Shemesh (Solar Light)	ShMSh	שמש
♀	Nogah (Glittering Splendor)	NOGH	נוגה
☿	Kokab (Stellar Light)	KOKB	כוכב
☽	Levanah (Lunar Flame)	LBNH	לבנה

2. *Dagymiel*—The Hebrew names for the signs of the Zodiac are:

♈	Teleth	TLH	טלה
♉	Sur	SVR	שור
♊	Tomim	ThAOMIM	תאומים
♋	Sattam (Sartan)	SRTN	סרטן
♌	Arih	ARIH	אריה
♍	Betulh	BThVLH	בתולה
♎	Maznim	MAZNIM	מאזנים
♏	Acrab	AQRB	אקרב
♐	Cheseth	QShTh	קשת
♑	Gedi	GDI	גדי
♒	Deli	DLI	דלי
♓	Dagim	DGIM	דגים

Based upon the Hebrew, Agrippa's angel of Cancer is incorrect. It should probably be Sartaniel.

The angel of Libra should probably be Maznimiel.

For the Hebrew names of the signs of the zodiac, see Regardie [1937–40] 1982, 1:171–4 (table). These names for the signs are to be found in the *Book of Raziel.* An illustration from a manuscript of this Hebrew magical text in the British Museum shows the names in 12 interlocking circles (see Budge [1930] 1968, 22:387).

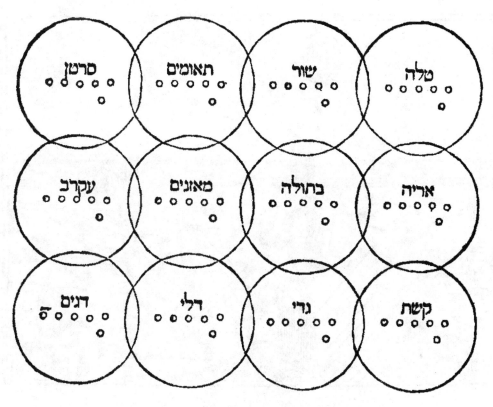

Hebrew Names of the Zodiac

from the *Book of Raziel*

Budge [1930] 1968, 22:387).

3. *in Esdras*—II Esdras 2:18.

4. *Phaniel*—Penuel. See Genesis 32:31.

5. *Lion of God*—אר״י, ARI (lion) + אל, AL (God).

6. *evil demon*—Milton ranks Ariel among the "Atheist crew" of the fallen angels (*Paradise Lost* 6, line 371). Robert H. West in his work *Milton and the Angels* (Athens, 1955) mentions that the name is used as an epithet of Jerusalem in Isaiah 29:1 and 33:7, where it is translated "valiant ones." He further says that in the translations of the Old Testament by Aquila and Symmachus, Ariel is the name given to the pagan city of Arina, or Ariopolis, which worshipped the idol *Ariel* (Mars). See West 1955, 154.

7. *dwelt giants*—Numbers 21:33. Ashtaroth was the name of a city of Bashan, presumably the capitol, since the king of Bashan, Og, is said to have dwelt there (Deuteronomy 1:4). Its full name was Ashteroth Karnaim, AaShThRVTh QRNIM, עשתרות קרנים, "the horned Astartes," perhaps after a temple or

statue of the goddess maintained there.

8. *Amorrhei*—Og was one of the two Amorite kings who ruled beyond Jordan. See Deuteronomy 4:47.

9. *Raphaim*—Isaiah 17:5.

10. *the Allophyli*—The Jerahmeelites are mentioned as a people in I Samuel 27:10 and 30:29. They occupied a section of the southern steppes of Palestine about 17 miles south of Hebron. *Allophyli* (Ἀλλόφυλοι) is Greek for "Philistines."

11. *Remma*—Rimmon. See II Kings 5:18.

12. *Chamos*—Chemosh, KMVSh, כמוש (Subduer), the national god of the Moabites and the Ammonites (Judges 11:24) worshipped by Solomon after he was corrupted by his wives (II Kings 23:13).

13. *Melchim*—Malcham, MLKM, מלכם, idol of the Moabites and Ammonites (Zephaniah 1:5).

14. *Bel*—BL, בל, a contraction of BAaL, בעל, the chief god of the Babylonians, worshipped in the

Dagon

from *Oedipus Aegyptiacus* by Athanasius Kircher (Rome, 1652)

by Greek and Roman writers to be the planet Jupiter *(stella Jovis).*

15. *Adramelech*—Adrammelech, ADRMLK, אדרמלך, "Magnificence of the King," an idol of the Sepharvites carried from Mesopotamia into Samaria (II Kings 17:31).

16. *Dagon*—DGVN, דגון, "Great Fish," an idol with the head and hands of a man and the tail of a fish worshipped by the Philistines at Ashdod (I Samuel 5:1–7).

17. *Amorrhei*—Amorites.

18. *Nimbroth*—Nisroch? If so, see Isaiah 37:38.

19. *Chodorlaomor*—Chedorlaomer, king of Elam. Genesis 14:1.

20. *Balach*—Balac, king of Moab. Numbers 22:4; Revelation 2:14.

21. *Amalech*—Amalek, an ancient people (Numbers 24:20) who dwelt in the south of Palestine (Numbers 13:29). They were perpetually persecuted by God (Exodus 17:14).

22. *Enakim*—Anakim, AaNQIM, עֲנָקִים, "Long Necked," a Canaanite nation famous for their great stature (Deuteronomy 9:2).

23. *Tochot*—

> For 130 years Adam kept separate from his wife and did not beget. After Cain killed Abel, Adam did not want to copulate with his wife. ... And two female spirits [Lilith and Naamah] would come and copulate with him and bear children. And those whom they bore are the evil spirits of the world and are called Plagues of Mankind. *(Zohar* [3-vol. ed., Vilna: Rome, 1894, 3:76b], quoted by Patai 1980, 456)

24. *is a devil*—See note 7, ch. XX, bk. III.

25. *adventitious*—Added from the outside; not essentially inherent.

26. *Behemoth, and the Leviathan*—The elephant (or hippopotamus) and the whale. See Job 40:15–24 and 41. They represent vast elemental powers beyond the edge of perception.

> And on that day were two monsters parted, a female monster named Leviathan, to dwell in the abysses of the ocean over the fountains of the waters. But the male is named Behemoth, who occupied with his breast a waste wilderness named Dûidâin, on the east of the garden where the elect and righteous dwell, where my grandfather [Enoch] was taken up, the seventh from Adam, the first man whom the Lord of Spirits created. And I besought the other angel that he should show me the might of these monsters, how they were parted on one day and cast, the one into the abysses of the sea, and the other into the dry land of the wilderness. And he said to me: "Thou son of man, herein thou dost seek to know what is hidden." *(Book of Enoch 60:7–10 [Charles 1913, 2:224])*

CHAPTER XXIX

Of the characters and seals of spirits.

We must now speak of the characters and seals of spirits. Characters therefore are nothing else than certain unknowable letters and writings, preserving the secrets of the gods, and names of spirits from the use and reading of prophane men, which the ancients called hieroglyphical,[1] or sacred letters, because devoted to the secrets of the gods only. For they did account it unlawful to write the mysteries of the gods with those characters with which prophane and vulgar things were wrote.

Whence *Porphyry* saith, that the ancients were willing to conceal God, and divine virtues by sensible figures, and by those things which were visible, yet signifying invisible things, as being willing to deliver great mysteries in sacred letters, and explain them in certain symbolical figures: as when they dedicated all round things to the world, the Sun, the Moon, hope, and fortune; a circle to the heaven, and parts of a circle to the Moon; pyramids and obelisks to the fire, and Olympian gods; a cylinder to the Sun and Earth; a man's yard to generation and *Juno,* to whom also by reason of the feminine sex the triangular figure.

Wherefore this kind of characters hath another root beside the pleasure, and authority of the institutor, of him I say, who received power of instituting, and consecrating these kind of letters, such as were many prelates amongst divers nations, and sects of religions, whose institutions came not to us, by reason that few of them were delivered by the authors scatteringly, and by fragments.

Of this kind of character therefore are those which *Peter Apponus* notes, as delivered by *Honorius* of Thebes,[2] the figures whereof are such, being related to our alphabet:

A	B	C	D	E	F	G	H
I	K	L	M	N	O	P	Q
R	S	T	V	X	Y	Z	Ω

Noτes—Chapτer XXIX

1. *hieroglyphical*—From the Greek ἱερος (sacred) γλυφη (carving). Plutarch first used the term in reference to writing.

2. *Honorius of Thebes*—This is perhaps the same Honorius of Thebes who is the reputed author of the *Sworn Book of Honorius.* In the 14th-century manuscripts of his work, it is said that in order to save their magic art from annihilation at the hands of the pope and his cardinals, 89 master magicians from Naples, Athens and Toledo assembled together and selected Honorius, son of Euclid, a master of Thebes, to condense their magical grimoires into a single book with 93 chapters. This was to be made into three copies and passed on from the deathbed only upon condition that the new owner of each volume swear an oath of fidelity—hence the name. However, the Theban alphabet does not appear in the *Sworn Book,* nor in the *Heptameron* of Pietro d'Abano. Perhaps it appears in Peter's *Conciliator,* which I have not had the opportunity to examine.

CHAPTER XXX

Another manner of making characters, delivered by Cabalists.

Amongst the Hebrews I find more fashions of characters, whereof one is most ancient, viz. an ancient writing which *Moses,* and the prophets used, the form of which is not rashly to be discovered to any, for those letters which they use at this day, were instituted by *Esdras.*[1]

There is also amongst them a writing which they call Celestial, because they show it placed and figured amongst the stars, no otherwise than the other astrologers produce images of signs from the lineaments of stars. There is also a writing which they call Malachim, or Melachim, i.e. Of Angels, or Regal. There is also another, which they call the Passing Through the River. And the characters and figures of all these[2] are such:

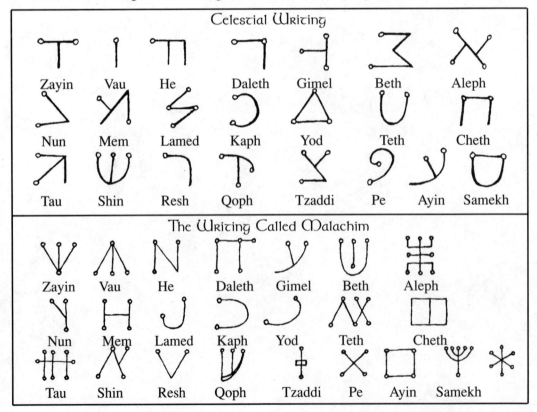

560

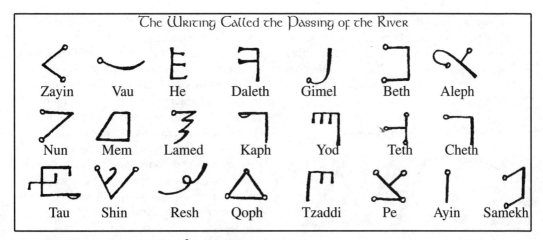

The Writing Called the Passing of the River

Zayin	Vau	He	Daleth	Gimel	Beth	Aleph
Nun	Mem	Lamed	Kaph	Yod	Teth	Cheth
Tau	Shin	Resh	Qoph	Tzaddi	Pe	Ayin	Samekh

characters and figures of all these[2] are such:

There is moreover another fashion amongst the Cabalists, formerly had in great esteem, but now it is so common, that it is placed amongst prophane things, and it is this. The twenty-seven characters of the Hebrews may be divided into three classes, whereof every one contains nine letters. The first, viz. אבגדהוזחט, which are the seals or marks of simple numbers, and of intellectual things, distributed into nine orders of angels. The second hath יכלמנסעפצ, the marks of tens, and of celestial things, in the nine orbs of the heavens. The third hath the other four letters, with the five final, by order, viz. קרשתךםןףץ, which are marks of hundreds, and inferior things, viz. four simple elements, and of five kinds of perfect compounds.[3]

They do now and then distribute these three classes into nine chambers, whereof the first is of unities, viz. intellectual, celestial and elemental; the second is of twos; the third of threes; and so of the rest: these chambers are framed by the intersection of four parallel lines, intersecting themselves into right angles, as is expressed in this following figure:

Out of which, being dissected into parts,

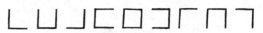

proceed nine particular figures, viz:

Which are of the nine chambers, characterizing their letters by the above written Notariacon: which if it be of one point, shows the first letter of that chamber; if of two, the second; if of three, the third letter: as if thou wouldest frame the character *Michael* מיכאל, that comes

forth thus, extended with five figures, viz:
Which then are contracted to three figures, after

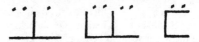

this manner:
Which then are contracted into one, yet the points Notariacon are wont to be omitted, and then there comes forth such a character of

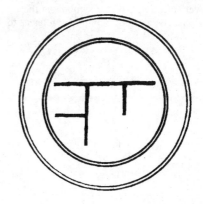

There is yet another fashion of characters, common to almost all letters, and tongues, and very easy, which is by the gathering together of letters; as if the name of the angel *Michael* be given, the characters thereof shall be framed thus:

In Hebrew   In Greek

In Latin

And this fashion amongst the Arabians is most received; neither is there any writing which is so readily, and elegantly joined to itself, as the Arabic.

Now you must know that angelical spirits, seeing they are of a pure intellect, and altogether incorporeal, are not marked with any marks or characters, and pingible[4] figures, or any other human signs; but we not knowing their essence, or quality, do from their names, or works, or otherwise, according to our fancies devote and consecrate to them figures, and marks, by which we cannot any way compel them to us, but by which we rise up to them; as not to be known by such characters, and figures.

And first of all we do set our senses both inward and outward, upon them; then by a certain admiration of our reason we are induced to a religious veneration of them, and then are wrapt with our whole mind into an ecstatical adoration, and then with a wonderful belief, an undoubted hope, quickening love, we calling upon them in spirit, and truth, by true names and characters do obtain from them that virtue, or power which we desire.

Notes—Chapter XXX

1. *Esdras*—Ezra.

2. *figures of all these*—The symbols in Celestial are clearly stylized Hebrew letters in their correct sequence. However those making up Malachim and Passing the River seem to be more extreme stylizations, but not in their proper sequence. For example the symbol for Gimel in Malachim is far more suggestive of Ayin. The symbol for Pe in Passing the River is the same as the Tzaddi symbol in Celestial; likewise the Qoph sign is the Yod sign in Celestial. However since many of the symbols in these latter two alphabets are not obviously related to the Hebrew letters, it would be a matter of guesswork to restore them to their true order.

3. *perfect compounds*—Perhaps this refers to the compound bodies listed in the table at the end of ch. VIII, bk. II: animal, plant, metal, stone, and plant-animal. This last category is curious. A better division would seem to be that given in the *Rasa'il*, an Islamic text of the 10th century: angel, man, animal, plant, mineral.

4. *pingible*—Gross, thick, coarse.

Magical Alphabets

from *The Magus* by Francis Barrett (London, 1801)

Chapter XXXI

There is yet another fashion of characters, and concerning marks of spirits which are received by revelation.

There is another kind of character received by revelation only, which can be found out no other way: the virtue of which characters is from the deity revealing, of whom there are some secret works, breathing out a harmony of some divinity: or they are as it were some certain agreements or compacts of a league between us and them.

Of this kind there was a mark or sign showed to *Constantine,*[1] which many did call the cross, writ upon in Latin letters, *In hoc vince,* i.e. In This Overcome; and there was another revealed to *Antiochus,* by surname *Soteris,* in the figure of a pentangle, which signifies health; for being resolved into letters it speaks the word ὑγίεια, i.e. Health:[2] in the faith, and virtue of which signs both kings obtained a great victory against their enemies. So *Judas,* who by reason of that was afterward surnamed *Machabeus,* being to fight with the Jews against *Antiochus Eupator,*[3] received from an angel that notable sign מכבי,[4] in the virtue of which they first slew 14,000 with an infinite number of elephants, then again 35,000 of their enemies: for that sign did represent the name *Jehovah* and was a memorable emblem of the name of seventy-two letters by the equality of number, and the exposition thereof is, מי כמיך באלים יהוה i.e. who is there amongst thee strong as *Jehovah?*[5]

The figures of these memorable signs are to be framed thus:

Moreover of those signs and characters *Porphyry* speaks in his book De Responsis,[6] saying that they did signify the gods themselves, by whom they did enjoy things, and by which they were called forth, and which were to be offered to them: and did show the figures of the images what they should be; and that he perceived these things concerning the oracle of *Proserpina.*

He saith moreover that *Hecate* commanded how images should be constituted to her, and that they were to be surrounded with wormwood, and that domestic mice were to be painted, and the finest ornaments such as were most pleasing to her, and so many mice as her forms were to be taken; then blood, myrrh, storax, and other things were to be burnt: which things if they were done, she would appear, and answer the worker thereof by dreams.

But we shall here under write the oracle of *Hecate,* for thus she speaks:[7]

> Mark I will teach what statue thou shalt make
> For me; boughs of the wood, and wormwood take,

Then garnish it, on it paint domestic
mice;
Let ornaments be fair, and of great price.
Then frankincense, myrrh, storax mixed
with blood
Of mice; then sing thou words secret and
good;
As thou seest shapes of mine, so on it lay,
As many real mice; then take the bay,
And out of the trunk thereof a case prepare
To put it in; then see thou have a care,
That to the statue thou devoutly pray,
Also thy debts, and vows take care thou
pay;
If that these things that here required be
Thou shalt perform, in dreams thou shalt
me see.

Such were in old times the secret mysteries of the gods and demons of the gentiles, by which they did persuade themselves to be compelled, detained, and bound by men. Hence *Jamblicus,* and *Porphyry* teach that he that calls upon sacred demons must observe them, with their proper honour, and to distribute to each what is convenient to every one, as thanks, oblations, gifts, sacrifices, with words, characters suitable to their conditions, and most like unto them;[8] or else he should never obtain the presence of the deities, and demons, and the desired effect; moreover if they were called upon, yet they shall be constrained to hurt them especially who did it negligently.

Notes—Chapter XXXI

1. *Constantine*—When the Emperor Constantine was marching against the larger army of Maxentius encamped at Rome, he and his troops saw in the noon sky a shining cross of light amid the clouds with the words "By this conquer" inscribed upon it in Greek. That night Christ appeared to him in a dream with a cross in his hand and told Constantine to have a standard made like it. When he awoke the Emperor gave orders for the making of a gilt pole and crossbar surmounted by a bejeweled golden crown. In the midst of the crown arose the Greek letters Chi (X) and Rho (P) atop a cross: From the crossbar hung a purple veil. This standard was called a *Labarum.* Constantine selected 50 of his best men to bear and defend it. He met Maxentius in the Quintian Fields near the Milvian Bridge on October 27, 312, and utterly defeated his foe. Maxentius drowned in the Tiber. See Brewer 1901, 72, and Gibbon [1776–88] 1830, ch. 20. Gibbon relates the story with more skepticism, but less charm.

2. *Health*—In the Latin *Opera* this Greek word is rendered ὑγιqα, which is how it appears on the seal itself. The fourth character appears to be a contraction of ει, made necessary because the word has six letters while the pentagram has only five points.

3. *Antiochus Eupator*—Probably should be Antiochus Epiphanes, king of Syria 175–164 BC. See the biographical note on Judas Maccabaeus.

4. מכבי—MKBI. The letters form the name Maccabee, also spelled MQBI, מקבי.

5. *strong as Jehovah*—Exodus 15:11, part of which reads MI KMKH BALM IHVH מי כמכה באלם יהוה. However, since the Hebrew in Agrippa is the same in both the Latin and English editions, I have let it stand. In the seal some, but not all, of the Hebrew letters around the edge were drawn backward, inverted left to right, while retaining their proper placement in the words they compose. This was probably done to disguise the words, but may simply have been a mistake in copying. The four initial letters of the phrase numerically total 72: M = 40, K = 20, B = 2, I = 10.

6. *De Responsis*—*De Responsis Hecate,* perhaps a part of *De philosophia ex oraculis haurienda* (On the philosophy of the oracles), preserved in fragments in the *Praeparatio Evangelica* of Eusebius. More than a dozen fragments of oracles of Hecate from Porphyry are preserved in Eusebius.

7. *thus she speaks*—See Eusebius, *Praeparatio Evangelica* 5.12.1–2 and 5.13.3.

8. *most like unto them*—"For there is not any thing which in the smallest degree is adapted to the Gods, to which the Gods are not immediately present, and with which they are not conjoined" (Iamblichus *On the Mysteries* 1.15 [Taylor, 63]).

CHAPTER XXXII

How good spirits may be called up by us, and how evil spirits may be overcome by us.

By the efficacy of religion the presence of spirits doth dispose the effect, neither can any work of wonderful efficacy in religion be done, unless some good spirit the ruler and finisher of the work be there present.

Now good spirits, if they may be divers ways called up, yet can by no bounds, or vary hardly be allayed by us, but we must by some sacred things beseech them, as we read in *Apuleius,* by the celestial stars, by the infernal deities, by the natural elements, by the silence of the night, by the increase of the country of Nilus, by the secrets of Memphis;[1] and elsewhere is *Porphyry:* thou who art risen out of the mud, who sittest in thy place, who sailest in ships, who every hour dost change thy shape, and art changed in each sign of the Zodiac.

By these, and such like symbolical orations and hymns, because they are signs of divine virtues, spirits did sometimes apply themselves to human uses: not as being compelled by any kind of necessity, but of their own accord; and by a kind of custom, did, being overcome by the prayers of them that called on them, more easily yield: whence *Porphyry* in his book De Responsis Hecate[2] saith:

I by thy prayers being overcome
Came thither————————

And in another place in the same book he saith:

Conquered by prayer the deities above
Come down on the Earth and future things
   foreshow.

Also the divining of suitable things works so with man's mind, that good spirits do assist us willingly, and communicate their power and virtue to us, daily helping us with illuminations, inspirations, oracles, prophesyings, dreams, miracles, prodigies, divinations, and auguries, and working upon and acting upon our spirits, as images like to them, by framing them by their influences, and making them most like to themselves even so far, as that oftentimes our spirit doth as surely work wonderful things as the celestial spirits are wont to do.

But evil spirits are overcome by us through the assistance of the good, especially when the petitioner is very pious and devout, and sings forth sacred words, and a horrible speech, as by conjuring the divine power by the venerable names, and signs of supernatural powers, by miracles, by sacraments, by sacred mysteries, and such like; which conjurations, or adurations, in as much as they are done by the name and power of religion, and divine virtue, those evil spirits are afraid of; whence also oftentimes prophane men do bind or allay by such kind of sacred conjurations, evil spirits not enduring such things.

Whence *Cyprian* in his book Quod Idola Dii Non Sunt,[3] saith, that spirits being adjured by the true God to presently yield to us, and confess, and are forced to go out of possessed bodies, and either presently leap out, or by degrees vanish, according as the faith of the patient is helping, or grace of the swearer aspires. And *Athanasius* in his book De Variis Questionibus saith that there is no word more terrible and more destructive to the power of devils than the beginning of the 68 psalm, arise O God, and let thine enemies be scattered; for as soon as that word is spoken, the devil vanisheth away howling. And *Origen* against *Celsus* saith, that the naming the name *Jesus* hath oftentimes cast many devils as well out of the souls of men as their bodies, and hath exercised much power in them out of whom the devils were cast.[4]

Also we do oftentimes with threats and revilings bind or repel evil spirits, especially the lesser, as hags,[5] incubi, and such like, as we read in *Lucan*[6] concerning that witch saying:

> I will now call you up by a true name,
> The Stygian dogs I in the light supreme
> Will leave, and follow you also through grave,
> From all the urns in death I will you save,
> Thee O Hecate, unto the gods will show,
> (To whom to address thyself in other hue,
> Thou wast wont) in wan form, and without grace,
> And thee forbid to change Erebus his face.

And in *Philostratus* we read, when *Apollonius* and his companions were traveling in a bright Moon-shining night, that the phantasm of a hag met them,[7] and sometimes changed itself into this shape, and sometimes into that, and sometimes vanished out of their sight. Now as soon as *Apollonius* knew what it was, grievously reviling it advised his companions to do the like: for he knew that that was the best remedy against such invasions. His companions did as he advised, and the phantasm presently with a noise vanished away like a shadow: for so fearful is this kind of spirits, that they are moved, tremble, and are compelled by a feigned terror, and false and impossible threats. Whence *Chereon* the holy scribe saith that these are those things by which especially the spirits are compelled.[8]

There is moreover as hath been above said, a certain kind of spirits not so noxious, but most near to men, so that they are even affected with human passions, and many of these delight in man's society, and willingly dwell with them: some of them dote upon women, some upon children, some are delighted in the company of divers domestic and wild animals, some inhabit woods and parks, some dwell about fountains and meadows.

So the fairies, and hobgoblins inhabit champian fields;[9] the naiades fountains; the potamides rivers; the nymphs marshes, and ponds; the oreades[10] mountains; the humedes meadows; the dryades and hamadryades the woods, which also satyrs and sylvani[11] inhabit, the same also take delight in trees and brakes; as do the naptae,[12] and agapae in flowers; the dodonae in acorns; the paleae and feniliae in fodder and the country.

He therefore that will call upon them, may easily do it in the places where their abode is, by alluring them with sweet fumes, with pleasant sounds, and by such instruments as are made of the guts of certain animals and peculiar wood, adding songs, verses, enchantments suitable to it, and that which is especially to be observed in this, the singleness of the wit, innocency of the mind, a firm credulity, and constant silence; wherefore they do often meet children, women, and poor and mean men. They are afraid of and fly from men of a constant, bold, and undaunted mind, being no way offensive to good and pure men, but to wicked and impure, noxious.

Of this kind are hobgoblins, familiars, and ghosts of dead men. Hence *Plotinus* saith,[13] that the souls of men are sometimes made spirits: and of men well deserving are made familiars which the Greeks call eudemons,[14] i.e. blessed spirits: but of ill deserving men, hags, and hobgoblins, which the Greeks call cacodemons,[15] i.e. evil spirits; but they may be called ghosts when it is uncertain whether they have deserved well or ill.

Of these apparitions there are divers examples; such was that which *Pliny* the Junior makes mention of concerning the house of *Athenodorus* the philosopher of Tharsis, in which there appeared with a sudden horrible noise the ghost of an old man.[16] And *Philostratus* tells of the like of a hag of *Menippus Lycius* the philosopher, turned into a beautiful woman of Corinth, whom *Tyaneus Apollonius* took to be a hobgoblin; the same at Ephesus, the like in the shape of an old beggar who was the cause of the pestilence, who therefore being by his command stoned, there appeared a mastiff dog, and presently the pestilence ceased.[17]

We must know this, that whosoever shall intellectually work in evil spirits, shall by the power of good spirits bind them; but he that shall work only worldlily, shall work to himself judgement and damnation.

Notes—Chapter XXXII

1. *secrets of Memphis*—The Egyptian prophet Zachlas is entreated by an old man to restore the life of his murdered son, that the son may accuse his murderer:

> O priest have mercy, have mercy I pray thee by the Celestiall Planets, by the Powers infernall, by the vertue of the naturall elements, by the silences of the night, by the buildings of Swallows nigh unto the town Copton, by the increase of the floud Nilus, by the secret mysteries of Memphis, and by the instruments and trumpets of the Isle Pharos, have mercy I say, and call againe to life this dead body, and make that his eyes which he closed and shut, may be open and see. (Apuleius *The Golden Asse* ch. 11)

2. *De Responsis Hecate*—See note 6, ch. XXXI, bk. III.

3. *Quod Idola Dii Non Sunt*—

> These [spirits], however, when adjured by us through the true God, at once yield and confess, and are constrained to go out from the bodies possessed. You may see them at our voice, and by the operation of the hidden majesty, smitten with stripes, burnt with fire, stretched out with the increase of a growing punishment, howling, groaning, entreating, confessing whence they came and when they depart, even in the hearing of those very persons who worship them, and either springing forth at once or vanishing gradually, even as the faith of the sufferer comes in aid, or the grace of the healer effects. (Cyprian "On the Vanity of Idols" 7. In the *Treatises* 6 [*Ante-Nicene Fathers,* 5:467])

This very brief treatise scarcely warrants Agrippa's calling it a "book."

4. *devils were cast*—

> And a similar philosophy of names applies also to our Jesus, whose name has already been seen, in an unmistakeable manner, to have expelled myriads of evil spirits from the souls and bodies (of men), so great was the power which it exerted upon those from whom the spirits were driven out. (Origen *Against Celsus* 1.25 [*Ante-Nicene Fathers,* 4:406])

See also 1.67 (*Ante-Nicene Fathers* 4:427).

5. *Hags*—Nocturnal fiends associated with the Furies and Harpies by some early writers. They come in the form of old women and suck the vitality from children. They squat on the chests of those asleep and give them nightmares—hence the term "hag-ridden." The Latin *Opera* has *lamias,* of which "hag" is a translation.

6. *read in Lucan*—The witch Erichtho is annoyed when the shade of a dead soldier is hesitant in returning to its putrefying corpse. She encourages the Furies and the Goddess of hell to hasten it along:

> This moment under your real name will I summon you forth, and, Stygian bitches, will leave you in the light of the upper world; amid graves will I follow you, amid funereal rites, your watcher; from the tombs will I expel you, from all the urns will I drive you away. And thee, Hecate, squalid with thy pallid form, will I expose to the Gods, before whom in false shape with other features thou art wont to come, and I will forbid thee to conceal the visage of Erebus. I will disclose, damsel of Enna, under the boundless bulk of the earth, what feasts are detaining thee, upon what compact thou dost love the gloomy sovereign, to what corruption having submitted, thy parent was unwilling to call thee back. (Lucan *Pharsalia* 6, lines 730–42 [Riley, 243–4])

7. *a hag met them*—

> While they were pursuing their journey by moonlight one night, their path was beset by the ghostly apparition of an Empusa,

which assumed first one shape and then another, sometimes vanishing altogether. Apollonius recognized its nature at once, and not only reviled the spectre himself, but exhorted his companions to do the same, as this is a safeguard against such visitations, whereupon the Empusa fled squeaking as ghosts do. (Philostratus *Life and Times of Apollonius of Tyana* 2.4 [Eells, 37])

8. *spirits are compelled*—

And why, which is much more absurd than this, are threats employed and false terrors, by any casual person, not to a daemon, or some departed soul, but to the sovereign Sun himself, or to the Moon, or some one of the celestial Gods, in order to compel these divinities to speak the truth? For does not he who says that he will burst the heavens, or unfold the secrets of Isis, or point out the arcanum in the adytum, or stop Baris, or scatter the members of Osiris to Typhon, or that he will do something else of the like kind, does not he who says this, by thus threatening what he neither knows nor is able to effect, prove himself to be stupid in the extreme? And what abjectness does it not produce in those who, like very silly children, are possessed with such vain fear, and are terrified at such fictions? And yet Chaeremon, who was a sacred scribe, writes these things, as disseminated by the Egyptians. It is also said that these, and things of the like kind, are of a most compulsive nature. (Porphyry *Letter to Anebo*, prefixed to Iamblichus *On the Mysteries* [Taylor, 10–1]).

See the biographical note on Chaeremon.

9. *champian fields*—Champaign fields, flat open grassland as distinguished from hills, woodlands and towns. Perhaps used here for commons.

10. *oreades*—Mountain nymphs.

11. *sylvani*—Silvanus is the Latin god of woodlands and field boundaries. He is depicted as a cheerful, lustful old man, and was identified by late Roman writers with Pan and Faunus. Hence the silvani are woodland nymphs.

12. *naptae*—From ναπη, a wooded dell or glen.

13. *Plotinus saith*—"… and again, not a few souls, once among men, have continued to serve them after quitting the body and by revelations, practically help-

ful, make clear, as well, that the other souls, too, have not ceased to be" (Plotinus *Enneads* 4.7.15 [Mackenna, 3:143]).

14. *eudemons*—Greek εὐ (happy) δαίμων (genius). Related to the name of the 11th house of the zodiac.

15. *cacodemons*—Greek κακὸς (evil) δαίμων (genius). The name of the 12th house of the zodiac.

16. *ghost of an old man*—Since this is perhaps the quintessential ghost story of the classical, or any other, age, I give it here in full:

In Athens there was a large and spacious mansion with the bad reputation of being dangerous to its occupants. At dead of night the clanking of iron and, if you listened carefully, the rattle of chains could be heard, some way off at first, and then close at hand. Then there appeared the spectre of an old man, emaciated and filthy, with a long flowing beard and hair on end, wearing fetters on his legs and shaking the chains on his wrists. The wretched occupants would spend fearful nights awake in terror; lack of sleep led to illness and then death as their dread increased, for even during the day, when the apparition had vanished, the memory of it was in their minds' eye, so that their terror remained after the cause of it had gone. The house was therefore deserted, condemned to stand empty and wholly abandoned to the spectre; but it was advertised as being to let or for sale in case someone was found who knew nothing of its evil reputation.

The philosopher Athenodorus came to Athens and read the notice. His suspicions were aroused when he heard the low price, and the whole story came out on inquiry; but he was none the less, in fact all the more, eager to rent the house. When darkness fell he gave orders that a couch was to be made up for him in the front part of the house, and asked for his notebooks, pen and lamp. He sent all his servants to the inner rooms, and concentrated his thoughts, eyes and hand on this writing, so that his mind would be occupied and not conjure up the phantom he had heard about nor other imaginary fears. At first there was nothing but the general silence of night; then came the clanking of iron and dragging of chains. He did not look up nor stop writing, but steeled his mind to shut out the sounds. Then the noise grew louder, came nearer, was heard in the doorway, and then inside the room. He looked around, saw and recognized the ghost described to him. It stood and beckoned, as if summoning him. Athenodorus in his turn signed it to wait a little, and again bent over his notes and pen, while it stood rattling its chains over his head as he wrote. He looked round again and saw it beckoning as before, so without further delay he picked up his lamp and followed. It moved slowly, as if weighted down with chains, and when it turned off into the courtyard of the house it suddenly vanished, leaving him alone. He then picked some grass and leaves and marked the spot. The following day he approached the magistrates, and advised them to give orders for the place to be dug up. There they found bones, twisted round with chains, which were left bare and corroded by the fetters when time and the action of the soil had rotted away the body. The bones were collected and given a public buriel, and after the shades had been duly laid to rest the house saw them no more. (Pliny the Younger *Letters* 7.27, trans. B. Radice [Middlesex: Penguin, 1963], 203–4)

17. *pestilence ceased*—Apollonius addresses the wedding guests:

"You will understand that better when I say that this fair bride is one of those fiends whom the people call a lamia. These beings love and are fond of sexual pleasure, but still more of eating human flesh, and they use the seduction of the senses to entice their victims whom they mean to feast upon." "Hold your tongue and leave the house!" shrieked the bride, pretending to be horrified by what she heard; and she was going on to revile philosophers as fools when suddenly all the show of gold cups and silver plate changed to airy nothings and vanished before their eyes, and the cooks and the butlers and the rest of the household evaporated under the exorcism of Apollonius. Then the lamia simulated weeping, and besought him not to torment her, or force her to confess what she was, but he insisted, never relaxing his compulsion, until she admitted that she was a lamia and that she was fattening up Menippus with dainties so that she might devour his body, and that she made a practice of feeding on bodies which were young and beautiful, because their blood was untainted. (Philostratus *Life and Times of Apollonius of Tyana* 4.25 [Eells, 106])

They found there what looked like an old beggar, slyly blinking his eyes, ragged and haggard, and carrying a wallet of breadcrusts. Apollonius stationed the Ephesians around this object, and commanded them: "Gather up all the stones you can find, and smite with them this thing which is hateful to the gods!" The Ephesians were taken aback by this order, and remained quiet, for they thought it would be a crime to put to death so woe-begone a stranger, for he was begging for life, and making many pleas for sympathy. Apollonius persisted in urging them to stone the intruder, and not to let him escape; so at last some of those on the outside of the ring began to throw stones, whereat the beggar, who had been blinking until then, glared savagely with flaming eyes. All knew him then for a demon, and hurled stones upon him until they piled up a great heap where he had been standing. After a short pause, Apollonius ordered them to remove the stones and see what a wild beast they had slain. When they did so, the beggarman whom they supposed they had stoned had vanished, but in his stead lay a dog shaped like a mastiff, and as large as the largest lion, which had been crushed by the stones, and foamed at the mouth as if rabid. (ibid. 4.10 [Eels, 96])

CHAPTER XXXIII

Of the bonds of spirits, and of their adjurations, and castings out.

The bonds by which spirits are bound, besought, or cast out, are three.[1]

Some of them are taken from the elemental world, as when we adjure a spirit by any inferior and natural things of affinity with or adverse to them, in as much as we would call upon or cast them out, as by flowers, and herbs, by animals, by snow, by ice, by hell, by fire, and such like, as these also are ofttimes mixed with divine praises, and blessings, and consecrations, as appears in the Song of the Three Children,[2] and in the psalm: praise ye the Lord from the heavens,[3] and in the consecration and blessing of the Paschal taper.[4] This bond doth work upon the spirits by an apprehensive virtue under the account of love, or hatred, in as much as the spirits are present with, or favour, or abhor anything that is natural or against nature, as these things themselves love or hate one the other. Hence that of *Proclus,* as the lion fears a cock, especially a white cock: so doth a spirit appearing in the form of a lion vanish away at the sight of a cock.[5]

The second bond is taken from the celestial world, viz. when we adjure them by the heaven, by stars, by their motions, rays, light, beauty, clearness, excellency, fortitude, influence, and wonders, and such like: and this bond works upon spirits by way of admonition, and example. It hath also some command, especially upon the ministering spirits, and those who are of the lowest orders.

The third bond is from the intellectual and divine world, which is perfected by religion, that is to say, when we swear by the sacraments, by the miracles, by the divine names, by the sacred seals, and other mysteries of religion; wherefore this bond is the highest of all and the strongest, working upon the spirits by command and power.

But this is to be observed, that as after the universal providence, there is a particular one; and after the universal soul, particular souls; so in the first place we invocate by the superior bonds, and by the names and powers which rule the things, then by the inferior, and the things themselves.

We must know further, that by these bonds not only spirits, but also all creatures are bound, as tempests, burnings, floods, plagues, diseases, force of arms, and every animal, by assuming them, either by the manner of adjuration, or by the way of deprecation or benediction; as in the charming of serpents, besides the natural and celestial, by rehearsing out of the mysteries and religion, the curse of the serpent[6] in terrestrial Paradise, the lifting up[7] of the serpent in the wilderness; moreover by assuming that verse of the psalm 91: Thou shalt walk upon the ape and the basilisk, and shalt tread upon the lion and dragon.[8]

Superstition also very much prevaileth in these, by the translating of some sacramental rites to that which we intend to bind or hinder, as of excommunication, buriel or exequies for the driving away of diseases, serpents, mice or worms, which thing we read to have been thus done in divers places, and it is wont to be done even as yet.

Notes—Chapter XXXIII

1. *are three*—Note the echoing in this chapter of the structure of Agrippa's work as a whole—the division into natural, celestial and divine.

2. *of the Three Children*—Song of the Three Holy Children 35–65.

3. *from the heavens*—Psalms 148:1.

4. *Paschal taper*—In Agrippa's day the paschal candle figured prominently in the Easter festival of the Roman Church. It was of impressive dimensions—at Salisbury Cathedral in 1517 the candle measured 36 feet, and at Westminster Cathedral in 1558 it weighed 300 pounds. Usually set on the north side just below the first ascent to the high altar, it rested in an elaborate candlestick. At Durham Cathedral the holder itself was called the paschal, and was 38 feet high. Coupled with the candle, it towered 70 feet. New fire was kindled with flint and steel on Easter Eve. From it were lit the three candles that formed the *lumen Christi*, and from these the paschal candle proper. It symbolized the victorious and risen Christ and burned during each service until Whitsuntide (eighth week after Easter), after which its remains were cut up to make funeral candles for the poor. Symbolically its fire continued throughout the year, embodied in the flames of the other lights in the church.

5. *sight of a cock*—

> Hence it is said, that a cock is very much feared, and as it were reverenced, by a lion; the reason of which we cannot assign from matter or sense, but from the contemplation alone of a supernal order. For thus we shall find that the presence of the solar virtue accords more with a cock than with a lion. … Sometimes too there are daemons with a leonine front, who, when a cock is placed before them, unless they are of a solar order, suddenly disappear; and this because those natures which have an inferior rank in the same order, always reverence their superiors …" (Proclus *De sacrificio et magia*, frag., Latin trans. Marsilius Ficinus, Venice, 1497. Quoted in full by Taylor in Iamblichus' *Life of Pythagoras* [Taylor, 216])

6. *curse of the serpent*—Genesis 3:14.

7. *lifting up*—John 3:14. See also II Kings 18:4.

8. *lion and the dragon*—Psalms 91:13.

CHAPTER XXXIV

Of the animastical order, and the heros.

After the quires of the blessed spirits, the anamastical order is the next, which the Hebrew theologians call Issim,[1] that is, Strong and Mighty Men; the magicians of the gentiles, call heros and demigods, or half gods half men: whom *Fulgentius,* an author not to be contemned, supposeth were so called, either because that for the meanness of their desert they are not judged worthy of heaven, nor yet are accounted terresterial for the reverence of grace; of this kind in old time were *Priapus,*[2] *Hippo,*[3] *Vertumnus:*[4] or because they being eminent in this life for divine virtues, and benefits for mankind, after this mortal man put off, are translated into the quire of the blessed gods;[5] always providing for mortal men the same virtues and benefits which they long since had in this life: or because they were procreated from the secret seed of the superiors, whom they think were begotten by the mixture of gods or angels with men, and therefore obtaining a certain middle nature, so as they are neither angels nor men: which opinion *Lactantius*[6] also followeth.

And there are even at this time those who have commerce and conjugal mixture with spirits; and all now believe that *Merlin,*[7] a British prophet, was the son of a spirit, and born of a virgin: and also they imagined, that *Plato* the prince of wisdom was born of a virgin, impregnated by a phantasm of *Apollo*. And it is delivered in histories, that certain women of the Goths (which they call Alrumna) eminent both for beauty and ingenuity, long since at Filimire, or (as others say) at Idanthresie, going forth out of the tents of the king of the Goths, wandered in the deserts of Scythia in Asia beyond the marshes of Meotis, and there being impregnated by fauni and satyrs, brought forth the first Huns;[8] moreover *Psellus* is the author, that spirits sometimes cast forth seed,[9] from the which certain little creatures arise.

Therefore these heros have no less power in disposing and ruling these inferior things, than the gods and angels, and have both their offices and their dignities distributed to them: and therefore to them no otherwise than to the gods themselves were temples, images, altars, sacrifices, vows, and other mysteries of religion dedicated. And their names invocated had divine and magical virtues for the accomplishing of some miracles: which thing *Eusebius* declareth[10] that many tried by the invocation of the name of *Apollonius* of Tyana; and more of this kind we read of, both in the poets, and also in the historians and philosophers, concerning *Hercules, Atlas, Aesculapius* and the other heros of the gentiles;[11] but these are the follies of the gentiles.

But as concerning our holy heros we believe that they excel in divine power, and that the soul of the Messiah[12] doth rule over them (as the theologians of the Jews also testify), that is *Jesus* Christ, who by divers of his saints, as it were by members fitted for this purpose, doth administer and distribute divers gifts of his grace in these inferior parts, and every one of the saints do enjoy a particular gift of working. Whence they being implored by us with divers prayers and supplications according to the manifold distribution of graces, every one doth most freely bestow their gifts, benefits, and graces on us much more readily, truly, and also more abundantly than the angelical powers by how much they are nigher to us, and more allied to our natures, as they who in times past were both men, and suffered human affections and infirmities; and their names, degrees and offices are more known to us.

Therefore out of the number of these almost infinite, there are twelve chief, viz. the twelve apostles of Christ, who (as the evangelical truth saith) sit upon twelve thrones,[13] judging the twelve tribes of Israel, who in the Revelations are distributed upon twelve foundations,[14] at the twelve gates of the heavenly city, who rule the twelve signs, and are sealed in the twelve precious stones,[15] and the whole world is distributed to them; but their true names are these: the first הכפי שמעון Symehon Hacephi,

this is *Peter;* the second אלעוזי *Alousi,* whom we call *Andrew;* the third יעקבה *Jahacobah,* this is *James* the greater; the fourth פוליפוש *Polipos,* whom we call *Philip;* the fifth ברכיה *Barachiah,* this is *Bartholomew;* the sixth יוהנה *Johanah,* whom we name *John;* the seventh is תמני *Thamni,* whom we call *Thomas;* the eighth is called מדון *Medon,* for whom we say *Matthew;* the ninth is יעקב *Jahacob,* this is *James* the less; the tenth is כטיפא *Catepha,* that is *Thadeus;* the eleventh שמאם *Samam,* who is *Simon* the Canaanite; the twelfth מתתיה *Matattiah,* who is called *Matthias.*[16]

After these are the seventy-two disciples[17] of Christ, who also themselves do rule so many quinaries of heaven, and tribes, people, nations, and tongues. After whom is an innumerable multitude of saints, who also themselves have received divers offices, places, nations and people into their protection and patronage, whose most apparent miracles at the faithful prayers of those that invoke them, we plainly see and confess.

Notes—Chapter XXXIV

1. *Issim*—See note 26, ch. XVII, bk. III.

2. *Priapus*—Son of Dionysus and Aphrodite. Out of spite against Aphrodite, Hera caused her child to be ugly. Priapus is the god of universal fertility, and by extension protector of flocks, bees, vines, gardens and fishing. He was usually represented in the form of a hermae carrying a cornucopia or sickle, and stained a bright red, giving him the name *rubicundus.*

3. *Hippo*—One of the daughters of Oceanus and Tethys who "have charge of young men over all the earth" (Hesiod *Theogony* c. line 350) But this can hardly be Agrippa's intention. Perhaps he means Hippothoon, son of Poseidon and the mortal woman Alope. Hippothoon was one of the "heros of the names" after whom the ten Attic *phylae,* or tribes, were called. He possessed a statue in the Round House, as mentioned by Pausanias *(Guide to Greece* 1.5.2).

4. *Vertumnus*—Or Vortumnus, said to have been originally an Etruscan deity carried to Rome by the ancient Vulsinian colony that occupied the Caelian Hill. He was credited with the power of changing his shape, and gained the hand of his wife, Pomona, by transforming himself into a handsome youth. His fes-

tival, the Vortumnalia, was held on August 23 and marked the transition of the seasons. As god of the harvest, first fruits were sacrificed to him.

5. *the blessed* —"And human souls, when they have attained to a beginning of immortal life, change into daemons, and thereafter pass on into the choral dance of the gods; that is the crowning glory of the soul" *(Corpus Hermeticum* 10.7 [Scott 1:191, 193]).

6. *Lactantius*—

Therefore, while they [the angels] abode among men, that most deceitful ruler of the earth, by his very association, gradually enticed them to vices, and polluted them by intercourse with women. ... But they who were born from these, because they were neither angels nor men, but bearing a kind of mixed nature, were not admitted into hell, as their fathers were not into heaven. Thus there came to be two kinds of demons; one of heaven, and the other of the earth. The latter are the wicked spirits, the authors of all the evils which are done, and the same devil is their prince. Whence

Trismegistus calls him the ruler of the demons. But grammarians say that they are called demons, as though *daemones,* that is, skilled and acquainted with matters: for they think that these are gods. (Lactantius *Divine Institutes* 2.15 [*Ante-Nicene Christian Library,* 21:127])

7. *Merlin*—Merlin was engendered in a virgin girl by a demon to become the Antichrist. But the resourceful confessor of the girl at once baptized the unnatural infant, rescuing him for Christianity. From his demon father Merlin gained the power of prophecy.

8. *the first Huns*—

For even Jornandes, who was Bishop of the Goths when Justinian was Emperor, did not hesitate in his book on the origin of the Getae to affirm that there were in Scythia witch women, called in their native tongue *Aliorumnae [Haliurunae],* who were driven by Filimer the Gothic king into the farthest deserts, where they were embraced by unclean spirits and gave birth to hideous, fierce dwarfs from whom the Huns are descended. (Nicolas Remy *Demonolatry* 1.6 [Ashwin, 17])

The work referred to by Remy is *De origine actibusque getarum,* written in 551 by the historian Jordanes (more correctly but less commonly rendered Jordanis, or Jordannis). Filimer was sixth king of the Goths, who migrated under him into Scythia and settled in the region they called Oium. Idanthyrsus was chief king of the Scythians in the time of Darius (6th century BC).

9. *cast forth seed*—Of the semen of spirits Psellus writes in his work *De daemonibus:* "If they ejaculate any semen it is, like the body from which it comes, so lacking in warmth that nothing can be more unfit or unsuitable for procreation" (In Remy *Demonolatry* 1.6 [Ashwin, 13]).

10. *Eusebius declareth*—

Yet even today Jesus demonstrates the worth of his divine might in expelling, just by the invocation of his wonderous name, any evil or bothersome demons that fasten on the souls or bodies of men, and we know this to be true from our experience. To expect such efficacy from the name of Apollonius, or even to inquire after it, is foolish. (Eusebius *Against the Life of Apollonius of Tyana by Philostratus* 4)]

"There are still men in our own time who assert that they have discovered superstitious amulets dedicated in the name of Apollonius." (ibid. 40; both quotes my paraphrase)

11. *of the gentiles*—

Others, on the other hand, claim superhuman powers for such children, and assert that they possess some attributes of divinity, such as the ancients used to ascribe to their heros, who, according to Lucian, were held to be neither gods nor men, but both. Of this we have the fullest proof in what we find written of the birth of Castor and Pollux, Bacchus, Alexander, Romulus, Aesculapius, and other such demigods: that they were begotten by those who were at that time called gods, but we call Demons, who hid themselves in an assumed shape and so embraced the mothers of these men. (Remy *Demonolatry* 1.4 [Ashwin, 20])

12. *Messiah*—MShICh, מָשִׁיחַ, the "anointed prince" (Daniel 9:25).

13. *twelve thrones*—Matthew 19:28.

14. *twelve foundations*—Revelation 21:14.

15. *twelve precious stones*—Revelation 21:19–20.

16. *is called Matthias*—Notice the omission of Judas from the group. His place is taken by Matthias, the 13th apostle. See Acts 1:26.

17. *seventy-two disciples*—Luke 10:1. The King James says "seventy," but 72 is intended, and Knox gives 72.

CHAPTER XXXV

Of the mortal and terrestrial gods.

Next after these are the mortal gods, whom in like manner also we call heros, and terrestrial gods, or companions of the superior gods: viz. kings, princes, and priests, by whom this world is governed, and disposed by their laws, whom therefore as gods we receive, worship and reverence, because God himself hath suffered his name to be communicated to them, and by a proper denomination hath confirmed it to them, calling them gods, even as he spake to *Moses,* saying, I have made thee a god to Pharaoh;[1] and elsewhere he hath commanded concerning them, saying, thou shalt not detract from the gods;[2] and again, if theft shall lie hid, the master of the house shall apply himself to the gods;[3] and the Psalmist saith, the princes of the people were gathered together with the God of *Abraham:* because that the mighty gods of the Earth are vehemently lifted up;[4] and elsewhere God stood in the councils of the gods, but in the midst he judgeth the gods;[5] and a little after, I have said ye are all gods, and sons of the Most High.[6]

Moreover he hath commanded concerning the worshipping and reverencing of them, decreeing tithes and first fruits for them, and giving them the power of the sword, and forbidding any to curse them, and commanding obedience to be yielded to them, though wicked. Hence all antiquity called their princes gods, and worshipped them as divine powers, as *Janus* testifieth[7] in *Ovid,* in his first book of Fasti, saying:

When the Earth of the gods was potent, I
did reign
And deities mixed were with seats humane.

And divine *Plato* in his third book De Republica appointed that princes both alive and dead should be celebrated with divine honours, which institution hath been received amongst all nations, even from the first age, viz. to deify their princes with divine honours, and to consecrate them with eternal memory.[8]

Hence they did impose their never dying names on cities, provinces, mountains, rivers, lakes, islands and seas; and dedicated to them with great pomp, pyramids, colossuses, triumphal arches, trophies, statues, temples, plays, feasts; and also called the heavens, stars, days and months by their names. Hence January from *Janus,* July from *Julius,* August from *Augustus;* so dies Mercurii from *Mercury Trismegist,* dies Jovis from *Jupiter,* which custom we read was observed not only by the Egyptians, Greeks and Romans, but also by the extreme barbarous people, as Goths, Danes and Teutons.

Hence *Saxo Grammaticus* being witness, what day the former call dies Mercurii, these do call Othin's day:[9] what day the former name from *Jupiter,* these call Thor's day,[10] from *Othin* and *Thor,* in times past kings of Gotland and Denmark; neither are they for any other reason called Goths, than that they call in their language their chiefest god *Got.*[11] Hence also the Dutch are thus called, because they named the

576

god *Mars,* whom they worshipped, *Teutan;*[12] by which name the Gauls also called *Mercury.*

Therefore are kings and priests (if they be just) companions of the gods, and endowed with the like power. Hence they cure diseases by their touch and word,[13] and sometimes command the times and the heavens, as *Virgil* sang[14] of *Augustus:*

> It rains all night, in the morn the rays return;
> Caesar with Jove divided hath the throne.

And the Scripture testifieth of *Joshuah,* who fighting in Gibeon, commanded the Sun and Moon, saying, Sun stand still in Gibeon and thou Moon in the valley of Ajalon;[15] and the Sun and the Moon stood still at his command, neither did the Sun set in the space of one day, until he had revenged himself of his enemies, and the Lord obeyed the voice of man; also *Moses* divided the Red Sea,[16] and *Joshua* Jordan,[17] and led the people over dryshod; the like did *Alexander* the Macedonian, leading forth his army.[18]

Sometimes also they are endowed with a prophetic spirit, as we read of *Chaiaphas*[19] in the holy Scripture, that he prophesied, for that he was High Priest that year.

Seeing therefore it is so that the Lord of the Earth would that kings and priests be called gods by communication of name and power, surely we ought also to deserve well of them, and to prefer their judgements before ours, and simply to obey, supplicate and adore, and worship with all kind of worship and reverence the most high God in them.

Notes—Chapter XXXV

1. *god to Pharaoh*—Exodus 7:1.

2. *detract from the gods*—Exodus 22:28.

3. *to the gods*—Exodus 22:8.

4. *vehemently lifted up*—Psalms 47:9.

5. *judgeth the gods*—Psalms 82:1.

6. *sons of the Most High*—Psalms 82:6.

7. *Janus testifieth*—"Then, too, was I reigning, when the earth was fit to receive the gods, and the divinities were interspersed among the abodes of men" (Ovid *Fasti* 1, lines 247–8 [Riley, 19]). The meaning is that the gods could tolerate the Earth before the pollution of human sin.

8. *eternal memory*—

> And so, when each generation has educated others like themselves to take their place as guardians of the state, they shall depart to the Islands of the Blessed and there dwell. And the state shall establish public memorials and sacrifices for them as to divinities if the Pythian oracle approves or, if not, as to divine and god-like men. (Plato *Republic* 8.540b [Hamilton and Cairns, 772])

There is no similar reference in book 3 of the *Republic.*

9. *Othin's*—Woden's or Odin's day: Wednesday.

10. *Thor's*—Thursday.

11. *Got*—On the name "Goth," Brewer comments: "Icelandic, *got* (a horseman); whence *Woden*—i.e., Gothen. Without doubt, *got,* a horseman, *good,* and the sacred name of *God* are all to be traced to *got* or *guth,* the Teutonic idea of God being that of a mighty warrior" (Brewer 1870, 357.)

12. *Teutan*—Again, Brewer: "Thuath-duiné (north men). Our word *Dutch* and the German *Deutsch* are variations of the same word, originally written *Theodisk*" (ibid., 884–5).

13. *touch and word*—Scrofula was called the king's evil because it was thought the royal touch could cure it. The last person "touched" in England was Doctor Samuel Johnson, at the age of two and a half, by Queen Anne in 1712. The French kings also claimed this power from the time of Anne of Clovis (481 AD). One Easter Sunday in 1686 Louis XIV touched 1,600 persons, at the same time speaking the words: *"Le roy te touche, Dieu te gnerisse"* (The King touches you, God heals you).

14. *as Virgil sang*—This quotation is not from Virgil.

15. *valley of Ajalon*—Joshua 10:12–3.

16. *divided the Red Sea*—Exodus 14:21.

17. *Joshua Jordan*—Joshua 3:17.

18. *forth his army*—

Encouraged by this accident, he [Alexander] proceeded to reduce the maritime ports of Cilicia and Phoenicia, and passed his army along the sea-coasts of Pamphylia with such expedition that many historians have described and extolled it with that height of admiration, as if it were no less than a miracle, and an extraordinary effect of divine favour, that the waves which usually come rolling in violently from the main, and hardly ever leave so much as a narrow beach under the steep, broken cliffs at any time uncovered, should on a sudden retire to afford him passage. (Plutarch "Life of Alexander." In *Lives* [Dryden, 812–3]).

19. *Chaiaphas*—Caiaphas. See John 11:49–51.

CHAPTER XXXVI

Of man, how he was
created after the image of God.

The most abundant God (as *Trismegistus* saith)[1] hath framed two images like himself viz. the world and man, that in one of these he might sport himself with certain wonderful operations: but in the other, that he might enjoy his delights.

Who, seeing he is one, hath created the world one; seeing that he is infinite, hath created the world round; seeing he is eternal, he hath created the world incorruptible and everlasting; seeing he is immense, he hath created the world the greatest of all things; seeing he is the chiefest life, he hath adorned the world with vital seeds, begetting all things out of himself; and seeing he is omnipotent, by his will alone, not by any necessity of Nature, he hath created the world, not out of any foregoing matter, but out of nothing; and seeing he is the chief goodness, embracing his Word, which is the first Idea of all things, with his choicest will and essential love, he hath fabricated this external world after the example of the internal, viz. ideal world, yet sending forth nothing of the essence of the Idea, but created of nothing that which he had from eternity by the Idea.

God also created man after his image; for as the world is the image of God, so man is the image of the world. Hence some think that it is spoken, that man is not created simply the image of God, but after the image, or the image of the image; therefore he is called Microcosm, that is the Lesser World.

The world is a rational creature, immortal;

man in like manner is rational but mortal, that is, dissolvable; for (as *Hermes* saith)[2] seeing the world itself is immortal, it is impossible that any part of it can perish. Therefore to die, is a vain name, and even as vacuum is nowhere, so also death; therefore we say a man dieth, when his soul and body are separated, not that anything of them perisheth or is turned into nothing.

Notwithstanding the true image of God is his Word.[3] The wisdom, life, light and truth existing by himself, of which image man's soul is the image, in regard of which we are said to be made after the image of God, not after the image of the world, or of the creatures; for as God cannot be touched, nor perceived by the ears, nor seen with the eyes; so the soul of man can neither be seen, heard nor touched. And as God himself is infinite, and cannot be compelled by any, so also the mind of man is free, and cannot be enforced or bounded. Further, as God comprehendeth this whole world, and whatsoever is in it, in his mind alone; so man's mind comprehendeth it even in thought;[4] and that which is peculiar to him alone with God, as God moveth and governeth all this world by his beck alone, so man's mind ruleth and governeth his body.

Therefore it was necessary, that the mind of man thus sealed by the Word of God, should put on also the corporeal man, after the most complete example of the world: therefore man is called the other world, and the other image of God, because he hath in himself all that is contained in the greater world, so that there remaineth nothing which is not found even truly and really in man himself, and all these things do perform the same duties in him, as in the great world.

There are in him the four elements, with the most true properties of their nature, and in him an ethereal body, the chariot of the soul in proportion corresponding to the heaven: there are in him the vegetative life of plants, the senses of animals, of celestial spirits, the angelical reason, and the divine understanding, and the true conjunction, and divine possession of all these things flowing together into one.

Hence in sacred letters man is called every creature, and not only man being made another world doth comprehend all the parts thereof in himself but also doth receive and contain even God himself. Hence *Xystus*[5] the Pythagorean saith, that the soul of man is the temple of God: which thing *Paul* also more clearly expressed, saying, ye art the temple of God;[6] and the same the sacred Scripture testifieth in many places: therefore man is the most express image of God, seeing man containeth in himself all things which are in God.

But God by a certain eminency containeth all things through his power, and simply, as the cause and beginning of all things; but he hath given this power to man, that he should in like manner contain all things, but by a certain act and composition, as the knot, tie, and bond of all things.

Therefore man only rejoiceth in this honour, that he hath similitude with all, operation with all, and conversation with all: he symbolizeth with the matter in a proper subject; with the elements in a fourfold body; with plants in a vegetative virtue; with animals in a sensitive faculty; with the heavens in an etherial spirit, and influx of the superior parts on the inferior; with the angels in understanding and wisdom; with God in containing all things: he is preserved with God, and the intelligences, by faith and wisdom; with the heavens and heavenly things, by reason and discourse; with all inferior things, by sense and dominion: and acteth with all, and hath power on all, even on God himself, by knowing and loving him.

And as God knoweth all things, so also man can know all things intelligible, seeing he hath for an adequate object, *Ens*[7] in general, or (as others say) Truth itself; neither is there anything found in man, nor any disposition, in which something of divinity may not shine forth; neither is there anything in God, which may not also be represented in man.

Whosoever therefore shall know himself, shall know all things in himself; especially he shall know God, according to whose image he was made; he shall know the world, the resemblance of which he beareth; he shall know all creatures, with whom he symbolizeth; and what comfort he can have and obtain from stones, plants, animals, elements, heavens, from spirits, angels, and every thing, and how all things may be fitted for all things, in their time, place, order, measure, proportion and harmony, and can draw and bring to himself, even as a loadstone iron.

And *Geber* in his Sum of Alchemy[8] teacheth, that no man can come to the perfection of this art, who shall not know the principles of it in himself; but by how much the more everyone shall know himself, by so much he obtaineth the greater power of attracting it, and by so much operateth greater and more wonderful things, and will ascend to so great a perfection, that he is made the son of God, and is transformed into that image which is God, and is united with him, which is not granted to angels, the world, or any creature, but to man only, viz. to have power to be made the son of God, and to be united to him.

But man being united to God, all things which are in man, are united, especially his mind, then he spirits and animal powers, and vegetative faculty, and the elements are to the matter, drawing with itself even the body, whose form it hath been, leading it forth into a better condition, and an heavenly nature, even until it be glorified into immortality. And this which we have spoken is the peculiar gift of man, to whom this dignity of the divine image is proper, and common to no other creature.

But there are some theologians,[9] who make those powers of man's memory, understanding, will, the image of the divine Trinity; and there are who going further, do place this image not only in these three faculties which they call first acts, but also in the second acts; and as the memory representeth the Father, the understanding the Son, the will the Holy Ghost; so also the word produced from our understanding, and love flowing from our will, and the understanding itself having a present object and producing it, do set forth the Son, Spirit and Father.

And the more mysterious theologians teach that moreover all our members do represent something in God whose image they bear; and that even in our passions we represent God, but by a certain analogy: for in the holy word we read of the wrath, fury, repentance, complacency, love, hatred, pleasure, delectation, delight, indignation of God, and such like, and we have spoken something of the members of God, which may be congruent here.

Also *Mercurius Trismegistus* confessing the divine Trinity, describeth it Understanding, Life and Brightness, which elsewhere he calleth the Word the Mind and the Spirit, and saith that man made after the image of God doth represent the same Trinity; for there is in him an understanding mind, a verifying word, and a spirit, as it were a divine brightness diffusing itself on every side, replenishing all things, moving and knitting them together.[10]

But this is not to be understood of the natural spirit which is the middle by the which the soul is united with the flesh and the body, by the which the body liveth and acteth, and one member worketh on another, of the which spirit we have spoken in the first book. But we here speak of the natural spirit, which yet in some sort is also corporeal, notwithstanding it hath not a gross body, tangible and visible, but a most subtile body and easy to be united with the mind, viz. that superior and divine one which is in us; neither let anyone wonder, if we say that the rational soul is that spirit, and a corporeal thing, or that it either hath or favoureth something of corporeality while it is in the body, and useth it as an instrument, if so be that ye shall understand, what, amongst the Platonists, that etherial body of the soul, and chariot[11] of the same may be.

Therefore *Plotine*[12] and all the Platonists, after *Trismegist,* in like manner, place three things in man, which they call the supreme, lowest and middle.

The supreme is that divine thing which they call the mind, or superior portion, or illuminated intellect. *Moses* in Genesis calleth it the breath of life,[13] viz. breath from God or his spirit inspired into us.

The lowest is the sensitive soul which they also call an image: *Paul* the apostle nameth it the animal man.[14]

The middle is the reasonable spirit knitting and tying together both extremes, viz. the animal soul with the mind, favouring of the nature of both extremes: yet it differeth from that supreme which is called the illuminated intellect, the mind, light, and supreme portion; it differeth also from the animal soul, from the which, the apostle teacheth us, that we ought to separate it, by the power of the word of God, saying, the Word of God is lively and powerful, more penetrating than a two-edged sword, piercing even to the dividing of the soul and spirit.[15]

For as that supreme portion never sinneth, never consenteth to evil, and always resisteth error and exhorteth to the best things; so that inferior portion and animal soul is always overwhelmed in evil, in sin and concupiscence, and draweth to the worst things, of the which *Paul* saith, I see another law in my members, leading me captive to the law of sin:[16] the mind therefore the supreme portion is never damned; but when its companions are to be punished, goeth away unhurt into its Original: but the spirit, which by *Plotinus* is called the reasonable soul,[17] seeing it is by its nature, free, and can according to his pleasure adhere to either of them, if it constantly adhere to the superior portion, is at length united and beautified with it, until it be assumed into God: if it adhere unto the inferior soul, it is depraved, and becomes vicious, until it be made a wicked spirit. But thus much concerning the mind and spirit.

Now let us see concerning the speech or Word. *Mercurius* thinketh this of the same value for immortality; for speech or Word is that without which nothing is done or can be done: for it is the expression of the expressor and of the thing expressed; and the speaking of the speaker, and that which speaketh, is speech or Word; and the conception of the conceiver and that which conceiveth, is the Word; and the writing of the writer and that which writeth, is the Word; and the forming of the former and that which formeth, is the Word; and the creation of the creator, and that which createth, is the Word; and the doing of the doer, and that which is done is the Word; and the knowledge of him that knoweth and the thing known is the Word: and everything that can be spoken is but a Word, and it's called equality, for it carrieth itself equally towards all; seeing that it is not one thing more than another, equally bestowing on all, that they may be, that which they are, neither more nor less; and itself being sensible, doth make itself and all things sensible, as light maketh itself and all things visible.

Therefore the Word is called by *Mercurius* the bright son of the mind;[18] for the conception by the which the mind conceived itself, is the intrinsical Word generated from the mind, viz. the knowledge of itself: but the extrinsical and vocal word, is the offspring and manifestation of that Word, and a spirit proceeding out of the mouth with sound and voice, signifying something: but every voice of ours, speech and word, unless it be formed by the voice of God, is mingled with the air and vanisheth; but the Spirit and Word of the Lord remaineth, life and sense accompanying it.

Therefore all our speech, words, spirit and voice have no power in magic, unless they be formed by the divine Word: and *Aristotle* himself in his Meteors,[19] and in the end of his Ethics,[20] confesseth that there is not any virtue either natural or moral, unless through God; and in his Secret Tenents,[21] he affirmeth that our understanding being good and sound can do very much on the secrets of nature if so be that the influence of the divine power be present, otherwise nothing at all: so also our words can do very many miracles, if they be formed by the Word of God, in which also our universal gen-

eration is perfected; as *Isay* saith,[22] by thy countenance, O Lord, we have conceived, as women rightly conceive by the countenance of their husbands, and have brought forth Spirit.

Hither in some sort belongeth that which is delivered by the gymnosophists of the Indians, viz. that *Budda* a prince of this opinion, brought forth a virgin out of his side; and amongst the Mohammedans there is a constant opinion, that many, whom in their tongues they call Nefesohli, are born by a certain occult manner of divine dispensation without carnal copulation, whose life is therefore wonderful and impassible and as it were angelical and altogether supernatural; but these trifles we leave.

Only the King Messiah, the Word of the Father made flesh, Christ *Jesus,* hath revealed this secret, and will further manifest it at a certain fullness of time: therefore a mind very like to himself (as *Lazarillus* sang in Crater of Hermes):[23]

> God gave man reason that like deities
> He might bring forth gods with capacity.
> O happy he that knows his worth, and how
> He equal is unto the gods above!
> They repress dangers, make diseases fly,
> They give presages, and from misery
> Deliver men, reward the good, and ill
> Chastise, and so the will of God fulfill;
> These are disciples, and the sons of God
> Most high————

Who are not born of the will of flesh, or of man, or of a menstruous woman, but of God: but it is an universal generation in which the Son is like the Father in all manner of similitude, and in the which, that which is begot is the same in specie with the begetter; and this is the power of the Word formed by the mind, and received into a subject rightly disposed, as seed into the matrix for the generation; but I say disposed and rightly received; because that all are not partakers of the Word after the same manner, but others otherwise; and these are the most hidden secrets of nature which ought not to be further published.

Notes—Chapter XXXVI

1. *Trismegistus saith—*

> For there are two images of God; the Kosmos is one, and man is another, inasmuch as he, like the Kosmos, is a single whole built up of diverse parts. *(Asclepius* 1.10 [Scott, 1:305])

> ... when, I say, God had made this being [Kosmos], his first and one and only creation, and when he saw that the being he had made was beautiful, and wholly filled with all things good, he rejoiced in him, and loved him dearly, as being his own offspring. Therefore, being wise and good himself, he willed that there should be another who might look upon the being whom he had begotten; and in that act of willing, he made man, to be an imitator of his wisdom and his fostering care. (ibid. 1.8 [Scott, 1:301])

> For it is man's function to contemplate the works of God; and for this purpose was he made, that he might view the universe with wondering awe, and come to know its Maker. *(Corpus Hermeticum* 4.2 [Scott, 1:151])

2. *Hermes saith—*"For seeing that the Kosmos is the second God, and an immortal being, it is impossible that a part of that immortal being should die; and all things in the Kosmos are parts of the Kosmos" *(Corpus Hermeticum* 8.1b [Scott, 1:175]).

3. *his Word—*A reference to the Logos (Greek: λόγος—word, speech, discourse, reason). Neoplatonists and Stoics used the term for the Intelligence of the Cosmos, a kind of mediator between God and the world. The apostle John adopted this technical Greek term to refer specifically to the second part of the Trinity, Christ (John 1:1, 14).

4. *even in thought—*

> Bid your soul travel to any land you choose, and sooner than you can bid it go, it will be there. Bid it pass on from land to ocean, and it will be there too no less quickly; it has not moved as one moves from place to place, but it *is* there. Bid it fly up to heaven, and it will have no need of wings; nothing can bar its way, neither the fiery heat of the sun, nor the swirl of planet-spheres; cleaving its way through all, it will fly up till it reaches the outermost of all corporeal things. And should

you wish to break forth from the universe itself, and gaze on the things outside the Kosmos (if indeed there is anything outside the Kosmos), even that is permitted to you. *(Corpus Hermeticum* 11(2).19 [Scott, 1:221])

5. *Xystus—*Perhaps Sextus. "You have in yourself something similar to God, and therefore use yourself as the temple of God, on account of that which in you resembles God" *(Select Sentences of Sextus the Pythagorean.* In Iamblichus *Life of Pythagoras* [Taylor, 192]).

6. *temple of God—*I Corinthians 3:16.

7. *Ens—*From the Latin *esse:* to be. Entity, in the original sense of essential being, or real existence.

8. *Sum of Alchemy—Summa perfectionus magisterii.* See biographical note on Geber.

9. *some theologians—*See Augustine *De trinitate* (The trinity) 10.2; also Aquinas *Summa theologica* 77.1.1.

10. *knitting them together—*"'Learn my meaning,' said he [Poimandres], 'by looking at what you yourself have in you; for in you too, the word is son, and the mind is father of the word. They are not separate one from the other; for life is the union of word and mind'" *(Corpus Hermeticum* 1.6 [Scott, 1:117]).

11. *chariot—*For Plato's lengthy allegory of the soul as a winged chariot, see the *Phaedrus* 246–56.

12. *Plotine—*Plotinus.

13. *breath of life—*Genesis 2:7.

14. *animal man—*Perhaps I Corinthians 15:32.

15. *soul and spirit—*Hebrews 4:12.

16. *law of sin—*Romans 7:23.

17. *reasonable soul—*"The lower soul must be always striving to attain to memory of the activities of the higher: this will be especially so when it is itself of a fine quality, for there will always be some that are better from the beginning and bettered here by the guidance of the higher." (Plotinus *Enneads* 4.3.32 [Mackenna, 3:46])

18. *son of the mind—*"'That Light,' said he [Poimandres], 'is I, even Mind, the first God, who was before

the watery substance which appeared out of the darkness; and the Word which came forth from the Light is son of God.'" *(Corpus Hermeticum* 1.6 [Scott, 1:117]). See also note 10 above.

19. *his Meteors—De meteoris* (Meteorology).

20. *his Ethics—Nicomachean Ethics* 10.9.1179b, lines 20–30.

21. *Secret Tenents—Secretum secretorum* of pseudo-Aristotle, which M. Gaster called "The most popular book of the middle ages" ("Introduction to a Hebrew version of the Secret of Secrets," *Journal of the Royal Asiatic Society,* 1908, P. II, pp. 1065–84). There were at least 207 Latin manuscripts circulating, and many more in many other languages. It was printed several times before 1500. The work consists of a collection of information on astrology, alchemy, enchantments, geomancy, medicine, government, and "something useful about almost every science," supposedly written by Aristotle at the urging of Alexander. See Thorndike, 2:267-76.

22. *Isay saith*—I do not find this in Isaiah.

23. *Crater of Hermes—Crater Hermetis,* a work written in 1494 or shortly prior to this date by Ludovico Lazzarelli, a contemporary of Agrippa (see his biographical note). It was published by Lefevre d'Etaples in his 1505 Paris edition of several Hermetic writings, and consists of a dialogue between Lazzarelli and King Ferdinand of Aragon. Through a series of mystical hymns the King is prepared for the revelation of a sacred mystery involving the technique of god-making hinted at by Hermes Trismegistus in his *Asclepius* (see Scott [1924] 1985, 1:339–40). D. P. Walker is convinced that Lazzarelli was talking about the creation of a familiar good daemon by an occult master for his disciple—see his *Spiritual and Demonic Magic from Ficino to Campanella* (University of Notre Dame Press, 1975), 70–1. The work was strongly influenced by the *Hymns of Orpheus.* The crater of Hermes referred to in the title is the mixing bowl, or basis, filled with mind, which God sent down to Earth, and in which he invited all human hearts to dip themselves if they would attain a portion of gnosis. See *Corpus Hermeticum* 4.4 [Scott, 1:151]).

CHAPTER XXXVII

Of man's soul and through what means it is joined to the body.

The soul of man is a certain divine light, created after the image of the world, the cause of causes and first example, and the substance of God, figured by a seal whose character is the eternal Word; also the soul of man is a certain divine substance, individual and wholly present in every part of the body, so produced by an incorporeal author, that it dependeth by the power of the agent only, not by the bosom of the matter.

The soul is a substantial number, uniform, conversive[1] unto itself, and rational, very far excelling all bodies and material things; the partition of which is not according to the matter, nor proceeding from inferior and grosser things, but from the efficient cause: for it is not a quantitative number, but removed from all corporeal laws, whence it is not divided nor multiplied by parts. Therefore the soul of man is a certain divine substance, flowing from a divine fountain, carrying along with itself number: not that divine one by the which the Creator hath disposed all things, but a rational number by the which, seeing it hath a proportion to all things, it can understand all things.

Therefore man's soul being such, according to the opinion of the Platonists, immediately proceeding from God, is joined by competent means to this grosser body;[2] whence first of all in its descent, it is involved in a celestial and aerial body, which they call the celestial vehicle of the soul, others the chariot of the soul:[3] through this middle thing, by the command of God who is the center of the world, it is first infused into the middle point of the heart, which is the center of man's body, and from thence it is diffused through all the parts and members of his body, when it joineth his chariot to the natural heat, being a spirit generated from the heart by heat; by this it plungeth itself into the humours, by the which it inhereth in all the members, and to all these is made equally the nighest, although it be diffused through one to another; even as the heat of fire adhereth most nigh to the air and water, although it be transferred by the air to the water; thus it is manifest, how the immortal soul, by an immortal body, viz. an ethereal vehicle, is included in a gross and mortal body.

But when by a disease or some mischief, these middle things are dissolved or fail, then the soul itself by these middle things recollecteth itself, and floweth back into the heart which was the first receptacle of the soul: but the spirit of the heart failing, and heat being extinct, it leaveth him, and man dieth, and the soul flieth away with this celestial vehicle, and the Genius his keeper and the demon[4] follow it being gone forth, and carry it to the judge,[5] where sentence being pronounced, God quietly leadeth forth the good souls to glory: the evil, the fierce Devil draggeth to punishment.

Notes—Chapter XXXVII

1. *conversive*—Having the power of conversion. See Aquinas *Summa contra gentiles* 2.4

2. *grosser body*—See Plato *Timaeus* 42e–43a (Hamilton and Cairns, 1171).

3. *chariot of the soul*—See note 11, ch. XXXVI, bk. III.

4. *keeper and the demon*—The good and evil spirits appointed for life to each human soul (see Origen *De principiis* 3.2.4). After death they appear before the judge of souls (see note 5 below) and dispute which shall have charge.

5. *Judge*—

> When the soul has quitted the body, there will be held a trial and investigation of its deserts. The soul will come under the power of the chief of the daemons. When he finds a soul to be devout and righteous, he allows it to abide in the region which is suited to its character; but if he sees it to be marked with stains of sin, and defiled with (incurable) vices, he flings it downward, and delivers it to the storms and whirlwinds of that portion of the air which is in frequent conflict with fire and water, that the wicked soul may pay everlasting penalty, being ever swept and tossed hither and thither between sky and earth by the billows of cosmic matter. *(Asclepius* 3.28 [Scott, 1:367])

See note 36, ch. XVIII, bk. III.

CHAPTER XXXVIII

What divine gifts man receiveth from above, from the several orders of the intelligences and the heavens.

By the seven planets as it were by instruments, all powers are diffused into man from the supreme fountain of good.[1]

By Saturn, a sublime contemplation and profound understanding, solidity of judgement, firm speculation, stability and an immovable resolution.

By Jupiter, an unshaken prudence, temperance, benignity, piety, modesty, justice, faith, grace, religion, equity, clemency, royalty.

By Mars, truth, not to be terrified, constant courage and fortitude, a fervent desire of animosity, the power of acting and the practice, and an inconvertible vehemency of the mind.

By the Sun, nobility of mind, perspicuity of imagination, the nature of knowledge and opinion, maturity, counsel, zeal, light of justice, reason and judgement distinguishing right from wrong, purging light from the darkness of ignorance, the glory of truth found out, and charity the queen of all virtues.

By Venus, a fervent love, most sweet hope, the motion of desire, order, concupiscence, beauty, sweetness, desire of increasing and propagation of itself.

By Mercury, a piercing faith and belief, clear reasoning, the vigour of interpreting and pronouncing, gravity of speech, acuteness of wit, discourse of reason, and the swift motions of the senses.

By the Moon, a peacemaking consonancy, fecundity, the power of generation and of growing greater, of increasing and decreasing, and a moderate temperance, and faith which being conversant in manifest and occult things yieldeth direction to all; also motion to the tilling of the Earth for the manner of life and giving growth to itself and others.

But these influences are principally drawn from those seven intelligences,[2] who stand before the face of God, who dispose the soul the seat of these virtues: but the planets dispose the body only, giving a tractable complexion proportionated and tempered for every good thing, and they are as it were the instruments of the intelligences; but God as the primary cause doth yield both the influence and increase to all.

They therefore who have sought out the virtues and divers dispositions of the soul, do judge, that they obtain divers natures, by reason of the diversity of means, by the which they have a passage to us, and that these souls are not joined with the bodies themselves unless they be proportioned by these stars;[3] so in a body brought to a temperament by Jupiter, they think that the soul infused is temperated by the power and intelligence of Jupiter, and so of the rest. According to which disposition if the soul work well in this body, when it's purged and expiated, it returneth to that divine power and mansion from whence it descended.

Furthermore, from the angelical orders man is strengthened with wonderful virtues, viz:

From the Angels, that he may be a messenger of the divine will and an interpreter of the mind of God.

From the Archangels, that he may rule over all beasts of the field, fish of the sea, and fowls of the air, over the which command is given him.

From the Principalities, that all things may be subdued to him, he comprehending the powers of all, and drawing all powers to himself by a certain force most secret and supercelestial.

From the Virtues, it receiveth power, by the which it constantly fighting is strengthened against the enemies of truth, for the reward of which we run a race in this life.

From the Powers, against the enemies of this earthly tabernacle.

From the Dominations, it hath help by the which we can subject any domestic enemy we carry along with us, and can obtain our desired end.

From the Thrones, we are knit together, and being collected into ourselves, we fix our memory on those eternal visions.

From the Cherubims, is light of mind, power of wisdom, very high phantasies and figures, by the which we are able to contemplate even the divine things.

From the Seraphims, that by the perfect flame of love we may at length inhere in them.

These are the degrees, these the ladders, by the which men easily ascend to all kinds of powers by a certain natural connection and chariot, according to the divers disposition of body and mind, and by the favour of the stars, in the disposing of the body, and of the intelligences ruling them, the nature of which the soul in its descent putteth on, even as light the colour of the glass, through which it passeth; the supreme power of the Creator favouring, from whom is all good, and without which no good nor perfect thing can be obtained.

Therefore all those do labour in vain, who trusting only on the course of nature, and the power and favour of inferior things, do think to attain to divine things; and those who faining to have a foot in the heavens, do endeavour to receive those things from the favour of the heavens, which ought to be received from God alone; for these inferiors, I mean animals, herbs, stones, metals have their power subservient to the heaven; but the heaven from the intelligences; but these from God, in whom all things pre-exist in the greatest power; as in man the little world[4] there is not a member which hath not correspondence with some element, plant, intelligence, and with some measure and numeration in the Archetype: as we have shown before.

Notes—Chapter XXXVIII

1. *fountain of good*—See note 1, ch. LIX, bk. II.

2. *seven intelligences*—Revelation 1:4.

3. *these stars*—

> For at the time when each one of us is born and made alive, the daemons who are at that moment on duty as ministers of birth take charge of us,—that is, the daemons who are subject to some one planet. For the planets replace one another from moment to moment; they do not go on working without change, but succeed one another in rotation. *(Corpus Hermeticum 16.15 [Scott, 1:271])*

4. *little world*—Microcosm.

CHAPTER XXXIX

How the superior influences, seeing they are good by nature, are depraved in these inferior things, and are made causes of evil.

Seeing every power and virtue is from above, from God, from the intelligences and stars, who can neither err nor do evil,[1] it is necessary, that all evil, and whatsoever is found disagreeing and dissonant in these inferior things, do proceed, not from the malice of the influence, but from the evil disposition of the receiver; thus *Chysippus* rightly sang:

> They do like fools accuse the gods falsely,
> Make them the cause of all their misery,
> When as their folly hurts themselves——

Hence *Jupiter* calling to mind the case of *Aegisthus* slain by *Orestes,* by *Homer*[2] in the council of the gods saith:

> Us gods do men accuse (what vice is this?)
> To be the cause, fountain of what's amiss,
> When they themselves by their own
>   wickedness
> Run into danger————

When therefore the perversity of the subject receiveth the influences of the perverse, or its debility cannot endure the efficacy of the superiors, then by the influence of the heavens thus received into a matter full of discords, doth result something dissonant, deformed and evil; yet the celestial powers always remain good, which while they exist in themselves, and from the Giver of Light have their influence by the holy intelligences and the heavens, even till they shall come to the Moon, their influence is good, as it were in the first degree; but then when it is received in a viler subject, it also is vilified; then also in respect of the different nature of the recipient it is received after divers manners, and by the qualities disagreeing in the same subject amongst themselves, it also is varied and patiently suffereth in the subject.

Whence from all comprehended in the subject, at length some other thing doth result than the superiors send down; therefore the hurtful quality in these inferiors, is far different from the influx of the heavens; and therefore as the distemper of the blear-eyed is not to be imputed to the light, nor burnings to the fire, nor wounds to the sword, nor fetters and prisons to the judge, but to the evil disposed and offenders; so neither is the fault of wicked ones to be cast on the celestial influences.

Therefore we being well disposed, the celestial influences cooperate all things for good; but being evil disposed, and having for our sins, that divine good, which was in us, departed from us, all things work for evil: therefore the cause of all our evils is sin, which is the disorder and distemper of our soul; from the which then, thus evilly governing, or falling down or declining from that which the celestial influences require, all things rebel, and are distempered for our destruction.

Then in man's body, otherwise most temperate and composed with most sweet harmony, the distemper of the elements beginneth, evil humours arise: and even the good being disordered and severed from one another, by a certain vicissitude both vex and torment the body: then is a most vehement dissonance perceived, either by superfluity or diminution, or some iatrinseral[3] accident, or by superfluous meat, whence superfluous humours are generated, and by the same cause infirmities follow; yea the animal spirits, the bridle being broken, do fall to contention.

Then the celestial influences, otherwise of themselves good, are made hurtful to us, even as the light of the Sun to eyes ill disposed: then Saturn darteth down anguish, tediousness, melancholy, madness, sadness, obstinacy, rigidness, blasphemy, desperation, lying, apparitions, affrightments, walkings of the dead, stirrings of devils: Jupiter then sendeth down covetousness, evil occasions to get wealth and tyranny: Mars, furious wrath, prophane arrogancy, violent boldness, fierce stubbornness: but the Sun imperious pride and insatiable ambition: Venus, the deceits of concupiscence,

lascivious loves and filthy lusts: Mercury, deceits, cozenages, lies, subtile desires of evil, propensity to sin; the Moon the inconstant progress of all things, and whatsoever is contrary to man's nature.

And by this means man himself by reason of his unlikeness with the heavenly things receiveth hurt, whence he ought to reap benefit: by reason of the same dissonancy with the heavenly things (as *Proclus* saith) men also are subjected even to wicked spirits who as the officers of God do discharge themselves in punishing them: then do they suffer grievances by evil spirits, even until they are again expiated, by due purgations, and man returneth to a divine nature.

Therefore an excellent magician can prohibit many mischiefs about to fall on him from the disposition of the stars, when he foreknoweth their nature by preventing, taking heed, and defending, lest they should meet him, and lest an ill disposed subject, as we have said, should receive hurt whence it ought to reap benefit.

Notes—Chapter XXXIX

1. *nor do evil*—Agrippa seems to contradict himself: see the first paragraph of ch. XV, bk . III, and note 2 of that chapter.

2. *by Homer*—*Odyssey* 1, lines 32–4.

3. *iatrinseral*—Iatrical; medical.

CHAPTER XL

That on every man a divine character is imprinted, by the virtue of which man can attain the working of miracles.

By no small experience it is found that a certain power of ruling and predominating is implanted in man by nature; for *(Pliny* testifieth)[1] that an elephant meeting a man wandering in a desert, is reported to show himself gentle and courteous, and to show the way to him; and the same creature also is said, before he seeth man, to tremble, to stand still, to look about, to quake at the steps of man, for fear of treachery: in like manner the tiger, the most fierce of all beasts, at the sight of man doth remove her young ones;[2] and more of this kind we read in divers authors, who have writ great volumes of creatures.

But from whence do these animals know, that man is to be feared, whom they never saw: and if they have seen and known, whence do they fear him, seeing they do excel him in greatness, force and swiftness?[3] What is this nature of man, striking this terror on wild beasts? All the historiographers of animals do find out and grant this, but have left to others to teach and prove it.

Concerning this therefore *Apollonius Tyaneus* (as we read in *Philostratus)* seeing a child leading a huge elephant, answered *Damus* asking him, whence came that obedience of so huge a creature to the little child: that it was from a certain active terror, implanted in man by his Creator, which inferior creatures and all animals perceiving, do fear and reverence man, which is as it were a terrifying character, and a seal of God imprinted on man, by the which everything is subject to him, and acknowledges him superior, whether it be servant or animal. For otherwise neither could a child rule his herd and elephants, neither could a king terrify his people, nor the judge the guilty.[4]

Therefore this character is imprinted on man from the divine Idea which the Cabalists of the Hebrew call Pahad[5] פחד, and the left hand, or sword, of God: furthermore man hath not only a seal by which he is feared, but also by the which he is beloved, the Idea of which in the divine numerations is called Hesed[6] חסד, which signifieth Clemency, and the right hand and scepter of God.

From these divine numerations, by the intelligences and stars, seals and characters are imprinted on us, to everyone according to his capacity and purity: which signs the first man created, without doubt did possess in all integrity and fullness, when all creatures being attracted by secret gentleness, and subjected by terror, came to him as to their Lord, that he might give them names:[7] but after the sin of prevarication he fell from that dignity with all his posterity.

Yet that character is not altogether extinct in us. But by how much everyone is laden with sin, by so much he is farther off from these divine characters and receiveth less of them; and whence he ought to receive friendship and reverence, he falleth into the slavery and terror of others, both of animals and also men and devils: which *Cain* perceiving feared, saying to God, everyone who findeth me, will kill me;[8]

for he feared beasts and devils, not only men, who were very few.

But in the old times, many men who lived innocently, a very good life, as yet did enjoy that obedience and power, as *Sampson,*[9] *David*[10] and *Daniel*[11] over the lions, *Elisha*[12] over the bear, *Paul*[13] over the viper; and many Anchorites[14] lived in the deserts, in caves and dens of wild beasts, not fearing, nor receiving any hurt; for as by sin that divine character is obscured, so sin being purged and expiated, it again more and more shineth forth.

Notes—Chapter XL

1. *Pliny testifieth*—

When an elephant happens to meet a man in the desert, who is merely wandering about, the animal, it is said, shows himself both merciful and kind, and even points out the way. But the very same animal, if he meets with traces of a man, before he meets the man himself, trembles in very limb, for fear of an ambush, stops short and scents the wind, looks around him, and snorts aloud with rage ... (Pliny 8.5 [Bostock and Riley, 2:248])

2. *remove her young ones*—

In the same way, too, the tigress, which is the dread of the other wild beasts, and which sees, without alarm, the traces even of the elephant itself, is said at once, upon seeing the footsteps of man, to carry off her whelps. (ibid.)

3. *force and swiftness*—

And, what is still more, why should they [elephant and tiger] dread even the very sight of man, seeing that they are so far superior to him in strength, size, and swiftness? No doubt, such is the law of Nature, such is the influence of her power—the most savage and the very largest of wild beasts have never seen that which they have reason to fear, and yet instantly have an instinctive feeling of dread, when the moment has come for them to fear. (ibid., 248–9)

4. *judge the guilty*—

This is by far the most docile of all animals, and when once it has been tamed by a man it lets him do anything to it, and always shows him the same obedience. It delights to take food from his hand like a puppy; it caresses him with its trunk when he comes near; it lets him put his head into its jaws, holding them open as long as he likes, as we saw done among the nomads. Yet it is said to lament over its bondage at night, not with its usual trumpeting but with a mournful and piteous moaning; yet if the man comes to it while mourning so, the elephant stops its complaining as if ashamed. Thus it is its own master, Damis, and its tractable disposition manages and rules it more than its rider does. (Philostratus *Life and Times of Apollonius of Tyana* 2.11 [Eells, 42–3])

5. *Pahad*—Pachad. See Appendix VI.

6. *Hesed*—Chesed. See Appendix VI.

7. *give them names*—Genesis 2:19.

8. *will kill me*—Genesis 4:14.

9. *Sampson*—Judges 14:5–6.

10. *David*—I Samuel 17:34–5.

11. *Daniel*—Daniel 6:22.

12. *Elisha*—II Kings 2:24.

13. *Paul*—Acts 28:3–6.

14. *Anchorites*—An *anachoret* is one who withdraws and goes to live a devout life of contemplation and prayer apart from other men, as opposed to a *coenobite,* who withdraws from the world into a closed community of the religious. On the submission of beasts to the Anchorites, see Brewer 1901, 360–7. Also in this context see Hosea 2:18; Job 5:23; Isaiah 11:9; Ezekiel 34:25–8.

CHAPTER XLI

What concerning man after death, divers opinions.

In general it is appointed for all men once to die; death is fatal to all; but one is natural, another violent, another voluntarily received, another inflicted by human laws for offences, or by God for sin, that they seem not to have rendered a due to nature, but a punishment for sins; which (as the Hebrew masters saith) God remitteth to none.

Whence the assembly delivered to *Ezechiah*,[1] that after the house of the Sanctuary was pulled down, although there remained not any order of judiciary execution, yet there should be a fourfold kind of punishment by the which they might be condemned, that no man guilty of death should escape without retaliation; for he which had deserved to be stoned to death, was, God dispensing, either cast down headlong from the house, or trodden in pieces by wild beasts, or overwhelmed by ruin or fall; but he which had deserved to be burned, was either consumed by burnings, or finished he life either by venomous bitings, or stings of a serpent, or by poison; but he which should die by the sword, was killed either by the violence of the jurisdiction, or by the tumult of the people or faction, or by the treachery of thieves; he that ought to be hanged, was suffocated either in the waters, or extinguished by some other strangling punishment: and by the ground of this doctrine, that great *Origen* supposed the Gospel of Christ to be declared, he who useth the sword shall perish by sword.[2]

Moreover the ethnic philosophers pronounced that retaliation of this kind is *adrastia*,[3] viz. an inevitable power of divine laws, by the which in courses to come, is recompensed to everyone according to the reason and merits of his former life; so, as he who unjustly ruled in the former life, in the other life should relapse into a servile state; he which hath polluted his hands with blood, should be compelled to undergo retaliation; he that lived a brutish life, should be precipitated and revolved into a brutish body.

Of these things *Plotinus* writeth in his book of the proper Genius of everyone; saying, whosoever hath kept human propriety, do again arise men: but whosoever have used sense only, do return brute animals; yet so, as those who use sense especially together with wrath, do arise wild beasts; but whosoever use sense by concupisence and pleasure, do return lecherous, and gluttonous beasts: but if they shall live, not by sense together with them, so much as by the degeneration of sense, plants grow up again with them; for the vitals only, or chiefly, are living, and all their care was that they might be turned into plants. But they which have lived being too much allured by music, not being depraved in other things, are born again musical animals; and they which have reigned without reason, become eagles, unless they have been tainted with any wickedness. But he which hath lived civilly and virtuously, returns a man.[4]

And *Solomon* himself in the Proverbs calls man sometimes a lion,[5] tiger, bear,[6] a boar;[7] sometimes a hare, a hunting dog,[8] a cony;[9]

sometimes a pismire,[10] a hedgehog, a serpent,[11] a spider;[12] sometimes an eagle,[13] a stork, a cock, or any other bird;[14] and many such as these.

But the Cabalists of the Hebrews do not admit that souls are turned into brutes: yet they do not deny but that they that have wholly lost their reason, shall in another life be left to a brutish affection and imagination: they assert also that souls are revolved hither thrice, and no more; because this number seems sufficiently to suffice for the purgation of sins, according to that of Job, he hath delivered my soul that it should not proceed to death, but should live, and see the light. Behold all these things doth God work three times through each, that he might reduce their souls from corruption, and illuminate them with the light of the living.[15]

But now let us see what the ancients' opinion is concerning the dead. When man dies, his body returns into the earth, from which it was taken: the spirit returns to the heavens, from whence it descended, as saith the Preacher,[16] the body returns to the earth from whence it was, and the spirit returns to God that gave it; which *Lucretius* hath expressed[17] in these verses:

What came from earth to earth returns again;
What came from God, returns from whence it came.

But *Ovid* expressed it better in these verses:

Four things of man there are; spirit, soul, ghost, flesh;
These four, four places keep and do possess.
The earth covers flesh, the ghost hovers o'er the grave,
Orcus hath the soul, stars do the spirit crave.

The flesh being forsaken, and the body being defunct of life, is called a dead carcass; which as say the divines of the Hebrews, is left in the power of the demon *Zazel,*[18] of whom it is said in the Scripture: Thou shalt eat dust[19] all thy days; and elsewhere, The dust of the Earth[20] is his bread. Now man was created of the dust of the Earth, whence also that demon is called the Lord of Flesh and Blood, whilst the body is not expiated and sanctified with due solemnities.

Hence not without cause the ancients ordained expiations of carcasses, that that which was unclean might be sprinkled with holy water, perfumed with incense, be conjured with sacred orations, have lights set by as long as it was above ground, and then at length be buried in a holy place. Hence *Elpenor* in *Homer,*[21] I beseech thee (saith he) *Ulysses,* be mindful of me, and leave me not unburied; left behind I become an object of the gods' wrath.

But the spirit of a man, which is of a sacred nature, and divine offspring, because it is always faultless, becomes incapable of any punishment; but the soul if it hath done well, rejoiceth together with the spirit, and going forth with its aerial chariot, passeth freely to the quires of the heros, or reacheth heaven, where it enjoys all its senses, and powers, a perpetual blessed felicity, a perfect knowledge of all things, as also the divine vision, and possession of the kingdom of heaven, and being made partaker of the divine power bestows freely divers gifts upon these inferiors, as if it were an immortal god.

But if it hath done ill, the spirit judgeth it, and leaves it to the pleasure of the Devil, and the sad soul wanders about hell without a spirit, like an image, as *Dido* complains[22] in *Virgil:*

And now the great image of me shall go Under the earth————

Wherefore then this soul being void of an intelligible essence, and being left to the power of a furious phantasy, is ever subjected by the torment of corporeal qualities, knowing that it is by the just judgement of God, forever deprived of the divine vision (to which it was created) for its sins: the absence of which divine vision, as the Scripture testifies, is the ground of all evils, and the most grievous punishment of all, which the Scripture calls the pouring down of the wrath of God.[23]

This image therefore of the soul enters into the ghost as an aerial body, with which being covered doth sometimes advise friends, sometimes stir up enemies, as *Dido* threatens[24] *Aeneas* in *Virgil,* saying:

I'll hunt thee, and thee tortures I will give.

For when the soul is separated from the body, the perturbations of the memory and sense remain.

The Platonists say that the souls, especially of them that are slain, stir up enemies, man's indignation not so much doing of it, as the divine *Nemesis,* and demon, foreseeing, and permitting of it. So the spirit of *Naboth* (as the masters of the Hebrews interpret it) because in the end of its life it went forth with a desire of revenge, was made to execute revenge, the spirit of a lie, and went forth, God permitting it, a lying spirit in the mouth of all the prophets, until it made *Achab* go up unto Ramoth-Gilead.[25]

And *Virgil* himself together with the Pythagoreans, and Platonists, to whom also our *Austin* assents, confesseth that separated souls retain the fresh memory of those things which they did in this life, and their will, whence he sings:[26]

What care they living had of horses brave
And arms, the same doth follow them to
the grave.

And *Agazel* in his book De Scientia Divina, and other Arabians, and Mohammedans which were philosophers, think that the operations of the soul, being common to the conjoined body, impress upon the soul a character of use and exercise, which it being separated will use, being strongly impressed to the like operations and passions which were not destroyed in life time. And although the body and organ be corrupted, yet the operation will not cease, but like affections and dispositions will remain.

And these souls the ancients call with a common name Manes, whereof those that were in this life innocent, and purified by moral virtues, were very happy; and of them, as *Virgil* sings:[27]

——————that did for their country die,
With priests who in their lives vowed
chastity,
And sacred poets, who pleased Phoebus
best,
Or by invented arts man's life assist,
And others in their memories renowned,

——————

Although they departed this life without the justification of faith, and grace, as many divines think, yet their souls were carried without any suffering into happy pleasant fields; and as saith *Virgil:*[28]

They went to places and to pleasant greens,
And pleasant seats, the pleasant groves
between.

Where they enjoy certain wonderful pleasures, as also sensitive, intellectual, and revealed knowledge.

Also perhaps they may be indoctrinated concerning faith, and justification, as those spirits long since to whom Christ preached the Gospel in prison. For as it is certain that none can be saved without the faith of Christ, so it is probable that this faith is preached to many pagans and Saracens after this life, in those receptacles of souls[29] unto salvation, and that they are kept in those receptacles, as in a common prison, until the time comes when the great Judge shall examine our actions. To which opinion *Lactantius, Ireneus, Clemens, Tertullian, Austin, Ambrose,* and many more Christian writers do assent.

But those souls which are impure, incontinent, depart wicked, do not enjoy such happy dreams, but wander full of most hideous phantasms, and in worser places, enjoying no free knowledge but what is obtained by concession, or manifestation, and with a continual fleshy desire are subjected by reason of their corporeal corruption to the sense of pain, and fear swords, and knives.

These without doubt *Homer* seemed to be sensible of, when in the eleventh book of his Odyssey he brings in the mother of *Ulysses* being dead, standing near to him offering sacrifice, but neither knowing him or speaking to him, whilst he with his sword drawn did keep off ghosts from the blood of the sacrifice.[30] But after that *Tyresia* the prophetess[31] advising of her, she had tasted of the sacrifice, and had drunk the blood, she presently knew her son, and crying spake to him. But the soul of *Tyresia* the prophetess, notwithstanding the drawn sword, even before she tasted the blood, knew

Ulysses and spake to him, and showed him the ghost of his mother standing near to him.

Whatsoever vices therefore souls have committed in the bodies unexpiated in this life, they are constrained, carrying the habits of them along with them, to purge themselves of them in hell, and to undergo punishment for them; which the Poet explains[32] in these verses:

> ———————when they die,
> Then doth not leave them all their misery.
> They having not repented of their crimes,
> Must now be punished for their misspent
>   times.

For as the manners and habits of men are in this life, such affections for the most part follow the soul after death, which then calls to mind those things which it did formerly do in its life, and then more intently thinks on them,[33] for as much as then the divers offices of life cease, as those of nourishing, growing, generating, and various occupations of senses, and human affairs, and comforts, and obstacles of a grosser body. Then are represented to the phantastic reason those species, which are so much the more turbulent and furious, by how much in such souls there lies hid an intellectual spark more or less covered, or altogether extinct, into which are then by evil spirits conveyed species either most false, or terrible.

Whence now it is tormented in the concupiscile faculty, by the concupiscence of an imaginary good, or of those things which it did formerly affect in its lifetime, being deprived of the power of enjoying them, although it may seem to itself sometimes almost to obtain its delights, but to be driven from them by the evil spirits into bitter torments, as in the poets,[34] *Tantalus*[35] from a banquet, *Sardanapalus*[36] from embraces, *Midas*[37] from gold, *Sisyphus*[38] from power; and they called these souls hobgoblins, whereof if any taking care of household affairs lives and inhabits quietly in the house, it is called a household god, or familiar.

But they are most cruelly tortured in the irascible faculty with the hatred of an imaginary evil, into the perturbations whereof, as also false suspicions, and most horrible phantasms

they then fall, and there are represented to them sad representations; sometimes of the heaven falling upon their head, sometimes of being consumed by the violence of flames, sometimes of being drowned in a gulf, sometimes of being swallowed up into the earth, sometimes of being changed into divers kinds of beasts, sometimes of being torn and devoured by ugly monsters, sometimes of being carried abroad through woods, seas, fire, air, and through fearful infernal places, and sometimes of being taken, and tormented by devils.

All which we conceive happens to them after death no otherwise than in this life to those who are taken with a phrensy, and some other melancholy distemper, or to those who are affrighted with horrible things seen in dreams; and are thereby tormented, as if those things did really happen to them, which truly are not real, but only species of them apprehended in imagination: even so do horrible representations of sins terrify those souls after death as if they were in a dream, and the guilt of wickedness drives them headlong through divers places; which therefore *Orpheus* calls the people of dreams, saying, the gates of *Pluto* cannot be unlocked; within is a people of dreams.

Such wicked souls therefore enjoying no good places, when wandering in an aerial body, they represent any form to our sight, are called hags, and goblins, inoffensive to them that are good, but hurtful to the wicked, appearing one while in thinner bodies, another time in grosser, in the shape of divers animals, and monsters, whose conditions they had in their lifetime, as sings the Poet:[39]

> Then divers forms, and shapes of brutes
>   appear;
> For he becomes a tiger, swine, and bear,
> A scaly dragon, and a lioness,
> Or doth from fire a dreadful noise express;
> He doth transmute himself to divers looks,
> To fire, wild beasts, and into running brooks.

For the impure soul of a man, who in this life contracted too great a habit to its body, doth by a certain inward affection of the elemental body frame another body to itself of the vapours of the elements, refreshing as it were from an easy matter as it were with a suck, that body which is continually vanishing; to which being moreover enslaved as to a prison, and sensible instrument by a certain divine law, doth in it suffer cold, and heat, and whatsoever annoys the body, spirit, and sense; as stinks, howlings, wailings, gnashings of the teeth, stripes, tearings, and bonds, as *Virgil* sang:[40]

————————and therefore for their crimes
They must be punished, and for misspent times
Must tortures feel; some in the winds are hung,
Others to cleanse their spotted sins are flung
Into vast gulfs, or purged in fire————

And in *Homer* in his Necromancy[41] *Alcinous* makes this relation to *Ulysses:*[42]

Of Tytius the dear darling of the Earth,
We saw the body stretched nine furlongs forth,
And on each side of whom a vulture great
Gnawing his bowels————

These souls sometimes do inhabit not these kinds of bodies only, but by a too great affection of flesh and blood transmute themselves into other animals, and seize upon the bodies of creeping things, and brutes, entering into them, what kind soever they be of, possessing them like demons. *Pythagoras* is of the same opinion, and before him *Trismegistus,* asserting that wicked souls do oftentimes go into creeping things, and into brutes,[43] neither do they as essential forms vivify and inform those bodies, but as an inmate dwell there as in a prison, or stand near them by a local indistance as an internal mover to the thing moved; or being tied to them are tormented, as *Ixion*[44] to the wheel of serpents, *Sysiphus* to a stone.

Neither do they enter into brutes only, but sometimes into men, as we have spoken concerning the soul of *Nabaoth* which went forth a lying spirit in the mouth of the prophets. Hence some have asserted that the lives, or spirits of wicked men going into the bodies of some men, have disturbed them, and sometimes slew them.

Which is more fortunately granted unto blessed souls that like good angels they should dwell in us, and enlighten us, as we read of *Elias,* that he being taken from men he spirit fell upon *Elisha:*[45] and elsewhere we read that God took of the spirit which was in *Moses,* and gave it to seventy men.[46] Here lies a great secret, and not rashly to be revealed.

Sometimes also (which yet is very rare) souls are driven with such a madness that they do enter the bodies not only of the living, but also by a certain hellish power wander into dead carcasses, and being as it were revived commit horrid wickednesses, as we read in *Saxo Grammaticus,*[47] that *Asuitus* and *Asmundus,* two certain men, vowed one to the other, that he that should live longest should be buried with him that was first dead: at length *Asuitus* being first dead, is buried in a great vault with his dog, and horse, with whom also *Asmundus* by reason of his oath of friendship, suffered himself to be buried alive (meat which he should for a long time eat, being brought to him); in process of time *Ericus,* King of Suecia, passing by that place with an army, breaking up the tomb of *Asuitus* (supposing that there was treasure), the vault being opened, brought forth *Asmundus:* whom, when he saw having a hideous look, being smeared over with filthy corrupt blood which flowed from a green wound (for *Asuitus* being revived in the nights, took off with often struggling his right ear), he commanded him to tell him the cause of that wound: which he declares in these verses:

Why doth my visage wan you thus amaze?
Since he that lives amongst the dead, the grace
Of beauty needs must lose; I know not yet
What daring Stygian fiend of Asuit
The spirit sent from hell, who there did eat
A horse, and dog, and being with this meat
Not as yet sufficed, then set his claws on me,
Pulled off my cheek, mine ear, and hence you see
My ugly, wounded, mangled, bloody face;
This monstrous wight returned not to his place
Without received revenge; I presently
His head cut off, and with a stake did I
His body through run————-

Pausanias tells a story[48] not unlike to this, taken out of the interpreters of the Delphi; viz. that there was a certain infernal demon, which they called *Eurinomus,* who would eat the flesh of dead men, and devour it so that the bones would scarce be left. We read also in the Chronicles of the Cretensians, that the ghosts which they call Catechanae were wont to return back into their bodies, and go to their wives, and lie with them; for the avoiding of which, and that they might annoy their wives no more, it was provided in the common laws that the heart of them that did arise should be thrust through with a nail, and their whole carcass be burnt. These without doubt are wonderful things, and scarce credible, but that those laws and ancient histories make them credible.

Neither is it altogether strange in Christian religion that many souls were restored to their bodies, before the universal resurrection. Moreover we believe that many by the singular favour of God are together with their bodies received to glory, and that many went down alive to hell. And we have heard that oftentimes the bodies of the dead were by the devils taken from the graves, without doubt for no other use than to be imprisoned, and tormented in their hands. And to these prisons and bonds of their bodies there are added also the possessions of most filthy and abominable places, where are Aetnean fires,[49] gulfs of water, the shakings of thunder, and lightning, gapings of the Earth, and where the region is void of light, and receives not the rays of the Sun, and knows not the light of the stars, but is always dark. Whither *Ulysses* is reported in *Homer*[50] to come, when he sings:

> Here people are that be Cimmerian named,
> Drowned in perpetual darkness, it is famed,
> Whom rising, nor the setting Sun doth see,
> But with perpetual night oppressed be.

Neither are those mere fables which many have recorded of the cave of *Patricius,*[51] of the den of *Vulcan,*[52] of the Aetnean caves, and of the den of *Nursia,* many that have seen and known them testifying the same. Also *Saxo Grammaticus* tells of greater things than these of the palace of *Geruthus,* and of the cave of *Ugarthilocus.*

Also *Pliny, Solinus, Pythias, Clearchus,* of the wonderful prodigies of the Northern Sea, of which *Tacitus* also in his History of Drusus[53] shows that in the German sea there wandered soldiers by whom divers miraculous unheard of things were seen, viz. the force of whirlpools, unheard of kinds of birds, sea monsters like men and beasts;[54] and in his book Of Germany he tells that the Heldusians and Axions, who had the face of men, but their other parts were equal to beasts, did dwell there.[55] Which without all doubt were the works of ghosts and devils.

Of these also *Claudianus* long time since sang:[56]

> In the extreme bounds of France there is a
>   place,
> Encompassed by the sea, where in his race
> Fame saith Ulysses having tasted blood,
> A secret people did descry, where loud
> And mournful plaints were heard of wan-
>   dering spirits
> Which did the country people much affright.

Aristotle relates of the Aeolian Islands near Italy, that in Lipara was a certain tomb, to which no man could go safe by night, and that there were cymbals and shrill voices with certain absurd loud laughters; also tumults and empty sounds made, as the inhabitants did strongly aver; and that upon a time a certain young man being drunk went thither, and about night fell asleep near the cave of the tomb, and was after the third day found by them that sought him, and was taken up for dead; who being brought forth, the solemnities of the funeral being ready, suddenly arose up, and told in order, to the great admiration of all, many things which he had seen and suffered.

There is also in Norvegia a certain mountain most dreadful to all, surrounded by the sea, which commonly is called Hethelbergius, representing hell, whence there are heard great bewailings, howlings, and screechings a mile round about, and over which great vultures and most black crows fly, making horrible noises, which forbid any to come near it: moreover from hence flow two fountains whereof the one is most intense cold, the other most intense hot, far exceeding all other elements. There is also in the same country toward the southern corner thereof a promontory called Nadhegrin, where the demons of the place are seen by all, in an aerial body. There is also in Scotland the mountain Dolorosus,[57] from whence are heard dreadful lamentations: and in Thuringia there is a mountain called Horrisonus, where dwelt sylvani, and satyrs, as fame and experience teacheth, and faithful writers testify. There are in divers countries and provinces such like miracles as these.

I will not relate here those things which I have seen with mine eyes, and felt with mine hands, lest by the wonderful admirableness and strangeness of them I should by the incredulous be accounted a liar.

Neither do I think it fit to pass by what many of our age think concerning the receptacles of souls, not much differing from these which we have now spoken of: of which *Tertullian* in his fourth book against the heresies of *Marcion*[58] saith, it is apparent to every wise man, which hath ever heard of the Elysian Fields that there is some local determination (which is called *Abraham's* bosom) for the receiving of the souls of his sons, and that that region is not celestial, yet higher than hell, where the souls of the just rest, until the consummation of things restore the resurrection of all things with fullness of reward.

Also *Peter* the apostle saith to *Clemens,* a king,[59] him of these things, thou dost constrain me O *Clemens* to publish something concerning things unutterable: yet as far as I may, I will. Christ who from the beginning and always was, was always through each generation, though secretly, present with the godly, with those especially by whom he was desired, and to whom he did most often appear. But it was not time, that the bodies then being resolved, there should be a resurrection: but this rather seemed a remuneration from God, that he that was found just, should remain longer in a body: or that the Lord should translate him (as we see clearly related in the Scripture of some certain just men). After the like example God dealt with others, who pleased him well, and fulfilling his will were being translated to Paradise reserved for a kingdom. But of those who could not fulfill the rule of justice, but had some relic of wickedness in their flesh, the bodies indeed are resolved, but souls are kept in good and pleasant regions, that in the resurrection of the dead, when they shall receive their bodies, being now purged by resolution, they may enjoy an eternal inheritance for those things which they have done well.

Iraneus also in the end of his book which he wrote against the heresies of the Valentinians, saith: whereas the Lord went in the middle of the shadow of death, where the souls of the dead were, and after rose again corporeally, and after resurrection was taken up, it is manifest that the souls of his disciples (for whom he worked these things) should go to some invisible place, appointed by God, and there tarry until the resurrection, afterwards receiving their bodies, and rising again perfectly, i.e. corporeally, as the Lord arose, so shall they come into the presence of God; for no disciple is above his Master; but every one shall be perfect as his Master. Therefore even as our Master did not presently fly and go away, but expected the time of his resurrection determined by the Father, which is also manifested by *Jonas,*[60] after three days arising he is taken up; so also ought we to expect the time of our resurrection determined by God, foretold by the prophets; and so rising again we shall be taken up, as many as the Lord shall account worthy of this honour.

Lactantius Firmianus also agreeth to this, in that book of Divine Institutions whose title is Of Divine Reward;[61] saying, let no man think, that the souls after death are presently judged; for they are all detained in one common custody, until the time cometh in which the great Judge shall examine deserts; then they whose righteousness shall be approved, shall receive the reward of immortality: but they whose sins and wickednesses are detected, shall not rise again, but being destinated for certain punishment, shall be shut up with the wicked angels into the same darkness.

Of the same opinion are *Austine,* and *Ambrose,* who saith in his Enchiridion, the time which is interposed betwixt the death of man and the last resurrection, containeth the soul in secret receptacles; as everyone is worthy of rest or sorrow, according to that which it obtained whilst it lived in the flesh.

But *Ambrose* in his book concerning the Benefits of Death, saith: The writing of *Esdras*[62] calleth the habitations of the souls, storehouses; which he meeting with the complaints of man (because that the just who have gone before, may seem, even to the day of judgement, viz. for a long time, to be wonderfully defrauded of their just recompense of reward) doth liken the day of judgement to a garland; for the day of reward is expected of all, that in the meantime both the conquered may be ashamed, and the conquerors may attain the palm of victory; therefore while the fullness of times is expected, the souls expect their due recompense; punishment remaining for some, glory for others; and in the same place he calleth hell a place which is not seen, which the souls go to, being separated from the bodies; and in his second book Of Cain and Abel, he saith, the soul is loosed from the body, and after the end of this life, is even as yet in suspense, being doubtful of the judgement to come.

To these assenteth that evangelical saying, concerning the last judgement, Christ saying in Matthew: Many shall say to me in that day, Lord, Lord, have we not prophesied in thy name, and in thy name cast out devils? And then I shall confess to them, that I never knew them;[63] by which speech it seemeth to be clear, that even until this day they were uncertain concerning their sentence, and by the confidence of miracles which they had performed in the name of *Jesus,* whilst they lived, to have been in some hope of salvation.

Therefore because the judgement of souls is deferred until the last day, many theologians think that satisfactory intercessions may help not only the justified, but also the damned, before the appointed day of judgement. So *Trajan* the Emperor was delivered from hell by Saint *Gregory,*[64] and justified to salvation, though some think that he was not freed from the guilt of punishment, but the justice of punishment was prolonged until the day of judgement; but *Thomas Aquinas* saith it seemeth more probable, that by the intercessions of S. *Gregory, Trajan* lived again, and obtained a gracious power by the which he was freed from the punishment and guilt of sin.

And there are some theologians who think, that by the dirges for the dead neither the punishment nor the guilt is taken away or detracted, but that only some ease and assuagement of the pains is procured; and this by the similitude of a sweating porter, who by the sprinkling of some water seemeth to be eased of the weight of his burden, or helped to carry it more easily, although nothing of the burden be taken off: yet the common opinion of theologians denieth that prayers or funeral dirges do cause any favour for the guilty within the gates of *Pluto.*

But seeing all these things are of an incomprehensible obscurity, many have vainly whet their wits on them: therefore we holding to the opinion of *Austine,* as he saith in the tenth book on Genesis, do affirm, that it is better to doubt concerning occult things, than to contend about uncertain things: for I doubt not but that that rich man is to be understood in the flames of pains, and that poor man in the refreshment of joys; but how that flame of hell, that bosom of *Abraham,* that tongue of the rich man, that torment of thirst, that drop of cooling,[65] are to be understood, it is hardly found out by the modest searcher, but by the contentious never.

But these things being for this present omitted, we hasten to further matters and will dispute concerning the restitution of souls.

Nozes—Chapzer XLI

1. *Ezechiah*—Ezekiel 5.

2. *perish by sword*—Matthew 26:52.

3. *adrastia*—Adrastus, king of Argos, led the war of the Seven Against Thebes. The first attempt on the city failed and he alone escaped alive. Ten years after

he attacked a second time with the sons of his dead comrades and was victorious, fulfilling a favorable oracle which had predicted this outcome.

4. *returns a man*—The above is a roughly accurate quotation from the tractate *On Our Allotted Guardian Spirit* by Plotinus. However Agrippa edits the end of the list, which I will give here: "... futile and flighty visionaries ever soaring skyward, become high-flying birds; observance of civic and secular virtue makes men again, or when the merit is less marked, one of the animals of communal tendency, a bee or the like" (Plotinus *Enneads* 3.4.2 [Mackenna, 2:47]).

5. *lion*—Proverbs 19:12.

6. *bear*—Proverbs 17:12.

7. *boar*—Proverbs 11:22.

8. *hunting dog*—Proverbs 30:31.

9. *cony*—Rabbit. Proverbs 30:26.

10. *pismire*—Ant. Proverbs 6:6.

11. *serpent*—Perhaps Proverbs 23:32.

12. *spider*—Proverbs 30:28.

13. *eagle*—Perhaps Proverbs 23:5.

14. *any other bird*—Proverbs 1:17.

15. *light of the living*—The notion of a threefold reincarnation derives from a passage in *The Discourse Of the Faithful Shepherd,* the text of which is incorporated into the *Zohar.* On this matter Waite comments: "According to the testimony in this text, incarnation may take place thrice, because of the words: 'Lo, all these things worketh God oftentimes with men.' Job xxxiii;29. The Zohar renders the passage: 'Behold what God doeth in respect of each man, even to the third time.'" (Waite 1929, 6.1.253, n. 7). See the *Zohar,* Cremona Edition, 3:178b.

16. *saith the Preacher*—Ecclesiastes 3:20-1.

17. *Lucretius hath expressed*—*On the Nature of Things* 2, c. line 1011.

18. *Zazel*—Azazel. See note 51, ch. XVIII, bk. III.

19. *shalt eat dust*—See note 52, ch. XVIII, bk. III.

20. *dust of the Earth*—See note 53, ch. XVIII, bk. III.

21. *Elpenor in Homer*—

> But now I pray you, by those you have yet
>   to see, who are not here,
> by your wife, and by your father, who
>   reared you when you were little,
> and by Telemachos whom you left alone in
>   your palace;
> for I know that after you leave this place
>   and the house of Hades
> you will put back with your well made ship
>   to the island, Aiaia;
> there at that time, my lord, I ask that you
>   remember me
> and do not go and leave me behind unwept,
>   unburied,
> when you leave, for fear I might become
>   the god's curse upon you;
> but burn me there with all my armour that
>   belongs to me,
> and heap up a grave mound beside the
>   beach of the gray sea;
> for an unhappy man, so that those to come
>   will know of me.
> (Homer *Odyssey* 11, lines 66–76 [Lattimore, 170])

22. *Dido complains*—"I have lived my life, and finished the course that fortune assigned me, and now great will be my phantom that will pass beneath the earth" (Virgil *Aeneid* 4, c. line 650 [Lonsdale and Lee, 141]).

23. *wrath of God*—Revelation 16:1.

24. Dido threatens—"With black fires I will pursue you, though I be far away; and when cold death has separated my limbs from my spirit, my shade shall be with you wherever you are. You shall receive your punishment, wicked one!" (Virgil *Aeneid* 4, c. line 385 [Lonsdale and Lee, 135]).

25. *unto Ramoth-Gilead*—I Kings 21:9–10; 22:20–2 and II Kings 9:25–6.

26. *whence he sings*—Virgil *Aeneid* 6, c. line 655.

27. *as Virgil sings*—Virgil *Aeneid* 6, line 660ff.

28. *as saith Virgil*—Virgil's description of Elysium, *Aeneid* 6, c. line 638.

29. *receptacles of souls*—Irenaeus regarded as heretical the notion that souls are glorified immediately after death, and Cyprian, Tertullian, Cyril of Jerusalem, Basil, Ambrose, Gregory of Nyassa, Chrysostom, Jerome, and the *Acts* of Saint Perpetua all imply a kind of middle holding place for souls and

advocate the saying of prayers for the dead. The references are unclear and influenced by the pagan Hades. Origen thought that even the perfect must pass through fire in the afterworld. Augustine wrote that it was not incredible that imperfect souls will be saved by purgatorial fire. However it was Pope Gregory I (?544–604) who first expressly formulated the doctrine of purgatory *(purgatorium)*, a word officially entered into the vocabulary of the Church by Pope Innocent IV (ruled 1243–1254) and affirmed at the Council of Lyons (1274). The biblical authority, such as it is, stems from the apocryphal II Maccabees 12:39–45, where prayers for the sinful dead are described as a "holy and good thought" and a "reconciliation for the dead, that they might be delivered from sin."

30. *blood of sacrifice*—"I see before me now the soul of my perished mother,/but she sits beside the blood in silence, and has not yet deigned/to look directly at her own son and speak a word to me" (Homer *Odyssey* 11, lines 141–3 [Lattimore, 171–2]).

31. *Tyresia the prophetess*—Teiresias the prophet, not prophetess. Somehow Agrippa has changed his sex. Of all the souls in Hades only Teiresias is wholly aware.

32. *which the Poet explains*—The shade of Anchises expounds to his son, Aeneas, the doctrine of punishment:

> Nay, even when life has left them with its latest ray, still every ill and all the plagues of the body do not utterly pass out from the wretches, and it must needs be that many defilements long-contracted grew deep into their being in wonderous wise. Therefore they suffer a probation of punishment, and pay the full penalty of past misdeeds; some hung aloft are exposed to the viewless winds; from some the taint of guilt is washed away beneath the boundless flood: we suffer each his own ghostly penance: after that, we are released, to range through the wide spaces of Elysium, and possess the happy fields, a scanty band: till a long course of time, when the full cycle is complete, has purged away the long-contracted stain, and leaves pure the etherial essence, and unadulterated fire of heaven. (Virgil *Aeneid* 6, c. line 734 [Lonsdale and Lee, 174]).

33. *intently thinks on them*—The residual affection of the shades for the actions and feelings of their past lives is apparent when Odysseus visits the land of the dead: "Only the soul of Telamonian Aias stood off/at a distance from me, angry still over that decision/I

won against him, when beside the ships we disputed/our cases for the arms of Achilleus" (Homer *Odyssey* 11, lines 543–6 [Lattimore, 182]). See also the reaction of Dido's ghost to her former lover, Aeneas, when he visits hell *(Aeneid* 6, c. line 450).

34. *in the poets*—Homer *Odyssey* 11, lines 568–600; Virgil *Aeneid* 6, lines 562–627.

35. *Tantalus*—The mythic King Tantalus is supposed to have tested the divine foreknowledge of Zeus by presenting the god a banquet of human flesh. By another account Tantalus was invited to a banquet by Zeus and later betrayed the divine secrets communicated to him over the table in confidence. By still a third version of the tale, Tantalus stole nectar and ambrosia from the table of the gods to give to his mortal friends. His punishment was to continually thirst and not be able to drink. See the *Odyssey* 11, lines 583–92.

36. *Sardanapalus*—See biographical note.

37. *Midas*—The wealthy and effeminate king of Phrygia, who was said to have been given the gift by Silenus of turning everything he touched into gold. When he discovered that he could not eat, he begged Silenus to remove the gift. Silenus told him to bathe in the spring that was the source of the river Pactolus, which cleansed Midas of the curse and turned the river sands golden.

38. *Sisyphus*—The fraudulent and avaricious king of Corinth, doomed to roll a great stone up a hill endlessly in Hades. According to the most common legend, he told his wife to leave his body unburied, then when in hell he asked Pluto for permission to return to Earth to punish her negligence. When Pluto complied, Sisyphus refused to return to the underworld and had to be carried off forcibly by Hermes. See the *Odyssey* 11, lines 593–600.

39. *as sings the Poet*—The river nymph Cyrene advises her son Aristaeus about the shape-shifting powers of Proteus:

> But when you have seized him, and hold him with your hands and chains, straightway manifold forms will seek to baffle you, and figures of wild beasts; for he will suddenly become a bristly boar, and a fell tiger, and a scaly dragon, and a lioness with tawny neck; or will give forth a fierce roar of flames, and so strive to slip away from the fetters, or melt away into fleeting water, and so make his escape. (Virgil *Georgics* 4, c. line 405 [Lonsdale and Lee, 74]).

40. *Virgil sang*—See note 32 above.

41. *in his Necromancy*—Book 11 of the *Odyssey,* where Odysseus performs a necromantic ritual according with the instructions of Circe for calling forth the shades of the dead, in order to elicit their oracular responses.

42. *relation to Ulysses*—*Odyssey* 11, lines 576–8. See also the *Aeneid* 6, c. line 602. Virgil has borrowed this passage intact from Homer. Tityos was the giant son of Gaea who at the instigation of Hera tried to rape Artemis. The goddess killed him with her bow. It is Odysseus who tells this tale to King Alcinous.

43. *into brutes*—The Hermetic books are divided as to whether the souls of men can be reincarnated as beasts. This is the passage to which Agrippa refers:

> But if a soul, when it has entered a human body, persists in evil, it does not taste the sweets of immortal life, but is dragged back again; it reverses its course, and takes its way back to the creeping things; and that ill-fated soul, having failed to know itself, lives in servitude to uncouth and noxious bodies. *(Corpus Hermeticum* 10.8a [Scott, 1:193])

Scott has placed a few pages later this passage, obviously from a different pen:

> But it can enter a human body only; for no other kind of body can contain a human soul. It is not permitted that a human soul should fall so low as to enter the body of an irrational animal; it is a law of God that human souls must be kept safe from such outrage as that. (ibid. 10:19b [Scott, 201])

Proclus writes somewhat ambiguously:

> True reason asserts that the human soul may be lodged in brutes, yet in such a manner, as that it may obtain its own proper life, and that the degraded soul may, as it were, be carried above it and be bound to the baser nature by a propensity and similitude of affection. And that this is the only mode of insinuation we have proved by a multitude of arguments in our Commentaries on the *Phaedrus.* (Intro. to *Theology of Plato,* trans. Thomas Taylor. In Mead [1896] 1965, 193)

44. *Ixion*—Ixion, the king of the Lapithae in Thessaly, married Dia and agreed to give her father, Deioneus, a costly present in exchange for her hand, but treacherously lured his father-in-law to a banquet,

then cast him into a fiery pit. As a punishment he went mad. Zeus took pity on him, cured his madness, and invited him up to Olympus. The unrepentant Ixion tried, unsuccessfully, to seduce Hera. So furious was Zeus that he bound Ixion to an endlessly rolling wheel of fire. His fate is briefly mentioned by Virgil *(Aeneid* 6, line 601) and Ovid *(Metamorphoses* 4, line 461).

45. *upon Elisha*—II Kings 2:15.

46. *seventy men*—Numbers 11:25.

47. *in Saxo Grammaticus*—This is surely one of the earliest accounts (circa 1200) of the killing of a vampire by cutting off its head and driving a stake through its heart.

48. *Pausanias tells a story*—

> Above all there is Eurynomos; the officials at Delphi say Eurynomos is a daemonic spirit in Hades, who eats away the flesh of the dead, and leaves them only their bones. But Homer's *Odyssey* and the *Minyad* and the *Homecomings,* all of which mention Hades and its horrors, know nothing about any daemonic Eurynomos. But I will explain what kind of Eurynomos is in the painting and what he looks like: his flesh is between blue and black, like the flies that settle on meat, he shows his teeth, and the hide of a vulture has been spread for him to sit on. (Pausanias *Guide to Greece* 10.28.4 [Levi, 1:479–80])

49. *Aetnean fires*—Mount Etna in Sicily is volcanic.

50. *reported in Homer*—*Odyssey* 11, lines 14–9.

51. *cave of Patricius*—The cave of Saint Patrick of Ireland, otherwise known as St. Patrick's Purgatory, is located on a small island in Lough Derg in Donegal, Ireland. The saint had the walls of the cave painted with scenes of hell and often retired there to pray and practice austerities. It became the center of an ever-changing community of ascetics, who would entomb themselves in six tiny chambers three feet wide for nine days to learn ahead of time what awaited them in hell. They were allowed to leave their cells three times a day to attend chapel, consumed only bread and water for eight days, and on the ninth day fasted. On the edge of the island was a small pilgrims' hut that acted as a kind of hotel. Strange as it seems, this place was very popular, largely because it induced trances in those who voluntarily undertook the hardships. In effect it acted as a Christian oracle.

52. *den of Vulcan*—Vulcan (Hephaestus) was believed to have his workshop in the interior of Mount Etna in Sicily. Here he forged thunderbolts for Zeus.

53. *History of Drusus*—That section of the *Annals* (bks. I and II) of Tacitus which deals with the German campaigns of Drusus Caesar (15 BC–19 AD), otherwise known as Drusus Junior or Germanicus Caesar to distinguish him from his father Nero Claudius Drusus (38 BC–9 BC).

54. *men and beasts*—When the fleet of Germanicus was dispersed by storm, Germanicus sent ships looking for his soldiers, who had been blown aground in Britain and the surrounding islands: "Every one, as he returned from some far-distant region, told of wonders, of violent hurricanes, and unknown birds, of monsters of the sea, of forms half-human, half beast-like, things they had really seen or in their terror believed" (Tacitus *Annals* 2.24 [Church and Brodribb, 66]).

55. *did dwell there*—"All else [stories of Germanic tribes] is fabulous, as that the Hellusii and Oxiones have the faces and expressions of men, with the bodies and limbs of wild beasts" (Tacitus *Germany* 46 [Church and Brodribb, 732]).

56. *since sang*—The quotation from Claudianus refers to the necromantic ritual conducted by Odysseus in the northern land of the dead, but it was the shades, not Odysseus, who drank the blood—see *Odyssey* bk. 11.

57. *Dolorosus*—Perhaps Dollar (Dolour) Law, a hill of 2680 feet in Borders, Scotland, between the headwaters of the Yarrow and the Tweed rivers, northwest of St. Mary's Lake.

58. *heresies of Marcion*—Tertullian *Against Marcion* 4.34.

59. *Clemens, a king*—Perhaps refers to an apocryphal work ascribed to Pope Clement I, or Clemens Romanus, who was regarded as a disciple of Simon Peter.

60. *Jonas*—Jonah. See Jonah 1:17. Also Revelation 11:9–12.

61. *Of Divine Reward*—

Nor, however, let any one imagine that souls are immediately judged after death. For all are detained in one and a common place of confinement, until the arrival of the time in which the great Judge shall make an investigation of their deserts. Then they whose piety shall have been approved of will receive the reward of immortality; but they whose sins and crimes shall have been brought to light will not rise again, but will be hidden in the same darkness with the wicked, being destined to certain punishment. (Lactantius *Divine Institutions* 7.21 [*Ante-Nicene Christian Library* 21:474]).

62. *Esdras*—Perhaps II Esdras 7:32.

63. *never knew them*—Matthew 7:22–3.

64. *by Saint Gregory*—There was a popular legend in the Middle Ages that Pope Gregory the Great (540–604) prayed that the good soul of the pagan Roman emperor Trajan might be delivered from hell. Such a deliverance was not possible directly, so God caused Trajan to be reborn long enough to profess his faith in Christ, which he could not do while in hell. Dante refers to this tale in two places in his *Divine Comedy*: "Here was storied the high glory of the Roman prince, whose worth incited Gregory to his great victory: I speak of Trajan the emperor ..." (*Divine Comedy:Purgatory* 10.74–6, trans. Charles Eliot Norton [1891] [Boston: Houghton Mifflin, 1941], 2:76–7).

For the one came back unto his bones from Hell, where there is never return to righteous will; and that was the reward of living hope; of living hope, which put its power into the prayers made to God to raise him up, so that it might be possible for his will to be moved. The glorious soul, of whom I speak, returning to the flesh, in which it was but little while, believed in Him who had power to aid it; and in believing was kindled to such fire of true love, that at its second death it was worthy to come unto this festivity. (*Divine Comedy: Paradise* 20:106–17 [Norton, 3:164])

65. *drop of cooling*—Luke 16:19–26.

By what ways the magicians, and necromancers do think they can call forth the souls of the dead.

By the things which have been already spoken, it is manifest that souls after death do as yet love their body which they left, as those souls do whose bodies want a due burial, or have left their bodies by violent death, and as yet wander about their carcasses in a troubled and moist spirit, being as it were allured by something that hath an affinity with them.

The means being known by the which in times past they were joined to their bodies, they may easily be called forth and allured by the like vapours, liquors and savours,[1] certain artificial lights being also used, songs, sounds and such like, which do move the imaginative and spiritual harmony of the soul; also sacred invocations, and such like, which belong to religion, ought not to be neglected, by reason of the portion of the rational soul, which is above nature.

So the witch is said to have called up *Samuel,*[2] and the Thessalian prophetess in *Lucan,* to have caused a carcass to stand upright:[3] hence we read in poets, and those who relate these things, that the souls of the dead cannot be called up without blood and a carcass: but their shadows to be easily allured by the fumigations of these things; eggs being also used, and milk, honey, oil, wine, water, flour, as it were yielding a fit medicine for the souls to reassume their bodies, as you may see in *Homer,* where *Circe* at large instructeth *Ulysses.*[4]

Yet they think, that these things can be done in those places only where these kinds of souls are known to be most conversant, either by reason of some affinity, as their dead body alluring them, or by reason of some affection imprinted in their life, drawing the soul itself to certain places, or by reason of some hellish nature of the place; and therefore fit for the punishing or purging of souls.

Places of this kind are best known by the meeting of nocturnal visions and incursions, and such like phantasms; some are sufficiently known by themselves, as burial places and places of execution, and where public slaughters have lately been made, or where the carcasses of the slain, not as yet expiated, nor rightly buried, were some few years since put into the ground; for expiation[5] and exorcisation[6] of any place, and also the holy right of burial being duly performed to the bodies, oftentimes prohibiteth the souls themselves to come up, and driveth them farther off the places of judgement.

Hence necromancy hath its name,[7] because it worketh on the bodies of the dead, and giveth answers by the ghosts and apparitions of the dead, and subterrany spirits, alluring them into the carcasses of the dead, by certain hellish charms, and infernal invocations, and by deadly sacrifices, and wicked oblations; such we read in *Lucan* of *Erichthone*[8] the witch, who called up the dead, who foretold to *Sextus Pompey* all the events of the Pharsalian war:[9] there were also in Phigalia a city of Arcadia, certain magicians, priests most skillful in sacred rites and raisers up of the souls of the dead: and the holy

Scriptures testify, that a certain woman, a witch, called up *Samuel's* soul: even so truly the souls of the saints do love their bodies, and hear more readily there, where the pledges of their relics are preserved.

But there are two kinds of necromancy, the one called *necyomancy,* raising the carcasses, which is not done without blood; the other *sciomancy,*[10] in which the calling up of the shadow only sufficeth. To conclude, it worketh all its experiments by the carcasses of the slain, and their bones and members, and what is from them, because there is in these things a spiritual power friendly to them.

Therefore they easily allure the flowing down of wicked spirits, being by reason of the similitude and propriety very familiar: by whom the necromancer strengthened by their help can do very much in human and terrestrial things, and kindle unlawful lusts, cause dreams, diseases, hatred and such like passions, to the which also they can confer the powers of these souls, which as yet being involved in a moist and turbid spirit, and wandering about their cast bodies, can do the same things that the wicked spirits commit.

Seeing therefore they experimentally find, that the wicked and impure souls violently plucked from their bodies, and of men not expiated, and wanting burial, do stay about their carcasses, and are drawn to them by affinity, the witches easily abuse them for the effecting of their witchcrafts, alluring these unhappy souls by the apposition[11] of their body or by the taking of some part thereof, and compelling them by their devilish charms, by entreating them by the deformed carcasses dispersed through the wide fields, and the wandering shadows of those that want burials, and by the ghosts sent back from Acheron,[12] and the guests of hell, whom untimely death hath precipitated into hell; and by the horrible desires of the damned, and proud devils revengers of wickednesses.

But he which would restore the souls truly to their bodies, must first know what is the proper nature of the soul from whence it went forth, with how many and how great degrees of perfection it is replenished, with what intelligence it is strengthened, by what means diffused into the body, by what harmony it shall be compacted with it; what affinity it hath with God, with the intelligences, with the heavens, elements, and all other things whose image and resemblance it holdeth.

To conclude, by what influences the body may be knit together again for the raising of the dead, requireth all these things which belong not to men but to God only, and to whom he will communicate them, as to *Elishai* who raised up the son of the Shunamite;[13] so also *Alcestis*[14] is reported to have been raised by *Hercules,* and to have lived long after; and *Apollonius Tyanensis* restored a dead maid to life.

And here is to be noted that sometimes it happeneth to men, that their vivifying spirit is retracted in them, and they appear as dead and without sense, when as yet the intellectual nature remaineth united to the body, and it hath the same form, and remaineth the same body, although the power of vivifying extendeth not itself into it actually, but remaineth retracted in the union with the intellectual nature; yet it ceaseth not to be; and although that man may truly be said to be dead, inasmuch as death is a want of a vivifying spirit, yet is it not truly separated; and that body can be wakened again and live.

And thus many miracles appear in these; and of this kind many have been seen amongst the gentiles and Jews in former ages, in the number of which is that which *Plato* reciteth in his tenth book De Republic, viz. that one *Phereus* of Pamphilia lay ten days amongst the slain in battle, and after that he had been taken away and laid to the fire two days, he revived and told many wonderful things which he had seen in the time of his death;[15] and concerning these things we have spoken partly in the first book, and shall yet speak further anon where we shall speak of oracles, which come forth in a rapture, ecstasy, and in the agony of dying men.

Notes—Chapter XLII

1. *vapours, liquors and savours*—Sacrifices of food and drink with a pleasing appearance, odor and taste.

2. *called up Samuel*—I Samuel 28:11.

3. *stand upright*—

> Forthwith the clotted blood grows warm, and nourishes the blackened wounds, and runs into the veins and the extremities of the limbs. Smitten beneath the cold breast, the lungs palpitate; and a new life creeping on is mingled with the marrow so lately disused. Then does every joint throb; the sinews are stretched; and not by degrees throughout the limbs does the dead body lift itself from the earth, and it is spurned by the ground and raised erect at the same instant. The eyes with their apertures distended wide are opened. In it not as yet is there the face of one living, but of one now dying. His paleness and his stiffness remain, and, brought back to the world, he is astounded. But his sealed lips resound with no murmur. A voice and a tongue to answer alone are granted unto him. (Lucan *Pharsalia* 6, lines 750–62 [Riley, 244–5])

The Thessalian prophetess is the witch Erichtho.

4. *instructeth Ulysses*—Circe describes to Odysseus the necromantic ritual for calling up the shades of the dead:

> Dig a pit of about a cubit in each direction, and pour it full of drink offerings for all the dead, first
> honey mixed with milk, then a second pouring of sweet wine,
> and the third, water, and over all then sprinkle white barley,
> and promise many times to the strengthless heads of the perished
> dead that, returning to Ithaka, you will slaughter a barren
> cow, your best, in your palace and pile the pyre with treasures,
> and to Teiresias apart dedicate an all-black ram, the one conspicuous in all your sheep-flocks.
> But when with prayers you have entreated the glorious hordes
> of the dead, then sacrifice one ram and one black female,
> turning them towards Erebos, but yourself turn away from them

> and make for where the river runs, and there the numerous
> souls of the perished dead will come and gather about you.
> (Homer *Odyssey* 10, lines 517–30 [Lattimore, 165–6]).

Circe does not say, but Odysseus understands, that he must fill the pit with the blood of the sacrificed male and female sheep:

> Now when, with sacrifices and prayers, I had so entreated
> the hordes of the dead, I took the sheep and cut their throats
> over the pit, and the dark-clouding blood ran in, and the souls
> of the perished dead gathered to the place, up out of Erebos …
> (ibid. 11, lines 34–7 [Lattimore, 169])

This is necessary because the shades of Hades are without energy, and blood is filled with the vital life-force. It not only attracts the ghosts, but gives them the strength to become aware of their surroundings and converse.

5. *expiation*—Purification of a person, place or thing from guilt by religious ceremony, especially to avert evil.

6. *exorcisation*—Exorcization or exorcism, the action of expelling an evil spirit from a person, place or thing by religious ceremony.

7. *necromancy hath its name*—Greek: νεκρο, corpse; μαντεια, divination.

8. *Erichthone*—Erichtho.

9. *Pharsalian war*—See Lucan *Pharsalia* 6, lines 777–800.

10. *sciomancy*—Greek: σκιο, shadow: μαντεια, divination. Calling up the ghosts of the dead to prophesy, as was done by the witch of Endor for Saul, and by Odysseus in the land of the dead.

11. *apposition*—Application.

12. *Acheron*—The great river of Hades, used here to signify all of the land of the dead.

13. *the Shunamite*—II Kings 4:32–5.

14. *Alcestis*—Alcestis was wife of Admetus, king of Pherae in Thessaly. When he fell sick Apollo made a

bargain with the Moerae (Fates) to spare his life if someone else would voluntarily take his place. Admetus assented to this arrangement, believing some servant or friend would fulfill the pact, but when the hour approached, no one stepped forward, until at last Alcestis volunteered to die in place of her husband. Admetus was horrified, but the die had been cast. Just as Death was about to carry the loving Alcestis away to Hades, Hercules arrived at the palace. He forced Death to release the queen, who was reunited with her husband. See the play *Alcestis* by Euripides.

15. *time of his death*—This story is told by Plato about a man called Er, the son of Armenius, by race a Pamphylian, in the *Republic* 10:614b–621b.

CHAPTER XLIII

Of the power of man's soul, in the mind, reason and imagination.

an's soul consisteth of a mind, reason and imagination; the mind illuminates reason, reason floweth into the imagination: all is one soul. Reason unless it be illuminated by the mind, is not free from error: but the mind giveth not light to reason, unless God enlighten, viz. the first light; for the first light is in God very far exceeding all understanding: wherefore it cannot be called an intelligible light; but this when it is infused into the mind, is made intellectual, and can be understood: then when it is infused by the mind to the reason, it is made rational, and cannot only be understood but also considered: then when it is infused by the reason into the phantasy of the soul, it is made not only cogitable, but also imaginable; yet it is not as yet corporeal; but when from hence it goeth into the celestial vehicle of the soul, it is first made corporeal; yet not manifestly sensible till it hath passed into the elemental body, either simple and aerial, or compound, in the which the light is made manifestly visible to the eye.

The Chaldean philosophers considering this progress of light, declare a certain wonderful power of our mind: viz. that it may come to pass, that our mind being firmly fixed on God, may be filled with the divine power; and being so replenished with light, its beams being diffused through all the media, even to this gross, dark, heavy, mortal body, it may endow it with abundance of light,[1] and make it like the stars,

and equally shining, and also by the plenty of its beams and lightness lift it on high, as straw lifted up by the flame of fire, and can presently carry the body as a spirit into remote parts.

So we read of *Philip* in the Acts of the Apostles, who baptizing the eunuch in India, was presently found, in Azotus.[2] The like we read of *Habacuc* in Daniel:[3] so others going through the doors being shut, escaped both their keepers and imprisonment; as we read of *Peter* the apostle[4] and of *Peter* the exorcist:[5] he may the less wonder at this, who hath seen those famous melancholic men, who walk in their sleeps and pass through places even unpassable, and ascend even unaccessible places, and exercise the works of those that are awake, which they themselves being awake could not do; of the which things there is no other reason in nature, than a strong and exalted imagination.

But this power is in every man, and it is in the soul of man from the root of his creation; but it is varied in divers men, in strength and weakness, and is increased and diminished according to his exercise and use, by the which it is drawn forth from power into act, which thing he that rightly knoweth, can ascend by his knowledge, even until his imaginative faculty doth transcend and is joined with the universal power, which *Alchindus, Bacon,* and *Gulielmus Parisiensis* do call the sense of nature; *Virgil* the etherial sense, and *Plato* the sense of the vehicle.

And his imagination is made most strong, when that etherial and celestial power is poured out upon it, by whose brightness it is comforted, until it apprehend the species, notions and knowledge of true things, so that that which he thought in his mind, cometh to pass even as he thought, and it obtaineth so great power, that it can plunge, join and insinuate itself into the minds of men, and make them certain of his thoughts, and of his will and desire, even through large and remote spaces, as if they perceived a present object by their senses;[6] and it can in little time do many things, as if they were done without time.

Yet these things are not granted to all, but to those whose imaginative and cogitative power is most strong and hath arrived to the end of speculation; and he is fitted to apprehend and manifest all things, by the splendour of the universal power, or intelligence and spiritual apprehension which is above him: and this is that necessary power, which everyone ought to follow and obey, who followeth the truth.

If therefore now the power of the imagination is so great, that it can insinuate itself unto whom it pleaseth, being neither hindered nor let by any distance of time or place, and can sometimes draw its heavy body along with it, whither it imagineth and dreameth: there is no doubt but that the power of the mind is greater, if at any time it shall obtain its proper nature, and being no way oppressed by the allurements of the senses, shall persevere both uncorrupted and like itself.

But now for example, that the souls abound with so plentiful light of the celestial stars, and hence, a very great abundance of light redoundeth into their bodies; so *Moses'* face did shine,[7] that the children of Israel could not behold him by reason of the brightness of his countenance; thus *Socrates* was transfigured, as we read, that in light he overcame the luciferous wheels of the Sun; so *Zoroastes* being transfigured, his body was taken up. So *Eliah*[8] and *Enoch*[9] ascended to heaven in a certain fiery chariot, so *Paul* was rapt up into the third heaven:[10] so our bodies after the judgement of the world, shall be called glorified, and in like manner be rapt up, and we may say by this means, shall shine as the Sun and Moon; which thing that it is possible, and hath formerly been done, *Avicebron* the Moor, and *Avicen* the Arabian, and *Hippocrates* of Cous, and all the school of the Chaldeans do acknowledge and confirm.

Moreover it is reported in histories, that *Alexander the Great,* being circumvented and in great danger in India, did so burn in mind, that he seemed to the barbarians to cast forth light;[11] the father of *Theodoricus* also is reported to have cast forth sparks of fire through his whole body;[12] the same thing a wise man also delivered concerning himself, so that sparkling flames did break forth here and there even with a noise; neither is this power of the soul found in men only, but sometimes even in beasts, as in the horse of *Tiberius,* who seemed to send forth flames out of his mouth.

But the mind is above fate in providence, therefore is not affected either with the influences of the heavenly bodies, or the qualities of natural things; religion therefore can only cure it; but the sensitiveness of the soul is in fate, above nature, which is in a certain manner the knot of the body and soul, and under fate, above the body; therefore it is changed by the influences of the heavenly bodies, and affected by the qualities of natural and corporeal things.

Now I call the sensitiveness of the soul, that vivifying and rectifying power of the body, the original of the senses; the soul itself doth manifest in this body its sensitive powers and perceiveth corporeal things by the body, and locally moveth the body, and governeth it in his place, and nourisheth it in a body.

In this sensitiveness two most principal powers predominate; viz. one which is called the phantasy, or imaginative or cogitative faculty, of whose power we have already spoken, where we have handled the passions of the soul:[13] the other which is called the sense of nature, of the which also we have spoken, where we made mention of witchcraft.[14]

Man therefore by the nature of his body is under fate; the soul of man, by the sensitiveness moveth nature in fate, but by the mind is above fate, in the order of providence; yet reason is free at its own choice; therefore the soul by reason ascendeth into the mind, where it is replenished with divine light; sometimes it descendeth into sensitiveness and is affected by the influences of the heavenly bodies, and qualities of natural things, and is distracted by the passions and the encountering of sensible objects: sometimes the soul revolveth itself wholly into reason, searching out other things either by discourse, or by contemplating itself.

For it is possible, that that part of the reason, which the Peripatetics call the possible intellect,[15] may be brought to this, that it may freely discourse and operate without conversion to his phantasms: for so great is the command of this reason, that as often as anything incurreth either into the mind, or into the sensitiveness, or into nature, or into the body, it cannot pass into the soul, unless reason apply itself to it.

By this means the soul perceiveth itself neither to see, nor hear, nor feel, nor that it suffereth any things by the external senses, until cogitative reason first apprehend it; but it apprehendeth it when it is at leisure, not when it earnestly gapeth after another thing, as we man-ifestly see by these who heed not those that they meet, when they more seriously think on something else.

Know therefore that neither the superior influences, nor natural affections, nor sensations, nor passions either of the mind or body, nor any sensible thing whatsoever, can work or penetrate into the soul unless by the judgement of reason itself. Therefore by its act, not by any extrinsical violence, can the soul be either affected or disturbed, which thing even innumerable martyrs have proved by their martyrdom.

So *Anasarchus* a philosopher of Abdera, who, by the command of *Nicocreontes* a tyrant of Cyprus, being cast into a concave stone, neglecting the pains of his body while he was pounded with iron pestles, is reported to have said: pound, pound the shell of *Anasarchus*, thou nothing hurteth *Anasarchus* himself: the tyrant commanded his tongue to be cut off, but he with his own teeth did bite it off, and did spit it in the face of the tyrant.[16]

Notes—Chapter XLIII

1. *abundance of light*—

> The Oracles of the Gods declare, that through purifying ceremonies, not the Soul only, but bodies themselves become worthy of receiving much assistance and health, for, they say, the mortal vestment of coarse Matter will by these means be purified. And this, the Gods, in an exhortatory manner, announce to the most holy of Theurgists. *(Chaldean Oracles of Zoroaster* [Westcott, 60])

2. *in Azotus*—Acts 8:27–40. But the eunuch was baptized somewhere between Jerusalem and Gaza.

3. *Habacuc in Daniel*—Daniel 14:32–5 in the Knox translation. Chapters 13 and 14 of the book of Daniel are present in the Septuagint Greek, but absent from the Hebrew text. Consequently they are not found in the King James version.

4. *Peter the apostle*—Acts 12:7–10.

5. *Peter the exorcist*—During the reign of the Roman emperor Diocletian (284–305), Peter the Exorcist was cast into jail by the judge Serenus. Artemius, the keeper of the prison, had a daughter who was possessed by an evil spirit. Peter suggested that he pray for his daughter's salvation to Jesus Christ. Artemius retorted that a god who could not get one of his own preachers out of prison would have little power to help his daughter. Peter maintained that God had the power both to free him and cure the girl, at which point Artemius decided to put the question to a test, and locked Peter in his deepest dungeon bound hand and foot in iron fetters. That night Peter appeared before Artemius and his wife in their home and healed their daughter, at the same time baptizing 300 persons who had gathered to watch. Serenus ordered Peter again to be locked up, but again he was set free by an angel and went to Artemius to instruct him in his new faith. The story has an unhappy ending— Artemius, his wife Candida, and Peter were all beheaded, and their souls borne to heaven by angels. See Brewer 1901, 91–2.

6. *by their senses*—Telepathy.

7. *face did shine*—Exodus 34:30.

8. *Eliah*—Elijah. II Kings 2:11.

9. *Enoch*—"And he was raised aloft on the chariots of the spirit and his name vanished among them" (Book of Enoch 70:2 [Charles 1913, 2:235]). See Genesis 5:24.

10. *third heaven*—II Corinthians 12:2.

11. *cast forth light*—See note 6, ch. LXIII, bk. I.

12. *his whole body*—See note 7, ch. LXIII, bk. I.

13. *passions of the soul*—See the beginning of ch. LXIII, bk. I.

14. *witchcraft*—See ch. L, bk. I.

15. *possible intellect*—

> Now it is clear that no matter how the intellect is united or joined to this or that man, the intellect has the primacy among all other things which pertain to man, for the sensitive powers obey the intellect, and are at its service" (Aquinas *Summa theologica* 76.2. In *Introduction to Saint Thomas Aquinas,* ed. Anton C. Pegis [New York: Random House {Modern Library}], 1948], 299).

"Now to be cognizant of the natures of sensible qualities does not pertain to the senses, but to the intellect" (ibid. 78.3 [Pegis, 328]). About the "possible intellect," a term that derives from Aristotle's *De anima* (On the soul) 3.4.429a, Aquinas says: "But the phantasm itself is not the form of the possible intellect; the intelligible species abstracted from phantasms is such a form" *(Summa theologica* 76.2 [Pegis, 300]).

And later he says: "But the intellect which is in potentiality to things intelligible, and which for this reason Aristotle calls the possible intellect, is not passive ..." (ibid. 76.2 [Pegis, 340]). And still farther:

> Therefore nothing prevents one and the same soul, inasmuch as it is actually immaterial, from having a power by which it makes things actually immaterial, by abstraction from the conditions of individual matter (this power is called the agent intellect), and another power, receptive of such species, which is called the possible intellect by reason of its being in potentiality to such species. (ibid. 79.4 [Pegis, 346]).

Agrippa seems to have had in mind specifically question 76, article 2, the Answer of Aquinas, but the reader should read question 76–9 of the *Summa theologica* in light of bk. 3 of Aristotle's *De anima.*

16. *face of the tyrant*—See the biographical note on Anaxarchus.

CHAPTER XLIV

Of the degrees of souls, and their destruction, or immortality.

The mind, because it is from God, or from the intelligible world, is therefore immortal and eternal; but reason is long lived by the benefit of its celestial original from the heaven; but the sensitive because it is from the bosom of the matter and dependeth on sublunary nature, is subject to destruction and corruption: therefore the soul by its mind is immortal, by its reason long lived in its etherial vehicle, but resolvable unless it be restored in the circuit of its new body;[1] therefore it is not immortal, unless it be united to an immortal mind.

Therefore the sensitiveness of the soul or the sensitive or animal soul, because it is produced out of the bosom of a corporeal matter, the body being resolved, perisheth together with it, or the shadow thereof remaineth not long in the vapours of its resolved body, partaking nothing of immortality, unless it be also united to a more sublimed power.

Therefore the soul which is united to the mind, is called the soul standing not falling; but all men obtain not this mind because (as *Hermes* saith)[2] God would propound it as it were a prize and reward of the souls, which they that shall neglect, being without mind, spotted with corporeal senses, and made like to irrational creatures, are allotted to the same destruction with them, as Ecclesiastes saith:[3] there is the same destruction of man and beasts, and the condition of both is equal; as man dieth, so also they die, yea they have all one breath, so that man hath no preeminence over a beast; thus far he.

Hence many theologians think, that the souls of men of this kind have no immortality after they have left their body, but an hope of the Resurrection only, when all men shall be restored. *Austin* relateth that this was the heresy of the Arabians, who affirmed that the souls perished together with their bodies; and in the day of judgement did arise again with them.

Whosoever therefore being upheld by the divine grace have obtained a mind, these according to the proportion of their works become immortal[4] (as *Hermes* saith), having comprehended all things by their understanding, which are in the earth, and in the sea, and in the heavens, and if there be anything besides these above heaven, so that they behold even goodness itself.

But they who have lived a middle life, though they have not obtained the divine intelligence, but a certain rational intelligence of it; these men's souls, when they shall depart from their bodies, are bound over to certain secret receptacles, where they are affected with sensitive powers, and are exercised in a certain kind of act; and by imagination, and the irascible and concupiscible virtues, do either extremely rejoice, or grievously lament. Of which opinion Saint *Austin* also was, in his book which he wrote Of the Spirit and Soul;[5] the wise men of the Indians, Persians, Egyptians and Chaldeans have delivered, that this soul superviveth much longer than its body, yet that it is not made altogether immortal, unless by transmigration.

But our theologians do philosophize far otherwise concerning these things, that although there be the same common original and beginning of all souls, yet they are distinguished by the Creator with divers degrees, not only accidental, but also intrinsical, founded in their very essence, by the which one soul differeth from another, by that which is proper to itself; which opinion *John Scotus* also holdeth, and the Parisian theologians have so decreed in their Articles.

Hence the Wise Man saith, I was an ingenuous child, and obtained a good soul, viz. a better than many others; and according to this inequality of souls, everyone is capable in their degree, of their charge; which gift is freely given by God, as we read in the Gospel,[6] that he gave to one five talents, to another two, to another one, to everyone according to his virtue; and the Apostle saith,[7] he hath given some to be apostles, some prophets, some evangelists and doctors, for the consummation of the saints in the work of the ministry, for the building up of the body of Christ.

For there are (saith *Origen*)[8] certain invisible perfections, to the which are committed those things which are dispensed here upon Earth, in which there is no small difference, as also is required in the men.

Wherefore someone attaineth the highest degree of wisdom and dignity; another little differeth from beasts, and feeding beasts is made half a beast; another aboundeth in virtues and in wealth; another hath even little or nothing, and oftentimes that little which he hath is taken away from him, and given to him that hath; and this is the divine justice in the distribution of gifts, that they may correspond to the virtues of every receiver, to whom also rewards are given according to their works: that what proportion there is, of gifts to gifts, and of deserts to deserts, there may be the same proportion of rewards to rewards.[9]

To conclude, we must know this, that every noble soul hath a fourfold operation; first divine, by the image of the divine propriety; the second intellectual, by formality of participation with the intelligences; the third rational, by the perfection of its proper essence; the fourth animal or natural, by communion with the body and these inferior things; so that there is no work in this whole world so admirable, so excellent, so wonderful, which the soul of man, being associated to his image of divinity, which the magicians call a soul standing and not falling, cannot accomplish by its own power without any external help. Therefore the form of all magical power is from the soul of man standing and not falling.

Notes—Chapter XLIV

1. *its new body*—A reference to transmigration of souls.

2. *Hermes saith*—"Tat. 'Tell me then, father, why did not God impart mind to all men?'—*Hermes.* 'It was his will, my son, that mind should be placed in the midst as a prize that human souls may win'" *(Corpus Hermeticum* 4.3 [Scott, 1:151]).

3. *Ecclesiastes saith*—Ecclesiastes 3:19.

4. *become immortal*—"But as many as have partaken of the gift [of mind] which God has sent, these, my son, in comparison with the others, are as immortal gods to mortal men" *(Corpus Hermeticum* 4.5 [Scott, 1:153]).

5. *spirit and soul*—Perhaps Augustine's *De anima et ejus origine.*

6. *in the Gospel*—Matthew 25:15.

7. *the Apostle saith*—Ephesians 4:11.

8. *saith Origen*—"There are also certain invisible powers to which earthly things have been entrusted for administration; and amongst them no small difference must be believed to exist, as is also found to be the case among men" (Origen *De principiis* 2.9.3 [*Ante-Nicene Fathers,* 4:290]).

9. *rewards to rewards*—

It is therefore possible to understand that there have been also formerly rational vessels, whether purged or not, i.e., which either purged themselves or did not do so, and that consequently every vessel, according to the measure of its purity or impurity, received a place, or region, or condition by birth, or an office to discharge, in this world. All of which, down to the humblest, God providing for and distinguishing by the power of His wisdom, arranges all things by His controlling judgement, according to a most impartial retribution, so far as each one ought to be assisted or cared for in conformity with his deserts. In which certainly every principle of equity is shown, while the inequity of circumstances preserves the justice of a retribution according to merit. (ibid. 2.9.8 [*Ante-Nicene Fathers*, 4:293]).

CHAPTER XLV

Of soothsaying, and phrensy.

Soothsaying is that which the priests or others were stricken withal, and discerned the causes of things, and foresaw future things, viz. when oracles and spirits descend from the gods or from demons upon them, and are delivered by them; which descendings the Platonists call the falling down of superior souls on our souls; and *Mercurius* calls them the senses of the demons, and the spirits of demons. Of which sort of demons the ancients called Eurideae and Pythonae,[1] who, as the ancients believed, were wont to enter into the bodies of men, and make use of the voices, and tongues, for the prediction of things to come; of which *Plutarch* also made mention in his dialogue of the causes of Defect of Oracles.[2]

But *Cicero,* following the Stoics, affirms that the foreknowing of future things belongs only to the gods;[3] and *Ptolomy* the astrologer saith, that they only that are inspired with a deity foretell particular things. To these *Peter*[4] the apostle consents, saying, prophesying is not made according to the will of man, but holy men spake as they were moved by the Holy Ghost. Now that the foretellings of things to come are properly the fallings down of the gods, *Isaiah*[5] affirms, saying: And tell unto us those things that are coming, and we will tell them, because ye are gods. But these kinds of fallings down, or senses, come not into our souls when they are more attently busied about anything else; but they pass into them, when they are vacant.

Now there are three kinds of this vacancy, viz. phrensy, ecstasy, and dreams, of each of which in their order.

Notes—Chapter XLV

1. *Eurideae and Pythonae*—See note 2 below.

2. *Defect of Oracles*—

> For it is a very childish and silly thing, to suppose that the god [Apollo] himself does, like the spirits speaking in the bowels of ventriloquists (which were anciently called Euryclees, and now Pythons), enter into the bodies of the prophets, and speak by their mouths and voices, as fit instruments for that purpose. For he that thus mixes God in human affairs has not respect and reverence which is due to so great a majesty, as being ignorant of his power and virtue. (Plutarch *De defectu oraculorum* [The obsolescence of oracles] 9, trans. Robert Midgley [Goodwin, 4:13])

The Athenian diviner Eurycles was a ventriloquist surnamed Engastromythes (speech in the belly). The name was also applied to the priestesses of Apollo. He is mentioned by Aristophanes in the *Wasps,* line 1019 ("… and like the prophetic Genius, who hid himself in the belly of Eurycles …"), and also by Plato in the *Sophist* 252c ("… and, like that queer fellow Eurycles, they carry about with them wherever they go a voice in their own bellies to contradict them.").

3. *only to the gods*—As is so often the case in his ref-

erences, Agrippa attributes a belief to his author which his author expresses, but does not claim as his own:

> You are defending, I reply, the very citadel of the Stoics, O Quintus, by asserting the reciprocal dependence of these two conditions on one another; so that if there be such an art as divination, then there are Gods, and if there be such beings as Gods, then there is such an art as divination. But neither of these points is admitted as easily as you imagine. For future events may possibly be indicated by nature without the intervention of any God; and, even although there may be such beings as Gods, still it is possible that no such art as divination may be given by them to the human race. (Cicero *De divinatione* 1.6 [Yonge, 146])

For the complete argument of the Stoics as presented by Cicero, see *De divinatione* 1.38.

4. *Peter*—II Peter 1:21.

5. *Isaiah*—Isaiah 41:23. The text of this verse differs significantly in King James and Knox from Agrippa's version.

CHAPTER XLVI

Of the first kind of phrensy from the Muses.

Phrensy is an illustration of the soul coming from the gods, or demons. Whence this verse of *Ovid:*

God is in us, commerces of the throne
Of God, that spirit from above came down.

Plato defines[1] this by alienation, and binding; for he abstracts from those by which the corporeal senses are stirred up, and being estranged from an animal man, adheres to a deity from whom it receives those things which it cannot search into by its own power; for when the mind is free, and at liberty, the reins of the body being loosed, and going forth as out of a close prison, transcends the bonds of the members, and nothing hindering of it, being stirred up by its own instigations, and instigated by a divine spirit, comprehends all things, and foretells future things.

Now there are four kinds of divine phrensy proceeding from several deities, viz. from the Muses, from *Dionysus,* from *Apollo,* and from *Venus.*

The first phrensy therefore proceeding from the Muses, stirs up and tempers the mind, and makes it divine by drawing superior things to inferior things by things natural. Now Muses are the souls of the celestial spheres, according to which there are found several degrees, by which there is an attraction of superior things to inferior.

The inferior of these resembling the sphere of the Moon, possesseth those things which are from vegetables, as plants, fruits of trees, roots, and those which are from harder matters, as stones, metals, their alligations[2] and suspensions.[3] So it is said that the stone selenites,[4] i.e. moonstone, and the stone of the civet cat[5] cause divination; also vervain,[6] and the herb theangelis[7] cause soothsaying, as hath been above said.

The second degree resembling Mercury, possesseth those things which are from animals, and which are compounded of the mixtion of divers natural things together, as cups, and meats; upon this account the heart of a mole,[8] if anyone shall eat it whilst it is warm and panting, conduceth, as it is said, to the foretelling of future events. And Rabbi *Moses* in his commentaries upon Leviticus tells, that there is an animal called יְדוּעַ *Jedua,* having a human shape, in the middle of whose navel comes forth a string, by which it is fastened to the ground like a gourd, and as far as the length of that string reacheth, it devours and consumes all that is green about it, and deceiving the sight, cannot be taken, unless that string be cut off by the stroke of a dart, which being cut off, it presently dies. Now the bones of this animal being after a certain manner laid upon the mouth,[9] presently he whose mouth they are laid on, is taken with a phrensy, and soothsaying.

The third degree answers to the sphere of Venus; this possesseth subtile powders, vapours, and odours, and ointments, and suffumigations, which are made of these of which we have spoke above.

618

The fourth degree belongs to the sphere of the Sun; this possesseth voices, words, singings, and harmonical sounds, by the sweet consonancy whereof it drives forth of the mind any troublesomeness therein, and cheers it up. Whence *Hermes, Pythagoras,*[10] *Plato,* advise us to compose a discontented mind, and cheer it up by singing and harmony. So *Timotheus*[11] is said to have with sounds stirred up King *Alexander* to a phrensy: so the priest of Calame *(Aurelius Augustus*[12] being witness) was wont at his pleasure by a certain shrill harmony to call himself forth out of his body into a rapture, and ecstasy; of these also we have before spoken.

The fifth degree is answerable to Mars: this possesseth vehement imaginations, and affections of the mind, conceits also, and motions thereof, of all which before.

The sixth degree answers to Jupiter: this possesseth the discourses of reason, deliberations, consultations, and moral purgations: of these we have spoken in part above, and further we shall speak afterwards; it possesseth also admirations, and venerations, at the astonishment of which, the phantasy, and reason are sometimes so restrained, that they suddenly let pass all their own actions: whence then the mind itself being free, and exposed to a deity only, whether to any god, or demon, doth receive supernal, and divine influences, viz. those concerning which it did deliberate before. So we read that the sibyls, and the priests of Pythia were wont to receive oracles in the caves of *Jupiter,* and *Apollo.*[13]

The seventh degree resembles Saturn: this possesseth the more secret intelligences, and quiet contemplations of the mind. I call here, the contemplation, the free perspicacity of the mind, suspended with admiration upon the beholding of wisdom. For that excogitation which is made by riddles, and images, is a certain kind of speculation, or discourse belonging to Jupiter, and not a contemplation.

The eighth degree resembles the starry heaven; this observes the situation, motion, rays, and light of the celestial bodies: it possesseth also images, rings, and such like, which are made after the rule of celestials, as we have above spoken.

The ninth degree answers to the primum mobile, viz. the ninth sphere, as the very universe: this possesseth things more formal, as numbers, figures, characters, and observes the occult influences of the intelligences of the heaven, and other mysteries, which because they bear the energies of celestial deities, and invocated spirits, easily allures them, and compelleth them being forced by a certain necessity of conformity to come to one, and detains them, that they shall not easily go back, of which we read in the oracles in *Porphyry:*[14]

> Cease now at length, spare words, to life
> give rest,
> Dissolve, and leave old shapes (I thee
> request),
> Disshape the members, and the winding
> sheet
> Unloose————

And in another place in the same book:

> Ye garlands loose the feet, with water clean
> Let them be sprinkled, and the laurel green
> Be taken off from the hands, and every line
> And character be blotted out————

Of these we have sufficiently treated already, and shall afterwards treat further of them.

Notes—Chapter XLVI

1. *Plato defines*—See Plato *Phaedrus* 244–50.

2. *alligations*—See note 1, ch. XLVI, bk. I.

3. *suspensions*—See note 2, ch. XLVI, bk. I.

4. *selenites*—

Philosophers say, if it be tasted, it giveth knowledge of certain things to come. If it be put under the tongue, specially in the first [day of the] Moon, it hath a virtue only for an hour. Therefore being in the tenth day of the Moon, it hath this virtue in the first or tenth hour. The method of divination is this: when it is under the tongue, if our thought be of any business, whether it ought to be or no, if it ought to be, it is fixed steadfastly in the heart so that it may not be plucked away, if not, the heart leapeth aback from it. *(Book of Secrets* 2.6 [Best and Brightman, 28])

5. *stone of the civet cat*—The hyænia, or hyena stone. See note 3, ch. XXXVIII, bk. I.

6. *vervain*—"The people in the Gallic provinces [druids] make use of them both [male and female vervain] for soothsaying purposes, and for the prediction of future events ..." (Pliny 25.59 [Bostock and Riley, 5:121]).

7. *theangelis*—See note 5, ch. XXXVIII, bk. I.

8. *heart of a mole*—See note 18, ch. LV, bk. I.

9. *laid upon the mouth*—See the commentary of Rashi, note 11, ch. XVI, bk. III.

10. *Pythagoras*—See Iamblichus *On the Mysteries* 2.9, and the accompanying notes by Thomas Taylor.

11. *Timotheus*—See note 14, ch. XXIV, bk. II.

12. *Aurelius Augustus*—Saint Augustine, who was called Aurelius Augustine, although he himself never used Aurelius as a first name, nor was he addressed in this way in the letters written to him. This same reference occurs in ch. L, bk. III. Calamae, or Kalamata, was an ancient town in Greece (present-day Kalamai in Peloponnisos). See note 5, ch. XLVIII, bk. III, where Iamblichus seems to make the same reference.

13. *Jupiter, and Apollo*—The most famous cave of Apollo was located on Mount Parnassus at Delphi, wherein was the Pythia, or priestess of Apollo. The most notable cave of Zeus was on Mount Dicte in eastern Crete, where the god was said to have been raised in concealment from the malice of his father, Cronos.

14. *oracles in Porphyry*—*Porphyrii de philosophia ex oraculis hauriendis,* a commentary on the Chaldean oracles that is preserved in part in the *Præparatio evangelica* of Eusebius.

CHAPTER XLVII

Of the second kind from Dionysus.

Now the second phrensy proceeds from *Dionysus:* this doth by expiations exterior, and interior, and by conjurations, by mysteries, by solemnities, rites, temples, and observations divert the soul into the mind, the supreme part of itself, and makes it a fit and pure temple of the gods, in which the divine spirits may dwell, which the soul then possessing as the associate of life, is filled by them with felicity, wisdom, and oracles, not in signs, and marks, or conjectures, but in a certain concitation[1] of the mind, and free motion: so *Bacchus* did soothsay to the Boeotians,[2] and *Epimenides* to the people of Cous,[3] and the sibyl *Erithea*[4] to the Trojans.[5]

Sometimes this phrensy happens through a clear vision, sometimes by an express voice: so *Socrates* was governed by his demon, whose counsel he did diligently obey, whose voice he did often hear with his ears, to whom also the shape of a demon[6] did often appear. Many prophesying spirits also were wont to show themselves, and be associates with the souls of them that were purified; examples of which there are many in sacred writ, as in *Abraham,* and his bondmaid *Hagar,* in *Jacob, Gideon, Elias, Tobias, Daniel,* and many more.

So *Adam*[7] had familiarity with the angel *Raziel. Shem* the son of *Noah* with *Jophiel; Abraham*[8] with *Zadkiel; Isaac* and *Jacob*[9] with *Peliel; Joseph, Joshua*[10] and *Daniel*[11] with *Gabriel; Moses*[12] with *Metattron; Elias* with *Malbiel; Tobias*[13] the younger with *Raphael; David* with *Cerniel; Mannoah*[14] with *Phadael; Cenez*[15] with *Cerrel; Ezekiel*[16] with *Hasmael; Esdras*[17] with *Uriel; Solomon* with *Michael.*

Sometimes the spirits by virtue of the souls, enter into and seize upon organical bodies, whether of brutes or men, and using the souls thereof as the basis, utter voices through organical instruments, as is manifest in *Baalam's* ass,[18] and in *Saul,*[19] on whom the spirit of the Lord fell, and prophesied. Of these *Apollo* in his answers in *Porphyry*[20] thus:

> Phoebean fulgor charmed, did from on high
> Come down, and through pure air was
>   silently
> Conveyed; came into souls well purified
> With a sonorous breath, a voice uttered
> Through a mortal throat————

Notes—Chapter XLVII

1. *concitation*—Stirring up, or agitation.

2. *to the Boeotians*—Dionysus (Bacchus) was a prophetic god whose oracle at Delphi rivaled in importance that of Apollo. The chief seats of his worship were Boeotia and Attica.

3. *people of Cous*—There seems to be no connection between Epimenides and Cous (see his biographical note). Perhaps Agrippa means Cnossus.

4. *Erithea*—The Erythraean, also called the Cumaean, sibyl, who is fabled to have sold the

Sibylline books to Tarquin the Proud. When the books were destroyed by fire in 83 BC, the Romans had a new collection of 1,000 oracular verses gathered at Erythrae (present-day Cesme, Turkey). These oracles appear to have been first collected in the time of Solon and Cyrus (6th century BC) at Gergis, on Mount Ida in the Troad, which is not far from Troy. They were attributed to the Hellespontine sibyl and kept in the temple of Apollo at Gergis. From Gergis they were carried to Erythrae, from Erythrae to Cumae by the sibyl Herophile, and from Cumae to Rome.

5. *to the Trojans*—This threefold reference by Agrippa was probably inspired by this sentence from Cicero:

> But those men, on the other hand, are devoid of art, who give way to presentiments of future events, not proceeding by reason or conjecture, nor on the observation and consideration of particular signs, but yielding to some excitement of mind, or to some unknown influence subject to no precise rule or restraint, (as is often the case with men who dream, and sometimes with those who deliver predictions in a frenzied manner,) as Bacis of Boeotia, Epimenides the Cretan, and the Erythrean Sibyl. (*De Divinatione* 1.18 [Yonge, 159–60])

6. *shape of a demon*—See note 3, ch. XXII, bk. III.

7. *Adam*—See note 3, ch. XXIV, bk. III.

8. *Abraham*—Presumably refers to Genesis 18, although the angel is not named.

9. *Isaac and Jacob*—Genesis 26:24 and 32:30. Peniel, PNVAL, פנואל, "the face of God."

10. *Joshua*—Joshua was visited by an angel (Joshua 1:1), and in several places it is said "the Lord was with Joshua" (Genesis 39:2, 21, 23), but the angel is not named.

11. *Daniel*—Daniel 8:16 and 9:21.

12. *Moses*—Metatron is identified with the Shekinah, or Holy Spirit, who is with Moses—see notes 19 and 61, ch. X, bk. III.

13. *Tobias*—Tobit 5:4.

14. *Mannoah*—Judges 13:3–21. Again, the name of the angel is not given. See Judges 13:18.

15. *Cenez*—The reference is probably to Kenaz, brother of Caleb, upon whom the spirit of the Lord descended (Judges 3:9–10).

16. *Ezekiel*—Ezekiel 1:26–8.

17. *Esdras*—II Esdras 4:1 and following.

18. *Baalam's ass*—Numbers 22:28.

19. *in Saul*—I Samuel 10:10–3.

20. *in Porphyry*—See note 14, ch. XLVI, bk. III.

CHAPTER XLVIII

Of the third kind of phrensy from Apollo.

Now the third kind of phrensy proceeds from *Apollo,* viz. from the mind of the world. This doth by certain sacred mysteries, vows, sacrifices, adorations, invocations, and certain sacred arts, or certain secret confections, by which the spirits of their god did infuse virtue, make the soul rise above the mind, by joining it with deities, and demons.

So we read concerning the ephod,[1] which being applied, they did presently prophesy: so we read in the books of the Senates in the chapter of *Eleazar,* that Rabbi *Israel* made certain cakes, writ upon with certain divine and angelical names, and so consecrated, which they that did eat with faith, hope, and charity, did presently break forth with a spirit of prophecy. We read in the same place that Rabbi *Johena,* the son of *Jochahad,* did after that manner enlighten a certain rude countryman, called *Eleazar,* being altogether illiterate, that being compassed about with a sudden brightness, did unexpectedly preach such high mysteries of the Law to an assembly of wise men, that he did even astonish all that were near him.

And it is reported of a certain man called *Herviscus,* an Egyptian, that he was endowed with such a divine nature, that at the very sight of images that had any deity in them, he was forthwith stirred up with a kind of divine phrensy.

We read also in the Scripture, that when *Saul* was amongst the prophets, the spirit of the Lord came upon him, and he prophesied, and when he went forth from the assembly of the prophets, he ceased to prophesy;[2] the same happened to those officers which *Saul* sent to catch *David:* who when they saw the company of the prophets, and *Samuel* standing in the midst of them, received the spirit of the Lord on them, and prophesied also.[3] So great is the abounding of divine light oftentimes in the prophets, taken with a divine phrensy, that it also seizeth on them that are near them, and makes them have the same spirit of phrensy.

It is not therefore incredible, that an ignorant man should presently be made wise, and again that a wise man become ignorant: for there is a certain art (known but to few) of informing, adorning, and illustrating a pure mind, so that it should presently be recovered out of the darkness of ignorance, and brought to the light of wisdom: and on the contrary, there is a way by certain hid secrets to make them that have unclean, and unbelieving minds to become ignorant again, although for the present they are learned and wise.

Man's mind also, especially when it is simple, and pure, may *(Apuleius* being witness)[4] by some sacred, and mysterious recreation, and appeasing, be so brought into a sleep, and astonished, that it may forget things present so utterly, as to be brought into its divine nature, and so be enlightened with the divine light, and inspired with a divine phrensy that it may foretell things to come, and withall receive the virtue of some wonderful effects. Whence *Jamblicus* saith, when the prophets are inspired with a deity, they fear nothing, for they go through ways unpassable, and are carried into the fire without any hurt, and pass over rivers.[5]

So we read of certain caves, as of *Apollo*,[6] *Trophonius*,[7] the three-footed stools,[8] dens, fountains, lakes, and such like, that were consecrated to the gods after this manner, or made by that mystery, that from thence the priests might draw the spirit of prophesying, as *Jamblicus* in *Porphyry:*[9] the Sibyl (saith he) in Delphi was wont to receive God after two ways: either by a subtile spirit, and fire, which did break forth somewhere out of the mouth of the cave, where she sitting in the entrance upon a brazen three-footed stool dedicated to a deity, was divinely inspired, and did utter prophesyings; or a great fire flying out of the cave did surround this prophetess, stirring her up, being filled with a deity, to prophesy, which inspiration also she received as she sat upon a consecrated seat, breaking forth presently into predictions.

Moreover there was a prophetess in Branchi[10] which sat upon an ax-tree, and either held a wand in her hand, given to her by some deity, or washed her feet, and sometimes the hem of her garment in the waters, or drew the vapour of fire from the waters. By all these she was filled with divine splendour, and did unfold many oracles.

We also read that in the country of Thracia there was a certain passage[11] consecrated to *Bacchus*, from whence predictions, and oracles were wont to be given: the priors of whose temples having drank wine abundantly did do strange things. Amongst the Clarians also, where the temple of *Clarius Apollo*[12] was, to whom it was given to utter divine things, they having drank much wine did strange things.

There was also a prophetical fountain of Father Achaia,[13] constituted before the temple of *Ceres,* where they that did enquire of the event of the sick did let down a glass by degrees tied to a small cord, to the top of the water, and certain supplications and fumes being made, the event of the thing did appear in the glass.[14]

There was also not far from Epidaurus a city of Laconia, a deep fen, which was called the Water of *Juno*,[15] into which cakes of corn being cast, answers were given, fortunate, if the waters did quietly retain what was cast in; but unhappy, if they did as it were, scorning of them, cast them back. The like they say do the caves of Aetna, into which money or sacrifices did show the same presage of good or ill, by being retained, or rejected.

The like things reports *Dion* in his Roman History, in a place which they call the Nymphs: where frankincense being cast into the flames, oracles were received concerning all those things which he did desire to know, especially concerning death, and those things which belonged to marriages.

Wonderful also is that which *Aristotle* relates of a certain fountain of the Paliscans of Sicilia,[16] to which they that did take an oath did go, and whatsoever they did affirm upon oath writ it upon tables, which they cast into the fountain. If those things were true, the tables would swim; if false, sink; then fire coming suddenly forth burned him that was perjured into ashes.

There was also in the city Dodona an oak,[17] which as soon as anyone entered in to receive an answer, did forthwith move, and make a sound; there was also a statue holding a wand, which did strike a basin, whereby the basin made answer by moderated strokes. Whence it is read in the epistle of *Austinus* to *Paulinus:*[18]

Answers did give the Dodonean brass,
With moderated strokes; so docile it was.

Noтes—Chapтeя XLVIII

1. *ephod*—The vestment of a Jewish priest. It was of linen, sleeveless, slit at the sides under the armpits, fastened with buckles at the shoulders and girdled at the waist. The colours of the ephod of the high priest were gold, purple and scarlet. David used it to prophesy. See I Samuel 23:9–11; 30:7–8.

2. *ceased to prophesy*—See note 19, ch. XLVII, bk. III.

3. *prophesied also*—I Samuel 19:20.

4. *Apuleius being witness*—After bathing himself

seven times in the ocean, Apuleius invokes the Goddess with prayer: "When I had ended this orison, and discovered my plaints to the Goddesse, I fortuned to fall asleepe, and by and by appeared unto me a divine and venerable face, worshiped even of the Gods themselves" *(The Golden Asse* ch. 47). The Goddess foretells the future of Apuleius.

On the subject of prophetic sleep, Iamblichus writes:

> But the dreams which are denominated *theopemptoi,* or *sent from God,* do not subsist after the manner which you mention; but they take place either when sleep is leaving us, and we are beginning to awake, and then we hear a certain voice, which concisely tells us what is to be done; or voices are heard by us, between sleeping and waking, or when we are perfectly awake. And sometimes, indeed, an invisible and incorporeal spirit surrounds the recumbents, so as not to be perceived by the sight, but by a certain other cosensation and intelligence. The entrance of this spirit, also, is accompanied with a noise, and he diffuses himself on all sides without any contact, and effects admirable works conducive to the liberation of the passions of the soul and body. But sometimes a bright and tranquil light shines forth, by which the sight of the eyes is detained, and which occasions them to become closed, though they were before open. The other senses, however, are in a vigilant state, and in a certain respect have a cosensation of the light unfolded by the Gods; and the recumbents hear what the Gods say, and know, by a consecutive perception, what is then done by them. This, however, is beheld in a still more perfect manner, when the sight perceives, when intellect, being corroborated, follows what is performed, and this is accompanied with the motion of the spectators. Such, therefore, and so many being the differences of these dreams, no one of them is similar to human dreams. (Iamblichus *On the Mysteries* 3.2 [Taylor, 115–6])

5. *pass over rivers*—

> Many, through divine inspiration, are not burned when fire is introduced to them, the inspiring influence preventing the fire from touching them. Many, also, though burned, do not apprehend that they are so, because they do not live an animal life. And some, indeed, though transfixed with spits, do not perceive it; but others that are

struck on the shoulders with axes, and others that have their arms cut with knives, are by no means conscious of what is done to them. Their energies, likewise, are not at all human. For inaccessible places become accessible to those that are divinely inspired; they are thrown into fire, and pass through fire, and over rivers, like the priest in Castabalis, without being injured. (ibid. 3.4 [Taylor, 122])

6. *Apollo*—See note 13, ch. XLVI, bk. III.

7. *Trophonius*—Trophonius was son of Erginus, king of Orchomenus. Along with his brother Agamedes he is credited in legend with building the temple at Delphi, a magnificent structure. After his death he was worshiped as a hero, and had a celebrated oracle of his own in a cave near Lebadea in Boeotia (just west of present-day Lake Voiviis). For a fascinating first-hand account of the oracle of Trophonius, see Pausanias *Guide to Greece* 9.39.4. Pausanias not only saw the oracle but actually underwent the involved ritual procedure in consulting it.

8. *three-footed stools*—The priestess at Delphi sat on a tripod—a three-legged stool—over a fissure in the cave of Apollo from which arose intoxicating fumes. Although it is seldom explicitly stated, the reason was that the fumes were believed to enter her, not by the throat, but through the womb.

9. *Jamblicus in Porphyry*—

> But the prophetess in Delphi, whether she gives oracles to mankind through an attenuated and fiery spirit, bursting from the mouth of the cavern, or whether being seated in the adytum on a brazen tripod, or on a stool with four feet, she becomes sacred to the God; whichsoever of these is the case, she entirely gives herself up to a divine spirit, and is illuminated with a ray of divine fire. And when, indeed, fire ascending from the mouth of the cavern circularly invests her in collected abundance, she becomes filled from it with a divine splendour. (Iamblichus, *On the Mysteries* 3.11 [Taylor, 143])

The premise of this work is that it is a reply given by Iamblichus to Porphyry to questions raised in Porphyry's *Letter to Anebo,* which prefaces *On the Mysteries*—thus Agrippa's reference to Porphyry.

10. *prophetess in Branchi*—

> The prophetic woman too in Brandchidae, whether she holds in her hand a wand,

which was at first received from some God, and becomes filled with a divine splendour, or whether seated on an axis, she predicts future events, or dips her feet or the border of her garment in the water, or receives the God by imbibing the vapours of the water; by all these she becomes adapted to partake externally of the God. (ibid. [Taylor, 144])

It is worth looking at the Wheel of Fortune card in the Visconti-Sforza Tarocchi Deck in light of the above description.

11. *certain passage*—Thrace was the chief seat of the worship of Dionysus, and it is probable the god was introduced from Thrace into Greece. The Thracian oracle of Dionysus (whom the Thracians called Bacchus) was located in a fissure, or cave, on one of the highest summits of the Rhodope Mountains (southern Bulgaria).

12. *Clarius Apollo*—Clarus was a small town on the Ionian coast, near Colophon (not far from Ephesus), famous only for its temple and oracle of Apollo, who was surnamed Clarius on its account. See Iamblichus *On the Mysteries* 2.10 (Taylor, 141–2).

13. *Father Achaia*—Patrai in Achaia (present-day Patrai, Greece).

14. *appear in the glass*—

There is a spring in front of Demeter's sanctuary with a dry stone wall on the temple side and a way down to the spring on the outer side. There is an infallible oracle here, not for all purposes but for the sick. They tie a mirror onto some thin kind of cord, and balance it so as not to dip it into the spring, but let the surface of the mirror just touch lightly on the water. Then they pray to the goddess and burn incense and look into the mirror, and it shows them the sick man either alive or dead. (Pausanias *Guide to Greece* 7.21.5 [Levi, 1:283–4]).

Levi believes this is the spring presently at the church of St. Andrew beside the cathedral of Patrai.

15. *Water of Juno*—

About a quarter of a mile farther on to the right is Ino's water, as they call it, the size of a small lake only that it goes deeper; they throw loaves of barley bread into this water at Ino's festival. When the water accepts the loaves and keeps them it means a good omen for whoever threw them in, but if it sends them up to the surface again, this is accepted to be a terribly bad sign. (ibid. 3.23.8 [Levi, 2:87–8])

Levi says a small pool was discovered in recent times about a quarter of a mile from the acropolis at Epidaurus that is more than 100 feet deep. Ino was the mortal daughter of Cadmus who bore two illegitimate children to Athamas. When Athamas was driven mad by the gods for his infidelity, Ino threw herself into the sea and was transformed into the goddess Leucothea. Agrippa has confused Ino with Juno.

16. *Paliscans of Sicilia*—At Palice in Sicily (southwest of present-day Lentini) were two sulfurous fountains called Deilloi that were sacred to the Palici, twin brother gods born of Zeus and the nymph Thalia, who was the daughter of Vulcan. In early times human sacrifices were offered to the gods. In classical times their sanctuary became the asylum for runaway slaves. Oaths were written on tablets and thrown into one of the two springs. If the tablets floated, the oaths were considered true; if they sank, the oaths were looked upon as lies and the oath-takers punished with blindness or death.

17. *Dodona an oak*—It is very uncertain how the oracle through brass was received in the sacred grove of Zeus at Dodona. There seems to have been a circle of vessels placed or hung from trees around the temple. The blowing of the wind caused these to sound with mellow tones. Perhaps light wands were hung in such a way as to strike against the brass vessels or gongs when moved by the breeze between the oaks. Or perhaps statues holding wands were placed near the gently swinging brass, which was moved by the wind in the boughs of the sacred oaks, the vessels being suspended from their limbs.

18. *Austinus to Paulinus*—The letter of Ausonius Decimus Magnus to Meropius Pontius Anicius Paulinus. See their separate biographical notes.

CHAPTER XLIX

Of the fourth kind of phrensy, from Venus.

Now the fourth kind of phrensy proceeds from *Venus,* and it doth by a fervent love convert, and transmute the mind to God, and makes it altogether like to God, as it were the proper image of God; whence *Hermes* saith:[1] O *Asclepius!* Man is a great miracle, an animal to be honoured and adored; for he passeth into the nature of God, whereby he becomes God: he knows the rise of demons, and he knows himself to have his original with them, despising the part of his human nature in himself, having a sure confidence of the divinity of the other; the soul therefore being converted, and made like to God, is so formed of God, that it doth above all intellect, know all things by a certain essential contract of divinity: therefore *Orpheus* describes love to be without eyes,[2] because it is above the intellect.

Now then the soul being so converted into God by love, and sublimated above the intellectual sphere, doth beside that it hath by its integrity obtained the spirit of prophecy, sometimes work wonderful things, and greater than the nature of the world can do, which works are called miracles. For as the heaven by its image, light, and heat, doth those things, which the force of the fire cannot do by its natural quality (which in alchemy[3] is most known by experience), so also doth God by the image and light of himself do those things, which the world cannot do by its innate virtue.

Now the image of God is man, at least such a man that by a phrensy from *Venus* is made like to God, and lives by the mind only, and receives God into himself. Yet the soul of man according to the Hebrew doctors and Cabalists, is defined to be the light of God, and created after the image of the Word, the cause of causes, the first example, and the substance of God, figured by a seal whose character is the eternal Word.[4] Which *Mercurius Trismegistus* considering, saith, that such a man is more excellent than they that are in heaven, or at least equal to them.[5]

Notes—Chapter XLIX

1. *Hermes saith*—See *Asclepius* 1.6a (Scott, 1:295).

2. *without eyes*—An observation echoed by Chaucer ("The Marchantes Tale," line 1598) and Shakespeare (*Merchant of Venice,* act 2, sc. 6, line 36).

3. *in alchemy*—"O those celestial natures, multiplying the natures of truth by the will of God! O that potent Nature, which overcame and conquered natures, and caused its natures to rejoice and be glad! This, therefore, is that special and spiritual nature to which the God thereof can give what fire cannot" (*Turba Philosophorum* 11 [Waite, (1896) 1976, 35]).

4. *eternal Word*—This applies more to the archetypal soul of Adam, which comprehends all other souls within it, than to individual human souls. The Word is IHVH. The seal is the interlocking hexagram.

5. *equal to them*—"Nay, if we are to speak the truth without fear, he who is indeed a man is even above the gods of heaven, or at any rate he equals them in power" *(Corpus Hermeticum* 10.24b [Scott, 1:205])

> Willing then that man should be at once a thing of earth and capable of immortality, God compacted him of these two substances, the one divine, the other mortal; and in that he is thus compacted, it is ordained by God's will that man is not only better than all mortal beings, but also better than the gods, who are made wholly of immortal substance. *(Asclepius* 3:22b [Scott, 1:337])

CHAPTER L

OF rapture, and ecstasy, and soothsayings, which happen to them which are taken with the falling sickness, or with a swoon, or to them in an agony.

A rapture is an abstraction, and alienation, and an illustration of the soul proceeding from God, by which God doth again retract the soul, being fallen from above to hell, from hell to heaven. The cause of this is in us a continual contemplation of sublime things, which as far as it conjoins with a most profound intention of the mind, the soul to incorporeal wisdom, doth so far recall itself with its vehement agitations from things sensible and the body, and (as *Plato* saith) in such a manner sometimes, that it even flyeth out of the body, and seemeth as it were dissolved: even as *Aurelius Austin* reporteth concerning a priest of Calamia;[1] (of whom we have made mention before) he lay (saith he) most like unto a dead man, without breath; and when he was burnt with fire and wounded, he felt it not.

So great therefore is the command of the soul: viz. when it hath obtained its own nature, and is not oppressed by the allurements of the senses, that by its own power it suddenly ascendeth, not only remaining in the body, but even sometimes loosed from its fetters, and flyeth forth of the body to the supercelestial habitations, where now it being most nigh, and most like to God, and made the receptacle of divine things, it is filled with the divine light and oracles.

Whence *Zoroastes* saith,[2] thou must ascend to the light itself, and to the beams of the Father, whence thy soul was sent thee, clothed with very much mind; and *Trismegistus* saith,[3] it is necessary that thou ascend above the heavens, and be far from the quire of spirits; and *Pythagoras* saith,[4] if thou by leaving the body shalt pass into the spacious heavens, thou shalt be an immortal god.

So we read that *Hermes, Socrates, Xenocrates, Plato, Plotine,*[5] *Heraclitus, Pythagoras* and *Zoroastes,* were wont to abstract themselves by rapture, and so to learn the knowledge of many things: also we read in *Herodotus,* that there was in Proconnesus a philosopher of wonderful knowledge, called *Atheus,*[6] whose soul sometimes went out of the body, and after the visitation of places far remote, returned again into the body more learned. *Pliny* reporteth the same thing, that the soul of *Harman Clazomenius*[7] was wont to wander abroad, his body being left, and to bring true tidings of things very far off.

And there are even to this day in Norway and Lapland[8] very many who can abstract themselves three whole days from their body, and being returned declare many things which are afar off; and in the meantime it is necessary to keep them, that not any living creature come upon them or touch them; otherwise they report that they cannot return into their body.

Therefore we must know, that (according to the doctrine of the Egyptians), seeing the soul is a certain spiritual light, when it is loosed from the body, it comprehendeth every place and time, in such a manner as a light enclosed in a lantern, which being open, diffuseth itself everywhere, and faileth not anywhere, for it is everywhere, and continually; and *Cicero* in his book Of Divination saith, neither doth the soul of man at any time divine, except when it is so loosed that it hath indeed little or nothing to do with the body;[9] when therefore it shall attain to that state, which is the supreme degree of contemplative perfection, then it is rapt from all created species, and understandeth not by acquired species, but by the inspection of the Ideas, and it knoweth all things by the light of the Ideas: of which light *Plato* saith few men are partakers in this life; but in the hands of the gods, all.[10]

Also they who are troubled with the syncope[11] and falling sickness, do in some manner imitate a rapture, and in these sicknesses sometimes as in a rapture do bring forth prophecy,[12] in which kind of prophesying we read that *Hercules*[13] and many Arabians were very excellent.

And there are certain kinds of soothsayings, which are a middle betwixt the confines of natural predictions, and supernatural oracles, viz. which declare things to come from some excess of passion, as too much love, sorrow, or amongst frequent sighs, or in the agony of death, as in *Statius,* of the mother of *Achilles:*[14]

————————nor she without parents dear
Under the glassy gulf the oars did fear.

For there is in our minds a certain perspicuous power, and capable of all things, but encumbered and hindered by the darkness of the body and mortality, but after death it having acquired immortality, and being freed from the body, it hath a full and perfect knowledge. Hence it cometh to pass, that they who are nigh to death, and weakened by old age, have sometimes somewhat of an unaccustomed light, because the soul being less hindered by the senses, understandeth very acutely, and being now as it were a little relaxed from its bands, is not altogether subject to the body, and being as it were nigher to the place, to the which it is about to go, it easily perceiveth revelations, which being mixed with its agonies, are then offered to it.

Whence *Ambrose* in his book of the Belief of the Resurrection, saith, which being free in the aerial motion, knoweth not whither it goeth, and whence it cometh; yet we know that it surviveth the body, and that it being freed, the chains of its senses being cast off, freely discerneth those things which it saw not before, being in the body, which we may estimate by the example of those who sleep, whose mind being quiet, their bodies being as it were buried, do elevate themselves to higher things, and do declare to the body the visions of things absent, yea even of celestial things.

Notes—Chapter L

1. *priest of Calamia*—See note 12, ch. XLVI, bk. III.

2. *Zoroastes saith*—"It becometh you to hasten unto the Light, and to the Rays of the Father, from whom was sent unto you a Soul (Psyche) endued with much mind (Nous)" *(Chaldean Oracles* 160 [Westcott, 58]).

3. *Trismegistus saith*—

And thereupon, having been stripped of all that was wrought upon him by the structure of the heavens, he ascends to the substance of the eighth sphere, being now possessed of his own proper power; and he sings, together with those who dwell there, hymning the Father; and they that are there rejoice with him at his coming. And being made like to those with whom he dwells, he hears the Powers, who are above the substance of the eighth sphere, singing praises

to God with a voice that is theirs alone. And thereafter, each in his turn, they mount upward to the Father; they give themselves up to the Powers, and becoming Powers themselves, they enter into God. (*Corpus Hermeticum* 1.26a [Scott, 129])

You see, my son, through how many bodily things in succession we have to make our way, and through how many troops of daemons and courses of stars, that we may press on to the one and only God. (ibid. 4.8b [Scott, 155])

4. *Pythagoras saith*—

But observe my laws, abstaining from the things
Which thy soul must fear, distinguishing them well;

Letting intelligence o'er thy body reign;
So that, ascending into the radiant Ether,
Midst the Immortals, thou shalt be thyself a
    God.
(*Golden Verses of Pythagoras,* French trans.
Fabre d'Olivet [1813], English trans. from
French by Nayan Louise Redfield [1917]
[New York: Samuel Weiser, 1975], 9)

5. *Plotine*—

Many times it has happened: Lifted out of
the body into myself; becoming external to
all other things and self-encentered;
beholding a marvellous beauty; then, more
than ever, assured of community with the
loftiest order; enacting the noblest life,
acquiring identity with the divine; station-
ing within It by having attained that activity; poised above whatsoever within the
Intellectual is less than the Supreme: yet,
there comes the moment of descent from
intellection to reasoning, and after that
sojourn in the divine, I ask myself how it
happens that I can now be descending, and
how did the soul ever enter into my body,
the soul which, even within the body, is the
high thing it has shown itself to be. (Plotinus *Enneads* 4.8.1 [Mackenna 3:143])

6. *Atheus*—

Aristeas also, son of Caustrobius, a native
of Proconnesus, says in the course of his
poem that rapt in Bacchic fury he went as
far as the Issedones. ... I will now relate a
tale which I heard concerning him both at
Proconnesus and at Cyzicus. Aristeas, they
said, who belonged to one of the noblest
families in the island, had entered one day
into a fuller's shop, when he suddenly
dropt down dead. Hereupon the fuller shut
up his shop, and went to tell Aristeas' kindred what had happened. The report of the
death had just spread through the town,
when a certain Cyzicenian, lately arrived
from Artaca [Erdek], contradicted the
rumour, affirming that he had met Aristeas
on his road to Cyzicus, and had spoken
with him. This man, therefore, strenuously
denied the rumour; the relations, however,
proceeded to the fuller's shop with all
things necessary for the funeral, intending
to carry the body away. But on the shop
being opened, no Aristeas was found,
either dead or alive. Seven years afterwards he reappeared, they told me, in Proconnesus, and wrote the poem called by the
Greeks "The Arimaspeia," after which he

disappeared a second time. (Herodotus
History 4 [Rawlinson, 209])

Pliny contributes this colorful detail: "It is stated
also, that in Proconnesus, the soul of Aristeas was
seen to fly out of his mouth, under the form of a
raven ..." (Pliny 7.53 [Bostock and Riley, 2:210–1]).

7. *Harman Clazomenius*—

With reference to the soul of man, we find,
among other instances, that the soul of Her-
motinus of Clazomenae was in the habit of
leaving his body, and wandering into distant countries, whence it brought back
numerous accounts of various things, which
could not have been obtained by any one
but a person who was present. The body, in
the meantime, was left apparently lifeless.
At last, however, his enemies, the Canthari-
dae, as they were called, burned his body,
so that the soul, on its return, was deprived
of its sheath, as it were. (ibid., 210)

Such was the soul of Hermodorus the Clazomenian, of which it is reported that for
several nights and days it would leave his
body, travel over many countries, and
return after it had viewed things and discoursed with persons at a great distance; til
at last, by the treachery of his wife, his
body was delivered to his enemies, and
they burnt the house while the inhabitant
was abroad. It is certain, this is a mere
fable. The soul never went out of the body,
but it loosened the tie that held the Daemon, and permitted it to wander; so that
this, seeing and hearing the various external occurrences, brought in the news to it
... (Plutarch *On the Sign of Socrates* 22,
trans. Creech [Goodwin, 2:411])

With regard to the case of Hermotimus,
they say that he used to be deprived of his
soul in his sleep, as if it wandered away
from his body like a person on a holiday
trip. His wife betrayed the strange peculiarity. His enemies, finding him asleep, burnt
his body, as if it were a corpse: when his
soul returned too late, it appropriated (I
suppose) to itself the guilt of the murder.
However the good citizens of Clazomenae
consoled poor Hermotimus with a temple,
into which no woman ever enters, because
of the infamy of this wife. (Tertullian *A
Treatise On the Soul* (De anima) 44 [*Ante-
Nicene Fathers*, 3:223])

8. *Norway and Lapland*—The reference here is to
shamanism, a prominent feature of which is astral

travel, or soul flight. The myth of Odin exhibits many shamanic aspects: "His body lay as though he were asleep or dead, and he then became a bird or a beast, a fish or a dragon, and went in an instant to far-off lands ..." (Snorri Sturluson "Ynglinga Saga." In *Heimskringka,* trans. Erling Monson [Cambridge, 1932], 5, as quoted by Eliade [1951] 1972, 381). Elsewhere Eliade writes:

> What concerns us in this instance is the fact that sorcerers and shamans are able, *here on earth* and *as often as they wish,* to accomplish "coming out of the body," that is, the death that alone has power to transform the rest of mankind into "birds;" shamans and sorcerers can enjoy the condition of "souls," of "discarnate beings," which is accessible to the profane only when they die. (Eliade [1951] 1972, 479).

9. *with the body*—"The mind of man, however, never exerts the power of natural divination, unless when it is so free and disengaged as to be wholly disentangled from the body, as happens in the case of prophets and sleepers" (Cicero *De Divinatione* 1.50 [Yonge, 191]). The English edition of the *Occult Philosophy* omits the word "unless" from its free translation of Cicero, which inverts the meaning of the passage. I have corrected this error.

10. *of the gods, all*—See Socrates' dream of the cave, Plato *Republic* 7.514–9.

11. *syncope*—A suspension of the action of the heart; a suspension of vitality.

12. *bring forth prophecy*—See notes 1 and 2, ch. LX, bk. I. See also Aristotle's *Problems* 30.

13. *Hercules*—The Orphic hymn to Hercules calls the hero "in divination skilled." *(Hymns of Orpheus* 11 [*Thomas Taylor the Platonist: Selected Writings,* 226]).

14. *of Achilles*—Perhaps from the *Achilleis.* See biographical note on Statius.

CHAPTER LI

Of prophetical dreams.

Now I call that a dream, which proceedeth either from the spirit of the phantasy and intellect united together, or by the illustration of the agent intellect above our souls, or by the true revelation of some divine power in a quiet and purified mind; for by this our soul receiveth true oracles, and abundantly yieldeth prophecies to us.

For in dreams we seem both to ask questions, and learn to read and find them out; also many doubtful things, many policies, many things unknown, and unwished for, nor ever attempted by our minds, are manifested to us in dreams; also the representations of unknown places appear, and the images of men both alive and dead, and of things to come are foretold; and also things which at any times have happened, are revealed, which we knew not by any report; and these dreams need not any art of interpretation, as those of which we have spoken in the first book, which belong to divination, not foreknowledge.

And it cometh to pass that they who see these dreams for the most part understand them not; for (as *Abdala* the Arabian saith) as to see dreams, is from the strength of imagination, so to understand them, is from the strength of understanding; whose intellect therefore, being overwhelmed by the too much commerce of the flesh, is in a dead sleep, or its imaginative or phantastic spirit is too dull and unpolished, that it cannot receive the species and representations which flow from the superior intellect, and retain them when received, this man is altogether unfit for the soothsaying by dreams.

Therefore it is necessary, that he who would receive true dreams, should keep a pure, undisturbed, and an undisquieted imaginative spirit, and so compose it, that it may be made worthy of the knowledge and government by the mind and understanding: for such a spirit is most fit for prophesying, and (as *Sinesius* saith) is a most clear glass of all the images which flow everywhere from all things.

When therefore we are sound in body, not disturbed in mind, not dulled by meat or drink, nor sad through poverty, nor provoked by any vice of lust or wrath, but chastly going to bed, fall asleep, then our pure and divine soul being loosed from all hurtful thoughts, and now freed by dreaming, is endowed with this divine spirit as an instrument, and doth receive those beams and representations which are darted down, and shine forth from the divine mind into itself; and as it were in a deifying glass, it doth far more certainly, clearly, and efficaciously behold all things, than by the vulgar inquiry of the intellect, and by the discourse of reason; the divine power instructing the soul, being invited to their society by the opportunity of the nocturnal solitariness; neither further will that deity be wanting to him when he is awaked, which ruleth all his actions.

Whosoever therefore doth, by quiet and religious meditation, and by a diet temperate and moderated according to nature, preserve his spirit pure, doth very much prepare himself, that by this means he may become divine, and knowing all things; but whosoever, on the contrary, doth languish with a phantastic spirit, receiveth not perspicuous and distinct visions, but even as the divine sight, by reason of its weakness, judgeth confusedly and indistinctly; and also when we are overcome with wine and drunkenness, then our spirit being oppressed with noxious vapours (as a troubled water is wont to appear in divers forms) is deceived and waxeth dull.

For which cause *Amphiarus* the prophet (as we read in *Philostratus)* commanded those, who would receive oracles, to abstain one whole day from meat, and three days from wine, that the soul could not rightly prophesy unless it were free from wine, and meat; for to sober and religious minds, attending on the divine worship, the gods are wont to give oracles; whence *Orpheus* crieth out:[1]

> ———————thou spirit great of prophecy
> Dost go to souls that sleep full quietly,
> And them inspire with knowledge of the
> gods,
> And makest them soothsay————

Hence it was a custom amongst the ancients, that they who should receive answers, certain sacred expiations and sacrifices being first celebrated, and divine worship ended, did religiously lie down even in a consecrated chamber, or at least on the skins of the sacrifices; of which ceremony *Virgil* makes mention[2] in these verses:

> ———————hence they sought
> Answers to doubts, when gifts the priests
> had brought,
> Here he reposed on skins of slaughtered
> sheep,
> And under silent night prepares to sleep.

And a little after he singeth:[3]

> ———————but now
> Here King Latinus oracles to know,
> They did a hundred choice sheep sacrifice,
> And on their skins, and spreading fleeces lies

And the rulers of the Lacedemonians (as *Cicero* saith)[4] were wont to lie down in the temple at Pasiphae, that they might dream. The same was done in the temple of *Aesculapius,*[5] from whom true dreams were thought to be sent forth. And Calabrians, consulting *Podalyrius*[6] the son of *Aesculapius,* did sleep near his sepulchre in lambs' skins; for so doing they were told in their dreams whatsoever they desired to know.

For the most usual time for dreams is the night, when the senses are freed from wandering objects, and meridian errors,[7] and vain affections; neither doth fear strike the mind, nor the thought tremble, and the mind being most quiet, doth steadfastly adhere to the deity.

For there are (as Rabbi *Johenan* in his book of Senators saith) four kinds of true dreams: the first matutine, which is made betwixt sleep and awaking: the second, which one seeth concerning another: the third, whose interpretation is shown to the same dreamer in the nocturnal vision: the fourth, which is repeated to the same dreamer, according to that which *Joseph* saith to Pharaoh,[8] but that thou hast seen the dream belonging to the same thing the second time, it is a sign of confirmation. But that dream is most sure which is concerning those things which one did meditate on, and revolve in his mind, when he goeth to bed, as it is written, thou O King didst think upon thy bed, what should become of these things.

But it is necessary, that he which interpreteth other men's dreams, hath the knowledge by the which he can distinguish and discern the similitudes of all things, and know the customs of all nations, according to the laws which they have received from God and his angels; further this must be known, that there is scarce any dream without some vanity, as no grain of corn without his chaff, which thing even the dream of *Joseph* the Patriarch manifesteth; which his father *Jacob* interpreted,[9] saying: what meaneth this dream, that thou hast seen? What, shall I, and thy mother, and thy brethren fall down and worship thee? Which effect concerning his mother, who shortly after died, followed not.

Also Rabbi *Johenan* in the forecited book, saith these things; and also Rabbi *Levi* affirmeth, that no prophetical dream can be kept back from his effect longer than twenty-two years;[10] so *Joseph* dreamed in the seventeenth year of his age, which was accomplished in the thirty-ninth year of his age.

Therefore whosoever would receive divine dreams, let him be well disposed in body, his brain free from vapours, and his mind from perturbations, and let him that day abstain from supper, neither let him drink that which will inebriate, let him have a clean and neat chamber, also exorcised and consecrated: in the which, a perfume being made, his temples anointed, things causing dreams being put on his fingers,[11]

and the representation of the heavens being put under his head,[12] and paper being consecrated, his prayers being said, let him go to bed, earnestly meditating on that thing he desireth to know: so he shall see most true and certain dreams with the true illumination of his intellect.

Whosoever therefore shall know to join together those things which here and there we have delivered concerning this matter in these books, he shall easily obtain the gift of oracles and dreams.

Notes—Chapter LI

1. *Orpheus crieth out—*

Thee I invoke, blest power of dreams divine,
Angel of future fates, swift wings are thine:
Great source of oracles to human kind,
When stealing soft, and whisp'ring to the mind,
Thro' sleep's sweet silence and the gloom of night,
Thy pow'r awake the intellectual sight;
To silent souls the will of heav'n relates,
And silently reveals their future fates.
("To the Divinity of Dreams." In *Hymns of Orpheus* 85 [*Thomas Taylor the Platonist: Selected Writings*, 290])

2. *Virgil makes mention—*

Hither the priest brings his gifts, and as silent night draws on, lies on a bed of skins and woos sleep; then he sees many phantoms flitting in wonderous wise, and hears manifold voices, and enjoys the converse of the gods, and addresses the powers of Acheron let loose through deep Avernus. Here too at this time father Latinus, coming for oracular response, offered in due form an hundred woolly sheep, and lay raised on their skins and on a bed of fleeces ... (Virgil *Aeneid* 7, c. line 90 [Lonsdale and Lee, 179])

3. *little after he singeth—*See note 2 above.

4. *Cicero saith—*

Moreover, the Spartan magistrates, not content with a careful superintendence of the state affairs, went occasionally to spend a night in the temple of Pasiphae,

which is in the country in the neighbourhood of their city, for the sake of dreaming there, because they considered the oracles received in sleep to be true. (Cicero *De Divinatione* 1.43 [Yonge, 184])

Pasiphae was daughter of Helios and wife of Minos.

5. *temple of Aesculapius*—See note 2, ch. VII, bk. III.

6. *Podalyrius*—Podalirius was the son of Aesculapius and Epione (or Arsinoe), and the brother of Marchaon. He led the Thessalians against Troy. Returning from the war, he was cast by storm onto the coast of Syros in Caria, where he practiced his miraculous and healing arts (see Pausanias *Guide to Greece* 3.26.10). Apart from legend, nothing is known of Syros (or Syrnos). It is not to be confused with the island of Syros (or Syrus) in the Aegean Sea (present-day Siros).

7. *meridian errors*—Midday, or waking errors.

8. *saith to Pharaoh*—Genesis 41:32.

9. *Jacob interpreted*—Genesis 37:10.

10. *twenty-two years*—There are 22 letters in the Hebrew alphabet, making it a mystical number of completion or totality.

11. *put on his fingers*—Presumably stones or other substances set in rings, or symbols inscribed on rings.

12. *under his head*—Perhaps an astrological chart for that particular night drawn on consecrated paper; or the chart of a genius or spirit—see ch. xxvi, bk. III.

CHAPTER LII

Of lots and marks
possessing the sure power of oracles.

There are also certain lots having a divine power of oracles, and as it were indices of divine judgement, being before sought for by earnest prayer, and sometimes commanded by God himself to be done, as is read in Leviticus concerning a goat to be offered to the Lord, and of the scapegoat;[1] and in the book of Numbers of the rods of the tribes[2] of Israel.

Now both *Moses*[3] and *Joshua*[4] did by lots in the presence of the Lord divide the lands, and inheritances to the tribes of Israel according to the command of God. The apostles of Christ, prayers going before, did by lot choose *Matthias*[5] into the place of *Judas* the traitor. *Jonas* the prophet when he flying from the presence of God did sail to Tharsus, a dangerous storm being raised, was by lot found out by the mariners to be the cause of the danger, and being cast into the sea, the tempest ceased.[6]

Caesar reports[7] of *M. Valerius Procillus*, being taken by his enemies, concerning whom it was consulted whether he should be presently burnt, or reserved to another time, that by lot he escaped safe. There was formerly at Bura, a town of Achaia, an oracle of *Hercules*[8] constituted by a chessboard, where he that went to consult of anything, after he had prayed, cast four dice, the cast of which the prophet observing, did find written in the chessboard what should come to pass: now all such dice were made of the bones of sacrifices.

Now this you must know, that the ancients were not wont upon every slight cause to cast lots, but either upon necessity, or for some advantageous end, and that not but with great devotion, reverence, expiations, fasting, purity, prayers, invocations, vows, sacrifices, consecrations, and such like sacred mysteries of religion. For these sacred ordinances were wont to go before our works, especially to procure the divine good will, and pleasure, and the presence of the divine spirits, by whose dispensation the lot being directed, we may receive a true judgement of the things sought for.

Everyone therefore that works by lots, must go about it with a mind well disposed, not troubled, nor distracted, and with a strong desire, firm deliberation, and constant intention of knowing that which shall be desired. Moreover he must, being qualified with purity, chastity, and holiness towards God, and the celestials, with an undoubted hope, firm faith, and sacred orations, invocate them, that he may be made worthy of receiving the divine spirits, and knowing the divine pleasure; for if thou shalt be qualified, they will discover to thee most great secrets by virtue of lots, and thou shalt become a true prophet, and able to speak truth concerning things past, present, and to come, of which thou shalt be demanded.

Now what we have spoken here concerning lots, is also to be observed in the auguries of all discernings, viz. when with fear, yet with a firm expectation we prefix to our souls for the sake of prophesying some certain works, or require a sign, as *Eleazar,*[9] *Abraham's* countryman, and *Gideon,*[10] judge in Israel, are read to have done.

There was once at Pharis, a city of Achaia, in the middle of the market a statue of *Mercury,* where he that went to receive any omen, did, frankincense being fumed, and candles being lighted, which were set before it, and that country's coin being offered on the right hand of the statue, whisper into the right ear of the statue whatsoever he would demand, and presently his ears being stopped with both his hands, did make haste away from the marketplace, which when he was past, did presently his ears being opened, observe the first voice he did hear from any man for a certain oracle given to him.[11]

Although therefore these kinds of lots seem to the ignorant to be casual, or fortuitous, and to have nothing of reason in them, yet they are disposed by God, and the higher virtues by certain reasons, neither they do fall beside the intention of him that moderates them. Was not the lot in choosing *Saul*[12] to be king of Israel, thought to fall upon him casually, and fortuitously? Yet he was before appointed by the Lord to be king, and anointed by the prophet *Samuel.* And God that appointed him king, disposed of the lot that it should fall upon him. And thus much of these.

Notes—Chapter LII

1. *scapegoat*—Leviticus 16:8.

2. *rods of the tribes*—Numbers 17:2–5.

3. *Moses*—Numbers 26:55.

4. *Joshua*—Joshua 13:6.

5. *Matthias*—Acts 1:26.

6. *tempest ceased*—Jonah 1:7–15.

7. *Caesar reports*—Julius Caesar, writing of Gaius Valerius Procillus: "Procillus recounted how, before his very eyes, the Germans had three times cast lots to decide whether he should be burnt to death at once or reserved for execution later, and how he owed his life to the way the lots had fallen" (Caesar *Conquest of Gaul* 2.2, trans. S. A. Handford [1951] [Harmondsworth: Penguin Books, 1967], 73). Earlier in the same chapter Caesar says that the German women cast lots to decide on a suitable time for battle. These lots were probably runes.

8. *oracle of Hercules*—

> On the way down from Boura towards the sea is the Boura river, with a small Herakles in a grotto called the Boura Herakles, who gives oracles with a board and dice. To consult the god you pray in front of the statue, and then take dice (Herakles has an enormous number of dice) and throw four on the table. For every throw of the dice there is an interpretation written on the board. (Pausanias *Guide to Greece* 7.25.6 [Levi, 1:298–9])

Herakles is the Greek name for Hercules. Bura was one of the 12 cities of Achaia (north of Kalavrita, Peloponnisos). Presumably Pausanias means the dice were cast one at a time, and the oracles written in the squares of the board upon which each landed read successively.

9. *Eleazar*—Refers to the vision of Abram, Genesis 15—notice verse 15:2.

10. *Gideon*—Judges 6:17; 36:40.

11. *oracle given to him*—

> The market-place of Pharai is an old-fashioned, big enclosure, with a stone statue of Hermes in the middle that has a beard: it stands on the mere earth, block-shaped, of no great size. It has an inscription too, saying it was dedicated by Simylos of Messene. They call it the Market Hermes and it has a traditional oracle. In front of the statue is a stone hearthstone, with bronze lamps stuck onto it with lead. You come in the evening to consult the god, burn incense on the hearthstone, and fill up the lamps with oil; then you light them all and put a local coin (which they call a bronze bit) on the altar to the right of the god; and then you whisper in the god's ear whatever your question is. Then you stop up your ears and go out of the market-place, and when you get out take your hands away from your ears and whatever phrase you hear next is the oracle. (Pausanias *Guide to Greece* 7.22.2 [Levi 1:285])

12. *choosing Saul*—I Samuel 10:1, 20–7.

CHAPTER LIII

How he that will receive oracles must dispose himself.

hosoever therefore being desirous to come to the supreme state of the soul, goeth to receive oracles, must go to them being chastly and devoutly disposed, being pure and clean go to them, so that his soul be polluted with no filthiness, and free from all guilt. He must also so purify his mind and body as much as he may from all diseases, and passions, and all irrational conditions, which adhere to it as rust to iron, by rightly composing and disposing those things which belong to the tranquility of the mind; for by this means he shall receive the truer and more efficacious oracles.

Now by what things the mind is purged, and reduced into a divine purity, we must learn by religion, and wisdom. For neither wisdom without religion, nor religion without wisdom is to be approved of: for wisdom (as saith *Solomon*)[1] is the tree of life to them that lay hold on it. And *Lucretius* saith[2] that it is the intention of God, or the breathings of God, where he sings:

Most famous Memmius! This that god is he,
The prince of life, who reason, which all we
Call wisdom, first found out, and who by art
The life from troubles, darkness, set apart
And freed, and unto light, and peace
  reduced.

He also understandeth that to be a divine illustration, whence *Democritus* thinketh that there are no men wise but they that are struck with some divine phrensy, as was *Menos* that Cretensian, whom they report learned all things of *Jupiter,* whence he had frequent converse with God in the mount Ida:[3] so also the Athenians report that *Melosagora Eleusinus* was taught by the nymphs; so also we read, that *Hesiod* when he was a shepherd in Beotia, and kept his flock near the mountain Helicon, had some pens given him by the Muses, which having received, he presently became a poet,[4] which to become so suddenly was not of man, but by a divine inspiration.

For God conveying himself into holy souls, makes men prophets, and workers of miracles, being powerful in work and speech, as *Plato* and *Mercurius* affirm, and also *Xistus*[5] the Pythagorean, saying that such a man is the temple of God, and that God is his guest: to whom assents our *Paul,*[6] calling man the temple of God; and in another place speaking of himself, I can do all things in him that strengtheneth me; for he is our power, without which (as he saith)[7] we can do nothing; which also *Aristotle* confesseth in his Meteors[8] and Ethics,[9] saying, that there is no virtue whether natural or moral but by God; and in his Secrets[10] he saith that a good and sound intellect can do nothing in the secrets of nature without the influence of divine virtue.

Now we receive this influence then only, when we do acquit ourselves from burdensome impediments, and from carnal and terrene occupations, and from all external agitation; neither can a blear or impure eye behold things too light, neither can he receive divine things who is ignorant of the purifying of his mind. Now we must come to this purity of mind by degrees; neither can anyone that is initiated newly unto those mysteries presently comprehend all clear things, but his mind must be accustomed by degrees, until the intellect becomes more enlightened, and applying itself to divine light, be mixed with it.

A human soul therefore when it shall be rightly purged, and expiated, doth then, being loosed from all impurity, break forth with a liberal motion, and ascends upwards, receives divine things, instructs itself, when happily it seems to be instructed from elsewhere; neither doth it then need any remembrance, or demonstration by reason of the industry of itself, as by its mind which is the head and the pilot of the soul, it doth, imitating by its own nature the angels, attain to what it desires, not by succession or time, but in a moment.

For *David* when he had not learning, was of a shepherd made a prophet,[11] and most expert of divine things. *Solomon* in the dream of one night, was filled with the knowledge of all things above and below.[12] So *Isaiah, Ezekiel, Daniel,* and the other prophets, and apostles were taught.

For the soul (which is the common opinion of the Pythagoreans, and Platonists) can by way of purification, without any other study, or searching, only by an easy, and adventitious collating on these intelligibles received from above, acquire the perfect knowledge of all things knowable. It can also by an extrinsical expiation attain to this, as to understand all things invisibly by its substantial form.

For the mind is purged, and expiated by cleansing, by abstinence, by penitency, by alms: and then also do thereunto conduce certain sacred institutions, as shall afterward be discovered. For the soul is to be cured by the study of religions, and indeed these which are commonly called occult, that being restored to its soundness, confirmed by truth, and fortified by divine graces, may not fear any rising shakings.

Notes—Chapter LIII

1. *saith Solomon*—Proverbs 3:18.

2. *Lucretius saith*—

For if we ought to speak as the known dignity of the subjects which he expounded requires, he [Epicurus] was a god, a god, I say, O illustrious Memmius, who first discovered that discipline of life which is now called wisdom; and who, by the science of philosophy, placed human existence, from amid so great waves of trouble, and so great darkness of the mind, in so tranquil a condition and so clear a light. (Lucretius *On the Nature of Things* 5, c. line 6, trans. John Selby Watson [London: George Bell and Sons, 1901], 194).

The poem is addressed by Lucretius to his friend Caius Memmius Gemellus.

3. *in the mount Ida*—King Minos of Crete was said to have been instructed in the art of lawgiving by Zeus, who was worshiped on Mount Ida in Crete.

4. *became a poet*—

The Muses once taught Hesiod to sing
Sweet songs, while he was shepherding his
    lambs

On holy Helicon; the goddesses
Olympian, daughters of Zeus who holds
The aegis, first addressed these words to
    me:
"You rustic shepherds, shame: bellies you
    are,
Not men! We know enough to make up lies
Which are convincing, but we also have
The skill, when we've a mind, to speak the
    truth."
So spoke the fresh-voiced daughters of
    great Zeus
And plucked and gave a staff to me, a shoot
Of blooming laurel, wonderful to see,
And breathed a sacred voice into my mouth
With which to celebrate the things to come
And things that were before.
(Hesiod *Theogony* lines 21–35 [Wender,
    23–4])

5. *Xistus*—Note 5, ch. XXXVI, bk. III.

6. *Paul*—See note 6, ch. XXXVI, bk. III.

7. *as he saith*—Philippians 4:13.

8. *Meteors*—See note 19, ch. XXXVI, bk. III.

9. *Ethics*—See note 20, ch. XXXVI, bk. III.

10. *Secrets*—See note 21, ch. XXXVI, bk. III.

11. *made a prophet*—I Samuel 16:13.

12. *things above and below*—I Kings 3:5–15.

CHAPTER LIV

Of cleanness, and how to be observed.

We must therefore first observe cleanness in food, in works, in affections, and to put away all filthiness, and perturbations of the mind, and whatsoever sense or spirit that offends, and whatsoever things are in mind unlike to the heavens, not only if they be in mind and spirit, but also if they be in the body, or about the body: for such an external cleanness is believed not to help a little to the purity of the mind.

For this cause the Pythagorean philosophers being taken with the desire of oracles, divine praises being celebrated, did wash themselves in a river as in a bath, and did put on white raiment and linen; for they did account wool a prophane clothing being the excrements of beasts, and they did inhabit in a pure chamber, and altogether unspotted.[1]

In like manner the Bragmanni, the wise men of the Indians, were wont to wash themselves naked in a fountain, which is called Dirce in Boeotia,[2] their heads being first annointed with amber drops, and odours fit for that purpose; then after they were according to custom sufficiently clean, they were to go forth about noon, clothed in white linen, with a white attire, having rings on their fingers and staves in their hands.

In like manner amongst the Gymnosophists[3] it was a custom to wash themselves thrice in a day, and twice in the night, in cold water, before they entered into the holy places. They did also every day use linen garments every day newly washed.

We read also of the manner of this kind of washing in *Hesiod*[4] in his books of Works and Days, where he sings:

None dare with hands unwashed unto Jove
Wine pour forth, nor unto the gods above;
For then they do refuse for to be heard,
Though being prayed unto————

And elsewhere:[5]

When wicked men the rivers do pass by
With hands unwashed, then are the gods
    angry
With them, and them afflict————

Hence in *Virgil, Aeneas* thus speaks[6] to his father:

O father, take the household gods, and hold
Them in thy sacred hands; to be so bold
As them to handle after so great fights
I dare not till that washed in streams most
    bright.

It was also a custom amongst the gentiles, when they were wont to perform any holy services to the gods, to cleanse their bodies by washing; and when they were to contend with the infernal gods, sprinkling only did suffice. Hence in *Virgil, Dido,*[7] when she did perform any solemnities to the gods, saith:

Cause that my sister Ann (my nurse most
    dear):
Come, and my body wash with water clear.

And in another place where *Aeneas* is brought in amongst the infernals bringing a bough to *Proserpina*,[8] he sings thus:

The passage doth Aeneas keep, and wash
His body with fresh water————

Also when he relates of *Misenus* to be buried,[9] he sings:

His friends he thrice did wash with water
    new,
And with an olive branch, wet in the dew,
He did them sprinkle————

Now man being made thus clean becomes celestial, and spiritual, and is fitted for the sight of and union with God, whilst he ministers to God with a clean body, and pure mind, and delights in the cleanness of all things, as inwards, skin, garments, houses, utensils, oblations, gifts, and sacrifices; the cleanness of all which even purifies the air, and attracts the most pure influence of celestial, and divine things, and allures the pure ministers of God, and good demons: although sometimes impure spirits, and ill demons, as the apes of the good demons, take upon them this kind of cleanness, that either they may be adored, or may deceive: therefore first of all we must observe that the mind be pure, and the heart pure, and then the impure powers cannot ascend.

Notes—Chapter LIV

1. *altogether unspotted*—

They also wore a white and pure garment. And in a similar manner they lay on pure and white beds, the coverlets of which were made of thread; for they did not use woolen coverlets. (Iamblichus *Life of Pythagoras* 21 [Taylor, 54])

He [Pythagoras] likewise exhorted them [his disciples] to abstain from such things as are an impediment to prophesy, or to the purity and chastity of the soul, or to the habit of temperance, or of virtue. And lastly, he rejected all such things as are adverse to sanctity, and which obscure and disturb the other purities of the soul, and the phantasms which occur in sleep. (ibid. 24 [Taylor, 57])

2. *Dirce in Boeotia*—Dirce, wife of Lycus, tyrant of Thebes in Boeotia, was tied to a bull and dragged to death, then her corpse was cast into a well (or a spring), which afterwards bore the name Dirce's Well (or Dirce's Spring). The exact location of this water was a local secret in Thebes in ancient times. How the brahmans of India came to be washing in a fountain in Boeotia would no doubt be made clear by Agrippa's source, whatever it may be.

3. *Gymnosophists*—The naked sages of Egypt.

4. *washing in Hesiod*—Hesiod *Works and Days* c. line 724.

5. *elsewhere*—Ibid. c. line 739.

6. *Aeneas thus speaks*—"You, my father, take in your hand the sacred vessels and the household gods of our country. For me to handle them is a crime now that I have come away from so bloody a strife and from recent carnage, until I have purified myself with running water" (Virgil *Aeneid* 2, c. line 717–20 [Lonsdale and Lee, 112]).

7. *Dido*—"Dear nurse, bring hither to me where I stand my sister Anna; tell her to haste and sprinkle her body with river-water, and bring with her the prescribed victims and propitiatory offerings; in such manner let her come: and you yourself shade your brow with the sacred fillet" (ibid. 4, c. line 634–5 [Lonsdale and Lee, 140–1]).

8. *bough to Proserpina*—"Aeneas gains the entrance, and sprinkles his body with fresh water, and hangs up the bough in the threshold opposite" (ibid. 6, c. line 635–6 [Lonsdale and Lee, 172]). Aeneas deposits the golden bough in the doorway of Pluto's palace.

9. *Misenus to be buried*—"He too thrice bore to his comrades all around clear water, sprinkling them with light dew from the branch of a fruitful olive, and purified the warriors, and spoke the farewell words" (ibid. 6, c. line 229–30 [Lonsdale and Lee, 164]).

CHAPTER LV

Of abstinence, fastings, chastity, solitariness, the tranquility and ascent of the mind.

Abstinence also doth commonly fortify, and defend the observers thereof against vices, and evil demons, and makes the mind an unpolluted temple of God, uniting it to God. For nothing doth more conduce to health, and temperence of the complexion, than not to heap together superfluities, and not to exceed the bounds of necessary food.

Neither is nutriment to be taken that is too strong for nature, but rather let nature be stronger than the meat, as some affirm of Christ, that he took meat in that proportion that it should not breed any excrement of the third concoction.[1] Many others also taking meat sparingly, enjoyed thereby health and agility of body, as *Moses,*[2] and *Elias,*[3] who fasted forty days: whence his face shined, and he lifted up, could easily guide his body as if it were a spirit.

For magicians, and philosophers affirm that our spirit is not as a terene thing, or body nourished by nutriment received through certain organs by the concoction of meat, and drink, but draws in their aliment[4] like sponges through the whole body, viz. from the thin vapours penetrating the body on all sides. Therefore they that desire to have this spirit pure, and potent, let them use drier meats, and extenuate this gross body with fastings, and they make it more easily penetrable; and lest, by the weight thereof, the spirit should either become thick, or be suffocated, let them preserve the body clean by lotions, frictions, exercises, and clothings, and corroborate their spirits by lights, and fumes, and bring it to a pure and thin fineness.

We must therefore in taking of meats be pure, and abstinent, as the Pythagorean philosophers, who keeping a holy and sober table, did protract their life in all temperance.[5] The temperance therefore of life and complexion, because thereby no superfluous humour is bred, which may dull the phantasy, makes, that our soul oftentimes dreaming, and sometimes watching, is always subjected to the superior influences. Moreover the Pythagoreans, if anyone doth by abstinence moderate prudently every motion of the mind, and body, promise perpetual health of both, and long life.

So the Bragmani did admit none to their college, but those that were abstinent from wine, from flesh, and vices, saying that none could understand God, but they that emulate him by a divine conversation: which also *Phraotes* in *Philostrates* taught the lower Indians.

Moreover we must abstain from all those things which infect either the mind, or spirit, as from covetousness, and envy, which are handmaids to injustice (as *Hermes* saith), enforcing the mind and the hand to evil practices; also from idleness, and luxury; for the soul being suffocated with the body, and lust, cannot foresee any celestial thing. Wherefore the priests of the Athenians who are called in Greek *hierophantae*[6] (as *Hierom* reports), that they might live more chastly in their sacred employments, and might follow their divine affairs without

643

lust, were wont to castrate themselves by drinking of hemlock. Moreover the chastity of a mind devoted to God doth make our mind (as *Orpheus* teacheth *Museus* in the hymn of all the gods)[7] a perpetual temple of God.

Also we must abstain from all multitude and variety of senses, affections, imaginations, opinions, and such like passions, which hurt the mind and pervert the judgement of reason, as we manifestly see in the lascivious, the envious, and ambitious. Wherefore *Cicero* (in his Tusculans' Questions)[8] calls these passions the sickness of the mind, and the pestiferous diseases thereof. But *Horace* calls them furies or madness,[9] where he sings:

Girls have a thousand furies, so have boys.

The same also seems to be of opinion that all men are fools in something. Whence is read in Ecclesiasticus, there are an infinite number of fools.[10] Therefore the Stoics deny that passions are incident to a wise man; I say such passions, which follow the sensitive apprehension: for rational, and mental passions, they yield a wise man may have. This opinion did *Boetius*[11] seem to be of, where he sings that some passions are to be laid aside in the inquisition of truth, in these verses:

If truth thou wouldst discover with clear
 sight,
And walk in the right path, then from thee
 quit
Joy, fear, grief, hope expel; for where
 these reign,
The mind is dark and bound————

We must therefore acquit and avert our minds from all multitudes,[12] and such like passions, that we may attain to the simple truth; which indeed many philosophers are said to have attained to in the solitude of a long time. For the mind by solitude being loosed from all care of human affairs is at leisure, and prepared to receive the gifts of the celestial deities.

So *Moses* the lawgiver to the Hebrews, and the greatest of prophets, and learned in all the knowledge of the Chaldeans and Egyptians, when he would abstract himself from senses, went into the vast wildernesses of Ethiopia, where all human affairs being laid aside, he applied his mind to the sole contemplation of divine things, in which thing he so pleased the omnipotent God, that he suffered him to see him face to face, and also gave him a wondrous power of miracles, as sacred writ testifies of him.[13] So *Zoroastes* the father and prince of the magicians, is said to attain to the knowledge of all natural and divine things by the solitude of twenty years,[14] when he wrote, and did very strange things concerning all the art of divining, and soothsaying. The like things do the writings of *Orpheus* to *Museus* declare him to have done in the deserts of Thracia. So we read that *Epimenides* of Crete became learned by a very long sleep, for they say that he slept fifty years, i.e. to have lay hid so long;[15] *Pythagoras* also in like manner to have lain hid ten years; and *Heraclitus,* and *Democritus* for the same cause were delighted with solitariness.

For by how much the more we have relinquished the animal and the human life, by so much the more we live like angels, and God, to which being conjoined, and brought into a better condition, we have power over all things, ruling over all.

Now how our mind is to be separated from an animal life, and from all multitude, and to be erected, until it ascend to that very one, good, true, and perfect, through each degree of things knowable, and knowledges, *Proclus* teacheth in his Commentaries upon Alcibiades,[16] showing how that first sensible things are to be shunned, that we may pass to an incorporeal essence, where we must exceed the order of souls yet multiplied by divers rules, habitudes, and various proportions, many bonds, and a manifold variety of forces, and to strive after an intellect, and intelligible kingdom, and to contemplate how far better these are than souls.

Moreover we must bear an intellectual multitude, although united, and individual, and come to the superintellectual and essential unity, absolute from all multitude, and the very fountain of good, and truth. In like manner we must avoid all knowledge that doth any ways distract, and deceive, that we may obtain the most simple truth.[17] The multitude therefore of affections, senses, imaginations, and opinions is to be left, which in itself is as different, as some things are contrary to others in any subject; and we must ascend to sciences, in which although there be a various multitude, yet there is no contrariety. For all are knit one to the other, and do serve one the other, under one the other, until they come to one, presupposed by all, and supposing none beyond it; to which all the rest may be referred.

Yet this is not the highest top of knowledges, but above it is a pure intellect. Therefore all composition, division, and various discourse being laid aside, let us, ascending to the intellectual life, and simple sight, behold the intelligible essence with individual and simple precepts, that we may attain to the highest being of the soul, by which we are one, and under which our multitude is united. Therefore let us attain to the First Unity, from whom there is a union in all things, through that One which is as the flower of our essence: which then at length we attain to, when avoiding all multitude we do arise into our very unity, are made one, and act uniformly.

Notes—Chapter LV

1. *third concoction*—The first concoction was digestion in the stomach and intestines; the second concoction was the transformation of the chyme formed by the previous process into blood; the third concoction was secretion of such things as sweat and tears. These last Burton calls "excrementitious humours of the third concoction" (Burton *Anatomy of Melancholy* 1.1.2.2 [1621] 1961, 1:148).

2. *Moses*—Exodus 34:28–9.

3. *Elias*—I Kings 19:4–8; II Kings 2:11.

4. *aliment*—Sustenance.

5. *in all temperance*—For a description of the evening meal among the Pythagoreans, see Iamblichus *Life of Pythagoras* 21 (Taylor, 52).

6. *hierophantae*—Hierophantes was the supreme priest of Attica and head of the Eleusinian Mysteries. He was chosen for life from the hieratic family of the Eumolpidae, and upon assuming his office ritually cast his old name into the sea, and was thereafter known only by his title. Presiding over the Mysteries, he declared an end to all warfare while they were being observed, revealed the secrets of the cult to initiates, and had power to bar the entry of those he considered unworthy. A headband and embroidered purple robe made up his ritual apparel.

7. *hymn of all the gods*—This reference is not in the hymn to Musaeus given by Taylor in his *Hymns of Orpheus*. Agrippa must have another Orphic work in mind.

8. *Tusculans' Questions*—*Tusculanarum disputationum libri V*.

9. *furies or madness*—Horace *Satires* 2.3.

10. *infinite number of fools*—This seems not to be a specific quote, but a reference to the book Ecclesiasticus in general.

11. *Boetius*—Boetius *Consolation of Philosophy* 1.7: "The Perturbations of Passion."

12. *multitudes*—Agrippa uses this term in very much the same way that *maya* is used by the Hindus and Buddhists. Reality is single, uniform and unvarying. All that is changeable, varied and multiple is therefore unreal, a passing illusion from the absolute perspective, and if we are to approach that God view, we also must so regard it. This is derived from Neoplatonism (see note 16 below).

13. *testifies of him*—Exodus 3; 33:11.

14. *twenty years*—Pliny mentions this 20 years in the desert, during which, he says, Zoroaster lived on cheese (Pliny 11.97). The Zoroastrians called this retirement of their leader into the wilderness his "journey to the throne of Ormuzd." Dio Chrysostom writes that out of a love for wisdom and righteousness, Zoroaster withdrew from other men and lived in solitude on a mountain. The mountain was consumed by fire, but the sage escaped injury and thereafter spoke to the multitude.

15. *lay hid so long*—See note 3, ch. XLVII, bk. III.

16. *upon Alcibiades*—

So, if you wish to travel by the various ways of knowing, ... flee all the objects of sense (since they are dispersed and divided and not subject to accurate apprehension) and lift yourself up away from these to incorporeal being. ... After the multiplicity in souls lift yourself up to the Intellect and the realms of intelligence in order that you may grasp the unification of things: ... Having ascertained and been initiated into the knowledge of the intelligent multiplicity that is undivided and unified, proceed in turn to another principle, and prior to the intelligent forms of being consider their henads and the unity that transcends the totalities. When you have arrived there, you will have left behind all multiplicity, you will have ascended to the very source of the Good. (Proclus *Commentary on the First Alcibiades* 248–9. In *Proclus: Alcibiades I*, trans. W. O'Neill [The Hague: Martinus Nijhoff, 1965], 163)

17. *most simple truth*—This is the argument Agrippa was later to expound at greater length in the *Vanity of the Sciences*.

CHAPTER LVI

Of penitency, and alms.

Now the greatest part of purgations is a voluntary penitency for faults: for (as saith *Seneca* in Thyeste)[1] he whom it grieves that he hath offended, is in a manner innocent. This brings to us the greatest expiation, whilst it opposeth afflictings to delights, and purgeth out of the soul a stupid joyfulness, and gives a certain peculiar power, reducing us to the things above. Penitency therefore is not only a mortification of vices, but a spiritual martyrdom of the soul; which with the sword of the spirit is on all sides mortified; now the sword of the spirit is the word of God; whence *Jeremiah*[2] the prophet saith, and also *Paul,* writing to the Ephesians,[3] cursed is he that withholdeth his sword from blood; and the Psalmist sings:[4] A sword is in their lips.

Therefore our cogitations, afflictions of our mind, and all evils that proceed from our heart and mouth, must be uttered to the priest in confession, that he may according to the word of God judge those things; and according to the power granted to him by God, penitency being joined with it, may purify, and purge them, and direct them to that which is good; neither is there found in religion for the expiating heinous offences a stronger sacrament. Hence the gods themselves *(Ovid* in Pontus[5] being witness):

Do often ease the pains, restore the lights
Which were caught away, when that mortal
    wights
They see repenting of their sins————

There is as yet another sacrament of expiation, viz. alms giving, of which as I remember I have read very little in philosophers, but the very truth taught us that, saying, give ye alms, and all things shall be clean to you;[6] and in Ecclesiasticus it is read, as water extinguisheth fire, so alms doth sin;[7] and *Daniel* taught the King of Babylon,[8] that he should redeem his sins by alms; and the angel *Raphael* testifieth to *Tobias,*[9] because alms frees from death, and is that which purgeth sins, and make us find eternal life.

Hence Christ commanded us to pray to the Father, forgive us as we forgive others, give to us as we give to others;[10] of which he said in another place, ye shall receive an hundredfold, and shall possess eternal life.[11] He shall when he comes to judge the quick and the dead, upbraid the wicked above all things for their neglect of alms and works of mercy, when he shall say, I was hungry, and thirsty, and ye gave me neither meat, nor drink;[12] and in another place he speaks of the poor, what ye have done to any one of them ye have done to me.[13]

Which *Homer* also seems to be sensible of, when he brings in a young man wooing, *Antinoe,*[14] saying these words: *Antinoe* how plausibly hast thou slain a poor begger! He shall destroy thee if God be in heaven, for the gods themselves being likened to strangers, and guests, go out into the whole world, overturning cities, and beholding the injuries, and wickedness of men.

Notes—Chapter LVI

1. *in Thyeste*—The *Thyestes* is one of the tragic plays written by the Roman philosopher Seneca.

2. *Jeremiah*—Jeremiah 48:10.

3. *to the Ephesians*—Ephesians 6:17.

4. *Psalmist sings*—Psalms 59:7.

5. *Ovid in Pontus*—

> I have beheld one who confessed that he had offended the Divinity of Isis, clothed in linen, sitting before the altars of Isis; another, deprived of his sight for a fault like his, was crying, in the middle of the road, that he had deserved it. The inhabitants of heaven rejoice that such public declarations are made, that they may prove by testimony how great is the extent of their power. Often do they mitigate the punishment, and restore the sight that has been taken away, when they see that a man has truly repented of his error. (Ovid *Ex Ponto* 1, lines 51–8 [Riley, 371])

6. *clean to you*—Luke 11:41.

7. *alms doth sin*—Apocryphal book of Ecclesiasticus 3:30.

8. *King of Babylon*—Daniel 4:27.

9. *to Tobias*—Apocryphal book of Tobit 12:9. See also 4:7–11.

10. *as we give to others*—Matthew 6:12.

11. *possess eternal life*—Matthew 19:29.

12. *neither meat, nor drink*—Matthew 25:42.

13. *done to me*—Matthew 25:40.

14. *Antinoe*—One of the suitors of Penelope reproves Antinoös for striking Odysseus, who is disguised as a beggar:

> "Antinoös, you did badly to hit the
> unhappy vagabond:
> a curse on you, if he turns out to be some
> god from heaven.
> For the gods do take on all sorts of trans-
> formations, appearing
> as strangers from elsewhere, and thus they
> range at large through the cities,
> watching to see which men keep the laws,
> and which are violent."

(Homer *Odyssey* 17, c. lines 483–7 [Lattimore, 265]).

CHAPTER LVII

Of those things which being outwardly administered conduce to expiation.

It is believed, and it is delivered by them that are skillful in sacred things, that the mind also may be expiated with certain institutions, and sacraments ministered outwardly, as by sacrifices, baptisms, and adjurations, benedictions, consecrations, sprinklings of holy water, by annointings, and fumes, not so much consecrated to this, as having a natural power thus to do.

Upon this account sulphur hath a place in religions, to expiate ill demons with the fume thereof. An egg also was wont to be used in purgations;[1] hence eggs are called holy, whence *Ovid:*[2]

> Let the old woman come, and purge the bed,
> And place, and bring sulphur and eggs sacred
> In her trembling hand————

Proclus also writes,[3] that the priests in purifyings were wont to use sulphur, and bitumen, or the washings of sea water: for sulphur purifies by the sharpness of its odour, and sea water by reason of its fiery part.

In like manner the herb cinquefoil:[4] wherefore by reason of its purity the ancient priests did use it in purifications.[5] Also the boughs of olives: for these are said to be of so great purity, that they report that an olive tree planted by an harlot is thereby forever made unfruitful, or else withers.[6]

In like manner, frankincense, myrrh, vervain, valarian, and the herb called phu[7] conduce to expiation. Also the blessed clove flower; and the gall of a black dog[8] being fumed is said to be very powerful in these, as well for expiating of ill spirits, as any bewitchings: also the feathers of a lapwing being fumed, drives away phantasms.

It is wonderful and scarce credible, but that that grave and worthy author *Josephus* relates it in his history of Jerusalem, of a root of Baaras,[9] so called from a place near Machernus, a town of Judea, being of a yellow colour, that in the night it did shine, and was hard to be taken, that it did oftentimes deceive the hands of them that went to take it, and go out of their sight, never stood still, till the urine of a menstrous woman was sprinkled on it. Neither yet being thus retained, is it pulled up without danger, but sudden death falls upon him that draws it up, unless he were fortified with an amulet of the said root; which they that want, sacrificing about the earth do bind the root to a dog by a cord, and presently depart: at length the dog with a great deal of pains draws up the root, and as it were supplying the place of his master presently dies, after which anyone may handle the root without danger; the power of which is much excellent in expiations, as is manifest for the delivery of those that are vexed with unclean spirits.

Now that these kind of matters should act upon spiritual substances by putting them to flight, or by alluring them, or mitigating them, or by inciting them, they are of no other opinion than that the fire of Sicilia[10] acts upon souls: which *(William of Paris* being witness) not hurting the bodies, doth most intolerably torment the souls of them that are near.[11] But of those in part we have treated before.

Notes—Chapter LVII

1. *in purgations*—Rotten eggs have a sulfurous smell.

2. *whence Ovid*—Ovid *Ars Amatoria* (Art of love) 2 line 329. Eggs and sulfur were used to purify the chambers of the sick, even the love-sick. One can easily imagine that the lingering stench would lift them from their melancholy. Apuleius mentions the purification of a ship by a priest of Isis with "a torch, an egge, and sulphur" *(Golden Asse* ch. 47, near the end).

3. *Proclus also writes*—

The heart of a mole is subservient to divination, but sulphur and marine water to purification. Hence the ancient priests, by the mutual relation and sympathy of things to each other, collected their virtues into one, but expelled them by repugnancy and antipathy; purifying when it was requisite with sulphur and bitumen, and sprinkling with marine water. For sulphur purifies, from the sharpness of its odour; but marine water on account of its fiery portion. (Proclus *De sacrificio et magia,* frag., Latin trans. Marsilius Ficinus [Venice, 1497]. Trans. Thomas Taylor, in Iamblichus *On the Mysteries* [Taylor, 346])

4. *cinquefoil*—Pliny says about cinquefoil: "This plant is also employed in the purification of houses" (Pliny 25.62 [Bostock and Riley, 5:123]).

5. *in purifications*—Ovid gives an extensive list of materials used for purification in the rites of the goddess Pales:

The blood of a horse will be the fumigation, and the ashes of a calf; and the third ingredient will be the stripped stalk of the hard bean. Shepherd, purify the full sheep at the beginning of twilight; let the water first sprinkle them, and let the broom, made of twigs, sweep the ground. Let the sheepfolds, too, be decorated with leaves and branches fastened up, and let the long garland shade the ornamented doors. Let a blue smoke arise from the native sulphur, and let the ewe bleat aloud while rubbed with the brimstone as it smokes. Burn, too, rosemary, and the pitch tree, and the Sabine herbs, and let the burnt laurel crackle in the midst of the hearth. (Ovid *Fasti* 4, lines 733–42 [Riley, 166])

6. *or else withers*—Pliny relates another version of this folk belief concerning the purity of the olive:

"According to M. Varro [*De re rustica* 1.2], an olive-tree which has been licked by the tongue of the she-goat, or upon which she has browsed when it was first budding, is sure to be barren" [Pliny 15.8 [Bostock and Riley, 3:291–2])

7. *phu*—*Valeriana phu,* the garden valerian or Cretan spikenard. Turner reports that it "groweth in Pontus" *(Herbal* 1562, 2:86 [*OED,* s.v. Phu]). Gerard says it "is put into counterpoisons and medicines preservative against the pestilence" (Gerard [1633] 1975, 2:440:1078)

8. *black dog*—The black dog is the beast of Hecate.

9. *root of Baaras*—

… but still in that valley which encompasses the city on the north side, there is a certain place called Baaras, which produces a root of the same name with itself; its colour is like to that of flame, and towards the evening it sends out a certain ray like lightning; it is not easily taken by such as would do it, but recedes from their hands, nor will yield itself to be taken quietly, until either the urine or a woman, or her menstrual blood, be poured upon it; nay, even then it is certain death to those that touch it, unless any one take and hang the root itself down from his hand, and so carry it away. It may also be taken another way without danger, which is this: they dig a trench quite round about it, till the hidden part of the root be very small, they then tie a dog to it, and when the dog tries hard to follow him that tied him, this root is easily plucked up, but the dog dies immediately, as if it were instead of the man that would take the plant away; nor after this need any one be afraid of taking it into their hands. Yet after all this pains in getting it, it is only valuable on account of one virtue it hath, that if it only be brought to sick persons, it quickly drives away those called Demons, which are no other than the spirits of the wicked, which enter into men that are alive, and kill them, unless they can obtain some help against them. (Josephus *Wars of the Jews* 7.6.3 [Whiston, 667–8])

Gerard identifies this as the peony, and lists variations of the same story found in Apuleius, Theophrastus, Pliny and Aelianus, observing that "the like fabulous tale hath been set forth of Mandrake" (Gerard [1633] 1975, 2:380:983).

10. *fires of Sicilia*—Volcanic Mount Aetna in Sicily.

11. *them that are near*—One might speculate that this torment was caused by invisible poisonous gases that enveloped the unwary climbers.

CHAPTER LVIII

OF ADORATIONS, AND VOWS.

Adorations, and vows, sacrifices, and oblations[1] are certain degrees in sacred things to find out God, and those things which principally provoke the divine pleasure, and procure a sacred and indissolvable communion of God with souls; for by prayers which we utter with true and sacred words sensibly, and affectionately, we obtain a great power, when by the application of them to any deity we do so far move it, that he may direct his speech and answer by a divine way, by which (as saith *Dionysius)*[2] God speaks with men, but so occultly that very few perceive it. But oftentimes that king and prophet *David* perceives it, when he saith, I will hear what the Lord will speak in me.[3]

Adoration therefore being a long time continued, and often frequented, perfects the intellect, and makes the soul more large for the receiving of divine lights, inflaming divine love, producing faith, hope, and sacred manners, purifieth the soul from all contrariety, and what is any away adverse to it, and doth also repel divers evils, which would otherwise naturally fall out. Hence *Ovid* sings:

———————with prayers moved is Jove;
I oftentimes have seen when from above
He would send dreadful lightnings, him to be
Appeased with frankincense———————

Now man is returned to God by prayers, by which coming he (saith *Plato* in Phaedrus)[4] stops horses, and enters into the chambers of repose, where he feeds upon ambrosia, and drinks nectar. Therefore they that desire to enjoy any virtue, must pray, and supplicate often to him who hath all virtue in himself. Now that is the best prayer, which is not uttered in words, but that which with a religious silence[5] and sincere cogitation is offered up to God, and that which with the voice of the mind and words of the intellectual world, is offered to him.

Now a vow is an ardent affection of a chaste mind given up to God, which by vowing wisheth that which seems good. This affection (as *Jamblicus,*[6] and *Proclus* testify) doth so join the soul to God, that the operation of the mind and of God is one; viz. of God as an artificer, of the mind as a divine instrument: all antiquity testifies that by vows sometimes miracles are done, diseases are cured, tempests are diverted, and such like. Hence we read that the most excellent and wise in all nations, the Bragmanni of the Indians, the magicians of the Persians, the Gymnosophists of the Egyptians, the divines of the Greeks,[7] and Chaldeans[8] which did excel in divine secrets, did apply themselves to divine vows, and prayers, and thereby did effect many wonderful things.

Now to the perfection of a vow, and adoration (for a vow cannot be perfect without an adoration, nor an adoration without a vow) there are two things especially required viz:

First the knowledge of the thing to be adored, and to which we must vow, and in what manner, and order, and by what mediums it

652

must be worshiped; for there are various coop-erators and instruments of God, viz. the heavens, stars, administrating spirits, the celestial souls, and heros, which we must implore as porters, interpreters, administrators, mediators, but first of all him, who goeth to the archetype God, who only is the utmost term of adoration; the other deities are as it were passages to that very God. Know therefore that adorations and vows must with a pure and pious mind be principally made to that one only God, the highest Father, King and Lord of all the gods. But when they shall come before to the inferior gods, let the intention of the administration be terminated in them. Therefore to adorations, and vows, when they be directed to the inferior deities, *Zoroastes,* and *Orpheus* thought fitting that suffumigations and characters should be used; but when they are erected to the majesty of the supreme God, they must not in any wise; which also *Hermes,* and *Plato* forbid to be done. Whence *Hermes* to *Tatius;*[9] this (saith he) is like to sacrilege when thou prayest to God to be willing to kindle frankincense,[10] and such like; for (saith *Porphyry*) they are not agreeable to piety. For there is not any material thing can be found, which to the immaterial God is not unclean.[11] Therefore neither is that prayer which is uttered by words agreeable to him, nor that prayer which is mental, if the mind be polluted with vice.

Secondly there is also required a certain assimilation of our life to the divine life, in purity, chastity and holiness, with a lawful desire of that which we wish for; for by this means we especially obtain the divine benevolence, and are subjected to the divine bounty; for unless we, having our minds purged, be worthy to be heard, and also those things which we desire, be worthy to be done, it is manifest that the gods will not hearken to our prayers; whence divine *Plato* saith, that God cannot be bound by our prayers or gifts to do unjust things;[12] therefore let us desire nothing of God, which we think uncomely to wish for: for by this means only, we see that very many are frustrated of their prayers and vows, because that neither they themselves are religiously disposed, nor are their desires and prayers made for those things which are well pleasing to God, neither do they know to discern in what order they ought to pray, and through what mediators they ought to go to God; the ignorance of which doth very oft reduce our prayers and supplications to nothing, and causeth our desires and wishes to be denied.

Noτes—Chapτer LVIII

1. *oblations*—Offerings of sacrifice, devotion, or thanksgiving to a deity.

2. *Dionysius*—Pseudo-Dionysius the Aeropagite.

3. *speak in me*—Psalms 85:8.

4. *Plato in Phaedrus*—Plato is referring to "that place beyond the heavens" where:

> ... true being dwells, without colour or shape, that cannot be touched; reason alone, the soul's pilot, can behold it, and all true knowledge is knowledge thereof. ... And when she [the soul] has contemplated likewise and feasted upon all else that has true being, she descends again within the heavens and comes back home. And having so come, her charioteer [reason] sets his steeds at their manger, and

puts ambrosia before them and draught of nectar to drink withal. *(Phaedrus* 247c–e [Hamilton and Cairns, 494])

5. *religious silence*—"O unspeakable, unutterable, to be praised with silence!" *Divine Pymander of Hermes Mercurius Trismegistis* 2.96 (Everard [1650, 1884] 1978, 17). From the prayer of Hermes. The Scott translation of this same passage is more diffuse.

6. *Jamblicus*—See Iamblichus *On the Mysteries* 5.26 regarding the various kinds of prayer and their benefits.

7. *divines of the Greeks*—The Hierophants of the Mysteries.

8. *Chaldeans*—In ancient times "Chaldean" denoted "magician," particularly an astrologer, and it was

almost forgotten that the name referred to a geographical people.

9. *Hermes to Tatius*—

> But when they had begun to pray, Asclepius whispered, "Tell me, Tat, shall we propose to your father that we should add to our prayer, as men are wont to do, an offering of incense and perfumes?" Trismegistus heard; and much disturbed, he said, "Hush, hush, Asclepius; it is the height of impiety to think of such a thing with regard to Him who alone is good. Such gifts as these are unfit for him; for he is filled with all things that exist, and lacks for nothing. Let us adore him rather with thanksgiving; for words of praise are the only offering that he accepts." *(Asclepius Epilogue 41a [Scott, 1:373]. See also Corpus Hermeticum 5.10b, 11 [Scott, 1:165])*

10. *frankincense*—"Although frankincense may appease the Gods and the angry Divinities; still it must not all be given to the flaming altars" (Ovid *De medicamine faciei* [On the care of the complexion] [Riley, 494]). Of the Egyptian offerings of incense that Hermes condemns in the case of the Supreme Deity, Plutarch writes: "Moreover, they offer incense to the sun three times a day; resin at his rising, myrrh when it is in the mid-heaven, and that they call Kephi about the time of his setting" *(Isis and Osiris 52. In Moralia [Goodwin, 4:112])*. Kyphi, or cyphi, was a compound of honey, wine, raisins, cyperus, resin, myrrh, aspalathus, seselis, mastich, bitumen, nightshade, sorrel, berries of large and small juniper, cardamun and calamus (ibid. 80–1 [Goodwin, 136–8]). The Harvard University Press translation of the *Moralia* gives sweet rush in place of nightshade.

11. *unclean*—"For the Kosmos is one mass of evil, even as God is one mass of good" *(Corpus Hermeticum 6.4a [Scott, 1:169])*.

12. *unjust things*—

> For the good man 'tis most glorious and good and profitable to happiness of life, aye, and most excellently fit, to do sacrifice and be ever in communion with heaven through prayer and offerings and all manner of worship, but for the evil, entirely the contrary. For the evil man is impure of soul, where the other is pure, and from the polluted neither good men nor God may ever rightly accept a gift; thus all this toil taken with heaven is but labour thrown away for the impious though ever seasonable in the pious. (Plato *Laws* 4.716d–e [Hamilton and Cairns, 1307–8])

CHAPTER LIX

Of sacrifices and oblations, and their kinds and manners.

A sacrifice is an oblation which is both holy by offering, and sanctifieth and maketh holy the offerer, unless either irreverence or some other sin be an impediment to him; therefore these sacrifices and oblations do yield us much hope, and make us of the family of God, and do repel from us many evils hanging over our heads, which the doctors of the Hebrews do especially confirm, saying by this that as we kill our living creatures, and dissipate our wealth by sacrifice, we turn away mischiefs which do hang over us.

For as this mortal priest sacrificeth in this inferior world the soul of irrational creatures to God, by the separating of the body from the soul: so *Michael* the archangel, the priest of the higher world, sacrificeth the souls of men,[1] and this by the separation of the soul from the body, and not of the body from the soul, unless perchance, as it happeneth in fury, rapture, ecstasy and sleep, and such like vacations of the soul, which the Hebrews call the death of the body.

But sacrifices and oblations are first of all and principally to be offered up to the most high God; but when they are to be directed to the secondary divine powers, this ought to be done even as we have spoken concerning prayers and vows.

But there are many kinds of sacrifices: one kind is called a burnt offering, when the thing sacrificed was consumed by fire; another, is an offering of the effusion of blood; moreover there are salutiferous sacrifices which are made for the obtaining of health; others pacifying for obtaining peace; others praising for the freeing from some evil; and for the bestowing of some good thing; others gratulatory, for divine worship and thanksgiving; but some sacrifices are made neither for the honour of God, nor out of good will, of which sort was that amongst the Hebrews, called the sacrifice of jealousy, which was made only for the detecting of occult adultery.

There was in times past amongst the gentiles the sacrifice of expiation, by the which cities were purged from famine, pestilence, or some horrible calamity; whose rites were to search out the most wicked man in that city, and to lead him to the place appointed carrying in his hands a cheese and wafers and dry figs; afterwards to whip him seven times with rods, and then to burn him to ashes with the same rods, and to cast the ashes into the sea; of these *Lycophron* and *Hipponax* make mention; neither doth *Philostratus* relate things much different from these, concerning *Apollonius* of Tyana while he chased away the pestilence from Ephesus.

Moreover there were many kind of sacrifices and offerings, as *Agonalia,*[2] *Dapsa,*[3] *Farreationes, Hecatombe,*[4] *Hostia,*[5] *Hyacinthia,*[6] *Armilustra,*[7] *Janualia,*[8] *Lucalia, Lupercalia,*[9] *Munychia,*[10] *Novendinalia,*[11] *Nyctiluca, Palatialia, Pastillaria, Popularia, Protervia, Scenopegia, Solitaurilia, Stata, Rubigalia,*[12] *Fontanalia,*[13] *Ormia, Parentalia,*[14] *Inferiae,*[15] *Consualia,*[16] *Lampteria, Amburbia,*[17] *Ambarvalia,*[18] *Vinalia,*[19] *Thyia,*[20] *Holocaustomata,*[21] *Orgia,*[22] *Latialia,*[23] *Dianetaurica,*[24] *Bacchana-*

lia,[25] *Trieterica, Liberalia,*[26] *Cocytia, Cerealia,*[27] *Thesmophoria,*[28] *Adonia,*[29] *Teonia, Laurentalia,*[30] *Opalia,*[31] *Palilia,*[32] *Quirinalia,*[33] *Vertumnalia,*[34] *Gynaecia, Panathenea,*[35] *Quinquatria,*[36] *Diapalia,*[37] *Diasia,*[38] *Horma, Hormea, Nemea,*[39] *Mytriaca,*[40] *Palogygia.*

And the offerings of these were proper and divers; for a goat and an ass were sacrificed to *Bacchus*, a sow to *Ceres*, an horse to the Sun, an hart and dogs to *Diana*, an ass to *Priapus*, a goose to *Isis*, a dunghill cock[41] to the Night, a shegoat to *Faunus*, a bull to *Neptune*, a shegoat to *Minerva*, a bull to *Hercules*, a child[42] to *Saturn*, a sow with pigs to *Maja*,[43] a cock to *Aesculpaius:* moreover they did sacrifice to *Hercules Gnidius* with scoldings and railings.

There were also divers orders of priests, as High Priests, Flamines,[44] Archiflamines,[45] Phylades, Salians,[46] Hierophantes;[47] and divers names of religions, and superstitions, and sacrifices, ceremonies, feasts, consecrations, dedications, vows, devotions, expiations, oaths, offerings, satisfactory works; by the which the seduced gentiles did sacrifice to false gods and devils.

But the true sacrifice, which purgeth any man, and uniteth him to God, is twofold; one which the high priest Christ offered for the remission of sins, purifying all things by the blood of his cross; the other, by the which a man offereth up himself clean, unspotted, for a living sacrifice to God, as Christ the high priest offered himself, and taught us to be offered together with him, as he was offered, saying of the sacrament of his body, and blood, do this in remembrance of me;[48] viz. that we should offer ourselves together, being mortified by the passion of his mortal body, and quickened in spirit.

Of the which *Porphyry* saith, let us labour to offer up holiness of life for a sacrifice; for no man can be a good priest of God, but he which bringeth forth himself for a sacrifice, and buildeth up his own soul, as it were for an image, and doth constitute both his mind, and understanding for a temple in the which he may receive the divine light; but eternal sacrifices (as *Heraclitus* saith) are certain cures of the soul,

instituted by the most high physician; for the evil spirit possesseth a man (as *Proclus* saith) even until he be expiated by sacrifices; therefore sacrifices are required to pacify God and the heavenly powers, and to expiate a man, who beareth the image both of God and the world.

But our lord *Jesus* Christ the true high priest concluded all sacrifices in bread and wine only, as in the primary substance of man's meat, needing further the offering up of no animals, nor other things, or the effusion of blood, in which we may be cleansed, being perfectly cleansed in his blood.

There were also amongst the Egyptians six hundred sixty-six[49] kinds of sacrifices; for they did appoint divine honours, and holy sacrifices to each star, and planet, because they were divine animals partaking of an intellectual soul and a divine mind; whence they say that the stars being humbly prayed unto, do hear our prayer, and bestow celestial gifts, not so much by any natural agreement, as by their own free will.

And this is that which *Iamblicus* saith,[50] that celestial bodies, and the deities of the world have certain divine and superior powers in themselves, as also natural and inferior, which *Orpheus* calls the keys to open and shut;[51] and that by those we are bound to the fatal influences, but by these to loose us from fate. Whence if any misfortune hang over anyone from Saturn, or from Mars, the magicians command that he must not forthwith fly to Jupiter, or Venus, but to Saturn or Mars themselves. So that Apuleian *Psyche* who was persecuted by *Venus* for equaling her in beauty, was forced to importune for favour, not from *Ceres*, or *Juno*, but from *Venus* herself.[52]

Now they did sacrifice to each star with the things belonging to them; to the Sun with solary things, and its animals, as a laurel tree, a cock, a swan, a bull; to Venus with her animals, as a dove, or turtle, and by her plants, as vervain; as *Virgil* sings:

—————water bring out
With garlands soft, the altar round about
Compass, and burn fat boughs and frankin-
    cense
That's strong and pure—————

Moreover the magicians when they made any confection either natural, or artificial, belonging to any star, this did they afterward religiously offer, and sacrifice to the same star, receiving not so much a natural virtue from the influence thereof being opportunely received, as by that religious oblation receiving it divinely confirmed and stronger. For the oblation of anything, when it is offered to God after a right manner, that thing is sanctified by God by the oblation as is a sacrifice, and is made part thereof.

Moreover to the celestial and etherial gods white sacrifices were offered; but to the terrestrial or infernal, black: but to the terrestrial upon the altars, but to the infernal in ditches; to the aerial and watery, flying things: but to these white, to those black.[53] Finally, to all the gods and demons besides terrestrial and infernal, flying things were offered, but to those only four-footed animals, for like rejoiceth in like. Of these only which were offered to the celestial, and etherial, it is lawful to eat, the extreme parts[54] being reserved for God, but of the other not.

Now all these the oracle of Apollo hath expressed in these verses:

A threefold sacrifice to the gods above,
White must be slain for them; for them below
Threefold also, but black for them; withal
With open altars gods celestial
Are taken, when the infernal gods require
Pits embrued with black blood, and filled with mire;
And are not pleased but with a sacrifice
That's buried; but of the air the deities
Delight in honey, and in wines most clear,
And that on altars kindled be the fire,
Require, with flying sacrifice, and white:
But of the Earth the deities delight
That earthly bodies should with frankincense
And wafers offered be in reverence.

But for the gods that rule the sea thou must
Thy sacrifices lay on the sea coasts,
And on the waves cast the whole animal.
But to the deities celestial
Give the extreme parts, and them consume with fire;
What then remains thou mayest if thou desire
Eat up, and let the air with vapours thick
And sweet smelling drop————

These doth *Porphyry* make mention of in his book of Answers,[55] to whom the rest assent. For they say that these sacrifices are certain natural mediums betwixt the gods and men; which *Aristotle* affirming saith, that to sacrifice to God is in a man naturally. They are therefore they say, mediums, which favour of the nature of both, and represent divine things analogically, and have with the deity to whom they are offered, certain convenient analogies, but so occult that a man's understanding can scarce conceive of them, which God, and the deities require in particular for our expiation, with which the celestial virtues are pleased, and withhold themselves from execution of the punishment which our sins deserve.

And these are (as *Orpheus* calls them) keys which open the gate of the elements,[56] and the heavens, that by them a man may ascend to the supercelestials; and the intelligences of the heavens, and the demons of the elements may descend to him.

Now men that are perfect, and truly religious need them not, but only they, who (saith *Trismegistus*)[57] being fallen into disorder, are made the servants of the heavens and creatures; who because they are subjected to the heavens, therefore think they may be corroborated by the favour of the celestial virtue, until they flying higher be acquitted from their presidency, and become more sublime than they.

Noτes—Chapτer LIX

1. *souls of men*—It is Michael who weighs souls in a great scale at the final judgement.

2. *Agonalia*—Ancient Roman festivals celebrated January 9, March 17, May 21 and December 11 in honor of various divinities. See Ovid *Fasti* 1, lines 317–36.

3. *Dapsa*—Latin: *daps*—a magnificent banquet on the occasion of a sacrifice.

4. *Hecatombe*—Originally a Greek festival to Apollo that took place in the midsummer month of Hekatombaion, consisting of the mass sacrifice of a hundred oxen. As early as the time of Homer the word was used more generally to signify any numerous sacrifice, and in this sense was practiced by the Romans also.

5. *Hostia*—Latin: *hostia*—a sacrifice.

6. *Hyacinthia*—The death of Hyacinthus, the beautiful youth accidentally killed by Apollo, was celebrated at his native city of Amyclae with the Hyacinthia, the second most important of the Spartan festivals. It was observed sometime in early summer during the Spartan month Hecatombeus and lasted three days, the tone of the rites passing from mourning to rejoicing.

7. *Armilustra*—The Armilustrium (purification of arms) was celebrated on October 19 in honor of Mars and the 12 Salii Palatini, the dancers of Mars. On this date the 12 *ancilia,* or sacred shields, were displayed, one of which was supposed to have fallen from heaven during the reign of King Numa.

8. *Janualia*—Perhaps the festival of Janus, celebrated at Rome on January 1. The name of this festival may have been displaced by the Agonium of January 9 (see note 2 above) and seems not to be known to modern writers.

9. *Lupercalia*—Roman festival celebrated on February 15 with the sacrifice of a goat, or goats, and a dog, at the cave called the Lupercal, located below the western corner of the Palatine, chief of the seven hills of ancient Rome. After the sacrifice youths clad only in a girdle made of the skin of the victims ran around the Palatine lashing whomever they met, but mainly women, with strips of goat skin. It appears to have been a combined fertility rite and the propitiation of a wolf deity.

10. *Munychia*—A fortified hill on the peninsula of Piraeus near Athens. At its foot lay a harbor of the same name, the most easterly of three harbors that served Athens. On the Munychia stood the temple of Artemis Munychia, in which those accused of crimes against the state of Athens might seek refuge. The festival of this Moon goddess, called the Munychia, was celebrated in the Athenian month of Munychion (April) with the ritual sacrifice of a fawn dressed up as a girl.

11. *Novendinalia*—The Novendiale was a *feriae imperativae,* a Roman festival appointed by the senate, magistrates, or priests to commemorate some great event or to avert disaster. The Novendiale was observed whenever stones fell from heaven.

12. *Rubigalia*—Robigalia, a Roman festival celebrated on April 25 to avert mildew *(robigo)* from blighting the crops. A procession left the city through the Flaminian gate, crossed the Milvian bridge and stopped at the fifth milestone on the Via Claudia, where a dog and a sheep were sacrificed to the goddess (or god) Mildew. Ovid says the sacrifices took place in "the grove of ancient Mildew," that the participants wore white, and that the entrails of the dog and sheep were cast into a fire by the *flamen quirinalis* (see note 44 below) along with wine and incense *(Fasti* 4, lines 905–42). Columella adds the gruesome detail that the dog was a sucking puppy, and Pliny says the festival was first instituted by Numa in the 11th year of his reign.

13. *Fontanalia*—Roman festival celebrated on October 13 in honor of Fontus, son of Janus, during which fountains were adorned with garlands. The name of the god indicates his nature, the personification of flowing waters *(fons).*

14. *Parentalia*—A Roman public state festival for honoring the dead, or as Ovid more accurately puts it, "for propitiating the ghosts, " lasting February 13–21. The last day bore the name "Feralia." During the term of the festival all temples remained closed, magistrates put off their insignia of office and marriage ceremonies were forbidden. See Ovid *Fasti* 2, lines 533–70.

15. *Inferiae*—The *inferi* were the gods of the underworld. The word was also used more generally to describe any being in Hades, including all departed souls.

16. *Consualia*—The festival in honor of the ancient Italian god of agriculture Consus was celebrated at Rome on August 21 and also on December 15. On the first date the *flamen quirinalis* and the Vestal Virgins offered sacrifice, and mule races were held in the Circus. Horses and mules received rest from work and were crowned with garlands. Various rustic amusements, such as running on oil-slicked ox hides, took place. The festival was believed to have been instituted by Romulus.

17. *Amburbia*—The Amburbium was a solemn procession of the people around the city of Rome performed in times of great danger to avert calamity.

18. *Ambarvalia*—Roman festival to protect crops that was observed May 29. An ox, a sheep and a pig (called *suovetaurilia)* intended for sacrifice to Ceres were first led around the Roman lands by the *Fratres Arvales* (Arval Brothers), a priesthood of 12 members. As the *ager Romanus* increased in size, this procession was discontinued.

19. *Vinalia*—A Roman festival dedicated to Jupiter in his office as protector of wine. It had two parts, the *Vinalia rustica*, celebrating the harvest of the grapes on August 19, and the *Vinalia urbana*, observed on April 21, the official birthday of Rome, when the wine made from the harvest of the previous autumn was first tasted.

20. *Thyia*—A Greek festival dedicated to Dionysus, celebrated each year in the neighborhood of the city of Elis. Thyia, daughter of Castalius (or Cephisseus), was the first to offer sacrifice to Dionysus. The Thyiades, frenzied female devotees of Dionysus, were supposed to derive their name from her.

21. *Holocaustomata*—Holocaust is a Greek word meaning "wholly burnt"; that is, a sacrificial offering completely consumed by fire.

22. *Orgia*—Nocturnal festival of Dionysus in which the Bacchae women tore a bull to pieces and ate its raw flesh beneath the flickering light of torches. The word was generally used to designate any rite of Dionysus, particularly the triennial festival that took place atop Mount Cithaeron. See Virgil *Aeneid* 4, line 302.

23. *Latialia*—The *feriae Latinae* was celebrated each year on the Alban Mount in honour of Jupiter Latialis (or Latiaris), the protecting god of the region of Latium. During the days of its observation a sacred truce was observed, and the entire senate of Rome, along with the higher magistrates, took part in the rites, which were presided over by one of the consuls. The date of its celebration varied with political circumstances, because of the truce that accompanied it.

24. *Dianetaurica*—Festival of the Tauric Artemis (Artemis Taurica), to whom in Taurus all strangers shipwrecked on the coast were sacrificed. When the goddess was brought to Attica, and worshiped at Sparta, the rite was softened so that young men were only scourged until their blood spattered the altar.

25. *Bacchanalia*—The Latin name for the Dionysiac Orgia. See note 22 above.

26. *Liberalia*—Fertility festival observed on March 17 in honour of the Italian deity Liber Pater, identified by the Romans with Dionysus. Cakes of meal, honey and oil were offered to the god. Youths laid aside their boys' togas *(toga praetexta)* and adopted men's togas *(toga libera)*. See Ovid *Fasti* 3, lines 713–91.

27. *Cerealia*—Roman festival of April 12–19 in honor of Ceres, during which games were held. See Ovid , *Fasti* 4, lines 393–620, which is the finest passage in this work.

28. *Thesmophoria*—Ancient Greek festival celebrated by women only in honor of Demeter, on different dates in different city-states. At Athens it was observed October 24–26. Women abstained from sex with their husbands for nine days prior to the rites and slept in beds strewn with agnus castus, pine boughs or other magical plants. Pigs were cast down into pits or natural chasms supposed to be filled with poisonous serpents. After three days of ritual purification certain women called Drawers *(antletriai)* descended into the pits, frightened the serpents away by clapping their hands, and brought up some of the decaying swine flesh. Whoever obtained a bit of this flesh from its place on the altar of Demeter and sowed it with seed in the fields was assured of a good crop.

29. *Adonia*—Annual festivals in honor of Adonis held at Byblus, Alexandria, Athens and other places. At Alexandria images of Adonis and Aphrodite were placed together in mock union surrounded by the fruits of the season, costly perfumes and cakes made in the shape of living things. The next day women with dishevelled hair and bared breasts cast the image of Adonis into the sea and sang a prayer for a good year. This ceremony, along with the one at Athens, took place late in summer; the one at Byblus was conducted in the spring.

30. *Laurentalia*—More properly Larentalia, a Roman festival honoring Acca Larentia on December 23. Various stories are told of this woman. She is said to have suckled Romulus and Remus; or to have been won by Hercules in a game of dice, and to have bequeathed to Rome the vast fortune of her dead husband, the wealthy Etruscan Tarutius, whom Hercules had advised her to marry; or to have been the mother of the Lares, with whom she was closely connected. See Ovid *Fasti* 3, lines 55–8.

31. *Opalia*—Roman festival held toward the close of December.

32. *Palilia*—More correctly Parilia, a Roman festival celebrated on April 21 in honor of the Italian goddess Pales, keeper of the flocks. On this date shepherds asked for forgiveness of their accidental profanation of holy places and leaped three times across a bonfire of hay. See also note 19 above concerning this date.

33. *Quirinalia*—Roman festival of February 18 in honor of Quirinus, the name first given to Romulus after he was raised to the rank of a divinity.

34. *Vertumnalia*—Roman festival honoring the Etruscan god Vertumnus (or Vortumnus) on August 23. He was a god of growing vegetation, and the festival marked the change of seasons.

35. *Panathenea*—Athenian festival in honor of Athena Polias held on Hecatombaeon 28–29 (around the middle of August). There was a Lesser Panathenaea held every year and a Greater Panathenaea held every fourth year. In earliest times there was a great procession in which a statue of Athena was ritually robed in a saffron-colored garment called a *peplus*. In later times the festival included gymnastic games, a music contest, and an equestrian contest. A large host of animals gathered from all parts of the empire was sacrificed.

36. *Quinquatria*—Roman festival in honor of Minerva held March 19–23, so called because it fell on the fifth day following the Ides of March. In later times the festival occupied five days, the last four being devoted to gladitorial shows. There was a Lesser Quinquatrus on June 13–14 celebrated chiefly by flute players. See Ovid *Fasti* 3, lines 809–50 and 6, lines 651–710.

37. *Diapalia*—Diipolia, a sacrifice of an ox to Zeus Polieus held on the Acropolis at Athens each year in June. The priest who killed the ox fled and remained in ritual exile for a prescribed period; the ax used was tried, condemned and thrown into the sea; and the hide of the ox was stuffed with hay, yoked to a plow, and treated as though it were alive. See Pausanias *Guide to Greece* 1.24.4.

38. *Diasia*—Greek festival of Zeus held in February.

39. *Nemea*—Nemea was a valley in Argolia where Hercules was fabled to have killed the Nemean lion. There was a large temple of Zeus Nemeus there surrounded by a sacred grove in which the Nemean games were held every second year. The prize of the games was a crown of wild celery.

40. *Mytriaca*—Perhaps the Matralia, a Roman festival celebrated on June 11 in honor of the Italian deity Mater Matuta, goddess of the dawn, who was in early times associated with childbirth. Only married women were admitted to her rites, and none that had married more than once was permitted to crown her statue with garlands. In later times this goddess was associated with the sea and navigation.

41. *Dunghill cock*—The common barnyard fowl, as opposed to the gamecock.

42. *child*—There was a tradition that in earliest times human sacrifices were made to Saturn.

43. *Maja*—Maia was worshiped at Rome. Sacrifice was offered to her on May 1 by a priest of Vulcan, which led to her being regarded by some as Vulcan's wife. In later times she was confused with Maia, daughter of Atlas. She was also called by the name Majesta.

44. *Flamines*—A group of 15 priests at Rome, 3 Greater and 12 Lesser. Each was assigned to oversee the cult of a particular god. Two of the Lesser Flamines are unknown, but the others are:

Greater

Flamen	God
Dialis	Jupiter
Martialis	Mars
Quirinalis	Quirinus

Lesser

Flamen	God
Volturnalis	Volturnus
Palatualis	Pales
Furinalis	Furrina
Floralis	Flora
Falacer	Falacer
Pomonalis	Pomona
Volcanalis	Volcanus
Cerialis	Ceres
Carmentalis	Carmentis
Portunalis	Portunus

45. *Archiflamines*—The three Greater *(maiores)* Flamines. See note 44 above.

46. *Salians*—The Salii, two groups each made up of 12 dancing priests of Mars. They were of noble birth, wore military dress and carried the sacred shields *(ancilia)* of Mars. At the Quinquatrus (March 19) and the Armilustrium (October 19), which marked the beginning and end of the military campaign season, they went in procession through Rome performing acrobatic ritual dances and singing in an ancient lost dialect. The Salii Palatini (see note 7 above) were always connected with Mars, but the Salii Collini (or Agonenses) may have originally been attached to Quirinus.

47. *Hierophantes*—See note 6, ch. LV, bk. III.

48. *remembrance of me*—Luke 22:19.

49. *six hundred sixty-six*—It is surely no coincidence that this is the number of the Beast of Revelation 13:18.

50. *Iamblicus saith*—"For the Gods, indeed, dissolve fate; but the last natures which proceed from them, and are complicated with the generation of the world and with body, give completion to fate" (Iamblichus *On the Mysteries* 8.7 [Taylor, 309]). On the subject of binding to, and loosing from, Fate, see sec. 8, chs. 6–8 of this work in their entirety.

51. *keys to open and shut*—Keys were the symbol of Pluto, as Pausanias mentions in his *Guide to Greece* 5.20.3. Perhaps Agrippa alludes to the Orphic hymn to Pluto:

Earth's keys to thee, illustrious king belong,
Its secret gates unlocking, deep and strong.
(Hymns of Orpheus 17 [*Thomas Taylor the
Platonist: Selected Writings,* 233])

52. *Venus herself*—The mortal girl Psyche excited
the jealousy of Venus, who for spite ordered her son
Cupid to cause Psyche to fall in love with the lowest
and ugliest man on Earth. Instead, Cupid fell in love
with her himself. They lived happily in secret for a
time, but through curiosity Psyche violated the trust
of her lover and he left her. She wandered incon-
solable and at last found herself a prisoner in the
palace of Venus, where she was tormented. Bravely
she persevered through all her ordeals. Jupiter took
pity on her, restored her to Cupid, and made her
immortal. The tale is charmingly told by Apuleius in
ch. 22 of *The Golden Ass.*

53. *to these white, to those black*—That is, to the airy
gods white birds, to the watery gods black birds.

54. *extreme parts*—The thigh bones were burned in
sacrifice to the gods, as Homer describes:

When they had made their prayer and
slaughtered the oxen and skinned them,
they cut away the meat from the thighs and
wrapped them in fat,
making a double fold, and laid shreds of
flesh upon them;

and since they had no wine to pour on the
burning offerings,
they made a libation of water, and roasted
all of the entrails;
but when they had burned the thigh pieces
and tasted the vitals,
they cut all the remainder into pieces and
spitted them.
(Odyssey 12, lines 359–65 [Lattimore, 194])

55. *book of Answers*—*De philosophia ex oraculis
hausta.* many oracles from which are quoted by
Eusebius in his *Præparatio evangelica,* bk. 21.

56. *gate of the elements*—See note 51 above.

57. *saith Trismegistus*—Perhaps this passage is
intended:

If then the rational part of a man's soul is
illuminated by a ray of light from God, for
that man the working of the daemons is
brought to naught; for no daemon and no
god has power against a single ray of the
light of God. But such men are few indeed;
and all others are led and driven, soul and
body, by the daemons, setting their hearts
and affections on the workings of the daemons. *(Corpus Hermeticum* 16.16 [Scott,
1:271]

Chapter LX

What imprecations, and rites the ancients were wont to use in sacrifices, and oblations.

Now let us see what imprecations they did join to oblations and sacrifices; for he that did offer any sacrifice to God, did say these, or the like things: I thy servant do offer and sacrifice these things to thee; I confess that thou art the author of all sanctity, and I call upon thee to sanctify this oblation, that thou wouldst pour upon it the virtue of thy high and excellent spirit, that by it we may obtain what we ask for. Moreover also as this thing present by any oblations is made thine, as to live, or die to thee, so also let me be made thine who by this oblation, and communion, by this thing which I come to offer, and sacrifice to thee, profess to be one of thy family, and worshippers.

Besides in offerings it was said, as that animal is in my power to be slain, if I pleased, or to be saved: so it is in thy power to take away in wrath, or to give in love that which we desire.

Lastly, when for expiation, or the avoiding of any evil, any sacrifice was to be made, it was said, as that animal dies in my hand, so die all vice in me, also all uncleanness; or so let die and be annihilated such or such an evil, or dis-

commodity. Also, as the blood of this animal is poured forth out of its body, so let all vice and uncleanness flow out from me.

In sacrifices laid on the altar to be burnt, it was said, as this oblation is consumed by this present fire, so that nothing remains of it; so let all evil be consumed in me, or let such or such an evil which we would repel and avoid be consumed.

It was also a custom when imprecation was made, to touch the altar with the hands of all those for whom such a sacrifice was made, or of them who did desire to be partakers of it, because prayer only cannot prevail, unless he that prays toucheth the altar with his hands; whence in *Virgil*:[1]

Those that in these words pray, and altar touch
The omnipotent doth hear————

And elsewhere:[2]

I touch the altars, and the middle fires,
And the deities beseech.

Notes—Chapter LX

1. *whence in Virgil*—The *Aeneid* 4, lines 219–20.   2. *and elsewhere*—The *Aeneid* 12, line 201.

CHAPTER LXI

How these things must be performed, as to God, so to inferior deities.

Every adoration therefore, oblation, or sacrifice, deprecation, invocation, are differenced thus, viz. either because they are made to God only, or to inferior deities, as angels, stars, heros. In these therefore such rules are to be observed:

That when any prayer is to be offered to God alone for the obtaining of any effect, it must be done with the commemoration of some work, miracle, sacrament, or promise, taken somewhere out of Scripture; as if there be a deprecation made for the destruction of enemies, let it be commemorated that God destroyed the giants in the deluge[1] of waters, and the builders of Babel[2] in the confusion of tongues, Sodom and Gomorrah[3] in raining of fire, the host of Pharaoh[4] in the Red Sea, and the like; adding to those some malediction out of the Psalms, or such as may be gathered out of other places of Scripture.

In like manner when we are to deprecate against dangers of waters, let us commemorate the saving of *Noah* in the flood,[5] the passing of the children of Israel through the Red Sea,[6] and Christ walking dryshod upon the waters,[7] and saving a ship from shipwreck,[8] commanding the winds and waves,[9] and lifting up *Peter*[10] sinking in the waves of the sea, and such like.

But if a prayer be necessary for obtaining oracles, or dreams, whether it be to God, angels, or heros, there are many places offer themselves out of the Old Testament, where God is said to talk with men, promising in very many places

presages, and revelations, besides the prophetical dreams of *Jacob,*[11] *Joseph,*[12] Pharaoh,[13] *Daniel,*[14] *Nebuchadnezzar,*[15] in the Old Testament, and the Revelation of *John,*[16] *Paul,*[17] in the New; also of holy magicians, as *Helen, Constantine*[18] and *Charles;*[19] also of later prophets, as *Methodius,*[20] *Cyrillus,*[21] *Joachim, Merlin,*[22] *Brigitta, Mechtindis, Hildegardis,* the deities of whom being piously invoked, render us oftentimes partakers of divine revelations.

Moreover we must invocate the sacred names of God, but those especially, which are significative of the thing desired, or any way applicable to it; as for the destruction of enemies we must invocate the name of God's wrath, of the revenge of God, fear of God, justice of God, fortitude of God: but for the avoiding of any danger we must invocate the names of pity, defense, salvation, goodness, and the like.

Moreover we must petition for and to the effectors of the thing desired, viz. such an angel, star, or hero on whom that office lies, but observing that our invocation on them must be made with due number, weight, and measure, and according to the rules delivered concerning enchantments. For betwixt these there is no difference, but that enchantments are such as affect our mind, disposing the passions thereof into a conformity to certain deities; but prayers are such as are exhibited to any deity by way of worship, and veneration; and from the same root also may the manner of consecrations be taken, of which we shall in the next place speak.

663

Notes—Chapter LXI

1. *giants in the deluge*—Genesis 6:4–7,

2. *builders of Babel*—Genesis 11:5–7.

3. *Sodom and Gomorrah*—Genesis 19:24.

4. *host of Pharaoh*—Exodus 14:28.

5. *Noah in the flood*—Genesis 8:1.

6. *through the Red Sea*—Exodus 14:22.

7. *dryshod upon the waters*—Matthew 14:25.

8. *ship from shipwreck*—Matthew 8:23–6.

9. *winds and waves*—Matthew 8:26; 14:32.

10. *lifting up Peter*—Matthew 14:31.

11. *Jacob*—Genesis 28:12–5.

12. *Joseph*—Genesis 37:5–10.

13. *Pharaoh*—Genesis 41:17–24.

14. *Daniel*—Daniel 2:19; 7; 8.

15. *Nebuchadnezzar*—Daniel 2:31–5; 4:10–7.

16. *Revelation of John*—Revelation 1:10.

17. *Paul*—II Corinthians 12:1–4.

18. *Constantine*—The Emperor Constantine dreamed a vision of Saint Nicholas, who told him that three men about to die on a charge of necromancy were innocent, and that if they were not released war would desolate the land. Constantine set them free. He also dreamed of Christ, who appeared with a cross in his hand and ordered the ruler to have a standard made like it. See note 1, ch. XXXI, bk. III.

19. *Charles*—Perhaps Charlemagne, who is fabled to be not dead, but merely asleep.

20. *Methodius*—Methodius the Martyr wrote about the Seven Sleepers. See note 19, ch. LVIII, bk. I.

21. *Cyrillus*—Saint Cyril, who shortly after his inauguration (9 AM, May 7, 368 AD) saw a flaming cross in the sky over Jerusalem that persisted for several hours and was brighter than the sun. He wrote of this phenomenon to the Emperor Constantine, saying it was visible to the entire city, and gave proof of the Christian doctrine.

22. *Merlin*—In addition to his prophetic powers, Merlin is another of those said not to be dead, but merely asleep. See note 9, ch. XIX, bk. III.

CHAPTER LXII

OF CONSECRATIONS, AND THEIR MANNER.

onsecration is a lifting up of experiments, by which a spiritual soul, being drawn by proportion and conformity, is infused into the matter of our works according to the tradition of magical art rightly and lawfully prepared, and our work is vivified by the spirit of understanding. The efficacy of consecrations is perfected by two things especially, viz. the virtue of the person himself consecrating, and the virtue of the prayer itself.

In the person himself is required holiness of life, and a power to consecrate; the former, nature and desert perform; the latter is acquired by imitation, and dignification, of which we have spoken elsewhere. Then it is necessary that he that sacrificeth must know this virtue and power in himself, with a firm and undoubted faith.

Now what things are required in prayer are these. There is also a certain power of sanctifying placed in it by God, as if it be so ordained of God for this or that very thing (of which sort we read of many in the holy writ) or instituted to this or that thing, by the virtue of the Holy Ghost, according to the ordination of the Church, of which sort are many everywhere extant: or this holiness is in the prayer itself, not by virtue of institution, but of the commemoration of sacred things, as of sacred letters, histories, miracles, works, effects, favours, promises, sacraments and such sacramental things, which shall seem to cohere with the thing to be consecrated, either

properly, or improperly, or analogically.[1]

And of these we shall now give some examples, by which a way easily may be laid open to the whole consideration of it.

So in the consecrating of water there is this commemoration made, viz. because God placed the firmament in the middle of waters;[2] because in the middle of the earthly paradise he made a holy fountain, from which through four rivers the whole Earth is watered;[3] because he made the waters an instrument of his justice, in the destruction of the giants, by the general deluge over the whole Earth;[4] and in the destruction of the army of Pharaoh in the Red Sea;[5] and because he led the people dryshod through the middle of the Red Sea,[6] and through the middle of Jordan;[7] and because he brought water miraculously out of a rock of the wilderness;[8] and brought forth a fountain of living water out of the jawbone of an ass at the prayers of *Sampson;*[9] and because he appointed the waters as an instrument of his pity,[10] and of salvation for remission of sins; and because Christ being baptized in Jordan, purified and sanctified the waters:[11] and the like also by invocating divine names suitable to these things, as when God is called a living fountain, living water, a living river.

In like manner in consecration of fire, let there be a commemoration that God created the fire to be an instrument of his justice for punishment, revenge, purgation of sins, and when he comes to judge the world he will command burning to go before;[12] and he appeared to *Moses* in a burning bush,[13] went before the chil-

665

dren of Israel in a pillar of fire,[14] and commanded that inextinguishable fire should be kept in the Tabernacle of the Covenant,[15] and kept fire unextinguished under the water.[16] Also we must use such divine names as offer themselves, as because God is a consuming fire, and a melting fire: and such as are proper to these, as the shining of God, the light of God, the brightness of God, and such like.

So in the consecration of oil such solemnities must be commemorated as belong to these, as in Exodus the oil of unction[17] and sweet perfumes, and sacred names suitable to these, such as is the name *Christ,* which signifies Annointed, and such as this, and that in the Apocalypse concerning the two olive trees distilling sanctified oil into lamps burning in the presence of God.[18]

So in the consecration of places let there be commemoration made of Mount Sinai, of the Tabernacle of the Covenant, of the Sanctum Sanctorum,[19] the temple of *Solomon,* and of the sanctification of the hill Golgotha through the mystery of the passion of Christ, and of the field which was bought with the price of Christ's blood; also of Mount Tabor, where the transfiguration and ascent into heaven was. Sacred names also being used, as of the place of God, the throne of God, the chair of God, the tabernacle of God, the altar of God, the seat of God, and the habitation of God, and of such like.

After the same manner we must proceed in the benediction of other things, by inquiring into holy writ by divine names, and profession of religion for such things which may seem to be after a manner suitable to this or that thing.

As for example, if there be a paper, or a book having some of the mysteries which we should commemorate, as the tables of the ten commandments given to *Moses* on Mount Sinai, and the sanctification of the Law, and of the prophets, and Scriptures promulgated by the Holy Spirit: and let the divine names of the testament of God, the book of God, the book of life, the knowledge of God, the wisdom of God, and of such like be commemorated.

So if a sword be to be consecrated, we may remember out of the Second of Maccabees there was a sword sent from God[20] to *Judas Macchabeus,* that he should destroy the children of Israel's enemies; also that in the prophets, take unto you two-edged swords;[21] also in the Gospel, coats being sold, swords must be bought;[22] and in the history of *David* an angel was seen hiding a bloody sword;[23] and many such like we shall find in the prophets, and Apocalypse, as also the sacred names of the sword of God, the rod of God, the staff of God, the vengeance of God, and such like.

And now let these things which have been exemplified concerning real consecrations, and benedictions suffice: by which personal consecrations, and benedictions may easily be understood.

But there is yet another powerful and efficacious rite of consecrating, and expiating, which is of the kinds of superstitious, viz: when the rite of any sacrament is transsumed to another thing, which is intended to be consecrated, or expiated, as the rite of baptism, confirmation, funeral, and such like.

Moreover we must know, that a vow, oblation, and sacrifice, have a certain power of consecration, as well real as personal, as the things or persons are vowed or offered.

Notes—Chapter LXII

1. *properly, or improperly, or analogically*—That is, intrinsically, extrinsically, or by analogy.

2. *middle of the waters*—Genesis 1:6.

3. *Earth is watered*—Genesis 2:10.

4. *deluge over the whole Earth*—See note 1, ch. LXI, bk. III. Genesis 7:19 may be specifically intended.

5. *Pharaoh in the Red Sea*—See note 4, ch. LXI, bk. III.

6. *middle of the Red Sea*—See note 6, ch. LXI, bk. III.

7. *middle of Jordan*—Joshua 3:17.

8. *rock of the wilderness*—Exodus 17:6.

9. *prayers of Sampson*—Judges 15:19.

10. *instrument of his piety*—Perhaps John 3:5 or I Peter 3:20–1.

11. *sanctified the waters*—Matthew 3:16; Mark 1:9.

12. *burning to go before*—Psalms 97:3.

13. *burning bush*—Exodus 3:2.

14. *pillar of fire*—Exodus 13:21.

15. *Tabernacle of the Covenant*—Exodus 27:20.

16. *under the water*—Perhaps I Kings 18:38.

17. *oil of unction*—Exodus 30:25.

18. *presence of God*—Revelation 11:4.

19. *Sanctum Sanctorum*—The holy of holies, the innermost part of the tabernacle where no one is admitted: "Now the whole temple was called *The Holy Place;* but that part which was within the four pillars, and to which none were admitted, was called *The Holy of Holies*" (Josephus *Antiquities of the Jews* 3.6.4 [Whiston, 80]).

20. *sword sent from God*—II Maccabees 15:15–6.

21. *two-edged swords*—Perhaps Psalms 149:6.

22. *swords must be bought*—Luke 22:36.

23. *bloody sword*—I Chronicles 21:27.

CHAPTER LXIII

What things may be called holy, what consecrated, and how these become so betwixt us and the deities; and of sacred times.

Now these things are called sacred, which are made holy by the gods themselves, or their demons, being (as I may say) dedicated to us by the gods themselves. By this account we call demons holy, because in them God dwells, whose name they are often said to hear. Whence it is read in Exodus: I will send my angel who shall go before thee; observe him, neither think that he is to be dispised, because my name is in him.[1]

So also mysteries are called sacred. For a mystery is that which hath a holy and an occult virtue, and favour given by the gods or demons, or dispensed by the most high God himself; such as are those sacred names and characters, which have been spoken of. So the cross is called holy and mysterious, being made so by the passion of *Jesus* Christ. Hence also certain prayers are called holy and mystical, which are not instituted by the devotion of man, but by divine revelation, as we read in the Gospel that Christ instituted the Lord's Prayer.[2]

In like manner certain confections are called holy, into which God hath put the especial beam of his virtue, as we read in Exodus of the sweet perfume, and oil of anointing,[3] and as with us there is a sacred fountain, and a sacred ointment.

There is also another kind of holiness, whereby we call those things holy which are dedicated and consecrated by man to God, as vows, and sacrifices, of which we have spoken already; whence *Virgil*:[4]

But Caesar with a triple triumph brought
Into the city Rome, as most devout,
Did dedicate unto the Italian gods
An immortal vow————

And Ovid in his Metamorphoses[5] sings thus:

A feast was kept, wherein Aeacides
For Cicnus' death with heifers' blood did
  please
Propitious Pallas, when the entrails laid
On burning altars, to the gods conveyed
An acceptable smell; a part addressed
To sacred use, the board received the rest.

In like manner the representations, resemblances, idols, statues, images, pictures, made after the similitudes of the gods, or dedicated to them, are called sacred, even as *Orpheus* singeth in his hymn to *Lycian Venus*:[6]

The chieftains that the sacred things protect
Of our country, did for our town erect
A sacred statue————

And *Virgil*:[7]

O father, take the household gods, and hold
Them in thy sacred hands————

Hence divine *Plato* in his eleventh book of Laws,[8] commanded that the sacred images and statues of the gods should be honoured, not for themselves, but because they represent the gods to us, even as the ancients did worship that image of *Jupiter*, thus interpreting it: for in that he bears the resemblance of a man, was signified that he is a mind which produceth all things by his seminary power; he is feigned to sit, that his immutable and constant power might be expressed; he hath the upper parts bare and naked, because he is manifest to the intelligences and the superiors; but the lower parts are covered, because he is hid from the inferior creatures; he holdeth a scepter in his left hand, because in these parts of the body the most spiritual habitation[9] of life is found, for the creator of the intellect is the king and the vivifying spirit of the world; but in his right hand he holdeth forth both an eagle and victory, the one because he is lord of all the gods, as the eagle is of other birds, the other because all things are subject to him.

In like manner we also reverence the image of a lamb, because it representeth Christ, and the picture of a dove, because it signifieth the Holy Ghost, and the forms of a lion, ox, eagle, and a man, signifying the Evangelists,[10] and such like things, which we find expressed in the revelations of the prophets, and in divers places of the holy Scripture: moreover those things confer to the like revelations and dreams, and therefore are called sacred pictures.

There are also sacred rites and holy observations, which are made for the reverencing of the gods, and religion, viz. devout gestures, genuflexions, uncoverings of the head, washings, sprinklings of holy water, perfumes, exterior expiations, humble processions, and exterior ornaments for divine praises, as musical harmony, burning of wax candles and lights, ringing of bells, the adorning of temples, altars and images, in all which there is required a supreme and special reverence and comeliness; wherefore there are used for these things, the most excellent, most beautiful and precious things, as gold, silver, precious stones, and such like: which reverences and exterior rites are as it were lessons and invitations to spiritual sacred things, for the obtaining the bounty of the gods; concerning which *Proserpina* beareth witness in these verses:

> Who ever did the brazen statues slight,
> The yellow gifts of gold, or silver white?
> Who would not wonder, and not say that
> these
> Are of the gods?————

The priests also are called sacred, and the ministers of the divine powers, and gods, and they themselves being consecrated do both administer all the holy things, and also consecrate them, whence *Lucan:*

> The consecrated priests, to whom great
> power
> Is granted————

And *Virgil* saith of *Helenus* the priest of *Apollo:*[11]

> He prays for peace of the gods, and doth
> unloose
> The garlands of his sacred head————

Those holy rites are as it were certain agreements betwixt the gods and us, exhibited with praise, reverence or obedience, by the means of which we very oft obtain some wonderful virtue from that divine power, on whom such reverence is bestowed; for there are sacred hymns, sermons, exorcisms, incantations, and words, which are compounded and dedicated for the praises and divine services of the gods, whence *Orpheus* in a verse composed for the stars,[12] saith:

> With holy words, now on the gods I call.

And the primitive Church did use certain holy incantations against diseases and tempests, which we either pronounce praying to some divine powers, or also sometimes carrying them along with us, written and hanged on our neck, or bound to us, we obtain very oft some power from such a saint, which men very much admire.

By this means also there are sacred names, figures, characters, and seals, which contemplative men, in purity of mind, for their secret vows, have devoted, dedicated and consecrated to the worship of God; which things truly, if any man afterwards shall pronounce with the same purity of mind, with the which they were first instituted, he shall in like manner do miracles; further also, the manner and rules delivered by the first institutor must be observed, for they who are ignorant of these things, lose their labour, and work in vain.

Thus not only by barbarous words, but also by Hebrew, Egyptian, Greek, Latin, and the names of other languages, being devoted to God, and attributed and dedicated to his essence, power or operation, we sometimes do wonders; such names there are in *Iamblicus*,[13] viz. *Osyris, Jcton, Emeph, Ptha, Epies, Amun;* so in *Plato,* and amongst the Greeks, ὧν τὸν ταυτὸν,[14] so the Greeks call *Jupiter* ζῆνα απὸ τõ ζῆν[15] which signifieth to live, because he giveth life to all things; in like manner Δία[16] which signifieth through, because through him are all things made; so ἀθάνατὸν[17] which signifieth immortal; so amongst the Latins he is called *Jupiter,* as it were an adjuvant father, and such like, and also certain names are devoted to men, as *Eutychis, Sofia, Theophilus,* that is, prosperous, servant, dear to God.[18]

In like manner certain material things receive no little sanctity and virtue by consecration, especially if done by a priest, as we see those waxen seals, in which are imprinted the figure of lambs, to receive virtue by the benediction of the Roman high priest, against lightnings and tempests, that they cannot hurt those who carry them, for a divine virtue is inspired into images thus consecrated, and is contained in them, as it were in a certain sacred letter, which hath the image of God.

The like virtue those holy waxed lights receive at Easter, and at the feast of the Purification of the Virgin;[19] in like manner bells by consecration and benediction receive virtue, that they drive away and restrain lightnings, and tempests, that they hurt not in those places where their sounds are heard; in like manner salt and water, by their benedictions and exorcisms receive power to chase and drive away evil spirits.

And thus in things of this kind, there are also sacred times always observed by the nations of every religion with very great reverence, which are either commanded that we should sanctify by the gods themselves, or are dedicated to them by our forefathers and elders, for the commemoration of some benefit received of the gods, and for a perpetual thanksgiving. Thus the Hebrews have received their sabbaths, and the heathens their holy days, and we the solemn days of our holy rites, always to be reverenced with the highest solemnity.

There are also times contrary to these, which they call penitential, and we black days, because that in those days the commonwealth hath suffered some notable blow, and calamity, of which sort amongst the Romans was the day before the fourth nones of August, because that on that day they suffered that extraordinary blow at the battle of Canna.[20] In like manner all postriduan days[21] are called black days, because that most commonly battles succeeded ill on these days: so amongst the Jews the black days are the seventeenth day of June, because on that day *Moses* broke the tables, *Manasses* erected an idol[22] in the Sanctum Sanctorum, and the walls of Jerusalem are supposed to have been pulled down by their enemies; likewise the ninth of July is a black day with them, because on that day the destructions of both the temples happened. By this reason they are called Egyptian days, in the old time observed by the Egyptians; and every nation by this way may easily make a like calculation of days fortunate or unfortunate to them.

And the magicians command that these holy and religious days be observed no less than the planetary days, and the celestial dispositions; for they affirm that they are far more efficacious, especially to obtain spiritual and divine virtues, because that their virtue is not from the elements and celestial bodies, but descendeth from the intelligible and supercelestial world, and being helped by the common suffrages of the saints, is not infringed by any adverse disposition of the heavenly bodies, nor frustrated by the corruptible contagion of the elements, if so be that firm belief and religious worship be not wanting, that is, joined with fear and trembling, for religion properly holdeth forth thus much; hence those days are called religious, which to violate is a sin, which if we carefully observe, we fear not any great mischief, which we may do, if we do otherwise.

Notes—Chapter LXIII

1. *my name is in him*—Exodus 23:20–1.

2. *Lord's Prayer*—Matthew 6:7–13; Luke 11:1–4.

3. *oil of anointing*—See note 17, ch. LXII, bk. III.

4. *whence Virgil*—Virgil *Aeneid* 8, lines 714–5.

5. *in his Metamorphoses*—

> And while a watchful guard was keeping
> the Phrygian walls, and a watchful guard
> was keeping the Argive trenches, a festival
> day had arrived, on which Achilles, the
> conqueror of Cygnus, appeased Pallas with
> the blood of a heifer, adorned with fillets.
> As soon as he had placed its entrails upon
> the glowing altars, and the smell, accept-
> able to the Deities, mounted up to the skies,
> the sacred rites had their share, the other
> part was served up at the table. (Ovid *Meta-
> morphoses* 12.3, c. line 147 [Riley, 421]).

6. *Lycian Venus*—I do not find this hymn in Taylor's *Hymns of Orpheus*.

7. *And Virgil*—This quotation is missing from the English edition. I have restored it from the Latin *Opera*. See note 6, ch. LIV, bk. III.

8. *eleventh book of Laws*—"Some of the gods of our worship are manifest to sight; there are others in whose likeness we set up images, believing that when we adore the lifeless image, we win the bountiful favor and grace of the living god for whom it stands" (Plato *Laws* 11.931a [Hamilton and Cairns, 1481]).

9. *spiritual habitation*—The heart, which is on the left side.

10. *the Evangelists*—See the table at the end of ch. VII, bk. II.

11. *priest of Apollo*—"Then Helenus first sacrificed steers in due form, and tries to gain a blessing from the gods, and unbinds the fillet of his holy head, and to thy threshold, Phoebus, he leads me [Aeneas] with his own hand, full of many a religious doubt …" (Virgil *Aeneid* 3, c. line 370 [Lonsdale and Lee, 121]).

12. *composed for the stars*—*Hymns of Orpheus*, hymn 6: "To The Stars," line 1.

13. *in Iamblicus*—Iamblichus treats of the barbarous names, without actually giving any, in *On the Mysteries* 7.4, 5. The names given by Agrippa are not barbarous names to Iamblichus, but names for the Egyptian gods: Osiris, Typhon (?), Kneph (?), Ptah, Aphis, Ammon. See Thomas Taylor's note to page 289 of his translation of *On the Mysteries*.

14. ὢν τὸν ταυτὸν—ON, TON, TAUTON.

15. ζῆνα ἀπὸ τō ζῆν—ZENA APO TO ZEN.

16. Δία—DIA.

> The name of Zeus … has also an excellent
> meaning, although hard to be understood,
> because really like a sentence, which is
> divided into two parts, for some call him
> Zena (Ζῆνα), and use the one half, and oth-
> ers who use the other half call him Dia
> (Δία); the two together signify the nature of
> the god, and the business of a name, as we
> were saying, is to express the nature. For
> there is none who is more the author of life
> to us and to all than the lord and king of all.
> Wherefore we are right in calling him Zena
> and Dia, which are one name, although
> divided, meaning the god through whom all
> creatures always have life (δί ὃν ζῆν ἀεὶ
> πᾶσι τοῖς ζῶσιν ὑπάρχει). (Plato *Craty-
> lus* 396a [Hamilton and Cairns, 433–4]).

17. ἀθάνατὸν—ATHANATON, "not subject to death; immortal."

18. *dear to God*—

> The names of heros and of men in general
> are apt to be deceptive because they are often
> called after ancestors with whose names, as
> we were saying, they may have no business,
> or they are the expression of a wish, like
> Eurychides (the son of good fortune), or
> Sosias (the Savior), or Theophilus (the
> beloved of God), and others. (Plato *Cratylus*
> 397b [Hamilton and Cairnes, 434]).

19. *Purification of the Virgins*—The Feast of the Purification of the Virgin Mary, held on February 2, also called Candlemas Day due to the large number of candles distributed by the Pope and used in the service.

20. *battle of Canna*—The Romans were defeated by Hannibal at Cannae, a village in Apulia, in 216 BC.

21. *postriduan days*—The day after.

22. *Manasses erected an idol*—Manasseh. See II Chronicles 33:7.

CHAPTER LXIV

Of certain religious observations, ceremonies, and rites of perfumings, unctions, and such like.

Whosoever therefore thou art, who desirest to operate in this faculty, in the first place implore God the Father, being one, that thou also mayest be one worthy of his favour.

Be clean, within and without, in a clean place, because it is written in Leviticus, every man who shall approach those things which are consecrated, in whom there is uncleanness, shall perish before the Lord;[1] therefore wash yourselves oft, and at the days appointed, according to the mysteries of number, put on clean clothes, and abstain from all uncleanness, pollution, and lust; for the gods will not hear that man (as *Porphyry* saith) who hath not abstained many days from venereous acts.

Be not thou coupled to a polluted or menstruous woman, neither to her who hath the hemorrhoids; touch not an unclean thing; nor a carcass, whence *Porphyry* saith, whosoever shall touch a dead man, may not approach the oracles, perhaps, because that by a certain affinity of the funeral ill odour, the mind is corrupted and made unfit to receive divine influences.

Thou shalt wash, and anoint, and perfume thyself, and shalt offer sacrifices: for God accepteth for a most sweet odour those things which are offered to him by a man purified and well disposed, and together with that perfume condescendeth to your prayer and oblation, as the Psalmist singeth: Let my prayer, O Lord, be directed to thee, as incense in thy sight.[2] Moreover, the soul being the offspring and image of God himself, is delighted in these perfumes and odours, receiving them by those nostrils, by the which itself also entered into this corporeal man, and by the which (as *Job* testifieth)[3] the most lively spirits are sometimes sent forth, which cannot be retained in man's heart, boiling either through choler, or labour; whence some think that the faculty of smelling is the most lively and spiritual of all the senses.

Further, perfumes, sacrifice, and unction penetrate all things, and open the gates of the elements and of the heavens, that through them a man can see the secrets of God, heavenly things, and those things which are above the heavens, and also those which descend from the heavens, as angels, and spirits of deep pits, and profound places, apparitions of desert places, and doth make them to come to you, to appear visibly, and obey you; and they pacify all spirits, and attract them as the loadstone iron, and join them with the elements, and cause the spirits to assume bodies: for truly the spiritual body is very much incrassated by them, and made more gross: for it liveth by vapours, perfumes and the odours of sacrifices.

Moreover whatsoever thou operatest, do it with an earnest affection and hearty desire; that the goodness of the heavens and heavenly bodies may favour thee, whose favour, that thou mayest more easily obtain, the fitness of the place, time, profession, custom, diet, habit, exercise and name also do wonderfully conduce: for by these the power of nature is not only changed, but also overcome.

For a fortunate place conduceth much to favour: neither without cause did the Lord speak to *Abraham* that he should come into the land which he would show him; and *Abraham* arose and journeyed towards the south:[4] in like manner, *Isaac* went to Gerarath, where he sowed and gathered an hundredfold, and waxed very rich.[5]

But what place is congruous to each one, must be found out by his nativity, which thing he that knoweth not, let him observe where his spirits are especially recreated, where his senses are more lively, where the health of his body and his strength is most vigorous, where his businesses succeed best, where most favour him, where his enemies are overthrown, let him know that this region, this place is preordained by God and his angels for him; and is also well disposed, and prepared by the heavens. Therefore reverence this place, and change it according to your time and business, but always fly an unfortunate place.

Fortunate names also make things more fortunate; but unfortunate, unhappy; hence the Romans in lifting their soldiers were wary, lest that the soldiers' first names should be in any measure unfortunate; and for paying tributaries, and musterings of their armies and colonies, they did choose censors[6] with good names. Moreover they believed, that if unfortunate names were changed into fortunate, that the fortune of things would also be changed into better; so Epidamnus,[7] lest that seamen going that way should suffer damage, they commanded to be called Dyrachius; for the same cause they called Maleoton,[8] lest it should cause some mischief, Beneventus; but they thought good to call Lacus, Lucrinus,[9] for the goodness of the name being the most happy place of all.

Make election also of hours and days for thy operations, for not without cause our Saviour spake, are there not twelve hours in the day?[10] and so forth; for the astrologers teach that times can give a certain fortune to our businesses; the magicians likewise have observed, and to conclude, all the ancient wise men consent in this, that it is of very great concernment, that in what moment of time, and disposition of the heavens,

everything, whether natural or artificial hath received its being in this world; for they have delivered, that the first moment hath so great power, that all the course of fortune dependeth thereon, and may be foretold thereby; and in like manner, by the successes of the fortune of everything, they both firmly believed, and experience also testifieth, that the beginning of anything may thereby be found out.

Even as *Sulla* the astrologer foretold, that a most certain destruction approached *Caligula,* who asked him advice concerning his nature;[11] *Metheon* the astrologer foresaw the calamity of the wars which happened afterward to the Athenians, making an expedition against the Syracusans:[12] to the same about to sail to Sicilia, *Meson* the astrologer foretold a great tempest. *Anaxagoras* by the knowledge of the times, forewarned on what days a great stone should fall from the Sun; as afterward, it happened at Aegos, a river of Thracia;[13] on the contrary, *L. Tarnucius Firmianus* by the acts and fortune of *Romulus,* found both the time of his conception and nativity; the same man found out also the nativity of the city of Rome, by marking the successes and fortunes of that city:[14] so *Maternus* reporteth,[15] that the beginning and creation even of this world was found out by the events of things.

For that times can do very much in natural things, may be manifested by many examples; for there are trees, which after the solstice do invert their leaves, as the poplar, elm, olive, limetree, white willow;[16] and shellfishes, crabs, and oysters do increase, the Moon increasing, and when the Moon decreaseth, do grow lean; and the seas in ebbing and flowing do observe the motions and times of the Moon; and Euripus in Euboea,[17] doth it not seven times with wonderful swiftness ebb and flow? And three days in every month, viz. the seventh, eighth, and ninth day of the Moon, it standeth still; and amongst the Troglotides there is a lake, which thrice in a day is made bitter and salt, and again sweet;[18] moreover in the winter time, when all things wither and dry, pennyroyal flourisheth; on the same day, they say, that blown bladders do break, and that the leaves of sallows[19] and pomegranates are turned and forced about; and it is known to all, that which I have seen both in France and Italy, and I know also the sowing thereof, viz. that a nut tree, which seemeth dry all the year, on the even of Saint John's Day[20] doth produce both leaves, and flowers, and ripe fruits: and this miracle doth wholly consist in the observation of the time of its sowing.

Moreover that times can yield some wonderful power to artificial things, the astrologers in their books of elections and images do constantly affirm; and by this means, we read in *Plutarch,* that there was an image amongst the Peleneans made with such art, that what way soever it did look, it did strike all things with terror and very great perturbation, so that no man durst through fear, behold it; and we read in the life of *Apollonius,* that the magicians of Babylon had tied to the roof of their house, four golden fowls, which they called the tongues of the gods; and that they had power to reconcile the minds of the multitude to the love and obedience of the king.[21] In the island Chios there was the face of *Diana* placed on high, whose countenance appeared sad to those which came in, but to those that went out, it appeared cheerful: in Troas, the sacrifices which were left about the image of *Minerva* did not putrify.[22]

In the temple of *Venus* at Paphos, it never rained in the court:[23] if anything was taken forth from the tomb of *Antheus,*[24] showers were poured down from heaven till that which was digged up, was restored into its place: in the tomb of King *Bibria* of Pontus, did arise a laurel, from which if anyone did break a branch and carry it on shipboard, quarrels would never cease until it was thrown over.[25] In the island Boristhenes, no bird did haunt the house of *Achilles:* at Rome, neither fly, nor dog did enter into the palace of *Hercules,* in the ox market.[26] In Olynthus of Thracia there was a place, into the which if a beetle had fallen, it could not get forth, but writhing itself every way it died.[27]

I could bring even innumerable examples, and far more wonderful than these, which antiquity reporteth to have been done by the art of images, and by the observation of times: but lest anyone should think them long since obsolete, and repute them for fables, I will bring more new things, and such as remain even to this time in some places, and I will join to these some artificial wonders.

For they say, that by the art of images it cometh to pass, that at Byzantine serpents hurt not, and that jackdaws fly not over within the walls; that in Crete there are no night owls; that about Naples grasshoppers are never heard; that at Venice, no kind of fly doth enter the public houses of barbers; that in Toledo in the public shambles, one only fly is seen all the year long, of a notable whiteness.

And we in the foregoing book have declared already both the fashions and times, by the observation of which, these things and such like may be done; moreover you ought especially to observe the virtue of speeches and words, for by these the soul is spread forth into inferior substances, into stones, metals, plants, animals, and all natural things, imprinting divers figures and passions on them, enforcing all creatures, or leading and drawing them by a certain affection.

So *Cato* testifieth, that weary oxen are refreshed by words, and also that by prayers and words, you may obtain of *Tellus,*[28] that it produce unusual trees; trees also may by this means be entreated to pass over to another place, and to grow in another ground: rapes[29] grow the greater, if they be entreated when they are sown, to be beneficial to them, their family, and neighbours; the peacock also being commended, presently extends his feathers.

But on the contrary, it is found by experience that the herb basil, being sown with cursings and railings, is more flourishing; also a kind of lobster doth cure burnings and scaldings, if so be that in the meantime his name be not named: further, they which use witchcraft, kill trees by praising them, and thus do hurt sown corn and children:[30] moreover they say that there is so great power in man's execrations, that they chase and banish even wicked spirits: *Eusebius* declareth that by this means *Serapis* amongst the Egyptians, did publish short sentences, by the which devils were expelled, and he taught also, how devils having assumed the forms of brute beasts, do ensnare men.

To conclude, in all businesses, put God before your eyes, for it is written in Deuteronomy, when you shall seek the Lord your God, you shall find him.[31] Whence we read in Mark, that whatsoever ye shall desire and pray for, believing that you shall receive it, it shall come to pass for you;[32] and in Matthew, if you shall have faith as a grain of mustard seed, nothing shall be impossible for you;[33] also the fervent prayer of a righteous man prevaileth much, for *Elias* (as *James* saith) was a man like unto us, subject unto passions, and he prayed earnestly, that it might not rain upon the Earth, and it rained not in three years and six months; and again he prayed, and the heaven gave rain, and the Earth brought forth its fruit.[34]

But take heed in your prayers, lest that you should desire some vain thing, or that which is against the will of God; for God would have all things good: neither shalt thou use the name of thy God in vain, for he shall not go unpunished, who taketh his name for a vain thing: be abstemious and give alms, for the angel saith to *Tobiah*, prayer is good with fasting and alms;[35] and we read in the Book of Judith: know ye, that the Lord will hear your prayers, if ye shall persevere in fastings and prayers in his sight.[36]

Notes—Chapter LXIV

1. *perish before the Lord*—Leviticus 22:3.

2. *incense in thy sight*—Psalms 141:2.

3. *Job testifieth*—Job 27:3.

4. *towards the south*—Genesis 12:1–9.

5. *waxed very rich*—Genesis 26:12.

6. *censors*—Two Roman officials who had the power of striking off from the list of Roman knights the names of those who had disgraced themselves.

7. *Epidamnus*—When the Romans took control of this Greek town, they associated the name with the Latin *damnum* (damage, loss, hurt, injury), which they considered unlucky, and changed it to Dyrrachinus.

8. *Maleoton*—Maleventum, so called because of its bad air, was one of the most ancient towns in Italy. When the Romans colonized it in 268 BC, they changed its name to Beneventum (good air).

9. *Lucrinus*—Latin: *lucrum*—advantage, profit. See the geographical note on Lucrinus Lacus.

10. *hours in the day*—John 11:9.

11. *concerning his nature*—"Also Sulla the astrologer, when Gaius [Caligula] asked his counsel and opinion as touching the horoscope of his nativity, told him plain that most certain and inevitable death approached near at hand" (Suetonius "Gaius Caesar Caligula" 57. In *History of the Twelve Caesars* [Holland, 220]).

12. *against the Syracusans*—The Athenians laid siege to the city of Syracuse in Sicily during the Peloponnesian war. In 413 BC the Athenian army was totally destroyed.

13. *river of Thracia*—

The Greeks boast that Anaxagoras, the Clazomenian, in the second year of the 78th Olympiad [467 BC], from his knowledge of what relates to the heavens, had predicted, that at a certain time, a stone would fall from the sun. And the thing accordingly happened, in the daytime, in a part of Thrace, at the river Aegos. The stone is now to be seen, a waggon-load in size and of a burnt appearance; there was also a comet shining in the night at that time. (Pliny 2.59 [Bostock and Riley, 1:88–9])

14. *fortunes of that city*—See biographical note on Firmanus Tarutius.

15. *Maternus reporteth*—

Those divine men, altogether worthy and admirable, Petosiris and Nechepso, who approached the very secrets of divinity, also handed down to us the birthchart of the universe in order to show us that man is made in the likeness of the universe according to those same principles by which the universe itself is ruled; and that he is sustained forever by those same everlasting fires. (Firmicus Maternus *Ancient Astrology [Matheseos libri VIII]* 3 Proem, trans. Jean Rhys Bram [Park Ridge, NJ: Noyes Press, 1975], 71)

16. *white willow*—*Salix alba,* also called Huntingdon willow.

17. *Euripus in Euboea*—Any part of the seacoast subject to violent tides was called Euripus, but the name was especially applied to the narrow strait separating Euboea from Boeotia:

> There are, however, some tides which are of a peculiar nature, as in the Tauromenian Euripus [Straits of Messina], where the ebb and flow is more frequent than in other places, and in Euboea, where it takes place seven times during the day and the night. The tides intermit three times during each month, being the 7th, 8th and 9th day of the moon. (Pliny 2.100 [Bostock and Riley, 1:127])

18. *salt, and again sweet*—"In the country of the Troglodytae, what they call the Fountain of the Sun, about noon is fresh and very cold; it then gradually grows warm, and, at midnight, becomes hot and saline" (Pliny 2.106 [Bostock and Riley, 1:134]). The name Troglodytae was applied by the Greek geographers to primitive peoples living in caves—especially to those dwelling on the western shore of the Red Sea in Upper Egypt and Ethiopia. This coast was called Troglodytice.

19. *sallows*—A name applied to several low-growing species of willow, such as the *Salix cinerae* and *Salix caprae*.

20. *Saint John's Day*—The Eve of Saint John's was celebrated on midsummer eve (summer solstice) by songs, dances, leaping over fires and burning flower garlands. Boughs were taken from living trees and hung over the doors of houses. The soul was believed to leave the body of those asleep and wander, for which reason people sat up all night and celebrated.

21. *of the king*—

> Damis tells of their entering the great hall [at Babylon], whose vaulted ceiling imitates the sky and is covered with sapphires of celestial blue, overlaid with images of their gods, done in gold and shining out from that background as if floating in air. The king usually holds his court in this hall, and four golden wry-necks hung from the ceiling, which birds are symbolic of the goddess of retribution, to admonish the king not to exalt himself above mankind. The Magi who frequent the palace claim to have suspended them there, and call them the tongues of the gods. (Philostratus *Life and Times of Apollonius of Tyana* 1.25 [Eels, 25–6])

22. *did not putrify*—See note 23 below.

23. *never rained in the court*—"There is at Paphos a celebrated temple of Venus, in a certain court of which it never rains; also at Nea, a town of Troas, in the spot which surrounds the statue of Minerva: in this place also the remains of animals that are sacrificed never putrefy" (Pliny 2.97 [Bostock and Riley, 1:123]).

24. *tomb of Antheus*—Antheus was one of the Trojan followers of Aeneas.

25. *was thrown over*—

> In the same country [Pontus], too, is the port of Amycus, rendered famous by the circumstance that King Bebryx was slain there. Since the day of his death his tomb has been covered by a laurel, which has obtained the name of the "frantic laurel," from the fact that if a portion of it is plucked and taken on board ship, discord and quarrelling are the inevitable result, until it has been thrown overboard. (Pliny 16.89 [Bostock and Riley, 3:431–2])

26. *in the ox market*—Perhaps the temple of Hercules that stood near the Porta Trigemina and contained a bronze statue and an altar upon which the hero himself was supposed to once have sacrificed. Every year the city praetor offered up a young cow, which was then eaten by the people within the temple.

27. *every way it died*—"In Thrace, near Olynthus, there is a small locality, the only one in which this animal cannot exist; from which circumstance it has received the name of 'Cantharolethus' ['Beetle-bane']." (Pliny 11.34 [Bostock and Riley, 3:34])

28. *Tellus*—Tellus was the Roman name for Gaea, goddess of the Earth. Her festival, the Fordicidia (or Hordicidia) was celebrated on April 15 with the sacrifice of cows.

29. *rapes*—Turnips.

30. *hurt sown corn and children*—On the subject of praise used as a curse, see Elworthy [1895] 1971, ch. 1.

31. *shall find him*—Deuteronomy 4:29.

32. *pass for you*—Mark 11:24.

33. *impossible for you*—Matthew 17:20.

34. *forth its fruit*—James 5:16–8.

35. *fasting and alms*—Apocryphal book of Tobit 12:8.

36. *prayers in his sight*—Apocryphal book of Judith 4:13.

CHAPTER LXV

The conclusion of the whole work.

These are the things, which for an introduction into magic we have collected out of the tradition of the ancients, and diversly compiled in this book, in short words, yet sufficient for those who are intelligent; some of these things are written in order, some without order, some things are delivered by fragments, some things are even hid, and left for the search of the intelligent, who more acutely contemplating these things which are written, and diligently searching, may obtain the complete rudiments of the magical art, and also infallible experiments.

For we have delivered this art in such a manner, that it may not be hid from the prudent and intelligent, and yet may not admit wicked and incredulous men to the mysteries of these secrets, but leave them destitute and astonished, in the shade of ignorance and desperation.

You therefore sons of wisdom and learning, search diligently in this book, gathering together our dispersed intentions, which in divers places we have propounded, and what is hid in one place, we make manifest in another, that it may appear to you wise men; for, for you only have we written, whose mind is not corrupted, but regulated according to the right order of living, who in chastity, and honesty, and in sound faith fear and reverence God: whose hands are free from sin and wickedness, whose manners are gentle, sober, and modest, you only shall find out this knowledge which is preserved for you, and the secrets which are hid by many enigmas cannot be perceived but by a profound intellect, which when you shall obtain, the whole science of the invincible magical discipline will insinuate itself into you: and those virtues will appear to you, which in times past *Hermes, Zoroastes, Apollonius,* and the others, who wrought miracles, obtained.

But ye, envious, calumniators, sons of base ignorance, and foolish lewdness, come not nigh our writings, for they are your enemies, and stand on a precipice, that ye may err and fall headlong into misery.

If any therefore through his incredulity or dullness of intellect, doth not obtain his desire, let him not impute the fault of his ignorance to me, or say that I have erred, or purposely written falsely and lied, but let him accuse himself, who understandeth not our writings; for they are obscure, and covered with divers mysteries, by the which it will easily happen, that many may err and lose their sense; therefore let no man be angry with me, if we have folded up the truth of this science with many enigmas, and dispersed it in divers places, for we have not hidden it from the wise, but from the wicked and ungodly, and have delivered it in such words which necessarily blind the foolish, and easily may admit the wise to the understanding of them.

Finis.

To the Reverend Father, and Doctor of Divinity Aurelius de Aquapendente, Austin Frier; Henry Cornelius Agrippa sendeth greeting.[1]

By those letters (most reverend Father!) which you sent me since the second of this month,[2] I understand your candidness towards me, and great learning, and indeed the curious searching after these things which lie hid in darkness; I did presently rejoice, and do bless myself that I have entered into acquaintance with such a friend, with whom I may improve my gifts; and now (this handwriting being my witness) I reckon you amongst the chiefest of my friends.

But oh, who are your leaders that you follow, daring to enter into the house of *Dadalus*,[3] from whence is no return, and of most dreadful *Minois,* and daring to go through the watches, and commit yourself to the sisters of destiny?[4] Who are your masters that you are conversant about such huge things, daring to attempt to make a wandering deity, stable; perfidious, faithful; and the most fugatious[5] of all the gods to be more constant than *Adrastia;*[6] take heed that you be not deceived by them that are deceived.

Neither can the great reading of books direct you here, since they are but as riddles. How great writings are there made of the irresistible power of the magical art, of the prodigious images of astrologers, of the monstrous transmutations of alchemists, of that blessed stone, by which, *Midas* like, all metals that were touched are presently transmuted into gold, or silver, all which are found vain, fictitious, and false, as often as they are practised according to letter. Yet such things are delivered, and writ by great and grave philosophers, and holy men, whose traditions, who dare say are false? Nay, it were impious to think that they were lies.

There is therefore another meaning than what is written in letters, and that is veiled with divers mysteries, and as yet clearly explained by none of the masters, and which I believe no man can attain to by reading of books only, without a skillful, and faithful master,[7] unless he be divinely illuminated, as very few are. Therefore it is a vanity for any man that searcheth into the secrets of nature to give himself to bare reading. For they that thus do, are, being ensnared in the gins of the exterior spirits, to whom it is given to rule, made dangerous slaves, not knowing themselves, and go back into the footsteps of their flocks, seeking without themselves, what they have in themselves.

And this is that which I would have you know, because in us is the operator of all wonderful effects, who knows how to discern, and effect, and that without any sin or offense to God, whatsoever the monstrous mathematicians, the prodigious magicians, the envious alchemists, and bewitching necromancers, can do by spirits. In us I say is the operator of miracles.

> Not the bright stars of the sky, nor flames of hell,
> But the spirit that these doth make; doth in us dwell.

But of these I shall discourse more fully, but in your presence (for these things are not to be written, but to be infused by a few sacred words, and with face to face), and that when I shall haply see you.

Now as concerning those books which you desire of me, some of them were sometimes in my custody, but now are not.[8] But as for those books which you have of mine which were made in my youth, being entitled Of Occult Philosophy, the two former of them were deficient in many things, the third is wholly imperfect, and contains but a certain epitome of my writings. But I will (God willing) set forth the whole work, being made entire, and revised, reserving the key thereof for most intimate friends only, one whereof you need not at all question but that I reckon you.

Farewell and prosper.

From Lyons the XXIV of September, anno Domini MDXXVII.

Notes—To Aurelius

1. *sendeth greeting*—In the Latin *Opera* this letter is represented in the Epistolarum 5.14.

2. *second of this month*—September 2, 1527.

3. *house of Dadalus*—Daedalus constructed the labyrinth at Cnosus to hold the Minotaur. See his biographical note.

4. *sisters of destiny*—The three Fates, Clotho, Lachesis and Atropos.

5. *fugatious*—Fleeting, fleeing. Perhaps the reference is to Fortune.

6. *Adrastia*—Surname for Nemesis, the goddess who metes out happiness and unhappiness to mortals and maintains a just balance. She was looked upon as an avenging deity who sooner or later would overtake the reckless sinner.

7. *faithful master*—It is an accepted tenet in magic that power, or initiation (the same, since knowledge is power) can only be conferred from master to disciple. However a disciple may have for his master one of the gods, and so may be solitary, yet not alone.

8. *now are not*—Agrippa could scarcely set down in writing that he possessed forbidden books, even if he still retained them.

Unto the Same Man.[1]

By your courteous letters (most reverend Father!) I have seen, as in a glass, your whole mind, which I heartily embrace, and I would have you know that you shall be welcome to me beyond expression, and that you are seated deeply in my affections, and that I am such an one (I write this out of the abundance of my heart) as am not wont upon any occasion to forsake my friends. Wherefore that you may obtain the desires, which are no less than mine, I will hasten to come to you. When we shall come face to face, hear and speak with one the other, I know our friendship will be indissoluble, and endure forever.

But now concerning that philosophy which you require to know, I would have you know, that it is to know God himself, the worker of all things, and to pass into him by a whole image of likeness (as by an essential contract, and bond) whereby thou mayest be transformed, and made as God, as the Lord spake concerning *Moses,* saying: Behold, I have made thee the god of Pharaoh.[2] This is that true, high occult philosophy of wonderful works.

The key thereof is the intellect, for by how much higher things we understand, with so much the sublimer virtues are we endowed, and so much greater things do work, and that more easily, and efficaciously. But our intellect being included in the corruptible flesh, unless it shall exceed the way of the flesh, and obtain a proper nature, cannot be united to these virtues (for like to like) and is in searching into these occult secrets of God, and nature, altogether ineffica-cious; for it is no easy thing for us to ascend to the heavens. For how shall he that hath lost himself in mortal dust, and ashes, find God? How shall he apprehend spiritual things that is swallowed up in flesh and blood? Can man see God, and live? What fruit shall a grain of corn bear if it be not first dead?

For we must die, I say die to the world, and to the flesh, and all senses, and to the whole man animal, who would enter into these closets of secrets, not because the body is separated from the soul, but because the soul leaves the body: of which death *Paul* wrote to the Colossians: Ye are dead, and your life is hid with Christ;[3] and elsewhere he speaks more clearly of himself: I know a man, whether in the body, or out of the body I cannot tell, God knows, caught up unto the third heaven,[4] etc.

I say by this death, precious in the sight of God, we must die, which happens to few, and perhaps not always. For very few whom God loves, and are virtuous, are made so happy. And first those that are born, not of flesh and blood, but of God. Secondly those that are dignified to it by the blessing of nature, and the heavens at their birth. The rest endeavour by merits, and art, of which more fully when I see you.

But this I will advise you, that you be not deceived concerning me, as if I at any time having received such divine things should boast of them to you, or should arrogate any such thing to myself, or could hope to have them granted to me, who hitherto have been a soldier, consecrated with man's blood, having been almost always belonging to the King's Court, bound to a most dear wife by the bond of flesh, exposed to all the blast of inconstant fortune, and being crossed in my flesh, in the world, and worldly affairs, and therefore could not obtain the sublime gifts of the immortal God. But I would be accounted as a director, who waiting always at the doors, shows to others which way they must go.

But as for my love to you, you are indeed a little deceived: I do not see how you are my debtor, seeing I have bestowed nothing upon you, only I am ready when occasion serves to bestow all things.

So farewell and prosper.

From Lyons XIX November, anno Domini MDXXVII.

Notes—Unto the Same Man

1. *Same Man*—See the Latin *Opera,* Epistolarum 5.19.

2. *god to Pharaoh*—Exodus 7:1.

3. *hid with Christ*—Colossians 3:3.

4. *unto the third heaven*—II Corinthians 12:2.

Henry Cornelius Agrippa
sendeth greeting to
a certain friend of the King's Court.[1]

The ancients were wont to brand notorious folly with this proverb, viz. to bring owls to Athens:[2] but it is not a part of less folly, but of most great impiety, to send devils to hell. You know what I call hell, viz. that school of wickednesses, which with much displeasure I have elsewhere in its colours notoriously showed the Court to be. But there was never so just an occasion of writing and of indignation given as now, if it were lawful to treat of the whole business as I should, yet I cannot contain but give you an argument of it.

Now therefore hear a thing both foolish and impious: there was sent for out of Germany with no small charges a certain master of spirits, that is a necromancer, who possesseth a power over spirits, that as *James* and *Jambres*[3] resisted *Moses,* so he should oppose *Caesar;*[4] for they were persuaded by the Father of Lies, that he could foretell all things to come, and disclose all secret counsels, and manifest even the thoughts; moreover that he was endowed with so great power, that he could bring back the King's children through the air, even as we read that *Habacuck* with his pulse was carried to the den of lions,[5] and that he could do as *Elisha* did being besieged in Dotham,[6] show mountains full of horsemen and fiery chariots, and a very great army; moreover that he could find out and fetch up the treasures of the Earth, and compel what marriages and affections he pleased, to break them off, and cure all desperate diseases,

by a Stygian medicine, as a confirmed hectic, a radicated dropsy, leprosy in the bones; and:

Who wisely can the knotty gout soon cure,
And health even to the desperate procure.

See where their faith is placed, where their hope is reposed, who endeavour to subject the elements, heaven, fate, nature, providence, God, and all things to the command of one magician: and seek for the preservation of a kingdom from devils, the enemies of public preservation; saying in their heart with *Ochozias,*[7] there is not a God in Israel, let us go and consult *Beelzebub* the god of Achron, and as *Saul* speaking to the witch,[8] saith, the Philistines fight against me, and God hath deserted me, and will not hear me, therefore am I come to you.

What, do they so much despair of God, that they have judged it requisite to desire the aid of the devils? Is not this according to the word of *Jude*[9] and *Peter,*[10] to deny God and *Jesus* Christ our Lord and saviour who hath redeemed us, and to bring upon themselves swift destruction? Do they not treasure up for themselves the fierce wrath of the Lord who will send it upon them by evil spirits? Are they not delivered over to a reprobate sense, who desire the certainty of secret counsels from the Devil, the father of lies, and hope for victory elsewhere than from the Lord of Hosts?

And further, this added boldness to this abominable worker of idolatry and sacrilege, that the orthodox mother doth very much favour those things, and the authority of her most Christian son is accommodated, and gifts bestowed out of the sacred pence; the pillars of the Church, bishops and cardinals, winking at, yea furthering this abominable work; and the wicked nobles applaud this operation of impiety, as the crows the works of the wolf.

What greater wickedness have Pharaoh, *Balack, Saul, Ahab* with his *Jezabel, Ochozias, Nabuchadnezzar, Balthazar, Sennacherib* and the other worshippers of *Balaam*, committed?

Pharaoh called forth his magicians against *Moses;*[11] they being convicted in the third plague, confessed the finger of God:[12] but the king being obstinate through the ten plagues perished in the Red Sea;[13] *Balack* the Moabite sent forth *Baalam* the sorcerer that he should curse Israel,[14] but God himself turned the curse into a blessing;[15] *Balack* is cursed;[16] what did the answers of *Samuel* or the witch profit *Saul?* Was he not slain in the mountain Gilboah?[17] *Ahab* and *Jezabel* being wickedly married together, did confide in the prophets of *Baal,*[18] and according to the word of the Lord, a lying spirit went forth into the mouths of all the prophets who promised prosperity to *Ahab* going up against Ramoth Gilead,[19] but *Ahab* fell, and *Jezabel* was thrown down headlong, and the dogs did eat her:[20] *Asa* a king of Juda is reproved by the prophet of the Lord, because that in his sickness he sought not the Lord, but trusted to the skill of his physician:[21] have not they committed a greater sin, who leave God the saviour, and the wholesome virtues of nature, and seek for help of Satan? *Ochozias*[22] did thus in times past, and therefore heard from the prophet of the Lord, thou shalt not descend from thy bed on which thou art, but shalt certainly die.

Let the series of the other unrighteous kings be run over, and also the histories of the gentiles. *Zoroastes, Diatharus, Croesus, Pompey, Pyrrhus, Crassus, Nero, Julian,* what have they gained by their magicians and diviners, who falsely feigned prosperity for them? Were they not all reduced to nothing, and did they not wickedly perish in their sins? So are all these ungodly follies wont to bring destruction to the admirers thereof; to the which truly, they who especially confide, are made the most unfortunate of all men.

I deny not but that there are natural sciences, metaphysical arts, occult ingenuities, which can, without offending God, or injuring faith or religion, preserve kingdoms, dive into councils, overcome enemies, deliver captives, increase wealth, obtain the good will of men, expel diseases, conserve health, prolong life, and restore strength of youth: there are moreover sacred religious intercessions, public supplications, private prayers of good men: by the which we may not only turn away the wrath of God, but also entreat him to be gracious unto us.

Besides if there be a certain art to foretell, and work miracles, which the ancients call *calomagia*[23] or *theurgia,*[24] surely it is unknown unto these fools and slaves of the Devil, for to find out things to come, and to pronounce truth concerning those things which hang over our heads, and are occult, and from heaven portended unto men; and to effect things which exceed the common course of nature, belongeth only to a man of profound and perfect knowledge, and of a most pure life and faith, and not to men most vain and unlearned.

But every creature serveth those who are innocent, and learned in the law of God, for their faith's sake; and whatsoever they shall ask they shall receive: so the ravens fed *Eliah,*[25] and at his prayers the Earth withheld her fruits, the heaven denied rain,[26] and showered down fire upon the wicked:[27] so the ravens served *Elisha,* the angels fought for him;[28] rivers are passed dry-foot;[29] the lions laying aside their fierceness, and not regarding their hunger, fawn on *Daniel;*[30] and the hot fiery furnace burneth not the children.[31] These are not works of necromancers and sorcerers, nor of devils, but of faithful and godly men; for not the devils, but the spirit of God doth assist them.

I confess there are some (perhaps many) even at this time, who are very wise, and of wonderful knowledge, virtue and power, and of a pure conversation, most prudent, and also disposed by age and strength, that they can very much profit the Commonwealth by their counsel and operations; but your courtiers contemn these men, as those who are very far from their purpose, who for wisdom have malice, guile and deceit; for counsel deceit, and craft for knowledge; guile, and perfidiousness for prudence.

Superstition is in the place of religion, and God is blasphemed in afflictions: and what faith (as saith the Apostle) is perfected in weakness[32] is contemned: but they run to the invocations of evil spirits. Every good man is mocked at by them, bold hypocrisy is promoted, truth is accounted a crime; praise and rewards are reserved for foolishness and wickedness.

O fools, and wicked, who by these arts would establish a kingdom, by which formerly most potent empires have fallen, and have been utterly overthrown; of whom it was truly spoken by *Jeremiah,* our crown is fallen, woe to us because we have sinned:[33] which I wish might not be so truly as fitly applied to you.

For truly that verse, the numeral letters being gathered together MCVI expresseth the year MDXXIV,[34] wherein according to the account your king was taken at Papia:[35] did not ye see these things, and admire at them, which before they were done you judged impossible? And as yet you are proud, and obdurate in your affliction. You dispise the prophets, and the threatenings of God are as tales to you.

Behold, it is at hand, and as yet you shall see, and feel the great things of God upon the whole Earth, and shall tremble because the misery which you know not shall come upon you suddenly; whither then will ye fly? Stand with your enchanters and with the multitude of your sorceries, if haply they can profit you, or you can be made thereby stronger. Will not that German sorcerer[36] that is sent for, save you, and make lying, prophets, and prevail against the wrath of the Lord, and deliver you from evil?

No, ye wicked, *no;* unless the Lord shall build, and keep the cities, and kingdom, all the keepers thereof labour and watch in vain. It is the work of God alone, not of devils, not of magicians, to suspend or change the sentence of the prophets.

But if you will with your whole heart turn unto his mercy, and will change your wickedness, then you may be freed from evil, as was *Nebuchadnezzar,* who by the counsel of *Daniel* redeeming his sins by alms, and his iniquities by taking pity on the poor,[37] avoided the imminent wrath of God for a time, until in the court at Babylon he with a proud speech recalled it back to himself again.[38]

Achab most impious, with his *Jezebel,* to whom the Lord threatened death by *Elias,* was, because he turned to God, made again the word of the Lord to *Eliah,* because *Achab* feared my face I will not bring the evil in his days.[39]

The Ninevites, because by the edict of the king and princes they repented at the preaching of *Jonas,* were totally freed from the imminent punishment.[40]

Esaias brought this sentence to *Ezechias,* that he should set his house in order, because he should die; he prayed and wept, and was healed, and fifteen years added to his life; for thus the Lord spake to the same man by the same prophet, I have seen thy tears and heard thy prayers, behold I will add to thy days fifteen years; moreover I will deliver thee from the hand of the King of Assyria and this city, and protect it;[41] so much could the conversion and prayer of this pious king do, who though he prayed for himself alone, yet obtained not only for himself, but also for the city and people.

It is the Lord only who preserveth the King and who giveth wisdom to the King's son; they ought to fly to this master, who seek salvation, and not to magicians and sorcerers: put on righteousness and fear of the Lord, you who desire prosperity.

If the stability of a kingdom be sought for, it is written; the just shall inherit the land,[42] the just shall be had in everlasting remembrance, he shall not be moved forever.[43] If security be sought for; they that fear the Lord shall not be afraid for evil tidings, but shall scorn all their enemies.[44] If honour, and wealth be sought for; in his house are glory, and riches.[45] If praise, and favour; the generation of the righteous shall be blessed.[46] If power; he shall be powerful on the Earth, and his seed also:[47] his strength shall be exalted in glory.[48] If marriage, and prosperity of wedlock;

he wife shall be as a vine flourishing on the house side, and his children as olive branches.[49] If health of body, and strength; the Lord will not suffer his holy one to see corruption.[50]

Lastly, blessed is the man in all things that fears the Lord, who is unspotted in the way, who goes not into the council of the wicked, who takes pity on the poor, and needy. For in an evil day the Lord shall deliver him, and shall not deliver him into the hands of his enemies. All the wicked shall see, and be vexed, and shall gnash their teeth, and pine away, their desire shall perish.

Let this suffice for admonition. For I will not more curiously prosecute this matter, lest haply the evilness of the subject should provoke me to write more than is expedient.

Farewell.

From Paris, XIII of February, Anno MDXXVIII after the Roman account.

Notes—To a Certain Friend

1. *King's Court*—See the Latin *Opera,* Epistolarum 5.26.

2. *owls to Athens*—See note 20, ch. LIV, bk. I.

3. *James and Jambres*—Jannes and Jambres. See II Timothy 3:8, with reference to Exodus 7:11.

4. *Caesar*—Emperor Charles V.

5. *den of lions*—Apocryphal book Bel and the Dragon 36; or in Knox, Daniel 14:35.

6. *besieged in Dotham*—Dothan. See II Kings 6:13; 7:6.

7. *Ochozias*—II Kings 1:2.

8. *speaking to the witch*—I Samuel 28:15, where Saul speaks to the ghost of Samuel, not the witch.

9. *Jude*—Jude 14–5.

10. *Peter*—II Peter 2:1.

11. *against Moses*—Exodus 7:11.

12. *finger of God*—Exodus 8:19.

13. *in the Red Sea*—Exodus 14:28.

14. *curse Israel*—Balaam. Numbers 22:6.

15. *into a blessing*—Numbers 23:20.

16. *Balack is cursed*—Balak. Numbers 24:9.

17. *mountain Gilboah*—Gilboa. II Samuel 31:4.

18. *prophets of Baal*—I Kings 16:31; II Chronicles 18:5.

19. *Ramoth Gilead*—II Chronicles 18:19–21.

20. *dogs did eat her*—II Kings 9:36.

21. *his physician*—II Chronicles 16:12.

22. *Ochozias*—That is, Ahaziah. II Kings 1:4.

23. *calomagia*—From the Greek καλο, beautiful; the magic of good spirits.

24. *theurgia*—Greek: θεός, god; εργός, working. Magic of god; white magic, as distinguished from goetia, black magic.

25. *ravens fed Eliah*—I Kings 17:6.

26. *heaven denied rain*—I Kings 17:1.

27. *fire upon the wicked*—II Kings 1:10.

28. *angels fought for him*—II Kings 7:6.

29. *passed dry-foot*—II Kings 2:8.

30. *fawn on Daniel*—Daniel 6:22.

31. *burneth not the children*—Daniel 3:25.

32. *perfected in weakness*—II Corinthians 12:9.

33. *we have sinned*—Lamentations of Jeremiah 5:16.

34. *the year MDXXIV*—The reader must solve this numerological puzzle, as I cannot.

35. *taken at Papia*—Charles V, king of Spain, became emperor of Germany upon the death of Maximilian in 1519. His title was disputed by Francis I of France, and the two went to war. At the long siege of

Pavia in Italy, the army of Charles, who was himself occupied in Spain at the time, took Francis I prisoner. The siege occurred in 1524, but the capture was actually made on February 24, 1525.

36. *German sorcerer*—Can this have been Faust? The German conjurer was certainly very active around this time, among other things casting spells on the head of Martin Luther. The Abbot Trithemius in a letter dated 1507 contemptuously refers to Faust as a fool and a mountebank who should be whipped, further saying that Faust fled the city rather than confront him. Faust is supposed to have died around 1525, but the date is not certain, and a student of Agrippa's, Johann Wierus, says that Faust was a drunken vagabond who had practiced and debased the beautiful art of magic "shamelessly up and down Germany, with unspeakable deceit, many lies and great effect" until 1540 *(De præstigiis dæmonum,* Basel, 1563).

37. *pity on the poor*—Daniel 4:27.

38. *back to himself again*—Daniel 4:30–1.

39. *evil in his days*—I Kings 21:29.

40. *imminent punishment*—Jonah 3:6–10.

41. *protect it*—Isaiah 38:1–6.

42. *inherit the land*—Psalms 37:29.

43. *not be moved forever*—Psalms 112:6.

44. *all their enemies*—Psalms 112:7.

45. *glory, and riches*—Psalms 112:3.

46. *shall be blessed*—Psalms 112:2.

47. *seed also*—Ibid.

48. *exalted in glory*—Psalms 112:9.

49. *olive branches*—Psalms 128:3.

50. *see corruption*—Psalms 16:10.

The censure, or retraction of *Henry Cornelius Agrippa*, concerning magic, after his declamation of the vanity of sciences, and the excellency of the word of God.

Of magic in general.[1]

This place doth require that we speak of magic; for it is so near joined to, and of affinity with astrology, in so much that he that professeth magic without astrology, doth nothing, but altogether is in an error.

Suidas[2] is of the opinion that magic had its name, and original from the Maguseans. It is the common opinion, that it is a Persian name, to which *Porphyry,* and *Apuleius* assent, and that in that tongue it signifies a priest, wise man, or philosopher.

Magic therefore comprehending all philosophy, natural and mathematical, joins the powers of religions to them. Hence also they contain in them goetia, and theurgia,[3] for which cause many divide magic into two parts, viz. natural, and ceremonial.

Notes—Of Magic in General

1. *Of Magic in General*—This forms ch. 41 of Agrippa's *De incertitudine et vanitate scientiarum.*

2. *Suidas*—Usually considered to be the name of a Greek lexicographer about whom nothing is known, who wrote an ancient dictionary of Greek words, both names and places, valuable because it preserves much scholarship and lore otherwise lost. In fact Suidas is the name of the book, not the author, a word from the Latin meaning "stronghold" or "fortress." The work has suffered so many interpolations that it is impossible to date.

3. *goetia, and theurgia*—Black and white magic.

Of natural magic.[1]

It is thought that natural magic is nothing else but the highest power of natural sciences, which therefore is called the height of natural philosophy, and the most absolute consummation thereof, and that which is the active part of natural philosophy, which by the help of natural virtues, from a mutual, and opportune application of them, brings forth operations even to admiration: which magic the Ethiopians, and Indians especially did use, where the virtue of herbs, and stones, and other things looking towards it was sufficient.

It is said that *Hierome* made mention of it to *Paulinus,* where he saith that *Apollonius* the Tyanean was a magician, or philosopher, as also the Pythagoreans;[2] of this kind were those wise men which came to worship Christ with gifts when he was born, which the interpreters of the Chaldeans expound the philosophers of the Chaldeans, such as were *Hiarchas*[3] amongst the Bragmanni, *Tespion*[4] amongst the Gymnosophists, *Budda*[5] amongst the Babylonians, *Numa Pompilius* amongst the Romans, *Zamolxides* amongst the Thracians, *Abbaris* amongst the Hyperboreans, *Hermes* amongst the Egyptians, *Zoroastes* the son of *Oromasus*[6] amongst the Persians.

For the Indians, Ethiopians, Chaldeans, and Persians chiefly did excel in this magic. With which therefore (as *Plato* relates in Alcibiades)[7] the sons of the Persian kings were instructed, that they might learn to administer, and distribute their image to the commonwealth of the world, and the commonwealth to it: and *Cicero* saith in his books Of Divination,[8] that there was none amongst the Persians did enjoy the kingdom, but he that first had learned magic.

Natural magic therefore is that which contemplates the powers of all natural and celestial things, and searching curiously into their sympathy, doth produce occult powers in nature into public view, so coupling inferior things as allurements to the gifts of superior things, by their mutual application, that from thence arise wonderful miracles, not so much by art as by nature, to which art becomes an assistant whilst it works these things.

For magicians, as the most curious searchers of nature, making use of those things which are prepared by nature, by applying active things to passive, produce oftentimes effects before the time ordained by nature, which the vulgar think are miracles, which indeed are natural works, the prevention of the time only coming betwixt: as if anyone should produce roses in the month of March, and ripe grapes, or sown beans, or make parsley to grow into a perfect plant within few hours, nay, and cause greater things, as clouds, rains, thunders, and animals of divers kinds, and very many transmutions of things, many of which sort *Roger Bacon* boasted that he did do by mere natural magic.

Of the works thereof wrote *Zoroastes, Hermes, Eranthes* king of Arabia, *Zacharias* the Babylonian, *Joseph* the Hebrew,[9] *Bocus, Aaron, Zenotenus, Kiramides, Almadal, Thetel, Alchin-*

dus, *Abel, Ptolomy, Geber, Zahel, Nazabarub*,[10] *Thebith, Berith, Solomon, Astaphon, Hipparchus, Alcmeon, Apollonius, Triphon*,[11] and many others, many of whose works are yet entire, and many fragments are yet extant, and have come into my hands.

Some modern men have also wrote of natural magic, but they but a few things, as *Albertus, Arnoldus de Villa Nova, Raimundus Lullie, Bacon*, and *Apponus*, and the author of the book to *Alfonsus*, set forth under the name of *Picatrix*, who also together with natural magic, mixeth much superstition, which indeed the rest have done.

Notes—Of Natural Magic

1. *Natural Magic*—*De incertitudine et vanitate*, ch. 42.

2. *also the Pythagoreans*—

> In accord with the visits of Apollonius to the Arabs were his studies among the Persians, by the same author's [Philostratus] account. We are told that he forbad Damis to consort with the Magi, even though Damis was his only student and companion, but went himself alone and at midnight to study with them in order to spare his comrade the practices of magic for which he had no liking. And when he went to talk with Vardan, the Babylonian king, it is said that he spoke as follows: "My philosophy is from Pythagoras of Samos, who instructed me in the way of worship, and how to know the gods, visible or invisible, and to hold regular communication with them." (Eusebius *Against the Life of Apollonius of Tyana by Philostratus* 11. My paraphrase)

3. *Hiarchus*—Iarchus, leader of the Brahmans, mentioned in Philostratus *Life of Apollonius* 3.16–51.

4. *Tespion*—Thespesion, leader of the Gymnosophists. See *Life of Apollonius* 6.10.

5. *Budda*—Buddha would be more properly placed in India.

6. *Oromasus*—Oromasdes, or Ahura-Mazda.

7. *in Alcibiades*—

> And at fourteen years of age he is handed over to the royal schoolmasters, as they are termed: these are four chosen men, reputed to be the best among the Persians of a certain age; and one of them is the wisest, another the justest, a third the most temperate, and a fourth the most valiant. The first instructs him in the magianism of Zoroaster, the son of Oromasus, which is the worship of the Gods, and teaches him also the duties of his royal office; the second, who is the justest, teaches him always to speak the truth; the third, or most temperate, forbids him to allow any pleasure to be lord over him, that he may be accustomed to be a freeman and king indeed,— lord of himself first, and not a slave; the most valiant trains him to be bold and fearless, telling him that if he fears he is to deem himself a slave ..."(Plato *Alcibiades I* 122a, trans. Benjamin Jowett [1892] [New York: Random House, 1937], 2:755)

8. *books Of Divination*—"And no man can become a king of Persia who is not previous initiated in the doctrine of the magi" (Cicero *De divinatione* 1.41 [Yonge, 182]).

9. *Joseph the Hebrew*—Flavius Josephus.

10. *Nazabarub*—That is, Naza the Arab. Perhaps the same as Norbar the Arab, who was said to have compiled the *Picatrix* (see Thorndike, 2:813)

11. *Triphon*—Perhaps Typhon. Tertullian mentions Typhon in a list of writers on, or practitioners of, magic in his *Treatise on the Soul*, ch. 57. There was a Roman grammarian in the age of Augustus named Tryphon, but he can hardly be intended.

Of mathematical magic.[1]

There are moreover other most witty emulators of nature and most bold inquisitors, which promise they can by the influences of the heavens, obtained without natural virtues, but only by mathematical learning, produce works like to those of nature, as walking, or talking bodies, which have not animal virtues: such was the wooden dove of *Architas*[2] which did fly, and the statue of *Mercury*[3] which did speak; and the brazen head[4] made by *Albertus Magnus,* which they say did speak.

Boetius, a man of a great wit and much learning, excelled in these things, to whom *Cassiodurus* writing concerning such like things, saith, to thee it is appointed to know hard things, and show miracles: by the ingenuity of thy art metals speak, *Diomedes* in brass trumpets, the brazen serpent hisseth, birds are feigned, and those which know no proper sound, are heard sending forth sweet melody; we relate small things of him, who hath power to imitate the heavens.

Concerning these arts I think that is spoken which we read in *Plato,* in the eleventh book of Laws:[5] there is an art given to mortal men by which they should generate certain latter things, not partaking of truth or divinity, but should deduce certain representations of affinity with them. And thus far have magicians gone, being men most bold to do all things, especially that old strong Serpent, the promiser of all sciences favouring them, that they like apes endeavour to emulate God, and nature.

Notes—Of Mathematical Magic

1. *Mathematical Magic—De incertitudine et vanitate scientiarum,* ch. 43.

2. *Architas*—See biographical note on Archytas.

3. *statue of Mercury*—See note 11, ch. LII, bk. III.

4. *brazen head*—See note 22, ch. I, bk. II.

5. *eleventh book of Laws*—See note 8, ch. LXIII, bk. III.

Of enchanting magic.[1]

There is moreover a kind of natural magic, which they call bewitching, medicinary, which is done by cups, love potions, and divers medicaments of sorcerers: of which sort *Democritus* is said to make some, whereby good, happy, and fortunate sons may be begotten: and another whereby we may rightly understand the voices of birds, as *Philostratus* and *Porphyry* relate of *Apollonius*. *Virgil* also[2] speaking of certain Pontic herbs, saith:

> I many times, with these have Moeris spied,
> Changed to a wolf, and in the woods to hide:
> From sepulchres would souls departed charm,
> And corn bear standing from another's farm.

And *Pliny* relates[3] that a certain man, *Demarchus Parrhasitus,* in a sacrifice which the Arcades made by a human sacrifice to *Jupiter Lyceus,* tasted of the entrails of a boy that was sacrificed, and turned himself into a wolf, by reason of which changing of men into a wolf, *Austin* thinks[4] that the name was put upon *Pan Lyceus,* and *Jupiter Lyceus.*

The same *Austin* relates, that whilst he was in Italy, there were certain women magicians like *Circe,* who by giving cheese to travellers turned them into cattle; and when they had carried what burdens they pleased, restored them into men again; and that the same happened to a certain father called *Prestantine*.[5]

But lest anyone should think these things to be but foolish toys, and things impossible, let him call to mind what Scripture mentions concerning *Nebuchadnezzar* the king, how he was turned into an ox,[6] and lived seven years with hay, and at length returned through the mercy of God into a man again, whose body after his death, his son *Evilmerodac* gave as a prey to the vultures, lest he should again rise from the dead, who returned from a beast into a man: and more of this kind doth Exodus relate of the magicians of Pharaoh.[7] But *Solomon* speaks of the same, whether magicians or sorcerers, when he saith, thou hast terrified them O God! because they have done horrible deeds by enchantments.

Moreover, this I would have you know, that these magicians do not search into natural things only, but also those things which do accompany nature, and after a manner put it off, as motions, numbers, figures, sounds, voices, concents,[8] lights, affections of the mind, and words.

So the Psylli, and Marsi[9] called together serpents, and others by other things depressing them, put them to flight. So *Orpheus* repressed the tempest of the Argonauts with a hymn;[10] and *Homer* relates of *Ulysses* that his blood was restrained with words. And in the law of the Twelve Tables[11] punishment was ordained for them who enchanted the corn: that without all doubt the magicians did produce wonderful effects by words, affections, and such like, not only upon themselves, but also upon extraneous things.

All which things are thought to put forth their innate virtue upon other things, draw them to them, or expel them from them, or any otherwise affecting of them, no otherwise than the loadstone draws iron, or jet chaff, or a diamond or garlic[12] bind them, so that by this gradual, and concatenated sympaty of things, not only natural, and celestial gifts, but also intellectual, and divine may, as *Jamblicus, Proclus,* and *Synesius* confirm by the opinion of magicians, be received from above, which *Proclus* in his book Of Sacrifice and Magic[13] confesseth, viz: that by the consent of these kinds of things, the magicians were wont to call up the deities themselves.

To such a height of madness some of them are grown, that from divers constellations of the stars, through intervals of times, and a certain rule of proportions being observed, think that an image of the gods can with a beck receive the spirit of life, and intellect, and so give an answer to them that ask counsel of it, and reveal the secrets of occult truth. Hence it is manifest that this natural magic is, sometimes inclining to goetia, and theurgia, entangled in the wiles and errors of evil spirits.

Notes—Of Enchanting Magic

1. *Enchanting Magic—De incertitudine et vanitate scientiarum*, ch. 44.

2. *Virgil also—*See note I, ch. XLI, bk. I.

3. *Pliny relates—*See note 13, ch. XLV, bk. I.

4. *Austin thinks—*"Nor does he [Varro] think that Pan and Jupiter were called Lycaei in the Arcadian history for any other reason than for their transforming of men into wolves; for this they held impossible to any but a divine power" (Augustine *City of God* 18.17 [Healey, 2:191])

5. *Prestantine—*See note 14, ch. XLV, bk. I.

6. *turned into an ox—*Daniel 4:32. But Nebuchadnezzar only ate grass like an ox—that is, went mad—he was not transformed into an ox.

7. *magicians of Pharaoh—*Exodus 7:11–2; 8:7.

8. *concents—*Musical harmonies; songs.

9. *Psylli, and Marsi—*See note 16, ch. LVIII, bk. I.

10. *with a hymn—*See note 42, ch. XI, B. III.

11. *Twelve Tables—*The Twelve tables contained the earliest code of Roman law. The were compiled from the common law in 450 BC and put up in the Forum for all to read. The original Tables were destroyed when Rome was burnt by the Gauls.

"And then besides, in the laws themselves of the Twelve Tables, do we not read the following words—'Whosoever shall have enchanted the harvest,' and in another place, 'Whosoever shall have used pernicious incantations'?" (Pliny 28.4 [Bostock and Riley, 5:281]).

12. *diamond or garlic—*See note 2, ch. XIII, bk. I.

13. *Of Sacrifice and Magic—*

Now the ancients, having contemplated this mutual sympathy of things, applied for occult purposes, both celestial and terrene natures, by means of which, through a certain similitude, they deduced divine virtues into this inferior abode. (Proclus *De sacrificio et magia,* frag., Latin trans. Ficinus [Venice, 1497], English trans. Thomas Taylor. In Iamblichus *Life of Pythagoras* [Taylor, note to p. 72 on p. 214])

Of goetia and necromancy.[1]

Now the parts of ceremonial magic are goetia and theurgia.

Goetia is unfortunate, by the commerces of unclean spirits made up of the rites of wicked curiosities, unlawful charms, and deprecations, and is abandoned and execrated by all laws. Of this kind are those which we nowadays call necromancers and witches:[2]

> A people envied by the gods, have skill,
> Begot by the Evil One, even at their will
> The heavens for to blemish, and the things
> Which are in heaven, and on Earth to bring
> Out of order, and the poles for to force,
> And of the rivers for to turn the course,
> The mountains level, and the sky to drive
> Under the Earth———

These therefore are they which call upon the souls of the dead, and those which the ancients called *Epodi*,[3] who enchant boys,[4] and bring them out into the speech of the oracle, and which carry about them familiar spirits, as we read of *Socrates* and such, as it is said, they fed in glasses, by which they feign themselves to prophesy. And all these proceed two ways.

For some endeavour to call and compel evil spirits, adjuring by a certain power, especially of divine names; for seeing every creature fears, and reverenceth the name of him who made it, no marvel, if goetians infidels, pagans, Jews, Saracens, and men of every prophane sect and society do bind devils by invocating the divine name.

Now there are some that are most impiously wicked indeed, that submit themselves to devils, sacrifice to, and adore them, and thereby become guilty of idolatry, and the basest abasement: to which crimes if the former are not obnoxious, yet they expose themselves to manifest dangers. For even compelled devils always deceive us whithersoever we go.

Now from the sect of the goetians have proceeded all those books of darkness, which *Vulpianus* the lawyer calls books disallowed to be read, and forthwith appointed them to be destroyed, of which sort the first is *Zabulus* reported to invent, who was given to unlawful arts, then *Barnabas*[5] a certain Cyprian; and now in these days there are carried about books with feigned titles, under the names of *Adam*,[6] *Abel*,[7] *Enoch*,[8] *Abraham*,[9] *Solomon*,[10] also *Paul*,[11] *Honorius*,[12] *Cyprianus*,[13] *Albertus*,[14] *Thomas*,[15] *Hierome*,[16] and of a certain man of York,[17] whose toys *Alphonsus* King of Castile, *Robert* an Englishman, *Bacon*,[18] and *Apponius,* and many other men of a deplored wit have foolishly followed. Moreover they have not made men only and saints, and patriarchs, and the angels of God, the authors of such execrable opinions, but they boast also that those books were delivered by *Raziel,* and *Raphael* the angels of *Adam* and *Tobias.*

Which books openly betray themselves to him that looks narrowly into them, to be a rule, rite, and custom of their precepts, and a kind of words, and characters, an order of extruction, an empty phrase, and to contain nothing but mere toys, and impostures, and to be made in latter times by men ignorant of all ancient magic, and forlorn artists of pernicious art, of prophane observations mixed with the ceremonies of our religion, with many unknown names, and seals intermixed, that thereby they may terrify and astonish the simple, and ignorant.

Moreover it doth not yet appear that these arts are fables: for unless there were such indeed, and by them many wonderful and hurtful things done, there would not be such strict divine, and human laws made concerning them, for the utter exterminating of them.

And why do the goetians use those evil spirits only, but because good angels will hardly appear, expecting the command of God, and come not but to men pure in heart, and holy in life: but the evil are easily called up, favouring him that is false, and counterfeiting holiness are always ready to deceive with their craft, that they may be worshipped, and adored.

And because women are most desirous of secrets, and less cautious, and prone to superstition, they are the more easily deceived, and therefore give up themselves the more readily to them, and do great prodigies. The poets sing of Circe,[19] Medea,[20] and others of this sort; Cicero, Pliny, Seneca, Austin, and many others, as well philosophers as Catholic doctors, and historians, also the Scriptures, testify the like.

For in the books of the Kings we read, that a woman who lived at Endor, called up the soul of Samuel the prophet,[21] although many interpret it not to be the soul of the prophet, but an evil spirit, which took upon him his shape. Yet the Hebrew masters say that Austin to Simplicianus doth not deny but it might be the true spirit of Samuel, which might easily be called up from its body before a complete year after his departure, as also the goetians teach. Also magician necromancers suppose that might be done by certain natural powers and bonds, as we have said in our books of Occult Philosophy.

Therefore the ancient Fathers, skillful of spiritual things, did not without cause ordain that the bodies of the dead should be buried in a holy place, and be accompanied with lights, and sprinkled with holy water, and be perfumed with frankincense, and incense, and be expiated by prayers as long as they continued above ground.

For as the masters of the Hebrews say, all our body and carnal animal, and whatsoever in us depends upon the matter of the flesh, being ill disposed, is left for meat to the Serpent, and as they called it, to Azazel,[22] who is the lord of the flesh and blood, and the prince of this world, and is called in Leviticus the prince of deserts, to whom it is said in Genesis: Thou shalt eat dust all the days of thy life; and in Isaiah: Dust thy bread, i.e. our body created of the dust of the Earth, so long as it shall not be sanctified, and turned into better, that it be no longer an effect of the Serpent, but of God, viz. a spiritual made of carnal, according to the word of Paul, saying, that which is sowed a carnal, shall arise a spiritual;[23] and elsewhere, all indeed shall rise, but all shall not be changed because many shall remain forever as meat of the Serpent.

This filthy and horrid matter of the flesh and meat of the Serpent we therefore cast off by death, changing it for a better and spiritual, which shall be in the resurrection of the dead; and is already done in those, who have tasted of the first fruits of the resurrection, and many have already attained to, by the virtue of the divine Spirit, in this life, as Enoch, Eliah and Moses, whose bodies were changed into a spiritual nature, and have not seen corruption; neither are their carcasses left to the power of the Serpent. And this was that dispute of the Devil with Michael the archangel concerning the body of Moses, of which Jude makes mention[24] in his Epistle.

But of goetia, and necromancy let this suffice.

Noɔes—Of Goeɔia and Necromancy

1. *Goetia and Necromancy—De incertitudine et vanitate scientiarum,* ch. 45.

2. *necromancers, and witches*—The following quotation is from Lucan *Pharsalia* 6, c. line 458.

3. *Epodi*—From the Greek ἐπάδω: those who charm by incantations.

4. *enchant boys*—The use of pre-pubescent boys as an undefiled medium for the communications of the gods is very old. It began in Babylonia and was carried to Egypt, where it still exists today. This is why Pythagoras said that children were loved by the gods: "… he observed that boys were most dear to divinity, and hence in times of great drought, they were sent by cities to implore rain from the Gods, in consequence of the persuasion that divinity is especially attentive to children …" (Iamblichus *Life of Pythagoras* 10 [Taylor, 24]). The same awareness may be seen in Christ (Matthew 19:14).

I cannot resist giving several examples which show the pervasiveness and persistence of this form of magic:

> Take a new knife with a black handle and make with it a circle in the earth so that you can sit in it with a boy or a girl less than nine years, and anoint the left hand of one of them with olive oil and the black of a pan, and warn them that they should not look outside the anointed place, and then whisper into his right ear: I adjure you … that you shall appear unto this lad, and you shall give him a proper answer to all that he asks for me, and all this he shall say three times. *(Babylonian Oil Magic,* text 3, trans. S. Daiches [London, 1913]. In *Three Works of Ancient Jewish Magic)*

> You take a new dish and fill it with clean Oasis oil and add to the dish gradually without producing cloudiness so that it becomes clear exceedingly; and you take a boy, pure, before he has gone with a woman, you speak down into his head while he stands, previously, to learn whether he will be profitable in going to the vessel. If he is profitable, you make him lie on his belly; you call down into his head … he gazing downwards into the oil, for seven times, his eyes being closed. When you have finished, you make him open his eyes, you ask him about what you desire …" *(Leyden Papyrus* 3.9–15, ed. Griffith and Thompson [New York: Dover,

1974], 35. Originally published as *The Demotic Magical Papyrus of London and Leiden* [London: H. Grevel and Co., 1904])

> After some time, a boy about twelve years old was brought in, and the performance began. He took the child's right hand in his, and described a square figure on its palm, on which he wrote some Arabic characters; while this was drying, he wrote upon a piece of paper an invocation to his familiar Spirits, which he burnt with some frankincense in a brazier at his feet. For a moment, a cloud of fragrant smoke enveloped the wizard and the cowering child who sate before him, but it had entirely disappeared before the phantasms made their appearance. Then, taking the boy's hand in his, he poured some ink into the hollow of it, and began to mutter rapidly; his countenance assumed an appearance of intense anxiety, and the perspiration stood upon his brow; occasionally he ceased his incantations, to inquire if the boy saw anything; and being answered in the negative, he went on more vehemently than before. Meanwhile, the little Arab gazed on the inky globule in his hand with an eager and fascinated look, and at length exclaimed, "I see them now!" (Warburton [1844] 1849, 1:100–1)

Warburton observed this divination in Cairo.

5. *Barnabas*—Joseph Barnabas, a Levite of Cyprus who sold his property and gave the money to the disciples of Christ. See Acts 4:36–7.

6. *Adam*—Adam was said to be the co-author with Daniel of two books of astrological divination by the days of the lunar cycle, written in the 14th century. This kind of work was called a *Lunarium,* or Moon Book. Magical works are attributed to Adam because he was the first man, and so the only conduit through which the wisdom of the angels might reach later generations.

7. *Abel*—Jerome Torrella published a work called *Opus præclarum de imaginibus astrologicis* (On astrological images) at Valencia in 1496, in which he makes mention of "a most ancient book written by Abel, son of Adam," who sealed it inside a stone, where it remained safe through the flood and was afterwards discovered by Hermes (Thorndike, 4:580). Another work, the *Essentiis essentiarum* (Essence of essences) attributed to Thomas Aquinas,

sheds a little more light on this book. Of the author Thorndike writes:

> He has also seen Abel's book of marvelous images which was preserved through the deluge with its names of the intelligences ruling the planets. The images are said to turn other metals to gold and enable one to become a king or prelate. Our author, however, has tested only one of them. Horses going past in the morning to water used to prevent his sleeping. But he made an image according to Abel's directions and buried it before his house, and after that no horse could pass. (Thorndike, 3:139)

8. *Enoch*—There was a magical work ascribed to Enoch on 15 stars, 15 stones, 15 herbs and 15 images to be engraved on the stones. See Thorndike, 3:139.

9. *Abraham*—A book of Abraham, or Abram, is cited several times by Firmicus Maternus in his *Mathesis* (see Thorndike, 1:537). There was a myth that Abraham was skilled in astrology, and had instructed Zoroaster in this art (ibid., 3:51).

10. *Solomon*—The number of magical works supposed to have been written by Solomon is large. Thorndike lists the *Almandel, Ars notoria, Cephar Raziel, Clavicula, Experiments, Idea et entocta, Jocalia, Novem candariis, Palmistry, Pentagon, Philosophy, Quatuor* and *Umbris idearum*, and mentions other works as well. See Thorndike, 2:1024, and all of ch. 49. To this list might be added the *Lemegeton*.

11. *Paul*—Paul was the reputed author of the *Pauline Art*, which was "discovered by the Apostle Paul after he had been snatched up to the third heaven, and delivered by him at Corinth" (Thorndike, 2:282). The *Pauline Art* is the name of the third work in a collection of five that comprises the *Lemegeton* of Solomon—English translation, British Museum Library, Sloane 2731.

12. *Honorius*—Honorius of Thebes, master magician and author of *The Sworn Book of Honorius*. He is not to be confused with Pope Honorius III, supposed author of the *Grimoire of Pope Honorius III*.

13. *Cyprianus*—Cyprian, Bishop of Antioch, was born a pagan and raised as a magician, but was converted to Christianity by the virtue of the virgin Justina—at least, this is the account given in his *Confessions,* which details his magical works. See Thorndike, vol. 1, ch. 18.

14. *Albertus*—Albertus Magnus is known as a magician largely because of the *Book of Secrets,* which was attributed to him and which contains extracts from his works.

15. *Thomas*—Since Thomas Aquinas was a pupil of Albertus Magnus, it is not surprising that he was credited with a number of alchemical works, including a commentary on the *Turba philosophorum,* a work called the *Blessed Lily Among Thorns,* and a work called *De essentiis essentiarum* (On the essence of essences). See Thorndike, 3:42, 65, 136.

16. *Hierome*—Saint Jerome is the reputed author of a work on precious stones that is preserved in a 12th-century Berlin manuscript (Thorndike, 2:236). I find nothing else that especially connects Jerome with goetia.

17. *certain man of York*—Robert of York. See biographical note.

18. *Bacon*—A number of spurious alchemical works were attributed to Roger Bacon, and despite Bacon's own claim in his *Epistola de secretis operibus* that magic is essentially a delusion, there are many magical references in his own works. A grimoire called the *De nigromancia of Roger Bacon,* derived from British Museum MS. Sloane 3885 and additional MS. 36674 (ed. and trans. M. A. Macdonald [Gillette, NJ: Heptangle Books, 1988]), claims in its introduction to have been discovered by the Franciscan brothers Robert Lombard and Roger Bacon in their studies at Alexandria, Egypt.

19. *Circe*—See Homer *Odyssey* 10, line 135ff.

20. *Medea*—See Ovid *Metamorphoses* 7.1, lines 1–158, and Apollonius of Rhodes *Argonautica* 3, c. line 442ff.

21. *Samuel the prophet*—I Samuel 28:7–20.

22. *Azazel*—See note 51, ch. XVIII, bk. III.

23. *arise a spiritual*—I Corinthians 15:44.

24. *Jude makes mention*—Jude 9.

Of Theurgia.[1]

Now many think that theurgia is not unlawful, as if this be governed by good angels, and a divine deity, when as yet oftentimes it is under the names of God, and the fallacies of evil angels obstringed[2] by the wicked fallacies of the devils.

For we do procure, and attract not by natural powers only, but also by certain rites, and ceremonies, celestials, and by them divine virtues to ourselves; of which together with many rules the ancient magicians did treat in many volumes.

But the greatest part of all ceremonies consists in observing cleanness, and purity, first of the mind, then of the body, and of those things which are about the body, as in the skin, in garments, in habitations, in vessels, utensils, oblations, sacrifices, the purity of which disposeth to the acquaintance with and beholding of divine things, and is very much required in sacred things, according to the word of *Isaiah,* be ye washed, and made clean, and take away the evil of your thoughts.[3]

Now impurity, because it oftentimes infects the air, and man, disturbs that most pure influence of celestial and divine things, and chaseth away the pure spirits of God. But sometimes impure spirits, and deceiving powers, that they be worshipped, and adored for gods, require also this purity. Therefore here is great need of caution, as we have lately discoursed at large in our books of Occult Philosophy.

But of this theurgia, or magic of divine things, *Porphyry* disputing at large, at length concludes that by theurgical consecrations the soul of man may be fitted to receive spirits, and angels, and to see God: but he altogether denies that we can by this art return to God.

Of his school therefore is the Art Almadel, the Notary Art, the Pauline Art, the Art of Revelations, and many suchlike superstitions, which are so much the more pernicious, by how much they seem the more divine to the ignorant.[4]

Notes—Of Theurgia

1. *Theurgia—De incertitudine et vanitate scientiarum,* ch. 46.

2. *obstringed*—Bound; put under obligation.

3. *evil of your thoughts*—Isaiah 1:16.

4. *divine to the ignorant*—Various systems of magic set forth in books of the same names.

Of cabalie.[1]

ere the words of *Pliny*[2] come into my mind, who saith the faction of magic depends upon *Moses* and *Latopea,* being Jews; which words put me in mind of the Cabalie of the Jews, which the Hebrews are of opinion was delivered to *Moses* by God himself on Mount Sinai, and then by degrees of succession without the monuments of letters was until the times of *Esdra*[3] delivered to others by word of mouth only: as the Pythagorean opinions were formerly delivered by *Archippus,* and *Lysiaus,*[4] who had schools at Thebes in Greece, in which the scholars keeping the precepts of their masters in their memory, did use their wit, and memory instead of books.

So certain Jews despising literature, placed this in memory, and observations, and vocal traditions, whence Cabalie was by the Hebrews called as it were the reception of any thing from another only by hearing.[5] That art (as it is reported) is very ancient, but the name was known but of late times amongst Christians.

They deliver a double science therefore, the one of *Bresith,*[6] which they call Cosmology, viz: explaining the powers of things created, natural, and celestial, and expounding the secrets of the Law and Bible by philosophical reasons: which truly upon this account differs nothing at all from natural magic, in which we believe King *Solomon* excelled. For it is read in the sacred histories of the Hebrews, that he was skilled in all things, even from the cedar of Lebanon, to the hyssop that grows upon the wall: also in cat-

tle, birds, creeping things, and fishes; all which show that he knew the magical virtues of nature. *Moses* the Egyptian, amongst the later writers followed after this in his exposition upon the Pentacles; also many more Talmudists.

They call the other science thereof of *Mercara,*[7] which is concerning the more sublime contemplations of divine and angelic virtues, and of sacred names, and seals, being a certain symbolical divinity, in which letters, numbers, figures, things, and names, and tops of elements, and lines, points, and accents, are all significative of most profound things, and great secrets.

This again they divide into Arithmancy, viz. that which is called *Notariacon,*[8] treating of angelical virtues, names, and seals, also of the conditions of spirits, and souls; and into Theomancy, which searcheth into the mysteries of divine majesty, as the emanations thereof, and sacred names, and pentacles, which he that knows may excel with wonderful virtues; as that when he pleaseth, he may foreknow all future things, and command whole nature, have power over devils, and angels, and do miracles.

By this they suppose, that *Moses* did show so many signs, and turned the rod into a serpent,[9] and the waters into blood,[10] and that he sent frogs,[11] flies,[12] lice,[13] locusts,[14] caterpillars,[15] fire with hail,[16] botches and boils[17] on the Egyptians, and slew every firstborn[18] of man and beast; and that he opened the seas,[19] and carried his through, and brought forth fountains[20] out of the rock, and quails from heaven;[21] and he sent before his, clouds and lightnings by day, a pillar of fire[22] by night, and called down from heaven the voice of the living God[23] to the people, and did strike the haughty with fire,[24] and those that murmured with the leprosy;[25] and on the ill deserving brought sudden destruction, the earth gaping and swallowing them up;[26] further he fed the people with heavenly food;[27] pacified serpents,[28] cured the envenomed,[29] preserved the numerous multitude from infirmity, and their garments from wearing out, and made them victors over their enemies.[30]

To conclude, by this art of miracles *Joshua* commanded the Sun to stand still;[31] *Eliah* called down fire from heaven[32] upon his enemies, restored a dead child[33] to life; *Daniel* stopped the mouths of the lions;[34] the three children sang songs in the fiery oven;[35] moreover by this art the incredulous Jews affirm that even Christ did do so many miracles; *Solomon* also very well knew this art, and delivered charms against devils, and their bonds, and the manner of conjurations, and against diseases, as *Joseph* reporteth.[36]

But as I doubt not but that God revealed to *Moses* many secrets contained under the bark of the words of the Law, which were not to be revealed to the prophane vulgar, so I acknowledge that this Cabalistical art, which the Hebrews brag of, and I sometimes diligently and laboriously sought after, is nothing else than a mere rhapsody of superstition, and a certain theurgical magic: but if it proceeded from God (as the Jews boast) and conduceth to the perfection of life, health of men, to the worship of God, and to the truth of understanding; truly that Spirit of Truth,[37] which hath left this synagogue, and come to teach us all truth, would not have concealed it from his Church even until these last times, which indeed knoweth all things that are of God, whose benediction, baptism, and other mysteries of salvation are revealed and perfected in every tongue.

For every tongue hath the same equal power, if so be that there be the same equal piety, neither is there any name, either in heaven or Earth, by the which we must be saved, and by which we work miracles, besides this one name, *Jesus,* in which all things are recapitulated and contained.

Hence it is, that the Jews who are most skillful in using the names of God, can operate little or nothing after Christ, as their ancient fathers did; but that we by experience find, and see, that by the revolution of the art (as they call them) oftentimes wonderful sentences, full of great mysteries, are wrested from the holy Scriptures, being nothing else than a certain playing upon allegories, which idle men, busying themselves with all the points, letters, and numbers, which this tongue and the custom of writing do easily suffer, do feign and disguise at their pleasures; which although sometimes they hold forth great mysteries, yet they can neither prove nor evince anything; but we may (according to the words of *Gregory)* with the same facility contemn them, as they are affirmed.

Rabanus the monk, by the same artifice hath feigned many things, but in Latin characters and verses, with certain pictures inserted, which being read any way by the delineations of the superficies and pictures, do declare some sacred mystery, representing the histories of the things painted; which also may without doubt be wrested from prophane writings, as everyone may know, who hath read the Cantones of *Valeria Proba,* composed out of the verses of *Virgil,* concerning Christ.

All things of this kind are the speculations of idle brains, but what belongeth to the working of miracles, there is none of you, I suppose, of so foolish an understanding, who believeth that they have any art or science of them.

Therefore this Cabala of the Jews is nothing else than a most pernicious superstition, by the which they gather at their pleasure, divide, transfer words, names and letters, scatteringly put in the holy Scriptures, and by making one thing out of another, they dissolve the connections of the truth, the speeches, inductions and parables, and here and there construing them by their own fictions, would bring the words of God to their follies, defaming the Scriptures, and saying that their fictions have foundation on them. They calumniate the Law of God, and by the supputations of words, syllables, letters, numbers impudently extorted, they assay to bring violent and blasphemous proofs for their unbelief.

Besides, they being puffed up by these trifles, do boast that they find and search out the unspeakable mysteries of God, and secrets, which are above the Scriptures, by the which also they impudently affirm, and without blushing, that they can even prophesy, and do miracles and wonders; but it happeneth to them, as to *Aesop's* dog,[38] who leaving his bread, and gaping after the shadow, lost his food; so this perfidious and stiff-necked people, being always busied in the shadows of the Scriptures, and about their own vanities, and doing violence by their artificial, but superstitious Cabala, do lose the bread of eternal life, and being fed with vain words, do destroy the word of truth.

From this Judaical ferment of Cabalistical superstition proceeded (as I suppose) the Ophitane,[39] Gnostican, and Valentinian[40] heretics, who together with their disciples, feigned a certain Greek Cabala, perverting all the mysteries of the Christian faith, and by their heretical corruption wresting them to the Greek letters and numbers, by the which they constituted a body of truth (as they call it), and taught, that without these mysteries of letters and numbers the truth could not be found in the Gospel, because that the writings thereof are various, and sometimes repugnant to themselves, and full of parables; that they who see, might not see, and that they who hear, might not hear, and that they who understand, might not understand, and that they are propounded to the blind and erroneous, according to the capacity of their blindness and error; but that the sincere truth lying hid under these things, is committed to the perfect only, not by writings, but by word of mouth, and that this is that alphabetary and arithmatical theology which Christ in private manifested to his apostles;[41] and which *Paul* speaketh to the perfect only;[42] for seeing that these are the highest mysteries, therefore they are not written, nor ought so to be, but to be kept in secret amongst wise men.

But no man is a wise man amongst them, who knoweth not to refrain the greatest monsters of heresy.

Notes—Of Cabalie

1. *Cabalie—De incertitudine et vanitate scientiarum,* ch. 47.

2. *words of Pliny*—"There is another sect, also, of adepts in the magic art, who derive their origin from Moses, Jannes, and Lotapea, Jews by birth, but many thousands of years posterior to Zoroaster ..." (Pliny 30.2 [Bostock and Riley, 5:425]). W.H.S. Jones points out in his note to this passage (Cambridge: Harvard University Press, 1963, 8:285) that for "Lotapes" Pliny should have written "Iotape" (ἰῶταπῆ), which equals Yahweh, the Jewish name for God. Jannes is one of the magicians of Pharaoh who contested with Moses (Exodus 7:11). His name occurs in Timothy 3:8.

3. *times of Esdra*—See I Esdras 8:1–7.

4. *Archippus and Lysiaus*—Iamblichus relates the history of these two disciples:

> At length, however, the Cylonians became so hostile to the men, that setting fire to the house of Milo in which the Pythagoreans were seated, and were consulting about warlike concerns; they burnt all the men except two, Archippus and Lysis. For these being in perfect vigour, and most robust, escaped out of the house. ... But of the two Pythagoreans that were saved, and both of whom were Tarentines, Archippus indeed returned to Tarentum; but Lysis hating the negligence of the cities went into Greece, and dwelt in the Achaia of Peloponnesus. Afterwards he migrated to Thebes, being stimulated by a certain ardent desire of retreating thither; and there he had for his auditor Epaminodas, who called Lysis his father. There also Lysis terminated his life. *(Life of Pythagoras* 35 [Taylor, 128–9])

Plutarch says it was Philolaus and Lysis who survived the arson of the house in which the Pythagoreans were assembled. Of the two he reports:

> Philolaus flying to the Lucanians was there protected by his friends, who rose for his defence and overpowered the Cylonians; but where Lysis was, for a long time nobody could tell; at last Gorgias the

Leontine, sailing from Greece to Italy, seriously told Arcesus that he met and discoursed Lysis at Thebes. *(On the Sign of Socrates* 13 [Goodwin, 2:393])

5. *only by hearing*—Kabbalah comes from the Hebrew root קבל, QBL: to receive, accept, admit; it signifies the oral tradition handed down from Moses.

6. *Bresith*—See note 7 below.

7. *Mercara*—בראשית, BRAShITh (in the beginning) is the first word in the Old Testament. *Ma'asch bereshit* is the name given to the first chapter of Genesis, about which many esoteric traditions and speculations grew up. מרכבה, MRKBH (war chariot) is the source of *Ma'asch merkabah,* the name given to the first chapter of Ezekiel, which concerns the chariot of God. Gershom Scholem writes:

> These two terms were subsequently used to describe those subjects dealing with these topics. Both Mishuah and Talmud (Hag. 2:1 and the corresponding Gemara in both the Babylonian and Jerusalem Talmud) show that, in the first century of the common era, esoteric traditions existed within these areas, and severe limitations were placed on public discussion of such subjects: "The story of creation should not be expounded before two persons, nor the chapter on the Chariot before one person, unless he is a sage and already has an independent understanding of the matter." (Scholem *Kabbalah* 1977, 11–2)

8. *Notariacon*—See Appendix VII.

9. *rod into a serpent*—Exodus 7:10.

10. *waters into blood*—Exodus 7:20.

11. *frogs*—Exodus 8:6.

12. *flies*—Exodus 8:24.

13. *lice*—Exodus 8:17.

14. *locusts*—Exodus 10:13.

15. *caterpillars*—There is no such plague, unless it is linked with the plague of locusts. But Rashi states most emphatically that the plague of locusts was locusts only, and no other species. See Rashi 1949, 2:89.

16. *fire with hail*—Exodus 9:23.

17. *botches and boils*—Exodus 9:10.

18. *slew every firstborn*—Exodus 12:29.

19. *opened the seas*—Exodus 14:21.

20. *brought forth fountains*—Exodus 17:6.

21. *quails from heaven*—Exodus 16:13.

22. *pillar of fire*—Exodus 13:21.

23. *voice of the living God*—Deuteronomy 5:24; Exodus 19:19.

24. *haughty with fire*—Numbers 16:35.

25. *murmured with leprosy*—Numbers 12:10. However Moses ended the leprosy of Miriam, he did not bring it.

26. *swallowed them up*—Numbers 16:32.

27. *heavenly food*—Exodus 16:15.

28. *pacified serpents*—Numbers 21:7.

29. *cured the envenomed*—Numbers 21:9.

30. *over their enemies*—Exodus 17:11.

31. *Sun to stand still*—Joshua 10:12.

32. *fire from heaven*—II Kings 1:10.

33. *restored a dead child*—I Kings 17:22.

34. *mouths of the lions*—Daniel 6:22.

35. *fiery oven*—Song of the Three Holy Children 28, with reference to Daniel 3:20–30.

36. *Joseph reporteth*—See note 9 to "Of Natural Magic," p. 691.

37. *Spirit of Truth*—Jesus Christ.

38. *Aesop's dog*—

> A Dog, crossing a little rivulet with a piece of meat in his mouth, saw his own shadow represented in the clear mirror of the limpid stream; and believing it to be another dog, who was carrying a larger piece of meat, he could not forbear catching at it; but was so far from getting anything by his greedy design, that he dropped the piece he had in his mouth, which immediately sank to the bottom, and was irrecoverably lost. *(Fables of Aesop* 118,

trans. Croxall and L'Estrange [London: Frederick Warne, n.d.], 262)

39. *Ophitane*—The Ophites, or Ophians, or Naasenes, were an early sect of Gnostics who honored the serpent and believed in a trinity of the Universal God or First Man, his conception the Second Man, and a female Holy Spirit. From her the Third Man, Christ, was begotten by the First and Second. Christ rose up with his mother and dropped a spark on the waters, from which came Ialdabaoth, the Demiurgos, who gave rise to six powers and with them created the seven heavens. When Man, created by the six powers, worshipped the First Man, Ialdabaoth in wrath created Eve to destroy him. But Sophia, or Prunikos (the Spark) sent the Serpent to free Adam and Eve from the power of Ialdabaoth. Mankind then waged war with Ialdabaoth, which is the secret meaning of the Old Testament writings, until the Holy Spirit sent Christ, united with his sister Prunikos, to enter the pure vessel, Jesus born of a virgin. Ialdabaoth instructed the Jews to kill Jesus Christ, but only Jesus died on the cross, as Christ and Prunikos had already left him. Christ later raised the spiritual body of Jesus for 18 months to teach his disciples. In heaven Christ sits on the right hand of Ialdabaoth, whom he has deprived of glory, and receives those souls dedicated to him.

40. *Valentinian*—See biographical note on Valentinus.

41. *manifested to his apostles*—Matthew 13:11.

42. *the perfect only*—I Corinthians 2:6.

Of juggling or legerdemain.[1]

But let us return to that magic, part of which is an art of juggling, i.e. delusions, which are made according to appearance only, by which magicians show phantasms, and play many miracles by circulatory frauds, and cause dreams, which they do not so much by geotic enchantments, and imprecations, and deceits of devils, as by certain vapours, perfumes, lights, love medicines, collyries, alligations, and suspensions, also by rings, images, glasses, and such like drugs, and instruments of magical art, and a natural and celestial power.

Also many things are done daily by slight of hand, of which sort we see some are done daily by stage players, and sporters which we call chirosophers,[2] i.e. skillful in slight of hand. There are extant concerning this art, books of the legerdemain of *Hermes,* and some others.

We read also of a certain man called *Paseton,*[3] a most notable juggler, that was wont to show a banquet to guests, and when he pleased, to make it vanish away again, all rising with hunger, and thirst, being deluded. We read that *Numa Pompilius*[4] did use these kinds of jugglings, and also that most learned *Pythagoras*[5] did sometimes do this toy: that what things he pleased, he would write in a glass, which being set against the full Moon, he would show to anyone that stood behind it, those things represented in the globe of the Moon.

Hither belongs whatsoever poets sing of the transmutations of men, which also is delivered by historians, and by some Christian divines, and also is recorded in the Scripture. So men may appear like asses, or horses,[6] or other animals, with fascinated eyes, or a troubled medium, and that by a natural art. Sometimes these are done by good and evil spirits, or by God himself at the request of some good man, as in the Scripture we read of *Elisha* the prophet beset by an army of the king fortifying Dotham.[7] But to pure eyes, and such as be opened by God, those cannot deceive; so that woman which was judged to be a kind of cattle, did seem to *Hilario*[8] to be not any such thing, but a woman.

These things therefore which are done according to appearance only, are called jugglings. But those things which are done by the art of transmuting, or translating, as of *Nebuchadnezzar,*[9] or of corn carried to another field, we have spoke of before.

But of this art of juggling, thus saith *Jamblicus,*[10] these things which are supposed to be juggled or bewitched, besides imagination, have no truth of action or essence. The end of these is but to hold forth things to the imagination according to appearance, of which there presently remains no footsteps or signs. Now by what hath been said, it is manifest that magic is nothing else but a collection of idolatry, astrology, and superstitious medicines.

And now there is by magicians raised a great company of heretics in the Church, who as *Jannes* and *Jambres* resisted *Moses,*[11] do in the like manner resist the apostolical truth. The chief of these was *Simon* the Samaritan,[12] on whom by reason of this art was bestowed at Rome in *Claudius Caesar's* time, a statue, with this inscription: To *Simon* the holy god. Of his blasphemies *Clemens,*[13] *Eusebius,*[14] and *Irenaeus*[15] make mention.

From this *Simon,* as from a seminary of all heresies proceeded by successions the monstrous Ophites,[16] the filthy Gnostics,[17] the impious Valentinians,[18] Cerdonians,[19] Marcionists,[20] Montanians,[21] and many other heretics, lying against God for gain and vain glory, doing no good to men, but deceiving them, and drawing them into destruction and error, to whom they that give credit shall be confounded in the judgement of God.

But of magic I wrote whilst I was very young three large books, which I called Of Occult Philosophy, in which what was then through the curiosity of my youth erroneous, I now being more advised, am willing to have retracted, by this recantation; I formerly spent much time and costs in these vanities. At last I grew so wise as to be able to dissuade others from this destruction.

For whosoever do not in the truth, nor in the power of God, but in the deceits of devils, according to the operation of wicked spirits persume to divine and prophesy, and practising through magical vanities, exorcisms, incantions and other demoniacal works and deceits of idolatry, boasting of delusions, and phantasms, presently ceasing, brag that they can do miracles, I say all these shall with *Jannes,* and *Jambres,* and *Simon Magus,* be destinated to the torments of eternal fire.

Of the Occult Philosophy of Henry Cornelius Agrippa,

finis.

Anno MDXXXIII in the month of July.

Notes—Of Juggling or Legerdemain

1. *Juggling or Legerdemain—De incertitudine et vanitate scientiarum,* ch. 48.

2. *chirosophers*—From the Greek χειρύσοφος: skilled with the hands.

3. *Paseton*—

We read that the sorcerer Pasetes by means of certain enchantments caused a sumptuous feast to appear, and again he made all vanish at his pleasure. He used also to buy things and count out the price, and shortly the money would be found to have passed back secretly from the seller to the buyer. (Francesco Maria Guazzo *Compendium Maleficarum* 1.3, trans. E. A. Ashwin [New York: Dover, {1608, 1929} 1988], 7).

4. *Numa Pompilius*—See Augustine *City of God* 7.35. The legend that Numa was a pupil of Pythagoras is mentioned by Livy *(History* 1.17).

5. *Pythagoras*—Some of the wonders attributed to Pythagoras are enumerated in Iamblichus *Life of Pythagoras* 28.

6. *horses*—

This is not unlike the account given by S. Vincent of Beauvais in his *Speculum majus,* Lib. XVIII, of a woman who, at the request of a Jew because she would not lend herself to his pleasure, a witch so apparently changed into a mare that she seemed to be such not only to everyone else but even to her husband; and only S. Macharius, since he was a man of the rarest sanctity, was not deceived by that illusion, and knew her throughout for the woman that she really was. (Nicolas Remy *Demonolatry* 2.5 [Ashwin, 111])

7. *fortifying Dotham*—II Kings 6:18.

8. *Hilario*—Many miracles are attributed to Saint

Hilarion in the *Vita St Helarionius Eremitae* by St. Jerome.

9. *Nebuchadnezzar*—Alluding to the supposed transformation of Nebuchadnezzar into an ox. Daniel 4:32.

10. *Jamblicus*—

We must say the same thing, therefore, concerning phantasms. For if these are not true, but other things are so which have a real existence, thus also in the appearances of spirits, they seem to be such as things which are true beings; at the same time they participate of falsehood and deception, in the same manner as the forms which present themselves to the view in mirrors; and thus vainly attract the mind about things which never take place in any of the more excellent genera. These phantasms, likewise, will consist in deceptive perversions. For that which is an imitation of being, and is an obscure assimilation, and becomes the cause of deception, pertains to no one of the true and clearly existing genera. (Iamblichus *On the Mysteries* 2.10 [Taylor, 106])

11. *resisted Moses*—II Timothy 3:8.

12. *Simon the Samaritan*—

In S. Clement of Rome we also read much concerning Simon Magus: that he made a new man out of air, whom he could render invisible at will; that he could pierce stones as if they were clay; that he brought statues to life; that when cast into the fire he was not burned; that he had two faces like another Janus; that he could change himself into a ram or a goat; that he flew in the air; that he suddenly produced a great quantity of gold; that he could set up kings and cast them down; that he commanded a scythe to go and reap of itself, and that it went and reaped ten times as much as the others; and that when a certain harlot named Selene was in a tower, and a great crowd had run to see her and had entirely surrounded that tower, he caused her to appear simultaneously at all the windows and exhibit herself to all the people.

Anastasius of Nicaea says: "Simon Magus made statues walk, and when thrown into the fire he did not burn, and he flew in the air, and made bread from stones. He changed himself into the form of a serpent and other beasts; he had two faces; he was changed into gold; he would cause all sorts

of spectres to appear at feasts; he caused many shades to go before him, which he said were the souls of the departed; he made the vessels in a house move as though of their own accord with apparently none to carry them." (Guazzo *Compendium Maleficarum* 1.3 [Ashwin, 7–8])

13. *Clemens*—The *Recognitions* of pseudo-Clementines, a Latin translation made by Rufinus around 400 AD from a Greek text called the *Clementine Homilies,* which concerns the doings of Simon Magus. See Thorndike, 1:17.

14. *Eusebius*—See the *Ecclesiastical History* 2.13, 14. Eusebius quotes Justin Martyr and Irenaeus, and throws in a few embellishments of his own.

15. *Irenaeus*—See *Against Heresies* 1.16.

16. *Ophites*—See note 39 to "Of Cabalie," p. 704.

17. *Gnostics*—The term is used by Agrippa for a specific sect in the same way it is used by Irenaeus (*Against Heresies* 1.29, 30). In the broader sense, all the sects here mentioned are Gnostic except Montanism.

18. *Valentinians*—See biographical note on Valentinus.

19. *Cerdonians*—

A certain man, however, by name Cerdon, who derived his first impulse from the followers of Simon, and who made some stay at Rome, under Hyginus the ninth, that held the episcopate in succession from the apostles, taught that the God who had been proclaimed by the law and prophets, was not the Father of our Lord Jesus Christ, for the latter was revealed, the other was unknown; the former also was just, but the other was good. Marcion, who was from Pontus, having succeeded Cerdon, augmented his school by uttering his blasphemies without a blush. (Eusebius *Ecclesiastical History* 4.11, trans. C. F. Cruse [London: Bell and Daldy, 1866], 126–7)

Eusebius is here quoting directly from Irenaeus *Against Heresies,* bk. 3.

20. *Marcionists*—

And there is Marcion, a man of Pontus, who is even at this day [circa 150 AD] alive, and teaching his disciples to believe in some other god greater than the Creator.

And he, by the aid of devils, has caused many of every nation to speak blasphemies, and to deny that God is the maker of this universe, and to assert that some other, being greater than He, has done greater works. (Justin Martyr *First Apology* 26 [*Ante-Nicene Christian Library* 2:29–30])

21. *Montanians*—Montanism was a sort of charismatic Christianity of the 2nd century.

There is said to be a certain village of Mysia in Phrygia, called Ardaba. There, they say, one of those who was but a recent convert, Montanus by name, when Cratus was proconsul in Asia [circa 156 AD], in the excessive desire of his soul to take the lead, gave the adversary occasion against himself. So that he was carried away in spirit, and wrought up into a certain kind of frenzy and irregular ecstasy, raving, and speaking, and uttering strange things, and proclaiming what was contrary to the institutions that had prevailed in the church, as handed down and preserved in succession from the earliest times. (Eusebius *Ecclesiastical History* 5.16 [Cruse, 184])

Soon two women, Prisca and Maximilla, also began to prophesy. The persecution of 177 AD spread Montanism from Phrygia throughout Asia Minor, Rome and even Gaul. The message of the sect was a stricter adherence to an ascetic morality.

APPENDIX I

Emerald Tablet

The Smaragdine, or Emerald Table *(Tabula Smaragdina)* is a short alchemical work attributed by medieval commentators to Hermes Trismegistus. It first occurs in the writings of the Arab Jabir ibn Hayyan (i.e., Geber) who lived in the 8th century, but it has been thought to be much older (see Burckhardt [1960] 1974, 196). There were many manuscripts of it circulating at the time of Agrippa. Ortolanus (or Hortulanus) the alchemist wrote a commentary devoted to the Emerald Tablet around 1350 (Thorndike, 3:183). It is worth noting that Trithemius quotes the Tablet in full in his letter to Germanus de Gonay, dated August 24, 1505 (ibid., 4:348).

Hargrave Jennings, in his introduction to a translation of the Hermetic writings by John Everard, relates the legend of the Tablet:

> In a treatise attributed to Albertus Magnus, we are told that the tomb of Hermes was discovered by Alexander the Great in a cave near Hebron. In this was found a slab of emerald, which had been taken, from the hands of the dead Hermes, by "Sarah, the wife of Abraham," and which had inscribed upon it, in Phoenician characters, the precepts of the great master concerning the art of making gold. This inscription consisted of thirteen sentences, and is to be found in numerous alchemical works. *(Divine Pymander* [Everard, viii–ix])

The subject of the Tablet is the alchemical Great Work, or as it is here described, "the work of the Sun." This may be regarded in the higher sense as the material death and spiritual rebirth of the soul, or in the lower sense as the physical transformation of base metal into gold. Agrippa admits in ch. XIV, bk. I, that he has participated in alchemical experiments and has succeeded in creating gold, but no more by weight than the quintessence of gold used in the experiment. But he certainly valued the Tablet more as a repository, in cryptic shorthand form, of the great Hermetic principles, particularly the second sentence, which sums up the entire philosophical ground of occultism in the Middle Ages in a few words.

The version of the Smaragdine given here is based upon several translations of the Latin text, which is the one Agrippa would have had before him. In composing this version, consideration was also given to the Arabic text. This differs from the Latin in a few points of emphasis, but it was not thought necessary to depart radically from the sense of the Latin version. The major variation between the two is in Sentence 10, which in the Arabic reads: "Thus the microcosm was framed on the macrocosm." The words that translate "of the operation of the Sun" in Sentence 13 can also mean "of the work of gold" *(de operatione solis),* emphasizing the double interpretation that is possible.

Some translators combine the first and second Sentences, making a total of 12, but I have preferred to separate the two to emphasize that the "truth" referred to in Sentence 1 applies to the entire Tablet.

ΘΕΟC

Hermes Trismegistus

from *De divinatione et magicis præstigiis* by Jacques Boissard (Oppenheim, 1605)

Emerald Tablet
of
Hermes Trismegistus

1. It is true, without falsehood, and most certain.

2. What is below is like that which is above; and what is above is like that which is below: to accomplish the miracle of the one thing.

3. As all things were formed from one, by the thought of one, so all things are born from this one thing, by choice.

4. Its father is the Sun, its mother the Moon, the Wind carries it in its belly, its nurse is the Earth.

5. It is the author of all perfection throughout the World.

6. The power is strong when changed into Earth.

7. Separate the Earth from the Fire, the subtle from the gross, gently and with care.

8. Ascend from Earth to Heaven, and descend again to Earth, to unite the power of higher and lower things; thus you will obtain the glory of the whole World, and the shadows will leave you.

9. This has more strength than strength itself, for it overcomes all subtle things and penetrates every solid.

10. Thus the world was framed.

11. Hence proceed wonders, which means are here.

12. Therefore I am Hermes Trismegistus, having the three parts of world philosophy.

13. That which I had to say of the operation of the Sun is perfected.

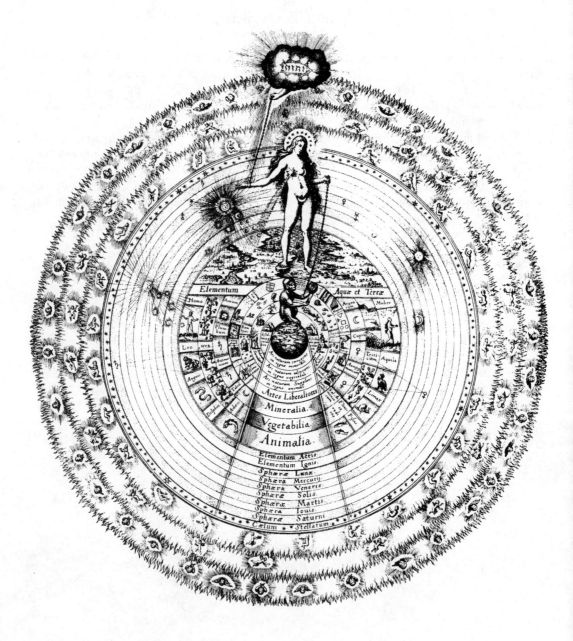

Soul of the World

from *Utriusque cosmi maioris scilicet et minoris metaphysica atque technica historia* by Robert Fludd
(Oppenheim, 1617)

APPENDIX II

The Soul of the World

Much of magic is based upon the premise, usually implicit, that the universe is a single living conscious being within whose body all things subsist. In consequence nothing is without life, and nothing is truly separate from everything else. This cosmic being was viewed as a god and was called by the ancients the Soul of the World. It will be useful to examine some of the qualities of this deity for the insights she will give into Agrippa's theory of magic.

In classical and medieval times "world" meant "universe." This must be emphasized as it tends to get lost in the modern astronomical perspective of vast distances, countless stars and planets, swirling galaxies and endless emptiness. Until a few short centuries ago the universe was a flat circle of earth and sea and the arching span of the heavens, in which moved the small disks of Sun and Moon, the five other wandering points of light called planets and a few hundred fixed points called stars.

A larger view of things was not unheard of—some philosophers speculated that the Earth was a sphere, and that the Sun was of great size, though they never imagined it a fraction as large as it turns out to be—but for the vast majority of educated people "Earth" and "world" were concentric ideas not too dissimilar in scope.

The doctrine of the World Soul is first expressed in its classical form by Plato. His writings became the foundation of all subsequent references. Later writers sometimes blur the distinction between the Soul of the World and the Great Mother, the goddess of the Earth. They sometimes are unclear as to the exact nature of the Soul. But in Plato himself these things are distinct and lucid.

For Plato, as he relates in the *Timaeus,* the highest god was the Creator, who was unknowable, eternal and perfect, the "best of causes." The world, fashioned in his image, is necessarily beautiful, and the beauty of the world is a mirror for the splendor of the Creator. Wishing to bring order to the chaos of the visible sphere so that "all things should be as like himself as they could be," out of pure goodness and free from all jealousy, he brought into being a copy of himself as exact as was possible for any secondary thing to be. The characteristics of this "fairest of creations" were determined by his own essential nature.

He made the world intelligent because intelligence is more beautiful than unintelligence. He gave the world a soul because intelligence cannot reside where a soul is lacking. He put the soul into a body because "that which is created is of necessity corporeal, and also visible and tangible."

The world is one and not many because the Creator is one, and the world is his image. That this single world might be visible he framed it of Fire. That it might be tangible he formed it from Earth. But these two elements could not be joined without a medium in the nature of an arithmetical mean. Had the world been planar

713

one mean would have sufficed, but because the world was solid, two means, Water and Air, were necessary. Fire is to Air as Air is to Water, and Air is to Water as Water is to Earth.

> And for these reasons, and out of such elements which are in number four, the body of the world was created, and it was harmonized by proportion, and therefore has the spirit of friendship, and having been reconciled to itself, it was indissoluble by the hand of any other than the framer. (Plato *Timaeus* 32c [Hamilton and Cairns])

The Creator formed the world in the most perfect of shapes, the sphere, "which comprehends within itself all other figures." The surface was fashioned with perfect smoothness, without eyes since there was nothing beyond the world to look upon, without ears since there was no sound outside to hear, without a nose since there was no air outside to breathe, without a mouth because the world was self-sufficient, "his own waste providing his own food, and all that he did or suffered taking place in and by himself," without hands since the world "had no need to take anything or defend himself against anyone," without feet since the motion of the world was circular rotation, the movement best suited to his spherical form and most appropriate to mind and intelligence.

In the center of the body of the world the Creator set the soul, which is older than the body. This is apparent since the soul rules the body, and the Creator would never permit the younger to rule the elder. The soul is diffused equally throughout all portions of the world, and also the "exterior environment of it," and is female, the mistress of the body of the world. She is framed out of harmonious numerical ratios, the mixture of which the Creator cut into an X and folded back upon itself into a double circle, both parts of which he set spinning in opposite directions, the outer circle to the right, the inner diagonally to the left. The inner circle he further subdivided into seven unequal circles in which move the seven planets.

Only after the Creator had "framed the soul according to his will" did he form within her the

material world and unite the two center to center. The body of the world is visible, but the soul invisible.

> And because she is composed of the same and of the different and of being these three, and is divided and united in due proportion, and in her revolutions returns upon herself, the soul, when touching anything which has being, whether dispersed in parts or undivided, is stirred through all her powers to declare the sameness or difference of that thing and some other, and to what individuals are related, and by what affected, and in what way and how and when, both in the world of generation and in the world of immutable being. (ibid. 37a)

Desiring to make the world as near a perfect copy of himself as possible, the Creator set the heavens in order and made them move according to number, thereby giving rise to time as a moving image of his own eternity. Time is a flawed model of eternity because eternity does not move, but "rests in unity." Plato says, "Now the nature of the ideal being was everlasting, but to bestow this attribute in its fullness upon a creature was impossible." However, time was as close as the Creator could come. "It was framed after the pattern of the eternal nature—that it might resemble this as far as was possible, for the pattern exists from eternity, and the created heaven has been and is and will be in all time. Such was the mind and thought of God in the creation of time" (ibid. 38b).

To mark and measure the numbers of time the Creator set the seven planets in the seven irregular divisions of the inner circle of the Soul of the World. He made the celestial gods of Fire and set them, after the figure of the world, in a circle "and made them follow the intelligent motion of the supreme, distributing them over the whole circumference of heaven, which was to be a true cosmos or glorious world spangled with them all over" (ibid. 40a).

The Earth, which is the nurse of humanity and the first and eldest of the gods in the interior of heaven, was set at the center of the universe on the axle of the world to be the "guardian and artificer of night and day." The Creator poured out the mingled elements with which he had made the Soul of the World, but diluted to the second and third degree, and divided it into souls equal in number to the fixed stars. Each soul he assigned a star. The celestial gods took the four elements from the world and fashioned bodies for these souls to reside in "not with the indissoluble chains by which they were themselves bound, but with little pegs too small to be visible" (ibid. 43a). Souls that lived righteously as men returned to their stars. Souls that did evil descended into the bodies of beasts.

That which is most perfect in men, the intellect and reason, was housed in a spherical body, the head, in imitation of the perfect sphere of the world. But the rest of the body was fashioned to meet the requirements of physical living. Man was given legs to move in the six directions—backwards, forwards; right, left; up, down. The seventh perfect motion, rotation on one place, was denied him due to his imperfection.

It was necessary to descend all the way to man in the genesis of Plato's *Timaeus* in order to show the link that exists between man, the Earth, the Soul of the World and the supreme Creator. Elsewhere, in his *Laws,* Plato has other things to say about the nature of the Soul of the World which are worth noting.

He defines Soul concisely as self-movement, and identifies it with the "primal becoming and movement of all that is, has been, or shall be, and of all their contraries, seeing it has disclosed itself as the universal cause of all change and motion" *(Laws* 896a [Hamilton and Cairns]). He goes on to say that it is the "first born of all things," which agrees with his *Timaeus;* and that Soul—meaning all soul, or the Soul of the World—is the cause of good and evil; and that it moves the heavens; and that individual souls, or parts of Soul, in heavenly bodies are esteemed as gods.

Agrippa was more familiar with the writings of Hermes Trismegistus than with those of Plato, if the quality of his quotations in the *Occult Philosophy* is any guide. The doctrine of the Soul of the World figures prominently in the Hermetica in several key ways.

Hermes emphasizes the distinction made by Plato between time, which is the duration of the world, and eternity, the duration of the Creator.

> The Kosmos is ever-living; for it is made immortal by the Father, who is eternal. "Ever-living" is not the same as "eternal." The Father has not been made by another; if he has been made at all, he has been made by himself; but it ought rather to be said that he has never been made, but ever is. But the Kosmos is ever being made. *(Corpus Hermeticum* 8.2 (Scott, 1:175)

He traces the link between God and man more directly than Plato, saying most succinctly: "There are these three then,—God, Kosmos, Man. The Kosmos is contained by God, and man is contained by the Kosmos. The Kosmos is son of God; man is son of the Kosmos, and grandson, so to speak, of God" (ibid. 10.14b [Scott, 197]).

Kosmos, or the world, is a sphere, as in Plato, but Hermes metaphorically calls this a "head." Those things closer to the outer surface of this head, its "cerebral membrane," have more soul than body and are thus immortal. These are the fixed stars and wandering planets. Those things nearer to the center have more body than soul and are mortal. These are the living things below the circle of the Moon. "Thus the universe is composed of a part that is material and a part that is incorporeal; and inasmuch as its body is made with soul in it, the universe is a living creature" (ibid. 10.11 [Scott, 195]).

Continuing this theme, Hermes observes that the world is in constant flux, changing from day to day as different parts of it pass from sight, yet the world as a whole never decomposes. He emphasizes that the forms which pass away are forms of the world itself, not merely forms contained in, yet separate from, the world. "And the Kosmos assumes all forms; it does not contain the forms as things placed in it, but the Kosmos itself changes."

In all this Hermes agrees with Plato. On another point he is in apparent disagreement, but this conflict is only superficial. Plato says quite definitely that the Soul of the World, as the most perfect image of God, is most perfectly good (Laws 898c; Timaeus 30b). Hermes takes an opposite position: "For the Kosmos is one mass of evil, even as God is one mass of good" (Corpus Hermeticum 6.4a [Scott, 169]). Later on he seems to contradict himself, saying: "The Kosmos is not indeed evil, but it is not good, as God is; for it is material, and subject to perturbation" (ibid. 10.l0b [Scott, 195]).

There is no real conflict of ideas in these statements, merely a difference of emphasis. Plato is referring to the Soul of the World, the incorporeal part of creation, as the highest good of created things, but he does not mean to imply that it is equal in goodness to God, whose goodness is beyond human comprehension. It is rather the highest good to which the term can rightly be applied. Hermes chooses to emphasize the vast distance that lies between God and even the most perfect of created things. He does this by considering the material part of the world, which is subject to change. He calls it all evil to point out that even the highest created good is evil in comparison to the good of God. Later he moderates this position, distinguishing the soul from the body of the world. In that the soul is everlasting, it is not evil in the human sense of the term; in that the body is ever-changing, it can never be good as the term is applied to eternal God.

Although Hermes is here referred to as though he were a single historical author, it is obvious that these two passages were written by different writers, the first more strongly influenced by Christian doctrine. Since there is a single philosophical harmony underlying the Hermetic writings it is not germane to this discussion that parts of the Corpus were written at different times by several hands. I mention it here so that the reader will not think I have overlooked the obvious.

The opinion of the Roman scholar Varro about the Soul of the World, as it is preserved in the commentary of Augustine in his City of God, is less abstract, more colloquial, as one would expect from a popularizer of ideas. Varro divides the Soul of the World into three degrees. The first degree of Soul is insensible, in the world wood, stones and earth, equivalent in man to fingernails, bones and hair. The second degree is sensible, in the world the Sun, Moon and stars, equivalent in man to ears, eyes, nose, mouth and touch. The third degree is intellectual, in the world the aether (which Agrippa calls the Spirit of the World, or quintessence), equivalent in man to the mind. This last highest level of Soul is in the world called a god, in man called the Genius—i.e., the guardian angel.

The Earth was regarded by Varro as a goddess, which the Soul of the World, here treated as a god, interpenetrated, impregnated and rendered fruitful. As Augustine writes, " the part of the world's soul (say they) 'contained in her, maketh her divine'" (City of God 7.23 [Healey]). According to Varro the masculine part of the world is called Tellus, the power of which is to produce, and the feminine part is called Tellumo, the power of which is to receive. The Roman priests add two other concepts, dividing the world into four powers, or deities. These two are Altor, which according to Augustine (i.e., Varro) is from alo, to nourish, because earth nourishes all things; and Rusor, from rursus, again, because all things return again to the earth. Although Augustine does not say, it would be reasonable to link Altor with Tellus and Rusor with Tellumo, forming pairs respectively of production and growth, and reception and decay.

All this Varro relates concerning the beliefs of his contemporaries and the priests. But elsewhere he gives his own views, which Augustine records (7.24):

> For Varro, as if feeling shame at this crew, would have Tellus to be but one goddess. They call her (says he) the great mother, and her timbrel is a sign of the earth's roundness: the turrets on her head, of the towns: the seats about her, of her eternal stability when all things else are moved: her galli, priests, signify that such as lack seed [they were castrated] must follow the earth that contains all: their violent motions about her [dances] do advise the tillers of earth not to sit idle, for there is still work for them. The cymbals signify the noises with plough-irons, etc., in husbandry; they are of brass, for so were these instruments

before iron was found out. The tame lion signified that the roughest land might by tillage be made fertile. And then he adds, that she was called mother earth, and many other names, which made them think her several gods.

In this second-hand account of Augustine, as in other writers, there is sometimes a vagueness in distinguishing between the active, occult, masculine face of the Soul of the World, and its receptive, manifest, feminine face. This is bound up with confusion between the world or universe and the material Earth. Confusion arises because these are not separate powers and bodies, but a single mingled and interpenetrated whole.

Plato makes clear that the Soul of the World is really neither masculine nor feminine in itself, but receives these polarities upon its blank surface in the same way that a mirror is not red or green, but reflects that color which passes into it:

> And the same argument applies to the universal nature which receives all bodies— that must be always called the same, for, inasmuch as she always receives all things, she never departs at all from her own nature and never, in any way or at any time, assumes a form like that of any of the things which enter into her; she is the natural recipient of all impressions, and is stirred and informed by them, and appears different from time to time by reason of them. (Plato *Timaeus* 50b)

Plato commonly speaks of the Soul of the World as feminine because of its relation to the Creator, who impresses forms upon the Soul, which forms are her children (see *Timaeus* 50d).

It is apparent that Augustine at least understood the distinction between the world and the Earth from this lucid and concise summary he gives, out of Plato, of the doctrine of the World Soul:

> They [Platonists] agree in this also, that earthly bodies cannot be eternal, and yet they hold the whole earth, which they regard as a central part of their great god (though not of their highest) the world, to be eternal. Seeing then their greatest God made another

god greater than all the rest beneath him, that is, the world, and seeing they hold that this is a creature having an intellectual soul included in it by which it lives, having the parts consisting of four elements, whose connection that great God (lest this other should ever perish) made indissoluble and eternal ... *(City of God* 13.17)

The threefold division of the Soul by Varro into an insensible degree, a sensible degree, and an intellectual degree seems to correspond to Plato's division of three natures that impress themselves on the Soul:

> ... first, that which is in process of generation; secondly, that in which the generation takes place; and thirdly, that of which the thing generated is a resemblance naturally produced. And we may liken the receiving principle to a mother, and the source or spring to a father, and the intermediate nature to a child, and may remark further that if the model is to take every variety of form, then the matter in which the model is fashioned will not be duly prepared unless it is formless and free from the impress of any of those shapes which it is hereafter to receive from without. *(Timaeus* 50c–d)

Varro's insensible degree is Plato's receptive nature, his intellectual degree is Plato's source of generation, and his sensible degree is Plato's intermediate nature of generated things. Thus the Sun, Moon and stars are the children born from the mother, the Soul of the World, by the father, the Creator.

The assertion by Varro that the Sun, Moon and stars are the world's senses would seem to be directly contradicted by Plato, who states at length that the world has no senses *(Timaeus* 33–4). The reason Plato is so adamant in denying the world senses is his wish to emphasize that there is nothing outside or apart from the world. Varro's world senses are directed inward, and seem inspired by astrological considerations. If the Sun, Moon and stars are to guide the destinies of men, they must be aware of what men are doing.

Implicate in this notion of Varro's is a separation between men and the Soul of the World. His World Soul must observe inwardly to be aware of what transpires on the Earth. Plato would have said this was unnecessary. The Soul of the World diffuses through every point on her sphere equally, allowing her to be aware of the actions of men as she is of her own thoughts—which, by the way, are not like the thoughts of men, but, as Hermes tells us, "mightier and less diversified" *(Corpus Hermeticum* 9.6 [Scott, 183]).

In closing, mention might be made of the survival of this doctrine into modern times. What is Mother Nature except the "great mother" of Varro, the goddess of the entire Earth who is its unifying and vivifying princi-

ple? That which impregnates her—Varro's intellectual degree, or Plato's source of generation— is hidden, seldom referred to in her popular mythology, yet constantly at work, as is manifest by her unceasing fecundity. Science has recently rediscovered Gaea and made her respectable, putting forward the theory that the physical Earth has not so much formed life, as life has formed the Earth, modifying its climate, atmosphere and surface. This theory, new in the West, is thousands of years old in the East, where the Hindu goddess Shakti, manifest power, is made fruitful by the action of Shiva, the unchanging universal consciousness.

APPENDIX III

The Elements

This examination of the elements relies upon the incomplete treatise *On the Nature of the Universe* by Ocellus Lucanus, *On Generation and Corruption* by Aristotle, and the *Timaeus* of Plato. Most modern critics assume the work attributed to Ocellus is bogus and that it was based upon Aristotle and written around 150 BC. There is good reason for this view. However, the older writers held that the work attributed to Ocellus was genuine and that Aristotle had taken many of his ideas about the elements from it. In this brief examination, which came first is not particularly important, so the older opinion, which Agrippa would have shared, has been nominally adopted.

The Pythagorean philosopher Ocellus Lucanus states that the first thing necessary for the world of generation to exist is a primal ground, base, or matter out of which all forms and qualities of things are shaped. This underlying strata has no tangible qualities in itself. Ocellus says it bears the same relationship to form as silence to sound, darkness to light, or pure water to taste: "… in matter [the intangible substratum] all things prior to generation are in capacity, but they exist in perfection when they are generated and receive their proper nature" (*On the Universe.* In *Ocellus Lucanus,* trans. Thomas Taylor [Los Angeles: Philosophical Research Society [1831], 1976], 11–2).

Following Ocellus, Aristotle emphasizes the point that this first ground of things cannot be tangible in itself.

But those thinkers are in error who postulate, beside the bodies we have mentioned, a single matter—and that a corporeal and separable matter. For this "body" of theirs cannot possibly exist without a "perceptible contrariety:" this "Boundless," which some thinkers identify with the "original real," must be either light or heavy, either cold or hot. … Our own doctrine is that although there is a matter of the perceptible bodies (a matter out of which the so-called "elements" come to be), it has no separate existence, but is always bound up with a contrariety. *(On Generation and Corruption* 2.1 [McKeon])

Regarding Plato's opinion of this primary matter, see the *Timaeus* 50b–d, which has been quoted in appendix II, p. 717.

The second thing needed for a world of generation is contrariety, which Ocellus says is required for two reasons: that change may take place in the forms impressed in passive primary matter, and that opposite powers may not come together and abolish each other—that is to say, the underlying existence of contrariety keeps opposing powers such as hot and cold from once and forever coming together and neutralizing each other, resulting in a uniform blandness.

Essences, or elements, are the third thing needed for a world of generation. These are Fire, Air, Water and Earth. Attributed to them are the powers, respectively, hot, moist, cold and dry. Ocellus says: "But essences differ from powers; for essences are locally corrupted by each other, but powers are neither corrupted nor generated, for the reasons of them are incorporeal" *(On the Universe* [Taylor, 12]). About this distinction Aristotle writes: "… for these bodies [elements] change into one another (they are not immutable as Empedocles and other thinkers assert, since 'alteration' would then have been impossible), whereas the contrarieties [powers] do not change" *(Generation and Corruption* 2.1).

Two of these powers, hot and cold, are active and, as Ocellus says, "subsist as causes and things of an effective nature …" *(On the Universe* [Taylor, 12]), whereas the other two, dry and moist, are passive. As Aristotle puts it: "On the other hand hot and cold, and dry and moist, are terms, of which the first pair implies power to act and the second pair susceptibility" *(Generation and Corruption* 2.2).

These four are the primary powers, or contrarieties, of tangibles. From them arise 12 others, for a total of 16, all of which affect the sense of touch. Aristotle explains:

> Since, then, we are looking for "originative sources," of perceptible body; and since "perceptible" is equivalent to "tangible," and "tangible" is that of which the perception is touch; it is clear that not all the contrarieties constitute "forms" and "originative sources" of body, but only those which correspond to touch. For it is in accordance with a contrariety—a contrariety, moreover, of tangible qualities—that the primary bodies are differentiated. That is why neither whiteness (and blackness), nor sweetness (and bitterness), nor any quality belonging to the other perceptible contrarieties either, constitutes an "element." *(Generation and Corruption* 2.2)

The 12 secondary elemental powers are, in pairs: heavy, light; rare, dense; smooth, rough; hard, soft; thin, thick (or fine, coarse); and acute, obtuse (or brittle, viscous). All these, according to Aristotle, derive from the moist and dry, and all may be reduced to the primary four powers, but no farther. "For the hot is not essentially moist or dry, nor the moist essentially hot or cold: nor are the cold and the dry derivative forms, either of one another or of the hot and moist. Hence these must be four" (ibid.).

If these four primary powers are combined into pairs, six pairs result. However, two of them, hot-cold and moist-dry, are composed of contrarieties which can never be joined, because opposites refuse to be coupled in stable harmony, for as Aristotle says, "it is impossible for the same thing to be hot and cold, or moist and dry" (ibid. 2.3). The four stable pairs attach themselves to the elements according to the manifest qualities of the elements. Fire is hot and dry, Air is hot and moist, Water is cold and moist and Earth is cold and dry.

Ocellus attributes four of the powers to each element. Fire is hot, dry, rare and acute. Air is soft, smooth, light and thin. Water is cold, moist, dense and obtuse. Earth is hard, rough, heavy and thick. However, where the elements are considered according to their interrelation, Ocellus agrees with Aristotle, saying: "Fire therefore, is hot and dry, but air is hot and moist; water is moist and cold, but earth is cold and dry. Hence heat is common to air and fire; cold is common to water and earth; dryness to earth and fire; and moisture to water and air" *(On the Universe* [Taylor, 14]).

Ocellus goes on to speak of the "peculiarity" of each element, saying: "heat is the peculiarity of fire, dryness of earth, moisture of air, and frigidity of water" (ibid., 15). Aristotle makes the same point: "Nevertheless, since they are four, each of them [each element] is characterized *par excellence* by a single quality: Earth by dry rather than by cold, Water by cold rather than by moist, Air by moist rather than by hot, and Fire by hot rather than by dry" *(Generation and Corruption* 2.3).

The elements may be divided into a number of contrasting pairs. Fire and Air both expand and rise, and are, Aristotle says, "forms of the body moving towards the limit" (ibid.). In contrast, Earth and Water contract and fall, and are "forms of the body which moves towards the centre" (ibid.). Fire and Earth form the pair of extremes, because in the natural order of the elements Fire rises to the top and Earth falls to the bottom. Aristotle says they are the "purest." Water and Air, on the other hand, form the pair of intermediaries and are "more like blends."

Also "the members of either pair are contrary to those of the other, Water being contrary to Fire and Earth to Air" (ibid.). That is to say, the powers of Fire, which are hot-dry, are contrary to the powers of Water, which are cold-moist, and so for Air and Earth.

These pairs may be illustrated by means of a simple diagram. Contrary powers are indicated by the diagonals:

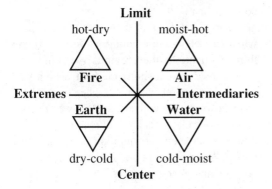

The question must be asked, why are the elements four in number? Though it is tempting to answer as Lear answered the Fool, when he was asked why the planets are seven ("Because they are not eight"), a more useful response can be made following Aristotle. He says that all philosophers postulate either one, two, three or four elements. Those that champion a single element say that it generates by the action of condensation and rarefaction, or cold and heat—thus they really propose two elements, and their single thing is the underlying matter, or "universal recipient" of Ocellus. Those such as Parmenides, who postulate two, the extremes Fire and Earth, make the intermediaries Water and Air their blends. Those who postulate three elements simply combine the intermediaries, and so differ very little from those who maintain that the elements are two. Finally there are philosophers who from the outset say there are four elements, such as Empedocles—yet he reduces them to two in effect by opposing all the others to Fire.

Aristotle does not consider why no one postulates five or more elements. Perhaps he assumes that this question does not need to be asked. Yet the quintessence, or aether, called by Agrippa the Spirit of the World, is sometimes treated as a fifth element, as the name implies (*quine:* five) and has not unreasonably been attributed to the fifth Platonic solid, the dodecahedron, which Plato says: "God used in the delineation of the universe with figures of animals" *(Timaeus* 55c).

In the *Epinomis* Plato treats aether as one of the elements, placing it between Fire and Air:

> Next to fire we will place aether, assuming that soul fashions from it creatures which, as with the other kinds, have in the main the character of its own substance, though with lesser portions of the other kinds as bonds of union, and that after aether soul fashions another sort of creature out of air and a third from water. *(Epinomis* 984b–c [Hamilton and Cairns])

However, this seems very out of keeping with the tone of the *Timaeus,* and indeed the authorship of the *Epinomis* is in doubt.

Aristotle asserts that the elements reciprocally come into being out of each other, and moreover each element can give rise to any other element.

> Now it is evident that all of them are by nature such as to change into one another: for coming-to-be is a change into contraries and out of contraries, and the "elements" all involve a contrariety in their mutual relations because their distinctive qualities are contrary. ... It is evident, therefore, if we consider them in general, that every one is by nature such as to come-to-be out of every one ... *(Generation and Corruption* 2.4)

As one would expect, Ocellus is in perfect accord with Aristotle's view.

Ocellus and Aristotle divide the transformations of elements into three groups.

The *first kind* of transformation occurs between elements that have one power in common. This is the most rapid and easiest change because only one power need be converted or overcome to transform the element containing it. This is the most frequent change in nature.

Fire (hot-dry) changes to Air (moist-hot) if the dryness in Fire is overcome by moisture. Air (moist-hot) changes to Water (cold-moist) if the heat in Air is overcome by cold. Water (cold-moist) changes to Earth (dry-cold) if the moisture in Water is overcome by dryness. Earth (dry-cold) changes to Fire (hot-dry) if the coldness of Earth is overcome by heat.

Aristotle says: "It is evident, therefore, that the coming-to-be of the simple bodies will by cyclical; and that this cyclical method of transformation is the easiest, because the consecutive elements contain interchangeable complementary factors" (Generation and Corruption 2.4). By "consecutive" he means in their natural order of separation one above the other. By "complementary factors" he is referring to the shared power in each pair.

Although it is implied, Aristotle does not state whether this cycle of transformation flows in both directions. Ocellus is more explicit on this point:

> Hence, when the moisture in air vanquishes the dryness in fire, but the frigidity in water, the heat in air, and the dryness in earth, the moisture in water, and vice versa, when the moisture in water vanquishes the dryness in earth, the heat in air, the coldness in water, and the dryness in fire, the moisture in air, then the mutations and generations of the elements from each other into each other are effected (On the Universe [Taylor, 15])

Fire (hot-dry) changes to Earth (dry-cold) if the heat of Fire is overcome by cold. Earth (dry-cold) changes to Water (cold-moist) if the dryness of Earth is overcome by moisture. Water (cold-moist) changes to Air (moist-hot) if the coldness of Water is overcome by heat. Air (moist-hot) changes to Fire (hot-dry) if the moisture of Air is overcome by dryness.

The *second kind* of transformation occurs between elements with no powers in common. Aristotle says that while this is possible, it is more difficult since it involves the change of more qualities, and therefore takes a longer period of time.

Fire (hot-dry) changes to Water (cold-moist) when the heat of Fire is overcome by cold and the dryness of Fire is overcome by moisture. Air (moist-hot) changes to Earth (dry-cold) when the moisture of Air is overcome by dryness and the heat of Air is overcome by cold.

Water (cold-moist) changes to Fire (hot-dry) when the cold of Water is overcome by heat and the moisture of Water is overcome by dryness. Earth (dry-cold) changes to Air (moist-hot) when the dryness of Earth is overcome by moisture and when the cold of Earth is overcome by heat.

The *third kind* of transformation occurs when two elements combine to form a single third element. In the previous two kinds we were considering a single element, which was changed into another element when one or both of its powers were converted. Here we are considering two elements brought together so that a power in one element annihilates, or as Ocellus puts it, "corrupts" a power in the other, leaving only a single pair of powers, which combine as a single element.

Fire (hot-dry) plus Water (cold-moist) change to Earth (dry-cold) when the heat of Fire and the moisture of Water pass away, but they change to Air (moist-hot) when the dryness of Fire and the cold of Water pass away.

Air (moist-hot) plus Earth (dry-cold) change to Fire (hot-dry) when the moisture of Air and the cold of Earth pass away, but they change to Water (cold-moist) when the heat of Air and the dryness of Earth pass away.

It is not possible to form a single new element by combining two consecutive elements in this way, because the result will be either contrary powers, which cannot coexist, or a single power, which does not in itself constitute an element. For example if the consecutive elements Fire (hot-dry) and Air (moist-hot) are combined, and the dryness of Fire along with the moisture of Air pass away, the remainder will be the heat of Fire and the heat of Air, which is not an element but a single power; if the heat of Fire and the heat of Air pass away, the remainder will be the dryness of Fire and the moisture of Air, contrary powers which cannot coexist; if the heat of Fire and the moisture of Air pass away, the remainder is dryness and heat, which constitute Fire; if the dryness of Fire and the heat of Air pass away, the remainder is heat and moisture, which constitute Air.

In fact, to transform two consecutive elements into a third element, it is necessary for more than one power in each to pass away. For example, to change Fire (hot-dry) and Air (moist-hot) into Water (cold-moist), the dryness of Fire must pass away, and also the heat of Air, and in addition the heat of Fire must be converted into cold. Aristotle regards this as possible, but since it is the most involved class of transformation it is the least common.

In his treatment of the elements Aristotle makes passing reference to Plato's opinion that not all the elements can be transformed into the others, dismissing it with the brief line, "Now it has been proved before that they must undergo reciprocal transformation" (Generation and Corruption 2.5). But he does not bother to give Plato's reasons. Since Plato's view of the elements is at least as important as that of Aristotle, it cannot be passed over in this way, but must be considered at length.

Most of what Plato has to say about the elements is in his Timaeus. He begins by speculating as to why the elements were necessary at all, and concludes that the tangibility of the world required it:

> Now that which is created is of necessity corporeal, and also visible and tangible. And nothing is visible where there is no fire, or tangible which has no solidity, and nothing is solid without earth. Wherefore also God in the beginning of creation made the body of the universe to consist of fire and earth. (Timaeus 31b)

Having arrived at these extremes, he says it is required that a third thing exist to act as a bond of union between them, in the way of a numerical mean. "And the fairest bond is that which makes the most complete fusion of itself and the things which it combines, and proportion is best adapted to effect such a union" (ibid. 31c). But one mean, or binding element, by itself is not enough.

> If the universal frame had been created a surface only and having no depth, a single mean would have sufficed to bind together itself and the other terms, but now, as the world must be solid, and solid bodies are always compacted not by one mean but by two, God placed water and air in the mean between fire and earth, and made them to have the same proportion so far as was possible—as fire is to air so is air to water, and as air is to water so is water to earth— and thus he bound and put together a visible and tangible heaven. (ibid. 32a–b)

To understand what Plato is saying, it is best to turn to Proclus and his Commentary on the Timaeus. Proclus first dismisses those who attribute only one power to each element; that is, heat to Fire, cold to Air, moisture to Water, and dryness to Earth. "For it is impossible for things to be co-adapted to each other, when they possess the most contrary powers, unless they have something in common" (Commentary on the Timaeus, quoted in an extensive note by Taylor in Ocellus On the Nature of the Universe [Taylor, 34]).

Having disposed of the theory of elements with only one power, he attacks that theory which postulates elements based upon two powers, specifically mentioning Ocellus and his treatise On Nature.

His first point is that the two-power theory results in elements that are equally hostile and harmonious to one another:

> What kind of world, therefore, will subsist from these; what order will there be of things which are without arrangement and most foreign, and of things which are most allied and co-arranged? For things which in an equal degree are hostile and peaceful, will in an equal mode dissolve and constitute communion. But this communion being similarly dissolved, and similarly implanted, the universe will no more exist than not exist. (Commentary on the Timaeus [Taylor, 35])

His second point is that, in the two power system of Ocellus and Aristotle, those elements naturally most distant from each other, Fire and Earth, do not, as one might reasonably expect, receive the attribution of the most contrary powers. That Fire and Earth are the most contrary elements is manifest in nature: "How, also, did she arrange the motions of them, since fire is most light and tends upward, but earth is most heavy and tends downward? But whence were the motions of them which are most contrary derived, if not from nature?" (ibid., 35). Yet in the face of this natural opposition, these philosophers gave the most contrary powers to Air (moist-hot) and Earth (dry-cold), and Fire (hot-dry) and Water (cold-moist).

And this may occasion some one to wonder at Aristotle, who, in what he says about motion, places earth as most contrary to fire; but in what he says about powers, he makes the most remote of similar natures to be more friendly [Fire (hot-dry) and Earth (dry-cold) share the power of dryness] than those which are proximate, when they are moved with most contrary motions [Fire (hot-dry) and Water (cold-moist) and Air (moist-hot) and Earth (dry-cold) are separated by only one element]. (ibid., 36)

His third point, the one pertinent to the quotation above from Plato, is that, accepting that elements are solids, it is not possible for them to be bound together by only one medium. "Hence those who assert these things neither speak mathematically nor physically, but unavoidably err in both these respects. For physical are derived from mathematical entities" (ibid.).

This sounds obscure but is really very simple. Since there are three dimensions of space—length, breadth, and height—and solids exist in space, they are related numerically to cube numbers (2 X 2 X 2 = 8), just as plane surfaces, with only two dimensions of length and breadth, are related to squares (2 X 2 = 4). The two smallest cubes, 8 (2 X 2 X 2) and 27 (3 X 3 X 3), which have great significance in Pythagorean and Platonic doctrines, have *two* means, which are 12 and 18. Thus 8 is to 12 as 12 is to 18, and 12 is to 18 as 18 is to 27. Each number is half again larger than the number preceding it.

The significance of these numbers will be apparent when they are related to the three powers of each element that Proclus extracts from Plato. He says:

Timaeus [the supposed narrator of the *Timaeus*] therefore alone, or any other who rightly follows him, neither attributes one or two powers alone to the elements, but triple powers; to fire indeed tenuity of parts, acuteness, and facility of motion; to air, tenuity of parts, obtuseness, and facility of motion; to water grossness of parts, obtuseness, and facility of motion; and to earth grossness of parts, obtuseness, and difficulty of motion. But this is in order that each of the elements may have two powers, each of which is common to the element placed next to it, and one power which is different, in the same manner as it was demonstrated in mathematical numbers and figures; this different power being assumed from one of the extremes; and also in order that earth, according to all the powers, may subsist opposite to fire; and that the extremes may have two media, and the continued quantities two; the latter having solids for the media, but the former, common powers. (ibid., 36–7)

This relationship can most clearly be shown in the form of a simple table:

△	subtle— sharp—quick	2 X 2 x 2 = 8
△	subtle— blunt—quick	2 X 3 x 2 = 12
▽	dense — blunt —quick	3 X 3 x 2 = 18
▽	dense — blunt —slow	3 X 3 x 3 = 27

Having stated his view on the origin of the elements and their relationship, Plato repeats the commonly accepted opinion that all four elements are changeable:

In the first place, we see that what we just now called water, by condensation, I suppose, becomes stone and earth, and this same element, when melted and dispersed, passes into vapor and air. Air, again, when inflamed, becomes fire, and, again, when condensed and extinguished, passes once more into the form of air, and once more, air, when collected and condensed, produces cloud and mist—and from these, when still more compressed, comes flowing water, and from water comes earth and stones once more—and thus generation appears to be transmitted from one to the other in a circle. (*Timaeus* 49c)

However this is not Plato's own opinion. He believes that the elements, as the most basic material things, must be formed from that simplest and most elegant of geometrical shapes, the triangle:

> In the first place, then as is evident to all, fire and earth and water and air are bodies. And every sort of body possesses volume, and every volume must necessarily be bounded by surfaces, and every rectilinear surface is composed of triangles, and all triangles are originally of two kinds, both of which are made up of one right and two acute angles; one of them has at either end of the base the half of a divided right angle, having equal sides, while in the other the right angle is divided into unequal parts, having unequal sides. (ibid. 53c–d)

The first figure referred to is the 45–45–90-degree isosceles triangle, of which there is only one. The second figure is the right angle scalene, of which, as Plato points out, there are an "infinite number." From this multitude Plato chooses for the elements the single right scalene triangle that is to him the most beautiful. "Now, the one which we maintain to be the most beautiful of all the many triangles—and we need not speak of the others—is that of which the double forms a third triangle which is equilateral" (ibid. 54a). This is a description of the 30–60–90-degree triangle. Thus the geometric building blocks of the elements are:

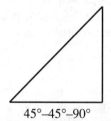 

45°–45°–90°   30°–60°–90°

These shapes should be familiar to everyone, as they are included in every set of mathematical drawing tools made for school use.

Plato goes on to elucidate:

> Now is the time to explain what was before obscurely said. There was an error in imagining that all the four elements might be generated by and into one another; this, I say, was an erroneous supposition, for there

are generated from the triangles which we have selected four kinds—three from the one which has the sides unequal, the fourth alone framed out of the isosceles triangle. Hence they cannot all be resolved into one another, a great number of small bodies being combined into a few large ones, or the converse. But three of them can be thus resolved and compounded, for they all spring from one, and when the greater bodies are broken up, many small bodies will spring up out of them and take their own proper figures. Or again, when many small bodies are dissolved into their triangles, by their total number, they can form one large mass of another kind. So much for their passage into one another. (ibid. 54c–d)

From the two triangles above Plato constructs the five regular solids, which are for this reason referred to as the Platonic solids, or Platonic bodies. Plato describes these as the solid forms which distribute into equal and similar parts the whole circle into which they are inscribed. That is to say, they are symmetrical in every dimension radially from their center points.

The 30–60–90-degree triangle is combined together in groups of six, each group forming a single equilateral triangle in this way:

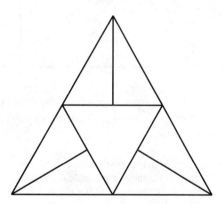

Four of these equilateral triangles compose the tetrahedron. Eight of them make up the octahedron. Twenty of them form the icosahedron. To these bodies Plato attributes the three elements which can be transformed one into the other, respectively Fire, Air and Water. To Fire is given the tetrahedron because of the three it is the most movable, the smallest and the sharpest.

To Air as the intermediate of the three is given the octahedron, which is second in mobility, size and acuteness. To Water is given the icosahedron because it is the least movable, the largest and the bluntest or least penetrating.

> Of all these elements, that which has the fewest bases must necessarily be the most movable, for it must be the acutest and most penetrating in every way, and also the lightest as being composed of the smallest number of similar particles, and the second body has similar properties in a second degree, and the third body, in the third degree. (ibid. 56b)

The 45–45–90-degree triangle is combined together in groups of four, each group forming a single square in this way:

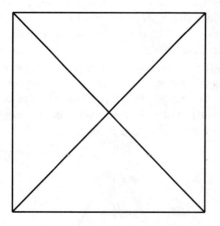

Six of these squares compose the cube, to which Plato attributes that element not subject to transformation, Earth.

> To earth, then, let us assign the cubic form, for earth is the most immovable of the four and the most plastic of all bodies, and that which has the most stable bases must of necessity be of such a nature. Now, of the triangles which we assumed at first, that which has two equal sides is by nature more firmly based than that which has unequal sides, and of the compound figures which are formed out of either, the plane equilateral quadrangle [square] has necessarily a more stable basis than the equilateral triangle, both in the whole and in the parts. (ibid. 55e)

The fifth regular solid, the dodecahedron, is composed from 12 pentagons. Plato says very little about this body, only: "There was yet a fifth combination which God used in the delineation of the universe with figures of animals" (ibid. 55c). The dodecahedron was accorded great reverence among the Pythagoreans, and indeed was said by Eudemus to have been discovered by Pythagoras himself, along with the other four regular bodies (see Diogenes Laertius *Lives of the Philosophers* 8.19). In fact, the tetrahedron, octahedron and cube were certainly known long before the time of Pythagoras by the Egyptians, but Pythagoras may have discovered the dodecahedron and icosahedron.

To the dodecahedron the ancients attributed Aether, the Quintessence (fifth essence) or Spirit of the World. The dodecahedron is mystically linked with the cube, and thus with the Earth, through geometry. If a line is divided into extreme and mean proportion, the whole line and the longer segment respectively measure the edges of a cube and dodecahedron concentrically inscribed in a single sphere. Iamblichus speaks of the Pythagorean Hippasus, who "in consequence of having divulged and described the method of forming a sphere from twelve pentagons, he perished in the sea, as an impious person ..." (*Life of Pythagoras* 18). Those curious about this method, by the way, should look in the tenth book of Euclid's *Elements*.

Based upon these underlying forms, Plato describes the transformations of the four elements this way:

> Earth, when meeting with fire and dissolved by its sharpness, whether the dissolution take place in the fire itself or perhaps in some mass of air or water, is borne hither and thither until its parts, meeting together and mutually harmonizing, again become earth, for they can never take any other form. But water, when divided by fire or by air, on reforming, may become one part fire and two parts air, and a single volume of air divided becomes two of fire. Again, when a small body of fire is contained in a larger body of air or water or earth, and both are moving, and the fire struggling is overcome and broken up, then two volumes of fire form one volume of

air, and when air is overcome and cut up into small pieces, two and a half parts of air are condensed into one part of water. *(Timaeus 56d–e)*

Fire, because it is more mobile, sharp and penetrating, naturally cuts up the other elements into their component triangles, which either disperse or are assimilated into Fire. To a lesser degree this is true of Air in relationship to Water. The more active naturally overcomes the more passive. In order for the conversion of the elements to flow in the opposite direction, from Fire to Air, and from Air to Water, it is necessary that small, and thus relatively weak, bits of the more active element be surrounded and overwhelmed by a greater volume of the more passive element, which is thus able to break it down and assimilate its parts in the case of Air and Water, or disperse it in the case of Earth. Earth can be broken up by the more active elements, or can itself surround and break up a smaller amount of a more active element by overwhelming it, but Earth never assimilates, nor is assimilated by, other elements.

This fundamental disagreement between Plato and Aristotle over whether all elements are convertible, or only some, is never really resolved in later centuries, and accounts for a good deal of the confusion concerning the properties of the elements. On the whole Aristotle's view gained the greater support, and exhibited itself in Arab medicine and alchemy, which carried over into Europe in the Middle Ages.

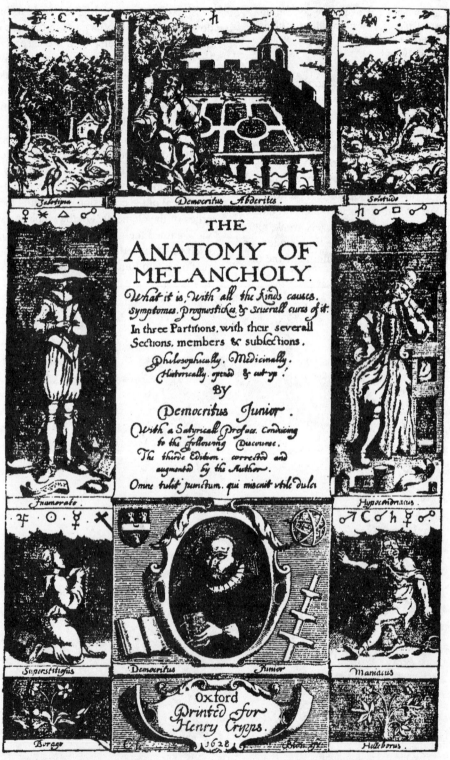

Title Page of The Anatomy of Melancholy *by Robert Burton (Oxford, 1628)*

APPENDIX IV

The Humors

The word "humor" is from the Latin *humorum,* meaning a fluid or moisture. It is in this sense that Shakespeare uses the term in his often quoted lines from *Julius Caesar:*

Is Brutus sick, and is it physical
To walk unbraced and suck up the humours
Of the dank morning? What! is Brutus sick,
And will he steal out of his wholesome bed
To dare the vile contagion of the night,
And tempt the rheumy and unpurged air
To add unto his sickness?
(Act 2, sc. 1, lines 261–7)

In this same sense Ben Jonson defines humor in his play *Every Man Out of His Humour:*

Why humour, as it is "ens," we thus define
    it,
To be a quality of air or water;
And in itself holds these two properties
Moisture and fluxure: as, for demonstration
Pour water on this floor. 'Twill wet and run.
Likewise the air forced through a horn or
    trumpet
Flows instantly away, and leaves behind
A kind of dew; and hence we do conclude
That whatsoe'er hath fluxture and humidity
As wanting power to contain itself
Is humour. So in every human body
The choler, melancholy, phlegm and blood
By reason that they flow continually
In some are part and are not continent
Receive the name of humours.
—The Induction

The most quoted author in the English language on the subject of the humors, Robert Burton, also returns to the source of the word in opening his examination of the humors in his *Anatomy of Melancholy:* "A humor is a liquid or fluent part of the body, comprehended in it, for the preservation of it ..." (1.1.2.2). Burton has already made the transition from general fluid, or vapor, to fluid inside a body, or juice. Any juice of plants or animals might be called a humor.

Agrippa refers to humors in a narrower medical sense derived from the teachings of Hippocrates and his disciples. According to this system there are two kinds: innate and adventitious. The innate, with which everyone is born, and which are necessary for sustaining life, are four in number, based upon the four elements of Fire, Air, Water and Earth. These four are called primary, or cardinal, humors, and bear the names yellow bile or choler, blood, phlegm and black bile or melancholy. No one has ever been able to describe them more concisely than Burton, and so I shall give his description here:

Blood is a hot, sweet, temperate, red humour, prepared in the meseraic veins [small veins that bring the chylus to the liver], and made of the most temperate parts of the chylus in the liver, whose office is to nourish the whole body, to give it strength and colour, being dispersed by the veins through every part of it. And from it spirits are first begotten in the heart, which afterwards by the arteries are communicated to the other parts.

Pituita, or phlegm, is a cold and moist humour, begotten of the colder part of the chylus (or white juice coming out of the meat digested in the stomach), in the liver; his office is to nourish and moisten the members of the body which, as the tongue, are moved, that they be not over-dry.

Choler is hot and dry, bitter, begotten of the hotter parts of the chylus, and gathered to the gall: it helps the natural heat and senses, and serves to the expelling of excrements.

Melancholy, cold and dry, thick, black, and sour, begotten of the more feculent part of nourishment, and purged from the spleen, is a bridle to the other two hot humours, blood and choler, preserving them in the blood, and nourishing the bones. These four humours have some analogy with the four elements, and to the four ages in man. (ibid. 1.1.2.2)

The spirits Burton alludes to in connection with blood make up, along with the humors, the category of parts contained in the body, as opposed to parts containing, such as the heart, liver, bones and so on. Burton defines spirit as "a most subtle vapour, which is expressed from the blood, and the instrument of the soul, to perform all his actions; a common tie or medium between the body and the soul, as some will have it ..." (ibid.). There are three spirits in the body.

The natural are begotten in the liver, and thence dispersed through the veins, to perform those natural actions. The vital spirits are made in the heart of the natural, which by the arteries are transported to all the other parts: if the spirits cease, then life ceaseth, as in a syncope or swooning. The animal spirits, formed of the vital, brought up to the brain, and diffused by the nerves to the subordinate members, give sense and motion to them all. (ibid. 1.1.2.2)

The "four ages in man" referred to by Burton are probably childhood, youth, maturity and old age, although he may also have in mind the Golden, Silver, Bronze and Iron ages of mankind. The humors can easily be attributed to both of these, as to many other fourfold divisions of man and nature. For example, John Wyclif, writing around 1380, says: "Blood is

moost kyndely umour, answeringe to the love of God, the othere uffours in man answeren to three other loves'' (OED s.v. humour).

The relationship of the humors to the elements is direct. Each humor shares the two powers of one of the elements according to the elemental scheme of Aristotle (see Appendix III):

FIRE (hot-dry) —Choler
AIR (moist-hot) —Blood
WATER (cold-moist)—Phlegm
EARTH (dry-cold) —Melancholy

This is perhaps more clearly shown in the following diagram:

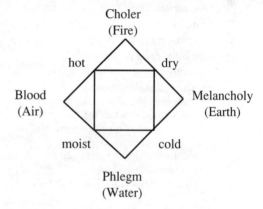

Each triangle of the larger square has an element and humor at its apex, and two contributing powers at its base.

According to the medical theories of the ancient Greeks, notably Hippocrates, and from them the Arabs, notably Avicenna, when the humors are in balance, the body enjoys perfect health. Each humor checks the harmful effects of the others, the result being a harmony in all the parts. Disease arises when this balance is disrupted. Plato puts it this way:

Now everyone can see whence diseases arise. There are four natures out of which the body is compacted—earth and fire and water and air—and the unnatural excess or defect of these, or the change of any of them from its own natural place into another, or, since there are more kinds than one of fire and of the other elements, the assumption by any of these of a wrong kind, or any similar irregularity, produces disorders and diseases. For when any of them is produced or changed in a manner contrary to nature, the parts which were previously cool grow warm, and those which are dry become moist, and the light become heavy, and the heavy light; all sorts of changes occur. *(Timaeus* 82a)

Plato describes some of the diseased humors which arise when the cardinal humors are thrown out of balance, such as "acid phlegm," which arises when "a secretion of black and acid bile is ... mingled by the power of heat with any salt substance" (ibid. 83c), and "white phlegm," which is:

> ... formed by the liquefaction of new and tender flesh when air is present, if inflated and incased in liquid so as to form bubbles which separately are invisible owing to their small size, but when collected are of a bulk which is visible and have a white color arising out of the generation of foam ... (ibid. 83d)

Disorders in the cardinal humors result in disorders in the soul, which is bound to the body and affected by its state.

> For where the acid and briny phlegm and other bitter and bilious humors wander about in the body and find no exit or escape, but are pent up within and mingle their own vapors with the motions of the soul, and are blended with them, they produce all sorts of diseases, more or fewer, and in every degree of intensity, and being carried to the three places of the soul, whichever they may severally assail, they create infinite varieties of ill temper and melancholy, of rashness and cowardice, and also of forgetfulness and stupidity. (ibid. 86e–87a)

From these imbalances, which practically speaking exist to some degree in everyone, since no man is perfect, arise the four temperaments of man, the sanguine (corresponding to blood), the choleric (choler), the phlegmatic (phlegm) and the melancholic (melancholy). The Elizabethan playwrights such as Shake-speare and Jonson made great capital of these human types. The admirable and happy man was one whose humors were in agreement. A man out of his humor became the butt of all manner of social censure and ridicule, and this was viewed as a natural and inevitable result of his one-sidedness. No pity was accorded such a creature, no quarter given. The perfect picture of a melancholic temperament is Jaques in *As You Like It*. The choleric temperament is exemplified in Hotspur in *Richard II*. Bottom in *A Midsummer Night's Dream* is a phlegmatic sort of soul. The most substantial sanguinary character in Shakespeare is gentle Falstaff in *Henry IV: Part I* and *The Merry Wives of Windsor*.

The choleric person is hot-tempered, combative, rash, thoughtless, bold, brave, active and flushed in face. Astrologically the planet corresponding to this disposition is Mars. The sanguinary person is optimistic, active, kind, just, cheerful, companionable and of a rosy complexion. His planet is Jupiter. The phlegmatic is dull, stolid, passive, methodical, lethargic and pale of face. His planet is the Moon. The melancholic is sad, unsuccessful, unfortunate, discontented, servile in station and dark complexioned. His planet is Saturn.

Melancholy must be given special notice because it was singled out and set apart from the other humors by some writers, including Agrippa. On the one hand it was the most base and ugly of the temperaments. On the other hand it was looked upon as something akin to the divine inspiration that possessed the oracles of the ancient world. Frances Yates *(Occult Philosophy in the Elizabethan Age,* ch. 6) traces this second current back to the 13th of pseudo-Aristotle's *Problems,* where melancholy is said to be the humor, or temperament, of heros and great men. According to this theory, the heroic frenzy, combined with black bile, produces genius. Agrippa expounds this view at length in ch. LX, bk. I.

To continue taking examples from Shake-speare, the character who best exemplifies the heroic madness of melancholy is Hamlet. Although Hamlet and Jaques are possessed by the same humor, they are completely different men. Hamlet is a great soul involved in great events. Jaques is a little—one might even say stunted—soul involved in futility, his only relief in fits of "black humor." But the greatness of Hamlet and other heroic melancholics is a dangerous and fearful greatness ever courting disaster. No man of balanced humors—Prospero, for example, in *The Tempest*—would ever voluntarily take upon himself melancholic genius. It is a gift, and curse, of the gods.

Magic Squares

A magic square in its purest form may be defined as a series of consecutive numbers beginning with one that is arranged in a square grid so that each row, column and diagonal of that grid has an equal sum. In the series 1 to n^2, n is the base, root, module or order of the square—"order" being the most common term. For example, a square of nine chambers (1 to 3^2) is called an order 3 square.

The most ancient square is the order 3 *Lo Shu* (scroll of Lo) of China, which occurs in manuscripts of the *I Ching* in this form:

Lo Shu

Legend says it was revealed to the Emperor Yu around 2200 BC, when a divine tortoise crawled from the River Lo with the square patterned on its shell. According to the *I Ching*

"the Lo gave forth the writing, of which the sages took advantage." Commenting on this passage, James Legge says: "To the hero sage it suggested 'the Great Plan,' an interesting but mystical document of the same classic, 'of Physics, Astrology, Divination, Morals, Politics, and Religion,' the great model for the government of the kingdom" (*I Ching*, trans. James Legge [New York: Dover, [1899] 1963], 17–8).

It will readily be seen that when the dots are transformed into numbers, the order 3 square results:

4	9	2
3	5	7
8	1	6

The ancient Chinese used this symbol to illustrate the unity of elemental principles. In their magic, as in that of the West, even numbers are passive and feminine, while odd numbers are active and masculine. The 4 and 9 stand for the element Metal; the 3 and 8, Wood; the 1 and 6, Water; and the 2 and 7, Fire. The central

5 represents the element Earth. Each of the elements in the outer cells of the square has both an odd and even number for the union of the female *yin* with the male *yang*.

The first appearance of the *Lo Shu* as a magic square proper is toward the end of the Chou Dynasty (951–1126). No doubt it is older, and may be a product of the numerical and astrological speculations of the ancient Babylonians. Wherever magic squares began, they have been used occultly around the world for centuries. In India they are inscribed on silver plates as amulets. It is conjectured that the Arabs, who used them as early as the 9th century as an adjunct to astrology, learned them from the Indians, and transmitted them through their mystical and astrological writings to the West. A magic square occurs in a Hebrew work by Abraham ben Ezra dated the 11th century. Skeat gives several examples of Malaysian magic squares in his *Malay Magic* (Skeat [1900] 1967, ch. 6, sec. 12, 555–8); however there is no way of knowing how ancient the Maylasian squares may be, or their place of origin.

Around the beginning of the 14th century Manuel Moschopulus (a nickname meaning "little calf"), a Byzantine commentator and grammarian, wrote a treatise devoted to magic squares. In view of the perennial fascination of the Abbot Trithemius for all ciphers and puzzles, it seems not unlikely that Agrippa would have been familiar with this work.

There are no order 2 squares, and only one order 3 square, which may be permuted eight ways. As the order increases, the number of possible squares and their permutations rises dramatically. There are 880 order 4 squares with 7,040 possible forms. There are 275,305,224 order 5 squares. The permutations of these have not been calculated.

Permutation is used here to refer to the way in which any square may be tipped, inverted, reflected, or otherwise played with to give the impression, at first glance, that a new square has been created. On closer examination it will be found that the essential structure of the permuted square is unchanged.

There are three classes of magic squares, each of which must be treated separately, as each has distinct methods of construction.

Odd Squares

Odd squares are those with an odd order, or root. The odd squares used by Agrippa are order 3, order 5, order 7, and order 9. All these may be constructed using the same techniques. There are several popular ways of making odd squares. The most common method will be described first to show how it relates to the technique used by Agrippa.

Odd squares of any order can be made by following these simple steps:

1. Construct the grid.

2. Place the number 1 in the middle cell of the top row.

3. Place the following numbers in order along the diagonal that slopes up and to the right, except—
   a. When the top row is reached write the next number in the bottom row *as if* it were above the top row.
   b. When the far right column is reached, put the next number in the far left column *as if* it were outside the right column.
   c. When a cell is reached that has already been filled, drop one square down and continue up and right diagonally as before.

These rules are difficult to follow in the abstract, but simple when applied graphically to a square:

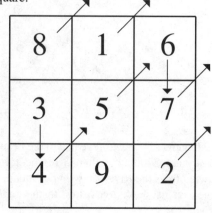

It is simplest to think of the square as simultaneously folded into a horizontal and a vertical cylinder, so that both the left and right edges and the top and bottom edges touch. As each diagonal ring of cells on this double cylinder is filled, the numbers drop down to the next ring until the square is complete.

Agrippa uses a slightly different but related technique for making odd squares that yields a different set of squares from those produced by the method given above, except of course in the case of the order 3 square, which is merely reflected by Agrippa's method.

He begins by placing the number 1 in the cell immediately below the middle cell of the square. Then he writes the numbers in order diagonally *down* and to the right, carrying them off the bottom back to the top row, and off the right back to the left column, as already described in the first method above. But when Agrippa reaches a filled cell, he jumps *down two* squares. When this carries him off the bottom of the square, he returns on the top:

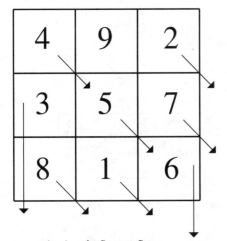

Agrippa's Saturn Square

It can readily be seen that Agrippa's square of Saturn is a reflection top to bottom (lake reflection) of the order 3 square arrived at by the first method. A permutation is inevitable since there is only one order 3 square. However, when the two methods are applied to the order 5 square of Mars, there is a different outcome. Here is the order 5 square generated by the first method:

17	24	1	8	15
23	5	7	14	16
4	6	13	20	22
10	12	19	21	3
11	18	25	2	9

By Agrippa's method, going down and right from the cell *below* the center cell, and dropping two cells, this square results:

11	24	7	20	3
4	12	25	8	16
17	5	13	21	9
10	18	1	14	22
23	6	19	2	15

Agrippa's Mars Square

Notice that the numbers in the rows of Agrippa's square form the diagonals running up-left to down-right on the first order 5 square; the up-left to down-right diagonals of Agrippa's are the down-left to up-right on the first square; and columns in both squares contain the same numbers, but in different ordering.

The same technique is used by Agrippa to generate the odd order 7 square of Venus and order 9 square of the Moon.

Doubly Even Squares

Doubly even squares are those which, when divided into four equal parts by a cross through the center, yield four squares of an even order, or root. The doubly even squares used by

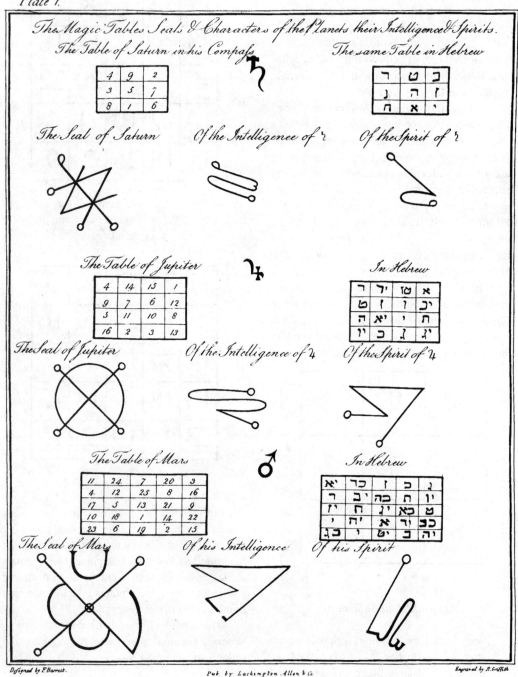

Magic Squares of Saturn, Jupiter and Mars

from *The Magus* by Francis Barrett (London, 1801)

Agrippa are the order 4 square of Jupiter and the order 8 square of Mercury.

This class of square is the easiest to construct. Agrippa has used the same method that is commonly used today. The rules are:

1. Construct the grid.

2. Place consecutive numbers in the cells beginning with 1 in the lower-left corner and going across to the right, then returning to the left to start the second row, and so on to the upper-right corner.

3. Invert all diagonal numbers with their opposites across the center intersection.

The order 4 square of Jupiter is constructed in this manner:

13	14	15	16
9	10	11	12
5	6	7	8
1	2	3	4

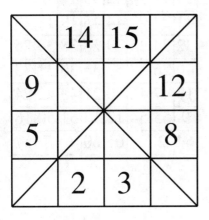

4	14	15	1
9	7	6	12
5	11	10	8
16	2	3	13

This is essentially the same square that is to be found in the famous engraving by Albrecht Dürer called *Melencholia I*. Dürer has rotated Agrippa's square onto its head, then interchanged the outer columns:

4	14	15	1
9	7	6	12
5	11	10	8
16	2	3	13

Agrippa

16	3	2	13
5	10	11	8
9	6	7	12
4	15	14	1

Dürer

Dürer inverted the square to get the number 1514 in the bottom row, which is the year the engraving was done. Why he interchanged the outer columns is less clear, unless it was to disguise the fact that his square and Agrippa's are the same. In his work Dürer borrowed shamelessly from the work of many other artists.

Karl Anton Nowotny states that there can be no doubt Dürer's Jupiter square "was taken from a treatise on magic squares, their relation to astrology and their magic influence when on talismans" ("The Construction of Certain Seals and Characters in the Work of Agrippa of Nettesheim," *Journal of the Warburg and Courtault Institutes* 12 [1949], 46). He goes on to say that "a version" of this treatise is bound up with a 15th-century Cracow manuscript of the *Picatrix,* and that another version differing in text with the squares "considerably distorted" appears in the pseudo-Paracelsian *Archidoxis Magica.*

Still it may be that Dürer's inspiration was Agrippa, not the *Picatrix* manuscript or the *Archidoxis Magica.* The *Occult Philosophy* was written in 1509 and circulated for many years in manuscript. Since Agrippa and Dürer were contemporary German intellectuals—Dürer died in 1528, Agrippa in 1535—it is reasonable to assume that they exchanged views on occult matters, especially as this was a passion of both.

Frances Yates puts forward the notion, which she says has been "proved" by various scholars, that Dürer's engraving is based on the manuscript version of ch. LX, bk. I of the *Occult Philosophy* (Yates [1979] 1983, pt. 1, ch. 6). It will be recalled that in this chapter Agrippa postulates three kinds of melancholy, which he sees as a type of possession, based on the three levels of the soul: imaginative, rational and mental. Thus the calling of the engraving *Melencholia I,* which represents the first type, imaginative melancholy. If this is true, it may be assumed that a set of three engravings was planned by Dürer, which unfortunately never materialized.

The other doubly even square is constructed in exactly the same way as the Jupiter square, with the minor difference that in the Mercury square the diagonals must be extended across each of the four quarter squares. Interchange of numbers still occurs around the center point of the great square:

57	58	59	60	61	62	63	64
49	50	51	52	53	54	55	56
41	42	43	44	45	46	47	48
33	34	35	36	37	38	39	40
25	26	27	28	29	30	31	32
17	18	19	20	21	22	23	24
9	10	11	12	13	14	15	16
1	2	3	4	5	6	7	8

	58	59			62	63	
49		52	53				56
41		44	45				48
	34	35			38	39	
	26	27			30	31	
17		20	21				24
9		12	13				16
	2	3			6	7	

8	58	59	5	4	62	63	1
49	15	14	52	53	11	10	56
41	23	22	44	45	19	18	48
32	34	35	29	28	38	39	25
40	26	27	37	36	30	31	33
17	47	46	20	21	43	42	24
9	55	54	12	13	51	50	16
64	2	3	61	60	6	7	57

Agrippa's Mercury Square

Melencolia I

engraving by Albrecht Dürer

Singly Even Squares

The third class of magic square is called singly even, because when it is divided into quarters by a cross through the center intersection, each quarter square is of an odd order, or root. Of all the squares used by Agrippa only the square of the Sun, which is an order 6 square, falls into this group. This is the most awkward of the three classes of squares to construct, and the least elegant, because it requires some fiddling.

Agrippa began by treating the order 6 square as a doubly even. First he constructed a grid and filled it with consecutive numbers, starting with 1 at the lower-left corner and going across the bottom row to the right, then continuing in the same way on the next higher row, and so on until he reached the final cell. As in the doubly even squares, he inverted the primary diagonals around the center point of the grid:

31	32	33	34	35	36
25	26	27	28	29	30
19	20	21	22	23	24
13	14	15	16	17	18
7	8	9	10	11	12
1	2	3	4	5	6

	32	33	34	35	
25		27	28		30
19	20			23	24
13	14			17	18
7		9	10		12
	2	3	4	5	

6	32	33	34	35	1
25	11	27	28	8	30
19	20	16	15	23	24
13	14	22	21	17	18
7	29	9	10	26	12
36	2	3	4	5	31

However, inverting the secondary diagonals of the quarter squares around the center point will not make the square magic. To make the final necessary substitutions it appears that Agrippa took his cue from the structure of the simplest square, the *Lo Shu,* or order 3 square of Saturn.

Treating the first quarter square—the one on the lower left—as an order 3 square, he superimposed the pattern of the Saturn seal, which is based upon the numerical structure of the Saturn square. It was necessary to rotate it 90 degrees to make the line that traces the diagonal of the Saturn square match the diagonal running through the quarter of the Sun square:

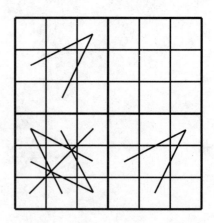

Saturn Seal

Relying on the seal of Saturn as his pattern, Agrippa made two inversions, each involving three pairs of numbers. The numbers beneath the points of the upward pointing angle of the Saturn seal he inverted left to right (mirror reflection) with the corresponding numbers in the lower-right quarter square. The numbers beneath the points of the downward pointing angle he inverted top to bottom (lake reflection) with their correspondents in the upper-left quarter square. It was not necessary to invert the numbers beneath the diagonal line, as these had already been inverted:

6	32	3↑	34	35	1
7↑	11	27	28	8	30
19	14↑	16	15	23	24
18	20↓	22	21	17	13→
25↓	29	10	9→	26	12
36	5←	33↓	4	2→	31

Agrippa's Sun Square

In the diagram above the underlined numbers have not moved on the grid. Small arrows indicate the direction of inversion of reflected pairs.

If Agrippa had chosen to invert the numbers under the upward pointing angle of the seal of Saturn *top to bottom* instead of left to right, and had likewise inverted the numbers under the points of the downward pointing angle *left to right* rather than top to bottom, the result would have been this square, which is also magic:

6	2↑	33	34	35	1
25	11	9↑	28	8	30
13↑	20	16	15	23	24
19↓	17←	22	21	14→	18
12←	29	27↓	10	26	7→
36	32↓	4←	3→	5	31

Inverted Agrippa

Why Agrippa chose the first of these two possibilities, if indeed he used this method, is not apparent, unless it is because, when reflected into the upper left and lower right quarters, each angle of the Saturn seal traces the position of the first three numbers in the Saturn square:

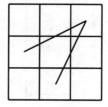
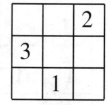

In addition to the basic characteristics that make a square magic, some squares have other qualities which have been noticed by mathematicians. A magic square is said to be symmetrical, or associated, when its skewly related numbers sum $n^2 + 1$, where n is the order of the square. Skewly related numbers are pairs opposite one another with respect to the center of the square. For example, in the order 4 Jupiter square, numbers 7 and 10 are skewly related about the center. Their sum ($4^2 + 1 = 17$) satisfies the requirement of an associated square, as does the sum of all other skewly related pairs.

All of the Agrippa squares are associative except the Sun square. In fact there are no associated magic squares of the singly even class.

Another special type of square is called pandiagonal. A pandiagonal magic square is one whose broken diagonals sum $\frac{1}{2} n (n^2 + 1)$, n being the order of the square. In other words, the broken diagonals are as magical as the solid diagonals. The diagrams below show what is meant by broken diagonals:

a	c	b	
c	b		a
b		a	c
	a	c	b

	e	f	d
d		e	f
f	d		e
e	f	d	

Pandiagonal Structure of the Order 4 Square

There are no pandiagonal squares of the singly even class, and the solitary order 3 square is not pandiagonal. Of the 880 distinct order 4 squares, 48 are pandiagonal. There are exactly 3,600 pandiagonal squares of order 5, more than 38 million of order 7, and over 6.5 billion of order 8. None of Agrippa's squares are pandiagonal. From the viewpoint of practical occultism this is unfortunate, since pandiagonal squares have the quality that, by shifting rows and columns around the center, any number can be made to occupy any cell.

At the beginning of this century a Professor Kielhorn discovered this pandiagonal order 4 square in a Jaina inscription of the 12th century in Khajuraho, India:

7	12	1	14
2	13	8	11
16	3	10	5
9	6	15	4

Jaina Square

It will readily be found by experiment that the sum of any broken diagonal equals 34, which fulfills the requirement of a pandiagonal square. At the same time observe that the Jaina square is not associated. For example, the skewly related pair 1 and 6 do *not* sum $4^2 + 1 = 17$.

Magic squares have been made with non-consecutive numbers and with prime numbers. A doubly magic square is magic for its numbers and the *squares* of those numbers. A trebly magic square is magic for its numbers, their squares, and their *cubes*. A magic cube is made up of layers of magic squares arranged so that each rank, file, column and cubic diagonal (or diameter) sums the same number. The diagonal of each individual square need not be magic to satisfy the requirements for a magic cube (see top of next page).

There are also magic stars in which the sums of numbers located on the interstices of rays are equal, and magic circles in which numbers are arranged magically in rays radially about a center point. Benjamin Franklin, in addition to his well known interest in magic squares, also constructed a magic circle with many interesting properties. There are even more elaborate magical geometries; for example, magic rings, magic spheres and magic octa-hedroids, which carry the magical properties of numbers into the fourth dimension, but these are far beyond the scope of this treatise.

Top

24	16	2
17	3	22
1	23	18

Middle

8	21	13
19	14	9
15	7	20

Bottom

10	5	27
6	25	11
26	12	4

Magic Cube with Nonconsecutive Numbers

With an understanding of the formation of the Agrippa squares, the seals of the planets that relate to those squares may be examined.

It is obvious at once that the Saturn seal is based upon the numerical structure of the Saturn square. The upward pointing angle traces the numbers 1, 2, 3; the diagonal covers 4, 5, 6; and the downward pointing angle touches 7, 8, 9.

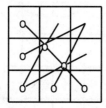

Seal of Saturn Set in Saturn Square

It is not clear what purpose, if any, is served by the small circles at the points of the seal. In Freake's edition seven circles are represented, two being absent from the horns of the downward pointing angle. In the Latin *Opera* of Agrippa, printed in Germany around 1600, the seal appears like this:

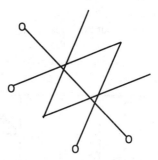

Saturn Seal in Latin Opera

The small triangular spaces generated by the misplaced diagonal may have inspired Freake to put circles at the interstices of the seal. On the whole I am inclined to think that the small circles in the seals have no occult meaning, and merely serve a decorative function.

The seal of Jupiter follows the same mathematical structure as the Saturn seal, echoing in its shape the method of forming the square of Jupiter. Those numbers touched by the circle are the ones in the original grid which have not moved from their consecutive placement. The numbers touched by the cross are the ones that were inverted around the central point of the square:

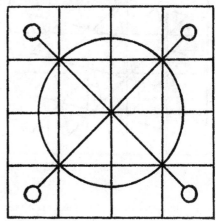

Seal of Jupiter Set in Jupiter Square

Notice again that all cells in the square are covered by some part of the seal.

With the seal of Mars the house of cards we have been building here comes crashing down. Not only is there no obvious relationship between the seal and the numerical structure of the Mars square, but the lines of the seal do not even touch every cell in the square. It seems that a totally different method has been used in designing this seal:

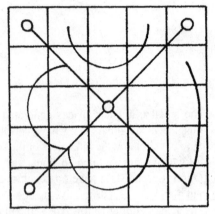

Seal of Mars Set in Mars Square

It is possible to construct a seal of Mars designed in a way similar to the seal of Saturn. It would look like this:

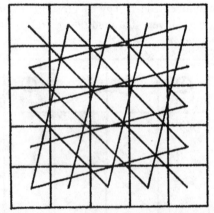

Hypothetical Seal of Mars Set in Mars Square

The diagonal of the Mars square that runs from upper left to bottom right traces the consecutive numbers 11 to 15 on the square, and the crescent attached to it bridges the distance between numbers 15 and 16, suggesting a structural application, The meaning of the three semicircles is less clear. Nowotny bases the construction of the odd squares on a chessboard pattern and says that each of these semicircles

defines three squares of the same color, but if this were true the single semicircle at the top of the seal would trace one color of squares and the other two semicircles the opposite color. Regarding the odd squares of Mars and Venus, he admits "besides the lines inherent in the diagram, symbolic figures are drawn over the chessboard pattern indicating the nature of the planet" (Nowotny 1949, 52).

Clearly there is a dynamic at work between the seal of Mars and the seal of Venus. In astrology, Mars (♂ or ♂) is the spouse of Venus (♀), and both are formed from the primary elemental properties of Sun (☉ or ○) and Earth (⊕ or +). The magic squares of Mars and Venus are both of the odd class, with an identical structure. The seals look as though they were formed with a single method, but what that method may be is obscure. Perhaps it is based on the Hebrew letter correspondents to numbers in the square, with a word key rather than a numerical key; or perhaps its structure is symbolic.

If the Mars seal is examined symbolically, the semicircle at once suggests the Moon, and the long arc on the right side the blade of Saturn's scythe. The two protrusions are not unlike testicles, calling up the myth of Uranus, who was castrated by his son, Cronus, who was identified with Saturn.

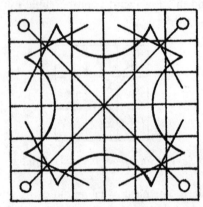

Seal of the Sun Set in Solar Square

The seal of the Sun is similar in construction to the Jupiter and Mercury seals, clearly expressing the structure of the magic square of the Sun. The large central cross covers the numbers that invert around the center point of the square. The smaller cross in the lower left quarter square may be superimposed over the seal of Saturn (see illustration, p. 740), echoing the method of forming the Sun square with the Saturn seal as a guide. Notice that each cell in the square is touched by some part of the seal.

The seal of Venus, as was true of its mate the seal of Mars, is completely different in structure, and presumably in concept, from the other seals:

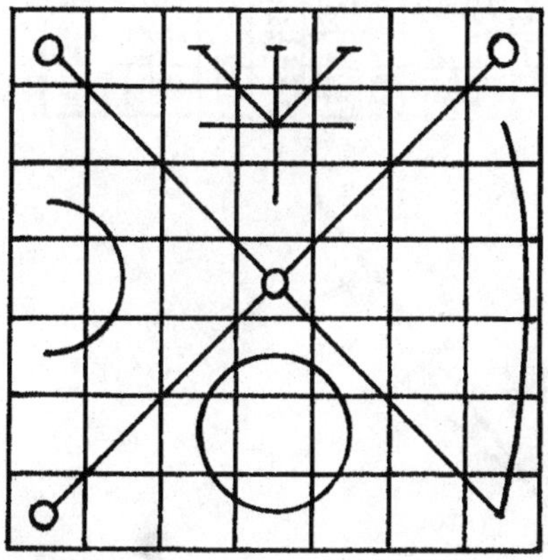

Seal of Venus Set in Venus Square

The same great cross and scythe that appear in the Mars seal are present here, along with the half circle or crescent. But the two bulges have given way to a circle and a figure with five branches. Symbolically at least this last might represent the letter V for Venus combined with the equal-armed cross (+), symbol of Earth. Along with the crescent of the Moon and the circle of the Sun, the three primary elements are present out of which all five lesser planets are constructed: ♀ = ○ plus +; ♁ (or ♂) = + plus ○; ♃ = ☽ plus +; ♄ = + plus ☽; and ☿ = ☽ plus ○ plus + . In this sense the seal of Venus embodies all seven planets, and indeed seven is the number of Venus.

Little need be said of the Mercury seal as it perfectly expresses the method of deriving the square of Mercury from a grid of consecutive numbers. In this it is an extension of the Jupiter seal, which it most closely resembles structurally:

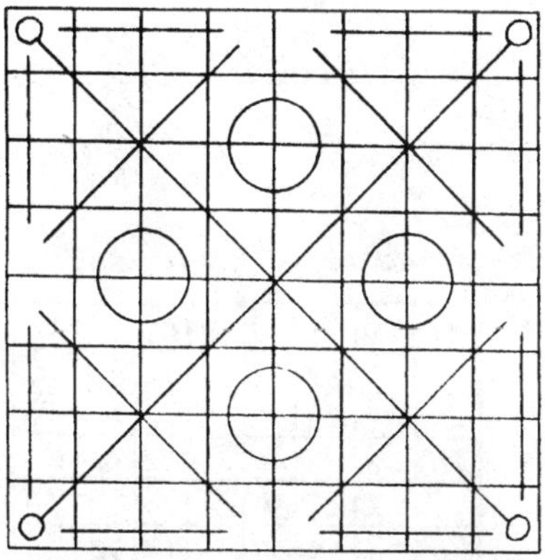

Seal of Mercury Set in Mercury Square

The seal of the Moon should be in the same style as the seals of Mars and Venus, if only its magic square, which is of the odd class, were considered. However, the astrological mate of Luna is Sol, and if the seals of the Moon and Sun are compared, similarities will be observed. Both have the great cross, and more significantly both contain four semicircles, or crescents, arranged symmetrically about the center with the horns pointing outward. The crescents of the Sun seal are single, while the crescents of the Moon seal are triple, perhaps so that they will touch on more of the cells in the square. Of course Hecate has three faces, one each for the waxing, full and waning phases of the Moon. There are 13 small circles in the seal and 13 months in the lunar year:

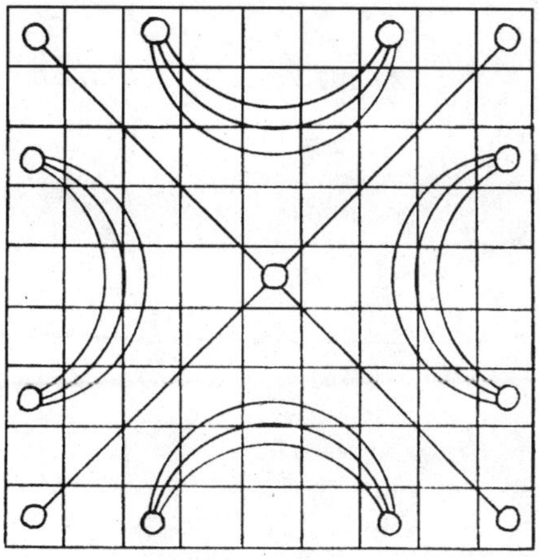

Seal of the Moon Set in the Lunar Square

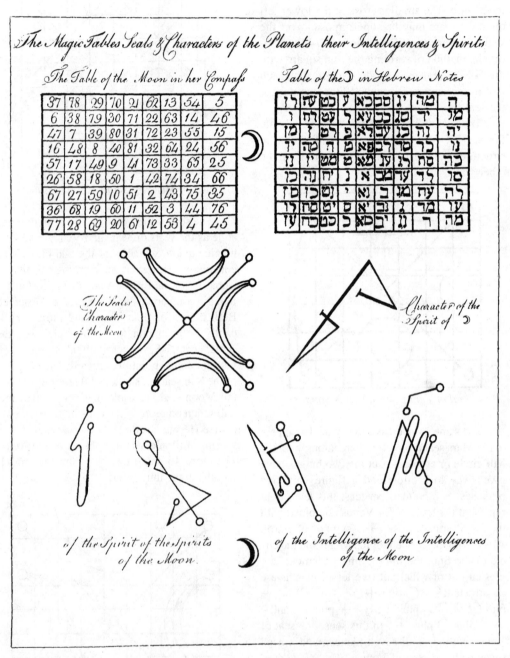

Magic Square of the Moon

from *The Magus* by Francis Barrett (London, 1801)

The lesser seals, or sigils, of the individual spirits and intelligences of the seven planets are formed by locating the Hebrew letters of each name, based on the numerical values of those letters, in their respective cells in the magic square of the planet to which that name attaches, then drawing a line from letter to letter in order.

The letters of each name connected with a planet sum one of the significant numbers in that planet's magic square. These numbers are based on the order of the square, the total number of cells, the sum of each row and the sum of the square. For example, the significant numbers of Saturn are 3, 9, 15 and 45. The Spirit of Saturn is Zazel, or in Hebrew זאזל, ZAZL, which numerically adds up to 7 + 1 + 7 + 30 = 45. Number values may be manipulated Kabbalistically where necessary through the technique of *Aiq Beker,* a grid of nine chambers each of which holds three Hebrew letters considered to be numerically interchangeable (22 letters plus 5 final forms equals 27 characters). In the example of Zazel, *lamed* (value 30) falls in the same chamber of *Aiq Beker* as *gimel* (value 3)—therefore ל, L, is located on the square of Saturn in the cell occupied by 3 (see Appendix VII: Practical Kabbalah).

Sigils may be disguised through the simple but effective tricks of rotating or reflecting them once they have been extracted from the squares. Without some grasp of how the sigils were created, it is then impossible to relate them to the squares directly.

Although it is a relatively simple matter to draw most of the sigils once the correct Hebrew spellings of the names are known, some of them are still quite difficult. Since all the sources of the Agrippa squares are corrupt, including the Latin *Opera,* the Freake translation and Barrett's *Magus*—which is the most frequently consulted source—the task effectively becomes impossible. Even the modern texts of well respected occultists such as Israel Regardie are full of mistakes. In fact I have yet to see one treatise on the squares, seals and sigils that is error free. This appendix may well be the first complete and accurate presentation of all the sigils of Agrippa in the five centuries that have passed since the work was written.

The following numerical breakdown of the restored names and graphic display of the sigils located in their respective squares will be found useful, particularly by the working occultist:

Saturn

Intelligence: Agiel; AGIAL; אגיאל.
  A G I A L
  $1 + 3 + 10 + 1 + 30 = 45$

Spirit: Zazel; ZAZL; זאזל
  Z A Z L
  $7 + 1 + 7 + 30 = 45$

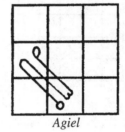 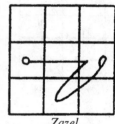

Agiel   *Zazel*

It will be observed in the case of Agiel that, since there is no *yod* (value 10) in the square, by *Aiq Beker, aleph* is substituted. Likewise *lamed* (30) becomes *gimel* (3)

Jupiter

Intelligence: Johphiel; IHPhIAL; יהפיאל.
  I H Ph I A L
  $10 + 5 + 80 + 10 + 1 + 30 = 136$

Spirit: Hismael; HSMAL; הסמאל
  H S M A L
  $5 + 60 + 40 + 1 + 30 = 136$

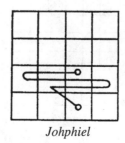 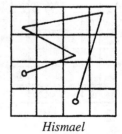

Johphiel   *Hismael*

In the sigil of Johphiel the two letters *yod* and *aleph* are doubled in the single cell that contains the number 11.

Mars

Intelligence: Graphiel; GRAPhIAL; גראפיאל.
  G   R   A Ph I   A   L
  3 +200 +1 +80 +10 + 1 + 30 = 325

Spirit: Barzabel; BRTzBAL; ברצבאל.
  B R Tz B A   L
  2 +200+90 +2 + 1 +30 = 325

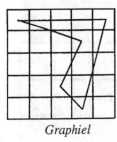 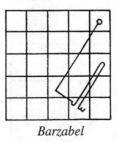

      Graphiel   *Barzabel*

Again in the Graphiel sigil *yod* and *aleph* are doubled in the cell that holds the number 11. The three small bumps on the Barzabel sigil emphasize that the cell holding number 2 is touched three times.

Sun

Intelligence: Nachiel; NKIAL; נכיאל.
  N   K   I   A   L
  50+20 +10 + 1 + 30 =111

Spirit: Sorath; SORTh; סורתה.
  S   O   R Th
  60 + 6 +200+400 = 666

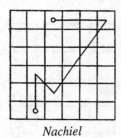 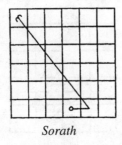

      Nachiel   *Sorath*

The sigil of Nachiel is tricky to draw in that the last segment leads to the cell of 3 rather than the cell of 30. The double bump at the beginning of the Sorath sigil indicates two letters occupying the same cell.

Venus

Intelligence: Hagiel; HGIAL; הגיאל.
  H   G   I   A   L
  5 + 3 +10 +1 +30 = 49

Spirit: Kedemel; QDMAL; קדמאל.
  Q   D   M   A   L
  100+4 + 40 + 1 +30 = 175

Intelligences: Bne Seraphim; BNI ShRPhIM; בני שרפים.
  B   N   I Sh R Ph I   M
  2 +50+10+300+200+80 +10+600=1252 (!)

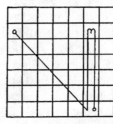 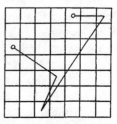

      Hagiel   *Kedemel*

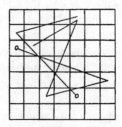

      Bne Seraphim

The sigil of the Bne Seraphim is based on the erroneous assumption that the sum of the numbers in the Venus square is 1252, when in fact the sum is 1225. In both the Latin *Opera* and the Freake translation the sum of 1252 is given. Obviously at some point the last two digits were transposed. A similar mistake occurs in the line above in the table in ch. XXII, bk. II, where the sum of a row in the Venus square was given as 157 instead of the correct 175. This error is also in both the Latin and English editions.

What is strange is that the name Bne Seraphim does numerically add up to 1252, and this name is used in the drawing of the sigil. This suggests that the original error was Agrippa's, and that he linked the name Bne Seraphim to the Venus square in the mistaken belief that the sum of the square was 1252. It is difficult to imagine how such an error might have occurred, particularly since the square of Venus is correctly given. On this point it would be interesting to consult the manuscript version of the *Occult Philosophy* to see if the error occurs there as well.

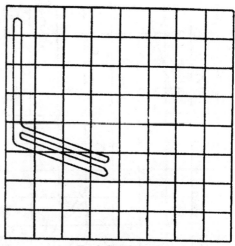

Taphthartharath

Mercury

Intelligence: Tiriel; TIRIAL; טיריאל.

T I R I A L
9 +10+200 +10 +1 +30 = 260

Spirit: Taphthartharath; ThPhThRThRTh; תפתרתרת.

Th Ph Th R Th R Th
400+80+400+200+400+200+400 = 2080

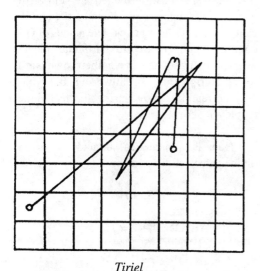

Tiriel

The double bump in the Tiriel sigil indicates the *yod* and *aleph* taken together in the cell containing number 11.

Moon

Intelligence: ?

Spirit: Hasmodai; ChShMODAI; חשמודאי.

Ch Sh M O D A I
8 +300+40 + 6 + 4 + 1 +10 = 369

Spirit of Spirits: Schedbarschemoth Schartathan; ShDBRShHMAaTh ShRThThN; שד ברשהמעת שרתתן.

Sh D B R Sh H M Aa Th
300+4 + 2 +200+300+5 +40+70+400 +
Sh R Th Th N
300+200+400+400+700 = 3321

Intelligency of the Intelligence: Malcha betharsithim hed beruah schehakim; MLKA BThRShIThIM AaD BRVCh ShChQIM; מלכא בתרשיתים עד ברוח שחקים.

M L K A B Th R Sh I Th
40+30+20 + 1 + 2 +400+200+300+10+400
I M Aa D B R V Ch
10 +600+70+ 4 + 2 +200+6 + 8
Sh Ch Q I M
300 +8 +100+10+600 = 3321

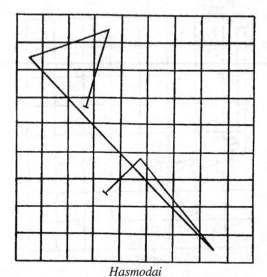

Hasmodai

In the sigil of Hasmodai, the *shin* (value 300, reduced by *Aiq Beker* to 30) and the *mem* (value 40) are combined in the cell containing the number 70.

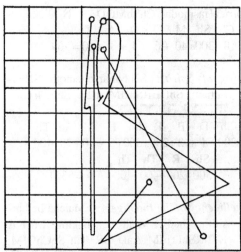

Schedbarschemoth Schartathan

In the sigil of Schedbarschemoth Schartathan, which might better be written Shad Barschemoth Schartathan, the second *shin* (value 300, reduced by *Aiq Beker* to 30) and the *he* (value 5) are doubled in the cell containing number 35.

In the sigil of the Intelligency of the Intelligence it appears that *kaph* (value 20) and *aleph* (value 1) of the first word have been doubled in the cell containing number 21, as this part of the sigil has only three points, and there are no words of three letters in the name. Due to the extreme complexity of the figure variations are possible, but this seems the most accurate form.

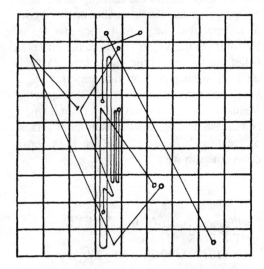

Malcha betharsithim hed beruah schehakim

Many other names may be applied to the squares to produce unique sigils that will be magically significant provided the sum of the letters in the names equals one of the significant numbers in the squares. The names of God connected numerically to particular planets through their squares have their own sigils which Agrippa has not drawn out, but which may be readily derived using the techniques employed above.

Here is a numerical breakdown of the divine names of the planets:

Saturn

3   Ab; AB; אב (1 + 2 = 3)

9   Hod; HD; הד (5 + 4 = 9)

15   Iah; IH; יה (10 + 5 = 15)

45   Hod; HVD; הוד (5 + 6 + 4 = 15)

45 Jehovah extended; IVD HA VAU HA;
יוד הא ואו הא (10 + 6 + 4 + 5 + 1 + 6
+ 1 + 6 + 5 + 1 = 45)

Jupiter

4   Aba; ABA; אבא (1 + 2 + 1 = 4)
16   —; HVH; הוה (5 + 6 + 5 = 16)
16   —; AHI; אהי (1 + 5 + 10 = 16)
34   El Ab; AL AB; אל אב (1 + 30 + 1 + 2 = 34)

Mars

5   He; H; ה (5)
25   —; IHI; יהי (10 + 5 + 10 = 25)
65   Adonai; ADNI; אדני (1 + 4 + 50 + 10 = 65)

Sun

6   Vau; V; ו (6)
6   He extended; HA; הא (5 + 1 = 6)
36   Eloh; ALH; אלה (1 + 30 + 5 = 36)

Venus

7   —; AHA; אהא (1 + 5 + 1 = 7)

Mercury

Asboga, eight extended; AZBVGH; אזבוגה
    ([1 + 7 = 8] + [2 + 6 = 8] + [3 + 5 = 8])
64 Din; DIN; דין (4 + 10 + 50 = 64)
64 Doni; DNI; דני (4 + 50 + 10 = 64)

Moon

9   Hod; HD; הד (5 + 4 = 9)
81   Elim; ALIM; אלים (1 + 30 + 10 + 40 = 81)

The names marked with a dash are presumably those to which Agrippa did not know the correct Latin pronunciation. The first name of Mercury, Asboga, is described as eight extended. Gershom Scholem *(Kabbalah,* 1977, 19) says that this is because each pair of letters adds up to 8. The fourth letter, *vau* (ו), has been inadvertently omitted from both the Latin and English texts, destroying the sense of the word. The error is here corrected.

APPENDIX VI

The Sephiroth

It is impossible to give even a brief summary of the ideas that make up the speculative Kabbalah *(Kabbalah iyyunit),* as these are too involved and extensive for a cursory treatment, but it is necessary to touch upon the doctrine of emanations referred to by Agrippa in ch. X, bk. III, so that those readers who are not students of the Kabbalah will have some notion of what he is talking about.

In their efforts to attain the highest and most perfect conception of God the Hebrew mecubalists divested the deity of all qualities, which they determined could not be a part of the primal God because each was limited by its definition and thus imperfect. They denied the deity a name, a face, a form and even a purpose. Everything that could be conceived was stripped away from this negative understanding of a God before, or apart from, the created world. The result they called *Ain Soph* (אֵין סוֹף), literally "not ending"; that is, unbounded.

Having attained this paragon, which is not unlike the Aristotelian Cause of All Causes, they were left in a quandary. The *Ain Soph* cannot be conceived in any way by anyone, not even through the most profound mystical meditation. More perplexing, being utterly without qualities, there is no involvement between the *Ain Soph* itself and the world of limited things. The writer of an early Kabbalistic work called *Ma'arekhet ha-Elohut* (see Scholem *Kabbalah* 1977, 1:3:89) put forward the not unreasonable position that since no notice is taken of the *Ain Soph* in either the Bible or the oral law, it was nonsensical to refer to this *deus absconditus* as God at all; that this title belonged to a being who was accessible to meditation and prayer. However this view was highly unpopular.

Philosophically the ultimate awareness of God as a being (or nonbeing) without limit who comprises all things in an undifferentiated way is inescapable. Also logically necessary is a supreme creator, or first cause. To explain the process of creation whereby a God who can neither be changed nor diminished puts forth the world of limited imperfect beings from, and yet still within, his own substance, recourse was had to a series of agents called Sephiroth, from the Hebrew for sapphire, the lucidity of which is likened to the radiance of God.

These Sephiroth, which are ten in number, act as vessels that convey the continuous emanation from the *Ain Soph* in successive stages down to the very world of creation. They should not be considered to be separate from God, as there is nothing which God is not—rather, they are the inherent tools through which the world is fashioned, made of the substance of the deity, yet in form at least differentiated each for its particular task. How they can be both one with God and yet distinguishable is one of the more-difficult insights in the philosophy of the Kabbalah, and at different periods in its history they have been regarded diversely as the very essence of God and as separate intermediate

752

beings unable to conceive the deity or approach Him except through prayer.

The process of emanation itself has been likened to the conception of a child which does not diminish the substance of the father in any way, but which conveys his qualities. Another metaphor regards the ten Sephiroth as mirrors of different colors which successively catch and reflect the light of a single flame. The flame itself is in no way diminished, though something appears to go out of it. This imagery arose to avoid any suggestion that in the act of creation something flowed away from God. Since God is perfect, and must always remain perfect, he can never be less than all.

For the same reason emanation was said not to proceed outward, but to occur inward in the depths of a kind of vortex at the heart of the *Ain Soph*. Thus all the universe remains within God, and nothing can ever separate from him and so reduce his majesty. The Sephiroth are thought of as various expressions of the single divinity, and each is given a different name of God to emphasize this unity in diversity, almost suggesting that they are no more than divine states of mind, or divine points of view.

Why a God who embodies the entire universe in potential would wish to create something imperfect is never adequately treated. The stock answer is that he did it for love, but as Scholem points out, "the assertion found in many books that God wished to reveal the measure of His goodness is there simply as an expedient that is never systematically developed" *(Kabbalah* 1977, 1:3:91). Just as unsatisfactory is the suggestion that God was in some manner required to create the world of necessity, for what necessity can exist for an omnipotent, all-sufficient being? Ultimately the question of why the universe was made is regarded in the Kabbalah as one of the unknowable mysteries.

Accepting that the impulse to create somehow came to be, it was necessary to postulate a creative force or instrument apart from the impassive *Ain Soph* yet still intimately bound up with it. This is Kether, the first Sephirah, the "infinite will" *(ha-razon ad ein-sof)* that the mind of man can never attain. It exists in a

dynamic balance with the *Ain Soph,* constantly going out from and returning to it, a mirror image of its source. Often Kether was identified with the *Ain Soph* in texts of the Kabbalah, so closely are they bound together. It is the external aspect of the *Ain Soph,* so exalted that it is scarcely just to speak of it as one of the Sephiroth; and indeed the list of Sephiroth sometimes begins with the second, Chokmah.

In the early Kabbalah Kether was the highest object of prayer, the ultimate source of life and of the remaining nine emanations, and therefore God. In later Kabbalah a distinction is made between the primal will to manifest and Kether, but it always remains the most exalted quality, beyond human conception.

From Kether emanate successively the other nine vessels, each going out from the one that precedes it, forming a ladder between the boundless and the material universe. This process occurs outside of time and space, the separation between each emanation and the next occurring in the "twinkling of an eye," an immeasurably brief moment that is actually an abstraction rather than a division of time.

The Sephiroth are called vessels because they hold the uniform radiance of God, which is obscured and colored by their successively coarser skins. The different degrees of veiling make the contents of each vessel appear different from all the others, but this is an illusion caused by the limitations of the human mind, which would be blasted if it were to see the full glory of this radiance unshielded even for an instant.

Linking one Sephirah to the next is a pathway, or channel, through which the light of the Sephiroth flows continually in both directions, from God to the world, and from the world to God. An interruption in the upward returning flux is called "breaking the channels" *(shevirat ha-zinnorot),* which is caused by sin. These channels may best be thought of as hollow tubes that connect transparent radiant spheres that glow with various colors. Through these channels it is possible for the devout mind in meditation to mount upward from one vessel to the next, experiencing the light of God with ever increasing purity. Attainment of one Sephirah makes mounting to the next higher possible, as the mind is conditioned to endure the awful glory of the light in bearable stages.

The two dimensional symbol of the ten Sephiroth linked by the channels is called the Tree of the Sephiroth. The first of the two accompanying illustrations is taken from the frontispiece of the book *Portae Lucis* by the Christianized Jew Paulus Ricius, which was published in Augsburg, Germany, in 1516. It shows 16 paths, or channels, one of which is bifurcated. The Tree continued to evolve and grow more complex as more associations were added to it, the major one being the assignment of the Hebrew alphabet to a system of 22 channels, designed to balance the ten numbers of the Sephiroth. This version, given by Athanasius Kircher in his *Oedipus Aegyptiacus,* published in Rome in 1652, is essentially the same as that used by Kabbalists in the modern day, a few details excepted.

By far the most important association with the Sephiroth is the series of ten divine names, because these are a constant reminder that the Sephiroth themselves are nothing other than names of God. As Scholem writes: "The God who 'called' His powers to reveal themselves named them, and, it could be said, called Himself also by appropriate names" (ibid., 99). These are the "ten names which must not be erased," in comparison with which all other names of God are mere epithets. In the early Kabbalah the actual words revealed to mankind by God are all-important. They supersede every other device which was used speculatively to obtain some grasp of truth. The power, the truth itself, is in the letters and words revealed by God.

The divine names are accompanied by descriptive names of the Sephiroth, which are also names of God. In the *Ain Soph* the deity has no name. The descriptive titles of the Sephiroth stand for the quality and quantity of the universal light that manifests itself through degrees of obscurity imposed by the vessels. More than one name may be applied to a single Sephirah where this is necessary to adequately suggest its nature. The titles of the Sephiroth are

in large measure based on the biblical verse I Chronicles 29:11. They also echo in the Lord's Prayer, Matthew 6:9–13.

Of far less philosophical importance are the other occult structures applied to the Sephiroth, such as the hierarchy of angels, the spheres of the heavens, the elements, the individual good and evil spirits, the Hebrew prophets and so on. These are later additions that accrued to the Tree after its shape began to solidify. However, these are extremely useful from the viewpoint of the practical Kabbalah. The sanctity of the Sephiroth is used to lend authority and power to particular elements in magical works.

Various divisions of the Sephiroth were made in an effort to comprehend their meaning. They were split into five upper and five lower, the hidden and manifest powers; on the same basis was made a division between upper three and lower seven, the lower being equated with the seven days of creation; they were split into three triangles, the upper of which (Kether, Chokmah, Binah) was linked with the intellect, the middle (Chesed, Geburah, Tiphareth) with the soul, and the lower (Netzach, Hod, Yesod) with nature.

The Tree was also divided into three pillars: the Right Pillar (Chokmah, Chesed, Netzach) of Mercy, the Middle Pillar (Kether, Tiphareth, Yesod, Malkuth) of Mildness and the Left Pillar (Binah, Geburah, Hod) of Severity. The right side of the Tree is considered to be masculine and the left side feminine. It must be pointed out here that the Tree of the Sephiroth is almost always represented as viewed from the *back*. Remember that Chokmah is on the right side of the Tree, and Binah on the left, and you will avoid the common error of confusing the sides.

There is an 11th Sephirah, which is not really a Sephirah at all, called Daath. It first occurs in the 13th century, as a mediator between the influences of Chesed and Binah, and is regarded as the manifest aspect of Kether. Located on the Middle Pillar between, and slightly below, Chokmah and Binah, it has the same balancing qualities as the other Middle Pillar Sephiroth.

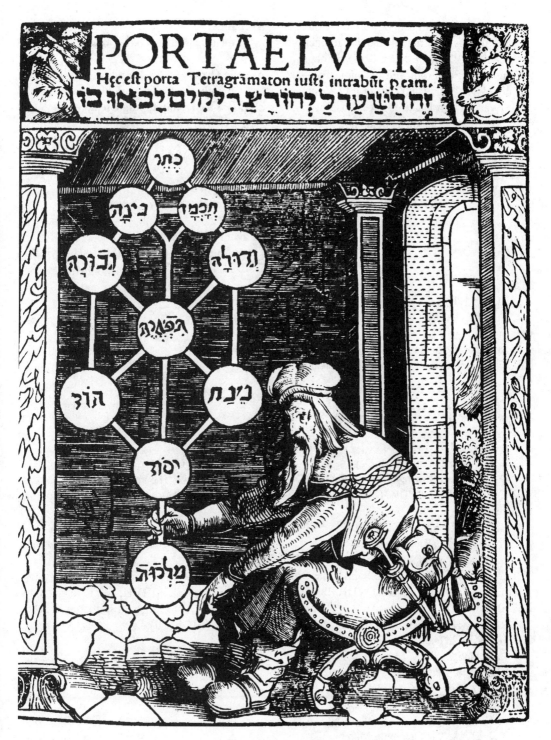

Sephirothic Tree

from *Portae Lucis* by Paulus Ricius (Augsburg, 1516)

The reason Daath cannot truly be regarded as a Sephirah is the strict and explicit injunction in the *Sepher Yetzirah:* "Ten is the number of the ineffable Sephiroth, ten and not nine, ten and not eleven" *(Sepher Yetzirah* 1.3 [Westcott, 15]). Even though Daath is a very useful concept, few are the Kabbalists bold enough to violate this clear decree from the oldest and most sacred Kabbalistic text.

KETHER

Number
    One.

Titles
    Kether, KThR, כתר, The Crown.
    Authiqa, AaThIQA, עתיקא, The Ancient One or The Aged.
    Authiqa Qadisha, AaThIQA QDISHA, עתיקא קדישא, The Most Holy Ancient One.
    Authiqa De-Authiqin, AaThIQA DAaThIQIN, עתיקא דעתיקין, The Ancient of the Ancient Ones.
    Authiq Iomin, AaThIQ IVMIN, עתיק יומין, The Ancient of Days.
    Temira De-Temirin, TMIRA DTMIRIN, טמירא דטמירין, The Concealed of the Concealed.
    Nequdah Rashunah, NQVDH RAShVNH, נקודה ראשונה, The Primordial Point.
    Nequdah Peshutah, NQVDH PShVTH, נקודה פשוטה, The Smooth Point. (MacGregor Mathers spells the name NQVDH PShVTh, נקודה פשות).
    Risha Havurah, RIShA HVVRH רישא הוורה, The White Head.
    Rom Meolah, RVM MAaLH, רום מעלה, The Inscrutable Height.
    Arikh Anpin, ARIK ANPIN, אריך אנפין, The Vast Countenance (Macroprosopus).
    Adam Auilah, ADM AaILAH, אדם עילאה, The Heavenly Man.

Divine Name
    Eheieh, AHIH, אה'ה, I Am.

Archangel
    Metatron, MTTRVN, מטטרון.

Angelic Order
    Chaioth ha-Qadesh, ChIVTh HQDSh, חיות הקדש, Holy Living Creatures.

Archdemons
    Satan and Moloch.

Demonic Order
    Thamiel, The Two Contenders.

Heavenly Sphere
    Rashith ha-Gilgalim, RAShITh HGLGLIM, ראשית הגלגלים, Primum Mobile.

Part of Man
    Head.

CHOKMAH

Number
    Two.

Titles
    Chokmah, ChKMH, חכמה, Wisdom.
    Ab, AB, אב, The Father.
    Abba, ABBA, אבבא, The Supernal Father.

Divine Names
    Jah, IH, י'.
    Jehovah, IHVH, יהוה, The Lord.
    Yod Jehovah, IIHVH, ייהוה (given by Agrippa, ch. X, bk. III, and in the table at the end of ch. XIII, bk. II).

Archangel
    Ratziel, RTzIAL, רציאל.

Angelic Order
    Auphanim, AVPNIM, אופנים, The Wheels.

Archdemon
    Beelzebub.

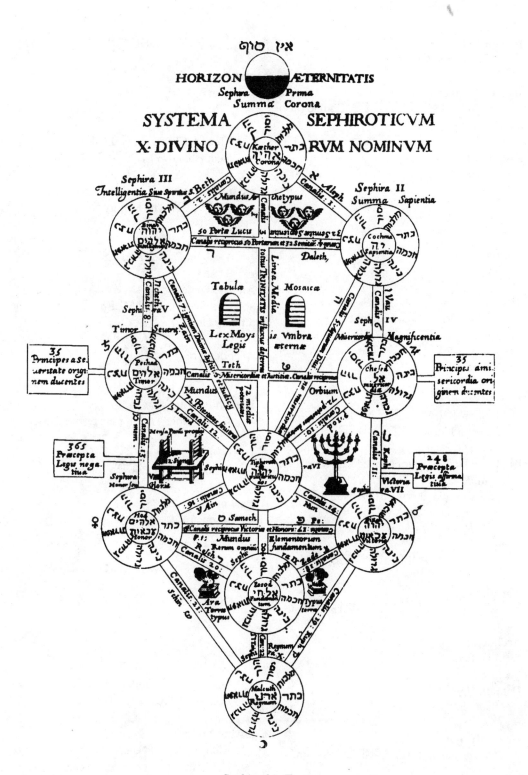

Sephirothic Tree

from *Oedipus Ægyptiacus* by Athanasius Kircher (Rome, 1652)

Demonic Order
    Ghogiel, The Hinderers.

Heavenly Sphere
    Masloth, MSLVTh, מסלות, Zodiac (also spelled MZLVTh, מזלות)

Part of Man
    Brain.

BINAH

Number
    Three.

Titles
    Binah, BINH, בינה, Intelligence.
    Ama, AMA, אמא, The Mother.
    Aima, AIMA, אימא, The Great Productive Mother.

Divine Names
    Elohim, ALHIM, אלהים, Lord.
    Jehovah Elohim, יהוה אלהים, The Lord God. Strictly speaking, the divine name is IHVH, which is pronounced Elohim (see Scholem, *Kabbalah* 1977, 108).
    Jehovah joined with *he,* HIHVH, היהוה (given by Agrippa, ch. XVII, bk. III).

Archangel
    Tzaphkiel, TzPQIAL, צפקיאל.

Angelic Order
    Aralim, ARALIM, אראלים, The Thrones.

Archdemon
    Lucifuge.

Demonic Order
    Satariel, the Concealers.

Heavenly Sphere
    Shabbathai, ShBThAI, שבתאי, Saturn.

Part of Man
    Heart.

CHESED

Number
    Four.

Titles
    Chesed, ChSD, חסד, Love.
    Gedulah, GDVLH, גדולה, Greatness.

Divine Name
    El, AL, אל, The Mighty One.

Archangel
    Tzadkiel, TzDQIAL, צדקיאל.

Angelic Order
    Chasmalim, ChShMLIM, חשמלים, The Shining Ones.

Archdemon
    Ashtaroth.

Demonic Order
    Agshekeloh, The Smiters or Breakers.

Heavenly Sphere
    Tzadekh, TzDQ, צדק, Jupiter.

Part of Man
    Right arm.

GEBURAH

Number
    Five.

Titles
    Geburah, GBVRH, גבורה, Strength.
    Din, DIN, דין, Judgment or Severity.
    Pachad, PChD, פחד, Fear.

Divine Names
    Eloh, ALH, אלה, The Almighty.
    Elohim Gibor, ALHIM GBVR, אלהים גבור, God of Battles. Agrippa spells this ALHIM GIBR, אלהים גיבר.

Archangel
Khamael, KMAL, כמאל.

Angelic Order
Seraphim, ShRPIM, שרפים, The Fiery Serpents.

Archdemon
Asmodeus.

Demonic Order
Golohab, The Burners or Flaming Ones.

Heavenly Sphere
Madim, MADIM, מאדים, Mars.

Part of Man
Left Arm.

TIPHARETH

Number
Six.

Titles
Tiphareth, ThPARTh, תפארת, Beauty.
Rahamim, RChMIM, רחמים, Compassion.
Melekh, MLK, מלך, The King.
Zauir Anpin, ZVIR ANPIN, זויר אנפין, The Lesser Countenance (Microprosopus). This title is also applied to the combined Sephiroth four through nine.

Divine Names
Eloah Va-Daath, ALVH VDAaTh, אלוה ודעת, God Manifest.
Elohim, ALHIM, אלהים, God.

Archangel
Raphael, RPAL, רפאל.

Angelic Order
Malachim, MLKIM, מלכים, Kings. Ginsburg ([1863] 1970) gives Shinanim, ShNANIM, שנאנים, Multitudes (see Psalms 68:17).

Archdemon
Belphegor.

Demonic Order
Tagiriron, The Disputers.

Heavenly Sphere
Shemesh, ShMSh, שמש, Sun.

Part of Man
Chest.

NETZACH

Number
Seven.

Titles
Netzach, NTzCh, נצח, Firmness or Victory.

Divine Names
Jehovah Sabaoth, IHVH TzBAVTh, יהוה צבאות, Lord of Hosts.

Archangel
Haniel, HANIAL, האניאל.

Angelic Order
Elohim, ALHIM, אלהים, Gods. Ginsburg ([1863] 1970) gives Tarshishim, ThRShIShIM, תרשישים, The Brilliant Ones (see Daniel 10:6).

Archdemon
Baal.

Demonic Order
Gharab Tzerek, The Raveners.

Heavenly Sphere
Nogah, NVGH, נוגה, Venus.

Part of Man
Right Leg.

HOD

Number
Eight.

Title
Hod, HVD, הוד, Splendor.

Divine Name
Elohim Sabaoth, ALHIM TzBAVTh, אלהים צבאות, God of Hosts.

Archangel
Michael, MIKAL, מיכאל.

Angelic Order
Beni Elohim, BNI ALHIM, בני אלהים, Sons of God.

Archdemon
Adrammelech.

Demonic Order
Samael, The False Accusers.

Heavenly Sphere
Kokab, KVKB, כוכב, Mercury.

Part of Man
Left Leg.

YESOD

Number
Nine.

Titles
Yesod, ISVD, יסוד, The Foundation.
Yesod Aalam, ISVD AaVLM, יסוד עולם, Eternal Foundation of the World.

Divine Names
Shaddai, ShDI, שדי, The Almighty.
El Chai, AL ChI, אל חי, Mighty Living One.

Archangel
Gabriel, GBRIAL, גבריאל.

Angelic Order
Cherubim, KRBIM, כרבים, The Strong. Ginsburg ([1863] 1970) places here the Ashim, AShIM, אשים. Agrippa spells Cherubim KRVBIM, כרובים.

Archdemon
Lilith, The Seducer.

Demonic Order
Gamaliel, The Obscene Ones.

Heavenly Sphere
Levanah, LBNH, לבנה, Moon.

Part of Man
Genitals.

MALKUTH

Number
Ten.

Titles
Malkuth, MLKVTh, מלכות, The Kingdom.
Atarah, AaTRH, עטרה, The Diadem. See Proverbs 12:4.
Shekinah, ShKINH, שכינה, The Manifest Glory Of God.
Kallah, KLH, כלה, The Bride (of Microprosopus).
Malkah, MLKH, מלכה, The Queen.

Divine Names
Adonai, ADNI, אדני, Lord.
Adonai Malekh, ADNI MLK, אדני מלך, Lord and King.
Adonai he-Aretz, ADNI HARTz, אדני הארץ, Lord of Earth.

Archangel
Metatron, MTTRVN, מטטרון, in his manifest aspect. The angel usually given is Sandalphon, SNDLPVN, סנדלפון, but Sandalphon is the angel of the Earth.

Angelic Order
Ashim (or Ishim), AShIM, אשים, Souls of

Flame: see Psalms 104:4. Agrippa spells this AIShIM, אישׁים.

Archdemon

Nahema, The Strangler of Children.

Demonic Order

Nahemoth, The Dolorous Ones.

Heavenly Sphere

Aulam Yesodoth, AaVLM ISVDVTh, עולם יסודות, The Elements. This is sometimes incorrectly given as Cholem Yesodoth, ChVLM ISVDVTh, חולם יסודות, The Breaker of Foundations.

Part of Man

The whole body.

There are various conflicting systems of demons and demonic orders in the literature of the Kabbalah. The one presented here is that given by S. L. MacGregor Mathers in the introduction to his translation of Knorr von Rosenroth's *Kabbalah Unveiled* (Mathers [1887] 1962), plate facing p. 30.

The archdemon of Malkuth, Nahema, is one of four demon queens. She is often confounded with Lilith in Kabbalistic writings. Lilith ruled over Rome, Agrath (or Agrat) ruled over Salamanca, Rahab (or Mahalath) ruled over Egypt, and Nahema ruled over Damascus. These four places symbolize, respectively, north, west, south and east.

APPENDIX VII

Practical Kabbalah

The esoteric speculations of Judaism known as the Kabbalah may for convenience be divided into two branches: the speculative Kabbalah *(Kabbalah iyyunit)*, which concerns the abstract philosophical doctrines on the nature of God, the universe and man; and the practical Kabbalah *(Kabbalah ma'asit)*, which involves magical practices intended to produce specific results. These branches are not entirely separate and often overlap, but may be considered independently on the basis of the goals to which they tend. The first seeks a transformation of the soul in accordance with the will of God, and is mystical; the second seeks a transformation of the world in accordance with the will of man, and is magical.

When the Kabbalah began to take shape as a metaphysical system, the techniques for making charms, amulets and talismans were absorbed into it. These were largely concerned with the magical powers of the letters of the Hebrew alphabet, particularly as they occurred in the words of the Torah, or sacred writings. A Jewish magician bore the title Ba'al Shem, בעל שם, Master of the Name, which referred to his ability to manipulate the names of God for magical purposes. That this title is Babylonian in origin is significant, as it points to the roots of Jewish magic in Babylonian demonology.

Because Jewish magic is so bound up in the manipulation of words and letters, the techniques through which this is done have themselves been called the practical Kabbalah.

However, this use is too narrow, as these techniques are also employed in abstract speculations and meditations on God.

In the main the significance of Hebrew letters derives from their numerical value. Each letter stands for one or more numbers, as may be seen in the accompanying table of the Hebrew alphabet, and by various systems these number values are interrelated. As many as 72 techniques have been listed (see Scholem, *Kabbalah*, 1977, 2:10:341), but the matter treated by Agrippa falls under the three headings of *gematria, notarikon,* and *temurah.*

Gematria, גמטריא, from the Greek γεωμετρία (geometry), not, as Ginsburg and after him Mathers erroneously assert, from γράμμα (a written character)—in the narrower sense used here is the rule by which a word or group of words is given meaning according to the total numerical value of the letters involved. One word may be linked with another that has the same value. For example the name of the angel Metatron, מטטרון, and the name of God, Shaddai, שדי, each total 314, allowing one to Kabbalistically stand for the other by the system of *gematria.* This is considered to explain Exodus 23:21. In the same manner a phrase may be made to stand for a word, or a word for a phrase, or a phrase for a phrase, provided that their numerical totals are equal.

Notarikon, נוטריקון, from the Latin *notarius,* a shorthand writer of ancient Rome who abbreviated words using single letters, is the

Hebrew Alphabet

Order	Letter	Transliteration	Value	Final	Name	Meaning	Kind
1.	א	A	1		Aleph	Ox	Mother
2.	ב	B, V	2		Beth	House	Double
3.	ג	G, Gh	3		Gimel	Camel	Double
4.	ד	D, Dh	4		Daleth	Door	Double
5.	ה	H	5		He	Window	Single
6.	ו	O, U, V	6		Vau	Nail	Single
7.	ז	Z	7		Zayin	Sword	Single
8.	ח	Ch	8		Cheth	Fence	Single
9.	ט	T	9		Teth	Snake	Single
10.	י	I, Y	10		Yod	Hand	Single
11.	כ	K, Kh	20	500 ך	Kaph	Fist	Double
12.	ל	L	30		Lamed	Ox-Goad	Single
13.	מ	M	40	600 ם	Mem	Water	Mother
14.	נ	N	50	700 ן	Nun	Fish	Single
15.	ס	S	60		Samekh	Prop	Single
16.	ע	Aa, Ngh, O	70		Ayin	Eye	Single
17.	פ	P, Ph	80	800 ף	Pe	Mouth	Double
18.	צ	Tz	90	900 ץ	Tzaddi	Hook	Single
19.	ק	Q, K	100		Qoph	Ear	Single
20.	ר	R	200		Resh	Head	Double
21.	ש	S, Sh	300		Shin	Tooth	Mother
22.	ת	T, Th	400		Tau	Cross	Double

rule by which the initial letters of the words in a phrase are combined to form a word, or words, with a related significance. Sometimes the final or medial letters are also used. For example, the phrase from Deuteronomy 30:12, "Who shall go up for us to heaven," מי יעלה לנו השמימה, yields letters from the beginning of each word that form the word for circumcision, מילה, and from the end of each word that form Jehovah, יהוה. This was considered to confirm the ordination by God of circumcision as the way to salvation. Inversely, by *notarikon* the individual letters in a word may become the initial letters in a phrase or sentence. The first word in the Bible, *Berashith,* בראשית, can be expanded into the sentence *Besrashith Rahi Elohim Sheyequebelo Israel Torah:*

בואשית ראה אלהים שיקבלו ישראל תורה

"In the beginning God saw that Israel would accept the Law."

Temurah, תמורה, permutation, which is also called *Tziruph,* צירוף, combination, is the rule by which letters are related and interchanged. By one technique the Hebrew alphabet is bent in the middle back upon itself to form eleven pairs of letters. By certain transpositions 22 sets of pairs are made that compose the "Table of the Combinations of Ziruph" given by Agrippa at the end of ch. XXV, bk. III. Each set derives its name from the first four letters, reading in the Hebrew way from right to left. For example, the upper row of the table shows the set called *Albath,* ALBTh, אלבת.

It will be easier to understand the method of Ziruph if the sets are written numerically, with each letter substituted for by its place in the Hebrew alphabet. Below is a numerical exposition of the Table of Ziruph, and also of the Rational Table of Ziruph, showing their structure:

ZIRUPH

11 10 9 8 7 6 5 4 3 2 1
13 14 15 16 17 18 19 20 21 22 12   Albath   (1.)

12 11 10 9 8 7 6 5 4 3 1
13 14 15 16 17 18 19 20 21 22 2   Abgath   (2.)

2 12 11 10 9 8 7 6 5 4 1
13 14 15 16 17 18 19 20 21 22 3   Agdath   (3.)

13 12 11 10 9 8 7 6 5 2 1
14 15 16 17 18 19 20 21 22 3 4   Adbag   (4.)

3 13 12 11 10 9 8 7 6 2 1
14 15 16 17 18 19 20 21 22 4 5   Ahbad   (5.)

14 13 12 11 10 9 8 7 3 2 1
15 16 17 18 19 20 21 22 4 5 6   Avbah   (6.)

4 14 13 12 11 10 9 8 3 2 1
15 16 17 18 19 20 21 22 5 6 7   Azbav   (7.)

15 14 13 12 11 10 9 4 3 2 1
16 17 18 19 20 21 22 5 6 7 8   Achbaz   (8.)

5 15 14 13 12 11 10 4 3 2 1
16 17 18 19 20 21 22 6 7 8 9   Atbach   (9.)

16 15 14 13 12 11 5 4 3 2 1
17 18 19 20 21 22 6 7 8 9 10   Aibat   (10.)

6 16 15 14 13 12 5 4 3 2 1
17 18 19 20 21 22 7 8 9 10 11   Achbi   (11.)

17 16 15 14 13 6 5 4 3 2 1
18 19 20 21 22 7 8 9 10 11 12   Albach   (12.)

7 17 16 15 14 6 5 4 3 2 1
18 19 20 21 22 8 9 10 11 12 13   Ambal   (13.)

18 17 16 15 7 6 5 4 3 2 1
19 20 21 22 8 9 10 11 12 13 14   Anbam (14.)

8 18 17 16 7 6 5 4 3 2 1
19 20 21 22 9 10 11 12 13 14 15   Asban   (15.)

19 18 17 8 7 6 5 4 3 2 1
20 21 22 9 10 11 12 13 14 15 16   Aabas   (16.)

9 19 18 8 7 6 5 4 3 2 1
20 21 22 10 11 12 13 14 15 16 17   Aphba   (17.)

20 19 9 8 7 6 5 4 3 2 1
21 22 10 11 12 13 14 15 16 17 18   Azbaph (18.)

10 20 9 8 7 6 5 4 3 2 1
21 22 **11 12 13 14 15 16 17 18 19** Akbaz (19.)

21 10 9 8 7 6 5 4 3 2 1
22 **11 12 13 14 15 16 17 18 19 20** Arbak (20.)

11 10 9 8 7 6 5 4 3 2 1
22 **12 13 14 15 16 17 18 19 20 21** Ashbar (21.)

11 10 9 8 7 6 5 4 3 2 1
12 13 14 15 16 17 18 19 20 21 22 Athbash (22.)

Also:

21 19 17 15 13 11 9 7 5 3 1
22 20 18 16 14 12 10 8 6 4 2 Abgad (23.)

11 10 9 8 7 6 5 4 3 2 1
22 21 20 19 18 17 16 15 14 13 12 Albam (24.)

RATIONAL ZIRUPH

12 11 10 9 8 7 6 5 4 3 1
13 14 15 16 17 18 19 20 21 22 **2** Abgath (1.)*

13 12 11 10 9 8 7 6 5 4 1
14 15 16 17 18 19 20 21 22 **2 3** Agdab (2.)

14 13 12 11 10 9 8 7 6 5 1
15 16 17 18 19 20 21 22 **2 3 4** Adhag (3.)

15 14 13 12 11 10 9 8 7 6 1
16 17 18 19 20 21 22 **2 3 4 5** Ahod (4.)

16 15 14 13 12 11 10 9 8 7 1
17 18 19 20 21 22 **2 3 4 5 6** Avzah (5.)

17 16 15 14 13 12 11 10 9 8 1
18 19 20 21 22 **2 3 4 5 6 7** Azcho (6.)

18 17 16 15 14 13 12 11 10 9 1
19 20 21 22 **2 3 4 5 6 7 8** Achto (7.)

19 18 17 16 15 14 13 12 11 10 1
20 21 22 **2 3 4 5 6 7 8 9** Atich (8.)

20 19 18 17 16 15 14 13 12 11 1
21 22 **2 3 4 5 6 7 8 9 10** Aikat (9.)

21 20 19 18 17 16 15 14 13 12 1
22 **2 3 4 5 6 7 8 9 10 11** Aklay (10.)

22 21 20 19 18 17 16 15 14 13 1
2 3 4 5 6 7 8 9 10 11 12 Almak (11.)

2 22 21 20 19 18 17 16 15 14 1
3 4 5 6 7 8 9 10 11 12 13 Amnal (12.)

3 2 22 21 20 19 18 17 16 15 1
4 5 6 7 8 9 10 11 12 13 14 Anmas (13.)

4 3 2 22 21 20 19 18 17 16 1
5 6 7 8 9 10 11 12 13 14 15 Asan (14.)

5 4 3 2 22 21 20 19 18 17 1
6 7 8 9 10 11 12 13 14 15 16 Aaphas (15.)

6 5 4 3 2 22 21 20 19 18 1
7 8 9 10 11 12 13 14 15 16 17 Aphza (16.)

7 6 5 4 3 2 22 21 20 19 1
8 9 10 11 12 13 14 15 16 17 18 Azkap (17.)

8 7 6 5 4 3 2 22 21 20 1
9 10 11 12 13 14 15 16 17 18 19 Akraz (18.)

9 8 7 6 5 4 3 2 22 21 1
10 11 12 13 14 15 16 17 18 19 20 Arshak (19.)

10 9 8 7 6 5 4 3 2 22 1
11 12 13 14 15 16 17 18 19 20 21 Ashthar (20.)

11 10 9 8 7 6 5 4 3 2 1
12 13 14 15 16 17 18 19 20 21 22 Athbash (21.)*

21 19 17 15 13 11 9 7 5 3 1
22 20 18 16 14 12 10 8 6 4 2 Abgad (22.)*

The number pairs in the above sets have been written top to bottom rather than side by side, as Agrippa has written the corresponding letters, to reflect the folding of the Hebrew alphabet back on itself. Letters that have been transposed out of their normal position are represented by numbers in bold type. The name of each set is given in English to the right. Appended to Ziruph are two sets mentioned by Ginsburg in his treatment of this subject ([1863]

1970, 137). The first of these appended sets is found at the end of the Rational Table of Ziruph given by Agrippa.

Notice that some of the pairs are necessarily repeated. For example in the Table of Ziruph the pair AL, אל, which occurs in the first place of the first set, called *Albath,* also occurs in the first place in the 12th set, *Albach.* Notice also that the first *(Abgath)* and 21st *(Athbash)* sets in the Rational Table occur in the regular Table of Ziruph, forming respectively the second and 22nd sets.

The use of the combinations of Ziruph is straightforward. In each particular set paired letters are considered to be Kabbalistically related and interchangeable. By substituting letters for their pairs, new words can be created that are occultly linked to the words that give them rise; also the numerical sums of words can be manipulated. This is done to yield insights into difficult speculations, or more commonly to furnish proofs for convictions previously arrived at by other means.

Also into the category of *temurah* fall the three Tables of Commutations called the Right, the Averse, and the Irregular. The Right Table takes its name from the upper row of letters, which is written in the normal Hebrew way, right to left. Its structure is so simple as to barely require comment. In the second row the *aleph,* א, is moved from its place to the end of the alphabet; in the third row the *aleph,* א, and *beth,* ב, are moved to the end; and so on down the table until in the bottom row the alphabet is completely transposed except for the letter *tau,* ת. Similarly, in the Averse Table, so-called because the upper row is written in reverse order, from left to right, letters are successively moved from the end of the alphabet to the beginning until the alphabet is completely transposed except for the letter *aleph,* א.

The Averse Irregular Table is more Complex and will require a numerical exposition, which is given on the opposite page. As is also true with the Right and Averse tables, the Irregular has a bilateral symmetry around the diagonal axis running from the lower left to upper right corners. Each row and column contains the complete Hebrew alphabet. The letters which were drawn oversized in the original table are here indicated by numbers in boldface type. If the structure of the table is examined it will be seen that these are the letters which it was necessary to shift at variance with the overall pattern in order to preserve the complete alphabet in both rows and columns. They represent breaks in the system. This is clearly shown when the pairs in boldface type in each row are inverted.

Why the Irregular table is also called Averse is not apparent to me, since the alphabet is written in its correct sequence on all four sides of the square in four different directions, the upper row being from right to left—but perhaps I have not correctly understood the use of this term in the previous table.

The method of using the tables of commutations must be conjectured—since I have not found it anywhere described—from their requirement to substitute one letter for another. The right outer column that has the alphabet in its normal sequence could be used as a key through which might be inserted the letters of a word or sentence desired to be transmuted. There would thus be 21 possible variations. I stress that this is only conjecture on my part.

Falling under the heading *temurah,* but important enough to be considered on its own, is the Kabbalah of Nine Chambers, or *Aiq Beker,* בכר איק, so-called from the first six letters that constitute it. The Hebrew alphabet is written into the nine cells of a grid formed by two pairs of parallel lines that intersect at right angles, resulting in three letters in each cell (22 letters plus 5 final forms equal 27 letters). The way of entering the letters is most easily shown by a diagram:

300	30	3	200	20	2	100	10	1
ש	ל	ג	ר	כ	ב	ק	י	א
Sh	L	G	R	K	B	Q	I	A
600	60	6	500	50	5	400	40	4
ם	ס	ו	ך	נ	ה	ת	מ	ד
M-f.	S	V	K-f.	N	H	Th	M	D
900	90	9	800	80	8	700	70	7
ץ	צ	ט	ף	פ	ח	ן	ע	ז
Tz-f.	Tz	T	P-f.	P	Ch	N-f.	Aa	Z

Any letter is occultly linked, and thus may be exchanged, with the other letters in its cell on the grid. For example, the letter *he, ה*, may be substituted for with either the letters *nun, נ*, or the final form of *kaph, ך*. Similarly their values may be interchanged in occult computations. Agrippa uses the *Aiq Beker* extensively in extracting his sigils for the spirits and intelligences of the planets from the magic squares in ch. XXII, bk. II. The *Aiq Beker,* and the system of secret writing that is based upon it, are described by Agrippa in ch. XXX, bk. III.

Another Kabbalistic technique for forming words with magical significance is that of writing verses from the Torah one over the other, and then extracting words from the vertical columns of letters. The most important use of this device involves Exodus 14:19–21, each verse of which contains 72 letters (see page 769).

Averse Irregular Table

22	21	20	19	18	17	16	15	14	13	12	11	10	9	8	7	6	5	4	3	2	1
21	12	1	22	20	19	18	17	16	15	14	13	11	10	9	8	7	6	5	4	3	2
20	13	2	1	22	21	19	18	17	16	15	14	12	11	10	9	8	7	6	5	4	3
19	3	13	2	1	22	21	20	18	17	16	15	14	12	11	10	9	8	7	6	5	4
18	14	4	3	2	1	22	21	20	19	17	16	15	13	12	11	10	9	8	7	6	5
17	4	14	5	3	2	1	22	21	20	19	18	16	15	13	12	11	10	9	8	7	6
16	15	5	6	4	3	2	1	22	21	20	19	18	17	14	13	12	11	10	9	8	7
15	5	16	7	6	4	3	2	1	22	21	20	19	18	17	14	13	12	11	10	9	8
14	16	6	8	7	5	4	3	2	1	22	21	20	19	18	17	15	13	12	11	10	9
13	6	17	21	8	7	5	4	3	2	1	22	9	20	19	18	16	15	14	12	11	10
12	17	7	10	9	8	6	5	4	3	2	1	22	21	20	19	18	16	15	14	13	11
11	7	18	13	10	9	8	6	5	4	3	2	1	22	21	20	19	17	16	15	14	12
10	18	8	14	12	11	9	7	6	5	4	3	2	1	22	21	20	19	17	16	15	13
9	8	19	15	13	12	11	10	7	6	5	4	3	2	1	22	21	20	18	17	16	14
8	11	9	16	14	13	12	19	10	7	6	5	4	3	2	1	22	21	20	18	17	15
7	20	10	17	15	14	13	12	11	9	8	6	5	4	3	2	1	22	21	19	18	16
6	10	15	18	16	20	14	13	12	11	9	8	7	5	4	3	2	1	22	21	19	17
5	19	21	11	17	16	15	14	13	12	10	9	8	7	6	4	3	2	1	22	20	18
4	9	12	20	11	18	17	16	15	14	13	10	21	8	7	6	5	3	2	1	22	19
3	22	11	12	21	15	10	9	19	8	18	7	17	6	16	5	14	4	13	2	1	20
2	1	22	9	19	10	20	11	8	18	7	17	6	16	5	15	4	14	3	13	12	21
1	2	3	4	5	6	7	8	9	10	11	12	13	14	15	16	17	18	19	20	21	22

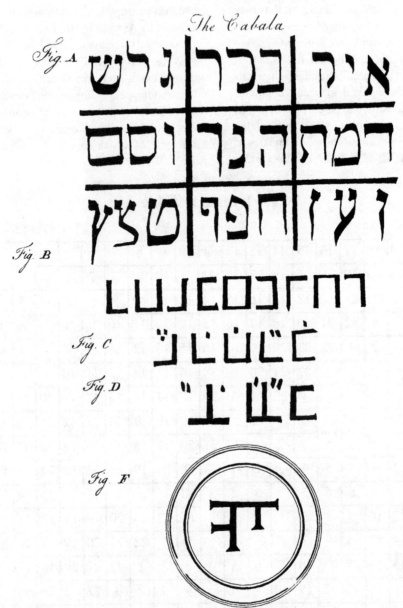

The Cabala

Fig. F The Cabalistic Character of the Spirit Michael as Composed out of the above Tables A B C D

Pub. by Lackington & Allen

Kabbalah of Nine Chambers

from *The Magus* by Francis Barrett (London, 1801)

The Schemhamphoras:

Exodus 14:19—

ויסע מלאך האלהים ההלך לפני מחנה
ישראל וילך מאחריהם ויסע עמוד הענן
מפניהם ויעמד מאחריהם:

Exodus 14:20—

ויבא בין מחנה מצרים ובין מחנה ישראל
ויהי הענן והחשך ויאר את הלילה ולא קרב
זה אל זה כל הלילה:

Exodus 14:21—

ויט משה את ידו על הים ויולך יהוה
את הים ברוח קדים עזה כל הלילה וישם
את הים לחרבה ויבקעו המים:

The first verse is written in the ordinary fashion right to left; the second, left to right beneath the first; and the third, right to left beneath the second. Each column of three letters, reading downwards on the column, yields one of the 72 names of God commonly called the Schemhamphoras, which are rendered additionally sacred by appending the divine suffixes El, AL, אל, or Yah, IH, יה. This is described by Agrippa at the end of ch. XXV, bk. III, and the result shown in the table of the Schemhamphoras appended to that chapter. For the sake of clarity the English transliteration of the letters is given below:

1	2	3	4	5	6	7	8	9	10	11	12
V	I	S	Aa	M	L	A	K	H	A	L	H
H	L	I	L	H	L	K	H	Z	L	A	H
V	I	T	M	Sh	H	A	Th	I	D	V	Aa

13	14	15	16	17	18	19	20	21	22	23	24
I	M	H	H	L	K	L	P	N	I	M	Ch
Z	B	R	Q	A	L	V	H	L	I	L	H
L	H	I	M	V	I	V	L;	K	I	H	V

25	26	27	28	29	30	31	32	33	34	35	36
N	H	I	Sh	R	A	L	V	I	L	K	M
Th	A	R	A	I	V	K	Sh	Ch	H	V	N
H	A	Th	H	I	M	B	R	V	Ch	Q	D

37	38	39	40	41	42	43	44	45	46	47	48
A	Ch	R	I	H	M	V	I	S	Aa	Aa	M
N	Aa	H	I	H	I	V	L	A	R	Sh	I
I	M	Aa	Z	H	K	L	H	L	I	L	H

49	50	51	52	53	54	55	56	57	58	59	60
V	D	H	Aa	N	N	M	P	N	I	H	M
H	N	Ch	M	N	I	B	V	M	I	R	Tz
V	I	Sh	M	A	Th	H	I	M	L	Ch	R

61	62	63	64	65	66	67	68	69	70	71	72
V	I	Aa	M	D	M	A	Ch	R	I	H	M
M	H	N	Ch	M	N	I	B	A	B	I	V
B	H	V	I	B	Q	Aa	V	H	M	I	M

Agrippa substitutes H, ה for Ch, ח and Ch, ח for K כ. I have changed the spelling to match the lettering of the texts of Exodus in the Hebrew bible and the sources on the Kabbalah I have consulted. Whether the spelling of Agrippa is an error, or whether, as seems more probable, it follows the lettering of his copy of the Hebrew, I am not certain. Those wishing to restore the spelling of the names as they appear in the English edition should make these substitutions.

Although Agrippa does not display it in the table, the four rows of Hebrew letters are associated with the letters of the Tetragrammaton, IHVH, which may be written on the right side of the table from top to bottom. Since the letters of the divine name are linked with the four elements *(yod* = Fire, first *he* = Water, *vau* = Air, second *he* = Earth), it becomes possible through this key to assign the 72 names to the elements and to the signs of the zodiac that are related to the elements in trines.

Each row of the table contains 18 names, divisible into three groups of six names each. Beginning at the right side of each row and reading left, the first group is given the cardinal sign of its element, the second group the fixed sign, and the third group the mutable sign. The names of each group are linked in order with the quinaries of each sign.

It must be stressed that this assignment of the Schemhamphoras to the zodiac is original with me. I have not seen it anywhere else, but it seems a logical extension of Agrippa's table.

The 19th-century French occultist Lenain in his work *La Science Cabalistique* (1823) gives an assignment of the names to the quinaries, but he makes the mistake, as it seems to me, of placing the names one after the other in order around the heavens without regard to their elemental associations.

Here is a corrected list of the names with a transliteration of the Hebrew letters into English, the numbering of the names, their elemental associations, and my own assignment of them to the signs of the zodiac:

Fire Trine

1. Vehuiah, VHV + IH, Fire, Aries 1°–5°
2. Yeliel, ILI + AL, Fire, Aries 6°–10°
3. Sitael, SIT + AL, Fire, Aries 11°–15°
4. Aulemiah, AaLM + IH, Fire, Aries 16°–20°
5. Mahasiah, MHSh + IH, Fire, Aries 21°–25°
6. Lelahel, LLH + AL, Fire, Aries 26°–30°

7. Akaiah, AKA + IH, Fire, Leo 1°–5°
8. Kahathel, KHTh + AL, Fire, Leo 6°–10°
9. Heziel, HZI + AL, Fire, Leo 11°–15°
10. Eladiah, ALD + IH, Fire, Leo 16°–20°
11. Laviah, LAV + IH, Fire, Leo 21°–25°
12. Hahauah, HHAa + IH, Fire, Leo 26°–30°

13. Yezalel, IZL + AL, Fire, Sagittarius 1°–5°
14. Mebahel, MBH + AL, Fire, Sagittarius 6°–10°
15. Hariel, HRI + AL, Fire, Sagittarius 11°–15°
16. Haqemiah, HQM + IH, Fire, Sagittarius 16°–20°
17. Leviah, LAV + IH, Fire, Sagittarius 21°–25°
18. Keliel, KLI + AL, Fire, Sagittarius, 26°–30°

Water Trine

19. Levoiah, LVV + IH, Water, Cancer 1°–5°
20. Paheliah, PHL + IH, Water, Cancer 6°–10°
21. Nelakel, NLK + AL, Water, Cancer 11°–15°
22. Yiaiel, III + AL, Water, Cancer 16°–20°
23. Melahel, MLH + AL, Water, Cancer 21°–25°
24. Chahuiah, ChHV + IH, Water, Cancer 26°–30°

25. Nethahiah, NThH + IH, Water, Scorpio 1°–5°
26. Haaiah, HAA + IH, Water, Scorpio 6°–10°

27. Yerathel, IRTh + AL, Water, Scorpio 11°–15°
28. Sheahiah, ShAH + IH, Water, Scorpio 16°–20°
29. Riyiel, RII + AL, Water, Scorpio, 21°–25°
30. Aumel, AVM + AL, Water, Scorpio 26°–30°

31. Lekabel, LKB + AL, Water, Pisces 1°–5°
32. Vesheriah, VShR + IH, Water, Pisces 6°–10°
33. Yechoiah, IChV + IH, Water, Pisces 11°–15°
34. Lehachiah, LHCh + IH, Water, Pisces 16°–20°
35. Keveqiah, KVQ + IH, Water, Pisces 21°–25°
36. Menadel, MND + AL, Water, Pisces 26°–30°

Air Trine

37. Aniel, ANI + AL, Air, Libra 1°–5°
38. Chaumiah, ChAaM + IH, Air, Libra 6°–10°
39. Rehauel, RHAa + AL, Air, Libra 11°–15°
40. Yeizel, IIZ + AL, Air, Libra 16°–20°
41. Hahahel, HHH + AL, Air, Libra 21°–25°
42. Mikael, MIK + AL, Air, Libra 26°–30°

43. Vevaliah, VVL + IH, Air, Aquarius 1°–5°
44. Yelahiah, YLH + AL, Air, Aquarius 6°–10°
45. Saeliah, SAL + IH, Air, Aquarius 11°–15°
46. Auriel, AaRI + AL, Air, Aquarius 16°–20°
47. Aushaliah, AaShL + IH, Air, Aquarius 21°–25°
48. Miahel, MIH + AL, Air, Aquarius 26°–30°

49. Vehuel, VHV + AL, Air, Gemini 1°–5°
50. Daniel, DNI + AL, Air, Gemini 6°–10°
51. Hachashiah, HChSh + IH, Air, Gemini 11°–15°
52. Aumemiah, AaMM + IH, Air, Gemini 16°–20°
53. Nanael, NNA + AL, Air, Gemini 21°–25°
54. Neithel, NITh + AL, Air, Gemini 26°–30°

Earth Trine

55. Mabehiah, MBH + IH, Earth, Capricorn 1°–5°
56. Poïel, PVI + AL, Earth, Capricorn 6°–10°
57. Nememiah, NMM + IH, Earth, Capricorn 11°–15°

58. Yeilel, IIL + AL, Earth, Capricorn 16°–20°
59. Harachel, HRCh + AL, Earth, Capricorn 21°–25°
60. Metzerel, MTzR + AL, Earth, Capricorn 26°–30°

61. Umabel, VMB + AL, Earth, Taurus 1°–5°
62. Yehahel, IHH + AL, Earth, Taurus 6°–10°
63. Aunuel, AaNV + AL, Earth, Taurus 11°–15°
64. Mechiel, MChI + AL, Earth, Taurus 16°–20°
65. Damebiah, DMB + IH, Earth, Taurus 21°–25°
66. Menaqel, MNQ + AL, Earth, Taurus 26°–30°

67. Aiauel, AIAa + AL, Earth, Virgo 1°–5°
68. Chebuiah, ChBV + IH, Earth, Virgo 6°–10°
69. Raahel, RAH + AL, Earth, Virgo 11°–15°
70. Yebemiah, IBM + IH, Earth, Virgo 16°–20°
71. Haïaiel, HII + AL, Earth, Virgo 21°–25°
72. Moumiah, MVM + IH, Earth, Virgo 26°–30°

The seven tables of Numerical Transpositions given at the end of ch. XXV, bk. III, appear incomplete at first glance, but an examination of their structure shows that they are complete and that they tabulate the different letter pairs in Hebrew that can be used to signify the same number (the use of letters for numbers is explained in ch. XIX, bk. II). Since different pairs of letters have the same numerical value, they are occultly linked, and thus may be interchanged.

The sixth table showing the pairs from 1100–1300 is drawn in a slightly different way from the other tables. It might easily be changed to conform in structure to the other tables. Why Agrippa has drawn it this way is not apparent to me. The last table contains no new information, and may have been added merely as a key to understanding the meaning of the previous tables.

It is easiest to grasp the structure of these tables by converting the letters to their number values:

Table of Ones

					1
				1 + 1	2
				2 + 1	3
			2 + 2	3 + 1	4
			3 + 2	4 + 1	5
		3 + 3	4 + 2	5 + 1	6
		4 + 3	5 + 2	6 + 1	7
	4 + 4	5 + 3	6 + 2	7 + 1	8
	5 + 4	6 + 3	7 + 2	8 + 1	9
5 + 5	6 + 4	7 + 3	8 + 2	9 + 1	10

11-19 by Ones

5 + 6	4 + 7	3 + 8	2 + 9	1 + 10
6 + 6	5 + 7	4 + 8	3 + 9	2 + 10
	6 + 7	5 + 8	4 + 9	3 + 10
	7 + 7	6 + 8	5 + 9	4 + 10
		7 + 8	6 + 9	5 + 10
		8 + 8	7 + 9	6 + 10
			8 + 9	7 + 10
			9 + 9	8 + 10
				9 + 10

Table of Tens

					10
				10+10	20
				20+10	30
			20+20	30+10	40
			30+20	40+10	50
		30+30	40+20	50+10	60
		40+30	50+20	60+10	70
	40+40	50+30	60+20	70+10	80
	50+40	60+30	70+20	80+10	90
50+50	60+40	70+30	80+20	90+10	100

110-190 by Tens

50+60	40+70	30+80	20+90	10+100
60+60	50+70	40+80	30+90	20+100
	60+70	50+80	40+90	30+100
	70+70	60+80	50+90	40+100
		70+80	60+90	50+100
		80+80	70+90	60+100
			80+90	70+100
			90+90	80+100
				90+100

Table of Hundreds

				100	
			100+100	200	
			200+100	300	
		200+200	300+100	400	
		300+200	400+100	500	
	300+300	400+200	500+100	600	
	400+300	500+200	600+100	700	
400+400	500+300	600+200	700+100	800	
500+400	600+300	700+200	800+100	900	
500+500	600+400	700+300	800+200	900+100	1000

1100–1300 by Hundreds

700+400	800+300	900+200
800+400	900+300	
900+400		

Key

5.	10.	10.	10.	10.
5	6 + 4	7 + 3	8 + 2	9 + 1
50.	100.	100.	100.	100.
50	60 + 40	70 + 30	80 + 20	90 + 10
500.	1000.	1000.	1000.	1000.
500	600+400	700+300	800+200	900+100

In closing these remarks on the practical Kabbalah, brief notice must be taken of the tables at the end of ch. XXVII, bk. III, for finding out the names of both good and evil angels of the planets and zodiac signs.

These two tables are formed by writing the letters of the Hebrew alphabet in the rows from the top to the bottom. When the alphabet is exhausted, it is begun again in the following cell. In the table of the planets, the letters are written right to left in each successive row. However, in the table of the zodiac, the letters are written right to left in every second row beginning with the top row, and at the same time left to right in every second row beginning with the row next to the top.

Any name or word can be converted into the name of an angel by finding the letters of the name or word individually in the alphabet that runs along the side of the table being used and reading across the row to the corresponding letter in the column under the planet, or zodiac sign, upon which the angelic name is to be based. Good angels are extracted by reading in the letters of the name from right to left—the natural direction of Hebrew writing. Evil angels are found by reading in the letters from left to right.

For example, if one wished to find the evil angel of Scorpio based upon the root name Ham, HM, חם, one would locate the letter H in the alphabet running up the left side of the table of the zodiac, then look across to the column above the sign Scorpio on the line of evil. The corresponding letter is Aa. Likewise, the corresponding letter for M of the root name is L. Thus the name of the evil angel is Aul, AaL, על. As always, vowels must be added to make the names pronounceable. Instructions on the use of these tables are given by Agrippa in ch. XXVII, bk. III.

APPENDIX VIII

Geomancy

Geomancy is a general term that covers any form of divination that employs, or is derived from, earth. There were a number of ancient methods (see ch. LVII, bk. I), but the one that Agrippa describes is the classical technique of divining by means of 16 figures generated by making series of holes in fine soft soil or sand. Agrippa's treatment of the subject in the *Occult Philosophy* is cursory to say the least, ch. XLVIII of bk. II being one of the shortest chapters in the entire work. He was, however, well schooled in the subject and wrote a separate treatise devoted to geomancy that served as one of the primary textbooks for later geomancers.

This essay he mentions in ch. XIII of his *De incertitudine et vanitate scientiarum,* where, referring to works of geomancy by Haly, Gerard of Cremona, Bartholomew of Parma and Tundinus, he says of his own treatise: "I too have written a geomancy quite different from the rest but no less superstitious and fallacious or if you wish I will even say 'mendacious'" (quoted by Thorndike, 5:8:131). It was written before 1526, but after the *Occult Philosophy*, and appears in the Latin *Opera* and in the collection of six occult works extracted from the *Opera* and translated into English under the title *Henry Cornelius Agrippa, His Fourth Book of Occult Philosophy.*

Actually the *Fourth Book* proper is only one of the six treatises, a spurious and inferior production very much in keeping with the quality of medieval grimoires. *Of Geomancy* seems to be genuine, if the style and content are any guide—it is completely in keeping with the tone and attitude Agrippa displays in the *Occult Philosophy*. Since the method of geomantic divination it describes is Agrippa's own, and differs from other methods, and since the work is difficult to decipher without a guide, I will give Agrippa's technique here.

He begins by declaring two opinions as to the source of the efficacy of this form of divination. The first, held by the ancients, is that it stems from the terrestrial spirits:

> … therefore they will have the projecting of the points of this art to be made with signs in the Earth, wherefore this art is appropriated to this element of Earth … and therefore they first used certain holy incantations and deprecations, with other rites and observations, provoking and alluring spirits of this nature hereunto. ("Of Geomancy," in *Fourth Book of Occult Philosophy,* 1–2)

The second opinion, which Agrippa himself favors, is that the efficacy comes from the strong desire in the soul of the diviner, and consequently "neither matters it where or how these points are projected …" (ibid., 2). On the question of which is the proximate source of the power in divination by lot to reveal things hidden, it is worth rereading ch. LIV, bk. II, where the matter is considered at length.

Then he gives the 16 figures as they are given in the *Occult Philosophy*. The attributing of the planets to the figures is the same; indeed

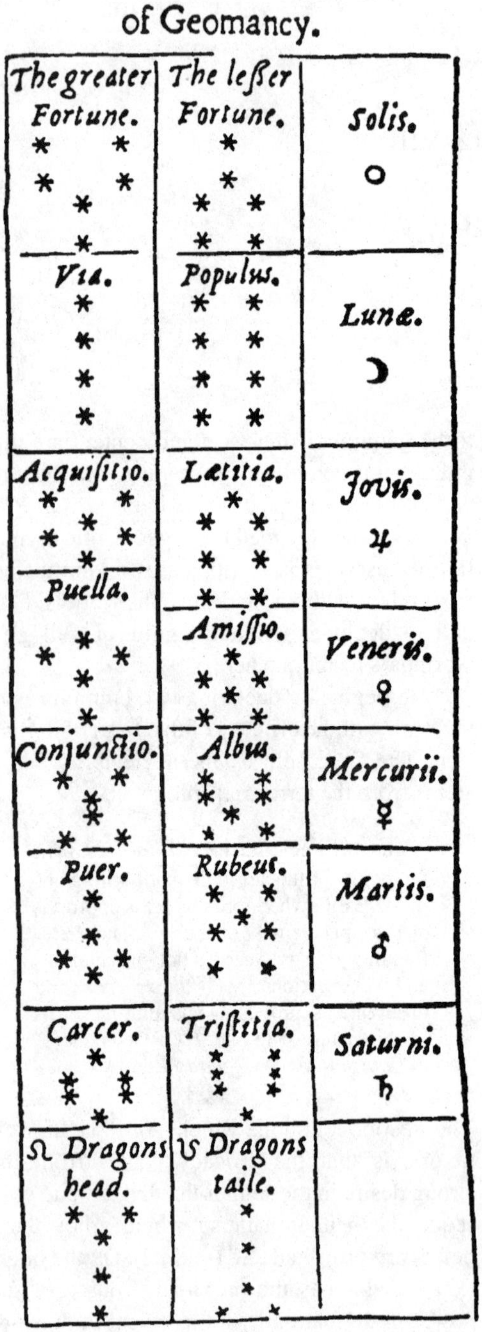
of Geomancy.
The greater Fortune.
The leſſer Fortune.
Solis.
Via.
Populus.
Lunæ.
Acquiſitio.
Lætitia.
Jovis.
Puella.
Amiſſio.
Veneris.
Conjunctio.
Albus.
Mercurii.
Puer.
Rubeus.
Martis.
Carcer.
Triſtitia.
Saturni.
Dragons head.
Dragons taile.

Geomantic Figures with Related Planets
from *Henry Cornelius Agrippa, His Fourth Book of Occult Philosophy* (London, 1655)

there is no disagreement among geomancers over the planets. But the assignment of the signs of the zodiac to the figures is completely different, as the accompanying comparative table will show (see facing page).

Since there appears to be no consensus on the numbering of the figures, I have ordered them according to their associated planets. The first column gives the figures themselves; the second, their names in Latin; the third, their planets; the fourth, their signs in the English translation of the *Occult Philosophy;* the fifth, the signs in the Latin *Opera;* the sixth, Agrippa's own attributions in *Of Geomancy,* which are made so that each sign attaches to its ruling planet, with the exception of the Head and Tail of the Dragon; the seventh, the vulgar or common attributions of the signs given by Agrippa in *Of Geomancy* for the sake of completeness; the eighth, the signs given by Gerard Cremonensis in his work *Astronomical Geomancy,* which is another of the tracts comprising the *Fourth Book of Occult Philosophy.*

Our author describes his method of ordering the zodiac to the figures in *Of Geomancy,* which I will quote here, mainly because it allows me to correct a confusing error in Turner's text:

> And these are the infallible comparisons of the figures, and from these we may easily discern the equality of their signs; therefore the Greater and Lesser Fortunes have the sign of Leo, which is the house of the Sun: Via and Populus have the sign of Cancer, which is the house of the Moon: Aquisitio hath for his sign Pisces, and Laetitia Sagitary, which are both the houses of Jupiter: Puella hath the sign of Taurus, and Amissio of Libra, which are the houses of Venus: Conjunctio hath for its sign Virgo, and Albus the sign Gemini, the houses of Mercury: Puer and Rubeus have for their signs Aries and Scorpio, the houses of Mars: Carcer hath the sign Capricorn, and Tristitia Aquary, the houses of Saturn: the Dragon's Head and Tail are thus divided, the Head to Capricorn, and the Dragon's Tail adhereth to Scorpio ... (Turner [1655] 1978, 4)

The strong similarity between Gerard's zodiacal attributions and those in the *Occult*

Geomantic Figures

| Figures | | Planets | Occult Philosophy | | Of Geomancy | | Gerard of Cremona |
Forms	Names		English	Latin	Agrippa	Common	
* * * * * *	Carcer	♄	♓	♓	♑	♓	♓
* * * * * * *	Tristitia	♄	♏	♒	♒	♐	♏
* * * * * *	Aquisitio	♃	♈	♈	♓	♈	♈
* * * * * * *	Laetitia	♃	♉	♉	♐	♊	♉
* * * * *	Puer	♂	♈	♈	♈	♏	♊
* * * * * * *	Rubeus	♂	♊	♊	♏	♋	♊
* * * * * *	Fortuna Major	☉	♒	♒	♌	♉	♒
* * * * * *	Fortuna Minor	☉	♉	♉	♌	♉	♉
* * * * *	Puella	♀	♎	♎	♉	♋	♎
* * * * * *	Amissio	♀	♎	♎	♎	♐	♏
* * * * * *	Conjunctio	☿	♍	♍	♍	♎	♍
* * * * * * *	Albus	☿	♋	♋	♊	♌	♋
* * * *	Via	☽	♌	♌	♋	♍	♌
* * * * * * * *	Populus	☽	♑	♑	♋	♒	♑
* * * * *	Caput Draconis	☊	♍	♍	♑	♎	♍
* * * * *	Cauda Draconis	☋	♐	♐	♏	♑	♐

Geomantic Characters

from *The Magus* by Francis Barrett (London, 1801)

Philosophy leads me to believe that Agrippa used Gerard as his source before he had completely formed his own understanding of geomancy. Later when he framed his own opinions, he did not bother to enter them into the revised edition of the *Occult Philosophy*.

It might be mentioned in passing that the attribution of the zodiac signs used in the Golden Dawn system of geomancy, which is the one most commonly used today, is identical to Agrippa's assignment by ruling planets, save only that the signs of Venus are inverted, as are the signs of Jupiter.

Although he does not appear to hold it in high regard, Agrippa goes on to describe the usual method of geomantic divination, beginning with an account of how to generate the figures:

> And now we come to speak of the manner of projecting or setting down these figures, which is thus; that we set down the points according to their course in four lines, from the right hand towards the left, and this in four courses: there will therefore result unto us four figures made in four several lines, according to the even or uneven marking every several line ... (ibid., 5)

This is not a particularly lucid description, but may have been typical. Gerard Cremonensis describes the same process:

> It is expedient therefore, to make four unequal lines, by the points casually set down; and to join together those points; and out of the points which are not joined together, which do remain in the heads of the lines (as it is done in geomancy), extract one figure ... ("Astronomical Geomancy." In *Fourth Book,* 155)

It did not really matter how clear the descriptions were, since everyone already knew how to generate the geomantic figures anyway.

You take a stick and poke four random series of holes in parallel lines in the ground, moving from right to left, stopping each series whenever it feels appropriate; i.e., when the Earth spirits tell you to stop. Then you count the holes in each line. An odd number of holes gen-erates one point, or star, on the geomantic figure; an even number of holes generates two stars. For example:

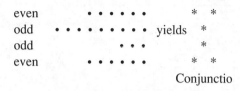

In the common form of geomancy Agrippa describes first, it is necessary to generate four figures, which are called the four *Matres,* or Mothers. These subsequently give birth to all the other figures generated. This is the reason Agrippa speaks of "four courses"; that is, four sets of four series of holes, resulting in four figures. In a hypothetical divination, these series might be poked out on the sand:

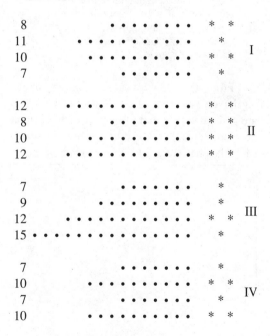

These Mothers are written right to left in a horizontal row:

*		*	*	*	* *	Level 1
* *	*	*	*	*	Level 2
*	* *	*	*	* *	Level 3
* *	*	*	*	*	Level 4
IV	III	II	I		

From the Mothers are born the Daughters, or *Filiae,* by combining the elements of each horizontal row of the Mothers right to left, and stacking them top to bottom to constitute each Daughter. Level 1 yields the first Daughter, level 2 the second, level 3 the third and level 4 the fourth. The Daughters are written to the left of the Mothers, also from right to left:

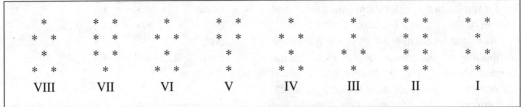

As Agrippa puts it:

> Of these four *Matres* are also produced four other secondary figures, which they call *Filiae,* or Succedents, which are gathered together after this manner; that is to say, by marking the four *Matres* according to their order, placing them by course one after another; then that which shall result out of every line, maketh the figure of *Filiae,* the order whereof is by descending from the superior points through both mediums to the lowest … ("Of Geomancy." In *Fourth Book,* 6)

From this row of eight figures, or as Agrippa terms them, "eight houses of heaven," are generated four more figures which Agrippa does not name, but which have been elsewhere called Nephews. Each Nephew is made by combining two adjacent Mothers or Daughters, the points of which are added together on each of the four levels to give either odd or even totals. An even total generates two points on the same level of the descendent Nephew, and an odd total one point. Agrippa says:

> … and the rest of the houses are found after this manner; that is to say, out of the first and second is derived the ninth; out of the third and fourth the tenth; out of the fifth and sixth the eleventh; and out of the seventh and eighth the twelfth: by the combination or joining together of two figures according to the rule of the even or uneven number in the remaining points of each figure. (ibid., 7)

This may be represented by continuing the example:

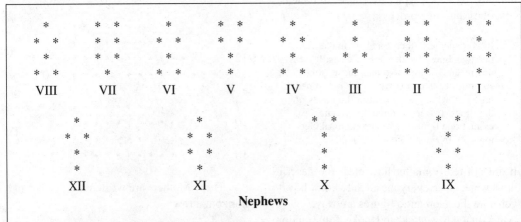

Nephews

Two more figures are generated by combining the Nephews in the same manner, which are called *Coadjuctrices* or *Testes*—in English, Witnesses. From the pair of Witnesses a single 15th figure is made, also by combination, called the Index by Agrippa, by others the Judge. Agrippa describes this procedure thus:

> After the same manner there are produced out of the last four figures; that is to say, of

the ninth, tenth, eleventh, and twelfth, two figures which they call Coadjutrices, or Testes; out of which two is also one constituted, which is called the Index of the whole figure, or thing generated ... (ibid., 7)

This may be demonstrated by continuing the example:

```
  *        * *        *         * *        *        *        * *        * *
* *        * *      * *        * *      * *      *        * *          *     Mothers
  *        * *        *          *        *      * *      * *        * *      and
* *          *      * *          *      * *      *        * *          *     Daughters
VIII        VII       VI         V        IV       III       II        I


       *                  *                 * *              * *
     * *                * *                *                *
       *                * *                *                * *         Nephews
       *                  *                *                  *
      XII                XI                 X                IX


              * *                              * *
              * *                              * *
                *                                *                      Witnesses
              * *                              * *
             XIV                             XIII


                        * *
                        * *
                        * *                                            Index
                        * *
                       XV
```

All these figures are used in the divination, but far more important than the rest are the Witnesses and the Index, which, because they are the focus of the entire work, concentrate occult potency in themselves.

There was a standard chart into which the 15 geomantic figures of a divination were entered. It served the same purpose as the astrological chart used in modern astrology, providing a framework that would set forth the figures clearly in their proper relationship so that they might be easily read. The version of this chart given by Agrippa is crude, but a more polished example such as might be expected to be used by diviners to the nobility during the Renaissance is represented by Robert Fludd in a plate in his work *Utriusque cosmi historia* (Oppenheim, 1619) which shows several principal methods of divination, geomancy among them. This plate is reproduced on the following page.

Our example would be entered into the chart after this manner:

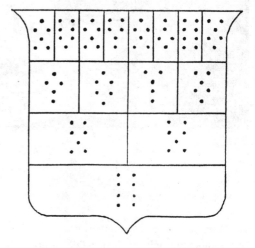

Stephen Skinner, in his useful book *The Oracle of Geomancy* (Prism, 1977, 350–2), rightly points out that, because of the inherent

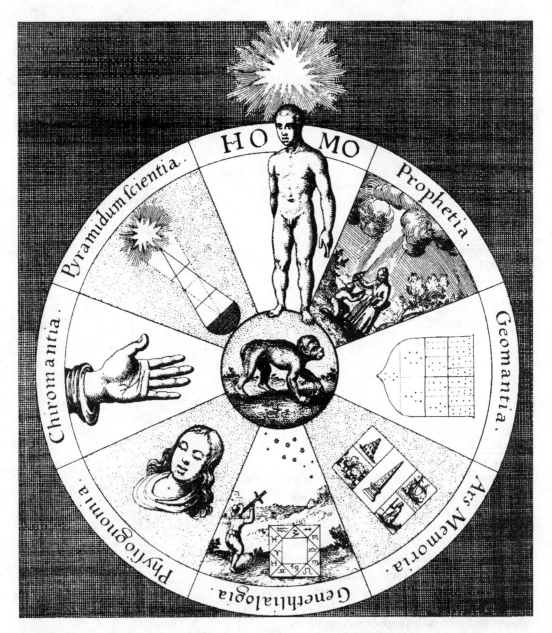

Methods of Divination, Showing Geomantic Chart

from *Tomus secundus de supernaturali, naturali, praeternaturali et contranaturali microcosmi historia* by
Robert Fludd (Oppenheim, 1619)

structure of the figures and their mode of generation, there are only eight possible figures that can occur in the Index: Acquisitio, Amissio, Fortuna Major, Fortuna Minor, Populus, Via, Conjunctio and Carcer. If any of the other forms appear in the position of the Index, an error has been made somewhere in the chart.

Agrippa was unenthusiastic about this conventional geomancy: "And this which we have declared is the common manner observed by geomancers, which we do not altogether reject neither extol ..." ("Of Geomancy." In *Fourth Book,* 8). He presents his own system of astrological geomancy wherein 12 of the geomantic figures are entered into the 12 houses of the zodiac on the standard astrological chart of his day. With each figure is also entered its related planet. The diviner then can draw upon both the meanings of the figures and the meanings of the houses, giving the divination a greater subtlety.

> As the former *Matres* do make the four Angles of an house, the first maketh the first Angle, the second the second Angle, the third maketh the third Angle, and the fourth the fourth Angle; so the four *Filiae* arising from the *Matres,* do constitute the four Succedent houses; the first maketh the second house, the second the eleventh, the third the eighth, and the fourth maketh the fifth house; the rest of the houses, which are Cadents are to be calculated according to the rule of their triplicity; that is to say, by making the ninth out of the first and fifth, and the sixth out of the tenth and second, of the seventh and eleventh the third, and of the fourth and eighth the twelfth. (ibid.)

For those completely unfamiliar with astrology a brief explanation is necessary. Each sign of the zodiac has a division on the circle of the heavens of 30 degrees with which it is associated. For early astrologers the house of a sign simply meant its natural place. The first house was the place of Aries, the second house the place of Taurus and so on. We need not consider here the later elaborations of astrologers on the use of the houses.

If a great cross is drawn upon the ring of the houses from horizon to horizon and midheaven to lower midheaven, it will divide the ring into four equal sections and touch, counting clockwise, the first, tenth, seventh and fourth houses, which for this reason are called the angles, or angular houses. The houses that follow after them in the ordinary counterclockwise motion of the planets are, counting clockwise, the second, eleventh, eighth and fifth, called for this reason the succedent houses. The second set of houses after the angles, again respectively, are the third, twelfth, ninth and

sixth, called the cadent houses.

By Agrippa's system, the four Mothers, generated in the way already described, are placed in the angular houses in order, beginning with the first house and proceeding clockwise to the tenth, seventh and fourth houses. The four Daughters, again generated in the usual way, are placed in the succedent houses clockwise beginning with the second, then the eleventh, the eighth and lastly the fifth.

The method for generating the four Nephews may have been invented by Agrippa— at least, I have not found it described by any previous writer. It is based upon the elemental trines which divide the zodiac and its corresponding houses into four groups of three, each allotted to an element. This is graphically represented by four equally spaced equilateral triangles centered on the axis of the Earth. Since the Mothers and Daughters have occupied two-points on each triangle, the figures for the cadent houses, the unoccupied points, are formed by combining the other two figures on each triangle.

This may be more readily grasped by means of a simple diagram:

The outer ring shows the houses, the inner ring their associated zodiacal signs; the elemental symbols indicate the trines, the exterior letters the geomantic figures and the Roman numerals beside them their order of generation. Agrippa does not explicitly state in what order the Nephews are to be generated. Although this may be implied in the sequence of his description, I have chosen to represent the numbering of the Nephews in the diagram following the same pattern that he gives for the Mothers and Daughters.

The geomantic figures having been set in the houses on the chart, it is a relatively simple matter to place the signs and planets, as Agrippa describes:

> ... the figure which shall be in the first house shall give you the sign ascending, which the first figure showeth; which being done, you shall attribute their signs to the rest of their houses, according to the order of the signs: then in every house you shall note the planets according to the nature of the figure: then from all these you shall build your judgement according to the signification of the planets in the signs and houses wherein they shall be found, and according to their aspects among themselves, and to the place of the querent and thing quosited; and you shall judge according to the natures of the signs ascending in their houses, and according to the natures and proprieties of the figures which they have placed in the several houses, and according to the commixture of other figures aspecting them ... (ibid., 8)

In other words, the figure that forms the first Mother, being placed in the first, or ascendent, house, determines which zodiac sign shall be placed in that house, according to the relationship already given between the 16 geomantic figures and the signs of the zodiac. Since the order of the zodiac is unvarying, the other signs are written in succession counterclockwise in the succeeding houses. For example, if the figure of the first Mother is the Greater Fortune, the zodiac sign entered in the first house is Leo, according to the system of attributing the signs by their ruling planets given by Agrippa in *Of Geomancy;* but it would be Aquarius according to the system derived from Gerard of Cremona and given in the *Occult Philosophy.* In any case, once the ascendent sign is established, the others are entered counterclockwise in order beginning with that sign; i.e., I—Leo, II—Virgo,

III—Libra and so on.

The planets are placed in the houses even more simply, according to their associated geomantic figures. The relationship between the figures and the planets is undisputed and never varies. If the Greater Fortune is in the first house, it always receives the Sun, and so for the rest.

The chart is then read in an astrological manner, with the admixture of the meanings of the geomantic figures. The positions of the querent and the thing questioned mentioned by Agrippa are determined from the meanings of the houses. The position of the thing inquired after depends upon its nature: if it was a money matter, it would probably be the second house; if a matter of communication, the third house; and so on. It would seem natural to locate the querent in the first house. In reading a geomantic chart it is not necessary to look up any astrological positions, but an understanding of the planets, signs, houses and aspects of astrology is essential.

It only remains to derive the Index, or Judge, and the chart is complete. The Witnesses are not consulted. The Index is found by counting the holes poked in the sand in the generation of the four Mothers, dividing by 12, then counting the number of the remainder counterclockwise from the first house. Wherever the count ends, the figure in that house is considered to be the Index. If there is no remainder after division, the Index is the figure in the 12th house.

> But here we shall give you the secret of the whole art, to find out the Index in the subsequent figure, which is thus: that you number all the points which are contained in the lines of the projections, and this you shall divide by twelve: and that which remaineth project from the Ascendent by the several houses, and upon which house there falleth a final unity, that figure giveth you a competent judgement of the thing quesited; and this together with the significations of the judgements aforesaid. But if on either part they shall be equal, or ambiguous, then the Index alone shall certify you of the thing quesited. (ibid., 8–9)

Remember that Agrippa begins to count on the first thing counted, not the second, as is the modern practice. In other words, if there were a remainder of three, the Index would be the geomantic figure in the third house, not the fourth.

On the principle that obscure matters are always more easily understood by example than by description, I will continue the example from the geomantic divination begun previously, extending it to the astrological system of Agrippa.

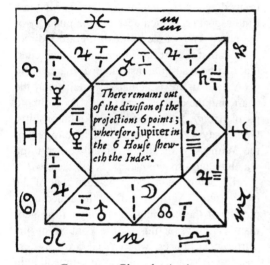

Geomancy Chart by Agrippa

from *Henry Cornelius Agrippa, His Fourth Book of Occult Philosophy* (London, 1655)

At the top of the next column is the square chart used during the Renaissance. The triangles represent the houses, which I have numbered. Within them are set the geomantic figures, signs and planets according to Agrippa's system of ruling planets. The Mothers and Daughters are the same as those previously derived. They combine according to their elemental trines to form the Nephews in the cadent houses. The ascendent sign is located by the first Mother and placed in the first house with the other signs following in order counterclockwise. The geomantic figures adhere to the houses, not the signs. The Index is determined by counting the total number of points in the 16 rows that generated the four Mothers, dividing by 12 and counting from the ascendent counterclockwise; or putting it another way, whatever the remainder is, the figure in the house of the same number is the Index.

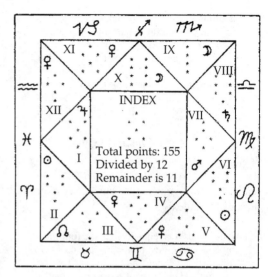

Gerard Cremonensis in his *Astronomical Geomancy* also gives a system of astrological divination by geomantic figures, and it may be that Agrippa derived his system from Gerard but modified it to suit his analytical mind.

Gerard begins by finding the zodiac sign to be placed in the first house by pricking four rows of dots to form a single geomantic figure:

It is expedient, therefore, to make four unequal lines, by the points casually set down; and to join together those points;

Geomancy Chart by Gerard Cremonensis

from *Henry Cornelius Agrippa, His Fourth Book of Occult Philosophy* (London, 1655)

and out of the points which are not joined together, which do remain in the heads of the lines (as it is done in Geomancy) extract one figure; and the sign of the zodiac that answereth to that figure [in Gerard's assignment: see the table], put for the Ascendent, for the word's sake. ("Astronomical Geomancy." In *Fourth Book*, 155)

The rest of the signs follow in order counterclockwise around the 12 houses.

Gerard assigns the planets to the houses individually in much the same way Agrippa locates the Index:

Afterwards it is requisite to make four lines by course for each planet, by points casually pricked down; and likewise for the Dragon's Head, as you have done for the Ascendent, and divide those points by twelve; and that which remaineth above twelve, or the twelfth itself, if a greater number doth not remain, retain, and the planet for which the projection was made, place in that House of which the superabounding number shall be; that is, if there remain twelve, let the planet be placed in the twelfth House; if ten, in the tenth House; if one, in the first House; if two, in the second House; and so of the rest. And you ought always to begin from the Sun, and afterwards from the Moon, then from Venus and Mercury, and from Saturn, Jupiter and Mars, and the Dragon's Head and Dragon's Tail ... (ibid., 157)

In Gerard's system nine figures are separately derived, each by pricking four rows of points in the sand; the first establishes the position of the zodiac signs in relation to the houses, the other eight the positions of the planets and the Dragon's Head and Tail. Since the Head and Tail of the Dragon are always opposite each other in the circle of houses, it is only necessary to establish the place of the Dragon's Head, and the Tail is 180 degrees around the circle of houses.

This, by the way, does not seem to have been understood by Skinner, who in describing Gerard's system incorrectly directs that geomantic figures be pricked for both the Head and Tail of the Dragon—indeed he represents them in his diagram *(Oracle of Geomancy,* 313) in a trine aspect (!), which destroys the integrity of the chart. The whole point of Gerard's directions is that they result in an astrological chart that can be read in an astrological manner. No geomantic figure is actually written upon the chart, and the chart is read strictly according to its planetary, zodiac and house relationships. Gerard says: "... neither are we here to regard the Witnesses, or Judge, or any other thing which belongs to geomancy ..." (ibid., 156).

By comparison it can be seen that of the two systems, Agrippa's offers the added complexity of the meanings attaching to the geomantic figures acting in the context of the astrological houses, whereas Gerard's system has simplicity and elegance to recommend it, in that no geomantic figures appear, each planet is written only once, and the Head and Tail of the Dragon are accurately represented 180 degrees apart on the chart.

Indeed, because of the frequent multiple occurrence of a single planet—in the example above Venus appears four times, and both the moon and sun twice—it is scarcely possible to read the aspects in a legitimate way in Agrippa's system, which might unkindly be characterized as an awkward hybrid of geomancy and astrology. For this reason it is liable to be anathema to astrologers, who will naturally prefer the system of Gerard.

Biographical Dictionary

A

ARON: The author of a book "of the nature of herbs, and stones" (*Book of Secrets* [Best and Brightman, 40]), along with Evax, called the *Book of Minerals* (ibid., 48). This work is cited many times in the *Book of Secrets* and also by Albertus Magnus in his writings. It is unknown, but has been presumed to have been a Jewish or Arabic work.

ABARIS: (6th or 8th century BC) The son of Seuthea, he was a priest of Apollo said to have fled from Hyperborea (the region north of the Caucasus), or from Scythia, to escape a plague in his own land. He traveled throughout Greece healing the sick with incantations, performed miracles, foretold the future and saved the city of Sparta from a plague. Legend says that he bore as an emblem a golden arrow given to him by the god Apollo, and that the arrow carried him through the air; furthermore, he took no earthly food. Herodotus comments: "As for the tale of Abaris, who is said to have been a Hyperborean, and to have gone with his arrow all round the world without once eating, I shall pass it by in silence. This much, however, is clear: if there are Hyperboreans, there must be hypernotions" (*History* 4 [Rawlinson, 215]). Suidas credits Abaris with four works: Scythian oracles, a poem on the visit of Apollo to Hyperborea, a collection of expiatory formulae and a prose theogony. These are no longer extant and are thought to have been spurious. Iamblichus

relates that Abaris was attracted to Pythagoras because of the resemblance of the Greek to Apollo, and that he gave Pythagoras his magic arrow as a gift. In return Pythagoras showed Abaris his "golden thigh," assured the Scythian that he was indeed the god incarnated upon the Earth to cure the ills of mankind and taught him various mysteries, including divination by numbers. See Iamblichus *Life of Pythagoras,* ch. 19.

ABBARIS: See ABARIS.

ABENEZRA: (1092–1167) Abraham Ben Meir Ibn Ezra, otherwise known as Abenezra, a Jewish philosopher born at Toledo. In the first half of his life he gained a reputation as a poet in his native Spain. Around 1140 he began to wander, traveling through North Africa, Egypt, Italy, France and England and stopping sometimes for years to write. He belonged to the school of Jewish philosophy based on Greek ideas, which was in conflict at that time with the mystical school that gave birth to the literature of the Kabbalah. His views were Neoplatonic, and he believed in astrology. Abenezra produced writings on mathematics and astronomy, as well as a Hebrew grammar and a commentary on the Bible.

ABRAHAM: See ABENEZRA.

ABU-MAASCHAR: (805–885) Arab astronomer born at Balkh, who lived and worked in Baghdad and died at Wasid in Central Asia. He maintained that the world had been created when the seven planets met in conjunction in the first degree of Aries, and that when they again conjoined in the final degree of Pisces the world would end—a view which seems to have had its origin in Stoic doctrine:

> The Stoics say that the planets, returning to the same point of longitude and latitude which each occupied when first the universe arose, at fixed periods of time bring about a conflagration and destruction of things, and that the universe again reverts anew to the same condition ... (Nemesius *Denatura hominus* 38. In Ptolemy *Tetrabiblos* [Robbins, 15, n. 3])

Three of the major works of Abu-Maaschar were printed around the time Agrippa was writing his *Occult Philosophy: De magnis conjunctionibus* (Augsburg, 1489), *Flores astrologici* (Augsburg, 1488) and *Introductorium in astronomiam* (Venice, 1506). The illustrations of the astrological spirits that appear in the *Astrolabium planum* of Pietro d'Abano, published by Johannes Angelus in 1488, are taken from a manuscript of Albumazar in the Vatican Library.

AESOP: (lived 600 BC) Famous writer of the fables who was born in Phrygia. He is said to have met his death at the hands of the jealous citizens of Delphi, who threw him from a cliff:

> And thus to gyder they machyned how and in what manere they myghte put hym to dethe
> but they durst not attempte ne falle on hym for the grete companyes of straungers whiche thenne were within the Cyte
> neuertheles as they aspyed and sawe that one of the seruaunts of Esope made the males and other gere redy for to ryde and departe thens
> they went & took a coupe of gold oute of the Temple of Appollo
> and secretely put and thrested it in to the male of Esope
> Esope thenne whiche ygnored and nothynge knewe of this trayson departed oute of delphye
> But he was not ferre whanne the traytours ranne after hym

> And with grete noyse and clamour took hym
> And as they tooke hym
> Esope said to hem
> My lordes why take yow me
> And they sayd to hym
> Ha a theef of celestyal ornaments
> Crokebacked and sacrylege
> wherfore has thou dyspoylled & robbed the Temple of Appollo. ...
> And thenne they casted and threwe hym doune fro the top of the hylle vnto the foot of hit
> And thus deyde Esope myseraby ...
> *(Caxton's Aesop* [Cambridge:Harvard University Press, 1967], 68, 71.)

Various plagues afflicted Delphi, and on the advice of the oracle the people paid a compensation to Aesop's nearest relative, whereupon the plagues ended. The story of his life is usually attributed to the 13th-century monk Maximus Planudes, but can be traced back to first-century Egypt.

AETLIUS: See SPARTIANUS.

AFRICANUS, P. CORNELIUS SCIPIO AEMILIANUS, MINOR: (?185–129 BC) The younger son of L. Aemilius Paulus, he was adopted by P. Cornelius Scipio Africanus, the elder son of Africanus the Great. A good soldier and leader of men—he fought his first war at 17—he was also a scholar. Perhaps he is best remembered for the capture of the city of Numantia in Spain in 133 BC. He had been appointed consul the previous year for the purpose of ending the war in Spain. The victim of political intrigue, he was murdered in his own room while composing a speech, perhaps by Fulvius Flaccus.

ALBERTUS MAGNUS: (?1206–1280) Also called Albert of Cologne, he was born at Laningen in Swabia of the noble family of Bollstadt, was educated at Padua in the works of Aristotle and became a Dominican brother in 1223, in which capacity he lectured on theology at Cologne. In 1245 he went to Paris to obtain his doctorate and remained there for a time to teach. In 1260 he became Bishop of Regensburg but resigned his office after three years to preach. Detractors contemptuously referred to him as the "ape of Aristotle," but his admirers surnamed him "Doctor Universalis" and "the Great." Thomas Aquinas was his pupil. His many works on philosophy occupied 36 volumes when printed at Paris in 1890. It is from these that *The Book of Secrets,* sometimes incorrectly attributed to Albertus, is in part drawn. The work Agrippa refers to is the *Speculum astronomiae,* attributed to Albertus. For a discussion of the authenticity of this work, see the article by Lynn Thorndike in *Speculum* 30 (1955), 413–33.

ALBUMASAR: See ABU-MAASCHAR.

ALCHINDUS: See ALKINDI.

ALCINOUS: (2nd century) Platonic philosopher who wrote the *Epitome of the Doctrines of Plato.*

ALCMAEON: (lived 500 BC) A physician and natural scientist from Croton who was a pupil of Pythagoras. He was the first to dissect animals and the first to operate on the human eye. He wrote several philosophical and medical works, of which only fragments survive.

ALEXANDER OF APHRODISIAS: (2nd century) Called the Expositor. He was born in Aphrodisias, in Caria. A pupil of Aristocles of Messene, he came to Athens toward the end of the second century and rose to the head of the Lyceum, where he lectured on peripatetic philosophy. The foremost commentator on the works of Aristotle, his writings are voluminous. Many were translated into Latin at the revival of learning in the Middle Ages, though others remained in Greek and Arabic. In addition to his commentaries, he wrote original works, notably *De fato* (On fate), which examines free will, and *De anima* (On the soul) which argues against immortality.

ALEXANDER OF MACEDONIA: (356–323 BC) Called the Great. Son of Philip II. In his youth he was instructed by Aristotle. At 16 he received the crown and immediately set about conquering the greater part of the known world. Handsome, courageous, physically powerful and skillful in combat, intelligent and honest, he had a quick temper that was easily inflamed by alcohol and lacked the prudence that might have made him a great ruler. Perhaps the best known story told about him concerns the knot of Gordium. It was fabled that he who could unbind the knot would be the conqueror of Asia. By most accounts Alexander cut it in twain with his sword, an act that has oppositely been characterized as sage, because it represents a Zenlike transcendence of thinking, and brutish, the proof of his barbarism. Plutarch tells a different story, that he merely slipped the knot off the yoke of the chariot to which it was fastened by pulling out the pin that held the yoke in place. His most lasting legacy was the founding of the great city of Alexandria at the mouth of the Nile in 331 BC. At the youthful age of 32 he died of fever in Babylon, which he had intended to make the capital of the world.

ALFARABIUS: (?870– 950) More properly Muhammad ibn Tarkhan ibn Uzlagh Abu Nasr al-Farabi, an Arabian philosopher born at Wasij near Farab in Turkestan. As a young man he journeyed to Baghdad, at that time the intellectual center of the world, where he learned Arabic and studied mathematics, philosophy and medicine. He attached himself to the court of Hamdanid Saif Addaula, from whom he received a small pension. He died in Damascus while traveling in company with his patron. The writings of al-Farabi on Aristotle formed the foundation for the philosophical system of Avicenna, and it is probable that Averroes also drew inspiration from his works, but the great acclaim accorded Avicenna led to the neglect of al-Farabi by later scholars.

AL GHAZALI: (1058–1111) Abu Hamid ibn Muhammad al-Ghazali, an Arabian philosopher and theologian who wrote profusely (69 works) on a wide variety of scholarly topics. His most important work is *Tahafut al-Falasifah* (Destruction of the philosophers).

ALGAZEL: See AL GHAZALI.

ALKINDI: (804–873) The Arab philosopher Abu Yusuf Ya'Qub Ibn Ishaq ul-Kindi, better known as Alkindi, al-Kindi, or simply Kindi. He was born in Kufa, where his father was governor, and studied in Bosra and Baghdad. Remaining to live in Baghdad, he obtained a government position to support himself and found time to write more than 200 works on all branches of the sciences. In addition he translated Aristotle. Roger Bacon held him in high regard as second only to Ptolemy on the subject of optics. He is referred to with honor as "The Philosopher of the Arabs."

ALMADEL: The name of a medieval magician mentioned by the Abbot Johann Trithemius in his *Antipalus maleficiorum* (c. 1500) as the author of an edition of the *Key of Solomon*. Also the name of the fourth book of the manuscript collection that goes under the collective name *Lesser Key of Solomon* or *Lemegeton;* it is specifically applied to the wax table described therein.

ALPHARUS: See ALFARABIUS.

ALPHONSUS: See PICATRIX THE SPANIARD.

AMBROSE: (?340–397) Bishop of Milan. A citizen of Rome, he was born in Treves of a wealthy and influential family and was educated for a political life by his father at Rome. When in 374 the Arian and orthodox parties of the Church contested with each other for the vacant bishopric of Milan, Ambrose delivered an address before them that was so well received, he was himself elected by acclamation as the only fit occupant of the see. Favoring the orthodox side, he spent the rest of his life waging doctrinal war with both the Arians and the pagans. He was an able administrator and an eloquent diplomat, of unshakable principles. His writings consist of commentaries, sermons, funeral orations and letters, but he is best remembered for his hymns, which formed a pattern for later times.

AMMONIUS SACCAS: (3rd century AD) Greek philosopher who founded the Neoplatonic school in Alexandria. He gained his surname from his work, which was carrying sacks of corn in his native Alexandria. Of humble Christian origins, he taught such celebrated men as Longinus, Herennius, Plotinus and Origen. In middle life he abandoned the faith of his birth in favor of philosophy, and left no written works—at least, this is what Porphyry asserts (as quoted by Eusebius *Ecclesiastical History* 6.19.6). Eusebius claims Ammonius remained Christian throughout his life and left two works behind: *The Harmony of Moses and Jesus* and *The Diatessaron* or *Harmony of the Four Gospels* (ibid.). There seems to have been a second Christian philosopher with the same name. It is to this man that Eusebius refers. The two are frequently confused. Ammonius probably died in 243 at an age of more than 80 years.

AMPHION: Semi-mythical son of Zeus and the Theban princess Antiope, who left him exposed along with his twin brother, Zethus, atop Mount Cithaeron out of fear of the wrath of her father, Nycteus. The boys were found and raised by shepherds. Hermes took an interest in Amphion and gave him a lyre, also teaching him to play it. Zethus, who grew into a man of great strength, occupied himself tending the herds and hunting. When Antiope was driven out of Thebes by the malice and cruelty of the usurper King Lycus and his wife Dirce, she made herself known to her sons, who returned to Thebes and revenged themselves on the pair. Masters of the city, they began to fortify the wall. Zethus carried great stones into place, scorning his brother's lack of manly prowess; in reply Amphion played on his lyre so magically that the stones danced out of the earth and assumed their ranks in the wall by themselves.

ANASARCHUS: See ANAXARCHUS.

ANAXAGORAS: (500–428 BC) Greek philosopher of Clazomenae in Ionia. At age 20 he gave up his property and went to Athens to devote himself to philosophy. Euripides and

Pericles were his pupils. In 450 BC he was accused of impiety but was rescued by the eloquence of Pericles. He retired to Lampsacus, where he died. He propounded the theory of a single higher cause independent of matter, which he considered to be mind.

ANAXARCHUS: (4th century BC) Greek philosopher born at Abdera, of the school of Democritus. He accompanied Alexander the Great (356–323 BC) on his Asiatic campaigns. One of his students was Pyrrhon the Skeptic. Alexander held Anaxarchus in great esteem, and the philosopher used this good will to occasionally remind the king of his humanity. Once when Alexander contemplated having himself elevated to the rank of a divinity, Anaxarchus pointed to a finger the king had recently cut and said, "See the blood of a mortal, not a god." When Nicocreon, the tyrant of Salamis in Cyprus, visited Alexander at Tyre, the philosopher insulted him, probably by refusing to grovel at his feet. There was nothing Nicocreon could do so long as Anaxarchus remained under the protection of Alexander, but the philosopher had the misfortune to be shipwrecked off the coast of Cyprus after Alexander's death and came into the power of his enemy, who tortured him to death by pounding him in a great mortar. This story is told by Cicero. Some later writers have accused Anaxarchus of flattering Alexander, but they may be confusing the philosopher with Cleon of Sicily, or be misled by the slanders of the Peripatetics, who were philosophical rivals of the Skeptics.

ANAXILAUS: (1st century BC) Physician and philosopher born at Larissa in Thessaly. In 28 BC he was banished from Italy by Augustus for practicing magic. The charge originated from his skill in natural philosophy, with which he apparently produced wondrous effects that the ignorant took to be the result of the magical arts.

ANGLICUS, ROBERTUS: (fl. c. 1260) English writer and translator, who wrote a commentary on the *Sphere* of Sacrobosco in 1271, a *Tractatus quadrantis* in 1276 and *Canons for*

the Astrolabe, which was printed around 1478. Lynn Thorndike suggests that Robert of England may be Robert of York (Thorndike, 4:520). But Agrippa speaks of "a certain man of York"—presumably Robert—and "Robert an Englishman" separately in his chapter on the Goetia from his *Incertitudine et vanitate scientiarum,* p. 695. It is possible, though less likely, that Robert an Englishman is Robert of Chester, a student of astronomy and geometry who translated the Koran in 1143, the *Judgements* of the astrologer Alkindi around the same time and a treatise on alchemy written for "Calid, king of Egypt" in 1144. According to Robert this last was the work of Hermes Triplex, who reigned in Egypt after the deluge.

ANSELME: See ANSELMI.

ANSELMI, GEORGIO: (?1400–?1450) Or Georgius de Anselmis, or George Anselm, of Parma, a physician and philosopher who was the son and grandson of physicians. Little is known about him other than that he had four sons and was named as one of the reformers of the statutes of the college of physicians at Parma in 1440. By later writers he was celebrated as one of Parma's most learned citizens, skilled in philosophy, the liberal arts and medicine. His writings on musical harmony were frequently cited by Franchino Gaffuri, who wrote about the same subject some 50 years later. He is also credited with a work on medicine in four books called *Theoremata radicalia,* an astrological treatise called *Astronomia* consisting of a series of brief explanations of astrological maxims, and a work on magic called *Opus de magia disciplina* in five parts. In this last work he defends magic and declares that a philosopher may be a magus if he uses magic only for good. He derives the word *magus* from the ancient Persian and says it is equivalent to the Greek *sacerdos,* or priest. The first part gives the categories of magic, part four is devoted to magical images for the signs of the zodiac and other heavenly bodies and part five is on recipes and antidotes for poison.

ANTIOCHUS SOTER: (3rd century BC) King of Syria, he reigned 280–261 BC. He was the son of Seleucus Nicator, and is perhaps best remembered for his passion for, and subsequent marriage to, his stepmother, Stratonice, whom his father voluntarily gave to him.

APION: (1st century) Greek grammarian who was born at Oasis Magna in Egypt and schooled at Alexandria. He taught rhetoric at Rome during the reigns of Tiberius and Claudius. When Caligula came to power he returned to Alexandria, but was sent back to Rome in 38 AD to make complaint against the Jews before Caligula on behalf of Alexandria. This gave rise to his work against the Jews, to which Josephus replied with *Against Apion*. He also wrote a recension of the Homeric poems, a Homeric dictionary and a work on Egypt in five books.

APOLLONIUS OF TYANA: (1st century AD) Pythagorean philosopher born in Tyana, he traveled widely to Nineveh, Babylon, Tibet and India and was accredited with many miracles. He won the favor of Vespasian but was later accused by Domitian of inciting insurrection. He is said to have escaped prison by magical means and to have proclaimed the death of Domitian the moment it occurred although he was physically far removed. Most of his life as recorded by his biographer Philostratus corresponds with the Gospel accounts of the life of Christ—a circumstance that raised the ire of the Church Fathers against his memory. It seems probable that the writers of the Gospels borrowed heavily from the fables that surrounded Apollonius. A spurious work, the *Nuctemeron,* carries his name and is reproduced by Eliphas Levi in his *Transcendental Magic.* Levi is said to have used this work in his famous evocation of the spirit of Apollonius in London in 1854. What the true history of the *Nuctemeron* is, I have not been able to ascertain. Cecco d'Ascoli in his *Sphera* mentions the *Book of Magic Art* and the *Angelic Faction* by Apollonius. There is also a work called the *Golden Flowers* under this authorship, and another called *The Secrets of Nature* (see Thorndike 2:43, 282).

APOLLONIUS PERGAEUS: (?262–?200 BC) Greek geometer of the Alexandrian school, a native of Perga, about whom almost nothing is known. His most famous work, *On Conic Sections* in eight books, is in parts highly original and earned him the name Great Geometer. He also wrote, among other mathematical works, *On the Burning Glass.* This has been lost, but is mentioned by ancient writers.

APOLLONIUS RHODIUS: (lived 100 AD) Poet and grammarian who was born at Alexandria in Egypt. He taught rhetoric at Rhodes and was later made chief librarian of the fabled library at Alexandria. His poem *Argonautica* is extant, but most of his other works are lost.

APPIOUS: See APION.

APPONUS: See PETRUS.

APULEIUS, LUCIUS: (2nd century AD) Born at Madaura in Numidia, he studied at Carthage and Athens, then traveled the East seeking occult knowledge and initiation. When he married a rich older woman of Alexandria, her family accused him of using sorcery to bewitch her mind. His successful trial defense has survived under the title *De magia.* The story of the *Golden Ass* was based on an earlier work, the *Metamorphoses* of Lucius of Petrae. Later in life Apuleius became a priest of the mysteries of Isis at Carthage and also gave lectures in philosophy.

AQUINAS, THOMAS: (?1227–1274) Catholic theologian and philosopher who was born of noble parents at Roccasecca, the castle of his father, the count of Aquino, in the territory of Naples. He got his early education at the monastery of Monte Cassino, where his classmates referred to him as the Dumb Ox, then went on to study at the University of Naples. At 16 he came under the influence of the Dominicans, much to the displeasure of his family, and assumed the habit of this order when he was 17. His superiors sent him to Cologne to be instructed by Albertus Magnus. In 1245 when Albertus was called to Paris, Thomas went with him and soon distinguished himself by his rhetorical skills. In 1257 he was made doctor of theology, and began to write, travel and lecture in Paris, Rome and London. The honors the Church tried to bestow upon him were refused— he declined the archbishopric of Naples and the abbasy of Monte Cassino. In January of 1274 he was summoned to Lyons by Pope Gregory X to settle a dispute between the Greek and Latin churches, but died of illness on the journey. Dante implies obliquely that he was poisoned by Charles of Anjou *(Divine Comedy: Purgatory* 20.69). The major works of Aquinas are *Summa theologiae* and *Summa catholicae fidei contra gentiles.* In addition he wrote commentaries on Aristotle, Boethius and Dionysius the pseudo-Areopagite. He is known by the titles Doctor Angelicus and Doctor Universalis.

ARATUS: (3rd century BC) Poet born in Soli (afterwards Pompeiopolis) in Cilicia, or by another account Tarsus, he spent most of his time at the court of Antigonus Gonatas, king of Macedonia. He wrote two astronomical poems: *Diosemeia,* which gives astronomical weather signs and the effects of weather on animals, and *Phænomena,* which introduces the constellations and describes their risings and settings. Aratus lists 44 constellations in his *Phænomena:* 19 northern (Ursa Major, Ursa Minor, Bootes, Draco, Cepheus, Cassiopeia, Andromeda, Perseus, Triangularum, Pegasus, Delphinus, Auriga, Hercules, Lyra, Cygnus, Aquila, Sagitta, Corona and Serpentarium), 13 central (Aries, Taurus, Gemini, Cancer, Leo, Virgo, Libra, Scorpio, Sagittarius, Capricornus, Aquarius, Pisces and the Pleiades) and 12 southern (Orion, Canus, Lepus, Argo, Cetus, Eridanus, Piscis Australis, Ara, Centaurus, Hydra, Crater and Corvus). The style of these poems was much admired by the Greeks and Romans. Ovid says, with his usual hyperbole: "… with the Sun and Moon Aratus will ever exist" *(Amours* 1.15, line 16 [Riley, 299]).

ARCHYTA: See ARCHYTAS.

ARCHYTAS: (lived 400 BC) Native of Tarentum, he was a philosopher, mathematician and general. In this last capacity he served his city seven times and was in all his campaigns victorious. Of the Pythagorean school of philosophy, he founded a sect of his own. His skill in mechanical inventions, particularly his wooden flying dove, was the admiration of his age. Both Plato and Aristotle are said to have borrowed from him. While on a voyage in the Adriatic Sea he was drowned.

ARION: (7th century BC) Greek musician of Methymna in Lesbos. He stayed for many years at the court of Periander, tyrant of Corinth, then felt the urge to travel and went to Italy and Sicily, where he won great renown and riches playing on his cithara. Returning by ship to Corinth, he was robbed by the sailors, who gave him the choice of either killing himself on the deck or jumping overboard. Arion chose the latter, but first asked to be allowed to play his harp on the bow of the ship. Delighted at the prospect of a free concert by the best musician and singer in the world, the sailors agreed. As Arion played, the sweetness of his music attracted a throng of dolphins, and when he at last flung himself in his musician's robes into the sea, one dolphin carried him safely on its back to Corinth. The whole affair was revealed to Periander, who punished the astonished sailors when they came into port. This story is related at length by Herodotus early on in the first book of his *History* and is mentioned by Pausanius, who describes seeing a bronze statue of Arion riding a dolphin at Tainaron *(Guide to Greece* 3.25.7 [Levi, 2:95]). Arion is also reputed to be the inventor of dithyrambic poetry and of the name "dithyramb."

ARISTOPHANES: (?444–?380 BC) Greek comic dramatist and poet. Very little is known about his personal life. His father, Philippus, was a landowner in Aegina. Aristophanes himself was an Athenian, although his rights of citizenship were more than once legally challenged by his enemy, Cleon. He is said to have been "almost a boy" when his first comedy, *The Banqueters,* was produced in 427 BC. According to Suidas, Aristophanes wrote 54 plays (or 44, depending on the reading of the text). His three sons, Philippus, Araros and Nicostratus, were all comic poets. Araros brought forth onto the stage two of his father's works posthumously. In his comedies Aristophanes exhibits his scorn for the modern decadence of Athens, as he sees it, brought on by the evils of the Peloponnesian war and exacerbated by the corrosive speculations of the Sophists, both of which serve to undermine patriotism and religion. His weapon is cutting personal satire against the leading men of his time of a type only possible in a true democracy. Eleven of his comedies have survived.

ARISTOTLE: (384–322 BC) The Greek philosopher was born at Stagira, a town in Chalcidice, Macedonia (now called Starros, on the Gulf of Strimon). His father, Nicomachus, was physician to the king of Macedonia, Amyntas II, and himself wrote several works on natural science. In 367 BC he went to Athens to study philosophy and became the pupil of Plato two years later, where he soon distinguished himself. Plato called him the "intellect of his school" and named his house the house of the "reader." He studied under Plato until the latter's death in 347 BC, after which he traveled to Atarneus and married Pythias, the adopted daughter of Prince Hermias. When his father-in-law was killed by the Persians, he removed to Mytilene and in 342 BC accepted an invitation from Philip of Macedonia to tutor his son Alexander, who was then 13 years old. The four years Aristotle spent teaching Alexander are in large measure the reason for any virtues this conqueror later may have exhibited.

Returning to Athens in 335 BC, Aristotle was assigned the Lyceum by the state and soon assembled a large number of students. He taught twice a day, in the morning lecturing on esoteric subjects to a select audience, in the evening speaking to a wider group on exoteric matters. His school soon became the most famous in Athens. He taught there for 13 years, until in 323 BC the death of Alexander allowed the suspicion and resentment that had been fermenting against him to express itself. He was suspected of being too much a friend to Macedonia, but since his behavior was above reproach, he was accused in 322 BC on a trumped up charge of impiety by the hierophant Eurymedon. Before he could be tried, Aristotle fled Athens and took refuge at Chalcis in Euboea, the hereditary city of his mother's family. He died there the same year from stomach trouble—probably cancer or bleeding ulcers. Physically he was unimpressive, being short and frail, with small eyes and an habitually sarcastic expression. A lisp in his speaking did nothing to counter these impediments. Even so, he rose to become the greatest philosopher in the Western world, rivaled only by his old master, Plato, who, despite rumors to the contrary, Aristotle always held in the highest regard.

ARISTOXENUS: (late 4th century BC) Greek philosopher and musician from Tarentum who was a disciple of Aristotle at Athens. Of his character we know nothing except that he is said to have been deeply annoyed when Theophrastus was appointed to succeed as head of the Peripatetics after Aristotle's death. Cicero (*Tusculanarum disputationum* 1.10) says that Aristoxenus held the soul to be a harmony of the body (see Plato's *Phaedo*). Suidas mentions that he wrote 453 works on all subjects open to literature. Only his *Elements of Harmony* has survived. It is a treatise on music in three books.

ARNOLDAS: See VILLA NOVA.

ARTEPHIUS: (12th century) A writer on alchemy and Hermetic philosophy who died in the 12th century but who was rumored to have lived more than a thousand years by means of his art, and to be in reality Apollonius of Tyana under an assumed name. He claims in the preface to one of his works, *De vita propaganda* (The art of prolonging life), to have written the document at the age of 1,025. Another work that circulated under his name was *The Key to Supreme Wisdom.* Yet another was on "the character of the planets, on the significance of the songs of birds, on things past and future, and on the Philosopher's Stone" (Spence [1920] 1968, 36). Girolamo Cardano (1501–1576) mentions these works and gives his opinion that they were written as a practical joke aimed at the credulity of would-be alchemists.

ASCLEPIADES: A lyric poet said to have invented the meter that bears his name *(Metrum Asclepiadeum).* Nothing is known about him. He is not to be confused with Asclepiades of Samos, a bucolic poet of the 3rd century who was a friend of Theocritus. Perhaps Agrippa has confounded the first Asclepiades above with Asclepiades the physician, a native of Bithynia born in 124 BC, who came to Rome as a rhetorician but found success as a healer. His treatment consisted of diet, exercise, massage, cold compacts and wine, which, if it did not always cure his patients, at least it did not kill them so quickly as the medical practices of his competitors. Consequently he enjoyed great acclaim.

ASCOLI, CECCO D': (1257–1327) The popular name of Francesco Degli Stabili, an Italian mathematician and astrologer born near Ancona. In 1322 he was made professor of astrology at the University of Bologna. He came into conflict with the Church when he published a controversial tract on the employment and agency of demons, and to elude its punishment he fled to Florence. But his unorthodox writings, as well as his public attacks on Dante's *Divine Comedy,* sealed his fate. He was burned at the stake in Florence. His best known work, the *Acerba,* is an encyclopedic poem on astrology, meteorology, stellar influences, physiognomy, vices and virtues, minerals, the love of animals, moral and physical problems and theology. It was printed many times, having reached 20 editions by 1546. The best edition is that of Venice, dated 1510. The earliest appeared in Brescia around 1473.

ASCULUS: see ASCOLI.

ATHANASIUS: (293–373) Bishop of Alexandria. He was born in that city. Nothing is known of his early life. In 326 he assumed his office and after a few short tranquil years became embroiled in the Arian controversy, opposing any compromise with that party. His iron principles caused him to be driven from his see no less than five times during the course of his life, but always he was able to resume the bishopric. He is best known for his *Discourse Against the Arians* and his *Orations,* both written during periods of exile.

ATHENAEUS: (3rd century) A Greek grammarian of Naucratis in Egypt who is remembered for his *Deipnosophistae* (Banquet of the learned), a collection of anecdotes in 15 books on a wide variety of topics.

ATHENODORUS CANANITES: (?74 BC–7 AD) Born at Canana near Tarsus, this philosopher was a personal friend of Strabo, who wrote about him. He taught Augustus at Apollonia in Epirus when the future emperor was a boy and followed him to Rome in 44 BC. He is credited with advising Augustus to recite the alphabet before acting in anger. When an old man, he returned to Tarsus to remodel the constitution of that city. None of his works survive. He is not to be confused with Athenodorus Cordylion (?120–?50 BC), the keeper of the library at Pergamum.

AUSONIUS DECIMUS MAGNUS: (?310–?390) Roman poet born at Burdigala (Bordeaux). He taught grammar and rhetoric in his native town and had the good fortune to be appointed tutor to Gratian, the son of the Emperor Valentinian. In 379 Gratian made him praefectus of Latium, Libya and Gaul, and in 383 raised Ausonius to the consulship. After the death of Gratian in that same year, he retired from public life and in 390 returned to his native Burdigala. He is thought to have been a Christian. Many of his writings are extant, mostly short poetical pieces. Agrippa refers to his *Epistolae,* a collection of 25 letters, some in verse and others in prose.

AVERROES: (1126–1198) Abu al-Walid Muhammad ibn-Rushd, an Arabian philosopher born at Cordova who studied theology, law, mathematics, medicine and philosophy under the greatest teachers of his time, and spent the latter part of his life in various judicial appointments in Spain and Morocco, and as a physician. For a time he enjoyed great favor; then, in reaction to his free-thinking views, he was banished to a place near Cordova. He enjoyed a resurgence of acclaim shortly before his death, which more or less coincided with the end of Moslem power and cultural pre-eminence. He gained his greatest reputation among Christian scholars for his commentaries on Aristotle. They did not realize that these were based on two centuries of prior wisdom and attributed every insight to Averroes himself. It is unclear to me why Agrippa calls him a Babylonian, unless the term denotes an astrologer.

AVICEBRON: See IBN GABRIOL.

AVICENNA: (980–1037) Abu 'Ali al-Husain ibn 'Abdallah ibn Sina, an Arabian philosopher and physician born at Afshena in the district of Bokhara (present-day Uzbekistan). His mother was a native of Afshena, his father a Persian by birth who worked as a tax collector. When Avicenna was quite young the family moved to the city of Bokhara (present-day Bukhara in Uzbekistan), which was a Moslem center of learning and culture at the time. At age ten the boy outdid his tutor and astonished the neighbors with his memorization of the complete Koran and a host of Arabic poems. He learned his arithmetic from a local grover and began the *Elements* of Euclid under a wandering scholar, but soon discarded his teachers in favor of solitary study of Aristotle and the other Greek philosophers. At 16 he was attending the sick for no payment in order to learn practical medicine. When he encountered a question he could not answer he would go to the mosque and pray all night until dawn, stimulating his mind with cups of wine. The *Metaphysics* of Aristotle remained impenetrable until one day he happened upon a commentary by al-Farabi, which at once illuminated the meaning.

When he cured the local emir of a dangerous illness in 997, he was granted access to the royal library of the Samanids, but after the

library was destroyed by a fire which Avicenna was accused of setting, he began to wander from town to town, finding employment for a time as physician to important officials, which allowed him the opportunity to write. He had a passion for wine and women and would intersperse his studies with sensual debauches. At Hamadan (in present Iran) he was raised to the administrative post of vizier, but even the tribulations of political life did not stop him from writing.

Driven by the upheavals of war to the city of Isfahan, Avicenna spent the last 12 years of his life in the service of Abu Ya'far 'Ala Addaula as physician and advisor and even accompanied the prince on his campaigns. He died in Hamadan after falling ill with colic on the military march to that city, and on his deathbed repented of his luxurious lifestyle, gave all his possessions to the poor and freed his slaves.

About 100 works are attributed to Avicenna, ranging in size from a few pages to several volumes. He owes his reputation in Europe to his *Canon of Medicine*, translated into Latin by Gerard of Cremona, which was used as a medical text in some French universities until the year 1650. He also wrote a book on animals that was translated by Michael Scot as well as works on theology, philology, mathematics, astronomy, physics, music, philosophy and alchemy.

BACON, ROGER: (?1214–?1294) English philosopher and alchemist born near Ilchester in Somerset. He studied at Oxford, then went to Paris, where he showed contempt for the sloth and credulity of the schoolmen of the day. Returning to Oxford about 1250, he entered the Franciscan order and began serious private study in languages and alchemy. Rumors began to fly that he was dealing in black arts. The play *Friar Bacon and Friar Bungay*, written by Robert Green in 1589, gives an entertaining account of these tales.

Bacon is credited with inventing the telescope and gunpowder and with predicting a host of modern inventions (in his tract *De secretis operibus naturae*). About 1257 he was driven from Oxford and placed under Church supervision in Paris, prohibited from writing for publication, but in 1265 Pope Clement IV requested that Bacon send him a treatise on the sciences. Bacon answered with *Opus majus, Opus minus* and *Opus tertium.* However in 1278 his books were condemned by Jerome de Ascoli, later to become Pope Nicholas IV, and Bacon was cast into prison for 14 years. He was released a few years before his death. *Opus minus* contained, or at least was intended to contain, a treatise on speculative and practical alchemy, which is not extant.

BASIL THE GREAT: (?330–379) Born at Caesarea, Cappadocia, into an eminent family, he studied at Constantinople and Athens with his friend and fellow student, Gregory of Nazianzus. Together they compiled an anthology of the writings of Origen, the *Philocalia.* Basil traveled in Syria and Arabia studying the most famous hermit saints, learning to mortify his body and increase the enthusiasm of his piety. He later became head of a convent at Pontus that contained his mother and sister. In 370 he was chosen bishop of Caesarea and pursued a vigorous attack against the Arian faction of the Church as well as reforming the monastic orders of the East.

BASILIUS: See BASIL THE GREAT.

BEDE: (672–735) English historian and theologian. At the age of seven he was given into the care of the monastery at Wearmouth and Jarrow, which consisted of two separate structures five or six miles apart under one abbot, to be raised and educated. His life was uneventful, a model for the vast majority of lives in that age. In 731 he wrote: "From that time I have spent the whole of my life within that monastery devoting all my pains to the study of the scriptures; and amid the observance of monastic discipline, and the daily charge of singing in the church, it has ever been my delight to learn or teach or write" (autobiographical note to *Ecclesiastical History of the English Nation*).

In 691 or the following year he was ordained deacon; in 702 or the following year,

priest. He visited Egbert in York in 733, but seems never to have gone out of England. Nonetheless his works had enormous influence, encompassing more of less the sum of human knowledge in Western Europe. His most widely read work was the *Ecclesiastical History*, which earned him the title "Father of English History." He was also called the Venerable Bede out of respect for his piety and learning.

BOCCHUS, CORNELIUS: Writer of a lapidary cited by Pliny in bk. 37 of his *Natural History.* Nothing is known about the author or the book.

BOCHUS: See BOCCHUS.

BOETHIUS, ANICIUS MANLIUS SEVERINUS: (?480–524) Roman philosopher and statesman who held the office of consul in 510 and saw his two sons elevated to the same position in 522. He became the object of political intrigue and was accused of treason against Theodoric the Great. His only crimes seem to have been fairness and judicial mercy. Theodoric threw him into prison, where he languished for many years before his execution. While there he wrote *De consolatione philosophiae*, a philosophical and theological work in five books that enjoyed an astounding success in the Middle Ages. He was a man of great learning, as his contemporaries attest.

When Gunibald, king of the Burgundians, visited Rome, Boethius showed him a water-clock and a sundial he had constructed. These so impressed the monarch that, at the request of Theodoric, Boethius duplicated them for Gunibald. In later centuries he was regarded, groundlessly, as a martyr, and pious Christian writings were falsely ascribed to him. Gibbon held Boethius in highest regard, calling him: "the last of the Romans whom Cato or Tully could have acknowledged for their countryman" (Gibbon [1776–88] 1830, 39:145).

BRENDAN: (6th century) Also called Brandon or Brandan. A native of Clonfert, he was the abbot of a Benedictine monastery he had founded at Clonfert in eastern Galway, Ireland, around 558. Nothing is known of his life.

He is the subject of a celebrated medieval saga that involves his voyage across the Atlantic to the promised land of the saints, afterwards called Saint Brendan's Island. Traditionally dated 565–573, it was translated into Latin, French, English, Saxon, Flemish, Welsh, Breton, Scottish and Gaelic and enjoyed such high repute that Saint Brendan's Island was regarded as a geographical fact at least until 1721, when the last of a long number of expeditions extending over centuries set off in search of it. More recently the legend is cited as evidence that the Irish travelled to the New World before the Vikings, but this opinion is likely to prove as chimerical as the island itself. He is not to be confused with his Irish contemporary, Saint Brendan of Birr.

BRIDGET, SAINT: Brigit (or Bridget or Brigid), a goddess of Ireland who was the daughter of the god Dagda, and the patroness of smiths, doctors and poets. She is linked with fires of purification. Her feast, Imbolc, comes on February 1. As was often the case, the Church absorbed her and turned her into a saint, whose dates are given as ?452–523 (or 436–523). Saint Bridget was said to have been born at Faughart in county Louth, daughter of a prince of Ulster. She was called St. Brigit Thaumaturge for her many miracles, a list of which ran to 25 folio chapters. In England she is worshiped as St Bride.

BRIGITTA: See BRIDGET.

CAIUS CAESAR: (12–41) Better known as Caligula, a nickname given to him by the Roman troops while he was a boy. He began his reign well enough, but suffered an illness in 38 AD that resulted in his madness, leading to such extravagances as declaring himself a god while alive and raising his horse to the position of consul. Mercifully for the Roman people, he was assassinated.

CALIGULA: see CAIUS CAESAR.

CASSIODORUS, FLAVIUS MAGNUS AURELIUS: (?490–585) Born of a Syrian family settled at Scyllacium in Bruttii, around 507 he became, through the influence of his father, quaestor (at that time, a kind of secretary) to Theodoric the Great, and continued to hold administrative positions until 540, when he retired as a monk. His passion was the promotion of classical learning, which he perceived to be threatened by the growing tide of barbarism. To this end he established two monasteries and set his monks copying and translating manuscripts. Like his contemporary Boethius he enjoyed building scientific toys such as the waterclock and the sundial. Most of his historical and theological writings have survived.

CATO CENSORIUS, MARCUS PORCIUS: (234–149 BC) Born at Tusculum (ancient city that stood near present-day Frascati, Italy), this Roman writer and politician was raised on his father's farm in the Sabine territory (central Italy). The practical and frugal lifestyle he learned there remained with him the rest of his life. He often upbraided the Romans for their extravagance. After distinguishing himself as a soldier, he was elected censor in 184 BC and remained vigorous in politics to the end, being one of the prime movers of the Third Punic War with his slogan *Delenda est Carthago* (down with Carthage). He wrote *De re rustica,* a treatise on agriculture, which is extant.

CELSUS, A. CORNELIUS: (1st century AD) Little of this Roman writer has survived except *De medicina,* a medical treatise in eight books that was highly regarded in the Middle Ages and during the Renaissance.

CHAEREMON OF ALEXANDRIA: (1st century AD) A Stoic philosopher and grammarian who was the custodian of the sacred books of the library of Alexandria, which were kept separately in the temple of Serapis. As the sacred scribe (ἱερογραμματεύς), it was his duty to expound on the meaning of these mystical writings. He must have belonged to the highest rank of the priesthood. In 49 AD he was called to Rome to tutor young Nero, the future emperor. In his own books he explains the occult teachings of Egypt as symbolic nature worship. These include a *History of Egypt,* a treatise on *Comets,* a work on *Egyptian Astrology* and one on *Hieroglyphics.* Only fragments of these works remain. Chaeremon's account of the system of Egyptian priesthood is given by Porphyry in his *De abstinentia* 4.6. He should not be confused with the Chaeremon who accompanied Aelius Gallus on an expedition into the interior of Egypt around 26 BC (see Strabo's *Geography,* the last book).

CHALCIDIUS: (6th century) Platonic philosopher who translated the *Timaeus* of Plato into Latin and added a voluminous commentary.

CHARLES OF BOHEMIA: (1316–1378) Son of John of Luxemburg, he succeeded to the throne when his father fell at the battle of Crecy fighting alongside the French.

CHIRAMIS: See KIRANUS.

CHRYSIPPUS: (280–207 BC) The third of the great Stoic philosophers, he was born at Soli in Cilicia, the son of Apollonius of Tarsus. While still a youth he was cheated out of his inheritance and came to Athens, where he studied under Cleanthes, and perhaps under Zeno as well. Later in life he combined the teachings of these two men into a unified system and defended them with his rhetorical skills against the attacks of the Middle Academy, causing Diogenes Laertius to write: "If the gods use dialectic, they can use no other than that of Chrysippus" *(Lives of the Philosophers,* bk. 7). He is said to have composed 705 (others say 750) works, of which only fragments survive.

CHYRANNIS: See KIRANUS.

CHYRANNIDES: See KIRANUS.

CICCLUS: See ASCOLI.

CLAUDIANUS, CLAUDIUS: (late 4th century AD) The last Latin classical poet, he was a pagan Egyptian, probably a native of Alexandria, born of Roman parents. In or before 395 he traveled to Rome and soon won the patronage of Stilicho, the general and minister of Honorius, young ruler of the Western Empire (ruled 395–423). As he was a court poet, his works consist chiefly of panegyrics upon the actions of his patron. His poems are distinguished by a surprising elegance and artistic judgement. It is presumed that he died with Stilicho in 408, as nothing is heard about him after 404, but this is only conjecture.

CLEANTHES: (?301–232 BC) The Stoic philosopher was born at Assos, an ancient Greek city on the north shore of the present-day Gulf of Edremit in Turkey. Originally a boxer, he came virtually penniless to Athens, where he attended the lectures first of Crates the Cynic and later of Zeno the Stoic. He supported himself by carrying water during the night. His dullness and patient endurance drew upon him the nickname "the Ass." However, after the death of Zeno in 263 BC he was held in high enough regard to become the head of the Stoic school.

All the while he refused grants of money and continued to support himself by manual labor. Contracting a stomach ulcer, he was advised that a fast would cure it. The ulcer soon healed, but Cleanthes still refused to eat. When asked why, he said that since he was already halfway along the road to death, he would not trouble to retrace his steps. In this way he starved himself. A large portion of his philosophical poem, the *Hymn to Zeus,* was preserved in the writings of Stobaeus. In it Cleanthes represents the Sun as the abode of God and vivifying fire of the universe. Some fragments of his works were recorded by Cicero, Seneca and Diogenes Laertius.

CLEARCHUS OF SOLI: (lived 300 BC) A pupil of Aristotle, he wrote numerous works on a wide variety of subjects. None are extant.

CROESUS: (reigned 560–546 BC) The last king of Lydia, he was famous for his wealth.

At the beginning of his reign he subdued all the surrounding nations. He then consulted the oracle at Delphi as to whether he should make war against the Persians. The oracle replied that if he marched against the Persians, he would overthrow a great empire. Croesus immediately collected an army and marched on the troops of Cyrus, never stopping to consider that the oracle might mean his own empire would be overthrown. After an indecisive battle at Sinope, Cyrus laid siege to Sardis and captured Croesus alive. At first Cyrus planned to burn Croesus, but oddly enough the two became friends. Croesus outlived Cyrus and even accompanied Cambyses in his expedition against Egypt.

CUSANUS, NICOLAUS: (1401–1464) Also called Nicholas of Cusa. A cardinal and theologian of the Catholic Church, he was the son of a fisherman of Cusa (or Kues) in the archbishopric of Treves. As a boy he showed much promise, causing a noble patron to pay for his education at the University of Padua, where he took a law degree. When he lost his very first case he abandoned law and took holy orders, quickly mounting up the hierarchy of the Church. From 1440–7 he served in Germany as papal legate. In recognition of his service Pope Nicholas V made him a cardinal in 1448 and appointed him bishop of Brixen in 1450. In 1451 he was sent back to Germany and the Netherlands to check ecclesiastical abuses and restore the poverty, chastity and obedience of monastic institutions. Pope Pius II respected him enough to make him governor of Rome during the Pope's absence from that city in 1459.

His most important writings are philosophical. In *De docta ignorantia* and *De conjecturis libri duo* (both 1440), he maintains that all human knowledge is conjecture, that wisdom lies in the recognition of ignorance and that God can be apprehended by intuition in an exalted state of consciousness. His beliefs were upheld a century later by Giordano Bruno, who called him "divine Cusanus."

CUSAUS: See CUSANUS.

CYPRIANUS, THASCIUS CAECILIUS (?200–258) Bishop of Carthage. It is thought that he was born at Carthage of a wealthy patrician family, received the best available classical education, then became a teacher of rhetoric. A pagan, he took pleasure in confounding the arguments of Christians, until Caecilius (or Caecilianus), a presbyter at Carthage, converted him in 246. At his baptism he adopted the name of this friend as his own. His energy in helping the poor with his own wealth, his piety and his brilliant rhetorical gifts caused him to be drafted by popular consent into the office of bishop in 248 (or 249).

The persecution by the Emperor Decius in 250 and 251 forced him to flee for his life. When Gallus came to power in 251, Cyprian returned to Carthage, but when the successor to Gallus, Valerianus, renewed the persecution, Cyprian was banished to the town of Curubis in Africa Proconsulasis in 257, where he remained 11 months. Recalled to Carthage, he was beheaded on the plain outside the wall of the city on September 14, 258, obtaining the dubious honor of being the first martyred African bishop.

CYRUS THE ELDER: (6th century BC) Founder of the Persian Empire. The Median king Astyages dreamed that a vine grew from the womb of his pregnant daughter Mandane and overshadowed with its leaves all Asia. He consulted the magi, who interpreted the dream to mean that his grandchild would rule Asia in his place. Alarmed, Astyages ordered the baby killed, but due to the kindness of the herdsman Mitradates and his wife Spaco, who cared for the baby, Cyrus was reared as a herdsman, and eventually fulfilled the prophecy of his birth.

Spaca is said to be the Median word for "bitch," which rendered into Greek is *cyno*. Herodotus, who relates this story at length, puts forth his explanation for the myth of the bitch, saying of the youthful Cyrus when he was reunited with his parents:

> "... he spoke of the cowherd's wife who had brought him up, and filled his whole talk with her praises; in all that he had to tell them about himself, it was always

Cyno—Cyno was everything. So it happened that his parents, catching the name at his mouth, and wishing to persuade the Persians that there was a special providence in his preservation, spread the report that Cyrus, when he was exposed, was suckled by a bitch. This was the sole origin of the rumor. (Herodotus *History* 1 [Rawlinson, 48])

DAEDALUS: Mythical Cretan sculptor and architect. Later writers represent him as an Athenian descended from the royal house of Erechtheus. He taught his mechanical arts to the son of his sister, Perdix, and when he saw that the skill of the boy surpassed his own killed him in envy. Condemned to death for his crime, he fled to Crete, where he obtained the friendship of King Minos, building for him a bronze man to repel the Argonauts.

When the wife of the king, Pasiphae, fell in love with a bull, Daedalus fashioned a wooden cow in which she lay and gratified her passion. The result of this peccant indiscretion was the man-bull monster called Minotaurus, for whom Daedalus built the labyrinth. Enraged by the part of the artisan in his wife's infidelity, Minos threw Daedalus into prison. Pasiphae released him, and he escaped Crete with his son Icarus on wings constructed of feathers and wax. Icarus flew too near the sun and the wax melted, precipitating him into the sea. (See Ovid *Metamorphoses* 8.3 and *Ars amatoria* 2, c. line 92.)

The Greeks attributed to Daedalus the saw, the ax, the gimlet, the geometer's compass and other tools, as well as the crude wooden statues, called *daidala,* found throughout Greece, the origins of which had been lost in antiquity. Their age and mystery lent them magical power. Pausanias describes a number of them *(Guide to Greece* 9.3.2).

DAGOBERT I: (?607–639). King of the Franks.

DAGOBERTUS: See Dagobert I.

DAMIGERON: (fl. 200 BC) Also called Amigeron. A famous magician. Tertullian lists him along with other legendary mages in his *De*

anima (200 AD). His prose lapidary formed the basis for the pseudo-Orphic *Lithica,* a poem of 770 lines on the magic of stones, as well as the lapidary of Marbod, the *Liber lapidum.* "An important Hellenistic lapidary is that ascribed to Damigeron. Some fragments of the original Greek text are preserved in the second book of the medical collections of Aetius, but the whole text survives only in a Latin translation ..." (Evans [1922] 1976, 20). The complete Latin text of the lapidary is given by Evans in Appendix A of her work. As nearly as I can gather, the work is usually ascribed to Evax, a Latin writer living in the time of Tiberius, who is more properly its translator from the Greek.

DARDANUS: (1st century BC) Stoic philosopher who, along with Mnesarchus, stood at the head of the Stoic school at Athens. He was the contemporary of the Academic philosopher Antiochus of Ascalon.

DEIOTARUS (?116–40 BC) Tetrarch of Galatia who supported the Romans in their wars in Asia against Mithradates In reward Pompey gave him part of east Pontus in 64 BC, and the senate added Lesser Armenia and most of Galatia around 51 BC, conferring upon him the title of king. When Caesar gained power he was for a time deprived of his gifts and accused of insubordination. Cicero defended him successfully in 45 BC. After the death of Caesar, Deiotarus switched his alliance to Anthony, thereby regaining his territories. By deserting Anthony at just the right moment, and by the subsequent murder of a rival tetrarch, he gained all Galatia.

DEMOCRITUS: (?460–?355 BC) Greek philosopher born at Abdera (near the mouth of the present-day Nestos river) in Thrace. He is fabled to have blinded himself as an aid to meditation, but is best remembered as the exponent of the theory of atoms. Born into great wealth, he spent it all on his extensive travels and studies and died at the scarcely credible age of 105.

DIATHARUS: See Deiotarus.

DIODORUS SICULUS: (1st century BC) Greek historian about whom little is known. He was born at Agyrium in Sicily. Between 60–57 BC he traveled in Egypt and later lived at Rome. He states that he spent 30 years traveling over the greater part of Europe and Asia collecting materials for his work *Bibliotheca historica* (Historical library), but this boast is generally discounted. The *History,* in 40 books, covered a span from the earliest legends to the beginning of Caesar's Gallic war. It is full of repetitions and contradictions but is valuable because it preserves elements from earlier sources that are otherwise lost. Only the books 1–5 and 11–20 are extant, although fragments survive of the missing books. The first five books treat of the mythic history of the Egyptians, Assyrians, Ethiopians and Greeks.

DIOMEDES: Son of Tydeus and Deipyle, he was king of Argos. He sailed with 80 ships in the Greek expedition against Troy and was the bravest hero in the Greek army after Achilles. Along with his companion Odysseus he carried off the magical palladium from Troy. He was worshiped as a divine being in Italy, where his statues were erected at Thurii, Argypipa, Metapontum and other places.

DION CASSIUS COCCEIANUS: (?155–?235) Also called Dio Cassius, or more correctly Cassius Dio. Roman historian born at Nicaea in Bithynia, the son of a Roman senator, he received the best possible education and traveled with his father to Cilicia, which his father governed. After his father's death (about 180) he went to Rome and was made a senator, in which capacity he pleaded legal suits in the courts. In 194 he became praetor and was made governor of Pergamus and Smyrna in 218. Around 220, upon his return to Rome, he became consul, an office he was to hold a second time in 229. Shortly after this date he retired to Nicaea. The date of his death is not known with certainty. He wrote a biography of Arrian, a work on the dreams and portents of Septimius Severus (both lost), and a history of Rome in 80 books, of which books 36–54 are relatively intact. The rest exists only in fragments and an epitome.

DIONYSIUS: A man converted to Christianity by Paul in Athens "Howbeit certain men clave unto him and believed: among the which was Dionysius the Areopagite ..." (Acts 17: 34). A series of mystical theological writings conjectured to have been written by some unknown Christian Platonist and Gnostic of the 5th century were attributed to Dionysius and formed the basis for the mystical theology of Western monasticism. The works treat such matters as divine essence, angels, holy spirits, ceremonies, the priestly hierarchy, and so on. Their titles are *Concerning the Celestial Hierarchy, Concerning the Ecclesiastical Hierarchy, Concerning Divine Names* and *Concerning Mystic Theology.* A collection of ten letters is also attributed to him. It is from the first of these works that the familiar orders of angels derive, namely: Seraphim, Cherubim, Thrones, Dominations, Virtues, Powers, Principalities, Archangels and Angels. Christ is placed at the head of this hierarchy.

DIONYSIUS THE ELDER: (430–367 BC). Tyrant of Syracuse. He defeated the Carthaginians and subdued the Greek cities in Italy, making himself the most powerful Greek prior to the time of Alexander. He is said to have died from excessive feasting, but by some accounts his death was hastened by his medical attendants at the order of his son.

DIOSCORIDES: (1st century) Called Pedacius (or Pedanius). A Greek physician of Anazarba, in Cilicia (region around present-day Adana, southern Turkey) who served as a military surgeon for the armies of Nero. In 77–78 AD he compiled a work describing the virtues of more than 400 plants and drugs in five books, called *De materia medica.* It became the standard work on the subject into the 17th century. Much material on the magical virtues of stones is also included. Other works were attributed to Dioscorides, but these are likely spurious. The *Materia medica* was translated as *The Greek Herbal of Dioscorides ... Englished by John Goodyer* (1655).

ENNIUS, QUINTUS: (239–170 BC) An ancient Latin poet, born at Rudiae in Calabria. He was a Greek subject of Rome and served in the Roman army. In 204 BC he held the rank of centurion while fighting at Sardinia during the Second Punic War. Cato the Elder noticed him and took him back to Rome. Ennius claimed descent from Messapus, one of the legendary kings of his native land, and had a noble, proud and upright character which drew the admiration of the Romans. He quickly gained the friendship of the great men of the city, notably Scipio the Elder and Fulvius Nobilior. Through the influence of Nobilior's son, Ennius was made a citizen of Rome.

To earn a living he taught Greek to the wealthy Roman youths and translated and adapted Greek plays into Latin for the stage, mainly the tragedies of Euripides, but he was chiefly celebrated for his *Annales,* an epic narrative poem based on the Roman national destiny. It was this that won him the popular title mentioned by Horace, *alter Homerus* (a second Homer)—see *Horace* Epistles 2.1, line 50.

He was regarded as the father of Latin poetry. Only fragments of his works survive. Cicero remembers him in his final days with affection: "Yet at the age of seventy, Ennius, who lived this many years, carried the two burdens thought to be the most pressing, poverty and age, and bore them in such a way that he seemed to derive enjoyment from them" *(De senectate* 5 [Yonge])

EPICTETUS: (1st century AD) Stoic philosopher, a native of Hierapolis in Phrygia. He was a slave of Epaphroditus, a freedman and favorite of Nero. After Epaphroditus give him his freedom, he continued to live and teach in Rome until Domitian banished the philosophers from that city. He then settled in Nicopolis in Epirus. Although the Emperor Hadrian held him in high regard, he never returned to Rome. He is said to have been lame and to have resided at a humble cottage in Nicopolis, living in poverty until his death. More concerned with life than philosophy, he lived his convictions, and was so honored that his earthenware lamp

sold for 3,000 drachmas after his death. He wrote nothing down. Arrian, one of his students, compiled the *Enchiridion* from the lectures he gave as an old man and collected the lectures of Epictetus in eight books, four of which are unfortunately lost.

EPIMENIDES: (lived 600 BC) Surnamed the Expiator, this semi-mythical priest, prophet and poet was a native of Phaestus, Crete, but was more closely associated with the Cretan town of Cnossus. He is said to have slept in a cave for 57 years (Pausanias says 40), to have lived to the various ripe old ages of 154, 157 or 229 years, and to have purified Athens by magic rites when it suffered a plague around 596 BC. This last story may have some historical basis, and is related in one form by Plato:

> You have presumably heard of Epimenides, an inspired person born in this city [Cnossus—but see above] and connected with my own family, who visited Athens ten years before the Persian Wars at the bidding of the [Delphic] oracle, and offered certain sacrifices enjoined by the god [Apollo], besides telling the citizens, who were alarmed by the Persian preparations, that the enemy would not come within ten years, and when they did, would depart again with their purpose uneffected after receiving more damage than they inflicted. *(Laws* 1.642d–e [Hamilton and Cairns, 1242])

Plato's date (Persian wars, circa 500 BC) is about a century later than the date given by Aristotle, who links the plague with an attempt by the Athenian nobleman Cylon to seize political control of the state. Suidas makes the interesting claim that Epimenides could travel outside his own body. A few fragments of poetry attributed to Epimenides survive, but his many mystical writings are lost.

EUDAMUS: (4th century BC) Peripatetic philosopher, a native of Rhodes, one of Aristotle's most important pupils. He edited many of Aristotle's works, one of which bears his name. Simplicius called him the most genuine of Aristotle's companions.

EUDOXUS: (4th century BC) Born at Cnidus, an ancient Greek city in the southwestern corner of present-day Turkey, he was a celebrated physician, geometer, legislator and astronomer. He studied under Plato at Athens but was dismissed by his teacher and traveled to Egypt, where he spent 16 months with the priests of Heliopolis. After teaching physics for a time, he returned to Athens with pupils of his own and later in life established an astronomical observatory in his native city of Cnidus.

Strabo says that Eudoxus was the one who discovered that six hours must be added to the 365-day year; Vitravius credits Eudoxus with the invention of the sundial. Aristotle writes:

> Eudoxus thought pleasure was the good because he saw all things, both rational and irrational, aiming at it, and because in all things that which is the object of choice is what is excellent, and that which is most the object of choice the greatest good; ... His arguments were credited more because of the excellence of his character than for their own sake; he was thought to be remarkably self-controlled, and therefore it was thought that he was not saying what he did say as a friend of pleasure, but that the facts really were so. *(Nicomachean Ethics* 10.2.1172b, trans. W. D. Ross [McKeon, 1094])

Few of his writings have survived. The *Phaenomena* of Aratus is a poem based on an astronomical prose work of Eudoxus. Fragments of Eudoxus are preserved in the writings of the astronomer Hipparchus.

EUDOXUS GUIDIUS: See EUDOXUS OF CNIDUS.

EURIPIDES: (480–406 BC) Greek dramatic poet, born on the island of Salamis in the Saronic Gulf on the very day of the Greek naval victory over the Persian fleet of Xerxes, which took place in the strait between the island and the coast. Although the comic playwright Aristophanes represented Euripides' mother as an herb seller of doubtful honesty, there is no reason to believe he was not of noble birth. As a youth he was cupbearer at the Thargelian festi-

val, an office requiring noble blood. He studied rhetoric under Producus, who charged a large fee, and sought out highborn pupils.

An oracle predicted he would one day be crowned with sacred garlands. Misunderstanding, Euripides' father had the boy trained as an athlete. He won the Eleusinian and Thesean games, but was turned away from the Olympic games because of his youth. Losing interest in gymnastics, he tried painting with little success, then studied philosophy under Anaxagoras and became an intimate friend of Socrates. The first play to bear his name was produced in 455 BC, but it was not until 441 BC that he won first prize and fulfilled the oracle. He continued to exhibit plays until 408 BC, then left Athens to enjoy the hospitality of the court of King Archelaus.

The rumors told about the poet are of questionable value. He is said to have left Athens because of the unfaithfulness of his wife and the resulting ridicule that was showered upon his head; to have as a consequence hated all women; to have been profligate in his personal behavior, and to have been torn apart by dogs set upon him by envious rival poets. Euripides died in Macedonia at the court of his royal patron. He was the reputed author of 75 plays, of which 18 have survived.

EUSEBIUS: (?260–?340) Bishop of Caesarea and ecclesiastical historian, he called himself Eusebius Pamphili out of devotion to his teacher Pamphilus. Eusebius was born in Palestine. He attached himself to the theological school of Pamphilus in Caesarea, where he studied the Bible and the writings of Origen. When his teacher was killed during the Diocletian persecutions in 309, he fled to Tyre and later to Egypt. He became bishop of Caesarea between 313 and 315, and was offered the patriarchate of Antioch in 331 but declined to accept it.

The most learned man of his age, and a friend of the Emperor Constantine, Eusebius was a power for moderation in the Church during a period of fanatical division. His most notable works are the *Chronicon,* an ancient history; *Praeparatio evangelica,* containing many valuable extracts from classical writers; and *Ecclesiastical History,* containing the history of Christianity from the time of Christ to 324 AD.

EVAX: A name mentioned eight times in *The Book of Secrets,* seven of those times in company with Aaron. Reference is made to the *Book of Minerals* of Aaron and Evax. It may be conjectured that these two authors were bound under one cover. The name Evax was associated in some manuscripts as either author or translator of a 6th-century Latin work, *De virtutibus lapidum* (On the power of stones). He was also linked with a later lapidary in Latin verse by Marbod (1035–1123). See the biographical note on Damigeron.

FIRMANUS TARUTIUS: (1st century BC) Mathematician and astrologer who was a friend to Varro and a contemporary of Cicero. It was at Varro's request that he cast an inverse horoscope of Romulus, working backwards from events to find the date of birth and so also the time of Rome's founding.

FIRMIANUS: See FIRMANUS.

FLACCUS, C. FULVIUS: (2nd century BC) Appointed consul with P. Cornelius Scipio Africanus Aemilianus II in 134 BC, he immediately set out for Sicily to end the slave revolt, called the Servile War, while Africanus was engaged fighting in Spain. He was defeated by the slave leader, Eunus.

FRANCIS, SAINT: (1182–1226) Of Assisi, the founder of the Franciscan order of friars.

FRANCISCUS: See FRANCIS.

FULGENTIUS, FABIUS PLANCIADES: (late 5th century) Latin grammarian who was born and lived in northern Africa. Other than that he was a Christian with Neoplatonic inclinations, nothing much is known about him. Four works are extant under his name. The one to which Agrippa probably refers is *Mytholo-*

giarum libri III ad Catum Presbyterum, a mythology in three books dedicated to Catus, a presbyter of Carthage. It relates 75 myths in a brief form, then explains them allegorically according to the mystical doctrines of the Stoics and Neoplatonists.

GALEN, CLAUDIUS: (130–?200) Greek physician born at Pergamum, an important town that stood at Bergama in present-day Turkey. When he was 17 years old his father had a dream which caused him to train Galen as a physician. About 150 works were either written by him or attributed to him, causing Galen to be the single most influential writer on medicine of all time.

GEBER: (8th or 9th century) This author of a number of Latin works on alchemy is usually supposed to be the same as Abu Abdallah Jaber ben Hayyam (Haiyan) ben Abdallah al-Kufi, an Arab credited with a 10th-century Arab historical work, the *Kitab-al-Fihrish,* with 500 other treatises, with skill in the art of making gold and silver and with having prepared the fabled alchemical elixir. However, there is considerable doubt that the Latin works of Geber are translations from the Arab Jaber. M. P. E. Barthelot *(Chimie au Moyen Age,* Paris, 1893) was convinced that the treatises were at least Arabic, translations from between the 9th and 12th centuries.

The most famous of the Latin works is the *Summa perfectionis magisterii* (Sum of perfection) and the *De investigatione perfectionis* (Investigation into the perfection of metals). Also attributed to Geber are the *De inventione veritatis,* the *Liber fornacum,* the *Testamentum Geberi regis Indiae* and the *Alchemia Geberi.*

The notion that Geber was a native Sabaean of Harran in Mesopotamia comes from the article under his name by d'Herbelot in the *Bibliotheque Orientale.* The other opinion that he was a Spanish Moor is from a single reference made by Albertus Magnus to a Geber "of Seville," probably the Arabian Jabir ben Aflah, a native of 11th-century Seville who wrote on astronomy and trigonometry.

GELLIUS, AULUS: (2nd century) A Roman grammarian. He wrote *Noctes Atticae* (Athenian nights), so called because it was composed in a country house near Athens during the long nights of winter. It is a loose collection of extracts in 20 books from Greek and Roman writers on history, antiquity, philosophy and philology, with observations and remarks by Gellius. The eighth book has been lost, but the rest is extant.

GERMA: I find no reference to Germa the Babylonian. The term "Babylonian" seems to have been used by Agrippa as a synonym for "astrologer." In this sense it seems to be applied to Averrois in bk. II, ch. II. There was a town in Persia called Germabad.

GRACCHUS, TIBERIUS SEMPRONIUS: (2nd century BC) Roman tribune and consul best remembered for his quelling of the Sardinian revolution in 176 BC. He married Cornelia, daughter of P. Scipio Africanus the Elder, and had by her 12 children. His daughter, also named Cornelia, married P. Scipio Africanus the Younger.

GREGORY OF NAZIANZUS: (329–389) Surnamed Theologus, this Father of the Eastern Church was born at Nazianzus, Cappadocia. Inclined toward Christianity by his mother, he studied grammar, mathematics, rhetoric and philosophy at Athens and Alexandria, and was a disciple of Origen and Athanasius. He received baptism at his father's house in Nazianzus in 360 and sought a retired, contemplative life as a monk. But the violent doctrinal clash between the Arian and orthodox parties of the Church drew him in. In 372 he was nominated, against his will, bishop of Sasima, and around 378 he went to Constantinople to shore up the debilitated remnants of the orthodox party, a task he performed with zealousness and much success. The ascent of Theodosius in 380 insured the triumph of his cause. Shortly thereafter he retired to a quiet life of literary composition, which at last he was permitted to enjoy. His works consist of poems, epistles and orations.

GREGORY THE GREAT, SAINT: (?540–604) Born in Rome of a wealthy family, he received the finest available education and excelled in grammar, rhetoric and dialectic. He began a political career and was prefect of Rome in 573, but shortly thereafter abandoned public life, used his wealth to establish six monasteries in Sicily and one in Rome, then retired into the last as a monk. In 578 he was sent as Church ambassador to the court at Constantinople, and in 586 became abbot of the monastery of St. Andrew.

At the death of Pelagius II in 590, Gregory was elected pope, very much against his will. He was the first monk to become pope, and may be called the first of the medieval popes because it was through his initiative that the papacy gained its great political power. Severe against pagans, heretics and clergy who violated the rule of the Church, he was uncharacteristically lenient with the Jews. His background as a monk made him highly supportive of monastic life, and he was accused of depleting the Church coffers with excessive charity to the needy. Nonetheless, under his skillful management the wealth of the Church increased and the power of the papacy was established.

GULIELMUS: See WILLIAM OF PARIS.

HADRIANUS, PUBLIUS AELIUS: (76–138) Better known as Hadrian, he was born at Italica in Hispania Baetica (some say at Rome). When he was about ten years old his father died, and he was placed under the care of his relative, Ulpius Trajanus, afterwards the Emperor Trajan. He spent five years at Rome, then embarked on a military career in Spain, but was soon recalled to Rome by his guardian, who appointed him to a succession of political posts.

Trajan had some doubts about Hadrian because of reports of his extravagance, but after becoming emperor, he was brought to think more highly of his young protege by his wife, the Empress Plotina, who arranged a marriage for Hadrian with Vibia Sabina, Trajan's great-niece. In 101 Hadrian was quaestor, in 105 tribune and in 106 praetor. He served with distinction in several military campaigns and held significant political posts in different parts of the Empire. Trajan was grooming Hadrian to be his successor, and when in 117 Trajan died, Plotina concealed the news of his death long enough to arrange a posthumous adoption of Hadrian by Trajan to insure his attainment of the throne. This was hardly necessary. Hadrian was acclaimed by the army and the senate.

His subsequent reign was one of the happiest times in Roman history. Rather than trying to extend the Empire by war, he strengthened its boundaries and improved its public works and social structures. He continued the tradition of building begun by Augustus and carried on by Trajan. Yet he could be grave or gay, cruel or gentle, mean or generous, impulsive or cautious, affectionate or mistrustful as the mood struck him. More feared than loved, he was highly intelligent, of strong and warped passions and grossly superstitious. With all his personal faults, he presided over a Golden Age of Rome and left enduring monuments to his energy and genius.

HAMA, RABBI: See HAMAI.

HAMAI, RABBI: (late 12th century) Commonly called Hamai Gaon, the pseudonym of a Kabbalist said to belong to the school of Isaac the Blind, who flourished around 1200. Two works on the Kabbalah that bear his name are *Sepher ha-Yihud,* "probably on the Tetragrammaton" *(Jewish Encyclopedia),* and *Safer ha-'Iyyun,* on the existence and unity of God.

HELENA, FLAVIA JULIA: (?247–?327) Christian saint, the mother of Constantine the Great. She was born at Drepanum, a town on the Gulf of Nicomedia (eastern end of the Sea of Marmara, Turkey), which her son later renamed Helenopolis in her honor. Legend credits her with the discovery both of the sepulchre of Christ and the true cross at Jerusalem. This fable arose because Constantine was the first Christian ruler to make extensive use of the cross as a symbol. Her body was said to reside at the abbey of Hautvilliers near Reims, which

was the center of her cult, but she was also popular in England. She is depicted in royal robes wearing a crown and carrying variously a model of the holy sepulchre, a large cross and the three nails that transfixed Christ. The festival of Saint Helena is August 18.

HENINA, RABBI: Various rabbis with this name are mentioned in the *Talmud, Midrash, Zohar* and Jewish folktales, notably Rav Hanina, who with Rav Oshaya "sat every Sabbath eve and studied the *Sepher Y'tzira* (Book of Creation), and created for themselves a three-year-old calf, which they then ate" (from the *Talmud,* as given by Patai 1980, 239).

HERACLITUS: (?540–?475 BC) Greek philosopher born at Ephesus of noble parents. Little is known of the events of his life. He declined the office of chief magistrate, which was his by right, giving it to his brother. It is evident that he held considerable political power—he compelled the usurper Melancomas to abdicate, and from time to time intervened in the affairs of Ephesus. However, he was by nature arrogant, sullen and solitary, his behavior earning him the nickname "he who rails at the people." He was also called the "Weeping Philosopher" and the "Dark Philosopher." Late in life he retired into the mountains and lived as a hermit on herbs, but was driven down to the city with sickness and soon after died.

Founded in the Ionic school, his philosophy is surprisingly modern. He held that all things are in a state of constant flux and becoming; that the senses are "bad witnesses" because they convey the fiction of a static universe and so cannot be trusted; that all things grow by a kind of condensation from a clear, fluid, primordial fire; and that true freedom is only attained by the subordination of the individual to the harmony of cosmic law. The single work of his that has survived is *On Nature,* which expresses his views. Fragments have also been preserved in the writings of later Greek philosophers such as Plato.

HERMANNUS OF WIED: (1477–1552) Educated by his father, Frederick, Count of Wied, for the Church, he became elector and archbishop of Cologne in 1515. At first hostile to the Protestant reform raging in Europe at the time, a dispute with the papacy changed his alliance, and he henceforth sought to bring about orderly reform from within the clergy, setting the example with reforms in his own diocese in 1536. When his efforts failed, he invited Martin Bucer, a friend of Luther, to Cologne in 1542. However, the victory of the Emperor Charles over William, Duke of Cleves, and the hostility of the citizens of Cologne ended the effort of Bucer. Hermann was summoned before the Emperor and Pope Paul III in 1546, deposed, and excommunicated. He returned to Weid, where he lived out his life.

HERMIPPUS: (2nd century BC) A native of Smyrna, this Greek Peripatetic philosopher and historian was a disciple of Callimachus of Alexandria, and is remembered chiefly for his biographical writings. He wrote a monograph on the *Disciples of Isocrates,* and is mentioned by Athenaeus.

HERODOTUS: (484–?425 BC) Greek historian born at Halicarnassus in Asia Minor to a prominent family. He traveled widely between 464-447 BC. In 457 BC he left Halicarnassus to escape the tyranny of Lygdamis and made his place of residence Samos, thus shifting his alliance from Persia to Greece. He helped ferment a rebellion against Lygdamis, and when Halicarnassus declared itself a member of the Athenian confederacy, Herodotus returned to his native town for a short while. In 447 BC the political climate changed again, and he went to live at Athens. His literary work was so well received by the Athenians, they voted him the large sum of ten talents in recognition of its merit. Ever restless, in 444 BC he sailed with the Athenian colonists to the new town of Thurii in Lucania, Italy. Little is known of the rest of his life. About 430 BC he revisited Athens, but he spent most of his time working on his great book, which earned him the title Father of History.

HESIOD: (8th century BC) Greek poet born in Ascra in Boeotia. He wrote *Works and Days* and the *Theogony.* Hesiod represents the Boeotian school of poetry, which was simple and didactic, as opposed to the Ionic school, represented by Homer, which was heroic.

HIERONYMUS, EUSEBIUS SOPHRONIUS: (?340–420) Better known as Saint Jerome. He was born at Strido, a town on the border of Dalmatia and Pannonia (present-day northwestern Yugoslavia), of Christian parents. He went to Rome, where he studied philosophy law, grammar and rhetoric, then traveled widely. At Antioch a serious illness changed his life. He had been very fond of the classics, but vowed to God that henceforth he would renounce them in favor of the Scriptures.

Adopting the life of a hermit at Chalcis in 374, he began to study Hebrew. This eventually led to his translation of the Scriptures, which became the Vulgate edition of the Bible used by the Roman Church. In 382 he was called to Rome by Pope Damasus to help in a theological dispute then raging at Antioch. The ladies of Rome were attracted to him and flocked to hear his teaching, which raised the ire of their male relations.

When Damasus died in 384, Jerome thought it expedient to leave Rome and travel east. The women followed him, determined to become nuns. With the money of Paula, a wealthy widow, he erected three nunneries and a monastery at Bethlehem. All the while he vehemently protested that he took no money or gifts, did not delight in fine silks or sparkling gems or gold ornaments, and was unmoved by the ladies except when they distinguished themselves by fasting and penitence.

At the end of his life he became embroiled in another Church controversy, and so inflamed his opponents that they attacked his monastery with force of arms. Jerome fled and hid himself for two years in fear of his life. He returned to Bethlehem in 418 but died two years later after a lingering illness. Jerome seems to have been devoid of the piety that marked so many of the Church Fathers. Luther said of him, "He teaches nothing either about faith, or love, or hope, or the works of faith."

HILARIUS: See HILARY.

HILARY, SAINT: (?300–367) Bishop of Pictavium (Poitiers) and an eminent doctor of the Western Church, he was called *malleus Arianorum* (hammer of the Arians) and the "Athanasius of the West." Born in Poitiers of an eminent family, he received an excellent education for the time, including some Greek. His study of the Bible texts caused him to abandon Neoplatonism for Christianity. In 353, although still married, he was elected bishop of Poitiers and at once secured the excommunication of the Arian bishop of Arles. For the rest of his life he kept up a vigorous campaign against Arianism, although at times he was accused by members of the orthodox faction of being too lenient in his doctrinal attacks on the Arians (demonstrating the rabid fanaticism of the time).

HILDEGARDES: (1098–1179) Daughter of the Count of Spanheim, she had revelations which the Holy Ghost told her to write down in a book. The book was shown to Pope Eugenius III, who had it investigated by the bishop of Verdun and St. Bernard of Clairvaux. The Church found the revelations to be genuine. They eventually filled three volumes, and the saint also wrote numerous other mystical works and 145 letters to various divines and rulers. Of her revelations, she says:

> From infancy to the present day, being now seventy years old, I have received without cessation visions and divine revelations. In these divine communications I seem to be carried away through the air to regions far, far away, and I see in my mind's eye the marvels shown to me. I do not see them with my bodily eyes, nor hear what is said by my bodily ears, nor do I discover them by the agency of any of my bodily senses, nor do they come into my thoughts, nor are they dreams, or trances, or ecstasies; but I see them with my eyes open, while I am awake, sometimes in the night, and sometimes by day. What I see, I see in my soul; and what I hear, I hear in my inner self. (quoted by Brewer 1901, 324)

HILDEGARDIS: See HILDEGARDES.

HIPPARCHUS: (?190–?120 BC) Greek astronomer born at Nicaea in Bithynia (present-day Iznik, Turkey). He introduced many bold innovations, including a method of representing the heavens on a plane, the notion of longitude and latitude in terrestrial geography, and the use of a table of chords similar to sines. His practical observations were much more accurate than those of his predecessors, allowing him to discover the precession of the equinoxes, the distance of the Sun and Moon from Earth, the exact length of the lunar month, and to compile a catalogue of more than 850 stars, which has been preserved in the *Almagest* of Ptolemy. Unfortunately all his writings are lost except *In eudoxi et Arati Phænomena,* a commentary on the *Phæmonena* of Aratus.

HIPPOCRATES: (?460–?375 BC) The most famous historical Greek physician, called the Father of Medicine, was born on the island of Cos (now Kos) in the Aegean Sea. Of the family of the Asclepiadae, he was said to be a direct descendant not only of Aesculapius, but of Hercules as well on his mother's side. His father, Heraclides, and the physician Herodicus of Selymbria trained him in medicine. Gorgias and Democritus taught him philosophy. He traveled widely and practiced his healing art at Athens, and perhaps also at Thrace, Thessaly, Delos and Cos at various times. It was at Larissa in Thessaly that he died in old age—precisely how old in not known. Ages of 85, 90, 104 and 109 are variously attributed to him at his death. Of these, the first seems most probable.

Both Plato and Aristotle make reference to him. Legend credits him with ending a plague at Athens by burning bonfires throughout the city. Descended from a line of priest-healers, he was the first to separate medicine from religion, and from philosophy also, introducing in their place natural remedies and practical observation.

Eighty-seven works pass under his name. Of these, perhaps as many as a dozen may be genuine. Some authorities believe that none were actually written by Hippocrates, but that some may have been composed by his descendants.

HIPPONAX: (lived 540 BC) This Greek poet and inventor of parody was born at Ephesus. When he was expelled from his native city by tyrants, he went to live at Clazomenae. A short, ugly, but powerful man, he became the object of ridicule of the brothers Bupalus and Athenis, who made a grotesque statue depicting him. In retaliation Hipponax skewered the sculptors in his satirical poetry, and is said (by Suidas) to have driven them to suicide. Hipponax turned his caustic wit on everyone—his fellow Ionians, his own parents, even the gods. Only fragments of his works survive. There was a philosopher of Samos of the same name, usually called Hippon to distinguish him from the poet.

HOMER: (9th century BC) Greek poet who is credited with the epics *Iliad* and *Odyssey*. No one really knows where or when he was born, but he is thought to have lived before Hesiod, and Smyrna (present-day Izmir in Turkey) is the most plausible of the seven ancient cities that claimed his origin. Legend says he was blind and poor. The 33 *Homeric Hymns* were not written by Homer but by the followers of his style, who were called Homerids. The Greeks once studied Homer with the same fervor that Calvinists used to read the Bible. He is the most influential poet of all time.

HORAPOLLO NILOUS: (c. 400 AD) The name is a combination of Horus and Apollo. Nilous may refer to the city of Middle Egypt or to the Nile itself. A Greek grammarian who lived in Egypt during the reign of Theodosius I (378–395). According to Suidas, he wrote commentaries on Sophocles, Alcaeus and Homer, and a work on places consecrated to the gods. Photius ascribes to him a history on the foundation of the city of Alexandria and its antiquities and calls him a dramatist. A work that carries his name, the *Hieroglyphics,* in two books, professes to be a translation from the Egyptian into Greek by Philippus, about whom nothing is known. Its genuineness has been questioned, and it has been assigned by some a date as late as the 15th century—however, by intrinsic evidence, it seems to convey a living tradition of the hieroglyphic symbols. It was much studied during the Renaissance as a source for mystical emblems.

HRABANUS MAURUS MAGENTIUS: (?776–856) Also called Rabanus, or Rhabanus, and sometimes incorrectly referred to as Saint Rabanus. Archbishop of Mainz who was born at Mainz of noble parents. He went to school at Fulda where he received his deacon's orders in 801, then studied at Tours under Alcuin, who named him Maurus after Saint Maur. From 804–14 he ran the school at Fulda with great skill, and composed his *Excerptio* of the grammar of Priscian, which became a standard medieval textbook. Ordained priest in 814, he became abbot at Fulda in 822 and served in this capacity for 20 years, at which time he tried to retire from public life. The retirement was short-lived—in 847 he was persuaded to become archbishop of Mainz, where he continued until his death. His works are numerous and include commentaries on the Scriptures and the *De institutione clericorum,* in which he expounds on the views of Augustine and Gregory the Great concerning clerical duties.

HYGINIUS: See HYGINUS.

HYGINUS: Nothing is known about the life of this writer. He is sometimes confused with the grammarian Gaius Julius Hyginus, who was a freedman of Caesar Augustus, but must have lived much later. He wrote two extant works: *Fabularum liber,* a series of short mythological legends with an introductory genealogy of divinities; and *Poeticon astronomicon libri IV.* It is the latter which contains the descriptions of constellations referred to by Agrippa in ch. XXVII, bk. II.

IAMBLICHUS: (4th century) According to his biographer, Eunapius, this Neoplatonic philosopher was born at Chalcis in Coele-Syria into a wealthy and prominent family and studied philosophy first under Anatolius, then under Porphyry. He gathered together many disciples from diverse nations and lived with them at

Chalcis in fraternal brotherhood, perhaps in an attempt to emulate the brotherhood of Pythagoras. By his contemporaries he was credited with miraculous powers, but Iamblichus himself denied this claim.

The Emperor Julian considered him the intellectual equal of Plato and said that he would give all the gold in Lydia for one epistle of Iamblichus. Most of his writings have been lost. What remains is five books of a greater work in ten books on Pythagorean philosophy, the first book of which is a biography of Pythagoras; and *On the Mysteries of the Egyptians, Chaldeans, and Assyrians,* which Proclus attributed to Iamblichus and which is certainly of his school. Iamblichus died during the reign of Constantine—according to Fabricius, before 333 AD.

IARCHAS: Leader of the Brahmans of India, who entertained Apollonius of Tyana on his journey through that country and initiated him by the "waters of Tantalus." When first he gave audience to Apollonius, Iarchas was seated on a lofty throne made of black bronze decorated with golden images. He proceeded to relate to Apollonius details of his family background and incidents of his travels that he had gained through his power of occult foresight. He confided to Apollonius that in a previous life he had been a king, and in the course of the sage's visit, performed various miracles such as driving out a demon that possessed a man, restoring sight to the blind and mobility and use to the lame. Before the departure of Apollonius, Iarchas gave him seven magic rings named after the seven planets, which Apollonius thereafter wore one at a time variously on the corresponding days of the week.

IAMBLICUS: See IAMBLICHUS.

IBN GABIROL, SOLOMON BEN JUDAH: (?1021–?1058) Jewish poet and philosopher born at Malaga, a town on the south coast of Spain. His parents died when he was a child. He was supported by Samuel ha-Nagid (or Nagdilah), prime minister of Spain and patron of the arts, with whom he frequently quarreled. At 16

he was already composing poems and was the first to popularize Arab poetic meters in Hebrew. His poetry is romantic in style and approach. The schoolmen of the 12th century knew him as Avicebron (also Avencebrol and Avicebrol) through the Latin translation of his philosophical work, *Fons vitae* (Fountain of life), which investigates the nature of created beings, the divine will and the intellect from the perspective of Neoplatonism, while exhibiting Kabbalistic overtones. This work influenced the philosophy of Duns Scotus.

ION: (5th century BC) The rhapsodist, or singer of poems, of Ephesus (ancient town on the Gulf of Kusada, eastern coast of Turkey). He was a contemporary of Socrates, and Plato uses him as a foil for the wit of the elder philosopher in his dialogue of the same title.

IRENAEUS: (2nd century AD) Bishop of Lyons, he was born around 130 at or near Smyrna in Asia Minor. Little is known of his early life. In 177 he was a presbyter of the church at Lyons. In that year or the next he traveled to Rome to plead for the Montanist sect, and upon his return became bishop of Lyons. Gregory of Tours says that in a short time he had converted all Lyons to Christianity (*Historia Francorum* 1.29). His moderation in dealing with various sects justified his name *Eirenaios* (Peacemaker). His main work, *Against the Heresies,* has survived intact in a Latin translation from the original Greek. It was produced around 180 and consists of five books. The first two describe and criticize heretical sects and the last three set forth Irenaeus' views on true Christianity. Gregory of Tours described his martyrdom under Septimius Severus (ruled 193–211), but the date of his death is uncertain.

ISAAC OF HOLLAND: (early 15th century) An alchemist who worked with his son on the manufacture of enamels and artificial gems. Paracelsus attached value to his researches. Isaac wrote two books: *De triplici ordine elixiris et lapidis theoria* and *Opera mineralia Joannis Isaaci Hollandi, sive de lapide philo-*

sophico. The latter is said to be the more important, setting forth with illustrations the method of changing base metal into *Sol* and *Luna*.

ISAAICK THE JEW: See ISAAC OF HOLLAND. It is also possible that, for "Isaac the Jew," Agrippa intends Isaac Ben Solomon Israeli, a medical writer and philosopher.

JAMBLICHUS: See IAMBLICHUS.

JAMBLICUS: See IAMBLICHUS.

JANUARIUS, SAINT: (late 2nd century) Also called San Gennaro. The patron saint of Naples. He is reputed to have been bishop of Benevento and to have suffered a martyr's death on September 19, 309. During the persecution of Diocletian and Maximian he was cast into a furnace by Timotheus, governor of Campania, but emerged unharmed. Undaunted, Timotheus threw him to the wild beasts in the arena. The beasts fawned at the saint's feet. When the governor again sentenced Januarius to death he was struck blind. The mercy of the saint restored his sight. However Timotheus was determined to see the end of this most resilient adversary and had him beheaded by the sword.

Centuries later when the relics of the saint were carried to Naples, Mount Vesuvius immediately stopped erupting. Various other charming fables are related about Januarius, but he is best known for the miracle of the liquefaction of his dried blood, preserved in two glass vessels in the church of Saint Gennaro, along with the head of the saint, which was donated by Charles II, duke of Anjou, in 1036. I cannot resist repeating an amusing anecdote related by Brewer:

> When Murat was king of Naples the blood would not liquify; whereupon the Frenchman planted two cannons opposite St. Gennaro and told the bishop he would blow the church to pieces unless he performed the "miracle." The bishop protested it could not be done; but seeing that Murat was in earnest, he produced the liquefaction as usual. (Brewer 1901, 184)

JARCHUS BRACHMANUS: See IARCHAS.

JEROME: See HIERONYMUS.

JOACHIM OF FLORIS: (?1145–1202) He was so called after the monastery of San Giovonni Fiore, of which he was abbot. While visiting holy places in Constantinople as a young man, his companions were killed by plague. This impelled him to adopt a devout and ascetic life as a monk. In 1177 he was abbot of the monastery of Corazzo near Martirano, but he left to found his own "ordo Florensis" with the help and approval of Pope Innocent III.

He was an extreme ascetic and mystic by nature who wrote a large number of prophetical works proclaiming three ages of the world, that of the Father, the Son, and the Spirit, the latter due to begin in the year 1260. His real influence began after his death, when innumerable commentators and followers of his works sprang up. They were called Spirituals and proclaimed St. Francis as the initiator of Joachim's Age of Spirit. In 1260 a council at Arles condemned Joachim's writings and his followers, but his supporters persisted. Joachim was held in high regard by such men as Roger Bacon, Arnaldus de Villa Nova, and Dante.

JOVIANUS: See JOVINIANUS.

JOVINIANUS: (late 4th century) Roman monk. All that is known about him is contained in St. Jerome's attack upon his heterodox opinions, *Adversum Jovinianum Libri II* (393), which says Jovinianus was living a pious and ascetic life at Rome in 388 when he underwent a heretical change of view and became a sensualist and an Epicurean. He was condemned by a Roman synod under Bishop Siricius in 390, and later excommunicated at Milan. Writing in 406, Jerome said Jovinianus was no longer alive. The only crime of Jovinianus seems to have been his dislike of the fanatical asceticism of his century. He should not be confounded with the Roman emperor of the same name, who died some four decades earlier.

JUDAS MACCABAEUS: (2nd century BC) The first great leader of the Maccabaean revolt against the attempt by Antiochus IV, surnamed Epiphanes, king of Syria (ruled 175–164 BC), to force Greek religion down the throats of the Jews. The revolt began in 168 BC when Mattathias, the father of Judas, refused to offer pagan sacrifice on the altar. Forced to flee into the hills with his five sons, he soon drew a large band of rebels around him. When he died in 166 BC, Judas took his place.

Not thinking the Jewish revolt of any importance, Antiochus Epiphanes took an army into Persia to raise tax money, and ordered his second in command, Lysias, to subdue Judaea, take its inhabitants for slaves and level Jerusalem. There followed a stunning series of defeats for Lysias and his handpicked noble-born generals. For example, in 165 BC Judas defeated a force of 60,000 footmen and 5,000 horsemen under the hapless Lysias with only 10,000 rebels.

Meanwhile, things were not going well for Antiochus in Persia. He tried to loot a rich temple of Diana in the city of Elymais. To his surprise the Persians resisted. When finally he lifted his siege they pursued his retreating army and decimated it. About this time the king got word of events in Judaea. The double shock brought on an illness that killed him.

Antiochus V, called Eupator (ruled 164–162 BC) ascended the throne while still a boy of nine, under the guardianship of Lysias, and immediately determined to attack Judaea and avenge his father's humiliation. In this he was more successful than Lysias and handed Judas a rare defeat. The young king laid siege to the temple of Jerusalem, where Judas kept up a stout resistance. Running low on provisions, however, the king made a peace with the rebels and hastened away to defend his crown against the pretender Philip, who had been one of his father's generals in Persia.

Judas died in battle against the superior force of Bacchides, the general of Demetrius Soter who assumed power in 162 BC and ruthlessly put both Lysias and the 11-year-old Antiochus to the sword.

JULIAN THE APOSTATE: (331–363) Roman emperor, the nephew of Constantine the Great. He was born at Constantinople and traveled to Athens in 355, where he studied Greek literature and philosophy. Later that same year he was given the title Caesar by the Emperor Constantius and sent to fight the Germans in Gaul. He had great success and won the love of his troops. At Paris in 360 they proclaimed him emperor.

Constantius marched against Julian in 361 but died en route in Cilicia, leaving Julian undisputed leader of the Empire. He at once proclaimed his apostasy from the Christian faith and declared himself a pagan. Nonetheless, he tolerated Christianity with an even hand and would perhaps not be so reviled by early Christian writers if he had not allowed the Jews to rebuild the temple at Jerusalem. In 362 he crossed the Tigris to make war against Persia, but was fatally wounded by an arrow and died on the battlefield.

His writings include the *Orations,* the *Letters,* a satire against the Caesars called *The Banquet,* and a satire against Antioch called *Misopogon.* His work *Against the Christians* is lost.

JUSTIN MARTYR: (?114–?165) This early Father of the Church was born in Flavia Neapolis in Samaria (modern-day Nablus in Jordan) of pagan parents and grew up with the study of Greek philosophy. By his own account he underwent a kind of mystical conversion when, while meditating by himself in a vacant field by the sea one day, he looked around and discovered a mysterious old man walking behind him. They began to talk philosophy, and the old man, using a method of argument not unlike that of Socrates, convinced Justin that philosophical knowledge was vain and that true knowledge was to be gained through the prophets of Christ.

> When he had spoken these and many other things, which there is no time for mentioning at present, he went away, bidding me attend to them; and I have not seen him since. But straightway a flame was kindled in my soul; and a love of the prophets, and

of those men who are friends of Christ, possessed me; and whilst revolving his words in my mind, I found this philosophy alone to be safe and profitable. *(Dialogue of Justin with Trypho, a Jew* 8 [*Ante-Nicene Christian Library,* 2:96])

He retained his philosopher's cloak and wandered about seeking converts to the Christian faith, staying a long while in Rome, where he established his own school. The pagan philosophers received him unfavorably, and his disciple Tatian goes so far as to assert that one of these, the Cynic philosopher Crescentius, was the one who brought the accusation against Justin that resulted in his martyrdom.

The most significant of his extant works are his *First* and *Second Apology,* the *Dialogue with Trypho* and the *Discourse* and *Hortatory Address* to the Greeks.

KIRAMIDES: See *Kiranus.*

KIRANUS: Or Cyranus, the supposed author of a book that is mentioned as a source in the first paragraph of *The Book of Secrets* and appears to have been well known in ancient times. Thorndike describes it as "a book of uncertain date and authorship, usually called the *Kiranides* of Kiranus, King of Persia" (Thorndike 1929, 2:46:229). The book appeared in English translation in 1685 under the title *The Magick of Kirani King of Persia, and of Harpocration.*

LACTANTIUS, LUCIUS COELIUS FIRMI-ANUS: (lived 300 AD) There is much confusion in manuscripts over the true form of his name. Coecilius is often given in place of Coelius, and the last two names are frequently inverted. A Father of the Church, born in Africa (or perhaps Italy at Firmum) around 260, he studied in Africa under Arnobius and taught rhetoric at Sicca, where his fame became so great he was invited by Diocletian to settle at Nicomedia. About the start of the 4th century he became a Christian and was invited by Constantine to Treves in Gaul around 310 to tutor his son, Crispus. He died around 330 or 340 at Treves.

A better stylist than theologian, his writings were attacked for containing unintentional heresy. His major work is *Divinatum institutionum* in seven books, an introduction to Christianity. He also wrote *De opificio dei sive de formatione hominis,* a pre-Christian work demonstrating the providence of God from the adaptability and beauty of the human body; *De ira dei,* a tract against Epicurianism; and *De mortibus persecutorum,* in which are described God's judgments of those who persecuted the Church. This last was very popular, and served as a model for many other writers.

LAZARILLUS: SEE LAZZARELLI.

LAZZARELLI, LUDOVICO: (?1450–?1500) A poet from San Severino, near Naples, who became a disciple of the wandering magician and prophet Giovanni Mercurio. He called himself "Lodovicus Enoch Lazarellus Septempedanus, once a poet but now by new rebirth the son of true wisdom" (Thorndike, 6:44:438). In his *Letter of Enoch* he describes how his master Giovanni Mercurio rode on horseback through the streets of Rome on April 11, 1484, wearing a crown of thorns, and how Giovanni was later examined before the college of cardinals.

Lazzarelli studied alchemy under John Richard de Branchiis of Burgundy, who began to instruct him in 1495. His *Tractatus de alchimia* contains his own treatise on alchemy, an alchemical sonnet, a secret recipe for the elixir invented by his teacher John Richard in 1494 at Sienna, a treatise by Raymond Lull and various chemical tables. He is best remembered for his *Crater Hermetis,* a dialogue of mystical rebirth that was edited and published by Jacques Lafevre d'Etaples at Paris in 1505 together with the *Pimander* and *Asclepius.* The *Crater* was reprinted in 1522, and in French translation in 1557.

The dates of birth and death given above come from Francisco Lancillotti, writing in 1765, and should be regarded only as approximations. It appears Lazzarelli may have lived some years into the following century.

LINUS: The mythic personification of a type of Greek dirge, or song of lamentation, mentioned by Homer. Of Semitic origin, the name derives from the words *ai lanu* (woe to us). Various stories grew up around the name.

Linus was said to be a beautiful youth, similar in type to Hyacinthus and Adonis, fond of rural life, the secret child of a muse (Calliope, Psamathe or Chalciope) and Apollo, who was exposed to die, was nourished by sheep, and finally torn apart by dogs. Pausanius relates this legend without naming the child in his *Guide to Greece* 1.43.5. A little farther on in the same work he gives another version, this time naming the hero: "The legend is that Linos is the son of Urania and Amphimaros, son of Poseidon, and the most glorious musician of his own or any earlier age, but Apollo murdered Linos for rivalling his singing" (ibid. 9.29.3 [Levi, 1:369]). Another legend relates that Linos was the music teacher of Herakles and was killed by his pupil when Linos rebuked him. This is mentioned by Pausanius (9.29.3) and also by Apollodorus *(Bibliotheca* 2.4.9).

Linus was said to have been the inventor of musical methods, the composer of prophecies and legends, and to have adapted the Phoenician letters introduced by Cadmus to the Greek language. He may generally be regarded as one of the many dying gods of vegetation.

LIVIA DRUSILLA: (?57 BC–29 AD) She was a woman of great beauty and political acumen. She married Tiberius Claudius Nero and had two sons by him, the future emperor Tiberius and Drusus, with whom she was six months pregnant when she divorced her first husband to marry Caesar Augustus in 38 BC. She is reputed to have poisoned two grandsons of Augustus to clear the way for Tiberius—and even to have dispatched Augustus himself. When Tiberius became emperor she tried to control the government but found her son stronger of will than she had calculated. He drove her from public affairs and exhibited a cold hatred toward her. When she lay on her deathbed he would not visit her, took no part in her funeral rites and forbad her consecration when the senate proposed it,

thereby demonstrating that he was not completely devoid of religious feeling.

LIVIUS ANDRONICUS: (?284–?204 BC) The earliest Roman poet and dramatist was by birth a Greek of Tarentum. When the Romans captured his city in 272 BC he was carried to Rome a slave and entered into the household of M. Livius Salinator, from whom he gained the Latin portion of his name. Later he gained a living by teaching Greek and Latin, having perfected his second tongue, and by translating Greek works such as the *Odyssey*. When he produced a Greek play in Latin in the year 240 BC, it changed the course of Roman drama, effectively killing the form that was native to Rome. He continued to produce Greek plays and to act in them, for 30 years. Cicero and Horace had no very high opinion of his talents, and he seems to have lacked originality. However, he set the pattern for Plautus, Ennius and all other Latin writers of comedies and tragedies, insuring that Roman drama would never be more than a pale shadow of the Greek.

LIVIUS, TITUS: (59 BC–17 AD) Better known as Livy, this Roman historian was born at Patavium (present-day Padua). He spent most of his life at Rome, where his literary talent secured him the patronage of the Emperor Augustus. It was Livy who induced the Emperor Claudius to try his hand at historical writing. Livy married and fathered at least two children, a son and a daughter. Toward the end of his life he returned to Patavium, where he died. During his lifetime he enjoyed considerable political power at court and great personal fame, but the only work of his that has survived is his *History of Rome,* which Livy himself called the *Annales,* in 142 books extending from the foundation of the city of Rome to the death of Drusus in 9 BC. Thirty-five books have survived intact; all but two of the others are represented by reliable epitomes.

LOMBARD, PETER: (?1100–?1160) Better known in the Middle Ages as *Magister Sententiarum* (Master of the Sentences). He was born in Novara of obscure parents and educated at Bologna. Traveling to France with only a letter of recommendation, he eventually established himself as a teacher in Paris and got a chair of theology in the cathedral school of St. Victor. In 1159 he became bishop of Paris, and probably continued in this post until his death, although there is some question as to his removal on a charge of simony—the selling of spiritual things, such as indulgences.

His great work *Sententiarum libri quatuor* is a collection of the opinions of the Church Fathers. The first book treats of God; the second of the created universe; the third of the incarnation, work of redemption, and virtues; and the fourth of the seven sacraments and eschatology. It was extraordinarily popular and became the standard theological school text, giving rise to numerous commentaries—more than 180 in England alone.

LUCANUS, M. ANNAEUS: (39–65) Better known as Lucan, this Roman poet was born in Corduba (now Cordova) in Spain. He traveled to Rome at an early age and studied under the best teachers, soon displaying precocious talent that awakened the jealousy of Nero, who forbad him to recite his poetry. Lucan first plotted against the Emperor, then basely turned informer on promise of pardon and denounced his own mother along with the others of the conspiracy. Nero proved that he was equally base by ordering Lucan's death in betrayal of his word. The only extant work of this poet is the *Pharsalia*, which describes the struggle between Caesar and Pompey in ten books. It is unfinished.

LUCAS PACIOLUS: (late 15th century) Also known as Lucas de Burgo, an Italian Minorite friar and mathematician who was a close friend of Leonardo da Vinci, and traveled with him in 1499 from Milan to Venice, where they occupied themselves with mathematical studies before moving on to Florence. Paciolus' principal work is *Summa de arithmetica geometria proportioni et proportionalita*, published in 1494. It is noteworthy for its systematic use of

symbols and was strongly influenced by another Leonardo—Leonardo of Pisa, an Italian mathematician who lived some three centuries earlier. Paciolus also wrote a treatise on accounting, published at Venice in 1495.

LUCRETIUS, CARUS: (?95–?51 BC) Roman poet, the author of *On the Nature of Things,* published around 56 BC, in which he derides superstition and expounds on the natural world. Not much is known of his life. According to an account in the additions made by St. Jerome to the *Eusebian Chronicle,* he was driven mad by a love potion and composed the poem during his lucid periods, committing suicide in his 44th year. However, this story may be a libel.

LULLIE: See LULLY.

LULLY, RAYMOND: (?1235–1315) Also called Ramon Lull, or Raimond Lulle, or Raymund Lull. Born at Palma on Majorca, this Christian visionary led the life of a courtier, wrote love poetry and generally lived what he later termed a dissipated life on the wealth inherited from his father until in 1266 he five times received a vision of Christ crucified. Converted, he devoted himself for nine years to the study of Arabic and mystical subjects generally so that he could fulfill the grand scheme he had conceived of converting the Moslems and rescuing the holy sepulcher. In fear for his sanity his wife had his estate entrusted to the administration of an official.

After serving as a professor of Arabic and philosophy, and writing and arguing about his ideas in Majorca and later at Paris, in 1291 he finally sailed to Tunis, where he preached Christianity for a year before being imprisoned and expelled. For a long time he contented himself with pursuing various projects in Europe, such as establishing missionary colleges and the teaching of Oriental languages at the universities, but had limited success. In 1305 he went to Bougie in Africa to preach and again was imprisoned for six months. After his release his persistence began to bear fruit. Some of his proposals were adopted, at least in principle, at the

Council at Vienna in 1311. By this time an old man, Lully sailed once more to Bougie to convert the Moslems, apparently determined to die the death of a martyr. In this he was successful. The citizens of Bougie stoned him to death outside the city walls on June 29, 1315. He left numerous mystical, philosophical and literary works, but the treatises on alchemy attributed to him are regarded as spurious.

LYCOPHRON: (born c. 320 BC) Greek poet and grammarian born at Chalcis in Euboea, the son of Socles, he was adopted later by Lycus of Rhegium and as a young man spent considerable time with the philosopher Menedemus. Ptolemy Philadelphus entrusted him with arranging the comedies collected for the library at Alexandria around 285–83 BC. Ovid says he was killed by an arrow *(Ibis* lines 529–30). He wrote 20 tragedies, all lost, and a treatise *On Comedy,* also lost, but is remembered for an extant poem of 1,474 lines called *Alexandra* (or *Cassandra),* which is filled with arcane lore and earned the poet the surname "The Obscure."

MACROBIUS, AMBROSIUS AURELIUS THEODOSIUS: (late 4th century) Greek grammarian. His *Saturnalia* is a series of discussions supposedly held during the Saturnalia. It is in seven books and contains much curious lore. He also wrote *Commentarius ex Cicerone in somnium Scipionis,* a commentary on a dream of Scipio related by Cicero in his *De republica,* in which Macrobius talks about the constitution of the universe according to the Neoplatonists. It was very popular in the Middle Ages.

MAGNUS: See ALBERTUS.

MAIMONIDES, MOSES: (1135–1204) Rabbi Moses ben Maimon, also called Rambam by an extraction of letters from his name, a Jewish philosopher born in Cordova, which was at that time enjoying the last glow of science, philosophy and art cultivated by its Arab rulers. He was taught Hebrew and Jewish scholarship by his father, and benefited from the climate of dis-

covery and free thought that pervaded the city. When in 1148 Cordova was captured by a more fanatical and intolerant sect of Islam, the persecutions began, and after ten years of hardship Maimonides took his family to Fez.

The Fez period (1160–1165) marked the beginning of his literary activities. His strong views against Jewish assimilation began to attract unfriendly notice. In 1165 he prudently left Fez and settled in Cairo, where he attained great prominence at court and within the Jewish community. Disciples flocked to him, and he was consulted for his wisdom. The shipwreck of his brother David, along with the loss of a consignment of gems intended for trade, ended the family fortune, and Maimonides was compelled to earn his living as a physician. Such was his success that he was able to refuse the request of Richard I that he become court physician in England.

His later life was made happy by marriage and the birth of a son, Abraham (in 1186). In these final years he sought to avoid controversy and wrote without ceasing. It was said of him, "From Moses unto Moses there arose not one like Moses," attesting to the veneration in which he was held. His great work is the *Moreh nebuhim* (Guide for the perplexed), written in 1190. He also wrote numerous other works and commentaries.

MARCELLUS, M. CLAUDIUS (?268–208 BC) Called the Sword of Rome because he gave Hannibal his first setback, Marcellus was five times consul. He is best remembered for his successful siege of Syracuse, where he overcame the mechanical ingenuity of Archimedes with typical Roman brute force and a prolonged blockade. After slaying him in battle, Hannibal gave the Roman general a funeral with full honors.

MARCUS THE VALENTINIAN: (2nd century AD) Also called Marcus the Gnostic, a native of south Gaul who exerted a wide influence extending into Asia Minor. Iranaeus *(Against Heresies* 1.7.2) calls him a magician because he filled the Eucharist cups with water and with incantations caused them to appear purple and red as though dyed with the blood of Christ. He also says that initiates into the mysteries of Marcus underwent a spiritual marriage in a specially constructed bridal chamber, where with certain invocations they were united with God "according to the likeness of the unions above."

MARGARET of AUSTRIA: (1480–1530) She was born at Brussels, the daughter of the archduke Maximilian of Austria, afterwards Emperor Maximilian I, who betrothed her at the age of two years to the son of Louis XI, who later became Charles VIII. The French king threw her over in 1489, and her father began to hunt for another match. In 1497 she married John, heir to the throne of Castile and Aragon, but he died a few months later. Undaunted, she became the wife of Philibert II, Duke of Savoy, in 1501. He also died after only three years. In 1507 Maximilian appointed her the guardian of her nephew, Charles, later to become Emperor Charles V. She became regent of the Netherlands in the same year and governed with great skill and prudence until her death.

It was Margaret who obtained for Agrippa the post of archivist and historiographer to the Emperor Charles V in 1528, earning the loyalty he expresses in his letter to Hermann of Weid at the beginning of the Second Book. Her death severely limited his influence at court.

MARIUS, C. GAIUS: (155–86 BC) Seven times consul of Rome, he distinguished himself by his skill in warfare and his great cruelty. Political conflict forced him to flee Rome under sentence of death in 88 BC. He was captured in the marsh near Minturnae in Latium (near the present-day town of Minturno) and his execution ordered by the magistrates. A Gaulish (or Cimbrian) soldier was ordered to perform the deed. The story is best told by Plutarch:

> The room itself was not very light, that part of it especially where he then lay was dark, from whence Marius's eyes, they say, seemed to the fellow to dart out flames at him, and a loud voice to say, out of the dark, "Fellow, darest thou kill Caius Marius?" The barbarian hereupon immediately

fled, and leaving his sword in the place, rushed out of doors, crying only this, "I cannot kill Caius Marius." At which they were all at first astonished, and presently began to feel pity, and remorse, and anger at themselves for making so unjust and ungrateful a decree against one who had preserved Italy, and whom it was bad enough not to assist. ("Caius Marius." In *Lives* [Dryden, 519])

Marius fled to Carthage and eventually was able to return briefly to power in Rome.

MARTIANUS MINNEUS FELIX CAPELLA: (early 5th century) Latin writer who was a native of Madaura in Africa. He appears to have been wealthy and to have practiced law at Carthage. His *Satyricon,* or *De nuptiis Philologiae et Mercurii et de septem artibus liberalibus libri novum,* is a curious kind of allegorical encyclopedia in nine books in a mixture of prose and verse. The first two books tell of the marriage between Mercury and the nymph Philologia, and the latter seven treat of the seven liberal arts: grammar, dialectics, rhetoric, geometry, arithmetic, astronomy and music. Each art is personified as a courtier of Mercury and Philologia. This work was very popular during the Middle Ages.

MATERNUS, JULIUS FIRMICUS (4th century AD) Astrologer born in Sicily, probably at Syracuse, into a prosperous and socially rising family. Here he received the education of a gentleman and gained a knowledge of Greek literature that he later drew upon in his writings. By his own account he served as a lawyer and hated it so much that he finally abandoned the profession, calling it, "the occupation of stealing, or rather of banditry" *(Matheseos* 4.3 [Bram, 117]). He is remembered for two works, the *Matheseos libri VIII* (c. 334), the last and most complete treatise on astrology that has survived from the ancient world, and *De errore profanarum religionum* (c. 346), an attack upon the mystery religions from the Christian point of view. This suggests that Maternus underwent a conversion during the decade spanning the two works, if they are indeed written by the same hand.

MAXIMILIAN I: (1459–1519) German emperor, the son of the Emperor Frederick III and Leonora, daughter of Edward, king of Portugal. In 1477 he married Mary, daughter of Charles the Bold, Duke of Burgundy, and embroiled himself in the defense of her lands from the French. This had a successful outcome in 1479, but the death of Mary in 1482 weakened his position and exacerbated his troubles in the Netherlands, which resented his authority. In 1485 he was chosen King of the Romans (i.e. German king). Marriage to Bianca Maria Sforza in 1494 brought him much needed funds to fuel his continual petty wars and grand schemes, such as driving the Turks from Europe.

In 1505 he reached the height of his power and cast his eyes on the title of emperor, but it was not until 1508 that he set out for Rome to be crowned. When Venice refused to let him pass, he declared himself Roman Emperor Elect, and this move was supported by Pope Julius II. Inevitably a war with Venice followed. It was not successful. Maximilian had a falling out with Julius soon after and seriously considered making himself pope. Nothing came of this notion, but it illustrates his mind. His life was filled with hastily conceived and poorly executed military and political endeavors. Rash rather than stupid, he could speak six languages and converse with understanding in the arts and sciences. He wrote books, some of which were illustrated by Albrecht Dürer, but none have singular merit.

MECHTHILD OF MAGDEBURG: (1207–1294) German saint who wrote a book called *Das Fliessende Licht der Gottheit,* a mystical work based on the teachings of Joachim of Floris.

MECHTINDIS: See MECHTHILD.

MELAMPUS: The first mortal endowed with prophetic powers, the first physician, and the one credited with establishing the worship of Dionysus in Greece. In front of his house grew an oak tree containing a nest of serpents. When the elders were killed, Melampus took pity on the young and reared them. One night while he lay asleep the serpents came to him and licked out his ears, after which he found that he could understand the language of birds. The name is carried by two extant Greek works, *Divinatio ex palpitatione* and *De naevis oleaceis in corpore,* believed to have been written by a resident of Alexandria in the 3rd century BC.

METHODIUS, SAINT: (?825–885) Monk native to Thessalonica. He traveled with his brother Cyril to Christianize the peoples of Moravia at the request of King Rastislav around 863. The two established a seminary and preached in the vernacular Slavonic with the approval of Pope John III, causing discord among the clergy. The brothers' sainthood is celebrated together by the Roman Church on March 9.

MILO: Titus Annius Milo Papinianus (1st century BC). He joined in a political revolt against Caesar and was killed in 48 BC in a battle near Thurii in Lucania, a region of southern Italy.

MITHRADATES VI: (131–64 BC) King of Pontus, surnamed the Great. He came to the throne in 120 BC at age eleven and immediately had to take strenuous measures to prevent himself from being poisoned or otherwise assassinated by his mother. He is said to have accustomed himself to the use of antidotes. Finally forced to flee into the mountains, he returned in 111 BC to claim his crown, throwing his mother into prison and executing his younger brother.

He proceeded to mount three wars against Rome, with remarkable success. Suffering setbacks against the masterly war skill of Pompey in 66 BC, he was finally brought down by the treachery of his troops and allies. He tried to poison himself in 64 BC, but was so inured to all popular poisons his body refused to die. In frustration he was forced to order a Gallic mercenary to dispatch him with a sword.

Many stories grew up around him. He was renowned for his love of art and learning, his mastery of 22 languages, his great strength and martial kill, his practice of magic, his invulnerability to poison and his vast capacity for food and drink. It was perhaps inevitable that books dealing with natural magic be attributed to him.

MITHRIDITES: See MITHRADATES.

MOSES THE EGYPTIAN: See MAIMONIDES.

MUSEUS: Semi-mythical Greek poet and prophet who lived in the time of Hercules at Eleusis, where he presided over the mystic rites of Demeter. He was said to be the son of Orpheus, and his disciple, and to have originated religious poetry in Attica. The most famous of the writings attributed to Museus is the *Oracles,* which were consulted by the ancients. Herodotus mentions them three times and tells the story of the "oracle-monger" Onomacritus:

> "... who set forth the prophecies of Musaeus in their order. ... He was banished from Athens by Hipparchus, the son of Pisistratus, because he foisted into the writings of Musaeus a prophecy that the islands which lie off Lemnos would one day disappear in the sea. Lasus of Hermione caught him in the act of so doing. For this cause Hipparchus banished him, though till then they had been the closest of friends. *(History* 7 [Rawlinson, 356–7]. See also 8 [Rawlinson, 460] and 9 [Rawlinson, 495])

Pausanias makes a brief mention of him in a geographical context: "The Museum is a small hill opposite the Akropolis, inside the ancient ring-wall, where they say Mousaios used to sing and died of old age and was buried ..." *(Guide to Greece* 1.25.6 [Levi, 1:72–3]). Museus is also credited with having written purificatory hymns, prose treatises, a *Titanomachia* concerning the war of the Titans, and a *Theogonia* on the genealogy of the gods.

NECTANEBUS II: (4th century BC) Also known as Nekhtnebf, the last native sovereign of Egypt and last king of the 30th Dynasty listed by Manetho in his *History of Egypt.* He ruled 360–343 BC, having assumed power during a military revolt against his predecessor, Teos, during an expedition against Persia that relied on the skill of a force of Greek mercenaries. Nectanebus did not take advantage of his opportunities, and when the Persian king Artaxerxes III Ochus subdued Egypt in 343 BC, Nectanebus fled, first to Memphis, and from there to Ethiopia.

Here the historical record of the king ends, but it is carried on in legend by the *Life of Alexander* of pseudo-Callisthenes, first written around 200 AD. According to this romance, Nectanebus was a great magician who ruled all other kings through the use of sympathetic magic. He made tiny figures of soldiers and warships to represent his armies and those of the foe, then recited words of power and caused his models to overcome the models of his enemies. When through his magic he saw that the tide of fate had turned against him and that the gods of Egypt favored his foes, he shaved off his hair and beard and fled to Pella in Macedonia, where he made a living as a physician and soothsayer. When Olympias, the wife of King Philip of Macedon, was ready to give birth to Alexander the Great, Nectanebus delayed her until the astrological aspects were more favorable.

NICOCREON: (4th century BC) King of Salamis, in Cyprus, during the period of Alexander the Great's Asian campaign (330 BC). After the death of Alexander he helped Ptolemy against Antigonus, and as a reward Ptolemy gave him command over all Cyprus. He is said by Cicero to have executed the philosopher Anaxarchus by pounding him to death in a great stone mortar to revenge an insult the latter had given him while the philosopher enjoyed the protection of Alexander.

NICOMACHUS: (1st century) This Pythagorean philosopher was called Gerasenus after the place of his birth, Gerasa in Arabia Petraea. Nothing is known about him personally. He wrote a life of Pythagoras and a mystical treatise on the decad, both lost. Two of his works have survived: *Introduction to Arithmetic,* a metaphysical account of the theory and proportions of numbers that was used as a schoolbook down to the Renaissance; and *Manual of Harmony,* which represents the oldest authority of the Pythagorean theory of music.

NUMA POMPILIUS: (late 8th century BC) The second king of Rome, whom Livy says reigned from 716–673 BC.

NUMENIUS OF APAMEA: (2nd century AD) Greek philosopher of Apamea in Syria who was a forerunner of the Neoplatonists. He followed the teachings of Pythagoras and Plato, whom he called an "Atticizing Moses," and was strongly influenced by the Valentinian gnostics and the Jewish-Alexandrian philosophers. Proclus in his *Commentary on Plato's Timaeus* says that Numenius believed in a trinity of gods that he named "father, "maker" and "that which is made." The first is pure intelligence, the second is the creator of the world (shakti) and the third *is* the world. His object was to syncretize the occult teachings of the Brahmans, Jews, Magi and Egyptians. Many fragments of his writings are preserved in the *Præparatio evangelica* of Eusebius.

ORIGEN: (186–?254) This Father of the Christian Church was born at Alexandria and carefully educated by his father, who was a devout Christian. Later he studied under Clement of Alexandria and became a teacher of grammar to feed and clothe himself. His life was harshly ascetic. When he aroused the ire of the bishop with his unorthodox opinions, he was forced to leave Egypt and ultimately was excommunicated. He settled in Palestine, where he taught. Gregory Thaumaturgus was one of his pupils, and left in his *Panegyric* an account of his teaching style and a portrait of Origen the man. Origen was highly skilled in Hebrew, as evidenced in his *Hexapla,* a commentary on the Old Testament and comparison of six versions of the text. Unfortunately only fragments of this work survive. His most important work is *De principiis,* which has survived in a defective Latin version of Rufinus.

ORPHEUS: A mythic figure, the first poet of the Greeks, said to be the son of Oeagrus, King of Thrace, and the muse Calliope. His master was the god Apollo. Many ancients considered him an historical figure, but Aristotle was of the opinion that he never existed. The collection of poems that goes under his name represents the forgeries of Christian grammarians and Alexandrian philosophers; however, some of the fragments are older and perhaps predate Plato. Orpheus is best known as the author of a fourth-century poem of 770 lines titled *Lithica* (Greek: *lithos* stone), the narrator of which, one Theodamas, describes the magical uses of 30 different gems to the author, whom he meets while Orpheus is on his way to sacrifice at the altar of the Sun.

ORUS APOLLO: See HORAPOLLO.

OSTANES: (3rd century) Called Ostanes the Mede, he was an alchemist supposed to have been the master of the pseudo-Democritus who wrote the alchemical work *Physica et mystica.* The name Ostanes is attached to a work that treats of a divine matter that cures all maladies —an early reference to the elixir of life. Saint Cyprian calls Ostanes the "chief" of the magi. The name occurs in the writings of Tertullian and Augustine, as well as in the *Leiden Papyrus.*

OSTHANES: See OSTANES.

PARISIENSIS: See WILLIAM OF PARIS.

PATRIARCHA, NICEPHORUS: (died 828) He was a secretary of state to the Emperor Constantine V Copronymus. He entered a monastery and later rose to the patriarchate of Constantinople, in 806. He wrote a *Byzantine History.*

PAUL THE HERMIT: (229–342) The first hermit of the Church, who lived deep in a cave in the Lower Thebaid, Egypt. As the story goes, when Saint Antony was 90 years old, he had a mystical vision informing him that he was not the only hermit, as he had believed, but that another lived who was both older and more holy than himself. Taking his staff, Antony set out to find this pious man. He walked for three days and received directions successively from a hippocentaur, a satyr and a wolf that led him to the depths of a cave. Here lay Paul the Eremite dying under the weight of his 113 years.

While they talked a crow came with a loaf of bread. Paul revealed that he had been fed by the bird for the last 60 years. Knowing that he was about to die and not wishing Antony to see his death, Paul sent the younger man away to fetch the cloak of Athenasius from a nearby convent where it was preserved. On his return Antony saw the soul of Paul borne into the heavens by angels and found the body of the saint kneeling in a position of prayer. He was too weak with age and fasting to dig a grave, but this lack was supplied by God, who sent two lions to bury Paul. After their work, Antony blessed them, and the lions went away with heads bowed in mourning. This charming story is told by Saint Jerome in his *Life of Paul, the First Hermit of Egypt,* written around 375.

PAULINUS, MEROPIUS PONTIUS ANICIUS: (?353–?431) Also called Paulinus Nolanus, bishop of Nola. He was born at Burdigala (Bordeaux), or perhaps at a nearby town he names Embromagum. His family was prominent and well off, allowing him the benefit of an excellent education. One of his tutors was the poet Ausonius (see biographical note). After a life of secular pursuits and honors he retired from the world and was made bishop of Nola in 409. His work include the *Epistolae,* a collection of 51 letters.

PAULUS DIACONUS: (?725–797) Also called Paulus Levita, Paulus Warnefridi and Paulus Casinensis. Born of a noble Lombard family at Friuli in Italy, as a young man he was secretary to the Lombard king Desiderius and educated the king's daughter Adelperga. Later (781) he became a monk at Monte Cassino, where he gained the notice and admiration of Charlemagne. He played a major part in the Carolingian renaissance. His major works are *Historia gentis Langobardorum* and *Historia Romana,* the latter composed at the urging of the Princess Adelperga. In addition he compiled a collection of homilies *(Homilarium)* at the request of Charlemagne, wrote many letters, poems, epigrams and a history of the bishops of Metz.

PAUSANIAS: (2nd century AD) Greek geographer who was a native of Lydia. He traveled over a large portion of the ancient world and wrote an account of what he had seen in the Peloponnesus and northern Greece. It is remarkable in that Pausanius actually visited and viewed the places and things he writes about rather than merely copying descriptions from older authors. In addition he gives much curious lore concerning fountains, rivers, mountains and temples, and relates folk legends of places with serious religious feeling. It was his description of the Lion gate and circuit wall of the Acropolis at Mycenae (2.16.4) that led to the discovery of that lost city by the archaeologist Heinrich Schliemann. Written in ten books during the reign of Marcus Aurelius, the *Description of Greece* has been called the "clue to the labyrinth" of the ruins of Greece.

PETER THE CRUEL: (1333–1369) King of Castile, son of Alphonso XI and Maria, daughter of Alphonso IV of Portugal. He came to the throne at age 16 while still under the thumb of his mother. At her coercion and that of the nobles who backed her, he reluctantly married Blanche of Bourbon in 1354, but almost at once deserted his wife in favor of a series of mistresses. It is to this time that the story of the girdle belongs. The story probably comes from the *Chronicle* of Lopez de Ayala, who had fought against Peter and had a low opinion of him. Peter had his wife imprisoned and murdered.

In 1356 he gained full political power and began to rule with an iron hand, confiding in no one except the Jews he employed as tax gatherers and the Mohammedans who acted as his personal guard. His enemies he murdered. Singularly inept and cowardly at warfare, his power was for a short time propped up by the Black Prince, but when this ally left him in disgust, he was easily overthrown by his own brother, Henry, who appropriately enough murdered him in the field tent of Bertrand du Guesclin on March 23, 1369.

PETILLIUS, L: (2nd century BC) In 181 BC the books of King Numa, the fabled second king of Rome who established the forms and ceremonies of the Roman religion, were supposedly dug up on the estate of one L. Petillius, who turned them over to Q. Petillius Spurinus, then praetor. Q Petellius Spurinus examined them and found that they consisted of 12 (or seven) Latin books of ecclesiastical law and the same number of Greek books on philosophy. He convinced the senate that the Greek works should be burned unread. The Latin books were preserved. The whole story of the finding of the books is said to be a forgery. In 176 Q. Petillius Spurinus fell in battle against the Ligurians.

PETRUS DE APONO: (1250–1316) Better known as Pietro d'Abano, or in its Anglicized form, Peter of Abano. Born near Padua, Italy, he studied philosophy and medicine at Paris, where he taught at the University and was regarded as a "second Aristotle." Returning to Padua to settle, he gained renown as a physician. His fondness for astrology caused him to be charged with the practice of magic, and he was accused of manufacturing money from the air and possessing the Philosopher's Stone. The first time he was brought before the Inquisition he was acquitted, but the second time was convicted posthumously, having died during the trial.

In his writings he presents the systems of Averroes and other Arabian philosophers and physicians. He was fabled to have learned the seven liberal arts from seven spirits which he kept in crystal vessels. The *Heptameron,* or *Magical Elements,* is a grimoire ascribed to him that was well known in the Middle Ages. It is said to have suggested to Boccaccio the name for his *Decameron.* The Abbot Trithemius, Agrippa's teacher, probably refers to it when he speaks of a *Clavicle* made by Abano, in his *Antipalus maleficiorum* (c. 1500).

PHALARIS: (6th century BC) Ruler and native of Agrigentum in Sicily. He appears to have held high office in his city, and from this vantage to have raised himself to a position of absolute authority. His rule (570–554 BC) was proverbial for cruelty even in ancient times: "Phalaris, ruthless in spirit, who burned his victims in his brazen bull, is whelmed for ever by a hateful infamy, and no lyres beneath the rooftree welcome him as a theme to be softly blended with the warbled songs of boys" (Pindar *Pythian Odes* 1, line 96, trans. John Sandys [London: William Heinemann, 1915], 167).

He is best remembered for the bronze bull in which he tortured and killed his victims, beginning with the unfortunate inventor of the bull, Perillus: "Phalaris, too, burnt in the bull the limbs of the cruel Perillus; the unhappy inventor was the first to make proof of his work" (Ovid *Ars Amatoria* 1, line 654 [Riley, 403]). The tyrant was killed in a popular uprising of his own people.

PHERECYDES: (6th century BC) Greek philosopher and theologian of Syros, an island in the Aegean. He was reputed to have studied the secret books of the Phoenicians and traveled in Egypt. With his occult knowledge he became the teacher of Pythagoras (Iamblichus *Life of Pythagoras* 2) and was perhaps responsible for the latter's belief in the immortality and transmigration of souls. One of his works which sets forth his views was extant during the Alexandrian period. He died of morbus pediculosus (lice). He should not be confused with the 5th-century-BC prose historian Pherecydes of Athens, which is perhaps the error committed by Agrippa.

PHILO JUDAEUS: (early 1st century AD) Jewish philosopher who was probably born in Alexandria, Egypt, around 15 BC, and lived in that city for the rest of his life. Little is known about him. Jerome says he came from a priestly family of distinction. He had a brother, Alexander, who was a chief tax collector, which suggests that his family was powerful and wealthy. In 40 AD he traveled from Alexandria to Rome at the head of a Jewish delegation to obtain exemption for the Jews from the necessity of worshiping the Emperor Caligula as a god. Eusebius, Jerome and other Church Fathers say that in the time of Claudius he met Saint Peter in Rome, but there is no evidence of this meeting.

The life work of Philo was an attempt to reconcile the philosophy of the Greeks, which he held in reverence, with the teachings in the books of Moses, to which he was bound by faith and blood. He did this by writing commentaries on the scriptures, particularly the Pentateuch, interpreting the Bible stories allegorically and extracting from them philosophical precepts in harmony with Greek metaphysical speculation. A product of his times, he possessed perfect Greek but very little Hebrew, and indeed was called by Clement of Alexandria a Pythagorean. He is the author of numerous extant works.

PICATRIX THE SPANIARD: *Picatrix* is the name of one the the most notorious grimoires of the middle ages. It is a translation of an Arabic book called *The Aim of the Sages* attributed to al-Maggriti (i.e., the man from Madrid), a Spanish-Arab mathematician of the 12th century. It was translated into Spanish for King Alfonso of Castile in 1256, then later into Latin, after which it circulated widely in manuscript. The Emperor Maximilian I (1459–1519) had a copy in his library.

The Abbot Trithemius attributes the name Picatrix to the writer of the work in his *Antipalus Maleficiorum,* as does Rabelais in his *Pantagruel,* and it seems that the book and its maker were always confounded. S. L. MacGregor Mathers, in his introduction to *The Sacred Magic of Abramelin the Mage* (Mathers 1975 [1900], xvi) refers to it as "Probably the same as Gio Peccatrix the Magician, the author of many Manuscripts on Magic." Casanova, who liked to play at being a magician, had a copy of the *Picatrix* in his library.

The content of the book is Hermetic and Gnostic set within a complex spirit hierarchy. One of its most interesting elements is its attribution of anthropomorphic figures to the 36 decans of the zodiac.

PLATO: (427–347 BC) The Greek philosopher was born at Athens, the son of Ariston, a descendent of Codrus. His mother, Perictione, was related to Solon by descent. Originally his name was Aristocles, but due to the great breadth of his chest he came to be called Plato. He also had a high forehead and very broad shoulders. As a youth he competed successfully in the games as a wrestler and spent the rest of his time writing poetry, which he is supposed to have burned the first time he heard Socrates speak.

When he was 20 Plato went to Socrates in the grove called Academus, where the elder philosopher taught his followers, and remained with him until his death in 399 BC. Then he traveled widely, going to Egypt, Sicily and lower Italy, and by a less trustworthy account to Asia, where he conversed with the sages of the Hebrews, Babylonians and Persians. One story relates that the elder Dionysius, tyrant of Sicily, gave Plato into the hands of the Spartan ambassador Pollis, who sold him as a slave into Aegina, but that he was given his liberty by Cyrenian Anniceris.

Returning to Athens around 389 BC, he taught philosophy without payment in the gymnasium of the Academy and in his own garden at Colonus. Soon he became the most influential teacher in Greece, numbering among his students Xenocrates of Chalcedon, Aristotle, Heraclides, Lycurgus, Isocrates and many other great men. He also accepted women as his disciples. Twice he traveled to Sicily on political missions to the younger Dionysius but had little success as an ambassador. His *Dialogues,* which have survived intact, are a towering monument to his lifelong pursuit of a mystical, perfect Truth upon which to base human living.

He died with his pen in his hand, and willed his garden to his school. It eventually descended to the Neoplatonists, who celebrated Plato's birthday, and that of Socrates, with festivals.

PLINIUS CAECILIUS SECUNDUS, CAIUS: (61–113) Better known as Pliny the Junior, or Pliny the Younger, he was the son of Pliny the Elder's sister Plinia and C. Caecilius, and was born at Novum Comum (present-day Como).

When he was quite young his father died and his uncle became his guardian. The author of the *Natural History* dedicated his nephew to the study of letters from the first. At 14, young Pliny wrote a Greek tragedy. He studied eloquence under Quintilian, and at 19 began to speak at the Forum. Soon he was appearing as legal advocate before the senate and the court of the Centumviri. While still young he served as a military tribune in Syria. He was praetor in 93 and consul in 100. Around 103 he became propraetor of the province of Pontica, where he served two years.

He was wealthy and generous, possessing a kind, moderate nature, but sickly in body. Twice married, he had no children. Among his friends he numbered Tacitus, Suetonius and Martial, and was himself known as one of the most learned men of his age. He is chiefly remembered for his *Letters,* which he seems to have written with an eye toward future publication, especially those to the Emperor Trajan. Also extant is an extended speech in honor of the Emperor, the *Panegyric on Trajan.*

PLINIUS SECUNDUS, CAIUS: (?23–79) Better known as Pliny the Elder, this natural historian was born at Novum Comum (Como) in northern Italy, where he later kept his estate. His father took him to Rome around 35 AD to be educated. Under the influence of Seneca he began practicing as an advocate. At age 23 he served in Lower Germany as a cavalry officer and traveled widely throughout this region. He used what he learned to write a history of the Germanic wars in 20 books.

Returning to Rome, he again took up as an advocate, with only moderate success, and appears to have spent the greater period of Nero's reign (54–68) in retirement on his estate, studying and writing. He read, or had books read to him, almost incessantly, and always made notes. After his death his son inherited 160 volumes of notes for the *Natural History,* closely written on both sides of the leaves.

During the reign of Vespasian, Pliny returned to Rome and the service of the state, but his true occupation was always writing. He was killed observing the eruption of Mount Vesuvius in 79 (see Pliny the Younger *Epistles* 6.16). Of his many works only his *Historia naturalis* survives, but it is his greatest achievement, comprising the full scope of the human science of that age.

PLOTINUS: (204–270) The greatest Neoplatonic philosopher was born of Roman parents at Lycopolis in Egypt. He attended the lectures of Ammonius Saccas, the founder of the Neoplatonic school, at Alexandria until 242, when he seized the opportunity to accompany the Emperor Gordian III in his expedition against Persia in order to study Persian and Indian philosophy. With his newfound knowledge he established a successful school at Rome in 244, and soon had many eager pupils, among them Porphyry, to whom he entrusted the editing of his philosophical writings. Porphyry edited the 54 books of Plotinus into six *Enneads,* or sets of nine books. After the death of Plotinus stories grew up crediting him with divine inspiration and the power to work miracles.

PLUTARCHUS: (?46—?120) This Greek writer of popular essays was born at Chaeronea in Boeotia (not far east of Mount Parnassus in central Greece) into a loving and stable family of four living generations. As a youth he attended the school of the philosopher Ammonius at Delphi, where he learned mathematics and philosophy. While still a youth he was appointed by his city to negotiate disputed matters with neighboring city states. He made his way to Rome seeking fame and fortune and probably delivered public lectures there on philosophical questions. He himself writes that he was so occupied with public business and private talks on philosophy that he did not have time to perfect his knowledge of Latin.

He championed the doctrines of Plato and attacked those of Epicurus with equal enthusiasm. There seems reason to doubt the story of Suidas that he was elevated to the rank of consul by Trajan, and the medieval legend that he supervised the education of young Hadrian is even more questionable. He seems to have lectured at Rome during the reign of Domitian and may have been driven out of the city when Domitian expelled all the philosophers in the year 89. At any rate he returned to his native Chaeronea, where he opened his own school. He traveled widely throughout Greece but never went back to Rome. He held the post of archon in his native town and was made a priest of Apollo at Delphi in the year 95.

We learn from his writings that he had at least four sons by his wife Timoxena and at some point was initiated into the mysteries of Dionysus. Plutarch is remembered for his *Parallel Lives,* 46 biographies of famous Greeks and Romans arranged in pairs for the purpose of comparison. Some of the original biographies have been lost. He is also known for a collection of about 60 essays on a wide range of topics generally given the title *Moralia.* Some of these essays are regarded as spurious. The writings of Plutarch are rich in the lore of religious customs, superstitions and magic.

POMPEIUS, MAGNUS: (106–48 BC) He began his military career in 89 BC under his father Pompeius Strabo and upheld the cause of the aristocrats against the Marians, fighting with great success under Sulla. He became consul in 71 BC and continued his military triumphs. When alienated from the senate, he threw in his lot with Caesar and formed with him and Crassus the first triumvirate. It was inevitable that such an ambitious man would eventually seek the highest power. When Pompey and Caesar met at Pharsalia to decide who should rule the empire, Pompey was soundly defeated. He fled to Egypt, where he was assassinated.

PONTANUS, JOVIANUS: (1426–1503) Italian scholar and poet, born at Cerreto in Spoleto. When still a boy, his father was murdered, depriving him of his inheritance. Penniless, he made his way to Naples and soon ingratiated himself into the favor of Alphonso the Magnanimous, king of Aragon, who made Pontanus his counselor. He established an academy of learned men at Naples that survived long after his death. His works include *Urania,* a treatise

on astronomy; *Eridanus,* a series of elegies; *De conjugali amore; De hortis Hesperidum,* a didactic poem on orange trees; and a history of the wars of Ferdinand I and John of Anjou.

PORPHYRIUS: See PORPHYRY.

PORPHYRY: (?233–?304) Born at Tyre, or perhaps Batanaea, in Syria, he studied grammar and rhetoric under Cassius Longinus. His original name was Malchus (king), in allusion to which his teacher called him Porphyrius (clad in purple), because purple was the royal color. In 262 he traveled to Rome and studied with Plotinus so diligently that he injured his mental balance and began to dream of suicide as a way of escaping the prison of the flesh.

It took five years of quiet living in Sicily for him to recover his mental equilibrium. Returning to Rome after the death of Plotinus, he set about making the doctrine of his master more readily known. His most famous student was Iamblichus. Late in life Porphyry married a widow with seven children. Nothing is known concerning his death. His great work, *Adversus Christianos,* has not survived. He also wrote celebrated lives of Plotinus and Pythagoras, a tract on vegetarianism called *De abstinentia* and numerous other works.

PROBA: See PROBUS.

PROBUS, VALERIUS: (1st century) Of Berytus (now Beirut), a Roman grammarian who wrote criticisms of classical authors by means of marginal notes or signs. He published little, but his lectures were partially preserved in the notes of his pupils. The commentary on Virgil, *Scholia in Bucolica et Georgica,* which bears his name, was likely written much later. However, he is the author of *De notis,* a fragment from a longer work, since lost, that lists abbreviations used in official and historical writings.

PROCLUS: (412–485) Called *Diadochus* (the Successor) because he was regarded as the natural champion of the teachings of Plato. Born in Byzantium, he studied at Alexandria and

Athens. He was an extreme ascetic and mystic who worshiped not only his own gods but those of other nations. Proclus studied the Orphic and Chaldic mysteries and was initiated into theurgy, or high magic, by Asclepegenia, daughter of Plutarchus, who was then the most perfect exponent of this wisdom, which had descended to her from Nestorius. Proclus claimed to have talked to gods and was said by Marinus to possess the power of calling down rain, stopping earthquakes and curing the sick. His greatest aspiration was to syncretize the wisdom of Plato with that of Orpheus, Pythagoras and Aristotle.

PTOLEMAEUS, CLAUDIUS: (100–178) Better known simply as Ptolemy, this celebrated Greek mathematician, astronomer and geographer was born at Ptolemais in Egypt. Little is known of his life. He observed the heavens for 40 years at Canopus, about 15 miles east of Alexandria, and died at the age of 78. The dates of his birth and death are not certain, but he himself records that the earliest observations made for his great astronomical work, the *Almagest,* were in 127, while the latest was made in 151, allowing his dates to be roughly fixed. His philosophy may be described as Aristotelian.

In ancient times he was held in almost idolatrous veneration. Hephaestion of Thebes called him "the divine Ptolemy" *(Catalogus codicum astrologicorum Graecorum* 8.2). In addition to the *Almagest,* which contains a catalog of the stars, he wrote the *Tetrabiblos,* an astrological treatise in four books; the *Geography,* being a description of the known world; the *Centiloquium,* a collection of astrological aphorisms; *On the Apparations of the Fixed Stars; On Music,* in three books; as well as other works of a more technical nature.

PTOLEMY: See PTOLEMAEUS.

PYRRHUS: (318–272 BC) King of Epirus and the most daring, if not the most prudent, military leader of his time. From the age of two, when he came under the protection of King Glaucias after the overthrow of his father, his life was a long list of political intrigues and military campaigns. Glaucus restored the boy to the throne of Epirus at age 12. He was driven out of the kingdom at 17, found allies in Egypt through marriage to the daughter of the wife of Ptolemy and regained his throne in 295 BC at age 23. He waged a campaign in Macedonia in 291 BC that resulted in his becoming co-ruler there for a few months in 286 BC. When he was forced out through political intrigue he decided to make war on Rome. This resulted in his famous "Pyrrhic victory" near Heraclea in 280 BC, in which he lost nearly as many of his officers and best troops as the defeated Romans. Surveying the field, he was heard to say, "Another such victory, and I must return to Epirus alone."

After a more or less successful campaign against Rome, he went to fight the Carthaginians in Sicily, was victorious despite the rebellion of his Greek troops, returned to Italy in 276 BC and was this time defeated by the Romans, invaded Macedonia in 273 BC and was crowned king there for the second time, attacked Sparta but was driven off, then, fatefully, decided to try his hand against Argos. An Argive woman dropped a roof tile on his head as he was retreating from the city, knocking him from his horse onto the swords of the Argive soldiers. Thus died the greatest warrior since Alexander.

PYTHAGORAS: (6th century BC) Greek philosopher, a native of Samos. He traveled widely in Egypt and the East acquiring occult knowledge. Said to possess the gift of prophecy, he believed in reincarnation and taught that the divine might be approached through the mystic power of numbers. In Crotona, Italy, he established a closely knit brotherhood of 300 bound together by vows to seek the perfection of their souls through ascetic and philosophical practices. Their work was kept secret, and admission to the brotherhood was very difficult to obtain. Pythagoras controlled all aspects of the life of his followers, prescribing diet, exercise and meditation that would yield inner harmony and self-control.

In time the political power of the brotherhood grew so great that the people of Crotona rose against them and burned the building in which they were assembled, killing many, including perhaps Pythagoras himself. By other accounts he fled to Tarentum and then to Metapontum, where he starved himself to death. Pythagoras wrote no books, but his disciples preserved fragments of his teachings, and these had a profound influence on later philosophers such as Plato.

PYTHEAS: (4th century BC) Greek navigator from Massilia (Marseilles) in Gaul. He wrote a work, *On the Ocean,* relating his discoveries on a voyage from Britain to Thule (perhaps the largest of the Shetland Islands), and a second work, *Periplus,* on his voyage from Gardira (Cadiz) to the Tanais (perhaps the river Don, which empties into the Sea of Azov). He mentions that in Thule the day and night are each six months long, leading some to speculate that he is speaking of Iceland. He further says that in these northern seas there is no distinction between air, earth and water, all together forming a gelatinous mass (ice) that renders progress impossible. It is a pity his works (or work— some maintain he took one voyage and wrote one treatise) have perished, as he was a remarkable astronomer, was the first to understand the tides, and actually visited the places he wrote about. What is known of him comes mainly from an extract from Polybius quoted by Strabo.

RABANUS: See HRABANUS.

ROBERT AN ENGLISHMAN: See ANGLICUS.

ROBERT OF YORK: (early 14th century) English Dominican friar and theologian who "scrutinized the hidden theorems of more secret medicine with such great care that he moved the most learned physicians to heartfelt admiration" (Thorndike. 3:105). Robert was called Perscrutator and was credited with the works *Correctorium alchimyae* and *De impressionibus aeris,* among others. See Thorndike, 3:6—particularly n. 3, p. 104. See also the biographical note on Robertus Anglicus.

RUBANUS: See HRABANUS.

RUFUS EPHESIUS: (fl. 100 AD) A celebrated Greek physician and medical writer who lived during the reign of Trajan (98–117). He was born at Ephesus, the chief of 12 Ionian cities that stood on the coast of Asia Minor (it was near present-day Selcuk, Turkey). He had a great interest in anatomy and made numerous experiments on living animals. Unfortunately the results of this branch of his study have survived only in the form of a list of anatomical names. The follower of no single school, he attempted to reconcile and blend the system of humors of Hippocrates, the method system of general symptoms of Themison, and the pneumatic system based on the operation of the universal soul of Athenaeus. He is the first to describe the symptoms of the bubonic plague, in a fragment of his writings preserved in the *Collections of Oribasius.* A number of the works of Rufus are extant.

SARDANAPALUS: (9th century BC) The last king of the Assyrian empire of Nineveh, he was proverbial for his luxury, effeminacy and licentiousness (see Dante *Divine Comedy: Paradiso* 15.107). He spent his time in the recesses of his palace dressed in feminine apparel and surrounded by his concubines. When the satrap of Media and the chief priest of the Chaldeans rebelled against his rule, he surprised the world by casting off his decadent ways and exhibiting himself as both a daring and successful general. Twice he defeated the rebel army and then endured a siege of Nineveh for two years. When it was clear he could not gain the victory, he gathered his concubines, wives, treasures and possessions into an immense pile, set it on fire and perished in the midst of the flames. The fall of the empire is supposed to have occurred in 876 BC. This story, as told by Ctesias, is preserved in the work of Diodorus Siculus. See also the tragedy *Sardanapalus* by Byron.

SAXO GRAMMATICUS: (?1150–?1206) Danish historian and poet. He was raised as a cleric and entered the service of the archbishop

Absalom around 1180. Absalom convinced him to undertake the writing of a history of the Danish kings, *Gesta Danorum* (or *Historia Danica),* which he began about 1185. Absalom died in 1201, and the history, finished in 1208, was dedicated to his successor, Archbishop Andreus. It was widely read during the Middle Ages in manuscript and first published at Paris in 1514. Saxo had limited learning and poor critical judgment. He is conjectured to have been a native of Zealand because of his effusive praise of the Zealanders, but nothing more is known of his personal life.

SCOT, MICHAEL: (1175–1235) An astrologer and magician, born in Scotland. He studied at Oxford and the Sorbonne, learned Arabic at Toledo, and became attached to the court of Ferdinand II of Sicily in the capacity of astrologer. Pope Honorius III held him in high regard, as did his successor, Gregory IX. Both petitioned the Archbishop of Canterbury to find a benefice for Scot. It is said that Scot introduced the works of Aristotle to England when he settled there in 1230. His best known work, on physiognomy, *De physiognomia et de hominis procreatione,* was reprinted many times. The legend grew up that he was a powerful magician. Dante mentions him in the *Inferno:* "That other who is so spare in the flanks was Michael Scot, who verily knew the game of magical deception" *(Inferno* 20 [Norton, 133]). It was said that he rode on a black demon horse as Scottish envoy to the king of France, and that when the horse stomped its hoof, all the bells of Notre Dame began to peal:

> A wizard of such dreaded fame
> That, when in Salamanca's cave
> Him listed his magic wand to wave,
> The bells would ring in Notre Dame!
> (W. Scott "Lay of the Last Minstrel" 2:13)

SCOTUS: See SCOT.

SCOTUS, JOHN DUNS: (?1265 - 1308) Also known as John Scot and Joannes Scotus Duns. A Franciscan theologian and scholastic, perhaps born in Duns in Berwickshire, who may have studied at Merton College, Oxford. He was learned in all branches of knowledge, particularly mathematics, and gained for himself the title Doctor Subtilis through his dialectical ingenuity while lecturing as professor of philosophy at the University of Paris in 1307. He vigorously defended, with great success, the doctrine of the Immaculate Conception against the Thomist Dominicans.

In 1308 Duns Scotus was sent to Cologne to found a university and died there that same year of apoplexy. One tradition maintains that he was buried alive. His works are *De modis significandi sive grammatica speculativa,* a philosophical grammar; *Quaestiones,* questions on logic; *De rerum principio,* a work of metaphysics; and *Opus Oxoniense,* a commentary on the *Sententiae* of Peter Lombard. The followers of Duns Scotus were called Dunsmen or Dunses, and in later times were held in low regard, giving birth to the word "dunce."

SENECA, LUCIUS ANNAEUS: (?4 BC—65 AD) Son of the famous Roman rhetorician Marcus Annaeus Seneca, the Roman philosopher was born in Corduba (Cordova), Spain, to a wealthy and distinguished equestrian family. As a small child he was taken to Rome by an aunt and received an education with a view to a career in the senate. In 32 AD or shortly after, he became quaestor, and soon received recognition as a writer and orator. In 41 his prospects suffered a setback when he was banished to Corsica for a supposed adultery, but in 49 he was recalled and made tutor to Nero, and the next year received the praetorship.

He became the more or less unwilling accomplice to Nero's crimes, composing Nero's explanation to the senate for the murder of Agrippina (59 AD). Three years later he attempted to retire to Campania to escape the intrigues of the court, but in 65 he was accused of conspiracy and forced to commit suicide. The extant writings of Seneca are too numerous to list. They include works of philosophy, natural history, many letters, a satire, and ten tragedies designed for reading rather than acting.

SERENUS, Q. SAMMONICUS: (early 3rd century) A learned Roman writer. His *De medicina praecepta* is an incomplete poem on medicine containing curious lore, ancient remedies and magical formulae—such as the Abracadabra charm—and was much used in the Middle Ages. Serenus was murdered while at supper in the year 212.

SERVIUS MAURUS (or MARIUS) HONORATUS: (late 4th century AD) A Latin grammarian about whom little is known. He is represented by Macrobius in his *Saturnalia* as a pagan. Were it not for his *Commentary on Virgil* Servius would be forgotten, but the *Commentary* is recognized as the most important Latin work of its kind. In it are preserved much lore and many customs of Roman life which would otherwise have been lost. Other works by Servius are *In secundam donati editionem interpretatio,* a collection of notes on the grammar of Aelius Donatus; *De ratione ultimarum syllabarum ad aquilinum liber,* a study of metrical endings; and *Ars de centum metris,* a tract on poetic meters.

SIMEON BEN YOHAI, RABBI: (2nd century AD) According to Talmudic tradition this Jewish scholar criticized Rome and was forced to hide in a cave for 12 years with his son, Rabbi Eleazar, awaiting the death of the Emperor Antoninus (ruled 138–161). During this time he dictated, and R. Eleazar wrote down, the *Zohar.* The story has some charming aspects. It is said the pair went naked for fear that otherwise their clothing would wear out. To cover their shame they sat buried in sand all day up to their necks, and only put on their robes at prayer.

SOCRATES: (469–399 BC) Greek philosopher born in the deme Alopece near Athens. His father was a statue maker and his mother a midwife. For a time he followed his father's craft and also served as a hoplite—a heavily armored infantry soldier—in the wars of Athens, where he distinguished himself. In 406 BC he became a member of the senate. It is not known when he devoted himself fully to philosophy, as he never

opened a school or delivered formal lectures or wrote books, preferring to wander the marketplace and gymnasiums talking about philosophy to anyone who would listen.

In appearance he was robust and rough, with homely features. He went barefoot summer and winter and wore the same simple clothing without regard to the weather, or indeed to the company he kept. This caused him to become the butt of the jokes of the Athenian playwrights.

Hated by men of power because he was totally incorruptible, fearless, and always spoke and acted as he believed, he was accused in a list of trumped-up charges, most notably of corrupting the youth of Athens and despising the gods (see Xenophon *Memorabilia of Socrates* 1.1). Had he chosen to grovel before his accusers he would have escaped harm, but instead he spoke proudly and was condemned to drink a poison concocted of hemlock. He died painlessly in his 70th year, without the least fear of death, surrounded by his many friends.

SOLINUS, CAIUS (GAIUS) JULIUS: (fl. 210) Latin historian who wrote, or rather compiled, *Collectanea rerum memorabilium,* a geographical history of the ancient world in 57 chapters. None of it is original. The largest part was taken directly from Pliny's *Natural History* and the geography of Pomponius Mela. Nothing is known about Solinus, but from the dedication of the *Collectanea* to Oclatinius Adventus, who was consul in 218 AD, it can be judged that the author lived in the first part of the third century. In the sixth century the *Collectanea* was revised under the title *Polyhistor,* and it is by this name that Solinus is sometimes erroneously called. The work was very popular in the Middle Ages. Two abridgements in hexameter verse circulated under the authors' names Theodericus and Petrus Diaconus.

SOPHOCLES: (495–406 BC) Greek dramatist who was born in the village of Colonus just northwest of Athens. He received the best education of the day and so far distinguished himself as to receive the prize of a garland in both music and gymnastics. As a youth he was admired both for his physical beauty and his skill in dancing. In 468 BC he competed in a drama contest against the elder Aeschylus, who was so humiliated to have been beaten by the newcomer that he retired for the remainder of his life to Sicily. After that Sophocles was unrivaled until 441 BC, when he himself was beaten in the drama contest by Euripides. The earliest of his tragedies that has survived, the *Antigone,* was written the following year. In all, seven plays are extant out of a possible 130.

There are various accounts of his death. By one he choked on a grape; by another he lost his breath fatally while reciting *Antigone;* a third story is that he was so overjoyed at obtaining a victory for one of his tragedies that he died.

SORANUS, QUINTUS VALERIUS: (1st century BC) Not much is known about this Roman writer. In 82 BC he was *tribunus plebis* (tribune of the people), an office in the Roman administration created to protect the interests of the plebeians from the patricians. A linguistic and antiquarian scholar, he was often quoted by Varro. Cicero mentions him in his *De oratore* (3.43) and his *Brutus* (ch. 169). An attempt has been made to identify Valerius Soranus with Valerius Aedituus (c. 100 BC), who wrote epigrams, many of them erotic, based on Greek models, but this identification is uncertain.

SPARTIANUS, AELIUS: (early 4th century) One of the six *Scriptores Historiae Augustae* who wrote the so-called *Augustan History,* a collection of lives of Roman emperors from Hadrian to Carinus, covering the period 117–284, which was written during the reigns of the emperors Diocletian (284–305) and Constantine (306–337), with later interpolations. Spartianus was responsible for the biographies of Hadrian, Aelius Verus, Didius Julianus, Septimius Severus, Pescennius Niger, Caracallus and Geta.

STATIUS, PUBLIUS PAPINIUS: (?61–?96) Roman poet born at Neapolis (Naples), the son of the distinguished grammarian Papinius Statius. He went with his father to Rome when the latter

became the teacher of Domitian, who later would be the patron of young Statius. The poet was particularly skillful at extemporaneous composition and at the public recitation of his works: "All flock in crowds to hear his sweet voice, and the tuneful strains of the *Thebais,* when Statius has gladdened the city, and fixed the day for reciting it" (Juvenal *Satires* 7, c. line 82).

Three times he won the annual prize for poetry at the festival at Alba, which was instituted by Domitian, but when he lost at the quinquennial Capitoline contest in 94 he returned in shame to Neapolis with his wife Claudia, where he remained the rest of his days. Nonetheless, he seems to have been comfortably well off and happy throughout his life, with very little to complain about. His extant works are the *Thebais,* an epic concerning the seven against Thebes, in 12 books; the *Achilleis,* an unfinished epic on the life of Achilles; and the *Silvae,* 32 poems in five books.

SULLA, L. CORNELIUS: (138–78 BC) Surnamed Felix, a Roman soldier and politician perhaps best remembered for the first use of the *proscriptio,* a death list, in Roman history. He died of a burst blood vessel while suffering from a morbid infestation of lice, known medically as *morbus pediculosus.*

SYLLA: See SULLA.

SYNESIUS: (?373–?414) Surnamed the Philosopher. Born in Cyrene (an ancient city in Libya) of wealthy parents, as a young man he traveled to Alexandria, where he became a Neoplatonist and disciple of Hypatia. In 397 he was chosen as ambassador by his native city to travel to Constantinople to plead with the Emperor Arcadius for a lowering of taxes. He stayed there three years, writing and no doubt learning something about politics, before his request was at last granted. Returning home, he spent the next ten years hunting and studying on his estate. During this period (403) he was married at Alexandria.

In 410 he was popularly chosen to become Bishop of Ptolemais. Since he was more of a Neoplatonist than a Christian, he was less than enthusiastic, but ultimately accepted the office thrust upon him with philosophic reservations—he refused to toe the Church line on the creation of the soul, the literal resurrection or the apocalypse and was allowed to retain his wife. His tenure as bishop was turbulent but successful. The date of his death is not known and may have been as late as 430. Many of his works have survived, including a large collection of letters, 12 Neoplatonic hymns and an alchemical work in the form of a commentary on pseudo-Democritus.

TACITUS, CAIUS (or PUBLIUS) CORNELIUS: (?55–?120) Roman historian. The time and place of his birth are unknown, but he must have been born sometime around 55 AD into a respectable family, as he himself writes *(Histories* 1.1) that he was noticed and promoted by the Emperor Vespasian, further elevated by Titus, and again advanced by Domitian. His prosperity continued under Nerva and Trajan. He was appointed along with his close friend, Pliny the Younger, to conduct the prosecution of Marius in 99. Nothing is recorded of his death. His works and their conjectured dates are the *Dialogue on Orators* (77), *Life of Agricola* (97), *Germany* (99), the *Histories* (116) and the *Annals* (118).

TARQUINIUS PRISCUS, LUCIAS: (658–578 BC) King of Rome, called the Elder. His father, Demaratus, fled political intrigue in Corinth, settled in Etruria and married an Etruscan wife, leaving his vast wealth to his first son, Lucumo, who despite his noble connection through his wife and his money was excluded from local politics. In discontent he set out for Rome in a chariot with his wife beside him. It was on this journey that the event of the eagle related by Agrippa is said to have occurred. Tarquinius was a great warrior and builder and is credited with the Roman sewer system, the Circus Maximus, the Forum and the Capitoline temple. He was assassinated in his 80th year.

TERENTIANUS MAURUS: (late 2nd century) Of Mauritania, he was a Roman poet who wrote an incomplete poem in four books called *De literis, syllabis, pedibus, metris* (On letters, syllables, feet, meters), which was based on a work of Caesius Bassus that the latter had dedicated to his friend, the Emperor Nero. Of the treatise of Bassus nothing remains but a few fragments. Terentianus was used as a source by later writers on prosody.

TERPANDER: (7th century BC) Of Antissa in Lesbos, he is regarded as the father of Greek classical music. According to Strabo he was the first to use a seven-string cithara, which until then had only four strings. Terpander traveled to Sparta in answer to a mandate from the Delphic oracle and with his music quelled a sedition that had been brewing. At the first recorded celebration of the Karneian festival at Sparta in 676 BC, Terpander won first prize in the music competition. He is credited with a variety of innovations, introducing several new rhythms and a new division of the ode, and was famous for his drinking songs. Only a few fragments of his poetry survive.

TEUCER: Semi-mythical founder and first king of Troy, said to be the son of the river god Scamander and the nymph Idaea. About the Babylonian mathematician of this name mentioned by Porphyry (p. 377) I have been able to learn nothing.

THALES: (?636–?546 BC) Ionic philosopher born at Miletus (a city once located on the west coast of Turkey near the mouth of the Menderes River). He is famed for having predicted an eclipse of the Sun in the reign of the Lydian king Alyattes, and is said to have studied in Egypt. His name stood at the head of the list of Seven Sages of antiquity.

THEBIT: See TOBIT BEN KORRA.

THEMISTIUS: (4th century) Philosopher native to Paphlagonia, he traveled first to Constantinople, then to Rome, enjoying the considerable favor of six successive emperors. He was made prefect of Constantinople by Theodosius in 384 and entrusted with the tutorship of Arcanius, the emperor's son, in 387. Libanius and Gregory Nazianzus were his friends and correspondents, the latter calling Themistius the "king of arguments." He wrote 36 orations, one of which is not extant, and died around 390.

THEOPHRASTUS: (?372–287 BC) Greek philosopher of Eresus in Lesbos, he studied in Athens under Plato, and later Aristotle, whom he succeeded as president of the Lyceum. Aristotle bequeathed his private library and the original manuscripts of his works to Theophrastus. He wrote many works, notably *On the History of Plants* in ten books; *On the Causes of Plants,* of which six of eight books survive; and *Of Stones.*

THEOPOMPOS: (?378–?300 BC) Greek historian and rhetorician born at Chios, where he studied under Isocrates. Cicero in his *Brutus* relates that Isocrates said of him and one of his fellow students, Ephorus the historian, that Ephorus required the spur, but Theopompos the bit. Around 352 BC he gained the prize for oratory given by Artemisia, competing against his old teacher, Isocrates, and beating him. When his father was exiled for supporting the cause of the Lacedaemonians, Theopompos went with him. He gained the friendship of Alexander the Great, who directed by letters that the Chians recall their exiles, and in 333 BC, when he was 45, Theopompos was able to return to his native land and take up the political power and wealth that was his by his birthright.

His impetuous temper earned him many enemies, but the power of Alexander protected him. Ultimately, at age 75, he was expelled from Chios on the charge of disturbing the public peace and found a cold haven in Egypt under Ptolemy in 305 BC. Ptolemy would have put Theopompos to death but for the strenuous intercession of the friends of the historian. Perhaps the main thing held against Theopompos was the truthfulness and impartiality of his writings. He is remembered for his *History of Philip,* his *Letter to Alexander*, his *Hellenics* (a large portion of which was discovered as recently as 1907) and his *Epitome of Herodotus' History,* the authorship of which is suspect.

THETEL: (or Techel, or Rechel, or Cehel) A Jewish writer chiefly known for a work concerning the magical powers of certain images engraved on precious or semiprecious stones. Thomas of Cantempre gives a Latin translation of this text in the 14th book of his *De natura rerum* (On the nature of things), written between 1228 and 1244. Thorndike (2:53:390) conjectures that Thetel is the same writer as Zethel (or Zachel, Zahel, Zehel, Zael, Zoel or Zebulis), whose name appears on a number of early astrological treatises, some of them listed by Albertus Magnus in his *Speculum astronomiae.* Zethel is also mentioned as an astronomical authority by Michael Scot (Thorndike, 2:322). Cecco d'Ascoli (ibid., 959) and Giovanni da Fontana (ibid., 4:171). For a list of manuscripts attributed to Thetel, see Thorndike 2:53, appendix 2.

TIBERIUS CLAUDIUS NERO CAESAR (42 BC–37 AD) Emperor of Rome from the death of Augustus in 14 AD until his own gently assisted demise in 37 AD.

TIBULLUS, ALBIUS: (54–18 BC) Roman poet. His *Elegies* are short love poems in four books. The first two books are undoubtedly his, the third book is by another author though attributed to him and the fourth book is partly Tibullus and partly another. Horace was a friend of the poet and has left a picture of him: "You were never body without soul. The gods have granted to you beauty, to you riches, and the art of enjoying them" (Horace *Epistles* 1.4 [Translation Publishing, 1961], 375).

TIMOTHEUS: (446–357 BC) A native of Miletus, this celebrated poet and musician enjoyed little early success because of his passion for innovation. Once when he was hissed from the stage, Euripides told him not to worry, that soon he would have the audience at his feet, which proved true not long after—the Ephesians paid him 1,000 pieces of gold for his hymn to Artemis. He is said to have increased the number of strings on the lyre (cithara), according to Pausanias adding four to the existing seven, but according to Suidas adding two to the existing nine.

TIRESIAS: Semi-mythical blind Theban seer. Two stories are told of his blindness. He is said to have seen Athene bathing, whereupon the goddess splashed water into his eyes and took away his sight. The mother of Tiresias, Chariclo, appealed to the mercy of Athene, who, relenting somewhat, granted him the power to know the speech of birds and gave him a magic golden staff to help him find his way.

According to the other tale, Zeus and Hera were arguing over who derived more pleasure from lovemaking, a man or a woman. They decided to ask Tiresias because he had been both sexes, a prodigy that came about this way: walking on Mount Cithaeron (some say Mount Cyllene), Tiresias saw two snakes together, a male and a female. He struck at them and, chancing to kill the female, was changed into a woman. Seven years later he again met two snakes and struck them with his staff, this time killing the male, which caused him to resume his masculine form.

Tiresias sided with Zeus in the debate and agreed that women derived nine times the pleasure of men from sex. This angered Hera, who "condemned the eyes of the umpire to eternal darkness. But the omnipotent father (for it is not allowed any God to cancel the acts of another Deity) gave him the knowledge of things to come, in recompense for his loss of sight, and alleviated his punishment by this honour." (Ovid *Metamorphoses* 3.5, c. line 334 [Riley, 100]).

TOBIT BEN KORRA: (836–901) Arabian mathematician and astronomer of Baghdad, a part of the great surge of Arab learning initiated in the 7th century by the unifying force of Mohammed. He worked at the observatory built in Baghdad in 829 by the Caliph al-Mamun and is remembered for his erroneous theory of the trepidation of the equinoxes, which attempts to explain the precession of the equinoxes as a libration, or rhythmic oscillation, of the ecliptic—a notion first suggested by Theon of Alexandria, who wrote a commentary on the *Almagest* of Ptolemy.

Tobit is also remembered for his translation of the *Elements* of Euclid, and his formula for deriving amicable numbers—pairs of numbers the factors of one added together equaling the other, and vice versa. The smallest pair is 220 and 284. Amicable numbers were known to the Pythagoreans and credited by them with mystical properties. Tobit appears to be the source of Agrippa's fixed stars, listed in ch. XXXI, bk. II, and ch. XXXII, bk. I.

TRAJANUS, MARCUS ULPIUS: (52–117) Better known as Trajan, he was born in Italica, in Spain. His father had begun as a common legionnaire and worked his way up through the ranks to the governorship of Asia. The father trained his son in his own principles of austerity and military discipline. Trajan traveled widely through the Empire as a soldier and gained a good reputation. When Nerva replaced the murdered Domitian as emperor in 96, Trajan became consular legate to Upper Germany. Needing a strong military ally, Nerva adopted Trajan as his son the following year, and in 98 Nerva died, making Trajan emperor.

His military powers insured his complete mastery of the army, and his simplicity and honesty won the love of the people. Insofar as he could without threatening his own power, he restored the honor and security of the senate. His wife, Plotina, was as simple and benevolent as her husband. There was no royal court, no imperial pomp and no intrigue during their reign. Military victory in the Docian war along the Danube brought seven years of peace.

In 113 Trajan set out to extend the Empire to the east. Although he had impressive victories, the campaign was ultimately a failure. It encouraged the Jewish uprising that was only finally quelled by Hadrian. Stricken by sickness in 117, Trajan returned by ship to Italy and died in August at Selinus in Cilicia.

TRITHEMIUS, JOHANNES: (1462–1516) German divine, historian and magician born at Trittenheim near Trier on the Moselle River. His birth name was von Heidenberg, but in accordance with the custom of his day he adopted the name of his place of birth. When he was a year old his father, a vine dresser, died, and his mother married a man who treated him harshly. This may account for his precociousness and mysticism. He claimed that while still a young child an angel appeared to him in a dream and offered him a choice of two tablets with letters written upon them. When he selected one of the tablets the angel promised to fulfill his prayers, and vanished. From that day he hungered after knowledge and taught himself to read German in the space of only a month. His need to learn became voracious. He went secretly to a neighbor at night, who taught him Latin by candlelight. Since he was unhappy at home in any case, he traveled, first to Trier and then to Heidelberg, where he received instruction from a mysterious stranger in the secret arts.

In 1482 he decided to return to Trittenheim, but became caught in a blizzard on the way and was forced to seek shelter in the Benedictine monastery of Saint Martin at Sponheim. Here he suddenly determined to become a monk. So successful was this resolution that in 1485 he was appointed abbot, much against his own wishes, at the tender age of 23 years.

He immediately set about repairing the decay of the buildings and rebuilding the library, which due to the negligence of the monks had shrunk to only 48 volumes. Over the next 23 years he raised this number to 2,000. The books covered all subjects. Many were rare and valuable. The fame of the library drew scholars from all over Europe, and students such as Agrippa, and his contemporary Paracelsus, came to study more esoteric subjects such as alchemy and natural magic. Members of royal families, even the Emperor Maximilian I, consulted Trithemius for his learning.

His effect on the art and science of his age is incalculable—how much he influenced the Kabbalistic writings of Reuchlin, for example, or the Neoplatonic proportions of the artist Dürer, can only be conjectured. Agrippa was with Trithemius when he wrote the first manuscript of the *Occult Philosophy* in 1509–10, which he originally dedicated to his teacher.

Inevitably Trithemius was accused of sorcery, a charge he vehemently denied all through his life. There is a fable that he once raised the ghost of Maria, the late wife of the Emperor Maximilian. Although she could not speak, the Emperor recognized her by a mole on her neck and was assured that the shade was not a demon impersonating his wife. The English dramatist Christopher Marlowe (1564–1593) used a version of this story in his play *Doctor Faustus* (act 3, sc. 2, lines 63–73).

In 1506 Trithemius resigned his position at Sponheim and was appointed soon after abbot of the monastery of Saint Jakob at Würzburg, where he remained for the final decade of his life. Trithemius is credited with around 70 works, the most important of which from a magical standpoint are his *Steganographia,* on the conjuration of spirits; *Polygraphia,* on ciphers and magical alphabets; *De septem secundeis,* on the planetary angels that rule the cycle of ages; and *Veterum sophorum sigilla et imagines magicae,* a series of descriptions of talismans or magical images.

TULLIUS, SERVIUS: (6th century BC) The sixth king of Rome, he ruled 578–534 BC. His mother was the slave of the wife of Tarquinius Priscus. Tullius was born and raised in the royal palace as the king's son and took the king's daughter in marriage. When the sons of the king murdered Tarquinius in an attempt to secure the throne they saw slipping into the hands of this favored slave, Tullius concealed the king's death until he had taken full control of the government. A wise and mild ruler, he always had the support of his people. He is credited with establishing the constitution and civil institutions of Rome. He is fabled to have been murdered by L. Tarquinius Priscus and his own daughter Aruns.

VALENTINUS: (2nd century AD) The most prominent leader of any of the Gnostic sects. He was born in Lower Egypt and brought up and educated at Alexandria. Around 135 he went to Rome as an orthodox Christian and was even a candidate for the bishopric of Rome, but when he was passed over for this office he began to reveal his heretical views—or it may have been his expression of these views that denied him his placement. Around 160 he left Rome and traveled to Cyprus, where his break with the Church was made irrevocable. Valentinian Gnosticism had an elaborate system of 30 aeons and shared with other Gnostic sects a deep reverence for the female creative principle. It is described in greater detail by Irenaeus in his *Adversus heraeses.*

VARRO, TERENTIUS: (116–28 BC) This celebrated writer was called the "most learned of the Romans." He was certainly one of the most prolific, composing by his own count 490 books, of which only two have survived: *De re rustica libri III,* a treatise on agriculture; and *De lingua Latina,* a grammatical treatise filled with curious lore of which only six of 24 books are extant. A large portion of his *De cultu deorum* has come down to us through the copious references made by Augustine in his *City of God.*

VAUGHAN, THOMAS: (1622–1666) English alchemist and mystical philosopher, was born of an ancient Welsh family at Newton St. Briget near Scethrog-by-Usk, Brecknockshire. He received a degree from Oxford in 1642, and subsequently pursued the art of alchemy with great diligence in Newton at the farm of his twin brother, the poet Henry Vaughan, and in various places of residence in London. Sir Robert Murray financed these researches. By his own account Vaughan succeeded in discovering the fabled Elixir, as he says, "an oyle with which I did miracles" (Waite 1888, ix). He died "when he was operating strong mercury, some of which by chance getting up his nose, killed him" (ibid., viii). Under the pseudonym Eugenius Philalethes he wrote *Anthroposophia theomagica, Anima magica abscondita, Magia Adamica* and *Coelum terrae,* all in 1650 while he was under the powerful influence of Agrippa's writings. Indeed, he virtually deifies Agrippa, so lavish is his praise. Later writings of Vaughan include *Aphorisimi magici eugeniani* (1651), *The Fame and Confession of the Fraternity of R.C.* (1652) and *Aula lucis* (1652).

VERRES, GAIUS (or CAIUS): (?120–43 BC) An unscrupulous Roman magistrate who made it his life business to become a fawning lapdog of some powerful man, obtain a political appointment from him and then pillage the unfortunate citizens who came under his rule, finally buying and conniving his own freedom from prosecution by betraying his former master. In 82 BC he was quaestor to Carbo and a member of the Marian party. He deserted Carbo and went over to Sulla, who gave him a present of land in Beneventum and, more importantly, made him safe from prosecution for his previous crimes of embezzlement.

In 80 BC he became quaestor to Dolabella, governor of Cilicia, which he helped to plunder. When Dolabella was brought to trial in 78 BC, Verres betrayed him in return for a pardon. In 74 BC, through lavish bribes and his association with Sulla, Verres became praetor of Rome and shamefully abused his authority for political ends. Sent as governor to Sicily, the richest province of Rome, he extorted so much money and misery from the people that it was said they suffered more under him than in three previous wars.

Driven beyond endurance, the Sicilians begged Cicero to prosecute Verres for his crimes before the senate. Cicero agreed. Verres boasted that he had stolen so much money from Sicily he could expend three quarters of it in bribes and still be a rich man. He chose Hortensius, the best Roman advocate, to defend him, and tried to get Cicero replaced by Caecilius, who was far less skilled. The Sicilians rejected this ploy. Fortunately the judge, city praetor Acilius Glabrio, was an honest man. He employed a technical process of Roman law called *divinatio* whereby the judices, without hearing evidence, determined who should be prosecutor. Cicero stayed. The last hope for Verro was to delay the trial until the next year when his friends would be in power. But working at a fever pitch, Cicero collected evidence and embodied the prosecution in a single oration, *Divinatio in Q. Caecilium,* and in a subsequent statement of the case. The defense was caught unprepared. Verres fled to Marseilles with as much of his loot as he could carry. Cicero eventually published the rest of the orations he had been planning for the trial but had not had time to deliver.

In 43 BC, Verres was proscribed by M. Anthony, who himself coveted some of his stolen art treasures. So ended the life of one of the most repulsive Romans remembered by history.

VILLA NOVA, ARNOLDAS DE: (?1235–1313) Also called Arnoldus de Villanueva, Arnoldus Villanovanus or Arnaud de Villeneuve. A Spanish alchemist, astrologer and physician, he gained a considerable reputation in Paris but was forced to flee to Sicily to escape the ire of the Church. About 1313 he was called to Avignon in his capacity as physician to treat the ailing Pope Clement V, but he died aboard ship before completing the voyage. Many alchemical writings were attributed to him on questionable authority. These were collected and published at Lyons in 1504 along with a biography of his life.

VITELLIUS: See VITELLO.

VITELLO: (13th century) Also written Witelo or Vitellio, a Polish natural philosopher who wrote the work *Optics* around 1270. In it he attempts to solve Aristotle's problem: "Why is it that when the sun passes through quadrilaterals, as for instance in wickerwork, it does not produce figures rectangular in shape but circular?" (*Problems* 15.6.911b [Hett, 1:333]). He was the first to put forward the notion that rainbows are caused by refraction through, rather than reflection from, raindrops, refuting the established view set down by Aristotle in his *Meteors.* The work of Vitello is to a large extent based on the Arabian philosopher Alhazen, who died in 1038.

WILLIAM OF PARIS: (?1180–1249) Also called William of Auvergne. He received a

degree in theology at the University of Paris. When as a deacon of the Church he went to Rome to appeal a disputed election, he so impressed the pope that he was raised to the rank of bishop. From 1228 until his death he served as Bishop of Paris. During this period he granted the Dominicans their first chair of theology in that city and took part in an attack upon the *Talmud.* His main work is *De universo* (On the universe), which treats of magic, divination, demons, astrology and the occult virtues.

XANTHUS: (5th century BC) Lydian historian. The *Four Books of Lydian History,* which has survived only in fragments and which was attributed to Xanthus, is thought to be the work of some later Alexandrian grammarian.

XENOCRATES: (396–314 BC) Philosopher of Chalcedon. He followed Plato to Sicily in 361 BC. Upon the death of Plato (347 BC) he attached himself to Aristotle and became head of the Academy at Athens from 339 to 314 BC. His philosophy closely follows Plato, but he believed that ideal numbers and mathematical numbers are the same, essentially a magical notion that was held by the Pythagoreans and which drew the criticism of Aristotle in his *Metaphysics* (13.1, 9). Only the titles of his works have survived, but he is frequently referred to and quoted by other writers.

ZACHALIAS THE BABYLONIAN: The author of an ancient lapidary used by Pliny as a source for book 37 of his *Natural History.* He and his work are otherwise unknown.

ZACHARIAS: See ZACHALIAS.

ZAHEL: See THETEL.

ZAMOLXIDES: See ZAMOLXIS.

ZAMOLXIS: Also called Zalmoxis or Gebeleizis. God of the Getae, a Thracian tribe than dwelt south of the mouths of the River Danube. Every five years the Getae chose a man to deliver messages to the god and dispatched him by casting him up into the air so that he fell upon spears held upright in the hands of other tribesmen. It was considered a good omen if the man died. Herodotus relates this story and goes on to say:

> I am told by the Greeks who dwell on the shores of the Hellespont and the Pontus, that Zalmoxis was in reality a man, that he lived at Samos, and while there was the slave of Pythagoras son of Mnesarchus. After obtaining his freedom he grew rich, and leaving Samos, returned to his own country. (Herodotus *The History* 4 [Rawlinson, 233])

Zalmoxis supposedly constructed a secret underground chamber in which he hid for three years, then suddenly and miraculously emerged to lend credence to his doctrine of immortality. To this, Herodotus skeptically comments: "I for my part neither put entire faith in this story of Zalmoxis and his underground chamber, nor do I altogether discredit it: but I believe Zalmoxis to have lived long before the time of Pythagoras" (ibid.). Plato briefly mentions him as one proverbially skilled in magic: "For if, as he declares, you have this gift of temperance already, and are temperate enough, in that case you have no need of any charms, whether of Zalmoxis or of Abaris the Hyperborean, and I may as well let you have the cure of the head at once" *(Charmides* 158-b [Jowett, 104]). Zalmoxis is said to be identical to Sabazius, the Thracian Dionysus. Mnaseas of Patrae identified him with the god Cronus.

ZENOTENUS: See ZENOTHEMIS.

ZENOTHEMIS: Author of a lapidary used as a source by Pliny in his *Natural History.* Nothing is known of the author or his work.

ZOROASTER: (fl. c. 1000 BC) Also called Zarathustra (Iranian) and Zardusht (Persian). The founder of the Magian religion, who was born in the northern part of present-day Iran. Nothing about his personal life is certain. He is responsible for abolishing the sensual worship of the devas and defining God as two abstract opposing principles—Ahura Mazda, the Wise Lord, and Angra Mainyu, the Evil Spirit. Of him Pliny says: "We find it stated that Zoroaster was the only human being who ever laughed on the same day on which he was born. We hear, too, that his brain pulsated so strongly that it repelled the hand when laid upon it, a presage of his future wisdom" (Pliny 7.16 [Bostock and Riley, 2:155]). He also says: "It is said that Zoroaster lived thirty years in the wilderness upon cheese, prepared in such a peculiar manner, that he was insensible to the advances of old age" (Pliny 11.97 [Bostock and Riley, 3:85]).

A collection of metaphysical aphorisms called the *Chaldean Oracles of Zoroaster* was popular in the Middle Ages, and it is certain Agrippa was familiar with at least some of these. According to Franz Cumont, the literature attributed to Zoroaster at the library of Alexandria amounted to two million lines, but none of these texts has survived.

Geographical Dictionary

A CHAIA: Land on the northern coast of Peloponnesus.

AEGOS-POTAMOS: Small river that flowed into the Hellespont (present-day Dardenelles) across Thracian Chersonesus (present-day peninsula of Gallipoli). There is a small town on the river of the same name.

AESCULANS: See ASCULUM.

AETNA: Volcanic mountain (present-day Etna) in northeast Sicily.

AGRA: One of the ancient divisions *(demus)* of Attica, it stood on the bank of the Ilissus River, which had its source on the slope of Mount Hymettus, not far southeast of Athens. Agra contained a temple of Artemis Agrotera.

AGRAS: See AGRA.

ALCOMENEUM: Perhaps Orchomenus. See separate note.

ALEXANDRIA: Also spelled Alexandrea. Seaport in Lower Egypt just west of the Nile delta. Founded by Alexander the Great in 332 BC. It served as the capitol under the Ptolemies.

ALEXANDRIA, LAKE OF: See MAREOTIS.

AMATHUS: Also spelled Amathuntis, an ancient town on the south coast of Cyprus (at present-day Limassol) that boasted a celebrated temple of Aphrodite, who in consequence bore the name Amathusia.

APOLLONIA: Important town in Ilyria (it stood near the mouth of the Vijose River in present-day Albania).

APULIA: The region on the southeastern coast of Italy (present-day Apulia). The heel of the boot of Italy was called by the Romans Calabria and distinguished from Apulia, which bordered it on the south.

ARABIA, HAPPY: Arabia was divided by the ancients into three parts: Arabia Petraea (Rocky Arabia—the present-day Sinai, Israel and western Jordan), Arabia Deserta (Desert Arabia—inland and northern Saudi Arabia, eastern Jordan and Iraq) and Arabia Felix (Happy Arabia —southwestern Saudi Arabia and Yemen). It derived its designation "Felix" from the fertile lowlands lying along the shore of the Red Sea.

ARACYNTHUS: Mountain on the southwest coast of Aetolia, near Pleuron (near present-day Mesolongion in central Greece). Later writers incorrectly placed the mountain on the border of Boeotia and Attica and identified it with the Boeotian hero Amphion: "I sing the songs which, whenever he called home his herds, Amphion of

Dirce used to sing on Attic Aracynth" (Virgil *Eclogues* 2, line 24 [Lonsdale and Lee, 14]).

ARCADIA: The mountainous country in the middle of Peloponnesus, Greece.

ARGOS: Town in Argolis, Peloponnesus (present-day Argos). It was celebrated for the worship of Hera. Her temple, called the Heraeum, lay between Argos and Mycenae.

ARHOS: See ARGOS.

ARIANA: The eastern provinces of the ancient Persian Empire (present-day central and eastern Iran).

ARICIA: Ancient town of Latium at the foot of the Alban Mount on the Appian Way, about 16 miles from ancient Rome. Near the town was a temple and sacred grove of Diana.

ARPINA: Ancient place in Elis near the Alpheus River (not too far from present-day Olimbia in Peloponnesus, Greece).

ARREPHINA: Perhaps Arpina. See the separate note.

ARRIANA: See ARIANA.

ASCULUM: The chief town of Picenum, a country of central Italy (present-day Ascoli Piceno).

ATTICA: The roughly triangular region in Greece surrounding Athens that lies south of Mount Parnis.

AVENTINUM: *Mons Aventinus,* one of the seven hills upon which ancient Rome was built. It supported the temple of Diana and for this reason Martial called it *Collis Dianae.*

AZOTUS: Free city of the Philistines near the seacoast (present-day Ashdod in Israel).

BACTRIA: Province of the Persian Empire that lay southwest of the headwaters of the Oxus

River (present-day Amu-Dar'ya), which divided it from the Persian province of Sogdiana on the northeastern bank. It occupied the northeastern corner of present-day Afghanistan. Agrippa calls it "Island Bractia," but it is not referred to in this way by Ptolemy, who groups it with Casperia and Serica *(Tetrabiblos* 2.3 [Robbins, 147, 159]).

BAEOTIANS: See BOEOTIA.

BASTARNIA: Region on the northern shore of the Euxine (Black Sea), between the rivers Tyras (present-day Dniester) and Borysthenes (Dnieper), extending as far south as the mouths of the Danube. Here lived a warlike German tribe who frequently battled the Romans in Macedonia until they were driven permanently north of the Danube in 30 BC. Roughly corresponds to the southern Ukraine.

BERECYNTHUS: Berecynthus Mons, a mountain in Phrygia sacred to Cybele, after which she received the name Cybele Berecynthia.

BITHEVIA: See BITHYNIA.

BITHYNIA: District of Asia Minor (Turkey) on the southern shore of the Pontus Euxinus (Black Sea) between Paphlagonia on the east and Mysia on the west.

BOEOTIA: District in ancient Greece, located in what is now central Greece. Thebes was its chief city.

BORISTHENES: See BORYSTHENES.

BORYSTHENES: Also spelled Borysthenis, a town at the mouth of the river of the same name (present-day Dnieper, in the Ukraine).

BRACTIA: See BACTRIA.

BYZANTINE: See BYZANTIUM.

BYZANTIUM: Town on the Thracian Bosporus which overlooked the entrance to the Euxine (Black Sea). The Emperor Constantine changed its name to Constantinopolis in 330 (it is present-day Istanbul, Turkey).

CALABRIA: Peninsula in southeast Italy; formed part of Apulia.

CALEDONIA: The Roman name for the north of Britain, still used in a poetic sense for Scotland.

CALIDONIA: See CALEDONIA.

CALLICHOROS: Perhaps Calycadnus. See separate note.

CALYCADNUS: River in Cilicia Tracheia (present-day Goksu on the southern coast of Turkey), which, however, is nowhere near Paphlagonia.

CANDY: Crete.

CANNA: See CANNAE.

CANNAE: A village in Apulia located northeast of Canusium (near present-day Andria, Italy). It is famous as the site of the victory of the Carthaginian general Hannibal over the Roman army in 216 BC.

CAPPADOCHIA: A mountainous region of Asia Minor with good pastureland for horses (it was located roughly in the center of present-day Turkey east of Lake Tuz).

CARCHEDONIA: See CARTHAGE.

CARTHAGE: Great city on the coast of northern Africa (near present-day Tunis), which at one point rivaled Rome in power and wealth. It controlled a region roughly corresponding to present-day Tunisia, which was called Carchedonia.

CASPIA: Land of the Caspii, Scythian tribes dwelling on the southern and southwestern shores of the Caspian Sea. Strabo places them on the western shore, Herodotus and Ptolemy on the south.

CATANA: Or Catina, a town on the east coast of Sicily at the foot of Mount Aetna (present-day Catania).

CATENIAN: See CATANA.

CELTICA: One of the three parts into which Julius Caesar divided Gaul. It corresponds to central and western France.

CHALDEA: A Babylonian province in what is now southeastern Iraq. In a wider sense the term applied to the whole of Babylonia.

CHONIA: District in the south of Italy around the town of Chone. Chonia is said to have included southeast Lucania and east Bruttium (the heel of Italy). It is thought its people may have been related to the Chaones of Epirus in northern Greece.

CHRYSA: A city on the coast of the Troad, near Thebes (it stood just south of the island of Bozcaada, Turkey, not far from the site of ancient Troy). There was a temple of Apollo Smintheus here.

CILICIA: That part of the southern coast of Asia Minor (Turkey) that projects into the Mediterranean Sea opposite the island of Cyprus, extending about as far east as the present-day town of Maras.

CIMMERII: The Cimmerians were a mythical people who dwelt in the far west on the ocean, enshrouded by mist and darkness. There was a real people of the same name who lived on the bank of the Palus Maeotis (Sea of Azov).

CITHAERON MONS: The highest summit of this range of mountains was sacred to Cithaeronian Zeus and the site of the festival called *Daedala*. It was located on the borders of Attica, Boeotia and Mygaris (roughly between present-day Thivai and Megara, in Greece).

CLAROS: See CLARUS.

CLARUS: Small town on the coast of Ionia near Colophon (at the east end of the Gulf of Kusada, Turkey). It was known for its temple and oracle of Apollo, who was surnamed Clarius.

CLAZOMENAE: An important city in Asia Minor located on the Gulf of Smyrna (present-day Gulf of Izmir, Turkey).

CNIDUS: See GNIDUS.

COANS: Chones. See CHONIA.

COLCHICA: Colchis, a country of Asia on the eastern shore of the Euxine (Black Sea) that roughly corresponds to present-day western Georgia in the former USSR.

COMAGENA: See COMMAGENE.

COMMAGENE: The northeastern district of Syria, notable in ancient times for its fertile farmlands.

CROTONA: City on the southernmost part of Italy, where Crotone is today. A Greek city founded in 710 BC, it flourished as the place Pythagoras chose to establish his school.

CROTONIENSIANS: See CROTONA.

CRUSTUMENSIANS: See CRUSTUMERIUM.

CRUSTUMERIUM: Ancient Sabine town in Latium, located in the mountains at the headwaters of the Allia River not far from the Tiber River (about 11 miles north of Rome).

CYMERIAN: See CIMMERII.

CYNOPS: Perhaps Cynopolis, a city of Middle Egypt located on an island in the Nile. It was a chief seat of the worship of Anubis. There was also a city of the same name on the Nile delta.

CYNTHUS: Mountain on the Isle of Delos (just west of the larger island of Mikonos in the Aegean Sea). Apollo and Artemis were said to have been born here.

CYRENAICA: District in northern Africa located on the coast of the Mediterranean between Marmaridae on the east and the Syrtis Major (Gulf of Sidra) on the west. Northeast corner of present-day Libya.

CYRENE: Chief town of Cyrenaica, a region in North Africa (it was at present-day Shahat in Libya).

CYTHERA: An island to the southwest of Laconia (present-day Kithira off the southern points of Peloponnesus). There was a town in the interior with the same name. The island was colonized by the Phoenicians, who introduced the worship of Aphrodite. The goddess was called for this reason Cytherea or Cythereis.

CYTHEREANS: See CYTHERA.

CYTHEROS: See CITHAERON MONS.

DELOS: Smallest island of the Cyclades. Legend says it was raised out of the sea by Poseidon and floated until Zeus fastened it down with adamantine chains to be the birthplace of Apollo and Artemis (it lies just west of present-day Mikonos).

DELPHI: Small town in Phocis (central Greece) renowned as the seat of the oracle of Apollo. Homer mentions it by its earlier name, Pytho. It was regarded as the center of the world and called "the navel of the Earth." Within the great temple of Apollo was a fissure that exhaled toxic fumes. Over this the Pythoness of Apollo sat upon a tripod and received the gift of prophecy whenever she breathed the vapors. No trace of this fissure exists in modern times.

DELPHOS: See DELPHI.

DINDYMUS: Or Dindyma, or Dindyorum, a mountain in Phrygia near the town of Pessinus (present-day Murat Dagi near the town of Usak in west-central Turkey). It was sacred to Cybele, who was called on that account Dindymene.

DOTHAM: See DOTHAN.

DOTHAN: Town in central Palestine. It is identified with present-day Tell Dothan, located about 60 miles north of Jerusalem.

ELA: See ELAM.

ELAM: Region of the Zagros Mountains in western Iran.

ELEUSIS: Town in Attica that lay northwest of Athens on the coast near the border with Megara. It possessed a temple of Demeter and was the site of the mysteries of Eleusinia held in honor of this goddess and the goddess Persephone.

ELIS: Country on the western coast of Peloponnesus, where Zeus was worshiped at Olympia near Pisa with a lavish festival every four years. In consequence Elis was held to be a sacred place. Its inhabitants had priestly honors, its cities were unwalled and it was free from the terrors of war.

ENNA: Also called Henna, an ancient fortified town in Sicily that was said to be the center of the island. A celebrated temple of Demeter was located here. Visitors were shown a meadow where Pluto was reputed to have carried off Persephone and a cave into which the pair was said to have vanished underground.

EPHESUS: Chief of the 12 Ionian cities on the coast of Asia Minor (it was located on the present-day Gulf of Kusada, Turkey). Beyond its walls stood a famous temple of Artemis.

EPIDAMNUS: Town in Greek Illyria (present-day Durres on the coast of Albania).

EPIDAURUS: Town in Argolis (on Peloponnesus) on the Sinus Saronicus (Saronic Gulf) which ruled a costal district called Epidauria independently until Roman times.

EPIDAURUS LIMERA: Town on the eastern shore of Laconia (on the eastern side of the southernmost projection of Peloponnesus). It is not to be confused with Epidaurus in Argolis.

EPIRUS: Northwest Greece.

ERCTA: Also called Ercte, or Hiercte (present-day Mount Pellegrino), a mountain near Palermo on the northern coast of Sicily. It played a part in the first Punic War as a fortified position for the Carthaginians.

ERICE: See ERCTA.

ETRURIA: A country in central Italy (present-day Tuscany), the heart of the Etruscan Empire, which was a great power before the rise of Rome.

FATHER ACHAIA: See PATRAI.

FREGELIA: See FREGELLANUS.

FREGELLANUS: An important town in Latium, which was in ancient times the region of central Italy south of the Tiber. It was destroyed by Optimius in 125 when it became involved in a revolt against Rome.

GAETULIA: A large region in the interior of northern Africa corresponding roughly to present-day central Algeria.

GETULIA: See GAETULIA.

GILBOA: Mountain at the northern end of a range of hills in Samoria (present-day Jelbun, Israel).

GNIDUS: Or Cnidus, a celebrated Lacedaemonian city on the west coast of Asia Minor (Turkey), located at the tip of the promontory south of the Sinus Ceramicus (Gulf of Kerme).

GORDIANA: Gordiaea, Gordyaei, Gordyene, or Corduene, a mountainous district in the south of Armenia Major between the Arsissa Palus (Lake Van in Turkey) and the Gordyaei Montes. It lay in present-day eastern Turkey and Armenia.

GRYNIA: Or Grynium, an ancient fortified city on the coast of Sinus Elaiticus (present-day Gulf of Candarli, Turkey). It was celebrated for its temple and oracle of Apollo Grynaeus.

HELIOPOLIS: Two ancient cities bore the name Heliopolis: (1) in Syria, chief seat of the worship of Baal, whose image was the Sun and whom the Greeks identified with Apollo and Zeus (it was located in present-day Lebanon not far east of Zegharta); (2) in Lower Egypt (just northeast of present-day Cairo). It was to this city that the phoenix returned to be reborn.

HELLESPONT: Strait connecting the Aegean Sea with the Sea of Marmara in present-day Turkey.

HERMOPOLIS MAGNA: One of the oldest cities in Egypt, it was a chief seat for the worship of Anubis and was the sacred burial place of the ibis, the bird symbol of Thoth (Hermes). The city was located on the west bank of the Nile just below the border of Upper Egypt (not far south of present-day El Minya)

HIRCANIA: See HYRCANIA.

HOMOLE: See HOMOLIUM.

HOMOLIUM: Town in Thessaly at the foot of Mount Ossa. It stood on the site of present-day Lamia.

HORMOPOLITES: See HERMOPOLIS MAGNA.

HYPAEPA: City in Lydia on the southern slope of Mount Tmolus, near the north bank of the Cayster (not far from present-day Tire in western Turkey).

HYPEPA: See HYPAEPA.

HYPERBOREA: Mythic region in which the Sun rose and set once a year, inhabited by a blessed people who worshiped Apollo and lived a thousand years. Originally it may have referred to the wilds of northern Thessaly, but as knowledge of geography expanded it was pushed farther north, to the very shores of the Hyperboreus Oceanus. The term "hyperborean" came to mean "the most northerly," and might in this sense be applied to anything.

HYRCANIA: Province of the ancient Persian Empire located on the southeastern coast of the Caspian Sea.

IDA: Two mountains bore this name: (1) in Crete, where Zeus was raised to adulthood; (2) in Mysia in Asia Minor (located about ten miles south of the innermost recess of the Gulf of Edremit in northwest Turkey). It was the scene of the rape of Ganymede and the judgment of Paris, and the ancient seat of the worship of Cybele, who was called on this account *Idaea Mater*.

IDALIAN GROVE: See IDALIUM.

IDALIUM: Town in Cyprus (present-day Dali) that was sacred to Aphrodite. The goddess carried the surname Idalia.

IDEA: See IDA.

IDUMIA: The Greek form of the biblical Edom, which in the time of the Romans extended along the eastern Mediterranean from Hebron in the north to Arabia Petrea in the south (corresponds to present-day southern Israel).

ILLYRIA: A region coequal with the western half of present-day Yugoslavia where it touches the Adriatic Sea. It was inhabited by numerous barbaric tribes.

IMBRES: See IMBROS.

IMBROS: An island in the north Aegean Sea (present-day Imroz). It was a seat of worship of the Cabiri, mystic divinities identified with Hephaestus. A town, also called Imbros, lay on the east of the island.

JUDEA: The Roman name for Palaestina (Palestine), which in the scriptures was called

Canaan. It corresponds more or less with present-day Israel.

LACEDAEMON: Another name for the city of Sparta, the chief city of the Greek Peloponnesus and the capitol of Laconia.

LACONIA: Southwest region of Peloponnesus.

LATIUM: Region of central Italy.

LAURENTUM: Ancient town of Latium that was located not far south of Rome.

LEMNOS: One of the largest islands in the Aegean Sea (present-day Limnos). There were two towns, Myrian (Mirina) on the west coast, and Hephaestia, or Hephaestias, on the northwest, the latter named after the god to whom the island was sacred. Hephaestus was fabled to have fallen to Lemnos when Zeus seized him by the heel and threw him down from heaven. In ancient times the island had a volcano named Mosychlus.

LEUCADIA: Also called Leucas (present-day Leukas), an island in the Ionian Sea.

LOCRENSIANS: See LOCRIS.

LOCRIS: Region of Greece between the Gulf of Corinth and the coast opposite the Isle of Euboea. The native Locrians were divided into eastern and western peoples, the latter being a colony of the former. Homer only mentions the eastern Locrians, while Thucydides calls the western people rude and barbarous.

LUCANIA: Region in southern Italy on the west side of the Sinus Tarentinus (Gulf of Taranto).

LUCRINUS LACUS: Originally a deep bay on the coast of Campania (in the present-day Gulf of Pozzuoli, Italy), it was separated from the sea by a volcanic upheaval in preclassical times and became a saltwater lake famous for its oyster beds. In 1538 a volcanic mountain

called Monte Nuovo rose up from the lake and obliterated it.

LYCIA: A district on the southwestern coast of Asia Minor that encompassed the semicircular projection lying between the present-day Gulf of Antalya, Turkey, and the island of Rhodes.

LYDIA: District occupying the middle coast of the western part of Asia Minor (western Turkey). Mysia lay to the north and Caria to the south on the peninsula, dividing it into three regions.

LYGURIA: Mountainous region in northwest Italy that was in ancient times of considerably greater extent than the province that now bears the name. Its northern boundary was the Po River.

MACEDONIA : A country that covered the north of present-day Greece, homeland of Alexander the Great.

MAEOTIS PALUS: The inland sea (present-day Sea of Azov) on the border of Europe and Asia. The ancients had only vague ideas of its size and form. The Scythian tribes living on its shore were collectively called Maeotae.

MAGNESIA: District in the eastern part of Thessalia in Greece. It was in the form of a narrow, mountainous strip along the coast bounded on the west by the Thessalian plain (it comprised the land roughly east of a line between present-day Larisa and Volos).

MALEA: A promontory on the southeast of Laconia between the Argolic and Laconic gulfs (present-day Cape Malea). It was a dreaded passage for sailors. Upon it stood a temple of Apollo Maleates. Agrippa seems to confuse this Malea with the southern promontory of the Isle of Lesbos, which was also called Malea.

MALEOTON: See MALEVENTUM.

MALEVENTUM: Ancient town in Samnium on the Roman road Appia Via. It was renamed by the Romans, after they conquered and colonized it, Beneventum (present-day Benevento, Italy).

MALLOIS: See MALEA.

MANTIANA: Mantiana Palus, also called Arsissa Palus (present-day Lake Van in Turkey), a large lake in the south of Armenia Major.

MAREOTIS: A lake on the western coast of Egypt separated from the Mediterranean only by the narrow neck of land upon which stood the city of Alexandria. The lake served the city as a port.

MARMARICA: District of northern Africa located between Cyrenaica on the west and ancient Egypt on the east. It corresponds to the northwestern corner of present-day Egypt.

MEDIA: A populous, fertile province of the Persian Empire that lay to the southwest of the Caspian Sea, in the northwestern extremity of present-day Iran.

MEGARIS: Small district of Greece between the Sinus Corinthiacus (Gulf of Corinth) and the Sinus Saronicus (Saronic Gulf).

MEMPHI: See MEMPHIS.

MEMPHIS: Ancient Egyptian city on the west bank of the lower Nile (not far south of present-day Cairo).

MEMPHITES: See MEMPHIS.

MEOTIS: See MAEOTIS PALUS.

MEROE: Once a district of Ethiopia, Meroe comprised the lands between the Blue Nile, the Nile and the Arbara River, and was so nearly surrounded by water that it was referred to as an island. The city of the same name, its capitol, stood at its northern point on the east bank of the Nile (near Ed Damer in the Sudan).

METAGONITIS: The northern coast of Mauretania Tingitana (present-day Morocco). The name Metagonium more properly applies to a single promontory on this coast.

METAGONIUM: See METAGONITIS.

METHANA: An ancient town in Troezenia, the southeastern district of Argolis, which occupied the peninsular thumb of Peloponnesus in Greece. The town lay opposite the island of Aegina at the foot of a volcanic mountain.

METHANENSES: See METHANA.

MILESIUS: Also called Miletus, a city on the coast of Asia Minor opposite the mouth of the Maeander (present-day Menderes) River.

MILETUS: See MILESIUS.

MINTURN: See MINTURNAE.

MINTURNAE: Town in Latium near the mouth of the Liris River, where the Italian town of Minturno stands today.

MYCENA: See MYCENAE.

MYCENAE: Or Mycene, an ancient town in Argolas about six miles northeast of Argos in Peloponnesus (at present-day Mikinai). During the reign of King Agamemnon it reached its height of glory and was the foremost city in all Greece.

NARNIA: Town on the Nera River, which flows into the Tiber (present-day Narni, Italy).

NARVENSIANS: Perhaps inhabitants of Nervi. See separate note.

NASAMONIA: The Nasamones were a warlike people of Libya who dwelt on the shore of the Syrtis Major (Gulf of Sidra). They were driven south deeper into Africa by the Greek and Roman settlers who came to Cyrenaica.

NAUCRATIS: A Greek city on the Nile delta that was founded around 550 BC. It was the only place in ancient Egypt where Greeks were permitted to settle and trade.

NAXOS: The largest of the isles of the Cyclades in the Aegean Sea. In classical times it was bound up with the legends of Dionysus, and was sometimes called Dionysias, probably because of the excellent wine produced there.

NAZIANZUS: City in Cappadocia that lay somewhere on the road from Archelais to Tyana. Its exact location is not known. It was the birthplace of the Father of the Christian Church, Gregory Nazianzen.

NEO: Roman name for the Isle of Ios, located south of Naxos in the cluster of the Sporades. The tomb of Homer was said to be located here.

NERVI: A coastal town of Liguria (near present-day Genoa, Italy).

NISE: See Nysa.

NORNIANS: See Narnia.

NORVEGIA: Norway.

NUMANTIA: Chief town of Celtiberia, a region of central Spain in Roman times. It sat on a low but very steep hill and could be reached only by a single path, rendering fortification walls unnecessary. The Celtiberians used it as their stronghold against the Romans. It was laid under siege, and after much trouble, destroyed by Scipio Africanus the Younger in 133 BC.

NUMIDIA: Land on the coast of northern Africa that corresponds with present-day northeastern Algeria.

NYSA: Also spelled Nyssa, the legendary place where Dionysus was nurtured by the Nyseides, or nymphs of Nysa. There were half a dozen places of this name in the ancient world, none of them in Arabia. Agrippa probably means to refer to the ancient city discovered by Alexander the

Great in the Peshawar valley of the present-day North West Frontier Province of Pakistan. Even down to the present century a section of the Kafir community claimed a Greek origin—as did the ancient Nysaeans—and chanted hymns to the god who sprang from Gir Nysa (the mountain of Nysa), identified as Koh-i-Mor.

OASIS: Two oases west of the Nile were claimed by the Egyptians: (1) Oasis Major (Kharga Oasis in Egypt); (2) Oasis Minor (Bahariya Oasis in Egypt). Oasis Major was a nome of Upper Egypt, while Oasis Minor was a nome of Middle Egypt. When the term Oasis is used by itself, Oasis Major is generally intended. A more famous oasis than either of these was that of Hammon, Ammon or Ammonium (Siwa in Egypt), so called because it contained an oracular shrine to the god Ammon. In ancient times this was in Libya, and it remained politically independent from Egypt down to the days of the Ptolemies. Alexander the Great visited its oracle, which hailed him as the son of Jupiter Ammon.

OCRICULUM: An important town in Umbria near the meeting of the Nera River with the Tiber River (at present-day Otricoli).

OLYNTHUS: Town of Macedonia in Chalcidice which lay at the head of the Toronaic Gulf slightly inland (it was located at the extreme head of the gulf just about equidistant from the two peninsulas that surround the Toronaic Gulf of Greece).

ORCHENIANS: Inhabitants of Orchenia, a land mentioned by Ptolemy in the *Tetrabiblos* 2.3 (Robbins, 143, 159) under the sign of Leo. It is not known to which region this refers, but it must be somewhere in the Middle East since it is grouped with such places as Idumaea, Syria, Judaea, Phoenicia, Arabia Felix and Chaldaea.

ORCHESTUS: See ORCHOMENUS.

ORCHOMENUS: City in the northwest corner of Boeotia on the southwest shore of Lake

Copais (less than ten miles northeast of present-day Levadhia in central Greece).

OTRICULANS: See OCRICULUM.

OXIANA: Refers to the lands of the Oxiani, a people dwelling on the northern bank of the Oxus River (present-day Amu-Dar'ya), which flows north into the Oxiana Palus (Aral Sea). Roughly corresponds to Uzbek in the former Soviet Union.

PAMPHYLIA: Narrow arched section on the southern coast of Asia Minor (Turkey) that lay on the Sinus Pamphylius (Gulf of Antalya). It was bounded on the west by Lycia and on the east by Cilicia.

PAPHLAGONIA: Region on the middle northern coast of Asia Minor (Turkey) occupying the gently rounded projection of the coast into the Euxine (Black Sea). Bithynia lay to the west and Pontus to the east.

PAPHOS: Old Paphos, a city of Cyprus situated near, but not on, the western coast of the island. It was the chief seat of the worship of Aphrodite. Another city of the same name, called New Paphos, lay more inland. Each year the priest of the temple of Aphrodite led a great procession from New to Old Paphos.

PAPIA: See PAVIA.

PARNASSUS: The highest part of the mountain range just north of Delphi, particularly the two peaks Tithorea and Lycorea. This region was densely wooded and contained many caves and glens. Parnassus was sacred to Apollo and the muses, and also to Bacchus.

PARTHIA: Inland region lying off the southeastern corner of the Caspian Sea which roughly occupied the northeastern bulge of present-day Iran. A part of the Persian Empire, it was inhabited by a warlike race noted for their skill of shooting the bow from horseback.

PATARA: One of the chief cities of Lycia, it stood on a promontory of the same name six miles to the east of the mouth of the Xanthus River (about 15 miles west of present-day Kastellorizon, Turkey). The city possessed an oracle of Apollo that gave responses only in the winter.

PATRAI: Town in Achaia (present-day Patrai, Greece).

PAVIA: Town in northern Italy not far south of Milan.

PERGA: Ancient city of Pamphylia located about ten miles east of Adalia, or Attalia (present-day Antalya) on the southern coast of Asia Minor (Turkey) on the Gulf of Antalya. It was famous as a seat of the.worship of Artemis. On a hill near the city stood a very old temple of the goddess where a yearly festival was celebrated. Coins of Perga bear the image of Artemis and her temple.

PERSIA: Iran.

PESSINUNTIUM: See PESSINUS.

PESSINUS: Or Pesinus, a city in Asia Minor on the slope of Mount Dindymus, or Agdistis, in the southwest corner of Galatia (near present-day Usak, Turkey). It was a chief seat of the worship of Cybele, who was surnamed Agdistis. Her lavish temple stood on a hill outside the city and contained a wooden (or stone) statue, which was carried off to Rome to satisfy an oracle in one of the Sibylline books.

PHALAESIAE: Town in Arcadia south of Megalopolis in Peloponnesus.

PHALISCIA: See PHALAESIAE.

PHAMPHILIA : See PAMPHYLIA.

PHARAI: Ancient town in western Achaea, one of the 12 Achaean cities. There was an oracle of Hermes located here. The town may have been situated about ten miles southwest of present-day Patrai.

PHARIS: See PHARAI.

PHARSALIA: The territory of the town of Pharsalus in Thessaly (present-day Farsala, Greece) upon which was fought in 48 BC the decisive battle between Julius Caesar and Pompey. Caesar was victorious.

PHAZANIA: District in the interior of Libya corresponding to present-day Fezzan.

PHENICIA: See PHOENICIA.

PHIGALIA: Town located midway along the Nedha River on the western shore of the Greek Peloponnesus.

PHOENICIA: Sea-trading nation that occupied a strip about ten miles wide running along the eastern coast of the Mediterranean Sea (coast of present-day Lebanon and Syria).

PHRYGIA: Region of Asia Minor (Turkey) bounded on the west by Mysia, Lydia and Caria, on the south by Lycia and Pisidia, on the north by Bithynia and on the east by Lycaonia and Galatia, which last was often considered a part of Phrygia (it corresponded roughly to the region of west-central Turkey).

PISA: Capitol of Pisatis, which was the middle region of Elis in Peloponnesus (it stood not far from present-day Olimbia).

PONTUS: Northern region of Asia Minor (Turkey) on the shore of the Pontus Euxinus (Black Sea) to the east of Paphlagonia. The Euxine was itself often called simply Pontus. Ovid applies this name to the shore of the Euxine between the mouths of the Istar River (Danube) and Mount Haemus (eastern coasts of present-day Rumania and Bulgaria).

PRAENESTE: Present-day Palestrina. One of the most ancient towns in Latium, it was con-

nected to Rome by a road called the Via Praenestina. Its inhabitants claimed it had been founded by Telegonus (Telemachos), son of Ulysses. It possessed a very famous and ancient temple of the goddess Fortuna, with an oracle which was called the Praenestine lots *(Praenestinae sortes)*. In the days of the empire the temple of Fortuna was enlarged to enormous proportions and the town became popular as a vacation resort for wealthy nobles. The oracle continued to be consulted down to Christian times until Constantine, and later Theodosius, banned it.

PRENESTE: See PRAENESTE.

PROCONNESUS: Island in the Propontis (present-day island of Marmara in the Sea of Marmara, Turkey).

PROSENNA: See PROSYMNA.

PROSYMNA: Ancient town in Argolis north of Argos, in Peloponnesus. It held a temple of Hera (Juno).

PYREUS: Perhaps Pyrrhi Castra, a fortified place in northern Laconia (southeast Peloponnesus) where Pyrrhus probably camped during his invasion of the country.

RAMOTH-GILEAD: Town in eastern Palestine, thought to have been located at present-day Tell Ramit, about a mile south of Er Ramtha, near the border between Jordan and Syria.

REATE: Town in Latium, Italy (present-day Rieti).

REATUM: See REATE.

SAMOS: Also spelled Samus, one of the islands in the Aegean Sea. A temple of Hera, called an *Heraeum,* was built two miles west of the city of Samos, which stood on the southeastern side of the island. This temple was the chief center for the worship of Hera among the Ionian Greeks.

SARMATIA: A large stretch of country extending from present-day Poland across southern Russia as far east as the Volga River. It was inhabited chiefly by Scythians, and in the west by Germans.

SAUROMATIAN COUNTRY: See SARMATIA.

SCYTHIA: A large region north of the Pontus Euxinus (Black Sea), bounded on the west by the Carpathian Mountains and on the east by the river Tanais (present-day Don). It corresponded roughly to the southernmost part of European Russia.

SEAS OF LITTLE ASIA: Seas of Asia Minor (Turkey), therefore the Euxine (Black Sea), the Propontis (Sea of Marmara) and perhaps the Maeotis Palus (Sea of Azov).

SERES: The far eastern land of the silkworm. To Ptolemy, Agrippa's source, it signified northwestern China and Tibet.

SICILIA: Sicily.

SORACTE: Mountain in Etruria near the Tiber, about 24 miles from Rome. The snow-covered summit was visible from the ancient city.

SPARTA: See LACEDAEMON.

SUTRINIANS: See SUTRIUM.

SUTRIUM: Ancient town of Etruria about 40 miles northwest of Rome (at present-day Sutri).

TAENARUM: Promontory in Laconia that forms the southern point of Peloponnesus (present-day Cape Tainaron). On it stood a temple of Poseidon. To the north of the point was a town of the same name.

TAMYRACA: According to Smith (1862, 852), "a town and promontory of European Sarmatia, at the innermost corner of the Sinus Carcinites, which was also called from this town Sinus Tamyraces." Unfortunately Smith neglects to mention where the Sinus Carcinites

was located—somewhere on the north shore of the Black Sea, perhaps around present-day Yeysk in the Sea of Azov.

TARENTUM: Ancient Greek town on the coast of southern Italy (present-day Taranto). It was captured by Hannibal during the Second Punic War in 212 BC.

TAURIS: Small island off the coast of Illyria in the Adriatic Sea between Pharus (present-day Hvar, off the coast of Yugoslavia) and Corcyra (present-day Kerkira, or Corfu).

TAURICA: See TAURIS.

TAURUS: Mountain of moderate height said to be steep and wooded at the summit. It is located in the Taurus range in southern Turkey (present-day Aladag).

TEGEA: City in Arcadia (nor far south of present-day Tripolis, Greece). At one period it was divided into four tribes, each of which kept a statue of Apollo Agyieus, who was held in special honor in the city.

TEGYRA: Perhaps Tegea. See separate note.

TENATUS: See TAENARUM.

TENEDOS: Small island in the Aegean Sea off the coast of Troas near the mouth of the Hellespont, located about six miles from the Isle of Lesbos and about four miles from the coast. It was celebrated in ancient times for its beautiful women and was reputed to be the place where the Greeks withdrew their fleet to induce the Trojans to accept the wooden horse.

THAMARITANS: See TAMYRACA.

THEBAIS: Upper Egypt.

THEBES: Several ancient cities bore this name, two of which are more important than the others: (1) Thebae in Egypt, the capitol of Thebais (Upper Egypt). It stood on the east bank of the

Nile (at present-day Luxor) and was fabled to be the oldest city in the world. Homer called it the "hundred-gated." (2) Thebae in Greece, an ancient city in Boeotia that stood in a plain southeast of Lake Helice (it was at present-day Thivai). Best known as the setting of *The Seven Against Thebes,* it was a flourishing city, fiercely independent, with seven gates set in a nearly circular wall nine miles in circumference. Dicaearchus (c. 300 BC) says it was a gloomy place with good water and beautiful gardens in the summer, but bitterly cold in the winter.

THERASIA: Small island just west of Thera (present-day Thira) in the Aegean Sea. It was once part of Thera but was separated from the larger island by a geological upheaval.

THERMA: Town in Macedonia (on the site of present-day Thessaloniki).

THERMODONIANS: See THERMA.

THRACIA: The land of Thrace lay between the Pontus Euxinus (Black Sea) and Macedonia. It was larger in extent than the part of Greece that presently bears this name, comprising as well the land between the Euxine and the Propontis (Sea of Marmara).

THURINGIA: Ancient district of Germany that lay in the southwestern corner of the former East Germany.

TIBER: One of the most ancient towns of Latium, it was located 16 miles northeast of Rome and in the days of the empire was a popular vacation resort where wealthy Roman nobles built lavish villas. There was a sacred grove and temple here to the sibyl, or nymph, Albunea, or Albuna, who gave oracles.

TREVERIS: Augusta Trevirorum (Trier in Germany), which has extensive Roman ruins.

TREZENIAN: See TROEZENIA.

TREZENIUM: See TROEZENIA.

TRITONES: See TRITONIS PALUS.

TRITONIS PALUS: Also called Tritonitis Palus (Latin: *palus*—marsh, swamp), a legendary river and lake on the ancient coast of Libya. By one account Athene was born on Lake Tritonis, the daughter of a nymph of the same name as the lake and of Poseidon: hence her surname Tritogenia. Early Greek writers identified Lake Tritonis with the Lesser Syrtis (present-day Gulf of Gabes, Tunisia). Later it was thought to be the great salt lake that lies inland from the gulf (Shott el Djerid). In ancient times this lake had a river flowing into it, but the shifting sands of the Sahara desert have made this difficult to identify. Some writers gave a different location and identified the legendary river with the river Lathon in Cyrenaica. Apollonius Rhodius even transferred the name to the Nile.

TROAD: See TROAS.

TROAS: Also called the Troad, the land around the ancient city of Troy in Asia Minor.

TROEZENIA: Region in the southwestern part of Argolis in Peloponnesus opposite the island of Calauria (present-day Poros). A town called Troezen lay a little distance inland from the sea. In earliest times Troezen was called Poseidonia, because of the worship of Poseidon that took place there.

TROGLODYS: See TROGLODYTICE.

TROGLODYTICE: Land of the *troglodytae,* or cave-dwellers, especially applied to the barbarous tribes living on the western coast of the Red Sea, the shores of Upper Egypt and Ethiopia.

TROGLOTIDES: See TROGLODYTICE.

TROY: Also called Ilium, ancient city in the northwest corner of Mysia in Asia Minor (it stood not far southeast of the mouth of the present-day Dardanelles, Turkey). Troy was conquered and destroyed by the Greeks and formed the subject of Homer's *Iliad*.

TUSCANA: See ETRURIA.

TUSCIA: See ETRURIA.

TYBUR: See TIBUR.

UMBRIA: District of central Italy that in ancient times was more far-reaching than that presently bearing the name, extending to the shores of the Adriatic.

Bibliography

Addis, W. E. *The Documents of the Hexateuch.* 2 vols. London: David Nutt, 1892.

Agrippa von Nettesheim, Heinrich Cornelius. *Opera.* 2 vols. Hildesheim and New York: Georg Olms Verlag, 1970.
A facsimile reprint of the Lyons edition, conjecturally dated by the publisher at 1600?. Strangely, the tables of the Kabbalah do not appear in this work, which severely limits its usefulness.

——————— *Three Books of Occult Philosophy.* Trans. from the Latin by J. F. [London: 1651]. London: Chthonios Books, 1986.
This is a photocopy facsimile of the London edition of 1651. I used it as the basis for the text of the present edition.

Allen, Richard Hinckley. *Star Names, Their Lore and Meaning.* New York: Dover Publications, 1963.
A reprint of *Star-Names and Their Meanings* published by G. E. Stechert, 1899.

Andrews, W. S. *Magic Squares and Cubes.* New York: Dover Publications, 1960.
A reprinting of the Open Court Publishing second edition of 1917. The book is made up of essays that appeared from 1905 to 1916 in the mathematical periodical *The Monist,* written by Andrews and others.

Angus, S. *The Mystery-Religions* [London: 1925]. New York: Dover Publications, 1975.
Originally published by John Murray under the title *The Mystery-Religions and Christianity.* A useful book, but the author has a tendency to moralize.

Anthon, Charles. *A Classical Dictionary.* New York: Harper and Brothers, 1843.
A massive volume treating a broad range of subjects in considerable depth.

——————— *A Latin-English and English-Latin Dictionary* [1849]. New York: Harper and Brothers, 1868.

The Apocrypha (authorized edition). Oxford: Univ. Press, n.d.

Apollonius Rhodius. *The Voyage of Argo.* Trans. E. V. Rieu [1959]. Harmondsworth: Penguin Books, 1985.

Apuleius, Lucius. *The Golden Asse.* Trans. William Adlington [1566], n.d.
Reprint of the edition of 1639. The publisher has not given his name, the date or any other information concerning this edition.

Aquinas, Thomas. *Introduction to Saint Thomas Aquinas.* Ed. Anton C. Pegis. New York: Random House, 1948.
A selection of the basic writings with a brief introduction and no index. This is the Modern Library edition.

——————— *Summa contra gentiles.* London: Burns, Oats and Washbourne, 1928.

Aristophanes. *The Eleven Comedies.* New York: Liveright Publishing Company, 1943.
This text was anonymously translated from the Greek and published in 1912 by the Athenian Society for subscribers only.

Aristotle. *The Basic Works.* Various translators. Compiled by Richard McKeon from the Oxford Univ. Press edition ed. by W. D. Ross. New York: Random House, 1941.
It stands in need of an index.

——————— *Problems.* Trans. E. S. Forster. Vol. 7 of *The Works of Aristotle.* Oxford: Clarendon Press, 1927.
This is not a genuine work by Aristotle but it has always carried his name.

——————— *Problems.* 2 vols. Trans. W. S. Hett. Cambridge: Harvard Univ. Press, various years.

Arnold, T. W. *The Little Flowers of St. Francis of Assisi.* Trans. from the Italian. London: Chatto and Windus, 1908.
A collection of popular fables that grew up around the memory of the saint.

Ars Notoria. Trans. Robert Turner [1657]. Seattle: Trident Books, 1987.
One of the more obtuse of the grimoires.

Augustine, Saint. *City of God.* 2 vols. Trans. John Healey [1610]. London: J. M. Dent and Sons, 1957.
Contains some of the original commentary of Joannes Vives. Unfortunately no index, making it difficult to use.

Bacon, Francis.*Essays* [1597]. Philadelphia: Henry Altemus Company, n.d.

Ball, W. W. R. *Mathematical Recreations and Essays* [1892]. London: Macmillan, 1905.
This excellent work contains a chapter on the magic squares, the best short treatment I have read.

Barham, Richard Harris. *The Ingoldsby Legends, or Mirth and Marvels* [1840]. London: Richard Bentley and Son, 1879.
The *Legends* were published anonymously, which seems a pity since they do the author so much credit.

Baring-Gould, Sabine. *The Book of Werewolves* [1865]. New York: Causeway Books, 1973.
Perhaps the best treatment of this subject in English.

Barrett, Francis. *The Magus, or Celestial Intelligencer* [London: 1801]. New York: Samuel Weiser, n.d.
Numbered, limited edition containing the facsimile text and colored plates of the original. A beautiful book. Virtually all of it is a plagiarism from the 1651 English translation by James Freake of the *Occult Philosophy.*

Bede. *A History of the English Church and People.* Trans. Leo Sherley-Price. Harmondsworth: Penguin Books, 1965.

Best, Michael R., and Frank H. Brightman. *The Book of Secrets of Albertus Magnus.* London: Oxford Univ. Press, 1974.
Appended to the main title is *The Book of the Marvels of the World.*

Blofeld, John. *I Ching.* New York: E. P. Dutton, 1968.
More accessible than the weightier Legge translation.

Boer, Charles. *The Homeric Hymns.* Chicago: The Swallow Press, 1970.

Boethius. *The Consolation of Philosophy* [523]. Trans. H. R. James. London: George Routledge and Sons, n.d.

Brewer, E. Cobham. *A Dictionary of Miracles.* London: Chatto and Windus, 1901.
——————— *Dictionary of Phrase and Fable* [1870]. London: Cassell and Company, n.d.

Browning, Robert. *Complete Poetic and Dramatic Works.* Boston and New York: Houghton Mifflin Company, 1895.

Budge, E. A. Wallis. *Amulets and Talismans.* New York: University Books, 1968.
Originally published in 1930 under the title *Amulets and Superstitions.* A useful collection because of its many illustrations and plates.

——————— *The Book of the Dead.* New York: University Books, 1970.
A translation of the Egyptian papyrus of Ani. Reproduction of the 1913 edition.

——————— *Egyptian Magic* [London: 1901]. New York: Dover Publications, 1971.
A brief overview of a complex subject, but very readable.

——————— *The Gods of the Egyptians* [London: 1904]. 2 vols. New York: Dover Publications, 1969.
A complete treatment of Egyptian mythology. Perhaps Budge's best work.

Bulfinch, Thomas. *Mythology.* New York: Random House, n.d.
This Modern Library edition contains the author's *Age of Fable* (1855), *Age of Chivalry* (1858) and *Legends of Charlemagne* (1863), which over the years have come to be regarded as parts of a single whole. Still one of the best books on the the subject.

Burckhardt, Titus. *Alchemy* [1960]. Trans. from the German by William Stoddart. Baltimore: Penguin Books, 1974.
Not an especially good book, but the most widely available general study of alchemy.

——————— *Mystical Astrology According to Ibn 'Arabi.* Trans. from the French by Bulent Rauf. Golcestershire: Beshara Publications, 1977.
A very slender treatment, but it contains some useful information of a basic type.

Burton, Robert. *The Anatomy of Melancholy* [1621]. 3 vols. London: J. M. Dent and Sons, 1961.
The amount of interesting lore in this vast work is astounding. A great book, the product of a lifetime.

Butler, E. M. *Ritual Magic* [1949]. Hollywood: New-castle Publishing Company, 1971.
This is a fine scholarly study of magical manu-scripts and books.

Byron, George Gordon. *The Poetical Works*. London: Oxford Univ. Press, 1926.

Caesar, Julius. *The Conquest of Gaul*. Trans. S. A. Handford [1951]. Harmondsworth: Penguin Books, 1967.
Some men can do everything well. Had Caesar not spent his time conquering the world he might have made an excellent full-time writer.

Canadian Oxford Atlas. Toronto: Oxford Univ. Press, 1951.
Useful in that it lists many ancient sites and has a clear topographical presentation.

Cary, M., A. D. Nock et al. *The Oxford Classical Dictionary*. Oxford: Clarendon Press, 1949.
The quality of writing in this work is disap-pointing. This is most glaringly apparent when it is compared with the much superior *Classical Dictionary* of Smith.

Chambers's Encyclopædia. 10 vols. London: W. and R. Chambers, 1868.
This work is chiefly useful in the area of botany. The engravings are excellent. The editors had not then decided, as they have in modern times, that all legends and fables must be omitted merely because they are not scientifically accurate.

Charles, R. H. *The Apocrypha and Pseudepigrapha of the Old Testament*. 2 vols. Oxford: Clarendon Press, 1913.

Chaucer, Geoffrey. *The Works*. Ed. F. N. Robinson. Boston: Houghton Mifflin, 1961.

Cicero. *De senectute, de amicitia, de divinatione*. Trans. W. A. Falconer. Cambridge: Harvard Univ. Press, 1959.

——— *The Treatises of M. T. Cicero*. Trans. C. D. Yonge. London: Bell and Daldy, 1872.

Cohen, A. *Everyman's Talmud*. New York: Schocken Books, 1975.
A general survey of the subjects contained in the *Talmud* with many quotations.

Crowley, Aleister. *Magick in Theory and Practice* [London: 1929]. New York: Dover Publica-tions, 1976.
This is Crowley's best work, with the possible exception of his *Book of Thoth*, the tarot deck he designed using the artist Lady Frieda Harris as his instrument.

Croxall, Samuel, and Roger L'Estrange. *The Fables of Aesop*. London: Frederick Warne, n.d.

Contains all of Croxall's fables and 50 addi-tional fables from the translation of L'Estrange.

Cruden, Alexander. *A Complete Concordance to the Holy Scriptures* [1736]. Boston: Gould, Kendall and Lincoln, 1847.
A condensation of the original edition.

Cyprian. *The Writings*. Trans. Ernest Wallis. In *The Ante-Nicene Fathers*. Buffalo: Christian Litera-ture Company, 1886.
Cyprian forms part of vol. 5 of this set.

D'Abano, Peter. *Heptameron: or, Magical Elements*. In the *Fourth Book of Occult Philosophy*. London: Askin Publishers, 1978.

Dauches, Samuel. *Babylonian Oil Magic in the Tal-mud and in Later Jewish Literature*. [London: 1913]. In *Three Works of Ancient Jewish Magic*. London: Chthonios Books, 1986.
The work is reprinted in facsimile in this collec-tion under the title *Ancient Jewish Oil-Magic*. It concerns techniques of divination.

Dante Alighieri. *The Divine Comedy*. Trans. Charles Eliot Norton [1891]. Boston: Houghton Mifflin Company, 1941.
A clear, if somewhat flat, prose translation.

——— *The Divine Comedy*. Trans. Laurence Grant White. New York: Pantheon Books, 1948.
A blank verse version illustrated with Doré's engravings.

David-Neel, Alexandra. *Initiations and Initiates in Tibet*. Trans. Fred Rothwell. New York: Univer-sity Books, 1959.
Many insights into Tibetan magic as it existed before the coming of the Chinese, observed firsthand by the author.

——— *Magic and Mystery in Tibet* [Paris: 1929]. Trans. from the French. New York: Dover Publications, 1971.
The original title is *Mystiques et magiciens du Thibet*. This is a reprinting of the English edi-tion of Claud Kendall, New York, 1932. The translator is not named, unless it is Kendall.

Dee, John. *A True and Faithful Relation of What Passed for Many Yeers Between Dr. John Dee and Some Spirits* [1659]. Ed. Meric. Casaubon. Glasgow: The Antonine Publishing Company, 1974.
A limited facsimile edition of the London edi-tion of 1659. Casaubon took a section of Dee's meticulous records of his scryings with Edward Kelly and other mediums and had them printed.

De Givry, Emile Grillot. *Illustrated Anthology of Sorcery, Magic and Alchemy* [1929]. Trans. from the French by J. Courtenay Locke [1931].

New York: Causeway Books, 1973.
The finest of all the picture books of occultism, thanks to its excellent structure and careful source references. An edition is also published by Dover, but the Causeway edition is superior.

D'Olivet, Fabre. *Golden Verses of Pythagoras* [1813]. Trans. from the French by Nayan Louise Redfield [1917]. New York: Samuel Weiser, 1975.
Extensive and somewhat tedious ruminations on the Pythagoric verses, useful because it gives the verses in Greek, in d'Olivet's French and in English.

Dryden, John. *The Best of Dryden*. Ed. Louis I. Bredvold. New York: Ronald Press Company, 1933.

Eliade, Mircea. *Shamanism* [Paris: 1951]. Princeton Univ. Press, 1972.
Revised edition. Originally published by Librairie Payot under the title *Le chamanisme et les techniques archaegues de l'estase*. This is an excellent book.

Elworthy, Frederick. *The Evil Eye* [London: 1895]. New York: Collier Books, 1971.
A classic that is notable for its numerous illustrations of magical objects and symbols.

Encyclopædia Britannica. 11th edition. 28 vols. plus index. New York: Cambridge Univ. Press, 1910–11.
Someone once said to me that the 11th was the last edition of the *Britannica* to possess any value. I tend to agree. It was still a scholarly instrument while in English hands, but after coming to America it lost its purpose.

Epictetus. *The Enchiridion*. Trans. Thomas W. Higginson [1948]. Indianapolis: Bobbs-Merrill, 1980.
This work is a compression of the ideas of Epictetus by Flavius Arrian, one of his students, who recorded a series of talks given by the great Stoic philosopher around the year 125 at Nicopolis.

Euripides. *The Complete Greek Tragedies*. Vols. 3 and 4. Ed. David Grene and Richmond Lattimore. Univ. of Chicago Press, 1960.

Eusebius. *Against the Life of Apollonius of Tyana Written by Philostratus*. Trans. F. C. Conybeare. In *Philostratus*. Vol. 2. Cambridge: Harvard Univ. Press, 1969.
The treatise is appended to the *Life of Apollonius* by Philostratus.

————— *The Ecclesiastical History*. 2 vols. Trans. Kirsopp Lake (vol. 1) and J. E. L. Oulton (vol. 2). Cambridge: Harvard Univ. Press, various years.

————— *The Ecclesiastical History of Eusebius Pamphilus*. Trans. C. F. Cruse. London: Bell and Daldy, 1866.
One of the Bohn Classical Library editions.

Evans, Joan. *Magical Jewels of the Middle Ages and the Renaissance* [1922]. New York: Dover Publications, 1976.
Reprinting of the Clarendon Press (Oxford) edition of 1922.

Evelyn, John. *John Evelyn's Diary* (abridged). Ed. Philip Francis. London: Folio Society, 1963.

Everard, Doctor John. *The Divine Pymander of Hermes Mercurius Trismegistus* [1650]. Trans. from the Arabic. San Diego: Wizards Bookshelf, 1978.
A reprint of the 1884 edition of Hargrave Jennings.

Fiske, N. W. *Manual of Classical Literature* [1836]. Philadelphia: W. S. Fortescue, 1843.
A useful reference, but the arrangement of its parts is poor, making it difficult to find in it what is wanted.

Flammel, Nicholas. *Alchemical Hieroglyphics* [1889]. Trans. Eirenaeus Orandus [1624]. Gillette, NJ: Heptangle Books, 1980.
This is a reprinting of the W. Wynn Westcott edition of 1889.

Franck, Adolphe. *The Kabbalah* [Paris: 1843]. Anonymously translated from the French. New York: Bell Publishing, 1940.
The original title is *La kabbale: ou la philosophie religieuse des Hebreaux*. The most readable of the older works on the Kabbalah.

Galen. *On the Natural Faculties*. Trans. Arthur John Brock. Pennsylvania: The Franklin Library, 1979.

Gaster, Moses. *The Sword of Moses* [London: 1896]. In *Three Works of Ancient Jewish Magic*. London: Chthonios Books, 1986.
A facsimile reproduction of the original translation and commentary by Gaster of this Hebrew magical work, along with the original Hebrew. It is concerned with magical names.

————— *The Wisdom of the Chaldeans* [1900]. In *Three Works of Ancient Jewish Magic*. London: Chthonios Books, 1986.
Originally published in the December 1900 issue of the *Proceedings of the Society of Biblical Archaeology*. Concerns the angels of the seven planets.

Gerard, John. *The Herbal or General History of Plants* [1633]. Revised by Thomas Johnson. New York: Dover Publications, 1975.
A facsimile reprint, enormous and beautiful, a thoroughly wonderful book.

Gesenius, William. *Hebrew and Chaldee Lexicon*. New York: John Wiley and Sons, 1890.
With additions and corrections by Samuel Prideaux Tregelles. An excellent work.

Gibbon, Edward. *The History of the Decline and Fall of the Roman Empire* [1776–1788]. London: Joseph Ogle Robinson, 1830.
A convenient, though hardly compact, one-volume edition of this mammoth work.

Ginsburg, Christian D. *The Essenes* [1864] and *The Kabbalah* [1863]. London: Routledge and Kegan Paul, 1974.
Two works bound under one cover.

Godwin, Joscelyn. *Robert Fludd*. Boulder: Shambhala, 1979.
A useful overview of Fludd, notable for the many illustrations taken from his books.

Goldsmith, Oliver. *A History of the Earth and Animated Nature* [1774]. London: Thomas Nelson, 1849.
A useful work only in that Goldsmith has preserved many of the fables and ancient lore of animals. Of course it is completely untrustworthy as a source of factual information.

Grant, Kenneth. *Cults of the Shadow*. New York: Samuel Weiser, 1976.
An examination of the major figures in Western occultism in the present century and the cults that have grown up around them.

Graves, Robert. *The Greek Myths*. 2 vols. Harmondsworth: Penguin Books, 1957.
Excellent. Graves is one of those scholars that make you wish the term of human life might be extended in special cases purely for professional purposes. He shares this distinction with Thomas Taylor.

———— *The White Goddess* [1948]. New York: Farrar, Straus and Giroux, 1973.

Green, Robert. *Friar Bacon and Friar Bungay*. In *Elizabethan Plays*. Ed. Arthur H. Nethercot, Charles R. Baskervill, and Virgil B. Heltzel. New York: Holt, Rinehart and Winston, 1971.
The play was probably written around 1592, likely before Marlowe's *Doctor Faustus*.

Gregory Thaumaturgus. *Writings*. Trans. S. D. F. Salmond. In *The Ante-Nicene Fathers*. Buffalo: The Christian Literature Company, 1886.
The writings of Gregory, which are not extensive, form part of vol. 6 of this set.

Griffith, F. L. and Herbert Thompson. *The Leyden Papyrus* [London: 1904]. New York: Dover Publications, 1974.
Originally titled the *Demotic Magical Papyrus of London and Leiden*. The text is in a very broken condition that makes it difficult to read.

Grimm's Complete Fairy Tales. New York: Nelson Doubleday, n.d.
The fairy tales were first published by the Grimm brothers Jacob and Wilhelm in Germany in 1812 and 1815. There is no indication in this edition as to who did the translation.

Grimoire of Pope Honorius III. Trans. B. J. H. King. Sut Anubis Books, 1984.
This is certainly not the true grimoire of Pope Honorius, which is described by Idries Shah in detail in his *Secret Lore of Magic* and by A. E. Waite in his *Book of Ceremonial Magic*. It bears some of the same symbols, but little or nothing of the text. What its origins are would be difficult to guess, especially as the publisher says nothing about the matter, but perhaps Idries Shah accurately describes this edition when he says that during the 19th century bogus works bearing this title were printed to deceive the ignorant into thinking they were getting the true grimoire, which at that time was almost impossible to come by. (See *Secret Lore of Magic*, ch. 14 [London: Abacus, 1972], 253–4)

Guazzo, Francesco Maria. *Compendium Maleficarum* [1608]. Trans. E. A. Ashwin. New York: Dover Publications, 1988.
A reprint of the 1929 edition of John Rodker, London, edited by Montague Summers.

Hamilton, Edith. *Mythology* [1940]. New York: Mentor Books. 40th printing, n.d.
It is surprising how useful this collection of the myths is—more often than not you will find what you are looking for in it, which is the ultimate test of any reference work.

Hansen, Harold A. *The Witch's Garden*. Trans. Muriel Crofts. York Beach, ME: Samuel Weiser, 1983.
Published in Danish in 1976 under the title *Heksens Urtegard*.

Herodotus. *The History*. Trans. George Rawlinson [1858]. New York: Tudor Publishing, 1947.
This edition is difficult to use because the paragraphs are not numbered.

Hesiod. *Hesiod and Theogonis*. Trans. Dorothea Wender. Harmondsworth: Penguin Books, 1973.
Contains the *Theogony* and *Works and Days* of Hesiod.

Hinnells, John R. *Persian Mythology*. New York: Hamlyn Publishing, 1973.
A picture book of Persian mythology.

Hippocrates. *Writings.* Pennsylvania: The Franklin Library, 1979.
The translator of this edition is not named. It originally appeared in one of the *Great Books of the Western World* published by Encyclopædia Britannica.

Homer. *The Iliad.* Trans. Richmond Lattimore. Univ. of Chicago Press, 1976.

——————— *The Odyssey.* Trans. Richmond Lattimore. New York: Harper and Row, 1977.
These translations of Homer are wonderful. It is difficult to imagine how they might be surpassed.

——————— *The Odyssey of Homer, with the Hymns, Epigrams, and Battle of the Frogs and Mice.* Trans. Theodore Alois Buckley. New York: Harper and Brothers, 1872.
This edition is useful because it gathers together all the bits and pieces popularly attributed to Homer, along with the earliest biography of Homer, attributed to Herodotus.

Hone, Margaret E. *The Modern Text Book of Astrology.* London: L. N. Fowler, 1975.
The best basic textbook on the subject.

Horace. *Complete Works.* Intro. J. Kendrick Noble. Translator not named. Translation Publishing, 1961.

Horapollo Nilous. *The Hieroglyphics of Horapollo Nilous* [1840]. Trans. Alexander Turner Cory. London: Chthonios Books, 1987.
A reprint of the original London 1840 edition.

How, W. W., and J. Wells. *A Commentary on Herodotus.* 2 vols. Oxford: Clarendon Press, 1928.
The maps are useful.

Hughes, Merritt Y. *John Milton: Complete Poems and Major Prose.* Indianapolis: Odyssey Press, 1975.
The notes in this edition are excellent.

Iamblichus. *Life of Pythagoras.* Trans. Thomas Taylor [1818]. London: John M. Watkins, 1926.
There is much useful Pythagorean material appended after the Life.

——————— *On the Mysteries of the Egyptians, Chaldeans, and Assyrians.* Trans. Thomas Taylor [1821]. London: Stuart and Watkins, 1968.
Perhaps the single most important text on neo-Pythagorean occultism.

Ishmael, Rabbi. *The Measure of the (Divine) Body Shiur Qoma.* From the *Book of the Angelic Secrets of the Great One (Sefer Raziel Hagadol).* In *Book of Enoch.* Vol. 3. Los Angeles: Work of the Chariot, 1970.
This work is also known as the *Proportion of the Height.* No information beyond what I have given is provided by the publisher. Shiur Qoma is the Hebrew for "measure of the height," but this is not explicitly stated. The work is concerned with the names and measurements of the various parts of the body of God.

Jacobi, Jolande. *Paracelsus: Selected Writings* [Zurich: 1942]. Trans. from the German by Norbert Guterman. Princeton Univ. Press, 1973.
The many woodcuts that illustrate this selection are attractive, though not particularly pertinent to the text.

Josephus, Flavius. *The Works of Flavius Josephus.* Trans. William Whiston. London: George Routledge and Sons, n.d.

Justin Martyr. *The Writings.* In *Ante-Nicene Christian Library.* Various translators. Edinburgh: T. and T. Clark, 1867.

Juvenal. *The Satires.* Trans. Lewis Evans. New York: Hinds, Noble and Eldredge, n.d.

Keightley, Thomas. *The World Guide to Gnomes, Fairies, Elves and Other Little People.* New York: Avenel Books, 1978.
Originally titled *The Fairy Mythology,* 1880.

King, Edw. G. *The Poem of Job.* New York: Cambridge Univ. Press, 1914.
A beautiful rendering of the book of Job in its original meter and accents.

Klibansky, Raymond; Erwin Panofsky; and Fritz Saxl. *Saturn and Melancholy.* London: Nelson, 1964.
Contains useful information on the humors.

Knight, Gareth. *A Practical Guide to Qabalistic Symbolism.* 2 vols. in one. New York: Samuel Weiser, 1980.
Good as a quick reference to the symbolism and correspondences of the Kabbalah that prevail in modern Western occultism.

Kramer, Heinrich, and James Sprenger. *The Malleus Maleficarum* [1486]. Trans. from the Latin by Montague Summers. New York: Dover Publications, 1971.
A reprint of the 1928 edition of John Rodker, London. As I said in the notes, an evil book.

Lactantius. *The Writings.* Trans. William Fletcher. In *Ante-Nicene Christian Library.* Edinburgh: T. and T. Clark, 1871.
Lactantius occupies volumes 21 and 22 of this set.

Larousse Encyclopedia of Mythology. New York: Prometheus Press, 1960.

Legaza, Laszb. *Tao Magic: The Chinese Art of the Occult.* New York: Pantheon Books, 1975.

A picture-book presentation of this interesting subject.

Legge, James. *The I Ching* [1899]. New York: Dover Publications, 1963.

Lemegeton; Clavicula Salomonis: or The Complete Lesser Key of Solomon the King. With a typed transcription and notes by Nelson and Anne White. Pasadena: The Technology Group, 1979.
This work consists of a poor photocopy of British Museum Sloane Ms. 2731, which is an English manuscript of the *Lemegeton,* coupled with an almost illegible transcription that is filled with careless and needless errors. The five books of the manuscript, which are really five separate works, are titled *The Goetia, The Theurgia Goetia, The Pauline Art, The Almadel of Solomon,* and *The Artem Novem.*

Lenaghan, R. T., ed. *Caxton's Aesop* [1484]. Cambridge: Harvard Univ. Press, 1967.
Caxton's edition contains a Life of Aesop taken from the Latin translation of the Italian humanist Rinuccio da Castiglione of Arezzo. This differs slightly from the Greek version of the 13th-century Byzantine monk Maximus Planudes, which was long thought to be its source.

Levi, Eliphas. *Transcendental Magic.* Trans. A. E. Waite [London: 1896]. New York: Samuel Weiser, 1979.
Contains the *Nuctameron of Apollonius of Tyana.*

Liddell, Henry George, and Robert Scott. *Greek-English Lexicon* (abridged) [1871]. Oxford Univ. Press, 1976.

Livy. *The Early History of Rome.* Trans. Aubrey de Selincourt [1960]. Harmondsworth: Penguin Books, 1982.
This is the first five books of Livy's *History.*

——————— *The History of Rome.* Trans. D. Spillan and Cyrus Edmonds. New York: Hinds, Noble and Eldredge, n.d.
Contains books 1 and 2 of the *History.*

Longfellow, Henry Wadsworth. *Poetical Works.* London: Ward Lock and Company, n.d.

Lucan. *Pharsalia.* Trans. Robert Graves. London: Cassell, 1961.
This is a spirited and readable translation, but the book lacks sufficient notes and an index.

——————— *Pharsalia.* Trans. H. T. Riley. London: Henry G. Bohn, 1853.
All of Riley's translations are good, but it is his notes that make them especially valuable.

Lucretius. *On the Nature of Things.* Prose trans. John Selby Watson. Verse trans. John Mason Good.

London: George Bell and Sons, 1901.
The Bohn's Classical Library edition.

——————— *On the Nature of Things.* Trans. H. A. J. Munro. New York: Washington Square Press, 1965.

Macdonald, Michael-Albion. *De Nigromancia of Roger Bacon.* Gillette, NJ: Heptangle Books, 1988.
An editing of British Museum Mss. Sloane 3885 and Additional 36674. The introduction of the manuscript asserts that it was discovered in Alexandria by the religious brothers Robert Lombard and Roger Bacon.

Maier, Michael. *Laws of the Fraternity of the Rosie Crosse* [1618]. Los Angeles: Philosophical Research Library, 1976.
The original Latin work, titled *Themis Aurea,* was translated into English in 1656 and dedicated to Elias Ashmole. This is one of the basic texts of the Rosicrucian movement, even though Maier himself never claimed to be a Rosicrucian.

Maimonides, Moses. *The Guide for the Perplexed.* Trans. from the Arabic by M. Friedlander. New York: Dover Publications, 1956.
Reprinted from the Routledge Kegan Paul edition of 1904.

Manetho. *History of Egypt.* Trans. W. S. Waddell. Cambridge: Harvard Univ. Press, 1964.
This work is bound under the same cover as earlier editions of the *Tetrabiblos* of Ptolemy.

Manhar, Nurho de. *Zohar* [1900–14]. San Diego: Wizards Bookshelf, 1980.
This is an incomplete translation from the Hebrew that was originally published in the Theosophical monthly magazine, *The Word.* It breaks off at Lekh Lekha (Genesis 17:27). In the margin the pagination of the Cremona folio, the *Great Zohar,* has been added for purposes of reference, as it is found in the 1933 Soncino English edition in five volumes.

Mann, A. T. *The Round Art.* New York: Mayflower Books, 1979.
One of the better general texts on modern astrology, notable for its attractive color illustrations and its useful glossary and index.

Marguerite of Navarre. *Heptameron.* Trans. from the French by Arthur Machen. London: George Routledge and Sons, n.d.
Margaret intended to write a *Decameron* in imitation of Boccaccio, but the plan was interrupted by her death.

Marlowe, Christopher. *The Tragical History of the Life and Death of Doctor Faustus.* In *Eliza-*

bethan Plays. New York: Holt, Rinehart and Winston, 1971.

Maternus, Firmicus. *Ancient Astrology Theory and Practice*. Trans. Jean Rhys Bram. Park Ridge, NJ: Noyes Press, 1975.
The work suffers from the lack of an index. The Latin title is *Matheseos*.

Mathers, Samuel Liddell MacGregor. *The Greater Key of Solomon* [1889]. Chicago: The DeLaurence Company, 1914.
A composite version based upon seven manuscripts in the British Museum Library: one in 16th century Latin, one in Italian and five in French. Unfortunately Mathers saw fit to expurgate the more diabolical passages.

——— *The Kabbalah Unveiled* [1887]. London: Routledge and Kegan Paul, 1962.
A translation of part of Knorr von Rosenroth's Latin work *Kabbala Denudata* (Sulzbach, 1677; Frankfort, 1684), which in turn is a translation of part of the *Zohar*. This edition was enormously influential upon English-speaking occultists around the turn of the century.

——— *The Book of the Goetia, or the Lesser Key of Solomon the King* [1903]. California: Health Research, 1976.
This goetic work, which is usually attributed to Aleister Crowley, but which seems actually to have been executed by Mathers, comprises the first book of the five-book collection that goes under the name *Lemegeton* or *Lesser Key of Solomon the King*. Although the title page boasts that it was compiled from "numerous manuscripts in Hebrew, Latin, French and English," it is actually a direct copying of the first book, called the *Goetia*, of British Museum Sloane Ms. 2731, which is a complete English edition of the *Lesser Key*. Thus no scholarship, beyond an ability to read English, was required.

——— *The Book of the Sacred Magic of Abramelin the Mage* [London: 1900]. New York: Dover Publications, 1975.
A translation of a French manuscript in the Bibliotheque de l'Arsenal that purports to have been written by Abraham the Jew to his younger son Lamech in 1458 in order to pass on to him the magical operation described in detail in the text. By far the most important of Mathers' contributions, it contains a truly effective technique for personal transformation.

Mauss, Marcel. *A General Theory of Magic*. Trans. Robert Brain. London: Routledge and Kegan Paul, 1972.

Useful for its background on the history of magical theories, but not for its conclusions.

McIntosh, Christopher. *The Devil's Bookshelf*. Northamptonshire: Aquarian Press, 1985.
Despite its promising title, this is a slender treatment of only the most famous of the grimoires and contains nothing original.

McKenzie, John L. *Dictionary of the Bible*. New York: Macmillan, 1976.

Mead, G. R. S. *Orpheus* [1896]. London: John M. Watkins, 1965.

Methodius. *The Writings*. In *The Ante-Nicene Fathers*. Buffalo: Christian Literature Company, 1886.
Methodius occupies part of vol. 6 of this set.

Morley, Henry. *The Life of Henry Cornelius Agrippa*. 2 vols. London: Chapman and Hall, 1856.
Until quite recently this was the only extensive biography of Agrippa in English. It is perhaps too uncritical, thanks to its reliance upon the letters of Agrippa as its primary source— Agrippa's own letters naturally paint a favorable portrait of him.

Murray, Margaret A. *The God of the Witches* [1931]. London: Oxford Univ. Press, 1979.

——— *The Witch-Cult in Western Europe* [London: 1921].Oxford: Clarendon Press, 1967.

Murray's Classical Atlas. Ed. G. B. Grundy [1904]. London: John Murray, 1959.

Myer, Isaac. *Qabbalah* [Philadelphia: 1888]. New York: Samuel Weiser, 1974.
A beautiful edition of this classic work, which was an important source of information about the Kabbalah in the early decades of this century.

Mylonas, George E. *Eleusis and the Eleusinian Mysteries*. New York: Princeton Univ. Press, 1974.

Nasr, Seyyed Hossein. *An Introduction to Islamic Cosmological Doctrines*. Boulder: Shambhala, 1978.
As the title implies, this is an overview of the great Muslim scholars of the past.

Nauert, Charles G. *Agrippa and the Crisis of Renaissance Thought*. Urbana, IL: University of Illinois Press, 1965.

Odeberg, Hugo. *Book of Enoch by R. Ishmael ben Elisha the High Priest*. New York: Cambridge Univ. Press, 1928.

Oesterreich, Traugott K. *Possession and Exorcism* [1921]. Trans. from the German by D. Ibberson. New York: Causeway Books, 1974.
Originally titled *Possession: Demonical and*

Other. This is the definitive work on demonic possession. It was the sourcebook for Peter Blatty's novel *The Exorcist*.

Origen. *The Writings*. Volume 4 of *The Ante-Nicene Fathers*. Buffalo: Christian Literature Publishing Company, 1885.
Contains *De principiis, Against Celsus* and several letters.

Ovid. *Fasti*. Trans. Sir James G. Frazer [1931]. Cambridge: Harvard Univ. Press, 1989.

——— *The Fasti, Tristia, Pontic Epistles, Ibis, and Halieuticon of Ovid*. Trans. Henry T. Riley. London: George Bell and Sons, 1881.

——— *The Heroides, The Amours, The Art of Love, The Remedy of Love, and Minor Works*. Trans. Henry T. Riley. London: George Bell and Sons, 1883.

——— *The Metamorphoses*. Trans. Henry T. Riley. London: George Bell and Sons, 1884.

——— *Tristia and Ex ponto*. Trans. A. L. Wheeler. Cambridge: Harvard Univ. Press, various years.

Oxford English Dictionary, Compact Edition. 2 vols. Oxford Univ. Press, 1971.

Pagals, Elaine. *The Gnostic Gospels*. New York: Vintage Press, 1981.

Papus. *The Qabalah* [1892]. Northamptonshire: Thorsons Publishers, 1977.
Bound up with the classic occult examination of the Kabbalah by the 18th-century French occultist Dr. Gerard Encausse (Papus) are many fragments from other writers, among them the assignment of the 72 names of God to the quines of the zodiac by Lenain.

Patai, Raphael. *Gates to the Old City*. New York: Avon Books, 1980.

——— *The Messiah Texts*. New York: Avon Books, 1979.
A presentation of the Jewish legends concerning the Messiah.

Pausanias. *Guide to Greece*. Trans. P. Levi. 2 vols. Harmondsworth: Penguin, 1971.

Pearce, Alfred John. *The Text-Book of Astrology* [1879]. Washington: American Federation of Astrologers, 1970.
This is a reprinting of the second edition. It contains a wealth of information but is poorly organized.

Pepys, Samuel. *The Diary*. 2 vols. London: J. M. Dent, 1906.
The Everyman Library edition.

Philostratus. *The Life of Apollonius of Tyana*. 2 vols. Trans. F. C. Conybeare [1912]. Cambridge: Harvard Univ. Press, various years.
The *Epistles of Apollonius* and the treatise of Eusebius, *Against the Life of Apollonius*, are appended to the end of the second volume.

——— *Life and Times of Apollonius of Tyana, Rendered into English from the Greek of Philostratus the Elder*. Trans. Charles P. Eells. Stanford, CA: Stanford Univ. Press, 1923.

Pindar. *The Odes of Pindar*. Trans. from the Greek by John Sandys. London: William Heinemann, 1915.

Plato. *The Collected Dialogues*. Ed. Edith Hamilton and Huntington Cairns. Various translators. Princeton, NJ: Princeton Univ. Press, 1973.
An excellent text, but it should contain the *Alcibiades*.

——— *The Dialogues of Plato*. 2 vols. Trans. Benjamin Jowett. New York: Random House, 1937.
First published by the Macmillan Company in 1892. It contains all the dialogues which in past centuries were generally attributed to Plato.

Pliny the Elder. *Natural History*. 10 vols. Vols. 1–5 and 9 trans. H. Rackham; vols. 6–8 trans. W. H. S. Jones; vol. 10 trans. D. E. Eichholz. Cambridge: Harvard Univ. Press, 1938–1986.

——— *The Natural History of Pliny*. 6 vols. Trans. John Bostock and H. T. Riley. London: Henry G. Bohn, 1855–7.
Only the first two of the 32 books of the Natural History were translated by Bostock. The rest is Riley's work, and it is excellent, although a bit more prolix than the recent Harvard University Press edition, with which I compared it line for line. Riley's notes are of great value.

Pliny the Younger. *The Letters*. Trans. Betty Radice. Harmondsworth: Penguin Books, 1963.

Plotinus. *The Enneads*. 7 vols. Trans. A. H. Armstrong. Cambridge: Harvard Univ. Press, various years.
This is a really excellent translation.

——— *Plotinus: The Ethical Treatises* (vol. 1), *Being the Treatises of the First Ennead with Porphyry's Life of Plotinus, and the Preller-Ritter Extracts Forming a Conspectus of the Plotinian System, Translated from the Greek by Stephen MacKenna*. London: Philip Lee Warner, Publisher to the Medici Society, Limited, 1917.

——— *Plotinus: Psychic and Physical Treatises* (vol. 2), *Comprising the Second and Third Enneads, Translated from the Greek by Stephen*

MacKenna. London: Philip Lee Warner, Publisher to the Medici Society, 1921.

———— *Plotninus: On the Nature of the Soul* (vol. 3), *Being the Fourth Ennead, Translated from the Greek by Stephen MacKenna*. London and Boston: The Medici Society, Limited, 1924.

———— *Plotinus: The Divine Mind* (vol. 4), *Being the Treatises of the Fifth Ennead, Translated from the Greek by Stephen MacKenna*. London and Boston: The Medici Society, Limited, 1926.

These four volumes, supplemented by B. S. Page's translation of the sixth and final Ennead, appeared as one of the Great Books series published by Encyclopaedia Britannica. MacKenna's translation suffers badly when it is compared, as I compared it, with the superior Harvard translation. It lacks clarity. I would have preferred to use the Harvard translation in the notes but was refused permission to do so.

Plutarch. *Moralia*. 16 vols. Vols. 1–5 trans. F. C. Babbitt; vol. 6 trans. W. C. Helmbold; vol. 7 trans. P. H. De Lacy and B. Einarson; vol. 8 trans. P. A. Clement and H. B. Hoffleit; vol. 9 trans. E. L. Minar Jr., F. H. Sandbach and W. C. Helmbold; vol. 10 trans. H. N. Fowler; vol. 11 trans. L. Pearson and F. H. Sandbach; vol. 12 trans. H. Cherniss and W. C. Helmbold; vol. 13, pts. 1 and 2, trans. H. Chernise; vol. 14 trans. P. H. DeLacy and B. Einarson; vol. 15 trans. F. H. Sandbach. Cambridge: Harvard Univ. Press, various years. This collection is made up of all the works of Plutarch apart from the *Lives*.

———— *Plutarch's Essays and Miscellanies: Comprising all his Works Collected Under the Title of "Morals;" Translated from the Greek by Several Hands, Corrected and Revised by William W. Goodwin*. 5 vols. London: Simpkin, Marshall, Hamilton, Kent and Co., 1974–8. This edition was first published in 1684–94, was reissued in 1704 and revised and corrected in 1718. The last edition formed the basis for this translation, which comprises the second half of a ten-volume *Plutarch's Lives and Writings*, edited by A. H. Clough and William W. Goodwin, with an introduction by Ralph Waldo Emerson.

———— *Plutarch's Moralia: Twenty Essays*. Trans. Philemon Holland [1603]. London: J. M. Dent and Sons, n.d. The Everyman Library edition, consisting of 20 essays extracted from Holland's translation of the *Moralia*.

———— *The Lives of the Noble Grecians and Romans*. Trans. John Dryden. New York: Modern Library, n.d.

Although Dryden is credited with the translation on the title page, the actual work of translation was done by someone else. A reprint of the 1874 revised edition of Arthur Hugh Clough and William W. Goodwin (see above).

Porphyry. *Epistle to Anebo*. In *On the Mysteries*. Trans. Thomas Taylor [1821]. London: Stuart and Watkins, 1968. This work is prefaced to *On the Mysteries* by Iamblichus and is quite short. It forms the structure for the work of Iamblichus, which was written in response to points raised in the letter.

———— *On the Life of Plotinus and the Arrangement of His Work*. In *Plotinus: The Ethical Treatises*. Trans. Stephen MacKenna. London: Philip Lee Warner, 1917. This work by Porphyry is prefixed to the *Enneads*.

Pough, Frederick H. A *Field Guide to Rocks and Minerals*. 4th ed. Boston: Houghton Mifflin, 1976.

Proclus. *Proclus: Alcibiades I*. Trans. William O'Neill. The Hague: Martinus Nijhoff, 1965. This commentary by Proclus on the *First Alcibiades* is arguably more important than the dialogue itself.

Ptolemy. *Almagest*. Great Books of the Western World, vol. 16. Chicago: Encyclopaedia Britannica, 1980.

———— *Tetrabiblos*. Trans. F. E. Robbins. Cambridge: Harvard Univ. Press, 1980.

Rabelais, Francois. *The Works of Mr. Francis Rabelais*. New York: Rarity Press, 1932. The translation is not identified, but seems to be that of Sir Thomas Urquhart (bks. 1–3, 1653 and 1693) and Peter Anthony Motteux (bks. 4–5, 1693–4).

Rashi. *The Pentateuch and Rashi's Commentary*. 5 vols. Trans. R. Abraham ben Isaiah, R. Benjamin Sharfman, Harry M. Orlinsky and R. Morris Charner. Brooklyn: S. S. and R. Publishing Company, 1949. This wonderful edition provides a linear translation of the text and commentary beside the original Hebrew.

Regardie, Israel. *The Golden Dawn* [1937-40]. St. Paul, MN: Llewellyn Publications, 1982. This is the single most important book ever written on magic. Regardie is really the editor. He gathered the working documents of the Hermetic Order of the Golden Dawn, a Victorian secret society devoted to the practice of magic. It is difficult to be certain who actually wrote the papers. The poet W. B. Yeats seems to have had a hand in some of them. S. L. MacGregor Mathers is usually said to be the primary author, yet in his other works Mathers displays no creativity. Aleister Crowley, who first published the papers in his periodical *The Equinox,* did not write any of them. Perhaps the rituals really were the writings of angels, or the "Secret Chiefs" as Mathers called them. Quite apart from its practical occult value the book is a monumental work of art. This has not yet been recognized by mainstream literary criticism.

Remy, Nicolas. *Demonolatry* [1595]. Trans. E. A. Ashwin. London: John Rodker, 1930.
It contains many interesting quotations from classical and medieval works, as well as Remy's firsthand accounts of witch trials.

Robinson, James M. *The Nag Hammadi Library.* Various translators. San Francisco: Harper and Row, 1981.
The Gnostic writings.

Rollin, Charles. *The Ancient History* [Paris: 1730–38]. 2 vols. Cincinnati: Applegate and Company, 1855.
Contains a large amount of material, but it is really not to be trusted where matters of fact are concerned. It is useful as a source of legends and fables.

Rose, H. J. *Religion in Greece and Rome.* New York: Harper and Brothers, 1959.
Originally published in two separate books, *Ancient Greek Religion* (1946) and *Ancient Roman Religion* (1948).

Saint-Germain, Comte C. de. *The Practice of Palmistry* [Chicago: 1897]. New York: Samuel Weiser, 1970.
A very clear and complete exposition of palm reading. The author is not to be confused with the alchemist of the 18th century, whose name he has adopted.

Sale, George. *The Koran.* Trans. from the original Arabic. London and New York: Frederick Warne, 1887.

Scholem, Gershom. *Kabbalah.* Jerusalem: Keter Publishing, 1974.

————— *On the Kabbalah and Its Symbolism* [1965]. New York: Schocken Books, 1977.
This is the best introduction I have read on the philosophy of the Kabbalah.

————— *Zohar* [1949]. New York: Schocken Books, 1978.
Selected passages from the *Zohar.*

Scott, Walter. *Hermetica* [1924]. 4 vols. Boston: Shambhala, 1985.
All of the Hermetic writings are contained in the first volume.

Scott, Sir Walter. *Scott's Poetical Works.* Philadelphia: G. and G. Evans, 1859.

Seznec, Jean. *The Survival of the Pagan Gods* [London: 1940]. Trans. from the French by Barbara F. Sessions. Princeton, NJ: Princeton Univ. Press, 1972.
Traces the gods of Greece and Rome through Renaissance art. Its many illustrations make it useful.

Shakespeare, William. *The Complete Works.* Ed. W. J. Craig. London: Oxford Univ. Press.
The Oxford India Paper edition of 1954.

Skeat, Walter William. *Malay Magic* [London: 1900]. New York: Dover Publications, 1967.

Skinner, Stephen. *The Oracle of Geomancy.* California: Prism Press, 1986.
Useful as a guide to the available works on the subject, but contains nothing original and reproduces a number of errors.

Seligmann, Kurt. *The History of Magic.* New York: Pantheon Books, 1948.
Originally published under the superior title *The Mirror of Magic.* Next to DeGivry, this is the best picture book on magic.

Smith, William. *A New Classical Dictionary.* Rev. and corr. Charles Anthon. New York: Harper and Brothers, 1862.
Although parts of it are out of date, the usefulness of this work cannot be overstated. It remains the best of its kind.

Sophocles. *The Complete Greek Tragedies,* vol 2. Ed. David Grene and Richmond Lattimore. Chicago: Univ. of Chicago Press, 1960.

Spence, Lewis. *An Encyclopædia of Occultism* [London: 1920]. New York: University Books, 1968.
A large work that contains a great deal of material. Unfortunately Spence was not careful about identifying his sources.

Spenser, Edmund. *The Works.* Ed. R. Morris. London: Macmillan and Company, 1910.
The Globe Edition.

Sturluson, Snorri. *The Prose Edda* (abridged). Trans. Jean J. Young. Cambridge: Bowes and Bowes, 1954.
The original work of Sturluson is in three parts, of which most of the second and all of the third—the parts not concerned with Norse mythology—are omitted.

Suetonius. *History of Twelve Caesars*. Trans. Philemon Holland [1606]. London: George Routledge and Sons, n.d.

Summers, Montague. *The Werewolf* [1923]. New York: Bell Publishing Company, 1966.

Sworn Book of Honorius the Magician. Trans. from the Latin by Donald J. Driscoll. Gillette, NJ: Heptangle Books, 1983.
This edition of the grimoire is a composite of British Museum manuscripts Sloane 313 and Royal 17-A xlii, the latter being a later incomplete transcription of the former in Latin and English with additional material not contained in Sloane 313.

Tacitus. *Complete Works*. Trans. Alfred John Church and William Jackson Brodribb. New York: Random House, Modern Library edition, 1942.

Tasso, Torquato. *Jerusalem Delivered* [Parma: 1581]. Trans. from the Italian by Edward Fairfax [1600]. New York: P. F. Collier and Son, 1901.

Taylor, Thomas. *Ocellus Lucanus* [1831]. Los Angeles: Philosophical Research Society, 1976.

———— *The Eleusinian and Bacchic Mysteries*. Ed. Alexander Wilder. New York: J. W. Bouton, 1875.

———— *Thomas Taylor the Platonist: Selected Writings*. Ed. Kathleen Raine and George Mills Harper. Princeton, NJ: Princeton Univ. Press. Contains Taylor's edition of the Orphic hymns, along with other important translations.

Tertullian. *The Writings*. Vols. 3 and 4 of *The Ante-Nicene Fathers*. Buffalo: Christian Literature Publishing Company, 1885.

Theocritus. *Theocritus, Bion and Moschus*. Trans. A. Lang. London: Macmillan, 1907.
A prose translation.

Theon of Smyrna. *Mathematics Useful for Understanding Plato*. Trans. Robert and Deborah Lawlor from the 1892 Greek/French edition of J. Dupuis. San Diego: Wizards Bookshelf, 1979.

Thomas, William, and Kate Pavitt. *The Book of Talismans, Amulets and Zodiacal Gems* [1914]. Hollywood: Wilshire Book Company, 1970.

Thorndike, Lynn. *A History of Magic and Experimental Science*. 8 vols. New York: Columbia Univ. Press, 1923–1958.
Volumes 1 and 2 are the most important. The commentary on Agrippa appears in volume 5.

———— *The Sphere of Sacrobosco and Its Commentators*. Chicago: Univ. of Chicago Press.
Thorndike provides an English translation of the *Sphere* and an English version of the commentary by Robertus Anglicus, making this book useful to the vast majority of the English-speaking population who do not read Latin. Unfortunately he has not carried this plan through to the other commentators. There is much matter here on ancient astrology.

Three Works of Ancient Jewish Magic. London: Chthonios Books, 1986.
A photocopy reprinting of the *Sword of Moses*, trans. from the Hebrew by M. Gaster (London, 1896); *The Wisdom of the Chaldeans*, trans. M. Gaster (1900); and *Babylonian Oil Magic in the Talmud and in Later Jewish Literature*, trans. S. Daiches (London: 1913). The last work is titled *Ancient Jewish Oil-Magic* in this collection.

Tibullus. *The Poems of Catullus and Tibullus*. Trans. from the Latin by Walter K. Kelly. London: George Bell and Sons, 1884.

Trithemius, Johannes. *The Steganographia*. Bk. 1 trans. from the Latin by Fiona Tait and Christopher Upton; bk. 3 and part of 4 trans. Dr. Walden. Edinburgh: Magnum Opus Hermetic Sourceworks, 1982.
The book is incomplete, omiting entirely bk. 2 with its complex spirit wheels. It is a pity so important a work could not have been published in its entirety.

Turner, Robert. *Henry Cornelius Agrippa His Fourth Book of Occult Philosophy* [1655]. London: Askin Publishers, 1978.
A facsimile reprint containing the apocryphal *Fourth Book;* Agrippa's treatise *Of Geomancy;* the *Magical Elements* of Peter de Abano; *Astronomical Geomancy* by Gerard Cremonensis; the *Isagoge* or *An Introductory Discourse of the Nature of Such Spirits as are exercised in the sublunary Bounds* by Geo. Pictorius Villinganus; and the first book of the *Arbatel of Magick*, also called the *Isagoge*. All these works appear at the end of the first volume of the two-volume Latin *Opera* of Agrippa.

Vaughan, Thomas. *The Magical Writings of Thomas Vaughan*. Ed. Arthur Edward Waite. London: George Redway, 1888.

Virgil. *The Works of Virgil*. Trans. James Lonsdale and Samuel Lee. London: Macmillan and Company, 1885.
The Globe Edition.

Waite, Arthur Edward. *The Alchemical Writings of Edward Kelly* [London: 1893]. New York: Samuel Weiser, 1976.
Trans. from the Hamburg edition of 1676.

————— *The Book of Ceremonial Magic* [London: 1911]. Secaucus, NJ: Citadel Press, 1961.

————— *The Holy Kabbalah* [1929]. Secaucus, NJ: University Books, 1975.
This is Waite's greatest work. It remains one of the best books on the Kabbalah ever written.

————— *The Turba Philosophorum, or Assembly of the Sages* [London: 1896]. New York: Samuel Weiser, 1976.
Waite's translation of this ancient Latin alchemical text.

Warburton, Eliot. *The Crescent and the Cross* [1844]. New York: P. Putnam, 1849.
A travel book describing the experiences of the author in the Middle East, primarily in Egypt and Syria.

Ward, J. S. M. *Signs and Symbols of Freemasonry* [1928]. New York: Land's End Press, 1969.
This work contains a wealth of symbolic imagery that ranges far beyond its title. It is concerned with the meanings of human posture and gestures, as preserved in painting, sculpture and other art.

Westcott, W. Wynn. *The Chaldean Oracles of Zoroaster* [1895]. Northamptonshire: Aquarian Press, 1983.

————— *Sepher Yetzirah* [London: 1887]. New York: Samuel Weiser, 1980.
This edition of the most ancient text of the Kabbalah has great importance in the history of magic because Westcott was a founding father of the Hermetic Order of the Golden Dawn.

Wilhelm, Helmut. *Change: Eight Lectures on the I Ching*. Trans. from the German by Cary F. Baynes. New York: Pantheon Books, 1960.

Woodroffe, John. *S'akti and S'akta* [1918]. Madras: Ganesh and Company, 1969.

Yates, Frances A. *The Occult Philosophy in the Elizabethan Age* [1979]. London: Ark Paperbacks, 1983.

————— *Theatre of the World*. Chicago: Univ. of Chicago Press, 1969.
The opening two chapters contain an excellent treatment of John Dee, and Appendix A is Dee's Preface to the *English Euclid*.

————— *Giordano Bruno and the Hermetic Tradition*. London: Routledge and Kegan Paul, 1964.

Xenophon. *The Anabasis or Expedition of Cyrus and the Memorabilia of Socrates*. Trans. J. S. Watson. London: George Bell and Sons, 1875.

Index to Biblical Texts

This index includes both direct quotations and allusions made by Agrippa to specific matters in the Bible and Apocrypha and biblical references occurring solely in the notes. Only texts cited in the notes are listed here. Where there is a degree of uncertainty in my mind as to whether my location of a text is correct, I have indicated this in the notes with a "perhaps." Page numbers in boldface refer to the notes. The other numbers refer to the text of the *Occult Philosophy.*

General Index

An effort was made to compose a comprehensive index to the text, while still providing an adequate reference to the notes and other supplemental materials. Considerations of space necessitated that the entries be weighted in favor of the *Occult Philosophy* itself.

Names of print and manuscript works are in capitals. Personal names are italicized. The page numbers in boldface refer to the notes, appendices, and introductory matter. The numbers in italics indicate references to quotations in the body of the text.

In using the index the reader should consult variants of spelling, and also entries on related topics, for the broadest overview. The more important cross references are given in the index itself.

Magic, ceremonial, 3, 435, 444, 450, 689, 695

Magic, Chinese, **733**

Magic, Egyptian, 140, 219, **220**

Magic, mathematical, 331, 692

Magic, natural, 3, 10, 216, 241, 331, 427, **470,** 689–91, 693–4, 700, **818, 833**

Magic cubes, **742–3**

MAGICAL ELEMENTS (Petrus de Apono), **821**

MAGICAL JEWELS OF THE MIDDLE AGES AND RENAISSANCE (Evans), **42, 411, 799**

MAGICAL WRITINGS OF THOMAS VAUGHAN (ed. A. E. Waite), **834**

Magician(s), li, liii, **25, 40, 42, 60, 68, 77–8,** 80, **81,** 108, 110, 112, **113, 126, 128,** 132, 145, **147, 151–2, 173,** 181, 213, 216–7, 221, 233, 250, 255, 303, 310, 318, 371, 400, 423, 430, 435, 441, 448, 451, 457, **459,** 467, 476–8, **480,** 499, 522, 532, **537,** 547, 554, 573, 590, 605, 614, **620,** 643–4, 652, **653,** 656–7, 663, 670, 673–4, 679, 683–5, 690, **691,** 692–4, 696, **698,** 699, **702,** 705, **750, 798–9, 815, 818–9, 827, 833**

MAGICK IN THEORY AND PRACTICE (Crowley), **482**

MAGICK OF KIRANI KING OF PERSIA, AND OF HARPOCRATION (English translation of the KIRANIDES), **812**

Magnesia (place), **843**

Magnesians, 492

Magnitude (astronomical), 362

Magoa (evil spirit), **536**

MAGUS THE (Barrett), **xiii, xl, xlii, 291, 329, 483, 508, 514–5, 563, 736, 746–7, 768, 776**

Maguseans, 689

Mahazael (devil of Earth), 259

Maia (daughter of *Atlas),* **660**

Maia (goddess), 656, **660**

Maidenhair (herb), 91, **92, 100**

Maier, Michael (writer), **207**

Maimonides, Moses (writer), **184,** 478, **478, 482,** 554, 618, 700, **815, 818**

Majesta (the goddess *Maia),* **660**

Malabar leaf (leaf Indum), **133**

Malachi (prophet), **408**

Malachim (angelic order), 289, 468, **473,** 506, **507, 759**

Malachim alphabet, 406, **408,** 560, **562–3**

MALAY MAGIC (Skeat), **734**

Malbiel (angel), 621

Malcha Betharsithim Hed Beruah Schehakim (intelligence of the intelligences of the Moon), 320, **749–50**

Malchidiel (angel of Aries), 294, 533, **536**

Malchuth—see Malkuth

Malea (promontory in Laconia), **843**

Maleoton—see Maleventum

Maleventum (town in Samnium), 673, **675, 843–4**

Malkuth (tenth Sephirah), 289, 469, **473, 754–5, 757, 760–1**

MALLEUS MALIFICARUM (Kramer and Sprenger), **xxiv–xxv, 115, 118, 205**

Mallians (people of India), **200**

Mallois (Malea), 491, **844**

Mammon (devil), 506, 510, **511, 514**

Manasseh (biblical), 670, **671**

Mandrake(s), 53, **57,** 83, **84–5,** 98, 108, 132, **650**

Manes (spirits of the dead), **219,** 595

Manetho (historian), **818**

Maniacal men, 134

Manilius, Marcus (writer), 417, **418,** 423

Manna (food), 265, 701

Manna (resin), 86, **87**

Manna ash (tree), **87**

Mannoah (biblical), 621

Mansions of the Moon, 299, 359, 368–70, **370,** 392–3, 533

Mantiana (Lake Van in Turkey), 97, **844**

Manto (daughter of *Tiresias),* **493**

MANUAL OF HARMONY (Nicomachus), **819**

Maracus the Syracusan (poet), 188, **190**

Marble, red, 94

Marbodus (writer), **61, 799, 803**

Marcasite, gold (stone), 83, **83**

Marcasite, silver (stone), 80, **81,** 94, **386**

Marcella (Roman matron), 474, **478**

Marcellinus (writer), 443

Marcellus, Gaius (Roman consul), 175, **177**

Marcellus, M. Claudius (Roman consul), **167,** 171, **173, 815**

Marcion (heretic), **707**

Marcionists (heretical sect), 706, **707**

Marcus the Valentinian, 519, **520, 815–6**

Mare(s), 53, **55,** 123–4, **125, 127, 253, 706**

Mareotis, Lake, 333, **334, 844**

Margaret of Austria, **xviii–xix, xxi, xxx–xxxii, xxxix,** xlix, 229, **816**

Margaret of Navarre, **xxvii**

Margari (pearl oyster), 76, **79**

Marinus (biographer of *Proclus),* **825**

Maris (god), 467

Marius, Gaius (Roman statesman), **87–8,** 162, **166,** 171, **174, 816, 830**

Marjoram (herb), **61,** 73, **74,** 76, 94, 99

Marjoram, wild, **55**

Mark Anthony, 522, **523**

Markab (star), **364**

Marks of stars, 73, **74,** 102

Marlowe, Christopher (playwright), **833**

Marmarica (place), 97, **844**

Marmorites (herb), 112, **113**

Marriage, wedlock, 262, **264,** 265, 315, **658,** 683, 685

Mars (god), **236,** 297, 313, 316, *423,* 423, 491, **493–5,** *524,* **555,** 577, **658, 660**

Mars (planet), 26, 52, 72–3, **74,** 80, 89, 96–9, **101,** 103, 132–3, 143, 146, 148, 154–5, 170, 210, 245, 258, 263, 265–6, 274, 283–5, 288, 312, 315, **317,** 318–20, 323, **328, 339–40,** *340,* **341–2,** 355, 357,

The Magician's Workbook
Practicing the Rituals of the Western Tradition
Donald Tyson

Contains everything that beginners need to start their esoteric training . . .

The Magician's Workbook has a single purpose: to present a graded and integrated series of practical exercises designed to teach the essentials of ritual magic.

It contains no history or theory—just forty exercises that anyone can do without prior training, special tools, or costly materials. The content ranges from simple mental exercises to complete rituals that form templates for future work in Western magic.

These exercises do not merely teach—they transform. When practiced regularly, they cause changes in the body, brain, perceptions, emotions, and the will—changes necessary for the successful working of magic in any of its ancient or modern traditions.

- A complete basic training manual for serious beginners who want to start performing ritual magic, rather than just reading about it
- Presents a progressive, forty-week schedule of daily study that fully integrates inner mental conditioning with external movements, gestures, and words
- Enables students to go on to study the Golden Dawn system in greater depth, or move forward with confidence to any other form of Western magic

0-7387-0000-2
7½ x 9⅛, 336 pp., illus.   **$17.95**

Enochian Magic for Beginners
The Original System of Angel Magic

Donald Tyson

The most remarkable artifact in the entire history of spirit communication is the legacy of the Enochian angels, who presented themselves to the famed Elizabethan mathematician Dr. John Dee through his seer, the infamous alchemist Edward Kelley, between the years 1582–1589. Enochian Magic is a method for summoning and commanding angelic beings and demons, although the angels gave Dee strict instructions never to use the magick for evoking evil spirits. Now, *Enochian Magic for Beginners* provides this system in its complete and original form.

Newcomers to Enochian Magic will not find a clearer or more comprehensive overview. Experienced Enochian scholars will be pleasantly surprised by how many gaps in the communications have finally been filled. Donald Tyson gives all of the essential magical teachings of the angels along with the necessary symbols, sigils, and letter squares required to put these teachings into practice. More importantly, he explains how these sigils and squares were derived and what they signify.

1-56718-747-1
408 pp., 5³⁄₁₆ x 8, illus.

$14.95

TO ORDER, CALL 1-877-NEW-WRLD
Prices subject to change without notice

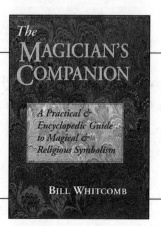

The Magician's Companion

A Practical and Encyclopedic Guide to Magical and Religious Symbolism

Bill Whitcomb

The Magician's Companion is a "desk reference" overflowing with a wide range of occult and esoteric materials absolutely indispensable to anyone engaged in the magickal arts!

The magical knowledge of our ancestors comprises an intricate and elegant technology of the mind and imagination. This book attempts to make the ancient systems accessible, understandable and useful to modern magicians by categorizing and cross-referencing the major magical symbol-systems (i.e., world views on inner and outer levels). Students of religion, mysticism, mythology, symbolic art, literature, and even cryptography will find this work of value.

0-87542-868-1,
522 pp., 7 x 10, illus., softcover $24.95

Sexual Alchemy
Magical Intercourse with Spirits
Donald Tyson

Sexual Alchemy is a system of ritual magic that allows you to initiate and sustain satisfying erotic relationships with loving spirits who are the active agents of the Goddess, the creative mother of the universe.

At the heart of sexual alchemy lies the most potent and jealously guarded of all occult mysteries—the method for using the forces liberated by the union with spiritual beings for self-empowerment and personal transformation.

Erotic unions with gods, angels, and demons have occurred throughout human history in all cultures, but the methods have been suppressed and lost, save for references and fragments in ancient alchemical and magical texts.

Sexual Alchemy is the first book exclusively devoted to a detailed examination of sex between human beings and spirits, and the uniquely transformed products of the human body that such unions generate. Most other books on sex magic focus on the Tantra of India and Tibet, or the Western magical practice of auto-eroticism.

1-56718-741-2
408 pp., 7½ x 9⅛, 17 illus.   **$19.95**

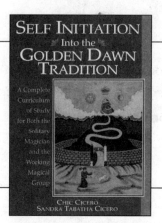

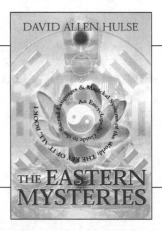

The Eastern Mysteries

An Encyclopedic Guide to the Sacred Languages & Magical Systems of the World

David Allen Hulse

Formerly titled The Key of It All–Book One

The Eastern Mysteries series clarifies and extends the knowledge established by all previous books on occult magick. Book One catalogs and distills, in hundreds of tables of secret symbolism, the true alphabet magick of every ancient Eastern magickal tradition. Unlike the current rash of publications which do no more than recapitulate Regardie or Crowley, *The Eastern Mysteries* series establishes a new level of competence in all fields of magick both East and West.

Cuneiform—the oldest tradition ascribing number to word; the symbolism of base 60 used in Babylonian and Sumerian Cuneiform; the first God and Goddess names associated to number.

Hebrew—a complete exposition of the rules governing the Hebrew Qabalah; the evolution of the Tree of Life; an analysis of the Book of Formation, the oldest key to the symbolic meaning of the Hebrew alphabet.

Arabic—the similarity between the Hebrew and Arabic Qabalahs; the secret Quranic symbolism for the Arabic alphabet; the Persian alphabet code; the philosophical numbering system of G.I. Gurdjieff.

Sanskrit—the secret Vedic number codes for Sanskrit; the digital word-numbers; the symbolism of the seven chakras and their numerical key.

Tibetan—the secret number lore for Tibetan as inspired by the Sanskrit codes; the secret symbols for the Tibetan alphabet; the six major schools of Tattva philosophy.

Chinese—the Taoist calligraphic stroke count technique for number Chinese characters; Chinese Taoist number philosophy; the I Ching, the Japanese language and its parallels to the Chinese number system.

1-56718-428-6
656 pp., 7 x 10, tables, charts $29.95

TO ORDER, CALL 1-800 THE MOON

Prices subject to change without notice

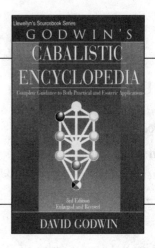

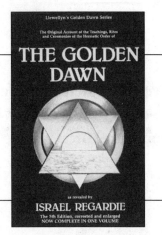

The Golden Dawn
*The Original Account of the Teachings, Rites
& Ceremonies of the Hermetic Order*

As revealed by Israel Regardie

Complete in one volume with further revision, expansion, and additional notes by Regardie, Cris Monnastre, and others. Expanded with an index of more than 100 pages!

Originally published in four bulky volumes of some 1,200 pages, this sixth revised and enlarged edition has been entirely reset in modern, less space-consuming type, in half the pages (while retaining the original pagination in marginal notation for reference) for greater ease and use.

Corrections of typographical errors perpetuated in the original and subsequent editions have been made, with further revision and additional text and notes by noted scholars and by actual practitioners of the Golden Dawn system of Magick, with an Introduction by the only student ever accepted for personal training by Regardie.

Also included are Initiation Ceremonies, important rituals for consecration and invocation, methods of meditation and magical working based on the Enochian Tablets, studies in the Tarot, and the system of Qabalistic Correspondences that unite the World's religions and magical traditions into a comprehensive and practical whole.

This volume is designed as a study and practice curriculum suited to both group and private practice. Meditation upon, and following with the Active Imagination, the Initiation Ceremonies are fully experiential without need of participation in group or lodge. A very complete reference encyclopedia of Western Magick.

0-87542-663-8
840 pp., 6 x 9, illus., softcover   **$29.95**

TO ORDER, CALL 1-800 THE MOON

Prices subject to change without notice

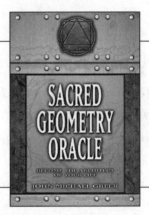

Sacred Geometry Oracle
Become the Architect of Your Life
John Michael Greer

Use the same tools that designed temples and pyramids to design your own life . . .

From the time of Stonehenge and the Pyramids, through the mystical teachings of Pythagoras to the cutting edge of advanced science, the cosmic patterns and universal truths of sacred geometry bridge past and future. Now, for the first time, you can put this ancient wisdom to work in your own life with the *Sacred Geometry Oracle*.

This kit contains thirty-three cards, each representing a basic figure in traditional sacred geometry, and each relating to one of the basic patterns of the universe—patterns that form the hidden structure of our everyday lives. Use the cards for divination, meditation, and self-exploration.

- The only divination system that draws on the traditions of sacred geometry
- The book Techniques for Geometric Transformation presents the meanings of each card, how to cast and interpret readings with several original layouts, and meditations
- Provides clear, insightful, and accurate readings about past, present, and future events
- A tool for expanding awareness of the patterns of reality that shape our lives

0-7387-0051-7
Boxed kit: 33-card deck and
6 x 9, 240-pp. illustrated guidebook   **$34.95**

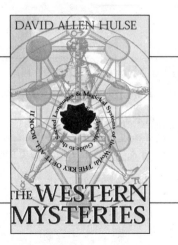

The Middle Pillar

The Balance Between Mind & Magic

Israel Regardie
edited and annotated with new material by Chic Cicero & Sandra Tabatha Cicero

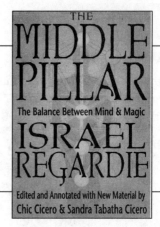

Here is a charming little grimoire of magical thought. Break the barrier between the conscious and unconscious mind through the Middle Pillar exercise, a technique that serves as a bridge into magic, chakra work, and psychology. This classic work introduces a psychological perspective on magic and occultism while giving clear directions on how to perform the Qabalistic Cross, The Lesser Banishing Ritual of the Pentagram, the Middle Pillar exercise, along with its accompanying methods of circulating the light, the Vibratory Formula, and the building up of the Tree of Life in the aura.

The Ciceros, who knew Regardie personally, have made his book much more accessible by adding an extensive and useful set of notes, along with chapters that explain Regardie's work in depth. They expand upon it by carrying it into a realm of new techniques that are directly related to Regardie's core material. Especially valuable is the chapter on psychology, which provides a solid frame of reference for Regardie's' numerous remarks on this subject.

1-56718-140-6
312 pp., 6 x 9, illus., softcover   **$12.95**